W9-AOR-212

THE NAVARRE BIBLE

CHRONICLES–MACCABEES

FOR THE ENGLISH EDITION
James Gavigan, Brian McCarthy
Thomas McGovern

VOLUMES IN THIS SERIES

Standard Edition

NEW TESTAMENT
St Matthew's Gospel
St Mark's Gospel
St Luke's Gospel
St John's Gospel
Acts of the Apostles
Romans and Galatians
Corinthians
Captivity Letters
Thessalonians and Pastoral Letters
Hebrews
Catholic Letters
Revelation

OLD TESTAMENT
The Pentateuch
Joshua–Kings [Historical Books 1]
Chronicles–Maccabees [Historical Books 2]
The Psalms and the Song of Solomon
Wisdom Books
Major Prophets
Minor Prophets

Reader's (Omnibus) Edition
The Gospels and Acts
The Letters of St Paul
Revelation, Hebrews and Catholic Letters

Single-volume, large-format New Testament

THE NAVARRE BIBLE

Chronicles–Maccabees

The Books of 1 and 2 Chronicles, Ezra, Nehemiah,
Tobit, Judith, Esther and 1 and 2 Maccabees
in the Revised Standard Version and New Vulgate
with a commentary by members of the
Faculty of Theology of the University of Navarre

FOUR COURTS PRESS • DUBLIN
SCEPTER PUBLISHERS • NEW YORK

Typeset by Carrigboy Typesetting Services for
FOUR COURTS PRESS LTD
7 Malpas Street, Dublin 8, Ireland
www.fourcourtspress.ie
and in North America for
SCEPTER PUBLISHERS, INC
P.O. Box 211, New York, NY 10018–0004
www.scepterpublishers.org

The translation of introductions and commentary was made by
Michael Adams and Coilín O hAodha.

Nihil obstat: Martin Hogan, LSS, PhD, *censor deputatus*
Imprimi potest: Desmond, Archbishop of Dublin, 17 July 2002

A catalogue record for this title is available from the British Library.

1st edition 2003; reprinted 2006, 2009, 2013.

ISBN 1–85182–677–7 (Four Courts Press)
ISBN 1–889334–84–7 (Scepter Publishers)

Library of Congress Cataloging-in-Publication Data [for first volume in this series]

Bible. O.T. English. Revised Standard. 1999.
The Navarre Bible. – North American ed.
p. cm
"The Books of Genesis, Exodus, Leviticus, Numbers, Deuteronomy in the Revised Standard Version and New Vulgate with a commentary by members of the Faculty of Theology of the University of Navarre."
Includes bibliographical references.
Contents: [1] The Pentateuch.
ISBN 1–889334–21–9 (hardback: alk. paper)
I. Title.
BS891.A1 1999.P75 99–23033
221.7'7—dc21 CIP

ACKNOWLEDGMENTS

Original title: *Sagrada Biblia: Libros históricas* [*Josué–2 Reyes*]
Quotations from Vatican II documents are based on the translation in *Vatican Council II: The Conciliar and Post Conciliar Documents*, ed. A. Flannery, OP (Dublin 1981).

Printed and bound by CPI Group (UK) Ltd, Croydon, CR0 4YY.

Contents

Contents

Preface and Preliminary Notes

The project of a new Spanish translation of the Bible, with commentary, was originally entrusted to the faculty of theology at the University of Navarre by St Josemaría Escrivá, the founder of Opus Dei and the university's first chancellor.

The main feature of the English edition, *The Navarre Bible*, is the commentary, that is, the notes and introductions provided by the editors; rarely very technical, these are designed to elucidate the spiritual and theological message of the Bible. Quotations from commentaries by the Fathers, and excerpts from other spiritual writers, not least St Josemaría, are provided to show how they read Scripture and made it meaningful in their lives. This edition also carries the Western Church's official Latin version of the Bible, the *editio typica altera* of the New Vulgate (1986).

For the English edition we consider ourselves fortunate in having the Revised Standard Version as the translation of Scripture and wish to record our appreciation for permission to use that text.[1]

PRELIMINARY NOTES

The headings in the biblical text have been provided by the editors (they are not taken from the RSV); this is true also of the cross references in the marginal notes. These headings are also listed together at the end of the book, to act as a sort of index.

References in the margin of the biblical text or its headings point to parallel passages or other passages which deal with the same theme. With the exception of the New Testament and Psalms, the marginal references are to the New Vulgate, that is, they are not normally adjusted to the RSV.

Some headings carry an asterisk; this means there is an asterisked note below, more general than the normal and one which examines the structure or content of an entire passage. To get an overview of each book, the reader may find it helpful to read the asterisked notes before reading the biblical text and the more specific notes. An asterisk *inside the RSV text* refers the reader to the Explanatory Notes at the end of the book.

1. Integral to which are the RSV footnotes, which are indicated by superior letters.

Abbreviations

1. BOOK OF HOLY SCRIPTURE

Acts	Acts of the Apostles	1 Kings	1 Kings
Amos	Amos	2 Kings	2 Kings
Bar	Baruch	Lam	Lamentations
1 Chron	1 Chronicles	Lev	Leviticus
2 Chron	2 Chronicles	Lk	Luke
Col	Colossians	1 Mac	1 Maccabees
1 Cor	1 Corinthians	2 Mac	2 Maccabees
2 Cor	2 Corinthians	Mal	Malachi
Dan	Daniel	Mic	Micah
Deut	Deuteronomy	Mk	Mark
Eccles	Ecclesiastes (Qohelet)	Mt	Matthew
Esther	Esther	Nah	Nahum
Eph	Ephesians	Neh	Nehemiah
Ex	Exodus	Num	Numbers
Ezek	Ezekiel	Obad	Obadiah
Ezra	Ezra	1 Pet	1 Peter
Gal	Galatians	2 Pet	2 Peter
Gen	Genesis	Phil	Philippians
Hab	Habakkuk	Philem	Philemon
Hag	Haggai	Ps	Psalms
Heb	Hebrews	Prov	Proverbs
Hos	Hosea	Rev	Revelation (Apocalypse)
Is	Isaiah	Rom	Romans
Jas	James	Ruth	Ruth
Jer	Jeremiah	1 Sam	1 Samuel
Jn	John	2 Sam	2 Samuel
1 Jn	1 John	Sir	Sirach (Ecclesiasticus)
2 Jn	2 John	Song	Song of Solomon
3 Jn	3 John	1 Thess	1 Thessalonians
Job	Job	2 Thess	2 Thessalonians
Joel	Joel	1 Tim	1 Timothy
Jon	Jonah	2 Tim	2 Timothy
Josh	Joshua	Tit	Titus
Jud	Judith	Wis	Wisdom
Jude	Jude	Zech	Zechariah
Judg	Judges	Zeph	Zephaniah

2. RSV ABBREVIATIONS

In the notes indicated by superior *letters* in the biblical text, the following abbreviations are used:

Cn	a correction made where the text has suffered in transmission and the versions provide no satisfactory restoration but the RSV Committee agrees with the judgment of competent scholars as to the most probable reconstruction of the original text
Heb	the Hebrew of the consonantal Masoretic Text of the Old Testament
Gk	Septuagint, Greek Version of the Old Testament
Lat	Latin Version of Tobit, Judith, and 2 Maccabees
Ms	manuscript
Mss	manuscripts
MT	the Hebrew of the pointed Masoretic Text of the Old Testament
Sam	Samaritan Hebrew text of the Old Testament
Syr	Syriac Version of the Old Testament
Tg	Targum
Vg	Vulgate, Latin Version of Old Testament

N.B. In the biblical text, the word LORD, when spelled with capital letters, stands for the divine name, Yhwh.

3. OTHER ABBREVIATIONS

ad loc.	*ad locum*, commentary on this passage
AAS	*Acta Apostolicae Sedis*
Apost.	Apostolic
can.	canon
chap.	chapter
cf.	*confer*, compare
CCC	*Catechism of the Catholic Church*
Const.	Constitution
Decl.	Declaration
Dz-Sch	Denzinger-Schönmetzer, *Enchiridion Biblicum* (4th edition, Naples & Rome, 1961)
Enc.	Encyclical
Exhort.	Exhortation
f	and following (*pl.* ff)
ibid.	*ibidem*, in the same place
in loc.	*in locum,* commentary on this passage
loc.	*locum*, place or passage
par.	parallel passages
Past.	Pastoral
RSV	Revised Standard Version
RSVCE	Revised Standard Version, Catholic Edition
SCDF	Sacred Congregation for the Doctrine of the Faith
sess.	session
v.	verse (*pl.* vv.)

THE HISTORY OF THE CHRONICLER

Introduction

The "history of the Chronicler" is the general name given to a collection of historical writings comprising the two books of Chronicles and the books of Ezra and Nehemiah, which are clearly a continuation of Chronicles. In fact, the first four verses of Ezra repeat the last verses of 2 Chronicles. It would seem as if, by starting a new roll of parchment with the same words as were used to finish the previous one, the editor wanted to show that he was not beginning a new book but continuing one already begun. This entire suite of books provides a general history of the chosen people that begins with the origins of man and ends (in the books of Ezra and Nehemiah) in the Persian era. That is how this history is arranged in the Christian canon of the Bible; however, in the Hebrew canon, 1 and 2 Chronicles come last in the series and are positioned after Ezra-Nehemiah, possibly because, being seen as repetitions of Samuel and Kings, it took time for them to be considered canonical.

1. STRUCTURE AND CONTENT

The "history of the Chronicler" follows the people of God from Adam down to the restoration of Judah in the Persian era, using a lot of material from other historical books of the Old Testament and other extrabiblical sources. Because it deals with events already covered in the preceding historical books, the works of the Chronicler were very little commented on by the Fathers or ecclesiastical writers. The first complete commentary—that of Rabanus Maurus—was not made until the ninth century. However, in recent years more attention has been paid to these works because scholars have come to realize that the Chronicles are not mere repetition: they are a reinterpretation and updating of previous recorded history that forms part of the Bible; that is, they are acknowledged to be the word of God. In other words, the author or authors of this work did not intend merely to repeat the same history and religious teaching: under the influence of the Holy Spirit, they were writing a theological book focusing on the identity of the people of God and set within the framework of temple worship and observances of the Law of Moses. The books pay special attention to the two most significant points in the temple's history—its construction under Solomon, and its restoration in the time of Ezra and Nehemiah. Also, in their genealogies they establish a line of continuity right back to Adam and the patriarchs and the people that came to live in the promised land many generations later. The temple and the splendour of its rites reflect the unity and identity of that people. Therefore, all the first part

of the history is an account of how that unity was achieved, its most perfect prototype being found in David's reign. When, after the death of Solomon, that unity was shattered and the very identity of the people was endangered, a long series of difficult situations arose which, despite some short-lived attempts to restore national unity and bring about religious reform, ultimately led to the destruction of the temple and the exile in Babylon. But Cyrus' edict opened the way for a return to the holy city, rebuilding of the temple, and national reconstruction based on the Law.

2. COMPOSITION

Since the early nineteenth century there has been growing acceptance of the view that these four books form a unit and were all written by the same author, probably a Levite, called "the Chronicler". The strong evidence in favour of this theory is: the continuity in the books' teaching about the unity of the people; the importance given to the temple; and the similarity in linguistic style and even vocabulary. However, in recent years some scholars have argued that Ezra and Nehemiah form a bloc distinct from 1 and 2 Chronicles and were written by various hands and at different times: 1 and 2 Chronicles would have been written in the fourth century BC with the purpose of stressing that Israel's very identity was tied in with worship in the temple of Jerusalem, and of showing that that was what ensured the survival of the kingdom that God promised David; whereas Ezra-Nehemiah would have been written around the year 100 BC, as a text dealing with the two figures most remembered as the protagonists of Jewish revival. However, the four books all have a fairly similar doctrinal thrust, so it still makes sense to speak in terms of the "Chronicler" and the "history of the Chronicler".

3. MESSAGE

The "history of the Chronicler" was written to meet the needs of one specific period in the history of Israel—when the nation was called on to face the challenge of staying true to its origins, and to its Covenant with God, in a paganized environment and at a time when another group, the Samaritans, were claiming to be the true Israel. The response to that challenge will be to put the stress on the identity of the people, and on faith in God, the Lord of history and the author of the Covenant. The people comprises those who returned from exile. The Covenant is spelt out in the Law.

The Chronicler highlights the figure of David as lawmaker and organizer of divine worship. Anything that might diminish the great king's stature is left unmentioned (the murder of Uriah, disputes about the succession, etc.) in the

interests of portraying David as a great ruler and, especially, a devout king who planned the building of the temple and laid down the rules of the liturgy and the duties of the various priests.

The other main thread running through this history is its teaching about the temple. In the Persian era, those who returned from exile and those who had never left Palestine managed to rebuild unity, thanks to the joint project of the reconstruction of the temple, and the reforming zeal of Ezra the priest and Nehemiah. All the previous history, with its emphasis on the temple, is a lesson the Israelites must remember now that they have to work together in rebuilding the centre of worship and engaging in its splendid rites.

Fidelity entails fulfilment of the Law and carefully orchestrated and devout worship which gives God due obeisance. The rites must be marked by all due splendour, and this affects not only the role of priests and Levites: even the services performed by lesser officials, such as porters and cantors, must be carried out perfectly. Everything—fidelity to the Law, conformity to the proper form of worship—expresses joy at the presence of God in the temple among his people.

But the basic message of the history contained in these books has to do with God himself, who never abandons his people. The long genealogical lists provided here all serve to show that the exile in Babylon did not involve any break in the links binding the people to their ancestors, the patriarchs, or even to the first man, created directly by God. Therefore, their own descendants must stay loyal to the Covenant that their fathers made; it establishes Israel as a holy nation set apart from the rest, to be devoted to God. That fidelity also involves a duty to maintain the identity of the chosen people from one generation to the next—hence their need to keep themselves separate from foreigners (Neh 9:2) and not to inter-marry with them (Neh 10:30).

In his care of his people God also grants a just reward, giving to each what he or she deserves. This teaching is very pronounced in the books of the Chronicler and it fosters hope in a continual beginning and beginning again. Each age, each king, each person sets out on his or her pilgrimage without carrying any burden of sin from their forebears. God is a just judge towards all. This teaching, already found in Jeremiah (cf. Jer 31:29–30) and Ezekiel (cf. Ezek 18:1–32), began to become clearer as people came to realize that divine justice did not have to manifest itself in this life but could involve waiting until the next.

These books contain many appeals for conversion, for personal responsibility as regards fidelity to the God of the Covenant and to the worship due him. An important part of the work of the Levites (the discreet protagonists of much of this history) is to call on the people to praise the Lord "for his steadfast love endures for ever!" (1 Chron 16:34, 41; 2 Chron 5:13; 7:3; 20:21).

The text also stresses in various ways that when a person stays true to God, he is rewarded with a joy which helps him cope with difficulties, "for the joy of the Lord is your strength" (Neh 8:10).

4. THE "HISTORY OF THE CHRONICLER" IN THE LIGHT OF THE NEW TESTAMENT

The spiritual meaning that inspires these books, and their emphasis on the primacy of the Law, constitute the very soul of Judaism: from the time they were written onwards, Judaism will often show signs of great vitality. It is true that, on occasions, zeal to ensure the ritual cleanliness needed for worship, and fidelity to the traditions of the elders of the people, gave rise to over-rigorous interpretation of the Law. We can see evidence in the New Testament of excesses in some Jewish circles at the start of the Christian era. However, one must remember that Jesus himself was born into and reared in that religion and cultural milieu; he went up to the temple to pray; he took part in services in synagogues; and he kept to many of the good traditions and customs of his people. But the universal nature of the salvation that he brought (its availability to all mankind), and his teaching about how inner commitment must accompany worship, served to correct and perfect what is only outlined in these books. That may be why Christian tradition has not given them very great attention.

Still, they have always had a place in the Christian canon of the Old Testament; that is, the Church recognizes them as an integral and necessary part of the deposit of Revelation. The teaching contained in the Chronicler's history applies not only to the needs obtaining at a particular point in Israel's history, but has a permanent value. Obviously it is not a matter of conforming to rules which had relevance in their time in Judaism; but it is important to be in tune with the spirit behind those laws—the importance of rendering due worship to the Lord, staying loyal to God despite difficulties, and seeking in the deposit of faith a valid answer to the questions that arise at different times.

1 AND 2 CHRONICLES

Introduction

In the Hebrew Bible this text is called *Dibre ha-yamin*, that is, "the events of the days", or "the journal". In the Septuagint its title is *Paraleipómena*, "the things left out", the books that complement the preceding ones. St Jerome, in his prologue to the books of Samuel and Kings (*Prologus Galeatus*), gives them the very suitable title of *Chronicon totius divinae historiae* (Chronicle of all divine history). Hence the name "Chronicles" that has become part of Christian tradition.

1. STRUCTURE AND CONTENT

As stated already, the books of the Chronicles cover the history of the people of God from Adam right up to the Babylonian captivity. They focus particularly on the building of the temple of Jerusalem and on temple ritual. In line with this, we can distinguish the following parts:

1. GENEALOGICAL LISTS PRIOR TO THE MONARCHY (1 CHRON 1:1—9:44). This part summarizes the history of mankind from Adam to Saul. The genealogies of the sons of Jacob, especially those of Judah and Levi, are particularly prominent, some of them extending as far as the period of exile.

2. THE HISTORY OF DAVID (1 CHRON 10:1—29:30). The narrative part of the book starts with the death of Saul, which is presented as being punishment for his infidelity. The author focuses on the figure of David, paying special attention to things to do with the transfer of the ark and the preparations for the building of the temple and the organization of its liturgy. The famous king is very much to the fore.

3. THE HISTORY OF SOLOMON (2 CHRON 1:1—9:31). David's successor is portrayed as a man of great wisdom and enormous wealth, whose honour it was to actually build the temple. Under Solomon the kingdom reached its zenith and all the plans devised by David were put into effect.

4. THE KINGS OF JUDAH (2 CHRON 10:1—35:27). The sacred writer has nothing in particular to say about the kings of the Northern kingdom (Israel), but he reviews all the kings of Judah, evaluating each against the example of David, and concentrating on the religious reforms undertaken by some of them—Asa, Jehoshaphat, Joash, Hezekiah, Josiah and Manasseh; regarding the last mentioned, it is put on record that, though he was undevout, he was later converted.

5. THE END OF THE KINGDOM OF JUDAH (2 CHRON 36:1–23). The book ends with reports on the fall of Judah, Cyrus' edict and the restoration of the temple.

2. COMPOSITION

The books of Chronicles include material drawn from earlier documents, and rounded off with the help of oral traditions. The principal sources used were:

a) *Sacred writings*. The genealogical lists given in the early chapters are based on material in Genesis, Exodus, Numbers, Joshua, Ruth etc. In the section to do with the kings, there are many complete accounts which are almost word for word with passages in the books of Samuel and Kings. Although the most widely held opinion is that Samuel and Kings had not been fully completed when 1 and 2 Chronicles were being edited, it is likely that the Chronicler had access to a fairly complete version of them.

b) *Official documents*. These are cited explicitly—the Book of the Kings of Judah (cf. 1 Chron 9:1; 2 Chron 27:7; 35:27; 36:8), the Book of the Kings of Judah and Israel (2 Chron 32:32), the Book of the Kings of Israel (1 Chron 9:1; 2 Chron 20:32), and the Chronicles of the Kings of Israel (2 Chron 33:18). The Commentary on the Book of the Kings is also cited (2 Chron 24:27). It is possible that these books were just compilations of documents and records rather than structured books in the normal sense.

c) *Other written sources*. These would usually have been accounts or collections of sayings connected with well-known figures, many of them revered as prophets. Thus, there is mention of Chronicles of Samuel the seer (1 Chron 29:29), Nathan the prophet (1 Chron 1:29; 2 Chron 9:29) and Gad the seer (1 Chron 29:29); Iddo the seer (2 Chron 9:29); the Chronicles of Shemaiah the prophet (2 Chron 12:15); Jehu the son of Hanani (2 Chron 20:34); the story of Iddo the prophet (2 Chron 13:22); the vision of Isaiah the prophet (2 Chron 32:32); Ahijah the Shilonite (2 Chron 9:29); and the acts of Uzziah written by Isaiah (2 Chron 26:22).

d) *Oral traditions*. These books record reminiscences preserved in Judah, which were passed on by the returned exiles and went back to the Persian era.

Working with all this material, the author set about writing up a history designed to transmit a religious message. It is highly likely that the books were written in Jerusalem, but when they were written is not so clear. Very probably it was before the invasion by Alexander the Great (333 BC) because there is no trace of references to Hellenism, and after the missions of Ezra and Nehemiah which end in 398 BC. So, they must have been written in the period 400–350 BC. Some scholars argue that the texts went through various editions, the first of which would have been prior to Nehemiah and the last (and definitive) edition made around 350 BC.

3. MESSAGE

The books of Chronicles see history as being religious in character. The fact that the accounts contained in them sometimes differ from those in "Deuteronomic history" does not mean that history is distorted here but that it is being written from a standpoint which allows the writer to omit certain items or to complement previous accounts of certain figures, as in the case of Manasseh (cf. the note on 2 Chron 33:1–20). The sacred writers are providing a theological reflection on past events, and they deduce from them teachings designed for their immediate readership.

In addition to the general features discussed on pages 13ff above, we might draw attention to the following points in Chronicles.

Firstly, there is the importance given to the figure of David, portrayed here as the ideal king. David's role in these books parallels that of Moses in the Pentateuch. David made Jerusalem a holy city, and he has provided Israel with cultic institutions fully in line with the Law. Fidelity to the Law is not something oppressive; rather, it fills the heart with a deep, interior joy. It is moreover a source of hope: the Davidic dynasty will disappear from the political stage, but its cultic institutions and its profound religious sensibility will endure forever. In placing the figure of David at the centre of these books, the author(s) may well have had in mind the ideal king, the expected Messiah. Or, at least, they are pointing out that the holy people established by David still exists and will endure.

Time and again the books of the Chronicles focus attention on the presence of God in the midst of his people, in the holy city. The Lord is always present among his own people. He is with David (1 Chron 11:9; 17:2, 8; 22:11, 16; 28:20), with Solomon (2 Chron 1:1), with Jehoshaphat (2 Chron 17:3) and with the whole people, especially in times of trial, as for example the siege suffered by Jerusalem in the reign of Hezekiah (2 Chron 32:22).

Another important aspect is personal retribution: God always rewards those who do good and punishes those who do evil. If bad things happen, it is because some evil has been committed. A good example of this is the version of Josiah's death given in 2 Chronicles 35:20–27 as compared with that in 2 Kings 23:28–30: Josiah dies prematurely, despite being a devout king. Since there seems to be no reason for this untoward event, the Chronicler tells the reader that it happened because Josiah failed to listen to the voice of God speaking through the pharaoh Neco when the pharaoh asked Josiah not to block his way north to Assyria.

Sometimes this immediate personal retribution might seem unwarranted. However, in the overall unfolding of Revelation, it marks an important advance. "Deuteronomic history" interprets the exile as a punishment that God cannot but impose on his people on account of the sins of their forebears. That is the thrust of the oracle we find in the book of Isaiah: "Comfort, comfort my

people, says your God. [. . .] cry to her [. . .] that she has received from the Lord's hand double for all her sins" (Is 40:1–2). However, Ezekiel's teaching says that there is no such thing as collective responsibility for sin and, therefore, no collective punishment, but, rather, that only "the soul that sins shall die" (Ezek 18:4). The Chronicler goes a step further and takes it as read that each king begins his reign enjoying divine protection and without having to carry any burden of his predecessors' sins. That is, the positive or negative final judgment on each king is based only on the way he himself has behaved; every new king, on coming to the throne, has an open road ahead of him. In this sense, the exile is not a punishment imposed for transgressions of others in the past; it is something deserved by those who undergo it. Thus, it becomes just another stage in history, a long "sabbath" (2 Chron 36:21) lasting some years, to be followed by a new stage, in which the people will enjoy the same protection as, they had in the reign of David. The Chronicler's teaching is, then, filled with hope, an as yet imperfect hope.

In this connexion we must draw attention to the joyful, festive nature of divine worship that comes across from 1 and 2 Chronicles—as witness, for example, the Levites with their "instruments for music to the Lord" (2 Chron 7:6). (From 1 Chronicles 6:16–38 one can deduce that there was a permanent establishment of Levite cantors—men "in charge of the service of song in the praise of the Lord.") The figure of David is also highly relevant here, given that many poems were attributed to him, and musical instruments for singing the praises of the Lord (cf. 1 Chron 23:5). The high points in this history—such as the dedication of the temple, the enthronement of the kings, the religious reforms or the passover festivities—are all celebrated with liturgical chants which express to God the prayerful feelings of individuals and of the entire people.

In the splendour of the liturgy and the attraction of the temple, the Levites played an essential and leading role. The Chronicler puts great stress on this because, when he was writing up these books, Levites had a key role as regards the teaching of the Law, the splendour of the liturgy, and the fostering of the people's religious hope and solidarity.

4. THE BOOKS OF CHRONICLES IN THE LIGHT OF THE NEW TESTAMENT

The books of Chronicles end with the divine decree to rebuild the temple of Jerusalem and send the exiles home (cf. 2 Chron 36:22–23). By the time these books were redacted (the fourth century BC), that decree had been put into effect, and the people once again were dwelling in the promised land and worshipping God in the temple in the manner laid down by David, according to these books. The people and its priests are now, therefore, the "successors" of David, and in the temple and its liturgy they discover their true identity and

the guarantee of divine protection. Chronicles, therefore, does not make it quite clear that this was a temporary situation and one that would remain so until the Messiah came, the successor of David; although the attention focused on David might seem to imply that outcome. Instead, this history gives the impression that God's Covenant with David is already being fulfilled, just as it was in the case of those successors of David who were faithful to God. In this sense one must say that there is no dimension of messianic hope in 1 and 2 Chronicles.

However, these books do mark an important stage in the unfolding of divine Revelation which will reach its climax in the New Testament. Perhaps more strongly than anywhere else in the Old Testament, they evidence awareness of the presence of God among his people through the temple of Jerusalem and the institutions connected with it, and the continuity of that presence as long as due worship is offered there. In this sense 1 and 2 Chronicles prepare the way for the Revelation of the New Testament, according to which God has become truly present in the midst of his people and all mankind through the incarnation of his Son Jesus Christ. The teaching contained in Chronicles gives us a better grasp of Jesus' zeal for the temple (cf. Mt 21:12–17) and of how he could even identify himself with the temple by describing himself as the definitive dwelling place of God among men (cf. Mt 12:6; Jn 2:21). The physical death of Jesus (cf. Jn 2:18–22), a true sacrifice and an act of worship to the Father, "presaged the destruction of the Temple, which would manifest the dawning of a new age in the history of salvation: 'The hour is coming when neither on this mountain nor in Jerusalem will you worship the Father' (Jn 4:21; cf. Jn 4:23–24; Mt 27:51; Heb 9:11, Acts 21:22)."[1] Jesus, then, is the new David who provides in himself the place where men—not just the Jews, but all mankind—truly meet God.

1. *Cathechism of the Catholic Church*, 586.

1. GENEALOGIES PRIOR TO THE MONARCHY*

Gen 5; 10:1–32
Lk 3:36–38

From Adam to Noah

1 *[1]Adam, Seth, Enosh; [2]Kenan, Ma-halalel, Jared; [3]Enoch, Methuselah, Lamech; [4]Noah, Shem, Ham, and Japheth.

Gen 10:2–4

The Japhethites

[5]The sons of Japheth: Gomer, Magog, Madai, Javan, Tubal, Meshech, and Tiras. [6]The sons of Gomer: Ashkenaz, Diphath, and Togarmah. [7]The sons of Javan: Elishah, Tarshish, Kittim, and Rodanim.

***1:1—9:44.** The genealogies given in these chapters consist of two lists, the first from Adam to Israel (1:1–34) and Esau (1:35–54), the second from the sons of Israel to David (2:1—9:44). Both lists are devised in line with the message that gives shape to the entire book—that is, to show that the people of God that has come back from exile has kept the same identity as it had from Adam and is, therefore, the heir of the promises of salvation; after the exile its life hinges on the figure of David and on the city of Jerusalem. The lists are based on lines of descent already to be found in the earlier books—from Genesis to Kings; but they do not follow them exactly, for they often omit names which might distract attention from the main genealogical tree (for example, they do not give the descendants of Cain listed in Genesis 4:17–24) and they add others, as is the case in the Levite genealogies.

Even though these chapters do not give much detail about the great events in the history of Israel, they do provide short items of information about some significant episodes, especially those to do with the settlement of the tribes in the various parts of the promised land. Even here, the account keeps focusing on the city of Jerusalem, the enduring continuity of the people and the roles proper to each tribe, particularly those of the Levites. Thus, no reference is made to Moses and the Exodus, for fear that would cloud the line of descent from Abraham; on the other hand, stress is put on events, persons or places which help to accentuate the identity of the people. And so, whereas in Genesis the tribe of Judah comes fourth among the sons of Jacob, that is, Israel (cf. Gen 29:35; 35:23; 46:12; 49:8; cf. also 1 Chron 2:1), here it moves to first place (cf. 1 Chron 2:3; 12:25), because it received Jerusalem as its inheritance and was the tribe of David. The same happens with the tribe of Levi, which had such an important role in the post-exilic period: a number of Levite genealogies are provided, and Levite cities are listed (cf. 6:1–70).

In the first great period (1:1–54), Jacob is called Israel (v. 34), probably because the Chronicler is thinking more about the unity of the people than about

---

[1] [1]Adam, Seth, Enos, [2]Cainan, Malaleel, Iared, [3]Henoch, Mathusala, Lamech, [4]Noe, Sem, Cham et Iapheth. [5]Filii Iapheth: Gomer, Magog, Madai et Iavan, Thubal, Mosoch, Thiras. [6]Porro filii Gomer: Aschenez et Riphath et Thogorma. [7]Filii autem Iavan: Elisa et Tharsis, Cetthim et Rodanim. [8]Filii

The Hamites

Gen 10:6–8

[8]The sons of Ham: Cush, Egypt, Put, and Canaan. [9]The sons of Cush: Seba, Havilah, Sabta, Raama, and Sabteca. The sons of Raamah: Sheba and Dedan. [10]Cush was the father of Nimrod; he began to be a mighty one in the earth.

Gen 10:13–18

[11]Egypt was the father of Ludim, Anamim, Lehabim, Naphtuhim, [12]Pathrusim, Casluhim (whence came the Philistines), and Caphtorim.

[13]Canaan was the father of Sidon his first-born, and Heth, [14]and the Jebusites, the Amorites, the Girgashites, [15]the Hivites, the Arkites, the Sinites, [16]the Arvadites, the Zemarites, and the Hamathites.

---

historical facts to do with its progenitor. Considerable attention is given to the descendants of Esau (vv. 35–53), but the book makes no further mention of them: this gives a degree of importance to the Edomites (descendants of Esau/Edom)—and yet very little compared with the Israelites (descendants of Jacob/Israel), who take up the rest of the book. There is only a passing reference to an historical event: "before any king reigned over the Israelites" (v. 43), thereby putting on record the fact that the monarchy marked a key stage in the history of the people of Abraham; one could say that everything prior to it was prehistory.

The second period (chaps. 2–7) covers the long years from the birth of the tribes in Israel to their eventual settlement in the various parts of Palestine. Here again the Chronicler's purpose dictates the form of the genealogical lists: he highlights the line of descent from Judah (chap. 2) and, particularly, the line of David (chap. 3), who marks the apex of the history and is the key reference point for the identity of the people. Importance is given also to the tribe of Benjamin, in whose territory the holy city of Jerusalem is located (7:6–12; 8:1–40). And, finally, the focus turns to the tribe of Levi (6:1–66), spelling out who its members are, what functions they perform in the temple, and what cities are theirs.

Chapters 8–9 are a sort of appendix dealing with the descendants of Benjamin (the most prominent of them being Saul, the first king of Israel) and with the inhabitants of Jerusalem before and after the exile. Prominent among those who returned and regained their ancient holdings are the Levite families. These last genealogies put much emphasis on the close connexion between the repatriates and the forebears of Saul and David; and therefore on their right to inherit the promises made to the patriarchs. The teaching that underlies these lists survives up to the New Testament, where the genealogies of Jesus (cf. Mt 1:1–16; Lk 3:23–28) link him to the patriarchs, to David, and to the repatriated exiles. By doing this, the

Cham: Chus et Mesraim, Phut et Chanaan. [9]Filii autem Chus: Saba et Hevila, Sabatha et Regma et Sabathacha. Porro filii Regma: Saba et Dedan. [10]Chus autem genuit Nemrod: iste coepit esse potens in terra. [11]Mesraim vero genuit Ludim et Anamim et Laabim et Nephthuim, [12]Phetrusim quoque et Chasluim, de quibus egressi sunt Philisthim et Caphtorim. [13]Chanaan vero genuit Sidonem primogenitum, Heth, [14]Iebusaeum quoque et Amorraeum et Gergesaeum [15]Hevaeumque et Aracaeum et Sinaeum, [16]Aradium quoque et Samaraeum et Emathaeum. [17]Filii Sem: Elam et Assur et Arphaxad

Gen 10:22–29

The Semites

[17]The sons of Shem: Elam, Asshur, Arpachshad, Lud, Aram, Uz, Hul, Gether, and Meshech. [18]Arpachshad was the father of Shelah; and Shelah was the father of Eber. [19]To Eber were born two sons: the name of the one was Peleg (for in his days the earth was divided), and the name of his brother Joktan. [20]Joktan was the father of Almodad, Sheleph, Hazarmaveth, Jerah, [21]Hadoram, Uzal, Diklah, [22]Ebal, Abima-el, Sheba, [23]Ophir, Havilah, and Jobab; all these were the sons of Joktan.

Gen 11:10–26
Lk 3:34–35

[24]Shem, Arpachshad, Shelah; [25]Eber, Peleg, Reu; [26]Serug, Nahor, Terah; [27]Abram, that is, Abraham.

The Ishmaelites

Gen 25:12–18
Gen 25:13–16

[28]The sons of Abraham: Isaac and Ishmael. [29]These are their genealogies: the first-born of Ishmael, Nebaioth; and Kedar, Adbeel, Mibsam, [30]Mishma, Dumah, Massa, Hadad, Tema, [31]Jetur, Naphish, and Kedemah. These are the sons of Ishmael. [32]The sons of Keturah, Abraham's concubine: she bore Zimran, Jokshan, Medan, Midian, Ishbak, and Shuah. The sons of Jokshan: Sheba and Dedan. [33]The sons of Midian: Ephah, Epher, Hanoch, Abida, and Eldaah. All these were the descendants of Keturah.

Gen 25:2–4

Gen 25:19
Mt 1:2
Gen 36:10–17

[34]Abraham was the father of Isaac. The sons of Isaac: Esau and Israel. [35]The sons of Esau: Eliphaz, Reuel, Jeush, Jalam, and

---

evangelists are saying that Jesus marks the plenitude of salvation history, a history which never suffered interruption.

1:5–16. The genealogies of Japheth (cf. Gen 10:2–4) and those of Ham (cf. Gen 10:6–9) are short compared with those of Shem (v. 28). In this way the sacred writer is able to focus on Noah and Abraham as two figures relevant to salvation history. Note that of the two sons of Abraham (v. 28) Israel is named before Ishmael, even though Ishmael was older than he.

et Lud et Aram. Filii autem Aram: Us et Hul et Gether et Mes. [18]Arphaxad autem genuit Sala, qui et ipse genuit Heber. [19]Porro Heber nati sunt duo filii: nomen uni Phaleg, quia in diebus eius divisa est terra, et nomen fratris eius Iectan. [20]Iectan autem genuit Elmodad et Saleph et Asarmoth et Iare, [21]Adoram quoque et Uzal et Decla, [22]Ebal etiam et Abimael et Saba necnon [23]et Ophir et Hevila et Iobab; omnes isti filii Iectan. [24]Sem, Arphaxad, Sala, [25]Heber, Phaleg, Reu, [26]Seruch, Nachor, Thare, [27]Abram: iste est Abraham. [28]Filii autem Abraham: Isaac et Ismael. [29]Et hae generationes eorum: primogenitus Ismaelis Nabaioth et Cedar et Adbeel et Mabsam, [30]Masma et Duma, Massa, Hadad et Thema, [31]Iethur, Naphis, Cedma; hi sunt filii Ismaelis. [32]Filii autem Ceturae concubinae Abraham, quos genuit: Zamran, Iecsan, Madan, Madian, Iesboc, Sue. Porro filii Iecsan: Saba et Dedan. Filii autem Dedan: Assurim et Latusim et Loommim. [33]Filii autem Madian: Epha et Opher et Henoch et Abida et Eldaa. Omnes hi filii Ceturae. [34]Generavit autem Abraham Isaac, cuius fuerunt filii Esau et Israel. [35]Filii Esau: Eliphaz, Rahuel, Iehus, Ialam, Core. [36]Filii Eliphaz: Theman, Omar, Sepho, Gatham, Cenez, Thamna, Amalec. [37]Filii Rahuel: Nahath, Zara, Samma, Meza. [38]Filii Seir: Lotan, Sobal, Sebeon, Ana, Dison, Eser, Disan. [39]Filii Lotan: Hori, Hemam; soror autem Lotan fuit Thamna. [40]Filii Sobal: Alvan et Manahath et Ebal et Sepho et

Korah. [36]The sons of Eliphaz: Teman, Omar, Zephi, Gatam, Kenaz, Timna, and Amalek. [37]The sons of Reuel: Nahath, Zerah, Shammah, and Mizzah. Gen 36:15–17

Sons of Seir

[38]The sons of Seir: Lotan, Shobal, Zibeon, Anah, Dishon, Ezer, and Dishan. [39]The sons of Lotan: Hori and Homam; and Lotan's sister was Timna. [40]The sons of Shobal: Alian, Manahath, Ebal, Shephi, and Onam. The sons of Zibeon: Aiah and Anah. [41]The sons of Anah: Dishon. The sons of Dishon: Hamran, Eshban, Ithran, and Cheran. [42]The sons of Ezer: Bilhan, Zaavan, and Jaakan. The sons of Dishan: Uz and Aran. Gen 36:20–28

Kings of Edom

Gen 36:31–39

[43]These are the kings who reigned in the land of Edom before any king reigned over the Israelites: Bela the son of Beor, the name of whose city was Dinhabah. [44]When Bela died, Jobab the son of Zerah of Bozrah reigned in his stead. [45]When Jobab died, Husham of the land of the Temanites reigned in his stead. [46]When Husham died, Hadad the son of Bedad, who defeated Midian in the country of Moab, reigned in his stead; and the name of his city was Avith. [47]When Hadad died, Samlah of Masrekah reigned in his stead. [48]When Samlah died, Shaul of Rehoboth on the Euphrates reigned in his stead. [49]When Shaul died, Baal-hanan, the son of Achbor, reigned in his stead. [50]When Baal-hanan died, Hadad reigned in his stead; and the name of his city was Pai, and his wife's name Mehetabel the daughter of Matred, the daughter of Mezahab. [51]And Hadad died.

The chiefs of Edom were: chiefs Timna, Aliah, Jetheth, [52]Oholibamah, Elah, Pinon, [53]Kenaz, Teman, Mibzar, [54]Magdi-el, and Iram; these are the chiefs of Edom. Gen 36:40–43

Onam. Filii Sebeon: Aia et Ana. [41]Filii Ana: Dison. Filii Dison: Hemdan et Eseban et Iethran et Charran. [42]Filii Eser: Bilhan et Zavan et Iacan. Filii Disan: Us et Aran. [43]Isti sunt reges, qui imperaverunt in terra Edom, antequam esset rex super filios Israel: Bela filius Beor, et nomen civitatis eius Denaba. [44]Mortuus est autem Bela, et regnavit pro eo Iobab filius Zarae de Bosra. [45]Cumque et Iobab fuisset mortuus, regnavit pro eo Husam de terra Themanorum. [46]Obiit quoque et Husam, et regnavit pro eo Adad filius Badad, qui percussit Madian in terra Moab; et nomen civitatis eius Avith. [47]Cumque et Adad fuisset mortuus, regnavit pro eo Semla de Masreca. [48]Sed et Semla mortuus est; et regnavit pro eo Saul de Rohoboth, quae iuxta amnem sita est. [49]Mortuo quoque Saul, regnavit pro eo Baalhanan filius Achobor. [50]Sed et hic mortuus est, et regnavit pro eo Adad, cuius urbis fuit nomen Phau; et appellata est uxor eius Meetabel filia Matred filiae Mezaab. [51]Adad autem mortuo, duces pro regibus in Edom esse coeperunt: dux Thamna, dux Alva, dux Ietheth, [52]dux Oolibama, dux Ela, dux Phinon, [53]dux Cenez, dux Theman, dux Mabsar, [54]dux Magdiel, dux Iram. Hi duces Edom. **[2]** [1]Filii autem Israel: Ruben, Simeon, Levi, Iuda, Issachar et Zabulon, [2]Dan, Ioseph, Beniamin, Nephthali, Gad, Aser. [3]Filii Iudae: Her, Onan et

Gen 35:23–26
Lk 3:32–34

Descendants of Judah

2 [1]These are the sons of Israel: Reuben, Simeon, Levi, Judah, Issachar, Zebulun, [2]Dan, Joseph, Benjamin, Naphtali, Gad, and Asher. [3]The sons of Judah: Er, Onan, and Shelah; these three Bath-shua the Canaanitess bore to him. Now Er, Judah's first-born, was wicked in the sight of the LORD, and he slew him. [4]His daughter-in-law Tamar also bore him Perez and Zerah. Judah had five sons in all.

Gen 38:2–5,7
Gen 38:27–30
Mt 1:3

[5]The sons of Perez: Hezron and Hamul. [6]The sons of Zerah: Zimri, Ethan, Heman, Calcol, and Dara, five in all. [7]The sons of Carmi: Achar, the troubler of Israel, who transgressed in the matter of the devoted thing; [8]and Ethan's son was Azariah.

Gen 46:12
1 Kings 5:11
Josh 7

[9]The sons of Hezron, that were born to him: Jerahmeel, Ram, and Chelubai. [10]Ram was the father of Amminadab, and Amminadab was the father of Nahshon, prince of the sons of Judah. [11]Nahshon was the father of Salma, Salma of Boaz, [12]Boaz of Obed, Obed of Jesse. [13]Jesse was the father of Eliab his first-born, Abinadab the second, Shimea the third, [14]Nethanel the fourth, Raddai the fifth, [15]Ozem the sixth, David the seventh; [16]and their sisters were Zeruiah and Abigail. The sons of Zeruiah: Abishai, Joab, and Asahel, three. [17]Abigail bore Amasa, and the father of Amasa was Jether the Ishmaelite.

Mt 1:4–6a
Num 1:7
Ruth 4:19–22
Lk 3:31

[18]Caleb the son of Hezron had children by his wife Azubah, and by Jerioth; and these were her sons: Jesher, Shobab, and Ardon. [19]When Azubah died, Caleb married Ephrath,[a] who bore him Hur. [20]Hur was the father of Uri, and Uri was the father of Bezalel.

Josh 14:6
1 Chron 2:24ff; 4:11ff

2:15. David is the foremost descendant of Judah. According to 1 Samuel 17:12, 14, he was the youngest of eight brothers, but here he is given the symbolically significant seventh place.

Sela; hi tres nati sunt ei de filia Sue Chananitide. Fuit autem Her primogenitus Iudae malus coram Domino, et occidit eum. [4]Thamar autem nurus eius peperit ei Phares et Zara; omnes ergo filii Iudae quinque. [5] Filii autem Phares: Esrom et Hamul. [6]Filii quoque Zarae: Zamri et Ethan et Heman, Chalchol quoque et Darda; simul quinque. [7]Filii Charmi: Achar, qui turbavit Israel et peccavit in furto anathematis. [8]Filii Ethan: Azarias. [9]Filii autem Esrom, qui nati sunt ei: Ierameel et Aram et Chaleb. [10]Porro Aram genuit Aminadab, Aminadab autem genuit Naasson principem filiorum Iudae, [11]Naasson quoque genuit Salmon, de quo ortus est Booz. [12]Booz vero genuit Obed, qui et ipse genuit Isai. [13]Isai autem genuit primogenitum Eliab, secundum Abinadab, tertium Samma, [14]quartum Nathanael, quintum Raddai, [15]sextum Asom, septimum David. [16]Quorum sorores fuerunt: Sarvia et Abigail; filii Sarviae: Abisai, Ioab et Asael, tres. [17]Abigail autem genuit Amasa, cuius pater fuit Iether Ismaelites. [18]Chaleb vero filius Esrom genuit de uxore sua nomine Azuba, de qua nati sunt Ierioth, Ieser et Sobab et Ardon. [19]Cumque mortua fuisset Azuba, accepit uxorem Chaleb Ephratha, quae peperit ei Hur. [20]Porro Hur genuit Uri, et Uri genuit Beseleel. [21]Post haec ingressus est Esrom ad filiam Machir patris Galaad et accepit eam, cum ipse esset annorum sexaginta; quae peperit ei Segub. [22]Sed et Segub genuit Iair, qui

a. Gk Vg: Heb *in Caleb Ephrathah*

[21]Afterward Hezron went in to the daughter of Machir the father of Gilead, whom he married when he was sixty years old; and she bore him Segub; [22]and Segub was the father of Jair, who had twenty-three cities in the land of Gilead. [23]But Geshur and Aram took from them Havvoth-jair, Kenath and its villages, sixty towns. All these were descendants of Machir, the father of Gilead. [24]After the death of Hezron, Caleb went in to Ephrathah,[a] the wife of Hezron his father, and she bore him Ashhur, the father of Tekoa.

Num 32:41–42

[25]The sons of Jerahmeel, the first-born of Hezron: Ram, his first-born, Bunah, Oren, Ozem, and Ahijah. [26]Jerahmeel also had another wife, whose name was Atarah; she was the mother of Onam. [27]The sons of Ram, the first-born of Jerahmeel: Maaz, Jamin, and Eker. [28]The sons of Onam: Shammai and Jada. The sons of Shammai: Nadab and Abishur. [29]The name of Abishur's wife was Abihail, and she bore him Ahban and Molid. [30]The sons of Nadab: Seled and Appa-im; and Seled died childless. [31]The sons of Appa-im: Ishi. The sons of Ishi: Sheshan. The sons of Sheshan: Ahlai. [32]The sons of Jada, Shammai's brother: Jether and Jonathan; and Jether died childless. [33]The sons of Jonathan: Peleth and Zaza. These were the descendants of Jerahmeel. [34]Now Sheshan had no sons, only daughters; but Sheshan had an Egyptian slave, whose name was Jarha. [35]So Sheshan gave his daughter in marriage to Jarha his slave; and she bore him Attai. [36]Attai was the father of Nathan and Nathan of Zabad. [37]Zabad was the father of Ephlal, and Ephlal of Obed. [38]Obed was the father of Jehu, and Jehu of Azariah. [39]Azariah was the father of Helez, and Helez of Ele-asah. [40]Ele-asah was the father of Sismai, and Sismai of Shallum. [41]Shallum was the father of Jekamiah, and Jekamiah of Elishama.

1 Sam 27:10

---

possedit viginti tres civitates in terra Galaad. [23]Cepitque Gesur et Aram oppida Iair ipsis et Canath et viculos eius sexaginta civitates. Omnes isti filii Machir patris Galaad. [24]Cum autem mortuus esset Esrom, ingressus est Chaleb ad Ephratha uxorem Esrom patris sui. Habuit quoque Esrom uxorem Abia, quae peperit ei Ashur patrem Thecue. [25]Nati sunt autem filii Ierameel primogeniti Esrom: Ram primogenitus eius et Buna et Aran et Asom et Ahia. [26]Duxit quoque uxorem alteram Ierameel nomine Atara, quae fuit mater Onam. [27]Sed et filii Ram primogeniti Ierameel fuerunt: Moos et Iamin et Acar. [28]Onam autem habuit filios: Sammai et Iada. Filii autem Sammai: Nadab et Abisur. [29]Nomen vero uxoris Abisur Abiail, quae peperit ei Ahobban et Molid. [30]Filii autem Nadab fuerunt Saled et Apphaim; mortuus est autem Saled absque liberis. [31]Filius vero Apphaim: Iesi, qui Iesi genuit Sesan; porro Sesan genuit Oholai. [32]Filii autem Iada fratris Semmei: Iether et Ionathan; sed et Iether mortuus est absque liberis. [33]Porro Ionathan genuit Phaleth et Ziza. Isti fuerunt filii Ierameel. [34]Sesan autem non habuit filios sed filias et servum Aegyptium nomine Ieraa; [35]deditque ei filiam suam uxorem, quae peperit ei Eththei. [36]Eththei autem genuit Nathan, et Nathan genuit Zabad; [37]Zabad quoque genuit Ophlal, et Ophlal genuit Obed. [38]Obed genuit Iehu, Iehu genuit Azariam; [39]Azarias genuit Helles, Helles genuit Elasa. [40]Elasa genuit Sisamoi, Sisamoi genuit Sellum; [41]Sellum genuit Iecemiam, Iecemias genuit Elisama. [42]Filii autem Chaleb fratris Ierameel: Mesa primogenitus eius, ipse est pater Ziph; et filius eius

a. Gk Vg: Heb *in Caleb Ephrathah*

Josh 14:6
1 Chron 2:18ff; 4:11ff

[42]The sons of Caleb the brother of Jerahmeel: Mareshah[b] his first-born, who was the father of Ziph. The sons of Mareshah: Hebron.[c] [43]The sons of Hebron: Korah, Tappuah, Rekem, and Shema. [44]Shema was the father of Raham, the father of Jorke-am; and Rekem was the father of Shammai. [45]The son of Shammai: Maon; and Maon was the father of Bethzur. [46]Ephah also, Caleb's concubine, bore Haran, Moza, and Gazez; and Haran was the father of Gazez. [47]The sons of Jahdai: Regem, Jotham, Geshan, Pelet, Ephah, and Shaaph. [48]Maacah, Caleb's concubine, bore Sheber and Tirhanah. [49]She also bore Shaaph the father of Madmannah, Sheva the father of Machbenah and the father of Gibe-a; and the daughter of Caleb was Achsah. [50]These were the descendants of Caleb.

Josh 15:16–19
1 Chron 2:19; 4:1ff

The sons[d] of Hur the first-born of Ephrathah: Shobal the father of Kiriath-jearim, [51]Salma, the father of Bethlehem, and Hareph the father of Beth-gader. [52]Shobal the father of Kiriath-jearim had other sons: Haroeh, half of the Menuhoth. [53]And the families of Kiriath-jearim: the Ithrites, the Puthites, the Shumathites, and the Mishra-ites; from these came the Zorathites and the Eshtaolites. [54]The sons of Salma: Bethlehem, the Netophathites, Atroth-beth-joab, and half of the Manahathites, the Zorites. [55]The families also of the scribes that dwelt at Jabez: the Tirathites, the Shime-athites, and the Sucathites. These are the Kenites who came from Hammath, the father of the house of Rechab.

Judg 13:2; 18:2
Num 24:31
2 Kings 10:15

Sons of David

2 Sam 3:2–5

3 [1]These are the sons of David that were born to him in Hebron: the first-born Amnon, by Ahino-am the Jezreelitess; the second Daniel, by Abigail the Carmelitess, [2]the third Absalom, whose

---

Maresa pater Hebron. [43]Porro filii Hebron: Core et Thapphua et Recem et Samma; [44]Samma autem genuit Raham patrem Iercaam, et Recem genuit Sammai. [45]Filius Sammai: Maon, et Maon pater Bethsur. [46]Epha autem concubina Chaleb peperit Charran et Mosa et Gezez; porro Charran genuit Gezez. [47]Filii Iahaddai: Regem et Iotham et Gesan et Phalet et Epha et Saaph. [48]Concubina Chaleb Maacha peperit Saber et Tharana. [49]Genuit autem Saaph pater Madmena Sue patrem Machbena et patrem Gabaa. Filia vero Chaleb fuit Achsa. [50]Hi erant filii Chaleb. Filii Hur primogeniti Ephratha: Sobal pater Cariathiarim, [51]Salmon pater Bethlehem, Hariph pater Bethgader. [52]Fuerunt autem filii Sobal patris Cariathiarim Raaia, dimidium Manahat [53]et cognationes Cariathiarim: Iethraei et Phutaei et Sumathaei et Maseraei. Ex his egressi sunt Saraitae et Esthaolitae. [54]Filii Salmon: Bethlehem et Netophathitae, Atarothbethioab et dimidium Manahat de Saraa, [55]cognationes quoque de Cariathsepher habitantes in Iabes: Therathaei, Semathaei et Suchathaei. Hi sunt Cinaei, qui orti sunt de Ammath patre domus Rechab. **[3]** [1]David vero hos habuit filios, qui ei nati sunt in Hebron: primogenitum Amnon ex Achinoam Iezrahelitide, secundum Daniel de Abigail de Carmel, [2]tertium Absalom filium Maacha filiae

b. Gk: Heb *Mesha* **c.** Heb *the father of Hebron* **d.** Gk Vg: Heb *son*

mother was Maacah, the daughter of Talmai, king of Geshur; the fourth Adonijah, whose mother was Haggith; [3]the fifth Shephatiah, by Abital; the sixth Ithream, by his wife Eglah; [4]six were born to him in Hebron, where he reigned for seven years and six months. And he reigned thirty-three years in Jerusalem. [5]These were born to him in Jerusalem: Shime-a, Shobab, Nathan and Solomon, four by Bath-shua, the daughter of Ammi-el; [6]then Ibhar, Elishama, Eliphelet, [7]Nogah, Nepheg, Japhia, [8]Elishama, Eliada, and Eliphelet, nine. [9]All these were David's sons, besides the sons of the concubines; and Tamar was their sister.

2 Sam 5:14–16
1 Chron 14:3–7
Mt 1:7–12
Lk 3:31
Sam 13:1ff

Sons of Solomon

[10]The descendants of Solomon: Rehoboam, Abijah his son, Asa his son, Jehoshaphat his son, [11]Joram his son, Ahaziah his son, Joash his son, [12]Amaziah his son, Azariah his son, Jotham his son, [13]Ahaz his son, Hezekiah his son, Manasseh his son, [14]Amon his son, Josiah his son. [15]The sons of Josiah: Johanan the first-born, the second Jehoiakim, the third Zedekiah, the fourth Shallum. [16]The

Mt 1:6b–11
2 Chron 36:1ff

3:1. The list of David's sons born in Hebron agrees with that in 2 Samuel 3:2–5, except that the second son, Chileab, is called Daniel in Chronicles; he could have had both names, and may have died very young; his brothers Amnon, Absalom and Adonijah, all aspirants to David's throne, achieved more prominence.

3:5–6. Solomon is named last among the sons of Bathsheba, not because he was the youngest, but because the author, by putting his name last in the list, wants to show that he was the most important of her children.

"Bath-shua, the daughter of Ammiel" (v. 5): this is how the name appears in the Hebrew text; it may be another form of Bathsheba; but in 2 Samuel 11:3 Bathsheba was the daughter of Eliam. Variants of this sort can be explained by the fact that the Chronicler probably used, in addition to Samuel and Kings, other, extrabiblical sources which have not come down to us. There also seems to be a repetition or confusion of the names Elishama and Eliphelet in v. 6.

3:10–24. Two lists are given for the descendants of Solomon. The first (vv. 10–16), gives the kings of Judah down to

Tholmai regis Gesur, quartum Adoniam filium Haggith, [3]quintum Saphatiam ex Abital, sextum Iethraam de Egla uxore sua. [4]Sex ergo nati sunt ei in Hebron, ubi regnavit septem annis et sex mensibus. Triginta autem et tribus annis regnavit in Ierusalem. [5]Porro in Ierusalem nati sunt ei filii: Samua et Sobab et Nathan et Salomon, quattuor de Bethsabee filia Ammiel; [6]Iebahar quoque et Elisama et Eliphalet [7]et Noga et Napheg et Iaphia [8]necnon Elisama et Eliada et Eliphalet, novem. [9]Omnes hi filii David absque filiis concubinarum; habueruntque sororem Thamar. [10]Filius autem Salomonis Roboam, cuius Abia filius genuit Asa; de hoc quoque natus est Iosaphat [11]pater Ioram; qui Ioram genuit Ochoziam, ex quo ortus est Ioas. [12]Et huius Amasias filius genuit Azariam, porro Azariae filius Ioatham [13]procreavit Achaz patrem Ezechiae, de quo natus est Manasses. [14]Sed et Manasses genuit Amon patrem Iosiae; [15]filii

2 Kings 24–25 Jer 22:24 Mt 1:12 descendants of Jehoiakim: Jeconiah his son, Zedekiah his son; [17]and the sons of Jeconiah, the captive: She-altiel his son, [18]Malchiram, Pedaiah, Shenazzar, Jekamiah, Hoshama, and Nedabiah; [19]and the Mt 1:12 sons of Pedaiah: Zerubbabel and Shime-i; and the sons of Zerubbabel: Meshullam and Hananiah, and Shelomith was their sister; [20]and Hashubah, Ohel, Berechiah, Hasadiah, and Jushab-hesed, five. [21]The sons of Hananiah: Pelatiah and Jeshaiah, his son[e] Rephaiah, his son[e] Arnan, his son[e] Obadiah, his son[e] Ezra 8:3 Shecaniah. [22]The sons of Shecaniah: Shemaiah. And the sons of Shemaiah: Hattush, Igal, Bariah, Neariah, and Shaphat, six. [23]The sons of Neariah: Eli-o-enai, Hizkiah, and Azrikam, three. [24]The sons of Eli-o-enai: Hodaviah, Eliashib, Pelaiah, Akkub, Johanan, Delaiah, and Anani, seven.

Descendants of Judah

1 Chron 2:3 4 [1]The sons of Judah: Perez, Hezron, Carmi, Hur, and Shobal. [2]Re-aiah the son of Shobal was the father of Jahath, and Jahath was the father of Ahumai and Lahad. These were the families of 1 Chron 2:50 the Zorathites. [3]These were the sons[f] of Etam: Jezreel, Ishma, and Idbash; and the name of their sister was Hazzelelponi, [4]and Penuel

---

the exile; the second (vv. 17–24), the leaders repatriated from Babylon. The exile is alluded to by the description of Jeconiah as "the captive" (v. 17); this serves to stress the link between the Chronicler's contemporaries and those who had been part of the kingdom of Judah.

4:1–23. This genealogy of Judah repeats, with some variants, that given in 2:3–55, and it shows the most important tribe to be that of Judah, from which David will be born in Bethlehem (v. 4).

Verses 9–10 indicate the importance of Jabez; in 2:55 Jabez is given as the name of a city. In the genealogical lists the geographical location of a family is often identified with the person who is thought to have been its founder or forebear. The Chronicler makes the point that the growth of the clans was due to special divine protection (v. 10).

autem Iosiae fuerunt: primogenitus Iohanan, secundus Ioachim, tertius Sedecias, quartus Sellum. [16]Filii Ioachim: Iechonias filius eius, Sedecias filius eius. [17]Filii Iechoniae captivi fuerunt: Salathiel filius eius, [18]Melchiram, Phadaia, Senasser et Iecemias, Hosama et Nadabias. [19]De Phadaia orti sunt Zorobabel et Semei. Zorobabel genuit Mosollam, Hananiam et Salomith sororem eorum, [20]Hasabamque et Ohol et Barachiam et Hasadiam, Iosabhesed, quinque. [21]Filii autem Hananiae: Pheltias, Iesaias, Raphaia, Arnan, Abdia et Sechenias. [22]Filii Secheniae: Semeia et Hattus et Igal et Baria et Naaria et Saphat, sex numero. [23]Filii Naariae: Elioenai et Ezechias et Ezricam, tres. [24]Filii Elioenai: Odovia et Eliasib et Pheleia et Accub et Iohanan et Dalaia et Anani, septem. **[4]** [1]Filii Iudae: Phares, Esrom et Charmi et Hur et Sobal. [2]Reaia vero filius Sobal genuit Iahath, de quo nati sunt Ahumai et Laad: hae cognationes

e. Gk Compare Syr Vg: Heb *sons of* **f.** Gk Compare Vg: Heb *father*

was the father of Gedor, and Ezer the father of Hushah. These were the sons of Hur, the first-born of Ephrathah, the father of Bethlehem. [5]Ashhur, the father of Tekoa, had two wives, Helah and Naarah; [6]Naarah bore him Ahuzzam, Hepher, Temeni, and Haahashtari. These were the sons of Naarah. [7]The sons of Helah: Zereth, Izhar, and Ethnan. [8]Koz was the father of Anub, Zobebah, and the families of Aharhel the son of Harum. [9]Jabez was more honourable than his brothers; and his mother called his name Jabez, saying, "Because I bore him in pain." [10]Jabez called on the God of Israel, saying, "Oh that thou wouldst bless me and enlarge my border, and that thy hand might be with me, and that thou wouldst keep me from harm so that it might not hurt me!" And God granted what he asked. [11]Chelub, the brother of Shuhah, was the father of Mehir, who was the father of Eshton. [12]Eshton was the father of Bethrapha, Paseah, and Tehinnah the father of Irnahash. These are the men of Recah. [13]The sons of Kenaz: Othni-el and Seraiah; and the sons of Othni-el: Hathath and Meonothai.[g] [14]Meonothai was the father of Ophrah; and Seraiah was the father of Joab the father of Ge-harashim,[h] so-called because they were craftsmen. [15]The sons of Caleb the son of Jephunneh: Iru, Elah, and Naam; and the sons of Elah: Kenaz. [16]The sons of Jehallelel: Ziph, Ziphah, Tiri-a, and Asarel. [17]The sons of Ezrah: Jether, Mered, Epher, and Jalon. These are the sons of Bithi-ah, the daughter of Pharaoh, whom Mered married;[i] and she conceived and bore[j] Miriam, Shammai, and Ishbah, the father of Eshtemoa.

Gen 35:18
1 Chron 2:55

Josh 14:6
1 Chron 2:9,18ff,42ff

Judg 1:13

Num 13:6
Neh 11:35

4:17–19. The Greek version of this passage is different from the Hebrew, and neither of them is easy to interpret.

Saraitarum. [3]Et ista stirps Etam: Iezrahel et Iesema et Iedebos, nomenque sororis eorum Asalelphuni. [4]Phanuel autem pater Gedor et Ezer pater Hosa: isti sunt filii Hur primogeniti Ephratha patris Bethlehem. [5]Ashur vero patris Thecue erant duae uxores: Halaa et Naara. [6]Peperit autem ei Naara Oozam et Hepher et Themani et Ahasthari: isti sunt filii Naara. [7]Porro filii Halaa: Sereth et Sohar et Ethnan. [8]Cos autem genuit Anob et Sobeba et cognationes Aharehel filii Arum. [9]Fuit autem Iabes inclitus prae fratribus suis; et mater eius vocavit nomen illius Iabes dicens: «Quia peperi eum in dolore». [10]Invocavit vero Iabes Deum Israel dicens: «Si benedicens benedixeris mihi et dilataveris terminos meos, et fuerit manus tua mecum, et feceris me a malitia non opprimi!». Et praestitit Deus quae precatus est. [11]Chelub autem frater Suaa genuit Mahir, qui fuit pater Esthon. [12]Porro Esthon genuit Bethrapha et Phasea et Tehinna patrem Hirnaas (id est urbis Naas): hi sunt viri Recha. [13]Filii autem Cenez: Othoniel et Saraia; porro filii Othoniel: Hathath et Maonathi. [14]Maonathi genuit Ophra, Saraia autem genuit Ioab patrem Geharasim (id est vallis Artificum): ibi quippe artifices erant. [15]Filii vero Chaleb filii Iephonne: Hir et Ela et Naham; filius quoque Ela: Cenez. [16]Filii quoque Iallelel: Ziph et Zipha, Thiria et Asarel. [17]Et filii Ezra: Iether et Mered et Epher et Ialon. Et genuit Iether Mariam et Sammai et Iesba patrem

g. Gk Vg: Heb lacks *Meonothai* **h.** That is *Valley of craftsmen* **i.** The clause: *These are . . . married* is transposed from verse 18

[18]And his Jewish wife bore Jered the father of Gedor, Heber the father of Soco, and Jekuthiel the father of Zanoah. [19]The sons of the wife of Hodiah, the sister of Naham, were the fathers of Keilah the Garmite and Eshtemoa the Ma-acathite. [20]The sons of Shimon: Amnon, Rinnah, Ben-hanan, and Tilon. The sons of Ishi: Zoheth and Ben-zoheth. [21]The sons of Shelah the son of Judah: Er the father of Lecah, Laadah the father of Mareshah, and the families of the house of linen workers at Beth-ashbea; [22]and Jokim, and the men of Cozeba, and Joash, and Saraph, who ruled in Moab and returned to Lehem[k] (now the records[l] are ancient). [23]These were the potters and inhabitants of Netaim and Gederah; they dwelt there with the king for his work.

1 Chron 2:3

Descendants of Simeon

Gen 46:10
Num 26:12
Gen 25:13–14
1 Chron 1:29–30
Josh 19:1–8

[24]The sons of Simeon: Nemuel, Jamin, Jarib, Zerah, Shaul; [25]Shallum was his son, Mibsam his son, Mishma his son. [26]The sons of Mishma: Hammu-el his son, Zaccur his son, Shime-i his son. [27]Shime-i had sixteen sons and six daughters; but his brothers had not many children, nor did all their family multiply like the men of Judah. [28]They dwelt in Beer-sheba, Moladah, Hazar-shual, [29]Bilhah, Ezem, Tolad, [30]Bethuel, Hormah, Ziklag, [31]Beth-marcaboth, Hazar-susim, Beth-biri, and Sha-araim. These were their cities until

---

4:24–43. The tribe of Simeon and that of Judah occupied the south, but Simeon never grew to the same extent. In addition to naming the descendants (vv. 24–27 and 34–40) the list gives the names not only of the cities that were Simeon's endowment but also of others which the tribe of Simeon annexed, both peaceably and by force of arms (vv. 28–33 and 41–43).

Esthemo. [18b]Hi autem sunt filii Bethiae filiae pharaonis, quam accepit Mered: [18a]peperit Iared patrem Gedor et Heber patrem Socho et Iecuthiel patrem Zanoa. [19]Filii autem uxoris eius Iudaicae sororis Naham patris Ceilae: Dalaia et Simeon pater Ioman. Filii autem Naham patris Ceilae: Garmitae et Esthemo Maachathitarum. [20]Filii quoque Simon: Ammon et Rinna, Benhanan et Thilon. Et filii Iesi: Zoheth et Benzoheth. [21]Filii Sela filii Iudae: Her pater Lecha et Laada pater Maresa et cognationes domus operantium byssum in Bethasbea [22]et Iochim virique Chozeba et Ioas et Saraph, qui principes fuerunt in Moab et qui reversi sunt in Bethlehem: hae autem sunt res veteres. [23]Hi sunt figuli habitantes Netaim et Gedera; apud regem in operibus eius commorati sunt ibi. [24]Filii Simeon: Namuel et Iamin, Iarib, Zara, Saul; [25]Sellum filius eius, Mabsam filius eius, Masma filius eius. [26]Filii Masma: Hamuel filius eius, Zacchur filius eius, Semei filius eius. [27]Filii Semei sedecim et filiae sex; fratres autem eius non habuerunt filios multos, et universa cognatio eorum non potuit adaequare summam filiorum Iudae. [28]Habitaverunt autem in Bersabee et Molada et Asarsual [29]et in Bilha et in Esem et in Tholad [30]et in Bathuel et in Horma et in Siceleg [31]et in Bethmarchaboth et in Asarsusim et in Bethberai et in Saarim:

j. Heb lacks *and bore* **k.** Vg Compare Gk: Heb *and Jashubi-lahem* **l.** Or *matters*

David reigned. [32]And their villages were Etam, Ain, Rimmon, Tochen, and Ashan, five cities, [33]along with all their villages which were round about these cities as far as Baal. These were their settlements, and they kept a genealogical record.

[34]Meshobab, Jamlech, Joshah the son of Amaziah, [35]Joel, Jehu the son of Joshibiah, son of Seraiah, son of Asi-el, [36]Eli-o-enai, Jaakobah, Jeshohaiah, Asaiah, Adi-el, Jesimiel, Benaiah, [37]Ziza the son of Shiphi, son of Allon, son of Jedaiah, son of Shimri, son of Shemaiah—[38]these mentioned by name were princes in their families, and their fathers' houses increased greatly. [39]They journeyed to the entrance of Gedor, to the east side of the valley, to seek pasture for their flocks, [40]where they found rich, good pasture, and the land was very broad, quiet, and peaceful; for the former inhabitants there belonged to Ham. [41]These, registered by name, came in the days of Hezekiah, king of Judah, and destroyed their tents and the Me-unim who were found there, and exterminated them to this day, and settled in their place, because there was pasture there for their flocks. [42]And some of them, five hundred men of the Simeonites, went to Mount Seir, having as their leaders Pelatiah, Ne-ariah, Rephaiah, and Uzziel, the sons of Ishi; [43]and they destroyed the remnant of the Amalekites that had escaped, and they have dwelt there to this day.

Num 1:2

Josh 6:17

Ex 17:8

Descendants of Reuben

5 [1]The sons of Reuben the first-born of Israel (for he was the first-born; but because he polluted his father's couch, his

Gen 35:22; 46:9
Num 26:5ff

5:1–10. The line of Reuben is the first one to be given for the Transjordanian tribes. By way of introduction, the Chronicler mentions some facts to justify three significant things—why the tribe of Reuben lost its privileges,

hae civitates eorum usque ad regem David. [32]Villae quoque eorum: Etam et Ain, Remmon et Thochen et Asan, civitates quinque. [33]Et universi viculi eorum per circuitum civitatum istarum usque ad Baal: haec est habitatio eorum et genealogia. [34]Masobab quoque et Iemlech et Iosa filius Amasiae [35]et Ioel et Iehu filius Iosabiae filii Saraiae filii Asiel [36]et Elioenai et Iacoba et Isuhaia et Asaia et Adiel et Isimiel et Banaia, [37]Ziza quoque filius Sephei filii Allon filii Iedaia filii Semri filii Samaia. [38]Isti nominatim inscripti erant principes in cognationibus suis; et familiae eorum expansae sunt vehementer, [39]et profecti sunt ad introitum Gedor usque ad orientem vallis, ut quaererent pascua gregibus suis. [40]Inveneruntque pascuas uberes et valde bonas et terram latissimam et quietam et fertilem, in qua ante habitaverunt de stirpe Cham. [41]Hi ergo venerunt, qui inscripti erant nominatim, in diebus Ezechiae regis Iudae, et percusserunt tabernacula eorum et Meunitas, qui inventi fuerunt ibi, et deleverunt eos usque in praesentem diem habitaveruntque pro eis, quoniam uberrimas ibidem pascuas reppererunt. [42]De filiis quoque Simeon abierunt in montem Seir viri quingenti habentes principes Pheltiam et Naariam et Raphaiam et Oziel filios Iesi, [43]et percusserunt reliquias, quae evadere potuerant Amalecitarum, et habitaverunt ibi pro eis usque ad diem hanc. **[5]** [1]Filii quoque Ruben primogeniti Israel: ipse quippe fuit primogenitus eius, sed, cum violasset torum patris sui, data sunt primogenita eius filiis Ioseph filii

Gen 49:8–10
Mic 5:2
Mt 2:6
Gen 46:9
Num 26:5

2 Kings 15:29; 16:7

Num 32:37ff

birthright was given to the sons of Joseph the son of Israel, so that he is not enrolled in the genealogy according to the birthright; [2]though Judah became strong among his brothers and a prince was from him, yet the birthright belonged to Joseph), [3]the sons of Reuben, the first-born of Israel: Hanoch, Pallu, Hezron, and Carmi. [4]The sons of Joel: Shemaiah his son, Gog his son, Shime-i his son, [5]Micah his son, Re-aiah his son, Baal his son, [6]Be-erah his son, whom Tilgath-pilneser king of Assyria carried away into exile; he was a chieftain of the Reubenites. [7]And his kinsmen by their families, when the genealogy of their generations was reckoned: the chief, Je-iel, and Zechariah, [8]and Bela the son of Azaz, son of Shema, son of Joel, who dwelt in Aroer, as far as Nebo and Baal-meon. [9]He also dwelt to the east as far as the entrance of the desert this side of the Euphrates, because their cattle had multiplied in the land of Gilead. [10]And in the days of Saul they made war on the Hagrites, who fell by their hand; and they dwelt in their tents throughout all the region east of Gilead.

Gen 46:16
Num 26:15–18
Deut 3:10
Josh 13:24–28

Descendants of Gad

[11]The sons of Gad dwelt over against them in the land of Bashan as far as Salecah: [12]Joel the chief, Shapham the second, Janai, and Shaphat in Bashan. [13]And their kinsmen according to their fathers'

---

even though Reuben was the first-born (v. 1; cf. Gen 35:22); the primacy of the tribe of Judah, for it was from this line that David, "a prince", the great king, would be born (v. 2); and the importance of the tribes of Ephraim and Manasseh which had more extensive territory because they inherited the birthright of Joseph, Jacob's favourite son. All this goes to show that the lists in Chronicles are based more on doctrinal criteria than on chronological exactness.

5:11–22. The tribe of Gad lived in Gilead, west of the Jordan, contiguous with the territory of Reuben. The Chronicler, more interested in the

Israel, ut non computaretur in primogenitum, [2]quia Iuda erat quidem fortissimus inter fratres suos et de stirpe eius principes germinati sunt, primogenita autem reputata sunt Ioseph. [3]Filii ergo Ruben primogeniti Israel: Henoch et Phallu, Hesron et Charmi. [4]Filii Ioel: Semeia filius eius, Gog filius eius, Semei filius eius, [5]Micha filius eius, Reaia filius eius, Baal filius eius, [6]Beera filius eius, quem captivum duxit Theglathphalasar rex Assyriorum, et fuit princeps in tribu Ruben. [7]Fratres autem eius in cognationibus eius, quando numerabantur in genealogiis suis, erant: caput Iehiel, deinde Zacharias; [8]porro Bela filius Azaz filii Samma filii Ioel, ipse habitavit in Aroer usque ad Nabo et Baalmeon. [9]Contra orientalem quoque plagam habitavit usque ad introitum eremi, quae est inde a flumine Euphrate, multum quippe gregum eorum numerus creverat in terra Galaad. [10]In diebus autem Saul proeliati sunt contra Agarenos et interfecerunt illos; habitaveruntque pro eis in tabernaculis eorum in omni plaga, quae respicit ad orientem Galaad. [11]Filii vero Gad e regione eorum habitaverunt in terra Basan usque Salcha: [12]Ioel in capite et Sapham secundus, porro Ianai et Saphat in Basan; [13]fratres vero eorum secundum familias suas: Michael et Mosollam et Seba et Iorai et Iachan et Zie et Heber, septem.

houses: Michael, Meshullam, Sheba, Jorai, Jacan, Zia, and Eber, seven. [14]These were the sons of Abihail the son of Huri, son of Jaroah, son of Gilead, son of Michael, son of Jeshishai, son of Jahdo, son of Buz; [15]Ahi the son of Abdi-el, son of Guni, was chief in their fathers' houses; [16]and they dwelt in Gilead, in Bashan and in its towns, and in all the pasture lands of Sharon to their limits. [17]All of these were enrolled by genealogies in the days of Jotham king of Judah, and in the days of Jeroboam king of Israel.

2 Kings 15:5,32; 16:7

[18]The Reubenites, the Gadites, and the half-tribe of Manasseh had valiant men, who carried shield and sword, and drew the bow, expert in war, forty-four thousand seven hundred and sixty, ready for service. [19]They made war upon the Hagrites, Jetur, Naphish, and Nodab; [20]and when they received help against them, the Hagrites and all who were with them were given into their hands, for they cried to God in the battle, and he granted their entreaty because they trusted in him. [21]They carried off their livestock: fifty thousand of their camels, two hundred and fifty thousand sheep, two thousand asses, and a hundred thousand men alive. [22]For many fell slain, because the war was of God. And they dwelt in their place until the exile.

Gen 25:15
Deut 33:20–21

Descendants of the half-tribe of Manasseh

[23]The members of the half-tribe of Manasseh dwelt in the land; they were very numerous from Bashan to Baal-hermon, Senir, and

Num 32:39

---

doctrinal content of his history than in geographical or chronological detail, pays special attention to the close alliance formed by Gad, Reuben and Manasseh to do battle with a common enemy, the Hagrites (vv. 18–22). The Lord will give them special protection and enable them to take over the livestock and territory of the vanquished because they combined forces to fight a "holy war", a war that was "of God" (cf. v. 22).

5:23–26. At the end of the genealogy of Manasseh (who occupied the most northerly part of Transjordan), we can

[14]Hi filii Abihail filii Huri filii Iaroe filii Galaad filii Michael filii Iesesi filii Ieddo filii Buz. [15]Ahi filius Abdiel filii Guni princeps familiarum eorum. [16]Et habitaverunt in Galaad et in Basan et in viculis eius et in cunctis suburbanis Saron usque ad terminos. [17]Omnes hi numerati sunt in diebus Ioatham regis Iudae et in diebus Ieroboam regis Israel. [18]Filii Ruben et Gad et dimidiae tribus Manasse viri bellatores scuta portantes et gladios et tendentes arcum eruditique ad proelia, quadraginta quattuor milia et septingenti sexaginta procedentes ad pugnam; [19]dimicaverunt contra Agarenos et Ituraeos et Naphisaeos et Nodabaeos. [20]Et datum est eis auxilium, traditique sunt in manus eorum Agareni et universi qui fuerant cum eis, quia Deum invocaverunt cum proeliarentur, et exaudivit eos, eo quod credidissent in eum. [21]Ceperuntque omnia, quae possederant, camelorum quinquaginta milia et ovium ducenta quinquaginta milia, asinos duo milia et animas hominum centum milia; [22]vulnerati autem multi corruerunt: fuit enim bellum Domini. Habitaveruntque pro eis usque ad transmigrationem. [23]Filii quoque dimidiae tribus Manasse possederunt terram a Basan usque Baalhermon et Sanir et montem

Mount Hermon. [24]These were the heads of their fathers' houses: Epher,[m] Ishi, Eliel, Azri-el, Jeremiah, Hodaviah, and Jahdi-el, mighty warriors, famous men, heads of their fathers' houses. [25]But they transgressed against the God of their fathers, and played the harlot after the gods of the peoples of the land, whom God had destroyed before them. [26]So the God of Israel stirred up the spirit of Pul king of Assyria, the spirit of Tilgath-pilneser king of Assyria, and he carried them away, namely, the Reubenites, the Gadites, and the half-tribe of Manasseh, and brought them to Halah, Habor, Hara, and the river Gozan, to this day.

Num 3:17–20
Josh 21:4–40
Gen 46:11
Ex 6:18
Num 26:59–60

Descendants of Levi

6 [1n]The sons of Levi: Gershom, Kohath, and Merari. [2]The sons of Kohath: Amram, Izhar, Hebron, and Uzziel. [3]The children of Amram: Aaron, Moses, and Miriam. The sons of Aaron: Nadab, Abihu, Eleazar, and Ithamar. [4]Eleazar was the father of Phinehas, Phinehas of Abishua, [5]Abishua of Bukki, Bukki of Uzzi, [6]Uzzi of Zerahiah, Zerahiah of Meraioth, [7]Meraioth of Amariah, Amariah

---

see another instance of the writer's religious interpretation of events. The cause of Assyria's invasion (in the years 733–732 BC; cf. 2 Kings 15:29) was the infidelity and idolatry of the tribes that made up the Northern kingdom; and the Assyrian king was the instrument God used to punish them. This application of the doctrine of retribution serves to explain why these tribes were dispossessed forever.

6:1–15. Special attention is given to the tribe of Levi: it gets more space than any other (6:1–81) and its genealogy is given a central position in the lists.

This first genealogy of Levi gives the high priests belonging to the family of Aaron and Eleazar (cf. Num 26:59–60); from certain things that are highlighted, we can see the special protection God gives this tribe: this is the only tribe involved in the temple of Solomon, so the building of the temple divides the list in two, almost symmetrical, parts; as in the other genealogy of Aaron given later (6:50–53), the figure of Zadok is mentioned (from whom the

Hermon; ingens quippe numerus erat. [24]Et hi fuerunt principes familiarum eorum: Epher et Iesi et Eliel et Azriel et Ieremia et Odovia et Iediel: viri bellatores fortissimi et nominati, duces in familiis suis. [25]Reliquerunt autem Deum patrum suorum et fornicati sunt post deos populorum terrae, quos abstulit Deus coram eis. [26]Et suscitavit Deus Israel spiritum Phul regis Assyriorum et spiritum Theglathphalasar regis Assur; et transtulit Ruben et Gad et dimidium tribus Manasse et adduxit eos in Hala et Habor et Ara et fluvium Gozan usque ad diem hanc. [27]Filii Levi: Gerson, Caath, Merari. [28]Filii Caath: Amram, Isaar, Hebron et Oziel. [29]Filii Amram: Aaron, Moyses et Maria. Filii Aaron: Nadab et Abiu, Eleazar et Ithamar. [30]Eleazar genuit Phinees, et Phinees genuit Abisue; [31]Abisue vero genuit Bocci, et Bocci genuit Ozi. [32]Ozi genuit Zaraiam, et Zaraias genuit Meraioth, [33]porro Meraioth genuit Amariam, et Amarias genuit Achitob; [34]Achitob genuit Sadoc, Sadoc genuit Achimaas, [35]Achimaas genuit Azariam, Azarias genuit Iohanan;

m. Gk Vg: Heb *and Epher* **n.** Ch 5:27 in Heb

of Ahitub, [8]Ahitub of Zadok, Zadok of Ahima-az, [9]Ahima-az of Azariah, Azariah of Johanan, [10]and Johanan of Azariah (it was he who served as priest in the house that Solomon built in Jerusalem). [11]Azariah was the father of Amariah, Amariah of Ahitub, [12]Ahitub of Zadok, Zadok of Shallum, [13]Shallum of Hilkiah, Hilkiah of Azariah, [14]Azariah of Seraiah, Seraiah of Jehozadak; [15]and Jehozadak went into exile when the LORD sent Judah and Jerusalem into exile by the hand of Nebuchadnezzar.

Other descendants of Levi

Num 3:17–20

[16] [o]The sons of Levi: Gershom, Kohath, and Merari. [17]And these are the names of the sons of Gershom: Libni and Shime-i. [18]The sons of Kohath: Amram, Izhar, Hebron, and Uzziel. [19]The sons of Merari: Mahli and Mushi. These are the families of the Levites according to their fathers. [20]Of Gershom: Libni his son, Jahath his son, Zimmah his son, [21]Joah his son, Iddo his son, Zerah his son, Je-atherai his son. [22]The sons of Kohath: Amminadab his son, Korah his son, Assir his son, [23]Elkanah his son, Ebiasaph his son, Assir his son, [24]Tahath his son, Uriel his son, Uzziah his son, and

Gen 46:11
Ex 6:18

Num 26:59–60

Zadokites—the Sadducees of the New Testament—took their name; it was these who held the priesthood at the time this book was written); and special stress is put on the continuity of the high priesthood from Aaron to Jehozadak, who was deported to Babylon (v. 15) and whose son Jeshua was the first high priest at the restoration, after the return from exile (cf. Ezra 3:2).

6:16–30. This second genealogy leads off with the descendants of Levi (vv. 16–19; cf. Ex 6:16–19; Num 3:17–20) without mentioning Miriam, the sister of Aaron, who was not a forebear of any priestly line. It goes on to list (vv. 20–30) other priestly families, distinct from the high priests, and does so to show that all those who exercised the priestly ministry in Israel were descendants of Levi. Specifically, Samuel and his father Elkanah (v. 26) are included here in the Levite genealogy despite the fact that they came from the tribe of Ephraim (cf. 1 Sam 1:1). On the other hand, there is no mention of Eli, the priest of Shiloh, from whom Samuel

[36]Iohanan genuit Azariam: ipse est qui sacerdotio functus est in domo, quam aedificavit Salomon in Ierusalem. [37]Genuit autem Azarias Amariam, et Amarias genuit Achitob, [38]Achitob genuit Sadoc, et Sadoc genuit Sellum; [39]Sellum genuit Helciam, et Helcias genuit Azariam. [40]Azarias genuit Saraiam, et Saraias genuit Iosedec; [41]porro Iosedec egressus est, quando transtulit Dominus Iudam et Ierusalem per manus Nabuchodonosor. **[6]** [1]Filii ergo Levi: Gerson, Caath et Merari. [2]Et haec nomina filiorum Gerson: Lobni et Semei. [3]Filii Caath: Amram et Isaar et Hebron et Oziel. [4]Filii Merari: Moholi et Musi. Hae autem cognationes Levi secundum familias eorum: [5]Gerson, Lobni filius eius, Iahath filius eius, Zimma filius eius, [6]Ioah filius eius, Addo filius eius, Zara filius eius, Iethrai filius eius. [7]Filii Caath: Aminadab filius eius, Core filius eius, Asir filius eius, [8]Elcana filius eius, Abiasaph filius eius, Asir filius eius, [9]Thahath filius eius, Uriel filius eius, Ozias filius eius, Saul filius eius. [10]Filii Elcana: Amasai et Achimoth, [11]Elcana filius

o. Ch 6:1 in Heb

Shaul his son. [25]The sons of Elkanah: Amasai and Ahimoth, [26]Elkanah his son, Zophai his son, Nahath his son, [27]Eliab his son, Jeroham his son, Elkanah his son. [28]The sons of Samuel: Joel[p] his first-born, the second Abijah.[q] [29]The sons of Merari: Mahli, Libni his son, Shime-i his son, Uzzah his son, [30]Shime-a his son, Haggiah his son, and Asaiah his son.

1 Sam 1:1
Ex 6:19
Num 26:58

Cantors

[31]These are the men whom David put in charge of the service of song in the house of the LORD, after the ark rested there. [32]They ministered with song before the tabernacle of the tent of meeting, until Solomon had built the house of the LORD in Jerusalem; and they performed their service in due order. [33]These are the men who served and their sons. Of the sons of the Kohathites: Heman the singer the son of Joel, son of Samuel, [34]son of Elkanah, son of Jeroham, son of Eliel, son of Toah, [35]son of Zuph, son of Elkanah, son of Mahath, son of Amasai, [36]son of Elkanah, son of Joel, son of Azariah, son of Zephaniah, [37]son of Tahath, son of Assir, son of Ebiasaph, son of Korah, [38]son of Izhar, son of Kohath, son of Levi, son of Israel; [39]and his brother Asaph, who stood on his right hand, namely, Asaph the son of Berechiah, son of Shime-a, [40]son of

inherited the priesthood, because Eli's sons, who they sinned gravely, did not inherit the priesthood from their father (cf. 1 Sam 2:34–36). The Chronicler blissfully overlooks the objections a meticulous historian might raise; he simply certifies the Levitical descent of all priests.

6:31–53. The cantors have an important place in the Levitical family, given their key role in the liturgy after the return from exile (cf. chap. 25). It is pointed out here that David personally charged them with the service of song (vv. 31–32); therefore this was a permanent ministry. The list also includes as descendants of Levi three wise men to whom some psalms are attributed (cf. 1 Kings 5:11; Ps 89, title)—Heman (vv. 33–38), Asaph (vv. 39–43) and Ethan (vv. 44–47); the cantors, then, had very high status as wise men and composers of psalms and they even had prophetical roles (cf. 25:2).

In addition to organizing the service of song, Levites of lesser degree helped in all the temple ministries (cf. Num 3:9); they were aides of the priests, who were in charge of offerings and sacrifices (cf. vv. 48–49).

eius, Sophai filius eius, Nahath filius eius, [12]Eliab filius eius, Ieroham filius eius, Elcana filius eius, Samuel filius eius. [13]Filii Samuel: primogenitus Ioel et secundus Abia. [14]Filii autem Merari: Moholi, Lobni filius eius, Semei filius eius, Oza filius eius, [15]Samaa filius eius, Haggia filius eius, Asaia filius eius. [16]Isti sunt quos constituit David super cantum domus Domini, ex quo collocata est arca; [17]et ministrabant coram habitatione tabernaculi conventus canentes, donec aedificaret Salomon domum Domini in Ierusalem; stabant autem iuxta ordinem suum in ministerio. [18]Hi vero sunt, qui assistebant

p. Gk Syr Compare verse 33 and 1 Sam 8:2: Heb lacks *Joel* **q.** Heb *and Abijah*

Michael, son of Ba-aseiah, son of Malchijah, [41]son of Ethni, son of Zerah, son of Adaiah, [42]son of Ethan, son of Zimmah, son of Shime-i, [43]son of Jahath, son of Gershom, son of Levi. [44]On the left hand were their brethren the sons of Merari: Ethan the son of Kishi, son of Abdi, son of Malluch, [45]son of Hashabiah, son of Amaziah, son of Hilkiah, [46]son of Amzi, son of Bani, son of Shemer, [47]son of Mahli, son of Mushi, son of Merari, son of Levi; [48]and their brethren the Levites were appointed for all the service of the tabernacle of the house of God.

Lev 1:4; 2:3

[49]But Aaron and his sons made offerings upon the altar of burnt offering and upon the altar of incense for all the work of the most holy place, and to make atonement for Israel, according to all that Moses the servant of God had commanded. [50]These are the sons of Aaron: Eleazar his son, Phinehas his son, Abishua his son, [51]Bukki his son, Uzzi his son, Zerahiah his son, [52]Meraioth his son, Amariah his son, Ahitub his son, [53]Zadok his son, Ahima-az his son.

Levite cities

Josh 21:4–40

Josh 21:4,10–19

[54]These are their dwelling places according to their settlements within their borders: to the sons of Aaron of the families of Kohathites, for theirs was the lot, [55]to them they gave Hebron in the land of Judah and its surrounding pasture lands, [56]but the fields of the

---

cum filiis suis. De filiis Caath: Heman cantor filius Ioel filii Samuel [19]filii Elcana filii Ieroham filii Eliel filii Thohu [20]filii Suph filii Elcana filii Mahath filii Amasai [21]filii Elcana filii Ioel filii Azariae filii Sophoniae [22]filii Thahath filii Asir filii Abiasaph filii Core [23]filii Isaar filii Caath filii Levi filii Israel. [24]Et frater eius Asaph, qui stabat a dextris eius, Asaph filius Barachiae filii Samaa [25]filii Michael filii Basaiae filii Melchiae [26]filii Athnai filii Zara filii Adaia [27]filii Ethan filii Zimma filii Semei [28]filii Iahath filii Gerson filii Levi. [29]Filii autem Merari fratres eorum ad sinistram: Ethan filius Cusi filii Abdi filii Melluch [30]filii Hasabiae filii Amasiae filii Helciae [31]filii Amsi filii Bani filii Somer [32]filii Moholi filii Musi filii Merari filii Levi. [33]Fratres quoque eorum Levitae, qui ordinati sunt in cunctum ministerium habitaculi domus Domini; [34]Aaron vero et filii eius adolebant super altare holocausti et super altare thymiamatis in omne opus sancti sanctorum, et ut expiarent pro Israel, iuxta omnia quae praecepit Moyses servus Dei. [35]Hi sunt autem filii Aaron: Eleazar filius eius, Phinees filius eius, Abisue filius eius, [36]Bocci filius eius, Ozi filius eius, Zaraia filius eius, [37]Meraioth filius eius, Amarias filius eius, Achitob filius eius, [38]Sadoc filius eius, Achimaas filius eius. [39]Et haec habitacula eorum per castra atque confinia, filiorum scilicet Aaron ex cognatione Caathitarum: ipsis enim sorte contigerat. [40]Dederunt igitur eis Hebron in terra Iudae et suburbana eius per circuitum; [41]agros autem civitatis et villas Chaleb filio Iephonne. [42]Porro filiis Aaron dederunt civitatem ad confugiendum: Hebron et Lobna et suburbana eius, [43]Iether quoque et Esthemo cum suburbanis eius, sed et Helon et Dabir cum suburbanis suis, [44]Asan quoque et Iutta et Bethsames et suburbana earum; [45]de tribu autem Beniamin: Gabaon et Gabaa et suburbana earum et Almath cum suburbanis suis, Anathoth quoque cum suburbanis suis: omnes civitates tredecim, singulae per cognationes suas. [46]Filiis autem Caath residuis de cognatione sua dederunt ex tribu Ephraim et ex tribu Dan et ex dimidia tribu Manasse in possessionem urbes decem. [47]Porro filiis Gerson per cognationes suas de tribu Issachar et de tribu Aser et de tribu Nephthali et de tribu Manasse in Basan urbes tredecim. [48]Filiis autem Merari per cognationes suas de tribu Ruben et de tribu Gad et de tribu Zabulon dederunt sorte civitates duodecim. [49]Dederunt quoque filii Israel Levitis civitates et suburbana earum; [50]dederuntque per sortem ex tribu filiorum Iudae et ex tribu filiorum Simeon et ex tribu filiorum Beniamin urbes has, quas vocaverunt nominibus suis. [51]Et his, qui erant ex cognationibus

city and its villages they gave to Caleb the son of Jephunneh. [57]To the sons of Aaron they gave the cities of refuge: Hebron, Libnah with its pasture lands, Jattir, Eshtemoa with its pasture lands, [58]Hilen with its pasture lands, Debir with its pasture lands, [59]Ashan with its pasture lands, and Beth-shemesh with its pasture lands; [60]and from the tribe of Benjamin, Geba with its pasture lands, Alemeth with its pasture lands, and Anathoth with its pasture lands. All their cities throughout their families were thirteen.

Josh 21:5–8

[61]To the rest of the Kohathites were given by lot out of the family of the tribe, out of the half-tribe, the half of Manasseh, ten cities. [62]To the Gershomites according to their families were allotted thirteen cities out of the tribes of Issachar, Asher, Naphtali, and Manasseh in Bashan. [63]To the Merarites according to their families were allotted twelve cities out of the tribes of Reuben, Gad, and Zebulun. [64]So the people of Israel gave the Levites the cities with their pasture lands. [65]They also gave them by lot out of the tribes of Judah, Simeon, and Benjamin these cities which are mentioned by name.

Josh 21:9

Josh 21:20–39

[66]And some of the families of the sons of Kohath had cities of their territory out of the tribe of Ephraim. [67]They were given the cities of refuge: Shechem with its pasture lands in the hill country

6:54–81. The history of the cities inherited by or ceded to the tribe of Levi is the same as that given in Joshua 21:1–42, except for minor changes. Levites and priests are based in all the regions where the other tribes were settled; this shows that they played an essential role in the life of the country. What we have here are: a) priestly cities in the territory of Judah and Simeon, with Hebron as the centre and the city of refuge (vv. 54–60; cf. Josh 21:9–19); b) Levitical cities in Ephraim, with Shechem as the centre and city of refuge (vv. 66–70; cf. Josh 21:20–26); c) Levitical cities of the north assigned to the Gershomites (vv. 71–76; cf. Josh 21:27–33); d) Levitical cities of the territory of Zebulun (vv. 77–81; cf. Josh 21:34–35). The centre of the passage (vv. 61–65) summarizes this distribution of the cities in terms of the great Levitical families—Kohath, Gershom and Merari (cf. Josh 21:5–8).

filiorum Caath, fuerunt civitates in terminis eorum de tribu Ephraim. [52]Dederunt ergo eis urbem ad confugiendum: Sichem cum suburbanis suis in monte Ephraim et Gazer cum suburbanis suis, [53]Iecmaam quoque cum suburbanis suis et Bethoron similiter; [54]necnon et Aialon cum suburbanis suis et Gethremmon in eundem modum. [55]Porro ex dimidia tribu Manasse Thenach et suburbana eius, Ieblaam et suburbana eius, his videlicet qui de cognationibus filiorum Caath reliqui erant. [56]Filiis autem Gerson de cognationibus dimidiae tribus Manasse: Golan in Basan et suburbana eius et Astharoth cum suburbanis suis. [57]De tribu Issachar Cedes et suburbana illius et Dabereth cum suburbanis suis, [58]Ramoth quoque et suburbana illius et Anem cum suburbanis suis. [59]De tribu vero Aser: Masal cum suburbanis suis et Abdon similiter, [60]Hucoc quoque et suburbana eius et Rohob cum suburbanis suis. [61]Porro de tribu Nephthali: Cedes in Galilaea et suburbana eius, Hamon cum suburbanis suis et

of Ephraim, Gezer with its pasture lands, [68]Jokme-am with its pasture lands, Beth-horon with its pasture lands, [69]Aijalon with its pasture lands, Gath-rimmon with its pasture lands, [70]and out of the half-tribe of Manasseh, Aner with its pasture lands, and Bile-am with its pasture lands, for the rest of the families of the Kohathites.

[71]To the Gershomites were given out of the half-tribe of Manasseh: Golan in Bashan with its pasture lands and Ashtaroth with its pasture lands; [72]and out of the tribe of Issachar: Kedesh with its pasture lands, Daberath with its pasture lands, [73]Ramoth with its pasture lands, and Anem with its pasture lands; [74]out of the tribe of Asher: Mashal with its pasture lands, Abdon with its pasture lands, [75]Hukok with its pasture lands, and Rehob with its pasture lands; [76]and out of the tribe of Naphtali: Kedesh in Galilee with its pasture lands, Hammon with its pasture lands, and Kiriathaim with its pasture lands. [77]To the rest of the Merarites were allotted out of the tribe of Zebulun: Rimmono with its pasture lands, Tabor with its pasture lands, [78]and beyond the Jordan at Jericho, on the east side of the Jordan, out of the tribe of Reuben: Bezer in the steppe with its pasture lands, Jahzah with its pasture lands, [79]Kedemoth with its pasture lands, and Mepha-ath with its pasture lands; [80]and out of the tribe of Gad: Ramoth in Gilead with its pasture lands, Mahanaim with its pasture lands, [81]Heshbon with its pasture lands, and Jazer with its pasture lands.

Descendants of Issachar

7 [1]The sons[r] of Issachar: Tola, Puah, Jashub, and Shimron, four. [2]The sons of Tola: Uzzi, Rephaiah, Jeri-el, Jahmai, Ibsam, and Shemuel, heads of their fathers' houses, namely of Tola, mighty

Gen 46:13
Num 26:21–24
Judg 10:1
2 Sam 24:1–2,9

7:1–40. The lists of the tribes of the north, except for those of Dan and Zebulun, completes the genealogical map of Israel. Even though the northerners occupied a very extensive area and had much history attaching to them, the Chronicler confines himself to genealogical lists, mentioning no particular

Cariathaim et suburbana eius. [62]Filiis autem Merari residuis de tribu Zabulon: Remmon et suburbana eius et Thabor cum suburbanis suis. [63]Trans Iordanem quoque ex adverso Iericho, contra orientem Iordanis de tribu Ruben: Bosor in solitudine cum suburbanis suis et Iasa cum suburbanis suis, [64]Cademoth quoque et suburbana eius et Mephaath cum suburbanis suis. [65]Necnon et de tribu Gad: Ramoth in Galaad et suburbana eius et Mahanaim cum suburbanis suis, [66]sed et Hesebon cum suburbanis eius, et Iazer cum suburbanis suis. **[7]** [1]Porro filii Issachar: Thola et Phua, Iasub et Semron, quattuor. [2]Filii Thola: Ozi et Raphaia et Ieriel et Iemai et Iebsem et Samuel, principes familiarum suarum; de stirpe Thola viri fortissimi numerati sunt iuxta genealogias suas in diebus David viginti duo

r. Syr Compare Vg: Heb *and to the sons*

warriors of their generations, their number in the days of David being twenty-two thousand six hundred. [3]The sons of Uzzi: Izrahiah. And the sons of Izrahiah: Michael, Obadiah, Joel, and Isshiah, five, all of them chief men; [4]and along with them, by their generations, according to their fathers' houses, were units of the army for war, thirty-six thousand, for they had many wives and sons. [5]Their kinsmen belonging to all the families of Issachar were in all eighty-seven thousand mighty warriors, enrolled by genealogy.

Gen 46:21
Num 26:38
1 Chron 8:1ff

Descendants of Benjamin

[6]The sons of Benjamin: Bela, Becher, and Jedia-el, three. [7]The sons of Bela: Ezbon, Uzzi, Uzziel, Jerimoth, and Iri, five, heads of fathers' houses, mighty warriors; and their enrollment by genealogies was twenty-two thousand and thirty-four. [8]The sons of Becher: Zemirah, Joash, Eliezer, Eli-o-enai, Omri, Jeremoth, Abijah, Anathoth, and Alemeth. All these were the sons of Becher; [9]and their enrollment by genealogies, according to their generations, as heads of their fathers' houses, mighty warriors, was twenty thousand two hundred. [10]The sons of Jedia-el: Bilhan. And the sons of Bilhan: Jeush, Benjamin, Ehud, Chenaanah, Zethan, Tarshish, and Ahishahar. [11]All these were the sons of Jedia-el according to the heads of their fathers' houses, mighty warriors, seventeen thousand and two hundred, ready for service in war. [12]And Shuppim and Huppim were the sons of Ir, Hushim the sons of Aher.

Josh 21:18

Num 26:38–39

historical episode. This evidences his conviction that only the descendants of the southern tribes, that is, the forebears of those who came back from the exile, had managed to keep their identity, whereas the northerners disappeared from the map as a punishment for their idolatry and other sins.

The Benjamin genealogy (vv. 6–12) is not fully in line with that given in 8:1–32. Various explanations have been offered for this discrepancy, but all that can be said is that a substantial number of those repatriated from Babylon belonged to this tribe. That may be why two different genealogies were conserved.

milia sescenti. [3]Filii Ozi: Izrahia, de quo nati sunt Michael et Obadia et Ioel et Iesia, quinque principes omnes. [4]Cumque eis erant secundum genealogias familiarum suarum turmae accinctae ad proelium, viri fortissimi, triginta sex milia; multas enim habuere uxores et filios. [5]Fratresque eorum per omnes cognationes Issachar robustissimi ad pugnandum octoginta septem milia numerati sunt. [6]Filii Beniamin: Bela et Bochor et Iedihel, tres. [7]Filii Bela: Esebon et Ozi et Oziel et Ierimoth et Urai, quinque principes familiarum et ad pugnandum robustissimi; numerus autem eorum viginti duo milia et triginta quattuor. [8]Porro filii Bochor: Zamira et Ioas et Eliezer et Elioenai et Amri et Ierimoth et Abia et Anathoth et Almath; omnes hi filii Bochor. [9]Numerati sunt autem in genealogiis suis principes familiarum suarum ad bella fortissimi viginti milia et ducenti. [10]Porro filii Iedihel: Bilhan; filii autem Bilhan: Iehus et Beniamin et Aod et Chanaana et Zethan et Tharsis et Ahisahar; [11]omnes hi filii Iedihel principes familiarum suarum viri fortissimi decem et septem milia et ducenti ad proelium procedentes. [12]Suphim quoque et Huphim filii Hir et Husim filii Aher. [13]Filii autem Nephthali: Iasiel et Guni et Ieser et Sellum,

Descendants of Naphtali

[13]The sons of Naphtali: Jahzi-el, Guni, Jezer, and Shallum, the offspring of Bilhah.

Gen 46:24
Num 26:48–50

Descendants of Manasseh

[14]The sons of Manasseh: Asri-el, whom his Aramean concubine bore; she bore Machir the father of Gilead. [15]And Machir took a wife for Huppim and for Shuppim. The name of his sister was Maacah. And the name of the second was Zelophehad; and Zelophehad had daughters. [16]And Maacah the wife of Machir bore a son, and she called his name Peresh; and the name of his brother was Sheresh; and his sons were Ulam and Rakem. [17]The sons of Ulam: Bedan. These were the sons of Gilead the son of Machir, son of Manasseh. [18]And his sister Hammolecheth bore Ishhod, Abi-ezer, and Mahlah. [19]The sons of Shemida were Ahian, Shechem, Likhi, and Aniam.

Num 26:29–33
Num 26:33
Judg 6:11

Descendants of Ephraim

[20]The sons of Ephraim: Shuthelah, and Bered his son, Tahath his son, Ele-adah his son, Tahath his son, [21]Zabad his son, Shuthelah his son, and Ezer and Ele-ad, whom the men of Gath who were born in the land slew, because they came down to raid their cattle. [22]And Ephraim their father mourned many days, and his brothers came to comfort him. [23]And Ephraim went in to his wife, and she conceived and bore a son; and he called his name Beriah, because evil had befallen his house. [24]His daughter was Sheerah, who built both Lower and Upper Beth-horon, and Uzzen-sheerah. [25]Rephah was his son, Resheph his son, Telah his son, Tahan his son, [26]Ladan his son, Ammihud his son, Elishama his son, [27]Nun his son, Joshua his son. [28]Their possessions and settlements were Bethel and its towns, and eastward Naaran, and westward Gezer

Num 26:35
2 Chron 8:13
Josh 16:3
Num 1:10
Ex 33:11

---

filii Bilhae. [14]Porro filius Manasse: Asriel, quem peperit concubina eius Syra; peperit quoque Machir patrem Galaad. [15]Machir autem accepit uxorem de Huphim et Suphim et habuit sororem nomine Maacha; nomen autem secundi Salphaad, nataeque sunt Salphaad filiae. [16]Et peperit Maacha uxor Machir filium vocavitque nomen eius Phares; porro nomen fratris eius Sares et filii eius Ulam et Recem. [17]Filius autem Ulam: Badan; hi sunt filii Galaad filii Machir filii Manasse. [18]Soror autem eius Ammalecheth peperit Isod et Abiezer et Maala. [19]Erant autem filii Semida: Ahin et Sechem et Leci et Aniam. [20]Filii autem Ephraim: Suthala, Bared filius eius, Thahath filius eius, Elada filius eius, Thahath filius eius, [21]et huius filius Zabad et huius filius Suthala et huius filius Ezer et Elad. Occiderunt autem eos viri Geth indigenae, quia descenderant, ut invaderent possessiones eorum. [22]Luxit igitur Ephraim pater eorum multis diebus, et venerunt fratres eius, ut consolarentur eum; [23]ingressusque est ad uxorem suam, quae concepit et peperit filium, et vocavit nomen eius Beria, eo quod in malis domus eius ortus esset. [24]Filia autem eius fuit Sara, quae aedificavit Bethoron inferiorem et superiorem et Ozensara. [25]Porro filius eius Rapha et Reseph et Thale filius eius, de quo natus est Thaan, [26]qui genuit Laadan; huius quoque filius Ammiud genuit Elisama, [27]de quo ortus est Nun, qui habuit filium Iosue. [28]Possessio autem eorum et habitationes: Bethel cum filiabus suis et contra orientem Noran, ad occidentalem

and its towns, Shechem and its towns, and Ayyah and its towns; [29]also along the borders of the Manassites, Beth-shean and its towns, Taanach and its towns, Megiddo and its towns, Dor and its towns. In these dwelt the sons of Joseph the son of Israel.

Descendants of Asher

Gen 46:17
Num 26:44ff

[30]The sons of Asher: Imnah, Ishvah, Ishvi, Beriah, and their sister Serah. [31]The sons of Beriah: Heber and Malchi-el, who was the father of Birzaith. [32]Heber was the father of Japhlet, Shomer, Hotham, and their sister Shua. [33]The sons of Japhlet: Pasach, Bimhal, and Ashvath. These are the sons of Japhlet. [34]The sons of Shemer his brother: Rohgah, Jehubbah, and Aram. [35]The sons of Helem his brother: Zophah, Imna, Shelesh, and Amal. [36]The sons of Zophah: Suah, Harnepher, Shual, Beri, Imrah, [37]Bezer, Hod, Shamma, Shilshah, Ithran, and Be-era. [38]The sons of Jether: Jephunneh, Pispa, and Ara. [39]The sons of Ulla: Arah, Hanniel, and Rizia. [40]All of these were men of Asher, heads of fathers' houses, approved, mighty warriors, chief of the princes. Their number enrolled by genealogies, for service in war, was twenty-six thousand men.

Num 1:2

Descendants of Benjamin

Gen 46:21
Num 26:38–40

8 [1]Benjamin was the father of Bela his first-born, Ashbel the second, Aharah the third, [2]Nohah the fourth, and Rapha the fifth. [3]And Bela had sons: Addar, Gera, Abihud, [4]Abishua, Naaman, Ahoah, [5]Gera, Shephuphan, and Huram. [6]These are the

---

plagam Gazer et filiae eius, Sichem quoque cum filiabus suis usque Hai et filias eius. [29]Iuxta filios quoque Manasse: Bethsan et filias eius, Thenach et filias eius, Mageddo et filias eius, Dor et filias eius. In his habitaverunt filii Ioseph filii Israel. [30]Filii Aser: Iemna et Iesua et Isui et Beria et Sara soror eorum. [31]Filii autem Beria: Heber et Melchiel, ipse est pater Barzaith. [32]Heber autem genuit Iephlat et Somer et Hotham et Suaa sororem eorum. [33]Filii Iephlat: Phosech et Bamaal et Asoth; hi filii Iephlat. [34]Porro filii Somer fratris sui: Roaga et Haba et Aram. [35]Filii autem Hotham fratris eius: Supha et Iemna et Selles et Amal. [36]Filii Supha: Sue, Harnapher et Sual et Beri et Iamra, [37]Bosor et Od et Samma et Salusa et Iethran et Beera. [38]Filii Iether: Iephonne et Phaspha et Ara. [39]Filii autem Olla: Area et Hanniel et Resia. [40]Omnes hi filii Aser, principes familiarum electi atque fortissimi, capita principum; numerus autem eorum, qui inscripti erant in exercitu ad bellum, viginti sex milia. **[8]** [1]Beniamin autem genuit Bela primogenitum suum, Asbel secundum, Ahara tertium, [2]Nohaa quartum et Rapha quintum. [3]Fueruntque filii Bela: Addar et Gera pater Aod, [4]Abisue quoque et Naaman et Ahoe, [5]sed et Gera et Sephuphan et Huram. [6]Hi sunt filii Aod principes familiarum habitantium in Gabaa, qui translati sunt in Manahath; [7]Naaman autem et Ahia et Gera: ipse transtulit eos et genuit Oza et Ahiud. [8]Porro Saharaim genuit in regione Moab, postquam dimisit Husim et Bara uxores suas; [9]genuit autem de Hodes uxore sua Iobab et Sebia et Mesa et Melcham, [10]Iehus quoque et Sechia et Marma; hi sunt filii eius principes in familiis suis. [11]De Husim vero genuit Abitob et Elphaal; [12]porro filii Elphaal Heber et Misaam et Samad; hic aedificavit Ono et Lod et filias eius. [13]Beria autem et Samma principes familiarum habitantium in Aialon; hi fugaverunt habitatores Geth. [14]Et Ahi et Sesac et Ierimoth [15]et Zabadia et Arad et Eder, [16]Michael quoque et Iespha et Ioha filii Beria. [17]Et Zabadia et Mosollam et Hezeci et Heber [18]et

sons of Ehud (they were heads of fathers' houses of the inhabitants of Geba, and they were carried into exile to Manahath): [7]Naaman,[s] Ahijah, and Gera, that is, Heglam,[t] who was the father of Uzza and Ahihud. [8]And Shaharaim had sons in the country of Moab after he had sent away Hushim and Baara his wives. [9]He had sons by Hodesh his wife: Jobab, Zibia, Mesha, Malcam, [10]Jeuz, Sachia, and Mirmah. These were his sons, heads of fathers' houses. [11]He also had sons by Hushim: Abitub and Elpaal. [12]The sons of Elpaal: Eber, Misham, and Shemed, who built Ono and Lod with its towns, [13]and Beriah and Shema (they were heads of fathers' houses of the inhabitants of Aijalon, who put to flight the inhabitants of Gath); [14]and Ahio, Shashak, and Jeremoth. [15]Zebadiah, Arad, Eder, [16]Michael, Ishpah, and Joha were sons of Beriah. [17]Zebadiah, Meshullam, Hizki, Heber, [18]Ishmerai, Izliah, and Jobab were the sons of Elpaal. [19]Jakim, Zichri, Zabdi, [20]Eli-enai, Zillethai, Eliel, [21]Adaiah, Beraiah, and Shimrath were the sons of Shime-i. [22]Ishpan, Eber, Eliel, [23]Abdon, Zichri, Hanan, [24]Hananiah, Elam, Anthothijah, [25]Iphdeiah, and Penuel were the sons of Shashak. [26]Shamsherai, Shehariah, Athaliah, [27]Ja-areshiah, Elijah, and Zichri were the sons of Jeroham. [28]These were the heads of fathers' houses, according to their generations, chief men. These dwelt in Jerusalem.

[29]Je-iel[u] the father of Gibeon dwelt in Gibeon, and the name of his wife was Maacah. [30]His first-born son: Abdon, then Zur, Kish,

1 Chron 7:23

1 Chron 9:34

1 Chron 9:35–38

8:1–32. The Benjamin genealogy given in this chapter contains brief notes on episodes which, although it is difficult to prove, are designed to add status, in some instances, to the tribe of Benjamin and, in others, to the city of Jerusalem. Ehud is the judge who rescued the sons of Benjamin from enslavement by Moab (according to Judges 3:12–30). Verse 6 may be a reference to the drama of Gibe-ah (here "Geba") narrated in detail in Judges 19:1—21:25; the flight of the Benjaminites (cf. Judg 20:45–47) would be seen as a type of deportation. In v. 28 the Benjaminites are said to have lived in Jerusalem, the future capital, from ancient times (cf. v. 32). But in Judges 21 we were told that the Benjaminites were unable to dislodge the Jebusites.

Iesamari et Iezlia et Iobab filii Elphaal [19]et Iacim et Zechri et Zabdi [20]et Elioenai et Selethai et Eliel [21]et Adaia et Baraia et Samarath filii Semei [22]et Iesphan et Heber et Eliel [23]et Abdon et Zechri et Hanan [24]et Hanania et Elam et Anathothia [25]et Iephdaia et Phanuel filii Sesac. [26]Et Samsari et Sohoria et Otholia [27]et Iersia et Elia et Zechri filii Ieroham. [28]Hi capita familiarum secundum genealogias, principes qui habitaverunt in Ierusalem. [29]In Gabaon autem habitaverunt Iehiel pater Gabaon, et nomen uxoris eius Maacha, [30]filiusque eius primogenitus Abdon et Sur et Cis et Baal et Ner et Nadab, [31]Gedor quoque et Ahio et Zacher et Macelloth; [32]et Macelloth genuit Samaa. Habitaveruntque ex adverso fratrum suorum

s. Heb *and Naaman* **t.** Or *he carried them into exile* **u.** Compare 9:35: Heb lacks *Jeiel*

Baal, Nadab, [31]Gedor, Ahio, Zecher, [32]and Mikloth (he was the father of Shime-ah). Now these also dwelt opposite their kinsmen in Jerusalem, with their kinsmen.

1 Sam 9:1–2; 14:49–51
1 Chron 9:39–43

Descendants of Saul

[33]Ner was the father of Kish, Kish of Saul, Saul of Jonathan, Malchishua, Abinadab, and Esh-baal; [34]and the son of Jonathan was Merib-baal; and Merib-baal was the father of Micah. [35]The sons of Micah: Pithon, Melech, Tarea, and Ahaz. [36]Ahaz was the father of Jehoaddah; and Jehoaddah was the father of Alemeth, Azmaveth, and Zimri; Zimri was the father of Moza. [37]Moza was the father of Bine-a; Raphah was his son, Ele-asah his son, Azel his son. [38]Azel had six sons, and these are their names: Azrikam, Bocheru, Ishmael, She-ariah, Obadiah, and Hanan. All these were the sons of Azel. [39]The sons of Eshek his brother: Ulam his first-born, Jeush the second, [40]The sons of Ulam were men who were mighty warriors, bowmen, having many sons and grandsons, one hundred and fifty. All these were Benjaminites.

Jerusalem after the exile

1 Chron 6:33
Neh 11:3–19

9 [1]So all Israel was enrolled by genealogies; and these are written in the Book of the Kings of Israel. And Judah was taken into exile in Babylon because of their unfaithfulness. [2]Now the first to

---

8:33–40. Outstanding among the descendants of Benjamin is Saul, the first king of Judah. His genealogy is repeated in 9:35–44; but here the stress is put on the Benjaminites' military valour and their archery skills (v. 40; cf. 2 Sam 1:22; 1 Chron 12:2). The Chronicler has very little to say about the events of Saul's life.

9:1–44. This chapter, which closes the first part of the book about the ancestors of David, contains lists of descendants of Judah and Benjamin (vv. 4–16) which are almost identical with those in Nehemiah 11:3–19. It then goes on to list the Levite doorkeepers, providing a description of their functions (vv. 17–34), and to give Saul's genealogy,

in Ierusalem cum fratribus suis. [33]Ner autem genuit Cis, et Cis genuit Saul. Porro Saul genuit Ionathan et Melchisua et Abinadab et Isbaal. [34]Filius autem Ionathan Meribbaal, et Meribbaal genuit Micha; [35]filii Micha Phithon et Melech et Tharaa et Ahaz. [36]Et Ahaz genuit Ioada, et Ioada genuit Almath et Azmaveth et Zamri; porro Zamri genuit Mosa. [37]Et Mosa genuit Banaa, cuius filius fuit Raphaia, de quo ortus est Elasa, qui genuit Asel. [38]Porro Asel sex filii fuere his nominibus: Ezricam primogenitus eius, Ismael, Saria, Azarias, Obdia et Hanan; omnes hi filii Asel. [39]Filii autem Esec fratris eius: Ulam primogenitus et Iehus secundus et Eliphalet tertius. [40]Fueruntque filii Ulam viri robustissimi ad bellum et magno robore tendentes arcum et multos habentes filios ac nepotes usque ad centum quinquaginta. Omnes hi filii Beniamin. **[9]** [1]Universus ergo Israel dinumeratus est, et summa eorum scripta est in libro regum Israel et Iudae. Translatique sunt in Babylonem propter delictum suum. [2]Qui autem habitaverunt primi in possessionibus et in urbibus suis: Israel et sacerdotes et Levitae et Nathinaei. [3]Commorati sunt in Ierusalem de filiis Iudae et de filiis Beniamin de filiis quoque Ephraim et Manasse.

dwell again in their possessions in their cities were Israel, the priests, the Levites, and the temple servants. [3]And some of the people of Judah, Benjamin, Ephraim, and Manasseh dwelt in Jerusalem: [4]Uthai the son of Ammihud, son of Omri, son of Imri, son of Bani, from the sons of Perez the son of Judah. [5]And of the Shilonites: Asaiah the first-born, and his sons. [6]Of the sons of Zerah: Jeuel and their kinsmen, six hundred and ninety. [7]Of the Benjaminites: Sallu the son of Meshullam, son of Hodaviah, son of Hassenuah, [8]Ibneiah the son of Jeroham, Elah the son of Uzzi, son of Michri, and Meshullam the son of Shephatiah, son of Reuel, son of Ibnijah; [9]and their kinsmen according to their generations, nine hundred and fifty-six. All these were heads of father's houses according to their fathers' houses.

[10]Of the priests: Jedaiah, Jehoiarib, Jachin, [11]and Azariah the son of Hilkiah, son of Meshullam, of Meraioth, son of Ahitub, the chief officer of the house of God; [12]and Adaiah the son of Jeroham, son of Pashhur, son of Malchijah, and Maasai the son of Adi-el, son of Jahzerah, son of Meshullam, son of Meshillemith, son of Immer; [13]besides their kinsmen, heads of their fathers' houses, one thousand seven hundred and sixty, very able men for the work of the service of the house of God.

Neh 11:10–14

[14]Of the Levites: Shemaiah the son of Hasshub, son of Azrikam, son of Hashabiah, of the sons of Merari; [15]and Bakbakkar, Heresh,

Neh 11:15–18

already covered in the previous chapter (8:33–40).

But before these last genealogies comes a short preface (vv. 1–3) containing the main doctrinal points that form the religious backbone of the book: first, the writer stresses, the lists provided are not the author's invention, for "all Israel" (v. 1), all the Israelites, were named in the Book of the Kings. This means that there was no discontinuity between those who came back from exile and those who made up the previous history of Israel. Secondly, the exile is interpreted as a punishment for the infidelities of those who were actually deported, not their ancestors. This in effect spells out the doctrine of

[4]Uthai filius Ammiud filii Amri filii Imri filii Bani: de filiis Phares filii Iudae; [5]et de Selanitis: Asaia primogenitus et filii eius; [6]de filiis autem Zara: Iehuel et fratres eorum sescenti nonaginta. [7]Porro de filiis Beniamin: Sallu filius Mosollam filii Odovia filii Asana [8]et Iobania filius Ieroham et Ela filius Ozi filii Mochori et Mosollam filius Saphatiae filii Rahuel filii Iebaniae [9]et fratres eorum secundum genealogias suas nongenti quinquaginta sex; omnes hi principes familiarum secundum familias suas. [10]De sacerdotibus autem: Iedaia, Ioiarib et Iachin, [11]Azarias quoque filius Helciae filii Mosollam filii Sadoc filii Meraioth filii Achitob principes domus Dei. [12]Porro Adaias filius Ieroham filii Phassur filii Melchiae et Maasai filius Adiel filii Iezra filii Mosollam filii Mosollamoth filii Emmer, [13]fratres quoque eorum principes per familias suas mille septingenti sexaginta, fortissimi robore ad faciendum opus ministerii in domo Dei. [14]De Levitis autem: Semeia filius Hassub filii Ezricam filii Hasabia de filiis Merari; [15]Bacbacar quoque, Hares et Galal et Matthania filius Micha filii Zechri filii Asaph [16]et Abdia filius Semeiae filii Galal filii Idithun et Barachia filius Asa filii Elcana, qui habitavit in atriis

Galal, and Mattaniah the son of Mica, son of Zichri, son of Asaph; [16]and Obadiah the son of Shemaiah, son of Galal, son of Jeduthun, and Berechiah the son of Asa, son of Elkanah, who dwelt in the villages of the Netophathites.

[17]The gatekeepers were: Shallum, Akkub, Talmon, Ahiman, and their kinsmen (Shallum being the chief), [18]stationed hitherto in the king's gate on the east side. These were the gatekeepers of the camp of the Levites. [19]Shallum the son of Kore, son of Ebiasaph, son of Korah, and his kinsmen of his fathers' house, the Korahites, were in charge of the work of the service, keepers of the thresholds of the tent, as their fathers had been in charge of the camp of the LORD, keepers of the entrance. [20]And Phinehas the son of Eleazar was the ruler over them in time past; the LORD was with him. [21]Zechariah the son of Meshelemiah was gatekeeper at the entrance of the tent of meeting. [22]All these, who were chosen as gatekeepers at the thresholds, were two hundred and twelve. They were enrolled by genealogies in their villages. David and Samuel the seer established them in their office of trust. [23]So they and their sons were in charge of the gates of the house of the LORD, that is, the house of the tent, as guards. [24]The gatekeepers were on the four sides, east, west, north, and south; [25]and their kinsmen who were in their villages were obliged to come in every seven days, from time to time, to be with these; [26]for the four chief gatekeepers, who were Levites, were in charge of the chambers and the

Neh 15:19

2 Kings 11:5

---

personal retribution. Finally, Jerusalem is the capital, and in it dwell both the tribes of the south (Judah and Benjamin) and those of the north (Ephraim and Manasseh). He wants to register the fact that the whole people, "all Israel", has been united, and that the division which obtained between the old kingdoms is no more.

9:20. "The Lord was with him" or "the Lord be with him": a form of words often found in later Judaism, to show respect for someone who was already

Netophathitarum. [17]Ianitores autem: Sellum et Accub et Telmon et Ahiman; et frater eorum Sellum princeps [18]et usque ad hoc tempus est in porta regis ad orientem. Hi erant ianitores castris filiorum Levi. [19]Sellum vero filius Core filii Abiasaph filii Core cum fratribus suis de domo patris sui: hi Coritae erant super opera ministerii custodes liminum tabernaculi; patres autem eorum super castra Domini custodiebant introitum, [20]et Phinees filius Eleazari princeps erat super eos olim—Dominus sit cum eo!—[21]Zacharias filius Mosollamia ianitor portae tabernaculi conventus. [22]Omnes hi electi in ostiarios liminum ducenti duodecim, et descripti in villis propriis, quos constituerunt David et Samuel videns in munus perpetuum, [23]tam ipsos quam filios eorum in ostiis domus Domini, domus tabernaculi, in custodias. [24]Per quattuor ventos erant ostiarii, id est ad orientem et ad occidentem, ad aquilonem et ad austrum. [25]Fratres autem eorum in viculis suis morabantur et veniebant per septem dies de tempore usque ad tempus, ut essent cum illis. [26]Nam munus habebant perpetuum hi quattuor principes ianitorum. Hi scilicet Levitae erant super exedras et thesauros domus Domini; [27]per gyrum quoque templi Domini

treasures of the house of God. [27]And they lodged round about the house of God; for upon them lay the duty of watching, and they had charge of opening it every morning.

[28]Some of them had charge of the utensils of service, for they were required to count them when they were brought in and taken out. [29]Others of them were appointed over the furniture, and over all the holy utensils, also over the fine flour, the wine, the oil, the incense, and the spices. [30]Others, of the sons of the priests, prepared the mixing of the spices, [31]and Mattithiah, one of the Levites, the first-born of Shallum the Korahite, was in charge of making the flat cakes. [32]Also some of their kinsmen of the Kohathites had charge of the showbread, to prepare it every sabbath.

Lev 2:4–7

[33]Now these are the singers, the heads of fathers' houses of the Levites, dwelling in the chambers of the temple free from other service, for they were on duty day and night. [34]These were heads of fathers' houses of the Levites, according to their generations, leaders, who lived in Jerusalem.

1 Chron 8:28

The family of Saul

1 Chron 8:29–38

[35]In Gibeon dwelt the father of Gibeon, Je-iel, and the name of his wife was Maacah, [36]and his first-born son Abdon, then Zur, Kish, Baal, Ner, Nadab, [37]Gedor, Ahio, Zechariah and Mikloth; [38]and Mikloth was the father of Shime-am; and these also dwelt opposite

---

dead; but this is the only place where it occurs in the Bible: Phinehas merited a special blessing from the Lord (cf. Num 25:6–13).

9:35–44. The repetition of Saul's genealogy brings to a close this first part of the book devoted to the ancestors of the tribes. A new dynasty now begins, that of David; it has no connexion with Saul, but its roots go back to the very origin of mankind.

pernoctabant in custodiis suis, ut et ipsi mane aperirent fores. [28]De horum genere erant et super vasa ministerii, ad numerum enim et inferebantur vasa et efferebantur; [29]de ipsis et, qui credita habebant utensilia et omnia utensilia sancta, praeerant similae et vino et oleo et turi et aromatibus. [30]Filii quidam autem sacerdotum unguenta ex aromatibus conficiebant; [31]et Matthathias Levites, primogenitus Sellum Coritae, munere perpetuo praefectus erat eorum, quae in sartagine frigebantur. [32]Porro de filiis Caath fratribus eorum super panes erant propositionis, ut semper novos per singula sabbata praepararent. [33]Hi sunt cantores, principes per familias Levitarum, qui in exedris vacantes morabantur, ita ut die et nocte iugiter suo ministerio deservirent. [34]Hi sunt capita Levitarum per familias suas secundum genealogias suas principes; hi habitaverunt in Ierusalem. [35]In Gabaon autem commorati sunt pater Gabaon Iehiel, et nomen uxoris eius Maacha. [36]Filius primogenitus eius Abdon et Sur et Cis et Baal et Ner et Nadab, [37]Gedor quoque et Ahio et Zacharias et Macelloth. [38]Porro Macelloth genuit Samaam; isti habitaverunt e regione fratrum suorum in Ierusalem cum fratribus suis. [39]Ner autem genuit Cis, et Cis genuit Saul. Et Saul genuit Ionathan et Melchisua et Abinadab et Isbaal. [40]Filius autem Ionathan Meribbaal, et

1 Chron 8:29–32

their kinsmen in Jerusalem, with their kinsmen. [39]Ner was the father of Kish, Kish of Saul, Saul of Jonathan, Malchishua, Abinadab, and Eshbaal; [40]and the son of Jonathan was Merib-baal; and Merib-baal was the father of Micah. [41]The sons of Micah: Pithon, Melech, Tahre-a, and Ahaz;[v] [42]and Ahaz was the father of Jarah, and Jarah of Alemeth, Azmaveth, and Zimri; and Zimri was the father of Moza. [43]Moza was the father of Bine-a; and Rephaiah was his son, Ele-asah his son, Azel his son. [44]Azel had six sons and these are their names: Azrikam, Bocheru, Ishmael, She-ariah, Obadiah, and Hanan; these were the sons of Azel.

2. THE REIGN OF DAVID

1 Sam 31:1–13

Death of Saul

10 [1]Now the Philistines fought against Israel; and the men of Israel fled before the Philistines, and fell slain on Mount Gilboa. [2]And the Philistines overtook Saul and his sons; and the Philistines slew Jonathan and Abinadab and Malchishua, the sons of Saul. [3]The battle pressed hard upon Saul, and the archers found him; and he was wounded by the archers. [4]Then Saul said to his armour-bearer, "Draw your sword, and thrust me through with it, lest these uncircumcised come and make sport of me." But his armour-bearer would not; for he feared greatly. Therefore Saul took his own sword, and fell upon it. [5]And when his armour-bearer

1 Sam 31:6

10:1–14. The Chronicler begins his account of the monarchy with a few lines about the reign of Saul and about his death, before going on to introduce the figure of David, who will be the protagonist and the model king in the rest of 1 Chronicles. There is no mention of Samuel or of military, social and religious events during the chequered life of Saul, as narrated in 1 Samuel.

The death of Saul (v. 1) draws a line under the first dynasty, which never managed to consolidate its position.

Meribbaal genuit Micha; [41]porro filii Micha: Phithon et Melech et Tharaa et Ahaz. [42]Ahaz autem genuit Iara, et Iara genuit Almath et Azmaveth et Zamri; Zamri autem genuit Mosa. [43]Mosa vero genuit Banaa, cuius filius Raphaia genuit Elasa, de quo ortus est Asel. [44]Porro Asel sex filios habuit his nominibus: Ezricam primogenitus eius, Ismael, Saria, Azarias, Obdia, Hanan; hi filii Asel. **[10]** [1]Philisthim autem pugnabant contra Israel, fugeruntque viri Israel a facie Philisthim et ceciderunt vulnerati in monte Gelboe; [2]cumque appropinquassent Philisthaei persequentes Saul et filios eius, percusserunt Ionathan et Abinadab et Melchisua filios Saul. [3]Et aggravatum est proelium contra Saul, inveneruntque eum sagittarii et vulneraverunt iaculis; [4]et dixit Saul ad armigerum suum: «Evagina gladium tuum et interfice me, ne forte veniant incircumcisi isti et illudant mihi». Noluit autem armiger eius hoc facere timore perterritus. Arripuit igitur Saul ensem et irruit in eum; [5]quod cum vidisset armiger eius, videlicet

v. Compare 8:35: Heb lacks *and Ahaz*

saw that Saul was dead, he also fell upon his sword, and died. [6]Thus Saul died; he and his three sons and all his house died together. [7]And when all the men of Israel who were in the valley saw that the army[w] had fled and that Saul and his sons were dead, they forsook their cities and fled; and the Philistines came and dwelt in them.

[8]On the morrow, when the Philistines came to strip the slain, they found Saul and his sons fallen on Mount Gilboa. [9]And they stripped him and took his head and his armour, and sent messengers throughout the land of the Philistines, to carry the good news to their idols and to the people. [10]And they put his armour in the temple of their gods, and fastened his head in the temple of Dagon. [11]But when all Jabesh-gilead heard all that the Philistines had done to Saul, [12]all the valiant men arose, and took away the body of Saul and the bodies of his sons, and brought them to Jabesh. And they buried their bones under the oak in Jabesh, and fasted seven days.

1 Sam 31:13

The way is open for a new dynasty, that of David, which will endure and which will raise the people to its proper dignity. The account taken from 1 Samuel 31:1–13 adds a new piece of information—that with the king died "all his house" (v. 6). By making this alteration, the Chronicler puts it on record that the disappearance of Saul's line was part of God's plan. David had nothing to do with it; he could not be accused of committing any crime in order to gain the throne.

The last verses in the chapter (vv. 13–14), not found in the books of Samuel, are couched like a legal sentence: Saul died "for his unfaithfulness" in not keeping the Lord's command and because he consulted a medium instead of the Lord (cf. 1 Sam 28:1–25). The Chronicler interprets the facts, applying the doctrine of personal retribution, whereby each man is punished for his own transgressions; but the Lord is still intent on his people's welfare. Both these ideas are contained in the final sentence: "the Lord slew him, and turned the kingdom over to David the son of Jesse" (v. 14).

The stress on personal responsibility for one's own actions is something new compared with the widespread notion

mortuum esse Saul, irruit etiam ipse in gladium suum et mortuus est. [6]Interiit ergo Saul et tres filii eius; omnis domus illius pariter concidit. [7]Quod cum vidissent omnes viri Israel, qui habitabant in campestribus, quod fugissent, et mortui essent Saul et filii eius, dereliquerunt urbes suas et huc illucque dispersi sunt; veneruntque Philisthim et habitaverunt in eis. [8]Die igitur altero venerunt Philisthim, ut spoliarent interfectos, et invenerunt Saul et filios eius iacentes in monte Gelboe; [9]cumque spoliassent eum et amputassent caput armisque nudassent, miserunt in terram suam per circuitum, ut annuntiaretur in idolorum templis et in populis. [10]Arma autem eius consecraverunt in fano Astharoth et caput affixerunt in templo Dagon. [11]Hoc cum audissent viri Iabes Galaad, omnia scilicet quae Philisthim fecerunt super Saul, [12]consurrexerunt omnes viri fortes et tulerunt cadavera Saul et filiorum eius attuleruntque ea in Iabes et sepelierunt ossa eorum subter quercum, quae erat in Iabes, et ieiunaverunt

w. Heb *they*

[13]So Saul died for his unfaithfulness; he was unfaithful to the LORD in that he did not keep the command of the LORD, and also consulted a medium, seeking guidance, [14]and did not seek guidance from the LORD. Therefore the LORD slew him, and turned the kingdom over to David the son of Jesse.

2 Sam 5:1–3

David is proclaimed king*

Mt 2:6

11 [1]Then all Israel gathered together to David at Hebron, and said, "Behold, we are your bone and flesh. [2]In times past, even when Saul was king, it was you that led out and brought in Israel; and the LORD your God said to you, 'You shall be shepherd of my people Israel, and you shall be prince over my people Israel.'" [3]So all the elders of Israel came to the king at Hebron; and David made a covenant with them at Hebron before the LORD, and they anointed David king over Israel, according to the word of the LORD by Samuel.

1 Sam 16:1–13

2 Sam 5:6–10

Capture of Jerusalem

[4]And David and all Israel went to Jerusalem, that is Jebus, where the Jebusites were, the inhabitants of the land. [5]The inhabitants of Jebus said to David, "You will not come in here." Nevertheless

---

at the time in the Eastern world that each individual is so much part of his family and his people that God punishes sons for the sins of parents (cf. "Introduction", p. 21f above). The doctrine that personal retribution will be meted out in the next life is a New Testament one. This teaching should help a person to live an upright life, conscious of eternity. "The reward of future transformation is promised to those who turn evil to good in this present life" (St Fulgentius of Ruspe, *De remissione peccatorum*, 2, 12).

***11:1—12:41.** The events of David's reign are going to be recounted in a way that makes the personality and qualities of the king the centre of attention; so, although almost all the data are taken from 2 Samuel, it is interesting to notice the variations in

septem diebus. [13]Mortuus est ergo Saul propter iniquitatem suam, eo quod praevaricatus sit mandatum Domini, quod praeceperat, et non custodierit illud, sed insuper etiam pythonissam consuluerit, [14]nec quaesierit Dominum; propter quod et interfecit eum et transtulit regnum eius ad David filium Isai. **[11]** [1]Congregatus est igitur omnis Israel ad David in Hebron dicens: «Os tuum sumus et caro tua. [2]Heri quoque et nudiustertius, cum adhuc regnaret Saul, tu eras qui educebas et introducebas Israel; tibi enim dixit Dominus Deus tuus: "Tu pasces populum meum Israel et tu eris princeps super eum"». [3]Venerunt ergo omnes maiores natu Israel ad regem in Hebron, et iniit David cum eis foedus in Hebron coram Domino; unxeruntque eum regem super Israel iuxta sermonem Domini, quem locutus est in manu Samuel. [4]Abiit quoque David et omnis Israel in Ierusalem, haec est Iebus, ubi erant Iebusaei habitatores terrae. [5]Dixeruntque, qui habitabant in Iebus, ad David: «Non ingredieris huc». Porro David cepit arcem Sion, quae est civitas David, [6]dixitque: «Omnis, qui percusserit Iebusaeum, in primis erit princeps et

David took the stronghold of Zion, that is, the city of David. [6]David said, "Whoever shall smite the Jebusites first shall be chief and commander." And Joab the son of Zeruiah went up first, so he became chief. [7]And David dwelt in the stronghold; therefore it was called the city of David. [8]And he built the city round about from the Millo in complete circuit; and Joab repaired the rest of the city. [9]And David became greater and greater, for the LORD of hosts was with him.

2 Sam 5:8

David's champions

[10]Now these are the chiefs of David's mighty men, who gave him strong support in his kingdom, together with all Israel, to make him king, according to the word of the LORD concerning Israel. [11]This is an account of David's mighty men: Jashobe-am, a Hachmonite, was chief of the three;[x] he wielded his spear against three hundred whom he slew at one time.

2 Sam 23:8–39

---

order to see the doctrinal approach the Chronicler takes.

As reported in this book, David's reign contains three outstanding events —his accession to the throne (chaps. 11–12), the transfer of the ark to Jerusalem (chaps. 13–16) and the preparatory work for the building of the temple (chaps. 17–29).

The account of David's rise to the throne includes his proclamation as king (11:1–3), the conquest of Jerusalem (11:4–9), and the list of his most faithful followers, first the men of valour (11:47) and then the representatives of the tribes (12:1–14). To heighten David's prestige, emphasis is put on the fact that he met no obstacles in his way to the throne and, especially, that from the very beginning he was king of "all Israel", not just king of the south.

11:1–3. In this brief account, which parallels 2 Samuel 5:1–3, we can easily notice, once again, the criteria being used to interpret David's reign. Firstly, nothing is said about north/south divisions: "all Israel" assemble at Hebron. The expression "all Israel", which appears for the first time in 9:1, will become a fixed formula (11:4, 10) that evidences the unity of the people.

But, also, David is king by the will of God ("according to the word of the Lord by Samuel": v. 3). The book constantly teaches that the Lord makes

dux». Ascendit igitur primus Ioab filius Sarviae et factus est princeps. [7]Habitavit autem David in arce, et idcirco appellata est civitas David. [8]Aedificavitque urbem in circuitu a Mello usque ad gyrum; Ioab autem reliqua urbis instauravit. [9]Proficiebatque David vadens et crescens, et Dominus exercituum erat cum eo. [10]Hi principes virorum fortium David, qui adiuverunt eum, ut rex fieret super omnem Israel iuxta verbum Domini, quod locutus est ad Israel; [11]et iste numerus robustorum David: Iesbaam filius Hachamon filius Hachamonitis princeps inter triginta; iste levavit hastam suam super trecentos, quos occidit impetu uno. [12]Et post eum Eleazar filius Dodo Ahohites, qui erat inter tres potentes; [13]iste fuit cum David in Aphesdommim, quando Philisthim congregati sunt ad locum illum in proelium. Et erat

x. Compare 2 Sam 23:8: Heb *thirty* or *captains*

[12]And next to him among the three mighty men was Eleazar the son of Dodo, the Ahohite. [13]He was with David at Pas-dammim when the Philistines were gathered there for battle. There was a plot of ground full of barley, and the men fled from the Philistines. [14]But he[y] took his stand in the midst of the plot, and defended it, and slew the Philistines; and the LORD saved them by a great victory.

1 Sam 17:1

[15]Three of the thirty chief men went down to the rock to David at the cave of Adullam, when the army of Philistines was encamped in the valley of Rephaim. [16]David was then in the stronghold; and the garrison of the Philistines was then at Bethlehem. [17]And David said longingly, "O that some one would give me water to drink from the well of Bethlehem which is by the gate!" [18]Then the three mighty men broke through the camp of the Philistines, and drew water out of the well of Bethlehem which was by the gate, and took and brought it to David. But David would not drink of it; he poured it out to the LORD [19]and said, "Far be it from me before my God that I should do this. Shall I drink the

---

his will known through the prophets; so here Samuel is being seen as a prophet rather than a judge or priest.

11:4–9. The account of the conquest of Jerusalem, which will become the political capital of "all Israel" (v. 4), is in line with information given in 2 Samuel 5:6–10 but omits anything which might not show David in the best light—for example, opposition from the blind and the lame. David makes a triumphal entry, taking over the city (formerly, Jebus) and setting about its government and repair: Joab is entrusted with lesser works of reconstruction and David himself sees to the building of the walls. On the Millo (v. 8), see the note on 2 Sam 5:9.

11:10–47. In the book of Samuel this listing of mighty men is a sort of appendix (cf. 2 Sam 23:8–38); by placing it here, the Chronicler is making the point that "all Israel" (v. 10) and all its most prominent people gave the new king their consent and support from the very start. This stress on nation-

---

ager regionis illius plenus hordeo, fugeratque populus a facie Philisthinorum. [14]Hic stetit in medio agri et defendit eum; cumque percussisset Philisthaeos, dedit Dominus salutem magnam populo suo. [15]Descenderunt autem tres de triginta principibus ad petram, in qua erat David, ad speluncam Odollam, quando Philisthim fuerant castrametati in valle Raphaim. [16]Porro David erat in praesidio, et statio Philisthinorum in Bethlehem; [17]desideravit igitur David et dixit: «O si quis daret mihi aquam de cisterna Bethlehem, quae est in porta!». [18]Tres ergo isti per media castra Philisthinorum perrexerunt et hauserunt aquam de cisterna Bethlehem, quae erat in porta, et attulerunt ad David, ut biberet. Qui noluit, sed magis libavit illam Domino [19]dicens: «Avertat a me Deus meus, ut hoc faciam et sanguinem virorum istorum bibam, quia in periculo animarum suarum attulerunt mihi aquam». Et ob hanc causam noluit bibere. Haec fecerunt tres robustissimi. [20]Abisai quoque frater Ioab; ipse erat princeps inter triginta et ipse

y. Compare 2 Sam 23:12: Heb *they . . . their*

lifeblood of these men? For at the risk of their lives they brought it." Therefore he would not drink it. These things did the three mighty men.

[20]Now Abishai, the brother of Joab, was chief of the thirty.[z] And he wielded his spear against three hundred men and slew them, and won a name beside the three. [21]He was the most renowned[a] of the thirty,[z] and became their commander; but he did not attain to the three.

[22]And Benaiah the son of Jehoiada was a valiant man[b] of Kabzeel, a doer of great deeds; he smote two ariels[c] of Moab. He also went down and slew a lion in a pit on a day when snow had fallen. [23]And he slew an Egyptian, a man of great stature, five cubits tall. The Egyptian had in his hand a spear like a weaver's beam; but Benaiah went down to him with a staff, and snatched the spear out of the Egyptian's hand, and slew him with his own spear. [24]These things did Benaiah the son of Jehoiada, and won a name beside the three mighty men. [25]He was renowned among the thirty, but he did not attain to the three. And David set him over his bodyguard.

[26]The mighty men of the armies were Asahel the brother of Joab, Elhanan the son of Dodo of Bethlehem, [27]Shammoth of Harod,[d] Helez the Pelonite, [28]Ira the son of Ikkesh of Tekoa, Abiezer of Anathoth, [29]Sibbecai the Hushathite, Ilai the Ahohite, [30]Maharai of Netophah, Heled the son of Baanah of Netophah, [31]Ithai the son of Ribai of Gibe-ah of the Benjaminites, Benaiah of

---

al unity was a call to the Chronicler's contemporaries, and it carries a message for all believers in every age: "When our ideas separate us from other people, when they weaken our communion, our unity with our brothers, it is a sure sign that we are not doing what God wants" (St J. Escrivá, *Christ Is Passing By*, 17).

levavit hastam suam contra trecentos, quos interfecit, et ipse erat inter tres nominatus, [21]inter triginta duplici honore eminens et princeps eorum; verumtamen usque ad tres non pervenerat. [22]Banaias filius Ioiadae vir robustissimus, qui multa opera perpetrarat, de Cabseel; ipse percussit duos Ariel de Moab et ipse descendit et interfecit leonem in media cisterna tempore nivis. [23]Et ipse percussit virum Aegyptium, cuius statura erat quinque cubitorum et habebat lanceam ut liciatorium texentium; descendit ergo ad eum cum virga et rapuit hastam, quam tenebat manu, et interfecit eum hasta sua. [24]Haec fecit Banaias filius Ioiadae, qui erat inter tres robustos nominatus, [25]inter triginta primus; verumtamen ad tres usque non pervenerat, posuit autem eum David super satellites suos. [26]Porro fortissimi in exercitu: Asael frater Ioab et Elchanan filius Dodo de Bethlehem, [27]Sammoth Harodites, Elica Harodites, Heles Phalonites, [28]Hira filius Acces Thecuites, Abiezer Anathothites, [29]Sobbochai Husathites, Ilai Ahohites, [30]Maharai Netophathites, Heled filius Baana Netophathites, [31]Ithai filius Ribai de Gabaa filiorum

z. Syr: Heb *three* **a.** Compare 2 Sam 23:19: Heb *more renowned among the two* **b.** Syr: Heb *the son of a valiant man* **c.** The meaning of the word *ariel* is unknown **d.** Compare 2 Sam 23:25: Heb *the Harorite*

Pirathon, [32]Hurai of the brooks of Gaash, Abiel the Arbathite, [33]Azmaveth of Baharum, Eliahba of Sha-albon, [34]Hashem[e] the Gizonite, Jonathan the son of Shagee the Hararite, [35]Ahiam the son of Sachar the Hararite, Eliphal the son of Ur, [36]Hepher the Mecherathite, Ahijah the Pelonite, [37]Hezro of Carmel, Naarai the son of Ezbai, [38]Joel the brother of Nathan, Mibhar the son of Hagri, [39]Zelek the Ammonite, Naharai of Be-eroth, the armour-bearer of Joab the son of Zeruiah, [40]Ira the Ithrite, Gareb the Ithrite, [41]Uriah the Hittite, Zabad the son of Ahlai, [42]Adina the son of Shiza the Reubenite, a leader of the Reubenites, and thirty with him, [43]Hanan the son of Maacah, and Joshaphat the Mithnite, [44]Uzzia the Ashterathite, Shama and Je-iel the sons of Hotham the Aroerite, [45]Jedia-el the son of Shimri, and Joha his brother, the Tizite, [46]Eliel the Mahavite, and Jeribai, and Joshaviah, the sons of Elna-am, and Ithmah the Moabite,[47] Eliel, and Obed, and Ja-asiel the Mezoba-ite.

David's first supporters

1 Sam 27:1–7

12 [1]Now these are the men who came to David at Ziklag, while he could not move about freely because of Saul the son of Kish; and they were among the mighty men who helped him in war. [2]They were bowmen, and could shoot arrows and sling stones with either the right or the left hand; they were Benjaminites, Saul's kinsmen. [3]The chief was Ahi-ezer, then Joash, both sons of

1 Chron 8:40

12:1–23. The "mighty men" include representatives of the various tribes who supported David—the northern as well as the southern tribes. Amasai, acting like a prophet ("the Spirit came upon" him: v. 18), solemnly confirms that David's monarchy is part of God's plan.

Beniamin, Banaia Pharathonites, [32]Hurai de torrentibus Gaas, Abiel Arbathites, [33]Azmaveth Bahurimites, Eliaba Saalbonites, [34]Asem Gezonites, Ionathan filius Sage Ararites, [35]Ahiam filius Sachar Ararites, Eliphal filius Ur, [36]Hepher Mecherathites, Ahia Phelonites, [37]Hesro de Carmel, Naarai filius Azbai, [38]Ioel frater Nathan, Mibahar filius Agarai, [39]Selec Ammonites, Naharai Berothites armiger Ioab filii Sarviae, [40]Hira Iethraeus, Gareb Iethraeus, [41]Urias Hetthaeus, Zabad filius Oholai, [42]Adina filius Siza Rubenites princeps Rubenitarum, et cum eo triginta; [43]Hanan filius Maacha et Iosaphat Matthanites, [44]Ozia Astharothites, Sama et Iehiel filii Hotham Aroerites, [45]Iedihel filius Semri et Ioha frater eius Thosaites, [46]Eliel Mahumites et Ieribai et Iosaia filii Elnaem et Iethma Moabites, [47]Eliel et Obed et Iasiel de Soba. **[12]** [1]Hi quoque venerunt ad David in Siceleg, cum adhuc fugeret Saul filium Cis; qui erant fortissimi et egregii pugnatores [2]tendentes arcum et utraque manu fundis saxa iacientes et dirigentes sagittas. De fratribus Saul ex Beniamin: [3]princeps Ahiezer et Ioas filii Samaa Gabaathites et Iaziel et Phalet filii Azmaveth et Baracha et Iehu Anathothites; [4]Iesmaias quoque Gabaonites fortissimus inter triginta et super triginta, [5]Ieremias et Iahaziel et Iohanan et Iozabad Gederothites, [6]Eluzai et Ierimoth et Baalia et Samaria et Saphatia Haruphites, [7]Elcana et Iesia et Azareel et Ioezer et Iesbaam Coritae, [8]Ioela quoque et Zabadia filii Ieroham de Gedor. [9]Sed et de Gad transfugerunt ad David, cum lateret in deserto, viri robustissimi et pugnatores optimi tenentes clipeum et hastam; facies

e. Compare Gk and 2 Sam 23:32: Heb *the sons of Hashem*

Shemaah of Gibe-ah; also Jezi-el and Pelet the sons of Azmaveth; Beracah, Jehu of Anathoth, [4]Ishmaiah of Gibeon, a mighty man among the thirty and a leader over the thirty; Jeremiah,[f] Jahaziel, Johanan, Jozabad of Gederah, [5]Eluzai,[g] Jerimoth, Bealiah, Shemariah, Shephatiah the Haruphite; [6]Elkanah, Isshiah, Azarel, Jo-ezer, and Jashobe-am, the Korahites; [7]and Joelah and Zebadiah, the sons of Jeroham of Gedor.

[8]From the Gadites there went over to David at the stronghold in the wilderness mighty and experienced warriors, expert with shield and spear, whose faces were like the faces of lions, and who were swift as gazelles upon the mountains: [9]Ezer the chief, Obadiah second, Eliab third, [10]Mishmannah fourth, Jeremiah fifth, [11]Attai sixth, Eliel seventh, [12]Johanan eighth, Elzabad ninth, [13]Jeremiah tenth, Machbannai eleventh. [14]These Gadites were officers of the army, the lesser over a hundred and the greater over a thousand. [15]These are the men who crossed the Jordan in the first month, when it was overflowing all its banks, and put to flight all those in the valleys, to the east and to the west.

Deut 33:20

[16]And some of the men of Benjamin and Judah came to the stronghold to David. [17]David went out to meet them and said to them, "If you have come to me in friendship to help me, my heart will be knit to you; but if to betray me to my adversaries, although there is no wrong in my hands, then may the God of our fathers see and rebuke you." [18]Then the Spirit came upon Amasai, chief of the thirty, and he said,

> "We are yours, O David;
> and with you, O son of Jesse!
> Peace, peace to you,
> and peace to your helpers!
> For your God helps you."

Then David received them, and made them officers of his troops.

---

eorum quasi facies leonis et veloces quasi capreae in montibus: [10]Ezer princeps, Abdias secundus, Eliab tertius, [11]Masmana quartus, Ieremias quintus, [12]Etthei sextus, Eliel septimus, [13]Iohanan octavus, Elzebad nonus, [14]Ieremias decimus, Machbanai undecimus. [15]Hi de filiis Gad principes exercitus, minimus contra centum praevalebat et maximus contra mille. [16]Isti sunt qui transierunt Iordanem mense primo, quando inundare consuevit super ripas suas, et omnes fugaverunt, qui morabantur in vallibus ad orientalem plagam et occidentalem. [17]Venerunt autem et de Beniamin et de Iuda ad praesidium, in quo morabatur David. [18]Egressusque est David obviam eis et ait: «Si pacifice venistis ad me, ut auxiliemini mihi, cor meum iungatur vobis; si autem insidiamini mihi pro adversariis meis, cum ego iniquitatem in manibus non habeam, videat Deus patrum nostrorum et iudicet». [19]Spiritus vero induit Amasai principem inter triginta, et ait: «Tui sumus, o David, / et tecum, fili Isai! / Pax, pax tibi / et pax adiutoribus tuis: / te enim adiuvat Deus tuus». Suscepit ergo eos David et constituit principes turmae. [20]Porro de Manasse transfugerunt ad David, quando veniebat cum Philisthim adversus Saul, ut

f. Heb verse 5 **g.** Heb verse 6

1 Sam 30:1–10

[19]Some of the men of Manasseh deserted to David when he came with the Philistines for the battle against Saul. (Yet he did not help them, for the rulers of the Philistines took counsel and sent him away, saying, "At peril to our heads he will desert to his master Saul.") [20]As he went to Ziklag these men of Manasseh deserted to him: Adnah, Jozabad, Jedia-el, Michael, Jozabad, Elihu, and Zillethai, chiefs of thousands in Manasseh. [21]They helped David against the band of raiders;[h] for they were all mighty men of valour, and were commanders in the army. [22]For from day to day men kept coming to David to help him, until there was a great army, like an army of God.

1 Sam 29

Warriors who assured David's kingship

2 Sam 2–4; 5:1

[23]These are the numbers of the divisions of the armed troops, who came to David in Hebron, to turn the kingdom of Saul over to him, according to the word of the LORD. [24]The men of Judah bearing shield and spear were six thousand eight hundred armed troops. [25]Of the Simeonites, mighty men of valour for war, seven thousand one hundred. [26]Of the Levites four thousand six hundred. [27]The prince Jehoiada, of the house of Aaron, and with him three thousand seven hundred. [28]Zadok, a young man mighty in valour, and twenty-two commanders from his own father's house. [29]Of the Benjaminites, the kinsmen of Saul, three thousand, of whom the majority had hitherto kept their allegiance to the house of Saul. [30]Of the Ephraimites twenty thousand eight hundred, mighty men of valour, famous men in their fathers' houses. [31]Of the half-tribe

12:24–41. The census of David's strong army shows that the monarchy is beginning with a great impetus: the soldiers are many and brave, there is a great sense of solidarity (v. 39), and there is no shortage of provisions (cf. v. 41). All this shows God's protection of David and his kingdom.

pugnaret; et non dimicavit cum eis, quia inito consilio remiserunt eum principes Philisthinorum dicentes: «Periculo capitis nostri revertetur ad dominum suum Saul». [21]Quando igitur reversus est in Siceleg, transfugerunt ad eum de Manasse Ednas et Iozabad et Iedihel et Michael et Iozabad et Eliu et Selathai principes milium in Manasse: [22]hi praebuerunt auxilium David adversus latrunculos; omnes enim erant viri fortissimi et facti sunt principes in exercitu. [23]Sed et per singulos dies veniebant ad David ad auxiliandum ei, usque dum fieret grandis numerus quasi exercitus Dei. [24]Iste quoque est numerus principum exercitus, qui venerunt ad David, cum esset in Hebron, ut transferrent regnum Saul ad eum iuxta verbum Domini: [25]Filii Iudae portantes clipeum et hastam sex milia octingenti expediti ad proelium. [26]De filiis Simeon virorum fortissimorum ad pugnandum septem milia centum. [27]De filiis Levi quattuor milia sescenti; [28]Ioiada quoque princeps de stirpe Aaron et cum eo tria milia septingenti; [29]Sadoc etiam iuvenis fortissimus et familia eius principes viginti duo. [30]De filiis autem Beniamin

h. Or *as officers of his troops*

of Manasseh eighteen thousand, who were expressly named to come and make David king. [32]Of Issachar men who had understanding of the times, to know what Israel ought to do, two hundred chiefs, and all their kinsmen under their command. [33]Of Zebulun fifty thousand seasoned troops, equipped for battle with all the weapons of war, to help David[i] with singleness of purpose. [34]Of Naphtali a thousand commanders with whom were thirty-seven thousand men armed with shield and spear. [35]Of the Danites twenty-eight thousand six hundred men equipped for battle. [36]Of Asher forty thousand seasoned troops ready for battle. [37]Of the Reubenites and Gadites and the half-tribe of Manasseh from beyond the Jordan, one hundred and twenty thousand men armed with all the weapons of war.

[38]All these, men of war, arrayed in battle order, came to Hebron with full intent to make David king over all Israel; likewise all the rest of Israel were of a single mind to make David king. [39]And they were there with David for three days, eating and drinking, for their brethren had made preparation for them. [40]And also their neighbours, from as far as Issachar and Zebulun and Naphtali, came bringing food on asses and on camels and on mules and on oxen, abundant provisions of meal, cakes of figs, clusters of raisins, and wine and oil, oxen and sheep, for there was joy in Israel.

2 Sam 6:1–11

The ark is brought back to Jerusalem*

13 [1]David consulted with the commanders of thousands and of hundreds, with every leader. [2]And David said to all the

---

fratribus Saul tria milia; magna enim pars eorum adhuc sequebatur domum Saul. [31]Porro de filiis Ephraim viginti milia octingenti, fortissimi robore viri nominati in familiis suis. [32]Et ex dimidia parte tribus Manasse decem et octo milia; singuli per nomina sua destinati, ut venirent et constituerent regem David. [33]De filiis quoque Issachar viri eruditi, qui norant singula tempora ad sciendum quid facere deberet Israel, principes ducenti et omnes fratres eorum ad iussa eorum. [34]Porro de Zabulon, qui egrediebantur ad proelium et stabant in acie instructi omnibus armis bellicis, quinquaginta milia venerunt, ut congregarentur non in corde duplici. [35]Et de Nephthali principes mille; et cum eis instructa clipeo et hasta triginta septem milia. [36]De Dan etiam praeparata ad proelium viginti octo milia sescenti. [37]Et de Aser egredientes ad pugnam et in acie procedentes quadraginta milia. [38]Trans Iordanem autem de filiis Ruben et de Gad et dimidia parte tribus Manasse, instructi omnibus armis bellicis, centum viginti milia. [39]Omnes isti viri bellatores expediti ad pugnandum corde perfecto venerunt in Hebron, ut constituerent regem David super universum Israel; sed et omnes reliqui ex Israel uno corde erant, ut rex fieret David. [40]Fueruntque ibi apud David tribus diebus comedentes et bibentes; praeparaverunt enim eis fratres sui. [41]Sed et qui iuxta eos erant, usque ad Issachar et Zabulon et Nephthali, afferebant panes in asinis et camelis et mulis et bobus, escam farinae, palathas, uvam passam, vinum, oleum, boves, oves ad omnem copiam; gaudium quippe erat in Israel. **[13]** [1]Iniit autem consilium David cum tribunis et centurionibus et universis principibus [2]et ait ad omnem coetum Israel: «Si placet vobis, et a Domino Deo nostro egreditur sermo, quem loquor, mittamus ad fratres nostros reliquos in universas regiones

i. Gk: Heb lacks *David*

assembly of Israel, "If it seems good to you, and if it is the will of the LORD our God, let us send abroad to our brethren who remain in all the land of Israel, and with them to the priests and Levites in the cities that have pasture lands, that they may come together to us. 3Then let us bring again the ark of our God to us; for we neglected it in the days of Saul." 4All the assembly agreed to do so, for the thing was right in the eyes of all the people.

1 Sam 5:10; 7:1–2

Judg 20:1

5So David assembled all Israel from the Shihor of Egypt to the entrance of Hamath, to bring the ark of God from Kiriath-jearim. 6And David and all Israel went up to Baalah, that is, to Kiriath-jearim which belongs to Judah, to bring up from there the ark of God, which is called by the name of the LORD who sits enthroned above the cherubim. 7And they carried the ark of God upon a new cart, from the house of Abinadab, and Uzzah and Ahio[j] were driving the cart. 8And David and all Israel were making merry before God with all their might, with song and lyres and harps and tambourines and cymbals and trumpets.

2 Sam 6:6

9And when they came to the threshing floor of Chidon, Uzzah put out his hand to hold the ark, for the oxen stumbled. 10And the

---

***13:1—16:43.** Following the account in the book of Samuel (cf. 2 Sam 5:1—6:23), after establishing Jerusalem as his political capital David also gives it the status of religious capital. This is the significance of the transfer of the ark of God to Jerusalem.

But the Chronicler adds his own doctrinal emphasis. First, there is the stress on unity: "all the assembly" and "all Israel" (cf. 13:2, 4–6; 15:3, 28; 16:3, 43) approve the king's decisions. Secondly, David himself is exemplary: he seeks no personal advantage in having the ark (13:13), he is well-regarded by neighbouring Tyre (14:1–2), God blesses him with many children (14:3–7), he is feared by his enemies, the Philistines (14:8–17). Thirdly, there is the importance given to the liturgy and the temple: the transfer of the ark is a very elaborate ceremony, conducted by Levites and priests—a preamble and even a prototype of the ceremonies that will later be held in the future temple, once the exiles return from Babylon.

13:1–14. The king's proposal about the transfer of the ark is readily accepted by "all the assembly", that is, by the

Israel et ad sacerdotes et Levitas, qui habitant in suburbanis urbium, ut congregentur ad nos. 3et reducamus arcam Dei nostri ad nos: non enim requisivimus eam in diebus Saul». 4Et respondit universa multitudo, ut ita fieret; placuerat enim sermo omni populo. 5Congregavit ergo David cunctum Israel a Sihor Aegypti usque ad introitum dum ingrediaris Emath, ut adduceret arcam Dei de Cariathiarim. 6Et ascendit David et omnis Israel in Baala, in Cariathiarim, quae est in Iuda, ut afferrent inde arcam Dei Domini sedentis super cherubim, ubi invocatum est nomen eius. 7Imposueruntque arcam Dei super plaustrum novum de domo Abinadab. Oza autem et Ahio minabant plaustrum. 8Porro David et universus Israel ludebant coram Deo omni virtute in canticis et in citharis et psalteriis et tympanis et cymbalis et

j. Or *and his brother*

anger of the LORD was kindled against Uzzah; and he smote him because he put forth his hand to the ark; and he died there before God. [11]And David was angry because the LORD had broken forth upon Uzzah; and that place is called Perez-uzza[k] to this day. [12]And David was afraid of God that day; and he said, "How can I bring the ark of God home to me?" [13]So David did not take the ark home into the city of David, but took it aside to the house of Obed-edom the Gittite. [14]And the ark of God remained with the household of Obed-edom in his house three months; and the LORD blessed the household of Obed-edom and all that he had.

David at Jerusalem

2 Sam 5:11–25

14 [1]And Hiram king of Tyre sent messengers to David, and cedar trees, also masons and carpenters to build a house for him. [2]And David perceived that the LORD had established him king over Israel, and that his kingdom was highly exalted for the sake of his people Israel.

1 Chron 3:5–8 Lk 3:31

[3]And David took more wives in Jerusalem, and David begot more sons and daughters. [4]These are the names of the children whom he had in Jerusalem: Shammua, Shobab, Nathan, Solomon,

---

people as a worshipping community (v. 4). This gets across the idea that the transfer is not a social or political act, but a religious one. The ark, the most sacred artefact in pre-monarchic worship, was a rectangular chest, made of acacia wood and covered inside and out with gold (cf. the note on Ex 25:10–22). Among other names given it was "the ark of God", because it symbolized the presence of God among his people. Although the Chronicler does not disguise the fact that disrespectful treatment of the ark could involve the risk of death, as happened to Uzzah (v. 10; cf. the note on 2 Sam 6:1–23), the account given in this book ends on a positive note, with a divine blessing on Obed-edom and his property (v. 14).

14:1–17. In these episodes, taken from 2 Samuel 5:11–25, David is respected and feared by the foreign kings (vv. 1, 17), but above all he is the devout king

tubis. [9]Cum autem pervenissent ad aream Chidon, tetendit Oza manum suam, ut sustentaret arcam; boves quippe lascivientes proruperunt. [10]Iratus est itaque Dominus contra Ozam et percussit eum, eo quod contigisset arcam; et mortuus est ibi coram Deo. [11]Contristatusque est David, eo quod dirupisset Dominus Ozam; et vocatus est locus ille Pharesoza (id est Diruptio Ozae) usque in praesentem diem. [12]Et timuit Deum tunc temporis dicens: «Quomodo possum ad me introducere arcam Dei?». [13]Et ob hanc causam non eam adduxit ad se, hoc est in civitatem David, sed avertit in domum Obededom Getthaei. [14]Mansit ergo arca Dei apud domum Obededom tribus mensibus; et benedixit Dominus domui eius et omnibus quae habebat. **[14]** [1]Misit quoque Hiram rex Tyri nuntios ad David et ligna cedrina et artifices parietum lignorumque, ut aedificarent ei domum. [2]Cognovitque David quod confirmasset eum Dominus in regem super Israel et sublevatum esset regnum suum propter populum eius Israel. [3]Accepit

k. That is *The breaking forth upon Uzzah*

2 Sam 5:16 [5]Ibhar, Elishu-a, Elpelet, [6]Nogah, Nepheg, Japhia, [7]Elishama, Beeliada, and Eliphelet.

2 Sam 5:7 [8]When the Philistines heard that David had been anointed king over all Israel, all the Philistines went up in search of David; and David heard of it and went out against them. [9]Now the Philistines had come and made a raid in the valley of Rephaim. [10]And David inquired of God, "Shall I go up against the Philistines? Wilt thou give them into my hand?" And the LORD said to him, "Go up, and I will give them into your hand." [11]And he went up to Baal-perazim, and David defeated them there; and David said, "God has broken through[l] my enemies by my hand, like a bursting flood." Therefore the name of that place is called Baal-perazim.[m] [12]And they left their gods there, and David gave command, and they were burned.

[13]And the Philistines yet again made a raid in the valley. [14]And when David again inquired of God, God said to him, "You shall not go up after them; go around and come upon them opposite the balsam trees. [15]And when you hear the sound of marching in the tops of the balsam trees, then go out to battle; for God has gone out before you to smite the army of the Philistines." [16]And David did as God commanded him, and they smote the Philistine army from Gibeon to Gezer. [17]And the fame of David went out into all lands, and the LORD brought the fear of him upon all nations.

2 Sam 5:25

Deut 2:25

---

who acknowledges the Lord's sovereignty (v. 2) and scrupulously does what the law lays down by destroying the idols of the Philistines (v. 12). The order to burn the idols, which is not found in the book of Samuel, is very significant for the Chronicler, an untiring opponent of idolatry and a defender of worship of the one true God: "To adore God is to acknowledge, in respect and absolute submission, the 'nothingness of the creature' who would not exist but for God. [. . .] The worship of the one God sets man free from turning in on himself, from the slavery of sin and the idolatry of the world" (*Catechism of the Catholic Church*, 2097).

quoque David alias uxores in Ierusalem genuitque filios et filias; [4]et haec nomina eorum, qui nati sunt ei in Ierusalem: Samua et Sobab, Nathan et Salomon, [5]Iebahar et Elisua et Eliphalet, [6]Noga quoque et Napheg et Iaphia, [7]Elisama et Beeliada et Eliphalet. [8]Audientes autem Philisthim quod unctus esset David in regem super universum Israel, ascenderunt omnes, ut quaererent eum; quod cum audisset David, egressus est obviam eis. [9]Porro Philisthim venientes diffusi sunt in valle Raphaim. [10]Consuluitque David Deum dicens: «Si ascendam contra Philisthaeos, et si trades eos in manu mea?». Et dixit ei Dominus: «Ascende, et tradam eos in manu tua». [11]Cumque illi ascendissent in Baalpharasim, percussit eos ibi David et dixit: «Dirupit Deus inimicos meos per manum meam sicut dirumpuntur aquae». Et idcirco vocatum est nomen loci illius Baalpharasim (id est Dominus diruptionum). [12]Dereliqueruntque ibi deos suos, quos David iussit exuri. [13]Alia etiam vice Philisthim irruerunt et diffusi sunt in valle; [14]consuluitque rursum David Deum, et dixit ei Deus: «Non ascendas post eos; circumdabis eos et venies contra illos ex adverso arborum celthium; [15]cumque audieris sonitum gradientis in cacumine arborum celthium, tunc egredieris ad bellum: egressus est enim Deus ante te, ut percutias castra Philisthim». [16]Fecit ergo David, sicut

l. Heb *paraz* **m.** That is *Lord of breaking through*

Enthronement of the ark in Jerusalem

15 [1]David built houses for himself in the city of David; and he prepared a place for the ark of God, and pitched a tent for it. [2]Then David said, "No one but the Levites may carry the ark of God, for the LORD chose them to carry the ark of the LORD and to minister to him for ever." [3]And David assembled all Israel at Jerusalem, to bring up the ark of the LORD to its place, which he had prepared for it. [4]And David gathered together the sons of Aaron and the Levites: [5]of the sons of Kohath, Uriel the chief, with a hundred and twenty of his brethren; [6]of the sons of Merari, Asaiah the chief, with two hundred and twenty of his brethren; [7]of the sons of Gershom, Joel the chief, with a hundred and thirty of his brethren; [8]of the sons of Elizaphan, Shemaiah the chief, with two hundred of his brethren; [9]of the sons of Hebron, Eliel the chief, with eighty of his brethren; [10]of the sons of Uzziel, Amminadab the chief, with a hundred and twelve of his brethren. [11]Then David summoned the priests Zadok and Abiathar, and the Levites Uriel, Asaiah, Joel, Shemaiah, Eliel, and Amminadab, [12]and said to them, "You are the heads of the fathers' houses of the

Num 1:50; 3:5ff; 4; 7:9
Deut 31:25

15:1–24. The preparations for the transfer of the ark involve leading figures in the life of the people and in the priesthood. Firstly, David himself, who makes arrangements about where it will be lodged (v. 1), calls the people together (v. 3), and gives all the necessary instructions (vv. 4, 11–12, 16); secondly, the Levites, chosen to be the only ones to carry the ark (vv. 2, 12) and organize the liturgical chant (v. 19); thirdly, the priests, particularly those appointed by David—Zadok and Abiathar (cf. 2 Sam 8:17; 15:24–27; 17:15; 19:12), who are sanctified along with the Levites (vv. 11, 14); and finally the entire people gathered in liturgical assembly.

The liturgy of the Church uses much of this passage in the Mass of the Vigil of the Assumption of the Blessed Virgin, thereby teaching that Mary is the true ark of the Covenant, the temple of God's enduring Presence on earth. Apropos of the Assumption, St John Damascene says, in a meaningful play on words: "Today, she who was the temple of the Lord is at rest in the divine temple that was not built by human hand" (*In Assumptionem*, 2).

praeceperat ei Deus, et percussit castra Philisthinorum de Gabaon usque Gazer. [17]Divulgatumque est nomen David in universis regionibus, et Dominus dedit pavorem eius super omnes gentes. **[15]** [1]Fecit quoque sibi domos in civitate David et praeparavit locum arcae Dei tetenditque ei tabernaculum. [2]Tunc dixit David: «Illicitum est, ut a quocumque portetur arca Dei, nisi a Levitis, quos elegit Dominus ad portandum eam et ad ministrandum sibi usque in aeternum». [3]Congregavitque David universum Israel in Ierusalem, ut afferretur arca Domini in locum suum, quem praeparaverat ei; [4]necnon et filios Aaron et Levitas. [5]De filiis Caath Uriel princeps fuit et fratres eius centum viginti; [6]de filiis Merari Asaia princeps et fratres eius ducenti viginti; [7]de filiis Gerson Ioel princeps et fratres eius centum triginta; [8]de filiis Elisaphan Semeias princeps et fratres eius ducenti; [9]de filiis Hebron Eliel princeps et fratres eius

Levites; sanctify yourselves, you and your brethren, so that you may bring up the ark of the LORD, the God of Israel, to the place that I have prepared for it. [13]Because you did not carry it the first time,[n] the LORD our God broke forth upon us, because we did not care for it in the way that is ordained." [14]So the priests and the Levites sanctified themselves to bring up the ark of the LORD, the God of Israel. [15]And the Levites carried the ark of God upon their shoulders with the poles, as Moses had commanded according to the word of the LORD.

Ex 25:14
Num 4:10; 7:9

[16]David also commanded the chiefs of the Levites to appoint their brethren as the singers who should play loudly on musical instruments, on harps and lyres and cymbals, to raise sounds of joy. [17]So the Levites appointed Heman the son of Joel; and of his brethren Asaph the son of Berechiah; and of the sons of Merari, their brethren, Ethan the son of Kushaiah; [18]and with them their brethren of the second order, Zechariah, Ja-aziel, Shemiramoth, Jehiel, Unni, Eliab, Benaiah, Ma-aseiah, Mattithiah, Eliphelehu, and Mikneiah, and the gatekeepers Obed-edom and Je-iel. [19]The singers, Heman, Asaph, and Ethan, were to sound bronze cymbals; [20]Zechariah, Aziel, Shemiramoth, Jehiel, Unni, Eliab, Ma-aseiah, and Benaiah were to play harps according to Alamoth; [21]but Mattithiah, Eliphelehu, Mikneiah, Obed-edom, Je-iel, and Azaziah were to lead with lyres according to the Sheminith. [22]Chenaniah, leader of the Levites in music, should direct the music, for he understood it. [23]Berechiah and Elkanah were to be gatekeepers for the ark. [24]Shebaniah, Joshaphat, Nethanel, Amasai, Zechariah, Benaiah, and Eliezer, the priests, should blow the trumpets before the ark of God. Obed-edom and Jehiah also were to be gatekeepers for the ark.

---

octoginta; [10]de filiis Oziel Aminadab princeps et fratres eius centum duodecim. [11]Vocavitque David Sadoc et Abiathar sacerdotes et Levitas Uriel, Asaiam, Ioel, Semeiam, Eliel et Aminadab [12]et dixit ad eos: «Vos, qui estis principes familiarum Leviticarum, sanctificamini cum fratribus vestris et afferte arcam Domini Dei Israel ad locum, quem praeparavi. [13]Quia a principio non eratis praesentes, fecit Dominus Deus Israel diruptionem in nobis; non enim quaesivimus eum, sicut fas erat». [14]Sanctificati sunt ergo sacerdotes et Levitae, ut portarent arcam Domini Dei Israel; [15]et tulerunt filii Levi arcam Dei, sicut praeceperat Moyses iuxta verbum Domini, umeris suis in vectibus. [16]Dixitque David principibus Levitarum, ut constituerent de fratribus suis cantores in organis musicorum, nablis videlicet et lyris et cymbalis, ut resonaret fortiter sonitus laetitiae. [17]Constitueruntque Levitae Heman filium Ioel et de fratribus eius Asaph filium Barachiae, de filiis vero Merari fratribus eorum Ethan filium Casaiae [18]et cum eis fratres eorum in secundo ordine Zachariam et Bani et Iaziel et Semiramoth et Iahiel et Ani, Eliab et Banaiam et Maasiam et Matthathiam et Eliphalu et Maceniam et Obededom et Iehiel ianitores. [19]Porro cantores Heman, Asaph et Ethan in cymbalis aeneis bene sonantibus, [20]Zacharias autem et Oziel et Semiramoth et Iahiel et Ani et Eliab et Maasias et Banaias in nablis secundum «Virgines». [21]Porro Matthathias et Eliphalu et Macenias et Obededom et Iehiel et Ozaziu in citharis super octavam, ut dirigerent; [22]Chonenias autem princeps Levitarum portantium arcam praeerat ad portandum, erat quippe

n. The meaning of the Hebrew word is uncertain

[25]So David and the elders of Israel, and the commanders of thousands, went to bring up the ark of the covenant of the LORD from the house of Obed-edom with rejoicing. [26]And because God helped the Levites who were carrying the ark of the covenant of the LORD, they sacrificed seven bulls and seven rams. [27]David was clothed with a robe of fine linen, as also were all the Levites who were carrying the ark, and the singers, and Chenaniah the leader of the music of the singers; and David wore a linen ephod. [28]So all Israel brought up the ark of the covenant of the LORD with shouting, to the sound of the horn, trumpets, and cymbals, and made loud music on harps and lyres.

2 Sam 6:12–19

2 Chron 3:14

[29]And as the ark of the covenant of the LORD came to the city of David, Michal the daughter of Saul looked out of the window, and saw King David dancing and making merry; and she despised him in her heart.

2 Sam 6:16–19

The ark is placed in the tent

16 [1]And they brought the ark of God, and set it inside the tent which David had pitched for it; and they offered burnt offerings and peace offerings before God. [2]And when David had finished offering the burnt offerings and the peace offerings, he

2 Sam 6:19

15:25–29. The procession includes the elders and the commanders of thousands, that is, all those with positions of some authority; the illustrious figure of David stands out, attired like all the Levites (cf. v. 27), that is, in the place of the highest honour in the liturgy. David is despised by Michal (v. 29), but unlike what we are told in the book of Samuel (2 Sam 6:20–23) there is no mention of his making any comment: the Michal incident is not allowed to sully the grandeur of the ceremony.

16:1–43. The Levites who brought the ark to Jerusalem are charged by David himself with organizing the liturgy and its music. This definition of their role will be a point of reference for those who succeed them, including those who were alive when this book was written.

valde sapiens. [23]Et Barachias et Elcana ianitores pro arca. [24]Porro Sebania et Iosaphat et Nathanael et Amasai et Zacharias et Banaias et Eliezer sacerdotes clangebant tubis coram arca Dei, et Obededom et Iehias erant ianitores pro arca. [25]Igitur David et maiores natu Israel et tribuni ierunt ad deportandam arcam foederis Domini de domo Obededom cum laetitia. [26]Cumque adiuvisset Deus Levitas, qui portabant arcam foederis Domini, immolati sunt septem tauri et septem arietes. [27]Porro David indutus pallio byssino et universi Levitae, qui portabant arcam, cantoresque et Chonenias princeps pro portanda arca—David autem indutus erat etiam ephod lineo—[28]universusque Israel deducebant arcam foederis Domini in iubilo et sonitu bucinae et tubis et cymbalis bene sonantibus et nablis et citharis. [29]Cumque pervenisset arca foederis Domini usque ad civitatem David, Michol filia Saul prospiciens per fenestram vidit regem David saltantem atque ludentem et despexit eum in corde suo. **[16]** [1]Attulerunt igitur arcam Dei et constituerunt eam in medio tabernaculi, quod tetenderat ei David, et obtulerunt holocausta et pacifica coram Deo. [2]Cumque complesset David offerens holocausta et pacifica, benedixit populo in

blessed the people in the name of the LORD, [3]and distributed to all Israel, both men and women, to each a loaf of bread, a portion of meat,[o] and a cake of raisins.

[4]Moreover he appointed certain of the Levites as ministers before the ark of the LORD, to invoke, to thank, and to praise the LORD, the God of Israel. [5]Asaph was the chief, and second to him were Zechariah, Je-iel, Shemiramoth, Jehiel, Mattithiah, Eliab, Benaiah, Obed-edom, and Je-iel, who were to play harps and lyres; Asaph was to sound the cymbals, [6]and Benaiah and Jahaziel the priests were to blow trumpets continually, before the ark of the covenant of God.

[7]Then on that day David first appointed that thanksgiving be sung to the LORD by Asaph and his brethren.

Ps 105:1–15

[8]O give thanks to the LORD, call on his name,
make known his deeds among the peoples!
[9]Sing to him, sing praises to him,
tell of all his wonderful works!
[10]Glory in his holy name;
let the hearts of those who seek the LORD rejoice!
[11]Seek the LORD and his strength,
seek his presence continually!
[12]Remember the wonderful works that he has done,

"To invoke, to thank and to praise the Lord" (v. 4), three essential elements of the liturgy, are spelt out also in the psalm that follows. Invocation includes the joyful remembrance of the wonders worked by the Lord (vv. 12, 15); thanksgiving means acknowledging God in all his works (vv. 8, 34, 35); and praise of the Lord means sharing in his glory, glorying in him (vv. 10, 25, 36). In Christian liturgy, as a response of faith and love to the spiritual blessings God gives us, "the Church, united with her Lord and 'in the Holy Spirit' (Lk 10:21), blesses the Father 'for his inexpressible gift (2 Cor 9:15) in her adoration, praise and thanksgiving" (*Catechism of the Catholic Church*, 1083).

16:8–36. This hymn is an ensemble of pieces that already existed at the time of writing—specifically, from Psalm 105:

nomine Domini. [3]Et divisit unicuique de Israel a viro usque ad mulierem tortam panis et laganum palmarum et palatham. [4]Constituitque coram arca Domini de Levitis ministros, qui recordarentur operum eius et glorificarent atque laudarent Dominum Deum Israel: [5]Asaph principem et secundum eius Zachariam, porro Iehiel et Semiramoth et Iahiel et Matthathiam et Eliab et Banaiam et Obededom et Iehiel in organis psalterii et citharis, Asaph autem, ut cymbalis personaret, [6]Banaiam vero et Iahaziel sacerdotes, ut canerent tubis iugiter coram arca foederis Dei. [7]In illo die, tunc fecit David prima vice confiteri Domino per manum Asaph et fratrum eius: [8]«Confitemini Domino, invocate nomen eius, / notas facite in populis opera eius. / [9]Canite ei et psallite / et narrate omnia mirabilia eius. / [10]Laudate nomen sanctum eius, / laetetur cor quaerentium Dominum. / [11]Quaerite Dominum et virtutem eius, / quaerite faciem eius semper. / [12]Recordamini mirabilium eius, quae fecit, / signorum illius et iudiciorum

o. Compare Gk Syr Vg: Heb uncertain

the wonders he wrought, the judgments he uttered,
[13] O offspring of Abraham his servant,
sons of Jacob, his chosen ones!
[14] He is the LORD our God;
his judgments are in all the earth.
[15] He is mindful of his covenant for ever,
of the word that he commanded, for a thousand generations,
[16] the covenant which he made with Abraham,
his sworn promise to Isaac,
[17] which he confirmed as a statute to Jacob,
as an everlasting covenant to Israel,
[18] saying, "To you I will give the land of Canaan,
as your portion for an inheritance."
[19] When they were few in number,
and of little account, and sojourners in it,
[20] wandering from nation to nation,
from one kingdom to another people,
[21] he allowed no one to oppress them;
he rebuked kings on their account,
[22] saying, "Touch not my anointed ones,
do my prophets no harm!"
[23] Sing to the LORD, all the earth!
Tell of his salvation from day to day.
[24] Declare his glory among the nations,
his marvellous works among all the peoples!

Is 26:9

Gen 13:15; 15:18–21

Ps 96

1–15 (vv. 8–22), Psalm 96:1–13 (vv. 23–33) and Psalm 106:1, 47–48 (vv. 34–36). It includes some important changes—for example, in v. 13; this is not apparent in the RSV (which has "offspring *of Abraham*"—the same wording as Ps 105:6) but the Hebrew has "offspring *of Israel*". Thus, the song is being sung by the Israel that has returned from exile in Babylon and is celebrating in its life and liturgy the marvels God performed in its regard in the past; it knows it has been gathered "from among the nations to give thanks to thy holy name" (cf. v. 35). Those who have returned from exile see the liturgy as a place where they can celebrate their identity as God's chosen people that exists "from everlasting to everlasting" (v. 36).

oris eius, / [13]semen Israel, servi eius, / filii Iacob, electi illius. / [14]Ipse Dominus Deus noster; / in universa terra iudicia eius. / [15]Recordamini in sempiternum pacti eius, / sermonis, quem praecepit in mille generationes, / [16]pacti, quod pepigit cum Abraham, / et iuramenti illius cum Isaac. / [17]Et constituit illud Iacob in praeceptum / et Israel in pactum sempiternum / [18]dicens: "Tibi dabo terram Chanaan / funiculum hereditatis vestrae", / [19]cum essent pauci numero, / parvi et coloni in ea. / [20]Et transierunt de gente in gentem / et de regno ad populum alterum; / [21]non dimisit quemquam calumniari eos, / sed increpuit pro eis reges: / [22]"Nolite tangere christos meos / et in prophetis meis nolite malignari". / [23]Canite Domino, omnis terra, / annuntiate ex die in diem salutare eius. / [24]Narrate in gentibus gloriam

[25] For great is the LORD, and greatly to be praised,
and he is to be held in awe above all gods.
[26] For all the gods of the peoples are idols;
but the LORD made the heavens.
[27] Honour and majesty are before him;
strength and joy are in his place.
Rev 19:7 [28] Ascribe to the LORD, O families of the peoples,
ascribe to the LORD glory and strength!
[29] Ascribe to the LORD the glory due his name;
bring an offering, and come before him!
Worship the LORD in holy array;
[30] tremble before him, all the earth;
yea, the world stands firm, never to be moved.
Rev 19:6 [31] Let the heavens be glad, and let the earth rejoice,
and let them say among the nations, "The LORD reigns!"
[32] Let the sea roar, and all that fills it,
let the field exult, and everything in it!
[33] Then shall the trees of the wood sing for joy
before the LORD, for he comes to judge the earth.
Ps 106:1, 47–48 [34] O give thanks to the LORD, for he is good;
for his steadfast love endures for ever!

Ps 105:1–15 Acts 26:17 [35]Say also:
"Deliver us, O God of our salvation,
and gather and save us from among the nations,
that we may give thanks to thy holy name,
and glory in thy praise.
1 Cor 14:16 [36]Blessed be the LORD, the God of Israel,
from everlasting to everlasting!"
Then all the people said "Amen!" and praised the LORD.

[37]So David left Asaph and his brethren there before the ark of the covenant of the LORD to minister continually before the ark as

---

eius, / in cunctis populis mirabilia illius. / [25]Quia magnus Dominus et laudabilis nimis / et horribilis super omnes deos; / [26]omnes enim dii populorum inania, / Dominus autem caelos fecit. / [27]Magnificentia et pulchritudo coram eo, / fortitudo et gaudium in loco eius. / [28]Afferte Domino, familiae populorum, / afferte Domino gloriam et imperium; / [29]date Domino gloriam nominis eius, / levate oblationem et venite in conspectu eius / et adorate Dominum in decore sancto. / [30]Commoveatur a facie illius omnis terra; / ipse enim fundavit orbem immobilem. / [31]Laetentur caeli, et exsultet terra, / et dicant in nationibus: "Dominus regnat!". / [32]Tonet mare et plenitudo eius, / exsultent agri et omnia, quae in eis sunt. / [33]Tunc laudabunt ligna saltus coram Domino, / quia venit iudicare terram. / [34]Confitemini Domino, quoniam bonus, / quoniam in aeternum misericordia eius. / [35]Et dicite: "Salva nos, Deus salvator noster, / et congrega nos et erue de gentibus, / ut confiteamur nomini sancto tuo / et exsultemus in carminibus tuis. / [36]Benedictus Dominus, Deus Israel, / ab aeterno usque in aeternum"». Et dixit omnis populus: «Amen!» et «Laus Domino!». [37]Dereliquit itaque ibi coram arca foederis Domini Asaph et fratres eius, ut ministrarent in conspectu arcae iugiter secundum ritum singulorum

each day required, [38]and also Obed-edom and his[p] sixty-eight brethren; while Obed-edom, the son of Jeduthun, and Hosah were to be gatekeepers. [39]And he left Zadok the priest and his brethren the priests before the tabernacle of the LORD in the high place that was at Gibeon, [40]to offer burnt offerings to the LORD upon the altar of burnt offering continually morning and evening, according to all that is written in the law of the LORD which he commanded Israel. [41]With them were Heman and Jeduthun, and the rest of those chosen and expressly named to give thanks to the LORD, for his steadfast love endures for ever. [42]Heman and Jeduthun had trumpets and cymbals for the music and instruments for sacred song. The sons of Jeduthun were appointed to the gate.

[43]Then all the people departed each to his house, and David went home to bless his household. 2 Sam 6:19–20

The prophecy of Nathan

2 Sam 7:1–17

17 [1]Now when David dwelt in his house, David said to Nathan the prophet, "Behold, I dwell in a house of cedar, but the ark of the covenant of the LORD is under a tent." [2]And Nathan said to David, "Do all that is in your heart, for God is with you."

[3]But that same night the word of the LORD came to Nathan, [4]"Go and tell my servant David, 'Thus says the LORD: You shall not Lk 1:69

17:1–27. The last section of the book begins here, the part to do with preparations for the building of the temple, the great enterprise which Solomon will carry out. Nathan's prophecy is faithfully transcribed from 2 Samuel 7:1–29. It is touched up in a few places to suit the period of the post-exile: whereas the oracle in the book of Samuel is messianic in tone, because it is applicable to the Davidic dynasty as such and to each of David's descendants, here it applies directly to Solomon and the temple he will build.

Thus, in v. 1 David is not portrayed as king of peace, and the words "the Lord had given him rest from all his enemies round about" are omitted; this

dierum. [38]Porro Obededom et fratres eius sexaginta octo et Obededom filium Idithun et Hosa constituit ianitores. [39]Sadoc autem sacerdotem et fratres illius sacerdotes coram habitaculo Domini in excelso, quod erat in Gabaon, [40]ut offerrent holocausta Domino super altare holocautomatis iugiter, mane et vespere, iuxta omnia, quae scripta sunt in lege Domini, quam praecepit Israeli. [41]Et cum eis Heman et Idithun et reliquos electos, qui nominatim memorati sunt ad confitendum Domino: «Quoniam in aeternum misericordia eius». [42]Et cum eis Heman et Idithun canentes tuba et quatientes cymbala bene sonantia et omnia musicorum organa ad canendum Deo; filios autem Idithun fecit esse portarios. [43]Reversusque est omnis populus unusquisque in domum suam et David, ut benediceret etiam domui suae. **[17]** [1]Cum autem habitaret David in domo sua, dixit ad Nathan prophetam: «Ecce ego habito in domo cedrina, arca autem foederis Domini sub pellibus est». [2]Et ait Nathan ad David: «Omnia, quae in corde tuo sunt, fac; Deus enim tecum est». [3]Igitur nocte illa factus est sermo Dei ad Nathan dicens:

p. Heb *their*

build me a house to dwell in. [5]For I have not dwelt in a house since the day I led up Israel to this day, but I have gone from tent to tent and from dwelling to dwelling. [6]In all places where I have moved with all Israel, did I speak a word with any of the judges of Israel, whom I commanded to shepherd my people, saying, "Why have you not built me a house of cedar?"' [7]Now therefore thus shall you say to my servant David, 'Thus says the LORD of hosts, I took you from the pasture, from following the sheep, that you should be prince over my people Israel; [8]and I have been with you wherever you went, and have cut off all your enemies from before you; and I will make for you a name, like the name of the great ones of the earth. [9]And I will appoint a place for my people Israel, and will plant them, that they may dwell in their own place, and be disturbed no more; and violent men shall waste them no more, as formerly, [10]from the time that I appointed judges over my people Israel; and I will subdue all your enemies. Moreover I declare to you that the LORD will build you a house. [11]When your days are fulfilled to go to be with your fathers, I will raise up your offspring

---

shows that the Lord is not opposed to the building of the temple, but only to its being built by David, who never managed to achieve peace with his neighbours. David will indeed make careful preparation for the temple's construction, but it will be Solomon who actually builds it. There is also a significant change in the question "Would you build me a house to dwell in" (2 Sam 7:4), to the definite negative "You shall not build me a house to dwell in" (v. 4). Instead, David is assured that Solomon will build the temple: in 2 Samuel 7:12 we read "I will raise up your offspring after you, who will establish his kingdom", whereas Chronicles says, "I will raise up your offspring after you, one of your own sons" (v. 11), thereby specifying that this means Solomon.

Another small variation has the effect of pointing out that God is not guaranteeing stability to the dynasty but only to the immediate succession. The promise "Your house and your kingdom shall be made sure for ever before me" (2 Sam 7:16) becomes "I will confirm him [Solomon] in my house and in my kingdom for ever"

[4]«Vade et loquere David servo meo: Haec dicit Dominus: Non aedificabis tu mihi domum ad habitandum; [5]neque enim mansi in domo ex eo tempore, quo eduxi Israel usque ad hanc diem, sed fui semper migrans de tabernaculo in tabernaculum et de habitatione in habitationem. [6]Ubicumque ambulabam in omni Israel, numquid locutus sum uni iudicum Israel, quibus praeceperam, ut pascerent populum meum, et dixi: Quare non aedificastis mihi domum cedrinam?' " [7]Nunc itaque, sic loqueris ad servum meum David: 'Haec dicit Dominus exercituum: Ego tuli te, cum in pascuis sequereris gregem, ut esses dux populi mei Israel; [8]et fui tecum, quocumque perrexisti, et interfeci omnes inimicos tuos coram te fecique tibi nomen quasi unius magnorum, qui celebrantur in terra. [9]Et dedi locum populo meo Israel et plantavi eum, ut habitaret in eo, et ultra non commovebitur, nec filii iniquitatis atterent eos sicut in principio [10]et ex diebus, quibus dedi iudices populo meo Israel et humiliavi universos inimicos tuos. Annuntio ergo tibi quod aedificaturus sit domum tibi Dominus. [11]Cumque impleveris dies tuos, ut vadas ad patres tuos, suscitabo semen tuum post te, quod erit de filiis tuis, et stabiliam regnum eius. [12]Ipse

after you, one of your own sons, and I will establish his kingdom. [12]He shall build a house for me, and I will establish his throne for ever. [13]I will be his father, and he shall be my son; I will not take my steadfast love from him, as I took it from him who was before you, [14]but I will confirm him in my house and in my kingdom for ever and his throne shall be established for ever.'" [15]In accordance with all these words, and in accordance with all this vision, Nathan spoke to David.

Heb 1:5

Heb 3:2

David's prayer

2 Sam 7:18–29

[16]Then King David went in and sat before the LORD, and said, "Who am I, O LORD God, and what is my house, that thou hast brought me thus far? [17]And this was a small thing in thy eyes, O God; thou hast also spoken of thy servant's house for a great while to come, and hast shown me future generations,[q] O LORD God! [18]And what more can David say to thee for honouring thy servant? For thou knowest thy servant. [19]For thy servant's sake, O LORD, and according to thy own heart, thou hast wrought all this greatness, in

2 Sam 7:21

(v. 14). After the exile, when there is no reigning monarch, the temple itself will endure and the Lord himself will guarantee the continuity of the people. The theological significance of the temple has been used to explain the remarkable event of the incarnation of Jesus Christ: "The entry of our Saviour into history was like the building of the divine temple, but with greater glory; this new temple, if it is compared to the old, is more excellent and illustrious in the same way as the evangelical worship of Christ is greater than the cult of the Law, or as reality transcends its symbols. Moreover, I believe it can also be said that there was only one old temple, established in only one place, Jerusalem, and only one people, the Israelites, could offer sacrifice there; whereas, by contrast, when the Only-begotten Son became like us [. . .], the world was filled with holy temples and countless worshippers, who venerate the Lord of the universe without ceasing, through their spiritual sacrifices and their prayers" (St Cyril of Alexandria, *In Aggaeum*, 14).

The changes made in the "prayer of David" (vv. 16–27) as compared with 2 Samuel 7:18–29 serve to stress the king's devoutness; he acknowledges that all his qualities and all his successes come from the Lord.

aedificabit mihi domum, et firmabo solium eius usque in aeternum. [13]Ego ero ei in patrem, et ipse erit mihi in filium; et misericordiam meam non auferam ab eo, sicut abstuli ab eo, qui ante te fuit. [14]Et statuam eum in domo mea et in regno meo usque in sempiternum, et thronus eius erit firmissimus in perpetuum». [15]Iuxta omnia verba haec et iuxta universam visionem istam, sic locutus est Nathan ad David. [16]Cumque venisset rex David et sedisset coram Domino, dixit: «Quis ego sum, Domine Deus, et quae domus mea, quia adduxisti me hucusque? [17]Sed hoc parum visum est in conspectu tuo, Deus; ideoque locutus es super domum servi tui etiam in futurum et aspexisti me excelsum super ordinem

q. Cn: Heb uncertain

making known all these great things. [20]There is none like thee, O LORD, and there is no God besides thee, according to all that we have heard with our ears. [21]What other[r] nation on earth is like thy people Israel, whom God went to redeem to be his people, making for thyself a name for great and terrible things, in driving out nations before thy people whom thou didst redeem from Egypt? [22]And thou didst make thy people Israel to be thy people for ever; and thou, O LORD, didst become their God. [23]And now, O LORD, let the word which thou hast spoken concerning thy servant and concerning his house be established for ever, and do as thou hast spoken; [24]and thy name will be established and magnified for ever, saying, 'The LORD of hosts, the God of Israel, is Israel's God,' and the house of thy servant David will be established before thee. [25]For thou, my God, hast revealed to thy servant that thou wilt build a house for him; therefore thy servant has found courage to pray before thee. [26]And now, O LORD, thou art God, and thou hast promised this good thing to thy servant; [27]now therefore may it please thee to bless the house of thy servant, that it may continue for ever before thee; for what thou, O LORD, hast blessed is blessed for ever."

Lk 1:69

David's victories

1 Sam 17:4
2 Sam 8:1–14

18 [1]After this David defeated the Philistines and subdued them, and he took Gath and its villages out of the hand of the Philistines.

18:1—20:8. The account of David's wars stresses that God blessed all the king's enterprises (cf. 17:27), including military ones. The king is not to be faulted, so the bloodier episodes reported in the book of Samuel are toned down here, or omitted altogether. The wars, in their way, helped to enhance the splendour of the temple: thanks to the plunder that resulted from them, Solomon had large

hominum, Domine Deus. [18]Quid ultra addere potest David, cum ita glorificaveris servum tuum et cognoveris eum? [19]Domine, propter famulum tuum iuxta cor tuum fecisti omnem magnificentiam hanc; et nota esse voluisti universa magnalia. [20]Domine, non est similis tui, et non est alius deus absque te secundum omnia, quae audivimus auribus nostris. [21]Quis autem est alius ut populus tuus Israel, gens una in terra, ad quam perrexit Deus, ut liberaret sibi populum, ut faceres tibi nomen magnum et terribile eiciens nationes a facie populi tui, quem de Aegypto liberasti? [22]Et posuisti populum tuum Israel tibi in populum usque in aeternum; et tu, Domine, factus es Deus eius. [23]Nunc igitur, Domine, sermo, quem locutus es super famulum tuum et super domum eius, confirmetur in perpetuum; et fac, sicut locutus es. [24]Permaneatque et magnificetur nomen tuum usque in sempiternum, et dicatur: "Dominus exercituum, Deus Israel, est Deus pro Israel, et domus David servi tui permanens coram te". [25]Tu enim, Deus meus, revelasti auriculam servi tui, ut aedificares ei domum; et idcirco invenit servus tuus fiduciam, ut oret coram te. [26]Nunc ergo, Domine, tu es Deus; et locutus es super servum tuum tanta beneficia [27]et coepisti benedicere domui servi tui, ut sit semper coram te: te enim, Domine, benedicente, benedicta erit in perpetuum». **[18]** [1]Factum est autem post haec, ut percuteret David Philisthim et humiliaret eos et

r. Gk Vg: Heb *one*

[2]And he defeated Moab, and the Moabites became servants to David and brought tribute.

[3]David also defeated Hadadezer king of Zobah, toward Hamath, as he went to set up his monument[s] at the river Euphrates. [4]And David took from him a thousand chariots, seven thousand horsemen, and twenty thousand foot soldiers; and David hamstrung all the chariot horses, but left enough for a hundred chariots. [5]And when the Syrians of Damascus came to help Hadadezer king of Zobah, David slew twenty-two thousand men of the Syrians. [6]Then David put garrisons[t] in Syria of Damascus; and the Syrians became servants to David, and brought tribute. And the LORD gave victory to David wherever he went. [7]And David took the shields of gold which were carried by the servants of Hadadezer, and brought them to Jerusalem. [8]And from Tibhath and from Cun, cities of Hadadezer, David took very much bronze; with it Solomon made the bronze sea and the pillars and the vessels of bronze.

1 Kings 7:15,23,27
1 Chron 22:3

[9]When Tou king of Hamath heard that David had defeated the whole army of Hadadezer, king of Zobah, [10]he sent his son Hadoram to King David, to greet him, and to congratulate him because he had fought against Hadadezer and defeated him; for Hadadezer had often been at war with Tou. And he sent all sorts of articles of gold, of silver, and of bronze; [11]these also King David dedicated to the LORD, together with the silver and gold which he had carried off from all the nations, from Edom, Moab, the Ammonites, the Philistines, and Amalek.

2 Sam 8:10

---

quantities of bronze for making the pillars and vessels (18:8). Also, there is no mention of David's adultery or of the death of Uriah (reported in Samuel in the context of the wars against the Ammonites: cf. 2 Sam 10:1–12, 31)—possibly to preserve Solomon's name from any trace of uncleanness, even an uncleanness inherited from his parents.

tolleret Geth et filias eius de manu Philisthim [2]percuteretque Moab, et fierent Moabitae servi David offerentes ei tributum. [3]Et percussit David etiam Adadezer regem Soba in regione ad Emath, quando perrexit, ut dilataret imperium suum usque ad flumen Euphraten. [4]Cepit ergo David mille quadrigas eius et septem milia equites ac viginti milia virorum peditum; subnervavitque omnes equos curruum, exceptis centum quadrigis, quas reservavit sibi. [5]Supervenit autem et Syrus Damascenus, ut auxilium praeberet Adadezer regi Soba; sed et huius percussit David viginti duo milia virorum [6]et posuit praesidium in Syria Damasci, ut Syria quoque serviret sibi et offerret tributum. Adiuvitque eum Dominus in cunctis, ad quae perrexerat. [7]Tulit quoque David arma aurea, quae habuerant servi Adadezer, et attulit ea in Ierusalem; [8]necnon de Tebah et Chun urbibus Adadezer aeris plurimum, de quo fecit Salomon mare aeneum et columnas et vasa aenea. [9]Quod cum audisset Thou rex Emath, percussisse videlicet David omnem exercitum Adadezer regis Soba, [10]misit Adoram filium suum ad regem David, ut salutaret eum et congratularetur, eo quod pugnasset cum Adadezer et percussisset eum; adversarius quippe erat Thou Adadezer. [11]Sed et omnia vasa aurea et argentea et aenea consecravit rex

s. Heb *hand* **t.** Gk Vg 2 Sam 8:6 Compare Syr: Heb lacks *garrisons*

1 Sam 26:6
1 Chron 19:11

[12]And Abishai, the son of Zeruiah, slew eighteen thousand Edomites in the Valley of Salt. [13]And he put garrisons in Edom; and all the Edomites became David's servants. And the LORD gave victory to David wherever he went.

2 Sam 8:15–18

[14]So David reigned over all Israel; and he administered justice and equity to all his people. [15]And Joab the son of Zeruiah was over the army; and Jehoshaphat the son of Ahilud was recorder;

2 Sam 8:17

[16]and Zadok the son of Ahitub and Ahimelech the son of Abiathar were priests; and Shavsha was secretary; [17]and Benaiah the son of Jehoiada was over the Cherethites and the Pelethites; and David's sons were the chief officials in the service of the king.

2 Sam 10:1–19

Victories over the Ammonites

19 [1]Now after this Nahash the king of the Ammonites died, and his son reigned in his stead. [2]And David said, "I will deal loyally with Hanun the son of Nahash, for his father dealt loyally with me." So David sent messengers to console him concerning his father. And David's servants came to Hanun in the land of the Ammonites, to console him. [3]But the princes of the Ammonites said to Hanun, "Do you think, because David has sent comforters to you, that he is honouring your father? Have not his servants come to you to search and to overthrow and to spy out the land?"

18:17. The king's sons, who in 2 Samuel 8:18, were priests, are portrayed here as having only political roles, leaving the liturgy the exclusive preserve of the Levites and priests. This separation of religion and politics would become important after the return from exile, and even more so in the New Testament. The evangelists report what Jesus said about the distinction between serving God and serving the political community: "Render to Caesar the things that are Caesar's, and to God the things that are God's" (cf. Mt 22:21).

19:1–19. This account of wars against the Ammonites and the Syrians is almost identical to that in 2 Samuel 10:1–19, and the few changes there are are due to the writer's desire to enhance David's reputation.

David Domino cum argento et auro, quod tulerat ex universis gentibus, tam de Idumaea et Moab et filiis Ammon, quam de Philisthim et Amalec. [12]Abisai vero filius Sarviae percussit Edom in valle Salis decem et octo milia [13] et constituit in Edom praesidium, ut serviret Idumaea David. Salvavitque Dominus David in cunctis, ad quae perrexerat. [14]Regnavit ergo David super universum Israel et faciebat iudicium atque iustitiam cuncto populo suo. [15]Porro Ioab filius Sarviae erat super exercitum, et Iosaphat filius Ahilud a commentariis. [16]Sadoc autem filius Achitob et Achimelech filius Abiathar sacerdotes et Susa scriba. [17]Banaias vero filius Ioiadae super legiones Cherethi et Phelethi; porro filii David primi ad manum regis. **[19]** [1]Accidit autem post haec, ut moreretur Naas rex filiorum Ammon, et regnaret filius eius pro eo. [2]Dixitque David: «Faciam misericordiam cum Hanon filio Naas; praestitit enim pater eius mihi gratiam». Misitque David nuntios ad consolandum eum super morte patris sui. Qui cum pervenissent in terram filiorum Ammon, ut consolarentur Hanon, [3]dixerunt principes filiorum Ammon ad Hanon: «Tu forsitan putas quod David honoris causa in patrem tuum miserit, qui consolentur te; nec animadvertis

[4]So Hanun took David's servants, and shaved them, and cut off their garments in the middle, at their hips, and sent them away; [5]and they departed. When David was told concerning the men, he sent to meet them, for the men were greatly ashamed. And the king said, "Remain at Jericho until your beards have grown, and then return."

[6]When the Ammonites saw that they had made themselves odious to David, Hanun and the Ammonites sent a thousand talents of silver to hire chariots and horsemen from Mesopotamia, from Aram-maacah, and from Zobah. [7]They hired thirty-two thousand chariots and the king of Maacah with his army, who came and encamped before Medeba. And the Ammonites were mustered from their cities and came to battle. [8]When David heard of it, he sent Joab and all the army of the mighty men. [9]And the Ammonites came out and drew up in battle array at the entrance of the city, and the kings who had come were by themselves in the open country.

[10]When Joab saw that the battle was set against him both in front and in the rear, he chose some of the picked men of Israel, and arrayed them against the Syrians; [11]the rest of his men he put in the charge of Abishai his brother, and they were arrayed against the Ammonites. [12]And he said, "If the Syrians are too strong for me, then you shall help me; but if the Ammonites are too strong for you, then I will help you. [13]Be of good courage, and let us play the man for our people, and for the cities of our God; and may the LORD do what seems good to him." [14]So Joab and the people who were with him drew near before the Syrians for battle; and they fled before him. [15]And when the Ammonites saw that the Syrians fled, they likewise fled before Abishai, Joab's brother, and entered the city. Then Joab came to Jerusalem.

---

quod, ut explorent et investigent et evertant terram tuam, venerint ad te servi eius». [4]Igitur Hanon pueros David tulit et rasit et praecidit tunicas eorum a natibus usque ad pedes et dimisit eos. [5]Qui cum abissent et hoc mandassent David, misit in occursum eorum—grandem enim contumeliam sustinuerant—et praecepit, ut manerent in Iericho, donec cresceret barba eorum, et tunc reverterentur. [6]Videntes autem filii Ammon quod odiosos se fecissent David, tam Hanon quam reliquus populus miserunt mille talenta argenti, ut conducerent sibi de Mesopotamia et de Syria Maacha et de Soba currus et equites; [7]conduxeruntque sibi triginta duo milia curruum et regem Maacha cum populo eius. Qui cum venissent, castrametati sunt e regione Medaba; filii quoque Ammon congregati de urbibus suis venerunt ad bellum. [8]Quod cum audisset David, misit Ioab et omnem exercitum virorum fortium. [9]Egressique filii Ammon direxerunt aciem iuxta portam civitatis; reges autem, qui ad auxilium venerant, separatim in agro steterunt. [10]Igitur Ioab intellegens bellum et ex adverso et post tergum contra se fieri elegit viros fortissimos de universo Israel et perrexit contra Syrum; [11]reliquam autem partem populi dedit sub manu Abisai fratris sui, et perrexerunt contra filios Ammon. [12]Dixitque: «Si vicerit me Syrus, auxilio eris mihi; si autem superaverint te filii Ammon, ero tibi in praesidium. [13]Confortare et agamus viriliter pro populo nostro et pro urbibus Dei nostri; Dominus autem, quod in conspectu suo bonum est. faciet». [14]Appropinquavit ergo Ioab et populus, qui cum eo erat, contra Syrum ad proelium, et fugerunt a facie eorum. [15]Porro filii Ammon videntes quod fugisset Syrus, ipsi quoque fugerunt Abisai fratrem eius et ingressi sunt civitatem. Reversusque est etiam Ioab in Ierusalem. [16]Videns autem Syrus quod cecidisset

[16]But when the Syrians saw that they had been defeated by Israel, they sent messengers and brought out the Syrians who were beyond the Euphrates, with Shophach the commander of the army of Hadadezer at their head. [17]And when it was told David, he gathered all Israel together, and crossed the Jordan, and came to them, and drew up his forces against them. And when David set the battle in array against the Syrians, they fought with him. [18]And the Syrians fled before Israel; and David slew of the Syrians the men of seven thousand chariots, and forty thousand foot soldiers, and killed also Shophach the commander of their army.[19]And when the servants of Hadadezer saw that they had been defeated by Israel, they made peace with David, and became subject to him. So the Syrians were not willing to help the Ammonites any more.

2 Sam 11:1; 12:26

Siege and capture of Rabbah

20 [1]In the spring of the year, the time when kings go forth to battle, Joab led out the army, and ravaged the country of the Ammonites, and came and besieged Rabbah. But David remained at Jerusalem. And Joab smote Rabbah, and overthrew it. [2]And

20:1–8. The wars against the Ammonites and the Philistines are interpreted as episodes which underline the extraordinary qualities of the king. Thus, in the conquest of the Ammonite capital, Rabbah, David is not depicted as being a greater strategist than his lieutenant Joab (cf. 2 Sam 12:26–28) but as the devout king who fights against idolatry and destroys Milcom the idol (cf. 1 Kings 11:5). And in the struggle against the giants, it is not David the daring youth who takes on Goliath (cf. 1 Sam 17:1–58) but the mature king who comes to dominate his enemies (v. 8), leaving it to his men to do the slaying. As victorious but peace-loving king, David is also a figure of Christ: "The word David means 'strong-armed'; and he was truly a great warrior. Trusting in the Lord his God, he waged war and defeated all his enemies; with God's help, he ruled over his empire; in all things he foreshadowed the one who was to come and cause his enemies to submit—the devil and his minions. The Church overcomes all these enemies. And she overcomes them by meekness,

coram Israel, misit nuntios et adduxit Syrum, qui erat trans fluvium; Sophach autem princeps militiae Adadezer erat dux eorum. [17]Quod cum nuntiatum esset David, congregavit universum Israel et transivit Iordanem venitque ad eos et direxit ex adverso aciem et pugnavit cum eis. [18]Fugit autem Syrus Israel, et interfecit David de Syris septem milia curruum et quadraginta milia peditum et Sophach exercitus principem. [19]Videntes autem servi Adadezer se ab Israel esse superatos, fecerunt pacem cum David et servierunt ei; noluitque ultra Syria auxilium praebere filiis Ammon. **[20]** [1]Factum est autem post anni circulum, eo tempore, quo solent reges ad bella procedere, eduxit Ioab robur exercitus et vastavit terram filiorum Ammon; perrexitque et obsedit Rabba. Porro David manebat in Ierusalem, quando Ioab percussit Rabba et destruxit eam. [2]Tulit autem David coronam Melchom de capite eius et invenit in ea auri pondo talentum et pretiosissimam gemmam, venitque super caput David; manubias quoque urbis plurimas tulit. [3]Populum autem, qui erat in ea. eduxit et condemnavit ad operam lapicidinarum et ad

David took the crown of their king[u] from his head; he found that it weighed a talent of gold, and in it was a precious stone; and it was placed on David's head. And he brought forth the spoil of the city, a very great amount. [3]And he brought forth the people who were in it, and set them to labour[v] with saws and iron picks and axes;[w] and thus David did to all the cities of the Ammonites. Then David and all the people returned to Jerusalem.

2 Sam 12:30–31
Rev 14:14

Other victories over the Philistines

[4]And after this there arose war with the Philistines at Gezer; then Sibbecai the Hushathite slew Sippai, who was one of the descendants of the giants; and the Philistines were subdued. [5]And there was again war with the Philistines; and Elhanan the son of Jair slew Lahmi the brother of Goliath the Gittite, the shaft of whose spear was like a weaver's beam. [6]And there was again war at Gath, where there was a man of great stature, who had six fingers on each hand, and six toes on each foot, twenty-four in number; and he also was descended from the giants. [7]And when he taunted Israel, Jonathan the son of Shime-a, David's brother, slew him. [8]These were descended from the giants in Gath; and they fell by the hand of David and by the hand of his servants.

Deut 2:10
Josh 10:33
2 Sam 21:18–22
1 Kings 16:9

The census

21 *[1]Satan stood up against Israel, and incited David to number Israel. [2]So David said to Joab and the commanders

2 Sam 24:1–9
Job 1:6–9; 2:1–4
Mt 4:10
1 Cor 7:5

for our King defeated the devil by his meekness" (St Augustine, *Enarrationes in Psalmos*, 131, 3).

21:1–30. The episode of the census, even though it implies an offence against God (v. 7; cf. 2 Sam 24:1), is interpreted here as a context which allows us to see David's religious piety: the king sincerely repents and acquires a site for the future temple.

So, deceived by Satan (v. 1), the king commissioned a census without realizing that he was committing a sin. But

secures et dolabras ferreas. Sic fecit David cunctis urbibus filiorum Ammon et reversus est cum omni populo suo in Ierusalem. [4]Post haec initum est bellum in Gazer adversum Philisthaeos, in quo percussit Sobbochai Husathites Saphai de genere Raphaim, et humiliavit eos. [5]Aliud quoque bellum gestum est adversus Philisthaeos, in quo percussit Elchanan filius Iair Lahmi fratrem Goliath Getthaeum, cuius hastae lignum erat quasi liciatorium texentium. [6]Sed et aliud bellum accidit in Geth, in quo fuit homo longissimus senos habens digitos, id est simul viginti quattuor, qui et ipse de Rapha fuerat stirpe generatus; [7]hic blasphemavit Israel, et percussit eum Ionathan filius Samma fratris David. Hi sunt filii Rapha in Geth, qui ceciderunt in manu David et servorum eius. **[21]** [1]Consurrexit autem Satan contra Israel et incitavit David, ut numeraret Israel. [2]Dixitque David ad Ioab et ad principes populi: «Ite et

u. Or *Milcom* See 1 Kings 11:5 **v.** Compare 2 Sam 12:31: Heb *he sawed* **w.** Compare 2 Sam 12:31: Heb *saws*

of the army, "Go, number Israel, from Beer-sheba to Dan, and bring me a report, that I may know their number." [3]But Joab said, "May the LORD add to his people a hundred times as many as they are! Are they not, my lord the king, all of them my lord's servants? Why then should my lord require this? Why should he bring guilt upon Israel?" [4]But the king's word prevailed against Joab. So Joab departed and went throughout all Israel, and came back to Jerusalem. [5]And Joab gave the sum of the numbering of the people to David. In all Israel there were one million one hundred thousand men who drew the sword, and in Judah four hundred and seventy thousand who drew the sword. [6]But he did not include Levi and Benjamin in the numbering, for the king's command was abhorrent to Joab.

---

as soon as he heard that God was going to punish Israel on account of this, the king realized the gravity of his action and how foolish he had been, and he humbled himself (v. 8); he accepted God's punishment, did penance (as did the elders: v. 16), and pleaded on behalf of the people, asking God to punish him and not them (v. 17). The prophet Gad then made known to the king that God had chosen the threshing floor of Ornan to be the site of the altar (v. 18), the place, too, where the temple would be built: the presence of the angel (vv. 15, 19) confirms this, and the fire that comes down from heaven shows that God indeed approves this site. David paid a huge price for the threshing floor—six hundred shekels (v. 25). According to the book of Samuel (2 Sam 24:24) he paid only fifty shekels: probably the Chronicler interpreted that as meaning fifty per each tribe, so that the costs were borne by all. At the end of the negotiations for the purchase, the king solemnly proclaimed: "Here shall be the house of the Lord God and here the altar of burnt offering for Israel" (22:1).

21:1. "Satan" is he who tempts man to commit evil. The book of Chronicles reflects a very advanced stage in revelation concerning the devil and angels. In previous books the Hebrew word *satan* refers to any adversary (cf. 1 Kings 5:4; 11:14–23), or to a deceiver (cf. 1 Kings 22:19–23); even in Job 1:6–12; 2:1–10 Satan plays this role of accusing someone before the Lord, and in Zechariah 3:1 he accuses the priest before God. But here the word *satan*, without the definite article, is a proper name: "He who machinates evil against men". In the New Testament he is given the Greek name "devil" both when he tempts Jesus (cf. Mt 4:1–11; cf. Lk 4:1–13) and when he exercises possession over individuals. Christian teaching is very clear about the devil being a real person, one who tries to lead men into sin. "Satan is the 'deceiver of the whole world' (Rev 12:9). Through him

numerate Israel a Bersabee usque Dan et afferte mihi numerum, ut sciam». [3]Responditque Ioab: «Augeat Dominus populum suum centuplum quam sunt. Nonne, domine mi rex, omnes servi tui sunt? Quare hoc quaerit dominus meus, quod in peccatum reputetur Israeli?». [4]Sed sermo regis magis praevaluit; egressusque est Ioab et circuivit universum Israel et reversus est Ierusalem. [5]Deditque David numerum census, et inventus est omnis Israel numerus mille milia et centum milia virorum educentium gladium; de Iuda autem quadringenta septuaginta milia bellatorum; [6]nam Levi et Beniamin non

Punishment for holding the census

2 Sam 24:10–17

[7]But God was displeased with this thing, and he smote Israel. [8]And David said to God, "I have sinned greatly in that I have done this thing. But now, I pray thee, take away the iniquity of thy servant; for I have done very foolishly." [9]And the LORD spoke to Gad, David's seer, saying, [10]"Go and say to David, 'Thus says the LORD, Three things I offer you; choose one of them, that I may do it to you.'" [11]So Gad came to David and said to him, "Thus says the LORD, 'Take which you will: [12]either three years of famine; or three months of devastation by your foes, while the sword of your enemies overtakes you; or else three days of the sword of the LORD, pestilence upon the land, and the angel of the LORD destroying throughout all the territory of Israel.' Now decide what answer I shall return to him who sent me." [13]Then David said to Gad, "I am in great distress; let me fall into the hand of the LORD, for his mercy is very great; but let me not fall into the hand of man."

2 Sam 24:13

[14]So the LORD sent a pestilence upon Israel; and there fell seventy thousand men of Israel. [15]And God sent the angel to Jerusalem to destroy it; but when he was about to destroy it, the LORD saw, and he repented of the evil; and he said to the destroying angel, "It is enough; now stay your hand." And the angel of the LORD was standing by the threshing floor of Ornan the Jebusite.

---

sin and death entered the world and by his definitive defeat all creation will be 'freed from the corruption of sin and death' (*Roman Missal*, Eucharistic Prayer IV)" (*Catechism of the Catholic Church*, 2852).

"The angel", on the other hand, is the faithful obeyer of the Lord's commands (vv. 12, 15–16, 20, 30). In this episode he has to implement the punishment laid down by God, which is why he is also called the "destroying angel" (v. 15; cf. Ex 12:23), and he fills men with dread (v. 3). God uses angels to influence human events: "In the meantime, the whole life of the Church benefits from the mysterious and powerful help of angels" (*Catechism of the Catholic Church*, 334).

numeravit in medio eorum, eo quod invitus exequeretur regis imperium. [7]Displicuit autem Deo, quod iussum erat, et percussit Israel. [8]Dixitque David ad Deum: «Peccavi nimis, ut hoc facerem; obsecro, aufer iniquitatem servi tui, quia valde insipienter egi». [9]Et locutus est Dominus ad Gad videntem David dicens: [10]«Vade et loquere ad David et dic: Haec dicit Dominus: Trium tibi optionem do: unum, quod volueris, elige, et faciam tibi». [11]Cumque venisset Gad ad David, dixit ei: «Haec dicit Dominus: Elige, quod volueris: [12]aut tribus annis famem aut tribus mensibus fugere te hostes tuos et gladium eorum non posse evadere aut tribus diebus gladium Domini et pestilentiam versari in terra et angelum Domini interficere in universis finibus Israel. Nunc igitur vide quid respondeam ei, qui misit me». [13]Et dixit David ad Gad: «Ex omni parte me angustiae premunt, sed melius mihi est, ut incidam in manus Domini, quia multae sunt miserationes eius, quam in manus hominum». [14]Misit ergo Dominus pestilentiam in Israel, et ceciderunt de Israel septuaginta milia virorum. [15]Misit quoque Deus angelum in Ierusalem, ut percuteret eam. Cumque percuteretur, vidit Dominus et misertus est super magnitudinem mali et imperavit

[16]And David lifted his eyes and saw the angel of the LORD standing between earth and heaven, and in his hand a drawn sword stretched out over Jerusalem. Then David and the elders, clothed in sackcloth, fell upon their faces. [17]And David said to God, "Was it not I who gave command to number the people? It is I who have sinned and done very wickedly. But these sheep, what have they done? Let thy hand, I pray thee, O LORD my God, be against me and against my father's house; but let not the plague be upon thy people."

2 Sam 24:18–25

[18]Then the angel of the LORD commanded Gad to say to David that David should go up and rear an altar to the LORD on the threshing floor of Ornan the Jebusite. [19]So David went up at Gad's word, which he had spoken in the name of the LORD. [20]Now Ornan was threshing wheat; he turned and saw the angel, and his four sons who were with him hid themselves. [21]As David came to Ornan, Ornan looked and saw David and went forth from the threshing floor, and did obeisance to David with his face to the ground. [22]And David said to Ornan, "Give me the site of the threshing floor that I may build on it an altar to the LORD—give it to me at its full price—that the plague may be averted from the people." [23]Then Ornan said to David, "Take it; and let my lord the king do what seems good to him; see, I give the oxen for burnt offerings, and the threshing sledges for the wood, and the wheat for a cereal offering. I give it all." [24]But King David said to Ornan, "No, but I will buy it for the full price; I will not take for the LORD what is yours, nor offer burnt offerings which cost me nothing." [25]So David paid Ornan six hundred shekels of gold by weight for the site. [26]And David built there an altar to the LORD and presented burnt offerings and peace offerings, and called upon the LORD, and

2 Sam 24:24

1 Kings 18:38

---

angelo, qui percutiebat: «Sufficit, iam cesset manus tua». Porro angelus Domini stabat iuxta aream Ornan Iebusaei. [16]Levansque David oculos suos vidit angelum Domini stantem inter terram et caelum et evaginatum gladium in manu eius et versum contra Ierusalem; et ceciderunt tam ipse quam maiores natu vestiti ciliciis proni in terram. [17]Dixitque David ad Deum: «Nonne ego sum, qui iussi, ut numeraretur populus? Ego qui peccavi, ego qui malum feci: iste grex quid commeruit? Domine Deus meus, vertatur, obsecro, manus tua in me et in domum patris mei; populus autem tuus non percutiatur». [18]Angelus autem Domini praecepit Gad dicere David, ut ascenderet exstrueretque altare Domino in area Ornan Iebusaei. [19]Ascendit ergo David iuxta sermonem Gad, quem locutus fuerat ex nomine Domini. [20]Porro Ornan, cum conversus vidisset angelum, quattuorque filii eius cum eo absconderunt se; nam eo tempore terebat in area triticum. [21]Igitur, cum veniret David ad Ornan, conspexit eum Ornan et processit ei obviam de area et adoravit illum pronus in terram. [22]Dixitque ei David: «Da mihi locum areae tuae, ut aedificem in ea altare Domino, ita ut quantum valet argenti accipias, et cesset plaga a populo». [23]Dixit autem Ornan ad David: «Tolle, et faciat dominus meus rex, quodcumque ei placet; sed et boves do in holocaustum et tribulas in ligna et triticum in sacrificium; omnia libens praebebo». [24]Dixitque ei rex David: «Nequaquam ita fiet, sed argentum dabo quantum valet; neque enim tibi auferre debeo et sic offerre Domino holocausta gratuita». [25]Dedit ergo David Ornan pro loco siclos auri iustissimi ponderis

he answered him with fire from heaven upon the altar of burnt offering. [27]Then the LORD commanded the angel; and he put his sword back into its sheath.

[28]At that time, when David saw that the LORD had answered him at the threshing floor of Ornan the Jebusite, he made his sacrifices there. [29]For the tabernacle of the LORD, which Moses had made in the wilderness, and the altar of burnt offering were at that time in the high place at Gibeon; [30]but David could not go before it to inquire of God, for he was afraid of the sword of the angel of the LORD.

Preparations for building the temple*

1 Chron 29:2–19
2 Chron 3:1

22 [1]Then David said, "Here shall be the house of the LORD God and here the altar of burnt offering for Israel."

1 Kings 5:31–32; 9–11
2 Chron 2:17

[2]David commanded to gather together the aliens who were in the land of Israel, and he set stonecutters to prepare dressed stones for building the house of God. [3]David also provided great stores of iron for nails for the doors of the gates and for clamps, as well as bronze in quantities beyond weighing, [4]and cedar timbers without number; for the Sidonians and Tyrians brought great quantities of cedar to David. [5]For David said, "Solomon my son is young and inexperienced, and the house that is to be built for the LORD must be exceedingly magnificent, of fame and glory throughout all lands; I will therefore make preparation for it." So David provided materials in great quantity before his death.

1 Kings 5:6
1 Kings 3:7
1 Chron 29:1

***22:1—29:30.** The last section of 1 Chronicles has no exact parallels in Samuel or Kings, though a few scattered pieces come from these books. The central theme here is the plan for building the temple. Being the last great enterprise of David, it is like a last will which his son Solomon, and the priests and Levites, will have to execute. The end of David's life parallels Moses' in a way: Moses did not get to enter the promised land, and he had to hand over to his lieutenant Joshua (cf. Deut 31:1–3); and David will not see the

sescentos [26]et aedificavit ibi altare Domino obtulitque holocausta et pacifica et invocavit Dominum. Et exaudivit eum in igne de caelo super altare holocausti, [27]praecepitque Dominus angelo, et convertit gladium suum in vaginam. [28]In illo ergo tempore David videns quod exaudisset eum Dominus in area Ornan Iebusaei immolavit ibi victimas. [29]Tabernaculum autem Domini, quod fecerat Moyses in deserto, et altare holocaustorum ea tempestate erat in excelso Gabaon; [30]et non praevaluit David ire, ut ibi obsecraret Deum; nimio enim fuerat timore perterritus videns gladium angeli Domini. **[22]** [1]Dixitque David: «Haec est domus Domini Dei, et hoc est altare holocausti pro Israel». [2]Et praecepit, ut congregarentur omnes advenae de terra Israel et constituit ex eis latomos ad caedendos lapides et poliendos, ut aedificaretur domus Dei. [3]Ferrum quoque plurimum ad clavos ianuarum et ad commissuras atque iuncturas praeparavit David et aeris pondus innumerabile. [4]Ligna quoque cedrina non poterant aestimari, quae Sidonii et Tyrii deportaverant ad David. [5]Et dixit David: «Salomon filius meus puer parvulus est et tener; domus autem, quae aedificanda est Domino, talis esse debet, ut in cunctis regionibus nominetur et glorificetur. Praeparabo ergo ei necessaria». Et ob hanc causam ante mortem

Acts 7:47
2 Sam 7:3
1 Chron 28:3
1 Kings 4:25; 5:4
2 Sam 7:13

[6]Then he called for Solomon his son, and charged him to build a house for the LORD, the God of Israel. [7]David said to Solomon, "My son, I had it in my heart to build a house to the name of the LORD my God. [8]But the word of the LORD came to me, saying, 'You have shed much blood and have waged great wars; you shall not build a house to my name, because you have shed so much blood before me upon the earth. [9]Behold, a son shall be born to you; he shall be a man of peace. I will give him peace from all his enemies round about; for his name shall be Solomon, and I will give peace and quiet to Israel in his days. [10]He shall build a house for my name. He shall be my son, and I will be his father, and I will establish his royal throne in Israel for ever.' [11]Now, my son, the LORD be with you, so that you may succeed in building the house

---

fulfilment of his great desire to build the temple: that will be Solomon's task. In both cases God weaves the web of history, using men as his loyal instruments.

There are three symmetrical parts to this section: the discourses of David to Solomon and the elders of the people (chap. 22), the lists of the temple servants (chaps. 23–27), and the final discourses about the building of the temple and about its future liturgy (chaps. 28–29).

22:1–19. David's discourse to Solomon (vv. 7–16) is a canticle in praise of peace: David's involvement in war is the real obstacle to his building the temple himself; this is not because all wars are morally wrong, but because only a "man of peace" could build the temple which is to be a "house of rest" (28:2). Solomon, the one chosen to build it, bears a name which is phonetically like *shalom* (peace); in the days of Solomon, God "will grant Israel peace and quiet" (v. 9). In this sense Solomon is also a figure of Christ: "Christ, the Word made flesh, the prince of peace, reconciled all men to God by the cross, and, restoring the unity of all in one people and one body, he abolished hatred in his own flesh; having been lifted up through his resurrection he poured forth the Spirit of love into the hearts of men" (Vatican II, *Gaudium et spes*, 78).

The second discourse, addressed to the leaders (vv. 18–19), is an exhortation to "seek the Lord" (v. 19), that is, to be committed to doing the will of God, specifically to build the temple. This testament of David, which will be executed by his subjects, will be re-enacted by the exiles returned from Babylon, whose duty it is to restore the profaned temple.

suam omnes paravit impensas. [6]Vocavitque Salomonem filium suum et praecepit ei, ut aedificaret domum Domino, Deo Israel; [7]dixitque David ad Salomonem: «Fili mi, voluntatis meae fuit, ut aedificarem domum nomini Domini Dei mei, [8]et factus est ad me sermo Domini dicens: "Multum sanguinem effudisti et magna bella bellasti. Non poteris aedificare domum nomini meo, tanto effuso sanguine coram me. [9]Filius, qui nascetur tibi, erit vir quietissimus; faciam enim eum requiescere ab omnibus inimicis suis per circuitum et ob hanc causam Salomon vocabitur, et pacem et otium dabo in Israel cunctis diebus eius. [10]Ipse aedificabit domum nomini meo et ipse erit mihi in filium, et ego ero ei in patrem; firmaboque solium regni eius super Israel in aeternum". [11]Nunc ergo, fili mi, sit Dominus

of the LORD your God, as he has spoken concerning you. [12]Only, may the LORD grant you discretion and understanding, that when he gives you charge over Israel you may keep the law of the LORD your God. [13]Then you will prosper if you are careful to observe the statutes and the ordinances which the LORD commanded Moses for Israel. Be strong, and of good courage. Fear not; be not dismayed. [14]With great pains I have provided for the house of the LORD a hundred thousand talents of gold, a million talents of silver, and bronze and iron beyond weighing, for there is so much of it; timber and stone too I have provided. To these you must add. [15]You have an abundance of workmen: stonecutters, masons, carpenters, and all kinds of craftsmen without number, skilled in working [16]gold, silver, bronze, and iron. Arise and be doing! The LORD be with you!"

Deut 31:23

[17]David also commanded all the leaders of Israel to help Solomon his son, saying, [18]"Is not the LORD your God with you? And has he not given you peace on every side? For he has delivered the inhabitants of the land into my hand; and the land is subdued before the LORD and his people. [19]Now set your mind and heart to seek the LORD your God. Arise and build the sanctuary of the LORD God, so that the ark of the covenant of the LORD and the holy vessels of God may be brought into a house built for the name of the LORD."

1 Kings 8:6
2 Chron 5:7; 6:11

Orders and functions of Levites

23 [1]When David was old and full of days, he made Solomon his son king over Israel.

Num 1:50; 3:6–10
1 Kings 1:1–2:1

23:1–6. David made the throne over to his son without any intrigue about the succession (v. 1); he established the functions of each Levite group (vv. 4–5), and allocated roles to the Levites (v. 6). This shows that his mental

tecum; et prosperare et aedifica domum Domino Deo tuo, sicut locutus est de te. [12]Tantum det tibi Dominus prudentiam et sensum, ut regere possis Israel et custodire legem Domini Dei tui; [13]tunc enim proficere poteris, si custodieris mandata et iudicia, quae praecepit Dominus Moysi super Israel. Confortare et viriliter age; ne timeas neque paveas. [14]Ecce ego in labore meo praeparavi impensas domus Domini: auri talenta centum milia et argenti mille milia talentorum, aeris vero et ferri non est pondus, vincitur enim numerus magnitudine. Ligna et lapides praeparavi; tu autem ad ea adicies. [15]Habes quoque plurimos artifices latomos et caementarios artificesque lignorum et omnium artium ad faciendum opus prudentissimos [16]in auro et argento et aere et ferro, cuius non est numerus. Surge igitur et fac, et erit Dominus tecum». [17]Praecepit quoque David cunctis principibus Israel, ut adiuvarent Salomonem filium suum: [18]«Cernitis, inquiens, quod Dominus Deus vester vobiscum sit et dederit vobis requiem per circuitum et tradiderit habitatores terrae in manu vestra, et subiecta sit terra coram Domino et coram populo eius. [19]Praebete igitur corda vestra et animas vestras, ut quaeratis Dominum Deum vestrum; et consurgite et aedificate sanctuarium Domini Dei, ut introducatur arca foederis Domini et vasa Deo consecrata in domum, quae aedificatur nomini Domini». **[23]** [1]Igitur David senex et plenus

[2]David assembled all the leaders of Israel and the priests and the Levites. [3]The Levites, thirty years old and upward, were numbered, and the total was thirty-eight thousand men. [4]"Twenty-four thousand of these," David said, "shall have charge of the work in the house of the LORD, six thousand shall be officers and judges, [5]four thousand gatekeepers, and four thousand shall offer praises to the LORD with the instruments which I have made for praise." [6]And David organized them in divisions corresponding to the sons of Levi: Gershom, Kohath, and Merari.

Num 4:3

Amos 6:5

[7]The sons of Gershom[x] were Ladan and Shime-i. [8]The sons of Ladan: Jehiel the chief, and Zetham, and Joel, three. [9]The sons of Shime-i: Shelomoth, Hazi-el, and Haran, three. These were the heads of the fathers' houses of Ladan. [10]And the sons of Shime-i: Jahath, Zina, and Jeush, and Beriah. These four were the sons of Shime-i. [11]Jahath was the chief, and Zizah the second; but Jeush and Beriah had not many sons, therefore they became a father's house in one reckoning.

1 Chron 26:21ff

[12]The sons of Kohath: Amram, Izhar, Hebron, and Uzziel, four. [13]The sons of Amram: Aaron and Moses. Aaron was set apart to consecrate the most holy things, that he and his sons for ever should burn incense before the LORD, and minister to him and

---

powers and administrative skills stayed with him till his death—as did his religious piety and interest in the liturgy, given that he laid the foundations for a properly functioning priesthood.

The minimum age for a Levite to execute his ministry was not always the same; it seems that initially it was thirty years (v. 3; cf. Num 4:3); at some point it was lowered to twenty-five (cf. Num 8:24), and at the time the Chronicler was writing it was further reduced to twenty years (cf. v. 27). Probably from the second century BC, adulthood was reached at the age of twenty, which is the age referred to in many of the Qumran documents (*Rule of the Assembly*, 1, 7–12). This means that when Jesus began his public life (at the age of around thirty: cf. Lk 3:23), he was considered a mature person.

dierum regem constituit Salomonem filium suum super Israel [2]et congregavit omnes principes Israel et sacerdotes atque Levitas. [3]Numeratique sunt Levitae a triginta annis et supra, et inventa sunt triginta octo milia virorum. [4]«Ex his, inquit, praesint ministerio domus Domini viginti quattuor milia, praepositi autem et iudices sex milia; [5]porro quattuor milia ianitores et totidem psaltae canentes Domino in organis, quae feci ad canendum». [6]Et distribuit eos David per vices filiorum Levi Gerson videlicet et Caath et Merari. [7]Filii Gerson: Ladan et Semei. [8]Filii Ladan: princeps Iahiel et Zetham et Ioel, tres. [9]Filii Semei: Salomith et Hoziel et Aran, tres; isti principes familiarum Ladan. [10]Porro filii Semei: Iahath et Ziza et Iehus et Beria; isti filii Semei, quattuor. [11]Erat autem Iahath prior, Ziza secundus; porro Iehus et Beria non habuerunt plurimos filios, et idcirco in una familia unaque domo computati sunt. [12]Filii Caath: Amram et Isaar, Hebron et Oziel, quattuor. [13]Filii Amram: Aaron et Moyses. Separatusque est

x. Vg Compare Gk Syr: Heb *to the Gershonite*

pronounce blessings in his name for ever. [14]But the sons of Moses the man of God were named among the tribe of Levi. [15]The sons of Moses: Gershom and Eliezer. [16]The sons of Gershom: Shebuel the chief. [17]The sons of Eliezer: Rehabiah the chief; Eliezer had no other sons, but the sons of Rehabiah were very many. [18]The sons of Izhar: Shelomith the chief. [19]The sons of Hebron: Jeriah the chief, Amariah the second, Jahaziel the third, and Jekameam the fourth. [20]The sons of Uzziel: Micah the chief and Isshiah the second.

Ex 2:22; 18:3–4

1 Chron 24:20–30

[21]The sons of Merari: Mahli and Mushi. The sons of Mahli: Eleazar and Kish. [22]Eleazar died having no sons, but only daughters; their kinsmen, the sons of Kish, married them. [23]The sons of Mushi: Mahli, Eder, and Jeremoth, three.

[24]These were the sons of Levi by their fathers' houses, the heads of fathers houses as they were registered according to the number of the names of the individuals from twenty years old and upward who were to do the work for the service of the house of the LORD. [25]For David said, "The LORD, the God of Israel, has given peace to his people; and he dwells in Jerusalem for ever. [26]And so the Levites no longer need to carry the tabernacle or any of the things for its service"—[27]for by the last words of David these were the number of the Levites from twenty years old and upward—[28]"but their duty shall be to assist the sons of Aaron for the service of the house of the LORD, having the care of the courts and the chambers, the cleansing of all that is holy, and any work for the service of the house of God; [29]to assist also with the showbread, the flour for the cereal offering, the wafers of unleavened bread, the baked offering, the offering mixed with oil, and all measures of quantity or size. [30]And they shall stand every morning, thanking and praising the

Num 1:22; 10:17,21
2 Chron 31:17

1 Chron 23:3–24

Aaron, ut sanctificaret sanctissima, ipse et filii eius in sempiternum, et adoleret Domino et serviret ei ac benediceret in nomine eius in perpetuum. [14]Moysi quoque hominis Dei filii annumerati sunt in tribu Levi. [15]Filii Moysi: Gersam et Eliezer. [16]Filii Gersam: Subael primus. [17]Fuerunt autem filii Eliezer: Rohobia primus, et non erant Eliezer filii alii; porro filii Rohobia multiplicati sunt nimis. [18]Filii Isaar: Salomoth primus. [19]Filii Hebron: Ieriau primus, Amarias secundus, Iahaziel tertius, Iecmaam quartus. [20]Filii Oziel: Micha primus, Iesia secundus. [21]Filii Merari: Moholi et Musi. Filii Moholi: Eleazar et Cis; [22]mortuus est autem Eleazar et non habuit filios sed filias acceperuntque eas filii Cis fratres earum. [23]Filii Musi: Moholi et Eder et Ierimoth, tres. [24]Hi filii Levi in familiis suis, principes familiarum per vices et numerum capitum singulorum, qui faciebant opera ministerii domus Domini a viginti annis et supra. [25]Dixit enim David: «Requiem dedit Dominus Deus Israel populo suo et habitat in Ierusalem usque in aeternum; [26]nec erit officii Levitarum, ut ultra portent tabernaculum et omnia vasa eius ad ministrandum. [27]Iuxta praecepta igitur David novissima, supputabitur numerus filiorum Levi a viginti annis et supra, [28]et erunt sub manu filiorum Aaron in cultum domus Domini pro atriis et exedris et in purificationem omnis rei sacrae et in ministerium templi Dei, [29]pro panibus propositionis et farina oblationis et laganis azymorum et pro sartagine et ad torrendum et super omne pondus atque mensuram. [30]Et stent mane ad confitendum et canendum Domino, similiterque ad vesperam [31]tam in oblatione holocaustorum Domini, quam in sabbatis et calendis et sollemnitatibus reliquis iuxta numerum et

Num 28; 29

LORD, and likewise at evening, [31]and whenever burnt offerings are offered to the LORD on sabbaths, new moons, and feast days, according to the number required of them, continually before the LORD. [32]Thus they shall keep charge of the tent of meeting and the sanctuary, and shall attend the sons of Aaron, their brethren, for the service of the house of the LORD."

Classification of the priests

Num 3:2–4; 26:60 Lev 10:1

2 Sam 8:17

24 [1]The divisions of the sons of Aaron were these. The sons of Aaron: Nadab, Abihu, Eleazar, and Ithamar. [2]But Nadab and Abihu died before their father, and had no children, so Eleazar and Ithamar became the priests. [3]With the help of Zadok of the sons of Eleazar, and Ahimelech of the sons of Ithamar,* David organized them according to the appointed duties in their service. [4]Since more chief men were found among the sons of Eleazar than among the sons of Ithamar, they organized them under sixteen heads of fathers' houses of the sons of Eleazar, and eight of the sons of Ithamar. [5]They organized them by lot, all alike, for there were officers of the sanctuary and officers of God among both the sons of Eleazar and the sons of Ithamar. [6]And the scribe Shemaiah the son of Nethanel, a Levite, recorded them in the presence of the king, and the princes, and Zadok the priest, and Ahimelech the son of Abiathar, and the heads of the fathers' houses of the priests and of the Levites; one father's house being chosen for Eleazar and one chosen for Ithamar.

24:1–19. The division of the priests into twenty-four turns (v. 4), attributed here to David, is an anachronism; in fact, this arrangement did not come into force until some years after Nehemiah (cf. Neh 7:39–42; 10:2–9; 12:1–7, 12–21). The sacred writer certainly saw the priesthood as being an institution fundamental to Israel after the return from exile. The division given here obtained right up to New Testament times: cf. the reference to Zechariah being part of the eighth (Abijah) division: Lk 1:5, 8.

caeremonias uniuscuiusque rei iugiter coram Domino. [32]Et custodiant observationes tabernaculi conventus et ritum sanctuarii et observationem filiorum Aaron fratrum suorum, ut ministrent in domo Domini». **[24]** [1]Porro filiis Aaron hae partitiones erant. Filii Aaron: Nadab et Abiu et Eleazar et Ithamar. [2]Mortui sunt autem Nadab et Abiu ante patrem suum absque liberis; sacerdotioque functus est Eleazar et Ithamar. [3]Et divisit eos David cum Sadoc de filiis Eleazari et cum Achimelech de filiis Ithamar, secundum vices suas et ministerium. [4]Inventique sunt multo plures filii Eleazar secundum capita virorum quam filii Ithamar; divisit igitur eis, hoc est filiis Eleazar principes per familias sedecim, et filiis Ithamar per familias et domos suas octo. [5]Porro divisit utrasque inter se familias sortibus; erant enim principes sanctuarii et principes Dei tam de filiis Eleazar quam de filiis Ithamar. [6]Descripsitque eos Semeias filius Nathanael scriba Levites coram rege et principibus et Sadoc sacerdote et Achimelech

[7]The first lot fell to Jehoiarib, the second to Jedaiah, [8]the third to Harim, the fourth to Se-orim, [9]the fifth to Malchijah, the sixth to Mijamin, [10]the seventh to Hakkoz, the eighth to Abijah, [11]the ninth to Jeshua, the tenth to Shecaniah, [12]the eleventh to Eliashib, the twelfth to Jakim, [13]the thirteenth to Huppah, the fourteenth to Jeshebe-ab, [14]the fifteenth to Bilgah, the sixteenth to Immer, [15]the seventeenth to Hezir, the eighteenth to Happizzez, [16]the nineteenth to Pethahiah, the twentieth to Jehezkel, [17]the twenty-first to Jachin, the twenty-second to Gamul, [18]the twenty-third to Delaiah, the twenty-fourth to Ma-aziah. [19]These had as their appointed duty in their service to come into the house of the LORD according to the procedure established for them by Aaron their father, as the LORD God of Israel had commanded him.

Lk 1:5

Other Levites

[20]And of the rest of the sons of Levi: of the sons of Amram, Shuba-el; of the sons of Shuba-el, Jehdeiah. [21]Of Rehabiah: of the sons of Rehabiah, Isshiah the chief. [22]Of the Izharites, Shelomoth; of the sons of Shelomoth, Jahath. [23]The sons of Hebron:[y] Jeriah the chief,[z] Amariah the second, Jahaziel the third, Jekameam the fourth. [24]The sons of Uzziel, Micah; of the sons of Micah, Shamir. [25]The brother of Micah, Isshiah; of the sons of Isshiah, Zechariah. [26]The sons of Merari: Mahli and Mushi. The sons of Ja-aziah: Beno. [27]The sons of Merari: of Ja-aziah, Beno, Shoham, Zaccur, and Ibri. [28]Of Mahli: Eleazar, who had no sons. [29]Of Kish, the sons of Kish: Jerahmeel. [30]The sons of Mushi: Mahli, Eder, and Jerimoth. These were the sons of the Levites according to their fathers' houses. [31]These also, the head of each father's house and

1 Chron 23:16ff

---

filio Abiathar, principibus quoque familiarum sacerdotalium et leviticarum: unam familiam pro Eleazar et unam pro Ithamar. [7]Exivit autem sors prima Ioiarib, secunda Iedaiae, [8]tertia Harim, quarta Seorim, [9]quinta Melchia, sexta Miamin, [10]septima Accos, octava Abia, [11]nona Iesua, decima Sechenia, [12]undecima Eliasib, duodecima Iacim, [13]tertia decima Hoppha, quarta decima Isbaab, [14]quinta decima Belga, sexta decima Emmer, [15]septima decima Hezir, octava decima Aphses, [16]nona decima Phethahia, vicesima Hezechiel, [17]vicesima prima Iachin, vicesima secunda Gamul, [18]vicesima tertia Dalaiau, vicesima quarta Maaziau. [19]Hae vices eorum secundum ministeria sua, ut ingrediantur domum Domini, et iuxta ritum suum sub manu Aaron patris eorum, sicut praecepit Dominus Deus Israel. [20]Porro filiorum Levi, qui reliqui fuerant: de filiis Amram Subael et de filiis Subael Iehedeia. [21]De filiis quoque Rohobiae princeps Iesias. [22]De Isaaritis vero Salomoth; de filiis Salomoth Iahath. [23]De Hebronitis: Ieriau, Amarias secundus, Iahaziel tertius, Iecmaam quartus. [24]Filius Oziel Micha; de filiis Micha Samir; [25]frater Micha Iesia; de filiis Iesiae Zacharias. [26]Filii Merari: Moholi et Musi. Filii eius: Iaziau et Bani. [27]Filius Merari: de Iaziau filio suo Soam et Zacchur et Hebri. [28]Porro de Moholi filius Eleazar, qui non habebat liberos. [29]Filius vero Cis Ierameel; [30]filii Musi: Moholi, Eder et Ierimoth. Isti filii Levi secundum familias suas. [31]Ipsi quoque miserunt sortes sicut fratres sui, filii Aaron coram David rege et Sadoc et Achimelech et principibus familiarum sacerdotalium et leviticarum tam maiores quam minores: omnes sors aequaliter

y. See 23:19: Heb lacks *Hebron* **z.** See 23:19: Heb lacks *the chief*

his younger brother alike, cast lots, just as their brethren the sons of Aaron, in the presence of King David, Zadok, Ahimelech, and the heads of fathers' houses of the priests and of the Levites.

Cantors

1 Chron 16:37–43
2 Chron 29:25

25 [1]David and the chiefs of the service also set apart for the service certain of the sons of Asaph, and of Heman, and of Jeduthun, who should prophesy with lyres, with harps, and with cymbals. The list of those who did the work and of their duties was: [2]Of the sons of Asaph: Zaccur, Joseph, Nethaniah, and Asharelah, sons of Asaph, under the direction of Asaph, who prophesied under the direction of the king. [3]Of Jeduthun, the sons of Jeduthun: Gedaliah, Zeri, Jeshaiah, Shime-i,[a] Hashabiah, and Mattithiah, six, under the direction of their father Jeduthun, who prophesied with the lyre in thanksgiving and praise to the LORD. [4]Of Heman, the sons of Heman: Bukkiah, Mattaniah, Uzziel, Shebuel, and Jerimoth, Hananiah, Hanani, Eliathah, Giddalti, and Romamti-ezer, Joshbekashah, Mallothi, Hothir, Mahazi-oth. [5]All these were the sons of Heman the king's seer, according to the

2 Kings 3:15

25:1–31. The cantors were spread over twenty-four divisions, like the priests. After the exile, when the liturgy became more splendid, the cantors were very highly regarded and were essential to the liturgy.

"Who prophesied" (v. 2): this means that as early as the Chronicler's time the composition of many psalms was attributed to cantor families, especially Asaph, Heman and Ethan. Certainly, it is a sign that musical composition was steadily becoming a more important part of the temple liturgy. Christianity has inherited appreciation for music in the liturgy: "The musical tradition of the universal Church is a treasure of inestimable value, greater even than that of any other art. The main reason for this pre-eminence is that, as a combination of sacred music and words, it forms a necessary or integral part of the solemn liturgy" (Vatican II, *Sacrosanctum Concilium*, 112).

In v. 3 the name Shime-i does not appear in the Hebrew (cf. RSV note), but it is found in many Greek manuscripts and is consistent with v. 17. As the text goes on to say, there were six sons of Jeduthun (v. 6).

dividebat. **[25]** [1]Igitur David et magistratus exercitus segregaverunt in ministerium filios Asaph et Heman et Idithun, qui prophetarent in citharis et psalteriis et cymbalis, secundum numerum suum dedicato sibi officio servientes. [2]De filiis Asaph: Zacchur et Ioseph et Nathania et Asarela filii Asaph erant sub manu Asaph prophetantis sub manu regis. [3]De Idithun; filii Idithun: Godolias, Sori, Iesaias et Hasabias et Matthathias, sex, sub manu patris sui Idithun, qui in cithara prophetabat ad confitendum et laudandum Dominum. [4]De Heman quoque; filii Heman: Bocciau, Matthaniau, Oziel, Subael et Ierimoth, Hananias, Hanani, Eliatha, Geddelthi et Romemthiezer et Iesbacasa, Mellothi, Othir, Mahazioth; [5]omnes isti filii Heman videntis regis iuxta sermones Dei, quod exaltaret cornu eius, deditque Deus Heman filios

a. One Ms Gk: Heb lacks *Shimei*

promise of God to exalt him; for God had given Heman fourteen sons and three daughters. [6]They were all under the direction of their father in the music in the house of the LORD with cymbals, harps, and lyres for the service of the house of God. Asaph, Jeduthun, and Heman were under the order of the king. [7]The number of them along with their brethren, who were trained in singing to the LORD, all who were skilful, was two hundred and eighty-eight. [8]And they cast lots for their duties, small and great, teacher and pupil alike.

[9]The first lot fell for Asaph to Joseph; the second to Gedaliah, to him and his brethren and his sons, twelve; [10]the third to Zaccur, his sons and his brethren, twelve; [11]the fourth to Izri, his sons and his brethren, twelve; [12]the fifth to Nethaniah, his sons and his brethren, twelve; [13]the sixth to Bukkiah, his sons and his brethren, twelve; [14]the seventh to Jesharelah, his sons and his brethren, twelve; [15]the eighth to Jeshaiah, his sons and his brethren, twelve; [16]the ninth to Mattaniah, his sons and his brethren, twelve; [17]the tenth to Shime-i, his sons and his brethren, twelve; [18]the eleventh to Azarel, his sons and his brethren, twelve; [19]the twelfth to Hashabiah, his sons and his brethren, twelve; [20]to the thirteenth, Shuba-el, his sons and his brethren, twelve; [21]to the fourteenth, Mattithiah, his sons and his brethren, twelve; [22]to the fifteenth, to Jeremoth, his sons and his brethren, twelve; [23]to the sixteenth, to Hananiah, his sons and his brethren, twelve; [24]to the seventeenth, to Joshbekashah, his sons and his brethren, twelve; [25]to the eighteenth, to Hanani, his sons and his brethren, twelve; [26]to the nineteenth, to Mallothi, his sons and his brethren, twelve; [27]to the twentieth, to Eliathah, his sons and his brethren, twelve; [28]to the twenty-first, to Hothir, his sons and his brethren, twelve; [29]to the twenty-second, to Giddalti, his sons and his

---

quattuordecim et filias tres. [6]Universi sub manu patris sui ad cantandum in templo Domini distributi erant in cymbalis et psalteriis et citharis, in ministeria domus Dei sub manu regis: Asaph et Idithun et Heman. [7]Fuit autem numerus eorum cum fratribus suis eruditis in cantando Domino, cuncti magistri, ducenti octoginta octo. [8]Miseruntque sortes pro ministerio ex aequo, tam maior quam minor, magister pariter et discipulus. [9]Egressaque est sors prima Ioseph, qui erat de Asaph. Secunda Godoliae, ipsi et fratribus eius et filiis eius, duodecim. [10]Tertia Zacchur, filiis et fratribus eius, duodecim. [11]Quarta Isari, filiis et fratribus eius, duodecim. [12]Quinta Nathaniau, filiis et fratribus eius, duodecim. [13]Sexta Bocciau, filiis et fratribus eius, duodecim. [14]Septima Isreela, filiis et fratribus eius, duodecim. [15]Octava Iesaiae, filiis et fratribus eius, duodecim. [16]Nona Matthaniau, filiis et fratribus eius, duodecim. [17]Decima Semei, filiis et fratribus eius, duodecim. [18]Undecima Azareel, filiis et fratribus eius, duodecim. [19]Duodecima Hasabiae, filiis et fratribus eius, duodecim. [20]Tertia decima Subael, filiis et fratribus eius, duodecim. [21]Quarta decima Matthathiae, filiis et fratribus eius, duodecim. [22]Quinta decima Ierimoth, filiis et fratribus eius, duodecim. [23]Sexta decima Hananiae, filiis et fratribus eius, duodecim. [24]Septima decima Iesbacasae, filiis et fratribus eius, duodecim. [25]Octava decima Hanani, filiis et fratribus eius, duodecim. [26]Nona decima Mellothi, filiis et fratribus eius, duodecim. [27]Vicesima Eliatha, filiis et fratribus eius, duodecim. [28]Vicesima prima Othir, filiis et fratribus eius, duodecim. [29]Vicesima secunda Geddelthi, filiis

brethren, twelve; [30]to the twenty-third, to Mahazi-oth, his sons and his brethren, twelve; [31]to the twenty-fourth, to Romamti-ezer, his sons and his brethren, twelve.

1 Chron 9:17–27

Gatekeepers

26 [1]As for the divisions of the gatekeepers: of the Korahites, Meshelemiah the son of Kore, of the sons of Asaph. [2]And Meshelemiah had sons: Zechariah the first-born, Jedia-el the second, Zebadiah the third, Jathni-el the fourth, [3]Elam the fifth, Jehohanan the sixth, Eli-e-ho-enai the seventh. [4]And Obed-edom had sons: Shemaiah the first-born, Jehozabad the second, Joah the third, Sachar the fourth, Nethanel the fifth, [5]Ammi-el the sixth, Issachar the seventh, Pe-ullethai the eighth; for God blessed him. [6]Also to his son Shemaiah were sons born who were rulers in their fathers' houses, for they were men of great ability. [7]The sons of Shemaiah: Othni, Repha-el, Obed, and Elzabad, whose brethren were able men, Elihu and Semachiah. [8]All these were of the sons of Obed-edom with their sons and brethren, able men qualified for the service; sixty-two of Obed-edom. [9]And Meshelemiah had sons and brethren, able men, eighteen. [10]And Hosah, of the sons of Merari, had sons: Shimri the chief (for though he was not the first-

2 Sam 6:10ff 1 Chron 15:21

Gen 48:13–20

26:1–19. The Levites charged with being temple gatekeepers also enjoyed high status, because they too were divided into twenty-four turns, like the priests. Obed-edom (v. 4) is probably the same person as kept the ark in his house (cf. 2 Sam 6:10–11; cf. 13:13). That is why, even though he was a foreigner (perhaps a Philistine), God blessed him with many offspring; and he was later treated like a Levite, by being given the additional job of guarding the storehouse.

26:20–32. The Levites, as Chronicles here attests, were enormously influential in post-exilic Israel. In addition to their key role in the liturgy, they were responsible for the temple treasures and, above all, had the functions of scribes who recorded administrative decisions in writing, and of judges who could hear cases (v. 29).

et fratribus eius, duodecim. [30]Vicesima tertia Mahazioth, filiis et fratribus eius, duodecim. [31]Vicesima quarta Romemthiezer, filiis et fratribus eius, duodecim. **[26]** [1]Divisiones autem ianitorum. De Coritis: Meselemia filius Core de filiis Abiasaph. [2]Filii Meselemiae: Zacharias primogenitus, Iedihel secundus, Zabadias tertius, Iathanael quartus, [3]Elam quintus, Iohanan sextus, Elioenai septimus. [4]Filii autem Obededom: Semeias primogenitus, Iozabad secundus, Ioah tertius, Sachar quartus, Nathanael quintus, [5]Ammiel sextus, Issachar septimus, Phollathi octavus, quia benedixit illi Deus. [6]Semeiae autem filio eius nati sunt filii praefecti familiarum suarum, erant enim viri fortissimi; [7]filii ergo Semeiae: Othni et Raphael et Obed, Elzabad, fratres eius viri fortissimi, Eliu quoque et Samachias; [8]omnes hi de filiis Obededom, ipsi et filii et fratres eorum fortissimi ad ministrandum sexaginta duo de Obededom. [9]Porro Meselemiae filii et fratres eorum robustissimi decem et octo. [10]De Hosa autem, de filiis Merari, erant filii: Semri princeps—non enim fuerat primogenitus, et idcirco posuerat eum pater eius in principem—

born, his father made him chief), [11]Hilkiah the second, Tebaliah the third, Zechariah the fourth: all the sons and brethren of Hosah were thirteen.

[12]These divisions of the gatekeepers, corresponding to their chief men, had duties, just as their brethren did, ministering in the house of the LORD; [13]and they cast lots by fathers' houses, small and great alike, for their gates. [14]The lot for the east fell to Shelemiah. They cast lots also for his son Zechariah, a shrewd counsellor, and his lot came out for the north. [15]Obed-edom's came out for the south, and to his sons was allotted the storehouse. [16]For Shuppim and Hosah it came out for the west, at the gate of Shallecheth on the road that goes up. Watch corresponded to watch. [17]On the east there were six each day,[b] on the north four each day, on the south four each day, as well as two and two at the storehouse; [18]and for the parbar[c] on the west there were four at the road and two at the parbar. [19]These were the divisions of the gatekeepers among the Korahites and the sons of Merari.

1 Chron 9:24

Other duties of the Levites

[20]And of the Levites, Ahijah had charge of the treasuries of the house of God and the treasuries of the dedicated gifts. [21]The sons of Ladan, the sons of the Gershonites belonging to Ladan, the heads of the fathers' houses belonging to Ladan the Gershonite: Jehieli.[d]

[22]The sons of Jehieli, Zetham and Joel his brother, were in charge of the treasuries of the house of the LORD. [23]Of the Amramites, the Izharites, the Hebronites, and the Uzzielites—[24]and Shebuel the son of Gershom, son of Moses, was chief officer in charge of the treasuries. [25]His brethren: from Eliezer were his son Rehabiah, and his son Jeshaiah, and his son Joram, and his son Zichri, and his son Shelomoth. [26]This Shelomoth and his brethren

Num 31:48–54
1 Chron 18:11

[11]Helcias secundus, Tabelias tertius, Zacharias quartus; omnes hi filii et fratres Hosa tredecim. [12]Hae divisiones ianitorum: secundum capita virorum habebant ministeria sicut et fratres eorum ad ministrandum in domo Domini. [13]Missae sunt ergo sortes ex aequo et parvis et magnis per familias suas in unamquamque portarum. [14]Cecidit igitur sors orientalis Selemiae; porro Zachariae filio eius consiliario prudentissimo et erudito sortito obtigit plaga septentrionalis; [15]Obededom vero australis, et filiis eius horreum; [16]Sephim et Hosa occidentalis iuxta portam Sallecheth apud viam ascensionis. Custodia iuxta custodiam: [17]ad orientem per diem sex et ad aquilonem quattuor per diem, atque ad meridiem similiter in die quattuor et pro horreo bini et bini, [18]pro Parbar quoque ad occidentem quattuor in via, duo pro Parbar. [19]Hae sunt divisiones ianitorum filiorum Core et Merari. [20]Porro Levitae fratres eorum super thesauros domus Dei ac thesauros rerum consecratarum: [21]De filiis Ladan Gersonitae principes familiarum Ladan Gersonitae erant Iahielitae. [22]Filii Iahiel et Zetham et Ioel fratrum eius erant super thesauros domus Domini. [23]De Amramitis et Isaaritis et Hebronitis et Ozielitis: [24]Subael filius Gersam filii Moysi praepositus thesauris. [25]Fratres quoque eius Eliezer, cuius filius Rohobia et huius filius Iesaias; et huius filius Ioram, huius quoque filius Zechri et huius filius Selemith. [26]Ipse Selemith

b. Gk: Heb *Levites* **c.** The meaning of the word *parbar* is unknown **d.** The Hebrew text of verse 21 is confused

were in charge of all the treasuries of the dedicated gifts which David the king, and the heads of the fathers' houses, and the officers of the thousands and the hundreds, and the commanders of the army, had dedicated. [27]From spoil won in battles they dedicated gifts for the maintenance of the house of the LORD. [28]Also all that Samuel the seer, and Saul the son of Kish, and Abner the son of Ner, and Joab the son of Zeruiah had dedicated—all dedicated gifts were in the care of Shelomoth[e] and his brethren.

1 Chron 29:29

[29]Of the Izharites, Chenaniah and his sons were appointed to outside duties for Israel, as officers and judges. [30]Of the Hebronites, Hashabiah and his brethren, one thousand seven hundred men of ability, had the oversight of Israel westward of the Jordan for all the work of the LORD and for the service of the king. [31]Of the Hebronites, Jerijah was chief of the Hebronites of whatever genealogy or fathers' houses. (In the fortieth year of David's reign search was made and men of great ability among them were found at Jazer in Gilead.) [32]King David appointed him and his brethren, two thousand seven hundred men of ability, heads of fathers' houses, to have the oversight of the Reubenites, the Gadites, and the half-tribe of the Manassites for everything pertaining to God and for the affairs of the king.

1 Chron 15:22
1 Chron 27:17

Military organization

27 [1]This is the list of the people of Israel, the heads of fathers' houses, the commanders of thousands and hundreds, and their officers who served the king in all matters concerning the

et fratres eius super omnes thesauros rerum consecratarum, quas sanctificavit David rex et principes familiarum et tribuni et centuriones et duces exercitus, [27]de bellis et, manubiis proeliorum, quas consecraverant ad sustentandum templum Domini. [28]Et universa, quae consecraverant Samuel videns et Saul filius Cis et Abner filius Ner et Ioab filius Sarviae, omnia donaria sacra erant sub manu Selemith et fratrum eius. [29]De Isaaritis vero erant Chonenias et filii eius ad opera forinsecus super Israel praefecti et iudices. [30]Porro de Hebronitis Hasabias et fratres eius viri strenui mille septingenti erant magistratus Israel trans Iordanem contra occidentem in cunctis operibus Domini et in ministerium regis; [31]Hebronitarum autem princeps fuit Ieria secundum cognationes et familias eorum. Quadragesimo anno regni David recensiti sunt et inventi viri fortes in Iazer Galaad [32]fratresque eius viri strenui duo milia septingenti principes familiarum; praeposuit autem eos David rex Rubenitis et Gadditis et dimidio tribus Manasse in omne ministerium Dei et regis. **[27]** [1]Filii autem Israel secundum numerum suum, principes familiarum, tribuni et centuriones et praefecti, qui ministrabant regi iuxta turmas suas ingredientes et egredientes per singulos menses in anno, unaquaeque turma viginti quattuor milia. [2]Primae turmae in primo mense Iesbaam praeerat filius Zabdiel, et sub eo viginti quattuor milia; [3]erat de filiis Phares princeps cunctorum principum in exercitu mense primo. [4]Secundi mensis habebat turmam Dudi Ahohites, et sub eo viginti quattuor milia. [5]Dux quoque turmae tertiae in mense tertio erat Banaias filius Ioiadae sacerdotis, et in divisione sua viginti quattuor milia; [6]ipse est Banaias fortissimus inter triginta et super triginta; praeerat autem turmae ipsius Amizabad filius eius. [7]Quartus, mense quarto, Asael frater Ioab et Zabadias filius eius post eum, et in turma eius viginti quattuor milia. [8]Quintus, mense quinto,

e. Heb *Shelomith*

divisions that came and went, month after month throughout the year, each division numbering twenty-four thousand:

[2]Jashobeam the son of Zabdi-el was in charge of the first division in the first month; in his division were twenty-four thousand. [3]He was a descendant of Perez, and was chief of all the commanders of the army for the first month. [4]Dodai the Ahohite[f] was in charge of the division of the second month; in his division were twenty-four thousand. [5]The third commander, for the third month, was Benaiah, the son of Jehoiada the priest, as chief; in his division were twenty-four thousand. [6]This is the Benaiah who was a mighty man of the thirty and in command of the thirty; Ammizabad his son was in charge of his division.[g] [7]Asahel the brother of Joab was fourth, for the fourth month, and his son Zebadiah after him; in his division were twenty-four thousand. [8]The fifth commander, for the fifth month, was Shamhuth, the Izrahite; in his division were twenty-four thousand. [9]Sixth, for the sixth month, was Ira, the son of Ikkesh the Tekoite; in his division were twenty-four thousand. [10]Seventh, for the seventh month, was Helez the Pelonite, of the sons of Ephraim; in his division were twenty-four thousand. [11]Eighth, for the eighth month, was Sibbecai the Hushathite, of the Zerahites; in his division were twenty-four thousand. [12]Ninth, for the ninth month, was Abi-ezer of Anathoth, a Benjaminite; in his division were twenty-four thousand. [13]Tenth, for the tenth month, was Maharai of Netophah, of the Zerahites; in his division were twenty-four thousand. [14]Eleventh, for the eleventh

1 Chron 11:11
1 Chron 11:12
1 Chron 12:28
2 Sam 2:18–23

27:1–34. The system of civil administration laid down by David was similar to that for the temple, showing that this was a very hierarchical and theocratic society. The administration consisted of four classes—the military (vv. 2–18) divided into twelve sections; the government of the tribes (vv. 16–24) which is reminiscent of the divisions in the first census held in the desert (cf. Num 1:5–16); the control of the royal treasuries (vv. 25–31); and, finally, the cabinet of royal advisers (vv. 32–34).

The fact that the census taken by Joab is mentioned (vv. 23–24; cf. 21:1–16) means that it was lawful to count the men fit for military service, that is, those aged twenty and over—but not all Israelites, because that would imply lack of trust in the Lord's promise to multiply them (cf. Gen 15:5; 22:17).

princeps Samaoth Zaraita, et in turma eius viginti quattuor milia. [9]Sextus, mense sexto, Hira filius Acces Thecuites, et in turma eius viginti quattuor milia. [10]Septimus, mense septimo, Helles Phalonites de filiis Ephraim, et in turma eius viginti quattuor milia. [11]Octavus, mense octavo, Sobbochai Husathites de stirpe Zara, et in turma eius viginti quattuor milia. [12]Nonus, mense nono, Abiezer Anathothites de filiis Beniamin, et in turma eius viginti quattuor milia. [13]Decimus, mense decimo, Maharai Netophathites de stirpe Zara, et in turma eius viginti quattuor milia. [14]Undecimus, mense undecimo, Banaias

f. Gk: Heb *Ahohite and his division and Mikloth the chief officer* **g.** Gk Vg: Heb *was his division*

month, was Benaiah of Pirathon, of the sons of Ephraim; in his division were twenty-four thousand. [15]Twelfth, for the twelfth month, was Heldai the Netophathite, of Othni-el; in his division were twenty-four thousand.

Civil organization

[16]Over the tribes of Israel, for the Reubenites Eliezer the son of Zichri was chief officer; for the Simeonites, Shephatiah the son of Maacah; [17]for Levi, Hashabiah the son of Kemuel; for Aaron, Zadok; [18]for Judah, Elihu, one of David's brothers; for Issachar, Omri the son of Michael; [19]for Zebulun, Ishmaiah the son of Obadiah; for Naphtali, Jeremoth the son of Azriel; [20]for the Ephraimites, Hoshea the son of Azaziah; for the half-tribe of Manasseh, Joel the son of Pedaiah; [21]for the half-tribe of Manasseh in Gilead, Iddo the son of Zechariah; for Benjamin, Ja-asiel the son of Abner; [22]for Dan, Azarel the son of Jeroham. These were the leaders of the tribes of Israel. [23]David did not number those below twenty years of age, for the LORD had promised to make Israel as many as the stars of heaven. [24]Joab the son of Zeruiah began to number, but did not finish; yet wrath came upon Israel for this, and the number was not entered in the chronicles of King David.

Gen 15:5

[25]Over the king's treasuries was Azmaveth the son of Adi-el; and over the treasuries in the country, in the cities, in the villages and in the towers, was Jonathan the son of Uzziah; [26]and over those who did the work of the field for tilling the soil was Ezri the son of Chelub; [27]and over the vineyards was Shime-i the Ramathite; and over the produce of the vineyards for the wine cellars was Zabdi the Shiphmite. [28]Over the olive and sycamore trees in the Shephelah was Baal-hanan the Gederite; and over the stores of oil was Joash. [29]Over

---

Pharathonites de filiis Ephraim, et in turma eius viginti quattuor milia. [15]Duodecimus, mense duodecimo, Holdai Netophathites de stirpe Othoniel, et in turma eius viginti quattuor milia. [16]Porro tribubus praeerant Israel: Rubenitis dux Eliezer filius Zechri; Simeonitis Saphatia filius Maacha; [17]Levitis Hasabias filius Camuel; Aaronitis Sadoc; [18]Iudae Eliu de fratribus David; Issachar Amri filius Michael; [19]Zabulon Iesmaias filius Abdiae; Nephthali Ierimoth filius Azriel; [20]filiis Ephraim Osee filius Ozaziu; dimidio tribus Manasse Ioel filius Phadaiae; [21]et dimidio tribus Manasse in Galaad Iaddo filius Zachariae; Beniamin autem Iasiel filius Abner; [22]Dan vero Azareel filius Ieroham: hi principes tribuum Israel. [23]Noluit autem David numerare eos a viginti annis inferius, quia dixerat Dominus ut multiplicaret Israel quasi stellas caeli. [24]Ioab filius Sarviae coeperat numerare nec complevit, quia super hoc ira irruerat in Israel, et idcirco numerus non est relatus in librum annalium regis David. [25]Super thesauros autem regis fuit Azmaveth filius Adiel; his autem thesauris, qui erant in regione, in urbibus et in vicis et in turribus praesidebat Ionathan filius Oziae. [26]Operi autem rustico et agricolis, qui exercebant terram, praeerat Ezri filius Chelub. [27]Vinearumque cultoribus Semei Ramathites; cellis autem vinariis in vineis Zabdi Sephamatites. [28]Nam super oliveta et ficeta, quae erant in Sephela, Baalhanan Gederites; super apothecas autem olei Ioas. [29]Porro armentis, quae pascebantur in Saron, praepositus fuit Setrai Saronites, et super boves in vallibus Saphat filius Adli. [30]Super camelos vero Ubil Ismaelites et super

the herds that pastured in Sharon was Shitrai the Sharonite; over the herds in the valleys was Shaphat the son of Adlai. [30]Over the camels was Obil the Ishmaelite; and over the she-asses was Jehdeiah the Meronothite. Over the flocks was Jaziz the Hagrite. [31]All these were stewards of King David's property.

[32]Jonathan, David's uncle, was a counsellor, being a man of understanding and a scribe; he and Jehiel the son of Hachmoni attended the king's sons. [33]Ahithophel was the king's counsellor, and Hushai the Archite was the king's friend. [34]Ahithophel was succeeded by Jehoiada the son of Benaiah, and Abiathar. Joab was commander of the king's army.

2 Sam 15:31ff; 16:15

Instructions for the building of the temple*

28 [1]David assembled at Jerusalem all the officials of Israel, the officials of the tribes, the officers of the divisions that served the king, the commanders of thousands, the commanders of hundreds, the stewards of all the property and cattle of the king and his sons, together with the palace officials, the mighty men, and all the seasoned warriors. [2]Then King David rose to his feet and said: "Hear me, my brethren and my people. I had it in my heart to build a house of rest for the ark of the covenant of the

2 Chron 6:7–11
Ps 132:7

***28:1—29:30.** The tone of the book's ending is very like that of a last will and testament. These chapters consist of various discourses of David, addressed to the assembly of the whole people (28:2–10 and 29:1–5), to his son Solomon (28:20–21) and to God himself, in a heartfelt prayer (29:10–19). Throughout these addresses we find the same teaching as forms the backbone of the entire book. In the first place, the unity of the kingdom, with no strife between north and south; hence the repetition of the already familiar expression, "all Israel" (28:4; 29:21, 23, 25–26). Secondly, the doctrine of divine election, interpreted in a somewhat unusual way. Thus, Solomon is the one "whom God has chosen" (29:1), just as earlier God chose Saul (cf. 1 Sam 10:24) and David (cf. 2 Sam 6:21), but in this case he is chosen for a particular task—to build the temple: "the Lord has chosen you to build a

asinas Iehedeia Meronathites; [31]super oves quoque Iaziz Agarenus: omnes hi principes substantiae regis David. [32]Ionathan autem patruus David consiliarius, vir prudens et litteratus, ipse et Iahiel filius Hachamonitis erant cum filiis regis. [33]Achitophel etiam consiliarius regis et Chusai Arachites amicus regis; [34]post Achitophel fuit Ioiada filius Banaiae et Abiathar. Princeps autem exercitus regis erat Ioab. **[28]** [1]Convocavit igitur David omnes principes Israel, duces tribuum et praepositos turmarum, qui ministrabant regi, tribunos quoque et centuriones et, qui praeerant substantiae et gregibus regis filiorumque suorum, cum eunuchis et fortibus et robustissimis quibusque in exercitu Ierusalem. [2]Cumque surrexisset rex et stetisset, ait: «Audite me, fratres mei et populus meus. Cogitavi ut aedificarem domum, in qua requiesceret arca foederis Domini et scabellum pedum Dei nostri, et ad aedificandum omnia praeparavi; [3]Deus autem dixit mihi: "Non aedificabis domum nomini meo, eo quod

2 Sam 7:5,13
1 Chron 22:8

LORD, and for the footstool of our God; and I made preparations for building. [3]But God said to me, 'You may not build a house for my name, for you are a warrior and have shed blood.' [4]Yet the LORD God of Israel chose me from all my father's house to be king over Israel for ever; for he chose Judah as leader, and in the house of Judah my father's house, and among my father's sons he took pleasure in me to make me king over all Israel. [5]And of all my sons (for the LORD has given me many sons) he has chosen Solomon my son to sit upon the throne of the kingdom of the LORD over Israel. [6]He said to me, 'It is Solomon your son who shall build my house and my courts, for I have chosen him to be my son, and I will be his father. [7]I will establish his kingdom for ever if he continues resolute in keeping my commandments and my ordinances, as he is today.' [8]Now therefore in the sight of all Israel, the assembly of the LORD, and in the hearing of our God, observe and seek out all the commandments of the LORD your God; that

2 Sam 7:13
1 Chron 17:12ff; 22:10ff

Deut 4:5

house for the sanctuary" (28:10; cf. 28:6, 20; 29:1). This brings us to the third and most important message of the book, the central place that the temple has in the life of Israel. Because he is a "warrior" (28:3), David cannot be the one who builds it, but as an inheritance to his son and the whole assembly he leaves the design for the temple and its dependencies (28:11–12, 19), just as Moses did when he gave the sons of Israel the pattern for the tabernacle (cf. Ex 25:8–9). In addition, David will pass over all the property of the royal house and his personal property (29:3–5) to be applied to the costs of the building and he will urge others to do the same (29:6–9).

Solomon will be able to build the temple because the Lord will give him peace (cf. 22:9) and Solomon will respond wholeheartedly and dutifully (29:19). Peace and virtue are preconditions for putting God's plans into effect, just as obedience to God's precepts (28:8–9) is a prerequisite for inheriting the land and sharing in the promises God has made. "Great peace have those who love thy law; nothing can make them stumble", sings Psalm 119:165. And St Leo the Great comments: "This peace is not to be found even within the bonds of intimate friendship nor in a deep similarity of character, if it is not all founded on the total union of our will with the will of God" (*De beatitudinibus*, 95, 9).

sis vir bellator et sanguinem fuderis". [4]Sed elegit Dominus Deus Israel me de universa domo patris mei, ut essem rex super Israel in sempiternum; Iudam enim elegit principem, porro in domo Iudae domum patris mei, et in filiis patris mei placuit ei, ut me eligeret regem super cunctum Israel. [5] Sed et de filiis meis—filios enim multos dedit mihi Dominus—elegit Salomonem filium meum, ut sederet in throno regni Domini super Israel. [6]Dixitque mihi: "Salomon filius tuus aedificabit domum meam et atria mea; ipsum enim elegi mihi in filium, et ego ero ei in patrem. [7]Et firmabo regnum eius usque in aeternum, si perseveraverit facere praecepta mea et iudicia, sicut et hodie". [8]Nunc igitur coram universo Israel coetu Domini, audiente Deo nostro, custodite et perquirite cuncta mandata Domini Dei vestri, ut possideatis terram bonam et relinquatis eam in hereditatem filiis vestris post vos usque in sempiternum. [9]Tu autem,

you may possess this good land, and leave it for an inheritance to your children after you for ever.

[9]"And you, Solomon my son, know the God of your father, and serve him with a whole heart and with a willing mind; for the LORD searches all hearts, and understands every plan and thought. If you seek him, he will be found by you; but if you forsake him, he will cast you off for ever. [10]Take heed now, for the LORD has chosen you to build a house for the sanctuary; be strong, and do it."

Jer 17:10; 29:13
Lk 16:15

[11]Then David gave Solomon his son the plan of the vestibule of the temple, and of its houses, its treasuries, its upper rooms, and its inner chambers, and of the room for the mercy seat; [12]and the plan of all that he had in mind for the courts of the house of the LORD, all the surrounding chambers, the treasuries of the house of God, and the treasuries for dedicated gifts; [13]for the divisions of the priests and of the Levites, and all the work of the service in the house of the LORD; for all the vessels for the service in the house of the LORD, [14]the weight of gold for all golden vessels for each service, the weight of silver vessels for each service, [15]the weight of the golden lampstands and their lamps, the weight of gold for each lampstand and its lamps, the weight of silver for a lampstand and its lamps, according to the use of each lampstand in the service, [16]the weight of gold for each table for the showbread, the

Ex 25:40
1 Kings 6:3

1 Chron 26:20
Ezek 42

Salomon, fili mi, scito Deum patris tui et servi ei corde perfecto et animo voluntario; omnia enim corda scrutatur Dominus et universas mentium cogitationes intellegit. Si quaesieris eum, invenies; si autem dereliqueris illum, proiciet te in aeternum. [10]Nunc ergo vide quia elegit te Dominus, ut aedificares domum sanctuarii; confortare et perfice». [11]Dedit autem David Salomoni filio suo descriptionem porticus et templi et cellariorum et cenaculorum et cubiculorum interiorum et domus propitiatorii [12]necnon et omnium, quae per Spiritum cum eo erant, de atriis domus Domini et de omnibus exedris per circuitum, de thesauris domus Dei et de thesauris rerum consecratarum [13]et de divisionibus sacerdotalibus et leviticis, de omni opere ministerii domus Domini et de universis vasis ministerii templi Domini, [14]de auro in pondere per singula vasa ministerii, de omnibus vasis argenteis in pondere per omnia vasa pro operum diversitate; [15]sed et ad candelabra aurea et ad lucernas eorum aurum pro mensura uniuscuiusque candelabri et lucernarum, similiter et in candelabris argenteis et in lucernis eorum pro diversitate mensurae, pondus argenti indicavit. [16]Aurum quoque in mensas propositionis pro diversitate mensarum, similiter et argentum in alias mensas argenteas; [17]ad fuscinulas quoque et phialas et crateras ex auro purissimo et scyphos aureos pro qualitate mensurae pondus distribuit in scyphum et scyphum; similiter et in scyphos argenteos diversum argenti pondus constituit, [18]altari autem, in quo adoletur incensum, aurum purissimum, et aurum pro structura quadrigae cherubim extendentium alas et velantium arcam foederis Domini. [19]«Omnia, inquit, venerunt scripta manu Domini ad me, ut intellegerem universa opera exemplaris». [20]Dixit quoque David Salomoni filio suo: «Viriliter age et confortare et fac, ne timeas et ne paveas; Dominus enim Deus meus tecum erit et non dimittet te, nec derelinquet, donec perficias omne opus ministerii domus Domini. [21]Ecce divisiones sacerdotum et Levitarum: parati erunt in omne ministerium domus Dei; et assistet tibi in omni opere quisquis in sapientia ad omne ministerium promptus fuerit, principes quoque et universus populus in negotiis tuis». **[29]** [1]Locutusque est David rex ad omnem ecclesiam: «Salomonem filium meum unum elegit Deus adhuc puerum et tenellum; opus autem grande est: neque enim homini praeparatur habitatio sed Domino Deo. [2]Ego autem totis viribus meis praeparavi impensas domus Dei mei: aurum ad vasa aurea et argentum in argentea, aes in aenea, ferrum in ferrea, ligna ad lignea, lapides onychinos et ad inserendum, durum

Ex 27:3
Num 4:14

silver for the silver tables, [17]and pure gold for the forks, the basins, and the cups; for the golden bowls and the weight of each; for the silver bowls and the weight of each; [18]for the altar of incense made of refined gold, and its weight; also his plan for the golden chariot of the cherubim that spread their wings and covered the ark of the covenant of the LORD. [19]All this he made clear by the writing from the hand of the LORD concerning it,[h] all the work to be done according to the plan.

[20]Then David said to Solomon his son, "Be strong and of good courage, and do it. Fear not, be not dismayed; for the LORD God, even my God, is with you. He will not fail you or forsake you, until all the work for the service of the house of the LORD is finished. [21]And behold the divisions of the priests and the Levites for all the service of the house of God; and with you in all the work will be every willing man who has skill for any kind of service; also the officers and all the people will be wholly at your command."

Ex 35:25; 36:1

Voluntary offerings

29 [1]And David the king said to all the assembly, "Solomon my son, whom alone God has chosen, is young and inexperienced, and the work is great; for the palace will not be for man but for the LORD God. [2]So I have provided for the house of my God, so far as I was able, the gold for the things of gold, the silver for the things of silver, and the bronze for the things of bronze, the iron for the things of iron, and wood for the things of wood, besides great quantities of onyx and stones for setting, antimony, colored stones, all sorts of precious stones, and marble. [3]Moreover,

---

caementum et lapides diversorum colorum omnemque pretiosum lapidem et marmor Parium abundantissime. [3]Et super haec, cum delectarer super domo Dei mei, de peculio meo aurum et argentum do in templum Dei mei, exceptis his, quae paravi in aedem sanctam: [4]tria milia talenta auri de auro Ophir et septem milia talentorum argenti probatissimi ad operiendos parietes templi; [5]et ubicumque opus est aurum pro aureis, et ubicumque opus est argentum pro argenteis et pro quolibet opere per manus artificum; et si quis sponte offert, impleat manum suam hodie et offerat, quod voluerit Domino». [6]Sponte obtulerunt itaque principes familiarum et proceres tribuum Israel, tribuni quoque et centuriones et principes operis regis; [7]dederuntque in opera domus Dei auri talenta quinque milia et solidos decem milia, argenti talenta decem milia et aeris talenta decem et octo milia, ferri quoque centum milia talentorum. [8]Et apud quemcumque inventi sunt lapides, dederunt in thesaurum domus Domini in manum Iahiel Gersonitis. [9]Laetatusque est populus super prompto animo eorum, quia corde toto offerebant ea Domino; sed et David rex laetatus est gaudio magno. [10]Et benedixit Domino coram universa multitudine et ait: «Benedictus es, Domine, Deus Israel patris nostri, / ab aeterno in aeternum. / [11]Tua est, Domine, magnificentia et potentia, / gloria, splendor atque maiestas. / Cuncta enim, quae in caelo sunt et in terra, tua sunt, / Tuum, Domine, regnum, et tu elevaris ut caput super omnia. / [12]De te sunt divitiae et gloria, / tu dominaris omnium. / In manu tua virtus et potentia, / in manu tua est

h. Cn: Heb *upon me*

in addition to all that I have provided for the holy house, I have a treasure of my own of gold and silver, and because of my devotion to the house of my God I give it to the house of my God: [4]three thousand talents of gold, of the gold of Ophir, and seven thousand talents of refined silver, for overlaying the walls of the house, [5]and for all the work to be done by craftsmen, gold for the things of gold and silver for the things of silver. Who then will offer willingly, consecrating himself today to the LORD?"

1 Chron 22:14

[6]Then the heads of fathers' houses made their freewill offerings, as did also the leaders of the tribes, the commanders of thousands and of hundreds, and the officers over the king's work. [7]They gave for the service of the house of God five thousand talents and ten thousand darics of gold, ten thousand talents of silver, eighteen thousand talents of bronze, and a hundred thousand talents of iron. [8]And whoever had precious stones gave them to the treasury of the house of the LORD, in the care of Jehiel the Gershonite. [9]Then the people rejoiced because these had given willingly, for with a whole heart they had offered freely to the LORD; David the king also rejoiced greatly.

Num 7

2 Cor 9:7

David's prayer

[10]Therefore David blessed the LORD in the presence of all the assembly; and David said: "Blessed art thou, O LORD, the God of Israel our father, for ever and ever. [11]Thine, O LORD, is the greatness, and the power, and the glory, and the victory, and the

Jas 3:9

1 Tim 1:17
Rev 4:11; 5:12–13

29:10–19. David's prayer is a beautiful song of thanksgiving, which accords more with the solemn liturgy of the reconstructed temple of the post-exile than with the ceremonial sobriety which one would expect to have found in David's time. It consists of three parts —solemn praise of God's sovereignty and power (vv. 10–13), humble recognition on David's part of his personal limitations and of the extent of his property, for all that he has is given him by God (vv. 14–17), and a plea for perseverance in righteousness (vv. 18–19). This prayer is the testament of a devout man and epitomizes David as a model for Israelites in all ages.

magnificare et firmare omnia. / [13]Nunc igitur, Deus noster, confitemur tibi / et laudamus nomen tuum inclitum. [14]Quis ego et quis populus meus, ut possimus haec tibi universa offerre? Tua sunt haec omnia, et, quae de manu tua accepimus, dedimus tibi. [15]Peregrini enim sumus coram te et advenae, sicut omnes patres nostri; dies nostri quasi umbra super terram, et nulla est spes. [16]Domine Deus noster, omnis haec copia, quam paravimus, ut aedificaretur domus nomini sancto tuo, de manu tua est et tua sunt omnia. [17]Scio, Deus meus, quod probes corda et simplicitatem diligas; unde et ego in simplicitate cordis mei laetus obtuli universa haec et populum tuum, qui hic repertus est, vidi cum ingenti gaudio sponte tibi offerre donaria. [18]Domine, Deus Abraham et Isaac et Israel patrum nostrorum, custodi in aeternum hanc voluntatem cordis eorum; et semper in venerationem tui mens ista permaneat. [19] Salomoni quoque filio meo da cor perfectum, ut custodiat mandata tua, testimonia tua et legitima tua et faciat universa et

majesty; for all that is in the heavens and in the earth is thine; thine is the kingdom, O LORD, and thou art exalted as head above all. [12]Both riches and honour come from thee, and thou rulest over all. In thy hand are power and might; and in thy hand it is to make great and to give strength to all. [13]And now we thank thee, our God, and praise thy glorious name.

[14]"But who am I, and what is my people, that we should be able thus to offer willingly? For all things come from thee, and of thy own have we given thee. [15]For we are strangers before thee, and sojourners, as all our fathers were; our days on the earth are like a shadow, and there is no abiding.[i] [16]O LORD our God, all this abundance that we have provided for building thee a house for thy holy name comes from thy hand and is all thy own. [17]I know, my God, that thou triest the heart, and hast pleasure in uprightness; in the uprightness of my heart I have freely offered all these things, and now I have seen thy people, who are present here, offering freely and joyously to thee. [18]O LORD, the God of Abraham, Isaac, and Israel, our fathers, keep for ever such purposes and thoughts in the hearts of thy people, and direct their hearts toward thee. [19]Grant to Solomon my son that with a whole heart he may keep thy commandments, thy testimonies, and thy statutes, performing all, and that he may build the palace for which I have made provision."

Job 14:2
Ps 39:11
Heb 11:13
2 Thess 3:5
1 Kings 8:61

[20]Then David said to all the assembly, "Bless the LORD your God." And all the assembly blessed the LORD, the God of their fathers, and bowed their heads, and worshipped the LORD, and did obeisance to the king. [21]And they performed sacrifices to the LORD, and on the next day offered burnt offerings to the LORD, a

Ex 24:5

---

aedificet aedem, cuius impensas paravi». [20]Praecepit autem David universae ecclesiae: «Benedicite Domino Deo vestro!». Et benedixit omnis ecclesia Domino, Deo patrum suorum; et inclinaverunt se et adoraverunt Deum et deinde regem. [21]Immolaveruntque victimas Domino et obtulerunt holocausta die sequenti, tauros mille, arietes mille, agnos mille cum libaminibus suis et sacrificia abundantissime in omnem Israel. [22]Et comederunt et biberunt coram Domino in die illo cum grandi laetitia; et fecerunt regem secundo Salomonem filium David atque unxerunt Domino in principem et Sadoc in pontificem. [23]Seditque Salomon super solium Domini, ut esset rex pro David patre suo, et prosperatus est et paruit illi omnis Israel. [24]Sed et universi principes et fortes et cuncti filii regis David dederunt manum subicientes se Salomoni regi. [25] Magnificavit ergo Dominus Salomonem in excelsum in conspectu omnis Israel et dedit illi gloriam regni, qualem nullus habuit ante eum rex Israel. [26]Igitur David filius Isai regnavit super universum Israel; [27]et dies, quibus regnavit super Israel, fuerunt quadraginta anni: in Hebron regnavit septem annis et in Ierusalem annis triginta tribus. [28]Et mortuus est in senectute bona plenus dierum et divitiis et gloria; et regnavit Salomon filius eius pro eo. [29]Gesta autem David regis priora et novissima scripta sunt in libro Samuel videntis et in libro Nathan prophetae atque in volumine Gad videntis, [30]universique regni eius et fortitudinis et temporum, quae transierunt sub eo sive in Israel sive in cunctis regnis terrarum.

i. Gk Vg: Heb *hope*

thousand bulls, a thousand rams, and a thousand lambs, with their drink offerings, and sacrifices in abundance for all Israel; [22]and they ate and drank before the LORD on that day with great gladness.

Ex 24:11
1 Kings 1:33–39

And they made Solomon the son of David king the second time, and they anointed him as prince for the LORD, and Zadok as priest.

Solomon proclaimed king

[23]Then Solomon sat on the throne of the LORD as king instead of David his father; and he prospered, and all Israel obeyed him. [24]All the leaders and the mighty men, and also all the sons of King David, pledged their allegiance to King Solomon. [25]And the LORD gave Solomon great repute in the sight of all Israel, and bestowed upon him such royal majesty as had not been on any king before him in Israel.

1 Kings 10:23
2 Chron 1:1,12; 9:22

Death of David

[26]Thus David the son of Jesse reigned over all Israel. [27]The time that he reigned over Israel was forty years; he reigned seven years in Hebron, and thirty-three years in Jerusalem. [28]Then he died in a good old age, full of days, riches, and honour; and Solomon his son reigned in his stead. [29]Now the acts of King David, from first to last, are written in the Chronicles of Samuel the seer, and in the Chronicles of Nathan the prophet, and in the Chronicles of Gad the seer, [30]with accounts of all his rule and his might and of the circumstances that came upon him and upon Israel, and upon all the kingdoms of the countries.

2 Sam 5:4
1 Kings 2:11
1 Sam 9:9; 12:1

29:23–25. According to the information given here, Solomon's proclamation as king is entirely peaceful, and meets with no opposition; no mention is made of Adonijah (cf. 1 Kings 2:13–25). All that matters is that it took place with all solemnity, in a liturgy in which the priest Zadok was also anointed (29:22). The reign of Solomon begins as a model of theocratic government, for the throne of Israel is now "the throne of the Lord" (v. 23). "Among the Israelites kings and priests were appointed by means of material anointing with oil; that is not to say that the anointing made them both kings and priests: some were anointed kings, others priests; only to Christ does entire perfection and fullness belong—Christ, who came to bring the Law to fulfilment" (Faustinus Luciferanus, *De Trinitate*, 39). Through the anointing received in the sacraments of baptism and confirmation, Christians are given a share in the mission of Jesus Christ: "By Confirmation, Christians, that is, those who are anointed, share more completely in the mission of Jesus Christ and the fullness of the Holy Spirit with which he is filled, so that their lives may give off 'the aroma of Christ' (cf. 2 Cor 2:15)" (*Catechism of the Catholic Church*, 1294).

3. THE REIGN OF SOLOMON*

Solomon's gift of wisdom

1 Kings 2:46

1 [1]Solomon the son of David established himself in his kingdom, and the LORD his God was with him and made him exceedingly great.*

1 Kings 3:14–15
1 Chron 16:39; 21:29

[2]Solomon spoke to all Israel, to the commanders of thousands and of hundreds, to the judges, and to all the leaders in all Israel, the heads of fathers' houses. [3]And Solomon, and all the assembly with him, went to the high place that was at Gibeon; for the tent of meeting of God, which Moses the servant of the LORD had made in the wilderness, was there. [4](But David had brought up the ark of God from Kiriath-jearim to the place that David had prepared for it, for he had pitched a tent for it in Jerusalem.) [5]Moreover the bronze altar that Bezalel the son of Uri, son of Hur, had made, was there before the tabernacle of the LORD. And Solomon and the

Ex 27:1–2; 31:2; 38:1
1 Chron 2:20

***1:1—9:31.** The first part of the book deals with the reign of Solomon, and in it the two doctrinal points noted in 1 Chronicles are even more pronounced: the first is that the king (in this case, Solomon, the first in David's line) has been chosen by God and therefore has all the qualities needed in a ruler; and has no faults or failings which might tarnish his image. The second is the importance of the temple of Jerusalem which in the Chronicler's time was seen as a kind of synthesis of all the wonders worked by God over the course of history, particularly the history of Israel.

In order to get these two ideas across, the first part of the book is built around the construction and dedication of the temple (chaps. 3–7). By way of introduction, Solomon is portrayed as a man endowed by God with wisdom and wealth (chap. 1) and acknowledged by the king of Tyre (chap. 2). After the account of the dedication of the temple, some aspects of Solomon's reign are covered (chap. 8) as well as the visit of the queen of Sheba who, like the king of Tyre, and despite being a foreigner, is full of praise for Solomon's wisdom and magnificence (chap. 9).

1:1—2:1. Ignoring the matter of intrigue about the succession (cf. 1 Kings 1:2), the Chronicler reports that Solomon's reign begins in a period of peace in "all Israel" (v. 2), and the first thing he does is to travel with "all the assembly" (v. 3) to Gibeon, where God grants him wisdom. In the book of Kings (1 Kings 3:4–15) God's gift is one of wisdom for governance, but here he is also given riches (v. 12) to enable him to build the

[1] [1]Confortatus est ergo Salomon filius David in regno suo, et Dominus Deus eius erat cum eo et magnificavit eum in excelsum. [2]Praecepitque Salomon universo Israeli, tribunis et centurionibus et iudicibus et ducibus omnis Israel et principibus familiarum [3]et abiit cum universa multitudine in excelsum Gabaon, ubi erat tabernaculum conventus Dei, quod fecit Moyses famulus Dei in solitudine. [4]Arcam autem Dei adduxerat David de Cariathiarim in locum, quem praeparaverat ei et ubi fixerat illi tabernaculum, hoc est in Ierusalem; [5]altare quoque aeneum, quod fabricatus fuerat Beseleel filius Uri filii Hur, ibi erat coram tabernaculo Domini; ibique requisivit eum Salomon et omnis ecclesia.

assembly sought the LORD. [6]And Solomon went up there to the bronze altar before the LORD, which was at the tent of meeting, and offered a thousand burnt offerings upon it.

1 Kings 3:5–14

[7]In that night God appeared to Solomon, and said to him, "Ask what I shall give you." [8]And Solomon said to God, "Thou hast shown great and steadfast love to David my father, and hast made me king in his stead. [9]O LORD God, let thy promise to David my father be now fulfilled, for thou hast made me king over a people as many as the dust of the earth. [10]Give me now wisdom and knowledge to go out and come in before this people, for who can rule this thy people, that is so great?" [11]God answered Solomon, "Because this was in your heart, and you have not asked possessions, wealth, honour, or the life of those who hate you, and have not even asked long life, but have asked wisdom and knowledge for yourself that you may rule my people over whom I have made you king, [12]wisdom and knowledge are granted to you. I will also give you riches, possessions, and honour, such as none of the kings had who were before you, and none after you shall have the like." [13]So Solomon came from the high place at Gibeon, from[a] before the tent of meeting, to Jerusalem. And he reigned over Israel.

Mt 6:33

Solomon's wealth

[14]Solomon gathered together chariots and horsemen; he had fourteen hundred chariots and twelve thousand horsemen, whom he stationed in the chariot cities and with the king in Jerusalem. [15]And the king made silver and gold as common in Jerusalem as stone, and he made cedar as plentiful as the sycamore of the Shephelah. [16]And Solomon's import of horses was from Egypt and

1 Kings 9:19; 10:26–29
2 Chron 9:25

temple, which will be the primary objective of his reign (2:1). This emphasizes the fact that the Lord's promise is being fulfilled, and the importance of the temple of Jerusalem. The Chronicler makes it quite clear that Solomon ruled over all Israel and the fact that the entire people assembled dispels any question of there being divisions in the realm.

[6]Ascenditque ibi Salomon ad altare aeneum coram tabernaculo conventus Domini et obtulit in eo mille hostias. [7]Ecce autem in ipsa nocte apparuit ei Deus dicens: «Postula, quod vis, ut dem tibi». [8]Dixitque Salomon Deo: «Tu fecisti cum David patre meo misericordiam magnam et constituisti me regem pro eo. [9]Nunc ergo, Domine Deus, impleatur sermo tuus, quem pollicitus es David patri meo; tu enim me fecisti regem super populum tuum multum, qui tam innumerabilis est quam pulvis terrae. [10]Da mihi sapientiam et intellegentiam, ut ingrediar et egrediar coram populo tuo; quis enim potest hunc populum tuum digne, qui tam grandis est, iudicare?». [11]Dixit autem Deus ad Salomonem: «Quia hoc magis placuit cordi tuo et non postulasti divitias et substantiam et gloriam neque animas eorum, qui te oderant,

a. Gk Vg: Heb *to*

Kue, and the king's traders received them from Kue for a price. [17]They imported a chariot from Egypt for six hundred shekels of silver, and a horse for a hundred and fifty; likewise through them these were exported to all the kings of the Hittites and the kings of Syria.

2 Chron 2:17
1 Kings 5:29–30

2 [1 b]Now Solomon purposed to build a temple for the name of the LORD, and a royal palace for himself.

1 Kings 5:15–20
1 Chron 14:1
Lev 24:6
Num 17:5; 28:29

Treaty with the king of Tyre

[2 c]And Solomon assigned seventy thousand men to bear burdens and eighty thousand to quarry in the hill country, and three thousand six hundred to oversee them. [3]And Solomon sent word to Huram the king of Tyre: "As you dealt with David my father and

---

2:2–18. Solomon's agreement with Huram of Tyre (cf. 1 Kings 5:15–32) is designed to ensure that the temple will have all the magnificence it deserves: "The house which I am to build will be great, for our God is greater than all gods" (v. 5). It must be built by highly skilled craftsmen, using the very best materials. In all its details the building must conform to the description of the sanctuary in the desert (cf. Ex 25:1—31:18) and to that of the temple of Ezekiel (Ez 40:1—48:35).

The king of Tyre appreciates the wisdom of Solomon (vv. 11–16), not because he has evidence of Solomon's expertise as a ruler (his reign has only begun) but rather on account of his decision to build a temple for the Lord (v. 12). When Jesus speaks about the construction/destruction of the temple as symbolizing his death and resurrection, he gives a sublime interpretation of the centrality of the temple in the period when the Chronicler was writing, to indicate that the true centre of the life of the people of God is he himself, Jesus, the Saviour (cf. Jn 2:19–21).

The name of the king of Tyre was Hiram (cf. 1 Kings 5:15, 22, 25, 32; 9:11, 14; etc.), but in Chronicles he is normally called Huram.

sed nec dies vitae plurimos, petisti autem sapientiam et scientiam, ut iudicare possis populum meum, super quem constitui te regem, [12]sapientia et scientia data sunt tibi; divitias autem et substantiam et gloriam dabo tibi, ita ut nullus in regibus nec ante te nec post te fuerit similis tui». [13]Venit ergo Salomon ab excelso Gabaon in Ierusalem coram tabernaculo conventus et regnavit super Israel. [14]Congregavitque sibi currus et equites, et facti sunt ei mille quadringenti currus et duodecim milia equitum, et fecit eos esse in urbibus quadrigarum et cum rege in Ierusalem. [15]Praebuitque rex argentum et aurum in Ierusalem quasi lapides et cedros quasi sycomoros, quae nascuntur in Sephela multitudine magna. [16]Adducebantur autem ei equi de Aegypto et de Coa; negotiatores regis de Coa emebant pretio [17]et faciebant ascendere et exire de Aegypto quadrigam sescentis argenteis et equum centum quinquaginta; similiter universis regibus Hetthaeorum et Syriae per manus suas educebant. [18]Decrevit autem Salomon aedificare domum nomini Domini et palatium sibi. **[2]** [1]Et numeravit septuaginta milia virorum portantium umeris et octoginta milia, qui caederent lapides in montibus, praepositosque eorum tria milia sescentos. [2]Misit quoque ad Hiram regem Tyri dicens: «Sicut egisti cum David patre meo et misisti ei ligna cedrina, ut aedificaret sibi domum ad habitandum in ea. [3]sic fac mecum, ut aedificem domum nomini Domini Dei mei, ut consecrem eam ad adolendum coram illo fumiganda aromata et ad propositionem panum sempiternam et ad holocautomata mane et vespere, sabbatis quoque et neomeniis

b. Ch 1:18 in Heb **c.** Ch 2:1 in Heb

sent him cedar to build himself a house to dwell in, so deal with me. [4]Behold, I am about to build a house for the name of the LORD my God and dedicate it to him for the burning of incense of sweet spices before him, and for the continual offering of the showbread, and for burnt offerings morning and evening, on the sabbaths and the new moons and the appointed feasts of the LORD our God, as ordained for ever for Israel. [5]The house which I am to build will be great, for our God is greater than all gods. [6]But who is able to build him a house, since heaven, even highest heaven, cannot contain him? Who am I to build a house for him, except as a place to burn incense before him? [7]So now send me a man skilled to work in gold, silver, bronze, and iron, and in purple, crimson, and blue fabrics, trained also in engraving, to be with the skilled workers who are with me in Judah and Jerusalem, whom David my father provided. [8]Send me also cedar, cypress, and algum timber from Lebanon, for I know that your servants know how to cut timber in Lebanon. And my servants will be with your servants, [9]to prepare timber for me in abundance, for the house I am to build will be great and wonderful. [10]I will give for your servants, the hewers who cut timber, twenty thousand cors of crushed wheat, twenty thousand cors of barley, twenty thousand baths of wine, and twenty thousand baths of oil."

2 Chron 6:18

[11]Then Huram the king of Tyre answered in a letter which he sent to Solomon, "Because the LORD loves his people he has made you king over them." [12]Huram also said, "Blessed be the LORD God of Israel, who made heaven and earth, who has given King David a wise son, endued with discretion and understanding, who will build a temple for the LORD, and a royal palace for himself.

Ex 31:2
1 Kings 7:14

[13]"Now I have sent a skilled man, endued with understanding, Huram-abi, [14]the son of a woman of the daughters of Dan, and his

---

et sollemnitatibus Domini Dei nostri in sempiternum, quae mandata sunt Israeli. [4]Domus enim, quam aedificare cupio, magna est; magnus est enim Deus noster super omnes deos. [5]Quis ergo poterit praevalere, ut aedificet ei dignam domum? Si caelum et caeli caelorum capere eum nequeunt, quantus ego sum, ut possim aedificare ei domum? Sed ad hoc tantum, ut adoleatur incensum coram illo. [6]Mitte ergo mihi virum eruditum, qui noverit operari in auro et argento, aere et ferro, purpura coccino et hyacintho, et qui sciat sculpere caelaturas cum his artificibus, quos mecum habeo in Iudaea et Ierusalem, quos praeparavit David pater meus. [7]Sed et ligna cedrina mitte mihi et arceuthina et pinea de Libano; scio enim quod servi tui noverint caedere ligna de Libano, et erunt servi mei cum servis tuis, [8]ut parentur mihi ligna plurima; domus enim, quam cupio aedificare, magna erit nimis et inclita. [9]Praeterea operariis, qui caesuri sunt ligna, servis tuis dabo in cibaria tritici choros viginti milia et hordei choros totidem et vini viginti milia batos, olei quoque batos viginti milia». [10]Dixit autem Hiram rex Tyri per litteras, quas miserat Salomoni: «Quia dilexit Dominus populum suum, idcirco te regnare fecit super eum». [11]Et addidit dicens: «Benedictus Dominus, Deus Israel, qui fecit caelum et terram, qui dedit David regi filium sapientem et eruditum et sensatum atque prudentem, ut aedificaret domum Domino et palatium sibi. [12]Misi ergo tibi virum prudentem et scientissimum Hiram magistrum meum, [13]filium mulieris de filiabus Dan, cuius pater fuit Tyrius, qui novit operari in auro et argento, aere et ferro et lapidibus et lignis, in purpura quoque et hyacintho et bysso et coccino, et qui scit caelare omnem sculpturam et adinvenire prudenter, quodcumque in opere necessarium est. cum

father was a man of Tyre. He is trained to work in gold, silver, bronze, iron, stone, and wood, and in purple, blue, and crimson fabrics and fine linen, and to do all sorts of engraving and execute any design that may be assigned him, with your craftsmen, the craftsmen of my lord, David your father. [15]Now therefore the wheat and barley, oil and wine, of which my lord has spoken, let him send to his servants; [16]and we will cut whatever timber you need from Lebanon, and bring it to you in rafts by sea to Joppa, so that you may take it up to Jerusalem."

1 Kings 5:22–26
1 Chron 22:2

[17]Then Solomon took a census of all the aliens who were in the land of Israel, after the census of them which David his father had taken; and there were found a hundred and fifty-three thousand six hundred. [18]Seventy thousand of them he assigned to bear burdens, eighty thousand to quarry in the hill country, and three thousand six hundred as overseers to make the people work.

2 Chron 2:1

Building of the temple

3 [1]Then Solomon began to build the house of the LORD in Jerusalem on Mount Moriah, where the LORD had appeared to David his father, at the place that David had appointed, on the threshing floor of Ornan the Jebusite. [2]He began to build in the second month of the fourth year of his reign. [3]These are Solomon's measurements[d] for building the house of God: the length, in cubits

Gen 22:2
1 Kings 6
1 Chron 21:15ff
Ezek 40:5

3:1–17. Despite the parallel with 1 Kings 6:1–38 and 7:15–22, in this passage the Chronicler has added little touches to enhance the splendour of the temple and highlight its religious character: the mention of Mount Moriah (v. 1) is significant, because this is the only biblical text that identifies the mount on which the temple was built with that on which God commanded Abraham to offer his son Isaac in sacrifice (Gen 22:2).

The introduction to this account (vv. 1–2) is written in a formal style, as befits the start of a new stage with a new temple, a new liturgy and a new society.

Parvaim (v. 6) is an unknown city, evocative perhaps of paradise, where gold was plentiful and very pure. The measurements of the temple (vv. 3–4,

artificibus tuis et cum artificibus domini mei David patris tui. [14]Triticum ergo et hordeum et oleum et vinum, quae pollicitus es, domine mi, mitte servis tuis. [15]Nos autem caedemus ligna de Libano, quot necessaria habueris, et applicabimus ea ratibus per mare in Ioppe; tuum autem erit transferre ea in Ierusalem». [16]Numeravit igitur Salomon omnes viros peregrinos, qui erant in terra Israel post dinumerationem, quam dinumeravit David pater eius; et inventi sunt centum quinquaginta milia et tria milia sescenti. [17]Fecitque ex eis septuaginta milia, qui umeris onera portarent, et octoginta milia, qui lapides in montibus caederent; tria autem milia et sescentos praepositos operum populi. **[3]** [1]Et coepit Salomon aedificare domum Domini in Ierusalem in monte Moria, qui demonstratus fuerat a David patre eius, in loco, quem paraverat David in area Ornan Iebusaei. [2]Coepit autem aedificare mense secundo anno quarto regni sui. [3]Et hae sunt mensurae, quas statuit Salomon, ut aedificaret domum Dei: longitudinis cubiti in mensura

d. Syr: Heb *foundations*

of the old standard, was sixty cubits, and the breadth twenty cubits. [4]The vestibule in front of the nave of the house was twenty cubits long, equal to the width of the house;[e] and its height was a hundred and twenty cubits. He overlaid it on the inside with pure gold. [5]The nave he lined with cypress, and covered it with fine gold, and made palms and chains on it. [6]He adorned the house with settings of precious stones. The gold was gold of Parvaim. [7]So he lined the house with gold—its beams, its thresholds, its walls, and its doors; and he carved cherubim on the walls.

[8]And he made the most holy place; its length, corresponding to the breadth of the house, was twenty cubits, and its breadth was twenty cubits; he overlaid it with six hundred talents of fine gold. [9]The weight of the nails was one shekel[f] to fifty shekels of gold. And he overlaid the upper chambers with gold.

[10]In the most holy place he made two cherubim of wood[g] and overlaid[h] them with gold. [11]The wings of the cherubim together extended twenty cubits: one wing of the one, of five cubits, touched the wall of the house, and its other wing, of five cubits, touched the wing of the other cherub; [12]and of this cherub, one wing, of five cubits, touched the wall of the house, and the other wing, also of five cubits, was joined to the wing of the first cherub. [13]The wings of these cherubim extended twenty cubits; the cherubim[i] stood on their feet, facing the nave. [14]And he made the veil of blue and purple and crimson fabrics and fine linen, and worked cherubim on it.

1 Kings 6:23–28

8, 11)—those of its site as well as floor area, buildings, cherubim—are greater than those given in the book of Kings. The writer probably exaggerates because this is the place where the glory of God resides: he is more interested in the religious significance of the building than in accurate measurement.

prima sexaginta, latitudinis cubiti viginti. [4]Porticum vero ante frontem, quae tendebatur in longum, iuxta mensuram latitudinis domus, cubitorum viginti; porro altitudo centum viginti cubitorum erat. Et deauravit eam intrinsecus auro mundissimo. [5]Domum quoque maiorem texit tabulis ligneis abiegnis et laminas auri obryzi affixit per totum; scalpsitque in eis palmas et quasi catenulas se invicem complectentes. [6]Stravit quoque pavimentum templi pretiosissimo marmore decore multo. [7]Porro aurum erat de Parvaim, de cuius laminis texit domum, et trabes eius et postes et parietes et ostia; et caelavit cherubim in parietibus. [8]Fecit quoque domum sancti sanctorum: longitudinem iuxta latitudinem domus cubitorum viginti et latitudinem similiter viginti cubitorum; et laminis auri optimi texit eam quasi talentis sescentis. [9]Sed et pro clavis usus est auro ponderis quinquaginta siclorum. Cenacula quoque texit auro. [10]Fecit etiam in domo sancti sanctorum cherubim duos opere statuario et texit eos auro. [11]Alae cherubim viginti cubitis extendebantur, ita ut una ala haberet cubitos quinque et tangeret parietem domus, et altera quinque cubitos habens alam tangeret alterius cherub. [12]Similiter cherub alterius ala quinque habebat cubitos et tangebat parietem, et ala eius altera quinque cubitorum alam cherub alterius contingebat. [13]Igitur alae utriusque cherubim expansae erant et extendebantur per cubitos viginti; ipsi autem stabant erectis pedibus, et facies eorum erant versae ad exteriorem domum. [14]Fecit

e. 1 Kings 6:3: Heb uncertain **f.** Compare Gk: Heb lacks *one shekel* **g.** Gk: Heb uncertain **h.** Heb *they overlaid* **i.** Heb *they*

1 Kings 7:15–22 2 Kings 25:17

[15]In front of the house he made two pillars thirty-five cubits high, with a capital of five cubits on the top of each. [16]He made chains like a necklace[j] and put them on the tops of the pillars; and he made a hundred pomegranates, and put them on the chains. [17]He set up the pillars in front of the temple, one on the south, the other on the north; that on the south he called Jachin, and that on the north Boaz.

Furnishings of the temple

1 Kings 7:23–26

4 [1]He made an altar of bronze, twenty cubits long, and twenty cubits wide, and ten cubits high. [2]Then he made the molten sea; it was round, ten cubits from brim to brim, and five cubits high, and a line of thirty cubits measured its circumference. [3]Under it were figures of gourds,[k] for thirty[l] cubits, compassing the sea round about; the gourds[k] were in two rows, cast with it when it was cast. [4]It stood upon twelve oxen, three facing north, three facing west, three facing south, and three facing east; the sea was set upon them, and all their hinder parts were inward. [5]Its thickness was a handbreadth; and its brim was made like the brim of a cup, like the flower of a lily; it held over three thousand baths.

4:1–22. The description of the temple furnishings is practically the same as that in 1 Kings 7:23–26, 38–51, especially from v. 11 onwards. The capacity of "the sea", or the tank, was about three thousand baths (v. 5). A bath (*bat*, in Hebrew) was approximately 21 litres (4.5 gallons), which meant that the tank could hold 63,000 litres (13,800 gallons). But it seems unlikely that a tank of the size given in v. 2 could have held as much as that. The writer's theological purpose leads him to exaggerate in order to convey the grandeur of the temple: all aspects of it, and even details of its ornamentation, must symbolize the greatness of God.

quoque velum ex hyacintho, purpura, cocco et bysso et intexuit ei cherubim. [15]Ante fores etiam templi duas columnas, quae triginta et quinque cubitos habebant altitudinis; porro capita earum quinque cubitorum. [16]Necnon et quasi catenulas in torque, et superposuit eas capitibus columnarum; malogranata etiam centum, quae catenulis interposuit. [17]Ipsas quoque columnas posuit ante faciem templi, unam a dextris et alteram a sinistris; eam, quae a dextris erat, vocavit Iachin et, quae ad laevam, Booz. **[4]** [1]Fecit quoque altare aeneum viginti cubitorum longitudinis et viginti cubitorum latitudinis et decem cubitorum altitudinis. [2]Mare etiam fusile decem cubitis a labio usque ad labium rotundum per circuitum; quinque cubitos habebat altitudinis, et funiculus triginta cubitorum ambiebat gyrum eius. [3]Similitudo quoque boum erat subter illud, in circuitu circumdabant illud—decem cubitis—duobus versibus alvum maris circuibant boves fusiles in una fusione cum mari. [4]Et ipsum mare super duodecim boves impositum erat, quorum tres respiciebant aquilonem et alii tres occidentem, porro tres alii meridiem et tres, qui reliqui erant, orientem habentes mare superpositum; posteriora autem boum erant intrinsecus sub mari. [5]Porro vastitas eius habebat mensuram palmi, et labium illius erat quasi labium calicis vel repandi lilii;

j. Cn: Heb *in the inner sanctuary* **k.** 1 Kings 7:24: Heb *oxen* **l.** Compare verse 2: Heb *ten*

[6]He also made ten lavers in which to wash, and set five on the south side, and five on the north side. In these they were to rinse off what was used for the burnt offering, and the sea was for the priests to wash in.

1 Kings 7:38–39

[7]And he made ten golden lampstands as prescribed, and set them in the temple, five on the south side and five on the north. [8]He also made ten tables, and placed them in the temple, five on the south side and five on the north. And he made a hundred basins of gold. [9]He made the court of the priests, and the great court, and doors for the court, and overlaid their doors with bronze; [10]and he set the sea at the southeast corner of the house.

1 Kings 7:49

1 Kings 7:50
1 Chron 28:16

1 Kings 7:12

[11]Huram also made the pots, the shovels, and the basins. So Huram finished the work that he did for King Solomon on the house of God: [12]the two pillars, the bowls, and the two capitals on the top of the pillars; and the two networks to cover the two bowls of the capitals that were on the top of the pillars; [13]and the four hundred pomegranates for the two networks, two rows of pomegranates for each network, to cover the two bowls of the capitals that were upon the pillars. [14]He made the stands also, and the lavers upon the stands, [15]and the one sea, and the twelve oxen underneath it. [16]The pots, the shovels, the forks, and all the equipment for these Huram-abi made of burnished bronze for King Solomon for the house of the LORD. [17]In the plain of the Jordan the king cast them, in the clay ground between Succoth and Zeredah. [18]Solomon made all these things in great quantities, so that the weight of the bronze was not ascertained.

1 Kings 7:40–51

[19]So Solomon made all the things that were in the house of God: the golden altar, the tables for the bread of the Presence, [20]the lampstands and their lamps of pure gold to burn before the inner sanctuary, as prescribed; [21]the flowers, the lamps, and the tongs, of

---

capiebatque tria milia batos. [6]Fecit quoque luteres decem et posuit quinque a dextris et quinque a sinistris, ut lavarent in eis omnia, quae in holocaustum oblaturi erant; porro in mari sacerdotes lavabantur. [7]Fecit autem et candelabra aurea decem secundum speciem, qua iussa erant fieri, et posuit ea in templo quinque a dextris et quinque a sinistris. [8]Necnon et mensas decem, et posuit eas in templo quinque a dextris et quinque a sinistris; phialas quoque aureas centum. [9]Fecit etiam atrium sacerdotum et atrium grande et ostia in atrio, quae texit aere. [10]Porro mare posuit in latere dextro contra orientem ad meridiem. [11]Fecit autem Hiram lebetes et vatilla et phialas et complevit omne opus regis Salomonis in domo Dei; [12]hoc est columnas duas et globos et capitella super caput columnarum duarum et serta duo, quae tegerent globos capitellorum; [13]malogranata quoque quadringenta et serta duo, ita ut bini ordines malogranatorum singulis sertis iungerentur, quae protegerent globos capitellorum columnarum. [14]Bases etiam fecit et luteres, quos superposuit basibus, [15]mare unum, boves quoque duodecim sub mari; [16]et lebetes et vatilla et fuscinulas: omnia vasa fecit regi Salomoni Hiram magister eius pro domo Domini ex aere mundissimo. [17]In regione Iordanis fudit ea rex in argillosa terra inter Succoth et Saredatha. [18]Fecitque Salomon multitudinem vasorum innumerabilem, ita ut ignoraretur pondus aeris. [19]Fecitque Salomon omnia vasa domus Dei et altare aureum et mensas et super eas panes propositionis; [20]candelabra quoque cum lucernis suis, ut lucerent ante Dabir iuxta ritum, ex auro purissimo, [21]et florem

purest gold; [22]the snuffers, basins, dishes for incense, and firepans, of pure gold; and the sockets[m] of the temple, for the inner doors to the most holy place and for the doors of the nave of the temple were of gold.

The ark is brought to the temple

1 Kings 7:51—8:11

5 [1]Thus all the work that Solomon did for the house of the LORD was finished. And Solomon brought in the things which David his father had dedicated, and stored the silver, the gold, and all the vessels in the treasuries of the house of God.

1 Kings 8:1–9

[2]Then Solomon assembled the elders of Israel and all the heads of the tribes, the leaders of the fathers houses of the people of Israel, in Jerusalem, to bring up the ark of the covenant of the LORD out of the city of David, which is Zion. [3]And all the men of Israel assembled before the king at the feast which is in the seventh month. [4]And all the elders of Israel came, and the Levites took up the ark. [5]And they brought up the ark, the tent of meeting, and all the holy vessels that were in the tent; the priests and the Levites brought them up. [6]And King Solomon and all the congregation of Israel, who had assembled before him, were before the ark, sacrificing so many sheep and oxen that they could not be counted or numbered. [7]So the priests brought the ark of the covenant of the LORD to its place, in the inner sanctuary of the house, in the most holy place, underneath the wings of the cherubim. [8]For the

---

5:1–14. This account of the transfer of the ark parallels 1 Kings 8:1–13, with this difference—here (cf. also 1 Chron 15:2, 16–24) the Levites have a more prominent role: they bear the ark, they are in charge of the chants and the music, and they are positioned beside the priests inside the temple (vv. 12–13). All this shows that the Levites played an important role in the life of Israel during the Persian period, when this book was being put together.

et lucernas et forcipes aureos: omnia de auro perfectissimo facta sunt; [22]cultros quoque et phialas et sartagines et turibula ex auro purissimo. Et ostia templi interiora in sancta sanctorum et ostia templi forinsecus aurea. **[5]** [1]Sicque completum est omne opus, quod fecit Salomon in domo Domini. Intulit igitur Salomon omnia, quae voverat David pater suus, argentum et aurum, et universa vasa posuit in thesauris domus Dei. [2]Post quae congregavit maiores natu Israel et cunctos principes tribuum et capita familiarum de filiis Israel in Ierusalem, ut adducerent arcam foederis Domini de civitate David, quae est Sion. [3]Venerunt igitur ad regem omnes viri Israel in die sollemni mensis septimi. [4]Cumque venissent cuncti seniorum Israel, portaverunt Levitae arcam [5]et intulerunt eam et tabernaculum conventus et omnem paraturam tabernaculi. Porro omnia vasa sanctuarii, quae erant in tabernaculo, portaverunt sacerdotes levitici generis. [6]Rex autem Salomon et universus coetus Israel, omnes, qui fuerunt congregati ad eum ante arcam, immolabant oves et boves absque ullo numero: tanta enim erat multitudo victimarum. [7]Et intulerunt sacerdotes arcam foederis Domini in locum suum ad Dabir templi, in sancta sanctorum subter alas cherubim, [8]ita ut cherubim expanderent alas suas super locum, in quo posita erat

m. 1 Kings 7:50: Heb *the door of the house*

cherubim spread out their wings over the place of the ark, so that the cherubim made a covering above the ark and its poles. [9]And the poles were so long that the ends of the poles were seen from the holy place before the inner sanctuary; but they could not be seen from outside; and they are there to this day. [10]There was nothing in the ark except the two tables which Moses put there at Horeb, where the LORD made a covenant with the people of Israel, when they came out of Egypt. [11]Now when the priests came out of the holy place (for all the priests who were present had sanctified themselves, without regard to their divisions; [12]and all the Levitical singers, Asaph, Heman, and Jeduthun, their sons and kinsmen, arrayed in fine linen, with cymbals, harps, and lyres, stood east of the altar with a hundred and twenty priests who were trumpeters; [13]and it was the duty of the trumpeters and singers to make themselves heard in unison in praise and thanksgiving to the LORD), and when the song was raised, with trumpets and cymbals and other musical instruments, in praise to the LORD,

"For he is good,
for his steadfast love endures for ever,"

the house, the house of the LORD, was filled with a cloud, [14]so that the priests could not stand to minister because of the cloud; for the glory of the LORD filled the house of God.

1 Kings 8:10–13

1 Chron 24

Rev 15:8

Solomon blesses the people

6 [1]Then Solomon said,
"The LORD has said that he would
dwell in thick darkness.

6:1–42. Solomon's prayer as given here is word for word the same as in 1 Kings 8:12–52; this applies to the introductory hymn (vv. 1–2), and the address to the people (vv. 4–11) and the prayer in the strict sense (vv. 12–42). But three significant nuances have been added: according to v. 11 the Lord made the Covenant "with the people of Israel" (an expression which includes

arca, et ipsam arcam tegerent cum vectibus suis ab alto. [9]Vectium autem, quibus portabatur arca, quia paululum longiores erant, capita parebant ante Dabir; si vero quis erat extrinsecus eos videre non poterat. Fuit itaque arca ibi usque in praesentem diem. [10]Nihilque erat aliud in arca, nisi duae tabulae, quas posuerat Moyses in Horeb, quando fecit Dominus foedus cum filiis Israel egredientibus ex Aegypto. [11]Egressis autem sacerdotibus de sanctuario—omnes enim sacerdotes, qui ibi potuerant inveniri, sanctificati sunt, non observantes vices et ministeriorum ordinem, [12]et Levitae cantores, omnes, qui sub Asaph erant et qui sub Heman et qui sub Idithun, filii et fratres eorum, vestiti byssinis, cymbalis et psalteriis et citharis stabant ad orientalem plagam altaris, et cum eis sacerdotes centum viginti canentes tubis—[13]igitur cunctis pariter et tubis et voce et cymbalis et organis et diversi generis musicorum concinentibus et vocem in sublime tollentibus, cum una voce Dominum laudare coepissent et dicere: «Confitemini Domino quoniam bonus, quoniam in aeternum misericordia eius», impleta est domus Dei nube, [14]nec potuerunt sacerdotes stare et ministrare propter nubem; compleverat enim gloria Domini domum Dei. **[6]** [1]Tunc

[2]I have built thee an exalted house,
place for thee to dwell in for ever."

1 Kings 8:14–21

[3]Then the king faced about, and blessed all the assembly of Israel, while all the assembly of Israel stood. [4]And he said, "Blessed be the LORD, the God of Israel, who with his hand has fulfilled what he promised with his mouth to David my father, saying, [5]'Since the day that I brought my people out of the land of Egypt, I chose no city in all the tribes of Israel in which to build a house, that my name might be there, and I chose no man as prince over my people Israel; [6]but I have chosen Jerusalem that my name may be there and I have chosen David to be over my people Israel.' [7]Now it was in the heart of David my father to build a house for the name of the LORD, the God of Israel. [8]But the LORD said to David my father, 'Whereas it was in your heart to build a house for my name, you did well that it was in your heart; [9]nevertheless you shall not build the house, but your son who shall be born to you shall build the house for my name.' [10]Now the LORD has fulfilled his promise

---

those who were alive after the exile) and not "with our fathers" (1 Kings 8:21); therefore, the Chronicler's contemporaries are the beneficiaries of that Covenant, which means that they are subject to what it lays down. According to v. 13, Solomon speaks from a platform built for the purpose, and not from the altar (1 Kings 8:22) which was reserved for priests. This has the effect of drawing a clear distinction between king and priest, between governmental and liturgical roles. And, vv. 41–42 are taken from Psalm 132:8–10, not 1 Kings 8:53 which made reference to Moses and deliverance from Egypt. The Chronicler prefers to see the divine promises as being fulfilled in the liturgy and in the Levites and priests rather than in the past history of the people; and he puts the emphasis more on the Covenant with David than on the Covenant made with Moses on Sinai. These little changes mean that Solomon's ancient prayer will lose none of its impact in the more complex society of the post-exilic period. This is a clear example of a re-reading of an ancient biblical text to suit new circumstances.

Salomon ait: «Dominus pollicitus est, ut habitaret in caligine; [2]ego autem aedificavi domum in habitaculum tuum, ut habitares ibi in perpetuum». [3]Et convertit rex faciem suam et benedixit universae multitudini Israel—nam omnis turba stabat intenta—et ait: [4]«Benedictus Dominus, Deus Israel, qui, quod locutus est ore suo David patri meo, opere complevit dicens: [5]'A die qua eduxi populum meum de terra Aegypti non elegi civitatem de cunctis tribubus Israel, ut aedificaretur in ea domus nomini meo, neque elegi quemquam alium virum, ut esset dux in populo meo Israel, [6]sed elegi Ierusalem, ut sit nomen meum in ea, et elegi David, ut constituerem eum super populum meum Israel". [7]Cumque fuisset voluntatis David patris mei, ut aedificaret domum nomini Domini, Dei Israel, [8]dixit Dominus ad eum: "Quia haec fuit voluntas tua, ut aedificares domum nomini meo, bene quidem fecisti huiuscemodi habere voluntatem, [9]sed non tu aedificabis domum, verum filius tuus, qui egredietur de lumbis tuis, ipse aedificabit domum nomini meo". [10]Complevit ergo Dominus sermonem suum, quem locutus fuerat, et ego surrexi pro David patre meo et sedi super thronum Israel, sicut locutus est Dominus, et aedificavi

which he made; for I have risen in the place of David my father, and sit on the throne of Israel, as the LORD promised, and I have built the house for the name of the LORD, the God of Israel. [11]And there I have set the ark, in which is the covenant of the LORD which he made with the people of Israel."

Solomon's prayer

[12]Then Solomon stood before the altar of the LORD in the presence of all the assembly of Israel, and spread forth his hands. [13]Solomon had made a bronze platform five cubits long, five cubits wide, and three cubits high, and had set it in the court; and he stood upon it. Then he knelt upon his knees in the presence of all the assembly of Israel, and spread forth his hands toward heaven; [14]and said, "O LORD, God of Israel, there is no God like thee, in heaven or on earth, keeping covenant and showing steadfast love to thy servants who walk before thee with all their heart; [15]who hast kept with thy servant David my father what thou didst declare to him; yea, thou didst speak with thy mouth, and with thy hand hast fulfilled it this day. [16]Now therefore, O LORD, God of Israel, keep with thy servant David my father what thou hast promised him, saying, 'There shall never fail you a man before me to sit upon the throne of Israel, if only your sons take heed to their way, to walk in my law as you have walked before me.' [17]Now therefore, O LORD, God of Israel, let thy word be confirmed, which thou hast spoken to thy servant David.

1 Kings 8:22–29

[18]"But will God dwell indeed with man on the earth? Behold, heaven and the highest heaven cannot contain thee; how much less this house which I have built! [19]Yet have regard to the prayer of thy servant and to his supplication, O LORD my God, hearkening to the cry and to the prayer which thy servant prays before thee; [20]that

---

domum nomini Domini, Dei Israel; [11]et posui in ea arcam, in qua est pactum Domini, quod pepigit cum filiis Israel». [12]Stetit ergo coram altari Domini ex adverso universae multitudinis Israel et extendit manus suas. [13]Siquidem fecerat Salomon basim aeneam et posuerat eam in medio atrii habentem quinque cubitos longitudinis et quinque cubitos latitudinis et tres cubitos altitudinis, stetitque super eam; et deinceps, flexis genibus contra universam multitudinem Israel et palmis in caelum levatis, [14]ait: «Domine, Deus Israel, non est similis tui Deus in caelo et in terra, qui custodis pactum et misericordiam cum servis tuis, qui ambulant coram te in toto corde suo, [15]qui praestitisti servo tuo David patri meo quaecumque locutus fueras ei, et, quae ore promiseras, opere complesti, sicut et praesens tempus probat. [16]Nunc ergo, Domine, Deus Israel, imple servo tuo patri meo David, quaecumque locutus es dicens: "Non deficiet ex te vir coram me, qui sedeat super thronum Israel, ita tamen si custodierint filii tui vias suas et ambulaverint in lege mea, sicut et tu ambulasti coram me". [17]Et nunc, Domine, Deus Israel, firmetur sermo tuus, quem locutus es servo tuo David! [18]Ergone credibile est, ut habitet Deus cum hominibus super terram? Si caelum et caeli caelorum non te capiunt, quanto magis domus ista, quam aedificavi! [19]Sed respice orationem servi tui et obsecrationem eius, Domine Deus meus, et audi clamorem et preces, quas fundit famulus tuus coram te, [20]ut aperias oculos tuos super domum istam

thy eyes may be open day and night toward this house, the place where thou hast promised to set thy name, that thou mayest hearken to the prayer which thy servant offers toward this place. [21]And hearken thou to the supplications of thy servant and of thy people Israel, when they pray toward this place; yea, hear thou from heaven* thy dwelling place; and when thou hearest, forgive.

1 Kings 8:30–51

[22]"If a man sins against his neighbour and is made to take an oath, and comes and swears his oath before thy altar in this house, [23]then hear thou from heaven, and act, and judge thy servants, requiting the guilty by bringing his conduct upon his own head, and vindicating the righteous by rewarding him according to his righteousness.

[24]"If thy people Israel are defeated before the enemy because they have sinned against thee, when they turn again and acknowledge thy name, and pray and make supplication to thee in this house, [25]then hear thou from heaven, and forgive the sin of thy people Israel, and bring them again to the land which thou gavest to them and to their fathers.

[26]"When heaven is shut up and there is no rain because they have sinned against thee, if they pray toward this place, and acknowledge thy name, and turn from their sin, when thou dost afflict them, [27]then hear thou in heaven, and forgive the sin of thy servants, thy people Israel, when thou dost teach them the good way[n] in which they should walk; and grant rain upon thy land, which thou hast given to thy people as an inheritance.

[28]"If there is famine in the land, if there is pestilence or blight or mildew or locust or caterpillar; if their enemies besiege them in any of their cities; whatever plague, whatever sickness there is; [29]whatever prayer, whatever supplication is made by any man or by all thy people Israel, each knowing his own affliction, and his

---

diebus ac noctibus, super locum in quo pollicitus es, ut ponas nomen tuum et exaudires orationem, quam servus tuus orat in eo. [21]Et exaudi preces famuli tui et populi tui Israel, qui oraverint ad locum istum; exaudi de habitaculo tuo, de caelis, exaudi et propitiare! [22]Si peccaverit quispiam in proximum suum, et ille exegerit ab eo iuramentum, ut se maledicto constringat coram altari in domo ista, [23]tu audies de caelo et facies iudicium servorum tuorum, ita ut reddas iniquo viam suam in caput proprium et ulciscaris iustum retribuens ei secundum iustitiam suam. [24]Si superatus fuerit populus tuus Israel ab inimicis, quia peccaturi sunt tibi, et conversi egerint paenitentiam et confitentes nomini tuo oraverint et fuerint deprecati in domo ista, [25]tu exaudies de caelo, et propitiare peccato populi tui Israel et reduc eos in terram, quam dedisti eis et patribus eorum. [26]Si clauso caelo pluvia non fluxerit propter peccata populi, et deprecati te fuerint in loco isto et confessi nomini tuo et conversi a peccatis suis, cum eos afflixeris, [27]exaudi de caelo, Domine, et dimitte peccata servorum tuorum et populi tui Israel, doce eos viam bonam, per quam ingrediantur, et da pluviam terrae, quam dedisti populo tuo ad possidendum. [28]Fames si orta fuerit in terra et pestilentia, uredo et aurugo et locusta etbruchus et hostes, vastatis regionibus, portas eius obsederint, omnisque plaga et infirmitas presserit, [29]si quis de populo tuo Israel fuerit

n. Gk Syr Vg: Heb *toward the good way*

own sorrow and stretching out his hands toward this house; [30]then hear thou from heaven thy dwelling place, and forgive, and render to each whose heart thou knowest, according to all his ways (for thou, thou only, knowest the hearts of the children of men); [31]that they may fear thee and walk in thy ways all the days that they live in the land which thou gavest to our fathers.

[32]"Likewise when a foreigner, who is not of thy people Israel, comes from a far country for the sake of thy great name, and thy mighty hand, and thy outstretched arm, when he comes and prays toward this house, [33]hear thou from heaven thy dwelling place, and do according to all for which the foreigner calls to thee; in order that all the peoples of the earth may know thy name and fear thee, as do thy people Israel, and that they may know that this house which I have built is called by thy name.

[34]"If thy people go out to battle against their enemies, by whatever way thou shalt send them, and they pray to thee toward this city which thou hast chosen and the house which I have built for thy name, [35]then hear thou from heaven their prayer and their supplication, and maintain their cause.

[36]"If they sin against thee—for there is no man who does not sin—and thou art angry with them, and dost give them to an enemy, so that they are carried away captive to a land far or near; [37]yet if they lay it to heart in the land to which they have been carried captive, and repent, and make supplication to thee in the land of their captivity, saying, 'We have sinned, and have acted perversely and wickedly'; [38]if they repent with all their mind and with all their heart in the land of their captivity, to which they were carried captive, and pray toward their land, which thou gavest to their fathers, the city which thou hast chosen, and the house which

---

deprecatus cognoscens plagam et infirmitatem suam et expanderit manus suas ad domum hanc, [30]tu exaudi de caelo, de loco habitationis tuae, et propitiare et redde unicuique secundum vias suas, quia nosti cor eius; tu enim solus nosti corda filiorum hominum, [31]ut timeant te et ambulent in viis tuis cunctis diebus, quibus vivunt super faciem terrae, quam dedisti patribus nostris. [32]Externum quoque, qui non est de populo tuo Israel, si venerit de terra longinqua propter nomen tuum magnum et propter manum tuam robustam et brachium tuum extentum, et oraverit in loco isto, [33]tu exaudies de caelo firmissimo habitaculo tuo et facies cuncta, pro quibus invocaverit te ille peregrinus, ut sciant omnes populi terrae nomen tuum et timeant te sicut populus tuus Israel et cognoscant quia nomen tuum invocatum est super domum hanc, quam aedificavi. [34]Si egressus fuerit populus tuus ad bellum contra adversarios suos per viam, in qua miseris eos, et oraverint te contra viam, in qua civitas haec est, quam elegisti, et domus, quam aedificavi nomini tuo, [35]tu exaudies de caelo preces eorum et obsecrationem, et facies iudicium eorum. [36]Si autem peccaverint tibi—neque enim est homo, qui non peccet—et iratus fueris eis et tradideris hostibus, et captivos duxerint eos in terram longinquam vel propinquam, [37]et conversi in corde suo in terra, ad quam captivi ducti fuerant, egerint paenitentiam et deprecati te fuerint in terra captivitatis suae dicentes: "Peccavimus, inique fecimus, iniuste egimus"; [38]et reversi fuerint ad te in toto corde suo et in tota anima sua in terra captivitatis suae, ad quam ducti sunt, et oraverint te

I have built for thy name, [39]then hear thou from heaven thy dwelling place their prayer and their supplications, and maintain their cause and forgive thy people who have sinned against thee.

1 Kings 8:52 [40]Now, O my God, let thy eyes be open and thy ears attentive to a prayer of this place.

Ps 132:8–10

[41] "And now arise, O LORD God, and go to thy resting place,
thou and the ark of thy might.
Let thy priests, O LORD God, be clothed with salvation,
and let thy saints rejoice in thy goodness.
[42] O LORD God, do not turn away the face of thy anointed one!
Remember thy steadfast love for David thy servant."

Dedication of the temple

1 Chron 21:26; Ex 24:16; 2 Chron 5:14; 2 Chron 5:13; Ps 136:1

7 [1]When Solomon had ended his prayer, fire came down* from heaven and consumed the burnt offering and the sacrifices, and the glory of the LORD filled the temple. [2]And the priests could not enter the house of the LORD, because the glory of the LORD filled the LORD's house. [3]When all the children of Israel saw the fire come down and the glory of the LORD upon the temple, they bowed down with their faces to the earth on the pavement, and worshipped and gave thanks to the LORD, saying,

"For he is good,
for his steadfast love endures for ever."

1 Kings 8:62–63

[4]Then the king and all the people offered sacrifice before the LORD. [5]King Solomon offered as a sacrifice twenty-two thousand oxen and a hundred and twenty thousand sheep. So the king and all the people dedicated the house of God. [6]The priests stood at

---

7:1–10. After the king's prayer, the holy rites begin. These include three basic elements—the manifestation of God both in the fire and in the glory which filled the temple (vv. 4–6); the solemn sacrifices and offerings (vv. 4–6); and the festival proper which, coinciding with the feast of Tabernacles, goes on for seven days more (vv. 8–10).

contra viam terrae suae, quam dedisti patribus eorum, et urbis, quam elegisti, et domus, quam aedificavi nomini tuo, [39]ut exaudias de caelo, de loco habitationis tuae, preces eorum et supplicationes eorum et facias iudicium et dimittas populo tuo, qui peccavit tibi; [40]tu es enim Deus meus. Aperiantur, quaeso, oculi tui, et aures tuae intentae sint ad orationem, quae fit in loco isto. [41]Nunc igitur consurge, Domine Deus, in requiem tuam, tu et arca fortitudinis tuae; sacerdotes tui, Domine Deus, induantur salutem, et sancti tui laetentur in bonis. [42]Domine Deus, ne averteris faciem christi tui; memento misericordiarum David servi tui». [7] [1]Cumque complesset Salomon fundens preces, ignis descendit de caelo et devoravit holocaustum et victimas, et maiestas Domini implevit domum. [2]Nec poterant sacerdotes ingredi templum Domini, eo quod implesset maiestas Domini templum Domini. [3]Sed et omnes filii Israel videbant descendentem ignem et gloriam Domini super domum et corruentes proni in terram super pavimentum stratum lapide adoraverunt et laudaverunt Dominum: «Quoniam bonus, quoniam in saeculum misericordia eius». [4]Rex autem et omnis populus immolabant victimas coram Domino.

their posts; the Levites also, with the instruments for music to the LORD which King David had made for giving thanks to the LORD—for his steadfast love endures for ever—whenever David offered praises by their ministry; opposite them the priests sounded trumpets; and all Israel stood.

Num 10:1–10
Ps 136:1

[7]And Solomon consecrated the middle of the court that was before the house of the LORD; for there he offered the burnt offering and the fat of the peace offerings, because the bronze altar Solomon had made could not hold the burnt offering and the cereal offering and the fat.

1 Kings 8:64–66

[8]At that time Solomon held the feast for seven days, and all Israel with him, a very great congregation, from the entrance of Hamath to the Brook of Egypt. [9]And on the eighth day they held a solemn assembly; for they had kept the dedication of the altar seven days and the feast seven days. [10]On the twenty-third day of the seventh month he sent the people away to their homes, joyful and glad of heart for the goodness that the LORD had shown to David and to Solomon and to Israel his people.

The manifestation of God (which is substituted for the second blessing given by Solomon: cf. 1 Kings 8:54–61) dramatically demonstrates that God accepts the temple building and Solomon's prayer (cf. 1 Chron 21:26); it is evocative of the dedication of the tabernacle in the desert (v. 3; cf. Ex 40:34–35); and it recalls the inauguration of the ministry of the priests (cf. Lev 9:22–24); a new stage of Israelite liturgy has begun with all due solemnity.

The priests, and not the king, are in charge of offering the sacrifices, and the Levites are in charge of the liturgy. A refrain, often found in Chronicles (1 Chron 16:34, 41; 2 Chron 5:13; etc.) and in the Psalms (106:1; 136:1, 3, 26; etc.), extols God's goodness: "For he is good, for his steadfast love endures for ever" (v. 3).

The feast of the Dedication will be revived when the Maccabees rededicate the altar profaned by Antiochus Epiphanes (cf. 1 Mac 4:59) and will be given the name of *Hanukkah* or "Feast of Lights"; it was still celebrated in Jesus' time, as it is indeed in Jewish communities to this day.

[5]Mactavit igitur rex Salomon hostias boum viginti duo milia, ovium centum viginti milia, et dedicavit domum Dei rex et universus populus. [6]Sacerdotes autem stabant in officiis suis et Levitae in organis carminum Domini, quae fecit David rex ad laudandum Dominum: «Quoniam in aeternum misericordia eius», hymnos David canentes per manus suas. Porro sacerdotes canebant tubis ante eos, cunctusque Israel stabat. [7]Sanctificavit quoque Salomon medium atrii ante templum Domini; obtulerat enim ibi holocausta et adipes pacificorum, quia altare aeneum, quod fecerat, non poterat sustinere holocausta et oblationes et adipes. [8]Fecit ergo Salomon sollemnitatem in tempore illo septem diebus, et omnis Israel cum eo, ecclesia magna valde ab introitu Emath usque ad torrentem Aegypti. [9]Feceruntque die octavo collectam magnam, eo quod dedicassent altare septem diebus et sollemnitatem celebrassent diebus septem. [10]Igitur in die vicesimo tertio mensis septimi dimisit populum ad tabernacula sua, laetantem

1 Kings 9:1–9

God's reply to Solomon

[11]Thus Solomon finished the house of the LORD and the king's house; all that Solomon had planned to do in the house of the LORD and in his own house he successfully accomplished. [12]Then the LORD appeared to Solomon in the night and said to him: "I have heard your prayer, and have chosen this place for myself as a house of sacrifice. [13]When I shut up the heavens so that there is no rain, or command the locust to devour the land, or send pestilence among my people, [14]if my people who are called by my name humble themselves, and pray and seek my face, and turn from their wicked ways, then I will hear from heaven, and will forgive their sin and heal their land. [15]Now my eyes will be open and my ears attentive to the prayer that is made in this place. [16]For now I have chosen and consecrated this house that my name may be there for ever; my eyes and my heart will be there for all time. [17]And as for you, if you walk before me, as David your father walked, doing according to all that I have commanded you and keeping my statutes and my ordinances, [18]then I will establish your royal throne, as I covenanted with David your father, saying, 'There shall not fail you a man to rule Israel.'

[19]"But if you[o] turn aside and forsake my statutes and my commandments which I have set before you, and go and serve other

---

7:11–22. The Lord's reply (almost identical with that recorded in 1 Kings 9:1–9) shows that God means the temple to be the symbol of his protection of the people as long as it still stands—and the symbol of their punishment once it is destroyed. It is also a symbol of the Lord's presence; he is always ready to listen to entreaties and to come to the aid of those who have recourse to him (vv. 13–15). The Lord's words in this passage are an invitation to put our trust in him. "If you don't leave him, he won't leave you" (St J. Escrivá, *The Way*, 730).

atque gaudentem super bono, quod fecerat Dominus Davidi et Salomoni et Israeli populo suo. [11]Complevitque Salomon domum Domini et domum regis; et in omnibus, quae disposuerat in corde suo, ut faceret in domo Domini et in domo sua, prosperatus est. [12]Apparuit autem ei Dominus nocte et ait: «Audivi orationem tuam et elegi locum istum mihi in domum sacrificii. [13]Si clausero caelum, et pluvia non fluxerit, et mandavero et praecepero locustae, ut devoret terram, et misero pestilentiam in populum meum, [14]humiliatus autem populus meus, super quos invocatum est nomen meum, deprecatus me fuerit et exquisierit faciem meam et egerit paenitentiam a viis suis pessimis, ego exaudiam de caelo et propitius ero peccatis eorum et sanabo terram eorum. [15]Nunc oculi mei erunt aperti et aures meae attentae ad orationem eius, qui in loco isto oraverit; [16]elegi enim et sanctificavi locum istum, ut sit nomen meum ibi in sempiternum, et permaneant oculi mei et cor meum ibi cunctis diebus. [17]Tu quoque, si ambulaveris coram me, sicut ambulavit David pater tuus, et feceris iuxta omnia, quae praecepi tibi, et decreta et iudicia mea servaveris, [18]stabiliam thronum regni tui, sicut pollicitus sum David patri tuo

o. The word *you* is plural here

gods and worship them, [20]then I will pluck you[p] up from the land which I have given you;[p] and this house, which I have consecrated for my name, I will cast out of my sight, and will make it a proverb and a byword among all peoples. [21]And at this house, which is exalted, every one passing by will be astonished, and say, 'Why has the LORD done thus to this land and to this house?' [22]Then they will say, 'Because they forsook the LORD the God of their fathers who brought them out of the land of Egypt, and laid hold on other gods, and worshipped them and served them; therefore he has brought all this evil upon them.'"

Building of cities

1 Kings 9:10–25

8 [1]At the end of twenty years, in which Solomon had built the house of the LORD and his own house, [2]Solomon rebuilt the cities which Huram had given to him, and settled the people of Israel in them.

[3]And Solomon went to Hamath-zobah, and took it. [4]He built Tadmor in the wilderness and all the store-cities which he built in Hamath. [5]He also built Upper Beth-horon and Lower Beth-horon,

---

8:1–6. In addition to the temple, Solomon built new cities and restored many others (cf. 1 Kings 9:10–18). According to 1 Kings 9:11–14, some of those cities were given by Solomon to Hiram as payment for his help in building the temple. But Hiram did not consider them to be of much value, and handed them back. The Chronicler prefers not to mention Hiram's dissatisfaction; he simply says that Solomon rebuilt both those cities handed over to him in times of peace and those acquired through war or which had been Israel's from early times. This serves to heighten the reputation of the great king: he did all things well.

Tadmor (v. 4) is Palmyra in Greek, that is, an oasis of palm trees and olive groves situated in the centre of the Syrian desert and a place which became an important hub of communications and of commercial and cultural interchange in Hellenistic times.

dicens: Non auferetur de stirpe tua vir, qui sit princeps in Israel. [19]Si autem aversi fueritis et dereliqueritis decreta mea et praecepta mea, quae proposui vobis, et abeuntes servieritis diis alienis et adoraveritis eos, [20]evellam vos de terra mea, quam dedi vobis, et domum hanc, quam sanctificavi nomini meo, proiciam a facie mea et tradam eam in parabolam et in fabulam cunctis populis. [21]Et super domo ista, quae erat excelsa, universi transeuntes stupebunt et dicent: "Quare fecit Dominus sic terrae huic et domui huic?" [22]respondebuntque: "Quia dereliquerunt Dominum, Deum patrum suorum, qui eduxit eos de terra Aegypti, et apprehenderunt deos alienos et adoraverunt eos et coluerunt, idcirco venerunt super eos universa haec mala"». **[8]** [1]Expletis autem viginti annis, postquam aedificavit Salomon domum Domini et domum suam, [2]civitates, quas dederat Hiram Salomoni, aedificavit et habitare ibi fecit filios Israel. [3]Abiit quoque in Emath Soba et obtinuit eam. [4]Et aedificavit Palmyram in deserto et omnes civitates horreorum, quas aedificavit in Emath. [5]Exstruxitque Bethoron superiorem et Bethoron inferiorem, civitates

p. Heb *them*

fortified cities with walls, gates, and bars, [6]and Baalath, and all the store-cities that Solomon had, and all the cities for his chariots, and the cities for his horsemen, and whatever Solomon desired to build in Jerusalem, in Lebanon, and in all the land of his dominion.

1 Kings 9:20–28

Solomon's administration

[7]All the people who were left of the Hittites, the Amorites, the Perizzites, the Hivites, and the Jebusites, who were not of Israel, [8]from their descendants who were left after them in the land, whom the people of Israel had not destroyed—these Solomon made a forced levy and so they are to this day. [9]But of the people of Israel Solomon made no slaves for his work; they were soldiers, and his officers, the commanders of his chariots, and his horsemen. [10]And these were the chief officers of King Solomon, two hundred and fifty, who exercised authority over the people.

[11]Solomon brought Pharaoh's daughter up from the city of David to the house which he had built for her, for he said, "My wife shall not live in the house of David king of Israel, for the places to which the ark of the LORD has come are holy."

Ex 23:14
Num 28–29

[12]Then Solomon offered up burnt offerings to the LORD upon the altar of the LORD which he had built before the vestibule, [13]as the

---

8:7–18. Solomon was a skilled administrator (cf. 1 Kings 9:20–28) of internal affairs and external commerce. This passage contains two pieces of information very much in line with the doctrinal thrust of the book. The first is that Solomon never used Israelites in the arduous work of building, (cf., on the contrary, 1 Kings 5:27). The second is that he built a palace for the pharaoh's daughter whom he had married (cf. 1 Kings 3:1; 9:16, 24), not as a present but for religious reasons—to preserve the temple and the royal palace from the uncleanness that would occur if a pagan woman lived there. These two decisions show that Solomon acted as a protector of his people and devoutly complied with ritual regulations. He was a model in every way because he acted "according to the commandment of Moses" (v. 13), and he also kept to the divisions of the priests laid down by David, his father (vv. 14–15).

munitas habentes muros et portas et vectes, [6]Baalath etiam et omnes urbes horreorum, quae fuerunt Salomonis, cunctasque urbes quadrigarum et urbes equorum. Omnia quaecumque voluit Salomon atque disposuit, aedificavit in Ierusalem et in Libano et in universa terra potestatis suae. [7]Omnem populum, qui derelictus fuerat de Hetthaeis et Amorraeis et Pherezaeis et Hevaeis et Iebusaeis, qui non erant de stirpe Israel, [8]de filiis eorum, qui remanserant post eos in terra, quos non interfecerant filii Israel, subiugavit Salomon in tributarios usque in diem hanc. [9]Porro de filiis Israel non posuit, ut servirent operibus regis; ipsi enim erant viri bellatores et principes pugnatorum eius et principes quadrigarum et equitum eius. [10]Omnes autem principes praefectorum regis Salomonis fuerunt ducenti quinquaginta, qui praefuerant populo. [11]Filiam vero pharaonis transtulit de civitate David in domum, quam aedificaverat ei; dixit enim rex: «Non habitabit mulier mihi in domo David regis Israel, eo quod sanctificata sit, quia ingressa est in eam arca Domini». [12]Tunc obtulit Salomon holocausta Domino

duty of each day required, offering according to the commandment of Moses for the sabbaths, the new moons, and the three annual feasts—the feast of unleavened bread, the feast of weeks, and the feast of tabernacles. [14]According to the ordinance of David his father, he appointed the divisions of the priests for their service, and the Levites for their offices of praise and ministry before the priests as the duty of each day required, and the gatekeepers in their divisions for the several gates; for so David the man of God had commanded. [15]And they did not turn aside from what the king had commanded the priests and Levites concerning any matter and concerning the treasuries.

1 Chron 23–26

[16]Thus was accomplished all the work of Solomon from[q] the day the foundation of the house of the LORD was laid until it was finished. So the house of the LORD was completed.

1 Kings 9:26–28

[17]Then Solomon went to Ezion-geber and Eloth on the shore of the sea, in the land of Edom. [18]And Huram sent him by his servants ships and servants familiar with the sea, and they went to Ophir together with the servants of Solomon, and fetched from there four hundred and fifty talents of gold and brought it to King Solomon.

1 Kings 10:1–13

Visit of the queen of Sheba

9 [1]Now when the queen of Sheba heard of the fame of Solomon she came to Jerusalem to test him with hard questions, having a very great retinue and camels bearing spices and very much gold

---

9:1–12. The visit of the queen of Sheba (the account here is the same as in 1 Kings 10:1–13) is designed to show that foreign monarchs, for example the king of Tyre (2:1–17) and the queen of Sheba herself, acknowledge and are in awe of the wealth and wisdom of Solomon. This is the last episode reported in the reign of Solomon. His wisdom and power are embodied in the temple for all to behold, both Israelite and foreigner.

Whereas 1 Kings (10:8) says "Happy are your wives", the Chronicler has "Happy are you men" (v. 7: cf. RSV note); this avoids giving too much importance to Solomon's harem, in case that might be interpreted as evidence of political or religious weakness on the king's part.

super altare Domini, quod exstruxerat ante porticum, [13]ut per singulos dies offerretur in eo iuxta praeceptum Moysi in sabbatis et in calendis et in festis diebus ter per annum, id est in sollemnitate Azymorum et in sollemnitate Hebdomadarum et in sollemnitate Tabernaculorum. [14]Et constituit iuxta dispositionem David patris sui officia sacerdotum in ministeriis suis et Levitas in ordine suo, ut laudarent et ministrarent coram sacerdotibus iuxta ritum uniuscuiusque diei, et ianitores in divisionibus suis per portam et portam: sic enim praeceperat David homo Dei. [15]Nec praetergressi sunt mandata regis

q. Gk Syr Vg: Heb *to*

and precious stones. When she came to Solomon, she told him all that was on her mind. [2]And Solomon answered all her questions; there was nothing hidden from Solomon which he could not explain to her. [3]And when the queen of Sheba had seen the wisdom of Solomon, the house that he had built, [4]the food of his table, the seating of his officials, and the attendance of his servants, and their clothing, his cupbearers, and their clothing, and his burnt offerings which he offered at the house of the LORD, there was no more spirit in her.

[5]And she said to the king, "The report was true which I heard in my own land of your affairs and of your wisdom, [6]but I did not believe the[r] reports until I came and my own eyes had seen it; and behold, half the greatness of your wisdom was not told me; you surpass the report which I heard. [7]Happy are your wives![s] Happy are these your servants, who continually stand before you and hear your wisdom! [8]Blessed be the LORD your God, who has delighted in you and set you on his throne as king for the LORD your God! Because your God loved Israel and would establish them for ever, he has made you king over them, that you may execute justice and righteousness." [9]Then she gave the king a hundred and twenty talents of gold, and a very great quantity of spices, and precious stones: there were no spices such as those which the queen of Sheba gave to King Solomon.

[10]Moreover the servants of Huram and the servants of Solomon, who brought gold from Ophir, brought algum wood and precious

---

de sacerdotibus et Levitis in omnibus et in custodiis thesaurorum. [16]Et firmatum est totum opus Salomonis ex eo die, quo fundavit domum Domini, usque in diem, quo perfecit eam. [17]Tunc abiit Salomon in Asiongaber et in Ailath ad oram maris Rubri, quae est in terra Edom. [18]Misit autem ei Hiram per manus servorum suorum naves et nautas gnaros maris; et abierunt cum servis Salomonis in Ophir tuleruntque inde quadringenta quinquaginta talenta auri et attulerunt ad regem Salomonem. **[9]** [1]Regina quoque Saba, cum audisset famam Salomonis, venit, ut tentaret eum in aenigmatibus in Ierusalem cum magno comitatu et camelis, qui portabant aromata et auri plurimum gemmasque pretiosas. Cumque venisset ad Salomonem, locuta est ei, quaecumque erant in corde suo. [2]Et exposuit ei Salomon omnia, quae proposuerat, nec quidquam fuit quod ei non perspicuum fecerit. [3]Quae postquam vidit, sapientiam scilicet Salomonis et domum, quam aedificaverat, [4]necnon et cibaria mensae eius et sessionem servorum et officia ministrorum eius et vestimenta eorum, pincernas quoque et vestes eorum et victimas, quas immolabat in domo Domini, non erat prae stupore ultra in ea spiritus. [5]Dixitque ad regem: «Verus est sermo, quem audieram in terra mea, de rebus tuis et sapientia tua: [6]non credebam narrantibus, donec ipsa venissem, et vidissent oculi mei, et probassem vix medietatem sapientiae tuae mihi fuisse narratam; vicisti famam, quam audivi. [7]Beati viri tui et beati servi tui, qui assistunt coram te omni tempore et audiunt sapientiam tuam! [8]Sit Dominus Deus tuus benedictus, qui voluit te ordinare super thronum suum regem Domini Dei tui! Quia diligit Deus tuus Israel et vult servare eum in aeternum, idcirco posuit te super eum regem, ut facias iudicia atque iustitiam». [9]Dedit autem regi centum viginti talenta auri et aromata multa nimis et gemmas pretiosissimas; non fuerunt aromata talia

r. Heb *their* **s.** Gk Compare 1 Kings 10:8: Heb *men*

stones. [11]And the king made of the algum wood steps[t] for the house of the LORD and for the king's house, lyres also and harps for the singers; there never was seen the like of them before in the land of Judah.

[12]And King Solomon gave to the queen of Sheba all that she desired, whatever she asked besides what she had brought to the king. So she turned and went back to her own land, with her servants.

Solomon's wealth

1 Kings 10:14–20
Mt 6:29

[13]Now the weight of gold that came to Solomon in one year was six hundred and sixty-six talents of gold, [14]besides that which the traders and merchants brought; and all the kings of Arabia and the governors of the land brought gold and silver to Solomon. [15]King Solomon made two hundred large shields of beaten gold; six hundred shekels of beaten gold went into each shield. [16]And he made three hundred shields of beaten gold; three hundred shekels of gold went into each shield; and the king put them in the House of the Forest of Lebanon. [17]The king also made a great ivory throne, and overlaid it with pure gold. [18]The throne had six steps and a footstool of gold, which were attached to the throne, and on

1 Kings 10:16–17

1 Kings 10:18–20

9:13–28. The reign of Solomon is summed up in v. 22 (cf. 1 Kings 10:14–29): the king's vast wealth (exaggerated as compared with the parallel passage in Kings) shows that God has blessed Solomon and made him a king who is a model of good government and personal piety. If the Chronicler omits or tones down mention of the king's failings (cf. 1 Kings 11:1–40), he does so to highlight the part played by God. The Lord never deceives; his plans are always fulfilled, as all can see who contemplate the temple, the crowning achievement of the great king. The temple became the symbol of the people that God brought into being in ancient times, and the palpable proof that he continues to shower his blessings on them.

ut haec, quae dedit regina Saba regi Salomoni. [10]Sed et servi Hiram cum servis Salomonis attulerunt aurum de Ophir et ligna thyina et gemmas pretiosissimas; [11]et fecit rex de lignis thyinis gradus in domo Domini et in domo regia, citharas quoque et psalteria cantoribus. Numquam visa sunt in terra Iudae ligna talia. [12]Rex autem Salomon dedit reginae Saba cuncta, quae voluit et quae postulavit, et multo plura quam attulerat ad eum. Quae reversa abiit in terram suam cum servis suis. [13]Erat autem pondus auri, quod afferebatur Salomoni per singulos annos, sescenta sexaginta sex talenta auri, [14]excepta ea summa, quae proveniebat ex tributis mercatorum et negotiatorum afferentium et omnium regum Arabiae et ducum terrae, qui comportabant aurum et argentum Salomoni. [15]Fecit igitur rex Salomon ducenta scuta aurea de summa sescentorum aureorum, qui in singulis scutis expendebantur, [16]trecentas quoque peltas aureas trecentorum aureorum, quibus tegebantur singulae peltae, posuitque ea rex in domo Saltus Libani. [17]Fecit quoque rex solium eburneum grande et vestivit illud auro mundissimo; [18]sex quoque

t. Gk Vg: The meaning of the Hebrew word is uncertain

each side of the seat were arm rests and two lions standing beside the arm rests, [19]while twelve lions stood there, one on each end of a step on the six steps. The like of it was never made in any kingdom. [20]All King Solomon's drinking vessels were of gold, and all the vessels of the House of the Forest of Lebanon were of pure gold; silver was not considered as anything in the days of Solomon. [21]For the king's ships went to Tarshish with the servants of Huram; once every three years the ships of Tarshish used to come bringing gold, silver, ivory, apes, and peacocks.[x]

1 Kings 10:21–25

[22]Thus King Solomon excelled all the kings of the earth in riches and in wisdom. [23]And all the kings of the earth sought the presence of Solomon to hear his wisdom, which God had put into his mind. [24]Every one of them brought his present, articles of silver and of gold, garments, myrrh, spices, horses, and mules, so much year by year. [25]And Solomon had four thousand stalls for horses and chariots, and twelve thousand horsemen, whom he stationed in the chariot cities and with the king in Jerusalem. [26]And he ruled over all the kings from the Euphrates to the land of the Philistines, and to the border of Egypt. [27]And the king made silver as common in Jerusalem as stone, and cedar as plentiful as the sycamore of the Shephelah. [28]And horses were imported for Solomon from Egypt and from all lands.

1 Kings 5:6; 10:26
2 Chron 1:14
1 Kings 5:1
1 Kings 10:27–28
2 Chron 1:15

Death of Solomon

[29]Now the rest of the acts of Solomon, from first to last, are they not written in the history of Nathan the prophet, and in the

1 Kings 11:41–43

9:29–31. The tailpiece of the chapters dealing with Solomon is taken from 1 Kings 11:41–43, and the same formula is used to sum up the lives of other kings. All that is added here is the mention of Nathan, Ahijah and Iddo. The writings of these men have not survived, but the Chronicler evidently wants to record that the prophets approved of Solomon and his doings.

gradus, quibus ascendebatur ad solium, et scabellum aureum et brachiola duo altrinsecus et duos leones stantes iuxta brachiola, [19]sed et alios duodecim leunculos stantes super sex gradus ex utraque parte: non fuit tale solium in universis regnis. [20]Omnia quoque vasa convivii regis erant aurea et vasa domus Saltus Libani ex auro purissimo; argentum enim in diebus Salomonis pro nihilo reputabatur. [21]Siquidem naves regis ibant in Tharsis cum servis Hiram; semel in annis tribus veniebant naves Tharsis portantes aurum et argentum et ebur et simias et pavos. [22]Magnificatus est igitur rex Salomon super omnes reges terrae divitiis et sapientia. [23]Omnesque reges terrarum desiderabant faciem videre Salomonis, ut audirent sapientiam, quam dederat Deus in corde eius, [24]et deferebant ei munera, vasa argentea et aurea et vestes et arma et aromata, equos et mulos per singulos annos. [25]Habuit quoque Salomon quattuor milia stabula equorum et curruum equitumque duodecim milia; constituitque eos in urbibus quadrigarum et, ubi erat rex, in Ierusalem. [26]Exercuit etiam potestatem super cunctos reges, a fluvio Euphrate usque ad terram

x. Or *baboons*

prophecy of Ahijah the Shilonite, and in the visions of Iddo the seer concerning Jeroboam the son of Nebat? [30]Solomon reigned in Jerusalem over all Israel forty years. [31]And Solomon slept with his fathers, and was buried in the city of David his father; and Rehoboam his son reigned in his stead.*

4. THE KINGS OF JUDAH*

The kingdom is split in two

10 [1]Rehoboam went to Shechem, for all Israel had come to Shechem to make him king. [2]And when Jeroboam the son of Nebat heard of it (for he was in Egypt, whither he had fled from King Solomon), then Jeroboam returned from Egypt. [3]And they sent and called him; and Jeroboam and all Israel came and said to Rehoboam, [4]"Your father made our yoke heavy. Now therefore lighten the hard service of your father and his heavy yoke upon us, and we will serve you." [5]He said to them, "Come to me again in three days." So the people went away.

1 Kings 12:1–19

[6]Then King Rehoboam took counsel with the old men, who had stood before Solomon his father while he was yet alive, saying, "How do you advise me to answer this people?" [7]And they said to

*__10:1—28:27.__ The second part of the book deals with the successors of Solomon as kings of Judah. Again, the main source the writer uses is the book of Kings. However, he omits practically all references to the Northern kingdom (despite the fact that it was really more important than the Southern), nor is there any mention of the prophets Elijah and Elisha, who lived there. Also, the writer's aim is not to provide a chronicle of events in the kingdom of Judah, much less give exact lists of the battles, pacts, victories or defeats involving each king; nor does he apply the Deuteronomic teaching that assesses each king by using the principle that the misfortunes of the people are God's

Philisthinorum et usque ad terminos Aegypti; [27]tantamque copiam praebuit argenti in Ierusalem quasi lapidum, et cedrorum tantam multitudinem velut sycomororum, quae gignuntur in Sephela. [28]Adducebantur autem ei equi de Aegypto cunctisque regionibus. [29]Reliqua vero operum Salomonis priorum et novissimorum scripta sunt in verbis Nathan prophetae et in prophetia Ahiae Silonitis, in visione quoque Addo videntis super Ieroboam filium Nabat. [30]Regnavit autem Salomon in Ierusalem super omnem Israel quadraginta annis; [31]dormivitque cum patribus suis, et sepelierunt eum in civitate David patris eius. Regnavitque Roboam filius eius pro eo. **[10]** [1]Profectus est autem Roboam in Sichem; illuc enim cunctus Israel convenerat, ut constituerent eum regem. [2]Quod cum audisset Ieroboam filius Nabat, qui erat in Aegypto—fugerat quippe illuc ante Salomonem—statim reversus est; [3]vocaveruntque eum, et venit cum universo Israel, et locuti sunt ad Roboam dicentes: [4]«Pater tuus durissimo iugo nos pressit; tu leviora impera patre tuo, qui nobis gravem imposuit servitutem, et paululum de onere subleva et serviemus tibi». [5]Qui ait: «Post tres dies revertimini ad me». Cumque abisset populus, [6]iniit rex Roboam consilium cum senibus, qui steterant coram patre eius Salomone, dum adhuc viveret, dicens:

him, "If you will be kind to this people and please them, and speak good words to them, then they will be your servants for ever." [8]But he forsook the counsel which the old men gave him, and took counsel with the young men who had grown up with him and stood before him. [9]And he said to them, "What do you advise that we answer this people who have said to me, 'Lighten the yoke that your father put upon us'?" [10]And the young men who had grown up with him said to him, "Thus shall you speak to the people who said to you, 'Your father made our yoke heavy, but do you lighten it for us'; thus shall you say to them, 'My little finger is thicker than my father's loins. [11]And now, whereas my father laid upon you a heavy yoke, I will add to your yoke. My father chastised you with whips, but I will chastise you with scorpions.'"

[12]So Jeroboam and all the people came to Rehoboam the third day, as the king said, "Come to me again the third day." [13]And the king answered them harshly, and forsaking the counsel of the old men, [14]King Rehoboam spoke to them according to the counsel of the young men, saying, "My father made your yoke heavy, but I will add to it; my father chastised you with whips, but I will chastise you with scorpions." [15]So the king did not hearken to the people; for it was a turn of affairs brought about by God that the

---

punishment for the reigning king's transgressions. The writer confines himself to reviewing the history of the temple and of the liturgical institutions established by David and Solomon, and underlining the fact that those remained in place despite often being at risk. The kings who caused disunion between North and South, for example, Rehoboam (chaps. 10–12), or who favoured idolatry, such as Ahaz (chap. 28), are painted in dark tones, whereas those who encouraged the correct, united, form of worship in the temple of Jerusalem are exalted and praised. In this book each monarch is approved or censured according to how he himself acted—in line with the doctrine of personal retribution (cf. Ezek 18:1–32), so much stressed by those who returned from exile. Thus, each king enjoys the Lord's protection when he begins his reign.

«Quid datis consilii, ut respondeam populo?». [7]Qui dixerunt ei: «Si placueris populo huic et lenieris eos verbis clementibus, servient tibi omni tempore». [8]At ille reliquit consilium senum et cum iuvenibus tractare coepit, qui cum eo nutriti fuerant et erant in comitatu illius. [9]Dixitque ad eos: Quid vobis videtur, vel respondere quid debemus populo huic, qui dixit mihi: "Subleva iugum, quod imposuit nobis pater tuus'?" [10]Et responderunt iuvenes, qui nutriti fuerant cum eo, atque dixerunt: «Sic loqueris populo, qui dixit tibi: "Pater tuus aggravavit iugum nostrum, tu subleva", et sic respondebis eis: Minimus digitus meus grossior est lumbis patris mei; [11]pater meus imposuit vobis iugum grave, et ego maius pondus apponam; pater meus cecidit vos flagellis, ego vero caedam scorpionibus». [12]Venit ergo Ieroboam et universus populus ad Roboam die tertio, sicut praeceperat eis rex dicens: «Revertimini ad me die tertio». [13]Responditque rex dura, derelicto consilio seniorum; [14]locutusque est iuxta iuvenum voluntatem: «Pater meus grave vobis imposuit iugum, / quod ego gravius faciam. / Pater meus cecidit vos flagellis,

LORD might fulfil his word, which he spoke by Ahijah the Shilonite to Jeroboam the son of Nebat.

[16]And when all Israel saw that the king did not hearken to them, the people answered the king,

"What portion have we in David?
We have no inheritance in the son of Jesse.
Each of you to your tents, O Israel!
Look now to your own house, David."

So all Israel departed to their tents.

[17]But Rehoboam reigned over the people of Israel who dwelt in the cities of Judah. [18]Then King Rehoboam sent Hadoram, who was taskmaster over the forced labour, and the people of Israel stoned him to death with stones. And King Rehoboam made haste to mount his chariot, to flee to Jerusalem. [19]So Israel has been in rebellion against the house of David to this day.

Rehoboam, king of Judah

1 Kings 12:21–24

11 [1]When Rehoboam came to Jerusalem, he assembled the house of Judah, and Benjamin, a hundred and eighty thousand chosen warriors, to fight against Israel, to restore the

---

10:1–19. The separation of the two kingdoms is reported on the basis of information contained in 2 Kings 12:1–25, but giving the impression that the schism was not really a total one. The text alludes to Jeroboam's revolt but does not mention his appointment as king (1 Kings 12:20 is omitted), or record that Israel became divided. Instead, the writer stresses that Rehoboam continues to be king over the Israelites, over "all Israel", who dwelt in the cities of Judah (vv. 1–3, 17). Although the author knows that a separate kingdom was established in the North (v. 19), he writes his account as he does in order to stress the continuity between the undivided Israel of David and Solomon, and the Israel of the post-exilic period.

The prophets and their policies play a key part in 2 Chronicles. In this account, the Northern breakaway is seen as the fulfilment of the prophecy of Ahijah the Shilonite (v. 15), whereas, according to 1 Kings 11:31, it was caused by the sins of Solomon. The Chronicler is at pains to show that it was God himself who willed that the rupture take place.

11:1–12. These verses parallel 1 Kings 12:21–24, but we can see three doctrinal features of Chronicles in them: firstly,

/ ego vero caedam scorpionibus». [15]Et non acquievit populi precibus. Erat enim voluntatis Dei, ut compleretur sermo eius, quem locutus fuerat per manum Ahiae Silonitis ad Ieroboam filium Nabat. [16]Israel autem universus videns quod noluisset eos audire rex, locutus est ad eum: «Non est nobis pars in David / neque hereditas in filio Isai! / Revertere in tabernacula tua, Israel! / Tu autem vide domum tuam, David!». Et abiit Israel in tabernacula sua. [17]Super filios autem Israel, qui habitabant in civitatibus Iudae, regnavit Roboam. [18]Misitque rex Roboam Adoram, qui praeerat servituti, et lapidaverunt eum filii Israel, et mortuus est. Porro rex Roboam currum festinavit ascendere et fugit in Ierusalem. [19]Recessitque Israel a domo David usque ad diem hanc. **[11]** [1]Venit autem Roboam in Ierusalem et

kingdom to Rehoboam. [2]But the word of the LORD came to Shemaiah the man of God: [3]"Say to Rehoboam the son of Solomon king of Judah, and to all Israel in Judah and Benjamin, [4]'Thus says the LORD, You shall not go up or fight against your brethren. Return every man to his home, for this thing is from me.'" So they hearkened to the word of the LORD, and returned and did not go against Jeroboam.

[5]Rehoboam dwelt in Jerusalem, and he built cities for defence in Judah. [6]He built Bethlehem, Etam, Tekoa, [7]Beth-zur, Soco, Adullam, [8]Gath, Mareshah, Ziph, [9]Adoraim, Lachish, Azekah, [10]Zorah, Aijalon, and Hebron, fortified cities which are in Judah and in Benjamin. [11]He made the fortresses strong, and put commanders in them, and stores of food, oil, and wine. [12]And he put shields and spears in all the cities, and made them very strong. So he held Judah and Benjamin.

Rehoboam's supporters

[13]And the priests and the Levites that were in all Israel resorted to him from all places where they lived. [14]For the Levites left their

---

there is no reference at all to the division into two kingdoms; thus the inhabitants of Judah are the true Israel, as can be seen from the nuance in v. 3, "all Israel in Judah and Benjamin" as compared with "to all the house of Judah and Benjamin, and to the rest of the people" in 1 Kings 12:23. Moreover, in Shemaiah's actual oracle the Northerners are referred to as "your brethren" (v. 4), omitting the description "the people of Israel" (1 Kings 12:24). Secondly, from now on stress is put on obedience to the word of God proclaimed by the prophets (v. 4): if one goes along with it, one prospers; if one rejects it, misfortune follows. Finally, Rehoboam, who listens to God's word, devotes himself to building and fortifying cities. In return for this good beginning to the kingdom of Judah, God protected Jerusalem, allowing the king to establish himself there, and the entire territory of Judah became strong.

11:13–17. In contrast to Jeroboam's wrong-headed policy (cf. 1 Kings

convocavit universam domum Iudae et Beniamin, centum octoginta milia electorum bellantium, ut dimicaret contra Israel et converteret ad se regnum suum. [2]Factusque est sermo Domini ad Semeiam hominem Dei dicens: [3]«Loquere ad Roboam filium Salomonis regem Iudae et ad universum Israel, qui est in Iuda et Beniamin: [4]Haec dicit Dominus: Non ascendetis neque pugnabitis contra fratres vestros. Revertatur unusquisque in domum suam, quia mea hoc gestum est voluntate». Qui cum audissent sermonem Domini, reversi sunt nec perrexerunt contra Ieroboam. [5]Habitavit autem Roboam in Ierusalem et aedificavit civitates muratas in Iuda. [6]Exstruxitque Bethlehem et Etam et Thecue, [7]Bethsur quoque et Socho et Odollam [8]necnon Geth et Maresa et Ziph, [9]sed et Aduram et Lachis et Azeca, [10]Saraa quoque et Aialon et Hebron, quae erant in Iuda et Beniamin civitates munitissimas. [11]Cumque clausisset eas muris, posuit in eis principes ciborumque horrea et olei et vini. [12]Sed et in singulis urbibus fecit armamentarium scutorum et hastarum firmavitque eas summa diligentia et imperavit super Iudam et Beniamin. [13]Sacerdotes autem et Levitae, qui erant in universo Israel, venerunt ad eum de cunctis

common lands and their holdings and came to Judah and Jerusalem, because Jeroboam and his sons cast them out from serving as priests of the LORD, [15]and he appointed his own priests for the high places, and for the satyrs, and for the calves which he had made. [16]And those who had set their hearts to seek the LORD God of Israel came after them from all the tribes of Israel to Jerusalem to sacrifice to the LORD, the God of their fathers. [17]They strengthened the kingdom of Judah, and for three years they made Rehoboam the son of Solomon secure, for they walked for three years in the way of David and Solomon.

Num 35:2

Lev 17:7
1 Kings 12:31

Ezra 2:43

Rehoboam's wives and family

[18]Rehoboam took as wife Mahalath the daughter of Jerimoth the son of David, and of Abihail the daughter of Eliab the son of Jesse; [19]and she bore him sons, Jeush, Shemariah, and Zaham.

[20]After her he took Maacah the daughter of Absalom, who bore him Abijah, Attai, Ziza, and Shelomith. [21]Rehoboam loved Maacah the daughter of Absalom above all his wives and concubines (he took eighteen wives and sixty concubines, and had twenty-eight sons and sixty daughters); [22]and Rehoboam appointed Abijah the son of Maacah as chief prince among his brothers, for he intended to make him king. [23]And he dealt wisely, and distributed some of his

1 Kings 15:2

12:26–33), Rehoboam could not be faulted in religious affairs: he promoted solidarity among the priests (v. 13), the Levites (v. 14) and all Israel (v. 16); he got the Levites to stay loyal (v. 14) and re-established the true cult of the Lord in Jerusalem (v. 16). God blessed Rehoboam's initial good behaviour by granting his kingdom stability.

11:18–23. God also blessed Rehoboam with a large family. The Absalom mentioned in v. 20 (called Abishalom in 1 Kings 15:1) cannot be the son of David who died without issue (cf. 2 Sam 18:18) but some relative of Rehoboam difficult to identify, as is true of many people included in the genealogical lists. The Lord's protection

sedibus suis. [14]Levitae relinquentes suburbana et possessiones suas transierunt ad Iudam et Ierusalem, eo quod abiecisset eos Ieroboam et posteri eius, ne sacerdotio Domini fungerentur. [15]Qui constituit sibi sacerdotes excelsorum et daemoniorum vitulorumque, quos fecerat. [16]Sed sequentes eos et de cunctis tribubus Israel quicumque dederant cor suum, ut quaererent Dominum, Deum Israel, venerunt Ierusalem ad immolandum victimas Domino, Deo patrum suorum. [17]Et roboraverunt regnum Iudae et confirmaverunt Roboam filium Salomonis per tres annos; ambulaverunt enim in viis David et Salomonis annis tantum tribus. [18]Duxit autem Roboam uxorem Mahalath filiam Ierimoth filii David et Abihail filiae Eliab filii Isai, [19]quae peperit ei filios Iehus et Samariam et Zoom. [20]Post hanc quoque accepit Maacha filiam Absalom, quae peperit ei Abia et Ethai et Ziza et Salomith. [21]Amavit autem Roboam Maacha filiam Absalom super omnes uxores suas et concubinas; nam uxores decem et octo duxerat, concubinas autem sexaginta. Et genuit viginti octo filios et sexaginta filias. [22]Constituit vero in capite Abiam filium Maacha ducem super fratres suos ipsum enim regem facere cogitabat. [23]Et sapienter filios suos dispersit in cunctis finibus Iudae et Beniamin in universis civitatibus muratis. Praebuitque eis escas

sons through all the districts of Judah and Benjamin, in all the fortified cities; and he gave them abundant provisions, and procured wives for them.[u]

1 Kings 14:21–31

Judah invaded by Egypt

1 Kings 14:22

12 [1]When the rule of Rehoboam was established and was strong, he forsook the law of the LORD, and all Israel with him. [2]In the fifth year of King Rehoboam, because they had been unfaithful to the LORD, Shishak king of Egypt came up against Jerusalem [3]with twelve hundred chariots and sixty thousand horsemen. And the people were without number who came with him from Egypt—Libyans, Sukki-im, and Ethiopians. [4]And he took the fortified cities of Judah and came as far as Jerusalem. [5]Then Shemaiah the prophet came to Rehoboam and to the princes of Judah, who had gathered at Jerusalem because of Shishak, and said to them, "Thus says the LORD, 'You abandoned me, so I have abandoned you to the hand of Shishak.'" [6]Then the princes of Israel and the king humbled themselves and said, "The LORD is

1 Kings 14:25

2 Chron 11:2

---

continues to be stressed: he favours the succession of Abijah (Abijam, in 1 Kings 15:1ff), the son of Maacah, Rehoboam's favourite wife; Abijah helped to place the king's sons all across the country.

12:1–16. The parallel passage (1 Kings 14:21–31) is used as a point of reference but its form is altered, to bring in the doctrine of personal, direct retribution and the importance of the prophet Shemaiah's message: thus, the king of Egypt attacks Jerusalem as punishment for Rehoboam's infidelity (vv. 1–5) but when the leaders of Judah do penance, the Egyptians desist. The prophet is charged with interpreting the cause of the Egyptian attack and making it known that God plans to preserve Jerusalem.

The terminology used here is very important, given that it continues to be used right into the New Testament: infidelity is referred to as "forsaking the law of the Lord" (vv. 1, 5; cf. Mt 23:23; Mk 7:8; etc.) and as "unfaithfulness" (v. 2; cf. Rom 2:8; Eph 5:6; etc.); whereas fidelity and conversion are translated as "seeking the Lord" (11:16; 12:14; cf. Mt 6:33; Lk 12:31; Jn 5:30; etc.), acknowledging in all humility that "the Lord is righteous", that is, just (vv. 6–7).

plurimas et multas petivit uxores. **[12]** [1]Cumque roboratum fuisset regnum Roboam et confortatum, dereliquit legem Domini, et omnis Israel cum eo. [2]Anno autem quinto regni Roboam ascendit Sesac rex Aegypti in Ierusalem—quia peccaverunt Domino—[3]cum mille ducentis curribus et sexaginta milibus equitum, nec erat numerus vulgi, quod venerat cum eo ex Aegypto, Libyes scilicet et Socciitae et Aethiopes. [4]Cepitque civitates munitissimas in Iuda et venit usque Ierusalem. [5]Semeias autem propheta ingressus est ad Roboam et principes Iudae, qui congregati fuerant in Ierusalem fugientes Sesac, dixitque ad eos: «Haec dicit Dominus: Vos reliquistis me, et ego reliqui vos in manu Sesac».

u. Cn: Heb *sought a multitude of wives*

righteous." [7]When the LORD saw that they humbled themselves, the word of the LORD came to Shemaiah: "They have humbled themselves; I will not destroy them, but I will grant them some deliverance, and my wrath shall not be poured out upon Jerusalem by the hand of Shishak. [8]Nevertheless they shall be servants to him, that they may know my service and the service of the kingdoms of the countries."

[9]So Shishak king of Egypt came up against Jerusalem; he took away the treasures of the house of the LORD and the treasures of the king's house; he took away everything. He also took away the shields of gold which Solomon had made; [10]and King Rehoboam made in their stead shields of bronze, and committed them to the hands of the officers of the guard, who kept the door of the king's house. [11]And as often as the king went into the house of the LORD, the guard came and bore them, and brought them back to the guardroom. [12]And when he humbled himself the wrath of the LORD turned from him, so as not to make a complete destruction; moreover, conditions were good in Judah.

1 Kings 14:26–28

[13]So King Rehoboam established himself in Jerusalem and reigned. Rehoboam was forty-one years old when he began to reign, and he reigned seventeen years in Jerusalem, the city which the LORD had chosen out of all the tribes of Israel to put his name there. His mother's name was Naamah the Ammonitess. [14]And he did evil, for he did not set his heart to seek the LORD.

1 Kings 14:21

Citing v. 6, the *Roman Catechism* teaches that the punishment inflicted on the Israelites by enemy kings ("the world", in the pejorative sense of the term) is permitted by God "in order to teach us that none are friends of God except those who are enemies of the world and pilgrims on earth [. . .]; and that, being brought to his service we should understand how much happier are those who serve God, than they who serve the world" (*Roman Catechism*, 3, 1, 13).

[6]Humiliatique principes Israel et rex dixerunt: «Iustus est Dominus!». [7]Cumque vidisset Dominus quod humiliati essent, factus est sermo Domini ad Semeiam dicens: «Quia humiliati sunt, non disperdam eos daboque eis mox effugium, et non effundetur furor meus super Ierusalem per manum Sesac. [8]Verumtamen servient ei, ut sciant distantiam servitutis meae et servitutis regni terrarum». [9]Ascendit itaque Sesac rex Aegypti in Ierusalem, sublatis thesauris domus Domini et domus regis; omniaque secum tulit et clipeos aureos, quos fecerat Salomon. [10]Pro quibus fecit rex Roboam aeneos et tradidit illos principibus cursorum, qui custodiebant vestibulum palatii. [11]Cumque introiret rex domum Domini, veniebant cursores et tollebant eos; iterumque referebant eos ad armamentarium suum. [12]Verumtamen, quia humiliatus est, aversa est ab eo ira Domini, nec deletus est penitus; siquidem et in Iuda inventa sunt opera bona. [13]Confortatus est igitur rex Roboam in Ierusalem atque regnavit. Quadraginta autem et unius anni erat, cum regnare coepisset, et decem septemque annis regnavit in Ierusalem urbe, quam elegit Dominus, ut confirmaret nomen suum ibi de cunctis tribubus Israel. Nomenque matris eius Naama Ammanitis. [14]Fecit autem malum et non praeparavit cor suum, ut quaereret Dominum. [15]Opera

1 Kings 14:29–31

[15]Now the acts of Rehoboam, from first to last, are they not written in the chronicles of Shemaiah the prophet and of Iddo the seer?[v] There were continual wars between Rehoboam and Jeroboam. [16]And Rehoboam slept with his fathers, and was buried in the city of David; and Abijah his son reigned in his stead.

The reign of Abijah

1 Kings 15:1–2,7

13 [1]In the eighteenth year of King Jeroboam Abijah began to reign over Judah. [2]He reigned for three years in Jerusalem. His mother's name was Micaiah the daughter of Uriel of Gibe-ah.

Now there was war between Abijah and Jeroboam. [3]Abijah went out to battle having an army of valiant men of war, four hundred thousand picked men; and Jeroboam drew up his line of battle against him with eight hundred thousand picked mighty warriors. [4]Then Abijah stood up on Mount Zemaraim which is in the hill country of Ephraim, and said, "Hear me, O Jeroboam and all Israel! [5]Ought you not to know that the LORD God of Israel gave

---

13:1–23. The reign of Abijah is covered very briefly in the book of Kings (1 Kings 15:1–8, where he is called Abijam), whereas Chronicles gives considerable space to his address to his northern brethren. The battle between North and South (cf. 1 Kings 15:6) becomes a religious argument involving the doctrinal principles covered in Abijah's address (cf. a similar speech, David's to Goliath: 1 Sam 17:45–47) and which sum up the message of Chronicles: the rightful kingdom is that of Judah (v. 5); the Northerners are rebellious (v. 6) and idolatrous (v. 8), and have unlawful priests (v. 9), whereas the men of Judah have not forsaken the Lord (v. 10) and their form of worship is the right one and their priests true priests (vv. 10–11).

The description of the battle is not so much military as liturgical; here are all the features of a liturgical procession—an opening prayer, the sounding of trumpets, war cries, engagement and then victory granted by the Lord to his faithful (vv. 14–18). The victory is, first and foremost, a religious one, and it means that not only will the line of David continue in power in Judah but so will the lawful priesthood and liturgy.

The passage also teaches that faithfulness to God and the service that is due to him guarantees victory. It is

vero Roboam prima et novissima scripta sunt in verbis Semeiae prophetae et Addo videntis, genealogia quoque et bella, quae erant inter Roboam et Ieroboam cunctis diebus. [16]Et dormivit Roboam cum patribus suis sepultusque est in civitate David; et regnavit Abia filius eius pro eo. **[13]** [1]Anno octavo decimo regis Ieroboam regnavit Abia super Iudam. [2]Tribus annis regnavit in Ierusalem. Nomenque matris eius Michaia filia Uriel de Gabaa. Et erat bellum inter Abiam et Ieroboam. [3]Cumque inisset Abia certamen et haberet bellicosissimos viros electorum quadringenta milia, Ieroboam instruxit e contra aciem octingenta milia virorum, qui et ipsi electi erant et ad bella fortissimi. [4]Stetit igitur Abia super montem Semaraim, qui est in monte Ephraim, et ait: «Audi, Ieroboam et omnis Israel: [5]Num ignoratis

v. Heb *seer, to enrol oneself*

the kingship over Israel for ever to David and his sons by a covenant of salt? [6]Yet Jeroboam the son of Nebat, a servant of Solomon the son of David, rose up and rebelled against his lord; [7]and certain worthless scoundrels gathered about him and defied Rehoboam the son of Solomon, when Rehoboam was young and irresolute and could not withstand them.

Deut 13:14

[8]"And now you think to withstand the kingdom of the LORD in the hand of the sons of David, because you are a great multitude and have with you the golden calves which Jeroboam made you for gods. [9]Have you not driven out the priests of the LORD, the sons of Aaron, and the Levites, and made priests for yourselves like the peoples of other lands? Whoever comes to consecrate himself with a young bull or seven rams becomes a priest of what are no gods. [10]But as for us, the LORD is our God, and we have not forsaken him. We have priests ministering to the LORD who are sons of Aaron, and Levites for their service. [11]They offer to the LORD every morning and every evening burnt offerings and incense of sweet spices, set out the showbread on the table of pure gold, and care for the golden lampstand that its lamps may burn every evening; for we keep the charge of the LORD our God, but you have forsaken him. [12]Behold, God is with us at our head, and his priests

1 Kings 12:31
Gal 4:8

2 Chron 11:14

Heb 9:2

Num 10:9

---

useless to take issue with God, as the words of v. 12 say: "O sons of Israel, do not fight against the Lord, the God of your fathers; for you cannot succeed"; and those who stay loyal to him will prevail (v. 18): "The men of Judah prevailed, because they relied upon the Lord." This episode remains an invitation to trust in almighty God: "Trust always in your God. He does not lose battles" (St J. Escrivá, *The Way*, 733).

God blesses Abijah by protecting his kingdom and granting him a large family (v. 21), that is, he rewarded him personally and immediately, because he stayed true.

13:5. "A covenant of salt", that is, an enduring covenant; just as salt preserves foodstuffs and retains its savour when mixed with food, the covenant must not lose its vigour; but rather, it should strengthen the connexion between the two contracting parties (cf. Lev 2:13; Num 18:19; Ezra 4:14).

quod Dominus, Deus Israel, dederit regnum David super Israel in sempiternum, ipsi et filiis eius, pactum salis? [6]Et surrexit Ieroboam filius Nabat servus Salomonis filii David et rebellavit contra dominum suum; [7]congregatique sunt ad eum viri vanissimi, filii Belial, et praevaluerunt contra Roboam filium Salomonis. Porro Roboam erat iuvenis et corde pavido, nec potuit resistere eis. [8]Nunc ergo vos dicitis quod resistere possitis regno Domini, quod possidet per filios David, habetisque grandem populi multitudinem atque vitulos aureos, quos fecit vobis Ieroboam in deos. [9]Et eiecistis sacerdotes Domini filios Aaron atque Levitas et fecistis vobis sacerdotes sicut populi terrarum. Quicumque venerit et initiaverit manum suam in tauro de bobus et in arietibus septem, fit sacerdos eorum, qui non sunt dii. [10]Noster autem Deus Dominus est, quem non reliquimus; sacerdotesque ministrant Domino de filiis Aaron, et Levitae sunt in ordine suo. [11]Holocausta quoque offerunt Domino per singulos dies, mane et vespere, et thymiama aromatum, et proponuntur panes in mensa mundissima. Estque apud nos candelabrum aureum et lucernae eius, ut

with their battle trumpets to sound the call to battle against you. O sons of Israel, do not fight against the LORD, the God of your fathers; for you cannot succeed."

Victory for Abijah

[13]Jeroboam had sent an ambush around to come on them from behind; thus his troops[w] were in front of Judah, and the ambush was behind them. [14]And when Judah looked, behold, the battle was before and behind them; and they cried to the LORD, and the priests blew the trumpets. [15]Then the men of Judah raised the battle shout. And when the men of Judah shouted, God defeated Jeroboam and all Israel before Abijah and Judah. [16]The men of Israel fled before Judah, and God gave them into their hand. [17]Abijah and his people slew them with a great slaughter; so there fell slain of Israel five hundred thousand picked men. [18]Thus the men of Israel were subdued at that time, and the men of Judah prevailed, because they relied upon the LORD, the God of their fathers. [19]And Abijah pursued Jeroboam, and took cities from him, Bethel with its villages and Jeshanah with its villages and Ephron[x] with its villages. [20]Jeroboam did not recover his power in the days of Abijah; and the LORD smote him, and he died. [21]But Abijah grew mighty. And he took fourteen wives, and had twenty-two sons and sixteen daughters. [22]The rest of the acts of Abijah, his ways and his sayings, are written in the story of the prophet Iddo.

1 Kings 14:20

1 Kings 15:7–8

The reign of Asa*

1 Kings 15:11–12

14 [1 y]So Abijah slept with his fathers, and they buried him in the city of David; and Asa his son reigned in his stead. In his

accendantur semper ad vesperam: nos quippe custodimus praecepta Domini Dei nostri, quem vos reliquistis. [12]Ergo in exercitu nostro dux Deus est et sacerdotes eius, qui clangunt tubis et resonant contra vos, filii Israel; nolite pugnare contra Dominum, Deum patrum vestrorum, quia non vobis expedit». [13]Ieroboam autem retro moliebatur insidias, ut venirent post eos, et erant ante Iudam, et insidiae post eos. [14]Respiciensque Iuda vidit instare bellum ex adverso et post tergum et clamavit ad Dominum, ac sacerdotes tubis canere coeperunt, [15]omnesque viri Iudae vociferati sunt; et ecce, illis clamantibus, perterruit Deus Ieroboam et omnem Israel coram Abia et Iuda. [16]Fugeruntque filii Israel Iudam, et tradidit eos Deus in manu eorum. [17]Percussit ergo eos Abia et populus eius plaga magna; et corruerunt vulnerati ex Israel quingenta milia virorum fortium. [18]Humiliatique sunt filii Israel in tempore illo, et confortati filii Iudae, eo quod sperassent in Domino, Deo patrum suorum. [19]Persecutus est autem Abia fugientem Ieroboam et cepit civitates eius Bethel et filias eius et Iesana cum filiabus suis, Ephron quoque et filias eius. [20]Nec invaluit ultra Ieroboam in diebus Abiae. Quem percussit Dominus, et mortuus est. [21]Abia autem confortatus est et accepit sibi uxores quattuordecim procreavitque viginti duos filios et sedecim filias. [22]Reliqua autem gestorum Abiae viarumque et sermonum eius scripta sunt in enarratione prophetae Addo. [23]Dormivit autem Abia cum patribus suis, et sepelierunt eum in civitate David; regnavitque Asa filius eius pro eo. In cuius diebus quievit terra annis decem. **[14]** [1]Fecit autem Asa, quod bonum et placitum erat in conspectu Domini Dei sui, et subvertit

w. Heb *they* **x.** Another reading is *Ephrain* **y.** Ch 13:23 in Heb

days the land had rest for ten years. [2] [z]And Asa did what was good and right in the eyes of the LORD his God. [3]He took away the foreign altars and the high places, and broke down the pillars and hewed down the Asherim, [4]and commanded Judah to seek the LORD, the God of their fathers, and to keep the law and the commandment. [5]He also took out of all the cities of Judah the high places and the incense altars. And the kingdom had rest under him. [6]He built fortified cities in Judah, for the land had rest. He had no war in those years, for the LORD gave him peace. [7]And he said to Judah, "Let us build these cities, and surround them with walls and towers, gates and bars; the land is still ours, because we have sought the LORD our God; we have sought him, and he has given us peace on every side." So they built and prospered. [8]And Asa had an army of three hundred thousand from Judah, armed with

Ex 23:24; 34:13
1 Sam 9:12
Deut 7:5
1 Kings 15:14
1 Chron 8:40

***14:2—16:14.** The report on Asa's reign follows that given in 1 Kings 15:9–24 but with some changes designed to stress the teaching about personal, immediate retribution: in the first ten years "the land had rest for ten years" (14:1) because "Asa did what was good and right in the eyes of the Lord" (14:2), and things would go on that way until the thirty-fifth year of his reign (15:19).

But from the thirty-sixth year (16:1), things would be different: the king plundered the temple (16:2), made a pact with Syria (16:3) and declared war on the cities of the North (16:4). As a consequence, the king fell seriously ill, did not seek the Lord's help, and died (16:12).

The thirty-five good years and five disastrous ones add up to forty, a number which symbolizes a complete life-cycle, leaving the way open for a new king to succeed. Each cycle and each king inherits the promise of divine protection and starts with a clean slate: there is no inherited debt or disadvantage attributable to sins of predecessors.

14:2–15. Two great projects occupied Asa in the early years of his reign—the struggle against idolatry (vv. 3–5) and the rebuilding of the cities of Judah (vv. 6–7). The Lord rewarded his efforts by listening to the king's heartfelt prayer (v. 11) and giving him victory in all his battles.

Asa's prayer contains the basic elements of piety and divine worship (v. 11)—acknowledgment of the sovereign power of God, full confidence in him, and, finally, a religious purpose in government and war.

altaria peregrini cultus et excelsa [2]et confregit lapides palosque succidit [3]ac praecepit Iudae, ut quaereret Dominum, Deum patrum suorum, et faceret legem et universa mandata, [4]et abstulit e cunctis urbibus Iudae excelsa et thymiateria et regnavit in pace. [5]Aedificavit quoque urbes munitas in Iuda, quia quievit terra et nulla temporibus eius bella surrexerant, pacem Domino ei largiente. [6]Dixit autem Iudae: «Aedificemus civitates istas et vallemus muris et roboremus turribus et portis et seris, donec a bellis quieta sunt omnia; quia quaesivimus Dominum Deum nostrum, quaesivit nos et dedit nobis pacem per gyrum». Aedificaverunt igitur et prosperati sunt. [7]Habuit autem Asa exercitum portantium scuta et hastas de Iuda trecenta milia, de Beniamin vero scutariorum et sagittariorum ducenta octoginta milia: omnes isti viri fortissimi. [8]Egressus est autem contra eos Zara Aethiops cum exercitu, decies centena

z. Ch 14:1 in Heb

bucklers and spears, and two hundred and eighty thousand men from Benjamin, that carried shields and drew bows; all these were mighty men of valour.

Victory over Zerah

[9]Zerah the Ethiopian came out against them with an army of a million men and three hundred chariots, and came as far as Mareshah. [10]And Asa went out to meet him, and they drew up their lines of battle in the valley of Zephathah at Mareshah. [11]And Asa cried to the LORD his God, "O LORD, there is none like thee to help, between the mighty and the weak. Help us, O LORD our God, for we rely on thee, and in thy name we have come against this multitude. O LORD, thou art our God; let not man prevail against thee." [12]So the LORD defeated the Ethiopians before Asa and before Judah, and the Ethiopians fled. [13]Asa and the people that were with him pursued them as far as Gerar, and the Ethiopians fell until none remained alive; for they were broken before the LORD and his army. The men of Judah[a] carried away very much booty. [14]And they smote all the cities round about Gerar, for the fear of the LORD was upon them. They plundered all the cities, for there was much plunder in them. [15]And they smote the tents of those who had cattle,[b] and carried away sheep in abundance and camels. Then they returned to Jerusalem.

Asa's regulations against idolatry

Num 24:2
Hos 3:4–5

15 [1]The Spirit of God came upon Azariah the son of Oded, [2]and he went out to meet Asa, and said to him, "Hear me,

milia et curribus trecentis, et venit usque Maresa. [9]Porro Asa perrexit obviam ei, et instruxerunt aciem ad bellum in valle, quae est ad septentrionem Maresa, [10]et invocavit Asa Dominum Deum suum et ait: «Domine, non est apud te ulla distantia, utrum paucis auxilieris an pluribus; adiuva nos, Domine Deus noster. In te enim et in tuo nomine habentes fiduciam venimus contra hanc multitudinem. Domine, Deus noster tu es, non praevaleat contra te homo». [11]Exterruit itaque Dominus Aethiopes coram Asa et Iuda; fugeruntque Aethiopes. [12]Et persecutus est eos Asa et populus, qui cum eo erat, usque Gerar; et ruerunt Aethiopes usque ad internecionem, quia Domino caedente contriti sunt et exercitu illius proeliante. Tulerunt ergo spolia multa [13]et percusserunt omnes civitates per circuitum Gerarae: terror quippe Domini eos invaserat. Et diripuerunt omnes urbes et multam praedam asportaverunt. [14]Sed et caulas ovium destruentes tulerunt pecorum infinitam multitudinem et camelorum reversique sunt Ierusalem. **[15]** [1]Azarias autem filius Oded, facto in se spiritu Dei, [2]egressus est in occursum Asa et dixit ei: «Audite me, Asa et omnis Iuda et Beniamin! Dominus vobiscum, quia fuistis cum eo. Si quaesieritis eum, invenietur a vobis; si autem dereliqueritis eum, derelinquet vos. [3]Transierunt autem multi dies in Israel absque Deo veritatis et absque sacerdote doctore et absque lege. [4]Cumque reversi essent in angustia sua ad Dominum, Deum Israel, et quaesivissent eum, inventus est ab eis. [5]In temporibus illis non erat pax egredienti et ingredienti, sed perturbatio magna multa in cunctis habitatoribus terrarum: [6]contundebatur enim gens contra gentem et civitas contra civitatem, quia Dominus conturbabat eos in

a. Heb *they* **b.** Heb obscure

Asa, and all Judah and Benjamin: The LORD is with you, while you are with him. If you seek him, he will be found by you, but if you forsake him, he will forsake you. [3]For a long time Israel was without the true God, and without a teaching priest, and without law; [4]but when in their distress they turned to the LORD, the God of Israel, and sought him, he was found by them. [5]In those times there was no peace to him who went out or to him who came in, for great disturbances afflicted all the inhabitants of the lands. [6]They were broken in pieces, nation against nation and city against city, for God troubled them with every sort of distress. [7]But you, take courage! Do not let your hands be weak, for your work shall be rewarded."

Deut 4:29–30
Is 19:2
Mt 24:7
Mk 13:8
Lk 21:10
Is 7:4
Jer 31:16
1 Cor 15:58

[8]When Asa heard these words, the prophecy of Azariah the son of Oded,[c] he took courage, and put away the abominable idols from all the land of Judah and Benjamin and from the cities which he had taken in the hill country of Ephraim, and he repaired the altar of the LORD that was in front of the vestibule of the house of the LORD.[d] [9]And he gathered all Judah and Benjamin, and those

---

15:1–19. Asa's reform of religion was far-reaching (vv. 8–18): he stamped out idolatry and fostered the lawful form of worship (v. 8; cf. 14:2–3); he called all his subjects to a liturgical assembly, to renew the Covenant (vv. 9–15); and he even removed his grandmother (*sic*) from the position of queen mother (v. 16). Azariah's prophecy (vv. 2–7) sums up the teaching contained in this section: "If you seek (the Lord), he will be found by you, but if you forsake him, he will forsake you" (v. 2). These words fuelled Asa's reform, which concentrated on rooting out every trace of idolatry (v. 8), restored the altar in front of the vestibule of the temple, and involved a commitment to seek the Lord wholeheartedly (v. 12). Seeking the Lord is the only way to attain salvation and true happiness: "May all who seek thee rejoice and be glad in thee" (Ps 70:4). And every good Christian should seek the Lord Jesus: "I have distinguished as it were four stages in our effort to identify ourselves with Christ—seeking him, finding him, getting to know him, loving him. It may seem clear to you that you are only at the first stage. Seek him then, hungrily; seek him within yourselves with all your strength. If you act with determination, I am ready to guarantee that you have already found him, and have begun to get to know him and to love him, and to hold your conversation in heaven" (St J. Escrivá, *Friends of God*, 300).

omni angustia. [7]Vos autem confortamini, et non dissolvantur manus vestrae; erit enim merces operi vestro». [8]Cum audisset Asa verba haec et prophetiam, confortatus est et abstulit idola de omni terra Iudae et Beniamin et ex urbibus, quas ceperat montis Ephraim, et dedicavit altare Domini, quod erat ante porticum Domini. [9]Congregavitque universum Iudam et Beniamin et advenas cum eis de Ephraim

c. Compare Syr Vg: Heb *the prophecy, Oded the prophet* **d.** Heb *the vestibule of the* LORD

from Ephraim, Manasseh, and Simeon who were sojourning with them, for great numbers had deserted to him from Israel when they saw that the LORD his God was with him. [10]They were gathered at Jerusalem in the third month of the fifteenth year of the reign of Asa. [11]They sacrificed to the LORD on that day, from the spoil which they had brought, seven hundred oxen and seven thousand sheep. [12]And they entered into a covenant to seek the LORD, the God of their fathers, with all their heart and with all their soul; [13]and that whoever would not seek the LORD, the God of Israel, should be put to death, whether young or old, man or woman. [14]They took oath to the LORD with a loud voice, and with shouting, and with trumpets, and with horns. [15]And all Judah rejoiced over the oath; for they had sworn with all their heart, and had sought him with their whole desire, and he was found by them, and the LORD gave them rest round about.

2 Kings 23:3
Neh 10:29
Neh 10:29

[16]Even Maacah, his mother, King Asa removed from being queen mother because she had made an abominable image for Asherah. Asa cut down her image, crushed it, and burned it at the brook Kidron. [17]But the high places were not taken out of Israel. Nevertheless the heart of Asa was blameless all his days. [18]And he brought into the house of God the votive gifts of his father and his own votive gifts, silver, and gold, and vessels. [19]And there was no more war until the thirty-fifth year of the reign of Asa.

1 Kings 15:13–15
2 Kings 23:6,15

Kings 15:16–22

Asa's war against Israel

16 [1]In the thirty-sixth year of the reign of Asa, Baasha king of Israel went up against Judah, and built Ramah, that he might

---

et de Manasse et de Simeon; plures enim ad eum confugerant ex Israel videntes quod Dominus Deus illius esset cum eo. [10]Cumque convenissent in Ierusalem mense tertio anno quinto decimo regni Asa, [11]immolaverunt Domino in die illa de manubiis, quas adduxerant: boves septingentos et oves septem milia. [12]Et inierunt foedus, ut quaererent Dominum, Deum patrum suorum, in toto corde et in tota anima sua: [13]si quis autem non quaesierit Dominum, Deum Israel, moriatur a minimo usque ad maximum, a viro usque ad mulierem. [14]Iuraveruntque Domino voce magna in iubilo et in clangore tubarum et in sonitu bucinarum. [15]Omnes, qui erant in Iuda, gavisi sunt de iuramento; in omni enim corde suo iuraverant et in tota voluntate quaesierat eum, et inventus fuerat ab eis. Praestititque eis Dominus requiem per circuitum. [16]Sed et Maacham matrem Asa rex amovit, ne esset domina, eo quod fecisset simulacrum Aserae; quod contrivit Asa et in frusta comminuens combussit in torrente Cedron. [17]Excelsa autem derelicta sunt in Israel; attamen cor Asa erat perfectum cunctis diebus eius. [18]Ea quae voverat pater suus et ipse, intulit in domum Dei, argentum et aurum vasorumque diversam supellectilem. [19]Bellum vero non fuit usque ad tricesimum quintum annum regni Asa. **[16]** [1]Anno autem tricesimo sexto regni eius ascendit Baasa rex Israel in Iudam; et muro circumdabat Rama, ut nullus tute posset egredi et ingredi de regno Asa. [2]Protulit ergo Asa argentum et aurum de thesauris domus Domini et domus regis misitque ad Benadad regem Syriae, qui habitabat in Damasco, dicens: [3]«Foedus inter me et te est et inter patrem meum et patrem tuum; quam ob rem misi tibi argentum et aurum, ut, rupto foedere, quod habes cum Baasa rege Israel, facias eum a me recedere». [4]Acquiescens Benadad regi Asa misit principes exercituum suorum ad urbes Israel, qui percusserunt Ahion et Dan et Abelmaim et universa horrea urbium

permit no one to go out or come in to Asa king of Judah. [2]Then Asa took silver and gold from the treasures of the house of the LORD and the king's house, and sent them to Ben-hadad king of Syria, who dwelt in Damascus, saying, [3]"Let there be a league between me and you, as between my father and your father; behold, I am sending to you silver and gold; go, break your league with Baasha king of Israel, that he may withdraw from me." [4]And Ben-hadad hearkened to King Asa, and sent the commanders of his armies against the cities of Israel, and they conquered Ijon, Dan, Abel-maim, and all the store-cities of Naphtali. [5]And when Baasha heard of it, he stopped building Ramah, and let his work cease. [6]Then King Asa took all Judah, and they carried away the stones of Ramah and its timber, with which Baasha had been building, and with them he built Geba and Mizpah.

[7]At that time Hanani the seer came to Asa king of Judah, and said to him, "Because you relied on the king of Syria, and did not rely on the LORD your God, the army of the king of Syria has escaped you. [8]Were not the Ethiopians and the Libyans a huge army with exceedingly many chariots and horsemen? Yet because you relied on the LORD, he gave them into your hand. [9]For the eyes of the LORD run to and fro throughout the whole earth, to show his might in behalf of those whose heart is blameless toward him. You have done foolishly in this; for from now on you will have wars."

1 Kings 16:1

2 Chron 14:8–14

Job 34:21
Ps 33:13–15
Jer 16:17; 32:19

16:1–14. The last stage of Asa's reign sharply contrasts with the early years—and he fails on an essential point: he does not put his trust in the Lord (v. 7) but instead relies on pacts with pagan kings (v. 3). As a punishment for this, his anger somehow gets the better of him and he now turns on his people (v. 10) and will be beset by wars (v. 9). The Lord punished the guilty king with death (vv. 12–13), but he still looked favourably on Judah, which gradually grew stronger under Jehoshaphat, Asa's son (17:1).

The sacred writer uses every opportunity to make the point that the true Israel dwells in the kingdom of Judah; therefore, when employing for the first time the formula frequently found in Kings to round off the account of a reign ("the rest of all the acts of Asa [. . .], are they not written in the Book of Chronicles of the Kings of Judah?": 1 Kings 15:23), he adds: "and Israel" (v. 11).

Nephthali. [5]Quod cum audisset Baasa, desivit aedificare Rama et intermisit opus suum. [6]Porro Asa rex assumpsit universum Iudam, et tulerunt lapides Rama et ligna, quibus aedificaverat Baasa, aedificavitque ex eis Gabaa et Maspha. [7]In tempore illo venit Hanani videns ad Asa regem Iudae et dixit ei: «Quia habuisti fiduciam in rege Syriae et non in Domino Deo tuo, idcirco evasit Syriae regis exercitus de manu tua. [8]Nonne Aethiopes et Libyes magnus exercitus erant quadrigis et equitibus et multitudine nimia, quos, cum Domino credidisses, tradidit in manu tua? [9]Oculi enim Domini contemplantur universam terram et praebent fortitudinem his, qui corde perfecto credunt in eum. Stulte igitur egisti in hoc, quia ex praesenti tempore contra te bella consurgent». [10]Iratusque Asa adversus videntem iussit eum mitti in

Jer 20:2 [10]Then Asa was angry with the seer, and put him in the stocks, in prison, for he was in a rage with him because of this. And Asa inflicted cruelties upon some of the people at the same time.

[11]The acts of Asa, from first to last, are written in the Book of the Kings of Judah and Israel. [12]In the thirty-ninth year of his reign Asa was diseased in his feet, and his disease became severe; yet even in his disease he did not seek the LORD, but sought help from physicians. [13]And Asa slept with his fathers, dying in the forty-first year of his reign. [14]They buried him in the tomb which he had hewn out for himself in the city of David. They laid him on a bier which had been filled with various kinds of spices prepared by the perfumer's art; and they made a very great fire in his honour.

1 Kings 15:24

The reign of Jehoshaphat*

1 Kings 15:24

17 [1]Jehoshaphat his son reigned in his stead, and strengthened himself against Israel. [2]He placed forces in all the fortified cities of Judah, and set garrisons in the land of Judah, and in the cities of Ephraim which Asa his father had taken. [3]The LORD was with Jehoshaphat, because he walked in the earlier ways of his father;[e] he did not seek the Baals, [4]but sought the God of his father and walked in his commandments, and not according to the ways of Israel. [5]Therefore the LORD established the kingdom in his hand; and

---

***17:1—20:37.** The reign of Jehoshaphat is very soberly reported in Kings (cf. 1 Kings 15:24b and 22:1–35, 41–51). The Chronicler may have had access to sources unknown to us, or he may simply have elaborated on the material in Kings, adding pieces which helped to emphasize his interpretation of history. Thus, he stresses that God protects the king as long as the king remains faithful, and that he will punish him if he does not. He repeats his message about how the nation advanced in the early part of the reign when Jehoshaphat behaved himself (17:3—18:1), and about the disasters at the end (20:37); about how the true Israel survives despite the misrule of Jehoshaphat, and,

nervum, valde quippe super hoc fuerat indignatus; et vexavit Asa quosdam de populo in tempore illo. [11]Opera autem Asa prima et novissima scripta sunt in libro regum Iudae et Israel. [12]Aegrotavit etiam Asa anno tricesimo nono regni sui dolore pedum vehementissimo et nec in infirmitate sua quaesivit Dominum, sed magis in medicorum arte confisus est. [13]Dormivitque Asa cum patribus suis et mortuus est anno quadragesimo primo regni sui. [14]Et sepelierunt eum in sepulcro suo, quod foderat sibi in civitate David; posueruntque eum super lectum plenum aromatibus et variis unguentis, quae erant pigmentariorum arte confecta, et fecerunt in exsequiis eius combustionem splendidam valde. **[17]** [1]Regnavit autem Iosaphat filius eius pro eo et invaluit contra Israel. [2]Constituitque militum numeros in cunctis urbibus Iudae, quae erant vallatae muris; praesidiaque disposuit in terra Iudae et in civitatibus Ephraim, quas ceperat Asa pater eius. [3]Et fuit Dominus cum Iosaphat, quia ambulavit in viis patris sui primis et non speravit in Baalim, [4]sed in Deo patris sui, et perrexit in praeceptis illius et non iuxta peccata Israel. [5]Confirmavitque Dominus regnum in manu eius, et dedit omnis Iuda munera

e. Another reading is *his father David*

all Judah brought tribute to Jehoshaphat; and he had great riches and honour. [6]His heart was courageous in the ways of the LORD; and furthermore he took the high places and the Asherim out of Judah.

Ex 34:13
1 Sam 9:12
1 Kings 22:43

[7]In the third year of his reign he sent his princes, Ben-hail, Obadiah, Zechariah, Nethanel, and Micaiah, to teach in the cities of Judah; [8]and with them the Levites, Shemaiah, Nethaniah, Zebadiah, Asahel, Shemiramoth, Jehonathan, Adonijah, Tobijah, and Tobadonijah; and with these Levites, the priests Elishama and Jehoram. [9]And they taught in Judah, having the book of the law of the LORD with them; they went about through all the cities of Judah and taught among the people.

2 Chron 19:8
Ezra 7:25

[10]And the fear of the LORD fell upon all the kingdoms of the lands that were round about Judah, and they made no war against Jehoshaphat. [11]Some of the Philistines brought Jehoshaphat presents, and silver for tribute; and the Arabs also brought him seven thousand seven hundred rams and seven thousand seven

Is 16:1

---

above all, the need to keep to a lawful form of worship and to put one's trust in the Lord.

Jehoshaphat's reign divides into five stages: it begins well, combating idolatry and rebuilding cities (chap. 17); then comes the alliance with Ahab and the battle against Syria (chap. 18), administrative reform, relying on priests and Levites (chap. 19), Jehoshaphat's prayer and his victory over the Ammonites and Moabites (20:1–30); and finally, the irreligious conduct of the king and consequent defeats and misfortunes (20:31–37). As a whole it was a good reign due to the many religious reforms instituted by the king.

17:1–19. The first stage is summarized in v. 3: "The Lord was with Jehoshaphat, because he walked in the earlier ways of his father David." In line with the doctrine of personal retribution, the sacred writer is delighted to record all the benefits God bestows on king and people—wealth, armies, buildings, etc. Everything thrives. This teaching about God's solicitous care of his people is later taken up by St Paul: "We know that in everything God works for good with those who love him" (Rom 8:28).

"The book of the law of the Lord" (v. 9): in the Persian period this was the name given to Deuteronomy and perhaps to the entire Pentateuch (cf. 2 Chron 34:14, 19). The Levites were in charge of instructing the people on matters to do with faith and morals contained in that book.

Iosaphat; factaeque sunt ei infinitae divitiae et multa gloria. [6]Cumque sumpsisset cor eius audaciam propter vias Domini, etiam excelsa et palos de Iuda abstulit. [7]Tertio autem anno regni sui misit principes suos Benhail et Abdiam et Zachariam et Nathanael et Michaiam, ut docerent in civitatibus Iudae, [8]et cum eis Levitas Semeiam et Nathaniam et Zabadiam, Asael quoque et Semiramoth et Ionathan Adoniamque et Thobiam Levitas et cum eis Elisama et Ioram sacerdotes. [9]Docebantque in Iuda habentes librum legis Domini et circuibant cunctas urbes Iudae atque erudiebant populum. [10]Itaque factus est pavor Domini super omnia regna terrarum, quae erant per gyrum Iudae, nec audebant bellare contra Iosaphat. [11]Sed et de Philisthim Iosaphat munera deferebant et vectigal argenti; Arabes quoque adducebant pecora arietum

hundred he-goats. [12]And Jehoshaphat grew steadily greater. He built in Judah fortresses and store-cities, [13]and he had great stores in the cities of Judah. He had soldiers, mighty men of valour, in Jerusalem. [14]This was the muster of them by fathers' houses: Of Judah, the commanders of thousands: Adnah the commander, with three hundred thousand mighty men of valour, [15]and next to him Jehohanan the commander, with two hundred and eighty thousand, [16]and next to him Amasiah the son of Zichri, a volunteer for the service of the LORD, with two hundred thousand mighty men of valour. [17]Of Benjamin: Eliada, a mighty man of valour, with two hundred thousand men armed with bow and shield, [18]and next to him Jehozabad with a hundred and eighty thousand armed for war. [19]These were in the service of the king, besides those whom the king had placed in the fortified cities throughout all Judah.

1 Chron 8:40

1 Kings 22:1–35

Alliance between Jehoshaphat and Ahab

18 [1]Now Jehoshaphat had great riches and honour; and he made a marriage alliance with Ahab. [2]After some years he went down to Ahab in Samaria. And Ahab killed an abundance of sheep and oxen for him and for the people who were with him, and induced him to go up against Ramoth-gilead. [3]Ahab king of Israel

18:1–34. The account of the alliance with Ahaz, king of Israel, and the battle against Syria (vv. 2–27) is taken almost word for word from 1 Kings 22:3–36. The intervention of Micaiah the son of Imlah is very much in line with the Chronicler's ideas. The word of the Lord communicated by the Lord's prophet is infallible and will always be fulfilled.

This prophet is different from Micah of Moresheth whose book is included among the minor prophets. The words of v. 16 are a call to the king to look after his people; they echo Moses' prayer to God to appoint Joshua in his place (Num 27:17) and also Ezekiel's inveighing against bad pastors (Ezek 34:5). The Gospel uses the same form of words: "like sheep without a

septem milia septingenta et hircos totidem. [12]Crevit ergo Iosaphat et magnificatus est usque in sublime atque aedificavit in Iuda castella urbesque horreorum. [13]Et multae copiae praesto erant ei in urbibus Iudae; viri quoque bellatores et robusti erant in Ierusalem, [14]quorum iste numerus per familias singulorum: in Iuda principes exercitus, Ednas dux, et cum eo robustissimorum trecenta milia; [15]et ad latus eius Iohanan princeps et cum eo ducenta octoginta milia; [16]ad latus quoque istius Amasias filius Zechri consecratus Domino et cum eo ducenta milia virorum fortium; [17]de Beniamin autem robustus ad proelia Eliada et cum eo tenentium arcum et clipeum ducenta milia; [18]et ad latus eius Iozabad et cum eo centum octoginta milia expeditorum militum. [19]Hi omnes erant ad manum regis, exceptis aliis, quos posuerat in urbibus muratis in universo Iuda. **[18]** [1]Fuit ergo Iosaphat dives et inclitus multum et affinitate coniunctus est Achab. [2]Descenditque post annos ad eum in Samariam, ad cuius adventum mactavit Achab oves et boves plurimos ipsi et populo, qui venerat cum eo; persuasitque illi, ut ascenderet in Ramoth Galaad. [3]Dixitque Achab rex Israel ad Iosaphat regem Iudae: «Veni mecum in Ramoth Galaad». Cui ille respondit: «Ut ego, et tu; sicut populus tuus, sic et populus meus, tecumque

said to Jehoshaphat king of Judah, "Will you go with me to Ramoth-gilead?" He answered him, "I am as you are, my people as your people. We will be with you in the war."

[4]And Jehoshaphat said to the king of Israel, "Inquire first for the word of the LORD." [5]Then the king of Israel gathered the prophets together, four hundred men, and said to them, "Shall we go to battle against Ramoth-gilead, or shall I forbear?" And they said, "Go up; for God will give it into the hand of the king." [6]But Jehoshaphat said, "Is there not here another prophet of the LORD of whom we may inquire?" [7]And the king of Israel said to Jehoshaphat, "There is yet one man by whom we may inquire of the LORD, Micaiah the son of Imlah; but I hate him, for he never prophesies good concerning me, but always evil." And Jehoshaphat said, "Let not the king say so." [8]Then the king of Israel summoned an officer and said, "Bring quickly Micaiah the son of Imlah." [9]Now the king of Israel and Jehoshaphat the king of Judah were sitting on their thrones, arrayed in their robes; and they were sitting at the threshing floor at the entrance of the gate of Samaria; and all the prophets were prophesying before them.

[10]And Zedekiah the son of Chenaanah made for himself horns of iron, and said, "Thus says the LORD, 'With these you shall push the Syrians until they are destroyed.'" [11]And all the prophets prophesied so, and said, "Go up to Ramoth-gilead and triumph; the LORD will give it into the hand of the king."

---

shepherd" (Mt 9:36; Mk 6:34), to describe the neglected state that Jesus found the people to be in.

Jehoshaphat is miraculously rescued, not so much on account of his cries (as 1 Kings 22:32 has it), but because the Lord heard his prayer and intervened (v. 31). The king's piety made up for his transgression in allying himself with Ahaz (v. 1) and allowed him to emerge from the battle unscathed—another instance of immediate retribution, for the Lord punished Ahaz and saved Jehoshaphat.

erimus in bello». [4]Dixitque Iosaphat ad regem Israel: «Consule, obsecro, impraesentiarum sermonem Domini». [5]Congregavitque rex Israel prophetarum quadringentos viros et dixit ad eos: «In Ramoth Galaad ad bellandum ire debemus an quiescere?». At illi: «Ascende, inquiunt, et tradet Deus in manu regis». [6]Dixitque Iosaphat: «Numquid non est hic et alius propheta Domini, ut ab illo etiam requiramus?». [7]Et ait rex Israel ad Iosaphat: «Adhuc est vir unus, a quo possumus quaerere Domini voluntatem; sed ego odi eum, quia non prophetat mihi bonum, sed malum omni tempore: est autem Michaeas filius Iemla». Dixitque Iosaphat: «Ne loquaris, rex, hoc modo». [8]Vocavit ergo rex Israel unum de eunuchis et dixit ei: «Voca cito Michaeam filium Iemla». [9]Porro rex Israel et Iosaphat rex Iudae uterque sedebant in solio suo vestiti cultu regio; sedebant autem in area iuxta portam Samariae, omnesque prophetae vaticinabantur coram eis. [10]Sedecias vero filius Chanaana fecit sibi cornua ferrea et ait: «Haec dicit Dominus: His ventilabis Syriam, donec conteras eam». [11]Omnesque prophetae similiter prophetabant atque dicebant: «Ascende in Ramoth Galaad et prosperaberis; et tradet Dominus in manu regis». [12]Nuntius autem, qui ierat ad vocandum Michaeam, ait illi: «En verba omnium

[12]And the messenger who went to summon Micaiah said to him, "Behold, the words of the prophets* with one accord are favourable to the king; let your word be like the word of one of them, and speak favourably." [13]But Micaiah said, "As the LORD lives, what my God says, that I will speak." [14]And when he had come to the king, the king said to him, "Micaiah, shall we go to Ramoth-gilead to battle, or shall I forbear?" And he answered, "Go up and triumph; they will be given into your hand." [15]But the king said to him, "How many times shall I adjure you that you speak to me nothing but the truth in the name of the LORD?" [16]And he said, "I saw all Israel scattered upon the mountains, as sheep that have *Mt 9:36* no shepherd; and the LORD said, 'These have no master; let each return to his home in peace.'" [17]And the king of Israel said to Jehoshaphat, "Did I not tell you that he would not prophesy good Rev 5:7 concerning me, but evil?" [18]And Micaiah said, "Therefore hear the word of the LORD: I saw the LORD sitting on his throne, and all the host of heaven standing on his right hand and on his left; [19]and the LORD said, 'Who will entice Ahab the king of Israel, that he may go up and fall at Ramoth-gilead?' And one said one thing, and another said another. [20]Then a spirit came forward and stood before the LORD, saying, 'I will entice him.' And the LORD said to him, 'By what means?' [21]And he said, 'I will go forth, and will be a lying spirit in the mouth of all his prophets.' And he said, 'You are to entice him, and you shall succeed; go forth and do so.' [22]Now therefore behold, the LORD has put a lying spirit in the mouth of these your prophets; the LORD has spoken evil concerning you."

[23]Then Zedekiah the son of Chenaanah came near and struck Micaiah on the cheek, and said, "Which way did the Spirit of the

---

prophetarum uno ore bona regi annuntiant; quaeso ergo te, ut et sermo tuus ab eis non dissentiat, loquarisque prospera». [13]Cui respondit Michaeas: «Vivit Dominus, quia, quodcumque dixerit Deus meus, hoc loquar». [14]enit ergo ad regem. Cui rex ait: «Michaea, ire debemus in Ramoth Galaad ad bellandum an quiescere?». Cui ille respondit: «Ascendite et prosperamini, ut tradantur hostes in manus vestras». [15]Dixitque rex: «Iterum atque iterum te adiuro, ut non mihi loquaris nisi, quod verum est, in nomine Domini». [16]At ille ait: «Vidi universum Israel dispersum in montibus sicut oves absque pastore. Et dixit Dominus: Non habent isti dominum; revertatur unusquisque in domum suam in pace!». [17]Et ait rex Israel ad Iosaphat: «Nonne dixi tibi quod non prophetaret iste mihi quidquam boni, sed ea, quae mala sunt?». [18]At ille idcirco ait: «Audite verbum Domini: Vidi Dominum sedentem in solio suo et omnem exercitum caeli assistentem ei a dextris et sinistris; [19] et dixit Dominus: "Quis decipiet Achab regem Israel, ut ascendat et corruat in Ramoth Galaad?". Cumque diceret unus hoc modo et alter alio, [20]processit spiritus et stetit coram Domino et ait: "Ego decipiam eum". Cui Dominus: "In quo, inquit, decipies?". [21]At ille respondit: "Egrediar et ero spiritus mendax in ore omnium prophetarum eius". Dixitque Dominus: "Decipies et praevalebis. Egredere et fac ita". [22]Nunc igitur, ecce dedit Dominus spiritum mendacii in ore omnium prophetarum tuorum et Dominus locutus est de te mala». [23]Accessit autem Sedecias filius Chanaana et percussit Michaeae maxillam et ait: «Per quam viam transivit spiritus Domini a me, ut loqueretur tibi?». [24]Dixitque Michaeas: «Tu ipse videbis

LORD go from me to speak to you?" [24]And Micaiah said, "Behold, you shall see on that day when you go into an inner chamber to hide yourself." [25]And the king of Israel said, "Seize Micaiah, and take him back to Amon the governor of the city and to Joash the king's son; [26]and say, 'Thus says the king, Put this fellow in prison, and feed him with scant fare of bread and water, until I return in peace.'" [27]And Micaiah said, "If you return in peace, the LORD has not spoken by me." And he said, "Hear, all you peoples!"

Death of Ahab

[28]So the king of Israel and Jehoshaphat the king of Judah went up to Ramoth-gilead. [29]And the king of Israel said to Jehoshaphat, "I will disguise myself and go into battle, but you wear your robes." And the king of Israel disguised himself; and they went into battle. [30]Now the king of Syria had commanded the captains of his chariots, "Fight with neither small nor great, but only with the king of Israel." [31]And when the captains of the chariots saw Jehoshaphat, they said, "It is the king of Israel." So they turned to fight against him; and Jehoshaphat cried out, and the LORD helped him. God drew them away from him, [32]for when the captains of the chariots saw that it was not the king of Israel, they turned back from pursuing him. [33]But a certain man drew his bow at a venture, and struck the king of Israel between the scale armour and the breastplate; therefore he said to the driver of his chariot, "Turn about, and carry me out of the battle, for I am wounded." [34]And the battle grew hot that day, and the king of Israel propped himself up in his chariot facing the Syrians until evening; then at sunset he died.

1 Kings 22:29–35

in die illo, quando ingressus fueris cubiculum intra cubiculum, ut abscondaris». [25]Praecepit autem rex Israel dicens: «Tollite Michaeam et ducite eum ad Amon principem civitatis et ad Ioas filium regis [26]et dicetis: Haec dicit rex: Mittite hunc in carcerem et date ei panis modicum et aquae pauxillum, donec revertar in pace». [27]Dixitque Michaeas: «Si reversus fueris in pace, non est locutus Dominus in me». Et ait: «Audite, populi omnes». [28]Igitur ascenderunt rex Israel et Iosaphat rex Iudae in Ramoth Galaad. [29]Dixitque rex Israel ad Iosaphat: «Mutabo habitum et sic ad pugnam vadam; tu autem induere vestibus tuis». Mutatoque rex Israel habitu venit ad bellum. [30]Rex autem Syriae praeceperat ducibus curruum suorum dicens: «Ne pugnetis contra minimum aut contra maximum, nisi contra solum regem Israel!». [31]Itaque, cum vidissent principes curruum Iosaphat, dixerunt: «Rex Israel est iste!». Et circumdederunt eum dimicantes. At ille clamavit ad Dominum, et auxiliatus est ei atque avertit eos Deus ab illo. [32]Cum enim vidissent duces curruum quod non esset rex Israel, reliquerunt eum. [33]Accidit autem, ut unus e populo sagittam in incertum iaceret et percuteret regem Israel inter iuncturas et loricam. At ille aurigae suo ait: «Converte manum tuam et educ me de acie, quia vulneratus sum». [34]Et aggravata est pugna in die illo; porro rex Israel stabat in curru suo contra Syros usque ad vesperam et mortuus est occidente sole.

Jehoshaphat's legal system

19 [1]Jehoshaphat the king of Judah returned in safety to his house in Jerusalem. [2]But Jehu the son of Hanani the seer went out to meet him, and said to King Jehoshaphat, "Should you help the wicked and love those who hate the LORD? Because of this, wrath has gone out against you from the LORD. [3]Nevertheless some good is found in you, for you destroyed the Asherahs out of the land, and have set your heart to seek God."

1 Kings 16:1; 22:45
2 Chron 14:4; 22:9

[4]Jehoshaphat dwelt at Jerusalem; and he went out again among the people, from Beer-sheba to the hill country of Ephraim, and brought them back to the LORD, the God of their fathers. [5]He appointed judges in the land in all the fortified cities of Judah, city by city, [6]and said to the judges, "Consider what you do, for you judge not for man but for the LORD; he is with you in giving judgment. [7]Now then, let the fear of the LORD be upon you; take heed what you do, for there is no perversion of justice with the LORD our God, or partiality, or taking bribes."

Deut 1:16–17; 16:19
Eph 6:7
Deut 10:17
Rom 2:11

[8]Moreover in Jerusalem Jehoshaphat appointed certain Levites and priests and heads of families of Israel, to give judgment for the LORD and to decide disputed cases. They had their seat at Jerusalem. [9]And he charged them: "Thus you shall do in the

Deut 17:8–13

19:1–11. This chapter has no parallel in the book of Kings; it deals with the institution of judges and draws its inspiration from information in Deuteronomy (cf. Deut 16:18–20; 17:8–13). Jehoshaphat "set his heart to seek God" and therefore, despite his defects, his reform of the judiciary worked out well. The king's appeal to the judges to have integrity is valid for all of us, because we should always be mindful of God when we judge people. Jesus confirmed this teaching and extended it to any situation which involves censuring one's neighbour: "Judge not, that you may not be judged. For with the judgment you pronounce you will be judged, and the measure you give will be the measure you get" (Mt 7:1–2; cf. Rom 2:1–3).

Priests and Levites are to try the more important cases, but lay people too, heads of families (vv. 8, 11), were to try civil cases or "the king's matters". This would have been the system that obtained in the fourth century BC.

[19] [1]Reversus est autem Iosaphat rex Iudae in domum suam pacifice in Ierusalem. [2]Cui occurrit Iehu filius Hanani videns et ait ad eum: «Impio praebes auxilium et his, qui oderunt Dominum, amicitia iungeris, et idcirco iram quidem Domini merebaris; [3]sed bona opera inventa sunt in te, eo quod abstuleris palos de terra et praeparaveris cor tuum, ut requireres Deum». [4]Habitavit ergo Iosaphat in Ierusalem. Rursumque egressus est ad populum de Bersabee usque ad montem Ephraim et revocavit eos ad Dominum, Deum patrum suorum. [5]Constituitque iudices terrae in cunctis civitatibus Iudae munitis per singula loca. [6]Et praecipiens iudicibus: «Videte, ait, quid faciatis. Non enim homini exercetis iudicium, sed Domino, qui vobiscum est, quando iudicaveritis. [7]Sit timor Domini vobiscum et caute cuncta facite; non est enim apud Dominum Deum nostrum iniquitas nec personarum acceptio nec cupido munerum». [8]In Ierusalem quoque constituit Iosaphat ex Levitis et sacerdotibus et principibus familiarum Israel pro iudicio Domini et pro causis habitatorum Ierusalem. [9]Praecepitque eis dicens: «Sic agetis in timore

fear of the LORD, in faithfulness, and with your whole heart: [10]whenever a case comes to you from your brethren who live in their cities, concerning bloodshed, law or commandment, statutes or ordinances, then you shall instruct them, that they may not incur guilt before the LORD and wrath may not come upon you and your brethren. Thus you shall do, and you will not incur guilt. [11]And behold, Amariah the chief priest is over you in all matters of the LORD; and Zebadiah the son of Ishmael, the governor of the house of Judah, in all the king's matters; and the Levites will serve you as officers. Deal courageously, and may the LORD be with the upright!"

Num 35:19
Deut 17:8

Jehoshaphat's victory over Ammonites and Moabites

20 [1]After this the Moabites and Ammonites, and with them some of the Me-unites,[f] came against Jehoshaphat for battle. [2]Some men came and told Jehoshaphat, "A great multitude is coming against you from Edom,[g] from beyond the sea; and, behold, they are in Hazazon-tamar" (that is, En-gedi). [3]Then Jehoshaphat feared, and set himself to seek the LORD, and proclaimed a fast throughout all Judah. [4]And Judah assembled to seek help from the LORD; from all the cities of Judah they came to seek the LORD.

1 Kings 21:9
Jer 36:6,9
Joel 1:14

20:1–30. Jehoshaphat's battle and victory over the Ammonites, Moabites and Me-unites is reported in the context of wars more to do with religious than political or territorial issues. In the first section of this account (vv. 3–5), when there is imminent danger of an enemy attack, the people are terrified, and their reaction, we are told, is to "seek the Lord" (v. 4). The harangue by the Levite Jahaziel (vv. 15–17) has the features of a prophetic oracle, reminiscent of Moses' exhortation prior to the crossing of the Red Sea (cf. Ex 14:13–14). The battle thus becomes a liturgical procession (cf. the notes on 13:1–23) in which the cantors (v. 21) and the Levites (vv. 14, 19) play a leading role. The victory ends with a pilgrimage to the temple, the fervour of the people expressing itself in songs and music: this entry into Jerusalem (vv. 27–28) is reminiscent of the general rejoicing when the ark was brought to the city in David's time (cf. 1 Chron 15:28).

Domini fideliter et corde perfecto. [10]Omnem causam, quae venerit ad vos fratrum vestrorum, qui habitant in urbibus suis, ubicumque quaestio est de homicidio, de lege, de mandato, de praeceptis et de iustificationibus, commonete eos, ut non peccent in Dominum, et ne veniat ira super vos et super fratres vestros; sic ergo agetis et non peccabitis. [11]Amarias autem sacerdos princeps super vos in omnibus, quae ad Deum pertinent, praesidebit; porro Zabadias filius Ismael, qui est dux in domo Iudae, super ea opera erit, quae ad regis officium pertinent; habetisque Levitas coram vobis ut scribas. Confortamini et agite diligenter, et sit Dominus cum bonis». **[20]** [1]Post haec congregati sunt filii Moab et filii Ammon et cum eis de Meunitis ad Iosaphat, ut pugnarent contra eum. [2]Veneruntque nuntii et indicaverunt Iosaphat

f. Compare 26:7: Heb *Ammonites* **g.** One Ms: Heb *Aram* (Syria)

[5]And Jehoshaphat stood in the assembly of Judah and Jerusalem, in the house of the LORD, before the new court, [6]and said, "O LORD, God of our fathers, art thou not God in heaven? Dost thou not rule over all the kingdoms of the nations? In thy hand are power and might, so that none is able to withstand thee. [7]Didst thou not, O our God, drive out the inhabitants of this land before thy people Israel, and give it for ever to the descendants of Abraham thy friend? [8]And they have dwelt in it, and have built thee in it a sanctuary for thy name, saying, [9]'If evil comes upon us, the sword, judgment,[h] or pestilence, or famine, we will stand before this house, and before thee, for thy name is in this house, and cry to thee in our affliction, and thou wilt hear and save.' [10]And now behold, the men of Ammon and Moab and Mount Seir, whom thou wouldest not let Israel invade when they came from the land of Egypt, and whom they avoided and did not destroy— [11]behold, they reward us by coming to drive us out of thy possession, which thou hast given us to inherit. [12]O our God, wilt thou not execute judgment upon them? For we are powerless against this great multitude that is coming against us. We do not know what to do, but our eyes are upon thee."

Deut 4:39
Dan 4:17
Is 41:8
Jas 2:23
1 Kings 8:37–39
Deut 2:4ff; 2:9ff; 2:18ff

---

dicentes: «Venit contra te multitudo magna de his locis, quae trans mare sunt, de Edom, et ecce consistunt in Asasonthamar, quae est Engaddi». [3]Iosaphat autem timore perterritus totum se contulit ad rogandum Dominum et praedicavit ieiunium universo Iudae. [4]Congregatusque est Iuda ad precandum Dominum; sed et de omnibus urbibus suis venerunt ad obsecrandum eum. [5]Cumque stetisset Iosaphat in medio coetu Iudae et Ierusalem in domo Domini ante atrium novum, [6]ait: «Domine, Deus patrum nostrorum, tu es Deus in caelo et dominaris cunctis regnis gentium; in manu tua est fortitudo et potentia, nec quisquam tibi potest resistere. [7]Nonne tu, Deus noster, expulisti habitatores terrae huius coram populo tuo Israel et dedisti eam semini Abraham amici tui in sempiternum? [8]Habitaveruntque in ea et exstruxerunt in illa sanctuarium nomini tuo dicentes: [9]"Si irruerint super nos mala, gladius iudicii, pestilentia et fames, stabimus coram domo hac in conspectu tuo, quia nomen tuum est in domo hac, et clamabimus ad te in tribulationibus nostris, et exaudies salvosque facies". [10]Nunc igitur ecce filii Ammon et Moab et mons Seir, per quos non concessisti Israeli ut transirent, quando egrediebantur de Aegypto, sed declinaverunt ab eis et non interfecerunt illos, [11]e contrario agunt et nituntur eicere nos de possessione tua, quam tradidisti nobis. [12]Deus noster, ergo non iudicabis eos? In nobis quidem non tanta est fortitudo, ut possimus huic multitudini resistere, quae irruit super nos; sed, cum ignoremus quid agere debeamus, hoc solum habemus residui, ut oculos nostros dirigamus ad te». [13]Omnis vero Iuda stabat coram Domino cum parvulis et uxoribus et liberis suis. [14]Erat autem Iahaziel filius Zachariae filii Banaiae filii Iehiel filii Matthaniae Levites de filiis Asaph, super quem factus est spiritus Domini in medio congregationis, [15]et ait: «Attendite, omnis Iuda et qui habitatis Ierusalem et tu rex Iosaphat: Haec dicit Dominus vobis: Nolite timere nec paveatis hanc multitudinem magnam; non est enim vestra pugna, sed Dei. [16]Cras descendetis contra eos; ascensuri enim sunt per clivum nomine Sis, et invenietis illos in summitate torrentis, qui est contra solitudinem Ieruel. [17]Non eritis vos, qui dimicabitis; sed tantummodo confidenter state et videbitis auxilium Domini super vos, o Iuda et Ierusalem. Nolite timere nec paveatis: cras egredimini contra eos, et Dominus erit vobiscum». [18]Iosaphat ergo inclinavit se super faciem suam in terra, et omnis Iuda et habitatores Ierusalem ceciderunt coram Domino et adoraverunt eum. [19]Porro Levitae de filiis Caath, de filiis Core scilicet, surrexerunt et laudabant Dominum, Deum Israel, voce magna in excelsum. [20]Cumque mane surrexissent, egressi sunt ad desertum Thecue; profectisque eis,

h. Or *the sword of judgment*

[13]Meanwhile all the men of Judah stood before the LORD, with their little ones, their wives, and their children. [14]And the Spirit of the LORD came upon Jahaziel the son of Zechariah, son of Benaiah, son of Je-iel, son of Mattaniah, a Levite of the sons of Asaph, in the midst of the assembly.[15]And he said, "Hearken, all Judah and inhabitants of Jerusalem, and King Jehoshaphat: Thus says the LORD to you, 'Fear not, and be not dismayed at this great multitude; for the battle is not yours but God's. [16]Tomorrow go down against them; behold, they will come up by the ascent of Ziz; you will find them at the end of the valley, east of the wilderness of Jeruel. [17]You will not need to fight in this battle; take your position, stand still, and see the victory of the LORD on your behalf, O Judah and Jerusalem.' Fear not, and be not dismayed; tomorrow go out against them, and the LORD will be with you."

1 Chron 9:15
Neh 11:17–22
Num 14:9
Deut 20:3–4
Is 8:10

[18]Then Jehoshaphat bowed his head with his face to the ground, and all Judah and the inhabitants of Jerusalem fell down before the LORD, worshipping the LORD. [19]And the Levites, of the Kohathites and the Korahites, stood up to praise the LORD, the God of Israel, with a very loud voice.

[20]And they rose early in the morning and went out into the wilderness of Tekoa; and as they went out, Jehoshaphat stood and said, "Hear me, Judah and inhabitants of Jerusalem! Believe in the LORD your God, and you will be established; believe his prophets, and you will succeed." [21]And when he had taken counsel with the people, he appointed those who were to sing to the LORD and praise him in holy array, as they went before the army, and say,

"Give thanks to the LORD,
for his steadfast love endures for ever."

2 Sam 14:2
Is 7:9
Ps 136:1

[22]And when they began to sing and praise, the LORD set an ambush against the men of Ammon, Moab, and Mount Seir, who had come

---

20:31–37. The last days of Jehoshaphat were marked by infidelity and the punishment it drew upon him. Compared with the parallel passage in Kings (1 Kings 22:41–46, 49–51), Chronicles adds the new alliance with the impious king of Israel, the oracle of the prophet Eliezer condemning that alliance, and the disaster that overtook the fleet (vv. 35–37). The sacred writer makes the point that anyone who fails to go along with the plans of God will be punished for it, even if he previously acted in an upright way—another reference to personal and immediate retribution.

stans Iosaphat in medio eorum dixit: «Audite me, Iuda et habitatores Ierusalem! Credite in Domino Deo vestro et permanebitis; credite prophetis eius, et cuncta evenient vobis prospera». [21]Habuitque consilium cum populo et statuit cantores Domini, ut laudarent eum in ornatu sancto et antecederent exercitum ac voce consona dicerent: «Confitemini Domino, quoniam in aeternum misericordia eius». [22]Cumque

against Judah, so that they were routed. [23]For the men of Ammon and Moab rose against the inhabitants of Mount Seir, destroying them utterly, and when they had made an end of the inhabitants of Seir, they all helped to destroy one another.

Josh 6:17
Ezek 38:21

[24]When Judah came to the watchtower of the wilderness, they looked toward the multitude; and behold, they were dead bodies lying on the ground; none had escaped. [25]When Jehoshaphat and his people came to take the spoil from them, they found cattle[i] in great numbers, goods, clothing, and precious things, which they took for themselves until they could carry no more. They were three days in taking the spoil, it was so much. [26]On the fourth day they assembled in the Valley of Beracah, [j]for there they blessed the LORD; therefore the name of that place has been called the Valley of Beracah to this day. [27]Then they returned, every man of Judah and Jerusalem, and Jehoshaphat at their head, returning to Jerusalem with joy, for the LORD had made them rejoice over their enemies. [28]They came to Jerusalem, with harps and lyres and trumpets, to the house of the LORD. [29]And the fear of God came on all the kingdoms of the countries when they heard that the LORD had fought against the enemies of Israel. [30]So the realm of Jehoshaphat was quiet, for his God gave him rest round about.

Deut 2:25

1 Kings
22:41–51

End of Jehoshaphat's reign

[31]Thus Jehoshaphat reigned over Judah. He was thirty-five years old when he began to reign, and he reigned twenty-five years in Jerusalem. His mother's name was Azubah the daughter of Shilhi. [32]He walked in the way of Asa his father and did not turn aside

---

coepissent laudes canere, vertit Dominus insidias eorum contra filios Ammon et Moab et montem Seir, qui egressi fuerant, ut pugnarent contra Iudam, et percussi sunt. [23]Et filii Ammon et Moab consurrexerunt adversum habitatores montis Seir, ut interficerent et delerent eos; cumque hoc opere perpetrassent, etiam in semetipsos versi mutuis concidere vulneribus. [24]Porro Iuda, cum venisset ad speculam, quae respicit solitudinem, vidit procul omnem late regionem plenam cadaveribus, nec superesse quemquam, qui necem potuisset evadere. [25]Venit ergo Iosaphat et omnis populus cum eo ad detrahenda spolia mortuorum inveneruntque iumenta multa et supellectilem, vestes quoque et vasa pretiosissima et diripuerunt, ita ut omnia portare non possent, et per tres dies spolia auferebant pro praedae magnitudine. [26]Die autem quarto congregati sunt in valle Baracha; etenim, quoniam ibi benedixerant Domino, vocaverunt locum illum vallis Benedictionis usque in praesentem diem. [27]Reversusque est omnis vir Iudae et Ierusalem et Iosaphat ante eos in Ierusalem cum laetitia magna, eo quod dedisset eis Dominus gaudium de inimicis suis; [28]ingressique sunt Ierusalem cum psalteriis et citharis et tubis in domum Domini. [29]Irruit autem pavor Dei super universa regna terrarum, cum audissent quod pugnasset Dominus contra inimicos Israel. [30]Quievitque regnum Iosaphat, et praebuit ei Deus eius pacem per circuitum. [31]Regnavit igitur Iosaphat super Iudam. Et erat triginta quinque annorum, cum regnare coepisset; viginti autem et quinque annis regnavit in Ierusalem. Nomen matris eius Azuba filia Selachi. [32]Et ambulavit in via patris sui Asa, nec declinavit ab ea. faciens quod rectum erat coram Domino. [33]Verumtamen excelsa non ablata sunt; et adhuc populus non direxerat cor suum

i. Gk: Heb *among them* **j.** That is *Blessing*

from it; he did what was right in the sight of the LORD. [33]The high places, however, were not taken away; the people had not yet set their hearts upon the God of their fathers. 2 Chron 17:6

[34]Now the rest of the acts of Jehoshaphat, from first to last, are written in the chronicles of Jehu the son of Hanani, which are recorded in the Book of the Kings of Israel. 1 Kings 16:1

[35]After this Jehoshaphat king of Judah joined with Ahaziah king of Israel, who did wickedly. [36]He joined him in building ships to go to Tarshish, and they built the ships in Ezion-geber. [37]Then Eliezer the son of Do-davahu of Mareshah prophesied against Jehoshaphat, saying, "Because you have joined with Ahaziah, the LORD will destroy what you have made." And the ships were wrecked and were not able to go to Tarshish.

The reign of Jehoram

21 [1]Jehoshaphat slept with his fathers, and was buried with his fathers in the city of David; and Jehoram his son reigned in his stead. [2]He had brothers, the sons of Jehoshaphat: Azariah, Jehiel, Zechariah, Azariah, Michael, and Shephatiah; all these were the sons of Jehoshaphat king of Judah. [3]Their father gave them great gifts, of silver, gold, and valuable possessions, together with fortified cities in Judah; but he gave the kingdom to Jehoram, because he was the first-born. [4]When Jehoram had ascended the throne of his father and was established, he slew all his brothers with the sword, and also some of the princes of Israel.

21:1–20. Jehoram's reign was dark in every sense: idolatry, alliances with the king of Israel, and straying from the path of the Lord, were responsible for humiliating defeats, a plague on the people and the king's own horrible illness. But even though God had to punish the king for his transgressions, he still kept the Covenant he made with David (v. 7). In his accounts of the less edifying reigns, the Chronicler never fails to make it clear that, even though the Lord inflicted punishment, he never forsook his people.

ad Deum patrum suorum. [34]Reliqua autem gestorum Iosaphat, priorum et novissimorum, scripta sunt in verbis Iehu filii Hanani, quae digesta sunt in libros regum Israel. [35]Post haec iniit amicitias Iosaphat rex Iudae cum Ochozia rege Israel, cuius opera fuerunt impiissima, [36]et particeps fuit, ut facerent naves, quae irent in Tharsis, feceruntque classem in Asiongaber. [37]Prophetavit autem Eliezer filius Dodiae de Maresa contra Iosaphat dicens: «Quia habuisti foedus cum Ochozia, percussit Dominus opera tua». Contritaeque sunt naves nec potuerunt ire in Tharsis. **[21]** [1]Dormivit autem Iosaphat cum patribus suis et sepultus est cum eis in civitate David; regnavitque Ioram filius eius pro eo. [2]Qui habuit fratres filios Iosaphat Azariam et Iahiel et Zachariam et Azariam et Michael et Saphatiam: omnes hi filii Iosaphat regis Israel. [3]Deditque eis pater suus multa munera argenti et auri et res pretiosas cum civitatibus munitissimis in Iuda; regnum autem tradidit Ioram, eo quod esset primogenitus. [4]Surrexit ergo Ioram super regnum patris sui; cumque se confirmasset, occidit omnes fratres suos gladio et quosdam de principibus Israel. [5]Triginta duorum annorum erat Ioram, cum regnare coepisset, et octo annis regnavit

[5]Jehoram was thirty-two years old when he became king, and he reigned eight years in Jerusalem. [6]And he walked in the way of the kings of Israel, as the house of Ahab had done; for the daughter of Ahab was his wife. And he did what was evil in the sight of the LORD. [7]Yet the LORD would not destroy the house of David, because of the covenant which he had made with David, and since he had promised to give a lamp to him and to his sons for ever.

2 Kings 8:17–22

1 Kings 11:36

An Edomite rebellion

2 Kings 8:20–22

[8]In his days Edom revolted from the rule of Judah, and set up a king of their own. [9]Then Jehoram passed over with his commanders and all his chariots, and he rose by night and smote the Edomites who had surrounded him and his chariot commanders. [10]So Edom revolted from the rule of Judah to this day. At that time Libnah also revolted from his rule, because he had forsaken the LORD, the God of his fathers.

Jehoram punished for his infidelity

[11]Moreover he made high places in the hill country of Judah, and led the inhabitants of Jerusalem into unfaithfulness, and made

---

"Jehoahaz, his youngest son" (v. 17): this was Ahaziah, who succeeded Jehoram (22:1). Maybe this is a copyist's error, for the Greek text does call him Ahaziah, or else it was an additional name the king had, as sometimes happens in the Bible.

21:2. "Jehoshaphat king of Judah": some manuscripts read "king of Israel", which is what the Hebrew has. If the Chronicler describes him as "king of Israel", it is because he regarded the kingdom of Judah as the heir of the ancient promises and, therefore, as the true Israel.

21:7. This verse parallels 2 Kings 8:19 but adds the reference to the "covenant with David" as being the reason why the Lord did not put an end to the dynasty. The Chronicler gives more importance to the Covenant with David than to any other, even that made with Moses on Sinai.

21:12–15. Elijah proclaims an oracle against Jehoram, in keeping with the

---

in Ierusalem. [6]Ambulavitque in viis regum Israel, sicut egerat domus Achab; filia quippe Achab erat uxor eius. Et fecit malum in conspectu Domini. [7]Noluit autem Dominus disperdere domum David propter pactum, quod inierat cum eo, et quia promiserat, ut daret ei lucernam et filiis eius omni tempore. [8]In diebus illis rebellavit Edom, ne esset subditus Iudae, et constituit sibi regem. [9]Cumque transisset Ioram cum principibus suis et cunctis curribus, qui erant secum, surrexit nocte et percussit Edom, qui eum circumdederat, et omnes duces curruum eius. [10]Attamen rebellavit Edom, ne esset sub dicione Iudae, usque ad hanc diem. Eo tempore et Lobna recessit, ne esset sub manu illius; dereliquerat enim Dominum Deum patrum suorum. [11]Insuper et excelsa fabricatus est in montibus Iudae et fornicari fecit habitatores Ierusalem et praevaricari Iudam. [12]Allatae sunt autem ei litterae ab Elia propheta, in quibus scriptum erat: «Haec dicit Dominus, Deus David patris tui: Quoniam non ambulasti in viis Iosaphat

Judah go astray. [12]And a letter came to him from Elijah the prophet, saying, "Thus says the LORD, the God of David your father, 'Because you have not walked in the ways of Jehoshaphat your father, or in the ways of Asa king of Judah, [13]but have walked in the way of the kings of Israel, and have led Judah and the inhabitants of Jerusalem into unfaithfulness, as the house of Ahab led Israel into unfaithfulness, and also you have killed your brothers, of your father's house, who were better than yourself; [14]behold, the LORD will bring a great plague on your people, your children, your wives, and all your possessions, [15]and you yourself will have a severe sickness with a disease of your bowels, until your bowels come out because of the disease, day by day.'"

[16]And the LORD stirred up against Jehoram the anger of the Philistines and of the Arabs who are near the Ethiopians; [17]and they came up against Judah, and invaded it, and carried away all the possessions they found that belonged to the king's house, and also his sons and his wives, so that no son was left to him except Jehoahaz, his youngest son.

2 Chron 14:8

[18]And after all this the LORD smote him in his bowels with an incurable disease. [19]In course of time, at the end of two years, his bowels came out because of the disease, and he died in great agony. His people made no fire in his honour, like the fires made for his fathers. [20]He was thirty-two years old when he began to

2 Chron 16:14

style of the prophets of Judah who also foretold the punishment that other kings would meet (cf. 16:7; 20:27). According to 2 Kings 3:11, Elijah was no longer alive by the time Jehoram was king, but the Chronicler mentions this oracle in order to give more authority to his denunciation of Jehoram. Also, this is the only time that he mentions the activity of a prophet of the Northern kingdom—a clear sign of the prestige that Elijah's memory still had when this book was being compiled.

patris tui et in viis Asa regis Iudae, [13]sed incessisti per iter regum Israel et fornicari fecisti Iudam et habitatores Ierusalem imitatus fornicationem domus Achab, insuper et fratres tuos domum patris tui meliores te occidisti: [14]ecce Dominus percutiet plaga magna populum tuum, filios et uxores tuas universamque substantiam tuam; [15]tu autem aegrotabis pessimo languore uteri tui, donec egrediantur vitalia tua paulatim per singulos dies». [16]Suscitavit ergo Dominus contra Ioram spiritum Philisthinorum et Arabum, qui confines sunt Aethiopibus, [17]et ascenderunt in terram Iudae et irruperunt in eam diripueruntque cunctam substantiam, quae inventa est in domo regis, insuper et filios eius et uxores, nec remansit ei filius nisi Ioachaz, qui minimus natu erat. [18]Et post haec omnia percussit eum Dominus alvi languore insanabili. [19]Cumque diei succederet dies, et temporum spatia volverentur, duorum annorum expletus est circulus; et sic longa consumptus tabe, ita ut egereret etiam viscera sua, languore pariter et vita caruit. Mortuusque est in infirmitate pessima, et non fecit ei populus eius secundum morem combustionis exsequias, sicut fecerat maioribus eius. [20]Triginta duorum annorum fuit, cum regnare coepisset, et octo annis regnavit in Ierusalem. Obiitque nullo relicto desiderio sui; et sepelierunt eum in civitate David, verumtamen non in sepulcro regum. **[22]** [1]Constituerunt autem habitatores Ierusalem

reign, and he reigned eight years in Jerusalem; and he departed with no one's regret. They buried him in the city of David, but not in the tombs of the kings.

2 Kings 8:24

The reign of Ahaziah

2 Kings 8:24–29

22 [1]And the inhabitants of Jerusalem made Ahaziah his youngest son king in his stead; for the band of men that came with the Arabs to the camp had slain all the older sons. So Ahaziah the son of Jehoram king of Judah reigned. [2]Ahaziah was forty-two years old when he began to reign, and he reigned one year in Jerusalem. His mother's name was Athaliah, the granddaughter of Omri. [3]He also walked in the ways of the house of Ahab, for his mother was his counsellor in doing wickedly. [4]He did what was evil in the sight of the LORD, as the house of Ahab had done; for after the death of his father they were his counsellors, to his undoing. [5]He even followed their counsel, and went with Jehoram the son of Ahab king of Israel to make war against Hazael king of Syria at Ramoth-gilead. And the Syrians wounded Joram, [6]and he returned to be healed in Jezreel of the wounds which he had received at Ramah, when he fought against Hazael king of Syria. And Ahaziah the son of Jehoram king of Judah went down to see Joram the son of Ahab in Jezreel, because he was sick.

2 Chron 10:6ff
Eccles 10:16

22:1–12. The reigns of Ahaziah and Athaliah were a dark time for Judah as far as both religious and secular history were concerned. The account given for Ahaziah (inspired by 2 Kings 8:25–27; 9:27–29) stresses the misfortunes of the people caused by the king's transgressions, specifically his pacts with Ahab, king of Israel. The account of Ahaziah's death is damning: it was "ordained by God" and brought about by Jehu "whom the Lord had anointed" (v. 7).

The crimes of Athaliah, the only woman who ruled over Judah (vv. 10–12), show that the Davidic dynasty was at a crisis point. This account, which parallels 2 Kings 11:1–3, exalts the figure of Jeho-shabe-ath, daughter of King Jehoram and therefore sister of Ahaziah. By rescuing Joash, she ensured that the Davidic dynasty would endure. The Chronicler stresses that she was the wife of the priest Jehoiada, thereby showing that the priesthood and the temple played a significant role in times of crisis.

Ochoziam filium eius minimum regem pro eo; omnes enim maiores natu interfecerat turba, quae irruerat cum Arabibus in castra. Regnavitque Ochozias filius Ioram regis Iudae. [2]Filius viginti duo annorum erat Ochozias, cum regnare coepisset, et uno anno regnavit in Ierusalem. Nomen matris eius Athalia filia Amri. [3]Sed et ipse ingressus est per vias domus Achab; mater enim eius impulit eum, ut impie ageret. [4]Fecit igitur malum in conspectu Domini sicut domus Achab; ipsi enim fuerunt ei consiliarii post mortem patris sui in interitum eius. [5]Ambulavitque in consiliis eorum et perrexit cum Ioram filio Achab rege Israel in bellum contra Hazael regem Syriae in Ramoth Galaad; vulneraveruntque Syri Ioram. [6]Qui reversus est, ut curaretur in Iezrahel a plagis, quas acceperat in supradicto certamine. Igitur Ochozias filius Ioram rex Iudae descendit, ut inviseret Ioram filium Achab in Iezrahel aegrotantem. [7]Voluntatis

[7]But it was ordained by God that the downfall of Ahaziah should come about through his going to visit Joram. For when he came there he went out with Jehoram to meet Jehu the son of Nimshi, whom the LORD had anointed to destroy the house of Ahab. [8]And when Jehu was executing judgment upon the house of Ahab, he met the princes of Judah and the sons of Ahaziah's brothers, who attended Ahaziah, and he killed them. [9]He searched for Ahaziah, and he was captured while hiding in Samaria, and he was brought to Jehu and put to death. They buried him, for they said, "He is the grandson of Jehoshaphat, who sought the LORD with all his heart." And the house of Ahaziah had no one able to rule the kingdom.

2 Kings 9:21; 10:12–14

2 Kings 9:27–29

The reign of Athaliah

2 Kings 11:1–3

[10]Now when Athaliah the mother of Ahaziah saw that her son was dead, she arose and destroyed all the royal family of the house of Judah. [11]But Jeho-shabe-ath, the daughter of the king, took Joash the son of Ahaziah, and stole him away from among the king's sons who were about to be slain, and she put him and his nurse in a bedchamber. Thus Jeho-shabe-ath, the daughter of King Jehoram and wife of Jehoiada the priest, because she was a sister of Ahaziah, hid him from Athaliah, so that she did not slay him; [12]and he remained with them six years, hid in the house of God, while Athaliah reigned over the land.

Joash proclaimed king. Death of Athaliah

2 Kings 11:4–16

23 [1]But in the seventh year Jehoiada took courage, and entered into a compact with the commanders of hundreds, Azariah

---

23:1–21. The proclamation of Joash as king and the death of Athaliah were part of God's plan of salvation; the account given here is very close to that in 2 Kings 11:4–20, but small changes serve to underline the key role played

quippe fuit Dei adversum Ochoziam, ut veniret ad Ioram et, cum venisset, egrederetur cum eo adversum Iehu filium Namsi, quem unxit Dominus, ut deleret domum Achab. [8]Cum ergo iudicium faceret Iehu in domum Achab, invenit principes Iudae et filios fratrum Ochoziae, qui ministrabant ei, et interfecit illos. [9]Ipsumque perquisivit Ochoziam, et comprehenderunt eum latentem in Samaria; adductumque ad se Iehu occidit. Et sepelierunt eum, eo quod dicebant eum esse filium Iosaphat, qui quaesierat Dominum in toto corde suo. Nec erat aliquis de stirpe Ochoziae, qui posset regnare. [10]Athalia autem mater eius videns quod mortuus esset filius suus surrexit et interfecit omnem stirpem regiam domus Iudae. [11]Porro Iosabeth filia regis tulit Ioas filium Ochoziae et furata est eum de medio filiorum regis, cum interficerentur, absconditque cum nutrice sua in cubiculo lectulorum. Iosabeth autem, quae absconderat eum, erat filia regis Ioram, uxor Ioiadae pontificis, soror Ochoziae; et idcirco Athalia non interfecit eum. [12]Fuit ergo cum eis in domo Dei absconditus sex annis, quibus regnavit Athalia super terram. **[23]** [1]Anno autem septimo confortatus Ioiada assumpsit centuriones, Azariam videlicet filium Ieroham et Ismael filium Iohanan,

the son of Jeroham, Ishmael the son of Jehohanan, Azariah the son of Obed, Ma-aseiah the son of Adaiah, and Elishaphat the son of Zichri. [2]And they went about through Judah and gathered the Levites from all the cities of Judah, and the heads of fathers' houses of Israel, and they came to Jerusalem. [3]And all the assembly made a covenant with the king in the house of God. And Jehoiada[l] said to them, "Behold, the king's son! Let him reign, as the LORD spoke concerning the sons of David. [4]This is the thing that you shall do: of you priests and Levites who come off duty on the sabbath, one third shall be gatekeepers, [5]and one third shall be at the king's house and one third at the Gate of the Foundation; and all the people shall be in the courts of the house of the LORD. [6]Let no one enter the house of the LORD except the priests and ministering Levites; they may enter, for they are holy, but all the people shall keep the charge of the LORD. [7]The Levites shall surround the king, each with his weapons in his hand; and whoever enters the house shall be slain. Be with the king when he comes in, and when he goes out."

---

by the priests and the temple: Jehoiada, as priest (22:11; 23:8, 11), convoked the Levites (v. 2) to involve them in the manoeuvre against Athaliah; since it was their job to supervise the proclamation ceremony, they were the only ones permitted to enter the temple (vv. 8–9).

After Athaliah disappeared from the scene, Jehoiada himself set about reforming the temple ministers to bring them into line with what David laid down (vv. 18–19). Once again the priesthood ensured the continuance of the Davidic dynasty.

23:13. "The people of the land" (vv. 20–21), the plain people, which the Greek translates here simply as *laos*. From that word comes the word "layman", meaning a member of the people who has not received any special consecration. In the New Covenant, Christians, by sharing in the priestly mission of Christ through faith and baptism, share in the priestly vocation of the People of God: "Christ the Lord, high priest taken from among men (cf. Heb 5:1–5), made the new people a kingdom of priests to God, his Father (Rev 1:6; cf. 5:9–10). The baptized, by regeneration and the anointing of the Holy Spirit are consecrated to be a spiritual house and a holy priesthood" (Vatican II, *Lumen gentium*, 10).

Azariam quoque filium Obed et Maasiam filium Adaiae et Elisaphat filium Zechri, et iniit cum eis foedus. [2]Qui circumeuntes Iudam congregaverunt Levitas de cunctis urbibus Iudae et principes familiarum Israel veneruntque in Ierusalem. [3]Iniit igitur omnis congregatio pactum in domo Dei cum rege. Dixitque ad eos Ioiada: «Ecce filius regis regnabit, sicut locutus est Dominus super filios David. [4]Hoc est ergo, quod facietis. [5]Tertia pars vestrum, qui veniunt ad sabbatum sacerdotum et Levitarum et ianitorum, erit in portis, tertia vero pars ad domum regis et tertia in porta, quae appellatur Fundamenti; omne vero reliquum vulgus sit in atriis domus Domini. [6]Nec quisquam alius ingrediatur domum Domini, nisi sacerdotes et qui ministrant de Levitis; ipsi tantummodo ingrediantur, quia sanctificati sunt.

l. Heb *he*

[8]The Levites and all Judah did according to all that Jehoiada the priest commanded. They each brought his men, who were to go off duty on the sabbath, with those who were to come on duty on the sabbath; for Jehoiada the priest did not dismiss the divisions. [9]And Jehoiada the priest delivered to the captains the spears and the large and small shields that had been King David's, which were in the house of God; [10]and he set all the people as a guard for the king, every man with his weapon in his hand, from the south side of the house to the north side of the house, around the altar and the house. [11]Then he brought out the king's son, and put the crown upon him, and gave him the testimony; and they proclaimed him king, and Jehoiada and his sons anointed him, and they said, "Long live the king."

1 Chron 24:19

[12]When Athaliah heard the noise of the people running and praising the king, she went into the house of the LORD to the people; [13]and when she looked, there was the king standing by his pillar at the entrance, and the captains and the trumpeters beside the king, and all the people of the land rejoicing and blowing trumpets, and the singers with their musical instruments leading in the celebration. And Athaliah rent her clothes, and cried, "Treason! Treason!" [14]Then Jehoiada the priest brought out the captains who were set over the army, saying to them, "Bring her out between the ranks; any one who follows her is to be slain with the sword." For the priest said, "Do not slay her in the house of the LORD." [15]So they laid hands on her; and she went into the entrance of the horse gate of the king's house, and they slew her there.

[16]And Jehoiada made a covenant between himself and all the people and the king that they should be the LORD's people. [17]Then

2 Kings 11:17–20

Et omne reliquum vulgus observet observationem Domini. [7]Levitae autem circumdent regem habentes singuli arma sua in manu. Et si quis alius ingressus fuerit templum, interficiatur. Sintque cum rege et intrante et egrediente». [8]Fecerunt igitur Levitae et universus Iuda iuxta omnia, quae praeceperat Ioiada pontifex; et assumpserunt singuli viros suos, qui veniebant sabbato cum his, qui sabbato egressuri erant: siquidem Ioiada pontifex non dimisit abire turmas, quae sibi per singulas hebdomadas succedere consueverant. [9]Deditque Ioiada sacerdos centurionibus lanceas clipeosque et peltas regis David, quae erant in domo Dei. [10]Constituitque omnem populum tenentium tela a parte templi dextra usque ad partem templi sinistram coram altari et templo per circuitum regis. [11]Et eduxerunt filium regis et dederunt ei diadema et testimonium et constituerunt eum regem. Unxerunt quoque illum Ioiada pontifex et filii eius; imprecatique sunt ei atque dixerunt: «Vivat rex!». [12]Quod cum audisset Athalia, vocem scilicet currentium atque laudantium regem, ingressa est ad populum in templum Domini. [13]Cumque vidisset regem stantem super gradum suum in introitu et principes tubasque circa eum omnemque populum terrae gaudentem atque clangentem tubis cantoresque cum diversi generis organis signum dantes ad laudandum, scidit vestimenta sua et ait: «Coniuratio, coniuratio!». [14]Praecepit autem Ioiada pontifex centurionibus, qui erant super exercitum, dicens: «Educite illam extra saepta templi! Qui autem sequetur eam, interficiatur foris gladio!». Dixerat enim sacerdos: «Non occidetis eam in domo Domini!». [15]Et imposuerunt ei manus; cumque intrasset portam Equorum domus regis, interfecerunt eam ibi. [16]Pepigit autem Ioiada foedus inter se universumque populum et regem, ut esset populus

2 Kings 10:26–27 all the people went to the house of Baal, and tore it down; his altars and his images they broke in pieces, and they slew Mattan the priest of Baal before the altars. [18]And Jehoiada posted watchmen for the house of the LORD under the direction of the Levitical priests and the Levites whom David had organized to be in charge of the house of the LORD, to offer burnt offerings to the LORD, as it is written in the law of Moses, with rejoicing and with singing, according to the order of David. [19]He stationed the gatekeepers at the gates of the house of the LORD so that no one should enter who was in any way unclean. [20]And he took the captains, the nobles, the governors of the people, and all the people of the land; and they brought the king down from the house of the LORD, marching through the upper gate to the king's house. And they set the king upon the royal throne. [21]So all the people of the land rejoiced; and the city was quiet, after Athaliah had been slain with the sword.

1 Chron 23:13; 25

1 Chron 26

2 Kings 12:1–17

The reign of Joash

24 [1]Joash was seven years old when he began to reign, and he reigned forty years in Jerusalem; his mother's name was Zibiah of Beer-sheba. [2]And Joash did what was right in the eyes of the LORD all the days of Jehoiada the priest. [3]Jehoiada got for him two wives, and he had sons and daughters.

[4]After this Joash decided to restore the house of the LORD. [5]And he gathered the priests and the Levites, and said to them, "Go out

---

24:1–27. The account of the reign of Joash is written with a clearly pedagogical purpose; we divide it into two stages, to help show the religious message it contains.

The first stage (vv. 1–16) is all about the collection of monies to pay for the restoration of the temple (it follows the parallel passage of 2 Kings 12:1–17). During these years the real protagonist is Jehoiada the priest, who implemented the king's initiatives to do with rebuilding the temple and returning it to its original splendour (v. 13). When

Domini. [17]Itaque ingressus est omnis populus domum Baal et destruxerunt eam et altaria ac simulacra illius confregerunt; Matthan quoque sacerdotem Baal interfecerunt ante aras. [18]Constituit autem Ioiada praepositos in domo Domini sub manibus sacerdotum et Levitarum, quos distribuit David in domo Domini, ut offerrent holocausta Domino, sicut scriptum est in lege Moysi, in gaudio et canticis iuxta dispositionem David. [19]Constituit quoque ianitores in portis domus Domini, ut non ingrederetur eam immundus in omni re. [20]Assumpsitque centuriones et fortissimos viros ac principes populi et omne vulgus terrae, et fecerunt descendere regem de domo Domini et introire per medium portae Superioris in domum regis et collocaverunt eum in solio regali. [21]Laetatusque est omnis populus terrae, et urbs quievit; porro Athalia interfecta est gladio. **[24]** [1]Septem annorum erat Ioas, cum regnare coepisset, et quadraginta annis regnavit in Ierusalem. Nomen matris eius Sebia de Bersabee. [2]Fecitque, quod bonum est coram Domino, cunctis diebus Ioiadae sacerdotis. [3]Accepit autem ei Ioiada uxores duas, e quibus genuit filios et filias. [4]Post quae placuit Ioas, ut instauraret domum Domini. [5]Congregavitque sacerdotes

to the cities of Judah, and gather from all Israel money to repair the house of your God from year to year; and see that you hasten the matter." But the Levites did not hasten it. [6]So the king summoned Jehoiada the chief, and said to him, "Why have you not required the Levites to bring in from Judah and Jerusalem the tax levied by Moses, the servant of the LORD, on[m] the congregation of Israel for the tent of testimony?" [7]For the sons of Athaliah, that wicked woman, had broken into the house of God; and had also used all the dedicated things of the house of the LORD for the Baals.

Ex 25:1–9; 30:12–16; 38:24–31

[8]So the king commanded, and they made a chest, and set it outside the gate of the house of the LORD. [9]And proclamation was made throughout Judah and Jerusalem, to bring in for the LORD the tax that Moses the servant of God laid upon Israel in the wilderness. [10]And all the princes and all the people rejoiced and

---

Jehoiada died, he was buried in the city of David, that is to say, he was accorded royal honours.

The second stage was marked by disloyalty to the Lord and by idolatry. The military defeats and conspiracies were forms of punishment for the king's transgressions (vv. 17–26). Joash's worst crime was the shameful execution of the son of Jehoiada, the prophet Zechariah (not the same person as the last of the minor prophets), who had dared to denounce the king's crimes. For this sin the king himself will lose his life at the hands of conspirators (v. 25). Once again we can see that God does not leave crimes unavenged.

This Zechariah is probably the prophet Jesus referred to as a prime example of an innocent victim sacrificed by his own people: "that upon you may come all the righteous blood shed on earth, from the blood of the innocent Abel to the blood of Zechariah the son of Barachiah, whom you murdered between the sanctuary and the altar" (Mt 23:35). The fact that Jesus calls him "son of Barachiah" instead of "son of Jehoiada" could be because different genealogies were being used, or else there may have been some error in the transmission of the text. Anyway, given that the book of Chronicles is the last book in the Hebrew Bible, Jesus is saying that all innocent victims, from the first (Abel) to the last (Zechariah), are figures of the Christian martyrs and share in the redemption Christ effected by his death

---

et Levitas et dixit eis: «Egredimini ad civitates Iudae et colligite de universo Israel pecuniam ad sartatecta templi Dei vestri per singulos annos. Festinatoque hoc facite». Porro Levitae non festinarunt. [6]Vocavitque rex Ioiadam principem et dixit ei: «Quare non tibi fuit curae, ut cogeres Levitas inferre de Iuda et de Ierusalem pecuniam, quae constituta est a Moyse servo Domini, ut inferret eam omnis congregatio Israel in tabernaculum testimonii? [7]Athalia enim impiissima et filii eius dissipaverunt domum Dei et de universis, quae sanctificata fuerant templo Domini, dedicaverunt Baalim». [8]Praecepit ergo rex, et fecerunt arcam posueruntque eam iuxta portam domus Domini forinsecus. [9]Et praedicatum est in Iuda et Ierusalem, ut deferrent singuli pretium Domino, quod constituit Moyses servus Dei super Israel in deserto. [10]Laetatique sunt cuncti principes et omnis populus et ingressi contulerunt in arcam

m. Compare Vg: Heb *and*

brought their tax and dropped it into the chest until they had finished. [11]And whenever the chest was brought to the king's officers by the Levites, when they saw that there was much money in it, the king's secretary and the officer of the chief priest would come and empty the chest and take it and return it to its place. Thus they did day after day, and collected money in abundance. [12]And the king and Jehoiada gave it to those who had charge of the work of the house of the LORD, and they hired masons and carpenters to restore the house of the LORD, and also workers in iron and bronze to repair the house of the LORD. [13]So those who were engaged in the work laboured, and the repairing went forward in their hands, and they restored the house of God to its proper condition and strengthened it. [14]And when they had finished, they brought the rest of the money before the king and Jehoiada, and with it were made utensils for the house of the LORD, both for the service and for the burnt offerings, and dishes for incense, and vessels of gold and silver. And they offered burnt offerings in the house of the LORD continually all the days of Jehoiada.

[15]But Jehoiada grew old and full of days, and died; he was a hundred and thirty years old at his death. [16]And they buried him in the city of David among the kings, because he had done good in Israel, and toward God and his house.

---

on the cross: "Moreover, my brothers, you must not think that all those good men who suffered persecution at the hands of the wicked—including those who were sent to announce the coming of the Lord—were not members of Christ's body. Any man who belongs to the city of which Christ is the king must be a servant of Christ. That city runs from the blood of the innocent Abel to the blood of Zechariah. And on from there, from the blood of John [the Baptist], through that of the apostles and martyrs and all those who were faithful to Christ: these people together make up the city of which we speak" (St Augustine, *Enarrationes in Psalmos*, 61, 3).

atque miserunt ita, ut impleretur. [11]Cumque tempus esset, ut deferrent arcam ad magistratus regis per manus Levitarum et viderent multam esse pecuniam, ingrediebatur scriba regis et quem primus sacerdos constituerat, effundebantque pecuniam, quae erat in arca; porro arcam reportabant ad locum suum. Sicque faciebant per singula tempora, et congregata est infinita pecunia, [12]quam dederunt rex et Ioiada his, qui praeerant operibus domus Domini. At illi conducebant ex ea caesores lapidum et artifices operum singulorum, ut instaurarent domum Domini, fabros quoque ferri et aeris, ut domus Dei fulciretur. [13]Egeruntque operarii, et obducebatur cicatrix operi per manus eorum, ac suscitaverunt domum Domini in statum pristinum et firme eam stare fecerunt. [14]Cumque haec complessent, detulerunt coram rege et Ioiada reliquam partem pecuniae, de qua facta sunt vasa templi in ministerium et ad holocausta, phialae quoque et cetera vasa aurea et argentea. Et offerebantur holocausta in domo Domini iugiter cunctis diebus Ioiadae. [15]Senuit autem Ioiada plenus dierum et mortuus est cum centum triginta esset annorum. [16]Sepelieruntque eum in civitate David cum regibus, eo quod fecisset bonum in Israel

Joash's infidelity

[17]Now after the death of Jehoiada the princes of Judah came and did obeisance to the king; then the king hearkened to them. [18]And they forsook the house of the LORD, the God of their fathers, and served the Asherim and the idols. And wrath came upon Judah and Jerusalem for this their guilt. [19]Yet he sent prophets among them to bring them back to the LORD; these testified against them, but they would not give heed.

Ex 34:13
1 Kings 14:23
Mt 21:34

[20]Then the Spirit of God took possession of[n] Zechariah the son of Jehoiada the priest; and he stood above the people, and said to them, "Thus says God, 'Why do you transgress the commandments of the LORD, so that you cannot prosper? Because you have forsaken the LORD, he has forsaken you.'" [21]But they conspired against him, and by command of the king they stoned him with stones in the court of the house of the LORD. [22]Thus Joash the king did not remember the kindness which Jehoiada, Zechariah's father, had shown him, but killed his son. And when he was dying, he said, "May the LORD see and avenge!"

Mt 23:35
Lk 11:51
Heb 11:37

[23]At the end of the year the army of the Syrians came up against Joash. They came to Judah and Jerusalem, and destroyed all the princes of the people from among the people, and sent all their spoil to the king of Damascus. [24]Though the army of the Syrians had come with few men, the LORD delivered into their hand a very great army, because they had forsaken the LORD, the God of their fathers. Thus they executed judgment on Joash.

2 Kings 12:18–22
Deut 32:30

[25]When they had departed from him, leaving him severely wounded, his servants conspired against him because of the blood of the son[o] of Jehoiada the priest, and slew him on his bed. So he died; and they buried him in the city of David, but they did not

2 Kings 12:20,21

cum Deo et cum domo eius. [17]Postquam autem obiit Ioiada, ingressi sunt principes Iudae et adoraverunt regem, qui delinitus obsequiis eorum acquievit eis. [18]Et dereliquerunt templum Domini, Dei patrum suorum, servieruntque palis et sculptilibus, et facta est ira contra Iudam et Ierusalem propter hoc peccatum. [19]Mittebatque eis prophetas, ut reverterentur ad Dominum, quos protestantes illi audire nolebant. [20]Spiritus itaque Dei induit Zachariam filium Ioiadae sacerdotis; et stetit in conspectu populi et dixit eis: «Haec dicit Deus: Quare transgredimini praecepta Domini, quod vobis non proderit? Quia dereliquistis Dominum, ipse dereliquit vos». [21]Qui coniuraverunt adversus eum et lapidaverunt eum iuxta regis imperium in atrio domus Domini. [22]Et non est recordatus Ioas rex misericordiae, quam fecerat Ioiada pater illius secum, sed interfecit filium eius. Qui cum moreretur, ait: «Videat Dominus et requirat!». [23]Cumque evolutus esset annus, ascendit contra eum exercitus Syriae venitque in Iudam et Ierusalem et exterminaverunt cunctos principes populi atque universam praedam miserunt regi Damascum. [24]Et certe, cum permodicus venisset numerus Syrorum, tradidit Dominus manibus eorum exercitum magnum valde, eo quod reliquissent Dominum, Deum patrum suorum; in Ioas quoque ignominiosa exercuere iudicia. [25]Et abeuntes dimiserunt eum in languoribus magnis. Coniuraverunt autem contra eum servi sui in ultionem sanguinis filii Ioiadae sacerdotis et occiderunt eum in lectulo

n. Heb *clothed itself with* **o.** Gk Vg: Heb *sons*

bury him in the tombs of the kings. [26]Those who conspired against him were Zabad the son of Shime-ath the Ammonitess, and Jehozabad the son of Shimrith the Moabitess. [27]Accounts of his sons, and of the many oracles against him, and of the rebuilding[p] of the house of God are written in the Commentary on the Book of the Kings. And Amaziah his son reigned in his stead.

The reign of Amaziah

2 Kings 14:2–6

25 [1]Amaziah was twenty-five years old when he began to reign, and he reigned twenty-nine years in Jerusalem. His mother's name was Jeho-addan of Jerusalem. [2]And he did what was right in the eyes of the LORD, yet not with a blameless heart. [3]And as soon as the royal power was firmly in his hand he killed his servants who had slain the king his father. [4]But he did not put their children to death, according to what is written in the law, in the book of Moses, where the LORD commanded, "The fathers shall not be put to death for the children, or the children be put to death for the fathers; but every man shall die for his own sin."

Ezek 18:20
Deut 24:16

[5]Then Amaziah assembled the men of Judah, and set them by fathers' houses under commanders of thousands and of hundreds for all Judah and Benjamin. He mustered those twenty years old

Num 1:3

25:1–28. The reign of Amaziah also divides into two stages, the first being one of faithfulness and promise (vv. 1–13) and the second one of irreligion and, following on that, misfortune and defeat (vv. 14–24). In each stage a prophet intervenes to announce God's plan: in the first, the king listens to him (vv. 9–10), in the second he refuses to do so (v. 16). The entire account is a lesson about personal, immediate retribution; and in this case the king's decision not to put to death the children of his father's assassins stems from the principle that every man should pay for his own crimes, not for those of his forebears (v. 4). The words quoted in v. 4 are taken from Deuteronomy 24:16 where they refer to human justice.

Amaziah's death at the hands of conspirators (v. 27), like the earlier victory of the king of Israel (v. 22), are not accidents but punishments for the king's idolatry and infidelity.

suo, et mortuus est. Sepelieruntque eum in civitate David, sed non in sepulcris regum. [26]Insidiati vero sunt ei Zabad filius Semath Ammanitidis et Iozabad filius Semarith Moabitidis. [27]Porro de filiis eius, de summa tributi, quod impositum fuerat sub eo, et de instauratione domus Dei scriptum est in commentariis libri regum. Regnavitque Amasias filius eius pro eo. **[25]** [1]Viginti quinque annorum erat Amasias, cum regnare coepisset, et viginti novem annis regnavit in Ierusalem. Nomen matris eius Ioaden de Ierusalem. [2]Fecitque bonum in conspectu Domini, verumtamen non in corde perfecto. [3]Cumque roboratum sibi videret imperium, iugulavit servos suos, qui occiderant regem patrem suum, [4]sed filios eorum non interfecit, sicut scriptum est in libro legis Moysi, ubi praecepit Dominus dicens: «Non occidentur patres pro filiis neque filii pro patribus suis, sed unusquisque in suo peccato morietur». [5]Congregavit igitur Amasias Iudam et constituit eos per familias tribunosque et centuriones in universo

p. Heb *founding*

and upward, and found that they were three hundred thousand picked men, fit for war, able to handle spear and shield. [6]He hired also a hundred thousand mighty men of valour from Israel for a hundred talents of silver. [7]But a man of God came to him and said, "O king, do not let the army of Israel go with you, for the LORD is not with Israel, with all these Ephraimites. [8]But if you suppose that in this way you will be strong for war,[q] God will cast you down before the enemy; for God has power to help or to cast down." [9]And Amaziah said to the man of God, "But what shall we do about the hundred talents which I have given to the army of Israel?" The man of God answered, "The LORD is able to give you much more than this." [10]Then Amaziah discharged the army that had come to him from Ephraim, to go home again. And they became very angry with Judah, and returned home in fierce anger.

[11]But Amaziah took courage, and led out his people, and went to the Valley of Salt and smote ten thousand men of Seir. [12]The men of Judah captured another ten thousand alive, and took them to the top of a rock and threw them down from the top of the rock; and they were all dashed to pieces. [13]But the men of the army whom Amaziah sent back, not letting them go with him to battle, fell upon the cities of Judah, from Samaria to Beth-horon, and killed three thousand people in them, and took much spoil.

2 Kings 14:7

Amaziah punished for his infidelity

[14]After Amaziah came from the slaughter of the Edomites, he brought the gods of the men of Seir, and set them up as his gods, and worshipped them, making offerings to them. [15]Therefore the LORD was angry with Amaziah and sent to him a prophet, who said to him, "Why have you resorted to the gods of a people, which did

---

Iuda et Beniamin. Et recensuit a viginti annis sursum invenitque trecenta milia iuvenum, qui egrederentur ad pugnam et tenerent hastam et clipeum. [6]Mercede quoque conduxit de Israel centum milia robustorum centum talentis argenti. [7]Venit autem homo Dei ad illum et ait: «O rex, ne egrediatur tecum exercitus Israel; non est enim Dominus cum Israel, cunctis filiis Ephraim. [8]Quod si putas in robore exercitus bella consistere, superari te faciet Deus ab hostibus: Dei quippe est et adiuvare et in fugam vertere». [9]Dixitque Amasias ad hominem Dei: «Quid ergo fiet de centum talentis, quae dedi militibus Israel?». Et respondit ei homo Dei: «Habet Dominus, unde tibi dare possit multo his plura». [10]Separavit itaque Amasias exercitum, qui venerat ad eum ex Ephraim, ut reverteretur in locum suum; at illi contra Iudam vehementer irati reversi sunt in regionem suam. [11]Porro Amasias confidenter eduxit populum suum et abiit in vallem Salinarum percussitque filios Seir decem milia. [12]Et alia decem milia virorum ceperunt filii Iudae et adduxerunt ad praeruptum cuiusdam petrae praecipitaveruntque eos de summo in praeceps, qui universi crepuerunt. [13]At ille exercitus, quem remiserat Amasias, ne secum iret ad proelium, diffusus est in civitatibus Iudae a Samaria usque Bethoron et, interfectis tribus milibus, diripuit praedam magnam. [14]Amasias vero, post caedem Idumaeorum et allatos deos filiorum Seir, statuit illos in deos sibi et adorabat eos et illis adolebat. [15]Quam ob rem iratus Dominus contra Amasiam

q. Gk: Heb *But if you go, act, be strong for the battle*

not deliver their own people from your hand?" [16]But as he was speaking the king said to him, "Have we made you a royal counsellor? Stop! Why should you be put to death?" So the prophet stopped, but said, "I know that God has determined to destroy you, because you have done this and have not listened to my counsel."

2 Kings 14:8–14

Amaziah defeated by the king of Israel

[17]Then Amaziah king of Judah took counsel and sent to Joash the son of Jehoahaz, son of Jehu, king of Israel, saying, "Come, let us look one another in the face." [18]And Joash the king of Israel sent word to Amaziah king of Judah, "A thistle on Lebanon sent to a cedar on Lebanon, saying, 'Give your daughter to my son for a wife'; and a wild beast of Lebanon passed by and trampled down the thistle. [19]You say, 'See, I have smitten Edom,' and your heart has lifted you up in boastfulness. But now stay at home; why should you provoke trouble so that you fall, you and Judah with you?"

Judg 9:7–15

[20]But Amaziah would not listen; for it was of God, in order that he might give them into the hand of their enemies, because they had sought the gods of Edom. [21]So Joash king of Israel went up; and he and Amaziah king of Judah faced one another in battle at Beth-shemesh, which belongs to Judah. [22]And Judah was defeated by Israel, and every man fled to his home. [23]And Joash king of Israel captured Amaziah king of Judah, the son of Joash, son of Ahaziah, at Beth-shemesh, and brought him to Jerusalem, and broke down the wall of Jerusalem for four hundred cubits, from the Ephraim Gate to the Corner Gate. [24]And he seized all the gold and silver, and all the vessels that were found in the house of God, and Obed-edom with them; he seized also the treasuries of the king's house, and hostages, and he returned to Samaria.

1 Chron 26:15

---

misit ad illum prophetam, qui diceret ei: «Cur adorasti deos, qui non liberaverunt populum suum de manu tua?». [16]Cumque haec ille loqueretur, respondit ei: «Num consiliarium regis fecimus te? Quiesce! Cur interficiam te?». Discedensque propheta: «Sed scio, inquit, quod decrevit Deus occidere te, quia fecisti hoc et non acquievisti consilio meo». [17]Igitur Amasias rex Iudae, inito consilio, misit ad Ioas filium Ioachaz filii Iehu regem Israel dicens: «Veni, videamus nos mutuo!». [18]At ille remisit nuntium dicens: «Carduus, qui est in Libano, misit ad cedrum Libani dicens: "Da filiam tuam filio meo uxorem". Et ecce bestiae agri, quae erant in Libano, transierunt et conculcaverunt carduum. [19]Dixisti: "Percussi Edom!". Et idcirco erigitur cor tuum in superbiam. Sede in domo tua! Cur malum adversum te provocas, ut cadas et tu et Iuda tecum?». [20]Noluit audire Amasias, eo quod Domini esset voluntas, ut traderetur in manibus hostium propter cultum deorum Edom. [21]Ascendit igitur Ioas rex Israel, et mutuos sibi praebuere conspectus: ipse et Amasias rex Iudae in Bethsames Iudae. [22]Corruitque Iuda coram Israel et fugit in tabernacula sua. [23]Porro Amasiam regem Iudae filium Ioas filii Ioachaz cepit Ioas rex Israel in Bethsames et adduxit in Ierusalem destruxitque murum eius a porta Ephraim usque ad portam Anguli quadringentis cubitis. [24]Omne quoque aurum et argentum et universa vasa, quae repererat in domo Dei et apud Obededom in thesauris etiam domus regiae, necnon et obsides reduxit Samariam. [25]Vixit autem Amasias filius Ioas rex Iudae, postquam mortuus est Ioas filius Ioachaz rex Israel,

End of Amaziah's reign

2 Kings 14:17–20

[25]Amaziah the son of Joash king of Judah lived fifteen years after the death of Joash the son of Jehoahaz, king of Israel. [26]Now the rest of the deeds of Amaziah, from first to last, are they not written in the Book of the Kings of Judah and Israel? [27]From the time when he turned away from the LORD they made a conspiracy against him in Jerusalem, and he fled to Lachish. But they sent after him to Lachish, and slew him there. [28]And they brought him upon horses; and he was buried with his fathers in the city of David.

The reign of Uzziah

2 Kings 14:21–22

26 [1]And all the people of Judah took Uzziah, who was sixteen years old, and made him king instead of his father Amaziah. [2]He built Eloth and restored it to Judah, after the king slept with his fathers. [3]Uzziah was sixteen years old when he began to reign, and he reigned fifty-two years in Jerusalem. His mother's name was Jecoliah of Jerusalem. [4]And he did what was right in the eyes of the LORD, according to all that his father Amaziah had done. [5]He set himself to seek God in the days of Zechariah, who instructed him in the fear of God; and as long as he sought the LORD, God made him prosper.

2 Kings 15:2–4

2 Kings 24:2

[6]He went out and made war against the Philistines, and broke down the wall of Gath and the wall of Jabneh and the wall of Ashdod; and he built cities in the territory of Ashdod and

---

26:1–23. The same two-stage structure of fidelity/infidelity also applies to the account of the reign of Uzziah, again with the emphasis on personal retribution, both when the king goes along with God's plans and when he goes against them. However, this account has some details of special note.

The Uzziah of this passage (Ozias, in Greek) is the king usually referred to as Azariah in the book of Kings (cf. 2 Kings 14:21–22 and 15:1–3, 5–7; but Uzziah in 15:34), and he is the one attested to in the prophets (cf. Is 6:1) and in the New Testament (cf. Mt 1:8–9). Maybe Uzziah was a second name or a diminutive.

quindecim annis. [26]Reliqua vero gestorum Amasiae priorum et novissimorum scripta sunt in libro regum Iudae et Israel. [27]Qui postquam recessit a Domino, tetenderunt ei insidias in Ierusalem; cumque fugisset Lachis, miserunt post eum in Lachis et interfecerunt eum ibi. [28]Reportantesque super equos sepelierunt eum cum patribus suis in civitate David. **[26]** [1]Omnis autem populus Iudae Oziam annorum sedecim constituit regem pro patre suo Amasia. [2]Ipse reaedificavit Ailath et restituit eam dicioni Iudae, postquam dormivit rex cum patribus suis. [3]Sedecim annorum erat Ozias, cum regnare coepisset, et quinquaginta duobus annis regnavit in Ierusalem. Nomen matris eius Iechelia de Ierusalem. [4]Fecitque, quod erat rectum in oculis Domini iuxta omnia, quae fecerat Amasias pater eius. [5]Et exquisivit Deum in diebus Zachariae, qui erudivit eum in timore Dei; et quamdiu requirebat Dominum, eum prosperari fecit Deus. [6]Denique egressus est et pugnavit contra Philisthim et destruxit murum Geth et murum Iabniae murumque Azoti. Aedificavit quoque oppida in regione Azoti et Philisthim. [7]Et adiuvit eum Deus contra

elsewhere among the Philistines. [7]God helped him against the Philistines, and against the Arabs that dwelt in Gurbaal, and against the Me-unites. [8]The Ammonites paid tribute to Uzziah, and his fame spread even to the border of Egypt, for he became very strong. [9]Moreover Uzziah built towers in Jerusalem at the Corner Gate and at the Valley Gate and at the Angle, and fortified them. [10]And he built towers in the wilderness, and hewed out many cisterns, for he had large herds, both in the Shephelah and in the plain, and he had farmers and vinedressers in the hills and in the fertile lands, for he loved the soil. [11]Moreover Uzziah had an army of soldiers, fit for war, in divisions according to the numbers in the muster made by Je-iel the secretary and Ma-aseiah the officer, under the direction of Hananiah, one of the king's commanders. [12]The whole number of the heads of fathers' houses of mighty men of valour was two thousand six hundred. [13]Under their command was an army of three hundred and seven thousand five hundred,

2 Chron 20:1

1 Chron 27:25–31

The buildings constructed, as also the victories over the Philistines and the Arabs and the strength of the army, are depicted as rewards for the king's fidelity to the advice of a man about whom all we know is that his name was Zechariah (v. 5), a different person from that mentioned in 22:20ff. Among the new buildings are the towers and cisterns in the wilderness (v. 10), probably the foundations of the later buildings of Qumran.

In line with the Chronicler's general message, emphasis is put on the importance of the priests and the temple: Zechariah educated the king in the fear of the Lord during the earlier part of his reign (v. 5); and the priest Azariah upbraided him for his infidelity in the latter part (vv. 17–18). The temple was the scenario for divine punishment, because this worst of all unclean diseases, leprosy, showed itself on the king in the temple and was a punishment for his having taken over temple functions which priests alone had the right to exercise.

The words "as long as he sought the Lord, God made him prosper" (v. 5) show how God rewards fidelity. When a person strives to do the will of God, the Lord will not fail to reward him: "The more generous you are for God, the happier you will be" (St J. Escrivá, *Furrow*, 18).

Philisthim et contra Arabas, qui habitabant in Gurbaal, et contra Meunitas. [8]Pendebantque Ammonitae munera Oziae; et divulgatum est nomen eius usque ad introitum Aegypti, quia confortatus est in excelsum. [9]Aedificavitque Ozias turres in Ierusalem super portam Anguli et super portam Vallis et super Angulum firmavitque eas. [10]Exstruxit etiam turres in solitudine et fodit cisternas plurimas, eo quod haberet multa pecora tam in Sephela quam in planitie; agricolas quoque habuit et vinitores in montibus et in campis fertilibus; erat quippe homo agriculturae deditus. [11]Fuit autem exercitus bellatorum eius, qui procedebant ad proelia in turmis secundum numerum census per manum Iehiel scribae Maasiaeque praefecti sub manu Hananiae, qui erat de ducibus regis. [12]Omnisque numerus principum per familias virorum fortium duorum milium sescentorum. [13]Et sub eis universus exercitus trecentorum et septem milium quingentorum, qui erant apti ad bella, ut pro rege contra adversarios dimicarent. [14]Praeparavit quoque eis Ozias, id est cuncto exercitui, clipeos et hastas et galeas et loricas arcusque et fundas ad

who could make war with mighty power, to help the king against the enemy. [14]And Uzziah prepared for all the army shields, spears, helmets, coats of mail, bows, and stones for slinging. [15]In Jerusalem he made engines, invented by skilful men, to be on the towers and the corners, to shoot arrows and great stones. And his fame spread far, for he was marvellously helped, till he was strong.

Uzziah punished for his infidelity

[16]But when he was strong he grew proud, to his destruction. For he was false to the LORD his God, and entered the temple of the LORD to burn incense on the altar of incense. [17]But Azariah the priest went in after him, with eighty priests of the LORD who were men of valour; [18]and they withstood King Uzziah, and said to him, "It is not for you, Uzziah, to burn incense to the LORD, but for the priests the sons of Aaron, who are consecrated to burn incense. Go out of the sanctuary; for you have done wrong, and it will bring you no honour from the LORD God." [19]Then Uzziah was angry. Now he had a censer in his hand to burn incense, and when he became angry with the priests leprosy broke out on his forehead, in the presence of the priests in the house of the LORD, by the altar of incense. [20]And Azariah the chief priest, and all the priests, looked at him, and behold, he was leprous in his forehead! And they thrust him out quickly, and he himself hastened to go out, because the LORD had smitten him. [21]And King Uzziah was a leper to the day of his death, and being a leper dwelt in a separate house, for he was excluded from the house of the LORD. And Jotham his son was over the king's household, governing the people of the land.

[22]Now the rest of the acts of Uzziah, from first to last, Isaiah the prophet the son of Amoz wrote. [23]And Uzziah slept with his

Num 16:40; 18:7

Num 12:10

Lev 13:46
Num 19:20
2 Kings 15:5–7

Is 1:1; 6:1

iaciendos lapides. [15]Et fecit in Ierusalem machinas excogitatas arte, quas in turribus collocavit et in angulis murorum, ut mitterent sagittas et saxa grandia; egressumque est nomen eius procul, eo quod mirabiliter auxiliaretur ei Dominus et corroborasset illum. [16]Sed, cum roboratus esset, elevatum est cor eius in interitum suum et deliquit contra Dominum Deum suum; ingressusque templum Domini adolere voluit incensum super altare thymiamatis. [17]Statimque ingressus post eum Azarias sacerdos et cum eo sacerdotes Domini octoginta viri fortissimi; [18]restiterunt regi atque dixerunt: «Non est tui officii, Ozia, ut adoleas incensum Domino, sed sacerdotum, hoc est filiorum Aaron, qui consecrati sunt ad huiuscemodi ministerium. Egredere de sanctuario, quia praevaricatus es; et non reputabitur tibi in gloriam hoc a Domino Deo». [19]Iratusque est Ozias et tenens in manu turibulum, ut adoleret incensum, minabatur sacerdotibus. Statimque orta est lepra in fronte eius coram sacerdotibus in domo Domini super altare thymiamatis. [20]Cumque respexisset eum Azarias pontifex et omnes reliqui sacerdotes, viderunt lepram in fronte eius et festinato expulerunt eum; sed et ipse acceleravit egredi, eo quod malo afflixisset eum Dominus. [21]Fuit igitur Ozias rex leprosus usque ad diem mortis suae et habitavit in domo separata plenus lepra, eo quod abscissus fuerat de domo Domini. Porro Ioatham filius eius rexit domum regis et iudicabat populum terrae. [22]Reliqua autem gestorum Oziae priorum et novissimorum scripsit Isaias filius Amos propheta. [23]Dormivitque Ozias cum patribus suis, et sepelierunt eum in agro regalium

fathers, and they buried him with his fathers in the burial field which belonged to the kings, for they said, "He is a leper." And Jotham his son reigned in his stead.

2 Kings 15:32–35

The reign of Jotham

27 [1]Jotham was twenty-five years old when he began to reign, and he reigned sixteen years in Jerusalem. His mother's name was Jerushah the daughter of Zadok. [2]And he did what was right in the eyes of the LORD according to all that his father Uzziah had done—only he did not invade the temple of the LORD. But the people still followed corrupt practices. [3]He built the upper gate of the house of the LORD, and did much building on the wall of Ophel. [4]Moreover he built cities in the hill country of Judah, and forts and towers on the wooded hills. [5]He fought with the king of the Ammonites and prevailed against them. And the Ammonites gave him that year a hundred talents of silver, and ten thousand cors of wheat and ten thousand of barley. The Ammonites paid him the same amount in the second and the third years. [6]So Jotham became mighty, because he ordered his ways before the LORD his God. [7]Now the rest of the acts of Jotham, and all his wars, and his ways, behold, they are written in the Book of the Kings of Israel and Judah. [8]He was twenty-five years old when he began to reign, and he reigned sixteen years in Jerusalem. [9]And Jotham slept with his fathers, and they buried him in the city of David; and Ahaz his son reigned in his stead.

2 Kings 15:36–38

27:1–9. Jotham was faithful and devout to the end of his days (cf. 2 Kings 15:32–38). The only thing that this book adds (vv. 4–6) serves to show that this king's building works and acquisition of territory were due to the fact that "he ordered his ways before the Lord his God" (v. 6).

sepulcrorum, eo quod dicebant: «Erat leprosus». Regnavitque Ioatham filius eius pro eo. **[27]** [1]Viginti quinque annorum erat Ioatham, cum regnare coepisset, et sedecim annis regnavit in Ierusalem. Nomen matris eius Ierusa filia Sadoc. [2]Fecitque, quod rectum erat coram Domino iuxta omnia, quae fecerat Ozias pater suus, excepto quod non est ingressus templum Domini, et adhuc populus delinquebat. [3]Ipse aedificavit portam domus Domini Superiorem et in muro Ophel multa construxit. [4]Urbes quoque aedificavit in montibus Iudae et in saltibus castella et turres. [5]Ipse pugnavit contra regem filiorum Ammon et vicit eos, dederuntque ei filii Ammon in anno illo centum talenta argenti et decem milia choros tritici ac totidem choros hordei; haec ei praebuerunt filii Ammon etiam in anno secundo et tertio. [6]Corroboratusque est Ioatham, eo quod direxisset vias suas coram Domino Deo suo. [7]Reliqua autem gestorum Ioatham et omnes pugnae eius et viae scriptae sunt in libro regum Israel et Iudae. [8]Viginti quinque annorum erat, cum regnare coepisset, et sedecim annis regnavit in Ierusalem. [9]Dormivitque Ioatham cum patribus suis, et sepelierunt eum in civitate David; et regnavit Achaz filius eius pro eo.

The reign of Ahaz

2 Kings 16:2–4

28 [1]Ahaz was twenty years old when he began to reign, and he reigned sixteen years in Jerusalem. And he did not do what was right in the eyes of the LORD, like his father David, [2]but walked in the ways of the kings of Israel. He even made molten images for the Baals; [3]and he burned incense in the valley of the son of Hinnom, and burned his sons as an offering, according to the abominable practises of the nations whom the LORD drove out before the people of Israel. [4]And he sacrificed and burned incense on the high places, and on the hills, and under every green tree.

Lev 18:21

War against Syria and Ephraim

2 Kings 16
Is 7–9

[5]Therefore the LORD his God gave him into the hand of the king of Syria, who defeated him and took captive a great number of his people and brought them to Damascus. He was also given into the hand of the king of Israel, who defeated him with great slaughter.

[6]For Pekah the son of Remaliah slew a hundred and twenty thousand in Judah in one day, all of them men of valour, because they had forsaken the LORD, the God of their fathers. [7]And Zichri, a mighty man of Ephraim, slew Ma-aseiah the king's son and Azrikam the commander of the palace and Elkanah the next in authority to the king.

[8]The men of Israel took captive two hundred thousand of their kinsfolk, women, sons, and daughters; they also took much spoil from them and brought the spoil to Samaria. [9]But a prophet of the

---

28:1–27. Ahaz was very much the opposite of his devout grandfather Uzziah: his entire reign was plagued with idolatry and irreligion; every battle he entered ended in defeat. But his worst sin and the one for which the Chronicler most severely denounces him was his profanation of the temple and its artefacts (vv. 20–24). The account given here of the war against Syria and Ephraim (vv. 5–15) has things not to be found in Kings (2 Kings 16:5–9) or in the book of Isaiah (Is 7:1–8, 23). Here, in order to punish Ahaz (v. 5) the Lord decides that he will suffer defeat, first at the hands of the Syrians and then by the Ephraimites (vv. 5–8). In this account intervention

[28] [1]Viginti annorum erat Achaz, cum regnare coepisset, et sedecim annis regnavit in Ierusalem. Non fecit rectum in conspectu Domini sicut David pater eius, [2]sed ambulavit in viis regum Israel. Insuper et simulacra fudit Baalim. [3]Ipse est, qui adolevit in valle filii Ennom et lustravit filios suos in igne iuxta abominationes gentium, quas expulit Dominus coram filiis Israel. [4]Sacrificabat quoque et thymiama succendebat in excelsis et in collibus et sub omni ligno frondoso. [5]Tradiditque eum Dominus Deus eius in manu regis Syriae, qui percussit eum multosque captivos de eo cepit et adduxit in Damascum. Manibus quoque regis Israel traditus est et percussus plaga grandi. [6]Occidit enim Phacee filius Romeliae de Iuda centum viginti milia in die uno, omnes viros bellatores, eo quod reliquissent Dominum, Deum patrum suorum. [7]Eodem tempore occidit Zechri vir potens ex Ephraim Maasiam filium regis et Ezricam praefectum domus, Elcanam quoque secundum a rege. [8]Ceperuntque filii Israel de fratribus suis ducenta milia mulierum, puerorum et puellarum, et infinitam praedam pertuleruntque eam in Samariam. [9]Erat

LORD was there, whose name was Oded; and he went out to meet the army that came to Samaria, and said to them, "Behold, because the LORD, the God of your fathers, was angry with Judah, he gave them into your hand, but you have slain them in a rage which has reached up to heaven. [10]And now you intend to subjugate the people of Judah and Jerusalem, male and female, as your slaves. Have you not sins of your own against the LORD your God? [11]Now hear me, and send back the captives from your kinsfolk whom you have taken, for the fierce wrath of the LORD is upon you." [12]Certain chiefs also of the men of Ephraim, Azariah the son of Johanan, Berechiah the son of Meshillemoth, Jehizkiah the son of Shallum, and Amasa the son of Hadlai, stood up against those who were coming from the war, [13]and said to them, "You shall not bring the captives in here, for you propose to bring upon us guilt against the LORD in addition to our present sins and guilt. For our guilt is already great, and there is fierce wrath against Israel." [14]So the armed men left the captives and the spoil before the princes and all the assembly. [15]And the men who have been mentioned by name

---

by a prophet and help from the people of the North (vv. 9–15) have the effect of assuaging the defeat; there was no terrible upheaval. All this goes to show God's loving-kindness towards the Jews and the conviction that they will never become the slaves of anyone, despite the fact that their kings are irreligious and deserving of severe punishment.

Ahaz' alliance with the Assyrians must have been a most humiliating experience (v. 19), because instead of helping him they set siege to Jerusalem and extorted huge tributes. The king himself was left unharmed, but such shameful idolatry took place in the temple (v. 23) and such dire profanation was done to it that it had to be closed down (v. 24).

In Chronicles' religious interpretation of history, this is the worst moment of all because it endangered the Davidic dynasty and the survival of the temple, that is, the very identity of the people.

In v. 19, Ahaz is called "king of Israel", though the Greek corrects this to "king of Judah". The Chronicler is more intent on depicting all Israel as one kingdom than on historical accuracy.

autem ibi propheta Domini nomine Oded, qui egressus obviam exercitui venienti in Samariam dixit eis: «Ecce, iratus Dominus, Deus patrum vestrorum, contra Iudam tradidit eos in manibus vestris, et occidistis eos atrociter, ita ut ad caelum pertingeret vestra crudelitas. [10]Insuper filios Iudae et Ierusalem vultis vobis subicere in servos et ancillas. Attamen nonne vos ipsi estis in culpa coram Domino Deo vestro? [11]Audite ergo consilium meum et reducite captivos, quos adduxistis de fratribus vestris, quia magnus furor Domini imminet vobis». [12]Steterunt itaque viri de principibus filiorum Ephraim, Azarias filius Iohanan, Barachias filius Mosollamoth, Ezechias filius Sellum et Amasa filius Adali, contra eos, qui veniebant de proelio, [13]et dixerunt eis: «Non introducetis huc captivos, quia ad culpam coram Domino, quae iam est super nos, vultis adicere super peccata nostra et culpam nostram. Grandis quippe culpa est nobis, et ira furoris Domini super Israel». [14]Dimiseruntque viri bellatores captivos et universa, quae ceperant, coram principibus et omni multitudine. [15]Et surrexerunt viri nominatim designati et

rose and took the captives, and with the spoil they clothed all that were naked among them; they clothed them, gave them sandals, provided them with food and drink, and anointed them; and carrying all the feeble among them on asses, they brought them to their kinsfolk at Jericho, the city of palm trees. Then they returned to Samaria.

Lk 10:25–37

Attack by the king of Assyria

[16]At that time King Ahaz sent to the king[r] of Assyria for help. [17]For the Edomites had again invaded and defeated Judah, and carried away captives. [18]And the Philistines had made raids on the cities in the Shephelah and the Negeb of Judah, and had taken Beth-shemesh, Aijalon, Gederoth, Soco with its villages, Timnah with its villages, and Gimzo with its villages; and they settled there. [19]For the LORD brought Judah low because of Ahaz king of Israel, for he had dealt wantonly in Judah and had been faithless to the LORD. [20]So Tilgath-pilneser king of Assyria came against him, and afflicted him instead of strengthening him. [21]For Ahaz took from the house of the LORD and the house of the king and of the princes, and gave tribute to the king of Assyria; but it did not help him.

2 Kings 16:7
Is 7–8

2 Kings 16:8

[22]In the time of his distress he became yet more faithless to the LORD—this same King Ahaz. [23]For he sacrificed to the gods of Damascus which had defeated him, and said, "Because the gods of the kings of Syria helped them, I will sacrifice to them that they may help me." But they were the ruin of him, and of all Israel. [24]And Ahaz gathered together the vessels of the house of God and cut in pieces the vessels of the house of God, and he shut up the doors of the house of the LORD; and he made himself altars in every

2 Kings 16:12–13
Is 10:20

2 Kings 16:17

---

confortaverunt captivos omnesque, qui nudi erant, vestierunt de spoliis. Cumque vestissent eos et calceassent et refecissent cibo ac potu unxissentque, deduxerunt eos sollicite, et quidem omnes vacillantes in iumentis, et adduxerunt Iericho civitatem Palmarum ad fratres eorum. Ipsique reversi sunt Samariam. [16]Tempore illo misit rex Achaz ad regem Assyriorum auxilium postulans. [17]Venerunt enim et Idumaei et percusserunt Iudam et ceperunt captivos. [18]Philisthim quoque diffusi sunt per urbes Sephelae et Nageb Iudae ceperuntque Bethsames et Aialon et Gederoth, Socho quoque cum viculis eius et Thamnan et Gamzo cum viculis earum et habitaverunt in eis. [19]Humiliaverat enim Dominus Iudam propter Achaz regem Israel, eo quod relaxasset ei frenum et contemptui habuisset Dominum. [20]Venitque contra eum Theglathphalasar rex Assyriorum, qui afflixit eum, non autem confortavit. [21]Achaz enim, spoliata domo Domini et domo regis et principum, dedit regi Assyriorum munera, et tamen nihil ei profuit. [22]Insuper et in tempore angustiae suae auxit contemptum in Dominum. Ipse rex Achaz [23]immolavit diis Damasci victimas percussoribus suis et dixit: «Dii regum Syriae auxiliantur eis; quos ego placabo hostiis, et aderunt mihi», cum e contrario ipsi fuerint ruina ei et universo Israel. [24]Direptis itaque Achaz omnibus vasis domus Dei atque confractis, clausit ianuas templi Dei et fecit sibi altaria in

r. Gk Syr Vg Compare 2 Kings 16:7: Heb *kings*

corner of Jerusalem. [25]In every city of Judah he made high places to burn incense to other gods, provoking to anger the LORD, the God of his fathers. [26]Now the rest of his acts and all his ways, from first to last, behold, they are written in the Book of the Kings of Judah and Israel. [27]And Ahaz slept with his fathers, and they buried him in the city, in Jerusalem, for they did not bring him into the tombs of the kings of Israel. And Hezekiah his son reigned in his stead.

2 Kings 16:17–20

5. THE GREAT REFORMS*

2 Kings 18:1–3

The reign of Hezekiah

29 [1]Hezekiah began to reign when he was twenty-five years old, and he reigned twenty-nine years in Jerusalem. His mother's name was Abijah the daughter of Zechariah. [2]And he did what was right in the eyes of the LORD, according to all that David his father had done.

2 Chron 28:24

Purification of the temple

[3]In the first year of his reign, in the first month, he opened the doors of the house of the LORD, and repaired them. [4]He brought in the priests and the Levites, and assembled them in the square on the east, [5]and said to them, "Hear me, Levites! Now sanctify yourselves, and sanctify the house of the LORD, the God of your

---

***29:1—32:32.** Hezekiah "did what was right in the eyes of the Lord, according to all that David his father had done"(v. 2). This very positive assessment of Hezekiah sets the tone for the extensive, four-chapter account that follows. With David as his model, Hezekiah will restore to Jerusalem its prestige as political and religious capital and will strive to unite the two kingdoms of Judah and Israel, offering a welcome to those groups that move south (30:25); he will successfully endeavour to get all the Israelites (literally, "all Israel": 3:1) to resolve on dismantling the high places right across the land; and he will convoke "all Israel" (30:5) to celebrate Passover at Jerusalem.

universis angulis Ierusalem. [25]In singulis quoque urbibus Iudae exstruxit excelsa ad adolendum diis alienis atque ad iracundiam provocavit Dominum, Deum patrum suorum. [26]Reliqua autem gestorum eius et omnium operum suorum priorum et novissimorum scripta sunt in libro regum Iudae et Israel. [27]Dormivitque Achaz cum patribus suis, et sepelierunt eum in civitate Ierusalem; non autem posuerunt eum in sepulcra regum Israel. Regnavitque Ezechias filius eius pro eo. **[29]** [1]Igitur Ezechias regnare coepit, cum viginti quinque esset annorum, et viginti novem annis regnavit in Ierusalem. Nomen matris eius Abi filia Zachariae. [2]Fecitque, quod erat placitum in conspectu Domini, iuxta omnia, quae fecerat David pater eius. [3]Ipse anno et mense primo regni sui aperuit valvas domus Domini et instauravit eas. [4]Adduxitque sacerdotes atque Levitas et congregavit eos in plateam orientalem [5]dixitque ad eos: «Audite me, Levitae! Nunc sanctificamini; mundate domum Domini, Dei patrum vestrorum, et auferte

fathers, and carry out the filth from the holy place. [6]For our fathers have been unfaithful and have done what was evil in the sight of the LORD our God; they have forsaken him, and have turned away their faces from the habitation of the LORD, and turned their backs. [7]They also shut the doors of the vestibule and put out the lamps, and have not burned incense or offered burnt offerings in the holy place to the God of Israel. [8]Therefore the wrath of the LORD came on Judah and Jerusalem, and he has made them an object of horror, of astonishment, and of hissing, as you see with your own eyes. [9]For lo, our fathers have fallen by the sword and our sons and our daughters and our wives are in captivity for this. [10]Now it is in my heart to make a covenant with the LORD, the God of Israel, that his fierce anger may turn away from us. [11]My sons, do not now be negligent, for the LORD has chosen you to stand in his presence, to minister to him, and to be his ministers and burn incense to him."

Lev 26:32
Deut 28:25
Jer 25:18

Num 3:6; 8:14; 18:14

[12]Then the Levites arose, Mahath the son of Amasai, and Joel the son of Azariah, of the sons of the Kohathites; and of the sons of Merari, Kish the son of Abdi, and Azariah the son of Jehallelel; and of the Gershonites, Joah the son of Zimmah, and Eden the son

---

As a devout and upright king he set in train a religious reform which covered all the main aspects of worship—the re-opening and cleansing of the temple (29:3–19), the re-establishment of the liturgy (29:20–36), a national celebration of Passover (30:1–27), and a reorganization of priestly rites and services at the temple (31:2–9). Hezekiah was one of the most remarkable kings of Judah, and the account of his reign ends with an assessment similar to that given at the start: everything he did, "seeking his God, he did with all his heart, and prospered" (31:21).

In the last scene of his life we can see how bravely (and religiously) he reacted to the Assyrian invasion (39:1–23), and the humility with which he prayed on behalf of his people (32:24–26).

These were years of great prosperity, marked by political and religious achievements, which the Chronicler interprets as God's blessing on the king's exemplary conduct.

29:3–36. The account of the religious reform (not to be found in the book of Kings) confirms the enormous influ-

omnem immunditiam de sanctuario. [6]Peccaverunt patres nostri et fecerunt malum in conspectu Domini Dei nostri derelinquentes eum; averterunt facies suas a tabernaculo Domini et praebuerunt dorsum. [7]Insuper clauserunt ostia, quae erant in porticu, et exstinxerunt lucernas incensumque non adoleverunt et holocausta non obtulerunt in sanctuario Deo Israel. [8]Concitatus est itaque furor Domini super Iudam et Ierusalem; tradiditque eos in commotionem et in stuporem et in sibilum, sicut ipsi cernitis oculis vestris. [9]En, corruerunt patres nostri gladiis, filii nostri et filiae nostrae et coniuges captivae ductae sunt propter hoc scelus. [10]Nunc igitur placet mihi, ut ineam foedus cum Domino, Deo Israel, et avertat a nobis furorem irae suae. [11]Filii mei, nolite neglegere; vos enim elegit Dominus, ut stetis coram eo et ministretis illi colatisque eum et adoleatis». [12]Surrexerunt ergo Levitae, Mahath filius Amasai et Ioel filius Azariae de filiis Caath; porro de filiis Merari Cis filius Abdi et Azarias filius Iallelel; de filiis autem

of Joah; [13]and of the sons of Elizaphan, Shimri and Jeuel; and of the sons of Asaph, Zechariah and Mattaniah; [14]and of the sons of Heman, Jehuel and Shime-i; and of the sons of Jeduthun, Shemaiah and Uzziel. [15]They gathered their brethren, and sanctified themselves, and went in as the king had commanded, by the words of the LORD, to cleanse the house. [16]The priests went into the inner part of the house of the LORD to cleanse it, and they brought out all the uncleanness that they found in the temple of the LORD into the court of the house of the LORD; and the Levites took it and carried it out to the brook Kidron. [17]They began to sanctify on the first day of the first month, and on the eighth day of the month they came to the vestibule of the LORD; then for eight days they sanctified the house of the LORD, and on the sixteenth day of the first month they finished. [18]Then they went in to Hezekiah the king and said, "We

2 Chron 15:16

ence priests and Levites had at the time when this book was being assembled. The account begins (v. 3) by making it clear that the temple and its gates are the same as were there before, in order to show continuity with the temple of Solomon.

The sanctification of persons and of the temple and its furnishings is carried out in accordance with the regulations given in Leviticus 13:1—16:34.

Hezekiah's speech (vv. 5–11) touches on all the main themes in the preaching of the prophets—the unfaithfulness of forefathers, the punishment that that deserved, a call to conversion, and ratification of the Covenant. This teaching will inspire the reform that Hezekiah institutes.

The elaborate sacrifices and the splendour of the songs and purification rites prefigure the liturgy of the Church and its sacraments: "The Chosen People received from God distinctive signs and symbols that marked its liturgical life. These are no longer solely celebrations of cosmic cycles and social gestures, but signs of the covenant, symbols of God's mighty deeds for his people. Among these liturgical signs from the Old Covenant are circumcision, anointing and consecration of kings and priests, laying on of hands, sacrifices, and, above all, the Passover. The Church sees in these signs a prefiguring of the sacraments of the New Covenant" (*Catechism of the Catholic Church*, 1150). As regards Vatican II's teaching on the role of music in the liturgy, see the quotation in the note on 1 Chronicles 25:1–31.

Gerson Ioah filius Zimma et Eden filius Ioah; [13]at vero de filiis Elisaphan Semri et Iehiel; de filiis quoque Asaph Zacharias et Matthanias; [14]necnon de filiis Heman Iahiel et Semei; sed et de filiis Idithun Semeias et Oziel. [15]Congregaveruntque fratres suos et sanctificati sunt et ingressi iuxta mandatum regis et imperium Domini, ut expiarent domum Dei. [16]Sacerdotes quoque ingressi intra templum Domini, ut mundarent illud, extulerunt omnem immunditiam, quam intro reppererant in vestibulum domus Domini, quam tulerunt Levitae et asportaverunt ad torrentem Cedron foras. [17]Coeperunt autem prima die mensis primi sanctificare et in die octava eiusdem mensis ingressi sunt porticum templi Domini et sanctificaverunt templum Domini diebus octo; et in die sexta decima mensis eiusdem, quod coeperant, impleverunt. [18]Ingressi quoque sunt ad Ezechiam regem et dixerunt ei: «Mundavimus omnem domum

have cleansed all the house of the LORD, the altar of burnt offering and all its utensils, and the table for the showbread and all its utensils. [19]All the utensils which King Ahaz discarded in his reign when he was faithless, we have made ready and sanctified; and behold, they are before the altar of the LORD."

Re-establishment of religious worship

[20]Then Hezekiah the king rose early and gathered the officials of the city, and went up to the house of the LORD. [21]And they brought seven bulls, seven rams, seven lambs, and seven he-goats for a sin offering for the kingdom and for the sanctuary and for Judah. And he commanded the priests the sons of Aaron to offer them on the altar of the LORD. [22]So they killed the bulls, and the priests received the blood and threw it against the altar; and they killed the rams and their blood was thrown against the altar; and they killed the lambs and their blood was thrown against the altar.

Lev 8:14—19:24

[23]Then the he-goats for the sin offering were brought to the king and the assembly, and they laid their hands upon them, [24]and the priests killed them and made a sin offering with their blood on the altar, to make atonement for all Israel. For the king commanded that the burnt offering and the sin offering should be made for all Israel.

Lev 4:23–24

[25]And he stationed the Levites in the house of the LORD with cymbals, harps, and lyres, according to the commandment of David and of Gad the king's seer and of Nathan the prophet; for the commandment was from the LORD through his prophets. [26]The Levites stood with the instruments of David, and the priests with the trumpets. [27]Then Hezekiah commanded that the burnt offering be offered on the altar. And when the burnt offering began, the song to the LORD began also, and the trumpets, accompanied by the

---

Domini et altare holocausti vasaque eius necnon et mensam propositionis cum omnibus vasis suis [19]cunctamque templi supellectilem, quam removerat rex Achaz in regno suo in praevaricatione sua, restituimus et sanctificavimus. Ecce exposita sunt omnia coram altari Domini». [20]Consurgensque diluculo Ezechias rex adunavit principes civitatis et ascendit domum Domini. [21]Attuleruntque simul tauros septem, arietes septem, agnos septem et hircos septem pro peccato, pro regno, pro sanctuario, pro Iuda; dixit quoque sacerdotibus filiis Aaron, ut offerrent super altare Domini. [22]Mactaverunt igitur tauros et susceperunt sacerdotes sanguinem et fuderunt illum super altare; mactaverunt etiam arietes et illorum sanguinem super altare fuderunt; immolaverunt agnos et fuderunt super altare sanguinem. [23]Applicaverunt hircos pro peccato coram rege et universa multitudine imposueruntque manus suas super eos, [24]et immolaverunt illos sacerdotes et asperserunt sanguinem eorum super altare pro piaculo universi Israelis; pro omni quippe Israel praeceperat rex, ut holocaustum fieret et pro peccato. [25]Constituit quoque Levitas in domo Domini cum cymbalis et psalteriis et citharis secundum dispositionem David et Gad videntis regis et Nathan prophetae; siquidem Domini praeceptum fuit per manum prophetarum eius. [26]Steteruntque Levitae tenentes organa David et sacerdotes tubas. [27]Et iussit Ezechias, ut offerrent holocaustum super altare; cumque offerretur holocaustum, coeperunt laudes

instruments of David king of Israel. [28]The whole assembly worshipped, and the singers sang, and the trumpeters sounded; all this continued until the burnt offering was finished. [29]When the offering was finished, the king and all who were present with him bowed themselves and worshipped. [30]And Hezekiah the king and the princes commanded the Levites to sing praises to the LORD with the words of David and of Asaph the seer. And they sang praises with gladness, and they bowed down and worshipped.

Ex 28:41
Lev 7:11–15
2 Chron 13:9
Heb 13:15

[31]Then Hezekiah said, "You have now consecrated yourselves to the LORD; come near, bring sacrifices and thank offerings to the house of the LORD." And the assembly brought sacrifices and thank offerings; and all who were of a willing heart brought burnt offerings. [32]The number of the burnt offerings which the assembly brought was seventy bulls, a hundred rams, and two hundred lambs; all these were for a burnt offering to the LORD. [33]And the consecrated offerings were six hundred bulls and three thousand sheep. [34]But the priests were too few and could not flay all the burnt offerings, so until other priests had sanctified themselves their brethren the Levites helped them, until the work was finished—for the Levites were more upright in heart than the priests in sanctifying themselves. [35]Besides the great number of burnt offerings there was the fat of the peace offerings, and there were the libations for the burnt offerings. Thus the service of the house of the LORD was restored. [36]And Hezekiah and all the people rejoiced because of what God had done for the people; for the thing came about suddenly.

1 Chron 15:12

Lev 3:1,16
Num 15:5–7

---

canere Domino et clangere tubis atque in diversis organis David regis Israel concrepare. [28]Omni autem turba adorante, cantores et ii, qui tenebant tubas, erant in officio suo, donec compleretur holocaustum. [29]Cumque finita esset oblatio, incurvatus est rex et omnes, qui erant cum eo, et adoraverunt. [30]Praecepitque Ezechias et principes Levitis, ut laudarent Dominum verbis David et Asaph videntis; qui laudaverunt eum magna laetitia et curvato genu adoraverunt. [31]Ezechias autem etiam haec addidit: «Nunc, impletis manibus vestris Domino, accedite et afferte victimas et sacrificia pro gratiarum actione in domo Domini». Attulit ergo universa multitudo hostias et sacrificia pro gratiarum actione et omnis voluntarius et proni animi holocausta. [32]Porro numerus holocaustorum, quae attulit multitudo, hic fuit: tauros septuaginta, arietes centum, agnos ducentos, in holocaustum Domino omnia haec. [33]Sanctificaveruntque Domino boves sescentos et oves tria milia. [34]Sacerdotes vero pauci erant nec poterant sufficere, ut pelles holocaustorum detraherent; unde et Levitae fratres eorum adiuverunt eos, donec impleretur opus et sanctificarentur sacerdotes; Levitae quippe recti corde, ut sanctificarentur magis quam sacerdotes. [35]Fuerunt igitur holocausta plurima, adipes pacificorum et libamina, quae pertinebant ad holocausta. Restitutus est ita cultus domus Domini. [36]Laetatusque est Ezechias et omnis populus de eo quod paravit Dominus populo; repente quippe hoc factum est.

Celebration of the Passover

30 [1]Hezekiah sent to all Israel and Judah, and wrote letters also to Ephraim and Manasseh, that they should come to the house of the LORD at Jerusalem, to keep the passover* to the LORD the God of Israel. [2]For the king and his princes and all the assembly in Jerusalem had taken counsel to keep the passover in the second month—[3]for they could not keep it in its time because the priests had not sanctified themselves in sufficient number, nor had the people assembled in Jerusalem—[4]and the plan seemed right to the king and all the assembly. [5]So they decreed to make a proclamation throughout all Israel, from Beer-sheba to Dan, that the people should come and keep the passover to the LORD the God of Israel, at Jerusalem; for they had not kept it in great numbers as prescribed. [6]So couriers went throughout all Israel and Judah with letters from the king and his princes, as the king had commanded, saying, "O people of Israel, return to the LORD, the God of Abraham, Isaac, and Israel, that he may turn again to the remnant of you who have escaped from the hand of the kings of Assyria. [7]Do not be like your fathers and your brethren, who were faithless

Ex 12:1

Ex 12:6,18
Num 9:6–13

Jer 4:1
Joel 2:12

30:1–27. The celebration of Passover was the clearest indication that religious worship was back to normal: the temple had been restored and its ministers sanctified (the Levites more assiduously than the priests: cf. v. 3; 29:34). All that remained was for "all Israel and Judah" (v. 1) to assemble to celebrate the central festival of the chosen people.

The preparations (vv. 1–12) clearly show that Hezekiah wanted his first Passover to involve everyone. The royal proclamation (vv. 6–9), inviting the Israelites of the North, gives the impression that it is a message the Chronicler wanted to be heard by the Samaritans and other dissenters of his time. It contains a moving appeal for reconciliation: only by turning to the Lord will it be possible for all Israelites to come together as one. It is a call equally valid for the ecumenical challenge of our own time: "There can be no ecumenism worthy of the name without interior conversion. For it is from newness of attitudes of mind, from self-denial and unstinted love,

[30] [1]Misit quoque Ezechias ad omnem Israel et Iudam scripsitque et epistulas ad Ephraim et Manassen, ut venirent ad domum Domini in Ierusalem et facerent Pascha Domino, Deo Israel. [2]Inito quoque consilio regis et principum et universi coetus in Ierusalem, decreverunt, ut facerent Pascha mense secundo. [3]Non enim potuerant facere in tempore suo, quia sacerdotes, qui possent sufficere, sanctificati non fuerant, et populus necdum congregatus erat in Ierusalem. [4]Placuit ergo sermo regi et omni multitudini, [5]et decreverunt, ut mitterent nuntios in universum Israel de Bersabee usque Dan, ut venirent et facerent Pascha Domino, Deo Israel, in Ierusalem; in plurima enim multitudine non fecerant, sicut lege praescriptum est. [6]Perrexeruntque cursores cum epistulis ex regis manu et principum eius in universum Israel et Iudam, iuxta quod rex iusserat, praedicantes: «Filii Israel, revertimini ad Dominum, Deum Abraham et Isaac et Israel, ut revertatur ad reliquias, quae effugerunt manum regum Assyriorum. [7]Nolite fieri sicut patres vestri et fratres, qui recesserunt a Domino, Deo patrum suorum, et tradidit eos

to the LORD God of their fathers, so that he made them a desolation, as you see. [8]Do not now be stiff-necked as your fathers were, but yield yourselves to the LORD, and come to his sanctuary, which he has sanctified for ever, and serve the LORD your God, that his fierce anger may turn away from you. [9]For if you return to the LORD, your brethren and your children will find compassion with their captors, and return to this land. For the LORD your God is gracious and merciful, and will not turn away his face from you, if you return to him."

1 Kings 8:50

[10]So the couriers went from city to city through the country of Ephraim and Manasseh, and as far as Zebulun; but they laughed them to scorn, and mocked them. [11]Only a few men of Asher, of Manasseh, and of Zebulun humbled themselves and came to Jerusalem. [12]The hand of God was also upon Judah to give them one heart to do what the king and the princes commanded by the word of the LORD.

[13]And many people came together in Jerusalem to keep the feast of unleavened bread in the second month, a very great

---

that desires of unity take their rise and develop in a mature way. We should therefore pray to the Holy Spirit for the grace to be genuinely self-denying, humble, gentle in the service of others and to have an attitude of brotherly generosity toward them" (Vatican II, *Unitatis redintegratio*, 7).

The Passover celebration properly speaking (vv. 13–22) is done with great formality and involves huge crowds of people. Since many had come great distances, they did not have time to purify themselves in advance—which meant that a greater number of Levites had to take part in order to perform the necessary number of sacrifices. In this context the king makes the significant point that cleanness of heart is more important than ritual purity.

So joyful an occasion was it (vv. 23–27), that the assembly decided to extend the festival for another week, as Solomon had done when the temple dedication was being celebrated (cf. 2 Chron 7:9). The Levites, the sacred writer points out again and again, were the main protagonists; they even joined the priests in blessing the people (v. 27), which went beyond their proper role.

On priests and Levites, see the notes on Num 3:5–10 and 18:1–7.

in interitum, ut ipsi cernitis. [8]Nolite nunc indurare cervices vestras sicut patres vestri. Tradite manus Domino et venite ad sanctuarium eius, quod sanctificavit in aeternum; servite Domino Deo vestro, ut avertatur a vobis ira furoris eius. [9]Si enim vos reversi fueritis ad Dominum, fratres vestri et filii habebunt misericordiam coram dominis suis, qui illos duxere captivos, et revertentur in terram hanc: misericors enim et clemens est Dominus Deus vester et non avertet faciem suam a vobis, si reversi fueritis ad eum». [10]Igitur cursores pergebant de civitate in civitatem per terram Ephraim et Manasse usque Zabulon, illis irridentibus et subsannantibus eos. [11]Attamen quidam viri ex Aser et Manasse et Zabulon se humiliaverunt et venerunt Ierusalem. [12]In Iuda quoque facta est manus Domini, ut daret eis cor unum, ut facerent praeceptum regis et principum iuxta verbum Domini. [13]Congregatus est ergo in Ierusalem

assembly. [14]They set to work and removed the altars that were in Jerusalem, and all the altars for burning incense they took away and threw into the Kidron valley. [15]And they killed the passover lamb on the fourteenth day of the second month. And the priests and the Levites were put to shame, so that they sanctified themselves, and brought burnt offerings into the house of the LORD. [16]They took their accustomed posts according to the law of Moses the man of God; the priests sprinkled the blood which they received from the hand of the Levites. [17]For there were many in the assembly who had not sanctified themselves; therefore the Levites had to kill the passover lamb for every one who was not clean, to make it holy to the LORD. [18]For a multitude of the people, many of them from Ephraim, Manasseh, Issachar, and Zebulun, had not cleansed themselves, yet they ate the passover otherwise than as prescribed. For Hezekiah had prayed for them, saying, "The good LORD pardon every one [19]who sets his heart to seek God, the LORD the God of his fathers, even though not according to the sanctuary's rules of cleanness." [20]And the LORD heard Hezekiah, and healed the people. [21]And the people of Israel that were present at Jerusalem kept the feast of unleavened bread seven days with great gladness; and the Levites and the priests praised the LORD day by day, singing with all their might[s] to the LORD. [22]And Hezekiah spoke encouragingly to all the Levites who showed good skill in the service of the LORD. So the people ate the food of the festival for seven days, sacrificing peace offerings and giving thanks to the LORD the God of their fathers.

[23]Then the whole assembly agreed together to keep the feast for another seven days; so they kept it for another seven days with

2 Kings 15:23; 18:4; 23:6
2 Chron 28:24–25

Ezra 9:6

Jn 11:55

Ex 12:43

1 Kings 8:65

---

populus multus, ut faceret sollemnitatem Azymorum in mense secundo, ecclesia magna valde. [14]Et surgentes destruxerunt altaria, quae erant in Ierusalem, atque universa thymiamateria subvertentes proiecerunt in torrentem Cedron. [15]Et mactaverunt Pascha quarta decima die mensis secundi; sacerdotes autem atque Levitae confusi sanctificati sunt et attulerunt holocausta in domum Domini. [16]Steteruntque in ordine suo iuxta dispositionem et legem Moysi hominis Dei, sacerdotes vero suscipiebant effundendum sanguinem de manibus Levitarum, [17]eo quod multi in coetu sanctificati non essent; idcirco Levitae mactaverunt victimas Paschae omnibus, qui non erant mundi, ut sanctificarent illas Domino. [18]Valde magna enim pars populi, de Ephraim et Manasse et Issachar et Zabulon, non erant mundati; et comederunt Pascha non iuxta, quod scriptum est. Et oravit pro eis Ezechias dicens: «Dominus bonus propitietur [19]cunctis, qui direxerunt cor suum, ut requirerent Dominum, Deum patrum suorum, quamvis non secundum munditiam sanctuarii». [20]Quem exaudivit Dominus, et placatus est populo. [21]Feceruntque filii Israel, qui inventi sunt in Ierusalem, sollemnitatem Azymorum septem diebus in laetitia magna, laudaverunt Dominum et per singulos dies Levitae et sacerdotes per organa benesonantia. [22]Et locutus est Ezechias ad cor omnium Levitarum, qui habebant intellegentiam bonam super Domino; et compleverunt sollemnitatem septem dierum immolantes victimas pacificorum et laudantes Dominum, Deum patrum suorum. [23]Placuitque universae multitudini, ut celebrarent etiam

s. Compare 1 Chron 13:8: Heb *with instruments of might*

gladness. [24]For Hezekiah king of Judah gave the assembly a thousand bulls and seven thousand sheep for offerings, and the princes gave the assembly a thousand bulls and ten thousand sheep. And the priests sanctified themselves in great numbers. [25]The whole assembly of Judah, and the priests and the Levites, and the whole assembly that came out of Israel, and the sojourners who came out of the land of Israel, and the sojourners who dwelt in Judah, rejoiced. [26]So there was great joy in Jerusalem, for since the time of Solomon the son of David king of Israel there had been nothing like this in Jerusalem. [27]Then the priests and the Levites arose and blessed the people, and their voice was heard, and their prayer came to his holy habitation in heaven.

Num 6:23–27
Deut 26:15

2 Kings 18:4

Organization of service in the temple

31 [1]Now when all this was finished, all Israel who were present went out to the cities of Judah and broke in pieces the pillars and hewed down the Asherim and broke down the high places and the altars throughout all Judah and Benjamin, and in Ephraim and Manasseh, until they had destroyed them all. Then all the people of Israel returned to their cities, every man to his possession.

[2]And Hezekiah appointed the divisions of the priests and of the Levites, division by division, each according to his service, the

1 Chron 9:19

31:1–21. Hezekiah's reform was primarily a religious one, to do with making the temple of Jerusalem the centre of all religious activity. The king laid down, in detail, the roles of priests and Levites in regard to liturgy (v. 2), as David and Solomon did in their time; but in addition he stipulated that part of the offerings must go to them "that they might give themselves to the law of the Lord" (v. 4). This made it clear that the Levites were in charge of teaching the Law.

The abundance of offerings that came to the temple (v. 10) was a clear sign that the reform had deeply affected the people, and that the Lord would bless them for all they had done. In line

alios dies septem, quod et fecerunt cum ingenti gaudio. [24]Ezechias enim rex Iudae praebuerat multitudini mille tauros et septem milia ovium; principes vero dederant populo tauros mille et oves decem milia; sanctificata est ergo sacerdotum plurima multitudo. [25]Et hilaritate perfusa est omnis turba Iudae, tam sacerdotum et Levitarum quam universae frequentiae, quae venerat ex Israel, advenae quoque, qui venerant de terra Israel vel habitabant in Iuda. [26]Factaque est grandis laetitia in Ierusalem, qualis a diebus Salomonis filii David regis Israel in ea urbe non fuerat. [27]Surrexerunt autem sacerdotes levitici generis benedicentes populo; et exaudita est vox eorum, pervenitque oratio eorum in habitaculum sanctum eius in caelum. **[31]** [1]Cumque haec fuissent rite celebrata, egressus est omnis Israel, qui inventus fuerat in urbibus Iudae, et fregerunt simulacra succideruntque palos, demoliti sunt excelsa et altaria destruxerunt non solum de universo Iuda et Beniamin, sed et de Ephraim quoque et Manasse, donec penitus everterent. Reversique sunt omnes filii Israel in possessiones et civitates suas. [2]Ezechias autem constituit turmas sacerdotales et leviticas per divisiones suas, unumquemque in officio

priests and the Levites, for burnt offerings and peace offerings, to minister in the gates of the camp of the LORD and to give thanks and praise. [3]The contribution of the king from his own possessions was for the burnt offerings: the burnt offerings of morning and evening, and the burnt offerings for the sabbaths, the new moons, and the appointed feasts, as it is written in the law of the LORD. [4]And he commanded the people who lived in Jerusalem to give the portion due to the priests and the Levites, that they might give themselves to the law of the LORD. [5]As soon as the command was spread abroad, the people of Israel gave in abundance the first fruits of grain, wine, oil, honey, and of all the produce of the field; and they brought in abundantly the tithe of everything. [6]And the people of Israel and Judah who lived in the cities of Judah also brought in the tithe of cattle and sheep, and the dedicated things[t] which had been consecrated to the LORD their God, and laid them in heaps. [7]In the third month they began to pile up the heaps, and finished them in the seventh month. [8]When Hezekiah and the princes came and saw the heaps, they blessed the LORD and his people Israel. [9]And Hezekiah questioned the priests and the Levites about the heaps. [10]Azariah the chief priest, who was of the house of Zadok, answered him, "Since they began to bring the contributions into the house of the LORD we have eaten and had enough and have plenty left; for the LORD has blessed his people, so that we have this great store left."

Num 28–29
1 Chron 29:3
Ezek 45:17

Num 18:8–24
Neh 13:10

Num 18:8–24
Deut 14:22

Neh
12:44–47;
13:10–13

Lev 25:19–22

---

with the Chronicler's thinking, we are being told once again that God generously rewards us for what we do in his service: "God does not let himself be out done in generosity" (St J. Escrivá, *Christ Is Passing By*, 40).

On the matter of tithes (v. 11), see the note on Deuteronomy 14:22–29.

The sacred writer ends his account of the religious reform (vv. 20–21) with a further consideration of Hezekiah and all he did for the temple, the Law and the commandments.

proprio tam sacerdotum videlicet quam Levitarum, ad holocausta et pacifica, ut ministrarent et confiterentur canerentque laudes in portis castrorum Domini. [3]Pars autem regis erat, ut de propria eius substantia offerretur holocaustum mane semper et vespere, sabbatis quoque et calendis et sollemnitatibus ceteris, sicut scriptum est in lege Moysi. [4]Praecepit etiam populo habitanti Ierusalem, ut darent partes sacerdotibus et Levitis, ut possent vacare legi Domini. [5]Quod cum percrebruisset in auribus multitudinis, plurimas obtulere primitias filii Israel frumenti, vini et olei, mellis quoque et omnium, quae gignit humus, et decimas obtulerunt de omnibus abundanter. [6]Sed et filii Israel et Iudae, qui habitabant in urbibus Iudae, obtulerunt decimas boum et ovium decimasque sanctorum, quae sanctificabant Domino Deo suo; atque universa portantes fecerunt acervos plurimos. [7]Mense tertio coeperunt acervorum iacere fundamenta et mense septimo compleverunt eos. [8]Cumque ingressi fuissent Ezechias et principes, viderunt acervos et benedixerunt Domino ac populo Israel. [9]Interrogavitque Ezechias sacerdotes et Levitas, cur ita iacerent acervi. [10]Respondit illi Azarias sacerdos primus de stirpe Sadoc dicens: «Ex quo coeperunt offerre donationem in domum Domini, comedimus et saturati sumus,

t. Heb *the tithe of the dedicated things*

[11]Then Hezekiah commanded them to prepare chambers in the house of the LORD; and they prepared them. [12]And they faithfully brought in the contributions, the tithes and the dedicated things. The chief officer in charge of them was Conaniah the Levite, with Shime-i his brother as second; [13]while Jehiel, Azaziah, Nahath, Asahel, Jerimoth, Jozabad, Eliel, Ismachiah, Mahath, and Benaiah were overseers assisting Conaniah and Shime-i his brother, by the appointment of Hezekiah the king and Azariah the chief officer of the house of God. [14]And Kore the son of Imnah the Levite, keeper of the east gate, was over the freewill offerings to God, to apportion the contribution reserved for the LORD and the most holy offerings. [15]Eden, Miniamin, Jeshua, Shemaiah, Amariah, and Shecaniah were faithfully assisting him in the cities of the priests, to distribute the portions to their brethren, old and young alike, by divisions, [16]except those enrolled by genealogy, males from three years old and upwards, all who entered the house of the LORD as the duty of each day required, for their service according to their offices, by their divisions. [17]The enrollment of the priests was according to their fathers' houses; that of the Levites from twenty years old and upwards was according to their offices, by their divisions. [18]The priests were enrolled with all their little children, their wives, their sons, and their daughters, the whole multitude; for they were faithful in keeping themselves holy. [19]And for the sons of Aaron, the priests, who were in the fields of common land belonging to their cities, there were men in the several cities who were designated by name to distribute portions to every male among the priests and to every one among the Levites who was enrolled.

1 Chron 23:3ff

1 Chron 23:7–23

[20]Thus Hezekiah did throughout all Judah; and he did what was good and right and faithful before the LORD his God. [21]And every

---

et remanserunt plurima, eo quod benedixerit Dominus populo suo; reliquiarum autem copia est ista, quam cernis». [11]Praecepit igitur Ezechias, ut praepararent cellas in domo Domini. Quod cum fecissent, [12]intulerunt tam donationem quam decimas et quaecumque sanctificaverant fideliter. Fuit autem praefectus eorum Chonenias Levita et Semei frater eius secundus, [13]post quem Iahiel et Azazias et Nahath et Asael et Ierimoth, Iozabad quoque et Eliel et Iesmachias et Mahath et Banaias praepositi sub manibus Choneniae et Semei fratris eius ex imperio Ezechiae regis et Azariae pontificis domus Dei. [14]Core vero filius Iemna Levites et ianitor orientalis portae praepositus erat iis, quae sponte offerebantur Domino, ad distribuendum donationem Domini et sanctissima. [15]Et sub cura eius Eden et Beniamin, Iesua et Semeias, Amarias quoque et Sechenias in civitatibus sacerdotum, ut fideliter distribuerent fratribus suis tam maioribus quam minoribus in divisionibus suis, [16]dummodo recensiti essent mares ab annis tribus et supra, cuncti qui ingrediebantur templum Domini, ut singulorum dierum ministeria observarent iuxta divisiones suas. [17]Sacerdotes recensiti erant per familias, et Levitae a vicesimo anno et supra per ministeria et turmas suas. [18]Et recensita erat universa familia omnis turmae, tam pro uxoribus quam liberis eorum utriusque sexus, quia in fidelitate servitii ipsorum sanctificati erant omnes. [19]Porro pro filiis Aaron, sacerdotibus in agris et suburbanis urbium singularum dispositi erant nominatim viri, qui partes distribuerent universo sexui masculino de sacerdotibus et omni, qui recensitus erat inter Levitas. [20]Fecit ergo Ezechias secundum haec in omni Iuda operatusque est bonum et rectum

work that he undertook in the service of the house of God and in accordance with the law and the commandments, seeking his God, he did with all his heart, and prospered.

Invasion by Sennacherib

32 [1]After these things and these acts of faithfulness Sennacherib king of Assyria came and invaded Judah and encamped against the fortified cities, thinking to win them for himself. [2]And when Hezekiah saw that Sennacherib had come and intended to fight against Jerusalem, [3]he planned with his officers and his mighty men to stop the water of the springs that were outside the city; and they helped him. [4]A great many people were gathered, and they stopped all the springs and the brook that flowed through the land, saying, "Why should the kings of Assyria come and find much water?" [5]He set to work resolutely and built up all the wall that was broken down, and raised towers upon it,[u] and outside it he built another wall; and he strengthened the Millo in the city of David. He also made weapons and shields in abundance. [6]And he set combat commanders over the people, and gathered them together to him in the square at the gate of the city and spoke encouragingly to them, saying, [7]"Be strong and of good courage. Do not be afraid or dismayed before the king of Assyria and all the horde that is with him; for there is one greater with us than with him. [8]With him is an arm of flesh; but with us is the LORD our God,

2 Kings 18:13
Is 36:1—37:38

Neh 2:17
Is 22:9–11

2 Chron 14:10; 20:6–12

Is 31:3

32:1–32. This chapter summarizes the three last episodes of Hezekiah's life which are covered in more detail elsewhere (cf. 2 Kings 18:9—20:21; Is 36:1—38:20)—the Assyrian invasions, the king's illness and his cure, and the prosperity of his reign. In this brief account, the accent, once more, is on the fact that the Lord blesses those who put their trust in him (v. 7).

et verum coram Domino Deo suo. [21]Et in universo opere, quod coepit in servitio domus Dei, et iuxta legem et praeceptum volens requirere Deum suum, in toto corde suo operatus et prosperatus est. **[32]** [1]Post quae et huiuscemodi fidem venit Sennacherib rex Assyriorum et ingressus Iudam obsedit civitates munitas volens eas capere. [2]Quod cum vidisset Ezechias, venisse scilicet Sennacherib et totum belli impetum verti contra Ierusalem, [3]inito cum principibus consilio virisque fortissimis, ut obturarent capita fontium, qui erant extra urbem, et, hoc omnium decernente sententia, [4]congregata est plurima multitudo, et obturaverunt cunctos fontes et rivum, qui fluebat in medio terrae, dicentes: «Ne veniant reges Assyriorum et inveniant aquarum abundantiam!». [5]Aedificavit quoque agens industrie omnem murum, qui fuerat dissipatus, et exstruxit turres de super et forinsecus alterum murum instauravitque Mello in civitate David et fecit iacula plurima et clipeos. [6]Constituitque principes belli super populum et convocavit illos ad se in platea portae civitatis ac locutus est ad cor eorum dicens: [7]«Viriliter agite et confortamini! Nolite timere, nec paveatis regem Assyriorum et universam multitudinem, quae est cum eo. Multo enim plures nobiscum sunt quam cum illo: [8]cum illo est brachium carneum, nobiscum autem

u. Vg: Heb *and raised upon the towers*

to help us and to fight our battles." And the people took confidence from the words of Hezekiah king of Judah.

2 Kings 18:17–37
Is 36:1–22

[9]After this Sennacherib king of Assyria, who was besieging Lachish with all his forces, sent his servants to Jerusalem to Hezekiah king of Judah and to all the people of Judah that were in Jerusalem, saying, [10]"Thus says Sennacherib king of Assyria, 'On what are you relying, that you stand siege in Jerusalem? [11]Is not Hezekiah misleading you, that he may give you over to die by famine and by thirst, when he tells you, "The LORD our God will deliver us from the hand of the king of Assyria"? [12]Has not this same Hezekiah

---

In anticipation of the Assyrian attack, the king acts with military astuteness by redirecting the waters of the spring of Gihon (vv. 3–30) into the city of Jerusalem through a channel (even today known as "Hezekiah's Channel"), in order to keep the city supplied with water during the siege. And, over and above everything else, the king's religious piety and trust in the Lord is evidenced by how he faces down the powerful Assyrian army. The end-result was that "the Lord saved Hezekiah and the inhabitants of Jerusalem from the hand of Sennacherib" and "gave them rest on every side" (v. 22), as happened also in the time of Solomon.

The king's illness was not a punishment of any kind (unlike the illnesses of Asah and Jehoram: cf. 16:12; 21:18–19) but an opportunity for the Lord to work "a sign" (v. 24). However, it could have spelt ruin for the king, because he failed, at first, to recognize the sign; but then he repented and punishment was averted (v. 26). The sacred writer is stressing the need to have humble and trusting recourse to the Lord as regards both public and personal matters. The king's good reaction anticipates New Testament teaching about always putting our trust in God: "This is the confidence which we have in him, that if we ask anything according to his will he hears us" (1 Jn 5:14). The liturgy of the Church reminds us of the same teaching in these simple and beautiful words: "God our Father, our strength in adversity, our health in weakness, our comfort in sorrow, be merciful to your people. As you have given us the punishment we deserve, give us also new life and hope as we rest in your kingdom" (*Roman Missal,* Mass for any need, B, collect prayer).

The prosperity enjoyed in Hezekiah's reign is a sign of God's blessing (vv. 27–29). The incident involving the embassy from Babylon (cf. 2 Kings 20:12–19; Is 39), reported briefly here (v. 31), shows the king's humility and religious devotion.

As regards the Millo, see the note on 2 Sam 5:9.

Dominus Deus noster, qui auxiliator est noster pugnatque pro nobis». Confortatusque est populus huiuscemodi verbis Ezechiae regis Iudae. [9]Quae postquam gesta sunt, misit Sennacherib rex Assyriorum servos suos Ierusalem—ipse enim cum universo exercitu obsidebat Lachis—ad Ezechiam regem Iudae et ad omnem populum, qui erat in urbe, dicens: [10]«Haec dicit Sennacherib rex Assyriorum: In quo habentes fiduciam sedetis obsessi in Ierusalem? [11]Nonne Ezechias decipit vos, ut tradat morti in fame et siti affirmans quod Dominus Deus vester liberet vos de manu regis Assyriorum? [12]Numquid non iste

taken away his high places and his altars and commanded Judah and Jerusalem, "Before one altar you shall worship, and upon it you shall burn your sacrifices"? [13]Do you not know what I and my fathers have done to all the peoples of other lands? Were the gods of the nations of those lands at all able to deliver their lands out of my hand? [14]Who among all the gods of those nations which my fathers utterly destroyed was able to deliver his people from my hand, that your God should be able to deliver you from my hand?

[15]Now therefore do not let Hezekiah deceive you or mislead you in this fashion, and do not believe him, for no god of any nation or kingdom has been able to deliver his people from my hand or from the hand of my fathers. How much less will your God deliver you out of my hand!'"

[16]And his servants said still more against the Lord GOD and against his servant Hezekiah. [17]And he wrote letters to cast contempt on the LORD the God of Israel and to speak against him, saying, "Like the gods of the nations of the lands who have not delivered their people from my hands, so the God of Hezekiah will not deliver his people from my hand." [18]And they shouted it with a loud voice in the language of Judah to the people of Jerusalem who were upon the wall, to frighten and terrify them, in order that they might take the city. [19]And they spoke of the God of Jerusalem as they spoke of the gods of the peoples of the earth, which are the work of men's hands.

2 Kings 19:9–13
Is 37:9–13

[20]Then Hezekiah the king and Isaiah the prophet, the son of Amoz, prayed because of this and cried to heaven. [21]And the LORD sent an angel, who cut off all the mighty warriors and commanders and officers in the camp of the king of Assyria. So he returned with shame of face to his own land. And when he came into the house of his god, some of his own sons struck him down there

2 Kings 11:15
Is 37:15

2 Kings 19:35–37
Is 37:36–38

---

est Ezechias, qui destruxit excelsa illius et altaria et praecepit Iudae et Ierusalem dicens: "Coram altari uno adorabitis et in ipso comburetis sacrificia"? [13]An ignoratis quae ego fecerim et patres mei cunctis terrarum populis? Numquid praevaluerunt dii gentium terrarum liberare regionem suam de manu mea? [14]Quis est de universis diis gentium, quas deleverunt patres mei, qui potuerit eruere populum suum de manu mea, ut possit etiam Deus vester eruere vos de hac manu? [15]Non vos ergo decipiat Ezechias nec vana persuasione deludat, neque credatis ei! Si enim nullus potuit deus cunctarum gentium atque regnorum liberare populum suum de manu mea et de manu patrum meorum, quanto minus Deus vester poterit eruere vos de manu mea!». [16]Sed et alia multa locuti sunt servi eius contra Dominum Deum et contra Ezechiam servum eius. [17]Epistulas quoque scripsit plenas blasphemiae in Dominum, Deum Israel, et locutus est adversus eum: «Sicut dii gentium terrarum non potuerunt liberare populos suos de manu mea, sic et Deus Ezechiae eruere non poterit populum suum de manu ista». [18]Insuper et clamore magno, lingua Iudaica, ad populum Ierusalem, qui sedebat in muro, personabant, ut terrerent et perturbarent eos et caperent civitatem. [19]Locutusque est Sennacherib contra Deum Ierusalem sicut adversum deos populorum terrae opera manuum hominum. [20]Oraverunt igitur Ezechias rex et Isaias filius Amos prophetes adversum hanc blasphemiam ac vociferati sunt in caelum. [21]Et misit Dominus angelum, qui percussit omnem virum robustum et bellatorem et principem in castris regis Assyriorum;

with the sword. [22]So the LORD saved Hezekiah and the inhabitants of Jerusalem from the hand of Sennacherib king of Assyria and from the hand of all his enemies; and he gave them rest on every side. [23]And many brought gifts to the LORD to Jerusalem and precious things to Hezekiah king of Judah, so that he was exalted in the sight of all nations from that time onward.

2 Chron 14:6

2 Kings 20:12

Hezekiah's illness and cure

2 Kings 20:1ff
Is 38:1ff

[24]In those days Hezekiah became sick and was at the point of death, and he prayed to the LORD; and he answered him and gave him a sign. [25]But Hezekiah did not make return according to the benefit done to him, for his heart was proud. Therefore wrath came upon him and Judah and Jerusalem. [26]But Hezekiah humbled himself for the pride of his heart, both he and the inhabitants of Jerusalem, so that the wrath of the LORD did not come upon them in the days of Hezekiah.

2 Kings 20:12–19
Is 39:1–8

Hezekiah's prosperity

2 Kings 20:13
Is 39:2

[27]And Hezekiah had very great riches and honour; and he made for himself treasuries for silver, for gold, for precious stones, for spices, for shields, and for all kinds of costly vessels; [28]storehouses also for the yield of grain, wine, and oil; and stalls for all kinds of cattle, and sheepfolds. [29]He likewise provided cities for himself, and flocks and herds in abundance; for God had given him very great possessions. [30]This same Hezekiah closed the upper outlet of the waters of Gihon and directed them down to the west side of the city of David. And Hezekiah prospered in all his works. [31]And so in the matter of the envoys of the princes of Babylon, who had been sent to him to inquire about the sign that had been done in the

2 Kings 20:20–21

---

reversusque est cum ignominia in terram suam. Cumque ingressus esset domum dei sui, filii, qui egressi fuerant de visceribus eius, interfecerunt eum ibi gladio. [22]Salvavit ergo Dominus Ezechiam et habitatores Ierusalem de manu Sennacherib regis Assyriorum et de manu omnium et praestitit eis quietem per circuitum. [23]Multi etiam deferebant munera Domino in Ierusalem et res pretiosas Ezechiae regi Iudae, qui exaltatus est post haec coram cunctis gentibus. [24]In diebus illis aegrotavit Ezechias usque ad mortem et oravit Dominum; exaudivitque eum et dedit ei signum. [25]Sed non iuxta beneficia, quae acceperat, retribuit, quia elevatum est cor eius; et facta est contra eum ira et contra Iudam et Ierusalem. [26]Humiliatusque est postea, eo quod exaltatum fuisset cor eius, tam ipse quam habitatores Ierusalem; et idcirco non venit super eos ira Domini in diebus Ezechiae. [27]Fuit autem Ezechias dives et inclitus valde; et thesauros sibi plurimos congregavit argenti, auri et lapidis pretiosi, aromatum et clipeorum omnisque generis rerum pretiosarum. [28]Apothecas quoque frumenti, vini et olei et praesepia omnium iumentorum caulasque pecoribus [29]et urbes exaedificavit sibi; habebat quippe greges ovium et armentorum innumerabiles, eo quod dedisset ei Deus substantiam multam nimis. [30]Ipse est Ezechias, qui obturavit superiorem exitum aquarum Gihon et avertit eas subter ad occidentem urbis David. In omnibus operibus suis prosperatus est. [31]Attamen sic in legatione principum Babylonis, qui missi fuerant ad eum, ut interrogarent de portento, quod acciderat super terram, dereliquit eum Deus, ut tentaretur, et nota fierent

land, God left him to himself, in order to try him and to know all that was in his heart.

[32]Now the rest of the acts of Hezekiah, and his good deeds, behold, they are written in the vision of Isaiah the prophet the son of Amoz, in the Book of the Kings of Judah and Israel. [33]And Hezekiah slept with his fathers, and they buried him in the ascent of the tombs of the sons of David; and all Judah and the inhabitants of Jerusalem did him honour at his death. And Manasseh his son reigned in his stead.

Is 36–38

The reign of Manasseh

2 Kings 21:1–18

33 [1]Manasseh was twelve years old when he began to reign, and he reigned fifty-five years in Jerusalem. [2]He did what was evil in the sight of the LORD, according to the abominable practices of the nations whom the LORD drove out before the people of Israel. [3]For he rebuilt the high places which his father Hezekiah had broken down, and erected altars to the Baals, and made Asherahs, and worshipped all the host of heaven, and served them. [4]And he built altars in the house of the LORD, of which the LORD had said, "In Jerusalem shall my name be for ever." [5]And he built altars for all the host of heaven in the two courts of the house of the LORD. [6]And he burned his sons as an offering in the valley of the son of Hinnom, and practised soothsaying and augury and sorcery, and dealt with mediums and with wizards. He did much evil in the sight of the LORD, provoking him to anger. [7]And the

Deut 18:10
Josh 18:16

33:1–20. The reign of Manasseh divides into two stages, but this time the first stage is one of irreligion (vv. 1–9) and the second, after the king's conversion, is marked by faithfulness to God (vv. 10–20). The account of the earlier period follows closely that given in 2 Kings 21:1–10, which depicts Manasseh as one of the most cruel and irreligious kings. But the second part is not found in Kings: once again the Chronicler is trying to provide a

omnia, quae erant in corde eius. [32]Reliqua autem gestorum Ezechiae et misericordiarum eius scripta sunt in visione Isaiae filii Amos prophetae et in libro regum Iudae et Israel. [33]Dormivitque Ezechias cum patribus suis, et sepelierunt eum in ascensu ad sepulcra filiorum David; et celebravit eius exsequias universus Iuda et omnes habitatores Ierusalem. Regnavitque Manasses filius eius pro eo. **[33]** [1]Duodecim annorum erat Manasses, cum regnare coepisset, et quinquaginta quinque annis regnavit in Ierusalem. [2]Fecit autem malum coram Domino iuxta abominationes gentium, quas expulit Dominus coram filiis Israel. [3]Et conversus instauravit excelsa, quae demolitus fuerat Ezechias pater eius, construxitque aras Baalim et fecit palos et adoravit omnem militiam caeli et coluit eam. [4]Aedificavit quoque altaria in domo Domini, de qua dixerat Dominus: «In Ierusalem erit nomen meum in aeternum». [5]Aedificavit autem ea cuncto exercitui caeli in duobus atriis domus Domini. [6]Transireque fecit filios suos per ignem in valle filii Ennom. Hariolatus est, sectabatur auguria, maleficis artibus inserviebat, habebat secum pythones et aruspices; multaque mala operatus est coram Domino, ut irritaret eum. [7]Posuit quoque sculptile, idolum, quod fecerat, in domo Dei, de qua locutus est Deus ad David et ad Salomonem filium eius dicens: «In domo hac et in Ierusalem, quam elegi de cunctis tribubus Israel, ponam nomen meum

image of the idol which he had made he set in the house of God, of which God said to David and to Solomon his son, "In this house, and in Jerusalem, which I have chosen out of all the tribes of Israel, I will put my name for ever; [8]and I will no more remove the foot of Israel from the land which I appointed for your fathers, if only they will be careful to do all that I have commanded them, all the law, the statutes, and the ordinances given through Moses." [9]Manasseh seduced Judah and the inhabitants of Jerusalem, so that they did more evil than the nations whom the LORD destroyed before the people of Israel.

[10]The LORD spoke to Manasseh and to his people, but they gave no heed. [11]Therefore the LORD brought upon them the commanders

---

religious interpretation of Manasseh's life. If the king stayed on the throne for forty-five years (698–642), that is, longer than either David or Solomon, it was because the king "humbled himself greatly before the God of his fathers" (v. 12) and therefore the Lord blessed him (v. 13). If idolatry continued to be practised, it was not the king's fault but the people's (v. 17). This is in line with the doctrine of personal retribution with which the whole book is imbued.

"(God) received his entreaty and heard his supplication" (v. 13). This passage may have inspired the "Prayer of Manasseh", a short apocryphal psalm which is to be found in some Greek codices at the end of the book of Psalms and which was used in Christian Lenten liturgy. This pious prayer, probably composed in the first or second century BC, deals with the infinite compassion of Almighty God and the effectiveness of true repentance: "I have sinned, Lord, I have sinned and I know my faults, but I beseech you: Do not rage against me, Lord, do not rage against me and do not let me fall to ruin through my sins. Do not be angered for eternity by the sight of my evildoings nor condemn me to the depths of the earth! For you, Lord, are the God of those who repent, and in me you will show your goodness, For although I am unworthy, you will save me out of the abundance of your mercy" (*Oratio Manassae*, 12–14).

33:3. Throughout the books of Chronicles, but particularly in the last chapters, there are continual references to irreligious men building "high places". These were originally Canaanite or unlawful altars, where acts of worship were performed in the belief that they were places where one could be nearer the godhead. In the times of the kings, they were probably artificial mounds, oval or circular platforms, built for purposes of worship. See also the note on 1 Kings 3:2–14.

in sempiternum. [8]Et moveri non faciam pedem Israel de terra, quam tradidi patribus eorum, ita dumtaxat si custodierint facere, quae praecepi eis, cunctamque legem et praecepta atque iudicia, per manum Moysi». [9]Igitur Manasses seduxit Iudam et habitatores Ierusalem, ut facerent malum super omnes gentes, quas subverterat Dominus a facie filiorum Israel. [10]Locutusque est Dominus ad eum et ad populum illius et attendere noluerunt. [11]Idcirco superinduxit eis principes exercitus regis Assyriorum; ceperuntque Manassen compedibus et vinctum catenis duxerunt Babylonem. [12]Qui, postquam

of the army of the king of Assyria, who took Manasseh with hooks and bound him with fetters of bronze and brought him to Babylon.* [12]And when he was in distress he entreated the favour of the LORD his God and humbled himself greatly before the God of his fathers. [13]He prayed to him, and God received his entreaty and heard his supplication and brought him again to Jerusalem into his kingdom. Then Manasseh knew that the LORD was God.

Ezek 19:9

[14]Afterwards he built an outer wall for the city of David west of Gihon, in the valley, and for the entrance into the Fish Gate, and carried it round Ophel, and raised it to a very great height; he also put commanders of the army in all the fortified cities in Judah. [15]And he took away the foreign gods and the idol from the house of the LORD, and all the altars that he had built on the mountain of the house of the LORD and in Jerusalem, and he threw them outside of the city. [16]He also restored the altar of the LORD and offered upon it sacrifices of peace offerings and of thanksgiving; and he commanded Judah to serve the LORD the God of Israel. [17]Nevertheless the people still sacrificed at the high places, but only to the LORD their God.

2 Chron 14:2

[18]Now the rest of the acts of Manasseh, and his prayer* to his God, and the words of the seers who spoke to him in the name of the LORD the God of Israel, behold, they are in the Chronicles of the Kings of Israel. [19]And his prayer, and how God received his entreaty, and all his sin and his faithlessness, and the sites on which he built high places and set up the Asherim and the images, before he humbled himself, behold, they are written in the

2 Sam 24:11
2 Kings 21:17–18

---

coangustatus est, oravit Dominum Deum suum et egit paenitentiam valde coram Deo patrum suorum. [13]Deprecatusque est eum, et placatus ei exaudivit orationem eius reduxitque eum Ierusalem in regnum suum; et cognovit Manasses quod Dominus ipse esset Deus. [14]Post haec aedificavit murum extra civitatem David ad occidentem Gihon in convalle et ad introitum portae Piscium per circuitum Ophel et exaltavit illum vehementer; constituitque principes exercitus in cunctis civitatibus Iudae munitis. [15]Et abstulit deos alienos et idolum de domo Domini, aras quoque, quas fecerat in monte domus Domini et in Ierusalem, et proiecit omnia extra urbem. [16]Porro instauravit altare Domini et immolavit super illud victimas pacificorum et pro gratiarum actione praecepitque Iudae, ut serviret Domino, Deo Israel. [17]Attamen adhuc populus immolabat in excelsis Domino Deo suo. [18]Reliqua autem gestorum Manasse et obsecratio eius ad Deum suum, verba quoque videntium, qui loquebantur ad eum in nomine Domini, Dei Israel, continentur in sermonibus regum Israel. [19]Oratio quoque eius et exauditio et cuncta peccata atque contemptus, loca etiam, in quibus aedificavit excelsa et fecit palos et statuas, antequam ageret paenitentiam, scripta sunt in sermonibus Hozai. [20]Dormivit ergo Manasses cum patribus suis, et sepelierunt eum in domo sua. Regnavitque pro eo filius eius Amon. [21]Viginti duorum annorum erat Amon, cum regnare coepisset, et duobus annis regnavit in Ierusalem. [22]Fecitque malum in conspectu Domini, sicut fecerat Manasses pater eius, et cunctis idolis, quae Manasses fuerat fabricatus, immolavit atque servivit. [23]Et non humiliavit se ante faciem Domini, sicut humiliaverat se Manasses pater eius, et multo maiora deliquit. [24]Cumque coniurassent adversus eum servi sui, interfecerunt eum in domo sua. [25]Porro populus terrae, caesis omnibus, qui conspiraverant contra regem Amon, constituit regem Iosiam filium eius pro eo. **[34]** [1]Octo annorum erat Iosias, cum regnare coepisset, et triginta et uno annis regnavit in Ierusalem. [2]Fecitque, quod erat rectum in conspectu Domini, et ambulavit in viis David

Chronicles of the Seers.[v] 20So Manasseh slept with his fathers, and they buried him in his house; and Amon his son reigned in his stead.

2 Kings 21:19–26

The reign of Amon

21Amon was twenty-two years old when he began to reign, and he reigned two years in Jerusalem. 22He did what was evil in the sight of the LORD, as Manasseh his father had done. Amon sacrificed to all the images that Manasseh his father had made, and served them. 23And he did not humble himself before the LORD, as Manasseh his father had humbled himself, but this Amon incurred guilt more and more. 24And his servants conspired against him and killed him in his house. 25But the people of the land slew all those who had conspired against King Amon; and the people of the land made Josiah his son king in his stead.

2 Kings 22:1–2

The reign of Josiah*

34 1Josiah was eight years old when he began to reign, and he reigned thirty-one years in Jerusalem. 2He did what was right in the eyes of the LORD, and walked in the ways of David his father; and he did not turn aside to the right or to the left.

2 Kings 23:4–20 2 Chron 14:1–4; 31:1

Josiah's early reforms

3For in the eighth year of his reign, while he was yet a boy, he began to seek the God of David his father; and in the twelfth year he began to purge Judah and Jerusalem of the high places, the Asherim, and the graven and the molten images. 4And they broke

---

33:21–25. Amon's was a short reign, but as disastrous as that of his father Manasseh. This passage gives the information contained in 2 Kings 21:19–24 but adds, "he did not humble himself before the Lord" (v. 23) to show that his premature death was punishment for his irreligion, even though it resulted from a conspiracy.

***34:1—35:27.** Josiah was the pious king who instituted a far-reaching religious reform and one of greater significance than that of Hezekiah, for Josiah had the honour of finding the book of the Law, that is, the nucleus of what now forms part of the book of Deuteronomy (cf. 2 Kings 22:1—23:30). The Chronicler's account keeps very

patris sui; non declinavit neque ad dextram neque ad sinistram. 3Octavo autem anno regni sui, cum adhuc esset puer, coepit quaerere Deum patris sui David; et duodecimo anno coepit mundare Iudam et Ierusalem ab excelsis et palis sculptilibusque et conflatilibus. 4Destruxeruntque coram eo aras Baalim; et thymiamateria, quae eis superposita fuerant, demolitus est; palos etiam et sculptilia et conflatilia succidit atque comminuit et super tumulos eorum, qui eis immolare consueverant, fragmenta dispersit.

v. One Ms Gk: Heb *of Hozai*

down the altars of the Baals in his presence; and he hewed down the incense altars which stood above them; and he broke in pieces the Asherim and the graven and the molten images, and he made dust of them and strewed it over the graves of those who had sacrificed to them. [5]He also burned the bones of the priests on their altars, and purged Judah and Jerusalem. [6]And in the cities of Manasseh, Ephraim, and Simeon, and as far as Naphtali, in their ruins[w] round about, [7]he broke down the altars, and beat the Asherim and the images into powder, and hewed down all the incense altars throughout all the land of Israel. Then he returned to Jerusalem.

2 Kings 23:4

1 Kings 13:2
2 Kings 23:20

Discovery of the book of the Law

[8]Now in the eighteenth year of his reign, when he had purged the land and the house, he sent Shaphan the son of Azaliah, and Maaseiah the governor of the city, and Joah the son of Joahaz, the recorder, to repair the house of the LORD his God. [9]They came to Hilkiah the high priest and delivered the money that had been

2 Kings 22:3–7

much to the content of that in Kings, but it arranges the material differently, to highlight the devoutness of Josiah, the leading part played by the Levites, and the central role of the temple. Thus, the first thing the king does is to destroy the idolatrous sites of Judah (34:3) and cleanse the other cities, including those of the North (34:6–7). When this purge was completed, he found the book (34:8ff). So the book did not give rise to the reform, but was by way of a reward for Josiah's initiative.

The Levites were essential to the reform: they were in charge of the restoration work on the temple (34:12–13); they acted as witnesses at the renewal of the Covenant (34:30); and, above all, they organized the celebration of Passover (33:3–16). At last, the temple again became the centre of religious worship and teaching. Significantly, the book of the Law came to light "while they were bringing out the money that had been brought into the house of the Lord" (34:14), that is, as God's reward for the care shown the House of God. Those of Israel as well as Judah flock to the passover celebration (35:18). The passover ceremonies described here probably lasted unchanged right up to Jesus' time.

[5]Ossa praeterea sacerdotum combussit in altaribus ipsorum; mundavitque Iudam et Ierusalem, [6]sed et in urbibus Manasse et Ephraim et Simeon usque Nephthali, in plateis eorum undique [7]dissipavit altaria et palos et sculptilia contrivit in frusta; cunctaque thymiamateria demolitus est de universa terra Israel et reversus est Ierusalem. [8]Igitur anno octavo decimo regni sui, cum mundaret terram et domum, misit Saphan filium Eseliae et Maasiam principem civitatis et Ioah filium Ioachaz a commentariis, ut instaurarent domum Domini Dei sui. [9]Qui venerunt ad Helciam sacerdotem magnum acceptamque ab eo pecuniam, quae illata fuerat in domum Domini et quam congregaverant Levitae ianitores de Manasse

w. Heb uncertain

2 Chron 24:8 brought into the house of God, which the Levites, the keepers of the threshold, had collected from Manasseh and Ephraim and from all the remnant of Israel and from all Judah and Benjamin and from the inhabitants of Jerusalem. [10]They delivered it to the workmen who had the oversight of the house of the LORD; and the workmen who were working in the house of the LORD gave it for repairing and restoring the house. [11]They gave it to the carpenters and the builders to buy quarried stone, and timber for binders and beams for the buildings which the kings of Judah had let go to ruin. [12]And the men did the work faithfully. Over them were set Jahath and Obadiah the Levites, of the sons of Merari, and Zechariah and Meshullam, of the sons of the Kohathites, to have oversight. The Levites, all who were skilful with instruments of music, [13]were over the burden bearers and directed all who did work in every kind of service; and some of the Levites were scribes, and officials, and gatekeepers.

2 Kings 22:8–13 [14]While they were bringing out the money that had been brought into the house of the LORD, Hilkiah the priest found the book of the law of the LORD given through Moses. [15]Then Hilkiah said to Shaphan the secretary, "I have found the book of the law in the house of the LORD"; and Hilkiah gave the book to Shaphan. [16]Shaphan brought the book to the king, and further reported to the king, "All that was committed to your servants they are doing. [17]They have emptied out the money that was found in the house of the LORD and have delivered it into the hand of the overseers and the workmen." [18]Then Shaphan the secretary told the king, "Hilkiah the priest has given me a book." And Shaphan read it before the king.

---

et Ephraim et universis reliquiis Israel ab omni quoque Iuda et Beniamin et habitatoribus Ierusalem, [10]tradiderunt in manibus opificum, qui praeerant in domo Domini, et illi dederunt eam operariis, qui operabantur in domo Domini, ut instaurarent templum et infirma quaeque sarcirent; [11]dederunt scilicet eam lignariis et caementariis, ut emerent lapides dolatos et ligna ad commissuras aedificii et ad contignationem domorum, quas destruxerant reges Iudae. [12]Qui fideliter cuncta faciebant. Erant autem praepositi operantium Iahath et Abdias Levitae de filiis Merari, Zacharias et Mosollam de filiis Caath, qui dirigebant opus. Omnes autem Levitae scientes organis canere [13]erant super eos, qui onera portabant et dirigebant omnes, qui varia opera faciebant. De Levitis quoque erant scribae et praefecti et ianitores. [14]Cumque efferrent pecuniam, quae illata fuerat in templum Domini, repperit Helcias sacerdos librum legis Domini per manum Moysi [15]et ait ad Saphan scribam: «Librum legis inveni in domo Domini». Et tradidit ei. [16]At ille intulit volumen ad regem et insuper nuntiavit ei dicens: «Omnia, quae dedisti in manu servorum tuorum, ecce complentur. [17]Argentum, quod repertum est in domo Domini, effuderunt, datumque est praefectis et operariis». [18]Et nuntiavit Saphan scriba regi dicens: «Librum tradidit mihi Helcias sacerdos». Et legebat illum Saphan coram rege. [19]Et factum est, cum audisset rex verba legis,

Huldah the prophetess is consulted

[19]When the king heard the words of the law he rent his clothes. [20]And the king commanded Hilkiah, Ahikam the son of Shaphan, Abdon the son of Micah, Shaphan the secretary, and Asaiah the king's servant, saying, [21]"Go, inquire of the LORD for me and for those who are left in Israel and in Judah, concerning the words of the book that has been found; for great is the wrath of the LORD that is poured out on us, because our fathers have not kept the word of the LORD, to do according to all that is written in this book."

2 Kings 22:12–14

[22]So Hilkiah and those whom the king had sent[x] went to Huldah the prophetess, the wife of Shallum the son of Tokhath, son of Hasrah, keeper of the wardrobe (now she dwelt in Jerusalem in the Second Quarter) and spoke to her to that effect. [23]And she said to them, "Thus says the LORD, the God of Israel: 'Tell the man who sent you to me, [24]Thus says the LORD, Behold, I will bring evil upon this place and upon its inhabitants, all the curses that are written in the book which was read before the king of Judah. [25]Because they have forsaken me and have burned incense to other gods, that they might provoke me to anger with all the works of their hands, therefore my wrath will be poured out upon this place and will not be quenched. [26]But to the king of Judah, who sent you to inquire of the LORD, thus shall you say to him, Thus says the

2 Kings 22:14–20

34:19–28. Impressed by the reading of the book, the king send an embassy to consult Huldah the prophetess; this showed his humble attitude in accepting what the book said as coming from God. This whole account follows 2 Kings 22:11–20 very closely but it adds, significantly, a reference to the "curses that are written in the book" (v. 24), an allusion to the last chapter of Deuteronomy (cf. Deut 30:7, 15–20). The Chronicler is taking it as read that "the book of the Law" was, in the Persian era, Deuteronomy in its entirety (and not just the central part of it, dealing with laws), and maybe even included the entire Pentateuch.

scidit vestimenta sua [20]et praecepit Helciae et Ahicam filio Saphan et Abdon filio Micha, Saphan quoque scribae et Asaiae servo regis dicens: [21]«Ite et consulite Dominum pro me et pro reliquiis Israel et Iudae super sermonibus libri, qui repertus est. Magnus enim furor Domini effusus est super nos, eo quod non custodierint patres nostri verba Domini, ut facerent iuxta omnia, quae scripta sunt in isto volumine». [22]Abiit igitur Helcias et hi, qui simul a rege missi fuerant, ad Holdam propheten uxorem Sellum filii Thecuae filii Haraas custodis vestium, quae habitabat in Ierusalem in secunda, et locuti sunt ei iuxta verba haec. [23]Et illa respondit eis: «Haec dicit Dominus, Deus Israel: Dicite viro, qui misit vos ad me: [24]Haec dicit Dominus: Ecce ego inducam mala super locum istum et super habitatores eius, cuncta maledicta, quae scripta sunt in libro hoc, quem legerunt coram rege Iudae, [25]quia dereliquerunt me et sacrificaverunt diis alienis, ut me ad iracundiam provocarent in cunctis operibus manuum suarum; idcirco effundetur furor meus super locum istum et non exstinguetur. [26]Ad regem autem Iudae, qui misit

x. Syr Vg: Heb lacks *had sent*

LORD, the God of Israel: Regarding the words which you have heard, [27]because your heart was penitent and you humbled yourself before God when you heard his words against this place and its inhabitants, and you have humbled yourself before me, and have rent your clothes and wept before me, I also have heard you, says the LORD. [28]Behold, I will gather you to your fathers, and you shall be gathered to your grave in peace, and your eyes shall not see all the evil which I will bring upon this place and its inhabitants.'" And they brought back word to the king.

2 Kings 23:1–3

The Covenant is renewed

[29]Then the king sent and gathered together all the elders of Judah and Jerusalem. [30]And the king went up to the house of the LORD, with all the men of Judah and the inhabitants of Jerusalem and the priests and the Levites, all the people both great and small; and he read in their hearing all the words of the book of the covenant which had been found in the house of the LORD. [31]And the king stood in his place and made a covenant before the LORD, to walk after the LORD and to keep his commandments and his testimonies and his statutes, with all his heart and all his soul, to perform the words of the covenant that were written in this book. [32]Then he made all who were present in Jerusalem and in Benjamin stand to it. And the inhabitants of Jerusalem did according to the covenant of God, the God of their fathers. [33]And Josiah took away all the abominations from all the territory that belonged to the people of Israel, and made all who were in Israel serve the LORD their God. All his days they did not turn away from following the LORD the God of their fathers.

2 Kings 23:4

---

vos pro Domino consulendo, sic loquimini: Haec dicit Dominus, Deus Israel: Quoniam audisti verba voluminis, [27]atque emollitum est cor tuum, et humiliatus es in conspectu Dei super his, quae dicta sunt contra locum hunc et habitatores Ierusalem, humiliatusque coram me scidisti vestimenta tua et flevisti coram me, ego quoque audivi, dicit Dominus. [28]Ecce colligam te ad patres tuos, et infereris in sepulcrum tuum in pace; nec videbunt oculi tui omne malum, quod ego inducturus sum super locum istum et super habitatores eius». Rettuleruntque itaque regi cuncta, quae dixerat. [29]At ille, convocatis universis maioribus natu Iudae et Ierusalem, [30]ascendit domum Domini, unaque omnes viri Iudae et habitatores Ierusalem, sacerdotes et Levitae et cunctus populus a minimo usque ad maximum. Quibus audientibus, in domo Domini legit rex omnia verba voluminis foederis inventi in domo Domini. [31]Et stans in gradu suo percussit foedus coram Domino, ut ambularet post eum et custodiret praecepta et testimonia et iustificationes eius in toto corde suo et in tota anima sua faceretque verba foederis scripta in hoc libro. [32]Adiuravit quoque super hoc omnes, qui reperti fuerant in Ierusalem et Beniamin; et fecerunt habitatores Ierusalem iuxta pactum Domini, Dei patrum suorum. [33]Abstulit ergo Iosias cunctas abominationes de universis regionibus filiorum Israel et fecit omnes, qui inventi erant in Israel, servire Domino Deo suo. Cunctis diebus eius non recesserunt a Domino, Deo patrum suorum.

Celebration of the Passover

35 [1]Josiah kept a passover to the LORD in Jerusalem; and they killed the passover lamb on the fourteenth day of the first month. [2]He appointed the priests to their offices and encouraged them in the service of the house of the LORD. [3]And he said to the Levites who taught all Israel and who were holy to the LORD, "Put the holy ark in the house which Solomon the son of David, king of Israel, built; you need no longer carry it upon your shoulders. Now serve the LORD your God and his people Israel. [4]Prepare yourselves according to your fathers' houses by your divisions, following the directions of David king of Israel and the directions of Solomon his son. [5]And stand in the holy place according to the groupings of the fathers' houses of your brethren the lay people, and let there be for each a part of a father's house of the Levites.[y] [6]And kill the passover lamb, and sanctify yourselves, and prepare for your brethren, to do according to the word of the LORD by Moses."

[7]Then Josiah contributed to the lay people, as passover offerings for all that were present, lambs and kids from the flock to the number of thirty thousand, and three thousand bulls; these were from the king's possessions. [8]And his princes contributed willingly to the people, to the priests, and to the Levites. Hilkiah, Zechariah, and Jehiel, the chief officers of the house of God, gave to the priests for the passover offerings two thousand six hundred lambs and kids and three hundred bulls. [9]Conaniah also, and

Ex 12:1–14,19
2 Kings 23:21

Deut 33:10
1 Chron 15:15
2 Chron 5:4
Ezra 7:10
Ml 2:7

1 Chron 24–27

Deut 12:18–19
2 Chron 30:17

Ex 12:5

Num 7
1 Chron 29:6–9

35:20–27. The tragic death of Josiah was something people found difficult to understand: why should an exemplary life like his end in tragedy? But, when noting that the king of Egypt sent messengers to explain that his incursion was not an attack on Judah (v. 21), the writer also points out that Josiah disobeyed by not listening to those words which "came from the mouth of God" (v. 22). It was this sin that caused the king's death, so the doctrine of personal retribution does apply. Cf. the note on 2 Kings 23:4–30.

[35] [1]Fecit autem Iosias in Ierusalem Pascha Domino, quod immolatum est quarta decima die mensis primi. [2]Et constituit sacerdotes in officiis suis confortavitque eos, ut ministrarent in domo Domini. [3]Levitis quoque, qui erudiebant omnem Israel et consecrati erant Domino, locutus est: «Ponite arcam sanctam in templum, quod aedificavit Salomon filius David rex Israel; nequaquam eam ultra umeris portabitis. Nunc ministrate Domino Deo vestro et populo eius Israel. [4]Et praeparate vos per familias vestras in divisionibus singulis, sicut scripsit David rex Israel, et descripsit Salomon filius eius; [5]et ministrate in sanctuario partibus familiarum fratrum vestrorum, filiorum populi, singulis pars familiae Levitarum. [6]Mactate ergo Pascha et sanctificamini et praeparate vos pro fratribus vestris, ut faciatis iuxta verbum, quod locutus est Dominus in manu Moysi». [7]Dedit praeterea Iosias omni populo, qui ibi inventus fuerat pro Pascha, agnos et haedos de gregibus triginta milia, boumque tria milia: haec de regis universa substantia. [8]Duces quoque eius sponte obtulerunt, tam populo quam sacerdotibus et Levitis; porro Helcias et Zacharias et Iahiel principes domus Domini dederunt sacerdotibus ad faciendum

y. Heb obscure

Shemaiah and Nethanel his brothers, and Hashabiah and Je-iel and Jozabad, the chiefs of the Levites, gave to the Levites for the passover offerings five thousand lambs and kids and five hundred bulls.

[10]When the service had been prepared for, the priests stood in their place, and the Levites in their divisions according to the king's command. [11]And they killed the passover lamb, and the priests sprinkled the blood which they received from them while the Levites flayed the victims. [12]And they set aside the burnt offerings that they might distribute them according to the groupings of the fathers' houses of the lay people, to offer to the LORD, as it is written in the book of Moses. And so they did with the bulls. [13]And they roasted the passover lamb with fire according to the ordinance; and they boiled the holy offerings in pots, in cauldrons, and in pans, and carried them quickly to all the lay people. [14]And afterward they prepared for themselves and for the priests, because the priests the sons of Aaron were busied in offering the burnt offerings and the fat parts until night; so the Levites prepared for themselves and for the priests the sons of Aaron. [15]The singers, the sons of Asaph, were in their place according to the command of David, and Asaph, and Heman, and Jeduthun the king's seer; and the gatekeepers were at each gate; they did not need to depart from their service, for their brethren the Levites prepared for them.

Ex 12:2–11
Deut 16:7

1 Chron 25:1

[16]So all the service of the LORD was prepared that day, to keep the passover and to offer burnt offerings on the altar of the LORD, according to the command of King Josiah. [17]And the people of Israel who were present kept the passover at that time, and the feast of unleavened bread seven days. [18]No passover like it had

2 Kings 23:22

Pascha pecora commixtim duo milia sescenta et boves trecentos. [9]Chonenias autem, Semeias etiam et Nathanael fratres eius necnon Hasabias et Iehiel et Iozabad principes Levitarum dederunt ceteris Levitis ad celebrandum Pascha quinque milia pecorum et boves quingentos. [10]Praeparatumque est ministerium, et steterunt sacerdotes in loco suo, Levitae quoque in turmis iuxta regis imperium. [11]Et mactatum est Pascha; asperseruntque sacerdotes manu sua sanguinem, et Levitae detraxerunt pelles holocaustorum [12]et separaverunt holocaustum, ut darent partibus familiarum populi, et offerretur Domino, sicut scriptum est in libro Moysi. De bobus quoque fecere similiter. [13]Et assaverunt Pascha super ignem, iuxta quod lege praeceptum est; pacificas vero hostias coxerunt in lebetis et caccabis et ollis et festinato distribuerunt universae plebi. [14]Sibi autem et sacerdotibus postea paraverunt; nam in oblatione holocaustorum et adipum usque ad noctem sacerdotes fuerant occupati, unde Levitae et sibi et sacerdotibus filiis Aaron paraverunt novissimis. [15]Porro cantores filii Asaph stabant in loco suo, iuxta praeceptum David et Asaph et Heman et Idithun prophetarum regis; ianitores vero per portas singulas observabant, ita ut ne puncto quidem discederent a ministerio, quia fratres eorum Levitae paraverunt eis cibos. [16]Omnis igitur cultus Domini rite praeparatus est in die illa, ut facerent Pascha et offerrent holocausta super altare Domini, iuxta praeceptum regis Iosiae. [17]Feceruntque filii Israel, qui reperti fuerant ibi, Pascha in tempore illo et sollemnitatem Azymorum septem diebus. [18]Non fuit simile huic in Israel a diebus Samuelis prophetae, sed nec quisquam de cunctis regibus Israel fecit Pascha sicut Iosias cum sacerdotibus et Levitis et omni Iuda et Israel, qui repertus fuerat, et habitantibus in

been kept in Israel since the days of Samuel the prophet; none of the kings of Israel had kept such a passover as was kept by Josiah, and the priests and the Levites, and all Judah and Israel who were present, and the inhabitants of Jerusalem. [19]In the eighteenth year of the reign of Josiah this passover was kept.

2 Kings 23:23,29–30

Death of Josiah

[20]After all this, when Josiah had prepared the temple, Neco king of Egypt went up to fight at Carchemish on the Euphrates and Josiah went out against him. [21]But he sent envoys to him, saying, "What have we to do with each other, king of Judah? I am not coming against you this day, but against the house with which I am at war; and God has commanded me to make haste. Cease opposing God, who is with me, lest he destroy you." [22]Nevertheless Josiah would not turn away from him, but disguised himself in order to fight with him. He did not listen to the words of Neco from the mouth of God, but joined battle in the plain of Megiddo. [23]And the archers shot King Josiah; and the king said to his servants, "Take me away, for I am badly wounded." [24]So his servants took him out of the chariot and carried him in his second chariot and brought him to Jerusalem. And he died, and was buried in the tombs of his fathers. All Judah and Jerusalem mourned for Josiah. [25]Jeremiah also uttered a lament for Josiah; and all the singing men and singing women have spoken of Josiah in their laments to this day. They made these an ordinance in Israel; behold, they are written in the Laments. [26]Now the rest of the acts of Josiah, and his good deeds according to what is written in the law of the LORD, [27]and his acts, first and last, behold, they are written in the Book of the Kings of Israel and Judah.

2 Kings 23:29
Is 10:9
Jer 46:2
2 Chron 18:33–34
1 Kings 22:34
Ezra 2:65

Ierusalem. [19]Octavo decimo anno regni Iosiae hoc Pascha celebratum est. [20]Postquam instauraverat Iosias templum, ascendit Nechao rex Aegypti ad pugnandum in Charchamis iuxta Euphraten. Et processit in occursum eius Iosias. [21]At ille, missis ad eum nuntiis, ait: «Quid mihi et tibi est, rex Iudae? Non adversum te hodie venio, sed contra aliam pugno domum, ad quam me Deus festinato ire praecepit. Desine adversum Deum facere, qui mecum est, ne interficiat te». [22]Noluit Iosias reverti, sed audacter praeparavit contra eum bellum, nec acquievit sermonibus Nechao ex ore Dei; verum perrexit, ut dimicaret in campo Mageddo. [23]Ibique vulneratus a sagittariis dixit pueris suis: «Educite me de proelio, quia oppido vulneratus sum». [24]Qui transtulerunt eum de curru in alterum currum eius et asportaverunt in Ierusalem. Mortuusque est et sepultus in sepulcris patrum suorum; et universus Iuda et Ierusalem luxerunt eum. [25]Ieremias fecit planctum super Iosiam; et omnes cantores atque cantrices usque in praesentem diem lamentationes super Iosia replicant, et quasi lex obtinuit in Israel: ecce scriptum fertur in Lamentationibus. [26]Reliqua autem gestorum Iosiae et misericordiae eius, quae lege praecepta sunt Domini, [27]gesta quoque illius prima et novissima scripta sunt in libro regum Israel et Iudae.

6. END OF THE KINGDOM OF JUDAH*

2 Kings 23:30–34

The reign of Jehoahaz

36 [1]The people of the land took Jehoahaz the son of Josiah and made him king in his father's stead in Jerusalem. [2]Jehoahaz was twenty-three years old when he began to reign; and he reigned three months in Jerusalem. [3]Then the king of Egypt deposed him in Jerusalem and laid upon the land a tribute of a hundred talents of silver and a talent of gold. [4]And the king of Egypt made Eliakim his brother king over Judah and Jerusalem, and changed his name to Jehoiakim; but Neco took Jehoahaz his brother and carried him to Egypt.

2 Kings 23:36–37

The reign of Jehoiakim

[5]Jehoiakim was twenty-five years old when he began to reign, and he reigned eleven years in Jerusalem. He did what was evil in the sight of the LORD his God. [6]Against him came up Nebuchadnezzar king of Babylon, and bound him in fetters to take him to Babylon. [7]Nebuchadnezzar also carried part of the vessels of the house of

2 Kings 24:1

Ezra 1:7

***36:1–21.** The reigns of the last kings of Judah are reported almost telegraphically, without even the standard formulaic introduction, ". . . began to reign", or conclusion, "The rest of the acts of . . .". The Chronicler simply reviews the irreligious conduct of each king and the deportation which is his punishment. So evil are their ways that they are chastised particularly severely: Jehoahaz was deported to Egypt on his own, but the people were unaffected (v. 4); Jehoiakim and Jehoiachin did what was evil and they were taken off to Babylon, as were many of the temple artefacts, but no hurt was done to anyone else (vv. 7 and 10); and, finally, Zedekiah, who led the people astray, who resolved not to turn back to the Lord, and who profaned the Lord's temple (v. 14), drew down the severest punishment of all: there was a general slaughter, the temple was destroyed, Jerusalem was laid waste, and the survivors were deported (vv. 17–20).

Thus, the exile is not interpreted as being a punishment inflicted on the whole people on account of infidelities committed down the years: it was a punishment inflicted on Zedekiah and his contemporaries on account of their own lives. The new generation that returns from exile will not bear the consequences of those transgressions; it will start afresh, counting on God's protection.

[36] [1]Tulit ergo populus terrae Ioachaz filium Iosiae et constituit regem pro patre suo in Ierusalem. [2]Viginti trium annorum erat Ioachaz, cum regnare coepisset, et tribus mensibus regnavit in Ierusalem. [3]Amovit autem eum rex Aegypti, cum venisset Ierusalem, et condemnavit terram centum talentis argenti et talento auri. [4]Constituitque regem pro eo Eliachim fratrem eius super Iudam et Ierusalem et vertit nomen eius Ioachim. Ipsum vero Ioachaz tulit secum et adduxit in Aegyptum. [5]Viginti quinque annorum erat Ioachim, cum regnare coepisset, et undecim annis regnavit in Ierusalem; fecitque malum coram Domino Deo suo. [6]Contra hunc ascendit Nabuchodonosor rex Chaldaeorum et vinctum catenis duxit in Babylonem, [7]ad quam et ex vasis Domini transtulit et posuit ea in templo suo. [8]Reliqua autem gestorum

the LORD to Babylon and put them in his palace in Babylon. [8]Now the rest of the acts of Jehoiakim, and the abominations which he did, and what was found against him, behold, they are written in the Book of the Kings of Israel and Judah; and Jehoiachin his son reigned in his stead.

2 Kings 24:5

The reign of Jehoiachin

[9]Jehoiachin was eight years old when he began to reign, and he reigned three months and ten days in Jerusalem. He did what was evil in the sight of the LORD. [10]In the spring of the year King Nebuchadnezzar sent and brought him to Babylon, with the precious vessels of the house of the LORD, and made his brother Zedekiah king over Judah and Jerusalem.

2 Kings 24:8–19

2 Kings 24:10–17

The reign of Zedekiah

[11]Zedekiah was twenty-one years old when he began to reign, and he reigned eleven years in Jerusalem. [12]He did what was evil in the sight of the LORD his God. He did not humble himself before Jeremiah the prophet, who spoke from the mouth of the LORD. [13]He also rebelled against King Nebuchadnezzar, who had made him swear by God; he stiffened his neck and hardened his heart against turning to the LORD, the God of Israel. [14]All the leading priests and the people likewise were exceedingly unfaithful, following all the abominations of the nations; and they polluted the house of the LORD which he had hallowed in Jerusalem.

[15]The LORD, the God of their fathers, sent persistently to them by his messengers, because he had compassion on his people and

2 Kings 24:18–20
Jer 52:1–3

Jer 37–39

Ezek 17:13–16,18

Heb 1:1

36:9. "Jehoiachin was eight years old". Many ancient manuscripts and translations have "eighteen years"; the Hebrew text, which does say "eight", seems to be mistaken: a person of that age could not have been responsible for evil in the eyes of the Lord.

Ioachim et abominationum eius, quas operatus est, et quae inventa sunt contra eum, continentur in libro regum Israel et Iudae. Regnavitque autem Ioachin filius eius pro eo. [9]Decem et octo annorum erat Ioachin, cum regnare coepisset, et tribus mensibus ac decem diebus regnavit in Ierusalem; fecitque malum in conspectu Domini. [10]Cumque anni circulus volveretur, misit Nabuchodonosor rex, qui adduxerunt eum in Babylonem, asportatis simul pretiosissimis vasis domus Domini; regem vero constituit Sedeciam fratrem eius super Iudam et Ierusalem. [11]Viginti et unius anni erat Sedecias, cum regnare coepisset, et undecim annis regnavit in Ierusalem. [12]Fecitque malum in oculis Domini Dei sui nec humiliavit se coram Ieremia propheta loquente ad se ex ore Domini. [13]Contra regem quoque Nabuchodonosor rebellavit, qui adiuraverat eum per Deum, et induravit cervicem suam et cor, ut non reverteretur ad Dominum, Deum Israel. [14]Sed et universi principes sacerdotum et populus multiplicaverunt praevaricationes suas iuxta universas abominationes gentium et polluerunt domum Domini, quam sanctificaverat in Ierusalem. [15]Mittebat autem Dominus, Deus patrum suorum, ad illos per manum nuntiorum suorum de nocte consurgens et cotidie commonens, eo quod parceret populo et

Lk 6:23 Acts 7:52 Heb 11:36 Mt 23:34–36

on his dwelling place; [16]but they kept mocking the messengers of God, despising his words, and scoffing at his prophets, till the wrath of the LORD rose against his people, till there was no remedy.

Lam 1:15; 5:11–14

Deportation. Destruction of Jerusalem

[17]Therefore he brought up against them the king of the Chaldeans, who slew their young men with the sword in the house of their sanctuary, and had no compassion on young man or virgin, old man or aged; he gave them all into his hand. [18]And all the vessels of the house of God, great and small, and the treasures of the house of the LORD, and the treasures of the king and of his princes, all these he brought to Babylon. [19]And they burned the house of God, and broke down the wall of Jerusalem, and burned all its palaces with fire, and destroyed all its precious vessels. [20]He took into exile in Babylon those who had escaped from the sword, and they became servants to him and to his sons until the establishment of the kingdom of Persia, [21]to fulfil the word of the LORD by the mouth of Jeremiah, until the land had enjoyed its sabbaths. All the days that it lay desolate it kept sabbath, to fulfil seventy years.

2 Kings 25:14ff

2 Kings 25:9ff

Jer 25:11; 29:10 Jer 27:7

Cyrus' edict

Ezra 1:1–3

[22]Now in the first year of Cyrus king of Persia, that the word of the LORD by the mouth of Jeremiah might be accomplished, the LORD

36:21. The mention of Jeremiah (cf. Jer 25:1–12; 29:10) indicates that his book was already seen in the Chronicler's time as being prophetical and holy; and it also underlines the fact that the exile was an event foreseen by God who kept the land in a long "sabbath", that is, a period of total rest, until the return of those who constituted the true Israel. By refraining from any mention of the governorship of Gedaliah (cf. 2 Kings 25:22–26) the writer avoids anything that would imply divisions between those who were deported and those who stayed on in Jerusalem.

36:22–23. The end of the book of Chronicles is identical with the start of that of Ezra (Ezra 1:1–3) and the repetition was probably inserted when Chronicles was finally separated from the books of Ezra and Nehemiah. But it

habitaculo suo. [16]At illi subsannabant nuntios Dei et parvipendebant sermones eius illudebantque prophetis, donec ascenderet furor Domini in populum eius, et esset nulla curatio. [17]Adduxit enim super eos regem Chaldaeorum et interfecit iuvenes eorum gladio in domo sanctuarii sui; non est misertus adulescentis et virginis et senis, nec decrepiti quidem, sed omnes tradidit in manibus eius. [18]Universaque vasa domus Dei tam maiora quam minora et thesauros templi et regis et principum transtulit in Babylonem. [19]Incenderunt hostes domum Dei destruxeruntque murum Ierusalem, universa palatia combusserunt et, quidquid pretiosum fuerat, demoliti sunt. [20]Si quis evaserat gladium, ductus in Babylonem servivit regi et filiis eius, donec imperaret rex Persarum, [21]ut compleretur sermo Domini ex ore Ieremiae: donec terra acciperet sabbata sua, cunctis diebus devastationis egit sabbatum, usque dum complerentur septuaginta anni. [22]Anno autem primo Cyri regis Persarum ad explendum sermonem

stirred up the spirit of Cyrus king of Persia so that he made a proclamation throughout all his kingdom and also put it in writing: [23]"Thus says Cyrus king of Persia, 'The LORD, the God of heaven, has given me all the kingdoms of the earth, and he has charged me to build him a house at Jerusalem, which is in Judah. Whoever is among you of all his people, may the LORD his God be with him. Let him go up.'"

---

does serve to reinforce the lesson, contained in the previous verses, that the exile does not mean the end, and that everything will continue as before the exile, because those who belong to the Lord's people will return, and the key conviction of faith will endure—that the Lord is with them, with *all* of those who, when this book was being assembled, were members of the people.

Domini, quem locutus fuerat per os Ieremiae, suscitavit Dominus spiritum Cyri regis Persarum, qui iussit praedicari in universo regno suo etiam per scripturam dicens: [23]«Haec dicit Cyrus rex Persarum: Omnia regna terrae dedit mihi Dominus, Deus caeli, et ipse praecepit mihi, ut aedificarem ei domum in Ierusalem, quae est in Iudaea. Quis ex vobis est de omni populo eius? Sit Dominus Deus suus cum eo, et ascendat».

EZRA AND NEHEMIAH

Introduction

The books of Ezra and Nehemiah are closely related to one another and are in many ways similar in style and approach to the books of Chronicles.[1] In the ancient Hebrew canon Ezra and Nehemiah formed a single book. This arrangement was carried into the Greek Septuagint version; the book is usually referred to as Ezra B (and in the Septuagint it follows what is called Ezra A, an apocryphal book found as an appendix in the Vulgate, where it is called as 3 Ezra). Christian commentators divided Ezra B in two, in line with its content: thus, as early as the Vulgate we find these books being called 1 Ezra and 2 Ezra. This division later came to be used in the Hebrew canon, and it is the one used in the New Vulgate, which calls the books "Ezra" and "Nehemiah".

1. STRUCTURE AND CONTENT

Unlike the books of "Deuteronomic history" and Chronicles, these books do not give a linear exposition of events: they deal only with the more outstanding episodes of the religious and civil reconstruction of Judah during the period when it formed part of the Persian empire. Taking them together, we can identify the following parts:

1. REBUILDING THE TEMPLE (EZRA 1:1—6:22). When Cyrus gave the go-ahead for the return of the Jewish exiles (Ezra 1:1–11), a caravan led by Sheshbazzar travelled from Babylon to Jerusalem (Ezra 2:1—3:6) and the new arrivals soon set about rebuilding the temple (Ezra 3:7—6:18). Once the building work was over and the temple re-dedicated, the festival of Passover was celebrated with much rejoicing (Ezra 6:19–22).

2. THE MISSION OF EZRA: TO RE-ESTABLISH THE LAW (EZRA 7:1—10:44). The account of the mission with which Ezra the scribe was charged begins with the letter of Ar-ta-xerxes empowering him to re-establish the Law (Ezra 7:1–26). It then goes on to describe the preparations for the return to Jerusalem, and the events of the journey (Ezra 8:1–36). Once they arrive, Ezra sees that many people are not complying with some precepts of the Law, and he makes a public penitential prayer acknowledging to God the sins of the people (Ezra 9:1–15). Then he takes radical steps to resolve the situation (Ezra 10:1–44).

1. Cf. "Introduction to the History of the Chronicles", pp 13–16 above.

3. THE MISSION OF NEHEMIAH: TO REBUILD THE CITY (NEH 1:1—13:31). Nehemiah was an official at the court of the king of Persia. The book of Nehemiah tells first why Nehemiah conceived the idea of rebuilding Jerusalem and how he managed to get the king's permission to embark on the project (Neh 1:1—2:20). Then comes a description of the building work (Neh 3:1—6:19) and the resettlement programme (Neh 7:1–72). The core of this part of the book is the proclamation of the Law by Ezra and the people's commitment to uphold it (Neh 8:1—10:40). Immediately after this come the arrangements as to who shall live in Jerusalem and who elsewhere in the territory (Neh 11:1–36), and the dedication of the new wall around Jerusalem (Neh 12:27–47). The last part of the book deals with the reorganization of civil life, which took place during a second mission carried out by Nehemiah.

2. COMPOSITION

The order of events in the books of Ezra and Nehemiah raises certain difficulties. The list of returned exiles is given twice (cf. Ezra 2:1–67 and Neh 7:6–72). In the passage running from Ezra 4:6 to 6:18, written in Aramaic, Darius is mentioned after Xerxes and Ar-ta-xerxes, whereas we know that they came after him. In the accounts given by Ezra and Nehemiah of their missions and activities, neither makes any mention of the other; on only two occasions does the writer mention their being in the same place at the same time (Neh 8:9; 12:26). It all gives the impression that when Ezra arrives on the scene, Nehemiah has already done his work, given that Ezra makes no mention of the ruinous state of the city which was what moved Nehemiah to take on the project of its reconstruction (cf. Neh 1:3). Moreover, how could Nehemiah have encountered disaster and irregularity, especially in the area of mixed marriages, if Ezra had been there first and had imposed the Law which he brought with him? All this leads one to suppose that the redactor of the book has combined reminiscences about Ezra (cf. Ezra 4:8—6:18) and reminiscences of Nehemiah written in the first person singular, and incorporated information from other sources, such as correspondence in Aramaic with the Persian kings, and lists of returned exiles (cf. Ezra 4:8—6:18); then he arranged all this material in an order which has more to do with doctrine rather than chronology.

In fact, although it is possible that Ezra was in Jerusalem prior to Nehemiah, or was there at the time of Nehemiah's second mission (cf. Neh 13:6), in the light of such information as is available (including an important papyrus from the period), scholars today think that the most probable explanation as regards the sequence of events is that Nehemiah's missions in Jerusalem took place between the years 445 and 424 BC, and that Ezra did not arrive in the city until

398. Nehemiah would have restored the wall, reorganized the social and political life of Judah, and built up the repatriates' sense of identity and solidarity by means of renewing the Covenant with God in line with Deuteronomy, promoting the celebration of the sabbath and banning certain kinds of mixed marriage. Ezra, on the other hand, would have brought in the Law and imposed it as the law of the state to be kept by all Jews. Nehemiah and Ezra would have been involved at different, successive, points in the re-establishement of the Jewish community of Jerusalem and its links with the diaspora.

The author of Ezra-Nehemiah amalgamated reminiscences of these two personalities that had been handed down independently. His aim in doing this was to enhance the figure of Ezra and at the same time record the achievements of Nehemiah. Ezra is extolled even more in the apocryphal 3 Ezra (see above), where Ezra is portrayed as the man who was to the fore in the later stages of the reforms begun by Josiah prior to the exile (cf. 2 Kings 23:1–3) and continued by Zerubbabel after the return—and in which Nehemiah is nowhere to be seen. The author of Ezra-Nehemiah also wants to give Ezra's mission pride of place, and then to show Nehemiah coming in to back up his efforts. To do this, he transfers the main episode in Ezra's life, the proclamation of the Law (cf. Neh 8:1–18), to a point in the reminiscences of Nehemiah, placing the two men in Jerusalem at the same time.

Possibly, given that his interests lay more in theological matters than in historical exactness, the author of Ezra-Nehemiah presented the facts in this order because he thought that the Ar-ta-xerxes, who in the seventh year of his reign gave Ezra permission to go to Jerusalem (cf. Ezra 7:1–10), was Ar-ta-xerxes I, who reigned from 465 to 424 BC, and who in the twentieth year of his reign allowed Nehemiah to go to Judea (cf. Neh 2:1–6). But in fact (as can be deduced from a papyrus of this period), the Ar-ta-xerxes who sent Ezra was Ar-ta-xerxes II, who reigned from 405 to 358 BC. The author of Ezra-Nehemiah may have set the missions of Nehemiah and Ezra in the reign of the same king, by failing to distinguish between the two kings of the same name.

Another way to explain the inconsistencies is that the reference in Ezra 7:7 to "the seventh year of Ar-ta-xerxes the king" should read "the thirty-seventh year": that would mean that the mission of Ezra took place in 428 BC and Ezra could have been in Jerusalem at the same time as Nehemiah.

Be that as it may, the author of Ezra-Nehemiah clearly wants to link the two figures because he, quite rightly, regards them as the revivers of Judaism—but giving more prominence to Ezra, the priest (cf. Ezra 7:1–6), who is the one who teaches and proclaims the Law. This has the effect of showing the Law to be the essential nucleus of Judaism. Nehemiah comes to aid Ezra and he concerns himself with seeing that the Law is kept and the city rebuilt. Given the vagueness about the sequence of events, the importance attributed to the teaching of the Law, and the fact that Ezra makes

no appearance in second century BC writings, such as the book of Ecclesiasticus and 2 Maccabees, in which Nehemiah, however, does appear, Ezra-Nehemiah is thought to have been written around the year 100 BC, although it must be said that some scholars put it in the fourth-to-third century BC.

3. MESSAGE

The books of Ezra and Nehemiah show that the events relating to the revival of social life in Judah after the exile form part of a single design by God, although they actually happened at separate points in time, during the reigns of a number of Persian kings.

These events constitute a new stage in salvation history which is part of an on-going process. This process, this continuity, is emphasized by the genealogies which all bear witness to the links between the Jews who were involved in the restoration and the people that had lived in Judea prior to the exile. Genealogies are provided for many different persons, but they are all members of the people that God chose for himself in earlier ages.

The Israel of the Persian and Greek period (these books are saying) is the same as existed before, though it has undergone profound change in relatively recent times—loss of national sovereignty, which meant that it was no longer ruled by a Davidic king although it was governed internally by a high priest. Its religious life had also undergone change: years of exile far away from Jerusalem meant that the usual sacrifices could not be offered in the temple. These circumstances gave rise to the synagogue as the Jewish place of meeting, and the Law was gradually playing a greater role in Jewish life.

While the city walls and the temple were being rebuilt, the national and religious life of the Jewish people also underwent reorganization. In this context it was important that they should be aware of the links between old and new institutions. The altar and the house of God were built on the same site as before (cf. Ezra 3:3; 6:7). The sacred vessels that the returned exiles brought back to Jerusalem were the same ones as Nebuchadnezzar had taken to Babylon as plunder (Ezra 5:14). The priests and the other personnel involved in the liturgy were descendants of the men who had had these functions prior to the exile (Ezra 2:36–63; Neh 7:39–65).

This continuity between the new and the old is something that these books are at pains to point out, for it bears witness to the fact that God guides the course of salvation history, providing new answers to fit changed circumstances, but ensuring that the link with the people's origins is never weakened.

As well as emphasizing this continuity, the books of Ezra-Nehemiah also put much stress on the importance of the people's identity; this must be ensured by severe prohibition of mixed marriage, and by Jews keeping their

distance from Gentiles. Such segregation was not always the order of the day, as can be seen from the books of Ruth and Jonah; but at this time, when the temptation of syncretism was particularly strong due to the political and social circumstances in which the Jews found themselves, the measures taken to maintain a distance from Gentiles were providential: they were needed in order to protect the religious identity of the "people of Israel", which at that time becomes synonymous with "the Jewish people". Thus, from the time of the reforms described in Ezra-Nehemiah, being a member of the people is no longer limited to living in a specific territory or having come from it; it is, rather a matter of being descended from a particular line (hence the importance of genealogies) and of submitting to a law which, while still being regarded as the Law given by God to Moses, is seen as having been laid down for all Jews on the authority of a foreign king.

4. THE BOOKS OF EZRA AND NEHEMIAH IN THE LIGHT OF THE NEW TESTAMENT

Within the canon of Holy Scripture, the books of Ezra and Nehemiah, as well as recording God's dealings with his people on the return from exile, also show the inspired writer's understanding of God and of the chosen people, and the sort of teachings he wanted to get across to his contemporaries. In this sense, Ezra-Nehemiah evidences a particular point in Old Testament revelation; contrary to what the Jewish canon of the Bible might lead us to think (for it ends with these books and Chronicles), that revelation was ongoing and it is to be found in later Jewish (and also canonical) books, such as 1 Maccabees or Wisdom, and it reaches its climax in the books of the New Testament. From this perspective, Ezra-Nehemiah should be seen and read as dealing with a preparatory and transitory stage of revelation prior to the New Testament. Preparatory, because both books allow us to see to a considerable extent (but not entirely, because there were other tendencies in Judaism not reflected here) the religious circumstances and mentality of the Jewish people, centred on obedience to the Law, in the period in which Jesus lived and the Church came into being. Transitory, in so far as the teachings in Ezra-Nehemiah about the Law being the only way to draw down the mercy of God, and about segregation from Gentiles as a way to protect the identity of the Jewish people, will undergo profound changes in the New Testament. For, according to the New Testament, although the Law still holds, God's mercy reaches man, all mankind, be they Jews or not, through Jesus Christ, the Messiah; the identity of the Church, the new people of God, is not a function of segregation from Gentiles: it derives from the fidelity and holiness of its members in the midst of the world.

Christian tradition has largely interpreted these books in a spiritual sense, seeking to draw from them lessons about the building-up of the City of God, that is, the Church. In addition to that general interpretation, Ezra's work is seen as anticipating what Jesus will fully bring about: just as Ezra instructed the people of God in the Law of Moses, Jesus taught that Law and brought it to perfection (cf. Mt 5:17).

1. REBUILDING OF THE TEMPLE*

The exiles return from Babylon

1 [1]In the first year of Cyrus king of Persia, that the word of the LORD by the mouth of Jeremiah might be accomplished, the LORD stirred up the spirit of Cyrus king of Persia so that he made a proclamation throughout all his kingdom and also put it in writing:

2 Chron 36:22–23
Jer 25:11–12; 29:10
Zech 1:12

***1:1—6:22.** The second book of Chronicles closed with an account of the fall of Jerusalem as a consequence of the city's repeated unfaithfulness to God (cf. 2 Chron 36:17–21), and with the news of Cyrus' calling, in God's name, for the rebuilding of the temple and the return of the exiles (cf. 2 Chron 36:22–23). The book of Ezra starts by covering the same ground (1:1–4) and then goes on to describe how Cyrus' decree was implemented. It deals with the preparation for the return to Jerusalem (1:5–11), and who these repatriates were (2:1–70); how the first thing they did at Jerusalem was to build an altar and start offering sacrifices (3:1–6), and about how, when they began to rebuild the temple, they met with opposition from the people in the land (4:1–5), who petitioned the Persian king, with the result that the rebuilding had to cease (4:6–24). But, encouraged by the prophets Haggai and Zechariah, those who had returned set about their task again (5:1–2) and kept at it, in the hope that the ban on building would be lifted (5:3–5). The authorities then sent a new letter to King Darius (5:6–17), who decreed that the Jews be allowed to build the temple in peace, as Cyrus had already instructed (6:1–12). This meant that they were able to finish the building and dedicate it to the Lord (6:13–18), and then celebrate joyfully their first Passover in their homeland (6:19–22).

This first part of the book shows how devout and tenacious these repatriates were—fully committed to the worship of the Lord and the reconstruction of his temple. But it also reveals the animosity shown towards them by those living in the country. Only God's will, expressed in decrees of the Persian kings, made it possible for this enterprise to succeed. The chosen people was springing up again in the promised land.

In Christian tradition, in the light of Jesus Christ's message, these pages are read as having a spiritual meaning to do with the advancement of the Church: just as the people of God in the Old Testament, was able to reconstitute itself after the bitter experience of the exile, and survived despite difficulties of all sorts, so too the new people of God manages to survive over the course of the centuries even though it encounters all kinds of obstacles. "If you do not trust words, believe in deeds. How many tyrants have tried to oppress the Church? How much boiling

[1] [1]In anno primo Cyri regis Persarum, ut compleretur verbum Domini ex ore Ieremiae, suscitavit Dominus spiritum Cyri regis Persarum, qui emisit edictum in omni regno suo etiam per scripturam

Is 45:1

[2]"Thus says Cyrus king of Persia:* The LORD, the God of heaven, has given me all the kingdoms of the earth, and he has charged me to build him a house at Jerusalem, which is in Judah. [3]Whoever is among you of all his people, may his God be with

---

oil! How many pyres and sharp teeth and raised swords . . . ! And they have not triumphed! Where are they now, those who waged war against her? And where is the Church? She shines brighter than the sun. The power of her enemies is spent, but the strength of the Church is endless. Even when there were very few Christians, the Church was not overcome; now that her faith and piety have spread throughout the world, do you think you can defeat her? 'Heaven will pass away but my words shall never fail'; it is clear: God loves the Church more than heaven itself. He did not take for himself a heavenly body but an ecclesial one. Heaven exists for the Church, not the Church for the sake of heaven" (St John Chrysostom, *Sermo antequam iret in exilium*, 2).

1:1–4. Cyrus was king of Persia from 559 to 529 BC. History portrays him as a ruler tolerant of the traditional customs of his subject peoples and respectful of their religious practices. When he entered Babylon in triumph in 539 BC, he established the cult of Marduk there, and when he heard about the position of the deportees from Jerusalem he facilitated their return to their country to rebuild the temple of their God.

But the sacred book, which looks beneath the surface of events, points out that Cyrus' decisions in favour of the Jews derived not just from the king's good disposition but from God himself. The Lord stirred up the spirit of Cyrus (v. 1) and the heads of the houses of Judah and Benjamin (1:5) so as to bring about in this new stage of salvation history the rebuilding of the temple and to re-establish the people in Jerusalem. God uses a pagan king to achieve his saving purpose for the chosen people. That is what Isaiah 45:1 means when it calls Cyrus "the Lord's anointed", even though the king does not realize he is forwarding the Lord's plans: "though you do not know me" (Is 45:4). Moreover, the "seventy years" of exile prophesied by Jeremiah (cf. 2 Chron 36:21) are shortened by Cyrus' decree which causes the return from exile to happen in 538 BC. It all goes to show that God is above kings and nations and that he is merciful to his people.

Unlike other passages which report Cyrus' decree (cf. 2 Chron 36:22–23; Ezra 6:3–12), here we are told that the king acknowledges that "the Lord, the God of heaven" (v. 2)—apparently the title given to the supreme Persian deity Ahura-Mazda—is one and the same as "Lord, the God of Israel who is in Jerusalem" (v. 3). This is a profession of faith in the one true God, the God

dicens: [2]«Haec dicit Cyrus rex Persarum: Omnia regna terrae dedit mihi Dominus, Deus caeli, et ipse praecepit mihi, ut aedificarem ei domum in Ierusalem, quae est in Iudaea. [3]Quis ex vobis est de omni populo eius? Sit Dominus Deus suus cum eo, et ascendat in Ierusalem, quae est in Iudaea, et aedificet domum Domini, Dei Israel: ipse est Deus, qui est in Ierusalem. [4]Et omnes reliqui in cunctis locis,

him, and let him go up to Jerusalem, which is in Judah, and rebuild the house of the LORD, the God of Israel—he is the God who is in Jerusalem; [4]and let each survivor, in whatever place he sojourns, be assisted by the men of his place with silver and gold, with goods and with beasts, besides freewill offerings for the house of God which is in Jerusalem."

[5]Then rose up the heads of the fathers' houses of Judah and Benjamin, and the priests and the Levites, every one whose spirit God had stirred to go up to rebuild the house of the LORD which is in Jerusalem; [6]and all who were about them aided them with

---

who revealed himself to the Jewish people, but whose power extends over all the nations.

1:5–11. Although the decree of Cyrus was addressed to all those belonging to the people of God (1:3) living in the Persian empire, already seen as "the remnant", the "survivors" of what was ancient Israel (1:4), now only the "heads of the houses of Judah and Benjamin" are mentioned (v. 5)—these being the two tribes that had made up the kingdom of the South, the kingdom of Judah. Those deported after the fall of the Northern kingdom (cf. 2 Kings 17:6) have disappeared from the writer's horizon in the same way as the author of 1 and 2 Chronicles put that kingdom out of his mind. The reconstruction of the people in this new stage of its existence that begins now is based solely on what had been the kingdom of Judah, including the priests and Levites who had been attached to the temple of Jerusalem: as this writer sees things, only the men of Judah were the true people of Israel and of these, in a special way, those Jews who gave up their position in Babylon and embarked on the adventure of returning to Jerusalem.

It is possible that Shesh-bazzar was a son of Jehoiachin (cf. 2 Chron 36:9–10), and that he held the title of king of Judah as a vassal when Cyrus was king of Persia. One gets the same impression from 1 Chronicles 3:17–18, although there he is called Shenazzar. He not only takes charge of the sacred vessels plundered by Nebuchadnezzar (cf. 2 Chron 36:10; 2 Kings 25:14–15) but heads up the first group of repatriates and lays the foundations of the temple (cf. 5:15–16). If this is who Shesh-bazzar was, then both he and his nephew Zerubbabel (cf. 1 Chron 3:19) were of the house of David. This would have been significant in the context of these events, for it would have meant that the line of David was continuing to play a key role. And yet there is nothing in the book of Ezra about Zerubbabel being of the house of David. This absence of information has led some

ubicumque habitant, adiuventur a viris de loco suo, argento et auro et substantia et pecore sicut et oblationibus spontaneis pro templo Dei, quod est in Ierusalem». [5]Et surrexerunt principes familiarum de Iuda et Beniamin et sacerdotes et Levitae et omnis, cuius Deus suscitavit spiritum, ut ascenderent ad aedificandum templum Domini, quod erat in Ierusalem. [6]Universique, qui erant in circuitu,

Ex 3:22; 11:2; 12:35

vessels of silver, with gold, with goods, with beasts, and with costly wares, besides all that was freely offered. [7]Cyrus the king also brought out the vessels of the house of the LORD which Nebuchadnezzar had carried away from Jerusalem and placed in the house of his gods. [8]Cyrus king of Persia brought these out in charge of Mithredath the treasurer, who counted them out to Shesh-bazzar the prince of Judah. [9]And this was the number of them: a thousand basins of gold, a thousand[a] basins of silver, twenty-nine censers, [10]thirty bowls of gold, two thousand[b] four hundred and ten bowls of silver, and a thousand other vessels; [11]all the vessels of gold and of silver were five thousand four hundred and sixty-nine.[c] All these did Shesh-bazzar bring up, when the exiles were brought up from Babylonia to Jerusalem.

---

scholars to think that Shesh-bazzar and Zerubbabel were one and the same person. On the other hand, the prophets Haggai (cf. Hag 1:20–23) and Zechariah (cf. Zech 4:6–10) are conscious that Zerubbabel was of the house of David and this feeds their messianic hopes. The author of Ezra focuses his attention on the continuity implied in the fact that the very same vessels as had been used in the temple before the exile found their way back to it.

In the account of the return of the exiles we find things reminiscent of events during the Exodus, albeit distinctions are drawn between the two situations. The first exodus began when the tyrannical king, the pharaoh, agreed to the Israelites' leaving his country, having been forced to do so by the plagues (cf. Ex 3:12; 7:26; etc.). But in this second exodus all that was needed was for God to stir the heart of Cyrus. Moreover, just as the Israelites did not leave Egypt empty-handed, but were able to despoil their neighbours of their gold and silver jewelry etc. (cf. Ex 3:21–22; 12:35–36), the deported Jews returned to Jerusalem loaded with gifts. In the first exodus Israel became a people; in the second it is portrayed as a coming back to life.

Everything we learn about here can be applied to all times in the future. Holy Scripture tells us, sometimes quite dramatically, others soberly, about many instances of God's saving intervention. Even though the social and political circumstances of the people of God change, the same people endures:

confortaverunt manus eorum cum vasis argenteis et aureis, substantia, pecore et pensitationibus, praeter oblationes spontaneas. [7]Rex quoque Cyrus protulit vasa templi Domini, quae tulerat Nabuchodonosor de Ierusalem et posuerat ea in templo dei sui; [8]protulit autem ea Cyrus rex Persarum per manum Mithridatis praepositi thesauri, qui enumeravit ea Sasabassar principi Iudae. [9]Et hic est numerus eorum: phialae aureae triginta, phialae argenteae mille, cultri viginti novem, scyphi aurei triginta, [10]scyphi quoque argentei quadringenti decem, vasa alia plurima; [11]omnia vasa aurea et argentea quinque milia quadringenta. Universa tulit Sasabassar cum his, qui ascendebant de transmigratione Babylonis in Ierusalem.

a. 1 Esdras 2:13: Heb *thirty* **b.** 1 Esdras 2:13: Heb *of a second sort* **c.** 1 Esdras 2:14: Heb *five thousand four hundred*

List of returning exiles

Neh 7:6–72

2 [1]Now these were the people of the province who came up out of the captivity of those exiles whom Nebuchadnezzar the king of Babylon had carried captive to Babylonia; they returned to Jerusalem and Judah, each to his own town. [2]They came with Zerubbabel, Jeshua, Nehemiah, Seraiah, Re-el-aiah, Mordecai, Bilshan, Mispar, Bigvai, Rehum, and Baanah.

The number of the men of the people of Israel: [3]the sons of Parosh, two thousand one hundred and seventy-two. [4]The sons of Shephatiah, three hundred and seventy-two. [5]The sons of Arah, seven hundred and seventy-five. [6]The sons of Pahath-moab, namely the sons of Jeshua and Joab, two thousand eight hundred and twelve. [7]The sons of Elam, one thousand two hundred and fifty-four. [8]The sons of Zattu, nine hundred and forty-five. [9]The sons of Zaccai, seven hundred and sixty. [10]The sons of Bani, six hundred and forty-two. [11]The sons of Bebai, six hundred and twenty-three. [12]The sons of Azgad, one thousand two hundred and twenty-two. [13]The sons of Adonikam, six hundred and sixty-six. [14]The sons of Bigvai, two thousand and fifty-six. [15]The sons of Adin, four hundred and fifty-four. [16]The sons of Ater, namely of

Rev 13:18

---

a remnant still remains, a new start is always possible. This can be applied to the Church down through history: circumstances change, and new forms of organization can emerge, but the Church continues to subsist as the same Church that Jesus Christ founded and established on the foundation of the apostles.

2:1–63. The beginning of the book of Exodus lists the sons of Israel who went down to Egypt with Jacob, to show that there was continuity between the generation that arrived in that country and the one that left it under the leadership of Moses (cf. Ex 1:1–7). Later, in the book of Numbers, we find two censuses of the people which list the members of each house—one in the wilderness of Sinai (Num 1:1–46 and 3:1–39) and the other in the mountains of Moab at the gates of the promised land (Num 26:1–65). Those censuses have to do with key moments in the story—the first being when the sons of Israel were constituted the people of

[2] [1]Hi sunt autem provinciae filii, qui ascenderunt de captivitate migrantium, quos transtulerat Nabuchodonosor rex Babylonis in Babylonem, et reversi sunt in Ierusalem et Iudam, unusquisque in civitatem suam. [2]Qui venerunt cum Zorobabel, Iesua, Nehemias, Saraia, Rahelaia, Mardochaeus, Belsan, Mesphar, Beguai, Rehum, Baana. Numerus virorum populi Israel: [3]filii Pharos duo milia centum septuaginta duo; [4]filii Saphatia trecenti septuaginta duo; [5]filii Area septingenti septuaginta quinque; [6]filii Phahathmoab, hi sunt filii Iesua et Ioab, duo milia octingenti duodecim; [7]filii Elam mille ducenti quinquaginta quattuor; [8]filii Zethua nongenti quadraginta quinque; [9]filii Zachai septingenti sexaginta; [10]filii Bani sescenti quadraginta duo; [11]filii Bebai sescenti viginti tres; [12]filii Azgad mille ducenti viginti duo; [13]filii Adonicam sescenti sexaginta sex; [14]filii Beguai duo milia quinquaginta sex; [15]filii Adin quadringenti quinquaginta quattuor; [16]filii Ater, qui erant ex Ezechia, nonaginta octo; [17]filii

Hezekiah, ninety-eight. [17]The sons of Bezai, three hundred and twenty-three. [18]The sons of Jorah, one hundred and twelve. [19]The sons of Hashum, two hundred and twenty-three. [20]The sons of Gibbar, ninety-five. [21]The sons of Bethlehem, one hundred and twenty-three. [22]The men of Netophah, fifty-six. [23]The men of Anathoth, one hundred and twenty-eight. [24]The sons of Azmaveth, forty-two. [25]The sons of Kiriatharim, Chephirah, and Be-eroth, seven hundred and forty-three. [26]The sons of Ramah and Geba, six hundred and twenty-one. [27]The men of Michmas, one hundred and twenty-two. [28]The men of Bethel and Ai, two hundred and twenty-three. [29]The sons of Nebo, fifty-two. [30]The sons of Magbish, one hundred and fifty-six. [31]The sons of the other Elam, one thousand

---

God by means of the Covenant, and the second when they were preparing to establish themselves in the land that God was going to make theirs. In both cases there was need to put on record the persons and houses that made up the people.

Now, when that people is being built up again in the land God gave them and from which they had been deported by the Babylonians, a new record is made of who the members of that new people are. The same list is to be found in the memoirs of Nehemiah (Neh 7:6–72), a source that the author of Ezra-Nehemiah could have used and adapted to the situation he is now describing. What he wants to do is to keep alive the memory of who the pioneers were who reconstructed the people and to show that they did indeed belong to it. The list begins with eleven names (Nehemiah 7:7 has twelve names) which may be meant to symbolize "all Israel". It then goes on to list the "men of the people", or laymen (vv. 3–35), giving the line from which they sprang or their place of origin; maybe to indicate that they have a lower social status. Then comes the list of priests (vv. 36–39)—adding up to a high number, as befitting the primary objective of the mission (to reactivate religious worship), and a list of Levites (v. 40)—a much smaller number, given that they were not as much needed there to provide instruction in the Law. Singers and gatekeepers (vv. 41–42) also had an important role in worship; and the *nethinim*, oblates ("temple servants": RSV), and "the sons of Solomon's servants" (vv. 43–58), descendants of prisoners of war who would have embraced Judaism (cf. Num 31:30, 47; Josh 9:19–27; 1 Kings 9:20–21), performed the more humble services associated with the liturgy.

The reference to the fact that some people could not prove their Jewish

Besai trecenti viginti tres; [18]filii Iora centum duodecim; [19]filii Hasum ducenti viginti tres; [20]filii Gebbar nonaginta quinque; [21]filii Bethlehem centum viginti tres; [22]viri Netopha quinquaginta sex; [23]viri Anathoth centum viginti octo; [24]filii Azmaveth quadraginta duo; [25]filii Cariathiarim, Cephira et Beroth septingenti quadraginta tres; [26]filii Rama et Gabaa sescenti viginti unus; [27]viri Machmas centum viginti duo; [28]viri Bethel et Hai ducenti viginti tres; [29]filii Nabo quinquaginta duo; [30]filii Megbis centum quinquaginta sex; [31]filii Elam alterius mille ducenti quinquaginta quattuor; [32]filii Harim trecenti viginti;

two hundred and fifty-four. [32]The sons of Harim, three hundred and twenty. [33]The sons of Lod, Hadid, and Ono, seven hundred and twenty-five. [34]The sons of Jericho, three hundred and forty-five. [35]The sons of Senaah, three thousand six hundred and thirty.

[36]The priests: the sons of Jedaiah, of the house of Jeshua, nine hundred and seventy-three. [37]The sons of Immer, one thousand and fifty-two. [38]The sons of Pashhur, one thousand two hundred and forty-seven. [39]The sons of Harim, one thousand and seventeen.

[40]The Levites: the sons of Jeshua and Kadmi-el, of the sons of Hodaviah, seventy-four. [41]The singers: the sons of Asaph, one hundred and twenty-eight. [42]The sons of the gatekeepers: the sons of Shallum, the sons of Ater, the sons of Talmon, the sons of Akkub, the sons of Hatita, and the sons of Shobai, in all one hundred and thirty-nine.

[43]The temple servants:[d] the sons of Ziha, the sons of Hasupha, the sons of Tabbaoth, [44]the sons of Keros, the sons of Siaha, the sons of Padon, [45]the sons of Lebanah, the sons of Hagabah, the sons of Akkub, [46]the sons of Hagab, the sons of Shamlai, the sons of Hanan, [47]the sons of Giddel, the sons of Gahar, the sons of Reaiah, [48]the sons of Rezin, the sons of Nekoda, the sons of Gazzam, [49]the sons of Uzza, the sons of Paseah, the sons of Besai, [50]the sons of Asnah, the sons of Me-unim, the sons of Nephisim, [51]the sons of Bakbuk, the sons of Hakupha, the sons of Harhur, [52]the sons of Bazluth, the sons of Mehida, the sons of Harsha, [53]the sons of Barkos, the sons of Sisera, the sons of Temah, [54]the sons of Neziah, and the sons of Hatipha.

---

descent (vv. 59–63) shows how seriously this matter was taken, especially if the people concerned figured among the priests. For if non-Jews took part in the offerings by eating the portion of the victim assigned to the priest, that would render the sacrifice invalid and unclean. Only God could determine whether these people were Jews or not: a priest ascertained this by resort to lots (*urim* and *tummim*).

[33]filii Lod, Hadid et Ono septingenti viginti quinque; [34]filii Iericho trecenti quadraginta quinque; [35]filii Senaa tria milia sescenti triginta. [36]Sacerdotes: filii Iedaia de domo Iesua nongenti septuaginta tres, [37]filii Emmer mille quinquaginta duo, [38]filii Phassur mille ducenti quadraginta septem, [39]filii Harim mille decem et septem. [40]Levitae: filii Iesua hi sunt filii Cadmihel, Bennui, Odoviae, septuaginta quattuor. [41]Cantores: filii Asaph centum viginti octo. [42]Ianitores: filii Sellum, filii Ater, filii Telmon, filii Accub, filii Hatita, filii Sobai: universi centum triginta novem. [43]Oblati: filii Siha, filii Hasupha, filii Tabbaoth, [44]filii Ceros, filii Siaa, filii Phadon, [45]filii Lebana, filii Hagaba, filii Accub, [46]filii Hagab, filii Semlai, filii Hanan, [47]filii Giddel, filii Gaher, filii Raaia, [48]filii Rasin, filii Necoda, filii Gazam, [49]filii Oza, filii Phasea, filii Besai, [50]filii Asena, filii Meunitarum, filii Nephusorum, [51]filii Bacbuc, filii Hacupha, filii Harhur, [52]filii Basluth, filii Mahida, filii Harsa, [53]filii Bercos, filii Sisara, filii Thema, [54]filii

d. Heb *nethinim*

[55]The sons of Solomon's servants: the sons of Sotai, the sons of Hassophereth, the sons of Peruda, [56]the sons of Jaalah, the sons of Darkon, the sons of Giddel, [57]the sons of Shephatiah, the sons of Hattil, the sons of Pochereth-hazzebaim, and the sons of Ami.

[58]All the temple servants[d] and the sons of Solomon's servants were three hundred and ninety-two.

[59]The following were those who came up from Tel-melah, Tel-harsha, Cherub, Addan, and Immer, though they could not prove their fathers' houses or their descent, whether they belonged to Israel: [60]the sons of Delaiah, the sons of Tobiah, and the sons of Nekoda, six hundred and fifty-two. [61]Also, of the sons of the priests: the sons of Habaiah, the sons of Hakkoz, and the sons of Barzillai (who had taken a wife from the daughters of Barzillai the Gileadite, and was called by their name). [62]These sought their registration among those enrolled in the genealogies, but they were not found there, and so they were excluded from the priesthood as unclean; [63]the governor told them that they were not to partake of the most holy food, until there should be a priest to consult Urim and Thummim.

2 Sam 17:27; 19:32–40
1 Kings 2:7
Num 3:10
Ex 28:30

[64]The whole assembly together was forty-two thousand three hundred and sixty, [65]besides their menservants and maidservants, of whom there were seven thousand three hundred and thirty-seven; and they had two hundred male and female singers. [66]Their horses were seven hundred and thirty-six, their mules were two hundred and forty-five, [67]their camels were four hundred and

---

2:64–67. The actual number who return to Jerusalem is very large, even though it represents only a small proportion of the Jews in the diaspora. Menservants and maidservants (though not many) are also mentioned—which would indicate that some of the returning families were quite well off. The number of beasts of burden used seems quite low, given the length of the journey and the number of people involved. Singers (male and female) are mentioned in v. 65, suggesting that the trek was liturgical in character, somewhat like a pilgrimage.

Nasia, filii Hatipha. [55]Filii servorum Salomonis: filii Sotai, filii Sophereth, filii Pheruda, [56]filii Iaala, filii Darcon, filii Giddel, [57]filii Saphatia, filii Hatil, filii Phochereth Hassebaim, filii Ami. [58]Omnes oblati et filii servorum Salomonis trecenti nonaginta duo. [59]Et hi, qui ascenderunt de Thelmela, Thelharsa, Cherub et Addon et Emmer et non potuerunt indicare domum patrum suorum et semen suum, utrum ex Israel essent: [60]filii Dalaia, filii Tobia, filii Necoda, sescenti quinquaginta duo. [61]Et de filiis sacerdotum: filii Hobia, filii Accos, filii Berzellai, qui accepit de filiabus Berzellai Galaaditis uxorem et vocatus est nomine eorum. [62] Hi quaesierunt tabulas genealogiae suae et non invenerunt, et eiecti sunt de sacerdotio. [63]Et dixit praepositus eis, ut non comederent de sanctificatis sanctuarii, donec surgeret sacerdos pro Urim et Tummim. [64]Omnis multitudo simul quadraginta duo milia trecenti sexaginta, [65]exceptis servis eorum et ancillis, qui erant septem milia trecenti triginta septem, insuper et cantores atque cantatrices ducenti. [66]Equi eorum septingenti triginta sex, muli eorum ducenti quadraginta quinque, [67]cameli eorum

d. Heb *nethinim*

thirty-five, and their asses were six thousand seven hundred and twenty.

The exiles arrive in Jerusalem

[68]Some of the heads of families, when they came to the house of the LORD which is in Jerusalem, made freewill offerings for the house of God, to erect it on its site; [69]according to their ability they gave to the treasury of the work sixty-one thousand darics of gold, five thousand minas of silver, and one hundred priests' garments.

1 Chron 29:7
Neh 7:70–72

[70]The priests, the Levites, and some of the people lived in Jerusalem and its vicinity;[e] and the singers, the gatekeepers, and the temple servants lived in their towns, and all Israel in their towns.

3 [1]When the seventh month came, and the sons of Israel were in the towns, the people gathered as one man to Jerusalem. [2]Then arose Jeshua the son of Jozadak, with his fellow priests, and Zerubbabel the son of She-alti-el with his kinsmen, and they built the altar of the God of Israel, to offer burnt offerings upon it, as it is written in the law of Moses the man of God. [3]They set the altar

Neh 7:72b; 8:1
1 Kings 8:64
Mt 1:12
Lk 3:27

2:68–70. One cannot but notice the generosity of this Jewish community. The fact that this group established itself in Jerusalem and in the towns of Judah shows that the whole exercise was a new settlement of the land by the people; "all Israel" is moving back. The author does not dwell on the difficulties of the journey or those involved in resettling the land. He simply says that they left Babylon, entered the land and settled it.

3:1–6. The seventh month was the first month of autumn (15 September or 15 October), when the feast of Tabernacles was celebrated in memory of the time the Israelites spent in the wilderness (cf. Lev 23:33–34). The repatriates felt an urgency to re-establish contact with God by means of offerings, especially those prescribed for that festival. This was why they immediately set about building an altar, following the example of the Israelites after leaving Egypt (cf. Ex 29:35–46). Jeshua and Zerubbabel, David's descendants, are specifically mentioned, though the latter is not given the prominence due him, perhaps because when the book of Ezra was

quadringenti triginta quinque, asini eorum sex milia septingenti viginti. [68]Nonnulli autem de principibus familiarum, cum ingrederentur templum domini, quod est in Ierusalem, sponte obtulerunt in domum Dei ad exstruendam eam in loco suo. [69]Secundum vires suas dederunt in aerarium operis auri solidos sexaginta milia et mille, argenti minas quinque milia et vestes sacerdotales centum. [70]Habitaverunt ergo ibi sacerdotes et Levitae et quidam de populo; cantores autem et ianitores et oblati in urbibus suis, universusque Israel in civitatibus suis. **[3]** [1]Iamque venerat mensis septimus, et erant filii Israel in civitatibus suis. Congregatus est ergo populus quasi vir unus in Ierusalem. [2]Et surrexit Iesua filius Iosedec et fratres eius sacerdotes et Zorobabel filius Salathiel et fratres eius et aedificaverunt altare Dei Israel, ut offerrent in eo holocautomata, sicut scriptum est in lege Moysi viri Dei. [3]Collocaverunt autem

e. 1 Esdras 5:46: Heb lacks *lived in Jerusalem and its vicinity*

in its place, for fear was upon them because of the peoples of the lands, and they offered burnt offerings upon it to the LORD, burnt offerings morning and evening. [4]And they kept the feast of booths, as it is written, and offered the daily burnt offerings by number according to the ordinance, as each day required, [5]and after that the continual burnt offerings, the offerings at the new moon and at all the appointed feasts of the LORD, and the offerings of every one who made a freewill offering to the LORD. [6]From the first day of the seventh month they began to offer burnt offerings to the LORD. But the foundation of the temple of the LORD was not yet laid.

Ex 23:14
Num 28:3–8

The rebuilding of the temple begins*

1 Chron 22:4
2 Chron 2:9–14

[7]So they gave money to the masons and the carpenters, and food, drink, and oil to the Sidonians and the Tyrians to bring cedar trees from Lebanon to the sea, to Joppa, according to the grant which they had from Cyrus king of Persia.

[8]Now in the second year of their coming to the house of God at Jerusalem, in the second month, Zerubbabel the son of She-alti-el and Jeshua the son of Jozadak made a beginning, together with the rest of their brethren, the priests and the Levites and all who had come to Jerusalem from the captivity. They appointed the Levites, from twenty years old and upward, to have the oversight of the work of the house of the LORD. [9]And Jeshua with his sons and his kinsmen, and Kadmi-el and his sons, the sons of Judah, together

---

being written the idea of a restoration of the monarchy had faded away. St Bede has this to say about the priority given to building the altar: "[those who returned from exile in Babylon] once they had built the altar, offered sacrifices daily to God, to purify themselves and become worthy to begin the rebuilding of the temple. Exactly the same holds for the spiritual rebuilding: those who are to teach must begin by teaching themselves; he who seeks to instruct his neighbour in the fear and love of God must first make himself worthy of the role of teacher by his own constant service to God" (*In Esdram et Nehemiam*, 1, 3).

altare super bases suas, deterrentibus eos per circuitum populis terrarum, et obtulerunt super illud holocaustum Domino mane et vespere. [4]Feceruntque sollemnitatem Tabernaculorum, sicut scriptum est, et holocaustum diebus singulis per ordinem, secundum praeceptum pro singulis diebus; [5]et praeter holocaustum sempiternum illa etiam pro calendis et universis sollemnitatibus, quae erant consecratae Domino, et pro omnibus, quae ultro offerebantur Domino. [6]A primo die mensis septimi coeperunt offerre holocaustum Domino; porro templum Dei nondum fundatum erat. [7]Dederunt autem pecunias latomis et fabris, cibum quoque et potum et oleum Sidoniis Tyriisque, ut deferrent ligna cedrina de Libano ad mare Ioppe, iuxta quod concesserat Cyrus rex Persarum eis. [8]Anno autem secundo adventus eorum ad templum Dei in Ierusalem mense secundo, coeperunt Zorobabel filius Salathiel et Iesua filius Iosedec et reliqui de fratribus eorum sacerdotes et Levitae et omnes, qui venerant de captivitate in Ierusalem, et constituerunt Levitas a viginti annis et supra, ut dirigerent opus templi Domini. [9]Stetitque Iesua et filii eius et fratres eius, Cadmihel, Bennui et Odovia quasi vir unus, ut dirigerent eos, qui faciebant opus in templo Dei; itemque filii Henadad et filii eorum et fratres eorum Levitae. [10]Fundato

took the oversight of the workmen in the house of God, along with the sons of Henadad and the Levites, their sons and kinsmen.

[10]And when the builders laid the foundation of the temple of the LORD, the priests in their vestments came forward with trumpets, and the Levites, the sons of Asaph, with cymbals, to praise the LORD, according to the directions of David king of Israel; [11]and they sang responsively, praising and giving thanks to the LORD,

"For he is good,
for his steadfast love endures for ever toward Israel."

And all the people shouted with a great shout, when they praised the LORD, because the foundation of the house of the LORD was laid. [12]But many of the priests and Levites and heads of fathers' houses, old men who had seen the first house, wept with a loud voice when they saw the foundation of this house being laid, though many shouted aloud for joy; [13]so that the people could not distinguish the sound of the joyful shout from the sound of the people's weeping, for the people shouted with a great shout, and the sound was heard afar.

Num 10:5
1 Chron 15:16; 25:1–2

Ps 100:5; 106:1; 136

Hag 2:3

***3:7—6:18.** This section is an account of the rebuilding of the temple. The sacred writer brings in material from different sources to show the obstacles that needed to be surmounted in the course of this project (4:1—6:12), and how they rejoiced and praised God at start (3:10–13) and finish (6:16–18). He does not assemble the material in strict chronological order, but he does make it clear that the building of the temple was a task that lasted some twenty years, from 536 BC, when the work began (3:8), to 515 when the new temple was dedicated (6:15). To justify this long time spent on the project, he brings in details from a later period to do with the building of the city walls (4:6–33).

3:7–13. Rather as David and Solomon had done, skilled building workers were contracted and materials imported from as far away as Phoenicia (cf. 1 Chron 22:1–5; 2 Chron 2:1–14). Zerubbabel and Jeshua are again mentioned as organizers of the work, but Shesh-bazzar (cf. 1:8) has disappeared from the scene. Some psalms (for example 100, 106 and especially 136) reflect the joy and praise of God associated with the enterprise, but they are tinged with sadness over the fact that the old temple had been destroyed.

igitur ab aedificatoribus templo Domini, steterunt sacerdotes in ornatu suo cum tubis, et Levitae filii Asaph in cymbalis, ut laudarent Deum iuxta mandatum David regis Israel. [11]Et concinebant in hymnis et gratiarum actione Domino: «Quoniam bonus, quoniam in aeternum misericordia eius» super Israel. Omnis quoque populus vociferabatur clamore magno in laudando Dominum, eo quod fundatum esset templum Domini. [12]Plurimi etiam senes de sacerdotibus et Levitis et principibus familiarum, qui viderant oculis suis prius templum in loco suo, flebant voce magna; et multi vociferantes in laetitia elevabant vocem. [13]Nec poterat quisquam agnoscere vocem clamoris laetantium et vocem fletus populi, quoniam populus vociferabatur clamore magno, et strepitus audiebatur procul.

Opposition to the rebuilding

Hag 1:2–4
Zech 8:9–10

2 Kings 17:24–41

4 [1]Now when the adversaries of Judah and Benjamin heard that the returned exiles were building a temple to the LORD, the God of Israel, [2]they approached Zerubbabel and the heads of fathers' houses and said to them, "Let us build with you; for we worship your God as you do, and we have been sacrificing to him ever since the days of Esar-haddon king of Assyria who brought us here." [3]But Zerubbabel, Jeshua, and the rest of the heads of fathers' houses in Israel said to them, "You have nothing to do with us in building a house to our God; but we alone will build to the LORD, the God of Israel, as King Cyrus the king of Persia has commanded us."

[4]Then the people of the land discouraged the people of Judah, and made them afraid to build,* [5]and hired counsellors against them to frustrate their purpose, all the days of Cyrus king of Persia, even until the reign of Darius king of Persia.

[6]And in the reign of Ahasu-erus, in the beginning of his reign, they wrote an accusation against the inhabitants of Judah and Jerusalem.

[7]And in the days of Ar-ta-xerxes, Bishlam and Mithredath and Tabeel and the rest of their associates wrote to Ar-ta-xerxes king of Persia; the letter was written in Aramaic and translated.[f]

4:1–7. Difficulties arise when the repatriates want to keep their distance from those that they found installed in the land when they returned. These "adversaries of Judah and Benjamin" (v. 1) were people who never belonged to the kingdom of Judah; that is, they were people the Assyrians settled in Samaria after the fall of the Northern kingdom (722 BC), and when Jerusalem fell and its inhabitants were deported to Babylon, they had moved into the south and intermingled with Jews who had not been deported. They would have accepted the cult of the Lord, God of Israel, as well as their own cults; so they would have practised a religious syncretism (cf. 2 Kings 17:24–41). By

[4] [1]Audierunt autem hostes Iudae et Beniamin, quia filii captivitatis aedificarent templum Domino Deo Israel, [2]et accedentes ad Zorobabel et ad principes familiarum dixerunt eis: «Aedificemus vobiscum, quia ita ut vos quaerimus Deum vestrum et immolavimus victimas a diebus Asarhaddon regis Assyriae, qui adduxit nos huc». [3]Et dixit eis Zorobabel et Iesua et reliqui principes familiarum Israel: «Non est vobis et nobis, ut aedificemus domum Deo nostro, sed nos ipsi soli aedificabimus Domino, Deo Israel, sicut praecepit nobis Cyrus rex Persarum». [4]Factum est igitur, ut populus terrae impediret manus populi Iudae et turbaret eos in aedificando. [5]Conduxerunt autem adversus eos consiliatores, ut destruerent consilium eorum omnibus diebus Cyri regis Persarum et usque ad regnum Darii regis Persarum. [6]In regno autem Asueri, in principio regni eius, scripserunt accusationem adversus habitatores Iudae et Ierusalem. [7]Et in diebus Artaxerxis scripsit Beselam, Mithridates et Tabel et reliqui, qui erant in consilio eorum, ad Artaxerxem regem Persarum; scriptura autem accusationis erat scripta litteris Syriacis et

f. Heb adds *in Aramaic*, indicating that 4:8—6:18 is in Aramaic. Another interpretation is *The letter was written in the Aramaic script and set forth in the Aramaic language*

A report sent to Artaxerxes

[8]Rehum the commander and Shimshai the scribe wrote a letter against Jerusalem to Ar-ta-xerxes the king as follows—[9]then wrote Rehum the commander, Shimshai the scribe, and the rest of their associates, the judges, the governors, the officials, the Persians, the men of Erech, the Babylonians, the men of Susa, that is, the Elamites, [10]and the rest of the nations whom the great and noble Osnappar deported and settled in the cities of Samaria and in the rest of the province Beyond the River, and now [11]this is a copy of the letter that they sent—"To Ar-ta-xerxes the king: Your servants, the men of the province Beyond the River, send greeting. And now [12]be it known to the king that the Jews who came up from you to us have gone to Jerusalem. They are rebuilding that rebellious and wicked city; they are finishing the walls and repairing the foundations. [13]Now be it known to the king that, if this city is rebuilt and the walls finished, they will not pay tribute, custom, or toll, and the royal revenue will be impaired. [14]Now because we eat the salt of the palace and it is not fitting for us to witness the kings dishonour, therefore we send and inform the king, [15]in order that search may be made in the book of the records of your fathers. You

---

taking part in the building of the temple they would have acquired a right to offer sacrifices to the God of Israel there—but for them he was just another local god. This was why the repatriates would have nothing to do with them. This led to confusion and, soon, open opposition from the people of the land not only to the rebuilding of the temple but also to the reconstruction of the city. The root cause of this opposition was religious—the assertion of Jewish belief in the one, true God, the God of Israel, who had chosen a people for himself. It was not a matter of racial discrimination, for we will be told later on that those people of the land who turned their back on idolatry celebrated the Passover with the Jews (cf. 6:21).

4:8–24. To show the sort of obstacles that got in the way of the project, the sacred text reproduces a letter petitioning the king of Persia to put a stop

composita sermone Syro. [8]Rehum praefectus et Samsai scriba scripserunt epistulam unam de Ierusalem Artaxerxi regi huiuscemodi: [9]«Rehum praefectus et Samsai scriba et reliqui socii eorum, iudices et duces, magistratus Persae, Erchuaei, Babylonii, Susanechaei, hoc est Elamitae, [10]et ceteri de gentibus, quas transtulit Asenaphar magnus et gloriosus et habitare fecit in civitatibus Samariae et in reliquis regionibus trans flumen in pace». [11]Hoc est exemplar epistulae, quam miserunt ad eum: «Artaxerxi regi, servi tui, viri, qui sunt trans fluvium. Igitur [12]notum sit regi quia Iudaei, qui ascenderunt a te ad nos, venerunt in Ierusalem civitatem rebellem et pessimam, quam aedificant, exstruentes muros eius, fundamenta iam componentes. [13]Nunc notum sit regi quia, si civitas illa aedificata fuerit et muri eius instaurati, tributum et annonam et vectigal non dabunt, et ad ultimum regibus noxa erit. [14]Nos autem, memores salis, quod in palatio comedimus, et quia laesiones regis videre nefas ducimus, idcirco misimus et nuntiavimus regi, [15]ut recenseas in libris historiarum patrum tuorum, et invenies in his historiis et scies quoniam urbs illa urbs rebellis est et nocens regibus et provinciis, et seditiones

will find in the book of the records and learn that this city is a rebellious city, hurtful to kings and provinces, and that sedition was stirred up in it from of old. That was why this city was laid waste. [16]We make known to the king that, if this city is rebuilt and its walls finished, you will then have no possession in the province Beyond the River."

Artaxerxes orders the building work to stop

[17]The king sent an answer: "To Rehum the commander and Shimshai the scribe and the rest of their associates who live in Samaria and in the rest of the province Beyond the River, greeting. And now [18]the letter which you sent to us has been plainly read before me. [19]And I made a decree, and search has been made, and it has been found that this city from of old has risen against kings, and that rebellion and sedition have been made in it. [20]And mighty kings have been over Jerusalem, who ruled over the whole province Beyond the River, to whom tribute, custom, and toll were paid. [21]Therefore make a decree that these men be made to cease, and that this city be not rebuilt, until a decree is made by me. [22]And take care not to be slack in this matter; why should damage grow to the hurt of the king?"

to the works (vv. 11–16). In the sacred (Hebrew) text, this letter is given in Aramaic, the language in which it was originally written. From here on, the rest of the vicissitudes of the project are recounted in Aramaic—until the time when the temple is dedicated (6:18); then the text reverts to Hebrew. The first letter and the king's reply mention the rebuilding of the wall and the city which in fact happened much later (vv. 12–21; cf. Neh 2:11–18). Certainly, the building of the temple was delayed until 520 BC, the second year of Darius' reign (v. 24), due not just to opposition from the people of the land but also perhaps to despondency among the repatriates when they realized that they were on their own (cf. 4:4). The letters written to the king identify those who held delegated authority from the king over the territory—the commander and the governor, who lived in Samaria (cf. v. 9; 5:3)—and give information on the background of the people who were living in the country at the time.

concitantur in ea ex diebus antiquis; quam ob rem et civitas ipsa destructa est. [16]Nuntiamus nos, regi quoniam, si civitas illa aedificata fuerit et muri ipsius instaurati, possessionem trans fluvium non habebis». [17]Verbum misit rex ad Rehum praefectum et Samsai scribam et ad reliquos, qui erant in consilio eorum, qui habitabant in Samaria et in regione trans fluvium: «Pax. Nunc igitur scriptura, [18]quam misistis ad nos, manifeste lecta est coram me. [19]Et a me praeceptum est, et recensuerunt inveneruntque quoniam civitas illa a diebus antiquis adversum reges rebellabat, et rebelliones et seditiones concitabantur in ea; [20]nam et reges fortissimi fuerunt in Ierusalem, qui et dominati sunt omni regioni, quae trans fluvium est, tributum quoque et annonam et vectigal accipiebant. [21]Nunc ergo praecipite, ut desistant isti homines, et urbs illa non aedificetur, donec forte a me iussum fuerit. [22]Videte,

[23]Then, when the copy of King Ar-ta-xerxes' letter was read before Rehum and Shimshai the scribe and their associates, they went in haste to the Jews at Jerusalem and by force and power made them cease. [24]Then the work on the house of God which is in Jerusalem stopped; and it ceased until the second year of the reign of Darius king of Persia.

Neh 1:3

The Jews start building again

5 *[1]Now the prophets, Haggai and Zechariah the son of Iddo, prophesied to the Jews who were in Judah and Jerusalem, in the name of the God of Israel who was over them. [2]Then Zerubbabel the son of She-alti-el and Jeshua the son of Jozadak arose and began to rebuild the house of God which is in Jerusalem; and with them were the prophets of God, helping them.

[3]At the same time Tattenai the governor of the province Beyond the River and Shethar-bozenai and their associates came to them and spoke to them thus, "Who gave you a decree to build this house and to finish this structure?" [4]They[g] also asked them this, "What are the names of the men who are building this building?" [5]But the eye of their God was upon the elders of the Jews, and they did not stop them till a report should reach Darius and then answer be returned by letter concerning it.

Ezra 6:14
Hag 1:14–29
Zech 4:9
1 Kings 6:1
Lk 3:27

5:1–5. These passages, written in Aramaic, also show the care God took of his own, and the help he gave them; they for their part stuck doggedly to their task. God's solicitude can be seen from the fact that he raises up new prophets (Haggai and Zechariah) and moves Jeshua and Zerubbabel to act. Soon after Darius comes to the throne, the Israelites set about their task again in defiance of the local authorities (vv. 3–5). God protected them so that they were able to carry on working until the new king's reply arrived.

ne negligenter hoc impleatis, et paulatim crescat malum contra reges». [23]Itaque exemplum edicti Artaxerxis regis lectum est coram Rehum praefectum et Samsai scriba et consiliariis eorum; et abierunt festini in Ierusalem ad Iudaeos et prohibuerunt eos in brachio et robore. [24]Tunc intermissum est opus domus Domini in Ierusalem et non fiebat usque ad annum secundum regni Darii regis Persarum. [5] [1]Prophetae autem Aggaeus et Zacharias filius Addo prophetaverunt ad Iudaeos, qui erant in Iudaea et Ierusalem, in nomine Dei Israel, quod erat super eos. [2]Tunc surrexerunt Zorobabel filius Salathiel et Iesua filius Iosedec et coeperunt aedificare templum Dei in Ierusalem; prophetae autem Dei adiuvabant eos. [3]In ipso autem tempore venit ad eos Thathanai, qui erat dux trans flumen, et Stharbuzanai et consiliarii eorum, sicque dixerunt eis: «Quis dedit vobis potestatem, ut domum hanc aedificaretis et materiam istam praepararetis? [4]Quae sunt nomina hominum auctorum aedificationis illius?». [5]Oculus autem Dei eorum factus est super senes Iudaeorum, et non obstiterunt eis, usque dum

g. Gk Syr: Aramaic *We*

Letter to Darius justifying the building work

[6]The copy of the letter which Tattenai the governor of the province Beyond the River and Shethar-bozenai and his associates the governors who were in the province Beyond the River sent to Darius the king; [7]they sent him a report, in which was written as follows: "To Darius the king, all peace. [8]Be it known to the king that we went to the province of Judah, to the house of the great God. It is being built with huge stones, and timber is laid in the walls; this work goes on diligently and prospers in their hands. [9]Then we asked those elders and spoke to them thus, 'Who gave you a decree to build this house and to finish this structure?' [10]We also asked them their names, for your information, that we might write down the names of the men at their head. [11]And this was their reply to us: 'We are the servants of the God of heaven and earth, and we are rebuilding the house that was built many years ago, which a great king of Israel built and finished. [12]But because our fathers had angered the God of heaven, he gave them into the hand of Nebuchadnezzar king of Babylon, the Chaldean, who destroyed this house and carried away the people to Babylonia. [13]However in the first year of Cyrus king of Babylon, Cyrus the king made a decree that this house of God should be rebuilt. [14]And the gold and silver vessels of the house of God, which Nebuchadnezzar had taken out of the temple that was in Jerusalem and brought into the temple of Babylon, these Cyrus the king took out of the temple of Babylon, and they were delivered to one whose name was Shesh-bazzar, whom he had made governor; [15]and he said to him, "Take these vessels, go and put them in the temple which is in Jerusalem, and let the house of God be rebuilt on its site." [16]Then this Shesh-bazzar came and laid the foundations of the house of

2 Kings 24:2; 25:8–11
2 Chron 36:16

---

res ad Darium referretur, et tunc sententia de hac re redderetur. [6]Exemplar epistulae, quam misit Thathanai dux regionis trans flumen et Stharbuzanai et consiliatores eius et duces, qui erant trans flumen, ad Darium regem. [7]Sermo, quem miserant ei, sic scriptus erat: «Dario regi pax omnis. [8]Notum sit regi isse nos ad Iudaeam provinciam, ad domum Dei magni, quae aedificatur lapide quadrato, et ligna ponuntur in parietibus; opusque illud diligenter exstruitur et crescit in manibus eorum. [9]Interrogavimus ergo senes illos et ita diximus eis: "Quis dedit vobis potestatem, ut domum hanc aedificaretis et materiam istam praepararetis?". [10]Sed et nomina eorum quaesivimus ab eis, ut nuntiaremus tibi, scripsimusque nomina eorum virorum, qui sunt principes in eis. [11]Huiuscemodi autem sermonem responderunt nobis dicentes: "Nos sumus servi Dei caeli et terrae et aedificamus templum, quod erat exstructum ante hos annos multos, quodque rex Israel magnus aedificaverat et exstruxerat. [12]Postquam autem ad iracundiam provocaverunt patres nostri Deum caeli, tradidit eos in manus Nabuchodonosor regis Babylonis Chaldaei, qui domum hanc destruxit et populum eius transtulit in Babylonem. [13]Anno autem primo Cyri regis Babylonis, Cyrus rex proposuit edictum, ut domus Dei haec aedificaretur. [14]Nam et vasa templi Dei aurea et argentea, quae Nabuchodonosor tulerat de templo, quod erat in Ierusalem, et asportaverat ea in templum Babylonis, protulit Cyrus rex de templo Babylonis et data sunt viro cuidam nomine Sasabassar, quem et principem constituit, [15]dixitque ei: 'Haec vasa tolle et vade et pone ea in templo, quod est in Ierusalem, et domus Dei aedificetur in loco suo'. [16]Tunc itaque Sasabassar ille venit et posuit fundamenta templi Dei in Ierusalem, et ex eo tempore usque nunc aedificatur et necdum completum

God which is in Jerusalem; and from that time until now it has been in building, and it is not yet finished.' [17]Therefore, if it seem good to the king, let search be made in the royal archives there in Babylon, to see whether a decree was issued by Cyrus the king for the rebuilding of this house of God in Jerusalem. And let the king send us his pleasure in this matter."

Darius allows the rebuilding to continue

6 [1]Then Darius the king made a decree, and search was made in Babylonia, in the house of the archives where the documents were stored. [2]And in Ecbatana, the capital which is in the province of Media, a scroll was found on which this was written: "A record. [3]In the first year of Cyrus the king, Cyrus the king issued a decree: Concerning the house of God at Jerusalem, let the house be rebuilt, the place where sacrifices are offered and burnt offerings are brought; its height shall be sixty cubits and its breadth sixty cubits, [4]with three courses of great stones and one course of timber; let the cost be paid from the royal treasury. [5]And also let the gold and silver vessels of the house of God, which Nebuchadnezzar took out of the temple that is in Jerusalem and brought to Babylon, be restored and brought back to the temple which is in Jerusalem, each to its place; you shall put them in the house of God."

Ezra 1:4

Completion of the building work

[6]"Now therefore, Tattenai, governor of the province Beyond the River, Shethar-bozenai, and your associates the governors who are in the province Beyond the River, keep away; [7]let the work on this

---

6:1–12. Eventually, God in his providence sorted the situation out and it became quite clear that the building work at Jerusalem had been legally authorized; so Darius gave his permission and every encouragement to push the project forward. The repatriates benefit from a special royal decree which reads as if the king not only recognized the Jews' rights in the

est". [17]Nunc ergo, si videtur regi bonum, recenseat in aerario regis, quod est in Babylone, utrumnam a Cyro rege potestas data fuerit, ut aedificaretur domus Dei in Ierusalem, et voluntatem regis super hac re mittat ad nos». **[6]** [1]Tunc Darius rex praecepit, et recensuerunt in tabulis aerarii, quod est in Babylone, [2]et inventum est in Ecbatanis, quod est castrum in Medena provincia, volumen unum, et sic scriptus erat in eo commentarius: [3]«Anno primo Cyri regis, Cyrus rex decrevit de domo Dei, quae est in Ierusalem: Aedificetur domus, ubi immolent et sacrificent; altitudo eius cubitorum sexaginta et latitudo eius cubitorum sexaginta, [4]ordines de lapidibus quadratis tres et ordo de lignis unus; sumptus autem de domo regis dabuntur. [5]Sed et vasa templi Dei aurea et argentea, quae Nabuchodonosor tulerat de templo Ierusalem et attulerat in Babylonem, reddantur et referantur in templum, quod est in Ierusalem, in locum suum, in templo Dei. [6]Nunc ergo, Thathanai dux regionis, quae est trans flumen, Stharbuzanai et consiliarii eius et duces, qui estis trans flumen, procul recedite ab illo loco, [7]dimittite fieri templum Dei

house of God alone; let the governor of the Jews and the elders of the Jews rebuild this house of God on its site. [8]Moreover I make a decree regarding what you shall do for these elders of the Jews for the rebuilding of this house of God; the cost is to be paid to these men in full and without delay from the royal revenue, the tribute of the province from Beyond the River. [9]And whatever is needed—young bulls, rams, or sheep for burnt offerings to the God of heaven, wheat, salt, wine, or oil, as the priests at Jerusalem require—let that be given to them day by day without fail, [10]that they may offer pleasing sacrifices to the God of heaven, and pray for the life of the king and his sons. [11]Also I make a decree that if any one alters this edict, a beam shall be pulled out of his house, and he shall be impaled upon it, and his house shall be made a dunghill. [12]May the God who has caused his name to dwell there overthrow any king or people that shall put forth a hand to alter this, or to destroy this house of God which is in Jerusalem. I Darius make a decree; let it be done with all diligence."

[13]Then, according to the word sent by Darius the king, Tattenai, the governor of the province Beyond the River, Shethar-bozenai, and their associates did with all diligence what Darius the king had

---

matter but also acknowledged the God whom they meant to worship in that temple. Darius invokes this God against anyone who might dare frustrate his wishes (v. 12). It is a kind of sign that the work the Jews are engaged in is desired by God, even though he makes his mind known through a foreign king. The same happened with Cyrus.

6:13–15. It is interesting that this last stage of building the temple is attributed to "the elders of the Jews". Maybe Jeshua and Zerubbabel are no longer around. It is also clear to see that the divine commandment is put into effect through decrees issued by Persian kings, who are now named in regnal order. Given the importance of the event, the exact date is naturally given—3 March 515 BC.

The New Testament says that the Church is "God's building" (1 Cor 3:9). "The Lord compared himself to the stone

---

illud; dux Iudaeorum et seniores eorum aedificent domum Dei illam in loco suo. [8]Sed et a me praeceptum est quomodo agere debeatis cum senioribus Iudaeorum illis, qui aedificant domum Dei illam: ut de arca regis, id est de tributis, quae dantur de regione trans flumen, studiose sumptus dentur viris illis sine intermissione. [9]Et si quid necesse fuerit, sive vituli et arietes et agni in holocaustum Deo caeli, sive frumentum, sal, vinum et oleum, secundum ordinationem sacerdotum, qui sunt in Ierusalem, detur eis per singulos dies sine neglegentia. [10]Et offerant oblationes suaves Deo caeli orentque pro vita regis et filiorum eius. [11]A me ergo positum est decretum, ut omnis homo, qui hanc mutaverit iussionem, tollatur lignum de domo ipsius et erigatur et configatur in eo; domus autem eius ponatur in sterquilinium. [12]Deus autem, qui habitare fecit nomen suum ibi, dissipet omnia regna et populum, qui extenderit manum suam, ut contemnat et dissipet domum Dei illam, quae est in Ierusalem. Ego Darius statui decretum, quod studiose impleri volo». [13]Igitur Thathanai dux regionis trans flumen et duces et

ordered. [14]And the elders of the Jews built and prospered, through the prophesying of Haggai the prophet and Zechariah the son of Iddo. They finished their building by command of the God of Israel and by decree of Cyrus and Darius and Ar-ta-xerxes king of Persia; [15]and this house was finished on the third day of the month of Adar, in the sixth year of the reign of Darius the king.

Dedication of the temple

[16]And the people of Israel, the priests and the Levites, and the rest of the returned exiles, celebrated the dedication of this house of God with joy. [17]They offered at the dedication of this house of God one hundred bulls, two hundred rams, four hundred lambs, and as a sin offering for all Israel twelve he-goats, according to the number of the tribes of Israel. [18]And they set the priests in their

1 Kings 8:62–65

1 Chron 23–24

which the builders rejected but which was made into the cornerstone (Mt 21: 42; cf. Acts 4:11; 1 Pet 2:7; Ps 117:22) On this foundation the Church is built by the apostles (cf. 1 Cor 3:11)" (Vatican II, *Lumen gentium*, 6). Christians are like living stones being used in the construction of the Church in this life (cf. 1 Pet 2:5). This building of God's rests on a sound foundation but it is something ongoing; there is always building to be done. It encounters external obstacles, and the builders themselves can grow tired; although the Lord allowed difficulties to arise with the building of the temple, it would in due course be completed; so too the Church will manage to make its way, thanks to the effort each Christian makes in his or her own place in the world.

6:16–18. Even though it is the climax in the whole story-line of the book, the dedication of the temple is described succinctly, especially when compared to the account of the dedication of Solomon's temple according to 2 Chronicles 5:1—7:22. It is probably done this way to show that this is not a new temple, but the continuation of the one that was there before. On the other hand, to legitimize the fact that there is a new altar and even a new temple, 2 Maccabees 1:18–36, which attributes the building to Nehemiah, records a different tradition about the dedication.

The Ezra text delights in noting the generous offerings made by the Israelites. In the Christian tradition, the ceremony of dedication survives in the dedication of churches, and pastors do

consiliarii eius, secundum quod praeceperat Darius rex, sic diligenter exsecuti sunt. [14]Seniores autem Iudaeorum prosperabantur in aedificatione iuxta prophetiam Aggaei prophetae et Zachariae filii Addo et perfecerunt aedificationem, iubente Deo Israel et iubente Cyro et Dario et Artaxerxe regibus Persarum, [15]et compleverunt domum Dei istam die tertia mensis Adar, qui est annus sextus regni Darii regis. [16]Fecerunt autem filii Israel, sacerdotes et Levitae et reliqui filiorum transmigrationis dedicationem domus Dei illius in gaudio. [17]Et obtulerunt in dedicationem domus Dei illius boves centum, arietes ducentos, agnos quadringentos, hircos caprarum pro peccato totius Israel duodecim, iuxta numerum tribuum Israel. [18]Et statuerunt sacerdotes in ordinibus suis et Levitas in vicibus suis in

divisions and the Levites in their courses, for the service of God at Jerusalem, as it is written in the book of Moses.

Ex 12:1

Celebration of the Passover

Lev 23:5

[19]On the fourteenth day of the first month the returned exiles kept the passover. [20]For the priests and the Levites had purified themselves together; all of them were clean. So they killed the passover lamb for all the returned exiles, for their fellow priests, and for themselves; [21]it was eaten by the people of Israel who had returned from exile, and also by every one who had joined them

---

not fail to encourage the faithful to make appropriate spiritual offerings: "Therefore, my beloved friends, if we wish to celebrate with joy the dedication of the temple, we must not destroy the living temple of God within us by evildoing. I will say it in a way that everybody can understand: we must prepare our souls in the same way as we would like the church to be prepared when we enter it. Do you want to visit a clean basilica? Then do not dirty your soul with sin. Just as you would like the basilica to be well-lit, God does not wish your soul to be in darkness, but rather he desires that the Lord's saying would prove true: that the light of good works may be shining within you so that he who lives in the heavens may be glorified" (St Caesarius of Arles, *Sermons*, 229, 3).

6:19–22. The account of the repatriates' return to Israel is reminiscent at times of events relating to the Exodus. One of these is the celebration of Passover. However, the context and the meaning of this celebration have nuances proper to each situation.

In the Exodus, Passover was celebrated prior to setting out on the journey, as a preparation for that great salvific intervention by God on behalf of his people. Here the Passover comes at the end, to show appreciation to God, who has allowed them to return from Babylon, rebuild the temple and begin to live normal lives again in the land he promised them. It is noteworthy that, alongside the repatriates, some "people of the land" (v. 21) also share in the passover meal.

Passover is the great festival that celebrates the saving action of God: that action is not just a past event, a memory of the escape from Egypt; it happens in various ways over the course of the life of the people down the ages. The celebration of this festival is a memorial of a past event which is made present at every Passover. All this helps us to appreciate the meaning of the paschal (Easter, Passover) mystery of Jesus, the greatest saving intervention by God on behalf of mankind, which brought to fullness the ancient passover celebrations. Every time that the memorial of the mystery

---

ministerium Dei in Ierusalem, sicut scriptum est in libro Moysi. [19]Fecerunt autem filii Israel transmigrationis Pascha quarta decima die mensis primi. [20]Levitae universi se purificaverunt; purificati autem cuncti immolaverunt Pascha universis filiis transmigrationis et fratribus suis sacerdotibus et sibi. [21]Et comederunt filii Israel, qui reversi fuerant de transmigratione, et omnes, qui a coinquinatione

and separated himself from the pollutions of the peoples of the land to worship the LORD, the God of Israel. [22]And they kept the feast of unleavened bread seven days with joy; for the LORD had made them joyful, and had turned the heart of the king of Assyria to them, so that he aided them in the work of the house of God, the God of Israel.

Ex 12:15; 13:16

2. EZRA'S MISSION—TO RE-ESTABLISH THE LAW*

Ezra travels from Babylon to Jerusalem

7 * [1]Now after this, in the reign of Ar-ta-xerxes king of Persia, Ezra the son of Seraiah, son of Azariah, son of Hilkiah, [2]son of Shallum, son of Zadok, son of Ahitub, [3]son of Amariah, son of

1 Chron 5:27–41
Neh 2:1

of Jesus' passion, death and resurrection is celebrated in the Eucharist, its salvific power takes effect.

***7:1—10:44.** The Persian authorities were quite tolerant of the traditional laws and customs of their subject peoples. This gained them their respect. Thus, just as Cyrus allowed the deported Jews to return to build the temple, Ar-ta-xerxes sent Ezra, an expert in the Law that the Lord God of Israel gave Moses, to see to it that that Law was put into effect in Jerusalem and the surrounding area. We do not know for certain whether this was Artaxerxes I (465–425 BC) or Artaxerxes II (405–399 BC), although the available information suggests it was more likely to have been the latter (cf. 'Introduction', p. 209).

The second part of the book Ezra tells what happened during the course of Ezra's mission. Most of the content probably derives from a document known as "the memoirs of Ezra" (which, in addition to what is here, would also have included Nehemiah 8). In this Ezra would have provided a report to the Persian imperial authorities telling how his mission had gone.

The "memoirs of Ezra" begins by outlining the mission he was charged with, and reproducing the document (written in Aramaic) whereby Ar-ta-xerxes conferred on him all the powers necessary to fulfil his assignment (7:11–26). Then comes a description of the committee that Ezra formed to accompany him to Jerusalem, with details of the material and spiritual preparations for the journey, and a description of it, which takes us to the Holy City (8:1–36). Once he arrived there, the main problem that concerned Ezra was that the prescriptions of the Law designed to protect the identity of the people were not being

gentium terrae transierunt ad eos, ut quaererent Dominum, Deum Israel. [22]Et fecerunt sollemnitatem Azymorum septem diebus in laetitia, quoniam laetificaverat eos Dominus et converterat cor regis Assyriae ad eos, ut adiuvaret manus eorum in opere domus Domini, Dei Israel. **[7]** [1]Post haec autem in regno Artaxerxis regis Persarum, Esdras filius Saraiae filii Azariae filii Helciae [2]filii Sellum filii Sadoc

Azariah, son of Meraioth, [4]son of Zerahiah, son of Uzzi, son of Bukki, [5]son of Abishu-a, son of Phinehas, son of Eleazar, son of Aaron the chief priest—[6]this Ezra went up from Babylonia. He was a scribe skilled in the law of Moses which the LORD the God of Israel had given; and the king granted him all that he asked, for the hand of the LORD his God was upon him.

Ezra 7:28 Neh 8:1–5,13; 12:26,36

[7]And there went up also to Jerusalem, in the seventh year of Ar-ta-xerxes the king, some of the people of Israel, and some of the priests and Levites, the singers and gatekeepers, and the temple servants. [8]And he came to Jerusalem in the fifth month, which was in the seventh year of the king; [9]for on the first day of the first month he began[h] to go up from Babylonia, and on the first day of the fifth month he came to Jerusalem, for the good hand of his God was upon him. [10]For Ezra had set his heart to study the law of the LORD, and to do it, and to teach his statutes and ordinances in Israel.

Neh 2:18

Powers given by Artaxerxes to Ezra

[11]This is a copy of the letter which King Ar-ta-xerxes gave to Ezra the priest, the scribe, learned in matters of the commandments of the LORD and his statutes for Israel: [12]"Ar-ta-xerxes, king of kings, to Ezra the priest, the scribe of the law of the God of heaven.[x] And now [13]I make a decree that any one of the people of Israel or their priests or Levites in my kingdom, who freely offers to go to Jerusalem, may go with you. [14]For you are sent by the king and his

Ezra 1:2

Esther 1:14

---

complied with: there had been a lot of intermarriage with foreigners and worship of these foreigners' gods. Things had come to such a pass that Ezra made a penitential prayer to God acknowledging the people's guilt (9:1–15). Then he set about righting the situation (10:1–44).

In the overall editorial plan of the books of Ezra and Nehemiah, this section is very important. As has already been said, the repatriates first of all attended to the service of God and they began to rebuild the temple (1:1—6:22). Now that that work was completed and religious worship was established again, the time had come to bring their personal lives into line with the Law of God. The chapters in this part of the book describe how they went about this.

filii Achitob [3]filii Amariae filii Azariae filii Meraioth [4]filii Zaraiae filii Ozi filii Bocci [5]filii Abisue filii Phinees filii Eleazar filii Aaron summi sacerdotis, [6]ipse Esdras ascendit de Babylone et ipse scriba velox in lege Moysi, quam dedit Dominus, Deus Israel. Cumque manus Domini Dei eius esset super eum, dedit ei rex omnem petitionem eius. [7]Et ascenderunt de filiis Israel et de filiis sacerdotum et de filiis

h. Vg See Syr: Heb *that was the foundation of the going up* **x.** Aramaic adds a word of uncertain meaning

seven counsellors to make inquiries about Judah and Jerusalem according to the law of your God, which is in your hand, [15]and also to convey the silver and gold which the king and his counselors have freely offered to the God of Israel, whose dwelling is in Jerusalem, [16]with all the silver and gold which you shall find in the whole province of Babylonia, and with the freewill offerings of the people and the priests, vowed willingly for the house of their God which is in Jerusalem. [17]With this money, then, you shall with

Ezra 8:28–30
2 Mac 3:2

7:1–10. One purpose of the genealogies given in the Bible is to show the importance of a person. Sometimes a family tree is given when his birth is mentioned (Gen 11:10–32; Mt 1:1–17) or when his mission begins (Ex 6: 14–27; Jud 8:1; Lk 3:23–28), as in this case (vv. 1–5), where we are told that Ezra is of the line of Aaron and, therefore, a priest. The text will often refer to this fact (cf. 10:10, 16; Neh 8:2, 9, etc.). But we are also told that he was "a scribe skilled in the law of Moses" (v. 6), and on many occasions he is referred to simply as "Ezra the scribe" (Neh 8:1, 4, 13, 15, etc.). This title probably stems from the fact that he was a counsellor and official of the Persian government dealing with Jewish affairs and, moreover, a specialist in Jewish texts and traditions. So, Ezra signals the start of a time when the priest who was expert in the Law wielded enormous influence in Jewry (by "Law" is meant a whole range of rules and prescriptions written down in various books). This heightened status of the priest developed during the exile in Babylon, and now it will be imposed over Judaism generally. That is why later tradition will point to Ezra as being the first compiler of the sacred books, the first to create the biblical canon.

Ezra felt moved by God to teach the Law in Israel and to see to its fulfilment. To this end, he began to assemble a group of people who would go with him to Jerusalem, and he sought the king's permission to put his plan into action. In this passage, we are twice told, "the hand of the Lord his God was upon him" (vv. 6 and 9). God gave him this help because his heart was in the right place: "Ezra had set his heart to study the Law of the Lord" (v. 10). The same idea is repeated later on: "The hand

Levitarum et de cantoribus et de ianitoribus oblatis in Ierusalem, anno septimo Artaxerxis regis. [8]Venit in Ierusalem mense quinto, ipse est annus septimus regis. [9]In primo die mensis primi coepit ascendere de Babylone et in primo die mensis quinti venit in Ierusalem, iuxta manum Dei sui bonam super se. [10]Esdras enim applicavit cor suum, ut investigaret et impleret legem Domini et faceret et doceret in Israel praeceptum et iudicium. [11]Hoc est autem exemplar epistulae, quam dedit rex Artaxerxes Esdrae sacerdoti, scribae erudito in mandatis Domini et praeceptis eius in Israel. [12]«Artaxerxes rex regum Esdrae sacerdoti, scribae legis Dei caeli, salutem. [13]A me decretum est, ut cuicumque placuerit in regno meo de populo Israel et de sacerdotibus eius et de Levitis ire in Ierusalem, tecum vadat. [14]A facie enim regis et septem consiliatorum eius missus es, ut visites Iudaeam et Ierusalem secundum legem Dei tui, quae est in manu tua, [15]et ut feras argentum et aurum, quod rex et consiliatores eius sponte obtulerunt Deo Israel, cuius in Ierusalem tabernaculum est. [16]Et omne argentum et aurum, quodcumque inveneris in universa provincia Babylonis simul cum oblationibus sponte oblatis a populo et a sacerdotibus pro domo Dei sui, quae est in Ierusalem, [17]igitur studiose eme de hac pecunia boves, arietes, agnos et

Num 15:4–13

all diligence buy bulls, rams, and lambs, with their cereal offerings and their drink offerings, and you shall offer them upon the altar of the house of your God which is in Jerusalem. [18]Whatever seems good to you and your brethren to do with the rest of the silver and gold, you may do, according to the will of your God. [19]The vessels that have been given you for the service of the house of your God, you shall deliver before the God of Jerusalem. [20]And whatever else is required for the house of your God, which you have occasion to provide, you may provide it out of the king's treasury.

Ezra 8:33–34

[21]"And I, Ar-ta-xerxes the king, make a decree to all the treasurers in the province Beyond the River: Whatever Ezra the priest, the scribe of the law of the God of heaven, requires of you, be it done with all diligence, [22]up to a hundred talents of silver, a hundred cors of wheat, a hundred baths of wine, a hundred baths of oil, and salt without prescribing how much. [23]Whatever is commanded by the God of heaven, let it be done in full for the

---

of our God is for good upon all that seek him" (8:22). St Bede comments that "Ezra becomes able to draw others to God by means of his teaching only when, by God's grace, he himself is made strong enough to overcome any obstacles to that holy venture" (*In Esdram et Nehemiam*, 1, 10). Christian tradition links Ezra to Jesus: just as Ezra instructed the people of God in the Law of Moses, Jesus taught that Law and brought it to fulfilment (cf. Mt 5:17).

7:11–26. Ezra is sent to Jerusalem endowed with truly remarkable powers. For one thing, he brings the Law, which the Persian king acknowledges to be the law of Judah and Jerusalem (v. 14), and the king also gives him authority to impose the Law on all Jews living west of the Euphrates (v. 25). Moreover, Ezra is entitled to channel funds to the temple of Jerusalem and to oversee how they are spent (vv. 16–18). This means that Ezra's activities were not confined to teaching the Law so as to bring about the religious renewal of the Jewish people: he had a wider brief, involving civil powers such as appointing judges and seeing that sentences were carried out (v. 26). We are seeing here the shape of official Judaism after the exile: kings and empires may come and go, but the high priest and the priestly class will continue to exercise these functions where possible.

oblationes et libamina eorum et offer ea super altare templi Dei vestri, quod est in Ierusalem. [18]Sed et, si quid tibi et fratribus tuis placuerit de reliquo argento et auro ut faciatis iuxta voluntatem Dei vestri, facite. [19]Vasa quoque, quae dantur tibi in ministerium domus Dei tui, trade in conspectu Dei in Ierusalem. [20]Sed et cetera, quibus opus fuerit in domum Dei tui, quantumcumque necesse est ut expendas, dabitur ab aerario regis. [21]Et ego Artaxerxes rex statui atque decrevi omnibus custodibus arcae publicae, qui sunt trans flumen, ut quodcumque petierit a vobis Esdras sacerdos, scriba legis Dei caeli, absque mora detis, [22]usque ad argenti talenta centum et usque ad frumenti coros centum et usque ad vini batos centum et usque ad batos olei centum; sal vero absque mensura. [23]Omne, quod requirit Deus caeli,

house of the God of heaven, lest his wrath be against the realm of the king and his sons. [24]We also notify you that it shall not be lawful to impose tribute, custom, or toll upon any one of the priests, the Levites, the singers, the doorkeepers, the temple servants, or other servants of this house of God.

[25]"And you, Ezra, according to the wisdom of your God which is in your hand, appoint magistrates and judges who may judge all the people in the province Beyond the River, all such as know the laws of your God; and those who do not know them, you shall teach. [26]Whoever will not obey the law of your God and the law of the king, let judgment be strictly executed upon him, whether for death or for banishment or for confiscation of his goods or for imprisonment."

Ezra's gratitude to God

[27]Blessed be the LORD, the God of our fathers, who put such a thing as this into the heart of the king, to beautify the house of the LORD which is in Jerusalem, [28]and who extended to me his steadfast love before the king and his counselors, and before all the king's mighty officers. I took courage, for the hand of the LORD my God was upon me, and I gathered leading men from Israel to go up with me.

7:27–28. From this point up to the end of chapter 9, there is a change of narrator. Now Ezra speaks in the first person. Recognizing what God has done in the king's heart, he joyfully exclaims: "Blessed be the Lord, the God of our fathers." As a good Israelite, when he sees the good things God has done for him and his people, he blesses the Lord, acknowledging that God, the source of all blessing, has worked wonders once again. Jesus too (whom Ezra prefigures) taught us to acknowledge the benefits God gives us, and to thank him for them. In his "hymn of praise" (Mt 11:25–27) he praises the Father, thanking him for the reception his teaching has had from humble folk: "I thank thee, Father, Lord of heaven and earth…". Later on, the apostles, in

tribuatur diligenter in domo Dei caeli, ne forte irascatur contra regnum regis et filiorum eius. [24]Vobis quoque notum facimus de universis sacerdotibus et Levitis et cantoribus et ianitoribus, oblatis et ministris domus Dei huius, ut tributum et annonas et vectigal non habeatis potestatem imponendi super eos. [25]Tu autem, Esdra, secundum sapientiam Dei tui, quae est in manu tua, constitue praesides et iudices, ut iudicent omni populo, qui est trans flumen, his videlicet, qui noverunt legem Dei tui; sed et imperitos docete. [26]Et omnis, qui non fecerit legem Dei tui et legem regis diligenter, iudicium erit de eo, sive in mortem sive in exsilium sive in damnum substantiae eius vel certe in carcerem». [27]Benedictus Dominus, Deus patrum nostrorum, qui dedit hoc in corde regis, ut glorificaret domum Domini, quae est in Ierusalem, [28]et in me inclinavit misericordiam regis et consiliariorum eius et cunctorum principum eius potentium. Et ego confortatus manu Domini Dei mei, quae erat in me, congregavi de Israel principes, qui ascenderent mecum.

Key men in Ezra's party

8 [1]These are the heads of their fathers' houses, and this is the genealogy of those who went up with me from Babylonia, in the reign of Ar-ta-xerxes the king: [2]Of the sons of Phinehas, Gershom. Of the sons of Ithamar, Daniel. Of the sons of David, Hattush, [3]of the sons of Shecaniah. Of the sons of Parosh, Zechariah, with whom were registered one hundred and fifty men. [4]Of the sons of Pahath-moab, Eli-e-ho-enai the son of Zerahiah, and with him two hundred men. [5]Of the sons of Zattu,[i] Shecaniah the son of Jahaziel, and with him three hundred men. [6]Of the sons of Adin, Ebed the son of Jonathan, and with him fifty men. [7]Of the sons of Elam, Jeshaiah the son of Athaliah, and with him seventy men. [8]Of the sons of Shephatiah, Zebadiah the son of Michael, and with him eighty men. [9]Of the sons of Joab, Obadiah the son of Jehiel, and with him two hundred and eighteen men. [10]Of the sons

1 Chron 24:3

imitation of their Master, will joyfully proclaim all the good things God has given us "in Christ": "Blessed be the God and Father of our Lord Jesus Christ, who has blessed us in Christ with every spiritual blessing in the heavenly places" (Eph 1:3). Thus, blessing becomes a beautiful form of prayer: "*Blessing* expresses the basic movement of Christian prayer: it is an encounter between God and man. In blessing, God's gift and man's acceptance of it are united in dialogue with each other. The prayer of blessing is man's response to God's gifts: because God blesses, the human heart can in return bless the One who is the source of every blessing. Two fundamental forms express this movement: our prayer ascends in the Holy Spirit through Christ to the Father—we bless him for having blessed us; it implores the grace of the Holy Spirit that descends through Christ from the Father—he blesses us" (*Catechism of the Catholic Church*, 2626–2627).

8:1–14. This new contingent of repatriates must have been a considerable reinforcement for those who had returned to the Holy City earlier: the latter had rebuilt the temple and perhaps the city walls, but the Jewish community still had to be reorganized and its religious identity reasserted. This new group includes, first, two priestly families (Phinehas and Ithamar); then a descendant of David (Zattu),

[8] [1]Hi sunt ergo principes familiarum et genealogia eorum, qui ascenderunt mecum in regno Artaxerxis regis de Babylone: [2]De filiis Phinees, Gersom. De filiis Ithamar, Daniel. De filiis David, Hattus filius Secheniae. [3]De filiis Pharos, Zacharias; et cum eo numerati sunt viri centum quinquaginta. [4]De filiis Phahathmoab, Elioenai filius Zaraiae, et cum eo ducenti viri. [5]De filiis Zethua, Sechenia filius Iahaziel, et cum eo trecenti viri. [6]De filiis Adin, Ebed filius Ionathan, et cum eo quinquaginta viri. [7]De filiis Elam, Iesaias filius Athaliae, et cum eo septuaginta viri. [8]De filiis Saphatiae, Zabadia filius Michael, et cum eo octoginta viri. [9]De filiis Ioab, Abdia filius Iahiel, et cum eo ducenti decem et octo viri. [10]De filiis

i. Gk 1 Esdras 8:32: Heb lacks *of Zattu*

of Bani,[j] Shelomith the son of Josiphiah, and with him a hundred and sixty men. [11]Of the sons of Bebai, Zechariah, the son of Bebai, and with him twenty-eight men. [12]Of the sons of Azgad, Johanan the son of Hakkatan, and with him a hundred and ten men. [13]Of the sons of Adonikam, those who came later, their names being Eliphelet, Jeuel, and Shemaiah, and with them sixty men. [14]Of the sons of Bigvai, Uthai and Zaccur, and with them seventy men.

Ezra's party prepares to leave

[15]I gathered them to the river that runs to Ahava, and there we encamped three days. As I reviewed the people and the priests, I found there none of the sons of Levi. [16]Then I sent for Eliezer, Ariel, Shemaiah, Elnathan, Jarib, Elnathan, Nathan, Zechariah, and Meshullam, leading men, and for Joiarib and Elnathan, who were men of insight, [17]and sent them to Iddo, the leading man at the place Casiphia, telling them what to say to Iddo and his brethren the temple servants[k] at the place Casiphia, namely, to send us ministers for the house of our God. [18]And by the good hand of our

---

although there is just this mention of him; and members of twelve families of Israel. These numbers and the order in which they are given may be meant to symbolize that all Israel was involved in the expedition.

8:15–30. Even in the first expedition there was a surprisingly small number of Levites (cf. 1:40). Now Ezra himself has to get involved in their recruitment, and the fact that they join the caravan at all is seen as a divine favour (v. 18). Probably their standard of living in Babylon was better than what they could expect in Jerusalem. The account of the journey shows how much Ezra and his companions rely on the Lord: in fact, just in case it might seem otherwise, they refrain from asking the king for protection though it would have been forthcoming (vv. 21–23). The account focuses largely on the enormous quantity of silver and gold they are bringing with them for the Lord's temple (vv. 24–30). It shows the very significant contribution made by the community in Babylon.

Bani, Selomith filius Iosphiae, et cum eo centum sexaginta viri. [11]De filiis Bebai, Zacharias filius Bebai, et cum eo viginti octo viri. [12]De filiis Azgad, Iohanan filius Eccetan, et cum eo centum et decem viri. [13]De filiis Adonicam ascenderunt iuniores, et haec nomina eorum: Eliphalet et Iehiel et Semeias, et cum eis sexaginta viri. [14]De filiis Beguai, Uthai filius Zabud, et cum eis septuaginta viri. [15]Congregavi autem eos ad fluvium, qui decurrit ad Ahava, et mansimus ibi tribus diebus. Recensui populum et sacerdotes; de filiis autem Levi non inveni ibi. [16]Itaque misi Eliezer et Ariel et Semeiam et Ioiarib et Elnathan et Nathan et Zachariam et Mosollam principes sapientes. [17]Et misi eos ad Eddo, qui est primus in Chasphiae loco, et posui in ore eorum verba, quae loquerentur ad Eddo et fratres eius, ut adducerent nobis ministros domus Dei nostri. [18]Et adduxerunt nobis per manum Dei nostri bonam super nos. virum

j. Gk 1 Esdras 8:36: Heb lacks *Bani* **k.** Heb *nethinim*

God upon us, they brought us a man of discretion, of the sons of Mahli the son of Levi, son of Israel, namely Sherebiah with his sons and kinsmen, eighteen; [19]also Hashabiah and with him Jeshaiah of the sons of Merari, with his kinsmen and their sons, twenty; [20]besides two hundred and twenty of the temple servants, whom David and his officials had set apart to attend the Levites. These were all mentioned by name.

Ezra 2:43

[21]Then I proclaimed a fast there, at the river Ahava, that we might humble ourselves before our God, to seek from him a straight way for ourselves, our children, and all our goods. [22]For I was ashamed to ask the king for a band of soldiers and horsemen to protect us against the enemy on our way; since we had told the king, "The hand of our God is for good upon all that seek him, and the power of his wrath is against all that forsake him." [23]So we fasted and besought our God for this, and he listened to our entreaty.

Neh 2:9

[24]Then I set apart twelve of the leading priests: Sherebiah, Hashabiah, and ten of their kinsmen with them. [25]And I weighed out to them the silver and the gold and the vessels, the offering for the house of our God which the king and his counsellors and his lords and all Israel there present had offered; [26]I weighed out into their hand six hundred and fifty talents of silver, and silver vessels worth a hundred talents, and a hundred talents of gold, [27]twenty bowls of gold worth a thousand darics, and two vessels of fine bright bronze as precious as gold. [28]And I said to them, "You are holy to the LORD, and the vessels are holy; and the silver and the gold are a freewill offering to the LORD, the God of your fathers.

Lev 21:6; 22:2–3

[29]Guard them and keep them until you weigh them before the chief priests and the Levites and the heads of fathers' houses in Israel at Jerusalem, within the chambers of the house of the LORD."

---

doctissimum de filiis Moholi filii Levi filii Israel nomine Serebiam et filios eius et fratres eius decem et octo [19]et Hasabiam et cum eo Iesaiam de filiis Merari filiosque eius et fratres eius viginti [20]et de oblatis, quos dederant David et principes ad ministeria Levitarum, ducentos viginti viros: omnes hi suis nominibus recensiti sunt. [21]Et praedicavi ibi ieiunium iuxta fluvium Ahava, ut affligeremur coram Deo nostro et peteremus ab eo iter prosperum nobis et filiis nostris universaeque substantiae nostrae. [22]Erubui enim petere a rege praesidium et equites, qui defenderent nos ab inimico in via, quia dixeramus regi: «Manus Dei nostri est super omnes, qui quaerunt eum in bonitate, et potentia eius et fortitudo eius super omnes, qui derelinquunt eum». [23]Ieiunavimus autem et rogavimus Deum nostrum per hoc, et evenit nobis prospere. [24]Et separavi de principibus sacerdotum duodecim, Serebiam et Hasabiam et cum eis de fratribus eorum decem, [25]appendique eis argentum et aurum et vasa: tributum domus Dei nostri, quod obtulerat rex et consiliatores eius et principes eius universusque Israel eorum, qui ibi inveniebantur. [26]Et appendi in manibus eorum argenti talenta sescenta quinquaginta et vasa argentea centum, quae habebant talenta duo, auri centum talenta, [27]et crateres aureos viginti, qui habebant solidos millenos, et vasa aeris fulgentis optimi duo pretiosa ut aurum. [28]Et dixi eis: «Vos sancti Domini et vasa sancta et argentum et aurum consecrata Domino, Deo patrum nostrorum; [29]vigilate et custodite, donec

[30]So the priests and the Levites took over the weight of the silver and the gold and the vessels, to bring them to Jerusalem, to the house of our God.

Ezra's party arrives in Jerusalem

[31]Then we departed from the river Ahava on the twelfth day of the first month, to go to Jerusalem; the hand of our God was upon us, and he delivered us from the hand of the enemy and from ambushes by the way. [32]We came to Jerusalem, and there we remained three days. [33]On the fourth day, within the house of our God, the silver and the gold and the vessels were weighed into the hands of Meremoth the priest, son of Uriah, and with him was Eleazar the son of Phinehas, and with them were the Levites, Jozabad the son of Jeshua and No-adiah the son of Binnui. [34]The whole was counted and weighed, and the weight of everything was recorded.

[35]At that time those who had come from captivity, the returned exiles, offered burnt offerings to the God of Israel, twelve bulls for all Israel, ninety-six rams, seventy-seven lambs, and as a sin offering twelve he-goats; all this was a burnt offering to the LORD.

Ezra presents his credentials

[36]They also delivered the king's commissions to the king's satraps and to the governors of the province Beyond the River; and they aided the people and the house of God.

Neh 2:7,9
Esther 3:12; 8:9

8:31–35. The journey goes very well, thanks to the Lord's protection. In Jerusalem the new arrivals are well received by those who have already settled in the city, but the narrative centres on their contributions to the temple and on their burnt offerings and sin offerings.

8:36. For the mission to succeed it is very important that the local governors accept Ezra's credentials; they do so and this is seen as a boon for the people and the temple.

appendatis coram principibus sacerdotum et Levitarum et ducibus familiarum Israel in Ierusalem, in habitaculis domus Domini». [30]Susceperunt autem sacerdotes et Levitae pondus argenti et auri et vasorum, ut deferrent Ierusalem in domum Dei nostri. [31]Promovimus ergo a flumine Ahava duodecimo die mensis primi, ut pergeremus Ierusalem; et manus Dei nostri fuit super nos et liberavit nos de manu inimici et insidiatoris in via, [32]et venimus Ierusalem et mansimus ibi tribus diebus. [33]Die autem quarta appensum est argentum et aurum et vasa in domo Dei nostri per manum Meremoth filii Uriae sacerdotis et cum eo Eleazar filius Phinees cumque eis Iozabad filius Iesua et Noadia filius Bennui Levitae, [34]iuxta numerum et pondus omnia; descriptumque est omne pondus. In tempore illo, [35]qui venerant de captivitate, filii transmigrationis, obtulerunt holocautomata Deo Israel, vitulos duodecim pro omni populo Israel, arietes nonaginta sex, agnos septuaginta septem, hircos pro peccato duodecim: omnia in holocaustum Domino. [36]Dederunt autem edicta regis satrapis regis et ducibus trans flumen et sublevaverunt populum et domum Dei.

Neh 13:23–28
Mal 2:10–12
Deut 7:1–4;
12:30

Ezra is pained to find the Law ignored

9 *[1]After these things had been done, the officials approached me and said, "The people of Israel and the priests and the Levites have not separated themselves from the peoples of the lands with their abominations, from the Canaanites, the Hittites, the Perizzites, the Jebusites, the Ammonites, the Moabites, the Egyptians, and the Amorites. [2]For they have taken some of their daughters to be wives for themselves and for their sons; so that the holy race has mixed itself with the peoples of the lands. And in this faithlessness the hand of the officials and chief men has been foremost." [3]When I heard this, I rent my garments and my mantle, and pulled hair from my head and beard, and sat appalled. [4]Then all who trembled at the words of the God of Israel, because of the faithlessness of the returned exiles, gathered round me while I sat appalled until the evening sacrifice. [5]And at the evening sacrifice I rose from my fasting, with my garments and my mantle rent, and fell upon my knees and spread out my hands to the LORD my God, [6]saying:

Ex 34:16
Neh 9:2
Is 66:2,5
Lev 18:24–27
Neh 1:6–9

"O my God, I am ashamed and blush to lift my face to thee, my God, for our iniquities have risen higher than our heads, and our guilt has mounted up to the heavens. [7]From the days of our fathers to this day we have been in great guilt; and for our iniquities we, our kings, and our priests have been given into the hand of the kings of the lands, to the sword, to captivity, to plundering, and to utter shame, as at this day. [8]But now for a brief moment favour has

Lk 21:24
Is 4:3

9:1–15. Ezra is deeply distressed to find that the people of God have intermarried with the local inhabitants, who do not belong to the people of God (the Law forbade such marriages: cf. Deut 7:3–4); Ezra acknowledges this sin and does penance for it.

[9] [1]Postquam autem haec completa sunt, accesserunt ad me principes dicentes: «Non est separatus populus Israel, sacerdotes et Levitae a populis terrarum et abominationibus eorum, Chananaei videlicet et Hetthaei et Pherezaei et Iebusaei et Ammonitarum et Moabitarum et Aegyptiorum et Amorraeorum. [2]Tulerunt enim de filiabus eorum sibi et filiis suis et commiscuerunt semen sanctum cum populis terrarum; manus etiam principum et magistratuum fuit in transgressione hac prima». [3]Cumque audissem sermonem istum, scidi vestimentum meum et pallium et evelli capillos capitis mei et barbae et sedi maerens. [4]Convenerunt autem ad me omnes, qui timebant verba Dei Israel pro transgressione eorum, qui de captivitate venerant; et ego sedebam tristis usque ad sacrificium vespertinum. [5]Et in sacrificio vespertino surrexi de afflictione mea et, scisso vestimento et pallio, curvavi genua mea et expandi manus meas ad Dominum Deum meum. [6]Et dixi: «Deus meus, confundor et erubesco levare faciem meam ad te, quoniam iniquitates nostrae multiplicatae sunt super caput nostrum, et delicta nostra creverunt usque ad caelum [7]a diebus patrum nostrorum. Peccavimus graviter usque ad diem hanc, et propter iniquitates nostras traditi sumus, ipsi et reges nostri et sacerdotes nostri, in manum regum terrarum et in gladium et in captivitatem et in rapinam et in confusionem vultus sicut et die hac. [8]Et nunc ad momentum invenimus gratiam apud Dominum Deum nostrum, ut servaret nobis reliquias et figeret nobis tentorium

been shown by the LORD our God, to leave us a remnant, and to give us a secure hold[l] within his holy place, that our God may brighten our eyes and grant us a little reviving in our bondage. [9]For we are bondmen; yet our God has not forsaken us in our bondage, but has extended to us his steadfast love before the kings of Persia, to grant us some reviving to set up the house of our God, to repair its ruins, and to give us protection[m] in Judea and Jerusalem.

[10]"And now, O our God, what shall we say after this? For we have forsaken thy commandments, [11]which thou didst command by thy servants the prophets, saying, 'The land which you are entering, to take possession of it, is a land unclean with the pollutions of the peoples of the lands, with their abominations which have filled it from end to end with their uncleanness. [12]Therefore give not your daughters to their sons, neither take their daughters for your sons, and never seek their peace or prosperity, that you may be strong, and eat the good of the land, and leave it for an inheritance to your children for ever.' [13]And after all that has come upon us for our evil deeds and for our great guilt, seeing that thou, our God, hast punished us less than our iniquities deserved and hast given us such a remnant as this, [14]shall we break thy commandments again and intermarry with the peoples who practise these abominations? Wouldst thou not be angry with us till thou wouldst consume us, so that there should be no remnant, nor any to escape? [15]O LORD the God of Israel, thou art just, for we are left a remnant that has escaped, as at this day. Behold, we are before thee in our guilt, for none can stand before thee because of this."

Lev 18:24
Ezek 36:17

Ex 23:32
Deut 7:3; 23:6

---

in loco sancto eius et illuminaret oculos nostros Deus noster et daret nobis solacium modicum in servitute nostra. [9]Quia servi sumus, et in servitute nostra non dereliquit nos Deus noster, sed inclinavit super nos misericordiam regum Persarum, ut darent nobis solacium, et erigeretur domus Dei nostri, et instaurarentur ruinae eius, et dedit nobis refugium in Iuda et Ierusalem. [10]Et nunc quid dicemus, Deus noster, post haec? Dereliquimus mandata tua, [11]quae praecepisti in manu servorum tuorum prophetarum dicens: "Terra, ad quam vos ingredimini, ut possideatis eam, terra immunda est, iuxta immunditiam populorum terrarum et abominationem eorum, qui repleverunt eam a fine usque ad finem coinquinatione sua. [12]Nunc ergo filias vestras ne detis filiis eorum et filias eorum ne accipiatis filiis vestris et non quaeratis pacem eorum et prosperitatem eorum usque in aeternum, ut confortemini et comedatis, quae bona sunt terrae, et heredes habeatis filios vestros usque in saeculum". [13]Et post omnia, quae venerunt super nos in operibus nostris pessimis et in delicto nostro magno, quia tu, Deus noster, non iudicasti secundum iniquitates nostras et dedisti nobis salutem, sicut est hodie, [14]numquid amplius irrita faciemus mandata tua et matrimonia iungemus cum populis abominationum istarum? Numquid iratus es nobis usque ad consummationem, ut non essent reliquiae et salus? [15]Domine, Deus Israel, tua clementia superstites sumus sicut die hac! Ecce coram te sumus in delicto nostro; non enim stari potest coram te propter hoc».

l. Heb *nail* or *tent-pin* **m.** Heb *a wall*

Neh 1:6
Dan 9:20
Neh 1:4

The people acknowledge their sin in marrying foreigners

10 [1]While Ezra prayed and made confession, weeping and casting himself down before the house of God, a very great assembly of men, women, and children, gathered to him out of Israel; for the people wept bitterly. [2]And Shecaniah the son of Jehiel, of the sons of Elam, addressed Ezra: "We have broken faith with our God and have married foreign women from the peoples of the land, but even now there is hope for Israel in spite of this. [3]Therefore let us make a covenant with our God to put away all these wives and their children, according to the counsel of my lord and of those who tremble at the commandment of our God; and let it be done according to the law. [4]Arise, for it is your task, and we are with you; be strong and do it."

Ezra calls on the people to assemble at Jerusalem

[5]Then Ezra arose and made the leading priests and Levites and all Israel take oath that they would do as had been said. So they took the oath.

10:1–44. The zeal shown by Ezra and the first group of deportees to conform to the Law on mixed marriage and to ensure that others conform to it (cf. 10:5–44) is not meant to promote isolationism or xenophobia. The point is that the people of Israel are a holy people, who have been given a Law by God, and to whom God has made certain promises: so they need to retain their identity, an identity which is bound up with their faithfulness to the Lord. To protect their identity and keep idolatry at bay it made sense for them to distance themselves to some degree from their neighbours—not an easy thing to do, as can be seen from vv. 12–17. This sacred text shows how important it is to take steps to protect the gifts God gives us, and to be faithful to him. However, stances were sometimes taken which evidenced a more open attitude; in the book of Ruth, which was also composed around this time, the Bible gives us the story of a Moabite woman who married an Israelite and, after being converted to the God of Israel, became no less than the grandmother of King David.

In the New Testament and in the practice of the Church, the dangers of mixed marriage or disparity of cult have never been lost sight of, but such marriages are also seen as a way of

[10] [1]Dum ergo oraret Esdras et imploraret flens et prostratus ante templum Dei, collectus est ad eum de Israel coetus grandis nimis virorum et mulierum et puerorum; et flevit populus fletu multo. [2]Et respondit Sechenias filius Iehiel de filiis Elam et dixit Esdrae: «Nos praevaricati sumus in Deum nostrum et duximus uxores alienigenas de populis terrae. Nunc autem spes est in Israel super hoc: [3]percutiamus foedus cum Domino Deo nostro, ut proiciamus universas uxores et eos, qui de his nati sunt, iuxta voluntatem Domini et eorum, qui timent praeceptum Domini Dei nostri, et secundum legem fiat. [4]Surge, tuum est decernere, nosque erimus tecum; confortare et fac». [5]Surrexit ergo Esdras et fecit

[6]Then Ezra withdrew from before the house of God, and went to the chamber of Jehohanan the son of Eliashib, where he spent the night,[n] neither eating bread nor drinking water; for he was mourning over the faithlessness of the exiles. [7]And a proclamation was made throughout Judah and Jerusalem to all the returned exiles that they should assemble at Jerusalem, [8]and that if any one did not come within three days, by order of the officials and the elders all his property should be forfeited, and he himself banned from the congregation of the exiles.

[9]Then all the men of Judah and Benjamin assembled at Jerusalem within the three days; it was the ninth month, on the twentieth day of the month. And all the people sat in the open square before the house of God, trembling because of this matter and because of the heavy rain.

The people confess their sin

[10]And Ezra the priest stood up and said to them, "You have trespassed and married foreign women, and so increased the guilt of Israel. [11]Now then make confession to the LORD the God of your fathers, and do his will; separate yourselves from the peoples

Josh 7:19

drawing spouses closer to the true faith. "Difference of confession between the spouses does not constitute an insurmountable obstacle for marriage, when they succeed in placing in common what they have received from their respective communities, and learn from each other the way in which each lives in fidelity to Christ. But the difficulties of mixed marriages must not be underestimated. They arise from the fact that the separation of Christians has not yet been overcome. The spouses risk experiencing the tragedy of Christian disunity even in the heart of their own home. Disparity of cult can further aggravate these difficulties. Differences about faith and the very notion of marriage, but also different religious mentalities, can become sources of tension in marriage, especially as regards the education of children. The temptation to religious indifference can then arise" (*Catechism of the Catholic Church*, 1634).

principes sacerdotum et Levitarum et omnem Israel iurare, ut facerent secundum verbum hoc, et iuraverunt. [6]Et surrexit Esdras ante domum Dei et abiit ad cubiculum Iohanan filii Eliasib et pernoctavit ibi; panem non comedit et aquam non bibit, lugebat enim transgressionem eorum, qui venerant de captivitate. [7]Et missa est vox in Iuda et in Ierusalem omnibus filiis transmigrationis, ut congregarentur in Ierusalem; [8]et omnis, qui non venerit in tribus diebus iuxta consilium principum et seniorum, auferetur universa substantia eius, et ipse abicietur de coetu transmigrationis. [9]Convenerunt igitur omnes viri Iudae et Beniamin in Ierusalem tribus diebus, ipse est mensis nonus vicesimo die mensis, et sedit omnis populus in platea domus Dei, trementes pro peccato et pluviis. [10]Et surrexit Esdras sacerdos et dixit ad eos: «Vos transgressi estis et duxistis uxores alienigenas, ut adderetis super delictum Israel. [11]Et

n. 1 Esdras 9:2: Heb *where he went*

of the land and from the foreign wives." [12]Then all the assembly answered with a loud voice, "It is so; we must do as you have said. [13]But the people are many, and it is a time of heavy rain; we cannot stand in the open. Nor is this a work for one day or for two; for we have greatly transgressed in this matter. [14]Let our officials stand for the whole assembly; let all in our cities who have taken foreign wives come at appointed times, and with them the elders and judges of every city, till the fierce wrath of our God over this matter be averted from us." [15]Only Jonathan the son of Asahel and Jahzeiah the son of Tikvah opposed this, and Meshullum and Shabbethai the Levite supported them.

Neh 10:34; 13:31

[16]Then the returned exiles did so. Ezra the priest selected men,[o] heads of fathers' houses, according to their fathers' houses, each of them designated by name. On the first day of the tenth month they sat down to examine the matter; [17]and by the first day of the first month they had come to the end of all the men who had married foreign women.

Foreign wives are sent away

[18]Of the sons of the priests who had married foreign women were found Ma-aseiah, Eliezer, Jarib, and Gedaliah, of the sons of Jeshua the son of Jozadak and his brethren. [19]They pledged themselves to put away their wives, and their guilt offering was a ram of the flock for their guilt. [20]Of the sons of Immer: Hanani and Zebadiah. [21]Of the sons of Harim: Ma-aseiah, Elijah, Shemaiah, Jehiel, and Uzziah. [22]Of the sons of Pashhur: Eli-o-enai, Ma-aseiah, Ishmael, Nethanel, Jozabad, and Elasah.

2 Kings 10:15

---

nunc date confessionem Domino, Deo patrum vestrorum, et facite placitum eius et separamini a populis terrae et ab uxoribus alienigenis». [12]Et respondit universa multitudo dixitque voce magna: «Iuxta verbum tuum ad nos, sic fiat. [13]Verumtamen quia populus multus est et tempus pluviae, et non sustinemus stare foris, et opus non est diei unius vel duorum—multi quippe peccavimus in sermone isto—[14]constituantur principes in universa multitudine; et omnes in civitatibus nostris, qui duxerunt uxores alienigenas, veniant in temporibus statutis, et cum his seniores per civitatem et civitatem et iudices eius, donec avertatur ira Dei nostri a nobis super peccato hoc». [15]Tantummodo Ionathan filius Asael et Iaasia filius Thecue steterunt contra hoc, et Mosollam et Sabethai Levites adiuverunt eos. [16]Feceruntque sic filii transmigrationis. Et elegit Esdras sacerdos viros principes familiarum iuxta domus patrum eorum, omnes autem per nomina eorum, et sederunt in die primo mensis decimi, ut quaererent rem. [17]Et absolverunt causam cunctorum, qui duxerant uxores alienigenas, intra diem primam mensis primi. [18]Et inventi sunt de filiis sacerdotum, qui duxerant uxores alienigenas. De filiis Iesua filii Iosedec et de fratribus eius: Maasia et Eliezer et Iarib et Godolia; [19]et dederunt manus suas, ut eicerent uxores suas et pro delicto suo arietem offerrent. [20]Et de filiis Emmer: Hanani et Zabadia. [21]Et de filiis Harim: Maasia et Elia et Semeia et Iehiel et Ozias. [22]Et de filiis Phassur: Elioenai, Maasia,

o. 1 Esdras 9:16 Syr: Heb *and there were selected Ezra*, etc.

[23]Of the Levites: Jozabad, Shime-i, Kelaiah (that is, Kelita), Petha-hiah, Judah, and Eliezer. [24]Of the singers: Eliashib. Of the gatekeepers: Shallum, Telem, and Uri.

Neh 8:7; 10:11

[25]And of Israel: of the sons of Parosh: Ramiah, Izziah, Malchijah, Mijamin, Eleazar, Hashabiah,[p] and Benaiah. [26]Of the sons of Elam: Mattaniah, Zechariah, Jehiel, Abdi, Jeremoth, and Elijah. [27]Of the sons of Zattu: Eli-o-enai, Eliashib, Mattaniah, Jeremoth, Zabad, and Aziza. [28]Of the sons of Bebai were Jehohanan, Hananiah, Zabbai, and Athlai. [29]Of the sons of Bani were Meshullum, Malluch, Adaiah, Jashub, Sheal, and Jeremoth. [30]Of the sons of Pahath-moab: Adna, Chelal, Benaiah, Ma-aseiah, Mattaniah, Bezalel, Binnui, and Manasseh. [31]Of the sons of Harim: Eliezer, Isshijah, Malchijah, Shemaiah, Shime-on, [32]Benjamin, Malluch, and Shemariah. [33]Of the sons of Hashum: Mattenai, Mattattah, Zabad, Eliphelet, Jeremai, Manasseh, and Shime-i. [34]Of the sons of Bani: Ma-adai, Amram, Uel, [35]Benaiah, Bedeiah, Cheluhi, [36]Vaniah, Meremoth, Eliashib, [37]Mattaniah, Mattenai, Jaasu. [38]Of the sons of Binnui:[q] Shime-i, [39]Shelemiah, Nathan, Adaiah, [40]Machnadebai, Shashai, Sharai, [41]Azarel, Shelemiah, Shemariah, [42]Shallum, Amariah, and Joseph. [43]Of the sons of Nebo: Je-iel, Mattithiah, Zabad, Zebina, Jaddai, Joel, and Benaiah. [44]All these had married foreign women, and they put them away with their children.[r]

Ismael, Nathanael, Iozabad et Elasa. [23]Et de filiis Levitarum: Iozabad et Semei et Celaia, ipse est Celita, Phethahia, Iuda et Eliezer. [24]Et de cantoribus: Eliasib. Et de ianitoribus: Sellum et Telem et Uri. [25]Et ex Israel de filiis Pharos: Remia et Iezia et Melchia et Miamin et Eleazar et Melchia et Banaia. [26]Et de filiis Elam: Matthania, Zacharias et Iehiel et Abdi et Ierimoth et Elia. [27]Et de filiis Zethua: Elioenai, Eliasib, Matthania et Ierimoth et Zabad et Aziza. [28]Et de filiis Bebai: Iohanan, Hanania, Zabbai, Athalai. [29]Et de filiis Beguai: Mosollam et Melluch et Adaia, Iasub et Saal et Ramoth. [30]Et de filiis Phahathmoab: Edna et Chalal, Banaias et Maasias, Matthanias, Beseleel, Bennui et Manasse. [31]Et de filiis Harim: Eliezer, Iesia, Melchias, Semeias, Simeon, [32]Beniamin, Melluch, Samarias. [33]Et de filiis Hasum: Matthanai, Matthatha, Zabad, Eliphalet, Iermai, Manasse, Semei. [34]De filiis Bani: Maaddi, Amram et Ioel, [35]Banaia et Badaias, Cheliau, [36]Vania, Meremoth et Eliasib, [37]Matthanias, Matthanai et Iasi. [38]Et de filiis Bennui: Semei [39]et Selemias et Nathan et Adaias [40]et Mechnedebai, Sisai, Sarai, [41]Azareel et Selemias, Samaria, [42]Sellum, Amaria, Ioseph. [43]De filiis Nabo: Iehiel, Matthathias, Zabad, Zabina, Ieddu et Ioel et Banaia. [44]Omnes hi acceperant uxores alienigenas et dimiserunt uxores et filios.

p. 1 Esdras 9:26 Gk: Heb *Malchijah* **q.** Gk: Heb *Bani*, *Binnui* **r.** 1 Esdras 9:36: Heb obscure

3. NEHEMIAH'S MISSION—TO REBUILD THE CITY*

Nehemiah's prayer for the reunification of Israel

Esther 1:2

1 [1]The words of Nehemiah the son of Hacaliah.
Now it happened in the month of Chislev, in the twentieth year, as I was in Susa the capital, [2]that Hanani, one of my brethren, came

---

***1:1—13:31**. The book of Nehemiah is of a piece with that of Ezra. Ezra recounted the return of the exiles from Babylon, the rebuilding of the temple (cf. Ezra 1:1—6:22) and the religious revival led by Ezra the scribe (cf. Ezra 7:1—10:44). The narrative now goes on to tell us about the reconstruction and resettlement of Jerusalem by the people of God, spearheaded by Nehemiah.

Nehemiah was an official of the Persian court whom King Ar-ta-xerxes authorized to go to Jerusalem, in the province of Judah, and rebuild the city. Most of this book probably derives from "the memoirs of Nehemiah", a document written by him some years after completing his mission and compiled on the basis of a short report written immediately after the events described. These memoirs survey the events of Nehemiah's mission in the light of belief in the God of Israel. The sacred author who gave the book its present form by combining memoirs of Ezra and Nehemiah rearranged their content, inserting material from the Ezra memoirs into the Nehemiah text (an example of this insertion is the passage about Ezra reading out the Law: chap. 8).

The account begins with the project of rebuilding Jerusalem, the main object of Nehemiah's first mission (1:1—2:20); it goes on to describe the restoration of the city (3:1—6:19) and what was done to repopulate it (7:1–72). However, the core of the book is the proclamation of the Law by Ezra and the people's confession of their sins and their promise to keep the Law (8:1—10:40). Once this central idea has been covered, the text describes the resettlement of the rest of the territory (11:1—12:26) and the dedication of the rebuilt wall (12:27–47). The book ends with a review of the revival of Jewish society in line with the Law of Moses, which was the main objective of Nehemiah's second mission (13:1–31). So, at the centre of the literary structure of the book we find its essential content—evaluation, in the light of the Law of God, of Nehemiah's personal life and of the history of the people of God, and acknowledgment of sins in the light of the Law.

1:1–11. The "memoirs of Nehemiah" begin by telling how the Lord used certain people to stir Nehemiah to ask the king for permission to go to Jerusalem and rebuild the Holy City. The text is written in the first person singular, with the spontaneity and gratefulness to God of someone who is

[1] [1]Verba Nehemiae filii Hachaliae. Et factum est in mense Casleu, anno vicesimo, et ego eram in castro Susan. [2]Et venit Hanani unus de fratribus meis, ipse et viri ex Iuda; et interrogavi eos de Iudaeis,

with certain men out of Judah; and I asked them concerning the Jews that survived, who had escaped exile, and concerning Jerusalem. [3]And they said to me, "The survivors there in the province who escaped exile are in great trouble and shame; the wall of Jerusalem is broken down, and its gates are destroyed by fire."

[4]When I heard these words I sat down and wept, and mourned for days; and I continued fasting and praying before the God of heaven. [5]And I said, "O LORD God of heaven, the great and terrible God who keeps covenant and steadfast love with those who love him and keep his commandments; [6]let thy ear be attentive, and thy eyes open, to hear the prayer of thy servant which I now pray before thee day and night for the people of Israel thy servants, confessing the sins of the people of Israel, which we have sinned against thee. Yea, I and my father's house have sinned. [7]We have acted very corruptly against thee, and have not kept the commandments, the statutes, and the ordinances which thou didst command thy servant Moses. [8]Remember the word which thou didst command thy servant Moses, saying, 'If you are unfaithful, I will

Ezra 9:3

Deut 7:9–12

2 Chron 6:40

Lev 26:33
Deut 4:25–28; 30:1–4

---

looking back at the past and recalling with emotion the efforts he made to serve his Lord.

As soon as Nehemiah learned that the city of Jerusalem was in ruins (due apparently to recent events unknown to us), he had a deeply religious reaction to the news: he realized that that situation resulted from infidelity to God, so he did penance and mourned in the presence of the Lord (v. 4). In this connexion, St Bede comments that just as Jerusalem at the time was a wasteland, "so, too, the Church is under siege; and those who reflect on their own lives and situation experience a saving sadness when they recognize that it is as a consequence of [their own] past sins, the vices of others and the negligence of those who could have made things better by correcting the faults of many people, that the devil has found it so easy to gain access to the Church as into a city whose walls are in ruins" (*In Esdram et Nehemiam*, 3, 15).

Nehemiah's prayer (vv. 4–11) includes acknowledgment of the sins committed, trust in God who listens to appeals made to him, and a conviction that one's God can change the course of events. Nehemiah reminds the Lord of the promise he made to Moses when he warned him that the people would be scattered out of the land (cf. Deut 30:1–4).

qui salvati erant et super erant de captivitate, et de Ierusalem. [3]Et dixerunt mihi: «Superstites, qui supererant de captivitate ibi in provincia, in afflictione magna sunt et in opprobrio; et murus Ierusalem dissipatus est, et portae eius combustae sunt igne». [4]Cumque audissem verba huiuscemodi, sedi et flevi et luxi diebus multis; ieiunabam et orabam ante faciem Dei caeli. [5]Et dixi: «Quaeso, Domine, Deus caeli, Deus fortis, magne atque terribilis, qui custodis pactum et misericordiam cum his, qui te diligunt et custodiunt mandata tua; [6]fiat auris tua auscultans et oculi tui aperti, ut audias orationem servi tui,

Lev 26:39–45 Deut 4:29–31; 12:5; 30:2,4
Deut 9:29

scatter you among the peoples; [9]but if you return to me and keep my commandments and do them, though your dispersed be under the farthest skies, I will gather them thence and bring them to the place which I have chosen, to make my name dwell there.' [10]They are thy servants and thy people, whom thou hast redeemed by thy great power and by thy strong hand. [11]O LORD, let thy ear be attentive to the prayer of thy servant, and to the prayer of thy servants who delight to fear thy name; and give success to thy servant today, and grant him mercy in the sight of this man."

Now I was cupbearer to the king.

Esther 3:7

Nehemiah is authorized to rebuild the wall of Jerusalem

2 [1]In the month of Nisan, in the twentieth year of King Artaxerxes, when wine was before him, I took up the wine and gave it to the king. Now I had not been sad in his presence. [2]And the king said to me, "Why is your face sad, seeing you are not sick? This is nothing else but sadness of the heart." Then I was very

---

2:1–20. Putting his trust entirely in the Lord, Nehemiah used every resource available to him to help his compatriots. He prayed for four months—from Chislev (1:1) to Nisan (v. 1)—and then used an opportunity that presented itself to outline his plans to the king; he managed not only to get Artaxerxes' authorization to go to Judah and rebuild Jerusalem, but also to requisition the necessary materials (vv. 1–9). The king referred to (v. 1) was probably Artaxerxes I (465–425 BC); and the twentieth year of his reign was 445 BC.

When Nehemiah reached the city of his ancestors, he initially met with opposition from the governor of Samaria, Sanbalat, and from Tobiah, a rich landowner who was related to priestly families (cf. 6:17–18). However, he did manage to get influential people in Jerusalem (vv. 16ff) to join in his project. Acting prudently and yet boldly, he was confident that God would help him in his endeavours (v. 20).

quam ego oro coram te hodie, die et nocte pro filiis Israel servis tuis, et confiteor pro peccatis filiorum Israel, quibus peccaverunt tibi. Ego quoque et domus patris mei peccavimus, [7]delinquentes deliquimus contra te et non custodivimus praecepta et mandata et iudicia, quae praecepisti Moysi famulo tuo. [8]Memento verbi, quod mandasti Moysi servo tuo dicens: "Cum transgressi fueritis, ego dispergam vos in populos; [9]si autem revertamini ad me et custodiatis praecepta mea et faciatis ea, etiamsi abducti fueritis in extrema caeli, inde congregabo vos et reducam in locum quem elegi, ut habitaret nomen meum ibi". [10]Ipsi enim sunt servi tui et populus tuus, quos redemisti in fortitudine tua magna et in manu tua valida. [11]Obsecro, Domine, sit auris tua attendens ad orationem servi tui et ad orationem servorum tuorum, qui volunt timere nomen tuum; et fac servum tuum prosperari hodie et da ei gratiam ante virum hunc». Ego enim eram pincerna regis. **[2]** [1]Factum est autem in mense Nisan, anno vicesimo Artaxerxis regis, dum biberet, levavi vinum et dedi regi; non enim eram ingratus coram eo. [2]Dixitque mihi rex: «Quare vultus tuus tristis est, cum te aegrotum non videam? Nihil est aliud nisi tristitia cordis». Et timui valde [3]et dixi regi: «Rex, in aeternum vive! Quare non maereat vultus meus, quia civitas sepulcrorum patrum meorum deserta est, et portae eius combustae sunt igne?». [4]Et ait mihi rex: «Pro qua re postulas?».

much afraid. [3]I said to the king, "Let the king live for ever! Why should not my face be sad, when the city, the place of my fathers' sepulchres, lies waste, and its gates have been destroyed by fire?" [4]Then the king said to me, "For what do you make request?" So I prayed to the God of heaven. [5]And I said to the king, "If it pleases the king, and if your servant has found favour in your sight, that you send me to Judah, to the city of my fathers' sepulchres, that I may rebuild it." [6]And the king said to me (the queen sitting beside him), "How long will you be gone, and when will you return?" So it pleased the king to send me; and I set him a time. [7]And I said to the king, "If it pleases the king, let letters be given me to the governors of the province Beyond the River, that they may let me pass through until I come to Judah; [8]and a letter to Asaph, the keeper of the king's forest, that he may give me timber to make beams for the gates of the fortress of the temple, and for the wall of the city, and for the house which I shall occupy." And the king granted me what I asked, for the good hand of my God was upon me.

Ezra 8:22

[9]Then I came to the governors of the province Beyond the River, and gave them the king's letters. Now the king had sent with me officers of the army and horsemen. [10]But when Sanballat the Horonite and Tobiah the servant, the Ammonite, heard this, it displeased them greatly that some one had come to seek the welfare of the children of Israel.

Neh 3:33; 4:1; 6:1–7

[11]So I came to Jerusalem and was there three days. [12]Then I arose in the night, I and a few men with me; and I told no one what my God had put into my heart to do for Jerusalem. There was no beast with me but the beast on which I rode. [13]I went out by night by the Valley Gate to the Jackal's Well and to the Dung Gate, and I inspected the walls of Jerusalem which were broken down and its gates which had been destroyed by fire. [14]Then I went on to the Fountain Gate and to the King's Pool; but there was no place for

---

Et oravi Deum caeli [5]et dixi ad regem: «Si videtur regi bonum, et si placet servus tuus ante faciem tuam, ut mittas me in Iudaeam ad civitatem sepulcrorum patrum meorum, et aedificabo eam». [6]Dixitque mihi rex, et regina sedebat iuxta eum: «Usque ad quod tempus erit iter tuum, et quando reverteris?». Et placuit regi mittere me; et constitui ei tempus. [7]Et dixi regi: «Si regi videtur bonum, epistulae dentur mihi ad duces regionis trans flumen, ut me transire permittant, donec veniam in Iudaeam; [8]et epistulam ad Asaph custodem saltus regis, ut det mihi ligna, ut contignare possim portas turris domus et muri civitatis et domus, in qua habitabo». Et dedit mihi rex, quia manus Dei mei bona super me. [9]Et veni ad duces regionis trans flumen dedique eis epistulas regis. Miserat autem rex mecum principes militum et equites. [10]Et audierunt Sanaballat Horonites et Thobias servus Ammanites et contristati sunt afflictione magna, quod venisset homo, qui quaereret prosperitatem filiorum Israel. [11]Et veni Ierusalem et eram ibi tribus diebus. [12]Et surrexi nocte ego, et viri pauci mecum, et non indicavi cuiquam quid Deus meus dedisset in corde meo, ut facerem in Ierusalem; et iumentum non erat mecum, nisi animal cui sedebam. [13]Et egressus sum per portam Vallis nocte et ad fontem Draconis et portam Sterquilinii et considerabam murum Ierusalem dissipatum et portas eius consumptas igne. [14]Et transivi ad portam

the beast that was under me to pass. [15]Then I went up in the night by the valley and inspected the wall; and I turned back and entered by the Valley Gate, and so returned. [16]And the officials did not know where I had gone or what I was doing; and I had not yet told the Jews, the priests, the nobles, the officials, and the rest that were to do the work.

Ezra 9:2

[17]Then I said to them, "You see the trouble we are in, how Jerusalem lies in ruins with its gates burned. Come, let us build the wall of Jerusalem, that we may no longer suffer disgrace." [18]And I told them of the hand of my God which had been upon me for good, and also of the words which the king had spoken to me. And they said, "Let us rise up and build." So they strengthened their hands for the good work. [19]But when Sanballat the Horonite and Tobiah the servant, the Ammonite, and Geshem the Arab heard of it, they derided us and despised us and said, "What is this thing that you are doing? Are you rebelling against the king?" [20]Then I replied to them, "The God of heaven will make us prosper, and we his servants will arise and build; but you have no portion or right or memorial in Jerusalem."

Zech 14:10
Jn 5:2

Those involved in rebuilding the wall

3 [1]Then Eliashib the high priest rose up with his brethren the priests and they built the Sheep Gate. They consecrated it and set its doors; they consecrated it as far as the Tower of the

---

3:1—4:6. Breaking the thread of the story, which is taken up again in v. 33, a list is given of the groups that took part in the rebuilding, specifying the area where each worked. The builders include priests and Levites; nobles and princes; representatives of guilds (goldsmiths, perfumers, merchants); rulers of provincial districts; and people from other cities like Jericho, Tekoah, Gibeon and Mizpah. All played their part in a co-operative effort, each in his assigned place. Thus, for the Lord's plan to work successfully, the co-

Fontis et ad piscinam Regis, et non erat locus iumento cui sedebam, ut transiret. [15]Et ascendi per torrentem nocte et considerabam murum; et iterum veni ad portam Vallis et reversus sum. [16]Magistratus autem nesciebant quo abissem aut quid ego facerem, sed et Iudaeis et sacerdotibus et optimatibus et magistratibus et reliquis, qui faciebant opus, usque ad id loci nihil indicaveram. [17]Et dixi eis: «Vos nostis afflictionem, in qua sumus, quia Ierusalem deserta est, et portae eius consumptae sunt igne; venite et aedificemus murum Ierusalem et non simus ultra opprobrium». [18]Et indicavi eis quod manus Dei mei bona esset super me et verba regis, quae locutus esset mihi, et dixerunt: «Surgamus et aedificemus!». Et confortatae sunt manus eorum in bonum. [19]Audierunt autem Sanaballat Horonites et Thobias servus Ammanites et Gosem Arabs et subsannaverunt nos et despexerunt dixeruntque: «Quae est haec res, quam facitis? Numquid contra regem vos rebellatis?». [20]Et dedi eis responsum dicens: «Deus caeli ipse nos facit prosperari, et nos servi eius sumus: surgamus et aedificemus. Vobis autem non est pars et ius et memoria in Ierusalem». **[3]** [1]Et surrexit Eliasib sacerdos magnus et fratres eius sacerdotes et

Hundred, as far as the Tower of Hananel. [2]And next to him the men of Jericho built. And next to them[a] Zaccur the son of Imri built.

Jer 31:38

[3]And the sons of Hassenaah built the Fish Gate; they laid its beams and set its doors, its bolts, and its bars. [4]And next to them Meremoth the son of Uriah, son of Hakkoz repaired. And next to them Meshullam the son of Berechiah, son of Meshezabel repaired. And next to them Zadok the son of Baana repaired. [5]And next to them the Tekoites repaired; but their nobles did not put their necks to the work of their LORD.[b]

2 Chron 33:14
Ezra 2:35

[6]And Joiada the son of Paseah and Meshullam the son of Besodeiah repaired the Old Gate; they laid its beams and set its doors, its bolts, and its bars. [7]And next to them repaired Melatiah the Gibeonite and Jadon the Meronothite, the men of Gibeon and of Mizpah, who were under the jurisdiction of the governor of the province Beyond the River. [8]Next to them Uzziel the son of Harhaiah, goldsmiths, repaired. Next to him Hananiah, one of the perfumers, repaired; and they restored[c] Jerusalem as far as the Broad Wall. [9]Next to them Rephaiah the son of Hur, ruler of half

---

ordinated efforts of many were needed; but the key factor was the Lord's support: he listened to their prayers (cf. 4:4) and blessed their work.

Today, also, building the Church and a better world runs into difficulties from people who take umbrage at the effort and energy of those who take this task seriously: "The enemies of the Church get angry when they see the elect setting about the restoration of the walls of the Church, that is, by their practice of the Catholic faith and the reformation of religious customs" (St Bede, *In Esdram et Nehemiam*, 3, 16). Their opponents' jeers did not defeat the builders of Jerusalem; similarly, we should remember that the Lord continues to back the work that the Church does, even when coping with obstacles entails effort and suffering.

aedificaverunt portam Gregis; contignaverunt eam et statuerunt valvas eius et usque ad turrim Meah et turrim Hananeel. [2]Et iuxta eos aedificaverunt viri Iericho, et iuxta eos aedificavit Zacchur filius Imri. [3]Portam autem Piscium aedificaverunt filii Asnaa; ipsi contignaverunt eam et statuerunt valvas eius et seras et vectes. [4]Et iuxta eos restauravit Meremoth filius Uriae filii Accos, et iuxta eum restauravit Mosollam filius Barachiae filii Mesezabel, et iuxta eum restauravit Sadoc filius Baana, [5]et iuxta eum restauraverunt Thecueni; optimates autem eorum non supposuerunt colla sua in opere Domini sui. [6]Et portam Veterem restauraverunt Ioiada filius Phasea et Mosollam filius Besodia; ipsi contignaverunt eam et statuerunt valvas eius et seras et vectes. [7]Et iuxta eos restauraverunt Meltias Gabaonites et Iadon Meronathites, viri de Gabaon et Maspha, qui erant ad solium ducis, qui erat in regione trans flumen; [8]et iuxta eos restauravit Oziel filius Araia de aurificibus, et iuxta eum restauravit Hananias de pigmentariis et firmaverunt Ierusalem usque ad murum latiorem. [9]Et iuxta eum restauravit Raphaia filius Hur,

a. Heb *him* **b.** Or *lords* **c.** Or *abandoned*

the district of[d] Jerusalem, repaired. [10]Next to them Jedaiah the son of Harumaph repaired opposite his house; and next to him Hattush the son of Hashabneiah repaired. [11]Malchijah the son of Harim and Hasshub the son of Pahath-moab repaired another section and the Tower of the Ovens. [12]Next to him Shallum the son of Hallohesh, ruler of half the district of[d] Jerusalem, repaired, he and his daughters.

2 Chron 26:9

[13]Hanun and the inhabitants of Zanoah repaired the Valley Gate; they rebuilt it and set its doors, its bolts, and its bars, and repaired a thousand cubits of the wall, as far as the Dung Gate.

[14]Malchijah the son of Rechab, ruler of the district of[d] Beth-haccherem, repaired the Dung Gate; he rebuilt it and set its doors, its bolts, and its bars.

[15]And Shallum the son of Colhozeh, ruler of the district of Mizpah, repaired the Fountain Gate; he rebuilt it and covered it and set its doors, its bolts, and its bars; and he built the wall of the Pool of Shelah of the king's garden, as far as the stairs that go down from the City of David. [16]After him Nehemiah the son of Azbuk, ruler of half the district of Beth-zur, repaired to a point opposite the sepulchres of David, to the artificial pool, and to the house of the mighty men. [17]After him the Levites repaired: Rehum the son of Bani; next to him Hashabiah, ruler of half the district of[d] Keilah, repaired for his district. [18]After him their brethren repaired: Bavvai the son of Henadad, ruler of half the district of[d] Keilah; [19]next to him Ezer the son of Jeshua, ruler of Mizpah, repaired another section opposite the ascent to the armoury at the Angle. [20]After him Baruch the son of Zabbai repaired another section from the Angle to the door of the house of Eliashib the high priest. [21]After him Meremoth the son of Uriah, son of Hakkoz

---

princeps dimidiae partis vici Ierusalem; [10]et iuxta eum restauravit Iedaia filius Haromaph contra domum suam, et iuxta eum restauravit Hattus filius Hasabneia. [11]Alteram partem restauravit Melchias filius Harim et Hassub filius Phahathmoab usque ad turrim Furnorum. [12]Et iuxta eos restauravit Sellum filius Alohes, princeps mediae partis vici Ierusalem, ipse et filiae eius. [13]Portam Vallis restauravit Hanun et habitatores Zanoa; ipsi aedificaverunt eam et statuerunt valvas eius et seras et vectes et mille cubitos in muro usque ad portam Sterquilinii. [14]Et portam Sterquilinii restauravit Melchias filius Rechab, princeps vici Bethcharem; ipse aedificavit eam et statuit valvas eius et seras et vectes. [15]Et portam Fontis restauravit Sellum filius Cholhoza princeps pagi Maspha; ipse aedificavit eam et texit et statuit valvas eius et seras et vectes et murum piscinae Siloae iuxta hortum regis et usque ad gradus, qui descendunt de civitate David. [16]Post eum restauravit Nehemias filius Azboc princeps dimidiae partis vici Bethsur usque contra sepulcra David et usque ad piscinam, quae repleta est, et usque ad domum Fortium. [17]Post eum restauraverunt Levitae, Rehum filius Bani; iuxta eum restauravit Hasabias princeps dimidiae partis vici Ceilae pro vico suo; [18]post eum aedificaverunt fratres eorum Bavai filius Henadad princeps dimidiae partis vici Ceilae. [19]Et restauravit iuxta eum Ezer filius Iesua princeps Maspha mensuram alteram contra ascensum armentarii in angulo. [20]Post eum restauravit Baruch filius Zachai mensuram alteram ab angulo usque ad portam domus Eliasib sacerdotis magni. [21]Post eum restauravit Meremoth filius Uriae filii Aecos mensuram secundam a porta domus Eliasib usque ad extremitatem domus

d. Or *foreman of half the portion assigned to*

repaired another section from the door of the house of Eliashib to the end of the house of Eliashib. [22]After him the priests, the men of the Plain, repaired. [23]After them Benjamin and Hasshub repaired opposite their house. After them Azariah the son of Ma-aseiah, son of Ananiah repaired beside his own house. [24]After him Binnui the son of Henadad repaired another section, from the house of Azariah to the Angle [25]and to the corner. Palal the son of Uzai repaired opposite the Angle and the tower projecting from the upper house of the king at the court of the guard. After him Pedaiah the son of Parosh [26]and the temple servants living[e] on Ophel repaired to a point opposite the Water Gate on the east and the projecting tower. [27]After him the Tekoites repaired another section opposite the great projecting tower as far as the wall of Ophel.

[28]Above the Horse Gate the priests repaired, each one opposite his own house. [29]After them Zadok the son of Immer repaired opposite his own house. After him Shemaiah the son of Shecaniah, the keeper of the East Gate, repaired. [30]After him Hananiah the son of Shelemiah and Hanun the sixth son of Zalaph repaired another section. After him Meshullam the son of Berechiah repaired opposite his chamber. [31]After him Malchijah, one of the goldsmiths, repaired as far as the house of the temple servants and of the merchants, opposite the Muster Gate,[f] and to the upper chamber of the corner. [32]And between the upper chamber of the corner and the Sheep Gate the goldsmiths and the merchants repaired.

Ezek 40:6

Jn 5:2

Enemies oppose the rebuilding of the wall

4 [1g]Now when Sanballat heard that we were building the wall, he was angry and greatly enraged, and he ridiculed the Jews. [2]And he said in the presence of his brethren and of the army of Samaria, "What are these feeble Jews doing? Will they restore things? Will they sacrifice? Will they finish up in a day? Will they revive the

Neh 2:10; 4:1

Eliasib. [22]Et post eum restauraverunt sacerdotes viri de campestribus. [23]Post eos restauravit Beniamin et Hassub contra domum suam; post eos restauravit Azarias filius Maasiae filii Ananiae iuxta domum suam. [24]Post eum restauravit Bennui filius Henadad mensuram alteram a domo Azariae usque ad angulum et flexuram. [25]Phalel filius Ozi contra angulum turris, quae eminet de domo regis excelsa in atrio carceris; post eum Phadaia filius Pharos restauravit [26]usque contra portam Aquarum ad orientem et turrim, quae prominebat. [27]Post eum restauraverunt Thecueni mensuram alteram a regione contra magnam turrim eminentem usque ad murum templi. [28]Sursum autem a porta Equorum restauraverunt sacerdotes, unusquisque contra domum suam. [29]Post eos restauravit Sadoc filius Emmer contra domum suam; et post eum restauravit Semeia filius Secheniae custos portae orientalis. [30]Post eum restauravit Hanania filius Selemiae et Hanun filius Seleph sextus mensuram alteram. Post eum restauravit Mosollam filius Barachiae contra cellam suam. [31]Post eum restauravit Melchias de aurificibus usque ad domum oblatorum et mercatorum, contra portam Iudicialem, et usque ad cenaculum anguli; [32]et inter cenaculum anguli et portam Gregis restauraverunt aurifices et negotiatores. [33]Factum est autem, cum

e. Cn: Heb *were living* **f.** Or *Hammippkad Gate*

stones out of the heaps of rubbish, and burned ones at that?" [3]Tobiah the Ammonite was by him, and he said, "Yes, what they are building—if a fox goes up on it he will break down their stone wall! [4]Hear, O our God, for we are despised; turn back their taunt upon their own heads, and give them up to be plundered in a land where they are captives. [5]Do not cover their guilt, and let not their sin be blotted out from thy sight; for they have provoked thee to anger before the builders.

Jer 18:23

[6]So we built the wall; and all the wall was joined together to half its height. For the people had a mind to work.

Obstacles to rebuilding the wall

[7h]But when Sanballat and Tobiah and the Arabs and the Ammonites and the Ashdodites heard that the repairing of the walls of Jerusalem was going forward and that the breaches were beginning to be closed, they were very angry; [8]and they all plotted together to come and fight against Jerusalem and to cause confusion in it. [9]And we prayed to our God, and set a guard as a protection against them day and night.

4:7–23. Those involved in rebuilding the walls met all kinds of difficulties. Firstly, from the peoples round about: the Ashdodites to the east, Sanbalat and the army of Samaria to the north, the Ammonites to the west and the Arabs of the desert to the south—they all combined against the inhabitants of Jerusalem. The city was surrounded; and the Jews began to feel demoralized and to complain they were exhausted, perhaps to dissuade their enemies from attacking (v. 10). But later, on receiving further reports of threats to the city, Nehemiah took steps to defend it, and when danger seemed more imminent, he set up a system designed to react immediately to any attack (vv. 15–23). In a spiritual reading of the text, these builders, who had a tool in one hand and a weapon in the other, symbolize the Christian who is called to build the Kingdom of God by works of love and charity, and at the same time to defend himself or herself against the snares of the enemy by means of an ascetical struggle.

audisset Sanaballat quod aedificaremus murum, iratus est et indignatus est nimis et subsannavit Iudaeos [34]et dixit coram fratribus suis et optimatibus Samariae: «Quid Iudaei faciunt imbecilles? Num hoc conceditur eis? Num, quia sacrificant, complebunt in una die? Numquid vivificare poterunt lapides de acervis pulveris, qui combusti sunt?». [35]Sed et Thobias Ammanites, qui erat ad latus eius, ait: «Sine aedificare; si ascenderit vulpes, diruet murum eorum lapideum». [36]Audi, Deus noster, quia facti sumus irrisio! Converte contumeliam eorum super caput eorum et da eos in irrisionem in terra captivitatis! [37]Ne operias iniquitatem eorum, et peccatum eorum coram facie tua non deleatur, quia offenderunt te coram aedificantibus. [38]Itaque aedificavimus murum, et compositus est totus murus usque ad partem dimidiam, et populus dabat cor suum, ut operaretur. **[4]** [1]Factum est autem cum audisset Sanaballat et Thobias et Arabes et Ammanitae et Azotii quod prosperaretur restauratio muri Ierusalem et quod coepissent

g. Ch 3:33 in Heb **h.** Ch 4:1 in Heb

[10]But Judah said, "The strength of the burden-bearers is failing, and there is much rubbish; we are not able to work on the wall." [11]And our enemies said, "They will not know or see till we come into the midst of them and kill them and stop the work." [12]When the Jews who lived by them came they said to us ten times, "From all the places where they live[i] they will come up against us."[j] [13]So in the lowest parts of the space behind the wall, in open places, I stationed the people according to their families, with their swords, their spears, and their bows. [14]And I looked, and arose, and said to the nobles and to the officials and to the rest of the people, "Do not be afraid of them. Remember the LORD, who is great and terrible, and fight for your brethren, your sons, your daughters, your wives, and your homes."

Num 14:9
Deut 7:21
Josh 23:9–10

The builders bear arms as they engage in their work

[15]When our enemies heard that it was known to us and that God had frustrated their plan, we all returned to the wall, each to his work. [16]From that day on, half of my servants worked on construction, and half held the spears, shields, bows, and coats of mail; and the leaders stood behind all the house of Judah, [17]who were building on the wall. Those who carried burdens were laden in such a way that each with one hand laboured on the work and with the other held his weapon. [18]And each of the builders had his sword girded at his side while he built. The man who sounded the trumpet was beside me. [19]And I said to the nobles and to the officials and to the rest of the people, "The work is great and widely spread, and we are separated on the wall, far from one another. [20]In the place where you hear the sound of the trumpet, rally to us there. Our God will fight for us."

Ex 14:14

---

interrupta concludi, irati sunt nimis; [2]et conspiraverunt omnes pariter, ut venirent et pugnarent contra Ierusalem et facerent confusionem. [3]Et oravimus Deum nostrum et posuimus custodiam die ac nocte contra eos. [4]Dixit autem Iudas: «Debilitata est fortitudo portantis, et humus nimia est; et nos non poterimus aedificare murum». [5]Et dixerunt hostes nostri: «Nesciant et ignorent, donec veniamus in medium eorum et interficiamus eos et cessare faciamus opus». [6]Factum est autem venientibus Iudaeis, qui habitabant iuxta eos, et dicentibus nobis per decem vices ex omnibus locis, quibus venerant ad nos. [7]statuimus nos in inferioribus post murum in locis apertis, et ordinavi populum secundum familias cum gladiis suis et lanceis suis et arcubus suis. [8]Et perspexi atque surrexi, et aio ad optimates et magistratus et ad reliquam partem vulgi: «Nolite timere a facie eorum: Domini magni et terribilis mementote et pugnate pro fratribus vestris, filiis vestris et filiabus vestris et uxoribus vestris et domibus vestris». [9]Factum est autem cum audissent inimici nostri nuntiatum esse nobis, dissipavit Deus consilium eorum, et reversi sumus omnes ad murum, unusquisque ad opus suum. [10]Et factum est a die illa, media pars iuvenum meorum faciebat opus, et media tenebat lanceas et scuta et arcus et loricas, et principes post omnem domum Iudae. [11]Aedificantium in muro et portantium onera et imponentium, una manu sua faciebat opus et altera tenebat gladium; [12]aedificantium enim unusquisque gladio erat accinctus renes,

i. Cn: Heb *you return* **j.** Compare Gk Syr: Heb uncertain

[21]So we laboured at the work, and half of them held the spears from the break of dawn till the stars came out. [22]I also said to the people at that time, "Let every man and his servant pass the night within Jerusalem, that they may be a guard for us by night and may labour by day." [23]So neither I nor my brethren nor my servants nor the men of the guard who followed me, none of us took off our clothes; each kept his weapon in his hand.[k]

Nehemiah's administration

Jer 34:8–22

5 [1]Now there arose a great outcry of the people and of their wives against their Jewish brethren. [2]For there were those who said, "With our sons and our daughters, we are many; let us get grain, that we may eat and keep alive." [3]There were also those who said, "We are mortgaging our fields, our vineyards, and our houses to

5:1–19. The second problem Nehemiah met with was the social situation of the Jews. The poorer Jews were unhappy because they had had to mortgage their lands to the better off in order to get food and pay the king's tax. Now they had no land and no resources, which meant that their sons and daughters were being enslaved. Their debts to their compatriots were too heavy to bear (vv. 1–5). Nehemiah, who by this time has great prestige and authority, cites the example he himself set (vv. 14–16), and initiates a significant social reform. He arranges for debts to be commuted and for alienated land to be restored to its original owners (in line with the system established in Deuteronomy 15:1–18 for sabbatical years) and, in addition, he proposes that every seven years lenders will forego interest on debts (cf. 10:31). These measures were not easily accepted, especially by landowners or nobles and officials (cf. v. 7), even though they must have realized that the existing situation could not go on indefinitely. Moreover, the costs involved in running the temple were largely met by the wealthier element in the community, which meant that they had the backing of the priests. Nehemiah cleverly makes the priests responsible for ensuring that these new measures are complied with; and in laying this charge on them he uses a gesture similar to that used by prophets (vv. 12–13; cf. Jer 18:1–12). As against this, to compensate the priests for the loss which these drastic measures might entail for themselves and for the temple economy, Nehemiah sets up a new system for financing temple worship and personnel (this is detailed in 10:32–39). This is a general temple tax, a system specifying when each family should provide fuel for the temple, and a commitment by the people to give the

et sic aedificabant; et qui clangebat bucina iuxta me. [13]Et dixi ad optimates et ad magistratus et ad reliquam partem vulgi: «Opus grande est et latum, et nos separati sumus in muro procul alter ab altero; [14]in loco quocumque audieritis clangorem tubae, illuc concurrite ad nos. Deus noster pugnabit pro

k. Cn: Heb *each his weapon the water*

get grain because of the famine." [4]And there were those who said, "We have borrowed money for the king's tax upon our fields and our vineyards. [5]Now our flesh is as the flesh of our brethren, our children are as their children; yet we are forcing our sons and our daughters to be slaves, and some of our daughters have already been enslaved; but it is not in our power to help it, for other men have our fields and our vineyards."

Ex 21:7
Lev 25:39

[6]I was very angry when I heard their outcry and these words. [7]I took counsel with myself, and I brought charges against the nobles and the officials. I said to them, "You are exacting interest, each

Ex 22:25

---

first fruits to the priests and tithes to the Levites (albeit under the supervision of priests).

These reforms instituted by Nehemiah lay the basis for reconstructing Jewish social and economic life for a period that extended right up to when the temple was destroyed. Similarly, his reconstruction of the city (the walls and previously the temple) establishes the temple as the spiritual centre of all Jewry. Later on, more specific (though somewhat idealized) laws will be enacted regarding sabbatical and jubilee years (cf. Lev 25:1–55), and the Law, together with Ezra's prescriptions, will determine the pattern of religious life (cf. Neh 8:1–18).

By showing social problems to be an obstacle to the building work (problems not caused by the building programme itself, for they were of earlier origin), the sacred text underlines how important it is not to neglect social justice or solidarity with the less-well-off on the excuse that all are engaged on a great common project. God had set his people free, and every member of that people has a personal dignity which must be respected. The same holds good nowadays: our faith tells us that human dignity needs to be recognized and protected—and the distribution of wealth must take account of this. "The exercise of solidarity *within* each society is valid when its members recognize one another as persons. Those who are more influential, because they have a greater share of goods and common services, should feel *responsible* for the weaker and be ready to share with them all they possess. Those who are weaker, for their part, in the same spirit of *solidarity*, should not adopt a purely passive attitude or one that is destructive of the social fabric, but, while claiming their legitimate rights, should do what they can for the good of all. The intermediate groups, in their turn, should not selfishly insist on their particular interests, but respect the interests of others. [. . .] Solidarity helps us to see the 'other'—whether a *person*, *people* or *nation*—not just as some kind of instrument, with a work capacity and physical strength to be exploited at low cost and then discarded when no longer useful, but as our 'neighbour', a 'helper' (cf. Gen 2: 18–20), to be made a sharer, on a par with ourselves, in the banquet of life to which all are equally invited by God" (John Paul II, *Sollicitudo rei socialis*, 39).

Lev 25:48

from his brother." And I held a great assembly against them, [8]and said to them, "We, as far as we are able, have bought back our Jewish brethren who have been sold to the nations; but you even sell your brethren that they may be sold to us!" They were silent, and could not find a word to say. [9]So I said, "The thing that you are doing is not good. Ought you not to walk in the fear of our God to prevent the taunts of the nations our enemies? [10]Moreover I and my brethren and my servants are lending them money and grain. Let us leave off this interest. [11]Return to them this very day their fields, their vineyards, their olive orchards, and their houses, and the hundredth of money, grain, wine, and oil which you have been exacting of them." [12]Then they said, "We will restore these and require nothing from them. We will do as you say." And I called the priests, and took an oath of them to do as they had promised. [13]I also shook out my lap and said, "So may God shake out every man from his house and from his labour who does not perform this promise. So may he be shaken out and emptied." And all the assembly said "Amen" and praised the LORD. And the people did as they had promised.

Jer 18:1
Acts 18:6

---

nobis». [15]Et sic nos fecimus opus, et media pars nostrum tenebat lanceas ab ascensu aurorae, donec egrediantur astra. [16]In tempore quoque illo dixi populo: «Unusquisque cum puero suo pernoctet in medio Ierusalem, et erit nobis custodia per noctem et opus per diem». [17]Ego autem et fratres mei et pueri mei et custodes, qui erant post me, non deponebamus vestimenta nostra; unusquisque tenebat gladium in dextera sua. **[5]** [1]Et factus est clamor populi et uxorum eius magnus adversus fratres suos Iudaeos. [2]Et erant qui dicerent: «Filios nostros et filias nostras pignoravimus, ut acciperemus frumentum et comederemus et viveremus!». [3]Et erant qui dicerent: «Agros nostros et vineas et domos nostras opposuimus, ut acciperemus frumentum in fame!». [4]Et alii dicebant: «Mutuo sumpsimus pecunias in tributa regis pro agris nostris et vineis nostris. [5]Et nunc sicut caro fratrum nostrorum sic caro nostra est. et sicut filii eorum ita et filii nostri; ecce nos subiugamus filios nostros et filias nostras in servitutem, et de filiabus nostris quaedam iam in servitute subiugatae sunt, nec habemus unde possint redimi, quia agros nostros et vineas nostras alii possident». [6]Et iratus sum nimis, cum audissem clamorem eorum secundum verba haec. [7]Cogitavique in corde meo et increpavi optimates et magistratus et dixi eis: «Usuras singuli a fratribus vestris exigitis!». Et congregavi adversum eos contionem magnam [8]et dixi eis: «Nos, ut scitis, redemimus fratres nostros Iudaeos, qui venditi fuerant gentibus, secundum possibilitatem nostram; quin potius et vos vendetis fratres vestros, ut vendentur nobis?». Et siluerunt nec invenerunt quid responderent. [9]Dixique ad eos: «Non est bona res, quam facitis. Quare non in timore Dei nostri ambulatis, ne exprobretur nobis a gentibus inimicis nostris? [10]Et ego et fratres mei et pueri mei commodavimus plurimis pecuniam et frumentum; non repetamus usuras istas. [11]Reddite eis hodie agros suos et vineas suas et oliveta sua et domos suas et centesimam pecuniae frumenti vini et olei, quam exigere soletis ab eis». [12]Et dixerunt: «Reddemus et ab eis nihil quaeremus; sicque faciemus, ut loqueris». Et vocavi sacerdotes et feci eos iurare, ut facerent, sicut dictum erat. [13]Insuper excussi sinum meum et dixi: «Sic excutiat Deus omnem virum, qui non compleverit verbum istud, de domo sua et de laboribus suis; sic excutiatur et vacuus fiat!». Et dixit universa multitudo: «Amen!». Et laudaverunt Deum. Fecit ergo populus, sicut erat dictum. [14]A die autem illa, qua praeceperat rex mihi, ut essem dux in terra Iudae, ab anno vicesimo usque ad annum tricesimum secundum Artaxerxis regis, per annos duodecim ego et fratres mei annonas, quae ducibus debebantur, non comedimus. [15]Duces autem priores, qui fuerant ante me, gravaverunt populum et acceperunt ab eis cotidie pro pane siclos

[14]Moreover from the time that I was appointed to be their governor in the land of Judah, from the twentieth year to the thirty-second year of Ar-ta-xerxes the king, twelve years, neither I nor my brethren ate the food allowance of the governor. [15]The former governors who were before me laid heavy burdens upon the people, and took from them food and wine, besides forty shekels of silver. Even their servants lorded it over the people. But I did not do so, because of the fear of God. [16]I also held to the work on this wall, and acquired no land; and all my servants were gathered there for the work. [17]Moreover there were at my table a hundred and fifty men, Jews and officials, besides those who came to us from the nations which were about us. [18]Now that which was prepared for one day was one ox and six choice sheep; fowls likewise were prepared for me, and every ten days skins of wine in abundance; yet with all this I did not demand the food allowance of the governor, because the servitude was heavy upon this people. [19]Remember for my good, O my God, all that I have done for this people.

1 Kings 4:22

Threats fail to prevent the rebuilding

Neh 2:10; 4:1

6 [1]Now when it was reported to Sanballat and Tobiah and to Geshem the Arab and to the rest of our enemies that I had built the wall and that there was no breach left in it (although up to that time I had not set up the doors in the gates), [2]Sanballat and

1 Chron 8:12

6:1–19. As the construction work progresses, so does opposition to it. Nehemiah's enemies call on him to meet with them, perhaps because they mean to kill him (vv. 1–4).

Rebuilding the wall meant that Jerusalem would become a strong city, a symbol of the revival of the Jewish people, a city with its own governor (Nehemiah) and one that could be closed to outsiders. Hence the opposition from inhabitants of Samaria and other neighbouring peoples—and also opposition from some Jews, who may have feared

argenti quadraginta; sed et ministri eorum depresserunt populum. Ego autem non feci ita propter timorem Dei, [16]quin potius in opere muri restauravi et agrum non emi; et omnes pueri mei congregati ad opus erant. [17]Iudaei quoque et magistratus, centum quinquaginta viri, et qui veniebant ad nos de gentibus, quae in circuitu nostro sunt, in mensa mea erant. [18]Parabatur autem mihi per dies singulos bos unus, arietes sex electi, exceptis volatilibus; et inter dies decem vina diversa multa. Insuper et annonas ducatus mei non quaesivi; gravis enim erat servitus populi huius. [19]Memento mei, Deus meus, in bonum, secundum omnia, quae feci populo huic. **[6]** [1]Factum est autem cum audisset Sanaballat et Thobias et Gosem Arabs et ceteri inimici nostri, quod aedificassem ego murum, et non esset in ipso residua interruptio—usque ad tempus autem illud valvas non posueram in portis—[2]miserunt Sanaballat et Gosem ad me dicentes: «Veni, et conveniamus in Cephirim in campo Ono». Ipsi autem cogitabant, ut facerent mihi malum. [3]Misi ergo ad eos nuntios dicens: «Opus grande ego facio et non possum descendere; cur cessare oportet opus, si desistero et descendero ad vos?». [4]Miserunt autem ad me secundum verbum hoc per quattuor vices, et respondi eis iuxta sermonem priorem. [5]Et misit ad me

Geshem sent to me, saying, "Come and let us meet together in one of the villages in the plain of Ono." But they intended to do me harm. [3]And I sent messengers to them, saying, "I am doing a great work and I cannot come down. Why should the work stop while I leave it and come down to you?" [4]And they sent to me four times in this way and I answered them in the same manner. [5]In the same way Sanballat for the fifth time sent his servant to me with an open letter in his hand. [6]In it was written, "It is reported among the nations, and Geshem[1] also says it, that you and the Jews intend to rebel; that is why you are building the wall; and you wish to become their king, according to this report. [7]And you have also set up prophets to proclaim concerning you in Jerusalem, 'There is a king in Judah.' And now it will be reported to the king according to these words. So now come, and let us take counsel together." [8]Then I sent to him, saying, "No such things as you say have been done, for you are inventing them out of your own mind." [9]For they all wanted to frighten us, thinking, "Their hands will drop from the work, and it will not be done." But now, O God, strengthen thou my hands.

[10]Now when I went into the house of Shemaiah the son of Delaiah, son of Mehetabel, who was shut up, he said, "Let us meet

---

their trading would be affected. The governors of these peoples threaten to approach the king, accusing Nehemiah of planning an insurrection and having himself proclaimed king. They also try to frighten him by telling him there is a plot to kill him, in the hope that he will take fright and go into hiding—which would mean he would lose face (vv. 10–13). However, their efforts are in vain, and at long last he can rejoice in seeing his mission completed, in early October 445 BC (v. 15).

Although the builders used all the human resources necessary for their task—sparing no effort in the building or in the defence of the work in progress—they acknowledge in all simplicity that the merit is not theirs, because the work was done "with the help of our God" (v. 16).

Sanaballat iuxta verbum prius quinta vice puerum suum, et epistulam non obsignatam habebat in manu sua, in qua erat scriptum: [6]«In gentibus auditum est, et Gosem dixit quod tu et Iudaei cogitetis rebellare, et propterea aedifices murum et levare te velis super eos regem; iuxta hanc vocem [7]et prophetas posueris, qui praedicent de te in Ierusalem dicentes: "Rex in Iudaea est!". Nunc autem auditurus est rex verba haec; idcirco nunc veni, ut ineamus consilium pariter». [8]Et misi ad eum dicens: «Non est factum secundum verba haec, quae tu loqueris; de corde enim tuo tu componis haec». [9]Omnes enim hi terrebant nos cogitantes: «Fatigabuntur manus eorum ab opere, et non complebitur». Quam ob causam magis confortavi manus meas. [10]Et ingressus sum domum Semeiae filii Dalaiae filii Meetabel, ubi erat detentus. Qui ait: «Tractemus nobiscum in domo Dei, in medio templi, et claudamus portas aedis, quia

1. Heb *Gashmu*

together in the house of God, within the temple, and let us close the doors of the temple; for they are coming to kill you, at night they are coming to kill you." [11]But I said, "Should such a man as I flee? And what man such as I could go into the temple and live?[m] I will not go in." [12]And I understood, and saw that God had not sent him, but he had pronounced the prophecy against me because Tobiah and Sanballat had hired him. [13]For this purpose he was hired, that I should be afraid and act in this way and sin, and so they could give me an evil name, in order to taunt me. [14]Remember Tobiah and Sanballat, O my God, according to these things that they did, and also the prophetess No-adiah and the rest of the prophets who wanted to make me afraid.

Jer 23:9–40
Zech 13:2ff

[15]So the wall was finished on the twenty-fifth day of the month Elul, in fifty-two days. [16]And when all our enemies heard of it, all the nations round about us were afraid[n] and fell greatly in their own esteem; for they perceived that this work had been accomplished with the help of our God. [17]Moreover in those days the nobles of Judah sent many letters to Tobiah, and Tobiah's letters came to them. [18]For many in Judah were bound by oath to him, because he was the son-in-law of Shecaniah the son of Arah: and his son Jehohanan had taken the daughter of Meshullam the son of Berechiah as his wife. [19]Also they spoke of his good deeds in my presence, and reported my words to him. And Tobiah sent letters to make me afraid.

Ps 118:22–23; 127:1

Census of the returned exiles

7 [1]Now when the wall had been built and I had set up the doors, and the gatekeepers, the singers, and the Levites had been

Ezra 2:1–70

---

venturi sunt, ut interficiant te; utique nocte venturi sunt ad occidendum te». [11]Et dixi: «Num quisquam similis mei fugit? Et quis ut ego ingredietur templum et vivet? Non ingrediar». [12]Et intellexi quod Deus non misisset eum, sed quasi vaticinans locutus esset ad me, quia Thobias et Sanaballat conduxerant eum. [13]Acceperat enim pretium, ut territus sic agerem et peccarem, et haberent malum, quod exprobrarent mihi. [14]Memento, Deus meus, Thobiae et Sanaballat iuxta opera eorum talia, sed et Noadiae prophetae et ceterorum prophetarum, qui terrebant me! [15]Completus est autem murus vicesimo quinto die mensis Elul, quinquaginta duobus diebus. [16]Factum est ergo, cum audissent omnes inimici nostri, et vidissent universae gentes, quae erant in circuitu nostro, ut conciderent intra semetipsos et scirent quod a Deo factum esset opus hoc. [17]Sed et in diebus illis, multae optimatum Iudaeorum epistulae mittebantur ad Thobiam, et a Thobia veniebant ad eos. [18]Multi enim in Iudaea coniurationem fecerunt cum eo, quia gener erat Secheniae filii Area, et Iohanan filius eius acceperat filiam Mosollam filii Barachiae. [19]Sed et laudabant eum coram me et verba mea nuntiabant ei; et Thobias mittebat epistulas, ut terreret me. **[7]** [1]Postquam autem aedificatus est murus, et posui valvas et recensui ianitores et cantores et Levitas, [2]praeposui Hanani fratrem meum et Hananiam principem arcis supra Ierusalem—ipse enim quasi vir verax et timens Deum plus ceteris videbatur—[3]et dixi eis: «Non aperiantur portae Ierusalem usque ad calorem solis. Dum adhuc calor permanet, claudantur portae et oppilentur; et ponant custodes de habitatoribus Ierusalem, singulos per vices suas et unumquemque

m. *Or would go into the temple to save his life* **n.** Another reading is *saw*

appointed, [2]I gave my brother Hanani and Hananiah the governor of the castle charge over Jerusalem, for he was a more faithful and God-fearing man than many. [3]And I said to them, "Let not the gates of Jerusalem be opened until the sun is hot; and while they are still standing guard[o] let them shut and bar the doors. Appoint guards from among the inhabitants of Jerusalem, each to his station and each opposite his own house." [4]The city was wide and large, but the people within it were few and no houses had been built.

[5]Then God put it into my mind to assemble the nobles and the officials and the people to be enrolled by genealogy. And I found the book of the genealogy of those who came up at the first, and I found written in it:

[6]These were the people of the province who came up out of the captivity of those exiles whom Nebuchadnezzar the king of Babylon had carried into exile; they returned to Jerusalem and Judah, each to his town. [7]They came with Zerubbabel, Jeshua, Nehemiah, Azariah, Raamiah, Nahamani, Mordecai, Bilshan, Mispereth, Bigvai, Nehum, Baanah.

7:1–72. Once the walls of the city are rebuilt and the gates put in place, steps are taken to guard the city and control access to it. Before recounting the formal dedication of the walls (cf. 12:27–47), the sacred text gives a fairly detailed account of how civic life was normalized, particularly the resettlement of Jerusalem and Judah. This subject will be taken up again in 11:1–36, but not before the writer reports on the renewal of the people's religious life, hingeing on the Law (chaps. 8–9) and the written pact the people make with God (chap. 10).

When Nehemiah sets about taking a census of the inhabitants of Jerusalem, in order to organize its resettlement, he comes across a list of the first contingent of repatriates (vv. 6–72). This is the same list as given in the book of Ezra (cf. Ezra 2:1–67); there are very few differences between the two lists. One significant change is that whereas Ezra 2:70 presupposes that Jerusalem has already been resettled, here (v. 72) it is recorded that the repatriates settled in their own cities but there is no mention of Jerusalem, because the resettlement of the city is something that is undertaken by Nehemiah, as we shall see later (11:1–24). The list of repatriates given here serves not only as a record of the first repatriates (which is its purpose in Ezra 2:1–67) but also to identify what

contra domum suam». [4]Civitas autem erat lata nimis et grandis, et populus parvus in medio eius, et non erant domus aedificatae. [5]Deus autem meus dedit in corde meo, et congregavi optimates et magistratus et vulgus, ut recenserem eos; et inveni librum census eorum, qui ascenderant primum, et inventum est scriptum in eo: [6]Isti filii provinciae, qui ascenderunt de captivitate migrantium, quos transtulerat Nabuchodonosor rex Babylonis, et reversi sunt in Ierusalem et in Iudaeam unusquisque in civitatem suam. [7]Qui venerunt cum Zorobabel, Iesua, Nehemias, Azarias, Raamias, Nahamani, Mardochaeus,

o. Heb obscure

The number of the men of the people of Israel: [8]the sons of Parosh, two thousand a hundred and seventy-two. [9]The sons of Shephatiah, three hundred and seventy-two. [10]The sons of Arah, six hundred and fifty-two. [11]The sons of Pahath-moab, namely the sons of Jeshua and Joab, two thousand eight hundred and eighteen. [12]The sons of Elam, a thousand two hundred and fifty-four. [13]The sons of Zattu, eight hundred and forty-five. [14]The sons of Zaccai, seven hundred and sixty. [15]The sons of Binnui, six hundred and forty-eight. [16]The sons of Bebai, six hundred and twenty-eight. [17]The sons of Azgad, two thousand three hundred and twenty-two. [18]The sons of Adonikam, six hundred and sixty-seven. [19]The sons of Bigvai, two thousand and sixty-seven. [20]The sons of Adin, six hundred and fifty-five. [21]The sons of Ater, namely of Hezekiah, ninety-eight. [22]The sons of Hashum, three hundred and twenty-eight. [23]The sons of Bezai, three hundred and twenty-four. [24]The sons of Hariph, a hundred and twelve. [25]The sons of Gibeon, ninety-five. [26]The men of Bethlehem and Netophah, a hundred and eighty-eight. [27]The men of Anathoth, a hundred and twenty-eight. [28]The men of Beth-azmaveth, forty-two. [29]The men of Kiriath-

---

house a person belonged to (and thereby his membership of the people). Some priests could not prove their genealogy and were suspended from their positions (vv. 64–65). The people is taken to be made up of the descendants of those who came back from exile (just as it was once made up of those who came up from Egypt) and those who are still living in exile. The fact that a person is of Hebrew descent (that is, of the line of Abraham) is of no account. Nor do those count who stayed on in Judah during the period of the Babylonian captivity or those who belonged to the Northern kingdom. Unlike what happened at the return from exile, when even foreigners who acknowledged the Lord were accepted as members of the people (cf. Is 56:1–8), Nehemiah's policy is now clearly isolationist. This comes across even more clearly in chapter 10, which deals with the covenant the people made with God. In the overall history of salvation, Nehemiah's reform can be seen as being designed to ensure the Jewish people's purity of faith until the time of our Lord's coming.

Belsan, Mespharath, Beguai, Nahum, Baana. Numerus virorum populi Israel: [8]filii Pharos duo milia centum septuaginta duo; [9]filii Saphatia trecenti septuaginta duo; [10]filii Area sescenti quinquaginta duo; [11]filii Phahathmoab, hi sunt filii Iesua et Ioab, duo milia octingenti decem et octo; [12]filii Elam mille ducenti quinquaginta quattuor; [13]filii Zethua octingenti quadraginta quinque; [14]filii Zachai septingenti sexaginta; [15]filii Bennui sescenti quadraginta octo; [16]filii Bebai sescenti viginti octo; [17]filii Azgad duo milia trecenti viginti duo; [18]filii Adonicam sescenti sexaginta septem; [19]filii Beguai duo milia sexaginta septem; [20]filii Adin sescenti quinquaginta quinque; [21]filii Ater, qui erant ex Ezechia, nonaginta octo; [22]filii Hasum trecenti viginti octo; [23]filii Besai trecenti viginti quattuor; [24]filii Hareph centum duodecim; [25]filii Gabaon nonaginta quinque; [26]filii Bethlehem et Netopha centum octoginta octo; [27]viri Anathoth centum viginti octo; [28]viri Bethazmaveth quadraginta duo; [29]viri Cariathiarim, Cephira et Beroth

jearim, Chephirah, and Be-eroth, seven hundred and forty-three. [30]The men of Ramah and Geba, six hundred and twenty-one. [31]The men of Michmas, a hundred and twenty-two. [32]The men of Bethel and Ai, a hundred and twenty-three. [33]The men of the other Nebo, fifty-two. [34]The sons of the other Elam, a thousand two hundred and fifty-four. [35]The sons of Harim, three hundred and twenty. [36]The sons of Jericho, three hundred and forty-five. [37]The sons of Lod, Hadid, and Ono, seven hundred and twenty-one. [38]The sons of Senaah, three thousand nine hundred and thirty.

[39]The priests: the sons of Jedaiah, namely the house of Jeshua, nine hundred and seventy-three. [40]The sons of Immer, a thousand and fifty-two. [41]The sons of Pashhur, a thousand two hundred and forty-seven. [42]The sons of Harim, a thousand and seventeen.

[43]The Levites: the sons of Jeshua, namely of Kadmi-el of the sons of Hodevah, seventy-four. [44]The singers: the sons of Asaph, a hundred and forty-eight. [45]The gatekeepers: the sons of Shallum, the sons of Ater, the sons of Talmon, the sons of Akkub, the sons of Hatita, the sons of Shobai, a hundred and thirty-eight.

[46]The temple servants:[p] the sons of Ziha, the sons of Hasupha, the sons of Tabbaoth, [47]the sons of Keros, the sons of Sia, the sons of Padon, [48]the sons of Lebana, the sons of Hagaba, the sons of Shalmai, [49]the sons of Hanan, the sons of Giddel, the sons of Gahar, [50]the sons of Re-aiah, the sons of Rezin, the sons of Nekoda, [51]the sons of Gazzam, the sons of Uzza, the sons of Paseah, [52]the sons of Besai, the sons of Me-unim, the sons of Nephushesim, [53]the sons of Bakbuk, the sons of Hakupha, the sons of Harhur, [54]the sons of Bazlith, the sons of Mehida, the sons of Harsha, [55]the sons of Barkos, the sons of Sisera, the sons of Temah, [56]the sons of Neziah, the sons of Hatipha.

[57]The sons of Solomon's servants: the sons of Sotai, the sons of Sophereth, the sons of Perida, [58]the sons of Jaala, the sons of

septingenti quadraginta tres; [30]viri Rama et Gabaa sescenti viginti unus [31]viri Machmas centum viginti duo; [32]viri Bethel et Hai centum viginti tres; [33]viri Nabo alterius quinquaginta duo; [34]viri Elam alterius mille ducenti quinquaginta quattuor; [35]filii Harim trecenti viginti; [36]filii Iericho trecenti quadraginta quinque; [37]filii Lod, Hadid et Ono septingenti viginti unus; [38]filii Senaa tria milia nongenti triginta. [39]Sacerdotes: filii Iedaia de domo Iesua nongenti septuaginta tres; [40]filii Emmer mille quinquaginta duo; [41]filii Phassur mille ducenti quadraginta septem; [42]filii Harim mille decem et septem. [43]Levitae: filii Iesua, hi sunt filii Cadmihel, Bennui et Odoviae, septuaginta quattuor. [44]Cantores: filii Asaph centum quadraginta octo. [45]Ianitores: filii Sellum, filii Ater, filii Telmon, filii Accub, filii Hatita, filii Sobai, centum triginta octo. [46]Oblati: filii Siha, filii Hasupha, filii Tabbaoth, [47]filii Ceros, filii Siaa, filii Phadon, [48]filii Lebana, filii Hagaba, filii Selmai, [49]filii Hanan, filii Giddel, filii Gaher, [50]filii Raaia, filii Rasin, filii Necoda, [51]filii Gazam, filii Oza, filii Phasea, [52]filii Besai, filii Meunitarum, filii Nephusorum, [53]filii Bacbuc, filii Hacupha, filii Harhur, [54]filii Basluth, filii Mahida, filii Harsa, [55]filii Bercos, filii Sisara, filii Thema, [56]filii Nasia, filii Hatipha. [57]Filii servorum Salomonis: filii Sotai, filii Sophereth, filii Pheruda,

p. Heb *nethinim*

Darkon, the sons of Giddel, [59]the sons of Shephatiah, the sons of Hattil, the sons of Pochereth-hazzebaim, the sons of Amon.

[60]All the temple servants and the sons of Solomon's servants were three hundred and ninety-two.

[61]The following were those who came up from Tel-melah, Tel-harsha, Cherub, Addon, and Immer, but they could not prove their fathers' houses nor their descent, whether they belonged to Israel: [62]the sons of Delaiah, the sons of Tobiah, the sons of Nekoda, six hundred and forty-two. [63]Also, of the priests: the sons of Hobaiah, the sons of Hakkoz, the sons of Barzillai (who had taken a wife of the daughters of Barzillai the Gileadite and was called by their name). [64]These sought their registration among those enrolled in the genealogies, but it was not found there, so they were excluded from the priesthood as unclean; [65]the governor told them that they were not to partake of the most holy food, until a priest with Urim and Thummim should arise.

[66]The whole assembly together was forty-two thousand three hundred and sixty, [67]besides their menservants and maidservants, of whom there were seven thousand three hundred and thirty-seven; and they had two hundred and forty-five singers, male and female. [68]Their horses were seven hundred and thirty-six, their mules two hundred and forty-five,[q] [69]their camels four hundred and thirty-five, and their asses six thousand seven hundred and twenty.

[70]Now some of the heads of fathers' houses gave to the work. The governor gave to the treasury a thousand darics of gold, fifty basins, five hundred and thirty priests' garments. [71]And some of

---

7:68. From here up to v. 72b (when they rejoin), the verse numbering of the New Vulgate is one figure different from the Masoretic text.

[58]filii Iaala, filii Darcon, filii Giddel, [59]filii Saphatia, filii Hatil, filii Phochereth Hassebaim, filii Amon. [60]Omnes oblati et filii servorum Salomonis trecenti nonaginta duo. [61]Hi sunt autem qui ascenderunt de Thelmela, Thelharsa, Cherub, Addon et Emmer, et non potuerunt indicare domum patrum suorum et semen suum, utrum ex Israel essent: [62]filii Dalaia, filii Thobia, filii Necoda sescenti quadraginta duo. [63]Et de sacerdotibus: filii Hobia, filii Accos, filii Berzellai, qui accepit de filiabus Berzellai Galaaditis uxorem et vocatus est nomine eorum. [64]Hi quaesierunt tabulas genealogiae suae et non invenerunt et eiecti sunt de sacerdotio; [65]dixitque praepositus eis, ut non manducarent de sanctificatis sanctuarii, donec staret sacerdos pro Urim et Tummim. [66]Omnis multitudo simul quadraginta duo milia trecenti sexaginta, [67]absque servis et ancillis eorum, qui erant septem milia trecenti triginta septem; insuper et cantores et cantatrices ducenti quadraginta quinque. [68]Equi eorum septingenti triginta sex, muli eorum ducenti quadraginta quinque, [69]cameli eorum quadringenti triginta quinque, asini sex milia septingenti viginti. [70]Nonnulli autem de principibus familiarum dederunt in opus: praepositus dedit in thesaurum auri drachmas mille, phialas quinquaginta, tunicas sacerdotales quingentas triginta; [71]et de principibus familiarum dederunt in thesaurum operis auri drachmas viginti milia et argenti minas duo milia

q. Ezra 2:66 and the margins of some Hebrew Mss: Heb lacks *their horses . . . forty-five*

the heads of fathers' houses gave into the treasury of the work twenty thousand darics of gold and two thousand two hundred minas of silver. [72]And what the rest of the people gave was twenty thousand darics of gold, two thousand minas of silver, and sixty-seven priests' garments.

[73]So the priests, the Levites, the gatekeepers, the singers, some of the people, the temple servants, and all Israel, lived in their towns.

The Law is read out. The feast of Tabernacles

Ezra 3:1; 7:6

8 And when the seventh month had come, the children of Israel were in their towns.* [1]And all the people gathered as one man into the square before the Water Gate; and they told Ezra the scribe to bring the book of the law of Moses which the LORD had given to Israel. [2]And Ezra the priest brought the law before the assembly, both men and women and all who could hear with understanding, on the first day of the seventh month. [3]And he read from it facing

---

8:1–18. The text of this chapter forms part of the "memoirs of Ezra" which the sacred writer has moved and positioned here in the account of the rebuilding of the city. By doing so, he highlights the importance of the Law in the new stage of the history of the chosen people (as the writer sees it, this stage begins with the reconstruction of their national and religious life spearheaded by Ezra the priest and Nehemiah the layman). We do not know the exact year when the events dealt with here occurred, nor the exact content of the Law proclaimed on this occasion. It is possible that a substantial part of the present Pentateuch was read out.

The reading and explanation of the Law did not take place inside the temple: the people gathered around the stage specially set up in front of that building. From the time of Solomon up to the fall of Jerusalem, religious activity centred on the temple liturgy. From the exile onwards it was built around the Law by means of the institution of the synagogue. Because they could not go up to the House of the Lord, exiles used to meet in private houses or in the open air to listen to the reading of legal and prophetical texts. The formal meeting described here, held in a square beside the city wall, shows that in this new stage, with Ezra to the fore, the Law of the Lord was

ducentas. [72]Et quod dedit reliquus populus, auri drachmas viginti milia et argenti minas duo milia et tunicas sacerdotales sexaginta septem. Habitaverunt autem ibi sacerdotes et Levitae; ianitores autem et cantores et quidam de populo et oblati et omnis Israel habitaverunt in civitatibus suis. Et venerat mensis septimus; filii autem Israel erant in civitatibus suis. **[8]** [1]Congregatusque est omnis populus quasi vir unus ad plateam, quae est ante portam Aquarum, et dixerunt Esdrae scribae, ut afferret librum legis Moysi, quam praeceperat Dominus Israeli. [2]Attulit ergo Esdras sacerdos legem coram multitudine virorum et mulierum cunctisque, qui poterant intellegere, in die prima mensis septimi. [3]Et legit in eo in platea, quae erat ante portam Aquarum, de mane usque ad mediam diem in conspectu virorum et

the square before the Water Gate from early morning until midday, in the presence of the men and the women and those who could understand; and the ears of all the people were attentive to the book of the law. [4]And Ezra the scribe stood on a wooden pulpit which they had made for the purpose; and beside him stood Mattithiah, Shema, Anaiah, Uriah, Hilkiah, and Ma-aseiah on his right hand; and Pedaiah, Misha-el, Malchijah, Hashum, Hash-baddanah, Zechariah, and Meshullam on his left hand. [5]And Ezra opened the book in the sight of all the people, for he was above all the people; and when he opened it all the people stood. [6]And Ezra blessed the LORD, the great God; and all the people answered, "Amen, Amen," lifting up their hands; and they bowed their heads and worshipped the LORD with their faces to the ground. [7]Also Jeshua, Bani, Sherebiah, Jamin, Akkub, Shabbethai, Hodiah, Ma-aseiah, Kelita, Azariah, Jozabad, Hanan, Pelaiah, the Levites,[r] helped

2 Chron 35:3

---

coming to occupy pride of place in the religious life of the people, and that it was already more important than the offering of victims for the purpose of sacrifice.

When they hear the commandments of the Law read out, the people weep because they have not been keeping some of them and they are afraid that God will punish them on that account. But Ezra and the Levites make them see that what they have to do is to start again, on that day, for it is a "holy" day. It was the festival day of the new civil year (cf. Lev 23:24–25; Num 29:1–6).

The proclamation of the Law seems to be linked to the celebration of the feast of Booths (or Tents, or Tabernacles). That celebration was already (briefly) mentioned in Ezra 3:4–6, but there is a new element here (which must be due to Ezra's interpretation)—the fact that the booths are made with branches cut in the hills (cf. Lev 23:39–43). No mention is made of the day of Atonement which was celebrated on the tenth day of the same month (cf. Lev 23:26–32). During the seven days of the feast of booths Ezra keeps reading out the Law as Deuteronomy 31:9–13 lays down must be done when the year is a sabbatical one. In these actions of Ezra and the Levites, the teachers of the Laws, we can see the origin of what will become the "Great Assembly", the official body which will, in the centuries to come, interpret the Law and identify which books form part of the canon. The reading of the books of the Law will from now on become the most important way of meeting God and listening to his word.

mulierum et eorum, qui intellegere poterant; et aures omnis populi erant erectae ad librum legis. [4]Stetit autem Esdras scriba super gradum ligneum, quem ad hoc fecerant; et steterunt iuxta eum Matthathias et Sema et Anaia et Uria et Helcia et Maasia ad dexteram eius, et ad sinistram Phadaia, Misael et Melchia et Hasum et Hasbadana, Zacharia et Mosollam. [5]Et aperuit Esdras librum coram omni populo—super universum quippe populum eminebat—et, cum aperuisset eum, stetit omnis populus. [6]Et

r. 1 Esdras 9:48 Vg: Heb *and the Levites* **s.** Or *with interpretation*

the people to understand the law, while the people remained in their places. [8]And they read from the book, from the law of God, clearly;[s] and they gave the sense, so that the people understood the reading.*

Ezra 7:6

[9]And Nehemiah, who was the governor, and Ezra the priest and scribe, and the Levites who taught the people said to all the people, "This day is holy to the LORD your God; do not mourn or weep." For all the people wept when they heard the words of the law. [10]Then he said to them, "Go your way, eat the fat and drink sweet wine and send portions to him for whom nothing is prepared; for this day is holy to our LORD; and do not be grieved, for the joy of the LORD is your strength." [11]So the Levites stilled all the people, saying, "Be quiet, for this day is holy; do not be grieved." [12]And all the people went their way to eat and drink and to send portions and to make great rejoicing, because they had understood the words that were declared to them.

[13]On the second day the heads of fathers' houses of all the people, with the priests and the Levites, came together to Ezra the scribe in order to study the words of the law. [14]And they found it written in the law that the LORD had commanded by Moses that the people of Israel should dwell in booths during the feast of the seventh month, [15]and that they should publish and proclaim in all their towns and in Jerusalem, "Go out to the hills and bring branches of olive, wild olive, myrtle, palm, and other leafy trees to make booths, as it is written." [16]So the people went out and brought them and made booths for themselves, each on his roof, and in their courts and in the courts of the house of God, and in the square at the Water Gate and in the square at the Gate of Ephraim.

Ex 22:14
Lev 23:33–36, 39–43
Deut 16:13

---

benedixit Esdras Domino Deo magno; et respondit omnis populus: «Amen, amen», elevans manus suas. Et incurvati sunt et adoraverunt Deum proni in terram. [7]Porro Iesua et Bani et Serebia, Iamin, Accub, Sabethai, Hodia, Maasia, Celita, Azarias, Iozabad, Hanan, Phalaia et Levitae erudiebant populum in lege; populus autem stabat in gradu suo. [8]Et legerunt in libro legis Dei distincte et aperierunt sensum et explicaverunt lectionem. [9]Dixit autem Nehemias, ipse est praepositus, et Esdras sacerdos et scriba et Levitae instruentes populum universo populo: «Dies iste sanctificatus est Domino Deo nostro! Nolite lugere et nolite flere». Flebat enim omnis populus, cum audiret verba legis. [10]Et dixit eis: «Ite, comedite pinguia et bibite mulsum et mittite partes his, qui non praeparaverunt sibi, quia sanctus dies Domini nostri est; et nolite contristari, gaudium etenim Domini est fortitudo vestra». [11]Levitae autem silentium faciebant in omni populo dicentes: «Tacete, quia dies sanctus est, et nolite dolere». [12]Abiit itaque omnis populus, ut comederet et biberet et mitteret partes et faceret laetitiam magnam, quia intellexerant verba, quae docuerat eos. [13]Et in die secundo congregati sunt principes familiarum universi populi, sacerdotes et Levitae ad Esdram scribam, ut intellegerent verba legis. [14]Et invenerunt scriptum in lege, quam praecepit Dominus per Moysen, ut habitent filii Israel in tabernaculis in die sollemni mense septimo [15]et ut praedicent et divulgent vocem in universis urbibus suis et in Ierusalem dicentes: «Egredimini in montem et afferte frondes olivae et frondes oleastri, frondes myrti et ramos palmarum et frondes ligni nemorosi, ut fiant tabernacula, sicut scriptum est». [16]Et egressus est populus, et attulerunt feceruntque sibi tabernacula, unusquisque in domate suo et in atriis suis et in atriis domus Dei et in platea portae

[17]And all the assembly of those who had returned from the captivity made booths and dwelt in the booths; for from the days of Jeshua the son of Nun to that day the people of Israel had not done so. And there was very great rejoicing. [18]And day by day, from the first day to the last day, he read from the book of the law of God. They kept the feast seven days; and on the eighth day there was a solemn assembly, according to the ordinance.

Deut 31:10–11

Fasting and confession of sins

9 [1]Now on the twenty-fourth day of this month the people of Israel were assembled with fasting and in sackcloth, and with earth upon their heads. [2]And the Israelites separated themselves from all foreigners, and stood and confessed their sins and the iniquities of their fathers. [3]And they stood up in their place and read from the book of the law of the LORD their God for a fourth of the day; for

Ezra 9:1–2; 10:11
Neh 13:3,30

9:1–37. After listening to the proclamation of the Law and joyfully celebrating the seven-day festival of Booths (cf. 8:1–18), the people confess their sins and acknowledge how good God has been to them. The order of feasts given in Leviticus 23:26–33 has been changed: the day of Atonement has been put after the reading of the Law, probably to underline the fact that the reading made the people conscious of their sin (v. 3).

The prayer recorded here (similar in style to Psalms 78, 105 and 106) begins by acknowledging all the blessings of God over the course of salvation history, beginning with the creation of the world, the election of Abraham and the promise that his descendants would be given the land they now inhabit (vv. 5–8). It goes on to focus on the deliverance of the sons of Abraham from bondage in Egypt, and how the Lord looked after them in the wilderness and gave them possession of the promised land (vv. 9–23). It recalls that, despite the prophets' warnings, the Israelites rebelled time and again, with the result that even though they continued to live in the land God gave their forebears, it was no longer theirs, because they were under the dominion of foreign kings (vv. 24–37).

Aquarum et in platea portae Ephraim. [17]Fecit ergo universa ecclesia eorum, qui redierant de captivitate, tabernacula et habitaverunt in tabernaculis. Non enim fecerant a diebus Iosue filii Nun taliter filii Israel usque ad diem illum: et fuit laetitia magna nimis. [18]Legit autem in libro legis Dei per dies singulos, a die primo usque ad diem novissimum; et fecerunt sollemnitatem septem diebus et in die octavo conventum iuxta ordinationem. **[9]** [1]In die autem vicesimo quarto mensis huius convenerunt filii Israel in ieiunio et in saccis, et humus super eos. [2]Et separatum est semen filiorum Israel ab omni alienigena; et steterunt et confitebantur peccata sua et iniquitates patrum suorum. [3]Et consurrexerunt ad standum et legerunt in volumine legis Domini Dei sui per quartam partem diei et per quartam partem confitebantur et adorabant Dominum Deum suum. [4]Surrexerunt autem super gradum Levitarum Iesua et Bani et Cadmihel, Sebania, Bunni, Serebia, Bani et Chanani et clamaverunt voce magna ad Dominum Deum suum. [5]Et dixerunt Levitae Iesua et Cadmihel, Bani, Hasabneia, Serebia, Hodia, Sebania, Phethahia: «Surgite, benedicite Domino Deo vestro / ab aeterno usque in aeternum, / et benedicant nomini / gloriae tuae excelso / super omnem benedictionem et laudem. / [6]Tu ipse, Domine, solus; / tu fecisti caelum et

another fourth of it they made confession and worshipped the LORD their God. [4]Upon the stairs of the Levites stood Jeshua, Bani, Kadmi-el, Shebaniah, Bunni, Sherebiah, Bani, and Chenani; and they cried with a loud voice to the LORD their God. [5]Then the Levites, Jeshua, Kadmi-el, Bani, Hashabneiah, Sherebiah, Hodiah, Shebaniah, and Pethahiah, said, "Stand up and bless the LORD your God from everlasting to everlasting. Blessed be thy glorious name which is exalted above all blessing and praise."

Ps 78
Dan 3:52

[6]And Ezra said:[t] "Thou art the LORD, thou alone; thou hast made heaven, the heaven of heavens, with all their host, the earth and all that is on it, the seas and all that is in them; and thou preservest all of them; and the host of heaven worships thee. [7]Thou art the LORD, the God who didst choose Abram and bring him forth out of Ur of the Chaldeans and give him the name Abraham; [8]and thou didst find his heart faithful before thee, and didst make with him the covenant to give to his descendants the land of the Canaanite, the Hittite, the Amorite, the Perizzite, the Jebusite, and the Girgashite; and thou hast fulfilled thy promise, for thou art righteous.

Deut 6:4; 10:14
2 Kings 19:15
Acts 4:24
Rev 10:6
Gen 12:1; 17:5
Gen 11:31; 12:7; 15:6,18; 17:7–9

[9]"And thou didst see the affliction of our fathers in Egypt and hear their cry at the Red Sea, [10]and didst perform signs and wonders against Pharaoh and all his servants and all the people of his land, for thou knewest that they acted insolently against our

Ex 2:23–24
Ex 7–12

The custom of beginning prayer by acknowledging the bounty of the Lord has a long tradition in Holy Scripture, as we can see from this text. It was a custom practised also by the early Christians. For example, when they meet together in Jerusalem to pray for Peter's release from prison, they address God in the same words as are used here: "Sovereign Lord, who didst make the heaven and the earth and the sea and everything in them..." (Acts 4:24; cf. v. 6).

The confession of sins reflects the feelings of those of the people who had lived on in Judah ever since their forebears reached that land, and not

caelum caelorum / et omnem exercitum eorum, / terram et universa, quae in ea sunt, / maria et omnia, quae in eis sunt; / et tu vivificas omnia haec, / et exercitus caeli te adorat. / [7]Tu ipse, Domine Deus, qui elegisti Abram / et eduxisti eum de Ur Chaldaeorum / et posuisti nomen eius Abraham. / [8]Et invenisti cor eius fidele coram te / et percussisti cum eo foedus, / ut dares terram Chananaei, Hetthaei et Amorraei / et Pherezaei et Iebusaei et Gergesaei, / nempe ut dares semini eius; / et implesti verba tua, / quoniam iustus es. / [9]Et vidisti afflictionem patrum nostrorum in Aegypto / clamoremque eorum audisti iuxta mare Rubrum. / [10]Et dedisti signa atque portenta in pharaone / et in universis servis eius et in omni populo terrae illius; / cognovisti enim quia superbe egerant contra eos / et fecisti tibi nomen, sicut et in hac die. / [11]Et mare divisisti ante eos, / et transierunt per medium maris in sicco; / persecutores autem eorum proiecisti in profundum, / quasi lapidem in aquas validas. / [12]Et in columna nubis ductor eorum fuisti per diem / et in columna ignis per noctem, / ut illuminaret eis viam, per quam ingrediebantur. / [13]Ad montem quoque Sinai descendisti / et locutus es cum eis de caelo; / et dedisti eis iudicia recta /

t. Gk: Heb lacks *and Ezra said*

fathers; and thou didst get thee a name, as it is to this day. [11]And thou didst divide the sea before them, so that they went through the midst of the sea on dry land; and thou didst cast their pursuers into the depths, as a stone into mighty waters. [12]By a pillar of cloud thou didst lead them in the day, and by a pillar of fire in the night to light for them the way in which they should go. [13]Thou didst come down upon Mount Sinai, and speak with them from heaven and give them right ordinances and true laws, good statutes and commandments, [14]and thou didst make known to them thy holy sabbath and command them commandments and statutes and a law by Moses thy servant. [15]Thou didst give them bread from heaven for their hunger and bring forth water for them from the rock for their thirst, and thou didst tell them to go in to possess the land which thou hadst sworn to give them.

Ex 14; 15:5,10
Ex 13:21ff
Ex 19
Deut 4:5–8
Ex 20:8
Ex 16:1,14; 17:1
Deut 1:8
Jn 6:31

[16]"But they and our fathers acted presumptuously and stiffened their neck and did not obey thy commandments; [17]they refused to obey, and were not mindful of the wonders which thou didst perform among them; but they stiffened their neck and appointed a leader to return to their bondage in Egypt. But thou art a God ready to forgive, gracious and merciful, slow to anger and abounding in steadfast love, and didst not forsake them. [18]Even when they had made for themselves a molten calf and said, 'This is your God who brought you up out of Egypt,' and had committed great blasphemies, [19]thou in thy great mercies didst not forsake

Ex 34:6
Num 14:1–4
Ex 32

---

those who had come back after having suffered exile. Unlike the latter, they are not well disposed towards the Persian kings (cf. vv. 36–37), and they make no reference to exile or to the subsequent restoration.

This dual dimension of prayer—gratefulness to God for his blessings, and petition for forgiveness of sins—is always to be found in saints' prayers and should always be present in every Christian's prayer.

et legem rectam, mandata et praecepta bona. / [14]Et sabbatum sanctificatum tuum ostendisti eis / et praecepta et mandata et legem praecepisti eis / in manu Moysi servi tui. / [15]Panem quoque de caelo dedisti eis in fame eorum / et aquam de petra eduxisti eis in siti eorum; / et dixisti eis, ut ingrederentur et possiderent terram, / super quam levasti manum tuam, ut traderes eis. / [16]Ipsi vero patres nostri superbe egerunt / et induraverunt cervices suas et non audierunt mandata tua. / [17]Et noluerunt audire / et non sunt recordati mirabilium tuorum, quae feceras eis, / et induraverunt cervices suas / et posuerunt caput suum, / ut reverterentur ad servitutem suam in Aegyptum. / Tu autem Deus propitius, clemens et misericors, / longanimis et multae miserationis, non dereliquisti eos. / [18]Et quidem, cum fecissent sibi vitulum conflatilem / et dixissent: "Iste est Deus tuus, / qui eduxit te de Aegypto" / feceruntque blasphemias magnas; / [19]tu autem in misericordiis tuis multis / non dimisisti eos in deserto: / columna nubis non recessit ab eis per diem, / ut duceret eos in viam; / et columna ignis per noctem, / ut

them in the wilderness; the pillar of cloud which led them in the way did not depart from them by day, nor the pillar of fire by night which lighted for them the way by which they should go. [20]Thou gavest thy good Spirit to instruct them, and didst not withhold thy manna from their mouth, and gavest them water for their thirst. [21]Forty years didst thou sustain them in the wilderness, and they lacked nothing; their clothes did not wear out and their feet did not swell. [22]And thou didst give them kingdoms and peoples, and didst allot to them every corner; so they took possession of the land of Sihon king of Heshbon and the land of Og king of Bashan. [23]Thou didst multiply their descendants as the stars of heaven, and thou didst bring them into the land which thou hadst told their fathers to enter and possess. [24]So the descendants went in and possessed the land, and thou didst subdue before them the inhabitants of the land, the Canaanites, and didst give them into their hands, with their kings and the peoples of the land, that they might do with them as they would. [25]And they captured fortified cities and a rich land, and took possession of houses full of all good things, cisterns hewn out, vineyards, olive orchards and fruit trees in abundance; so they ate, and were filled and became fat, and delighted themselves in thy great goodness.

[26]"Nevertheless they were disobedient and rebelled against thee and cast thy law behind their back and killed thy prophets, who had warned them in order to turn them back to thee, and they committed great blasphemies. [27]Therefore thou didst give them into the hand of their enemies, who made them suffer; and in the time of their suffering they cried to thee and thou didst hear them from heaven; and according to thy great mercies thou didst give them saviours who saved them from the hand of their enemies.

Deut 2:7; 8
Num 21:21–35
Deut 1:4; 2:26–3:11
Deut 1:10
Deut 3:5; 6:10–11; 32:15
1 Kings 18:4
Wis 2:10–20
Mt 21:36; 23:37
Acts 7:52

---

illuminaret eis iter, per quod ingrederentur. / [20]Et spiritum tuum bonum dedisti, qui doceret eos, / et manna tuum non prohibuisti ab ore eorum / et aquam dedisti eis in siti eorum. / [21]Quadraginta annis pavisti eos in deserto, / nihilque eis defuit; / vestimenta eorum non inveteraverunt, / et pedes eorum non intumuerunt. / [22]Et dedisti eis regna et populos / et partitus es eis sortes; / et possederunt terram Sehon et terram regis Hesebon / et terram Og regis Basan. / [23]Et multiplicasti filios eorum sicut stellas caeli; / et adduxisti eos ad terram, de qua dixeras patribus eorum, / ut ingrederentur et possiderent. / [24]Et venerunt filii et possederunt terram, / et humiliasti coram eis habitatores terrae Chananaeos; / et dedisti eos in manu eorum / et reges eorum et populos terrae, / ut facerent eis, sicut placebat illis. / [25]Ceperunt itaque urbes munitas et humum pinguem; / et possederunt domos plenas cunctis bonis, / cisternas ab aliis fabricatas, vineas et oliveta / et ligna pomifera multa. / Et comederunt et saturati sunt et impinguati sunt / et delectati sunt in bonitate tua magna. / [26]Vexaverunt autem te et rebellaverunt contra te / et proiecerunt legem tuam post terga sua; / et prophetas tuos occiderunt, / qui contestabantur eos, ut reverterentur ad te: / feceruntque blasphemias grandes. / [27]Et dedisti eos in manu hostium suorum, / et afflixerunt eos; / et in tempore tribulationis suae clamaverunt ad te, / et tu de caelo audisti / et secundum miserationes tuas multas dedisti eis salvatores, / qui salvarent eos da manu hostium suorum. / [28]Cumque requievissent, reversi sunt, / ut facerent malum in conspectu tuo; / et dereliquisti eos in manu

[28]But after they had rest they did evil again before thee, and thou didst abandon them to the hand of their enemies, so that they had dominion over them; yet when they turned and cried to thee thou didst hear from heaven, and many times thou didst deliver them according to thy mercies. [29]And thou didst warn them in order to turn them back to thy law. Yet they acted presumptuously and did not obey thy commandments, but sinned against thy ordinances, by the observance of which a man shall live, and turned a stubborn shoulder and stiffened their neck and would not obey. [30]Many years thou didst bear with them, and didst warn them by thy Spirit through thy prophets; yet they would not give ear. Therefore thou didst give them into the hand of the peoples of the lands. [31]Nevertheless in thy great mercies thou didst not make an end of them or forsake them; for thou art a gracious and merciful God.

Jer 4:27

[32]"Now therefore, our God, the great and mighty and terrible God, who keepest covenant and steadfast love, let not all the hardship seem little to thee that has come upon us, upon our kings, our princes, our priests, our prophets, our fathers, and all thy people, since the time of the kings of Assyria until this day. [33]Yet thou hast been just in all that has come upon us, for thou hast dealt faithfully and we have acted wickedly; [34]our kings, our princes, our priests, and our fathers have not kept thy law or heeded thy commandments and thy warnings which thou didst give them. [35]They did not serve thee in their kingdom, and in thy great goodness which thou gavest them, and in the large and rich land which thou didst set before them; and they did not turn from their wicked works. [36]Behold, we are slaves this day; in the land that thou gavest to our fathers to enjoy its fruit and its good gifts, behold, we are slaves. [37]And its rich yield goes to the kings whom

Sir 36:1–9
Lam 5

---

inimicorum suorum, / et dominati sunt eis. / Conversique sunt et clamaverunt ad te; / tu autem de caelo exaudisti / et liberasti eos in misericordiis tuis multis vicibus. / [29]Et contestatus es eos, ut reduceres eos ad legem tuam; / ipsi vero superbe egerunt et non audierunt mandata tua / et in iudicia tua peccaverunt, quae si fecerit homo vivet in eis, / et dederunt umerum rebellem / et cervicem suam induraverunt, nec audierunt. / [30]Et pepercisti eis annos multos / et contestatus es eos in spiritu tuo / per manum prophetarum tuorum, / et non audierunt; / et tradidisti eos in manu populorum terrarum. / [31]In misericordiis autem tuis plurimis / non fecisti eos in consumptionem nec dereliquisti eos; / quoniam Deus misericors et clemens es tu. / [32]Nunc itaque, Deus noster magne, fortis et terribilis, / custodiens pactum et misericordiam, / ne parvipendas omnem laborem, / qui invenit nos, reges nostros et principes nostros, / et sacerdotes nostros et prophetas nostros / et patres nostros et omnem populum tuum, / a diebus regum Assyriae usque in diem hanc. / [33]Et tu iustus es in omnibus, quae venerunt super nos, / quia recte fecisti, / nos autem impie egimus. / [34]Reges nostri, principes nostri, sacerdotes nostri / et patres nostri non fecerunt legem tuam / et non attenderunt mandata tua et testimonia tua, / quae testificatus es in eis. / [35]Et ipsi in regnis suis et in bonitate tua multa, quam dederas eis, / et in terra latissima et pingui, / quam tradideras in conspectu eorum, / non servierunt tibi nec reversi sunt a studiis suis pessimis. / [36]Ecce nos ipsi hodie servi sumus, / et in terra, quam dedisti patribus nostris, / ut comederent fructum eius et bona eius, nos ipsi servi sumus. / [37]Et fruges eius multiplicantur regibus, /

thou hast set over us because of our sins; they have power also over our bodies and over our cattle at their pleasure, and we are in great distress."

2 Kings 23:3
Ezra 10:3

Commitment to keep the Law

38[u]Because of all this we make a firm covenant and write it, and our princes, our Levites, and our priests set their seal to it.

Neh 10;
12:12–26

10 [1v]Those who set their seal are Nehemiah the governor, the son of Hacaliah, Zedekiah, [2]Seraiah, Azariah, Jeremiah, [3]Pashhur, Amariah, Malchijah, [4]Hattush, Shebaniah, Malluch, [5]Harim, Meremoth, Obadiah, [6]Daniel, Ginnethon, Baruch, [7]Meshullam, Abijah, Mijamin, [8]Ma-aziah, Bilgai, Shemaiah; these are the priests. [9]And the Levites: Jeshua the son of Azaniah, Binnui of the sons of Henadad, Kadmi-el; [10]and their brethren, Shebaniah, Hodiah, Kelita, Pelaiah, Hanan, [11]Mica, Rehob, Hashabiah, [12]Zaccur, Sherebiah, Shebaniah, [13]Hodiah, Bani, Beninu. [14]The chiefs of the people: Parosh, Pahath-moab, Elam, Zattu, Bani, [15]Bunni, Azgad, Bebai, [16]Adonijah, Bigvai, Adin,

---

9:38—10:39. This chapter, which takes up the theme of chapter 5, describes the people's commitment to the reform proposed by Nehemiah. However, the sacred writer positions this covenant after the people have listened to Ezra's proclamation of the Law, and after they have acknowledged their sins before God (cf. 9:1–37). This has the effect of emphasizing that Ezra's work and that of Nehemiah are of a piece, and of making it clear that the covenant was based on the Law proclaimed by Ezra. First in the list of signatories (9:38—10:28) come those who are now the intermediaries of the people's pact with God, in the same way as Moses, Joshua or the king were intermediaries in earlier times. As in Deuteronomy 5:27; 6:25; Joshua 24:16, the entire people commits itself to keep this Law (vv. 28–29). The intermediaries of the covenant with the people are its institutions and those who represent them. Undoubtedly this pact with God suited the situation in which the people found themselves, and that does not mean that it could not change; this can be seen in

quos posuisti super nos propter peccata nostra, / et corporibus nostris dominantur et iumentis nostris / secundum voluntatem suam, / et in tribulatione magna sumus». **[10]** [1]«Super omnibus ergo his nos ipsi percutimus foedus et scribimus, et signant principes nostri, Levitae nostri et sacerdotes nostri». [2]Signatores autem fuerunt: Nehemias praepositus, filius Hachaliae, et Sedecias, [3]Saraias, Azarias, Ieremias, [4]Phassur, Amarias, Melchias, [5]Hattus, Sebania, Melluch, [6]Harim, Meremoth, Abdias, [7]Daniel, Genthon, Baruch, [8]Mosollam, Abia, Miamin, [9]Maazia, Belgai, Semeia; hi sacerdotes. [10]Porro Levitae: Iesua filius Azaniae, Bennui de filiis Henadad, Cadmihel [11]et fratres eorum Sebania, Hodia, Celita, Phalaia, Hanan, [12]Micha, Rohob, Hasabia, [13]Zacchur, Serebia, Sebania, [14]Hodia, Bani, Baninu. [15]Capita populi: Pharos, Phahathmoab, Elam, Zethua, Bani, [16]Bunni, Azgad, Bebai, [17]Adonia, Beguai, Adin,

u. Ch 10:1 in Heb **v.** Ch 10:2 in Heb

[17]Ater, Hezekiah, Azzur, [18]Hodiah, Hashum, Bezai, [19]Hariph, Anathoth, Nebai, [20]Magpiash, Meshullam, Hezir, [21]Meshezabel, Zadok, Jaddu-a, [22]Pelatiah, Hanan, Anaiah, [23]Hoshea, Hananiah, Hasshub, [24]Hallohesh, Pilha, Shobek, [25]Rehum, Hashabnah, Maaseiah, [26]Ahiah, Hanan, Anan, [27]Malluch, Harim, Baanah.

[28]The rest of the people, the priests, the Levites, the gatekeepers, the singers, the temple servants, and all who have separated themselves from the peoples of the lands to the law of God, their wives, their sons, their daughters, all who have knowledge and understanding, [29]join with their brethren, their nobles, and enter into a curse and an oath to walk in God's law which was given by Moses the servant of God, and to observe and do all the commandments of the LORD our Lord and his ordinances and his statutes. [30]We will not give our daughters to the peoples of the land or take their daughters for our sons; [31]and if the peoples of the land bring in wares or any grain on the sabbath day to sell, we will not buy from them on the sabbath or on a holy day; and we will forego the crops of the seventh year and the exaction of every debt.

[32]We also lay upon ourselves the obligation to charge ourselves yearly with the third part of a shekel for the service of the house of

Deut 29:12–14

Neh 13:23–27

Ex 20:8
Neh 13:15–22

Ex 30:11ff
2 Cro 24:6–9

---

the books of the Old Testament, especially that of Daniel (Dan 7:15; 9:24–27), which predict a new intervention on God's part. The specific clauses in the pact refer to matters especially relevant at the time when Nehemiah reached Jerusalem and which do not appear to have been considered significant earlier. Nehemiah urges the Jews not to intermarry with the peoples of the land (v. 30), in line with what Deuteronomy 7:3–4 says about the Gentiles. This measure was designed to protect the religious identity of the people; now it applied to the exiles returned from Babylon. Nehemiah also stipulates things to do with sabbath observance which was being neglected and with the application of jubilee year rules about loans (v. 31). He also establishes a system for financing the costs of the liturgy and the personnel involved in it, applying laws to be found in the book of Deuteronomy and in 2 Chronicles (cf. Deut 14:22–28; 26:1–5; 2 Chron 24:6–9).

[18]Ater, Ezechia, Azur, [19]Hodia, Hasum, Besai, [20]Hareph, Anathoth, Nebai, [21]Megphias, Mosollam, Hezir, [22]Mesezabel, Sadoc, Ieddua, [23]Pheltia, Hanan, Anaia, [24]Osee, Hanania, Hassub, [25]Alohes, Phalea, Sobec, [26]Rehum, Hasabna, Maasia, [27]Ahia, Hanan, Anan, [28]Melluch, Harim, Baana. [29]Et reliqui de populo, sacerdotes, Levitae, ianitores et cantores, oblati et omnes, qui se separaverunt de populis terrarum ad legem Dei, uxores eorum, filii eorum et filiae eorum, omnes, qui poterant sapere, [30]adhaeserunt fratribus suis optimatibus pollicentes et iurantes, ut ambularent in lege Dei, quam dederat in manu Moysi servi Dei, et ut facerent et custodirent universa mandata Domini Dei nostri et iudicia eius et praecepta eius, [31]et ut non daremus filias nostras populo terrae et filias eorum non acciperemus filiis nostris. [32]Et si populi terrae importaverint venalia et omnia cibaria per diem sabbati, ut vendant, non accipiemus ab eis in sabbato et in die sanctificato; et dimittemus annum septimum et omnem

Lev 1:4; 24:5–9
Num 28–29
Gen 22:1
Ex 23:19; 34:26
Deut 26:1–2
Neh 13:31
Ex 13:11
Lev 23:17; 27:30
Num 15:19
Deut 18:4
Num 18:21,24–26
Deut 14:22
Neh 13:10–14
Num 18:26

our God: [33]for the showbread, the continual cereal offering, the continual burnt offering, the sabbaths, the new moons, the appointed feasts, the holy things, and the sin offerings to make atonement for Israel, and for all the work of the house of our God. [34]We have likewise cast lots, the priests, the Levites, and the people, for the wood offering, to bring it into the house of our God, according to our fathers' houses, at times appointed, year by year, to burn upon the altar of the LORD our God, as it is written in the law. [35]We obligate ourselves to bring the first fruits of our ground and the first fruits of all fruit of every tree, year by year, to the house of the LORD; [36]also to bring to the house of our God, to the priests who minister in the house of our God, the first-born of our sons and of our cattle, as it is written in the law, and the firstlings of our herds and of our flocks; [37]and to bring the first of our coarse meal, and our contributions, the fruit of every tree, the wine and the oil, to the priests, to the chambers of the house of our God; and to bring to the Levites the tithes from our ground, for it is the Levites who collect the tithes in all our rural towns. [38]And the priest, the son of Aaron, shall be with the Levites when the Levites receive the tithes; and the Levites shall bring up the tithe of the tithes to the house of our God, to the chambers, to the storehouse. [39]For the people of Israel and the sons of Levi shall bring the contribution of grain, wine, and oil to the chambers, where are the vessels of the sanctuary, and the priests that minister, and the gatekeepers and the singers. We will not neglect the house of our God.

---

exactionem. [33]Et statuimus super nos praecepta, ut demus tertiam partem sicli per annum ad opus domus Dei nostri, [34]ad panes propositionis et ad oblationem sempiternam et in holocaustum sempiternum in sabbatis, in calendis, in sollemnitatibus et in sanctificata et in sacrificium pro peccato, ut expietur pro Israel, et in omnem usum domus Dei nostri. [35]Sortes ergo misimus super oblationem lignorum inter sacerdotes et Levitas et populum, ut inferrentur in domum Dei nostri per domos patrum nostrorum, in temporibus constitutis ab anno in annum, ut arderent super altare domini Dei nostri, sicut scriptum est in lege; [36]et ut afferremus primogenita terrae nostrae et primitiva universi fructus omnis ligni ab anno in annum in domo Domini, [37]et primitiva filiorum nostrorum et pecorum nostrorum, sicut scriptum est in lege, et primitiva boum nostrorum et ovium nostrarum, ut afferrentur in domum Dei nostri sacerdotibus, qui ministrant in domo Dei nostri; [38]et primitias ciborum nostrorum et libaminum nostrorum et poma omnis ligni, vindemiae quoque et olei, afferemus sacerdotibus ad gazophylacium Dei nostri, et decimam partem terrae nostrae Levitis. Ipsi Levitae decimas accipient ex omnibus civitatibus agriculturae nostrae. [39]Erit autem sacerdos filius Aaron cum Levitis in decimis Levitarum colligendis, et Levitae offerent decimam partem decimae in domo Dei nostri ad gazophylacium thesauri. [40]Ad gazophylacium enim deportabunt filii Israel et filii Levi primitias frumenti, vini et olei; et ibi erunt vasa sanctificata et sacerdotes, qui ministrabant, et ianitores et cantores. Et non dimittemus domum Dei nostri.

Repopulation of Jerusalem and Jordan

Neh 7:4

11 [1]Now the leaders of the people lived in Jerusalem; and the rest of the people cast lots to bring one out of ten to live in Jerusalem the holy city, while nine tenths remained in the other towns. [2]And the people blessed all the men who willingly offered to live in Jerusalem.

Rev 21:1

[3]These are the chiefs of the province who lived in Jerusalem; but in the towns of Judah every one lived on his property in their towns: Israel, the priests, the Levites, the temple servants, and the descendants of Solomon's servants. [4]And in Jerusalem lived certain of the sons of Judah and of the sons of Benjamin. Of the sons of Judah: Athaiah the son of Uzziah, son of Zechariah, son of Amariah, son of Shephatiah, son of Mahalalel, of the sons of Perez; [5]and Ma-aseiah the son of Baruch, son of Col-hozeh, son of Hazaiah, son of Adaiah, son of Joiarib, son of Zechariah, son of the Shilonite. [6]All the sons of Perez who lived in Jerusalem were four hundred and sixty-eight valiant men.

1 Chron 9:2–19
Ezra 2:55
1 Chron 9:4–17

[7]And these are the sons of Benjamin: Sallu the son of Meshullam, son of Joed, son of Pedaiah, son of Kolaiah, son of Ma-aseiah, son of Ithi-el, son of Jeshaiah. [8]And after him Gabbai, Sallai, nine hundred and twenty-eight. [9]Joel the son of Zichri was their overseer; and Judah the son of Hassenu-ah was second over the city.

[10]Of the priests: Jedaiah the son of Joiarib, Jachin, [11]Seraiah the son of Hilkiah, son of Meshullam, son of Zadok, son of Meraioth, son of Ahitub, ruler of the house of God, [12]and their brethren who

1 Chron 9:10–13

11:1–36 In chapter 7 of this book, in the account of the rebuilding of the walls of Jerusalem, we were told that the city was almost depopulated (cf. 7:1–4) and a list was provided of those returned from exile (cf. 7:5–72). The text then went off at a tangent, to give a lengthy description of the religious reform brought about by Ezra with the help of Nehemiah (cf. 8:1—10:39). Now the point has come to explain how Jerusalem and the rest of Judah were

[11] [1]Habitaverunt autem principes populi in Ierusalem; reliqua vero plebs misit sortem, ut adducerent unum virum de decem ad habitandum in Ierusalem civitate sancta, novem vero partes in civitatibus· [2]Benedixit autem populus omnibus viris, qui se sponte obtulerant, ut habitarent in Ierusalem. [3]Hi sunt itaque principes provinciae, qui habitaverunt in Ierusalem et in civitatibus Iudae. Habitavit autem unusquisque in possessione sua, in urbibus suis, Israel, sacerdotes, Levitae, oblati et filii servorum Salomonis. [4]Et in Ierusalem habitaverunt de filiis Iudae et de filiis Beniamin. De filiis Iudae: Athaias filius Oziam filii Zachariae filii Amariae filii Saphatiae filii Malaleel, de filiis Phares; [5]et Maasia filius Baruch filius Cholhoza filius Hazia filius Adaia filius Ioiarib filius Zachariae filius Silonitis. [6]Omnes filii Phares, qui habitaverunt in Ierusalem, quadringenti sexaginta octo viri fortes. [7]Hi sunt autem filii Beniamin: Sallu filius Mosollam filius Ioed filius Phadaia filius Colaia filius Maasia filius Etheel filius Iesaia; [8]et fratres eius viri fortes, nongenti viginti octo. [9]Et Ioel filius Zechri praepositus eorum, et Iudas filius Asana super civitatem secundus. [10]Et de sacerdotibus: Iedaia filius Ioiarib filius [11]Saraia filius Helciae filius Mosollam filius Sadoc filius Meraioth filius Achitob princeps domus Dei; [12]et fratres

did the work of the house, eight hundred and twenty-two; and Adaiah the son of Jeroham, son of Pelaliah, son of Amzi, son of Zechariah, son of Pashhur, son of Malchijah, [13]and his brethren, heads of fathers' houses, two hundred and forty-two; and Amashsai, the son of Azarel, son of Ahzai, son of Meshillemoth, son of Immer, [14]and their brethren, mighty men of valour, a hundred and twenty-eight; their overseer was Zabdiel the son of Haggedolim.

Chron 9:14–17 [15]And of the Levites: Shemaiah the son of Hasshub, son of Azrikam, son of Hashabiah, son of Bunni; [16]and Shabbethai and Jozabad, of the chiefs of the Levites, who were over the outside work of the house of God; [17]and Mattaniah the son of Mica, son of Zabdi, son of Asaph, who was the leader to begin the thanksgiving in prayer, and Bakbukiah, the second among his brethren; and Rev 21:1 Abda the son of Shammua, son of Galal, son of Jeduthun. [18]All the Levites in the holy city were two hundred and eighty-four.

---

resettled. The material in these chapters would have come largely from the "memoirs of Nehemiah".

Jerusalem is called "the holy city" (v. 1), a name which will often be used from this time onwards. The name is given to the city twice in the Gospel of St Matthew (4:5; 27:53) but especially in the book of Revelation (11:2; 21:2, 10; 22:19) where the new Jerusalem is depicted as the bride of the Lamb, a wonderful city where God the Father and Christ reign, and which is a symbol of mankind reborn.

Just as the Law prescribes that a tithe of the produce of the land and of livestock shall be offered to the Lord (cf. Lev 27:30–33; cf. Deut 14:22–29), it is now established that one in every ten of the people shall reside in the Holy City dedicated to the Lord (v. 1).

The list of those who settled in Jerusalem and Judah given in vv. 3–20 refers to the situation in Nehemiah's time. This list, with some slight changes, was reproduced in 2 Chronicles 9:2–17 in order to show, as it does here, the continuity between the population in earlier times and the new inhabitants after the restoration. Added to the first list are some complementary data to do with people involved in the temple (vv. 21–24), and a list of the cities settled in the territory of Judah and Benjamin (vv. 25–36).

eorum facientes opera templi, octingenti viginti duo. Et Adaia filius Ieroham filius Phelelia filius Amsi filius Zachariae filius Phassur filius Melchiae; [13]et fratres eius principes familiarum ducenti quadraginta duo. Et Amassai filius Azareel filius Ahazi filius Mosollamoth filius Emmer; [14]et fratres eorum potentes nimis, centum viginti octo; et praepositus eorum Zabdiel vir nobilis. [15]Et de Levitis: Semeia filius Hassub filius Ezricam filius Hasabia filius Bunni; [16]et Sabethai et Iozabad super omnia opera, quae erant forinsecus in domo Dei, de principibus Levitarum; [17]et Matthania filius Micha filius Zebedaei filius Asaph magister chori incohabat orationem; et Becbecia secundus de fratribus eius, et Abda filius Sammua filius Galal filius Idithun. [18]Omnes Levitae in civitate sancta ducenti octoginta quattuor. [19]Et

[19]The gatekeepers, Akkub, Talmon and their brethren, who kept watch at the gates, were a hundred and seventy-two. [20]And the rest of Israel, and of the priests and the Levites, were in all the towns of Judah, every one in his inheritance. [21]But the temple servants lived on Ophel; and Ziha and Gishpa were over the temple servants.

1 Chron 9:17–27

1 Chron 9:2

[22]The overseer of the Levites in Jerusalem was Uzzi the son of Bani, son of Hashabiah, son of Mattaniah, son of Mica, of the sons of Asaph, the singers, over the work of the house of God. [23]For there was a command from the king concerning them, and a settled provision for the singers, as every day required. [24]And Pethahiah the son of Meshezabel, of the sons of Zerah the son of Judah, was at the king's hand in all matters concerning the people.

1 Chron 9:33

[25]And as for the villages, with their fields, some of the people of Judah lived in Kiriath-arba and its villages, and in Dibon and its villages, and in Jekabzeel and its villages, [26]and in Jeshua and in Moladah and Beth-pelet, [27]in Hazar-shual, in Beer-sheba and its villages,[28]in Ziklag, in Meconah and its villages, [29]in En-rimmon, in Zorah, in Jarmuth, [30]Zanoah, Adullam, and their villages, Lachish and its fields, and Azekah and its villages. So they encamped from Beer-sheba to the valley of Hinnom. [31]The people of Benjamin also lived from Geba onward, at Michmash, Aija, Bethel and its villages, [32]Anathoth, Nob, Ananiah, [33]Hazor, Ramah, Gittaim, [34]Hadid, Zeboim, Neballat, [35]Lod, and Ono, the valley of craftsmen. [36]And certain divisions of the Levites in Judah were joined to Benjamin.

---

ianitores: Accub, Telmon et fratres eorum, qui custodiebant ostia, centum septuaginta duo. [20]Et reliqui ex Israel sacerdotes et Levitae in universis civitatibus Iudae, unusquisque in possessione sua. [21]Et oblati habitabant in Ophel; et Siha et Gaspha super oblatos. [22]Et praefectus Levitarum in Ierusalem Ozi filius Bani filius Hasabiae filius Matthaniae filius Michae de filiis Asaph, cantores in ministerio domus Dei. [23]Praeceptum quippe regis super eos erat, et ordo in cantoribus per dies singulos. [24]Et Phethahia filius Mesezabel de filiis Zara filii Iudae, legatus regis in omni negotio populi. [25]Et in viculis per omnes regiones eorum, de filiis Iudae habitaverunt in Cariatharbe et in pagis eius et in Dibon et in pagis eius et in Cabseel et in viculis eius [26]et in Iesua et in Molada et in Bethpheleth [27]et in Asarsual et in Bersabee et in pagis eius [28]et in Siceleg et in Mochona et in pagis eius [29]et in Remmon et in Saraa et in Ierimoth, [30]Zanoa, Odollam et in villis earum, Lachis et regionibus eius et Azeca et pagis eius. Et habitaverunt a Bersabee usque ad vallem Ennom. [31]Filii autem Beniamin in Gabaa, Machmas et Hai et Bethel et pagis eius, [32]Anathoth, Nob, Anania, [33]Asor, Rama, Getthaim, [34]Hadid, Seboim et Neballat, [35]Lod et Ono et valle Artificum. [36]Et de Levitis portiones in Iuda et Beniamin.

Priests and Levites who returned with Zerubbabel and Jeshua

Ezra 2:1–2

12 [1]These are the priests and the Levites who came up with Zerubbabel the son of She-alti-el, and Jeshua: Seraiah, Jeremiah, Ezra, [2]Amariah, Malluch, Hattush, [3]Shecaniah, Rehum, Meremoth, [4]Iddo, Ginnethoi, Abijah, [5]Mijamin, Ma-adiah, Bilgah, [6]Shemaiah, Joiarib, Jedaiah, [7]Sallu, Amok, Hilkiah, Jedaiah. These were the chiefs of the priests and of their brethren in the days of Jeshua.

Lk 1:5

[8]And the Levites: Jeshua, Binnui, Kadmi-el, Sherebiah, Judah, and Mattaniah, who with his brethren was in charge of the songs of thanksgiving. [9]And Bakbukiah and Unno their brethren stood opposite them in the service. [10]And Jeshua was the father of Joiakim, Joiakim the father of Eliashib, Eliashib the father of Joiada, [11]Joiada the father of Jonathan, and Jonathan the father of Jaddu-a.

12:1–26. Before the account of the dedication of the wall comes the list of priests and Levites who came back in the first repatriation; Ezra 2:1–67 gives a similar list prior to dealing with the revival of worship at Jerusalem; and Nehemiah 7:1–72 gives the same list prior to the solemn proclamation of the Law. The present list of priests and Levites is a lead-up to another important milestone in the events covered in Ezra-Nehemiah—the dedication of the wall, in which these play a foremost part, because it is an act of great religious significance.

From the way it is presented, the list shows signs of having been adapted by the sacred writer (cf. v. 26). It may originally have been devised to safeguard ancient rights acquired by some priests and Levites. Be that as it may, v. 10 gives us an interesting piece of information as regards chronology, because it tells us that Eliashib, who was a contemporary of Nehemiah (cf. 13:4), was the grandson of Jeshua, the priest who came to Jerusalem from Babylon with Zerubbabel.

[12] [1]Hi sunt autem sacerdotes et Levitae, qui ascenderunt cum Zorobabel filio Salathiel et Iesua: Saraia, Ieremias, Esdras, [2]Amaria, Melluch, Hattus, [3]Sechenias, Rehum, Meremoth, [4]Addo, Genthon, Abia, [5]Miamin, Maadia, Belga, [6]Semeia et Ioiarib, Iedaia, [7]Sallu, Amoc, Helcias, Iedaia. Isti principes sacerdotum et fratrum eorum in diebus Iesua. [8]Porro Levitae: Iesua, Bennui, Cadmihel, Serebia, Iuda, Matthanias, super hymnos ipse et fratres eius; [9]et Becbecia atque Hanni fratres eorum coram eis per vices suas. [10]Iesua autem genuit Ioachim, et Ioachim genuit Eliasib, et Eliasib genuit Ioiada, [11]et Ioiada genuit Ionathan, et Ionathan genuit Ieddua. [12]In diebus autem Ioachim erant sacerdotes principes familiarum: Saraiae Maraia, Ieremiae Hanania, [13]Esdrae Mosollam, Amariae Iohanan, [14]Milicho Ionathan, Sebaniae Ioseph, [15]Harim Edna, Meraioth Helci, [16]Adaiae Zacharia, Genthon Mosollam, [17]Abiae Zechri, Miamin Maadiae Phelti, [18]Belgae Sammua, Semeiae Ionathan, [19]Ioiarib Matthanai, Iedaiae Ozi, [20]Sellai Celai, Amoc Heber, [21]Helciae Hasabia, Iedaiae Nathanael. [22]Levitae in diebus Eliasib et Ioiada et Iohanan et Ieddua scripti principes familiarum et sacerdotes usque ad regnum Darii Persae. [23]Filii Levi principes familiarum scripti in libro Chronicorum usque ad dies Ionathan filii Eliasib. [24]Et principes Levitarum Hasabia, Serebia, Iesua, Bennui et Cadmihel et fratres eorum coram eis, ut laudarent et confiterentur iuxta praeceptum David viri Dei per vices suas: [25]Matthania et Becbecia, Abdia, Mosollam, Telmon, Accub ianitores ad custodiam horreorum iuxta portas. [26]Hi in

[12]And in the days of Joiakim were priests, heads of fathers' houses: of Seraiah, Meraiah; of Jeremiah, Hananiah; [13]of Ezra, Meshullam; of Amariah, Jeho-hanan; [14]of Malluchi, Jonathan; of Shebaniah, Joseph; [15]of Harim, Adna; of Meraioth, Helkai; [16]of Iddo, Zechariah; of Ginnethon, Meshullam; [17]of Abijah, Zichri; of Miniamin, of Moadiah, Piltai; [18]of Bilgah, Shammu-a; of Shemaiah, Jehonathan; [19]of Joiarib, Mattenai; of Jedaiah, Uzzi; [20]of Sallai, Kallai; of Amok, Eber; [21]of Hilkiah, Hashabiah; of Jedaiah, Nethanel.

Neh 10:3–14; 12:1

Lk 1:5

[22]As for the Levites, in the days of Eliashib, Joiada, Johanan, and Jaddu-a, there were recorded the heads of fathers' houses; also the priests until the reign of Darius the Persian. [23]The sons of Levi, heads of fathers' houses, were written in the Book of the Chronicles until the days of Johanan the son of Eliashib. [24]And the chiefs of the Levites: Hashabiah, Sherebiah, and Jeshua the son of Kadmi-el, with their brethren over against them, to praise and to give thanks, according to the commandment of David the man of God, watch corresponding to watch. [25]Mattaniah, Bakbukiah, Obadiah, Meshullam, Talmon, and Akkub were gatekeepers standing guard at the storehouses of the gates. [26]These were in the days of Joiakim the son of Jeshua son of Jozadak, and in the days of Nehemiah the governor and of Ezra the priest the scribe.

Ezra 10:6

1 Chron 23:1ff
2 Chron 5:13
Ezra 2:40

Neh 11:17

Dedication of the wall of Jerusalem

[27]And at the dedication of the wall of Jerusalem they sought the Levites in all their places, to bring them to Jerusalem to celebrate

1 Chron 15:16–24

12:27–43. At last the moment has arrived—long awaited by the repatriates who came back to rebuild the city. The building work is over, the city and its hinterland has been resettled; now comes the solemn dedication of the walls. Two processions go round the city in opposite directions, chanting songs; they meet at the temple, where at the climax of the celebration great sacrifices are offered. The whole passage shows that everyone is delighted.

St Bede interprets these festivities marking the repossession of the city, as being an allegory of the Church's triumphal entry in heaven at the end of her mission on earth: "Once the Holy City has been completely restored, the dedication (of the temple) takes place. In the same way, at the end of time, when the full number of the elect has been assembled, the whole Church will enter into heaven to contemplate her Founder" (*In Esdram et Nehemiam*, 3, 33).

diebus Ioachim filii Iesua filii Iosedec et in diebus Nehemiae ducis et Esdrae sacerdotis scribaeque. [27]In dedicatione autem muri Ierusalem requisierunt Levitas de omnibus locis suis, ut adducerent eos in Ierusalem et facerent dedicationem in laetitia in actione gratiarum et cantico et cymbalis, psalteriis et

the dedication with gladness, with thanksgivings and with singing, with cymbals, harps, and lyres. [28]And the sons of the singers gathered together from the circuit round Jerusalem and from the villages of the Netophathites; [29]also from Beth-gilgal and from the region of Geba and Azmaveth; for the singers had built for themselves villages around Jerusalem. [30]And the priests and the Levites purified themselves; and they purified the people and the gates and the wall.

[31]Then I brought up the princes of Judah upon the wall, and appointed two great companies which gave thanks and went in procession. One went to the right upon the wall to the Dung Gate; [32]and after them went Hoshaiah and half of the princes of Judah, [33]and Azariah, Ezra, Meshullam, [34]Judah, Benjamin, Shemaiah, and Jeremiah, [35]and certain of the priests' sons with trumpets: Zechariah the son of Jonathan, son of Shemaiah, son of Mattaniah, son of Micaiah, son of Zaccur, son of Asaph; [36]and his kinsmen, Shemaiah, Azarel, Milalai, Gilalai, Maai, Nethanel, Judah, and Hanani, with the musical instruments of David the man of God; and Ezra the scribe went before them. [37]At the Fountain Gate they went up straight before them by the stairs of the city of David, at the ascent of the wall, above the house of David, to the Water Gate on the east.

1 Chron 23:5
Amos 6:5

[38]The other company of those who gave thanks went to the left, and I followed them with half of the people, upon the wall, above the Tower of the Ovens, to the Broad Wall, [39]and above the Gate of

---

Those men who under Nehemiah's leadership rebuilt the city of Jerusalem had to overcome many obstacles before they could enjoy this moment; but thanks to their tenacity and their trust in God, they were able to see the successful outcome of their endeavours on behalf of God and their fellow citizens. They had done their duty and now they were deservedly happy. "To begin is easy; to persevere is sanctity. Let your perseverance not be a blind consequence of the first impulse, the work of inertia: let it be a reflective perseverance" (St J. Escrivá, *The Way*, 983).

citharis. [28]Congregati sunt autem cantores de campestribus circa Ierusalem et de villis Netophathitarum [29]et de Bethgalgala et de regionibus Gabaa et Azmaveth, quoniam villas aedificaverunt sibi cantores in circuitu Ierusalem. [30]Et mundati sunt sacerdotes et Levitae et mundaverunt populum et portas et murum. [31]Ascendere autem feci principes Iudae super murum et statui duos magnos choros laudantium, quorum unus ivit ad dexteram super murum ad portam Sterquilinii. [32]Et ivit post eos Osaias et media pars principum Iudae [33]et Azarias, Esdras et Mosollam, [34]Iudas et Beniamin et Semeia et Ieremias. [35]Et de sacerdotibus cum tubis et Zacharias filius Ionathan filius Semeiae filius Matthaniae filius Michaiae filius Zacchur filius Asaph; [36]et fratres eius Semeia et Azareel, Malalai, Galalai, Maai, Nathanael et Iudas et Hanani cum musicis David viri Dei; et Esdras scriba ante eos et in porta Fontis. [37]Processerunt per gradus civitatis David in ascensu muri super domum David et usque ad portam Aquarum ad orientem. [38]Et chorus secundus gratias referentium ibat ex adverso, et ego post eum, et media pars populi super murum et super turrim Furnorum et usque ad murum latissimum [39]et super portam

Ephraim, and by the Old Gate, and by the Fish Gate and the Tower of Hananel and the Tower of the Hundred, to the Sheep Gate; and they came to a halt at the Gate of the Guard. [40]So both companies of those who gave thanks stood in the house of God, and I and half of the officials with me; [41]and the priests Eliakim, Ma-aseiah, Miniamin, Micaiah, Eli-o-enai, Zechariah, and Hananiah, with trumpets; [42]and Ma-aseiah, Shemaiah, Eleazar, Uzzi, Jehohanan, Malchijah, Elam, and Ezer. And the singers sang with Jezrahiah as their leader. [43]And they offered great sacrifices that day and rejoiced, for God had made them rejoice with great joy; the women and children also rejoiced. And the joy of Jerusalem was heard afar off.

Jn 5:2

The people rejoice. Gentiles are kept at a distance

[44]On that day men were appointed over the chambers for the stores, the contributions, the first fruits, and the tithes, to gather into them the portions required by the law for the priests and for the Levites according to the fields of the towns; for Judah rejoiced over the priests and the Levites who ministered. [45]And they performed the service of their God and the service of purification, as did the singers and the gatekeepers, according to the command of David and his son Solomon. [46]For in the days of David and Asaph of old there was a chief of the singers, and there were songs of praise and thanksgiving to God. [47]And all Israel in the days of

Neh 13:10f
1 Chron 23–26
2 Chron 8:14
2 Chron 29:30; 35:15
Neh 10:39; 13:10ff
Num 18:26

12:44—13:3. The sacred writer paints an idealized picture. The people are happy because they see that everything to do with the temple is working properly. Its costs are being met and everyone makes his contribution. This was the way David wanted it to be, and it was in line with the system Zerubbabel and the repatriates re-established; and now Nehemiah in his time has reformed it once more. The fact that Ezra is not mentioned here may be because, as would make sense, he does not figure in the "memoirs of Nehemiah".

The idealized picture of Nehemiah's reform ends with the application of

Ephraim et super portam Antiquam et super portam Piscium et turrim Hananeel et turrim Meah et usque ad portam Gregis; et steterunt in porta Custodiae. [40]Steteruntque duo chori laudantium in domo Dei, et ego et dimidia pars magistratuum mecum. [41]Et sacerdotes Eliachim, Maasia, Miamin, Michaia, Elioenai, Zacharia, Hanania in tubis; [42]et Maasia et Semeia et Eleazar et Ozi et Iohanan et Melchia et Elam et Ezer. Et clare cecinerunt cantores et Izrahia praepositus. [43]Et obtulerunt in die illa sacrificia magna et laetati sunt; Deus enim laetificaverat eos laetitia magna; sed et uxores eorum et liberi gavisi sunt, et audita est laetitia Ierusalem procul. [44]Praeposuerunt quoque in die illa viros super gazophylacia ad thesaurum, ad libamina et ad primitias et ad decimas, ut colligerent in ea de agris civitatum partes legitimas pro sacerdotibus et Levitis; quia laetificatus est Iuda in sacerdotibus et Levitis, qui adstiterunt [45]et servierunt in ministerio Dei sui et in ministerio purificationis simul cum cantoribus et ianitoribus iuxta praeceptum David et Salomonis filii eius; [46]quia in diebus David et Asaph ab exordio erant catervae cantorum et carmina laudis et actionis gratiarum Deo. [47]Et omnis Israel in diebus Zorobabel et

Zerubbabel and in the days of Nehemiah gave the daily portions for the singers and the gatekeepers; and they set apart that which was for the Levites; and the Levites set apart that which was for the sons of Aaron.

Deut 23:4–6

13 [1]On that day they read from the book of Moses in the hearing of the people; and in it was found written that no Ammonite or Moabite should ever enter the assembly of God; [2]for they did not meet the children of Israel with bread and water, but hired Balaam against them to curse them—yet our God turned the curse into a blessing. [3]When the people heard the law, they separated from Israel all those of foreign descent.

Num 22:5; 23:11; 24:10 2 Pet 2:15

Neh 13:4–9, 23–28

Nehemiah's second mission—to establish the Law of Moses

[4]Now before this, Eliashib the priest, who was appointed over the chambers of the house of our God, and who was connected with Tobiah, [5]prepared for Tobiah a large chamber where they had previously put the cereal offering, the frankincense, the vessels,

Neh 12:44

Deuteronomy 23:4–7 which prohibits admission to the assembly of any Ammonite or Moabite (these nations tried to block Israel's entry into the promised land: cf. Num 22:2—24:25). This ban is now extended to cover all non-Jews—going much further than that which Nehemiah laid down during his first mission (cf. 10:31); it may be something which came in later but it certainly derived from Nehemiah's reform.

The picture drawn is highly coloured and refers to a particular context; however, the passage does allow us to see that all society benefits if there are people consecrated to God and to divine service and prayer. It also shows the need to keep at bay anything which is likely to endanger one's fidelity and one's personal vocation.

13:4–31. The book ends with some "memoirs of Nehemiah" in which he speaks about his second mission to Judah after returning to the Persian court in 433 BC (v. 6). This mission took place in 424 BC, the year in which Artaxerxes died.

We can see that the regulations set in place by Nehemiah on his first mission were not having the desired effect, or at least not all of them were being complied with. When his back was turned, the influence of Tobiah the Ammonite (cf. 6:17–19) managed to reassert itself in Jerusalem, in fact in the temple itself,

---

in diebus Nehemiae dabant partes cantoribus et ianitoribus per dies singulos partem suam et partes consecrabant Levitis, et Levitae consecrabant filiis Aaron. **[13]** [1]In die autem illo lectum est in volumine Moysi, audiente populo, et inventum est scriptum in eo quod non debeant introire Ammonites et Moabites in ecclesiam Dei usque in aeternum, [2]eo quod non occurrerint filiis Israel cum pane et aqua et conduxerint adversum eos Balaam ad maledicendum eis, et convertit Deus noster maledictionem in benedictionem. [3]Factum est autem, cum audissent legem, separaverunt omnem promiscuum ab Israel. [4]Ante hoc autem erat Eliasib sacerdos, qui fuerat praepositus in gazophylacio domus Dei nostri et proximus Thobiae; [5]fecerat ei gazophylacium grande, ubi antea reponebant munera et tus et vasa et

and the tithes of grain, wine, and oil, which were given by commandment to the Levites, singers, and gatekeepers, and the contributions for the priests. [6]While this was taking place I was not in Jerusalem, for in the thirty-second year of Ar-ta-xerxes king of Babylon I went to the king. And after some time I asked leave of the king [7]and came to Jerusalem, and I then discovered the evil that Eliashib had done for Tobiah, preparing for him a chamber in the courts of the house of God. [8]And I was very angry, and I threw all the household furniture of Tobiah out of the chamber. [9]Then I gave orders and they cleansed the chambers; and I brought back thither the vessels of the house of God, with the cereal offering and the frankincense.

[10]I also found out that the portions of the Levites had not been given to them; so that the Levites and the singers, who did the work, had fled each to his field. [11]So I remonstrated with the officials and said, "Why is the house of God forsaken?" And I gathered them together and set them in their stations. [12]Then all Judah brought the tithe of the grain, wine, and oil into the

Mt 21:12–13
Jn 2:13–17

2 Chron 31:4
Neh
12:44–47
Mal 3:8

Neh 10:38ff

---

with the help of Eliashib the priest, a relative of Tobiah's (cf. vv. 4–7). The levies and tithes that were meant for the temple and its staff were being siphoned off (vv. 10–13) and the sabbath rest was being broken by trading (vv. 15–22). But worst of all, and probably the cause of these irregularities (cf. vv. 26–27), was the intermarriage of Jewish men with foreign women: the loss of identity that this implied could be seen from the fact that some Jews could not even speak their own language (vv. 23–25). Nehemiah is quick to take action—as the family of the high priest Eliashib (a relative of Sanballat) discover to their cost. But he does not succeed in dissolving all those mixed marriages and expelling the foreign wives and their children (as Ezra will do: cf. Ezra 10:3, 44). It is likely that the priest whom Nehemiah dismissed from his presence (v. 28) managed to get support in Samaria and established himself there; from him and others another branch of the Jewish people would develop—the Samaritans.

As elsewhere in his "memoirs" (cf. 5:19; 6:14), Nehemiah breaks off now and then to address a prayer to the Lord, asking him not to forget all the good he has done: "Remember me, O my God" (vv. 14, 22, 31).

decimam frumenti vini et olei, partes Levitarum et cantorum et ianitorum et tributa sacerdotum. [6]In omnibus autem his non fui in Ierusalem, quia anno tricesimo secundo Artaxerxis regis Babylonis veni ad regem et in fine dierum rogavi, ut abirem a rege, [7]et veni in Ierusalem. Et intellexi malum, quod fecerat Eliasib Thobiae: fecerat enim ei thesaurum in vestibulis domus Dei. [8]Et malum mihi visum est valde, et proieci vasa domus Thobiae foras de gazophylacio; [9]praecepique, et emundaverunt gazophylacia, et rettuli ibi vasa domus Dei, oblationem et tus. [10]Et cognovi quod partes Levitarum non fuissent datae, et fugisset unusquisque in campum suum de Levitis et cantoribus, qui ministrabant. [11]Et egi causam adversus magistratus et dixi: «Quare dereliquimus domum Dei?». Et congregavi eos et feci stare in stationibus suis. [12]Et omnis Iuda apportabat decimam frumenti, vini et olei in horrea. [13]Et

storehouses. [13]And I appointed as treasurers over the storehouses Shelemiah the priest, Zadok the scribe, and Pedaiah of the Levites, and as their assistant Hanan the son of Zaccur, son of Mattaniah, for they were counted faithful; and their duty was to distribute to their brethren. [14]Remember me, O my God, concerning this, and wipe not out my good deeds that I have done for the house of my God and for his service.

Ex 20:8
Neh 10:32

[15]In those days I saw in Judah men treading wine presses on the sabbath, and bringing in heaps of grain and loading them on asses; and also wine, grapes, figs, and all kinds of burdens, which they brought into Jerusalem on the sabbath day; and I warned them on the day when they sold food. [16]Men of Tyre also, who lived in the city, brought in fish and all kinds of wares and sold them on the sabbath to the people of Judah, and in Jerusalem. [17]Then I remonstrated with the nobles of Judah and said to them, "What is this evil thing which you are doing, profaning the sabbath day? [18]Did not your fathers act in this way, and did not our God bring all this evil on us and on this city? Yet you bring more wrath upon Israel by profaning the sabbath."

[19]When it began to be dark at the gates of Jerusalem before the sabbath, I commanded that the doors should be shut and gave orders that they should not be opened until after the sabbath. And I set some of my servants over the gates, that no burden might be brought in on the sabbath day. [20]Then the merchants and sellers of all kinds of wares lodged outside Jerusalem once or twice. [21]But I warned them and said to them, "Why do you lodge before the wall? If you do so again I will lay hands on you." From that time on they did not come on the sabbath. [22]And I commanded the Levites that they should purify themselves and come and guard the gates, to keep the sabbath day holy. Remember this also in my

---

constitui super horrea Selemiam sacerdotem et Sadoc scribam et Phadaiam de Levitis et iuxta eos Hanan filium Zacchur, filium Matthaniae, quoniam fideles comprobati sunt; et ipsi curam habebant distribuendi partes fratribus suis. [14]Memento mei, Deus meus, pro hoc; et ne deleas opera mea bona, quae feci in domo Dei mei et in ministeriis eius! [15]In diebus illis vidi in Iuda calcantes torcularia in sabbato, portantes acervos et onerantes super asinos vinum et uvas et ficus et omne onus et inferentes in Ierusalem die sabbati; et contestatus sum, quando vendebant cibaria. [16]Et ibi Tyrii habitaverunt in ea inferentes pisces et omnia venalia et vendebant in sabbatis filiis Iudae in Ierusalem. [17]Et obiurgavi optimates Iudae et dixi eis: «Quae est haec res mala, quam vos facitis, et profanatis diem sabbati? [18]Numquid non haec fecerunt patres nostri, et adduxit Deus noster super nos omne malum hoc et super civitatem hanc? Et vos additis iracundiam super Israel profanando sabbatum!». [19]Factum est autem cum obscuratae essent portae Ierusalem ante diem sabbati, dixi, et clauserunt ianuas; et praecepi, ut non aperirent eas usque post sabbatum. Et de pueris meis constitui super portas, ut nullus inferret onus in die sabbati. [20]Et manserunt negotiatores et vendentes universa venalia foris Ierusalem semel et bis. [21]Et contestatus sum eos et dixi eis: «Quare manetis ex adverso muri? Si iterum hoc feceritis, manum mittam in vos». Itaque ex tempore illo non venerunt in sabbato. [22]Dixi quoque Levitis, ut mundarentur et

favour, O my God, and spare me according to the greatness of thy steadfast love.

[23]In those days also I saw the Jews who had married women of Ashdod, Ammon, and Moab; [24]and half of their children spoke the language of Ashdod, and they could not speak the language of Judah, but the language of each people. [25]And I contended with them and cursed them and beat some of them and pulled out their hair; and I made them take oath in the name of God, saying, "You shall not give your daughters to their sons, or take their daughters for your sons or for yourselves. [26]Did not Solomon king of Israel sin on account of such women? Among the many nations there was no king like him, and he was beloved by his God, and God made him king over all Israel; nevertheless foreign women made even him to sin. [27]Shall we then listen to you and do all this great evil and act treacherously against our God by marrying foreign women?"

Neh 10:31; 13:1–3

Ezra 10:5

2 Sam 12:25
1 Kings 11:1–8

[28]And one of the sons of Jehoiada, the son of Eliashib the high priest, was the son-in-law of Sanballat the Horonite; therefore I chased him from me. [29]Remember them, O my God, because they have defiled the priesthood and the covenant of the priesthood and the Levites.

Neh 2:10; 13:1–3
Mal 2:4

[30]Thus I cleansed them from everything foreign, and I established the duties of the priests and Levites, each in his work; [31]and I provided for the wood offering, at appointed times, and for the first fruits. Remember me, O my God, for good.

---

venirent ad custodiendas portas et sanctificandam diem sabbati. Et pro hoc ergo memento mei, Deus meus, et parce mihi secundum multitudinem miserationum tuarum! [23]Sed et in diebus illis vidi Iudaeos, qui duxerant uxores Azotidas, Ammonitidas et Moabitidas. [24]Et filii eorum ex media parte loquebantur Azotice et nesciebant loqui Iudaice vel loquebantur iuxta linguam unius vel alterius populi. [25]Et obiurgavi eos et maledixi et cecidi quosdam ex eis et decalvavi eos; et adiuravi in Deo, ut non darent filias suas filiis eorum et non acciperent de filiabus eorum filiis suis et sibimetipsis dicens: [26]«Numquid non in huiuscemodi re peccavit Salomon rex Israel? Et certe in gentibus multis non erat rex similis ei et dilectus Deo suo erat, et posuit eum Deus regem super omnem Israel; et ipsum ergo duxerunt ad peccatum mulieres alienigenae. [27]Numquid et vobis obsequentes faciemus omne malum grande hoc, ut praevaricemur in Deo nostro et ducamus uxores peregrinas?». [28]Unus autem de filiis Ioiada filii Eliasib sacerdotis magni gener erat Sanaballat Horonites, quem fugavi a me. [29]Recordare, Domine Deus meus, adversum eos, qui polluunt sacerdotium et pactum sacerdotale et leviticum! [30]Igitur mundavi eos ab omnibus alienigenis et constitui ordines pro sacerdotibus et Levitis, unumquemque in ministerio suo [31]et pro oblatione lignorum in temporibus constitutis et pro primitiis. Memento mei, Deus meus, in bonum.

THE LAST HISTORICAL BOOKS OF THE OLD TESTAMENT

Introduction

In Christian Bibles the book of Nehemiah is followed by those of Tobit, Judith and Esther. The historical books are rounded off by 1 and 2 Maccabees, which some of these Bibles (the RSV, for example) place right at the end of the Old Testament. These various books, which the *Navarre* Bible groups together, do not in any sense form a homogenous bloc; however, they all have features that make them different from the earlier historical texts (Joshua, Judges, Samuel, Kings, Chronicles, Ezra, Nehemiah).

All the books we place at the end of the Historical Books sequence were written in a later period, when Hellenistic culture had become quite well established in Palestine—a time close to when Jesus lived. Although the authors are true believers in the religion of Israel, they often use a language and a way of writing history in which it is easy to detect the influence of Greek culture.

Only one of these books (Esther) eventually became part of the Hebrew canon of Scripture—and probably that did not happen until the Christian era had begun. And, even then, only the chapters written in Hebrew found their way into the Hebrew Bible; passages in Greek were excluded. The other books never entered the Hebrew canon, but they were accepted as canonical by the early Church.

1. HISTORICAL ACCOUNTS IN HELLENISTIC JUDAISM

The previous introductions to the historical books of the Old Testament have made reference to what history meant to the people of Israel. These books are not simply a record of past events: the record that they contain acts as a point of reference for religious reflection, with the help of the Holy Spirit, on the situation in which Israel found itself as history unfolded. "Deuteronomic history", specifically, provides an assessment of the history of Israel in terms of the faithfulness or otherwise to the Law of God of its leading personalities; this history explains how it came about that the people were exiled in Babylon; and its teaching kept the people's hope alive. And, towards the end of the Persian era, the religious reflections of the authors of the "history of the Chronicler" helped people to make sense of the new situation in which they found themselves, and to revere and obey the God of the Covenant.

As time went by, much of Jewish culture came to be imbued with Hellenism. Of course, there were aspects of Greek culture that a good Jew could not accept because they involved idolatry. However, most expressions of

that new culture were perfectly compatible with what being a Jew involved; for example, new Greek literary forms were capable of conveying very deep religious feelings. Openness to this new way of understanding things, of expressing oneself or of writing works of literature did not imply denying one's ancient religious heritage; on the contrary, it enriched it. The very same people who were ready to die for the custom of circumcision (cf. 1 Mac 1:60; 2 Mac 6:10), or the orthodox form of worship (cf. 1 Mac 4:44ff; 2 Mac 10:1ff), or to avoid eating meat forbidden by the Law (cf. 2 Mac 6:18; 7:1), were quite prepared to write heroic tales in Greek, using new literary forms of great narrative and rhetorical power—new ways of narrating events and conveying spiritual messages by means of stories.

For example, the literary genre of "dramatic history", which belongs to this period, could write up a story very vividly and make events and personalities (and emotions) come alive. And Hellenistic historians were skilled in influencing their readers' opinions and behaviour by describing events and people in such a way that readers could identify with good example and be put off by vicious behaviour. Second Maccabees is written very much in that style: the writer wants to convince his reader to follow the example of heroes whose lives were completely in line with their (Jewish) faith.

Another popular Hellenist genre was stories elaborated on historical fact and in a real geographical scenario which are designed to be edifying and at the same time a pleasant read. The books of Tobit, Judith and Esther, though different from one another in style and other ways, are written more or less in this genre.

The later historical books of the Old Testament were written in this historical and literary context: this is something one needs to be aware of to understand them properly. They take traditions and events and write them up in a vivid way to show how people managed to stay faithful to God in an age of change.

2. THE CONTRIBUTION OF THESE BOOKS TO BIBLICAL REVELATION

If we read these books carefully, we will see that they differ from other historical books of the Old Testament and not only in terms of literary style or structure. Divine Revelation took place gradually, and these books have more than a few doctrinal aspects which are more pronounced than those found in earlier texts. In this way they act as a kind of bridge between the Old Testament and the New, presaging the fullness of time (cf. Gal 4:4) when God's self-manifestation would reach its climax in human history in the incarnation of the Son of God, an event not now far off.

The advances in content and style were not the result of an uncritical assimilation of Hellenistic culture; they did not involve anything inconsistent

with the character of the chosen people or their religion. In fact, their beliefs and their trust in God (to the point of heroism: cf. 1 Mac 2:49–64) were reinforced by these accounts of former times. The fact that the Jews adopted Hellenistic culture showed the vitality of the people of God: their ability to adapt and yet not lose their identity was one of their great strengths.

An example of advance in revelation is the doctrine of personal retribution. It continues to be true that God rewards or punishes a person depending on his or her actions. However, that does not always happen in this life. Sometimes the righteous die because they stay true to God; this does not mean that God is unjust, for he will reward them in the next life. That is the message contained in the words of one of the seven brothers to his executioner (2 Mac 7:9): "You accursed wretch, you dismiss us from this present life, but the King of the universe will raise us up to an everlasting renewal of life, because we have died for his laws" (2 Mac 7:9).

This greater conviction about there being a life after death is linked to new insights the Spirit was giving to the Jews' contemplation of creation. In Tobias 8:5 we read, for example, "Let the heavens and all thy creatures bless thee" (Tob 8:5). Statements like this derive from the conviction that all created things depend on God: "God did not make them out of things that existed" (2 Mac 7:28). And it was this grasp of the creative power of God that underpinned belief in resurrection: as another of the seven brothers testifies, "I got these [hands] from Heaven, and because of his laws I disdain them, and from him I hope to get them back again" (2 Mac 7:11; cf. 2 Mac 7:22–23).

The revelation that the horizon of human life goes beyond death gave a whole new insight into the nature of man and made for a greater understanding of the mystery of suffering. Suffering can be expiatory, and it is something one can take in one's stride for the sake of others; this is something another of the brothers realizes: "I , like my brothers, give up body and life for the laws of our fathers, appealing to God to show mercy soon to our nation" (2 Mac 7:37).

So, gradually and slowly the way was being prepared for people to understand Jesus and his mission. The development of Revelation evidenced in these books helped people to see that the sufferings of one just man, Jesus, could benefit all mankind; it also made it possible to speak in terms of resurrection, not only that of Jesus but that of all men; and it made it possible for people to nourish a desire to "be with Christ" (Phil 1:23) prior to the time of the general resurrection.

TOBIT

Introduction

The story of Tobit has come down to us in three different forms. One of these, in the Codex Sinaiticus (fourth–fifth century BC), is the longest of the three; and the Latin versions are closely in line with it. Another form is in the Vatican B and Alexandrine A manuscripts (fourth and fifth centuries AD); it is shorter than the Sinaiticus and its Greek is more elegant; many scholars regard it as a corrected form of the Sinaiticus version. There is a third, intermediary version in some miniscule Greek codices and in the Syriac version, but this is regarded as secondary to the other two. The translation given in the *Navarre Bible* Spanish edition is based on the Greek text of the Sinaitic Codex and takes in some phrases or terms from the other codices because that is what the New Vulgate has done and it helps to make the text a bit clearer. The New Vulgate follows the text of the Old Latin (Vetus Latina) version taken from a ninth-century codex (Vercellensis XXII) which differs slightly from the Greek versions and which changes the number of verses in a few places. The *Navarre Bible* (English edition) basically follows the RSV. The notes of the RSVCE contain interesting information about variants in the Vulgate.

In addition to the Greek text, a few fragments of Tobit in Aramaic have been found at Qumran. This, and the Semiticized nature of the Greek of the Sinaiticus, has fuelled a debate among scholars as to whether this book was originally written in Greek, Aramaic or Hebrew. Be that as it may, the Greek text is the one accepted by the Church as canonical, but it has not come down on the side of any one of the three forms of that text. Jews and Protestants do not regard the book of Tobit as canonical; the King James version and the RSV classify it among the Apocrypha.

1. STRUCTURE AND CONTENT

The book of Tobit can be divided as follows:

1. TOBIT'S MISFORTUNE. HIS PRAYER IN NINEVEH AND SARAH'S PRAYER IN MEDIA (1:1—3:17). Tobit and his family lived in Nineveh, and Sarah lived with her people in Ecbatana, in Media. Both families were made up of devout Jews deported from Israel (cf. 1 Kings 17:5–6), who experienced misfortune despite their faithfulness to God and his law. In the case of Tobit we are told in some detail that despite his assiduous practice of the works of mercy, he became blind and his standard of living declined dramatically. On top of that, his wife showed little understanding. Things became so bad that he prayed to

God to let him die. Sarah's plight was that she had buried seven husbands, each killed by the demon on the wedding-night. On this account her maid jeered at her. She, too, prayed to God to take her life. Both prayers reached God at the same time, and he decided to help them by sending the angel Raphael.

2. TOBIAS' JOURNEY TO MEDIA ACCOMPANIED BY THE ARCHANGEL RAPHAEL (4:1—10:12). The text goes on to describe the journey of Tobit's son, Tobias, to Media in the company of the angel Raphael. He goes there to collect money that Tobit left on deposit when times were good. Raphael is not known to be an angel, because he appeared on the scene in the guise of a young man and was simply hired to act as Tobias' guide. In the first stage of the journey they catch a fish which had attacked Tobias in the river Tigris; on the angel's instructions, Tobias keeps the fish's heart, liver and gall in order to fend off evil spirits and cure blindness. When they draw near to Ecbatana, where Sarah lives, the angel tells Tobias that according to the Law he should take the young woman as his wife because she is his closest relative. Tobias is not keen on this, given the fate of Sarah's seven husbands, but the angel tells him how to chase away the evil spirit. Everything goes smoothly. When they reach Sarah's house, they ask for her hand in marriage; Tobias and Sarah are married and nothing untoward happens. Tobias then sends Raphael off to collect the money owing to his father; then, calling to mind his father and mother (a cameo piece shows them waiting eagerly for his return), Tobias, Raphael and Sarah, with all their entourage, leave for Nineveh.

3. TOBIT IS CURED AND EVENTUALLY DIES (11:1—14:15). The last part of the book describes what happened in Nineveh when Tobias and his party arrived. Tobias cures his father with the fish's gall; Tobit blesses his daughter-in-law, and the angel reveals who he really is and then disappears. Tobit bursts into a song in praise of God; later he leaves his son a spiritual testament. Finally, after the death of his mother, Tobias and Sarah go back to Media to live, as Tobit had told them to do, because he was aware of and believed in the prophecies about the destruction of Nineveh.

2. COMPOSITION

If at first sight, Tobit seems to be a history, it is not history in the proper sense of the word. It is in fact closer to a "moralistic" novel; it could be categorized as a "sapiential narrative". Although the author sets his story in the time when the Israelites were captive in Assyria and Media (eighth–seventh centuries BC), one can see that he is writing much later, for he makes reference to the fall of Jerusalem and the captivity in Babylon (Tob 13:9–12; 14–15). In fact what we have here is a story about a Jewish family in the diaspora which could be

anytime, anywhere in the fourth to second century BC. The story is designed to encourage the Jews of the time to put their trust in God, to praise him, to practise works of mercy within their community, and to protect their Jewish identity by marrying people of their own religion.

It is a lovely, well-written story, and they all live happily ever after. When misfortunes arise, they are not dwelt on, and no deep questions are asked about why a just man should suffer if he did not sin. The author is more interested in showing that God helps people and provides for them; so, from the very start, when he sent the angel Raphael, he had already decided that everything was going to be sorted out. Also, the writer is not so much interested in the storyline as in the religious message, and he sprinkles his narrative with prayers (Tob 3:2–6, 11–15; 8:5–7, 15–17; etc.), discourses (Tob 4:1–21; 12:6–15; etc.), and even conversations which the reader will find amusing because he already knows the truth (Tob 5:1–23).

In the early part of the book the author writes in the first person (Tob 1:3—3:6), as if he were the main character, Tobias; this is a device to make the story sound more authentic.

There are things in the book of Tobit which make it rather like a sapiential work known as the "Wisdom of Ahikar", a book which was very popular among the Jews of the diaspora even though it was not of Jewish origin. The author of Tobit seems to have been familiar with that book and he depicts Tobit as being an uncle of Ahikar, which has the effect of giving Tobit more status (Tob 1:21–22; 14:10–11). The sacred writer wants to show what true wisdom is for a devout Jew in the diaspora, and how he should conduct himself before God and in his family relationships, in line with the Law.

3. MESSAGE

The main idea running through the book is that God protects the righteous and saves them from any misfortunes which overtake them, provided they have recourse to him in heartfelt prayer. The story of Tobias and Sarah shows this very clearly. But the book also teaches that God exercises his protection by means of his angels. In this case the angel is Raphael, a name which means "God has cured", because he performs cures: Tobit is cured of his blindness and Sarah is relieved of the presence of the demon. The book leaves the way open for us to see how God can intervene in human affairs through other angels whose names also indicate their mission.

God acts in such a way that initially man does not notice him. Even misfortunes, which God allows to happen, have some good reason behind them which one does not perceive at the time but only later on: Tobit's blindness and the death of Sarah's husbands are all part of Providence—designed to bring about the marriage of Sarah and Tobias, and so the Law is fulfilled and

everything works out well. The book of Tobit teaches that God is providentially at work in the life of every family and every individual, and not just in the life of the community as a whole. Thus, the journey undertaken by Tobias and the angel—leading to Media and marriage—is a symbol showing that God leads man through the course of his life, and that man can co-operate with God provided he makes good use of the resources available to him to pursue noble objectives.

Man is not being asked to make sense of his misfortunes but rather to have recourse to God and to put himself in God's hands and not give way to despair. Man's attitude to God should always be one of praise, even in his prayer of petition. The good Jew is also being asked to practise the works of mercy, even to an heroic degree—particularly those of almsgiving and burying the dead. The book also puts a long stress on children's duties towards their parents in their old age and at the moment of death.

On another level, the book of Tobias carries the lesson that a Jew needs to be very conscious that he is a member of the people of God and he should feel and show solidarity with all other Jews. He needs to protect his Jewish identity by keeping the laws about clean and unclean food, and should look for a wife within his family circle; in the same connexion he should look forward to and pray for the reunification of God's people in a rebuilt Jerusalem (Tob 13:9–18; 14:3–7).

4. THE BOOK OF TOBIT IN THE LIGHT OF THE NEW TESTAMENT

The Christian reader can learn from the book of Tobit that God listens to and responds to prayer that comes from the heart, as our Lord Jesus Christ teaches (cf. Mt 6:6; 7:7–11; etc.). But the words of the Gospel also help him learn the main lesson from the story—that in everything God works for the good of those who love him (cf. Rom 8:28). Jesus' teaching about divine providence and the trust that man should place in it confirms the message of the book of Tobit, and it goes even deeper than that: he tells us that God knows what we need even before we ask him for it (cf. Mt 6:8, 32), and he invites us to seek first the Kingdom of God (cf. Mt 6:33).

Our Lord also confirms Tobit's exhortations about almsgiving and the works of mercy; these should be done not only with one's co-religionists (Tob 2:2) but with all those in need (cf. Mt 25:31–46; Lk 10:29–37), and one must always have the right intention (cf. Mt 6:1–4).

The book's teaching about God working through his angels is confirmed in the New Testament, where angels also are sent by God on special missions (cf. Lk 1:26; 22:43) and which speaks about the angel that each human being has as a guardian (cf. Mt 18:10).

Finally, we should point out that Tobit's prayer for the rebuilding of Jerusalem is fulfilled with the coming of our Lord Jesus Christ, not in the sense that a physical city is built but in the sense that all mankind, Jews and Gentiles, is assembled in the Church, the new Jerusalem which will appear in all its glory at the end of time (cf. Rev 21:1—22:5).

1. TOBIT'S MISFORTUNE. HIS PRAYER IN NINEVEH AND SARAH'S PRAYER IN MEDIA*

Tobit's ancestors and place of origin

1 [1]The book of the acts[a] of Tobit the son of Tobiel, son of Ananiel, son of Aduel, son of Gabael, of the descendants of Asiel and the tribe of Naphtali, [2]who in the days of Shalmaneser,[b] king of the Assyrians, was taken into captivity from Thisbe, which is to the south of Kedesh Naphtali in Galilee above Asher.

***1:1—3:17.** The first part of the book of Tobit introduces the main characters in the story—Tobit, his wife, his son Tobias, Sarah, her parents, and the angel Raphael—and describes the dire situation of Tobit in Nineveh (Assyria) and Sarah in Ecbatana (Media). Although they are living about a thousand kilometres (625 miles) apart, and their circumstances are different, they have a lot in common: they are both members of the Jewish people in the diaspora, and members of the same tribe; both are righteous and pure in the eyes of God—Tobit because he keeps to the letter of the Law, and Sarah because she faithfully obeys her parents; both of them seem to be in a hopeless position; and at the very same moment they have recourse to God in prayer, placing themselves in his hands; and both of them are going to be rescued from their plight through the help of God's messenger, the angel Raphael. The plot of the story is well organized, even though the outcome is known from the start. Already, the central message of the book is easy to see: God helps those who trust in him and try to do what is good for the right reasons.

1:1–2. The main character begins by introducing himself—Tobit, the father of Tobias. He tells us the tribe he comes from, his place of origin, and the time in which he lives (the last years of the eighth century BC). The name Tobias (cf. 1:9) means "my God is the Lord", and that is what the story bears out: God and the observance of his Law are what matters to Tobit, when things go well and also when misfortune strikes; that is why God's goodness and mercy will come to his aid to rescue him when all seems lost.

[1] [1]Liber sermonum Thobis filii Thobiel filii Ananiel filii Aduel filii Gabael filii Raphael filii Raguel ex semine Asiel, ex tribu Nephthali, [2]qui captivus ductus est in diebus Salmanasar regis Assyriorum ex Thisbe, quae est a dextera parte Cades Nephthali in superiori Galilaea supra Asor post occidentem solem a sinistra parte Phogor. [3]Ego Thobi in viis veritatis ambulabam et in iustitiis omnibus diebus vitae meae et eleemosynas multas feci fratribus meis et nationi meae, qui abierant mecum in captivitatem in regionem Assyriorum in Nineven. [4]Et cum essem in regione mea in terra Israel et cum essem iunior, omnis tribus Nephthali patris mei recessit de domo David patris mei et ab Ierusalem civitate, quae est electa ex omnibus tribubus Israel; et sanctificatum est templum habitationis Dei et aedificatum est in ipsa, ut sacrificarent omnes tribus Israel in omnes generationes saeculi. [5]Omnes fratres mei omnisque

a. Gk *words* **b.** Gk *Enemessarus*

Tobit's religious piety and works of mercy

[3]I, Tobit, walked in the ways of truth and righteousness all the days of my life, and I performed many acts of charity to my brethren and countrymen who went with me into the land of the Assyrians, to Nineveh. [4]Now when I was in my own country, in the land of Israel, while I was still a young man, the whole tribe of Naphtali my forefather deserted the house of Jerusalem. This was the place which had been chosen from among all the tribes of Israel, where all the tribes should sacrifice and where the temple of the dwelling of the Most High was consecrated and established for all generations for ever.

Num 18:8–24

[5]All the tribes that joined in apostasy used to sacrifice to the calf[c] Baal, and so did the house of Naphtali my forefather. [6]But I alone went often to Jerusalem for the feasts, as it is ordained for all Israel by an everlasting decree. Taking the first fruits and the tithes of my produce and the first shearings, I would give these to the priests, the sons of Aaron, at the altar. [7]Of all my produce I would give a tenth to the sons of Levi who ministered at Jerusalem; a second tenth I would sell, and I would go and spend the proceeds each year at Jerusalem; [8]the third tenth I would give to those to whom it was my duty, as Deborah my father's mother had

1 Kings 12:26–32
Deut 12:1–18; 14:22; 16:16

Num 14:22–27; 18:12ff
Deut 18:3–5

Deut 14:22–24, 28–29

1:3–22. At this point Tobit himself begins to recount his life, emphasizing that he has always dutifully kept the law of God, despite the fact that his compatriots, the Israelites of the Northern kingdom, kept it neither at home nor in exile. Prior to the exile, Tobit had continued to go up to Jerusalem to worship God, as the Law commanded (cf. Deut 12:1–18), and he never offered sacrifice to the golden calves set up by Jeroboam (cf. 1 Kings 12:26–32); he was also meticulous about the three tithes (cf. Num 18:12ff; Deut 14:22–23, 28–29); and, in keeping with the Law, he married a wife of his own nation (cf. Deut 7:3). Later, exiled far from his country, he never ate the unclean food of the Gentiles (cf. Lev 11:1–49; Deut 14:3–21); and now that he cannot bring tithes to the temple, he gives alms to the poor and heroically

domus Nephthali patris mei sacrificabant vitulo, quem fecit Ieroboam rex Israel in Dan, in omnibus montibus Galilaeae. [6]Ego autem solus ibam aliquotiens in Ierusalem diebus festis, sicut scriptum est in toto Israel in praecepto sempiterno; primitias et primogenita et decimas armentorum et pecorum et initia tonsurae ovium mecum portabam in Ierusalem [7]et dabam ea sacerdotibus, filiis Aaron, ad aram, et decimam tritici et vini et olei et malorum granatorum et ceterorum pomorum filiis Levi servientibus in Ierusalem et secundam decimationem computabam in pecunia sex annorum et ibam et consummabam illa in Ierusalem unoquoque anno. [8]Et dabam ea orphanis et viduis et proselytis appositis ad filios Israel inferebam et dabam illis in tertio anno, et manducabamus illa secundum praeceptum, quod praeceptum est de eis in lege Moysis, et secundum mandata, quae mandaverat Debora mater patris

c. Other authorities read *heifer*

Deut 7:3 commanded me, for I was left an orphan by my father. [9]When I became a man I married Anna, a member of our family, and by her I became the father of Tobias.

[10]Now when I was carried away captive to Nineveh, all my brethren and my relatives ate the food of the Gentiles; [11]but I kept myself from eating it, [12]because I remembered God with all my heart. [13]Then the Most High gave me favour and good appearance in the sight of Shalmaneser,[b] and I was his buyer of provisions. [14]So I used to go into Media, and once at Rages in Media I left ten talents of silver in trust with Gabael, the brother of Gabrias. [15]But when Shalmaneser[b] died, Sennacherib his son reigned in his place; and under him the highways were unsafe, so that I could no longer go into Media.

Lev 11:1–47
Deut 14:3–21
Dan 2:48–49

performs the works of mercy, especially as regards burying the dead. The type of piety described here is not in fact in keeping with the period in which the writer implies Tobit to have lived; the rules referred to stem from the reform instituted by Josiah in 622 BC and from the time of the return from the Babylonian exile. But the sacred writer uses them to depict Tobit as an example of a pious Jew, be he in the land of Israel or in the diaspora. In this respect, the teaching in the book of Tobit contrasts with that of the Gospel, which extends the concept of neighbour to include anyone, of whatever nation, race or religion (cf. Lk 10:29–37).

1:15–18. The author of the book of Tobit is not interested in exact historical detail. Shalmaneser V (727–722) was succeeded by Sargon II (722–705), and it was the latter who conquered Samaria and deported the Israelites. Sargon II was succeeded by Sennacherib (704–681). On Sennacherib's unsuccessful siege of Jerusalem, cf. 2 Kings 18:13—19:37 and Is 37:36–37.

mei Ananiel patris nostri, quia orphanum me reliquit pater et mortuus est. [9]Et, postquam vir factus sum, accepi uxorem Annam ex semine patriae nostrae et genui ex illa filium et vocavi nomen eius Thobiam. [10]Et, postquam in captivitatem deveni ad Assyrios, cum captivus morarer, ibam in Nineven; et omnes fratres mei et, qui de genere meo erant, manducabant de panibus gentium, [11]ego autem custodivi animam meam, ne manducarem de panibus gentium. [12]Et quoniam memor eram Dei mei in tota anima mea, [13]dedit mihi Excelsus gratiam et speciem penes Salmanasar, et comparabam illi omnia, quaecumque erant in usum; [14]et ibam in Mediam, usque dum moreretur, et commendavi Gabael fratri Gabriae in Rages, in regione Mediae, saccellos decem talenta argenti. [15]Et postquam mortuus est Salmanasar, et regnavit Sennacherib filius eius pro eo, et viae Mediae secesserunt, et non potui iam ire in Mediam. [16]Et in diebus Salmanasar multas eleemosynas feci fratribus meis, qui erant ex genere meo. [17]Panes meos dabam esurientibus et vestimenta nudis et, si quem videbam mortuum et proiectum post murum Nineves ex natione mea, sepeliebam illum. [18]Et, si quem occidebat Sennacherib rex, ubi venit de Iudaea fugiens in diebus iudicii, quod fecit Rex caeli ex illo de blasphemiis, quibus blasphemaverat—multos enim filiorum Israel occidit in ira sua—ego autem corpora illorum involabam et sepeliebam; et

b. Gk *Enemessarus*

[16]In the days of Shalmaneser[b] I performed many acts of charity to my brethren. [17]I would give my bread to the hungry and my clothing to the naked; and if I saw any one of my people dead and thrown out behind the wall of Nineveh, I would bury him. [18]And if Sennacherib the king put to death any who came fleeing from Judea, I buried them secretly. For in his anger he put many to death. When the bodies were sought by the king, they were not found. [19]Then one of the men of Nineveh went and informed the king about me, that I was burying them; so I hid myself. When I learned that I was being searched for, to be put to death, I left home in fear. [20]Then all my property was confiscated and nothing was left to me except my wife Anna and my son Tobias.

Job 31:16–20

2 Kings 18:13—19:37
Is 37:36–37

[21]But not fifty[d] days passed before two of Sennacherib's[e] sons killed him, and they fled to the mountains of Ararat. Then Esarhaddon, his son, reigned in his place; and he appointed Ahikar, the son of my brother Anael, over all the accounts of his kingdom and over the entire administration. [22]Ahikar interceded for me, and I returned to Nineveh. Now Ahikar was cupbearer, keeper of the signet, and in charge of administration of the accounts, for Esarhaddon[f] had appointed him second to himself.[g] He was my nephew.

Tobit's misfortune

2 [1]When I arrived home and my wife Anna and my son Tobias were restored to me, at the feast of Pentecost, which is the

Ex 23:14

1:21–22. Ahikar is the protagonist of a wisdom book, originating in Assyria, which circulated widely in ancient times even among Jews, and which shares some features with the book of Tobit. By saying here that Ahikar was Tobit's nephew, the writer is implying that Tobit was wiser than Ahikar and, as it were, the source Ahikar used.

2:1–14. The festival of the Seven Weeks or Pentecost, so-called because

quaesivit illa Sennacherib et non invenit illa. [19]Et abiit quidam ex Ninevitis et indicavit regi de me quoniam ego sepelio illos, et abscondi me et, ubi cognovi quod rex sciebat de me et quod inquiror, ut occidar, timui et refugi. [20]Et direpta est omnis substantia mea, et nihil mihi derelictum est, quod non assumptum esset in fiscum regis, nisi uxor mea Anna et Thobias filius meus. [21]Et non transierunt dies quadraginta, quousque occiderent illum duo filii ipsius et fugerunt in montes Ararat; et regnavit Asarhaddon filius eius pro illo et constituit Achicarum filium fratris mei Anael super omnem exactionem regni eius, et ipse habebat potestatem super omnem regionem. [22]Tunc petiit Achicarus pro me, et descendi in Nineven. Achicarus enim erat praepositus pincernarum et super anulum et procurator et exactor sub Sennacherib rege Assyriorum; et constituit illum Asarhaddon. Erat enim ex fratribus meis et ex cognatione mea. **[2]** [1]Et sub Asarhaddon rege descendi in domum meam, et reddita est mihi uxor

b. Gk *Enemessarus* **d.** Other authorities read *fifty-five* **e.** Gk *his* **f.** Gk *Sacherdonus* **g.** Or *a second time*

Lk 14:13

Amos 8:1

sacred festival of the seven weeks, a good dinner was prepared for me and I sat down to eat. [2]Upon seeing the abundance of food I said to my son, "Go and bring whatever poor man of our brethren you may find who is mindful of the Lord, and I will wait for you." [3]But he came back and said, "Father, one of our people has been strangled and thrown into the market place." [4]So before I tasted anything I sprang up and removed the body[h] to a place of shelter until sunset. [5]And when I returned I washed myself and ate my food in sorrow. [6]Then I remembered the prophecy of Amos, how he said,

"Your feasts shall be turned into mourning,
and all your festivities into lamentation."

And I wept.

---

it was held fifty days after Passover (cf. Deut 16:9–12; Lev 23:16), was one of the festivals involving pilgrimage to Jerusalem: during the exile it seems to have been commemorated by a special meal held as a remembrance rite for the feast. By looking after the needy, Tobit is fulfilling what the Law laid down should be done during this festival—taking an interest in strangers, orphans and widows (cf. Deut 16:14), although he is applying it to "brethren . . . mindful of the Lord" (v. 2). Despite his devoutness and ritual purity (v. 5; cf. Neh 19:11–12), Tobit has to share in the suffering inflicted on the people on account of their sins (v. 6; cf. Amos 8:10). But it gets worse than that: his works of mercy bring him misfortune (first blindness and then penury), to the point that his wife has to take paid work to make ends meet. Later, she queries whether he deserves to be suffering in the way that he is. He can put up with physical blindness because his family comes to his aid; but his wife's criticism casts a shadow on his soul.

Tobit's situation parallels that of everyone who strives to be faithful. As St Paul says in 2 Corinthians 4:8–10, "We are afflicted in every way, but not crushed; perplexed, but not driven to despair; persecuted, but not forsaken; struck down, but not destroyed; always carrying in the body the death of Jesus, so that the life of Jesus may also be manifested in our bodies." The Vulgate version of the Bible includes after v. 10 some reflections on why Tobit should have had to suffer in this way: see the RSVCE note on p. 615.

mea Anna et filius meus Thobias. In Pentecoste, die festo nostro, qui est sanctus a Septimanis, factum est mihi prandium bonum, et discubui, ut pranderem. [2]Et apposita est mihi mensa, et vidi pulmentaria complura. Et dixi Thobiae filio meo: «Vade et, quemcumque pauperem inveneris ex fratribus nostris, qui sunt captivi in Nineve, qui in mente habet Dominum in toto corde suo, hunc adduc, et manducabit pariter mecum; ecce sustineo te, fili, donec venias». [3]Et abiit Thobias quaerere aliquem pauperem ex fratribus nostris et reversus dixit mihi: «Pater!». Et ego dixi illi: «Ecce ego, fili». Et respondens ait: «Ecce unus ex natione nostra occisus est et proiectus est in foro et nunc ibidem laqueo suffocatus est». [4]Et exsiliens reliqui prandium, antequam ex illo gustarem, et sustuli eum de platea in unam domum, donec sol caderet, et illum sepelirem. [5]Et reversus lavi et manducavi panem meum cum luctu [6]et

h. Gk *him*

[7]When the sun had set I went and dug a grave and buried the body.[h] [8]And my neighbours laughed at me and said, "He is no longer afraid that he will be put to death for doing this; he once ran away, and here he is burying the dead again!" [9]On the same night I returned from burying him, and because I was defiled I slept by the wall of the courtyard, and my face was uncovered. [10]I did not know that there were sparrows on the wall and their fresh droppings fell into my open eyes and white films formed on my eyes. I went to physicians, but they did not help me. Ahikar, however, took care of me until he[i] went to Elymais.*

Mk 5:26

[11]Then my wife Anna earned money at women's work. [12]She used to send the product to the owners. Once when they paid her wages, they also gave her a kid; [13]and when she returned to me it began to bleat. So I said to her, "Where did you get the kid? It is not stolen, is it? Return it to the owners; for it is not right to eat what is stolen." [14]And she said, "It was given to me as a gift in addition to my wages." But I did not believe her, and told her to return it to the owners; and I blushed for her. Then she replied to me, "Where are your charities and your righteous deeds? You seem to know everything!"

Job 2:9

Tobit's prayer in Nineveh

3 [1]Then in my grief I wept, and I prayed in anguish, saying, [2]"Righteous art thou, O Lord; all thy deeds and all they ways

Ps 25:10; 119:137
Dan 3:27–32

---

rememoratus sum sermonis prophetae Amos, quem locutus est, in Bethel dicens: «Convertentur omnes dies festi vestri in luctum et omnia cantica vestra in lamentationem». [7]Et lacrimatus sum. Et, postquam sol occidit, abii et fodiens sepelivi illum. [8]Et proximi mei deridebant me dicentes: «Non timet adhuc hic homo; iam enim inquisitus est huius rei causa, ut occideretur, et fugit et ecce iterum sepelit mortuos». [9]Et lavi ea nocte, postquam illum sepelivi, et introivi in atrium meum et obdormivi circa parietem atrii, et facies mea nuda erat propter aestum. [10]Et ignorabam quoniam passeres in pariete super me erant, quorum stercora insederunt in oculos meos calida et induxerunt albugines. Et ibam ad medicos, ut curarer, et, quanto inunxerunt me medicamentis, tanto magis oculi mei excaecabantur maculis, donec perexcaecatus sum. Et eram inutilis meis oculis annis quattuor, et omnes fratres mei dolebant pro me. Achicarus autem pascebat me annis duobus, priusquam iret in Elymaida. [11]In illo tempore Anna uxor mea mercede deserviebat operibus mulierum lanam faciens. [12]Et remittebat dominis eorum, et dabant ei mercedem. Septima autem die mensis Dystri detexuit texturam et reddidit illam dominis, et dederunt ei mercedem totam et dederunt ei pro textura haedum de capris. [13]Et cum introisset ad me haedus, coepit clamare. Et vocavi eam et dixi: «Unde est hic haedus? Ne forte furtivus sit, redde illum dominis suis; nobis enim non licet manducare quidquam furtivum». [14]Et illa mihi dixit: «Munere mihi datus est supra mercedem». Et ego non credebam ei, sed dicebam, ut restitueret illum dominis, et erubescebam coram illa huius rei causa. Et respondens dixit mihi: «Et ubi sunt eleemosynae tuae? Ubi sunt iustitiae tuae? Ecce, omnia tibi nota sunt». **[3]** [1]Et contristatus animo et suspirans ploravi et coepi orare cum gemitibus: [2]«Iustus es, Domine, et omnia opera tua iusta sunt et omnes viae tuae misericordia et veritas, et tu iudicas saeculum. [3]Et nunc, Domine, memor esto mei et respice in me; ne vindictam sumas de me pro peccatis meis et pro neglegentiis meis et parentum meorum, quibus peccaverunt ante te, [4]quoniam

h. Gk *him* **i.** Other authorities read *I*

Ex 34:7
Bar 1:17–18

Bar 1:17–18; 2:4; 3:8
Dan 9:5–6

Num 11:15
Kings 19:4
Job 7:15
Jon 4:3,8

are mercy and truth, and thou dost render true and righteous judgment for ever. [3]Remember me and look favourably upon me; do not punish me for my sins and for my unwitting offences and those which my fathers committed before thee. [4]For they disobeyed thy commandments, and thou gavest us over to plunder, captivity, and death; thou madest us a byword of reproach in all the nations among which we have been dispersed. [5]And now thy many judgments are true in exacting penalty from me for my sins and those of my fathers, because we did not keep thy commandments. For we did not walk in truth before thee. [6]And now deal with me according to thy pleasure; command my spirit to be taken up, that I may depart and become dust. For it is better for me to die than to live, because I have heard false reproaches, and great is the sorrow within me. Command that I now be released from my distress to go to the eternal abode; do not turn thy face away from me."

3:1–6. Tobit does not reply to his wife's criticism; instead he entreats God in language reminiscent of the Psalms—but whereas the Psalms always pray for health and salvation, Tobit ends up praying for death. In this he is like Job (cf. Job 3:20–23), although Tobit acknowledges that God is right to punish him for his sins and those of his fathers, for which he feels responsible.

From the Greek text (where the RSV follows) one cannot deduce that Tobit envisages eternal life as a place of repose and joy in the presence of God; he sees it a place where the dead will dwell for all eternity. But the Latin version of the Vulgate implies that Tobit looks forward to being with the Lord. In any event, Tobit puts his trust in God, which means he can desire death, in the same sort of way that "the Christian can experience a desire for death like St Paul's: 'My desire is to depart and be with Christ' (Phil 1:23). He can transform his own death into an act of obedience and love towards the Father, after the example of Christ" (*Catechism of the Catholic Church*, 1011).

3:7–10. The narrator now takes over again (cf. 1:1–2), to introduce another Jewish family in exile which also finds itself in great difficulty. Tobit's and Sarah's are two stories in parallel but, pointing out that their prayers are

non oboedivimus praeceptis tuis, et tradidisti nos in direptionem et captivitatem et mortem et in parabolam et fabulam et improperium in omnibus nationibus, in quas nos dispersisti. [5]Et nunc multa sunt iudicia tua vera, quae de me exigas pro peccatis meis et parentum meorum, quia non egimus secundum praecepta tua et non ambulavimus sinceriter coram te. [6]Et nunc secundum quod tibi placet fac mecum et praecipe recipi spiritum meum, ut dimittar a facie terrae et fiam terra, quia expedit mihi mori magis quam vivere, quoniam improperia falsa audivi, et tristitia multa est in me. Praecipe, Domine, ut dimittar ab hac necessitate, et dimitte me in locum aeternum et noli avertere a me faciem tuam, Domine, quia expedit mihi mori magis quam videre tantam necessitatem in vita mea, et ne improperia audiam». [7]Eadem die contigit Sarae filiae Raguel, qui erat Ecbatanis Mediae, ut et ipsa audiret improperia ab una ex ancillis patris sui, [8]quoniam tradita erat viris septem, et Asmodeus daemonium

Sarah's misfortune

7On the same day, at Ecbatana in Media, it also happened that Sarah, the daughter of Raguel, was reproached by her father's maids, 8because she had been given to seven husbands, and the evil demon Asmodeus had slain each of them before he had been with her as his wife. So the maids[j] said to her, "Do you not know that you strangle your husbands? You already have had seven and have had no benefit from[k] any of them. 9Why do you beat us? If they are dead, go with them! May we never see a son or daughter of yours!"

10When she heard these things she was deeply grieved, even to the thought of hanging herself. But she said, "I am the only child

Gen 37:35; 42:38; 44:29,31 Tob 6:15

spoken on the same day, the writer makes it clear that they meet in God.

Sarah's goodness can be seen from the fact that she is obedient to her father and is worried on his account (v. 10). The demon's name, Asmodeus (v. 8), is reminiscent of *Aeshma Deva*, one of the seven evil spirits the Persians believed in, but it may also come from a Hebrew word (*smd*) which means "to destroy, to annihilate". Asmodeus is the demon who destroys Sarah's husbands.

The text does not say that the demon was infatuated with Sarah, as some have interpreted; what he seems to want is to drive her to despair, as happened in the case of Job. In fact Sarah is on the edge of committing the grave sin of suicide, but her love for her father holds her back. To avoid tainting Sarah with the thought of suicide, the Vulgate says that "she went into an upper chamber of her house: and for three days and three nights did neither eat nor drink: but continuing in prayer with tears besought God, that he would deliver her from this reproach."

Suicide very rarely appears in the Bible (cf. 2 Sam 17:23), and Scripture makes no moral judgment on it; but from the fifth commandment (cf. Ex 20:15; Deut 5:17) one can deduce that it is condemned: "Suicide contradicts the natural inclination of the human being to preserve and perpetuate his life. It is gravely contrary to the just love of self. It likewise offends love of neighbour because it unjustly breaks the ties of solidarity with family, nation and other human societies to which we continue to have obligations. Suicide is contrary to love for the living God" (*Catechism of the Catholic Church*, 2281).

nequissimum occidebat eos, antequam cum illa fierent, sicut est solitum mulieribus. Et dixit illi ancilla: «Tu es, quae suffocas viros tuos! Ecce iam tradita es viris septem, et nemine eorum fruita es. 9Quid nos flagellas causa virorum tuorum, quia mortui sunt? Vade cum illis, nec ex te videamus filium aut filiam in perpetuum». 10In illa die contristata est animo puella et lacrimata est et ascendens in superiorem locum patris sui voluit laqueo se suspendere. Et cogitavit iterum et dixit: «Ne forte improperent patri meo et dicant: "Unicam habuisti filiam carissimam, et haec laqueo se suspendit ex malis"; et deducam senectam patris mei cum tristitia ad inferos. Utilius mihi est non me laqueo suspendere, sed deprecari

j. Gk *they* **k.** Other authorities read *have not borne the name of*

of my father; if I do this, it will be a disgrace to him, and I shall bring his old age down in sorrow to the grave.[l]

1 Kings 8:44,48
Ps 5:7; 28:2; 134:2; 138:2
Dan 6:11
Tob 3:6

Sarah's prayer in Media

[11]So she prayed by her window and said,* "Blessed art thou, O Lord my God, and blessed is thy holy and honoured name for ever. May all thy works praise thee for ever. [12]And now, O Lord, I have turned my eyes and my face toward thee. [13]Command that I be released from the earth and that I hear reproach no more. [14]Thou knowest, O Lord, that I am innocent of any sin with man, [15]and that I did not stain my name or the name of my father in the land of my captivity. I am my father's only child, and he has no child to be his heir, no near kinsman or kinsman's[m] son for whom

3:11–15. The gesture of praying at the window with arms outstretched probably means that she was holding them towards Jerusalem, as any good Jew should do when praying (cf. Dan 6:10). Sarah's prayer begins with praise of God and then she immediately goes on to pray for death (v. 10). She explains her predicament to God: she is innocent (vv. 14–15) and yet she is being condemned to have no heirs—and, according to Jewish thinking at the time, life holds no meaning for someone in that situation; even her maidservants jeer at her. But Sarah leaves it up to God to sort things out; to her, death seems the only solution (v. 15). God can indeed come to our aid in unexpected ways, for "Providence is the care God provides for everything that exists. [. . .] Moreover, divine providence has countless ways of working: so many, that they can not be accounted for in words or comprehended by the mind. It cannot be denied that all the calamities that befall men work for the salvation of those who endure them giving thanks and thus win great reward for themselves. For God, according to his will that informs all things, desires that all be saved and come to be members of his kingdom (cf. 1 Tim 2:4): he has not created us in order to punish us, but rather, being good, he wants us to partake of his goodness" (St John Damascene, *Expositio fidei orthodoxae*, 2, 29).

Dominum, ut moriar et iam improperia non audiam in vita mea». [11]Eodem tempore, porrectis manibus ad fenestram, deprecata est et dixit: «Benedictus es, Domine Deus misericors, et benedictum est nomen tuum sanctum et honorabile in saecula. Benedicant tibi omnia opera tua in aeternum. [12]Et nunc, Domine, ad te faciem meam et oculos meos direxi. [13]Iube me dimitti desuper terram, et ne audiam iam improperia. [14]Tu scis, Domine, quoniam munda sum ab omni immunditia viri [15]et non coinquinavi nomen meum neque nomen patris mei in terra captivitatis meae. Unica sum patri meo, et non habet alium filium, qui possideat hereditatem illius, neque frater est illi proximus neque propinquus illi, ut custodiam me illi uxorem. Iam perierunt mihi septem, et ut quid mihi adhuc vivere? Et si non tibi videtur, Domine, occidere me, impera, ut respiciatur in me et misereatur mei, et ne iam improperium

l. Gk *to Hades* **m.** Gk *his*

I should keep myself as wife. Already seven husbands of mine are dead. Why should I live? But if it be not pleasing to thee to take my life, command that respect be shown to me and pity be taken upon me, and that I hear reproach no more."*

The prayers of Tobit and Sarah are heard

[16]The prayer of both was heard in the presence of the glory of the great God. [17]And Raphael[n] was sent to heal the two of them: to scale away the white films of Tobit's eyes; to give Sarah the daughter of Raguel in marriage to Tobias the son of Tobit, and to bind Asmodeus the evil demon, because Tobias was entitled to possess her. At that very moment Tobit returned and entered his house and Sarah the daughter of Raguel came down from her upper room.

Tob 12:12

Tob 4:12–13; 6:12

2. TOBIT'S JOURNEY TO MEDIA ACCOMPANIED BY THE ARCHANGEL RAPHAEL*

Tobit's appeal to his son

4 [1]On that day Tobit remembered the money which he had left in trust with Gabael at Rages in Media, and he said to himself; [2]"I have asked for death. Why do I not call my son Tobias so that I may explain to him about the money[o] before I die?" [3]So he called

---

3:16–17. Two things are stressed: God listens to prayers when they come from the heart; and he responds with mercy, wisdom and providence in ways that exceed man's expectations. Now, by one and the same action (the despatch of the angel Raphael) he comes to the rescue of Sarah and Tobit. The angel's name, meaning "God has cured" or "God's medicine", indicates the remedy God is going to provide: in a way it reveals the final outcome of the story.

***4:1—10:13.** The second part of the book deals with Tobias' journey to Media under the protection of the angel. The preparations are described and the leave-taking (chaps. 4–5), incidents on

audiam». [16]In ipso tempore exaudita est oratio amborum in conspectu claritatis Dei, [17]et missus est Raphael angelus sanare duos, Thobin desquamare ab albuginibus oculorum eius, ut videret oculis lumen Dei, et Saram filiam Raguel dare Thobiae filio Thobis uxorem, et colligare Asmodeum daemonium nequissimum, quoniam Thobiae contigit possidere eam prae omnibus, qui volebant accipere eam. In illo tempore reversus est Thobi de atrio in domum suam, et Sara filia Raguel descendit et ipsa de loco superiori. **[4]** [1]In illa die rememoratus est Thobi pecuniae, quam commendaverat Gabael in Rages Mediae. [2]Et dixit in corde suo: «Ecce ego postulavi mortem. Quid non voco Thobiam filium meum et indicabo illi de hac pecunia, quam commendavi, antequam moriar?». [3]Et vocavit Thobiam filium suum,

n. Other authorities read *the great Raphael. And he* **o.** Other authorities omit *about the money*

Ex 20:12 Prov 23:22 Sir 7:27 Mt 8:21 Tob 13:6 Jn 3:21 Eph 4:15 Deut 15:7—8:11 Tob 12:8–10 Prov 9:17 Sir 4:1–6 1 Jn 3:17 Mt 6:20

him and said, "My son, when I die, bury me, and do not neglect your mother. Honour her all the days of your life; do what is pleasing to her, and do not grieve her. [4]Remember, my son, that she faced many dangers for you while you were yet unborn. When she dies bury her beside me in the same grave.

[5]"Remember the Lord our God all your days, my son, and refuse to sin or to transgress his commandments. Live uprightly all the days of your life, and do not walk in the ways of wrong-doing. [6]For if you do what is true, your ways will prosper through your deeds. [7]Give alms from your possessions to all who live uprightly, and do not let your eye begrudge the gift when you make it. Do not turn your face away from any poor man, and the face of God will not be turned away from you. [8]If you have many possessions, make your gift from them in proportion; if few, do not be afraid to give according to the little you have. [9]So you will be laying up a

---

the way (6:1–8), the arrival at Ecbatana (6:9–17), Tobias' marriage to Sarah (7:1—8:21), the recovery of the money (chap. 9), and farewells prior to the return journey (10:8–12), not before a cameo account of how things are going in Nineveh (10:1–7). The story is all very touching, and the more it unfolds the more the reader gets, the message (through references to the final outcome): man's view of people and events is very blinkered; divine providence can see exactly where they lead. The young companion of Tobias turns out to be an angel, but neither Tobit nor his son knows this; the innards of the predatory fish prove to be effective medicine; and even the death of Sarah's seven husbands has a positive side, because it allows the law on marriage to be observed. Divine providence is at work all the time.

4:1–21. The assignment Tobit gives his son, to collect money deposited in Media, is part of the plot of the story (cf. 1:14), but the sacred writer also uses it to bring in an exhortation, which is a sort of testamentary speech to his son. In it Tobit explains what being a true Israelite entails, by quoting the Law of Moses and Wisdom books, particularly Proverbs.

Tobit's advice, especially as regards almsgiving, has become deeply etched in Christian traditions: "When you have

---

et venit ad illum, et dixit illi: «Fili, cum mortuus fuero, sepeli me diligenter et honorem habe matri tuae et noli derelinquere illam omnibus diebus vitae suae et fac, quod bonum est in conspectu eius, et noli contristare spiritum eius in ullo. [4]Memor esto eius, fili, quoniam multa pericula vidit propter te in utero. Cum mortua fuerit, sepeli illam iuxta me in uno sepulcro. [5]Et omnibus diebus tuis, fili, Dominum in mente habe et noli velle peccare et praeterire praecepta illius. Iustitiam fac omnibus diebus vitae tuae et noli ire in vias iniquitatis, [6]quoniam, agente te veritatem, prospera erunt itinera in operibus tuis et in omnibus, qui faciunt iustitiam. [7]Ex substantia tua, fili, fac eleemosynam et noli avertere faciem tuam ab ullo paupere, ne a te avertatur facies Dei. [8]Quomodo habueris, fili, secundum multitudinem fac ex ipsis eleemosynam. Si tibi fuerit largior substantia, plus ex illa fac eleemosynam. Si exiguum habueris, secundum exiguum ne timueris facere eleemosynam: [9]praemium enim bonum reponis tibi in diem

good treasure for yourself against the day of necessity. [10]For charity* delivers from death and keeps you from entering the darkness; [11]and for all who practise it charity is an excellent offering in the presence of the Most High.

Sir 3:30; 29:12
Jas 2:13

[12]"Beware, my son, of all immorality.* First of all take a wife from among the descendants of your fathers and do not marry a foreign woman, who is not of your father's tribe; for we are the sons of the prophets. Remember, my son, that Noah, Abraham, Isaac, and Jacob, our fathers of old, all took wives from among their brethren. They were blessed in their children, and their posterity will inherit the land. [13]So now, my son, love your brethren, and in your heart do not disdain your brethren and the sons and daughters of your people by refusing to take a wife for yourself from among them. For in pride there is ruin and great confusion; and in shiftlessness there is loss and great want, because shiftlessness is the mother of famine. [14]Do not hold over till the next day the wages of any man who works for you, but pay him at once; and if you serve God you will receive payment.

Gen 11:31; 24:3–4; 25:20; 28:1–2; 29:15–30
Judg 14:3
Tob 6:12

Lev 19:13
Deut 24:15
Jas 5:4

"Watch yourself, my son, in everything you do, and be disciplined in all your conduct. [15]And what you hate, do not do to any one. Do not drink wine to excess or let drunkenness go with you on your way. [16]Give of your bread to the hungry, and of your clothing to the naked. Give all your surplus to charity, and do not let your eye begrudge the gift when you make it. [17]Place your

Mt 7:12
Lk 6:31

Is 58:7
Mt 25:35–36

---

the opportunity to do good, do not spurn it, because charity frees [you] from death. Serve one another, be irreproachable in your dealings with pagans, so that you may be rewarded for your good works and God will not be offended by your faults" (St Polycarp, *Ad Philippenses*, 10, 2). Verse 17 refers to some sort of rite which was practised at the tombs of loved ones; see the RSVCE note on p. 615.

necessitatis, [10]quoniam eleemosyna a morte liberat et non sinit ire in tenebras. [11]Munus enim bonum est eleemosyna omnibus, qui faciunt illam coram Excelso. [12]Attende tibi, fili, ab omni fornicatione. Uxorem primum accipe ex semine parentum tuorum et noli sumere uxorem alienam, quae non est ex tribu patris tui, quoniam filii prophetarum sumus: Noe et Abraham et Isaac et Iacob patres nostri a saeculo. Rememorare, fili, quoniam hi omnes acceperunt uxores ex semine patrum suorum et benedicti sunt in filiis suis, et semen illorum possidebit hereditatem terrae. [13]Et tu, fili, dilige fratres tuos et noli fastidire in corde tuo a fratribus tuis et a filiis et filiabus populi tui, ut accipias uxorem ex illis, quoniam in fastidio perditio et inconstantia magna est, et in nugacitate diminutio et exiguitas magna est. Nugacitas enim mater est famis. [14]Merces omnis hominis, quicumque penes te operatus fuerit, non maneat penes te, sed redde ei statim, et merces tua non minorabitur; si servieris Deo in veritate, reddetur tibi. Attende tibi, fili, in omnibus operibus tuis et esto sapiens in omnibus sermonibus tuis [15]et, quod oderis, nemini feceris. Noli bibere vinum in ebrietatem, et non comitetur te ebrietas in via tua. [16]De pane tuo communica esurienti et de vestimentis tuis nudis; ex omnibus, quaecumque tibi abundaverint, fac eleemosynam, et non invideat oculus tuus, cum facis eleemosynam. [17]Frange panem tuum et effunde

Deut 15:10; 26:14
2 Cor 9:7
Deut 4:6
1 Sam 2:7
Ps 119:10–12,26f,33f

bread* on the grave of the righteous, but give none to sinners. [18]Seek advice from every wise man, and do not despise any useful counsel. [19]Bless the Lord God on every occasion; ask him that your ways may be made straight and that all your paths and plans may prosper. For none of the nations has understanding; but the Lord himself gives all good things, and according to his will he humbles whomever he wishes.

"So, my son, remember my commands, and do not let them be blotted out of your mind. [20]And now let me explain to you about the ten talents of silver which I left in trust with Gabael the son of Gabrias at Rages in Media. [21]Do not be afraid, my son, because we have become poor. You have great wealth if you fear God and refrain from every sin and do what is pleasing in his sight."

1 Tim 6:6–8

Tobias meets the archangel Raphael

5 [1]Then Tobias answered him, "Father, I will do everything that you have commanded me; [2]but how can I obtain the money when I do not know the man?" [3]Then Tobit gave him the receipt, and said to him, "Find a man to go with you and I will pay him

5:1–21. The preparations for the journey are described in four scenes, each involving a dialogue, which make clear that divine providence sees much further than man. The whole chapter is built around the angel Raphael whom God has sent (cf. 3:17).

The first scene, the dialogue between Tobit and his son, deals with the objections raised by Tobias and the solutions his father has worked out. After this stage is completed, events will unfold in line with God's plan. It shows that we should always act as if everything depended on us: "God is the sovereign master of his plan. But to carry it out he also makes use of his creatures' co-operation. This use is not a sign of

vinum tuum super sepulcra iustorum et noli dare peccatoribus. [18]Consilium ab omni sapiente inquire et noli contemnere omne consilium utile. [19]Omni tempore benedic Dominum et postula ab illo, ut dirigantur viae tuae et omnes semitae tuae et consilia bene disponantur, quoniam omnes gentes non habent consilium bonum, sed ipse Dominus dabit ipsis bonum consilium. Quem enim voluerit, allevat et, quem voluerit, Dominus de mergit usque ad inferos deorsum. Et nunc, fili, memor esto praeceptorum meorum, et non deleantur de corde tuo. [20]Et nunc, fili, indico tibi commendasse me decem talenta argenti Gabael filio Gabriae in Rages Mediae. [21]Noli vereri, fili, quia pauperem vitam gessimus. Habes multa bona, si timueris Deum et recesseris ab omni peccato et bene egeris in conspectu Domini Dei tui». **[5]** [1]Tunc Thobias respondens Thobi patri suo dixit: «Omnia, quae cumque mihi praecepisti, pater, faciam. [2]Quomodo autem potero hanc pecuniam recipere ab illo? Neque ille me novit neque ego novi illum. Quod signum dabo illi, ut me cognoscat et credat et det mihi hanc pecuniam? Sed neque vias, quae ad Mediam, novi, ut eam illuc». [3]Tunc respondens Thobi Thobiae filio suo dixit: «Chirographum dedit mihi, et chirographum meum dedi illi et divisi in duas partes, et unusquisque unam accepimus, et posui cum ipsa pecunia. Et ecce nunc anni sunt viginti, ex quibus penes illum commendavi hanc pecuniam. Et nunc, fili, inquire tibi hominem fidelem, qui eat tecum, et dabimus illi mercedem, donec venias. Et,

wages as long as I live; and go and get the money." [4]So he went to look for a man; and he found Raphael, who was an angel, [5]but Tobias[p] did not know it. Tobias[p] said to him, "Can you go with me to Rages in Media? Are you acquainted with that region?" [6]The angel replied, "I will go with you; I am familiar with the way, and I have stayed with our brother Gabael." [7]Then Tobias said to him, "Wait for me, and I shall tell my father." [8]And he said to him, "Go, and do not delay." So he went in and said to his father, "I have found some one to go with me." He said, "Call him to me, so that I may learn to what tribe he belongs, and whether he is a reliable man to go with you."

Tob 3:17

---

weakness, but rather a token of almighty God's greatness and goodness. For God grants his creatures not only their existence, but also the dignity of acting on their own, of being causes and principles for each other, and thus of co-operating in the accomplishment of his plan" (*Catechism of the Catholic Church*, 306).

The second scene (vv. 4–8) is the meeting and conversation between Tobias and a young man (the angel Raphael) who, remarkably, has all the qualifications to be his guide, including the fact that he knows Gabael. The sacred text shows that God exercises his providence through angels, though no one sees their dazzling presence. "From the beginning (cf. Mt 18:10) to death (cf. Lk 16:22) human life is surrounded by the angels watchful care (cf. Ps 34:7; 91:10–13) and intercession (cf. Job 33:23–24; Zech 1:12; Tob 12:12) 'Beside each believer stands an angel as protector and shepherd leading him to life.' Already here on earth the Christian life shares by faith in the blessed company of angels and men united in God" (*Catechism of the Catholic Church*, 336).

The third scene has the dialogue between Tobit and the angel (vv. 9–15). Tobit is concerned that the guide should not just be able to lead his son to Media but should be a good companion for him, a good Jew. The names the angel mentions to Tobit are significant: Azarias means "God helps", and Ananias "God is merciful". Tobit takes them to refer to relatives of his, but the angel intends them to refer to God's protection of men. It is a play on words. Tobit treats the angel as if he were his son: he not

dum vivo, recipe pecuniam ab illo». [4]Et exiit Thobias quaerere hominem, qui iret cum ipso in Mediam et qui haberet notitiam viae. Et invenit Raphael angelum stantem ante ipsum et nesciebat illum angelum Dei esse. [5]Et dixit illi: «Unde es, iuvenis?». Et dixit illi: «Ex filiis Israel fratribus tuis et veni huc, ut operer». Et dixit illi Thobias: «Nosti viam, quae ducit in Mediam?». [6]Et ille dixit: «Utique, aliquotiens fui ibi et habeo notitiam et scio omnes vias et aliquotiens ibam in Mediam et manebam penes Gabael fratrem nostrum, qui commoratur in Rages Mediae, et abest iter bidui statuti ex Ecbatanis usque Rages. Nam posita est in monte et Ecbatana in medio campo». [7]Et dixit illi Thobias: «Sustine me, iuvenis, donec intrans patri meo nuntiem. Necessarium est enim mihi, ut eas mecum, et dabo tibi mercedem tuam». [8]Et dixit illi: «Ecce sustineo; tantum noli tardare». [9]Et introiens Thobias renuntiavit Thobi patri

p. Gk *he*

[9]So Tobias[p] invited him in; he entered and they greeted each other. [10]Then Tobit said to him, "My brother, to what tribe and family do you belong? Tell me." [11]But he answered, "Are you looking for a tribe and a family or for a man whom you will pay to go with your son?" And Tobit said to him, "I should like to know, my brother, your people and your name." [12]He replied, "I am Azarias the son of the great Ananias, one of your relatives." [13]Then Tobit said to him, "You are welcome, my brother. Do not be angry with me because I tried to learn your tribe and family. You are a relative of mine, of a good and noble lineage. For I used to know Ananias and Jathan, the sons of the great Shemaiah, when we went together to Jerusalem to worship and offered the first-born of our

---

only offers to pay him a fair fee but gives him the same expenses as he gives his son (v. 14).

The blessing Tobit gives the angel, and his prayer that God will provide an angel to go with them (cf. Ps 91:11–12), is paradoxical, because God has already sent his angel to bring blessings for Tobit. God has anticipated his prayers. God knows what we need even before we petition him (cf. Mt 6:8).

The fourth scene (vv. 17–21) covers Tobit's conversation with his wife. We can see that their love for their son is far above their interest in material things; they have the right scale of values. But once more Tobit shows his trust in God's help; the Lord, he says, will listen to his prayer (cf. v. 16) and an angel will accompany his son (v. 21). The reader, who already knows that Raphael is an angel, can see that Tobit's words are being fulfilled: God certainly exercises his protection in ways man could never suspect.

suo et dixit ei: «Ecce inveni hominem ex fratribus nostris, de filiis Israel, qui eat mecum». Et dixit illi: «Roga mihi hominem, ut sciam quid sit genus eius, et ex qua tribu sit et an fidelis sit, ut eat tecum, fili». [10]Et exivit Thobias et vocavit illum et dixit ei: «Iuvenis, pater te rogat». Et introivit ad eum, et prior Thobis salutavit eum. Et ille dixit ei: «Gaudium tibi magnum sit!». Et respondens Thobi dixit illi: «Quid mihi adhuc gaudium est? Homo sum inutilis oculis et non video lumen caelorum, sed in tenebris positus sum sicut mortui, qui non amplius vident lumen. Vivus ego sum inter mortuos. Vocem hominum audio et ipsos non video». Et dixit ei: «Forti esto animo; in proximo est, ut a Deo cureris. Forti animo esto!». Et respondit illi Thobi: «Thobias filius meus vult ire in Mediam. Nonne poteris ire cum illo et ducere illum? Et dabo tibi mercedem tuam, frater». Et dixit illi: «Potero ire cum illo, quoniam novi omnes vias et aliquotiens ivi in Mediam et perambulavi omnes campos eius et montes et omnes commeatus scio». [11]Et dixit ei: «Frater, ex qua patria es et ex qua tribu? Narra mihi, frater». [12]Et ille dixit: «Quid tibi necesse est tribus?». Et dixit ei: «Volo scire ex veritate cuius sis et nomen tuum». [13]Et dixit: «Ego sum Azarias Ananiae magni filius, ex fratribus tuis». [14]Et dixit illi Thobi: «Salvus et sanus venias, frater, sed ne irascaris, frater, quod voluerim verum scire et patriam tuam. Tu frater meus es et de genere bono et optimo! Noveram Ananiam et Nathan duos filios Semeliae magni; et ipsi mecum ibant in Ierusalem et adorabant ibi mecum et non exerraverunt. Fratres tui viri optimi sunt; ex bona radice es. Et gaudens venias!». [15]Et dixit ei: «Ego tibi dabo mercedis nomine drachmam diurnam et, quaecumque necessaria sunt tibi et filio meo, similiter; et vade cum illo, [16]et adiciam tibi ad mercedem». [17]Et dixit illi: «Ibo cum illo, ne timueris; salvi ibimus et salvi revertemur ad te, quoniam via tuta est». Et dixit ei: «Benedictio sit

p. Gk *he*

flocks and the tithes of our produce. They did not go astray in the error of our brethren. My brother, you come of good stock. [14]But tell me, what wages am I to pay you—a drachma a day, and expenses for yourself as for my son? [15]And besides, I will add to your wages if you both return safe and sound." So they agreed to these terms.

Mt 20:2

[16]Then he said to Tobias, "Get ready for the journey, and good success to you both." So his son made the preparations for the journey. And his father said to him, "Go with this man; God who dwells in heaven will prosper your way, and may his angel attend you." So they both went out and departed, and the young man's dog was with them.

[17]But Anna,[q] his mother, began to weep, and said to Tobit, "Why have you sent our child away? Is he not the staff of our hands as he goes in and out before us? [18]Do not add money to money, but consider it as rubbish as compared to our child. [19]For the life that is given to us by the Lord is enough for us." [20]And Tobit said to her, "Do not worry, my sister; he will return safe and sound, and your eyes will see him. [21]For a good angel will go with him; his journey will be successful, and he will come back safe and sound." So she stopped weeping.

Gen 24:7,40
Ex 23:20

1 Cor 4:1

Tobias sets out for Media. The fish from the Tigris river

6 [1]Now as they proceeded on their way they came at evening to the Tigris river and camped there. [2]Then the young man went

---

6:1–8. The incident of the fish and Tobias' conversation with the angel help to show that everything that happens to them is part of divine providence: the fish's innards will be used to cure Tobit's blindness (11:8–12) and to cause the demon to flee (8:3). We can also see a deeper symbolism in this episode: the waters of the river and the fish are adverse forces which attract

tibi, frater!». Et vocavit filium suum et dixit illi: «Fili, praepara, quae ad viam, et exi cum fratre tuo. Deus autem, qui in caelo est, protegat vos ibi et reducat vos ad me salvos; et angelus illius comitetur vos cum sanitate, fili!». Et exiit, ut iret viam suam, et osculatus est patrem suum et matrem. Et dixit illi Thobi: «Vade sanus!». [18]Et lacrimata est mater illius et dixit Thobi: «Quid dimisisti filium meum? Nonne ipse est virga manus nostrae et ipse intrat et exit coram nobis? [19]Pecunia ne adveniat pecuniae, sed purgamentum sit filii nostri. [20]Quomodo datum est nos a Domino vivere, hoc sufficiebat nobis». [21]Et dixit illi: «Noli computare: salvus ibit filius noster et salvus revertetur ad nos, et oculi tui videbunt eum illa die, qua venerit ad te sanus. Ne computaveris, ne timueris de illis, soror. [22]Angelus enim bonus ibit cum illo, et bene disponetur via illius, et revertetur sanus». **[6]** [1]Et cessavit plorare. [2]Et profectus est puer et angelus cum illo; et canis exiit cum illo et secutus est eos. Et abierunt ambo, et comprehendit

q. Other authorities omit *Anna*

down to wash himself. A fish leaped up from the river and would have swallowed the young man; [3]and the angel said to him, "Catch the fish." So the young man seized the fish and threw it up on the land. [4]Then the angel said to him, "Cut open the fish and take the heart and liver and gall and put them away safely." [5]So the young man did as the angel told him; and they roasted and ate the fish.

And they both continued on their way until they came near to Ecbatana. [6]Then the young man said to the angel, "Brother Azarias, of what use is the liver and heart and gall of the fish?" [7]He replied, "As for the heart and liver, if a demon or evil spirit gives trouble to any one, you make a smoke from these before the man or woman, and that person will never be troubled again. [8]And as for the gall, anoint with it a man who has white films in his eyes, and he will be cured."

Arrival in Media

Tob 8:4–8

[9]When they approached Ecbatana,[r] [10]the angel said to the young man, "Brother, today we shall stay with Raguel. He is your

---

and at the same time spell danger for the young and inexperienced Tobias; but he manages to control them and press them into service by doing what the angel says.

6:9–17. According to the Law (cf. Num 36:1–13), when a daughter inherits from her father (cf. Num 27:1–11) she should marry a man of her own tribe, in order to ensure that her inheritance does not (as a dowry) become the property of another tribe. It is up to Tobias to marry Sarah because he is the closest relative (the text does not say whether the earlier husbands were relatives). The angel points out the advantages of complying with that law: Tobias will get Sarah's inheritance, but he will also get a beautiful and sensible wife; he encourages him not to delay (v. 12).

Tobias raises weighty objections, not just because he is afraid he will suffer the fate of the other husbands but

illos prima nox; et manserunt super flumen Tigrin. [3]Et descendit puer lavare pedes in flumen, et exsiliens piscis de aqua magnus volebat gluttire pedem pueri, et exclamavit. [4]Et ait illi angelus: «Comprehende et tene!». Et comprehendit puer piscem et eduxit illum in terram. [5]Et dixit angelus illi: «Exintera hunc piscem et tolle fel et cor et iecur illius et repone ea tecum et interanea proice. Sunt enim fel et cor et iecur eius ad medicamentum utilia». [6]Et exinterans puer piscem illum collegit fel, cor et iecur; et piscem assavit et manducavit et reliquit ex illo salitum. Et abierunt ambo pariter, donec appropinquarent ad Mediam. [7]Et tunc interrogavit puer angelum et dixit ei: «Azaria frater, quod remedium est in corde et iecore piscis et in felle?». [8]Et dixit illi: «Cor et iecur piscis fumiga coram viro aut muliere, qui occursum daemonii aut spiritus nequissimi habet, et fugiet ab illo omnis occursus, et ne maneant cum illo in aeternum. [9]Et fel ad inungendos oculos hominis, in quos ascenderunt albugines, ad flandum in ipsis super albugines, et ad sanitatem perveniunt». [10]Et postquam intravit in Mediam et iam

r. Other authorities read *Rages*

relative, and he has an only daughter named Sarah. I will suggest that she be given to you in marriage, [11]because you are entitled to her and to her inheritance, for you are her only eligible kinsman. [12]The girl is also beautiful and sensible. Now listen to my plan. I will speak to her father, and as soon as we return from Rages we will celebrate the marriage. For I know that Raguel, according to the law of Moses, cannot give her to another man without incurring the penalty of death, because you rather than any other man are entitled to the inheritance."

Deut 25:5–10

Num 36:1–13

[13]Then the young man said to the angel, "Brother Azarias, I have heard that the girl has been given to seven husbands and that each died in the bridal chamber. [14]Now I am the only son my father has, and I am afraid that if I go in I will die as those before

---

because he feels a duty to his elderly parents (vv. 14–15)—as indeed the Law lays down. The angel tells him how these difficulties can be dealt with: he reminds Tobias of his father's instruction (v. 15; 4:12) and tells him how to deal with the demon (vv. 16–17), not only by using parts of the fish but also by having recourse to prayer (v. 17). The words "she was destined for you from all eternity" (v. 17) show that the love between the two young people which leads them to marriage is being guided by divine providence and is part of a mysterious plan of God's, an eternal plan. This is borne out by the fact that Tobias falls in love with the girl even before meeting her (v. 18). St J. Escrivá advises young people to put themselves under the protection of the archangel Raphael: "How frankly you laughed when I advised you to put the years of your youth under the protection of Saint Raphael: 'so that he'll lead you, like young Tobias, to a holy marriage, with a girl who is good and pretty and rich', I told you, jokingly. And then how thoughtful you became! . . . when I went on to advise you to put yourself also under the patronage of that young apostle John; in case God were to ask more of you" (*The Way*, 360).

The Vulgate, after v. 16, adds the following: "For they who in such manner receive matrimony, as to shut out God from themselves, and from their mind,

appropinquabat ad Ecbatana, [11]dixit Raphael puero: «Thobia frater!». Et dixit ei: «Ecce ego». Et dixit illi: «In eis, quae sunt Raguel, hac nocte manere nos oportet. Et homo est propinquus tuus et habet filiam nomine Saram, [12]sed neque masculum neque filiam aliam praeter Saram solam habet, et tu proximus es illius prae omnibus hominibus, ut possideas eam; et iustum est, ut possideas, quae sunt patri eius. Et haec puella sapiens et fortis et bona valde, et pater ipsius diligit illam». [13]Et dixit: «Iustum est, ut accipias illam. Et audi me, frater, et loquar de puella hac nocte, ut accipiamus illam tibi uxorem et, cum reversi fuerimus ex Rages, faciemus nuptias eius. Scio autem quoniam Raguel non potest denegare illam tibi. Novit enim quia, si dederit illam viro alteri, morte periet, secundum iudicium libri Moysis, quia tibi aptum est accipere hereditatem et filiam illius magis quam omni homini. Et nunc, frater, audi me, et loquemur de hac puella hac nocte et desponsabimus illam tibi et, cum reversi fuerimus ex Rages, accipiemus illam et ducemus eam nobiscum in domum tuam». [14]Tunc respondens Thobias dixit Raphael: «Azaria frater, audivi quoniam iam tradita est viris septem, et mortui sunt in cubiculis suis noctu; cum intrabant ad illam, moriebantur. Audivi etiam quosdam dicentes quoniam daemonium illos

Tob 3:10 me did, for a demon is in love with her, and he harms no one except those who approach her. So now I fear that I may die and bring the lives of my father and mother to the grave in sorrow on my account. And they have no other son to bury them."

Tob 4:12–13 [15]*But the angel said to him, "Do you not remember the words with which your father commanded you to take a wife from among your own people? Now listen to me, brother, for she will become your wife; and do not worry about the demon, for this very night she will be given to you in marriage. [16]When you enter

Gen 24:44 the bridal chamber, you shall take live ashes of incense and lay upon them some of the heart and liver of the fish so as to make a smoke. [17]Then the demon will smell it and flee away, and will never again return. And when you approach her, rise up, both of you, and cry out to the merciful God, and he will save you and have mercy on you. Do not be afraid, for she was destined for you from eternity. You will save her, and she will go with you, and I suppose that you will have children by her." When Tobias heard these things, he fell in love with her and yearned deeply for her.

---

and to give themselves to their lust, as the horse and mule, which have not understanding: over them the devil hath power. But thou, when thou shalt take her, go into the chamber: and for three days keep thyself continent from her, and give thyself to nothing else but to prayers with her. And on that night lay the liver of the fish on the fire: and the devil shall be driven away. But the second night, thou shalt be admitted into the society of the holy Patriarchs. And the third night, thou shalt obtain a blessing that sound children may be born of you. And when the third night is past, thou shalt take the virgin with the fear of the Lord, moved rather for love of children than for lust: that in the seed of Abraham thou mayst obtain a blessing in children."

occidit [15]et timeo nunc, quoniam diligit illam et ipsam quidem non vexat, sed eum, qui illi voluerit propinquare, ipsum occidit. Unicus sum patri meo; ne forte moriar et deducam patris mei vitam et matris meae cum dolore super me in sepulcrum eorum. Sed neque alium filium habent, qui sepeliat illos». [16]Et dixit illi angelus: «Non es memor mandatorum patris tui, quoniam praecepit tibi accipere uxorem ex domo patris tui? Et nunc audi me, frater: noli computare daemonium illud, sed accipe illam, et scio quoniam dabitur tibi hac nocte uxor. [17]Et cum intraveris in cubiculum, tolle de iecore piscis et cor et impone super cinerem incensi. Et odor manabit, et odorabitur illud daemonium et fugiet et non apparebit circa illam omnino in perpetuo. [18]Et, cum coeperis esse cum illa, surgite primum ambo et orate et deprecamini Dominum caeli, ut detur vobis misericordia et sanitas. Noli timere: tibi enim destinata est ante saeculum, et tu illam sanabis, et ibit tecum, et credo quoniam habebis ex illa filios, et erunt tibi sicut fratres. Noli computare». Et cum audisset Thobias sermones Raphael quoniam soror est illius et de semine patris illius, dilexit eam valde, et cor eius haesit illi. **[7]** [1]Et cum venisset in Ecbatana,

Sarah's hand is sought in marriage

7 [1]When they reached Ecbatana and arrived at the house of Raguel, Sarah met them and greeted them. They returned her greeting, and she brought them into the house. [2]Then Raguel said to his wife Edna, "How much the young man resembles my cousin Tobit!" [3]And Raguel asked them, "Where are you from, brethren?" They answered him, "We belong to the sons of Naphtali, who are captives in Nineveh." [4]So he said to them, "Do you know our brother Tobit?" And they said, "Yes, we do." And he asked them, "Is he in good health?" [5]They replied, "He is alive and in good health." And Tobias said, "He is my father." [6]Then Raguel sprang up and kissed him and wept. [7]And he blessed him and exclaimed, "Son of that good and noble man!" When he heard that Tobit had lost his sight, he was stricken with grief and wept. [8]And his wife Edna and his daughter Sarah wept. They received them very warmly; and they killed a ram from the flock and set large servings of food before them.

Gen 29:4–6; 43:27–30

Gen 33:4; 45:14
Lk 15:20

Then Tobias said to Raphael, "Brother Azarias, speak of those things which you talked about on the journey, and let the matter be settled." [9]So he communicated the proposal to Raguel. And Raguel

---

7:1–12. At this point Tobias takes the initiative and asks the angel to speak on his behalf (v. 8). Raguel is clearly an upright man; he does not hide the situation from Tobias; he does not want the young man to die, so he tries to delay doing what the Law lays down (v. 10). Eventually he consents to the marriage: he will obey the law of Moses (v. 13), despite the possible consequences.

In the Vulgate, Raguel's decision is influenced by something the angel says to him: "Be not afraid to give her to this man, for to him who feareth God is thy daughter due to be his wife. Therefore another could not have her. Then Raguel said: I doubt not but God hath regarded my prayers and tears in his sight. And I believe he hath therefore made you come to me, that this maid

dixit illi: «Azaria frater, duc me ad Raguel, fratrem nostrum, viam rectam». Et duxit eum ad domum Raguel, et invenerunt illum sedentem circa ostium atrii sui et salutaverunt illum priores. Et ille dixit eis: «Bene valeatis, fratres, intrate salvi et sani». Et induxit eos in domum suam. [2]Et dixit Ednae uxori suae: «Quam similis est hic iuvenis Thobi fratri meo!». [3]Et interrogavit illos Edna et dixit eis: «Unde estis, fratres?». Et dixerunt illi: «Ex filiis Nephthali nos sumus captivis in Nineve». [4]Et dixit eis: «Nostis Thobin fratrem nostrum?». Et dixerunt ei: «Novimus illum». Et dixit eis: «Fortis est?». [5]Et dixerunt illi: «Fortis est et vivit». Et Thobias dixit: «Pater meus est». [6]Et exsilivit Raguel et osculatus est illum lacrimans [7]et dixit: «Benedictio tibi sit, fili, boni et optimi patris fili. O infelicitas malorum, quia excaecatus est vir iustus et faciens eleemosynas!». Et incubuit lacrimans super collum Thobiae filii fratris sui. [8]Et Edna uxor eius lacrimata est super eum et Sara filia eorum lacrimata est et ipsa. [9]Et occidit arietem ex ovibus et suscepit illos libenter. Et, postquam laverunt et se purificaverunt et discubuerunt ad cenandum, dixit Thobias ad Raphael: «Azaria frater, dic Raguel, ut det mihi Saram sororem meam». [10]Et audivit Raguel hunc sermonem et dixit puero: «Manduca et bibe et suaviter tibi sit hac nocte. Non

Lk 12:19 said to Tobias, "Eat, drink, and be merry; [10]for it is your right to take my child. But let me explain the true situation to you.

Gen 24:33 [11]I have given my daughter to seven husbands, and when each came to her he died in the night. But for the present be merry." And Tobias said, "I will eat nothing here until you make a binding agreement with me." [12]So Raguel said, "Take her right now, in accordance with the law. You are her relative, and she is yours. The merciful God will guide you both for the best." [13]Then he called his daughter Sarah, and taking her by the hand he gave her to Tobias to be his wife, saying, "Here she is; take her according to the law of Moses, and take her with you to your father." And he blessed them.* [14]Next he called his wife Edna, and took a scroll and wrote out the contract; and they set their seals to it. [15]Then they began to eat.

Gen 24:50–51

Tob 6:12 Gen 24:54

[16]And Raguel called his wife Edna and said to her, "Sister, make up the other room, and take her into it." [17]so she did as he said, and took her there; and the girl[s] began to weep. But the mother comforted her daughter in her tears, and said to her, [18]"Be brave, my child; the Lord of heaven and earth grant you joy[t] in place of this sorrow of yours. Be brave, my daughter."

---

might be married to one of her own kindred, according to the law of Moses: and now doubt not but I will give her to thee."

7:14–18. This is the first time we find in the Bible a formal marriage contract involving a written document. In time, this document will be called by Jews the *Ketubah*. For Sarah's parents the wedding is almost a mournful affair, but they still hope that things will work out well because they have done everything according to the Law of the Lord, whom they invoke.

est enim homo, quem oporteat accipere Saram filiam meam nisi tu, frater. Similiter et mihi non licet eam dare alii viro nisi tibi, quia tu proximus mihi es. Verum autem tibi dicam, fili. [11]Tradidi illam viris septem fratribus nostris et omnes mortui sunt nocte, cum intrabant ad eam. Et nunc, fili, manduca et bibe, et Dominus faciet in vobis». Et dixit Thobias: «Hinc non edam neque bibam, donec, quae sunt ad me, confirmes». Et Raguel dixit ei: «Facio; et ipsa datur tibi secundum iudicium libri Moysis, et de caelo iudicatum est tibi illam dari. Duc sororem tuam; amodo tu illius frater es, et haec tua soror est. Datur tibi ex hodierno et in aeternum. Et Dominus caeli bene disponat vobis, fili, hac nocte et faciat misericordiam et pacem». [12]Et accersivit Raguel Saram filiam suam, et accessit ad illum. Et, apprehensa manu illius, tradidit eam illi et dixit: «Duc secundum legem et iudicium, quod scriptum est in libro Moysis dari tibi uxorem. Habe et duc ad patrem tuum sanus. Et Deus caeli det vobis bonum iter et pacem». [13]Et vocavit matrem eius et praecepit afferri chartam, ut faceret conscriptionem coniugii et quemadmodum tradidit illam uxorem ei secundum iudicium legis Moysis. Et attulit mater illius chartam, et ille scripsit et signavit. [14]Et ex illa hora coeperunt manducare et bibere. [15]Et vocavit Raguel Ednam uxorem suam et dixit illi: «Soror, praepara cubiculum aliud et introduc eam illuc». [16]Et abiens stravit, sicut illi dixit, et introduxit eam illuc et lacrimata est causa illius et extersit lacrimas et dixit illi: [17]«Forti animo esto, filia. Dominus caeli det tibi gaudium pro taedio tuo. Forti animo esto!». Et exiit.

s. Gk *she* **t.** Other authorities read *favour*

Tobias' and Sarah's wedding night

8 [1]When they had finished eating, they escorted Tobias in to her. [2]As he went he remembered the words of Raphael, and he took the live ashes of incense and put the heart and liver of the fish upon them and made a smoke. [3]And when the demon smelled the odor he fled to the remotest parts of Egypt, and the angel bound him. [4]When the door was shut and the two were alone, Tobias got up from the bed and said, "Sister, get up, and let us pray that the Lord may have mercy upon us."* [5]And Tobias began to pray,

"Blessed art thou, O God of our fathers,
and blessed be thy holy and glorious name for ever.
Let the heavens and all thy creatures bless thee.
[6]Thou madest Adam and gavest him Eve his wife
as a helper and support.
From them the race of mankind has sprung.

Tob 6:8,17

Mt 12:22–30, 43–45

Dan 3:26

Gen 2:18

8:1–12. Three things happen in parallel here: the demon flees, chased off by a puff of smoke (which shows how weak he is when man lets himself be guided by the word of God), and the angel binds him; Sarah's father digs a grave for Tobias (this symbolizes those who are guided by human prudence, not trusting in divine providence; they are proved wrong); and Tobias and Sarah spend the night in prayer and win the Lord's blessing: their prayer praises God, recalling the creation of man and woman (cf. Gen 2:18) and implores his blessing.

The Church offers this passage (vv. 5–7) as a reading for the rite of marriage, because it touches on the divine and human aspects of married love. The Second Vatican Council says that "married love is eminently human love because it is an affection between two rooted in the will and it embraces the good of the whole person; it can enrich the sentiments of the spirit and their physical expression with a unique dignity and ennoble them as the special elements and signs of the friendship proper to marriage. The Lord, wishing to bestow special gifts of grace and divine love on it, has restored, perfected, and elevated it. A love like that, bringing together the human and the divine, leads the partners to a free and mutual giving of self, experienced in tenderness and action,

[8] [1]Et cum consummaverunt manducare et bibere, voluerunt dormire et deduxerunt iuvenem et induxerunt eum in cubiculum. [2]Et rememoratus est Thobias sermonum Raphael et sustulit de saccello, quem habebat, cor et iecur piscis et imposuit super cinerem incensi. [3]Et odor piscis prohibuit et refugit daemonium in superiores partes Aegypti. Et abiens Raphael colligavit eum ibi et reversus est continuo. [4]Et exierunt et clauserunt ostium cubiculi. Et exsurrexit Thobias de lecto et dixit ei: «Surge, soror! Oremus et deprecemur Dominum nostrum, ut faciat super nos misericordiam et sanitatem. [5]Et surrexit, et coeperunt orare et deprecari Dominum, ut daretur illis sanitas. Et coeperunt dicere: «Benedictus es, Deus patrum nostrorum, et benedictum nomen tuum in omnia saecula saeculorum! Benedicant tibi caeli et omnis creatura tua in omnia saecula! [6]Tu fecisti Adam et dedisti illi adiutorium firmum Evam, et ex ambobus factum est semen hominum. Et dixisti non esse bonum hominem solum: "Faciamus ei

Thou didst say, 'It is not good that the man should be alone;
let us make a helper for him like himself.'

[7]And now, O Lord, I am not taking this sister of mine because of lust, but with sincerity. Grant that I may find mercy and may grow old together with her." [8]And she said with him, "Amen." [9]Then they both went to sleep for the night.

But Raguel arose and went and dug a grave, [10]with the thought, "Perhaps he too will die." [11]Then Raguel went into his house [12]and said to his wife Edna, "Send one of the maids to see whether he is alive; and if he is not, let us bury him without any one knowing about it."

Surprise shown by Sarah's parents. Their prayer of thanksgiving

[13]So the maid opened the door and went in, and found them both asleep. [14]And she came out and told them that he was alive. [15]Then Raguel blessed God and said,

"Blessed art thou, O God, with every pure and holy blessing.
Let thy saints and all thy creatures bless thee;
let all thy angels and thy chosen people bless thee for ever.
[16]Blessed art thou, because thou hast made me glad.
It has not happened to me as I expected;
but thou hast treated us according to thy great mercy.

---

and permeates their whole lives; besides, this love is actually developed and increased by the exercise of it. This is a far cry from mere erotic attraction, which is pursued in selfishness and soon fades away in wretchedness.

"Married love is uniquely expressed and perfected by the exercise of the acts proper to marriage. Hence the acts in marriage by which the intimate and chaste union of the spouses take place are noble and honourable; the truly human performance of these acts fosters the self-giving they signify and enriches the spouses in joy and gratitude" (*Gaudium et spes*, 49).

8:13–21. The first reaction of Sarah's parents when they see what has happened is to give thanks to God and bless him, praying for the happiness of the young couple. Everything else

adiutorium simile sibi". [7]Et nunc non luxuriae causa accipio hanc sororem meam, sed in veritate. Praecipe, ut miserearis mei et illius, et consenescamus pariter sani». [8]Et dixerunt: «Amen, amen!». [9]Et dormierunt per noctem. Et surgens Raguel accersivit servos secum, et abierunt et foderunt foveam. [10]Dixit enim: «Ne forte moriatur, et omnibus simus derisio et opprobrium». [11]Et, ut consummaverunt fossuram, reversus est Raguel domum et vocavit uxorem suam [12]et dixit: «Mitte unam ex ancillis, et intrans videat an vivat; et, si mortuus est, ut sepeliamus illum, nemine sciente». [13]Et miserunt ancillam et accenderunt lucernam et aperuerunt ostium, et intravit et invenit illos iacentes et pariter dormientes. [14]Et reversa puella nuntiavit eis illum vivere et nihil mali esse. [15]Et benedixerunt Deum caeli et dixerunt: «Benedictus es, Deus, in omni benedictione sancta et munda, et benedicant tibi omnes sancti tui et omnis creatura tua; et omnes angeli tui et electi tui benedicant tibi in omnia saecula! [16]Benedictus es quoniam laetificasti me, et non contigit mihi, sicut putabam, sed secundum magnam misericordiam

[17] Blessed art thou, because thou hast had compassion
on two only children.
Show them mercy, O Lord;
and bring their lives to fulfilment in health and
happiness and mercy."

[18]Then he ordered his servants to fill in the grave.

[19]After this he gave a wedding feast for them which lasted fourteen days. [20]And before the days of the feast were over, Raguel declared by oath to Tobias[u] that he should not leave until the fourteen days of the wedding feast were ended, [21]that then he should take half of Raguel's[v] property and return in safety to his father, and that the rest would be his "when my wife and I die."

Gen 24:54–55
Judg 14:10–18

Further services rendered by Raphael

9 [1]Then Tobias called Raphael and said to him, [2]"Brother Azarias, take a servant and two camels with you and go to

follows on from this: they correct their mistake (v.18) and organize a proper wedding feast. This one goes on twice as long as normal (v. 20), to show what a signal favour the Lord has done. The marriage makes Tobias part of the family. The joy that fills this marriage hints at the joy Christians will have when marriage becomes a sacrament: "Who can find words to describe the happiness of marriage, which the Church joins and commitment confirms, which the blessing seals and angels proclaim, and which God the Father celebrates? [. . .] The two spouses are like siblings, each the servant of the other; they are not separated in any way, neither in body nor in spirit. For truly the two form one flesh, and where there is only one body, there should be only one spirit. [. . .] Christ rejoices in the contemplation of these homes and sends them his peace; where there are two, He is present with them, and where He is, there can be no evil" (Tertullian, *Ad uxorem*, 2, 9).

9:1–6. In the midst of the celebrations, Tobias does not forget the original reason for his journey; he remembers

tuam egisti nobiscum. [17]Et benedictus es, quoniam misertus es duorum unicorum. Fac illis, Domine, misericordiam et sanitatem et consumma vitam illorum cum misericordia et laetitia». [18]Tunc praecepit servis suis, ut replerent fossam priusquam lucesceret. [19]Et praecepit uxori suae, ut faceret panes multos; et abiens ipse ad gregem adduxit vaccas duas et quattuor arietes et iussit consummari eos, et coeperunt praeparare. [20]Et vocavit Thobiam et iuravit illi et dixit ei: «Diebus quattuordecim hinc non recedes, sed hic manebis, manducans et bibens mecum, et laetificabis animam filiae meae multis afflictam doloribus. [21]Et ex eo, quod possideo, accipe partem dimidiam et vade sanus ad patrem tuum. Et alia dimidia pars, cum mortui fuerimus ego et uxor mea, vestra erit. Forti animo esto, fili! Ego pater tuus sum et Edna mater tua; et tui sumus nos et sororis tuae amodo et in perpetuum. Forti animo esto, fili!». **[9]** [1]Tunc accersivit Thobias Raphael et dixit illi: [2]«Azaria frater, adsume tecum hinc servos quattuor et camelos duos et perveni in Rages et vade ad Gabael et da illi chirographum et recipe pecuniam et adduc illum

u. Gk *him* **v.** Gk *his*

Tob 10:1

Gabael at Rages in Media and get the money for me; and bring him to the wedding feast. [3]For Raguel has sworn that I should not leave; [4]but my father is counting the days, and if I delay long he will be greatly distressed." [5]So Raphael made the journey and stayed over night with Gabael. He gave him the receipt, and Gabael[w] brought out the money bags with their seals intact and gave them to him. [6]In the morning they both got up early and came to the wedding feast. And Gabael blessed Tobias and his wife.[x]*

Gen 44:18–34
Lk 15:20

Tobias' parents are concerned over his continued absence

10 Now his father Tobit was counting each day, and when the days for the journey had expired and they did not arrive, [2]he

---

his parents and his duty towards them. Once again the angel comes to his aid, now acting as a faithful servant to do the young man's bidding. Everything goes according to plan. The sacred writer has no interest in the time-scale (Ecbatana was 360 km.—225 miles—from Rages; and the journey would have taken about twenty days): he wants to show how helpful the angel is, and how upright a man Gabael is and how he joins in the wedding celebrations. Prayer flows spontaneously from Gabael's lips, as happens right through the book. The presence of the angel has proved to be the main factor in accomplishing what Tobias set out to do: "I ask our Lord that, during our stay on this earth of ours, we may never be parted from our divine travelling companion. To ensure this, let us also become firmer friends of the Holy Guardian Angels. We all need a lot of company, company from heaven and company on earth. Have great devotion to the Holy Angels! Friendship is a very human thing, but it is also very much a thing of God; just as our life is both human and divine. Don't you remember what our Lord says? 'I no longer call you servants, but friends'" (St J. Escrivá, *Friends of God*, 315).

10:1–7. Back at Nineveh, Tobit is hopeful, inventing reasons why his son

tecum ad nuptias. [3]Scis enim quoniam numerat dies pater et, si tardavero diem unum, contristabo eum valde. [4]Sed vides quomodo Raguel iuraverit, cuius iuramentum spernere non possum». [5]Et abiit Raphael et quattuor pueri et duo cameli in Rages Mediae, et manserunt penes Gabael, et dedit illi Raphael chirographum eius et indicavit illi de Thobia filio Thobis quoniam accepit uxorem filiam Raguel et quia rogat illum ad nuptias. Et surrexit Gabael et protulit folles cum sigillis suis et numeravit pecuniam et composuit supra camelos. [6]Et vigilaverunt simul et venerunt ad nuptias et intraverunt in ea, quae Raguel, et invenerunt Thobiam discumbentem. Et exsiliit et salutavit illum et lacrimatus est et benedixit eum et dixit illi Gabael: «Benedictus Dominus, qui dedit tibi pacem, quoniam boni et optimi et iusti viri et eleemosynas facientis filius es! Det tibi benedictionem Dominus caeli et uxori tuae et patri tuo et matri tuae et patri et matri uxoris tuae. Et benedictus Deus, quoniam video Thobiam consobrinum meum similem illi!». **[10]** [1]Et cotidie ex illo die computabat Thobi dies, in quibus iret et in quibus reverteretur filius eius. Et, postquam consummati sunt dies, et filius eius non veniebat, [2]dixit: «Numquid detentus est ibi? Aut numquid Gabael mortuus est, et nemo illi reddit pecuniam?». [3]Et contristari coepit.

w. Gk *he* **x.** Cn: Gk *And Tobias blessed his wife*

said, "Is it possible that he has been detained?[y] Or is it possible that Gabael has died and there is no one to give him the money?" [3]And he was greatly distressed. [4]And his wife said to him, "The lad has perished; his long delay proves it." Then she began to mourn for him, and said,[5] "Am I not distressed, my child, that I let you go, you who are the light of my eyes?" [6]But Tobit said to her, "Be still and stop worrying; he is well." [7]And she answered him, "Be still and stop deceiving me; my child has perished." And she went out every day to the road by which they had left; she ate nothing in the daytime, and throughout the nights she never stopped mourning for her son Tobias, until the fourteen days of the wedding feast had expired which Raguel had sworn that he should spend there.

Gen 45:26

Gen 24:54–61

Farewells in Media

At that time Tobias said to Raguel, "Send me back, for my father and mother have given up hope of ever seeing me again." [8]But his father-in-law said to him, "Stay with me, and I will send

---

should be so long in returning; but Anna can only think the worst. Tobit is the one who is blind (physically), but his wife's soul is blind because she has lost confidence in God. Christian ascetical tradition points to this paradox: someone who trusts in the Lord can always see clearly even though external factors present a different picture: "Therefore, we must be completely convinced and cry aloud not only from our mouths but also with our hearts: *the Lord is my light and my salvation, whom shall I fear?* If it is he who enlightens and saves me, of whom will I be afraid? When the darkness of deception falls: *the Lord is my light*. It may come, but it comes in vain; for although darkness may attack our hearts it will not triumph. And the blindness of evil desires may come: *the Lord is my light*. He is, above all, our strength; he who gives himself to us, and to whom we give ourselves. Seek out the doctor while you can; a time may come when you will want to see him but be unable to go" (St John Mediocre of Naples, *Sermons*, 18).

[4]Et Anna uxor illius dixit: «Periit filius meus et iam non est inter vivos. Quare tardat?». Et coepit plorare et lugere filium suum et dixit: [5]«Vae mihi, fili, quia te dimisi ire, lumen oculorum meorum!». [6]Cui Thobi dicebat: «Tace, noli computare, soror; salvus est filius noster, sed certe mora fuit illis ibi, et homo, qui cum illo ivit, fidelis est et est ex fratribus nostris. Noli taediare pro illo, soror, iam veniet». [7]Et illa dixit: «Tace a me; noli me seducere! Periit filius meus». Et exsiliens circumspiciebat cotidie viam, qua filius eius profectus erat, et nihil gustabat; et, cum occidisset sol, introibat et lugebat lacrimans tota nocte et non dormiebat. Et, ut consummati sunt quattuordecim dies nuptiarum, quos iuraverat Raguel facere filiae suae, exiit ad illum Thobias et dixit: «Dimitte me. Scio enim quia pater meus et mater mea non credunt se adhuc visuros me. Nunc itaque peto, pater, ut dimittas me, et eam ad patrem meum; iam tibi indicavi quomodo illum reliquerim». [8]Et dixit Raguel Thobiae: «Remane, fili, remane penes me, et

y. One Gk Ms Lat: Gk *they are put to shame* or *they are disappointed*

Gen 24:35; 30:43

Gen 45:28

messengers to your father, and they will inform him how things are with you." [9]Tobias replied, "No, send me back to my father." [10]So Raguel arose and gave him his wife Sarah and half of his property in slaves, cattle, and money. [11]And when he had blessed them he sent them away, saying, "The God of heaven will prosper you, my children, before I die." [12]He said also to his daughter, "Honour your father-in-law and your mother-in-law; they are now your parents. Let me hear a good report of you. " And he kissed her. And Edna said to Tobias, "The Lord of heaven bring you back safely, dear brother, and grant me to see your children by my daughter Sarah, that I may rejoice before the LORD. See, I am entrusting my daughter to you; do nothing to grieve her."

3. IN NINEVEH AGAIN. TOBIT'S CURE. HIS OLD AGE*

Arrival in Nineveh and cure of Tobit

11 [1]After this Tobias went on his way, praising God because he had made his journey a success. And he blessed Raguel and his wife Edna.

10:8–13. Here again Tobias' love for his parents is very evident, and his determination to do his duty by them, despite Raguel's efforts to have him delay his departure (v. 8). The words of farewell and sound advice from Sarah's parents underline the respect and love due to parents and in-laws, as also the care and affection a husband should have for his wife. Although they are sad to see their daughter leave, Sarah's parents cherish the hope that they will see her again, once Tobias has done his filial duty (v. 12). As regards honouring one's parents, the *Catechism of the Catholic Church*, 2197, says: "The fourth commandment opens the second table of the Decalogue. It shows us the order of charity. God has willed that, after him, we should honour our parents to whom we owe life and who have handed on to us the knowledge of God. We are obliged to honour and respect all those whom God, for our good, has vested with his authority."

ego nuntios mitto ad Thobin patrem tuum, et indicabunt illi de te». [9]Et dixit illi: «Minime; peto, ut dimittas me hinc ad patrem meum». [10]Et surgens Raguel tradidit Thobiae Saram uxorem eius et dimidiam partem substantiae suae, pueros et puellas, oves et boves, asinos et camelos, vestem et pecuniam et vasa. [11]Et dimisit illos et vale illi fecit et dixit illi: «Sanus sis, fili, et vade sanus! Dominus caeli bene dirigat vias vestras; et videam ex vobis filios, antequam moriar». [12]Et osculatus est Saram filiam suam et dixit illi: «Filia, honorem habe socero tuo et socrui tuae, quia ipsi amodo sunt parentes tui tamquam hi qui te genuerunt. Vade in pacem, filia! Audiam de te auditionem bonam in vita mea». Et osculatus est eam et dimisit illos. Et Edna dixit Thobiae: «Fili et frater dilecte, te restituat Dominus caeli, et videam filios tuos et Sarae filiae meae, antequam moriar, ut delecter coram Domino. Ego trado tibi filiam meam tamquam depositum, ut non vexes eam omnibus diebus vitae tuae. Vade, fili, in pacem.

So he continued on his way until they came near to Nineveh. [2]Then Raphael said to Tobias, "Are you not aware, brother, of how you left your father? [3]Let us run ahead of your wife and prepare the house. [4]And take the gall of the fish with you." So they went their way, and the dog went along behind them.

Gen 46:28

[5]Now Anna sat looking intently down the road for her son. [6]And she caught sight of him coming, and said to his father, "Behold, your son is coming, and so is the man who went with him!"

[7]Raphael said, "I know, Tobias, that your father will open his eyes. [8]You therefore must anoint his eyes with the gall; and when they smart he will rub them, and will cause the white films to fall away, and he will see you."

***11:1—14:15.** This last part of the story takes us back to Nineveh. The author tells about Tobias' arrival home with Sarah and the angel, and how Tobit is cured of his blindness (11:1–19). The angel has completed his mission (cf. 3:16–17) and can now reveal who he is, and go back to God (12:1–22). Tobit praises God in a long prayer of rejoicing (13:1–18), and, in due course, after giving his son his spiritual testament, he dies (14:1–11). Having done all that piety demands in Nineveh, Tobias and Sarah move to Media to be with Sarah's parents (14:12–15).

The story has a happy ending, befitting Tobit's good works and the mercy of God, who never neglects the righteous. There have been severe trials, but trust in God has been rewarded by special intervention of divine providence through the angel Raphael. This is the main message of the book of Tobias. True, not all painful situations are resolved by angels in the same remarkable way as in the story of Tobit. But we always have angels with us, and they will comfort us if we put our trust in God. We can see this in the life of our Lord: during his passion, an angel of heaven comforted him in the garden of olives (cf. Lk 22:43); but Jesus still had to drink the chalice of suffering and death in order to do his Father's will and bring about the redemption of mankind.

11:1–15a. The scene prior to the travellers' entry into Nineveh (vv. 1–8)

Ego mater tua amodo, et Sara soror tua. Bene dirigamur omnes in ipso omnibus diebus vitae nostrae». Et osculata est ambos et dimisit illos sanos. [13]Et discessit Thobias a Raguel gaudens et benedicens Dominum caeli et terrae, regem omnium, quia direxerat viam eius. Et benedixit Raguel et Ednae uxori eius et dixit eis: «Fiat mihi honorare vos tamquam parentes meos omnibus diebus vitae vestrae». **[11]** [1]Et abierunt viam suam et pervenerunt Charran, quae est contra Nineven. [2]Tunc dixit Raphael: «Scis quomodo dereliquerimus patrem tuum. [3]Praecedamus uxorem tuam et praeparemus domum, dum veniunt». [4]Et processerunt ambo pariter. Et dixit illi: «Tolle tecum fel». Et abiit cum illis canis ex eis, qui sequebantur eum et Thobiam. [5]Et Anna sedebat circumspiciens viam filii sui. [6]Et cognovit illum venientem et dixit patri eius: «Ecce filius tuus venit, et homo, qui cum illo ierat». [7]Et Raphael dixit Thobiae, antequam appropinquaret patri: «Scio quia oculi eius aperientur. [8]Asperge fel piscis in oculis eius; et detrahet medicamentum et decoriabit albugines de oculis eius. Et respiciet pater tuus et videbit lumen». [9]Et occurrit ei Anna et irruit collo filii sui et dixit illi: «Fili, video te; amodo moriar!». Et lacrimata est. [10]Et surrexit Thobi et offendebat pedibus et egressus est ad ostium atrii. Et occurrit illi

Gen 33:4; 45:14; 46:29–30 Lk 2:29; 15:20 Acts 9:18 Tob 10:5 Deut 32:39 Tob 13:2

[9]Then Anna ran to meet them, and embraced her son, and said to him, "I have seen you, my child; now I am ready to die." And they both wept. [10]Tobit started toward the door, and stumbled. But his son ran to him [11]and took hold of his father, and he sprinkled the gall upon his father's eyes, saying, "Be of good cheer, father." [12]And when his eyes began to smart he rubbed them, [13]and the white films scaled off from the corners of his eyes. [14]Then he saw his son and embraced him, and he wept and said, "Blessed art thou, O God, and blessed is thy name for ever, and blessed are all thy holy angels. [15]For thou hast afflicted me, but thou hast had mercy upon me; here I see my son Tobias!" And his son went in rejoicing, and he reported to his father the great things that had happened to him in Media.

Tobit blesses Sarah

[16]Then Tobit went out to meet his daughter-in-law at the gate of Nineveh, rejoicing and praising God. Those who saw him as he

---

is similar to that described earlier, when Tobias and the angel were nearing Ecbatana (cf. 6:10–17), and it connects up with the passage about the start of the journey through the mention of the dog (cf. 5:16). Once again the angel takes the initiative, by telling Tobit how to cure his father. Then (vv. 9–15) everything happens very quickly. Anna is cured of her spiritual blindness on seeing her son, and Tobit of his physical blindness thanks to the angel's wisdom and Tobias' obedience. Tobit launches into a spontaneous prayer, blessing God and all his angels, still not knowing who Raphael is.

11:15b–19. The recovery of the money deposited at Rages (which was why Tobias set off in the first place) pales in importance when Tobias tells his father about his marriage to Sarah (v. 15). Tobit rejoices at his good fortune (v. 16) and welcomes his daughter-in-law, and a new wedding feast is held (vv. 17–19).

Nadab was the nephew of Ahikar. According to the work previously

Thobias, [11]et fel piscis in manu sua, et insufflavit in oculis illius et apprehendit illum et dixit: «Forti animo esto, pater!». Et iniecit medicamentum super eum et imposuit. [12]Et decoriavit duabus manibus suis albugines ab angulis oculorum illius. [13]Et videns filium suum irruit collo eius [14]et lacrimatus est et dixit ei: «Video te, fili, lumen oculorum meorum!». Et dixit: «Benedictus Deus, et benedictum nomen illius magnum, et benedicti omnes sancti angeli eius in omnia saecula, [15]quoniam ipse flagellavit me, et ecce ego video Thobiam filium meum!». Et introivit Thobi et Anna uxor eius in domum gaudentes et benedicentes Deum toto ore suo pro omnibus, quae sibi evenerant. Et indicavit patri suo Thobias, quoniam perfecta erat via illius bene a Domino Deo, et quia attulerat pecuniam et quemadmodum acceperat Saram filiam Raguel uxorem, et quia ecce venit et ipsa in proximo est portae Nineves. Et gavisi sunt Thobi et Anna [16]et exierunt in obviam nurui suae ad portam Nineves. Et videntes Thobin, qui erant in Nineve, venientem et ambulantem cum omni vir tute sua et a nemine manu deductum mirabantur, [17]et confitebatur Thobi et benedicebat magna voce Deum coram illis, quoniam misertus est illius Deus et aperuit oculos eius. Et appropinquavit Thobi ad Saram uxorem Thobiae filii sui et

went were amazed because he could see. [17]And Tobit gave thanks before them that God had been merciful to him. When Tobit came near to Sarah his daughter-in-law, he blessed her, saying, "Welcome, daughter! Blessed is God who has brought you to us, and blessed are your father and your mother." So there was rejoicing among all his brethren in Nineveh. [18]Ahikar and his nephew Nadab[z] came, [19]and Tobias' marriage was celebrated for seven days with great festivity.

The archangel Raphael reveals himself

12 [1]Tobit then called his son Tobias and said to him, "My son, see to the wages of the man who went with you; and he must also be given more." [2]He replied, "Father, it would do me no harm to give him half of what I have brought back. [3]For he has led me back to you safely, he cured my wife, he obtained the money for me, and he also healed you." [4]The old man said, "He deserves it." [5]So he called the angel and said to him, "Take half of all that you two have brought back."

Gen 30:25–31

mentioned (the "Wisdom of Ahikar": cf. the note on 1:21–22) and according to the book of Tobit also (cf. 14:10), Nadab betrayed his uncle. The author of the book of Tobit seems to say that that happened after the events narrated here.

12:1–22. Giving the angel half the money brought from Media shows Tobit's great generosity and Tobias' appreciation of the angel's good offices. The young man attributes all the various favours to the angel (v. 3). But now the focus turns to what Raphael has to say—angelic words and therefore of special significance. Commenting on this book, St Ambrose highlights the virtues that make Tobit a model of righteousness and good works: "But that holy man Tobit [. . .] understood that the servant too must be paid a just wage. He offered half of what he owned, and it is no coincidence that the

benedixit illi et dixit ei: «Intres sana, filia! Et benedictus Deus tuus, qui adduxit te ad nos, filia! Et benedictus pater tuus et benedictus Thobias filius meus et benedicta tu, filia! Intra in domum tuam sana in benedictione et gaudio; intra, filia!». In illo die factum est gaudium omnibus Iudaeis, qui erant in Nineve. [18]Et venerunt Achicarus et Nadab ex fratribus illius gaudentes ad Thobiam. Et consummatae sunt nuptiae cum gaudio septem diebus, et data sunt illi munera multa. **[12]** [1]Et, postquam consummatae sunt nuptiae, vocavit Thobi filium suum Thobiam et dixit illi: «Homini illi, qui tecum ivit, reddamus honorem et adiciamus ad mercedem suam». [2]Et dixit illi: «Pater, quantam illi dabo mercedem? Non laedor, si dedero illi ex his, quae mecum contulit, dimidiam partem. [3]Duxit me sanum et uxorem meam curavit et pecuniam mecum attulit et te curavit! Quantam illi dabo mercedem adhuc?». [4]Et dixit illi Thobi: «Iustum est illum, fili, dimidium omnium horum, quae tecum attulit, accipere». [5]Et vocavit illum et dixit: «Accipe dimidium omnium horum, quae tecum attulisti, in mercedem tuam et vade sanus». [6]Tunc Raphael vocavit ambos abscondite et dixit illis: «Deum benedicite et illi confitemini

z. Other authorities read *Nasbas*

Tob 4:7–11
Prov 11:4; 16:8
Sir 29:8–13
Acts 10:2

Sir 3:30
Dan 4:24

Job 33:23–24
Zech 1:12

[6]Then the angel[a] called the two of them privately and said to them: "Praise God and give thanks to him; exalt him and give thanks to him in the presence of all the living for what he has done for you. It is good to praise God and to exalt his name, worthily declaring the works of God. Do not be slow to give him thanks. [7]It is good to guard the secret of a king, but gloriously to reveal the works of God. Do good, and evil will not overtake you. [8]Prayer is good when accompanied by fasting, almsgiving, and righteousness. A little with righteousness is better than much with wrongdoing. It is better to give alms than to treasure up gold. [9]For almsgiving delivers from death, and it will purge away every sin. Those who perform deeds of charity* and of righteousness will have fulness of life; [10]but those who commit sin are the enemies of their own lives.

[11]"I will not conceal anything from you. I have said, 'It is good to guard the secret of a king, but gloriously to reveal the works of

---

servant he hired was an angel. As for you, if you deny a just man his due reward, or worse still a weak man—Woe to him who scandalizes one of these, the least of my little ones—how do you know that you are not defrauding an angel? From the moment that Christ became a child, it became impossible for us to doubt that our servant could be an angel. Give your servant his due, do not deprive him of the reward for his labour, because you yourself are a servant of Christ, who has brought you into his vineyard and has prepared a place in heaven for you" (St Ambrose, *De Tobia*, 24, 91–92).

Tobit and his son feel a reverential fear on finding themselves in the presence of an angel, but Raphael puts them at ease, telling them not to be afraid and showing them that it has all been by the will of God: they should praise God, and put the whole story down in writing (vv. 17–21). Tobit and Tobias do confess the wonderful works of God (v. 22) and the sacred author has done the writing.

Many psalms in the Bible, particularly those of thanksgiving, bear witness to what God has done in the personal life of the psalmist, but the most splendid instance of all is to be found in the Magnificat, the Virgin Mary's prayer of praise after the Annunciation (cf. Lk 1:46–55).

coram omnibus viventibus, quae fecit nobiscum bona, ut benedicatis et decantetis nomini eius; sermones Dei honorifice ostendite et ne cunctemini confiteri illi. [7]Sacramentum regis bonum est abscondere, opera autem Dei revelare et confiteri honorificum est. Bonum facite, et malum non inveniet vos. [8]Bona est oratio cum ieiunio, et eleemosyna cum iustitia. Melius est modicum cum iustitia quam plurimum cum iniquitate. Bonum est facere eleemosynam magis quam thesauros auri condere. [9]Eleemosyna a morte liberat et ipsa purgat omne peccatum. Qui faciunt eleemosynam, saturabuntur vita; [10]qui faciunt peccatum et iniquitatem, hostes sunt animae suae. [11]Omnem veritatem vobis manifestabo et non abscondam a vobis ullum sermonem. Iam demonstravi vobis et dixi: Sacramentum regis bonum est

a. Gk *he*

God.' [12]And so, when you and your daughter-in-law Sarah prayed, I brought a reminder of your prayer before the Holy One; and when you buried the dead, I was likewise present with you. [13]When you did not hesitate to rise and leave your dinner in order to go and lay out the dead, your good deed was not hidden from me, but I was with you. [14]So now God sent me to heal you and your daughter-in-law Sarah. [15]I am Raphael, one of the seven holy angels who present the prayers of the saints and enter into the presence of the glory of the Holy One."

[16]They were both alarmed; and they fell upon their faces, for they were afraid. [17]But he said to them, "Do not be afraid; you will be safe. But praise God for ever. [18]For I did not come as a favour on my part, but by the will of our God. Therefore praise him for ever. [19]All these days I merely appeared to you and did not eat or drink, but you were seeing a vision. [20]And now give thanks to God, for I am ascending to him who sent me. Write in a book everything that has happened." [21]Then they stood up; but they saw him no more. [22]So they confessed the great and wonderful works of God, and acknowledged that the angel of the Lord had appeared to them.

Acts 10:4
Rev 8:3–4
Job 1–2
Tob 3:17
Zech 4:10
Mt 18:10
Lk 1:19
Rev 8:2
Judg 13:20–22
Judg 13:16,20
Lk 24:41–43
Jn 16:5
Jn 20:17

Tobias' song of praise

13 [1]Then Tobit wrote a prayer of rejoicing, and said:
"Blessed is God who lives for ever,
and blessed is his kingdom.
[2] For he afflicts, and he shows mercy;
he leads down to Hades, and brings up again,
and there is no one who can escape his hand.

1 Chron 29:10
Tob 3:11; 8:5,15
Ps 144:1
Dan 3:26
Lk 1:68
Eph 1:3
Deut 32:39
1 Sam 2:6
Wis 16:13,15
Dan 3:26

13:1–18. The content of this canticle, as can be seen from v. 9 onwards, is not in line with the historical context in which the writer has set his story, that is, the time when the Israelites were deported to Assyria in the eighth century BC. The hymn implies that Jerusalem has been destroyed and the Jews are captive in Babylon (which happened in the sixth century BC). It is couched in such terms that it can be recited by Jews of the diaspora in any set of circumstances—and that may explain why the text varies so much from one ancient codex to another. (There is in fact considerable divergence between

abscondere, opera autem Dei revelare honorificum est. [12]Et nunc, quando orabas tu et Sara, ego obtuli memoriam orationis vestrae in conspectu claritatis Domini; et, cum sepeliebas mortuos, similiter. [13]Et quia non es cunctatus exsurgere et relinquere prandium tuum et abisti et sepelisti mortuum, tunc missus sum ad te tentare te. [14]Et iterum me misit Deus curare te et Saram nurum tuam. [15]Ego sum Raphael, unus ex septem angelis sanctis, qui assistimus et ingredimur ante claritatem Domini». [16]Et conturbati sunt ambo et ceciderunt in faciem suam et timuerunt. [17]Et dixit illis: «Nolite timere; pax vobis. Deum

Deut 30:3
Wis 14:3
Sir 23:1,4
Is 63:16; 64:7
Jer 3:4
Mt 6:9

Deut 30:2
1 Tim 1:17

[3] Acknowledge him before the nations, O sons of Israel;
for he has scattered us among them.
[4] Make his greatness known there,
and exalt him in the presence of all the living;
because he is our Lord and God, he is our Father for ever.
[5] He will afflict us for our iniquities;
and again he will show mercy,
and will gather us from all the nations
among whom you[b] have been scattered.
[6] If you turn to him with all your heart and with all your soul,
to do what is true before him,
then he will turn to you and will not hide his face from you.
But see what he will do with you;
give thanks to him with your full voice.

---

the RSV and the New Vulgate, and also among the ancient Greek manuscripts. The New Vulgate follows the Old Latin version, using manuscripts which predate the Vulgate.) Verses 11–18 echo phrases from the Psalms and the book of Isaiah which reflect the joy of the exiles on their return to the promised land (cf. Is 66:1–24), the pilgrimages of all the nations to Jerusalem (cf. Is 2:1–5; 60:1), the good fortune of those who have mourned over the city (cf. Is 66:10), and its reconstruction (cf. Is 49:17; 61:4). The passages cited, and the Canticle of Tobit, look forward to the day when all the people will be re-united in a marvellous, newly built Jerusalem (vv. 17–18). This hope will endure until the coming of our Lord Jesus Christ, and the New Testament will project it onto the Church, the new Jerusalem which will appear in glory at the end of time (cf. Rev 21:2—22:15).

benedicite in omne aevum. [18]Cum essem vobiscum, non mea gratia eram vobiscum, sed voluntate Dei. Ipsi benedicite omnibus diebus, decantate ei. [19]Et videbatis me quia nihil manducabam, sed visus vobis videbatur. [20]Et nunc benedicite Dominum super terra et confitemini Deo. Ecce ego ascendo ad eum, qui me misit. Scribite omnia haec, quae contigerunt vobis». Et ascendit. [21]Et surrexerunt et iam non poterant illum videre. [22]Et benedicebant et decantabant Deo et confitebantur illi in omnibus his magnis operibus illius, quia apparuerat illis angelus Dei. **[13]** [1]Et scripsit orationem Thobi in laetitiam et dixit: [2]«Benedictus Deus vivens in aevum, / et regnum illius, / quia ipse flagellat et miseretur, / deducit usque ad inferos deorsum / et reducit a perditione maiestate sua, / et non est qui effugiat manum eius. / [3]Confitemini illi, filii Israel, coram nationibus, / quia ipse dispersit vos in illis / [4]et ibi ostendit maiestatem suam. / Et exaltate illum coram omni vivente, / quoniam Dominus noster, et ipse est pater noster / et ipse est Deus noster in omnia saecula. / [5]Flagellabit vos ob iniquitates vestras / et omnium miserebitur vestrum / et colliget vos ab omnibus nationibus, / ubicumque dispersi fueritis. / [6]Cum conversi fueritis ad illum / in toto corde vestro et in tota anima vestra, / ut faciatis coram illo veritatem, / tunc revertetur ad vos / et non abscondet a vobis faciem suam amplius. / Et nunc aspicite, quae fecit vobiscum, / et confitemini illi in toto ore vestro. / Benedicite Dominum iustitiae / et exaltate regem saeculorum. / Ego in terra captivitatis meae confiteor illi / et ostendo virtutem et maiestatem eius genti

b. Other authorities read *we*

Praise the Lord of righteousness,
and exalt the King of the ages.
I give him thanks in the land of my captivity,
and I show his power and majesty to a nation of sinners.
Turn back, you sinners, and do right before him;
who knows if he will accept you and have mercy on you?
[7] I exalt my God;
my soul exalts the King of heaven,
and will rejoice in his majesty.
[8] Let all men speak,
and give him thanks in Jerusalem.
[9] O Jerusalem, the holy city,
he will afflict you for the deeds of your sons,
but again he will show mercy to the sons of the righteous.
[10] Give thanks worthily to the Lord,
and praise the King of the ages,
that his tent may be raised for you again with joy.
May he cheer those within you who are captives,
and love those within you who are distressed,
to all generations for ever.
[11] Many nations will come from afar to the name of the Lord God,
bearing gifts in their hands, gifts for the King of heaven.
Generations of generations will give you joyful praise.
[12] Cursed are all who hate you;
blessed for ever will be all who love you.
[13] Rejoice and be glad for the sons of the righteous;
for they will be gathered together,
and will praise the Lord of the righteous.
[14] How blessed are those who love you!
They will rejoice in your peace.
Blessed are those who grieved over all your afflictions;

Is 60
Mic 7:19
Rev 21

Is 44:26,28
Amos 9:11
Zech 1:16

Ps 22:27
Is 2:3; 9:1; 49:6; 60:1
Mic 4:2
Zech 8:20–22
1 Tim 1:17
Rev 21:1

Bar 4:31ff

Is 2:3
Mic 4:2
Zech 8:20

Ps 122:6
Is 66:10
Bar 4:31

---

peccatorum. / Convertimini, peccatores, et facite iustitiam coram illo. / Quis scit, si velit vos et faciat vobis misericordiam? / [7]Ego et anima mea regi caeli laetationes dicimus, / et anima mea laetabitur omnibus diebus vitae suae. / [8]Benedicite Dominum, omnes electi, / et, omnes, laudate maiestatem illius. / Agite dies laetitiae et confitemini illi. / [9]Ierusalem, civitas sancta, / flagellabit te in operibus manuum tuarum. / [10]Confitere Domino in bono opere et benedic regem saeculorum, / ut iterum tabernaculum tuum aedificetur in te cum gaudio / et laetos faciat in te omnes captivos / et diligat in te omnes miseros in omnia saecula saeculorum. / [11]Lux splendida fulgebit in omnibus finibus terrae; / nationes multae venient tibi ex longinquo / et a novissimis partibus terrae ad nomen sanctum tuum / et munera sua in manibus suis habentes regi caeli. / Generationes generationum dabunt in te laetitiam, / et nomen electae erit in saecula saeculorum. / [12]Maledicti omnes, qui dixerint verbum durum. / Maledicti erunt omnes, qui deponunt te / et destruunt muros tuos, / et omnes, qui subvertunt turres tuas / et qui incendunt habitationes tuas. / Et benedicti erunt omnes, qui timent te in aevum. / [13]Tunc gaude et laetare in filiis iustorum, / quoniam omnes colligentur / et benedicent Domino aeterno. / [14]Felices, qui diligunt te, / et felices, qui gaudebunt in pace tua. / Et beati omnes homines, / qui contristabuntur in omnibus flagellis

Is 54:11; 62:1–2
Bar 5:1
Hag 2:9
Rev 21:10–21

Rev 19:1

for they will rejoice for you upon seeing all your glory,
and they will be made glad for ever.
[15] Let my soul praise God the great King.
[16] For Jerusalem will be built with sapphires and emeralds,
her[c] walls with precious stones,
and her towers and battlements with pure gold.
[17] The streets of Jerusalem will be paved[d] with beryl and ruby
and stones of Ophir;
[18] all her lanes will cry 'Hallelujah!' and will give praise,
saying, 'Blessed is God, who has exalted you for ever.'"

Tobias' will and death

Gen 47:29
Tob 4:2–3
Is 5:13; 64:10
Jer 9:15
Ezek 12:15; 23
Nahum 1–3
Mt 23:38
Lk 13:35

14 [1]Here Tobit ended his words of praise. [2]He was fifty-eight years old when he lost his sight, and after eight years he regained it. He gave alms, and he continued to fear the Lord God and to praise him. [3]When he had grown very old he called his son and grandsons, and said to him, "My son, take your sons; behold, I have grown old and am about to depart this life. [4]Go to Media, my son, for I fully believe what Jonah the prophet said about Nineveh, that it will be overthrown. But in Media there will be

14:1–11. Tobit is portrayed as having some of the features of the ancient patriarchs: he died at a great age and his last testament is similar to Testaments of the Twelve Patriarchs in an apocryphal book bearing that name. Like those testaments, this one here contains a very short summary of the protagonist's life and then gives his last will, in which he speaks of things which will happen soon and also of later events, when God's promises will finally be fulfilled (vv. 3–7). And, as in the earlier testaments too, Tobit exhorts his heirs to live good lives (vv. 8–11).

Bearing trials, giving alms and blessing God—these features show that there was an excellent balance to

tuis, / quoniam in te gaudebunt / et videbunt omne gaudium tuum in aeternum. / [15]Anima mea, benedic Domino regi magno, / [16]quia in Ierusalem civitate aedificabitur / domus illius in omnia saecula. / Felix ero, si fuerint reliquiae seminis mei / ad videndam claritatem tuam / et confitendum regi caeli. / Ostia Ierusalem sapphiro et smaragdo aedificabuntur, / et lapide pretioso omnes muri tui; / et turres Ierusalem auro aedificabuntur, / et propugnacula eius auro mundo. / [17]Plateae Ierusalem carbunculo sternentur / et lapide Ophir; / [18]et ostia Ierusalem cantica laetitiae dicent, / et omnes vici eius loquentur: "Alleluia. / Benedictus Deus Israel, / et benedicti, qui benedicent nomen sanctum, / in aeternum et adhuc!"». **[14]** [1]Et consummati sunt sermones confessionis Thobis. Et mortuus est in pace annorum centum duodecim et sepultus est praeclare in Nineve. [2]Sexaginta autem et duorum annorum erat, cum invalidus oculis factus est; et, postquam lucem recepit, vixit in bonis et fecit eleemosynas et proposuit benedicere Deum et confiteri magnitudini Dei. [3]Et, cum moreretur, vocavit Thobiam filium suum et praecepit illi dicens: «Fili, duc filios tuos [4]et recurre in Mediam, quoniam credo ego verbo Dei, quod locutus est Nahum in Nineven quia omnia erunt et venient super Assyriam et Nineven, quae locuti sunt prophetae

c. Gk *your* **d.** Or *inlaid*

peace for a time. Our brethren will be scattered over the earth from the good land, and Jerusalem will be desolate. The house of God in it will be burned down and will be in ruins for a time. [5]But God will again have mercy on them, and bring them back into their land; and they will rebuild the house of God,[e] though it will not be like the former one until the times of the age are completed. After this they will return from the places of their captivity, and will rebuild Jerusalem in splendour. And the house of God will be rebuilt there with a glorious building for all generations for ever, just as the prophets said of it. [6]Then all the Gentiles will turn to fear the Lord God in truth, and will bury their idols. [7]All the

Ezra 3:12
Is 35:8–10
Jer 31:38
Ezek 36:24ff
Hag 2:3
Mk 1:15
Gal 4:4

Is 18:7; 19:22
Jer 16:19
Ezek 40–42
Hag 2:9

Tobit's life. His advice to his son—to leave Nineveh and go to Media—stems from Tobit's conviction that the words of the prophets will be fulfilled. He cites Nahum specifically, whose oracles against Nineveh are recorded in the book that bears his name and which is part of the collection of the twelve minor prophets; but the text also reminds one of the prophets in general, including those who later on foretold the fall of Jerusalem, the Babylonian captivity, etc. (Isaiah, Jeremiah, etc.). Tobit's testament also has echoes of voices we know from apocryphal literature, such as the books of Enoch, and which regard the temple rebuilt after the exile as being something provisional. In this sense Tobit is speaking about a distant future when the temple will be built according to the pattern announced by the prophet (cf. Ezek 40–44), and when all the nations of the earth will be converted, all the scattered Israelites brought back, and there will be no more sin (vv. 5–7). Similar ideas occur in the Testaments of the Twelve Patriarchs—and (in even more symbol-laden language) in the book of Daniel (cf. Dan 9:24). Tobit's advice to his son when he warns him about the future catastrophe that will strike Nineveh is somewhat like what Jesus says when he tells his disciples to leave Jerusalem, forewarning them about the misfortunes that will befall the Holy City, which he links with events that will occur at the end of time (cf. Mt 24:15–28 and par.).

Tobit repeats his exhortation to Tobias to leave Nineveh—as soon as he has buried his mother (v. 10); and this time he cites the example of what happened to Ahikar. According to the "Wisdom of Ahikar" (cf. the note on

Israel, quos misit Deus; omnia evenient, nihilque minuetur ex omnibus verbis, sed omnia contingent temporibus suis. Et in Media erit salus magis quam in Assyriis et quam in Babylone, quia scio ego et credo quoniam omnia, quae dixit Deus, erunt. Et perficientur, et non excidet verbum de sermonibus. Et fratres nostri, qui habitant in terra Israel, omnes dispergentur et captivi ducentur a terra optima. Et erit omnis terra Israel deserta, et Samaria et Ierusalem erit deserta, et domus Dei in tristitia erit et incendetur et erit deserta usque in tempus. [5]Et iterum misericordiam faciet illorum Deus et convertetur ad illos Deus in terram Israel, et iterum aedificabunt domum, sed non sicut prius, quoadusque repleatur tempus maledictionum. Et postea revertentur a captivitate sua omnes et aedificabunt Ierusalem honorifice, et domus Dei aedificabitur in ea, sicut locuti sunt de illa omnes prophetae Israel. [6]Et omnes nationes in

e. Gk *house*

Is 60:4,21
Jer 32:37
Ezek 34:28;
36:12;
37:25; 39:26

Gentiles will praise the Lord, and his people will give thanks to God, and the Lord will exalt his people. And all who love the Lord God in truth and righteousness will rejoice, showing mercy to our brethren.

Tob 1:21

[8]"So now, my son, leave Nineveh, because what the prophet Jonah said will surely happen. [9]But keep the law and the commandments, and be merciful and just, so that it may be well with you. [10]Bury me properly, and your mother with me. And do not live in Nineveh any longer. See, my son, what Nadab[f] did to Ahikar who had reared him, how he brought him from light into darkness, and with what he repaid him. But Ahikar was saved, and the other received repayment as he himself went down into the darkness. Ahikar[g] gave alms and escaped the deathtrap which Nadab[h] had set for him; but Nadab fell into the trap and perished.

1:21–22), Ahikar was condemned to death by King Sennacherib through the treachery of his nephew Nadab, but he managed to escape with the help of a friend, and to hide from his nephew. Later on, the king had need of his advice and he rehabilitated him. The reference in the book of Tobit to the case of Ahikar attributes his escape to the fact that he gave alms. This is a theme that runs right through the book: prayer is heard when it is backed up by good works, especially almsgiving: "Those who pray cannont place themselves in the presence of God with empty petitions and no fruit to show. A barren request is worthless in God's eyes. Just as a tree that does not bear fruit is cut down and thrown on the fire, so too an empty promise, prayer that is not rooted in good works, is of no value to God. Thus we are taught in Scripture: '*Prayer is good when accompanied by fasting and almsgiving*' [Tob 12:8]. Prayers watered by the merits of good works rise up directly to God. The angel Rafael testified as much to Tobias" (St Cyprian, *De oratione dominica*, 32–33).

tota terra convertentur et timebunt Deum vere et relinquent omnes idola sua, quae seducunt false seductione eorum. [7]Et benedicent Deo aeterno in iustitia. Omnes filii Israel, qui liberabuntur in diebus illis, memores Dei in veritate, colligentur et venient in Ierusalem et habitabunt in aeternum in terra Abraham cum tutela, et tradetur eis. Et gaudebunt, qui diligunt Deum in veritate; qui autem faciunt iniquitatem et peccatum, deficient de terris omnibus. [8]Et nunc, filii, mando vobis: Servite Deo in veritate et facite coram illo, quod ipsi placet. Et filiis vestris mandabitur, ut faciant iustitias et eleemosynam et ut sint memores Dei et benedicant nomini ipsius in omni tempore in veritate et in tota virtute sua. [9]Nunc vero, fili, exi a Nineve et noli manere hic, [10]sed, quocumque die sepelieris matrem tuam circa me, eodem die noli manere in finibus eius. Video enim quia multa iniquitas est in illa, et fictio multa perficitur in illa, et non confunduntur. Vide, fili, quae fecit Nadab Achicaro, qui eum nutrivit. Nonne vivus deductus est in terram? Sed tradidit Deus infamiam ante faciem ipsius, et Achicarus exiit ad lucem, Nadab autem intravit in tenebras aeternas, quia quaesivit occidere Achicarum. Cum faciebat eleemosynam, exiit de laqueo mortis, quem fixerat ei Nadab, et Nadab cecidit in laqueum mortis, et

f. Other authorities read *Aman* **g.** Other authorities read *Manasses* **h.** Gk *he*

[11]So now, my children, consider what almsgiving accomplishes and how righteousness delivers." As he said this he died in his bed. He was a hundred and fifty-eight years old; and Tobias[h] gave him a magnificent funeral.

Tobit and Sarah move to Media

[12]And when Anna died he buried her with his father. Then Tobias returned with his wife and his sons to Ecbatana, to Raguel his father-in-law. [13]He grew old with honour, and he gave his father-in-law and mother-in-law magnificent funerals. He inherited their property and that of his father Tobit. [14]He died in Ecbatana of Media at the age of a hundred and twenty-seven years. [15]But before he died he heard of the destruction of Nineveh, which Nebuchadnezzar and Ahasuerus had captured. Before his death he rejoiced over Nineveh.

Gen 49:31
Tob 4:4

Ps 137:8
Nahum 1–3

14:12–15. The book ends by showing Tobias to be a model son towards his parents and in-laws, and that for this he is rewarded (vv. 13–14). By pointing out that the prophecies about the fall of Nineveh came true (the city was destroyed by Kyaxares, king of the Medes, in alliance with Nebuchadnezzar of Babylon, in 612 BC), the sacred writer is effectively saying that the other prophecies will also come true—those concerning the rebuilding of the temple and the reunification of all the Jews: hence Tobias' rejoicing.

perdidit illum. [11]Et nunc, filii, videte quid faciat eleemosyna et quid faciat iniquitas, quoniam occidit. Et ecce anima mea deficit!». Et posuerunt eum super lectum, et mortuus est et sepultus est praeclare. [12]Et, cum mortua est mater eius, Thobias sepelivit eam iuxta patrem suum et abiit ipse et uxor eius in Mediam et habitavit in Ecbatanis cum Raguel socero suo. [13]Et curam habuit senectutis eorum honorifice et sepelivit illos in Ecbatanis Mediae et hereditatem percepit domus Raguel et Thobis patris sui. [14]Et mortuus est annorum centum decem et septem cum claritate. [15]Et, antequam moreretur, vidit et audivit perditionem Nineves et vidit captivitatem illius in Mediam adductam, quam adduxit Asuerus rex Mediae, et benedixit Deum in omnibus, quae fecit filiis Nineves et Assyriae. Et gavisus est, antequam moreretur, in Nineve, et benedixit Dominum Deum in omnia saecula saeculorum.

h. Gk *he*

JUDITH

Introduction

The book of Judith is one of the "deutercanonical" books of the Old Testament, that is, it does not form part of the Hebrew canon. The extant manuscripts are in Greek and are thought to be a translation of an original Semitic text (Hebrew or Aramaic). Some translations, such as the old translation into Latin (the Vetus Latina) and the Syriac, derive from the Greek (as does the RSV). St Jerome's Vulgate seems to have been a revision of earlier Latin translations made with an eye on an Aramaic text.

1. STRUCTURE AND CONTENT

This book is a paean expressing hope in God who does not forget his people, particularly when they are in difficulty, and who comes to their rescue when he is invoked with an upright heart.

The book could be said to divide into two parts:

1. THE ISRAELITES ARE BESET BY A POWERFUL ENEMY (1:1—7:32). The text describes the campaign of a powerful army headed for Jerusalem; not far from its objective, it besieges the Israelites in the city of Bethulia. First we are told how fear-stricken everyone was by Nebuchadnezzar's military might (1:1–16) and of the impressive advance of his army led by Holofernes (2:1—3:10), drawing ever closer to the Israelites—and how they implored God to help them (4:1–15). When Holofernes draws near Bethulia and is discussing strategy with various commanders, one of them, Achior, the Ammonite leader, tells him about the greatness of the God of Israel (5:1—6:21). Eventually, the siege of Bethulia becomes so severe that its inhabitants are at the point of surrendering (7:1–32).

2. GOD CONFOUNDS HIS ENEMIES THROUGH THE ACTION OF JUDITH (8:1—16:25). In this desperate situation, Judith prays trustingly to God, begging him to back her plans to save her people (8:1—9:14). She embarks on a daring and dangerous venture. She goes out of the city and heads for the enemy camp, where she manages to gain access to Holofernes. After a banquet given by Holofernes, when the general is in a drunken sleep, Judith seizes the opportunity to cut off his head, which she then brings to Bethulia in a bag (10:1—13:20). Achior the Ammonite was given refuge by the Israelites after

his expulsion from the enemy camp by Holofernes, and, as soon as he sees what has happened, he professes his faith in God and is made a member of the house of Israel (14:1–10). The huge army, which had overrun many cities and threatened Israel, disintegrates (14:11—15:7). The book ends by exalting the figure of Judith. She, for her part, after going up to Jerusalem with all the people, dedicates her share of the booty to God; then she returns to Bethulia where she spends the rest of her long life a contented woman, honoured and esteemed by all the people (15:8—16:25).

2. COMPOSITION

It is very difficult to say exactly when this book was written, because its literary genre is so unusual that the story itself provides no reliable points of reference. For example, it speaks of Nebuchadnezzar, king of Nineveh, as reigning shortly after the Jews returned from exile and rebuilt the temple, whereas in fact Nebuchadnezzar was king of Babylon and it was he who sent the Jews into exile. There are expressions in the text which are typical of the Persian period—"prepare earth and water" (2:7), "the God of heaven" (5:8), the names of Holofernes and Bagoas (cf. 13:1) etc.—but there are also many Greek elements—the *gerusia* (senate) of Jerusalem (cf. 11:14), the use of garlands (cf. 3:7), the reference to a king (Nebuchadnezzar) being a god (cf. 3:8), etc. Besides, it is difficult to work out the geography of the story and the place-names (including "Bethulia").

In other words, this is not a history book in the sense that we use that word today. Its very particular literary style is full of symbolism: the little city of Bethulia, which resists so heroically, symbolizes all Israel; Judith (whose name means "the Jewess"), young and beautiful, devout and intrepid, stands for the entire people which, armed only with its faith and trust in God, faces up to powerful and skilled enemies, symbolized by Nebuchadnezzar and his lieutenant Holofernes.

The book must have been written around the second half of the second century BC, in the context of the persecution unleashed by Antiochus IV Epiphanes and the Maccabean revolt.

3. MESSAGE

Judith's prayer to the Lord (cf. 9:1–14) holds the theological key to the book: he who has sought to seduce Israel and lead her into idolatry, is himself seduced and vanquished; whereas those who are true to their commitments to God can always count on the Lord's fidelity. The entire story sends a message of hope in the God of Israel, who guides the course of his people's history.

Judith symbolizes faith, whereas Holofernes epitomizes force. Judith has no weapons nor is she skilled in their use, but she is resourceful and strong, thanks to her trust in God. These two characters are a paradigm of the difference between those who rely on human power and those who hope in God. It is the same teaching as given in Psalm 20:8: "Some boast of chariots, and some of horses; but we boast of the name of the Lord our God."

Judith is beautiful and wise (cf. 8:26–28). She is, then, a model of the woman endowed with a wisdom that gives her faith and confidence in God far beyond any human wisdom, be it Babylonian or Greek. But, above all, she is a model of the devout person who undertakes risk in order to help her or his brethren.

Even though human logic would lead one to think that the world is at the mercy of the powerful, the book of Judith invites us to use the logic of God, of which St Paul has this to say: "God chose what is weak in the world to shame the strong, God chose what is low and despised in the world, even things that are not, to bring to nothing things that are, so that no human being might boast in the presence of God" (1 Cor 1:27–28).

However, faith in God does not exclude the need for man to play his part. According to the story, the defeat of the Assyrians results from the resourcefulness of Judith, and not from any spectacular intervention by God. She cleverly uses all the resources available to her, and God enables her to succeed in an enterprise which, humanly speaking, seemed doomed to fail.

4. THE BOOK OF JUDITH IN THE LIGHT OF THE NEW TESTAMENT

Neither the book of Judith nor its heroine is cited explicitly in the New Testament. However, there is a significant allusion to it in the Gospel of St Luke when Elizabeth addresses the Blessed Virgin with the same greeting as Uzziah makes to Judith: "Blessed are you among women" (Lk 1:42; cf. Jud 13:18). On account of this expression, and other qualities of Judith's stressed in the text, the tradition of the Church sees Judith as a type of Mary, because "throughout the Old Covenant the mission of many holy women '*prepared*' for that of Mary".[1] In fact in the Divine Office some passages which sing of this Jewish heroine are applied to the Blessed Virgin (cf. 13:18–20; 15:9).

The Fathers of the Church have seen the book of Judith (and other Old Testament narratives) as an example of the Providence of God, who never leaves his people unprotected. Their writings, like the book of Judith, are very aware of God's preference for what is humble, for what seems of no account, in order to bring to nothing that which seems to be very strong: here, a woman,

1. *Catechism of the Catholic Church*, 489.

who is weaker than man as far as physical strength goes, proves to be stronger on account of her valour and her reliance on God.[2]

Judith is also seen as a model of other virtues. She is an example of courage, of chastity, of trusting prayer in God, and, on account of her firmness in rejecting suitors, she is a model for widows who decide to dedicate their lives to God.

2. St Clement of Rome, *Ad Corinthios*, 55, 3–5; St Ambrose, *De viduis*, 38ff.

1. THE ISRAELITES BESET BY A POWERFUL ENEMY*

Nebuchadnezzar's aggressiveness

1 [1]In the twelfth year of the reign of Nebuchadnezzar, who ruled over the Assyrians in the great city of Nineveh, in the days of Arphaxad, who ruled over the Medes in Ecbatana—[2]he is the king who built walls about Ecbatana with hewn stones three cubits thick and six cubits long; he made the walls seventy cubits high and fifty cubits wide; [3]at the gates he built towers a hundred cubits high and sixty cubits wide at the foundations; [4]and he made its gates, which were seventy cubits high and forty cubits wide, so that his armies could march out in force and his infantry form their ranks—[5]it was in those days that King Nebuchadnezzar made war against King Arphaxad in the great plain which is on the borders of Ragae. [6]He was joined by all the people of the hill country and all those who lived along the Euphrates and the Tigris and the Hydaspes and in

***1:1—7:32.** The book of Judith is an invitation to Israel to place its hope in the Lord, who never fails to come to its aid provided it stays faithful to him. The story it tells ignores history and geography, but it succeeds admirably in its purpose—to convey a theological message. The first part of the book tells of a military campaign in which a powerful foreign army tries to conquer Jerusalem. The army advances, sweeping all before it, and then it comes to Bethulia, a small city, the last defensive position on the way to the Holy City; the army besieges the city, which is on the point of surrendering.

The text stresses that the havoc wrought by the troops derives from King Nebuchadnezzar's vindictiveness: his pride has been wounded, and this he cannot abide. From the very start of the story, our attention is being drawn to the might of the Assyrian army: unaided (because no one wants to be Assyria's ally) it managed to win the war it had embarked on (1:1–16); once victory is achieved, Nebuchadnezzar turns on those who refused to be his allies, sending his general Holofernes with an army to pick off these (now) enemies one by one (2:1—3:10). When the army reaches Jewish territory, the Jews

[1] [1]Anno duodecimo regni Nabuchodonosor, qui regnavit in Assyriis in Nineve civitate magna, in diebus Arphaxad, qui regnavit in Medis in Ecbatanis [2]et aedificavit in Ecbatanis et in circuitu muros ex lapidibus excisis in latitudinem cubitorum trium et in longitudinem cubitorum sex et fecit altitudinem muri cubitorum septuaginta et latitudinem eius cubitorum quinquaginta [3]et turres eius constituit super portas eius cubitorum centum et latitudinem earum fundavit in cubitos sexaginta. [4]Et fecit portas eius portas exsurgentes in altitudinem cubitorum septuaginta et in latitudinem earum cubitis quadraginta in exitum virtutis potentium eius et in dispositiones peditum eius. [5]Et fecit bellum in diebus illis rex Nabuchodonosor ad Arphaxad regem in campo magno, hic est campus in finibus Ragau. [6]Et convenerunt in pugnam omnes inhabitantes montanam et omnes inhabitantes Euphraten et Tigrin et Hidaspen et campos Arioch regis Elymaeorum. Et convenerunt gentes multae valde ad bellum filiorum

the plain where Arioch ruled the Elymaeans. Many nations joined the forces of the Chaldeans.

[7]Then Nebuchadnezzar king of the Assyrians sent to all who lived in Persia and to all who lived in the west, those who lived in Cilicia and Damascus and Lebanon and Antilebanon and all who lived along the seacoast, [8]and those among the nations of Carmel and Gilead, and Upper Galilee and the great Plain of Esdraelon, [9]and all who were in Samaria and its surrounding towns, and beyond the Jordan as far as Jerusalem and Bethany and Chelous and Kadesh and the river of Egypt, and Tahpannes and Ra-amses and the whole land of Goshen, [10]even beyond Tanis and Memphis, and all who lived in Egypt as far as the borders of Ethiopia. [11]But all who lived in the whole region disregarded the orders of

---

are terrified, but they prepare to face him and they implore God to protect them (4:1–15). The situation seems hopeless, yet the reader begins to see light on the horizon. When the enemy commanders are making their plan of attack against the Israelites, a man of influence in the Assyrian camp, Achior the Ammonite, warns that whenever this people stays faithful to its God it never fails to win (5:1—6:21). Despite this, the Assyrians press on; they lay siege to Bethulia, and things get so bad that the inhabitants decide that they must either win within five days or else surrender (7:1–32).

1:1–16. The enemy is portrayed as an amalgam of the powers that caused the fall of Israel and later of Judah—the military might of Assyria (cf. 2 Kings 17:5–6) and the overweening pride of Babylon (cf. 2 Kings 24—25:21). Nebuchadnezzar was not in fact the king of the Assyrians in Nineveh (v. 1). But he was the prototype of the powerful, tyrannical, proud ruler. The sacred author, who is writing a story to convey a message, and is not very interested in history or chronology, uses Nebuchadnezzar as a symbol for the despotic Seleucids who dominated the Jews when this book was being written. The monarch described here is depicted as a proud and powerful king whose rule is expanding right across the Middle East. First he attacks King Arphaxad (whose power is indicated by the size of the walls around his capital, Ecbatana). Nebuchadnezzar tried to get allies to join him in his siege of the city, but he failed to do so, and resolved to take revenge for this in due course. But his army in fact took Ecbatana on its own, which serves to show how strong it was.

Chaldaeorum. [7]Et misit Nabuchodonosor rex Assyriorum ad omnes inhabitantes Persidem et ad omnes inhabitantes ad occasum: inhabitantes Ciliciam et Damascum et Libanum et Antilibanum et ad omnes inhabitantes circa faciem maritimae; [8]et ad eos, qui sunt in nationibus Carmeli et Galaad, et ad superiorem Galilaeam et ad campum magnum Esdrelon; [9]et ad omnes, qui in Samaria et civitatibus eius, et trans Iordanen usque in Ierusalem et Bathanam et Chelus et Cades et flumen Aegypti et Taphnas et Ramesses et omnem terram Gessen, [10]usquedum veniatur supra Tanim et Memphin et ad omnes inhabitantes Aegyptum, usquedum veniatur ad fines Aethiopiae. [11]Et contempserunt omnes inhabitantes

Nebuchadnezzar king of the Assyrians, and refused to join him in the war; for they were not afraid of him, but looked upon him as only one man,[a] and they sent back his messengers empty-handed and shamefaced.

[12]Then Nebuchadnezzar was very angry with this whole region, and swore by his throne and kingdom that he would surely take revenge on the whole territory of Cilicia and Damascus and Syria, that he would kill them by the sword, and also all the inhabitants of the land of Moab, and the people of Ammon, and all Judea, and every one in Egypt, as far as the coasts of the two seas. [13]In the seventeenth year he led his forces against King Arphaxad, and defeated him in battle, and overthrew the whole army of Arphaxad, and all his cavalry and all his chariots. [14]Thus he took possession of his cities, and came to Ecbatana, captured its towers, plundered its markets, and turned its beauty into shame. [15]He captured Arphaxad in the mountains of Ragae and struck him down with hunting spears; and he utterly destroyed him, to this day. [16]Then he returned with them to Nineveh, he and all his combined forces, a vast body of troops; and there he and his forces rested and feasted for one hundred and twenty days.

Esther 1:3–4

Holofernes' campaign

2 [1]In the eighteenth year, on the twenty-second day of the first month, there was talk in the palace of Nebuchadnezzar king of the Assyrians about carrying out his revenge on the whole region,

---

***2:1—3:10.** In search of revenge, Nebuchadnezzar sends Holofernes, his commander-in-chief, on a punitive campaign. "The eighteenth year" of Nebuchadnezzar was 587 BC, the very year when Babylonian troops took Jerusalem, profaned the temple and set it on fire, and deported part of the population (cf. Jer 52:29). The date is highly symbolic: for the sacred writer the destruction of the temple of Jerusalem implied that Nebuchadnezzar

universam terram verbum Nabuchodonosor regis Assyriorum et non convenerunt cum eo in pugnam, quoniam non timuerunt eum, sed erat adversus eos quasi vir unus. Et remiserunt legatos eius vacuos in despectu faciei eorum. [12]Et indignatus est rex Nabuchodonosor ad omnem terram istam vehementer. Et iuravit per thronum et regnum suum se vindicaturum esse omnes fines Ciliciae et Damascenae et Syriae, sublaturum se gladio suo et omnes inhabitantes Moab et filios Ammon et omnem Iudaeam et omnes, qui in Aegypto, usquedum veniatur ad fines duorum marium. [13]Et praeparavit se in virtute sua adversus regem Arphaxad in anno septimo decimo et invaluit in pugna sua et evertit omnem virtutem Arphaxad et omnem equitatum eius et omnes currus ipsius [14]et dominatus est civitatibus eius. Et abiit usque ad Ecbatana et obtinuit turres et praedavit plateas eius et ornatum eius posuit in improperium illius. [15]Et cepit Arphaxad in montibus Ragau et iaculatus est eum iaculis suis et disperdidit eum usque in illum diem. [16]Et reversus est postea in Nineven ipse et commixtura eius, multitudo hominum pugnatorum multa valde. Et erat ibi requiescens et epulans ipse et virtus eius per dies centum viginti. **[2]** [1]Et in anno octavo decimo, secundo et vicesimo die mensis primi factum est verbum Nabuchodonosor regis

a. Or *a man*

just as he said. [2]He called together all his officers and all his nobles and set forth to them his secret plan and recounted fully, with his own lips, all the wickedness of the region;[b] [3]and it was decided that every one who had not obeyed his command should be destroyed. [4]When he had finished setting forth his plan, Nebuchadnezzar king of the Assyrians called Holofernes, the chief general of his army, second only to himself, and said to him,

[5]"Thus says the Great King, the lord of the whole earth: When you leave my presence, take with you men confident in their strength, to the number of one hundred and twenty thousand foot soldiers and twelve thousand cavalry. [6]Go and attack the whole west country, because they disobeyed my orders. [7]Tell them to prepare earth and water, for I am coming against them in my anger, and will cover the whole face of the earth with the feet of my armies,

---

was assuming the prerogatives of divinity, as can also be seen from the fact that he called himself "lord of the whole earth" (2:5).

Holofernes assembles a huge army and sets out on his campaign of destruction and death. The order to "prepare earth and water" (2:7) is a Persian expression meaning everything necessary for a conquering army to move in and establish itself in a country. So, Nebuchadnezzar's intention was to seize these people's territories. Even those who did not resist him were subject to his wrath, the worst aspect of which was that they were forced to worship Nebuchadnezzar and invoke him as a god (cf. Dan 3:1–7). Therefore, the danger that threatened Jerusalem was particularly insidious: not only might its inhabitants be killed or made subject to a foreign power, but they could be forced to render to a man the worship that was due to God alone (3:8). During the period when the Seleucid kings dominated Judea (the first half of the second century BC), the sort of situation described in the book was very much the order of the day—military oppression and attempts to impose king-worship.

The route of the march described in 2:21—3:10 is geographically impossible. The author is exaggerating the feats of Holofernes, to prepare the ground for the religious message he wants to convey.

Assyriorum, ut vindicaret omnem terram, sicut locutus est. [2]Et convocavit omnes famulos suos et omnes magnates suos et posuit cum eis secretum consilii sui et consummavit omne malum terrae ex ore suo; [3]et ipsi iudicaverunt exterminare omnem carnem eorum, qui non sunt obsecuti verbo oris eius. [4]Et factum est, cum consummasset consilium suum, vocavit Nabuchodonosor rex Assyriorum Holofernen principem militiae virtutis suae, qui erat secundus post se, [5]et dixit ad eum: «Haec dicit rex magnus, universae terrae dominus. Ecce tu exies a facie mea et accipies tecum viros fidentes in virtute sua: in centum viginti milia peditum et multitudinem equorum cum ascensoribus duodecim milia; [6]et exies in obviam universae terrae ad occasum, quia non crediderunt verbo oris mei. [7]Et denuntiabis eis, ut praeparent mihi terram et aquam, quoniam ego exeam in ira mea ad eos et cooperiam omnem faciem

b. The meaning of the Greek of the last clause of this verse is uncertain

and will hand them over to be plundered by my troops,[c] [8]till their wounded shall fill their valleys, and every brook and river shall be filled with their dead, and overflow; [9]and I will lead them away captive to the ends of the whole earth. [10]You shall go and seize all their territory for me in advance. They will yield themselves to you, and you shall hold them for me till the day of their punishment. [11]But if they refuse, your eye shall not spare and you shall hand them over to slaughter and plunder throughout your whole region. [12]For as I live, and by the power of my kingdom, what I have spoken my hand will execute. [13]And you—take care not to transgress any of your sovereign's commands, but be sure to carry them out just as I have ordered you; and do not delay about it."

[14]So Holofernes left the presence of his master, and called together all the commanders, generals, and officers of the Assyrian army, [15]and mustered the picked troops by divisions as his lord had ordered him to do, one hundred and twenty thousand of them, together with twelve thousand archers on horseback, [16]and he organized them as a great army is marshaled for a campaign. [17]He collected a vast number of camels and asses and mules for transport, and innumerable sheep and oxen and goats for provision; [18]also plenty of food for every man, and a huge amount of gold and silver from the royal palace. [19]So he set out with his whole army, to go ahead of King Nebuchadnezzar and to cover the whole face of the earth to the west with their chariots and horsemen and picked troops of infantry. [20]Along with them went a mixed crowd like a swarm of locusts, like the dust of the earth—a multitude that could not be counted.

Judg 7:12
Joel 2:2–7,11

[21]They marched for three days from Nineveh to the plain of Bectileth, and camped opposite Bectileth near the mountain which

---

terrae in pedibus virtutis meae et dabo eos in rapinam, [8]et vulnerati illorum replebunt valles eorum, et omnis torrens et flumen inundans mortuis eorum replebuntur. [9]Et adducam captivitatem eorum ad extrema universae terrae. [10]Tu autem exiens praeoccupabis mihi omnem finem eorum, et tradent se tibi, et reservabis mihi in diem redargutionis eorum. [11]Super eos autem, qui non oboediunt, non parcet oculus tuus, ut des eos in occisionem et rapinam in tota terra tua, [12]quoniam vivo ego et potestas regni mei: locutus sum et faciam omnia haec in manu mea. [13]Et tu non praeteries unum verbum domini tui, sed consummans consummabis, sicut praecepi tibi, et non prolongabis, ut facias ea». [14]Et exiit Holofernes a facie domini sui et vocavit omnes praefectos et duces et magistratus virtutis Assyriae [15]et numeravit electos viros in expeditionem, quemadmodum praeceperat ei dominus suus, in centum viginti milia et equitum sagittariorum duodecim milia. [16]Et disposuit eos, quemadmodum belli multitudo constituitur. [17]Et accepit camelos et asinos et mulos ad utensilia eorum, multitudinem magnam valde, et oves et boves et capras in praeparationem eorum, quorum non erat numerus, [18]et epimenia omni viro in multitudinem. Et aurum et argentum de domo regis multum valde. [19]Et exiit a Nineve ipse et omnis virtus eius in profectionem, ut praecederet regem Nabuchodonosor et cooperiret omnem faciem terrae, quae est ad occasum, in quadrigis et equitibus et peditibus electis suis. [20]Et multa mixtura sicut locusta convenerunt cum eis et sicut arena terrae; non enim erat numerus prae multitudine eorum. [21]Et exierunt

c. Gk *them*

is to the north of Upper Cilicia. [22]From there Holofernes[d] took his whole army, his infantry, cavalry, and chariots, and went up into the hill country [23]and ravaged Put and Lud, and plundered all the people of Rassis and the Ishmaelites who lived along the desert, south of the country of the Chelleans. [24]Then he followed[e] the Euphrates and passed through Mesopotamia and destroyed all the hilltop cities along the brook Abron, as far as the sea. [25]He also seized the territory of Cilicia, and killed every one who resisted him, and came to the southern borders of Japheth, fronting toward Arabia. [26]He surrounded all the Midianites, and burned their tents and plundered their sheepfolds. [27]Then he went down into the plain of Damascus during the wheat harvest, and burned all their fields and destroyed their flocks and herds and sacked their cities and ravaged their lands and put to death all their young men with the edge of the sword.

Gen 10:6,13,22

Ex 15:15–16

[28]So fear and terror of him fell upon all the people who lived along the seacoast, at Sidon and Tyre, and those who lived in Sur and Ocina and all who lived in Jamnia. Those who lived in Azotus and Ascalon feared him exceedingly.

3 [1]So they sent messengers to sue for peace, and said, [2]"Behold, we the servants of Nebuchadnezzar, the Great King, lie prostrate before you. Do with us whatever you will. [3]Behold, our buildings, and all our land, and all our wheat fields, and our flocks and herds, and all our sheepfolds with their tents, lie before you; do with them whatever you please. [4]Our cities also and their inhabitants are your slaves; come and deal with them in any way that seems good to you."

---

ex Nineve viam dierum trium super faciem campi Bectileth et posuerunt tabernacula sua a Bectileth iuxta montem, qui est in sinistra superioris Ciliciae. [22]Et accepit omnem virtutem suam, pedites et equites et quadrigas suas et abiit inde in montanam [23]et concidit Phut et Lud et praedaverunt omnes filios Rassis et filios Ismael, qui erant contra faciem deserti ad austrum Chelaeorum. [24]Et trans gressus est Euphraten et transiit Mesopotamiam et diruit omnes civitates excelsas, quae erant ad torrentem Abronam, usquequo veniatur ad mare. [25]Et occupavit terminos Ciliciae et concidit omnes adversantes sibi et venit usque ad terminos Iapheth, qui sunt ad austrum contra faciem Arabiae. [26]Et circuivit omnes filios Madian et succendit tabernacula eorum et praedavit stabula eorum. [27]Et descendit in campum Damasci in diebus messis frumenti et succendit omnes agros eorum; greges et armenta dedit in exterminium et civitates eorum spoliavit et campos eorum ventilavit et percussit omnes iuvenes eorum in ore gladii. [28]Et incidit timor et tremor eius super inhabitantes maritimam, qui erant in Sidone et Tyro, et inhabitantes Sur et Ochina et omnes, qui incolebant Iamniam; et habitantes in Azoto et Ascalone et Gaza timuerunt eum valde. **[3]** [1]Et miserunt ad eum legatos verbis pacificis dicentes: [2]«Ecce nos pueri Nabuchodonosor regis magni adstamus coram te; utere nobis, quemadmodum placet faciei tuae. [3]Ecce villae nostrae et omnis locus noster et omnis campus frumenti et greges et armenta et omnia stabula iumentorum nostrorum adstant ante faciem tuam; utere, quemadmodum placet tibi. [4]Ecce et civitates nostrae et, qui inhabitant in eis, servi tui sunt; veniens occurre eis, sicut est bonum in oculis tuis». [5]Et

d. Gk *he* **e.** Or *crossed*

[5]The men came to Holofernes and told him all this. [6]Then he went down to the seacoast with his army and stationed garrisons in the hilltop cities and took picked men from them as his allies. [7]And these people and all in the country round about welcomed him with garlands and dances and tambourines. [8]And he demolished all their shrines[f] and cut down their sacred groves; for it had been given to him to destroy all the gods of the land, so that all nations should worship Nebuchadnezzar only, and all their tongues and tribes should call upon him as god.

Ex 34:13
2 Chron 17:6

[9]Then he came to the edge of Esdraelon, near Dothan, fronting the great ridge of Judea; [10]here he camped between Geba and Scythopolis, and remained for a whole month in order to assemble all the supplies for his army.

Judea on the alert

2 Chron 36:17–20

4 [1]By this time the people of Israel living in Judea heard of everything that Holofernes, the general of Nebuchadnezzar the king of the Assyrians, had done to the nations, and how he had plundered and destroyed all their temples; [2]they were therefore very greatly terrified at his approach, and were alarmed both for Jerusalem and for the temple of the Lord their God. [3]For they had only recently returned from the captivity, and all the people of

4:1–15. The Israelites are terrified when they hear of Holofernes' advance, and they take steps to resist him—establishing fortresses, stockpiling provisions and stationing their men in strategic positions (vv. 4–8); but they also try to win God's help by means of prayer and penance (vv. 9–15).

The book's message becomes ever more clear: this is primarily a struggle about religion. The enemy army symbolizes the huge impiety and pride of someone who thinks he is almighty and has no need of God; whereas the sons of Israel are devout men who know full well that their strength can come from

venerunt viri ad Holofernen et nuntiaverunt ei secundum verba haec. [6]Et descendit ad maritimam ipse et virtus eius et custodivit civitates excelsas et accepit ex eis in auxilium viros electos. [7]Et exceperunt eum ipsi et omnis circumregio eorum cum coronis et choris et tympanis. [8]Et destruxit omnes fines eorum et lucos eorum excidit, et datum ei erat omnes deos terrae exterminare, ut ipsi soli Nabuchodonosor servirent omnes gentes et omnes linguae et omnes tribus eorum invocarent eum deum. [9]Et venit contra faciem Esdrelon prope Dothain, quae est contra descensum magnum Iudaeae, [10]et castra posuerunt inter Gabaa et Scytharum civitatem. Et erat ibi mensem dierum, ut colligeret omnia utensilia virtutis suae. **[4]** [1]Et audierunt filii Israel, qui habitabant in Iudaea, omnia, quaecumque fecerat gentibus Holofernes princeps militiae Nabuchodonosor regis Assyriorum, et quemadmodum spoliaverat omnia sancta eorum et dederat ea in exterminium. [2]Et timuerunt multum valde a facie eius et pro Ierusalem et pro templo Domini Dei sui turbati sunt, [3]quoniam nuper ascenderant de captivitate et nuper omnis populus Iudaeae collectus erat, et vasa et altare et domus ex commaculatione sanctificata erant.

f. Syr: Gk *borders*

Judea were newly gathered together, and the sacred vessels and the altar and the temple had been consecrated after their profanation. [4]So they sent to every district of Samaria, and to Kona and Beth-horon and Belmain and Jericho and to Choba and Aesora and the valley of Salem, [5]and immediately seized all the high hilltops and fortified the villages on them and stored up food in preparation for war—since their fields had recently been harvested. [6]And Joakim, the high priest, who was in Jerusalem at the time, wrote to the people of Bethulia and Betomesthaim, which faces Esdraelon opposite the plain near Dothan, [7]ordering them to seize the passes up into the hills, since by them Judea could be invaded, and it was easy to stop any who tried to enter, for the approach was narrow, only wide enough for two men at the most.

[8]So the Israelites did as Joakim the high priest and the senate of the whole people of Israel, in session at Jerusalem, had given order. [9]And every man of Israel cried out to God with great fervour, and they humbled themselves with much fasting. [10]They and their wives and their children and their cattle and every resident alien

Acts 12:5
Jon 3:7–8

God alone, and that prayer is the best way to acknowledge their dependence on God: "by prayer of petition we express awareness of our relationship with God. We are creatures who are not our own beginning, not the masters of adversity, not our own last end. We are sinners who as Christians know that we have turned away from our Father. Our petition is already a turning back to him" (*Catechism of the Catholic Church*, 2629).

4:6. There is no geographical evidence that Bethulia existed. What we have here is probably another instance of the freedom taken by the author. He perhaps used some existing stories of heroic deeds to set a scene to convey his message. Some writers think that the name Bethulia may have a symbolic meaning and have the sense of "virgin", "house of the Lord God" or "house of the ascent".

4:9. "Humbled themselves with much fasting": literally, "humbled their souls with fervour": the Greek translation of a Hebrew expression to do with fasting (cf. 4:13; Lev 16:29, 31; 23:27). The Law prescribed fasting only for the day

---

[4]Et miserunt in omnem finem Samariae et in vicos et Bethoron et Abelmain et Iericho et Choba et Aisora et convallem Salem. [5]Et praeoccupaverunt omnes vertices montium excelsorum et muris circumdederunt vicos, qui in eis sunt, et reposuerunt epimenia in praeparationem pugnae, quoniam nuper erant campi eorum demessi. [6]Et scripsit Ioachim sacerdos magnus, qui erat in diebus illis in Ierusalem, inhabitantibus Betuliam et Betomesthaim, quae est supra descensum contra Esdrelon, contra faciem campi prope Dothain, [7]dicens ut obtinerent ascensus montanae, quoniam per eos erat introitus in Iudaeam et erat facile prohibere ascendentes, eo quod angustus esset accessus viris plus quam duobus. [8]Et fecerunt filii Israel, sicut constituerat illis Ioachim sacerdos magnus et seniores totius plebis Israel, qui sedebant in Ierusalem. [9]Et exclamavit omnis vir Israel ad Deum in instantia magna, et humiliaverunt animas suas in ieiunio magno; [10]ipsi et mulieres eorum et infantes eorum et iumenta

and hired labourer and purchased slave—they all girded themselves with sackcloth. [11]And all the men and women of Israel, and their children, living at Jerusalem, prostrated themselves before the temple and put ashes on their heads and spread out their sackcloth before the Lord. [12]They even surrounded the altar with sackcloth and cried out in unison, praying earnestly to the God of Israel not to give up their infants as prey and their wives as booty, and the cities they had inherited to be destroyed, and the sanctuary to be profaned and desecrated to the malicious joy of the Gentiles. [13]So the LORD heard their prayers and looked upon their affliction; for the people fasted many days throughout Judea and in Jerusalem before the sanctuary of the Lord Almighty. [14]And Joakim the high priest and all the priests who stood before the Lord and ministered to the Lord, with their loins girded with sackcloth, offered the continual burnt offerings and the vows and freewill offerings of the people. [15]With ashes upon their turbans, they cried out to the Lord with all their might to look with favour upon the whole house of Israel.

Esther 4:1ff

Esther 4:16

Esther 4:1ff
Joel 2:17

---

of Atonement (Yom Kippur); but according to the teaching of the prophets, fasting as a sign of penance was linked (cf. Joel 1:14; 2:12, 15; Zech 8:19) to other forms of penance, such as prayer, the wearing of sackcloth, putting dust or ashes on one's head, sleeping on the floor, etc. It was meant to show repentance and self-abasement. The prophet Isaiah reminds people that fasting is meant to show one is determined to avoid committing evil (cf. Is 58:3–5). In the post-exilic period, fasting became a common practice among devout Jews, who fasted two days a week (cf. Lk 18:12). We find traces of that custom in 8:5–6 and in Tobias 12:8 and Esther 4:16. When there was a threat of grave public calamity, people had recourse to fasting and prayer to implore God's mercy (cf. Jon 3:5; 2 Mac 13:12).

eorum et omnis advena et mercennarius et argento emptus eorum posuerunt cilicia super lumbos suos. [11]Et omnis vir Israel et mulier et pueri, qui habitabant in Ierusalem, prociderunt ante faciem templi et cineraverunt capita sua et extenderunt cilicia sua contra faciem templi Domini. [12]Et altare cilicio cooperuerunt et clamaverunt ad Deum Israel unanimes instanter, ut non daret in rapinam infantes eorum et mulieres in praedam et civitates hereditatis eorum in exterminium et sancta in maculationem et in improperium, gaudium gentibus. [13]Et audivit Dominus vocem eorum et vidit angustiam eorum; et erat populus ieiunans dies plures in tota Iudaea et Ierusalem, et prociderunt contra faciem sanctorum Domini omnipotentis. [14]Et Ioachim sacerdos magnus et omnes adstantes ante conspectum Domini sacerdotes et deservientes Domino praecincti ciliciis lumbos suos offerebant holocaustum instantiae et vota et voluntaria munera populi. [15]Et erat cinis super cidares eorum, et clamabant ad Dominum ex omni virtute, ut in bonum visitaret omnem domum Israel.

Achior proclaims the greatness of the God of Israel

5 [1]When Holofernes, the general of the Assyrian army, heard that the people of Israel had prepared for war and had closed the passes in the hills and fortified all the high hilltops and set up barricades in the plains, [2]he was very angry. So he called together all the princes of Moab and the commanders of Ammon and all the governors of the coastland, [3]and said to them, "Tell me, you Canaanites, what people is this that lives in the hill country? What cities do they inhabit? How large is their army, and in what does their power or strength consist? Who rules over them as king, leading their army? [4]And why have they alone, of all who live in the west, refused to come out and meet me?"

Num 20:23

Jud 11:9–19

[5]Then Achior, the leader of all the Ammonites, said to him, "Let my lord now hear a word from the mouth of your servant, and I will tell you the truth about this people that dwells in the nearby mountain district. No falsehood shall come from your servant's mouth. [6]This people is descended from the Chaldeans.

[7]At one time they lived in Mesopotamia, because they would not follow the gods of their fathers who were in Chaldea. [8]For they had left the ways of their ancestors, and they worshipped the God of heaven, the God they had come to know; hence they drove them out from the presence of their gods; and they fled to Mesopotamia,

---

5:1—6:21. The account sets Holofernes and his army close to the Israelites, who are ready to repel his attack on their city. To this foreign general the sons of Israel are a people of no significance; he seems to know nothing about them, for before launching his attack he asks for a report, in order to work out his strategy.

Achior, whose name means "my brother is light", gives Holofernes a broad-brush summary of the history of Israel from the time of the patriarchs up to the settlement of Canaan, making reference also to Nebuchadnezzar II's sack of Jerusalem. The Israelites are a special people, he explains; they have not survived through force of arms. His

[5] [1]Et renuntiatum est Holoferni principi militiae virtutis Assyriae quoniam filii Israel praeparaverant se ad pugnam et transitus montanae concluserant et muris cinxerant omnem verticem montis excelsi et posuerant in campis offendicula. [2]Et iratus est iracundia valde et convocavit omnes principes Moab et duces Ammon et omnes magistratus maritimae [3]et dixit eis: «Renuntiate mihi, filii Chanaan: Quis est iste populus, qui sedet in montanis? Quae sunt autem, quas inhabitant, civitates, et quae est multitudo virtutis eorum? Et in quo est potestas et fortitudo eorum, et quis praeest super eos rex, dux militiae eorum? [4]Et quare terga verterunt, ne venirent in obviam mihi prae omnibus, qui inhabitant ad occasum?». [5]Et dixit ad eum Achior dux filiorum Ammon: «Audiat dominus meus verbum ex ore servi tui, et referam tibi veritatem de populo isto, qui inhabitat montana ista iuxta te, et non exibit mendacium ex ore servi tui. [6]Populus hic est ex progenie Chaldaeorum [7]et inhabitaverunt primum in Mesopotamia, quoniam noluerunt sequi deos patrum suorum, qui fuerunt in terra Chaldaeorum praeclari. [8]Et declinaverunt de via parentum suorum et adoraverunt Deum caeli, Deum, quem cognoverunt; et eiecerunt eos a facie deorum suorum et fugerunt in Mesopotamiam et inhabitaverunt ibi dies multos.

and lived there for a long time. [9]Then their God commanded them to leave the place where they were living and go to the land of Canaan. There they settled, and prospered, with much gold and silver and very many cattle. [10]When a famine spread over Canaan they went down to Egypt and lived there as long as they had food; and there they became a great multitude—so great that they could not be counted. [11]So the king of Egypt became hostile to them; he took advantage of them and set them to making bricks, and humbled them and made slaves of them. [12]Then they cried out to their God, and he afflicted the whole land of Egypt with incurable plagues; and so the Egyptians drove them out of their sight. [13]Then

Gen 11:31—12:5
Gen 42:1–5; 46:1–7
Ex 1:7
Ex 1:8–14
Ex 7–12

speech divides into three parts—history of the Jewish people (5:5–16); their strength comes from their faithfulness to God (5:17–19); Holofernes would be wise to ponder carefully before he takes them on (5:20–21). In this summary, no personalities are mentioned and God is not given his specific name but is referred to generally as "God" or "God of heaven" (cf. Ezra 5:11–12). What we have here is a theological view of history, akin to that found in some Psalms (cf. Ps 78; 105; 106; cf. also Neh 9:6–37), as can be seen towards the end of Achior's speech (5:17–18, 21); but one does not have to be an Israelite to understand it. This passage about Achior, a foreigner who so accurately tells an enemy audience about God's dealings with the Israelite people, is reminiscent of the episode where the pagan Balaam (cf. Num 22:1—24:25) blesses the people of Israel in the presence of those who called him in to curse them. Achior's words show that God is the refuge of Israel and that the Israelites need never fear, provided they stay true to the Lord.

Holofernes follows Achior's speech with one of his own in which he exalts the divine power of Nebuchadnezzar in typically prophetical language (cf. Is 44:6; 45:21; Ps 18:31). Religious values are plainly at stake in the confrontation that lies ahead: Nebuchadnezzar's desire for vengeance is at odds with the will and might of the God of Israel. This is confirmed by the phrase "he [Nebuchadnezzar] has spoken; none of his words shall be in vain" (6:4)—an idea refuted by statements made by the prophets (cf. Is 55:10–11; Jer 1:22; Ezek 12:28; 2 Kings 10:10).

Holofernes is so enraged that he punishes Achior by handing him over to the Israelites (6:1–13). When they hear what he has to say, they become even more conscious of the need to have recourse to God; and they treat Achior with kindness.

[9]Et dixit Deus eorum, ut exirent de peregrinatione ipsorum et irent in terram Chanaan. Et inhabitaverunt ibi et repleti sunt auro et argento et pecoribus multis valde. [10]Et descenderunt in Aegyptum—cooperuerat enim fames faciem terrae Chanaan—et commorati sunt ibi, usquedum enutriti sunt et facti sunt ibi in multitudinem magnam, nec erat numerus generis eorum. [11]Et insurrexerunt super eos Aegyptii et circumvenerunt eos in luto et latere, humiliaverunt eos et posuerunt eos in servos. [12]Et clamaverunt ad Deum suum, et percussit totam terram Aegypti plagis, in quibus non erat medicina, et eiecerunt eos Aegyptii a facie sua. [13]Et exsiccavit Deus Rubrum mare ante eos [14]et eduxit eos in viam

Ex 14:21–22 Num 21:21–32 Josh 3 Deut 7:1 Deut 28–30 Ps 106:40–46 Is 59:2 2 Kings 25 Jud 11:10

God dried up the Red Sea before them, [14]and he led them by the way of Sinai and Kadesh-barnea, and drove out all the people of the wilderness. [15]So they lived in the land of the Amorites, and by their might destroyed all the inhabitants of Heshbon; and crossing over the Jordan they took possession of all the hill country. [16]And they drove out before them the Canaanites and the Perizzites and the Jebusites and the Shechemites and all the Gergesites, and lived there a long time. [17]As long as they did not sin against their God they prospered, for the God who hates iniquity is with them. [18]But when they departed from the way which he had appointed for them, they were utterly defeated in many battles and were led away captive to a foreign country; the temple of their God was razed to the ground, and their cities were captured by their enemies. [19]But now they have returned to their God, and have come back from the places to which they were scattered, and have occupied Jerusalem, where their sanctuary is, and have settled in the hill country, because it was uninhabited. [20]Now therefore, my master and lord, if there is any unwitting error in this people and they sin against their God and we find out their offence, then we will go up and defeat them. [21]But if there is no transgression in their nation, then let my lord pass them by; for their Lord will defend them, and their God will protect them, and we shall be put to shame before the whole world."

[22]When Achior had finished saying this, all the men standing around the tent began to complain; Holofernes' officers and all the men from the seacoast and from Moab insisted that he must be put to death. [23]"For," they said, "we will not be afraid of the Israelites; they are a people with no strength or power for making war. [24]Therefore let us go up, Lord Holofernes, and they will be devoured by your vast army."

Sinai et Cadesbarne. Et eiecerunt omnes inhabitantes in eremo [15]et habitaverunt in terra Amorraeorum et omnes Hesebonitas exstirpaverunt in virtute sua. Et transeuntes Iordanem possederunt totam montanam [16]et eiecerunt a facie sua Chananaeum et Pherezaeum et Iebusaeum et Sichem et omnes Gergesaeos et habitaverunt in ea diebus multis. [17]Et, usquedum non peccarent in conspectu Dei sui, erant cum ipsis bona, quia Deus odiens iniquitatem cum ipsis est. [18]Sed, cum recesserunt a via, quam disposuerat illis, exterminati sunt in bellis multis multum valde et captivi ducti sunt in terram non suam, et templum Dei eorum devenit ad solum, et civitates eorum comprehensae sunt ab adversariis. [19]Et nunc revertentes ad Deum suum ascenderunt a dispersione, qua dispersi fuerant, et possederunt Ierusalem, ubi sanctuarium eorum est, et inhabitaverunt in montana, quia erat deserta. [20]Et nunc, dominator domine, siquidem est ignorantia in populo isto, et peccant in Deum suum, inspiciemus quoniam est in illis offendiculum hoc et ascendemus et expugnabimus eos; [21]si autem non est iniquitas in ipsa gente, transeat dominus meus, ne forte protegat eos Dominus eorum et Deus eorum, et erimus in improperium coram omni terra». [22]Et factum est, ut desiit loqui Achior verba haec, murmuravit omnis populus, qui erat in circuitu tabernaculi. Et dixerunt magnates Holoferni et omnes, qui habitabant maritimam et Moab, ut configerent eum: [23]«Non enim timebimus a filiis Israel; ecce enim populus, in quo non est virtus neque potestas in pugnam validam. [24]Propter hoc ascendemus, et erunt in escam militiae tuae, dominator Holofernes».

6 [1]When the disturbance made by the men outside the council died down, Holofernes, the commander of the Assyrian army, said to Achior and all the Moabites in the presence of all the foreign contingents:

[2]"And who are you, Achior, and you hirelings of Ephraim, to prophesy among us as you have done today and tell us not to make war against the people of Israel because their God will defend them? Who is God except Nebuchadnezzar? [3]He will send his forces and will destroy them from the face of the earth, and their God will not deliver them—we the king's[f] servants will destroy them as one man. They cannot resist the might of our cavalry. [4]We will burn them up,[g] and their mountains will be drunk with their blood, and their fields will be full of their dead. They[h] cannot withstand us, but will utterly perish. So says King Nebuchadnezzar, the lord of the whole earth. For he has spoken; none of his words shall be in vain.

Jud 3:8
Dan 3:14–18

Is 36:18–20; 37:4,16–20

[5]"But you, Achior, you Ammonite hireling, who have said these words on the day of your iniquity, you shall not see my face again from this day until I take revenge on this race that came out of Egypt. [6]Then the sword of my army and the spear[i] of my servants shall pierce your sides, and you shall fall among their wounded, when I return. [7]Now my slaves are going to take you back into the hill country and put you in one of the cities beside the passes, [8]and you will not die until you perish along with them. [9]If you really hope in your heart that they will not be taken, do not look downcast! I have spoken and none of my words shall fail."

Jud 5:12; 16:12

[10]Then Holofernes ordered his slaves, who waited on him in his tent, to seize Achior and take him to Bethulia and hand him over

---

[6] [1]Et, cum cessasset tumultus virorum, qui erant in circuitu concilii, dixit Holofernes princeps militiae virtutis Assyriae ad Achior coram omni populo alienigenarum et ad omnes filios Moab: [2]«Et quis es tu, Achior, et mercennarii Ephraim, quoniam prophetasti nobis sicut hodie et dixisti quoniam genus filiorum Israel non expugnatur, quoniam Deus eorum proteget eos? Et quis est Deus nisi Nabuchodonosor rex omnis terrae? Hic mittet potestatem suam et disperdet eos a facie terrae, et non liberabit eos Deus eorum. [3]Sed nos servi illius percutiemus eos sicut hominem unum, nec sustinebunt vim equorum nostrorum. [4]Inundabimus enim eos in ipsis, et montes eorum inebriabuntur sanguine eorum, et campi eorum replebuntur mortuis eorum, et non resistet vestigium pedum eorum contra faciem nostram, sed perditione peribunt. Dicit rex Nabuchodonosor, dominus universae terrae: dixit enim, et non frustrabuntur verba oris eius. [5]Tu autem, Achior, mercennari Ammon, qui locutus es verba haec in die iniquitatis tuae, non videbis faciem meam iam ex hac die, quoadusque ulciscar in genus illorum, qui ascenderunt ex Aegypto. [6]Et tunc pertransiet ferrum militiae meae et populus famulorum meorum latera tua et cades cum vulneratis eorum, cum venero. [7]Et deducent te servi mei in montanam et ponent te in una civitatum ascensuum [8]et non peries, donec extermineris cum eis. [9]Et, si speras corde tuo quoniam non capientur, non concidat facies tua. Locutus sum, et nihil decidet verborum meorum». [10]Et praecepit Holofernes servis suis, qui erant adstantes in tabernaculo eius, ut comprehenderent Achior

f. Gk *his* **g.** Other authorities add *with it* **h.** *Gk The track of their feet* **i.** Lat Syr: Gk *people*

to the men of Israel. [11]So the slaves took him and led him out of the camp into the plain, and from the plain they went up into the hill country and came to the springs below Bethulia. [12]When the men of the city saw them,[j] they caught up their weapons and ran out of the city to the top of the hill, and all the slingers kept them from coming up by casting stones at them. [13]However, they got under the shelter of the hill and they bound Achior and left him lying at the foot of the hill, and returned to their master.

[14]Then the men of Israel came down from their city and found him; and they untied him and brought him into Bethulia and placed him before the magistrates of their city, [15]who in those days were Uzziah the son of Micah, of the tribe of Simeon, and Chabris the son of Gothoniel, and Charmis the son of Melchiel. [16]They called together all the elders of the city, and all their young men and their women ran to the assembly; and they set Achior in the midst of all their people, and Uzziah asked him what had happened. [17]He answered and told them what had taken place at the council of Holofernes, and all that he had said in the presence of the Assyrian leaders, and all that Holofernes had said so boastfully against the house of Israel. [18]Then the people fell down and worshipped God, and cried out to him, and said,

[19]"O Lord God of heaven, behold their arrogance, and have pity on the humiliation of our people, and look this day upon the faces of those who are consecrated to thee."

[20]Then they consoled Achior, and praised him greatly. [21]And Uzziah took him from the assembly to his own house and gave a banquet for the elders; and all that night they called on the God of Israel for help.

---

et ducerent eum in Betuliam et traderent in manus filiorum Israel. [11]Et comprehenderunt eum servi eius et duxerunt illum extra castra in campum et promoverunt ex medio campo in montanam et advenerunt ad fontes, qui erant sub Betulia. [12]Et, ut viderunt eos viri civitatis super verticem montis, acceperunt arma sua et exierunt extra civitatem supra cacumen montis, et omnis vir fundibalarius occupavit ascensus eorum et mittebat lapides super eos. [13]Et accedentes sub monte alligaverunt Achior et reliquerunt proiectum sub radice montis et reversi sunt ad dominum suum. [14]Descendentes autem filii Israel de civitate sua adstiterunt ei et solventes eum perduxerunt in Betuliam et adduxerunt eum ad principes civitatis suae, [15]qui erant in diebus illis Ozias filius Michae de tribu Simeon et Chabris filius Gothoniel et Charmis filius Melchiel. [16]Et convocaverunt omnes seniores civitatis et concurrerunt omnes iuvenes eorum et mulieres et pueri eorum in ecclesiam et statuerunt Achior in medio omnis populi ipsorum, et interrogavit eum Ozias, quid contigisset. [17]Et respondens indicavit eis verba consilii Holofernis et omnia verba, quaecumque locutus est in medio principum filiorum Assyriae, et quaecumque magniverbatus est Holofernes adversus domum Israel. [18]Et procidens omnis populus adoraverunt Deum et clamaverunt dicentes: [19]«Domine, Deus caeli, respice ad superbiam eorum et miserere humilitatis generis nostri et respice ad faciem eorum, qui sanctificati sunt tibi in hac die». [20]Et consolati sunt Achior et laudaverunt eum valde. [21]Et suscepit eum Ozias de ecclesia in domum suam et fecit cenam senioribus, et invocaverunt Deum Israel in adiutorium per totam noctem illam.

j. Other authorities add *on the top of the hill*

The Israelites besieged in Bethulia

7 [1]The next day Holofernes ordered his whole army, and all the allies who had joined him, to break camp and move against Bethulia, and to seize the passes up into the hill country and make war on the Israelites. [2]So all their warriors moved their camp that day; their force of men of war was one hundred and seventy thousand infantry and twelve thousand cavalry, together with the baggage and the foot soldiers handling it, a very great multitude. [3]They encamped in the valley near Bethulia, beside the spring, and they spread out in breadth over Dothan as far as Balbaim and in length from Bethulia to Cyamon, which faces Esdraelon.

[4]When the Israelites saw their vast numbers they were greatly terrified, and every one said to his neighbour, "These men will now lick up the face of the whole land; neither the high mountains nor the valleys nor the hills will bear their weight." [5]Then each man took up his weapons, and when they had kindled fires on their towers they remained on guard all that night.

1 Mac 12:28–29

7:1–32. Holofernes at last sets siege to Bethulia. Despite beseeching God's help (v. 19), the Israelites become terrified when they find themselves surrounded. Seeing no way out, the people ask their leaders to consider surrendering. Their appeal to Uzziah, the main ruler (cf. 6:15), and the council of elders shows just how despairing they are; it is as if they have lost faith in God, and it is reminiscent of the complaints the Israelites in the desert made against Moses (cf. Ex 16:2–3; Num 11:4–6; 14:2–4; 20:2–5). Such is the pressure, that all Uzziah can do is delay the decision to surrender for five days, in the hope that God may still show his mercy in the interval. This dramatically told story reflects the dire straits in which the Jews found themselves in the time of Antiochus IV Epiphanes and the Seleucid kings in general, but it also prepares the ground for God's wondrous intervention, just as he also came to their rescue during the Exodus.

[7] [1]Crastina autem die praecepit Holofernes omni militiae suae et omni populo suo, qui affuerunt in auxilium illius, ut pararent se ad Betuliam et ascensus montanae praeoccuparent et facerent pugnam adversus filios Israel. [2]Et paraverunt se in illa die omnis vir potens eorum; et virtus eorum virorum bellatorum erat centum septuaginta milia peditum et equitum duodecim milia, praeter impedimenta et viros, qui erant pedites in eis, multitudo magna valde. [3]Et castra collocaverunt in convallem iuxta Betuliam ad fontem et praetenderunt in latitudinem contra Dothain usque ad Abelmain et in longitudinem a Betulia usque Chyamonem, quae est contra Esdrelon. [4]Filii autem Israel, ut viderunt multitudinem eorum, turbati sunt valde et dixerunt unusquisque ad proximum suum: «Nunc lingent isti faciem totius terrae, nec montes alti neque valles neque colles sustinebunt pondus eorum». [5]Et accipientes unusquisque vasa sua bellica et accendentes ignem in turribus murorum suorum manebant custodientes per totam noctem illam. [6]Altera autem die eduxit Holofernes omnem equitatum suum contra faciem filiorum Israel, qui erant in Betulia, [7]et visitavit ascensus civitatis eorum et fontes aquarum perambulavit et praeoccupavit eos. Et praeposuit eis castra virorum bellatorum et ipse convertit in populum suum. [8]Et accedentes ad eum omnes principes filiorum Esau et omnes duces populi Moab

[6]On the second day Holofernes led out all his cavalry in full view of the Israelites in Bethulia, [7]and examined the approaches to the city, and visited the springs that supplied their water, and seized them and set guards of soldiers over them, and then returned to his army.

[8]Then all the chieftains of the people of Esau and all the leaders of the Moabites and the commanders of the coastland came to him and said, [9]"Let our lord hear a word, lest his army be defeated. [10]For these people, the Israelites, do not rely on their spears but on the height of the mountains where they live, for it is not easy to reach the tops of their mountains. [11]Therefore, my lord, do not fight against them in battle array, and not a man of your army will fall. [12]Remain in your camp, and keep all the men in your forces with you; only let your servants take possession of the spring of water that flows from the foot of the mountain—[13]for this is where all the people of Bethulia get their water. So thirst will destroy them, and they will give up their city. We and our people will go up to the tops of the nearby mountains and camp there to keep watch that not a man gets out of the city. [14]They and their wives and children will waste away with famine, and before the sword reaches them they will be strewn about in the streets where they live. [15]So you will pay them back with evil, because they rebelled and did not receive you peaceably."

1 Kings 20:23,28
Ps 68:14,16

[16]These words pleased Holofernes and all his servants, and he gave orders to do as they had said. [17]So the army of the Ammonites moved forward, together with five thousand Assyrians, and they encamped in the valley and seized the water supply and the springs of the Israelites. [18]And the sons of Esau and the sons of Ammon went up and encamped in the hill country opposite

---

et magistratus maritimae dixerunt: [9]«Audiat verbum dominator noster, ne fiat confractio in virtute tua. [10]Populus enim hic filiorum Israel non fidit in lanceis suis, sed in altitudinibus montium, in quibus inhabitant; non enim est facile ascendere vertices montium ipsorum. [11]Et nunc, dominator, noli pugnare ad eos sicut pugna fit belli, et non cadet ex populo tuo vir unus; [12]sed mane in castris tuis custodiens omnem virum virtutis tuae, et obtineant pueri tui fontem aquarum, qui emanat a radice montis, [13]quia inde hauriunt aquas omnes inhabitantes Betuliam. Et interficiet eos sitis, et tradent civitatem suam, et nos et populus tuus ascendemus super vertices montium proximos et obsidebimus in eis in custodiam, ut non exeat de civitate vir unus. [14]Et destilliscent in fame et siti ipsi et mulieres eorum et filii eorum et, priusquam veniat gladius super eos, prosternentur in plateis habitationis suae, [15]et retribues eis retributionem malam, eo quod secesserunt et non obviaverunt faciei tuae in pace». [16]Et placuerunt verba eorum coram Holoferne et coram omnibus famulis eius, et constituit facere, ut locuti sunt. [17]Et promoverunt castra filii Moab et cum eis quinque milia filiorum Assyriae et castra constituerunt in convalle et praeoccupaverunt aquas et fontes aquarum filiorum Israel. [18]Et ascenderunt filii Ammon et filii Esau et castra constituerunt in montana contra Dothain. Et miserunt ex eis ad austrum et orientem contra Egrebel, quae est iuxta Chus, quae est ad rivum Mochmur. Et reliqua militia Assyriorum castra

Dothan; and they sent some of their men toward the south and the east, toward Acraba, which is near Chusi beside the brook Mochmur. The rest of the Assyrian army encamped in the plain, and covered the whole face of the land, and their tents and supply trains spread out in great number, and they formed a vast multitude.

[19]The people of Israel cried out to the Lord their God, for their courage failed, because all their enemies had surrounded them and there was no way of escape from them. [20]The whole Assyrian army, their infantry, chariots, and cavalry, surrounded them for thirty-four days, until all the vessels of water belonging to every inhabitant of Bethulia were empty; [21]their cisterns were going dry, and they did not have enough water to drink their fill for a single day, because it was measured out to them to drink. [22]Their children lost heart, and the women and young men fainted from thirst and fell down in the streets of the city and in the passages through the gates; there was no strength left in them any longer.

[23]Then all the people, the young men, the women, and the children, gathered about Uzziah and the rulers of the city and cried out with a loud voice, and said before all the elders, [24]"God be judge between you and us! For you have done us a great injury in not making peace with the Assyrians. [25]For now we have no one to help us; God has sold us into their hands, to strew us on the ground before them with thirst and utter destruction. [26]Now call them in and surrender the whole city to the army of Holofernes and to all his forces, to be plundered. [27]For it would be better for us to be captured by them;[k] for we will be slaves, but our lives will be spared, and we shall not witness the death of our babes before our

Lam 2:11

---

constituerunt in campo et operuerunt omnem faciem terrae; et tabernacula et impedimenta eorum constituerunt in turba multa, et erant in multitudinem magnam valde. [19]Et filii Israel clamaverunt ad Dominum Deum suum, quoniam minorabatur spiritus eorum, quoniam circumdederant eos omnes inimici eorum, et non poterant effugere de medio eorum. [20]Et manserunt in circuitu eorum omnia castra Assyriae, pedites et quadrigae et equites eorum per dies triginta quattuor. Et deficiebant omnibus inhabitantibus Betuliam omnia vasa aquarum eorum, [21]et cisternae eorum evacuabantur, et non habebant quod biberent in satietatem aquam unam diem, quoniam in mensura dabant eis bibere. [22]Et anxiati sunt infantes eorum, et mulieres et iuvenes deficiebant a siti et cadebant in plateis civitatis et in transitu portarum, et non erat virtus adhuc in eis. [23]Et collegit se omnis populus ad Oziam et ad principes civitatis, iuvenes et mulieres et infantes et clamaverunt voce magna et dixerunt coram omnibus senioribus: [24]«Iudicet Deus inter vos et nos, quoniam fecistis in nobis iniquitatem magnam non loquentes pacifica cum filiis Assyriae. [25]Et nunc non est qui nos adiuvet, sed vendidit nos Deus in manus eorum, ut prosterneremur ante eos in siti et perditione magna. [26]Et nunc convocate eos et tradite civitatem totam in captivitatem populo Holofernis et omni virtuti eius. [27]Melius est enim nos fieri illis in rapinam; erimus enim eis in servos et ancillas, et vivet anima nostra, et non videbimus mortem infantium nostrorum in oculis nostris et mulieres et filios nostros deficientes in animabus suis. [28]Contestamur vobis caelum et terram et Deum eorum et Dominum patrum nostrorum, qui ulciscitur in

k. Other authorities add *than to die of thirst*

eyes, or see our wives and children draw their last breath. [28]We call to witness against you heaven and earth and our God, the Lord of our fathers, who punishes us according to our sins and the sins of our fathers. Let him not do this day the things which we have described!"

[29]Then great and general lamentation arose throughout the assembly, and they cried out to the Lord God with a loud voice. [30]And Uzziah said to them, "Have courage, my brothers! Let us hold out for five more days; by that time the Lord our God will restore to us his mercy, for he will not forsake us utterly. [31]But if these days pass by, and no help comes for us, I will do what you say."

[32]Then he dismissed the people to their various posts, and they went up on the walls and towers of their city. The women and children he sent home. And they were greatly depressed in the city.

2. GOD CONFOUNDS HIS ENEMIES BY MEANS OF JUDITH*

Judith appeals for divine protection

8 [1]At that time Judith heard about these things: she was the daughter of Merari the son of Ox, son of Joseph, son of Oziel, son of Elkiah, son of Ananias, son of Gideon, son of Raphaim, son of Ahitub, son of Elijah, son of Hilkiah, son of Eliab, son of Nathanael, son of Salamiel, son of Sarasadai, son of Israel.* [2]Her husband Manasseh, who belonged to her tribe and family, had died

---

***8:1—16:25.** The second part of the book describes how the situation was saved. It begins with the entrance on the scene of a young, God-fearing widow who, despite the general collapse of morale, still puts all her trust in God and is determined to take action to save her people. First, she prays trustingly to God: he will make her plan succeed (8:1—9:14). Then she boldly

nos secundum peccata nostra et secundum peccata patrum nostrorum, ut non faciat secundum verba haec in hac die». [29]Et factus est fletus magnus in medio ecclesiae omnium unanimiter, et clamaverunt ad Dominum Deum voce magna. [30]Et dixit ad eos Ozias: «Aequo animo estote, fratres, et sustineamus adhuc dies quinque, in quibus convertet Dominus Deus noster misericordiam suam super nos; non enim derelinquet nos in consummationem. [31]Si autem transierint isti quinque dies, et non fuerit super nos adiutorium, faciam secundum verba vestra». [32]Et dispersit plebem unumquemque in castra sua, et super muros et turres civitatis abierunt, et mulieres et filios in domus suas dimiserunt; et erant in magna humilitate valde. **[8]** [1]Et erat in civitate commorans in diebus illis Iudith filia Merari filii Ox filii Ioseph filii Oziel filii Elchiae filii Ananiae filii Gedeon filii Rafain filii Achitob filii Eliab filii Nathanael filii Salamiel filii Surisaddai filii Simeon filii Israel. [2]Et vir eius Manasses erat ex tribu eius et patria eius; et mortuus est in diebus messis hordiariae. [3]Steterat enim super alligantes manipulos in campo, et aestus introivit in caput eius, et incidit in lectum et mortuus est in Betulia civitate sua. Et sepelierunt eum cum

during the barley harvest. [3]For as he stood overseeing the men who were binding sheaves in the field, he was overcome by the burning heat, and took to his bed and died in Bethulia his city. So they buried him with his fathers in the field between Dothan and Balamon. [4]Judith had lived at home as a widow for three years and four months. [5]She set up a tent for herself on the roof of her house, and girded sackcloth about her loins and wore the garments of her widowhood. [6]She fasted all the days of her widowhood, except the day before the sabbath and the sabbath itself, the day before the new moon and the day of the new moon, and the feasts and days of rejoicing of the house of Israel. [7]She was beautiful in appearance, and had a very lovely face; and her husband Manasseh had left her gold and silver, and men and women slaves, and cattle, and fields; and she maintained this estate. [8]No one spoke ill of her, for she feared God with great devotion.

Judg 3:20
2 Kings 4:10
Lk 2:36–37

---

heads for the enemy encampment and manages to speak with Holofernes, who is captivated by her beauty and common sense, and gives her a good reception. After a banquet at which Holofernes has too much to drink, Judith goes to his bed and cuts off his head. She leaves the camp while it is still dark and returns to Bethulia with her trophy, the head of Holofernes (10:1—13:20). When Achior, the Ammonite leader given hospitality by the Israelites, learns what has happened, he believes in God and becomes part of the house of Israel (14:1–10). Meanwhile, when the besieging troops discover that their general has been killed, they panic and flee (14:11—15:7). The book ends by exalting the figure of Judith, for through her and thanks to her faith and trust in God, the Lord has done wonders for his people (15:8—16:25).

8:1–8. In Hebrew the name Judith means "the Jewess": it is an instance of a national name being used as a proper name. The only precedent for this name in the Bible is the Judith (the daughter of Beeri the Hittite) who was a wife of Esau (cf. Gen 26:34); perhaps for that reason and in order to make it clear that Judith is a member of the chosen people, the writer gives her genealogy back as far as Jacob. All this leads one to think that he means Judith to stand for the whole Jewish nation. And in fact, in the hymn

patribus suis in agro, qui est inter Dothain et Balamon. [4]Et erat Iudith in domo sua vidua per annos tres et menses quattuor. [5]Et fecit sibi tabernaculum super tectum domus suae et imposuit super lumbos suos cilicium, et erant super eam vestimenta viduitatis suae, [6]et ieiunabat per omnes dies viduitatis suae praeter pridie sabbatorum et sabbata et pridie neomeniarum et neomenias et dies festos et gaudimonia domus Israel. [7]Et erat bona in aspectu et formosa facie valde et prudens in corde et bona in sensu et erat honesta valde, quia reliquerat ei Manasses vir eius filius Ioseph filii Achitob filii Melchis filii Eliab filii Nathanael filii Surisaddai filii Simeon filii Israel aurum et argentum et pueros et puellas et pecora et praedia, et manebat in eis; [8]et non erat qui inferret ei verbum malum, quia timebat Deum valde. [9]Et audivit verba populi maligna super principem quoniam defecerunt animo super penuriam aquarum. Et

[9]When Judith heard the wicked words spoken by the people against the ruler, because they were faint for lack of water, and when she heard all that Uzziah said to them, and how he promised them under oath to surrender the city to the Assyrians after five days, [10]she sent her maid, who was in charge of all she possessed, to summon[l] Chabris and Charmis, the elders of her city. [11]They came to her, and she said to them,

Job 38:2; 40:2,7; 42:3

"Listen to me, rulers of the people of Bethulia! What you have said to the people today is not right; you have even sworn and pronounced this oath between God and you, promising to surrender the city to our enemies unless the Lord turns and helps us within so many days. [12]Who are you, that have put God to the test this day, and are setting yourselves up in the place of[m] God

---

at the end of the book, the personality of Judith fuses with that of the chosen people. In the genealogy there is no mention of which tribe she belonged to, but further on (9:2) we are told that she was of the tribe of Simeon. The names of Salamiel and Sarasadai occur in Numbers 1:6 (in a more Hebrew form) as leading men of that tribe. The dead husband of Judith, Manasseh, belonged to the same tribe and family (it was customary for devout Jews to marry within their own clan: cf. Tob 4:12).

Judith has all the qualities that might be desired in a woman, ranging from beauty to wealth and exemplary piety. In order to live a secluded life and devote herself to prayer, she had had a kind of hut or tent set up on the roof of her house. Constructions of this type were not uncommon (cf. Judg 3:20; 2 Sam 18:33; 2 Kings 4:10; Neh 8:16).

8:9–27. We could say that there are three parts to Judith's speech, dealing with three different ideas. First (vv. 11–17) she makes the point that one must not impose conditions on God: one must pray with faith and confidence. Secondly (vv. 18–24) she says that there are very good reasons why the people of Bethulia should put their trust in the Lord and not lose heart on account of difficulties; besides, their city is of unique strategic importance for the defence of Jerusalem and the temple: if they surrendered, they would be responsible for the destruction of the Holy City and the sanctuary. Finally (vv. 25–27), they must realize that God

audivit omnia verba Iudith, quae locutus est ad eos Ozias, quemadmodum iuraverat eis, ut post quinque dies traderet civitatem Assyriis. [10]Et mittens abram suam, quae erat super omnia bona eius, vocavit Oziam et Chabrin et Charmin seniores civitatis suae. [11]Et venerunt ad eam. Et dixit ad eos: «Audite me, principes inhabitantium in Betulia, quoniam non est rectum verbum vestrum, quod locuti estis coram plebe in hac die et statuistis iuramentum istud, quod locuti estis inter Deum et vos, et dixistis tradituros vos civitatem inimicis nostris, si non in illis diebus converterit Dominus Deus noster adiutorium nobis. [12]Et nunc qui estis vos, qui tentastis Deum in hodierno die et astitistis pro Deo in medio filiorum hominum? [13]Et nunc Dominum omnipotentem tentatis et nihil intellegetis usque in sempiternum. [14]Quoniam altitudinem cordis hominis non invenietis et cogitatus sensus eius non comprehendetis,

l. Some authorities add *Uzziah and* (See verses 28 and 35) **m.** Or *above*

among the sons of men? [13]You are putting the Lord Almighty to the test—but you will never know anything! [14]You cannot plumb the depths of the human heart, nor find out what a man is thinking; how do you expect to search out God, who made all these things, and find out his mind or comprehend his thought? No, my brethren, do not provoke the Lord our God to anger. [15]For if he does not choose to help us within these five days, he has power to protect us within any time he pleases, or even to destroy us in the presence of our enemies. [16]Do not try to bind the purposes of the Lord our God; for God is not like man, to be threatened, nor like a human being, to be won over by pleading. [17]Therefore, while we wait for his deliverance, let us call upon him to help us, and he will hear our voice, if it pleases him.

Ps 139:16–17
Prov 14:10
Rom 11:33–34
1 Cor 2:11

[18]"For never in our generation, nor in these present days, has there been any tribe or family or people or city of ours which

Jud 5:20–21; 11:10

---

sends men trials in order to purify them and then come to their rescue, as he did in the case of the patriarchs.

Three religious ideas back up what Judith has to say: no one knows the mind of God (vv. 13–14); when God sent punishment, it was on account of his people's idolatry and infidelity (vv. 18–20); and God tries with fire those who draw close to him (vv. 25–27). These convictions can be found in many passages elsewhere in Holy Scripture: for example, in Isaiah's canticles of consolation (cf. Is 40:12–26; 44:24–28; 46:8–13); in the Psalms dealing with the history of Israel (cf. Ps 78:56–66; 106:34–46); and in the book of Job. However, Judith's speech has a more lofty appreciation of suffering than that found in the book of Job; it is closer to that in the book of Wisdom (cf. Wis 3:1–9), and especially to that found in Christian tradition, as regards suffering being a warning and a call to greater perfection: "Suffering must serve for *conversion*, that is, *for the rebuilding of goodness* in the subject, who can recognize the divine mercy in this call to repentance. The purpose of penance is to overcome evil, which under different forms lies dormant in man. Its purpose is also to strengthen goodness both in man himself and in his relationship with others and especially with God" (John Paul II, *Salvifici doloris*, 12).

quomodo Deum, qui fecit omnia ista, inquiretis et sensum eius cognoscetis et cogitationem eius inspicietis? Minime, fratres, nolite exacerbare Dominum Deum nostrum, [15]quoniam, si noluerit in his quinque diebus adiuvare nos, ipse habet potestatem, in quibus diebus velit, protegere aut disperdere nos ante faciem inimicorum nostrorum. [16]Vos autem nolite praepignorare voluntates Domini Dei nostri, quoniam non sicut homo Deus est, ut minis terreatur, aut sicut filius hominis, ut iudicetur. [17]Propter quod sustinentes salvationem ab eo, invocemus ipsum in adiutorium nostrum, et exaudiet vocem nostram, si fuerit ipsi placitum. [18]Quoniam non exsurrexit in progenie nostra, nec est in hodierna die neque tribus neque patria neque populus neque civitas ex nobis, qui adorent deos manufactos, sicut factum est in primis diebus, [19]pro quibus traditi sunt in gladium et in rapinam patres nostri et ceciderunt casum magnum ante conspectum inimicorum nostrorum. [20]Nos autem alium Deum nescimus praeter

Ps 78:56ff; 106:13ff Jer 7:17–20; 14:7—15:9 Ezek 16:15–58

worshipped gods made with hands, as was done in days gone by—[19]and that was why our fathers were handed over to the sword, and to be plundered, and so they suffered a great catastrophe before our enemies. [20]But we know no other god but him, and therefore we hope that he will not disdain us or any of our nation. [21]For if we are captured all Judea will be captured and our sanctuary will be plundered; and he will exact of us[n] the penalty for its desecration. [22]And the slaughter of our brethren and the captivity of the land and the desolation of our inheritance—all this he will bring upon our heads among the Gentiles, wherever we serve as slaves; and we shall be an offence and a reproach in the eyes of those who acquire us. [23]For our slavery will not bring us into favour, but the Lord our God will turn it to dishonour.

Gen 22:1–19; 28:5; 29:22–30; 31 Acts 15:4

Deut 4:7

[24]"Now therefore, brethren, let us set an example to our brethren, for their lives depend upon us, and the sanctuary and the temple and the altar rest upon us. [25]In spite of everything let us give thanks to the Lord our God, who is putting us to the test as he did our forefathers. [26]Remember what he did with Abraham, and how he tested Isaac, and what happened to Jacob in Mesopotamia in Syria, while he was keeping the sheep of Laban, his mother's brother. [27]For he has not tried us with fire, as he did them, to search their hearts, nor has he taken revenge upon us; but the Lord scourges those who draw near to him, in order to admonish them."

[28]Then Uzziah said to her, "All that you have said has been spoken out of a true heart, and there is no one who can deny your words. [29]Today is not the first time your wisdom has been shown, but from the beginning of your life all the people have recognized your understanding, for your heart's disposition is right. [30]But the people were very thirsty, and they compelled us to do for them

---

eum, a quo speramus quia non despiciet nos, nec auferet salutare suum a genere nostro. [21]Quoniam in eo quod capti sumus, sic et capietur omnis Iudaea, et praedabuntur sancta nostra, et exquiret Deus coinquinationem eorum ex sanguine nostro [22]et mortem fratrum nostrorum et captivitatem terrae et desertionem hereditatis nostrae reducet in caput nostrum in gentibus, ubicumque servierimus. Et erimus in offendiculum et in improperium ante omnes, qui possidebunt nos, [23]quoniam non dirigetur servitus nostra in gratiam, sed in inhonorationem ponet eam Dominus Deus noster. [24]Et nunc, fratres, ostendamus fratribus nostris quoniam ex nobis pendet anima eorum, et sancta et domus et altare incumbit in nobis. [25]Praeter haec omnia gratias agamus Domino Deo nostro, qui tentat nos sicut et patres nostros. [26]Memores estote quanta fecerit cum Abraham et Isaac, et quanta facta sint Iacob in Mesopotamia Syriae pascenti oves Laban fratris matris suae. [27]Quia non sicut illos combussit in inquisitionem cordis illorum et in nos non ultus est, sed in monitionem flagellat Dominus appropinquantes sibi». [28]Et dixit ad eam Ozias: «Omnia, quaecumque dixisti, in bono corde locuta es, et non est qui resistat verbis tuis, [29]quoniam non ex hodierna die sapientia tua manifesta est, sed ab initio dierum tuorum scit omnis populus sensum tuum, quoniam bona sunt figmenta cordis tui. [30]Sed populus sitiit valde, et coegerunt nos sic facere, ut locuti sumus eis, et inducere super nos iuramentum, quod non praeteriemus. [31]Et nunc ora pro nobis, et forte exaudiet te Deus noster, quoniam tu mulier sancta es,

n. Gk *our blood*

what we have promised, and made us take an oath which we cannot break. [31]So pray for us, since you are a devout woman, and the Lord will send us rain to fill our cisterns and we will no longer be faint."

[32]Judith said to them, "Listen to me. I am about to do a thing which will go down through all generations of our descendants. [33]Stand at the city gate tonight, and I will go out with my maid; and within the days after which you have promised to surrender the city to our enemies, the Lord will deliver Israel by my hand. [34]Only, do not try to find out what I plan; for I will not tell you until I have finished what I am about to do."

Mk 5:34

[35]Uzziah and the rulers said to her, "Go in peace, and may the Lord God go before you, to take revenge upon our enemies." [36]So they returned from the tent and went to their posts.

Esther 4:1–9
Ex 30:7–8
Ps 141:2

9 [1]Then Judith fell upon her face, and put ashes on her head, and uncovered the sackcloth she was wearing; and at the very time when that evening's incense was being offered in the house of God in Jerusalem, Judith cried out to the Lord with a loud voice, and said, [2]"O Lord God of my father Simeon, to whom thou gavest a sword to take revenge on the strangers who had loosed the girdle[o] of a virgin to defile her, and uncovered her thigh to put her to shame, and polluted her womb to disgrace her; for thou hast said, 'It shall not be done'—yet they did it. [3]So thou gavest up their rulers to be slain, and their bed, which was ashamed of the deceit they had practised, to be stained with blood, and thou didst strike down slaves along with princes, and princes on their thrones; [4]and thou gavest their wives for a prey and their daughters to captivity, and all their booty to be divided among thy beloved sons, who

Gen 34
Jud 6:15

---

et dimittet Dominus pluviam in repletionem lacuum nostrorum, et non deficiemus iam». [32]Et dixit ad eos Iudith: «Audite me, et faciam opus prudentiae, quod perveniet in generationes generationum filiis generis nostri. [33]Vos enim stabitis ad portam hac nocte, et exeam ego cum abra mea, et in diebus, post quos dixistis civitatem tradituros vos inimicis nostris, visitabit Dominus Israel in manu mea, sicut ego fido. [34]Vos autem non scrutabitis actum meum; non enim renuntiabo vobis, quousque consummentur, quae ego facio». [35]Et dixit Ozias et principes ad eam: «Vade in pacem, et Dominus Deus sit ante te in ultionem inimicorum nostrorum». [36]Et revertentes descenderunt de tabernaculo eius et abierunt ad dispositiones suas. **[9]** [1]Iudith autem procidit in faciem suam et imposuit cinerem super caput suum et scidit tunicam suam et denudavit, quod induerat, cilicium; et, in ipso quod oblatum erat in Ierusalem in domum Dei incensum vespere illo, clamavit Iudith voce magna ad Dominum et dixit: [2]«Domine, Deus patris mei Simeon, cui dedisti in manu gladium in ultionem alienigenarum, qui solverunt cingulum virginis in coinquinationem et denudaverunt femur in confusionem et coinquinaverunt matricem in improperium. Dixisti enim: "Non sic erit!"; et fecerunt. [3]Pro quibus dedisti principes eorum in occisionem et torum eorum, qui erubuit seductione eorum, seductum in sanguinem; et percussisti servos super potentes et potentes super thronos eorum. [4]Et dedisti mulieres eorum in praedam et filias in captivitatem et omnia spolia in divisionem filiorum a te delectorum, qui zelaverunt zelum tuum et abominaverunt coinquinationem sanguinis sui et invocaverunt te in adiutorium. Deus, Deus meus,

o. Cn: Gk *womb*

Ps 115:3; 135:6
Is 44:7
Job 38:35
Is 46:9–13
Bar 3:35

were zealous for thee, and abhorred the pollution of their blood, and called on thee for help—O God, my God, hear me also, a widow.

[5]"For thou hast done these things and those that went before and those that followed; thou hast designed the things that are now, and those that are to come. Yea, the things thou didst intend came to pass, [6]and the things thou didst will presented themselves and said, 'Lo, we are here'; for all thy ways are prepared in advance, and thy judgment is with foreknowledge.

9:1–14. Judith's prayer expressed in very poetic language is full of typical Jewish piety, as can be seen from many prayers recorded in the historical books of the Old Testament, especially those which cover the post-exilic period (cf. Ezra 9:6–15; Neh 9:6–37; Tob 3:2–6, 11–15; Esther *14:13–9*). We can distinguish three parts: 1) the reference to the episode of the rape of Dinah, the daughter of Jacob, by Shechem, and the revenge taken by Simeon and Levi (Gen 34:1–31); in Judith's prayer that event symbolizes all offences suffered by the people of Israel, including those still fresh in their memory—especially the fall and destruction of Jerusalem (vv. 2–6). 2) A description of the military might of Assyria, and an appeal for victory over them at the hands of a woman (vv. 7–11). 3) Prayer for her plan to work (vv. 12–14). Right through her prayer Judith keeps calling for the God of Israel to be exalted and his enemies to be confounded—an appeal which becomes especially intense when she refers to the goodness and providence of God (v. 11) and his omnipotence (v. 12). God is invoked in language typical of Old Testament piety: he is the "Lord" (v. 9) who can win battles and scatter his enemies like a mighty warrior (cf. Ex 15:3 Greek; Jud 16:2); the "God of the inheritance of Israel, Lord of heaven and earth, Creator of the waters, King of all creation" (v. 12); and above all he is the "God of the lowly, helper of the oppressed, upholder of the weak, protector of the forlorn, saviour of those without hope" (v. 11).

Concern for the sanctuary and the Holy City is always at the forefront of Judith's mind as can be seen from the fact she was at prayer at the very time incense was being offered in the temple (v. 1; cf. Ex 29:41; Ezra 9:4–5), and from the references to Zion, the altar and the sanctuary (vv. 8 and 13).

From what she says we can divine part of her plan—to rescue her people. The enemies of Israel—Nebuchadnezzar and his general, Holofernes—are God's enemies. The confrontation narrated in this book is a ruthless religious war aimed at depriving the chosen people of its faith, its form of worship and even its identity. Hence Judith's appeal to God to bring to naught this idolatrous and blasphemous onslaught. Judith deceives and seduces Holofernes, but at

exaudi me viduam. [5]Tu enim fecisti priora illorum et illa et, quae postea et quae nunc et quae futura sunt, cogitasti, et facta sunt, quae cogitasti. [6]Et astiterunt, quae voluisti, et dixerunt: "Ecce adsumus". Omnes enim viae tuae paratae, et creatura tua in praescientia. [7]Ecce enim Assyrii repleti sunt in virtute

[7]"Behold now, the Assyrians are increased in their might; they are exalted, with their horses and riders; they glory in the strength of their foot soldiers; they trust in shield and spear, in bow and sling, and know not that thou art the Lord who crushest wars; the Lord is thy name. [8]Break their strength by thy might, and bring down their power in thy anger; for they intend to defile thy sanctuary, and to pollute the tabernacle where thy glorious name rests, and to cast down the horn of thy altar with the sword. [9]Behold their pride, and send thy wrath upon their heads; give to me, a widow, the strength to do what I plan. [10]By the deceit of my lips strike down the slave with the prince and the prince with his servant; crush their arrogance by the hand of a woman.

[11]"For thy power depends not upon numbers, nor thy might upon men of strength; for thou art God of the lowly, helper of the oppressed, upholder of the weak, protector of the forlorn, saviour of those without hope. [12]Hear, O hear me, God of my father, God of the inheritance of Israel, Lord of heaven and earth, Creator of the waters, King of all thy creation, hear my prayer! [13]Make my deceitful words to be their wound and stripe, for they have planned

Jud 5:23; 6:2; Mac 8:18
Ps 33:16–17
Ps 46:9; 76:3
Judg 7:4–7
1 Sam 14:6
Acts 4:24
Jud 10:4; 11:20,23; 16:6,9

---

no point in the story is she praised for this. In fact, the heroine herself feels obliged to reassure the elders and the people of Bethulia that she has done nothing blameworthy (cf. 13:16). Judith is the heroine raised up by God to save his people when they are at their wits' end. As Christian tradition sees it, the key thing is that God's enemy and Israel's has been defeated by a woman. The Church's liturgy is aware of this when it applies to the Blessed Virgin the praise that Uzziah heaps on Judith: "The Lord has blessed you with his power because through you he has overcome our enemies. The Lord has blessed you, my daughter, more than any other woman in the world" (*Divine Office*, 15 August, shorter reading; cf. 13:18); "You are the glory of Jerusalem! The joy of Israel! The pride of our race!" (Common of the Blessed Virgin Mary; *Ad Laudes*, second antiphon; cf. 15:9).

sua et exaltati sunt in equo et ascensore, gloriati sunt in brachio peditum, speraverunt in clipeis et lancea et arcu et fundibula et nescierunt quoniam tu es Dominus, qui conteris bella; [8]Dominus nomen est tibi. Tu allide illorum vires, aeterne Deus, comminue illorum plenitudinem in virtute tua et deduc fortitudinem eorum in ira tua. Voluerunt enim polluere sancta tua, coinquinare tabernaculum requiei nominis maiestatis tuae et deicere ferro cornu altaris tui. [9]Respice in superbiam eorum, dimitte iram tuam in capita eorum; da in manu mea viduae, quam cogitavi, virtutem, [10]et percute servum ex labiis seductionis meae super principem et principem super servum eius; quassa elationem in manu viduae. [11]Non enim in multitudine virtus tua, nec potentia tua neque datum tuum in fortibus, sed humilium es Deus et minorum adiutorium, infirmorum susceptor, abiectorum protector, desperatorum salvator. [12]Etiam, etiam, Deus patris mei et Deus hereditatis Israel, dominator caelorum et terrae, creator aquarum, rex totius creaturae tuae, exaudi deprecationem meam [13]et da verbum meum et suasionem in vulnus et livorem eorum, qui adversum testamentum tuum et domum tuam sanctam et verticem Sion et domum retentionis filiorum tuorum cogitaverunt dura. [14]Et fac super omnem gentem tuam et omnem

cruel things against thy covenant, and against thy consecrated house, and against the top of Zion, and against the house possessed by thy children. [14]And cause thy whole nation and every tribe to know and understand that thou art God, the God of all power and might, and that there is no other who protects the people of Israel but thou alone!"

Judith defeats Holofernes

Jud 8:6

10 [1]When Judith[p] had ceased crying out to the God of Israel, and had ended all these words, [2]she rose from where she lay prostrate and called her maid and went down into the house where she lived on sabbaths and on her feast days; [3]and she removed the sackcloth which she had been wearing, and took off her widow's garments, and bathed her body with water, and anointed herself with precious ointment, and combed her hair and put on a tiara, and arrayed herself in her gayest apparel, which she used to wear while her husband Manasseh was living. [4]And she put sandals on her feet, and put on her anklets and bracelets and rings, and her

Jud 9:13

10:1—12:9. "When her city was surrounded, that holy woman Judith asked the elders for their permission to go out to the enemy camp. Through love for her country and her people, she undertook the dangerous task and went out, and God delivered Holofernes' life into the hands of a woman" (St Clement of Rome, *Ad Corinthios*, 55, 4–5).

Judith continues to put all her trust in God and to keep the precepts of the Law. Determined to decline any food offered her by Holofernes (cf. 12:1–14), because it is unclean according to the traditions of devout Jews (cf. Tob 1:10–12; Dan 1:8), she makes a point of bringing provisions with her. The text mentions wine, in a leather bottle; oil, in a small flask; and food in the form of dried fruit (figs and raisins) and toasted cereal (in Hebrew, *qali:* cf. Ruth 2:14; 1 Sam 25:18), which was eaten mixed with water and flavoured with oil: all this food was clean and it will be all that Judith eats; she is sure that the Lord will quickly come to his people's aid (12:1–4).

Before putting her plan into action, but already inside the enemy camp, Judith keeps up her religious practice—by prayer, ritual bathing and fasting (12:5–9). Christian tradition depicts Judith as a model of how to deal with difficulties: "Having raised her entreaty up to God, Judith defeated Holofernes with His help; thus did one Hebrew woman, on her own, bring to shame the house of Nebuchadnezzar" (Origen, *De oratione*, 13, 2).

---

tribum scientiam, ut sciant quoniam tu Deus es universae potestatis et virtutis, et non est alius defensor generis Israel praeter te». **[10]** [1]Et factum est, ut cessavit clamans ad Deum Israel et consummavit omnia verba ista, [2]surrexit de prostratione sua et vocavit abram suam et descendit in domum suam, in

p. Gk *she*

earrings and all her ornaments,* and made herself very beautiful, to entice the eyes of all men who might see her. [5]And she gave her maid a bottle of wine and a flask of oil, and filled a bag with parched grain and a cake of dried fruit and fine bread; and she wrapped up all her vessels and gave them to her to carry.

Lev 17:10–14
Esther 4:17

[6]Then they went out to the city gate of Bethulia, and found Uzziah standing there with the elders of the city, Chabris and Charmis. [7]When they saw her, and noted how her face was altered and her clothing changed, they greatly admired her beauty, and said to her, [8]"May the God of our fathers grant you favour and fulfil your plans, that the people of Israel may glory and Jerusalem may be exalted." And she worshipped God.

[9]Then she said to them, "Order the gate of the city to be opened for me, and I will go out and accomplish the things about which you spoke with me." So they ordered the young men to open the gate for her, as she had said. [10]When they had done this, Judith went out, she and her maid with her; and the men of the city watched her until she had gone down the mountain and passed through the valley and they could no longer see her.

[11]The women[q] went straight on through the valley; and an Assyrian patrol met her [12]and took her into custody, and asked her, "To what people do you belong, and where are you coming from, and where are you going?" She replied, "I am a daughter of the Hebrews, but I am fleeing from them, for they are about to be handed over to you to be devoured. [13]I am on my way to the

Jud 5:5

---

qua commorabatur in diebus sabbatorum et in diebus festis suis. [3]Et abstulit cilicium, quod induerat, et exuit se vestimenta viduitatis suae et lavit corpus suum aqua et unxit se unguento spisso et pectinavit capillos capitis sui et imposuit mitram super caput suum et induit se vestimenta iucunditatis suae, quibus vestiebatur in diebus vitae viri sui Manasses. [4]Et accepit soleas in pedes suos et imposuit periscelides et dextralia et anulos et inaures et omnem ornatum suum et composuit se nimis in seductionem oculorum virorum, quicumque viderent eam. [5]Et porrexit abrae suae ascopam vini et vas olei et peram implevit alphitis et massa fici et panibus et caseo et plicavit omnia vasa sua et imposuit ei. [6]Et abierunt ad portam civitatis Betuliae et invenerunt adstantem ad eam Oziam et seniores civitatis Chabrin et Charmin. [7]Qui cum vidissent eam, et erat mutata facies eius, et vestem mutatam, mirati sunt valde et dixerunt ei: [8]«Deus patrum nostrorum det te in gratiam et consummet cogitationes tuas in gloriam filiorum Israel et in exaltationem Ierusalem». [9]Et procidens in faciem adoravit Deum et dixit ad eos: «Praecipite aperiri portam civitatis, et exeam in consummationem verborum, quae locuti estis mecum». Et constituerunt iuvenibus aperiri ei, sicut locuti sunt; [10]et fecerunt sic. Et exiit Iudith, ipsa et ancilla eius cum ea; et speculabantur eam viri civitatis, quoadusque descendit montem, usquedum transiit convallem, et iam non videbant eam. [11]Et ibant in convallem in directum, et obviavit ei prima custodia Assyriorum. [12]Et comprehenderunt eam et interrogaverunt eam: «Quorum es et unde venis et quo vadis?». Dixitque eis: «Filia sum ego Hebraeorum et recedo a facie ipsorum, quoniam incipiunt tradi vobis in devorationem. [13]Et ego venio ad faciem Holofernis principis militiae virtutis vestrae, ut renuntiem ei verba veritatis et ostendam ante faciem ipsius viam, per quam vadat, et dominetur

q. Gk *They*

presence of Holofernes the commander of your army, to give him a true report; and I will show him a way by which he can go and capture all the hill country without losing one of his men, captured or slain."

[14]When the men heard her words, and observed her face—she was in their eyes marvellously beautiful—they said to her, [15]"You have saved your life by hurrying down to the presence of our lord. Go at once to his tent; some of us will escort you and hand you over to him. [16]And when you stand before him, do not be afraid in your heart, but tell him just what you have said, and he will treat you well."

[17]They chose from their number a hundred men to accompany her and her maid, and they brought them to the tent of Holofernes. [18]There was great excitement in the whole camp, for her arrival was reported from tent to tent, and they came and stood around her as she waited outside the tent of Holofernes while they told him about her. [19]And they marvelled at her beauty, and admired the Israelites, judging them by her, and every one said to his neighbour, "Who can despise these people, who have women like this among them? Surely not a man of them had better be left alive, for if we let them go they will be able to ensnare the whole world!"

[20]Then Holofernes' companions and all his servants came out and led her into the tent. [21]Holofernes was resting on his bed, under a canopy which was woven with purple and gold and emeralds and precious stones. [22]When they told him of her he came forward to the front of the tent, with silver lamps carried before him. [23]And when Judith came into the presence of Holofernes[r] and his servants, they all marvelled at the beauty of her face; and she prostrated herself and made obeisance to him, and his slaves raised her up.

---

universae montanae, et non discumveniat ex viris eius caro una, nec spiritus vitae». [14]Et, ut audierunt viri verba eius et inspexerunt faciem eius—et erat in conspectu eorum mirabilis specie valde—dixerunt ad eam: [15]«Salvasti animam tuam in bonum festinans descendere ad faciem domini nostri. Et nunc accede ad tabernaculum eius; et ex nostris praemittent te, quousque tradant te in manibus eius. [16]Si autem steteris in conspectu eius, noli timere corde tuo, sed renuntia illi secundum verba tua, et bene tibi faciet». [17]Et elegerunt ex seipsis viros centum et adiunxerunt ei et abrae eius et perduxerunt eas ad tabernaculum Holofernis. [18]Et factus est concursus in omnibus castris; innotuit enim in tabernaculis adventus eius. Et venerunt et circumdederunt eam stantem extra tabernaculum Holofernis, quoadusque nuntiaverunt ei de ea. [19]Et mirabantur ad speciem eius et percipiebant verba eius, quia erant bona valde, et laudabant filios Israel propter eam. Et dixit unusquisque ad proximum suum: «Quis contemnet populum hunc, qui habet in se mulieres tales? Quoniam non est bonum derelinquere virum unum ex eis, qui relicti possint decipere totam terram». [20]Et exierunt omnes cubicularii Holofernis et omnes famuli eius et induxerunt eam in tabernaculum eius. [21]Et erat Holofernes requiescens in lectu suo in conopeo, quod erat ex purpura et auro et smaragdo et lapidibus pretiosissimis contextum. [22]Et nuntiaverunt ei de ea. Qui cum audisset, exiit in proscaenium; et lampades argenteae praecedentes eum multae valde. Et induxerunt eam ad eum. [23]Cum autem venit contra faciem eius Iudith et famulorum eius, laudaverunt

r. Gk *him*

11 [1]Then Holofernes said to her, "Take courage, woman, and do not be afraid in your heart, for I have never hurt any one who chose to serve Nebuchadnezzar, the king of all the earth. [2]And even now, if your people who live in the hill country had not slighted me, I would never have lifted my spear against them; but they have brought all this on themselves. [3]And now tell me why you have fled from them and have come over to us—since you have come to safety. [4]Have courage; you will live, tonight and from now on. No one will hurt you, but all will treat you well, as they do the servants of my lord King Nebuchadnezzar."

[5]Judith replied to him, "Accept the words of your servant, and let your maidservant speak in your presence, and I will tell nothing false to my lord this night. [6]And if you follow out the words of your maidservant, God will accomplish something through you, and my lord will not fail to achieve his purposes. [7]Nebuchadnezzar the king of the whole earth lives, and as his power endures, who had sent you to direct every living soul, not only do men serve him because of you, but also the beasts of the field and the cattle and the birds of the air will live by your power under Nebuchadnezzar and all his house. [8]For we have heard of your wisdom and skill, and it is reported throughout the whole world that you are the one good man in the whole kingdom, thoroughly informed and marvellous in military strategy.

[9]"Now as for the things Achior said in your council, we have heard his words, for the men of Bethulia spared him and he told them all he had said to you. [10]Therefore, my lord and master, do not disregard what he said, but keep it in your mind, for it is true: our nation cannot be punished, nor can the sword prevail against them, unless they sin against their God.

Jud 10:13

Jer 27:6
Bar 3:16–17
Dan 2:38

Jud 5:5

---

omnes speciem faciei eius; procidensque in faciem adoravit eum, et suscitaverunt eam servi eius. **[11]** [1]Dixitque ad eam Holofernes: «Aequo animo esto, mulier, et noli pavere corde tuo, quoniam ego non nocui viro cuicumque placuit servire Nabuchodonosor regi totius terrae. [2]Et nunc plebs tua, quae habitat montanam, nisi sprevissent me, non elevassem lanceam meam super ipsos, sed sibi ipsi fecerunt haec. [3]Et nunc dic mihi: Qua ex causa recessisti ab eis et venisti ad nos? Venisti enim ad salutem. Aequo animo esto, in hac nocte vives et deinceps. [4]Non enim est qui tibi noceat, sed bene tibi faciam, sicut fit servis domini mei». [5]Et dixit ad eum Iudith: «Sume verba ancillae tuae, et loquatur ancilla tua ante faciem tuam et non nuntiabo mendacium domino meo in hac nocte. [6]Et, si secutus fueris verba ancillae tuae, consummabis omnia in manibus tuis, quae faciet Deus tecum, et non excidet dominus meus de adinventionibus suis quoadusque vivit. [7]Vivit enim Nabuchodonosor rex totius terrae, et vivit virtus eius, qui misit te in correctionem omnium animarum, quoniam non solum homines per te servient ei, sed et bestiae agri et iumenta et volatilia caeli et per virtutem tuam vivent in Nabuchodonosor et omni domo eius. [8]Audivimus enim sapientiam tuam et adinventiones animi tui, et nuntiatum est universae terrae quoniam tu solus bonus in universo regno et potens in prudentia et admirabilis in militia belli. [9]Et nunc, domine meus, verbum, quod locutus est Achior in consilio tuo, audivimus verba eius quoniam susceperunt viri in Betulia, et nuntiavit eis omnia, quae locutus est apud te. [10]Propter quod, dominator

[11]"And now, in order that my lord may not be defeated and his purpose frustrated, death will fall upon them, for a sin has overtaken them by which they are about to provoke their God to anger when they do what is wrong. [12]Since their food supply is exhausted and their water has almost given out, they have planned to kill their cattle and have determined to use all that God by his laws has forbidden them to eat. [13]They have decided to consume the first fruits of the grain and the tithes of the wine and oil, which they had consecrated and set aside for the priests who minister in the presence of our God at Jerusalem—although it is not lawful for any of the people so much as to touch these things with their hands. [14]They have sent men to Jerusalem, because even the people living there have been doing this, to bring back to them permission from the senate. [15]When the word reaches them and they proceed to do this, on that very day they will be handed over to you to be destroyed.

Deut 14:22

[16]"Therefore, when I, your servant, learned all this, I fled from them; and God has sent me to accomplish with you things that will astonish the whole world, as many as shall hear about them. [17]For your servant is religious, and serves the God of heaven day and night; therefore, my lord, I will remain with you, and every night your servant will go out into the valley, and I will pray to God and he will tell me when they have committed their sins. [18]And I will come and tell you, and then you shall go out with your whole army, and not one of them will withstand you. [19]Then I will lead you through the middle of Judea, till you come to Jerusalem; and I will set your throne[s] in the midst of it; and you will lead them like sheep that have no shepherd, and not a dog will so much as open its mouth to growl at you. For this has been told me, by my foreknowledge; it was announced to me, and I was sent to tell you."

Jud 11:5

Mt 9:36

---

domine, non transeas verbum eius, sed conde illud in corde tuo, quia est verum. Non enim ultio cadit in genus nostrum, neque dominatur gladius super eos, nisi peccent in Deum suum. [11]Et nunc, ne fiat dominus meus frustratus et sine actu, cadet mors super faciem eorum, et comprehendet eos peccatum magnum, in quo exacerbaverint Dominum suum; mox ut fecerint illud, erunt tibi in consummationem. [12]Postquam enim defecerunt eis escae, et vacuefactae sunt ab eis aquae, voluerunt inicere manus iumentis suis et omnia, quae praecepit eis Deus legibus suis, ne manducarent, cogitaverunt consummare. [13]Et primitias frumenti et decimas vini et olei, quae conservaverunt sanctificantes sacerdotibus, qui praesunt in Ierusalem ante faciem Dei nostri, iudicaverunt consumere, quae nec manibus licet tangere neminem ex populo. [14]Et miserunt in Ierusalem—quia et, qui ibi inhabitant, fecerunt omnia haec—eos, qui transtulerint eis illationem a senioribus. [15]Et erit ut, cum nuntiatum fuerit, et fecerint, dentur tibi in perditionem in illa die. [16]Unde ego ancilla tua, cum cognovissem haec omnia, refugi a facie eorum, et misit me Deus facere tecum rem, in qua mirabitur tota terra, quicumque audierint ea. [17]Quoniam ancilla tua Deum colit et servit nocte ac die Deo caeli. Et nunc manebo penes te, domine meus, et exiet ancilla tua per noctem ad vallem et orabo ad Deum, et indicabit mihi quando fecerint peccata eorum. [18]Et veniens indicabo illud tibi, et exies in omni virtute tua, et non erit, qui resistat tibi ex eis. [19]Et adducam te per mediam Iudaeam, usque veniam contra Ierusalem et ponam sedem tuam in medio eius,

s. Or *chariot*

[20]Her words pleased Holofernes and all his servants, and they marveled at her wisdom and said, [21]"There is not such a woman from one end of the earth to the other, either for beauty of face or wisdom of speech!" [22]And Holofernes said to her, "God has done well to send you before the people, to lend strength to our hands and to bring destruction upon those who have slighted my lord. [23]You are not only beautiful in appearance, but wise in speech; and if you do as you have said, your God shall be my God, and you shall live in the house of King Nebuchadnezzar and be renowned throughout the whole world."

12 [1]Then he commanded them to bring her in where his silver dishes were kept, and ordered them to set a table for her with some of his own food and to serve her with his own wine. [2]But Judith said, "I cannot eat it, lest it be an offence; but I will be provided from the things I have brought with me." [3]Holofernes said to her, "If your supply runs out, where can we get more like it for you? For none of your people is here with us." [4]Judith replied, "As your soul lives, my lord, your servant will not use up the things I have with me before the Lord carries out by my hand what he has determined to do."

Jud 10:5
Esther *14:17*
Dan 1:8

12:10—13:20. The time for action is approaching. Holofernes organizes a banquet, which Judith attends dressed in all her finery because this is the opportunity offered by God's providence. Yet her inner attitude is one of humility and trust in the Lord and she acts in a very self-composed way. The text implies that Holofernes and his aides used to eat reclining on low couches or divans draped with pelts—a style reproved by the prophets (cf. Amos 6:4; Ezek). Judith, on the other hand, reclines on fleeces piled on the floor, as if to imply a degree of austerity on her part. She was fully in control of herself: "What shall I say about sobriety? [...] If Judith had drunk (wine), she would have slept with the adulterer, but since she did not drink, the sobriety of that woman alone brought about an easy victory over the

et adduces eos sicut oves, quibus non est pastor. Et non muttiet canis lingua sua contra te, quoniam haec dicta sunt mihi secundum praescientiam meam et renuntiata sunt mihi, et missa sum nuntiare tibi». [20] Et placuerunt verba eius coram Holoferne et coram omnibus famulis eius, et mirati sunt in specie et in sapientia eius et dixerunt: [21]«Non est talis mulier a summo usque ad summum terrae in specie faciei et sensu verborum». [22]Et dixit Holofernes ad eam: «Bene fecit Deus, qui misit te ante filios plebis tuae, ut fiat in manibus nostris virtus, in eis autem, qui spreverunt dominum meum perditio. [23]Et nunc tu es speciosa in aspectu et bona in verbis tuis. Quoniam, si feceris secundum quod locuta es, Deus tuus erit Deus meus, et tu in domo Nabuchodonosor regis sedebis et eris nominata per omnem terram». **[12]** [1]Et iussit introduci eam, ubi reponebatur argentum ipsius. Et praecepit sterni ei et dare ei ex obsoniis suis et ex vino suo bibere. [2]Et dixit Iudith: «Non manducabo ex eis, ne fiat mihi offensio, sed ex eis, quae allata sunt, praebebitur mihi». [3]Et dixit ad eam Holofernes: «Si autem defecerint, quae tecum sunt, unde afferemus et dabimus tibi similia eis? Non enim est homo nobiscum ex genere tuo, qui habeat similia». [4]Dixitque ad eum Iudith: «Vivit anima tua, domine mi, quoniam non impendet

[5]Then the servants of Holofernes brought her into the tent, and she slept until midnight. Along toward the morning watch she arose [6]and sent to Holofernes and said, "Let my lord now command that your servant be permitted to go out and pray." [7]So Holofernes commanded his guards not to hinder her. And she remained in the camp for three days, and went out each night to the valley of Bethulia, and bathed at the spring in the camp.[t] [8]When she came up from the spring she prayed the Lord God of Israel to direct her way for the raising up of her people. [9]So she returned clean and stayed in the tent until she ate her food toward evening.

1 Thess 3:11

[10]On the fourth day Holofernes held a banquet for his slave only, and did not invite any of his officers. [11]And he said to

---

drunken armies" (St Ambrose, *De viduis*, 7, 40); but Holofernes drank so much that he became senseless. This gave Judith the providential opportunity to act to save her people. Before she does the deed, she again says a short prayer to God. There is no trace of hatred or vengeance here: she is simply acting to defend the chosen people and the house of God. Her words are reminiscent of the Psalms of national lamentation (cf. Ps 79:6–7; 83:9–15). A similar but lengthier prayer is to be found in Sirach 36:1–17.

Judith cuts off Holofernes' head with a "sword"; the Greek word is *akinate*, a sword of Persian origin, short, worn in the belt by archers and light infantry. There are parallels with the account of the death of Sisera (Judg 4:21) and the death of Goliath (1 Sam 17:49–51), where those who rely on their own might are defeated by those who count only on God's help.

Before the enemy discover what has happened, Judith makes her way back to Bethulia carrying the head of Holofernes. The reference in Uzziah's speech to striking the enemy's head contains a slight echo of the protoevangelium (Gen 3:15).

This is another reason why we find in Christian tradition references to similarities between Judith and the Blessed Virgin. Note the parallel between Uzziah's blessing in 13:18 and Elizabeth's in Luke 1:42: "Blessed are you among women, and blessed is the fruit of your womb." On the use of the book of Judith in the liturgy for feasts of the Blessed Virgin, see the note on 9:1–14.

ancilla tua, quae sunt mecum, quousque faciat Dominus in manu mea, quae voluit». [5]Et induxerunt eam servi Holofernis in tabernaculum, et dormivit usque in mediam noctem. Surrexitque ante vigiliam matutinam [6]et misit ad Holofernen dicens: «Praecipiat nunc dominus meus permitti ancillam suam exire ad orationem». [7]Et praecepit Holofernes custodibus suis, ne prohiberent eam. Et permansit in castris triduum. Et exiebat per noctem in vallem Betuliae et baptizabat se in fontem aquae. [8]Et, ut ascendebat, orabat Dominum, Deum Israel, ut dirigeret viam eius in exaltationem populi sui. [9]Et introiens munda manebat in tabernaculo, usque dum afferretur esca eius in vesperum. [10]Et factum est, in quarta die fecit Holofernes cenam famulis suis solis et neminem eorum, qui erant super officia, vocavit ad convivium.

t. Other authorities omit *in the camp*

Bagoas, the eunuch who had charge of his personal affairs, "Go now and persuade the Hebrew woman who is in your care to join us and eat and drink with us. [12]For it will be a disgrace if we let such a woman go without enjoying her company, for if we do not embrace her she will laugh at us." [13]So Bagoas went out from the presence of Holofernes, and approached her and said, "This beautiful maidservant will please come to my lord and be honoured in his presence, and drink wine and be merry with us, and become today like one of the daughters of the Assyrians who serve in the house of Nebuchadnezzar." [14]And Judith said, "Who am I, to refuse my lord? Surely whatever pleases him I will do at once, and it will be a joy to me until the day of my death!" [15]So she got up and arrayed herself in all her woman's finery, and her maid went and spread on the ground for her before Holofernes the soft fleeces which she had received from Bagoas for her daily use, so that she might recline on them when she ate.

[16]Then Judith came in and lay down, and Holofernes' heart was ravished with her and he was moved with great desire to possess her; for he had been waiting for an opportunity to deceive her, ever since the day he first saw her. [17]So Holofernes said to her. "Drink now, and be merry with us!" [18]Judith said, "I will drink now, my lord, because my life means more to me today than in all the days since I was born." [19]Then she took and ate and drank before him what her maid had prepared. [20]And Holofernes was greatly pleased with her, and drank a great quantity of wine, much more than he had ever drunk in any one day since he was born.

13 [1]When evening came, his slaves quickly withdrew, and Bagoas closed the tent from outside and shut out the atten-

Judg 4:17–22

---

[11]Et dixit Bagoae spadoni, qui erat praepositus super omnia ipsius: «Vadens suade mulieri Hebraeae, quae est apud te, ut veniat ad nos et manducet et bibat nobiscum. [12]Ecce enim turpe est in conspectu nostro, ut mulierem talem dimittamus non fabulantes ei, quoniam, si non eam attraxerimus, deridebit nos». [13]Et exiit Bagoas a facie Holofernis et introivit ad eam et dixit ei: «Non pigeat puellam bonam hanc introeuntem ad dominum meum glorificari ante faciem eius et bibere nobiscum vinum in iucunditatem et fieri in hodierno die honorificam sicut unam filiarum magnatorum Assyriae, quae assistunt in domo Nabuchodonosor». [14]Dixitque ad eum Iudith: «Et quae sum ego, ut contradicam domino meo? Quoniam omne, quod erit optimum in oculis eius, festinans faciam, et erit hoc mihi gaudium usque ad diem mortis meae». [15]Et surgens exornavit se vestimento suo et omni muliebri ornatu, et praecessit ancilla eius et stravit ei contra Holofernen in terra stragula, quae acceperat a Bagoa in cotidianum usum, ut manducaret discumbens super ea. [16]Et introiens Iudith discubuit. Et obstupuit cor Holofernis in eam, et commota est anima eius et erat concupiscens valde, ut concumberet cum ea; quaerebatque tempus seducendi eam ex die, quo viderat illam. [17]Et dixit ad eam Holofernes: «Bibe et esto nobiscum in iucunditatem». [18]Et dixit Iudith: «Bibam, domine, quia magnificata est vita mea in me hodie prae omnibus diebus nativitatis meae». [19]Et accipiens manducavit et bibit coram illo ea, quae praeparaverat ipsi ancilla sua. [20]Et iucundatus est Holofernes de ea et bibit multum vinum, quantum numquam bibit in uno die, ex quo natus est. **[13]** [1]Et, ut vesper factus est, festinaverunt servi eius abire, et Bagoas conclusit tabernaculum a foris et dimisit adstantes a facie domini sui. Et abierunt omnes

dants from his master's presence; and they went to bed, for they all were weary because the banquet had lasted long. [2]So Judith was left alone in the tent, with Holofernes stretched out on his bed, for he was overcome with wine.

[3]Now Judith had told her maid to stand outside the bedchamber and to wait for her to come out, as she did every day; for she said she would be going out for her prayers. And she had said the same thing to Bagoas. [4]So every one went out, and no one, either small or great, was left in the bedchamber. Then Judith, standing beside his bed, said in her heart, "O Lord God of all might, look in this hour upon the work of my hands for the exaltation of Jerusalem. [5]For now is the time to help thy inheritance, and to carry out my undertaking for the destruction of the enemies who have risen up against us."

[6]She went up to the post at the end of the bed, above Holofernes' head, and took down his sword that hung there. [7]She came close to his bed and took hold of the hair of his head, and said, "Give me strength this day, O Lord God of Israel!" [8]And she struck his neck twice with all her might, and severed it from his body. [9]Then she tumbled his body off the bed and pulled down the canopy from the posts; after a moment she went out, and gave Holofernes' head to her maid, [10]who placed it in her food bag.

Judg 4:21

Then the two of them went out together, as they were accustomed to go for prayer; and they passed through the camp and circled around the valley and went up the mountain to Bethulia and came to its gates. [11]Judith called out from afar to the watchmen at the gates, "Open, open the gate! God, our God, is still with us, to show his power in Israel, and his strength against our enemies, even as he has done this day!"

Ex 15:1–2
Ps 48:7–11; 68; 98:1–3

---

in cubilia sua; erant enim omnes fatigati, quoniam plurimus factus erat potus. [2]Derelicta est autem sola Iudith in tabernaculo, et Holofernes prociderat in lectum suum; circumfusum enim erat ei vinum. [3]Et dixit Iudith ancillae suae, ut staret extra cubiculum et observaret exitum eius sicut cotidie; exire enim se dixit ad orationem suam, et Bagoae locuta est secundum verba haec. [4]Discesseruntque omnes a facie, et nemo relictus est in cubiculo eius, a minimo usque ad magnum. Et stans Iudith ad caput eius dixit: «Domine, Domine, Deus omnium virtutum, respice in hac hora ad opera manuum mearum, ut exaltetur Ierusalem. [5]Quia nunc est tempus, ut suscipias hereditatem tuam et facias cogitationem meam in quassationem inimicorum, qui in surrexerunt super nos». [6]Et accedens ad columnam lectus, quae erat ad caput Holofernis, deposuit pugionem illius ab illa. [7]Et accedens ad lectum comprehendit comam capitis eius et dixit: «Deus Israel, confirma me, Domine, Deus Israel, in hoc die». [8]Et percussit in cervicem eius bis in virtute sua et abstulit caput eius ab eo. [9]Et volutavit corpus eius a toro et abstulit conopeum eius a columnis; et post pusillum exiit et tradidit abrae suae caput Holofernis, [10]et misit illud in peram escarum suarum. Et exierunt ambae simul secundum consuetudinem suam quasi ad orationem. Transeuntesque castra gyraverunt totam vallem illam et subascenderunt montem Betuliae et venerunt ad portas eius. [11]Et dixit Iudith a longe eis, qui custodiebant in portis: «Aperite, aperite portam! Nobiscum est Deus, Deus noster, ut faciat adhuc virtutem in Israel et potentiam adversus inimicos nostros, sicut et hodie fecit».

[12]When the men of her city heard her voice, they hurried down to the city gate and called together the elders of the city. [13]They all ran together, both small and great, for it was unbelievable that she had returned; they opened the gate and admitted them, and they kindled a fire for light, and gathered around them. [14]Then she said to them with a loud voice, "Praise God, O praise him! Praise God, who has not withdrawn his mercy from the house of Israel, but has destroyed our enemies by my hand this very night!"

[15]Then she took the head out of the bag and showed it to them, and said, "See, here is the head of Holofernes, the commander of the Assyrian army, and here is the canopy beneath which he lay in his drunken stupor. The Lord has struck him down by the hand of a woman. [16]As the Lord lives, who has protected me in the way I went, it was my face that tricked him to his destruction, and yet he committed no act of sin with me, to defile and shame me."

[17]All the people were greatly astonished, and bowed down and worshipped God, and said with one accord, "Blessed art thou, our God, who hast brought into contempt this day the enemies of thy people."

[18]And Uzziah said to her, "O daughter, you are blessed by the Most High God above all women on earth; and blessed be the Lord God, who created the heavens and the earth, who has guided you to strike the head of the leader of our enemies. [19]Your hope will never depart from the hearts of men, as they remember the power of God. [20]May God grant this to be a perpetual honour to you, and may he visit you with blessings, because you did not spare your own life when our nation was brought low, but have avenged our ruin, walking in the straight path before our God." And all the people said, "So be it, so be it!"*

Judg 5:24
Lk 1:28,42,48

---

[12]Et factum est, ut audierunt viri civitatis vocem eius, festinaverunt descendere ad portam civitatis suae et convocaverunt seniores civitatis. [13]Et concurrerunt omnes a minimo usque ad magnum, quoniam mirum erat eis illam reversam esse. Et aperuerunt portam et receperunt eas et accendentes ignem ad lumen congyraverunt eam. [14]Quae dixit ad eos voce magna: «Laudate Dominum nostrum, laudate, quia non abstulit misericordiam suam a domo Israel, sed conteruit inimicos nostros per manum meam in hac nocte». [15]Et proferens caput de pera sua ostendit et dixit eis: «Ecce caput Holofernis principis militiae virtutis Assyriorum et ecce conopeum, in quo recumbebat in ebrietate sua. Et percussit eum Dominus in manu feminae. [16]Et vivit Dominus, qui custodivit me in via mea, qua profecta sum, quoniam seduxit eum facies mea in perditionem eius, et non fecit peccatum mecum in coinquinationem et confusionem». [17]Et obstupuit omnis populus valde et inclinantes se adoraverunt Deum et dixerunt unanimes: «Benedictus es, Deus noster, qui ad nihilum redegisti inimicos populi tui in hodierna die». [18]Et dixit ad eam Ozias: «Benedicta tu es, filia, a Deo excelso prae omnibus mulieribus, quae sunt super terram. Et benedictus Dominus Deus noster, qui creavit caelum et terram, qui direxit te in vulnus capitis principis inimicorum nostrorum. [19]Quoniam non discedet laus tua a corde hominum memorantium virtutis Dei usque in sempiternum. [20]Et faciat tibi ea Deus in exaltationem aeternam, ut visitet te in bonis, pro eo quod non pepercisti animae tuae propter humilitatem generis nostri, sed prosilisti in ruinam nostram in directum ambulans in conspectu Dei nostri». Et dixit omnis populus: «Fiat, fiat!».

Achior's conversion

14 [1]Then Judith said to them, "Listen to me, my brethren, and take this head and hang it upon the parapet of your wall. [2]And as soon as morning comes and the sun rises, let every valiant man take his weapons and go out of the city, and set a captain over them, as if you were going down to the plain against the Assyrian outpost; only do not go down. [3]Then they will seize their arms and go into the camp and rouse the officers of the Assyrian army; and they will rush into the tent of Holofernes, and will not find him. Then fear will come over them, and they will flee before you, [4]and you and all who live within the borders of Israel shall pursue them and cut them down as they flee. [5]But before you do all this, bring Achior the Ammonite to me, and let him see and recognize the man who despised the house of Israel and sent him to us as if to his death."

[6]So they summoned Achior from the house of Uzziah. And when he came and saw the head of Holofernes in the hand of one of the men at the gathering of the people, he fell down on his face and his spirit failed him. [7]And when they raised him up he fell at Judith's feet, and knelt before her, and said, "Blessed are you in every tent of Judah! In every nation those who hear your name will be alarmed. [8]Now tell me what you have done during these days."

14:1–10. The events covered in the central chapters of this book bear out what Achior the Ammonite said in his speech to Holofernes (cf. 5:6–19). Now, as the story draws to a close, we meet Achior again: when he hears what has happened, he is converted and becomes a member of the nation that enjoys such divine favour.

14:11—15:7. The army that had swept all before it and was on the verge of attacking the Israelites (5:1ff), breaks up in confusion when they find that the

[14] [1]Et dixit Iudith ad illos: «Audite me, fratres, et accipientes caput hoc suspendite illud super propugnaculum muri nostri. [2]Et, cum aurora illuxerit, et exierit sol super terram, accipite unusquisque vasa bellica vestra et exietis omnis vir potens extra civitatem et dabitis initium adversus eos tamquam descendentes in campum ad primam custodiam filiorum Assyriae; et non descendetis. [3]Et accipientes illi arma sua ibunt in castra sua et suscitabunt duces virtutis Assyriae concurrentque ad tabernaculum Holofernis et non invenient illum, et incidet in illos timor, et fugient a facie vestra. [4]Et subsecuti vos et omnes, qui incolunt omnem finem Israel, prosternite illos in viis illorum. [5]Ante autem quam faciatis ista, vocate mihi Achior Ammoniten, ut videns recognoscat eum, qui vituperavit domum Israel et ipsum quasi in mortem misit ad nos». [6]Et vocaverunt Achior de domo Oziae, qui, ut venit et vidit caput Holofernis in manu viri unius in ecclesia populi, cecidit in faciem, et resolutus est spiritus ipsius. [7]Ut autem resuscitaverunt eum, procidit ad pedes Iudith et adoravit faciem ipsius et dixit: «Benedicta tu in omni tabernaculo Iudae et in omni gente, quicumque audientes nomen tuum turbabuntur. [8]Et nunc annuntia mihi, quaecumque fecisti in diebus istis». Et rettulit illi Iudith in medio populi omnia, quaecumque fecerat, ex qua die exivit usque in diem, qua loquebatur illis. [9]Ut autem desiit loqui, exsultavit omnis populus voce magna et dedit vocem iucunditatis in civitate sua. [10]Videns autem Achior

Then Judith described to him in the presence of the people all that she had done, from the day she left until the moment of her speaking to them. [9]And when she had finished, the people raised a great shout and made a joyful noise in their city. [10]And when Achior saw all that the God of Israel had done, he believed firmly in God, and was circumcised, and joined the house of Israel, remaining so to this day.

Deut 23:4–5

The enemy army flees

[11]As soon as it was dawn they hung the head of Holofernes on the wall, and every man took his weapons, and they went out in companies to the passes in the mountains. [12]And when the Assyrians saw them they sent word to their commanders, and they went to the generals and the captains and to all their officers. [13]So they came to Holofernes' tent and said to the steward in charge of all his personal affairs, "Wake up our lord, for the slaves have been so bold as to come down against us to give battle, in order to be destroyed completely."

[14]So Bagoas went in and knocked at the door of the tent, for he supposed that he was sleeping with Judith. [15]But when no one answered, he opened it and went into the bedchamber and found

---

power of the God of Israel has used a woman to assassinate their general. It is a case of every man for himself. The Israelites give pursuit and they obtain a great victory and much booty. Mighty men of war who relied on their own resources have been undone by the power of the Lord. Judith is praised for her valour but also for her wisdom: "By her hand, Holofernes alone was overcome, but an entire army of the enemy was defeated by her intelligence. By cutting off the head of Holofernes—an act that the wisdom of men did not even think of doing—she raised the spirits of her people and trod the enemy's underfoot, filling her people with a sense of honour and striking terror into the heart of the enemy, who were defeated and fled. The temperance and sobriety of that widow not only gave her command over her own nature, but—more important still—it made men stronger" (St Ambrose, *De viduis,* 7, 41).

omnia, quaecumque fecit Deus Israel, credidit Deo valde et circumcidit carnem praeputii sui, et appositus est ad domum Israel usque in diem hanc. [11]Postquam autem aurora orta est, suspenderunt caput Holofernis super murum; et accepit omnis vir arma sua, et exierunt secundum cohortes ad ascensiones montis. [12]Filii autem Assyriae, ut viderunt illos, miserunt ad praepositos suos, et illi venerunt ad duces et ad tribunos et ad omnes principes suos. [13]Et venerunt ad tabernaculum Holofernis et dixerunt Bagoae, qui erat super omnia eius: «Suscita dominum nostrum, quoniam ausi sunt Iudaei descendere ad nos in bellum, ut pereant usque ad finem». [14]Introivitque Bagoas et pulsavit cortinam; suspicabatur enim illum cum Iudith dormire. [15]Cum autem nemo responderet, aperiens cortinam intravit in cubiculum et invenit illum in scabello proiectum, mortuum, nudum, et caput illius sublatum ab eo.

Acts 14:14
Judg 9:54
Jud 13:15; 16:5–9

him thrown down on the platform dead, with his head cut off and missing. [16]And he cried out with a loud voice and wept and groaned and shouted, and rent his garments. [17]Then he went to the tent where Judith had stayed, and when he did not find her he rushed out to the people and shouted, [18]"The slaves have tricked us! One Hebrew woman has brought disgrace upon the house of King Nebuchadnezzar! For look, here is Holofernes lying on the ground, and his head is not on him!"

[19]When the leaders of the Assyrian army heard this, they rent their tunics and were greatly dismayed, and their loud cries and shouts arose in the midst of the camp.

15 [1]When the men in the tents heard it, they were amazed at what had happened. [2]Fear and trembling came over them, so that they did not wait for one another, but with one impulse all rushed out and fled by every path across the plain and through the hill country. [3]Those who had camped in the hills around Bethulia also took to flight. Then the men of Israel, every one that was a

---

15:8—16:25. The book of Judith began by describing the arrogance of Nebuchadnezzar. God, through Judith, has defeated him. The book ends by exalting Judith, the humble widow who put all her trust in God (16:21–24). St Ambrose praises the simple, unaffected life led by Judith in later days: "Ever faithful to her state as a widow, she spurned the requests of those who desired to marry her, removing the feast-day garments and, putting on once more her widow's dress, she placed no value on the glories of her triumph, believing that the rewards for the victory won over bodily vices are of greater worth than those given for defeating the weapons of the enemy" (*De viduis*, 7, 42).

The New Testament helps us understand the divine logic at work in the book of Judith: the Lord "has put down the mighty from their thrones, and exalted those of low degree" (Lk 1:52) for, as Jesus taught, "everyone who exalts himself will be humbled, but he who humbles himself will be exalted" (Lk 14:11;18:14; Mt 23:12).

[16]Et exclamavit voce magna cum fletu et gemitu et clamore magno et scidit vestimenta sua. [17]Et intravit in tabernaculum, ubi Iudith fuerat hospitata, et non invenit eam. Et exsilivit ad populum et clamavit: [18]«Inique gesserunt servi! Fecit confusionem una mulier Hebraeorum in domum regis Nabuchodonosor, quoniam ecce Holofernes in terra, et caput ipsius non est in illo!». [19]Ut autem audierunt verba haec, principes virtutis Assyriae sciderunt tunicas suas, et conturbata est anima eorum valde, et factus est clamor et ululatus magnus in medio castrorum. **[15]** [1]Ut autem audierunt hi, qui in tabernaculis erant, obstupuerunt super quod factum erat. [2]Et incidit in illos timor et tremor, et non erat homo, qui maneret contra faciem proximi sui adhuc, sed effusi simul fugiebant in omnem viam campi et montanae. [3]Et qui castra collocaverant in montana circa Betuliam, in fugam conversi sunt. Et tunc filii Israel, omnis vir bellator eorum, diffusi sunt in illos. [4]Et misit Ozias Betomesthaim et Bemen et Chobam et Cholam in omnem finem Israel, qui renuntiarent de his rebus, quae consummata erant, et ut omnes in hostes effunderentur in interfectionem eorum. [5]Ut autem audierunt filii Israel, omnes simul irruerunt in illos et

soldier, rushed out upon them. [4]And Uzziah sent men to Betomasthaim and Bebai and Choba and Kola, and to all the frontiers of Israel, to tell what had taken place and to urge all to rush out upon their enemies to destroy them. [5]And when the Israelites heard it, with one accord they fell upon the enemy,[u] and cut them down as far as Choba. Those in Jerusalem and all the hill country also came, for they were told what had happened in the camp of the enemy; and those in Gilead and in Galilee outflanked them with great slaughter, even beyond Damascus and its borders. [6]The rest of the people of Bethulia fell upon the Assyrian camp and plundered it, and were greatly enriched. [7]And the Israelites, when they returned from the slaughter, took possession of what remained, and the villages and towns in the hill country and in the plain got a great amount of booty, for there was a vast quantity of it.

Esther 9:5–6

Judith's song of praise

[8]Then Joakim the high priest, and the senate of the people of Israel who lived at Jerusalem, came to witness the good things which the Lord had done for Israel, and to see Judith and to greet her. [9]And when they met her they all blessed her with one accord and said to her, "You are the exaltation of Jerusalem,* you are the great glory of Israel, you are the great pride of our nation! [10]You have done all this singlehanded; you have done great good to Israel, and God is well pleased with it. May the Almighty Lord bless you for ever!" And all the people said, "So be it!"

[11]So all the people plundered the camp for thirty days. They gave Judith the tent of Holofernes and all his silver dishes and his beds and his bowls and all his furniture; and she took them and loaded her mule and hitched up her carts and piled the things on them.

---

concidebant illos usque Chobam. Similiter autem et, qui in Ierusalem erant, advenerunt ex omni montana; renuntiata enim sunt illis, quae facta sunt in castris inimicorum illorum. Et qui in Galaad et qui in Galilaea erant, persecuti sunt illos et percusserunt eos plaga magna, donec transirent Damascum et terminos eorum. [6]Reliqui autem, qui inhabitabant Betuliam, irruerunt in castra Assyriae et exspoliaverunt eos et locupletati sunt valde. [7]Filii autem Israel regressi a caede dominati sunt reliquiis; et vici et villae in montana et in campestri multa spolia possederunt: multitudo enim magna erat. [8]Et venit Ioachim sacerdos magnus et seniores filiorum Israel, qui inhabitabant Ierusalem, ut viderent bona, quae fecit Dominus Israel, et ut viderent Iudith et loquerentur cum illa in pace. [9]Et, ut exiit ad illos Iudith, benedixerunt simul eam omnes et dixerunt ad illam: «Tu exaltatio Ierusalem, tu gloria magna Israel, tu laus magna generis nostri. [10]Fecisti omnia haec in manu tua, fecisti bona cum Israel, et complacuit in illis Deus. Benedicta esto tu, mulier, apud Deum omnipotentem in aeternum tempus». Et dixit omnis populus: «Fiat, fiat!». [11]Et exspoliavit populus castra per dies triginta, et dederunt Iudith tabernaculum Holofernis et omne argentum et lectus et vasa et omnem apparatum illius. Et accipiens

u. Gk *them*

Ex 15:20
Judg 11:34
1 Sam 18:6
Jer 31:4,13

[12]Then all the women of Israel gathered to see her, and blessed her, and some of them performed a dance for her; and she took branches in her hands and gave them to the women who were with her; [13]and they crowned themselves with olive wreaths, she and those who were with her; and she went before all the people in the dance, leading all the women, while all the men of Israel followed, bearing their arms and wearing garlands and with songs on their lips.

Ex 15
Judg 5
1 Sam 2:1–10
Ps 81:1–3; 135:1–3; 149:1–3

16 [1]Then Judith began this thanksgiving before all Israel, and all the people loudly sang this song of praise. [2]And Judith said,

Ex 15:3
Jud 9:7
Ps 46:9; 68:30; 76:3

Begin a song to my God with tambourines,
sing to my Lord with cymbals.
Raise to him a new psalm;[v]
exalt him, and call upon his name.

16:2–17. The song of Judith is one of the most poetic passages in the Old Testament—rich in imagery, profound in meaning. There is a brief introduction which calls for praise of God and summarizes why he is being thanked (vv.2–3); then comes an account of the events from the time the Assyrians invaded up to the victory won by Judith (vv. 4–12), and a song in praise of God for his wondrous works (vv. 13–15); and an invitation to trust in the Lord, and a warning to Israel's enemies (vv. 16–17).

The hymn begins in the same kind of way as Psalms of praise and thanksgiving (cf. Ps 81:1–3; 149:1–3). Tambourines and cymbals (cf. Ps 150:4–5) were used to accompany festive singing. The expression "the Lord who crushes wars" (v. 3) is a reference to an attribute of God mentioned in some Psalms (cf. Ps 46:9; 68:30; 76:3) and which Judith used earlier in her prayer (cf. 9:7).

The last part of the hymn has many parallels in other poetic passages of the Old Testament. Many Psalms, for example, begin with an exhortation to sing a new song to the Lord (Ps 95:1; 96:1; 144:9; 149:1). Likewise God the Creator is praised in terms similar to those used here, for example, in Psalm 86:9–10; 148:5, and particularly in Psalm 33:6–9 and 104:1–8, 29–30.

illa imposuit in mulas et iunxit currus suos et congessit illa in ipsis. [12]Et concurrit omnis mulier Israel, ut videret eam, et benedixerunt eam et fecerunt ei chorum de se. Et accepit thyrsos in manibus suis et dedit mulieribus, quae secum erant. [13]Et coronatae sunt oliva, ipsa et quae cum illa erant. Et antecessit omni populo in chorea dux omnium mulierum, et sequebatur omnis vir Israel armatus, cum coronis et hymnis in ore ipsorum. [14]Et exordiebatur Iudith confessionem hanc in omni Israel, et acclamabat omnis populus laudationem hanc Domini. **[16]** [1]Dixitque Iudith: «Incipite Deo meo in tympanis, / cantate Domino meo in cymbalis, / modulamini illi psalmum novum, / exaltate et invocate nomen ipsius. / [2]Tu es Deus conterens bella, / qui ponis castra in medio populi tui, / ut eripias me de manu persequentium me. / [3]Venit Assur a montibus, a borra, / venit in milibus virtutum suarum, / quorum multitudo obturavit torrentes, / et equitatus ipsorum texit colles. / [4]Et dixit incensurum se fines meos / et iuvenes meos

v. Other authorities read *a psalm and praise*

[3] For God is the Lord who crushes wars;
for he has delivered me out of the hands of my pursuers,
and brought me to his camp, in the midst of the people.

[4] The Assyrian came down from the mountains of the north;
he came with myriads of his warriors;
their multitude blocked up the valleys,
their cavalry covered the hills.
[5] He boasted that he would burn up my territory,
and kill my young men with the sword,
and dash my infants to the ground
and seize my children as prey,
and take my virgins as booty.

[6] But the Lord Almighty has foiled them
by the hand of a woman.
For their mighty one did not fall by the hands of the young men,
nor did the sons of the Titans smite him,
nor did tall giants set upon him;
but Judith the daughter of Merari undid him
with the beauty of her countenance.

[8] For she took off her widow's mourning
to exalt the oppressed in Israel.
She anointed her face with ointment
and fastened her hair with a tiara
and put on a linen gown to deceive him.
[9] Her sandal ravished his eyes,
her beauty captivated his mind,
and the sword severed his neck.
[10] The Persians trembled at her boldness,
the Medes were daunted at her daring.

---

occisurum gladio / et mammantes meos daturum ad solum / et infantes meos daturum in partitionem / et virgines spoliaturum. / [5]Dominus omnipotens sprevit illos / et confudit illos in manu feminae! / [6]Non enim cecidit potens eorum a iuvenibus, / nec filii Titanum percusserunt illum, / nec alti gigantes superposuerunt se illi, / sed Iudith filia Merari / in specie faciei suae dissolvit illum. / [7]Dispoliavit enim se stola viduitatis suae / in exaltationem dolentium in Israel. / Unxit faciem suam unguento / [8]et colligavit capillos suos in mitra / et accepit stolam lineam in seductionem eius. / [9]Sandalum eius rapuit oculum ipsius, / et species eius captivam fecit animam illius, / et transiit gladius cervicem eius. / [10]Horruerunt Persae audaciam eius, / et Medi turbati sunt constantia ipsius. / [11]Tunc ululaverunt humiles mei, / et exclamaverunt aegrotantes et territi sunt, / in altum extulerunt vocem suam / et conversi sunt. / [12]Filii puellarum compunxerunt illos / et tamquam pueros ultroneos vulnerabant; / perierunt a praelio

[11] Then my oppressed people shouted for joy;
my weak people shouted[w] and the enemy[x] trembled;
they lifted up their voices, and the enemy[x] were turned back.

Jud 5:23; 6:6

[12] The sons of maidservants have pierced them through;
they were wounded like the children of fugitives,
they perished before the army of my Lord.

Ps 86:10; 144:9; 147:5

[13] I will sing to my God a new song:
O Lord, thou are great and glorious,
wonderful in strength, invincible.

Esther 4:17b

Ps 33:9; 104:30; 148:5

[14] Let all thy creatures serve thee,
for thou didst speak, and they were made.
Thou didst send forth thy Spirit,[y] and it formed them;
there is none that can resist thy voice.

Ps 25:14; 97:5; 103:13

[15] For the mountains shall be shaken to their
foundations with the waters;
at thy presence the rocks shall melt like wax,
but to those who fear thee
thou wilt continue to show mercy.

Ps 51:16
Sir 34:13–17

[16] For every sacrifice as a fragrant offering is a small thing,
and all fat for burnt offerings to thee is a very little thing,
but he who fears the Lord shall be great for ever.

Judg 5:31
Sir 7:17
Is 66:24
Joel 4:1–4
Mt 11:22
Mk 9:48
Acts 12:23
Jas 5:3

[17] Woe to the nations that rise up against my people!
The Lord Almighty will take vengeance on them
in the day of judgment;
fire and worms he will give to their flesh;
they shall weep in pain for ever.

Conclusion

[18]When they arrived at Jerusalem they worshipped God. As soon as the people were purified, they offered their burnt offerings, their

Domini mei. / [13]Cantabo Deo meo hymnum novum: / Domine, magnus es tu et clarus, / mirabilis in virtute et insuperabilis. / [14]Tibi serviat omnis creatura tua, / quoniam dixisti, et facta sunt, /misisti spiritum tuum, et aedificata sunt, / et non est qui resistat voci tuae. / [15]Montes enim a fundamentis agitabuntur cum aquis, / petrae autem a facie tua tamquam cera liquescent. / Illis autem qui timent te / propitius adhuc eris. / [16]Quoniam pusillum omne sacrum ad odorem suavitatis, / et minimus omnis adeps in holocaustum tibi. / Qui autem timet Dominum, / magnus apud eum semper. / [17]Vae gentibus assurgentibus generi meo! / Dominus omnipotens vindicabit illos, / in die iudicii visitabit eos, / ut det ignem et vermes in carnes eorum, / et comburentur, ut sentiant usque in aeternum». [18]Ut autem venerunt in Ierusalem, adoraverunt Deum; et, postquam mundatus est populus, rettulerunt holocaustum Domino

w. Other authorities read *feared* **x.** Gk *they* **y.** Or *breath*

freewill offerings, and their gifts. [19]Judith also dedicated to God all the vessels of Holofernes, which the people had given her; and the canopy which she took for herself from his bedchamber she gave as a votive offering to the Lord. [20]So the people continued feasting in Jerusalem before the sanctuary for three months, and Judith remained with them.

Num 31:48–54
Josh 6:17
Ps 66:13–15

Lev 27:28–29
Deut 13:13–19

[21]After this every one returned home to his own inheritance, and Judith went to Bethulia, and remained on her estate, and was honoured in her time throughout the whole country. [22]Many desired to marry her, but she remained a widow all the days of her life after Manasseh her husband died and was gathered to his people. [23]She became more and more famous, and grew old in her husband's house, until she was one hundred and five years old. She set her maid free. She died in Bethulia, and they buried her in the cave of her husband Manasseh, [24]and the house of Israel mourned for her seven days. Before she died she distributed her property to all those who were next of kin to her husband Manasseh, and to her own nearest kindred. [25]And no one ever again spread terror among the people of Israel in the days of Judith, or for a long time after her death.*

Gen 23:19; 49:29–32

Lev 27:28

Judg 3:11,30; 5:31; 8:28

---

et voluntaria sua et munera. [19]Et attulit Iudith omnia vasa Holofernis, quaecumque dederat ei populus, et conopeum, quod sustulerat de cubiculo ipsius, in consecrationem Domino dedit. [20]Et populus laetabatur in Ierusalem contra faciem sanctorum per menses tres, et Iudith cum illis mansit. [21]Post illos autem dies rediit unusquisque in hereditatem suam, et Iudith abiit in Betuliam et demorata est in possessione sua. Et facta est secundum tempus suum clara in omni terra, [22]et multi concupierunt eam, et non cognovit vir illam omnibus diebus vitae eius, ex qua die mortuus est Manasses maritus illius et appositus est ad populum suum. [23]Et procedens magna facta est valde et senuit in domo mariti sui Manasses annos centum quinque; et dimisit abram suam liberam. Et mortua est in Betulia, et sepelierunt eam in spelunca. [24]Et planxit eam omnis Israel diebus septem. Divisitque bona sua, priusquam moreretur, omnibus proximis viri sui Manasses et proximis ex genere suo. [25]Et non fuit adhuc, qui in timorem mitteret filios Israel in diebus Iudith et post mortem eius diebus multis.

ESTHER

Introduction

In the Vulgate Latin version of the Bible the book of Esther comes immediately after those of Tobit and Judith. It closes that short sequence of pleasant stories filled with religious meaning which follow the books of Ezra and Nehemiah. In most codices of the Greek translation of the Septuagint it is placed at the end of the historical books of the Old Testament, though before Tobit and Judith. In the Hebrew Bible it is included among the "Writings". It is one of the five *megil·lot*, that is, the five parchment rolls read out on certain Jewish feast-days. The book of Esther is read in synagogues on the feast of Purim, a festival which Jews celebrate with special meals and the exchange of gifts.

1. THE TEXT OF ESTHER

The manuscripts of the Hebrew text and the Greek text differ from one another, as do early translations. The Greek is not a straight translation of the Hebrew: it is filled out with additions which are quite lengthy. Moreover, there are differences from one Greek codex to the next.

The solution adopted by the RSV is to print the translation of the Hebrew in roman type, and to insert in *italics* passages translated from Greek codices (these are inserted in places that fit the chronology; and they carry a completely different chapter-and-verse sequence: cf. the RSVCE note on 11:2 on p. 616). The New Vulgate (and the Spanish original of the *Navarre Bible*) inserts these "Greek" passages in their logical places but instead of using that different chapter-and-verse numeration, it retains the Hebrew numbering system and identifies verses by number and letters, not solely by numbers: cf. the New Vulgate text. The RSV and the New Vulgate do not run in exact parallel.

2. STRUCTURE AND CONTENT

In its Christian canonical version (which is the version provided in the RSV) the book of Esther tells the story of how God listened to the prayers of his people and delivered them from a persecution unleashed by their enemies. He did this by providentially guiding the course of events rather than by some dramatic intervention.

The story-line is summarized in the account of Mordecai's dream recorded at the start of the book and explained at the end. The various protagonists are

introduced by stages, and the tension builds up until eventually Haman, the enemy of the Jews, is disgraced, and the king changes his policy and authorizes the Jews to protect themselves from their enemies. The structure of the story is as follows:

PROLOGUE (*11:2–12*). The content of Mordecai's dream.

1. ESTHER BECOMES A QUEEN (1:1—2:18). King Ahasu-erus decides to repudiate his wife Vashti (1:1–22), and her place is taken by Esther, a Jewish maiden, an orphan who was brought up by her uncle Mordecai (2:1–18).

2. CONFRONTATION BETWEEN MORDECAI AND HAMAN (2:19—3:6). Here we meet Mordecai, the most prominent Jew, and his enemy Haman. Mordecai reports a conspiracy against the king but derives no benefit from doing so (2:19–23). Haman is promoted by the king, and comes to hate the Jews because Mordecai refuses to do obeisance to him (3:1–6).

3. A DECREE TO EXTERMINATE THE JEWS (3:7–13; *13:1–7*; 3:14–15). Haman uses his influence over the king to have him issue an edict calling for the extermination of all Jews throughout the empire on a particular day, the thirteenth of the month of Adar (3:7–13).

4. THE JEWS IMPLORE GOD'S HELP (4:1–17; *13:8—14:19*). When they learn about the decree, the Jews are thrown into consternation, and they pray to God (4:1–3; this is more evident in verses that are not found in the Greek codices, but which do exist in ancient Latin translations: cf. New Vulgate 3:15b–15i). Mordecai asks Esther to intercede on her people's behalf (4:1–17); and both Mordecai (*13:8–17*) and Esther (*14:1–19*) address God in prayer.

5. MORDECAI GAINS THE UPPER HAND OVER HAMAN (5:1–2; *15:1–16*; 5:3—6:14). Supported by her own prayer and that of all the people, Esther enters the king's presence to invite him to a dinner she has prepared and at which she plans to intercede on her people's behalf (5:1ff). That night, when he cannot sleep, the king remembers the favour done him by Mordecai and resolves to reward him for it (6:1–14).

6. GOD SAVES HIS PEOPLE FROM THE THREAT HANGING OVER THEM (7:1–10; 8:1–12; *16:1–24*: 8:13—10:3). Haman is disgraced and executed (7:1–10), and Mordecai is appointed in his place (8:1–8). Using powers delegated by the king, he issues an edict in the king's name authorizing the Jews to take steps to defend themselves (8:9–12; *16:1–24*; 8:13–17). On the

day fixed for their extermination, the Jews turn the tables on their persecutors (9:1–19). To celebrate the joy of their deliverance, the annual feast of Purim is established (9:20—10:3).

EPILOGUE (*10:4—11:1*). The book ends with an interpretation of Mordecai's dream reported at the start of the book (*11:2–12*).

3. COMPOSITION

The differences in the manuscripts of this book must all go back to its long and complicated process of composition. The core of the plot may derive from memories of some persecution suffered by Jews scattered across the Persian empire. The sacred writer could have used that material to compose this narrative meant to be read on the feast of Purim to instill in them the need to always be faithful to God, who is never forgetful of them.

Later on, some author or authors rewrote the text, translating the original Hebrew into Greek, and filling the narrative out to explain God's intervention in history and to show the importance of prayer for obtaining God's help. We do not know exactly when this rewriting took place but it was probably around the start of the first century AD.

4. MESSAGE

In the *Hebrew* text of the book of Esther, God is not named nor is the temple mentioned or indeed any of the institutions of the Jewish people—which indicates that the book was written in a pagan environment and was meant to be read by both Jews and non-Jews. But, although the Lord does not seem to be involved in the events narrated, divine Providence is at work, watching over his people and protecting them from their enemies. Things may seem to happen by chance or at random (even the date fixed for the massacre of the Jews is decided by the casting of lots: cf. 3:7), but if one reflects on the course of events one can see that the hand of God is at work quietly and effectively. This is the first lesson to be drawn from the book.

The *Greek* additions to the text make it very explicit that God is listening to the prayers of his people and hastens to their aid. However, he expects his faithful to take what steps they can. The faith shown by Esther and Mordecai is strong and undaunted. Acting in line with the customs in pagan courts of the time, Esther comes to be queen, but she does not lose her Jewish identity. She and Mordecai put all their trust in the Lord, doing penance and praying intensely, but they also act very responsibly and use all their initiative. They

manage to intercede with the king for their people to remove the threat hanging over them. Their trust in God is not a retreat into inaction: it gives them strength to make bold decisions.

The conflict between the Jews and their enemies was essentially a religious one: the Jews did not want to comply with requirements imposed on them by the civil authorities when these demanded an obedience that was due to God alone. The entire book, as far as Jewish readers are concerned, is a call to be resolute and put their trust in the Lord and not be drawn away from him by pressures of the environment: they should stay loyal to God and not be afraid of the difficulties that this causes. No matter how weak and powerless people may be, if they keep the faith they will win in the end.

The story of Esther does acquaint the reader with the reality of oppression and persecution; but it is also a hymn to hope in God who will never fail to listen to those who rely on him, and who will, in the long run, prevent injustice from triumphing. The book serves to keep alive in the chosen people the conviction that God will never abandon them. St Paul will later explain that "to the (Israelites) belong the sonship, the glory, the covenants, the giving of the law, the worship, and the promises; to them belong the patriarchs" (Rom 9:4–5a) and that "as regards election they are beloved for the sake of their forefathers. For the gifts and the call of God are irrevocable" (Rom 11:28b–29).

The two protagonists of the story, Esther and Mordecai, epitomize the person who is faithful to God: they are not cowed by difficulties; rather, their great faith in God and their recourse to prayer and penance are a source of strength.

5. THE BOOK OF ESTHER IN THE LIGHT OF THE NEW TESTAMENT

The book of Esther is not explicitly quoted in the New Testament, but in their teaching on the Christian life the Fathers and ecclesiastical writers do draw on it. The events narrated in the book are seen as a paradigm of God's providence towards his people: he delivers Israel from a powerful enemy by causing men unexpectedly to change their policies. But the book also stresses that God expects co-operation; Esther is often praised for risking her life on behalf of other members of her people (4:16).[1]

The book is also a summary of the virtues necessary for winning God's favour: it does not fail to show Esther's humility, her fidelity to God's commandments, how she fasts in order to support her prayer (4:16), etc.

In the liturgy of the church Esther is seen as a figure of the Virgin Mary on account of her royal dignity, her greatness of soul and the effectiveness of her

1. Cf. St Clement of Rome, *Ad Corinthios*, 55, 3, 6.

intercession with the king. The liturgical memorial of our Lady of Lourdes applies to our Lady words taken from this book.

For all these reasons Esther is seen in the tradition of the church as one of the links in the chain of God's paradoxes in salvation history: "Above all, the poor and humble of the Lord (cf. Zeph 2:3) will bear this hope. Such holy women as Sarah, Rebecca, Rachel, Miriam, Deborah, Hannah, Judith and Esther kept alive the hope of Israel's salvation. The purest figure among them is Mary (4 Lk 1:38)."[2]

2. *Cathechism of the Catholic Church*, 64.

PROLOGUE

Mordecai's dream

11 * [2]*In the second year of the reign of Ahasu-erus*[a] *the Great, on the first day of Nisan, Mordecai the son of Jair, son of Shime-i, son of Kish, of the tribe of Benjamin, had a dream.* [3]*He was a Jew, dwelling in the city of Susa, a great man, serving in the court of the king.* [4]*He was one of the captives whom Nebuchadnezzar king of Babylon had brought from Jerusalem with Jeconiah king of Judea. And this was his dream:*

2 Kings 24:8,15

[5]*Behold, noise*[a2] *and confusion, thunders and earthquake, tumult upon the earth!* [6]*And behold, two great dragons came forward, both ready to fight, and they roared terribly.* [7]*And at their roaring every nation prepared for war, to fight against of the nation of the righteous.* [8]*And behold, a day of darkness and gloom, tribulation and distress, affliction and great tumult upon the earth!* [9]*And the whole righteous nation was troubled; they feared the evils that threatened them, and were ready to perish.* [10]*Then they cried to God; and from their cry, as though from a tiny spring, there came a great river, with abundant water;* [11]*light came, and the sun rose, and the lowly were exalted and consumed those held in honour.*

Rev 4:5

Dan 5:15

[12]*Mordecai saw in this dream what God had determined to do, and after he awoke he had it on his mind and sought all day to understand it in every detail.*

11:2–12. The use of dreams or visions to reveal God's plans is a feature of apocalyptic writing, a genre used in this and in other books of Holy Scripture. In a veiled way, Mordecai's dream tells us in advance what the whole book is about, and yet leaves us wondering what it all means. Our uncertainty will disappear gradually, and only in the end, when the dream is interpreted, will everything become clear (*10:4–13*). Bit by bit the reader will see that the noise and confusion stood for a great battle, and what was meant by the tiny stream becoming a river, and who the two dragons were—and how it was that one prevailed over the other. However, it is better not to go into this now lest it spoil the story.

[1a] Anno secundo, regnante Artaxerxe rege magno, prima die mensis Nisan vidit somnium Mardochaeus filius Iair filii Semei filii Cis de tribu Beniamin, [1b]vir magnus, qui ministrabat in aula regia. [1c]Et hoc eius somnium fuit: apparuerunt voces et tumultus et tonitrua et terraemotus et conturbatio magna super terram. [1d]Et ecce duo dracones magni parati prodierunt uterque luctari; [1e]et facta est illorum magna pugna, et dominabantur, et congregatae sunt nationes [1f]in die tenebroso et malo, et fuit perturbatio magna in habitantibus super terram. [1g]Et timuerunt perditionem [1h]clamaveruntque ad Deum. Et a voce clamoris eorum factus est fons parvus, qui crevit in fluvium maximum et in aquas plurimas redundavit. [1i]Lux et sol ortus est. et humiles exaltati sunt et devoraverunt inclitos. [1k]Quod cum vidisset somnium Mardochaeus et surrexisset de strato, cogitabat quid Deus facere vellet; et fixum habebat in animo, quousque revelaretur. **[1]** [1]Et fuit in diebus Asueri, qui regnavit ab India usque Aethiopiam super

a. Gk *Artaxerxes* **a2.** Or *voices*

12 *Now Mordecai took his rest in the courtyard with Gabatha and Tharra, the two eunuchs of the king who kept watch in the courtyard.* [2]*He overheard their conversation and inquired into their purposes, and learned that they were preparing to lay hands upon Ahasu-erus*[a] *the king; and he informed the king concerning them.* [3]*Then the king examined the two eunuchs, and when they confessed they were led to execution.* [4]*The king made a permanent record of these things, and Mordecai wrote an account of them.* [5]*And the king ordered Mordecai to serve in the court and rewarded him for these things,* [6]*But Haman, the son of Hammedatha, a Bougaean, was in great honour with the king, and he sought to injure Mordecai and his people because of the two eunuchs of the king.*

1. ESTHER BECOMES QUEEN

Queen Vashti repudiated

1 [1]In the days of Ahasu-erus, the Ahasu-erus who reigned from India to Ethiopia over one hundred and twenty-seven provinces, [2]in those days when King Ahasu-erus[a] sat on his royal throne in

12:1–6. Cf. the note on 2:19–23.

1:1–22. The scene introduces one of the sides in the struggle referred to in Mordecai's dream (*11:5–12*)—a powerful kingdom, the largest empire to be found in the Old Testament, running from India to Ethiopia, beyond Upper Egypt. Its 127 provinces show just how extensive it is (ten by twelve, plus seven—a combination of these numbers, each of which symbolizes fullness, plenitude). Its wealth seems to be past all reckoning, to judge from the grandeur and duration of the banquet given by its ruler—and from the number of guests, the richness of the palace and the goblets, and the abundance of wine.

The king of this splendid empire is Ahasu-erus (Xerxes), a capricious man and one not to be crossed. At the height of the feast, when the king is merry with wine, he takes it into his head to call his queen, Vashti, to dazzle his guests with her beauty. When she refuses to comply, the king becomes furious. Both this reaction and the advice given by his counsellors point to this being a rather unsophisticated and intolerant society. The king's request shows him to be empty-headed and fickle (v. 11); his advisors are not interested in justice: they tell him what he wants to hear.

This is the description given of the first contender—a fearsome, very powerful, kingdom, not to be tangled with.

centum viginti septem provincias, [2]quando sedit in solio regni sui in castris Susan, [3]tertio igitur anno imperii sui, fecit grande convivium cunctis principibus et pueris suis, fortissimis Persarum et Medorum, inclitis et praefectis provinciarum coram se, [4]ut ostenderet divitias gloriae regni sui ac splendorem atque iactantiam magnitudinis suae multo tempore, centum videlicet et octoginta diebus. [5]Cumque implerentur

a. Gk *Artaxerxes*

Susa the capital,[3] in the third year of his reign he gave a banquet for all his princes and servants, the army chiefs[a] of Persia and Media and the nobles and governors of the provinces being before him, [4]while he showed the riches of his royal glory and the splendour and pomp of his majesty for many days, a hundred and eighty days. [5]And when these days were completed, the king gave for all the people present in Susa the capital, both great and small, a banquet lasting for seven days, in the court of the garden of the king's palace. [6]There were white cotton curtains and blue hangings caught up with cords of fine linen and purple to silver rings[b] and marble pillars, and also couches of gold and silver on a mosaic pavement of porphyry, marble, mother-of-pearl and precious stones. [7]Drinks were served in golden goblets, goblets of different kinds, and the royal wine was lavished according to the bounty of the king. [8]And drinking was according to the law, no one was compelled; for the king had given orders to all the officials of his palace to do as every man desired. [9]Queen Vashti also gave a banquet for the women in the palace which belonged to King Ahasu-erus.

Dan 5:1–4

[10]On the seventh day, when the heart of the king was merry with wine, he commanded Mehuman, Biztha, Harbona, Bigtha and Abagtha, Zethar and Carkas, the seven eunuchs who served King Ahasu-erus as chamberlains, [11]to bring Queen Vashti before the king with her royal crown, in order to show the peoples and the princes her beauty; for she was fair to behold. [12]But Queen Vashti refused to come at the king's command conveyed by the eunuchs. At this the king was enraged, and his anger burned within him.

[13]Then the king said to the wise men who knew the times—for this was the king's procedure toward all who were versed in law and judgment, [14]the men next to him being Carshena, Shethar,

---

dies convivii, invitavit omnem populum, qui inventus est in Susan, a maximo usque ad minimum; et septem diebus iussit convivium praeparari in vestibulo horti palatii regis. [6]Et pendebant ex omni parte tentoria lintea et carbasina ac hyacinthina sustentata funibus byssinis atque purpureis, qui argenteis circulis inserti erant et columnis marmoreis fulciebantur; lectuli quoque aurei et argentei dispositi erant super pavimentum smaragdino et pario stratum lapide aliisque varii coloris. [7]Bibebant autem, qui invitati erant, aureis poculis, aliis atque aliis; vinum quoque, ut magnificentia regia dignum erat, abundans et praecipuum ponebatur. [8]Nec erat qui cogeret ad bibendum, quoniam sic rex statuerat omnibus praepositis domus suae, ut facerent secundum uniuscuiusque voluntatem. [9]Vasthi quoque regina fecit convivium feminarum in palatio regio, ubi rex Asuerus manere consueverat. [10]Itaque die septimo, cum rex esset hilarior potione meri, praecepit Mauman et Bazatha et Harbona et Bagatha et Abgatha et Zethar et Charchas, septem eunuchis, qui in conspectu eius ministrabant, [11]ut introducerent reginam Vasthi coram rege, posito super caput eius diademate regni, ut ostenderet cunctis populis et principibus pulchritudinem illius: erat enim pulchra valde. [12]Quae renuit et ad regis imperium, quod per eunuchos mandaverat, venire contempsit; unde iratus rex et nimio furore succensus [13]interrogavit sapientes, qui tempora noverant, et illorum faciebat cuncta consilio scientium leges ac iura maiorum

a. Heb *the army* **b.** Or *rods*

Admatha, Tarshish, Meres, Marsena, and Memucan, the seven princes of Persia and Media, who saw the king's face, and sat first in the kingdom—: [15]"According to the law, what is to be done to Queen Vashti, because she has not performed the command of King Ahasu-erus conveyed by the eunuchs?" [16]Then Memucan said in presence of the king and the princes, "Not only to the king has Queen Vashti done wrong, but also to all the princes and all the peoples who are in all the provinces of King Ahasu-erus. [17]For this deed of the queen will be made known to all women, causing them to look with contempt upon their husbands, since they will say, 'King Ahasu-erus commanded Queen Vashti to be brought before him, and she did not come.' [18]This very day the ladies of Persia and Media who have heard of the queen's behaviour will be telling it to all the king's princes, and there will be contempt and wrath in plenty. [19]If it please the king, let a royal order go forth from him, and let it be written among the laws of the Persians and the Medes so that it may not be altered, that Vashti is to come no more before King Ahasu-erus; and let the king give her royal position to another who is better than she. [20]So when the decree made by the king is proclaimed throughout all his kingdom, vast as it is, all women will give honour to their husbands, high and low." [21]This advice pleased the king and the princes, and the king did as Memucan proposed; [22]he sent letters to all the royal provinces, to every province in its own script and to every people in its own language, that every man be lord in his own house and speak according to the language of his people.

Esther 3:12; 8:5,8 Dan 6:8,10, 13,16

Dan 3:4; 6:26

Ahasu-erus chooses Esther as his queen

2 [1]After these things, when the anger of King Ahasu-erus had abated, he remembered Vashti and what she had done and what had been decreed against her. [2]Then the king's servants who attended him said, "Let beautiful young virgins be sought out for

---

[14]—erant autem ei proximi Charsena et Sethar et Admatha et Tharsis et Mares et Marsana et Mamuchan, septem duces Persarum atque Medorum, qui videbant faciem regis et primi sedebant in regno—: [15]«Secundum legem quid oportet fieri Vasthi reginae, quae Asueri regis imperium, quod per eunuchos mandaverat, facere noluit?». [16]Responditque Mamuchan, audiente rege atque principibus: «Non solum regem laesit regina Vasthi, sed et omnes principes et populos, qui sunt in cunctis provinciis regis Asueri. [17]Egredietur enim sermo reginae ad omnes mulieres, ut contemnant viros suos et dicant: "Rex Asuerus iussit, ut regina Vasthi intraret ad eum, et illa noluit". [18]Atque hac ipsa die dicent omnes principum coniuges Persarum atque Medorum quem audierint sermonem reginae principibus regis; unde despectio et indignatio. [19]Si tibi, rex, placet, egrediatur edictum a facie tua et scribatur inter leges Persarum atque Medorum, quas immutari illicitum est, ut nequaquam ultra Vasthi ingrediatur ad regem, sed regnum illius altera, quae melior illa est, accipiat. [20]Et hoc in omne, quod latissimum est, provinciarum tuarum divulgetur imperium, et cunctae uxores, tam maiorum quam minorum, deferent maritis suis honorem». [21]Placuit consilium eius regi et principibus, fecitque rex iuxta consilium

the king. [3]And let the king appoint officers in all the provinces of his kingdom to gather all the beautiful young virgins to the harem in Susa the capital, under custody of Hegai the king's eunuch who is in charge of the women; let their ointments be given them. [4]And let the maiden who pleases the king be queen instead of Vashti." This pleased the king, and he did so.

Esther 1:1
2 Kings 24:14–16
Jer 24:1

[5]Now there was a Jew in Susa the capital whose name was Mordecai, the son of Jair, son of Shime-i, son of Kish, a Benjaminite, [6]who had been carried away from Jerusalem among the captives carried away with Jeconiah king of Judah, whom Nebuchadnezzar king of Babylon had carried away. [7]He had brought up Hadassah, that is Esther, the daughter of his uncle, for she had neither father nor mother; the maiden was beautiful and lovely, and when her father and her mother died, Mordecai

---

2:1–18. In the midst of this powerful nation dwell members of a lowly and oppressed people—Jews deported from their land and now living scattered across the empire. Among them is a young girl of no property or prospects—Esther, an orphan, brought up by her uncle Mordecai. In her simplicity she has the beauty of the "tiny spring" that figured in Mordecai's dream (*11:10*).

The helplessness of the Jews contrasts sharply with the might of the empire. Given the resources each has, any conflict between the two would spell the ruin of the Jews. Yet the Jews in their humility have a quality which can win people over. The king is very taken by Esther, who asks nothing of him, and soon she is made his queen.

Esther and Mordecai are Babylonian names connected with the goddess Ishtar and the god Marduk. It was quite common for Jews in the diaspora to have foreign names (cf. Dan 1:7). In addition, they usually had another, Jewish, name. Esther is also called Hadassah (v. 7), a Hebrew word meaning "myrtle".

Mamuchan. [22]Et misit epistulas ad universas provincias regni sui, ut quaeque gens audire et legere poterat, diversis linguis et litteris, esse viros principes ac maiores in domibus suis et subditas habere omnes mulieres, quae essent cum eis. **[2]** [1]His ita gestis, postquam regis Asueri deferbuerat indignatio, recordatus est Vasthi, et, quae fecisset vel quae passa esset. [2]Dixeruntque pueri regis ac ministri eius: «Quaerantur regi puellae virgines ac speciosae, [3]et constituantur, qui considerent per universas provincias puellas speciosas et virgines et adducant eas ad civitatem Susan et tradant in domum feminarum sub manu Egei eunuchi, qui est praepositus et custos mulierum regiarum; et accipiant mundum muliebrem. [4]Et quaecumque inter omnes oculis regis placuerit, ipsa regnet pro Vasthi». Placuit sermo regi; et ita, ut suggesserant, iussit fieri. [5]Erat vir Iudaeus in Susan civitate vocabulo Mardochaeus filius Iair filii Semei filii Cis de tribu Beniamin, [6]qui translatus fuerat de Ierusalem cum captivis, qui ducti fuerant cum Iechonia rege Iudae, quem Nabuchodonosor rex Babylonis transtulerat. [7]Qui fuit nutricius filiae patrui sui Edissae, quae altero nomine Esther vocabatur et utrumque parentem amiserat: pulchra aspectu et decora facie. Mortuisque patre eius ac matre, Mardochaeus sibi eam adoptavit in filiam. [8]Et factum est, cum percrebruisset regis imperium, et iuxta mandatum illius multae virgines pulchrae adducerentur Susan et Egeo traderentur, Esther quoque in domum regis in manus Egei custodis feminarum tradita est. [9]Quae placuit ei et invenit gratiam in conspectu illius; et acceleravit mundum muliebrem et tradidit ei partes suas et septem puellas speciosissimas de domo regis, et tam ipsam quam

adopted her as his own daughter. [8]So when the king's order and his edict were proclaimed, and when many maidens were gathered in Susa the capital in custody of Hegai, Esther also was taken into the king's palace and put in custody of Hegai who had charge of the women. [9]And the maiden pleased him and won his favour; and he quickly provided her with her ointments and her portion of food, and with seven chosen maids from the king's palace, and advanced her and her maids to the best place in the harem. [10]Esther had not made known her people or kindred, for Mordecai had charged her not to make it known. [11]And every day Mordecai walked in front of the court of the harem, to learn how Esther was and how she fared.

Dan 1:3–20

[12]Now when the turn came for each maiden to go in to King Ahasu-erus, after being twelve months under the regulations for the women, since this was the regular period of their beautifying, six months with oil of myrrh and six months with spices and ointments for women—[13]when the maiden went in to the king in this way she was given whatever she desired to take with her from the harem to the king's palace. [14]In the evening she went, and in the morning she came back to the second harem in custody of Sha-ashgaz the king's eunuch who was in charge of the concubines; she did not go in to the king again, unless the king delighted in her and she was summoned by name.

Esther 4:11

[15]When the turn came for Esther the daughter of Abihail the uncle of Mordecai, who had adopted her as his own daughter, to go in to the king, she asked for nothing except what Hegai the king's eunuch, who had charge of the women, advised. Now Esther found favour in the eyes of all who saw her. [16]And when Esther was taken to King Ahasu-erus into his royal palace in the tenth month, which is the month of Tebeth, in the seventh year of his reign, [17]the king loved Esther more than all the women, and

Gen 41:42
Dan 4:17

---

pedisequas eius transtulit in optimam partem domus feminarum. [10]Quae non indicaverat ei populum et cognationem suam; Mardochaeus enim praeceperat, ut de hac re omnino reticeret. [11]Qui deambulabat cotidie ante vestibulum domus, in qua electae virgines servabantur, curam agens salutis Esther et scire volens quid ei accideret. [12]Cum autem venisset tempus singularum per ordinem puellarum, ut intrarent ad regem, expletis omnibus, quae ad cultum muliebrem pertinebant, per menses duodecim; ita dumtaxat, ut sex mensibus oleo ungerentur myrrhino et aliis sex feminarum pigmentis et aromatibus uterentur, [13]ingredientesque ad regem, quidquid postulassent, accipiebant, ut portarent secum de triclinio feminarum ad regis cubiculum. [14]Et quae intraverat vespere, mane iterum in domum feminarum deducebatur, sub manu Sasagazi eunuchi, qui concubinis praesidebat. Nec habebat potestatem ad regem ultra redeundi, nisi voluisset rex et eam venire iussisset ex nomine. [15]Evoluto autem tempore per ordinem, instabat dies, quo Esther filia Abihail patrui Mardochaei, quam sibi adoptaverat in filiam, intrare deberet ad regem. Quae non quaesivit quidquam nisi, quae voluit Egeus eunuchus custos feminarum, et omnium oculis gratiosa et amabilis videbatur. [16]Ducta est itaque ad cubiculum regis Asueri mense decimo, qui vocatur Tebeth, septimo anno regni eius. [17]Et amavit eam rex plus quam

she found grace and favour in his sight more than all the virgins, so that he set the royal crown on her head and made her queen instead of Vashti. [18]Then the king gave a great banquet to all his princes and servants; it was Esther's banquet. He also granted a remission of taxes[c]to the provinces, and gave gifts with royal liberality.

2. MORDECAI AND HAMAN, ENEMIES

Mordecai exposes a plot against the king

Esther 2:14

[19]When the virgins were gathered together the second time, Mordecai was sitting at the king's gate. [20]Now Esther had not made known her kindred or her people, as Mordecai had charged her; for Esther obeyed Mordecai just as when she was brought up by him. [21]And in those days, as Mordecai was sitting at the king's gate, Bigthan and Teresh, two of the king's eunuchs, who guarded the threshold, became angry and sought to lay hands on King Ahasu-erus. [22]And this came to the knowledge of Mordecai, and he told it to Queen Esther, and Esther told the king in the name of Mordecai. [23]When the affair was investigated and found to be so, the men were both hanged on the gallows. And it was recorded in the Book of the Chronicles in the presence of the king.

Dan 3:8–12
Acts 16:20

Esther 9:24–26

Mordecai refuses to do obeisance to Haman

3 [1]After these things King Ahasu-erus promoted Haman the Agagite, the son of Hammedatha, and advanced him and set his seat above all the princes who were with him. [2]And all the king's

2:19–23. In this book Mordecai is the prototypical Jew, a man of wisdom and discretion, not unaware of the intrigues of the Persian courtiers. Esther keeps faith with her people and even though she is the queen she listens dutifully to Mordecai's advice. He, for his part, keeps in touch with her and is *au courant* with events at court.

omnes mulieres; habuitque gratiam et favorem coram eo super omnes virgines, et posuit diadema regni in capite eius fecitque eam regnare in loco Vasthi. [18]Et iussit convivium praeparari magnificum cunctis principibus et servis suis, convivium Esther; et dedit remissionem tributi universis provinciis ac dona largitus est iuxta magnificentiam principalem. [19]Mardochaeus autem manebat ad regis ianuam, [20]necdum prodiderat Esther cognationem et populum suum iuxta mandatum eius; quidquid enim ille praecipiebat, observabat Esther, ut eo tempore solita erat, quo eam parvulam nutriebat. [21]Eo igitur tempore, quo Mardochaeus ad regis ianuam morabatur, irati sunt Bagathan et Thares, duo eunuchi regis, qui ianitores erant volueruntque in regem mittere manus. [22]Quod Mardochaeum non latuit; statimque nuntiavit reginae Esther, et illa regi ex nomine Mardochaei. [23]Quaesitum est et inventum, et appensus

c. Or *a holiday*

servants who were at the king's gate bowed down and did obeisance to Haman; for the king had so commanded concerning him. But Mordecai did not bow down or do obeisance. [3]Then the king's servants who were at the king's gate said to Mordecai, "Why do you transgress the king's command?" [4]And when they spoke to him day after day and he would not listen to them, they

---

3:1–6. Haman is the worst example of someone hostile to the Jews; he abhors them and there is nothing he will not do to harm them. The sacred text depicts him as being proud and overbearing. He insists on people showing him maximum respect and is furious when Mordecai refuses to do him obeisance. The reason for Mordecai's refusal is a religious one: obeisance is a kind of adoration and according to Mosaic law that is due to God alone (cf. Ex 20:3–4). By adopting this attitude Mordecai was putting his social position and even his life at risk; but he preferred to put loyalty to God first. Today, too, in their everyday lives members of God's people feel conscience-bound to take decisions and do things which collide with the paganized world in which they live, and this may create difficulties for them; but they should not on that account change their stance: "When the defence of truth is at stake, how can one desire neither to displease God nor to clash with one's surroundings? These two things are opposed: it is either the one or the other! The sacrifice has to be a holocaust where everything is burned up, even the thought: 'What will they say?', even what we call our reputation" (St J. Escrivá, *Furrow*, 34).

In line with the broad theme of the book given in Mordecai's dream, one can see the persecution that threatens to overwhelm the Jews: the "two great dragons" (*11:6*) are preparing to fight. Haman and Mordecai are the protagonists. Haman is called "the Agagite" (v. 1), that is, of the house of Agag the Amalekite. Mordecai is the son of Kish, of the tribe of Benjamin (2:5), to which Saul belonged (1 Sam 9:1–2). In the background of this present story is the victory of Saul over Agag, king of the Amalekites, recounted in the first book of Samuel (1 Sam 15:7–9). So, there is a chink of hope. In line with the apocalyptic genre of this story, the oblique reference to the struggle between the Israelites and the Amalekites alludes to the confrontation between the people of God and the powers of this world.

uterque eorum in patibulo; mandatumque est libro annalium coram rege. **[3]** [1]Post haec rex Asuerus exaltavit Aman filium Amadathi, qui erat de stirpe Agag, et posuit solium eius super omnes principes, quos habebat. [2]Cunctique servi regis, qui in foribus palatii versabantur, flectebant genua et adorabant Aman; sic enim praeceperat rex pro illo. Solus Mardochaeus non flectebat genu neque adorabat eum. [3]Cui dixerunt pueri regis, qui ad fores palatii praesidebant: «Cur non observas mandatum regis?». [4]Cumque hoc crebrius dicerent, et ille nollet audire, nuntiaverunt Aman scire cupientes utrum perseveraret in sententia; dixerat enim eis se esse Iudaeum. [5]Cumque Aman experimento probasset quod Mardochaeus non sibi flecteret genu nec se adoraret, iratus est valde [6]et pro nihilo duxit in unum Mardochaeum mittere manus suas—audierat enim quod esset gentis Iudaeae—magisque voluit omnem Iudaeorum, qui erant in regno Asueri, perdere nationem. [7]Mense primo, cuius vocabulum est Nisan, anno duodecimo regni Asueri, missa est in urnam sors, quae dicitur Phur, coram Aman, quo die et quo

told Haman, in order to see whether Mordecai's words would avail; for he had told them that he was a Jew. [5]And when Haman saw that Mordecai did not bow down or do obeisance to him, Haman was filled with fury. [6]But he disdained to lay hands on Mordecai alone. So, as they had made known to him the people of Mordecai, Haman sought to destroy all the Jews, the people of Mordecai, throughout the whole kingdom of Ahasu-erus.

3. A DECREE ORDERING EXTERMINATION OF THE JEWS

Esther 9:24–26

[7]In the first month, which is the month of Nisan, in the twelfth year of King Ahasu-erus, they cast Pur, that is the lot, before Haman day after day; and they cast it month after month till the twelfth month, which is the month of Adar. [8]Then Haman said to King Ahasu-erus, "There is a certain people scattered abroad and dispersed among the peoples in all the provinces of your kingdom; their laws are different from those of every other people, and they do not keep the king's laws, so that it is not for the king's profit to tolerate them. [9]If it please the king, let it be decreed that they be destroyed, and I will pay ten thousand talents of silver into the hands of those who have charge of the king's business, that they may put it into the king's treasuries." [10]So the king took his signet ring from his hand and gave it to Haman the Agagite, the son of

Esther *13:4–5*
Wis 2:14–15
Dan 3:8–12

Esther 7:4

Gen 41:42

3:7–13; *13:1–6*; 3:14–15. The "fight" (cf. *11:6*) now begins. Haman gets the king to decree the extermination of the Jews. A royal edict is sent to the provincial governors and a date is fixed for the massacre. The day was chosen by the casting of lots—the thirteenth day of the month of Adar. Now we know the meaning of the "day of darkness and gloom" mentioned in the dream (*11:8*).

In *13:6* the fixed day is given as the fourteenth of Adar; the discrepancy is probably due to the complicated career of the text and it may have something to do with the celebration mentioned in 9:18.

The arguments put forward for the genocide are the same as are found in other books dating from the period when the book of Esther was written—

mense gens Iudaeorum deberet interfici; et exivit dies tertia decima mensis duodecimi, qui vocatur Adar. [8]Dixitque Aman regi Asuero: «Est populus per omnes provincias regni tui dispersus, segregatus inter populos alienisque utens legibus, quas ceteri non cognoscunt, insuper et regis scita contemnens; non expedit regi, ut det illis requiem. [9]Si tibi placet, scriptis decerne, ut pereat, et decem milia talentorum argenti appendam arcariis gazae tuae». [10]Tulit ergo rex anulum, quo utebatur, de manu sua et dedit eum Aman filio Amadathi de progenie Agag, hosti Iudaeorum. [11]Dixitque ad eum: «Argentum, quod polliceris, tuum sit; de populo age, quod tibi placet». [12]Vocatique sunt scribae regis mense primo, tertia decima die eius, et scriptum est, ut iusserat Aman, ad omnes satrapas regis et duces provinciarum et

Hammedatha, the enemy of the Jews. [11]And the king said to Haman, "The money is given to you, the people also, to do with them as it seems good to you."

[12]Then the king's secretaries were summoned on the thirteenth day of the first month, and an edict, according to all that Haman commanded, was written to the king's satraps and to the governors over all the provinces and to the princes of all the peoples, to every province in its own script and every people in its own language; it was written in the name of King Ahasu-erus and sealed with the king's ring. [13]Letters were sent by couriers to all the king's provinces, to destroy, to slay, and to annihilate all Jews, young and old, women and children, in one day, the thirteenth day of the twelfth month, which is the month of Adar, and to plunder their goods.

Dan 3:4,7

for example, Daniel, Judith, Wisdom: the Jews are a dispersed people who have laws and customs different from those of the people among whom they live (v. 8 and 13:5; cf. Dan 3:10–12; Wis 2:12–13). However, what their enemies find reprehensible is something the chosen people are proud of: what makes them different from others derives from their faithfulness to God and his Law; they are not afraid to be criticized for not adapting to the way other people live (cf. the note on Num 15:37–41). The reasons behind this planned attack on the Jews are not much different from anti-Semitic prejudices in evidence over the course of history until recent times: "The Church reproves every form of persecution against whomsoever it may be directed. Remembering, then, her common heritage with the Jews and moved not by any political consideration, but solely by the religious motivation of Christian charity, she deplores all hatreds, persecutions, displays of antisemitism levelled at any time or from any source against the Jews" (Vatican II, *Nostra aetate*, 4).

The planned pogrom causes the Jews to fast and lament (cf. 4:3)—which is in sharp contrast to life among the Persians (cf. New Vulgate, 3:15a). But our Lord proclaims that things will be different: "Blessed are you that weep now, for you shall laugh" (Lk 6:21); "Woe to you that laugh now, for you shall mourn and weep" (Lk 6:25).

Apropos of 3:15b–15i in the New Vulgate (this passage does not appear in the RSV), when news spread of the edict instigated by Haman "the whole righteous nation was troubled [. . .]. Then they cried out to God" (*11:9–10*). Mordecai's

principes diversarum gentium, ut quaeque gens legere poterat et audire pro varietate linguarum, ex nomine regis Asueri; et litterae ipsius signatae anulo. [13]Missae sunt epistulae per cursores ad universas provincias regis, ut perderent, occiderent atque delerent omnes Iudaeos, a puero usque ad senem, parvulos et mulieres uno die, hoc est tertio decimo mensis duodecimi, qui vocatur Adar, et bona eorum diriperent. [13a]Epistulae autem hoc exemplar fuit: «Rex magnus Artaxerxes centum viginti septem ab India usque Aethiopiam provinciarum satrapis et ducibus, qui eius imperio subiecti sunt, haec scribit: [13b]Cum plurimis gentibus imperarem et universum orbem meae dicioni subiugassem, volui nequaquam

Jud 2:5
Dan 3:31

13 *This is a copy of the letter: "The Great King, Ahasu-erus,*[c2] *to the rulers of the hundred and twenty-seven provinces from India to Ethiopia and to the governors under them, writes thus:*

[2]*"Having become ruler of many nations and master of the whole world, not elated with presumption of authority but always acting reasonably and with kindness, I have determined to settle the lives of my subjects in lasting tranquillity and, in order to make my kingdom peaceable and open to travel throughout all its extent, to re-establish the peace which all men desire.*

[3]*"When I asked my counsellors how this might be accomplished, Haman, who excels among us in sound judgment, and is*

---

dream continues to make more sense to the reader and now we learn of the clamour of prayer addressed to God by the Jews (3:15b–15i), by Mordecai, who sends details to Esther (4:1–17) and who prays to the Lord (*13:9–17*), and by Esther herself (*14:3–19*).

The prayer of the Jewish people (New Vulgate 3:15b–15i), which is to be found only in some ancient translations, is full of simplicity and trust in God. They acknowledge God's sovereignty over all things and confess their own infidelities, admitting that God would not be unjust if he were to abandon them, yet they confidently trust in his mercy. "Humility is the foundation of prayer" (*Catechism of the Catholic Church*, 2559), and "the first movement of the prayer of petition is *asking forgiveness*, like the tax collector in the parable: 'God, be merciful to me a sinner!' (Lk 18:13) It is a prerequisite for righteous and pure prayer. A trusting humility brings us back into the light of communion between the Father and his Son Jesus Christ and with one another (cf. 1 Jn 1:7–2:2) so that 'we receive from him whatever we ask' (1 Jn 3:22)" (ibid., 2631).

abuti potentiae magnitudine, sed semper clementer et leniter agens gubernare subiectorum vitam absque ullo terrore, regnumque quietum et usque ad fines pervium praestans, optatam cunctis mortalibus pacem renovare. [13c]Quaerente autem me a consiliariis meis, quomodo hoc posset impleri, unus qui prudentia, bona voluntate et fide stabili ceteros praecellit, et est post regem secundus, Aman nomine, [13d]indicavit mihi in totius orbis terrarum tribubus populum hostilem esse dispersum, qui, legibus suis contra omnium gentium faciens consuetudinem, regum iussa in perpetuum contemnat, ne consistat concordia nationum a nobis consolidata. [13e]Quod cum didicissemus, videntes unam hanc gentem rebellem adversus omne hominum genus perversis uti legibus nostrisque negotiis contraire, pessima conficere et regni impedire pacem, [13f]iussimus, ut quoscumque Aman, qui negotiis publicis praepositus est et quem patris loco colimus, per litteras monstraverit, cum coniugibus ac liberis radicitus deleantur inimicorum gladiis, nullusque eorum misereatur, quarta decima die duodecimi mensis Adar anni praesentis; [13g]ut, qui iam olim sunt nefarii homines, uno die violenter ad inferos descendentes stabiles in posterum et quietas reddant nobis plene res publicas. [13h]Qui autem celaverit genus eorum, inhabitabilis erit non solum inter homines, sed nec inter aves, et igne sancto comburetur; et substantia eorum in regnum conferetur. Valete». [14]Exemplar autem epistularum ut lex in omnibus provinciis promulgandum erat, ut scirent omnes populi et pararent se ad praedictam diem. [15]Festinabant cursores, qui missi erant, regis imperium explere; statimque in Susan pependit edictum, rege et Aman celebrante convivium, dum civitas ipsa esset conturbata. [15a]Et convivium fecerunt omnes gentes; rex autem et Aman, cum introisset

c2. Artaxerxes

distinguished for his unchanging good will and steadfast fidelity, and has attained the second place in the kingdom, [4]pointed out to us that among all the nations in the world there is scattered a certain hostile people, who have laws contrary to those of every nation and continually disregard the ordinances of the kings, so that the unifying of the kingdom, which we honourably intend cannot be brought about. [5]We understand that this people, and it alone, stands constantly in opposition to all men, perversely following a strange manner of life and laws, and is ill-disposed to our government, doing all the harm they can so that our kingdom may not attain stability.

Esther 3:8

[6]*"Therefore we have decreed that those indicated to you in the letters of Haman, who is in charge of affairs and is our second father, shall all, with their wives and children, be utterly destroyed by the sword of their enemies, without pity or mercy, on the fourteenth day of the twelfth month, Adar, of this present year, [7]so that those who have long been and are now hostile may in one day go down in violence to Hades, and leave our government completely secure and untroubled hereafter."*

Gen 45:8
Esther 8:12

3 [14]A copy of the document was to be issued as a decree in every province by proclamation to all the peoples to be ready for that day. [15]The couriers went in haste by order of the king, and the decree was issued in Susa the capital. And the king and Haman sat down to drink; but the city of Susa was perplexed.

Mordecai asks Esther to intercede for the Jews

4 [1]When Mordecai learned all that had been done, Mordecai rent his clothes and put on sackcloth and ashes, and went out into the midst of the city, wailing with a loud and bitter cry; [2]he went up to the entrance of the king's gate, for no one might enter the king's gate clothed with sackcloth. [3]And in every province, wherever the king's command and his decree came, there was

Lk 10:13

regiam, cum amicis luxuriabatur. [15b]Ubicumque igitur proponebatur exemplum epistulae, ploratio et luctus ingens fiebat apud omnes Iudaeos. [15c]Et invocabant Iudaei Deum patrum suorum et dicebant: [15d]«Domine Deus, tu solus Deus in caelo sursum, / et non est alius Deus praeter te. / [15e]Si enim fecissemus legem tuam et praecepta, / habitassemus cum securitate et pace / per omne tempus vitae nostrae. / [15f]Nunc autem, quoniam non fecimus praecepta tua, / venit super nos omnis tribulatio ista. / [15g]Iustus es et clemens et excelsus et magnus, / Domine, et omnes viae tuae iudicia. / [15h]Et nunc, Domine, non des filios tuos in captivitatem / neque uxores nostras in violationem neque in perditionem, / qui factus es nobis propitius ab Aegypto usque nunc. / [15i]Miserere principali tuae parti / et non tradas in infamiam hereditatem tuam, / ut hostes dominentur nostri». **[4]** [1]Cum comperisset Mardochaeus omnia, quae acciderant, scidit vestimenta sua et indutus est sacco spargens cinerem capiti. Et in platea mediae civitatis voce magna et amara clamabat [2]usque ad fores palatii gradiens; non enim erat licitum indutum sacco aulam regis intrare. [3]In omnibus quoque provinciis, quocumque edictum et dogma regis pervenerat, planctus ingens erat apud Iudaeos, ieiunium, ululatus et fletus, sacco et cinere multis pro strato utentibus. [4]Ingressae sunt autem puellae Esther et eunuchi nuntiaveruntque ei. Quod audiens

great mourning among the Jews, with fasting and weeping and lamenting, and most of them lay in sackcloth and ashes.

[4]When Esther's maids and her eunuchs came and told her, the queen was deeply distressed; she sent garments to clothe Mordecai, so that he might take off his sackcloth, but he would not accept them. [5]Then Esther called for Hathach, one of the king's eunuchs, who had been appointed to attend her, and ordered him to go to Mordecai to learn what this was and why it was. [6]Hathach went out to Mordecai in the open square of the city in front of the king's gate, [7]and Mordecai told him all that had happened to him, and the exact sum of money that Haman had promised to pay into the king's treasuries for the destruction of the Jews. [8]Mordecai also gave him a copy of the written decree issued in Susa for their destruction, that he might show it to Esther and explain it to her and charge her to go to the king to make supplication to him and entreat him for her people.* [9]And Hathach went and told Esther what Mordecai had said. [10]Then Esther spoke to Hathach and gave him a message for Mordecai, saying, [11]"All the king's servants and the people of the king's provinces know that if any man or woman goes to the king inside the inner court without being called, there is but one law; all alike are to be put to death, except the one to

---

4:1–17. When Mordecai learns of the impending disaster, he does penance and looks for a way to ward it off. He makes contact with Esther indirectly, to influence her to intercede with the king (vv. 8, 13–14), and she agrees to do so, despite the risks involved. Mordecai's request to Esther is an invitation to those with influence in public life to do what they can to advance the common good. "Thus one would hope that all those who, to some degree or other, are responsible for ensuring a 'more human life' for their fellow human beings, whether or not they are inspired by a religious faith, will become fully aware of the urgent need *to change the spiritual attitudes* which define each individual's relationship with self, with neighbour, with even the remotest human communities, and with nature itself; and all of this in view of higher values such as the *common good* or, to quote the felicitous expression of the encyclical *Populorum progressio*, the full development 'of the whole individual and of all people'" (John Paul II, *Sollicitudo rei socialis*, 38). Esther puts her trust in God and, before approaching the king, she fasts and does penance, and asks the Jews to intercede with the Lord by fasting on her behalf.

consternata est valde et misit vestem, ut, ablato sacco, induerent eum; quam accipere noluit. [5]Accitoque Athach eunucho, quem rex ministrum ei dederat, praecepit ei, ut iret ad Mardochaeum et disceret ab eo cur hoc faceret. [6]Egressusque Athach ivit ad Mardochaeum stantem in platea civitatis ante ostium palatii. [7]Qui indicavit ei omnia, quae ei acciderant, quantum Aman promisisset, ut in thesauros regis pro

whom the king holds out the golden sceptre that he may live. And I have not been called to come in to the king these thirty days." [12]And they told Mordecai what Esther had said. [13]Then Mordecai told them to return answer to Esther, "Think not that in the king's palace you will escape any more than all the other Jews. [14]For if you keep silence at such a time as this, relief and deliverance will rise for the Jews from another quarter, but you and your father's house will perish. And who knows whether you have not come to the kingdom for such a time as this?" [15]Then Esther told them to reply to Mordecai, [16]"Go, gather all the Jews to be found in Susa, and hold a fast on my behalf, and neither eat nor drink for three days, night or day. I and my maids will also fast as you do. Then I will go to the king, though it is against the law; and if I perish, I perish." [17]Mordecai then went away and did everything as Esther had ordered him.

Gen 45:7

Mordecai's prayer

13 [8]*Then he prayed to the Lord, calling to remembrance all the works of the Lord. He said:*

[9]*"O Lord, Lord, King who rulest over all things, for the universe is in thy power and there is no one who can oppose thee if it is thy will to save Israel.* [10]*For thou hast made heaven and earth and every wonderful thing under heaven,* [11]*and thou art Lord of all, and there is no one who can resist thee, who art the Lord.* [12]*Thou knowest all things; thou knowest, O Lord, that it was not*

Ex 19:5
2 Chron 20:6–7
Jud 16:14
Is 41:10–16
2 Kings 19:15
Is 40:21–26

13:8–18. Mordecai's prayer has similarities with some Psalms and other Old Testament prayers. He proclaims the power of the Lord and his dominion over all things (*13:9–12*; cf. 2 Chron 20:6–7) which is grounded on the fact that he made all things (cf. Is 40:21–26) and which he manifests over the course

Iudaeorum nece inferret argentum. [8]Exemplar quoque edicti, quod pendebat in Susan ad perdendum eos, dedit ei, ut reginae ostenderet et moneret eam, ut intraret ad regem et deprecaretur eum et rogaret pro populo suo. [8a]«Memor, inquit, dierum humilitatis tuae, quando nutrita sis in manu mea, quia Aman secundus a rege locutus est contra nos in mortem. Et tu invoca Dominum et loquere regi pro nobis et libera nos de morte». [9]Regressus Athach nuntiavit Esther omnia, quae Mardochaeus dixerat. [10]Quae respondit ei et iussit, ut diceret Mardochaeo: [11]«Omnes servi regis et cunctae, quae sub dicione eius sunt, norunt provinciae, quod cuique sive viro sive mulieri, qui non vocatus interius atrium regis intraverit, una lex sit, ut statim interficiatur, nisi forte rex auream virgam ad eum tetenderit, ut possit vivere; ego autem triginta iam diebus non sum vocata ad regem». [12]Quod cum audisset Mardochaeus, [13]rursum mandavit Esther dicens: «Ne putes quod animam tuam tantum liberes, quia in domo regis es, prae cunctis Iudaeis. [14]Si enim nunc silueris, aliunde Iudaeis liberatio et salvatio exsurget, et tu et domus patris tui peribitis; et quis novit utrum idcirco ad regnum veneris, ut in tali tempore parareris?». [15]Rursumque Esther haec Mardochaeo verba mandavit: [16]«Vade et congrega omnes Iudaeos, qui in

Joel 4:2 · Ex 3:6 · Ps 47:9 · Deut 9:26; 32:9 · 1 Kings 8:51 · Jer 10:16 · Is 38:18–20 · Ps 6:5; 115:17ff

in insolence or pride or for any love of glory that I did this, and refused to bow down to this proud Haman. [13]For I would have been willing to kiss the soles of his feet, to save Israel! [14]But I did this, that I might not set the glory of man above the glory of God, and I will not bow down to any one but to thee, who art my Lord; and I will not do these things in pride. [15]And now, O Lord God and King, God of Abraham, spare thy people; for the eyes of our foes are upon us[c] *to annihilate us, and they desire to destroy the inheritance that has been thine from the beginning. [16]Do not neglect thy portion, which thou didst redeem for thyself out of the land of Egypt. [17]Hear my prayer, and have mercy upon thy inheritance; turn our mourning into feasting, that we may live and sing praise to thy name, O Lord; do not destroy the mouth of those who praise thee."*

[18]And all Israel cried out mightily, for their death was before their eyes.

---

of salvation history. The God of Abraham will surely come to their aid as he did when he redeemed the people from Egypt.

However, unlike other petitionary prayers in the Old Testament, Mordecai's mentions his own attitudes. He tells that his refusal to bow down to Haman was done from the highest of motives, seeking only the glory of God; it was not a prideful act.

In Mordecai's prayer, and in Esther's which follows it, there is a tone of familiarity with and trust in God that is not so evident in earlier Old Testament prayers. Not only do they remind God of things he has done on behalf of the people, and plead for themselves and others (*13:10–11, 16–18*), but they reflect in God's presence on their own personal actions, speaking from the heart (*13:12–15*). This type of prayer will come into its own with Jesus Christ, who invites us to relate to God as Father.

Susan reperiuntur; et ieiunate pro me. Non comedatis et non bibatis tribus diebus et tribus noctibus, et ego cum ancillis meis similiter ieiunabo; et tunc ingrediar ad regem contra legem faciens: si pereo, pereo». [17]Ivit itaque Mardochaeus et fecit omnia, quae ei Esther mandaverat. [17a]Mardochaeus autem scidit vestimenta sua et substravit cilicium et cecidit super faciem suam in terram, et seniores populi a mane usque ad vesperam, [17b]et dixit: «Deus Abraham et Deus Isaac et Deus Iacob, benedictus es. / [17c]Domine, Domine rex omnipotens, / in dicione enim tua cuncta sunt posita, / et non est qui possit tuae resistere voluntati, / si decreveris salvare Israel. / [17d]Tu enim fecisti caelum et terram / et quidquid mirabile caeli ambitu continetur; /[17e]Dominus omnium es, / nec est qui resistat maiestati tuae. / [17f]Tu scis, Domine, quia libenter adorarem / plantas pedum Aman pro salute Israel; / [17g]hoc autem non feci, / ne gloriam hominis ponerem super gloriam Dei mei, / et alium non adorabo nisi te, Domine, Deus meus. / [17h]Et non facio ea in arrogantia / neque in gloriae cupiditate, Domine. / Appare, Domine; manifestare, Domine! / [17i]Et nunc, Domine rex, Deus Abraham et Deus Isaac et Deus Iacob, / parce populo tuo, / quia volunt nos inimici nostri perdere / et delere hereditatem tuam. / [17k]Ne despicias partem tuam, / quam redemisti tibi de terra Aegypti. / [17l]Exaudi deprecationem meam / et propitius esto sorti tuae; / et converte luctum nostrum in gaudium, / ut viventes laudemus nomen tuum, Domine, / et

c. *Gk* for they are looking upon us

Esther's prayer

14 [1]*And Esther the queen seized with deathly anxiety, fled to the Lord;* [2]*she took off her splendid apparel and put on the garments of distress and mourning, and instead of costly perfumes she covered her head with ashes and dung, and she utterly humbled her body, and every part that she loved to adorn she covered with her tangled hair.* [3]*And she prayed to the Lord God of Israel, and said:*

"O my Lord, thou art our King; help me, who am alone and have no helper but thee, [4]*for my danger is in my hand.* [5]*Ever since I was born I have heard in the tribe of my family that thou, O Lord, didst take Israel out of all the nations, and our fathers from among all their ancestors, for an everlasting inheritance, and that thou didst do for them all that thou didst promise.* [6]*And now we have sinned before thee, and thou hast given us into the hands of our enemies,* [7]*because we glorified their gods. Thou art righteous, O Lord!* [8]*And now they are not satisfied that we are in bitter slavery, but they have covenanted with their idols* [9]*to abolish what thy mouth has ordained and to destroy thy inheritance, to stop the mouths of those who praise thee and to quench thy altar and the glory of thy house,* [10]*to open the mouths of the nations for the praise of vain idols, and to magnify for ever a mortal king.* [11]*O Lord, do not surrender thy sceptre to what has no being; and do*

14:1–19. Esther's prayer is an example of the new tone of trusting prayer noticeable in this book and which is quite close to the New Testament style of prayer. Also, there is a kind of litany in it reminiscent of the style of Psalm 136. In all simplicity, Esther implores God's help, confident that he who has done so much for his people over the course of history will not leave them unprotected in their present need.

ne claudas ora te canentium». [17m]Omnis quoque Israel ex totis viribus clamavit ad Dominum, eo quod eis certa mors impenderet. [17n]Esther quoque regina confugit ad Dominum pavens periculum mortis, quod imminebat. [17o]Cumque deposuisset vestes gloriae, suscepit indumenta luctus et pro unguentis superbiae implevit caput suum cinere et corpus suum humiliavit ieiuniis valde. [17p]Et cecidit super terram cum ancillis suis a mane usque ad vesperam et dixit: [17q]«Deus Abraham et Deus Isaac et Deus Iacob, benedictus es. / Suffraga mihi soli / et non habenti defensorem praeter te, Domine, / [17r]quoniam periculum in manu mea est. / [17s]Ego audivi ex libris maiorum meorum, Domine, / quoniam tu Noe in aqua diluvii conservasti. / [17t]Ego audivi ex libris maiorum meorum, Domine, / quoniam tu Abrahae in trecentis et decem octo viris / novem reges tradidisti. / [17u]Ego audivi ex libris maiorum meorum, Domine, / quoniam tu Ionam de ventre ceti liberasti. / [17v]Ego audivi ex libris maiorum meorum, Domine, / quoniam tu Ananiam, Azariam et Misael de camino ignis liberasti. / [17x]Ego audivi ex libris maiorum meorum, Domine, / quoniam tu Daniel de lacu leonum eruisti. / [17y]Ego audivi ex libris maiorum meorum, Domine, / quoniam tu Ezechiae, regi Iudaeorum, / morte damnato et oranti pro vita misertus es / et donasti ei vitae annos quindecim. / [17z]Ego audivi ex libris maiorum meorum, Domine, / quoniam tu Annae petenti in desiderio animae / filii generationem donasti. / [17aa]Ego audivi ex libris maiorum meorum, Domine, / quoniam tu omnes complacentes tibi liberas, Domine, / usque in finem. / [17bb]Et nunc adiuva me solitariam / et neminem habentem nisi te, / Domine, Deus meus. / [17cc]Tu nosti / quoniam abominata est ancilla tua concubitum incircumcisorum. / [17dd]Deus, tu nosti / quoniam non

not let them mock at our downfall; but turn their plan against themselves, and make an example of the man who began this against us. [12]Remember, O Lord; make thyself known in this time of our affliction, and give me courage, O King of the Gods and Master of all dominion! [13]Put eloquent speech in my mouth before the lion, and turn his heart to hate the man who is fighting against us, so that there may be an end of him and those who agree with him. [14]But save us by thy hand, and help me, who am alone and have no helper but thee, O Lord. [15]Thou hast knowledge of all things; and thou knowest that I hate the splendour of the wicked and abhor the bed of the uncircumcised and of any alien. [16]Thou knowest my necessity—that I abhor the sign of my proud position, which is upon my head on the days when I appear in public. I abhor it like a menstruous rag, and I do not wear it on the days when I am at leisure. [17]And thy servant has not eaten at Haman's table, and I have not honoured the king's feast or drunk the wine of the libations. [18]The servant has had no joy since the day that I was brought here until now, except in thee, O Lord God of Abraham. [19]O God, whose might is over all, hear the voice of the despairing, and save us from the hands of evildoers. And save me from my fear!"

4. MORDECAI GETS THE BETTER OF HAMAN

Esther approaches the king

5 [1]On the third day Esther put on her royal robes and stood in the inner court of the king's palace, opposite the king's hall. The

---

5:1–2; *15:1–16*; 5:3–14. The "tiny spring" of Mordecai's dream (*11:10*) grew into "a great river, with abundant water" (ibid.) As already mentioned (cf. the note on 2:1–18), that spring represents Esther. She enjoyed God's favour and grew to become queen. Now, thanks to Esther's prayer and that

manducavi de mensa exsecrationum / et vinum libationum eorum non bibi. / [17ee]Tu nosti / quoniam a die translationis meae / non sum laetata, Domine, / nisi in te solo. / [17ff]Tu scis, Deus, / quoniam, ex quo vestimentum hoc super caput meum est, / exsecror illud tamquam pannum menstruatae / et non indui illud in die bona. / [17gg]Et nunc subveni orphanae mihi / et verbum concinnum da in os meum in conspectu leonis / et gratam me fac coram eo / et converte cor eius in odium oppugnantis nos, / in perditionem eius et eorum, qui consentiunt ei. / [17hh]Nos autem libera de manu inimicorum nostrorum; / converte luctum nostrum in laetitiam / et dolores nostros in sanitatem. / [17ii]Surgentes autem supra partem tuam, Deus, / fac in exemplum. / [17kk]Appare, Domine; manifestare, Domine!». **[5]** [1]Et factum est die tertio, induta Esther regalibus vestimentis stetit in atrio domus regiae, quod erat interius contra basilicam regis. At ille sedebat super solium suum in consistorio palatii contra ostium domus. [2]Et factum est cum vidisset Esther reginam stantem, placuit oculis eius, et extendit contra eam virgam

king was sitting on his royal throne inside the palace opposite the entrance to the palace; [2]and when the king saw Queen Esther standing in the court, she found favour in his sight and he held out to Esther the golden sceptre that was in his hand. Then Esther approached and touched the top of the sceptre.

15 **On the third day, when she ended her prayer, she took off the garments in which she had worshipped, and arrayed herself in splendid attire. [2]Then, majestically adorned, after invoking the aid of the all-seeing God and Saviour, she took her two maids with her, [3]leaning daintily on one, [4]while the other followed carrying her train. [5]She was radiant with perfect beauty, and she looked happy, as if beloved, but her heart was frozen with fear. [6]When she had gone throgh all the doors, she stood before the king. He was seated on his royal throne, clothed in the full array of his majesty, all covered with gold and precious stones. And he was most terrifying.*

[7]Lifting his face, flushed with splendour, he looked at her in fierce anger. And the queen faltered, and turned pale and faint, and collapsed upon the head of the maid who went before her. [8]Then God changed the spirit of the king to gentleness, and in alarm he sprang from his throne and took her in his arms until she came to herself. And he comforted her with soothing words, and said to her,

---

of the people, the moment has arrived when that river will overflow to the benefit of the Jews.

Unlike the other Greek passages added to the Hebrew text elsewhere in the book (shown in italics in the RSV), *15:1–16* is not an addition which fills out the Hebrew (cf. 5:1–2): it repeats it and develops it with much more drama and detail. Both the New Vulgate and the RSV provide the two passages even though some repetition is involved.

The key to the passage lies in the fact that "God changed the spirit of the king to gentleness" (*15:8*). This intervention by God is clearly an answer to Esther's prayer. St Augustine, interpreting the passage as an answer to her petition in *14:13–14*, reflects on prayer's ability to influence God to move the hearts of men:

aurean, quam tenebat manu; quae accedens tetigit summitatem virgae eius. [2a]Cumque regio fulgeret habitu et invocasset omnium rectorem et salvatorem Deum, assumpsit duas famulas [2b]et super unam quidem innitebatur, quasi in deliciis; [2c]altera autem sequebatur dominam defluentia in humum indumenta sustentans. [2d]Ipsa autem roseo vultu colore perfusa et gratis ac nitentibus oculis tristem celabat animum et mortis timore contractum. [2e]Ingressa igitur cuncta per ordinem ostia, stetit in aula interiore contra regem, ubi ille residebat super solium regni sui indutus vestibus regiis auroque fulgens et pretiosis lapidibus: eratque terribilis aspectu, et virga aurea in manu eius. [2f]Cumque elevasset faciem, vidit eam sicut taurus in impetu irae suae et cogitans eam perdere clamavit ambiguus: «Quis ausus est introire in aulam non vocatus?». Et regina corruit et, in pallorem colore mutato, lassa se reclinavit super caput ancillulae, quae antecedebat. [2g]Convertitque Iudaeorum Deus et universae creaturae Dominus spiritum regis in mansuetudinem, et festinus ac metuens exilivit de solio; et sustentans eam ulnis suis,

[9]*"What is it, Esther? I am your brother. Take courage;* [10]*you shall not die, for our law applies only to the people.*[d] *Come near."*

[11]*Then he raised the golden sceptre and touched it to her neck;* [12]*and he embraced her, and said, "Speak to me."* [13]*And she said to him, "I saw you, my lord, like an angel of God, and my heart was shaken with fear at your glory.* [14]*For you are wonderful, my lord, and your countenance is full of grace."* [15]*But as she was speaking, she fell fainting.* [16]*And the king was agitated, and all his servants sought to comfort her.*

Esther 5:6; 7:2; 9:12 Mk 6:23

[3]And the king said to her, "What is it, Queen Esther? What is your request? It shall be given you, even to the half of my kingdom." [4]And Esther said, "If it please the king, let the king and Haman come this day to a dinner that I have prepared for the king." [5]Then said the king, "Bring Haman quickly, that we may do as Esther desires." So the king and Haman came to the dinner that Esther had prepared. [6]And as they were drinking wine, the king said to Esther, "What is your petition? It shall be granted you. And

---

"Why did she make this petition to God, if God does not change the will hidden in the heart of men? It could be that this woman made her prayer in vain. We see that if prayer is rooted in the selfish interests of the one who prays, the petition comes to nothing. She made her petition to the king. In brief: forced by the seriousness of the situation, she went into the presence of the king unexpectedly; in the passage it is written that the king gave her the look of an enraged bull. The queen was filled with fear, the colour went from her face, and she rested her head on the one who had precedence over her. The Lord changed him, converting his wrath into gentleness. In recording what followed, Scripture bears witness to the fact that God granted what the woman had prayed for by changing the intention of the king's heart, in such a way that the king ordered that the wishes of the queen be carried out" (St Augustine, *Contra duas epistulas pelagianorum*, 1, 20, 38).

donec rediret ad se, verbis pacificis ei blandiebatur: [2h]«Quid habes, Esther regina, soror mea et consors regni? Ego sum frater tuus, noli metuere. [2i]Non morieris; non enim pro te, sed pro omnibus haec lex constituta est. [2k]Accede!». [2l]Et elevans auream virgam posuit super collum eius et osculatus est eam et ait: «Loquere mihi». [2m]Quae respondit: «Vidi te, domine, quasi angelum Dei, et conturbatum est cor meum prae timore gloriae tuae; [2n]valde enim mirabilis es, domine, et facies tua plena est gratiarum». [2o]Cumque loqueretur, rursus corruit et paene exanimata est. [2p]Rex autem turbabatur, et omnes ministri eius. [3]Dixitque ad eam rex: «Quid vis, Esther regina? Quae est petitio tua? Etiamsi dimidiam partem regni petieris, dabitur tibi». [4]At illa respondit: «Si regi placet, obsecro, ut venias ad me hodie et Aman tecum ad convivium, quod paravi». [5]Statimque rex: «Vocate, inquit, cito Aman, ut fiat verbum Esther». Venerunt itaque rex et Aman ad convivium, quod eis regina paraverat. [6]Dixitque ei rex, postquam vinum biberat: «Quid petis, ut detur tibi, et pro qua re postulas? Etiamsi dimidiam partem regni mei petieris, impetrabis». [7]Cui respondit Esther: «Petitio mea et preces: [8]Si inveni in conspectu regis gratiam, et si

d. *The meaning of the Greek text of this clause is obscure*

what is your request? Even to the half of my kingdom, it shall be fulfilled." [7]But Esther said, "My petition and my request is: [8]If I have found favour in the sight of the king, and if it please the king to grant my petition and fulfil my request, let the king and Haman come tomorrow[d] to the dinner which I will prepare for them, and tomorrow I will do as the king has said."

[9]And Haman went out that day joyful and glad of heart. But when Haman saw Mordecai in the king's gate, that he neither rose nor trembled before him, he was filled with wrath against Mordecai. [10]Nevertheless Haman restrained himself, and went home; and he sent and fetched his friends and his wife Zeresh. [11]And Haman recounted to them the splendour of his riches, the number of his sons, all the promotions with which the king had honoured him, and how he had advanced him above the princes and the servants of the king. [12]And Haman added, "Even Queen Esther let no one come with the king to the banquet she prepared but myself. And tomorrow also I am invited by her together with the king. [13]Yet all this does me no good, so long as I see Mordecai the Jew sitting at the king's gate." [14]Then his wife Zeresh and all his friends said to him, "Let a gallows fifty cubits high be made, and in the morning tell the king to have Mordecai hanged upon it; then go merrily with the king to the dinner." This counsel pleased Haman, and he had the gallows made.

The king remembers Mordecai

6 [1]On that night the king could not sleep; and he gave orders to bring the book of memorable deeds, the chronicles, and they

---

6:1–14. In Mordecai's dream the climax comes when the "two great dragons came forward, both ready to fight" (*11:6*)—and then "light came, and the sun rose" (*11:11*). The Jews had placed their trust in the Lord, just

regi placet, ut det mihi, quod postulo et meam impleat petitionem, veniat rex et Aman ad convivium, quod parabo eis, et cras faciam secundum verbum regis». [9]Egressus est itaque illo die Aman laetus et alacer corde. Cumque vidisset Mardochaeum sedentem in foribus palatii, et non solum non assurrexisse sibi, sed nec motum quidem de loco sessionis suae, indignatus est valde. [10]Et, dissimulata ira, reversus in domum suam convocavit ad se amicos suos et Zares uxorem suam [11]et exposuit illis magnitudinem divitiarum suarum filiorumque turbam et quanta eum gloria super omnes principes et servos suos rex elevasset. [12]Et post haec ait: «Regina quoque Esther nullum alium vocavit ad convivium cum rege praeter me; apud quam etiam cras cum rege pransurus sum. [13]Et cum omnia haec habeam, nihil me habere puto, quamdiu videro Mardochaeum Iudaeum sedentem in foribus regis». [14]Responderuntque ei Zares uxor eius et ceteri amici: «Iube parari excelsam trabem habentem altitudinis quinquaginta cubitos et dic mane regi, ut appendatur super eam Mardochaeus; et sic ibis cum rege laetus ad convivium». Placuit ei consilium et iussit excelsam parari trabem. **[6]** [1]Noctem illam duxit rex insomnem iussitque afferri sibi librum memorialium, annales priorum temporum. Quae cum illo praesente legerentur,

d. Gk: Heb lacks *tomorrow*

Esther 2:21–23

were read before the king. [2]And it was found written how Mordecai had told about Bigthana and Teresh, two of the king's eunuchs, who guarded the threshold, and who had sought to lay hands upon King Ahasu-erus. [3]And the king said, "What honour or dignity has been bestowed on Moredecai for this?" The king's servants who attended him said, "Nothing has been done for him." [4]And the king said, "Who is in the court?" Now Haman had just entered the outer court of the king's palace to speak to the king about having Mordecai hanged on the gallows that he had prepared for him. [5]So the king's servants told him, "Haman is there, standing in the court." And the king said, "Let him come in." [6]So Haman came in, and the king said to him, "What shall be done to the man whom the king delights to honour?" And Haman said to himself, "Whom would the king delight to honour more than me?" [7]and Haman said to the king, "For the man whom the king delights to honour, [8]let royal robes be brought, which the king has worn, and the horse which the king has ridden, and on whose head a royal crown is set; [9]and let the robes and the horse be handed over to one of the king's most noble princes; let him array the man whom the king delights to honour, and let him[e] conduct the man

Eccles 9:13–16

Gen 41:42ff

---

as the Psalm advises: "Commit your way to the Lord, trust in him, and he will act. He will bring forth your vindication as the light, and your right as the noonday" (Ps 37:5–6). He has responded to their prayer and fasting.

God's intervention on his people's behalf is beginning to be seen. The king's insomnia leads him to have the book of memorable deeds of his reign read out, and he is moved to reward Mordecai for the service he did him in the past. At this point Haman's power begins to wane, and the king's regard for Mordecai increases.

Haman in his pride thinks he is the only one deserving to be honoured by the king; now he is humiliated by having to proclaim the greatness of a man he hates. The passage bears out our Lord's teaching: "whoever exalts himself will be humbled, and whoever humbles himself will be exalted" (Mt 23:12).

[2]ventum est ad eum locum, ubi scriptum erat quomodo nuntiasset Mardochaeus insidias Bagathan et Thares duorum eunuchorum ianitorum, qui voluerant manus mittere in regem Asuerum. [3]Quod cum audisset rex, ait: «Quid pro hac fide honoris ac praemii Mardochaeus consecutus est?». Dixeruntque ei servi illius ac ministri: «Nihil omnino mercedis accepit». [4]Statimque rex: «Quis est, inquit, in atrio?». Aman quippe exterius atrium domus regiae intraverat, ut suggereret regi, ut iuberet Mardochaeum suspendi in patibulo, quod ei fuerat praeparatum. [5]Responderunt pueri: «Ecce Aman stat in atrio». Dixitque rex: «Ingrediatur». [6]Cumque esset ingressus, ait illi: «Quid debet fieri viro, quem rex honorare desiderat?». Cogitans autem in corde suo Aman et reputans quod nullum alium rex nisi se vellet honorare [7]respondit: «Homo, quem rex honorare cupit, [8]debet indui vestibus regiis, quibus rex indutus

e. Heb *them*

on horseback through the open square of the city, proclaiming before him: 'Thus shall it be done to the man whom the king delights to honour.'" [10]Then the king said to Haman, "Make haste, take the robes and the horse, as you have said, and do so to Mordecai the Jew who sits at the king's gate. Leave out nothing that you have mentioned." [11]So Haman took the robes and the horse, and he arrayed Mordecai and made him ride through the open square of the city, proclaiming, "Thus shall it be done to the man whom the king delights to honour."

1 Kings 1:33
Dan 5:29

[12]Then Mordecai returned to the king's gate. But Haman hurried to his house, mourning and with his head covered. [13]And Haman told his wife Zeresh and all his friends everything that had befallen him. Then his wise men and his wife Zeresh said to him, "If Mordecai, before whom you have begun to fall, is of the Jewish people, you will not prevail against him but will surely fall before him."

[14]While they were yet talking with him, the king's eunuchs arrived and brought Haman in haste to the banquet that Esther had prepared.

5. GOD SAVES HIS PEOPLE FROM EXTERMINATION

Haman is disgraced

7 [1]So the king and Haman went in to feast with Queen Esther. [2]And on the second day, as they were drinking wine, the king again said to Esther, "What is your petition, Queen Esther? It shall

---

7:1–10. The efforts of the people of God to defend themselves from their enemies (personified in Haman) have reached the moment of truth. Esther has prepared her banquet and her strategy to the last detail: the moment has come for her to present her petition to the king, and unmask Haman. She speaks

erat, et imponi super equum, qui de sella regis est, et acceperit regium diadema super caput suum; [9]et primus de regiis principibus nobilissimis induat eum et teneat equum eius et per plateam civitatis incedens clamet et dicat: "Sic honorabitur quemcumque voluerit rex honorare"». [10]Dixitque ei rex: «Festina et, sumpta stola et equo, fac, ut locutus es, Mardochaeo Iudaeo, qui sedet in foribus palatii; cave, ne quidquam de his, quae locutus es, praetermittas». [11]Tulit itaque Aman stolam et equum; indutumque Mardochaeum et impositum equo praecedebat in platea civitatis atque clamabat: «Hoc honore condignus est quemcumque rex voluerit honorare». [12]Reversusque est Mardochaeus ad ianuam palatii; et Aman festinavit ire in domum suam lugens et operto capite. [13]Narravitque Zares uxori suae et amicis omnia, quae evenissent sibi; cui responderunt sapientes, quos habebat in consilio, et uxor eius: «Si de semine Iudaeorum est Mardochaeus, ante quem cadere coepisti, non poteris praevalere contra eum, sed cades in conspectu eius». [14]Adhuc illis loquentibus, venerunt eunuchi regis et cito eum ad convivium, quod regina paraverat, pergere compulerunt. **[7]** [1]Intravit itaque rex et Aman, ut biberent cum regina. [2]Dixitque ei rex etiam in secundo die, postquam vino incaluerat: «Quae est petitio tua,

Mk 6:23 be granted you. And what is your request? Even to the half of my kingdom, it shall be fulfilled." [3]Then Queen Esther answered, "If I have found favour in your sight, O king, and if it please the king, let my life be given me at my petition, and my people at my request. [4]For we are sold, I and my people, to be destroyed, to be slain, and to be annihilated. If we had been sold merely as slaves, men and women, I would have held my peace; for our affliction is not to be compared with the loss to the king." [5]Then King Ahasuerus said to Queen Esther, "Who is he, and where is he, that would presume to do this?" [6]And Esther said, "A foe and enemy! This wicked Haman!" Then Haman was in terror before the king and the queen. [7]And the king rose from the feast in wrath and went into the palace garden; but Haman stayed to beg his life from Queen Esther, for he saw that evil was determined against him by the king. [8]And the king returned from the palace garden to the place where they were drinking wine, as Haman was falling on the couch where Esther was; and the king said, "Will he even assault the queen in my presence, in my own house?" As the words left the mouth of the king, they covered Haman's face. [9]Then said Harbona, one of the eunuchs in attendance on the king, "Moreover, the gallows which Haman has prepared for Mordecai, whose word saved the king, is standing in Haman's house, fifty cubits high." [10]And the king said, "Hang him on that." So they hanged Haman on the gallows which he had prepared for Mordecai. Then the anger of the king abated.

Esther 3:8–9

---

so convincingly that the king comes to realize the wickedness of Haman, and he orders him to be put to death.

Justice has won out in the end, and the man who plotted an ignominious death for Mordecai is hanged on the very gallows he set up for that purpose. As the Psalm says, "The wicked shall perish; the enemies of the Lord are like the glory of the pastures, they vanish—like smoke they vanish away" (Ps 37:20).

Esther, ut detur tibi, et quid vis fieri? Etiamsi dimidiam regni mei partem petieris, impetrabis». [3]Ad quem illa respondit: «Si inveni gratiam in oculis tuis, o rex, et si tibi placet, dona mihi animam meam, pro qua rogo, et populum meum, pro quo obsecro. [4]Traditi enim sumus, ego et populus meus, ut conteramur, iugulemur et pereamus. Atque utinam in servos et famulas venderemur: tacuissem, quia tribulatio haec non esset digna conturbare regem». [5]Respondensque rex Asuerus ait: «Quis est iste et ubi est, ut haec audeat facere?». [6]Dixit Esther: «Hostis et inimicus noster pessimus iste est Aman». Quod ille audiens ilico obstupuit coram rege ac regina. [7]Rex autem surrexit iratus et de loco convivii intravit in hortum palatii. Aman quoque surrexit, ut rogaret Esther reginam pro anima sua; intellexit enim a rege sibi decretum esse malum. [8]Qui cum reversus esset de horto et intrasset convivii locum, repperit Aman super lectulum corruisse, in quo iacebat Esther, et ait: «Etiam reginam vult opprimere, me praesente, in domo mea?». Necdum verbum de ore regis exierat, et statim operuerunt faciem eius. [9]Dixitque Harbona, unus de eunuchis, qui stabant in ministerio regis: «En etiam lignum, quod paraverat

Mordecai is given Haman's position

8 [1]On that day King Ahasu-erus gave to Queen Esther the house of Haman, the enemy of the Jews. And Mordecai came before the king, for Esther had told what he was to her; [2]and the king took off his signet ring, which he had taken from Haman, and gave it to Mordecai. And Esther set Mordecai over the house of Haman.

[3]Then Esther spoke again to the king; she fell at his feet and besought him with tears to avert the evil design of Haman the Agagite and the plot which he had devised against the Jews. [4]And the king held out the golden sceptre to Esther, [5]and Esther rose and stood before the king. And she said, "If it please the king, and if I have found favour in his sight, and if the thing seem right before the king, and I be pleasing in his eyes, let an order be written to revoke the letters devised by Haman the Agagite, the son of Hammedatha, which he wrote to destroy the Jews who are in all the provinces of the king. [6]For how can I endure to see the calamity that is coming to my people? Or how can I endure to see the destruction of my kindred?" [7]Then King Ahasu-erus said to Queen Esther and to Mordecai the Jew, "Behold, I have given Esther the house of Haman, and they have hanged him on the gallows, because he would lay hands on the Jews. [8]And you may write as you please with regard to the Jews, in the name of the

Prov 11:8; 26:27
Mt 7:2
Prov 13:22
Dan 2:48–49
Esther 1:19; 3:12

8:1–12; *16:1–24*; 8:13–17. Whereas Haman is disgraced, Mordecai is heaped with honours. However, in the Persian empire decrees issued by the king were irrevocable: no one, not even the king himself, could rescind them. This meant that Ahasu-erus could not agree to Esther's request that he set aside the decree sent out by Haman fixing the day for the massacre of the Jews. However, he instructed that new edicts be despatched post-haste to all the provinces authorizing the Jews to defend themselves and kill anyone who attacked them (8:11).

Mardochaeo, qui locutus est bonum pro rege, stat in domo Aman habens altitudinis quinquaginta cubitos». Cui dixit rex: «Appendite eum in eo». [10]Suspensus est itaque Aman in patibulo, quod paraverat Mardochaeo; et regis ira quievit. **[8]** [1]Die illo dedit rex Asuerus Esther reginae domum Aman adversarii Iudaeorum, et Mardochaeus ingressus est ante faciem regis; confessa est enim ei Esther quid esset sibi. [2]Tulitque rex anulum suum, quem ab Aman recipi iusserat, et tradidit Mardochaeo; Esther autem constituit Mardochaeum super domum Aman. [3]Et adiecit Esther loqui coram rege et procidit ad pedes eius flevitque et locuta ad eum oravit, ut malitiam Aman Agagitae et machinationes eius pessimas, quas excogitaverat contra Iudaeos, iuberet irritas fieri. [4]At ille ex more sceptrum aureum protendit manu; illaque consurgens stetit ante eum [5]et ait: «Si placet regi et si inveni gratiam coram eo, et deprecatio mea non ei videtur esse contraria, et accepta sum in oculis eius, obsecro, ut novis epistulis veteres litterae Aman filii Amadathi, Agagitae, insidiatoris et hostis Iudaeorum, quibus eos in cunctis regis provinciis perire praeceperat, corrigantur. [6]Quomodo enim potero sustinere malum, quod passurus est populus meus, et interitum cognationis meae?». [7]Responditque rex Asuerus Esther reginae et Mardochaeo Iudaeo: «Domum Aman concessi Esther et ipsum iussi appendi in patibulo, quia ausus est manum in

king, and seal it with the king's ring; for an edict written in the name of the king and sealed with the king's ring cannot be revoked."

The Jews are authorized to defend themselves

[9]The king's secretaries were summoned at that time, in the third month, which is the month of Sivan, on the twenty-third day; and an edict was written according to all that Mordecai commanded concerning the Jews to the satraps and the governors and the princes of the provinces from India to Ethiopia, a hundred and twenty-seven provinces, to every province in its own script and to every people in its own language, and also to the Jews in their script and their language. [10]The writing was in the name of King Ahasu-erus and sealed with the king's ring, and letters were sent by mounted couriers riding on swift horses that were used in the king's service, bred from the royal stud. [11]By these the king allowed the Jews who were in every city to gather and defend their lives, to destroy, to slay, and to annihilate any armed force of any people or province that might attack them, with their children and women, and to plunder their goods, [12]upon one day throughout all the provinces of King Ahasu-erus, on the thirteenth day of the twelfth month, which is the month of Adar.

16 *The following is a copy of this letter:*
"The Great King, Ahasu-erus,[e2] to the rulers of the provinces from India to Ethiopia, one hundred and twenty-seven satrapies, and to those who are loyal to our government, greeting.

Iudaeos mittere. [8]Scribite ergo Iudaeis sicut vobis placet, ex regis nomine, signantes litteras anulo meo, quia epistulae ex regis nomine scriptae et illius anulo signatae non possunt immutari». [9]Accitisque scribis regis—erat autem tempus tertii mensis, qui appellatur Sivan, vicesima et tertia illius die—scriptae sunt epistulae, ut Mardochaeus voluerat, ad Iudaeos et ad satrapas procuratoresque et principes, qui centum viginti septem provinciis ab India usque ad Aethiopiam praesidebant, provinciae atque provinciae, populo et populo, iuxta linguas et litteras suas, et Iudaeis iuxta linguam et litteras suas. [10]Ipsaeque epistulae, quae ex regis nomine mittebantur, anulo ipsius obsignatae sunt et missae per veredarios electis equis regiis discurrentes. [11]Quibus permisit rex Iudaeis in singulis civitatibus, ut in unum congregarentur et starent pro animabus suis et omnes inimicos suos cum coniugibus ac liberis interficerent atque delerent et spolia eorum diriperent; [12]et constituta est per omnes provincias una ultionis dies, id est tertia decima mensis duodecimi, qui vocatur Adar. [12a]Quomodo praecepit eis uti suis legibus in omni civitate et auxiliari illis et uti inimicis et adversariis ipsorum, sicut vellent, in uno die, [12b]in omni regno Artaxerxis, quarta decima die duodecimi mensis, id est Adar. [12c]Hoc est exemplar epistulae: [12d]«Rex magnus Artaxerxes ab India usque Aethiopiam centum viginti septem provinciarum satrapis ac omnibus, qui nostrae iussioni oboediunt, salutem dicit. [12e]Multi nimia bonitate principum et honore, qui in eos collatus est, abusi sunt in superbiam; [12f]et non solum subiectos regibus nituntur opprimere, sed datam sibi gloriam non ferentes in ipsos, qui dederunt, moliuntur insidias. [12g]Nec contenti sunt gratiarum actionem ex hominibus auferre, sed etiam vaniloquiis eorum, qui bono imperiti sunt inflati, Dei quoque cuncta cernentis et malum odientis arbitrantur se posse fugere sententiam.

e2. Gk Artaxerxes

[2]"The more often they are honoured by the too great kindness of their benefactors, the more proud do many men become. [3]They not only seek to injure our subjects, but in their inability to stand prosperity they even undertake to scheme against their own benefactors. [4]They not only take away thankfulness from men, but, carried away by the boasts of those who know nothing of goodness, they suppose that they will escape the evil hating justice of God, who always sees everything. [5]And often many of those who are set in places of authority have been made in part responsible for the shedding of innocent blood, and have been involved in irremediable calamities, by the persuasion of friends who have been entrusted with the administration of public affairs, [6]when these men by the false trickery of their evil natures beguile the sincere good will of their sovereigns,

[7]"What has been wickedly accomplished through the pestilent behaviour of those who exercise authority unworthily, can be seen not so much from the more ancient records which we hand on as from investigation of matters close at hand. [8]For the future we will take care to render our kingdom quiet and peaceable for all men, [9]by changing our methods and always judging what comes before our eyes with more equitable consideration. [10]For Haman, the son of Hammedatha, a Macedonian (really an alien to the Persian blood, and quite devoid of our kindness), having become our guest, [11]so far enjoyed the good will that we have for every nation that he was called our father and was continually bowed down to by all as the person second to the royal throne. [12]But, unable to restrain his arrogance, he undertook to deprive us of our kingdom

---

[12h]Saepe autem et multi in potestate constituti, amicorum, quibus credita erant officia consilio, participes facti sunt effusionis sanguinis innocentis et implicati calamitatibus insanabilibus, [12i]cum isti perversis et mendacibus cuniculis deciperent sinceram principum benignitatem. [12k]Quae res non tam ex veteribus probatur historiis quam ex his, quae in promptu sunt, intuentibus, quae pestilentia indigne dominantium perpetrata sunt. [12l]Unde in posterum providendum est paci omnium provinciarum. [12m]Si diversa iubeamus, quae sub oculis veniunt, discernimus semper cum clementissima attentione. [12n]Aman enim filius Amadathi, Macedo, alienusque a Persarum sanguine et a pietate nostra multum distans, a nobis hospitio susceptus est. [12o]Et tantam in se expertus humanitatem, quam erga omnem gentem habemus, ut pater noster publice vocaretur et adoraretur ab omnibus post regem semper secundus. [12p]Qui in tantum arrogantiae tumorem sublatus est. ut regno nos privare niteretur et spiritu. [12q]Nam nostrum servatorem et permanentem benefactorem Mardochaeum et irreprehensibilem consortem regni nostri Esther cum omni gente ipsorum tortuosis quibusdam atque fallacibus machinis expetivit in mortem; [12r]hoc cogitans, ut, illis interfectis, insidiaretur nostrae solitudini et regnum Persarum transferret in Macedonas. [12s]Nos autem a pessimo mortalium Iudaeos neci destinatos in nulla penitus culpa repperimus; sed e contrario iustissimis utentes legibus [12t]et filios altissimi et maximi semperque viventis Dei, cuius beneficio et nobis et patribus nostris regnum est optima dispositione directum. [12u]Bene igitur facietis non utentes litteris, quas Aman filius Amadathi direxerat. [12v]Pro quo scelere ante portas huius urbis, id est Susan, ipse, qui machinatus est cum omni cognatione sua, pendet in patibulo, Deo qui gubernat omnia celeriter ei reddente quod meruit. [12x]Exemplar autem huius edicti, quod nunc mittimus,

and our life, [13]and with intricate craft and deceit asked for the destruction of Mordecai, our saviour and perpetual benefactor, and of Esther, the blameless partner of our kingdom, together with their whole nation. [14]He thought that in this way he would find us undefended and would transfer the kingdom of the Persians to the Macedonians.

[15]"But we find that the Jews, who were consigned to annihilation by this thrice accursed man, are not evildoers but are governed by most righteous laws [16]and are sons of the Most High, the most mighty living God, who has directed the kingdom both for us and for our fathers in the most excellent order.

[17]"You will therefore do well not to put in execution the letters sent by Haman the son of Hammedatha, [18]because the man himself who did these things has been hanged at the gate of Susa, with all his household. For God, who rules over all things, has speedily inflicted on him the punishment he deserved.

[19]"Therefore post a copy of this letter publicly in every place, and permit the Jews to live under their own laws. [20]And give them reinforecements, so that on the thirteenth day of the twelfth month, Adar, on that very day they may defend themselves against those who attack them at the time of their affliction. [21]For God, who rules over all things, has made this day to be a joy to his chosen people instead of a day of destruction for them.

[22]"Therefore you shall observe this with all good cheer as a notable day among your commemorative festivals, [23]so that both now and hereafter it may mean salvation for us and the loyal Persians, but that for those who plot against us it may be a reminder of destruction.

[24]"Every city and country, without exception, which does not act accordingly, shall be destroyed in wrath with spear and fire. It shall be made not only impassable for men, but also most hateful for all time to beasts and birds."

8 [13]A copy of what was written was to be issued as a decree in every province, and by proclamation to all peoples, and the

---

in cunctis urbibus proponatur, ut liceat Iudaeis uti legibus suis. [12y]Quibus debetis esse adminiculo, ut contra eos, qui in tempore tribulationis eos aggrediuntur, se possint defendere quarta decima die mensis duodecimi, qui vocatur Adar. [12z]Hanc enim diem omnipotens Deus destinatam in interitum electi generis eis vertit in gaudium. [12aa]Unde et vos inter sollemnes vestros dies hanc habetote diem insignem et celebrate eam cum omni laetitia, [12bb]ut nunc et in posterum illa nobis et benevolis Persis sit salus, illis autem, qui nobis insidiantur, memoria perditionis. [12cc]Omnis autem civitas et provincia, quae noluerit sollemnitatis huius esse particeps, gladio et igne in ira pereat; et sic deleatur, ut non solum hominibus invia, sed etiam bestiis et volatilibus in sempiternum abominabilis relinquatur. Valete». [13]Exemplar epistulae in forma legis in omnibus provinciis promulgandum erat, ut omnibus populis notum fieret

Jews were to be ready on that day to avenge themselves upon their enemies. [14]So the couriers, mounted on their swift horses that were used in the king's service, rode out in haste, urged by the king's command; and the decree was issued in Susa the capital.

[15]Then Mordecai went out from the presence of the king in royal robes of blue and white, with a great golden crown and a mantle of fine linen and purple, while the city of Susa shouted and rejoiced. [16]The Jews had light and gladness and joy and honour. [17]And in every province and in every city, wherever the king's command and his edict came, there was gladness and joy among the Jews, a feast and a holiday. And many from the peoples of the country declared themselves Jews, for the fear of the Jews had fallen upon them.

The Jews avenge themselves

9 [1]Now in the twelfth month, which is the month of Adar, on the thirteenth day of the same, when the king's command and edict were about to be executed, on the very day when the enemies of

9:1–19. At the end of his dream Mordecai had seen that "the lowly were exalted and consumed those held in honour" (*11:11*). The new edicts arrive in time, and what was to have been a day of lamentation for the Jews becomes a day of victory. The number of those slain is exaggerated for the sake of effect.

Gory though the proceedings were, the account makes it clear that the Jews acted in self-defence and not to enrich themselves: "they laid no hand on the plunder" (vv. 10, 15–16). This restraint is significant if one bears in mind the fact that in the background lies the battle between Saul and Agag (cf. the note on 3:1–6); in that battle Saul and his men held on to the booty and they were rejected by God for doing so (cf. 1 Sam 7–23); but now the members of God's people are very careful not to plunder their enemies. In this we can see the great difference between the two sides: Haman had estimated that by plundering the Jews he could acquire an enormous amount of money (10,000 talents of silver, one talent being the

paratos esse Iudaeos in diem illam ad capiendam vindictam de hostibus suis. [14]Egressique sunt veredarii celeres nuntios perferentes, et edictum regis pependit in Susan. [15]Mardochaeus autem de palatio et de conspectu regis egrediens fulgebat vestibus regiis, hyacinthinis videlicet et albis, coronam magnam auream portans in capite et amictus pallio serico atque purpureo; omnisque civitas exsultavit atque laetata est. [16]Iudaeis autem nova lux oriri visa est. gaudium, honor et tripudium. [17]Apud omnes populos, urbes atque provincias, quocumque regis iussa veniebant, Iudaeis fuit exsultatio, epulae atque convivia et festus dies, in tantum ut plures alterius gentis et sectae eorum religioni et caeremoniis iungerentur; grandis enim cunctos Iudaici nominis terror invaserat. **[9]** [1]Igitur duodecimi mensis—id est Adar—tertia decima die, quando verbum et edictum regis explendum erat, et hostes Iudaeorum sperabant quod dominarentur ipsis, versa vice Iudaei superaverunt adversarios suos. [2]Congregatique sunt per singulas civitates, ut extenderent manum contra inimicos et persecutores suos; nullusque ausus est resistere, eo

Gen 22:17

Jud 15:7,11; 16:19
Esther 3:13; 9:15

the Jews hoped to get the mastery over them, but which had been changed to a day when the Jews should get the mastery over their foes, [2]the Jews gathered in their cities throughout all the provinces of King Ahasu-erus to lay hands on such as sought their hurt. And no one could make a stand against them, for the fear of them had fallen upon all peoples. [3]All the princes of the provinces and the satraps and the governors and the royal officials also helped the Jews, for the fear of Mordecai had fallen upon them. [4]For Mordecai was great in the king's house, and his fame spread throughout all the provinces; for the man Mordecai grew more and more powerful. [5]So the Jews smote all their enemies with the sword, slaughtering, and destroying them, and did as they pleased to those who hated them. [6]In Susa the capital itself the Jews slew and destroyed five hundred men, [7]and also slew Par-shan-datha and Dalphon and Aspatha [8]and Poratha and Adalia and Aridatha [9]and Parmashta and Arisai and Aridai and Vaizatha, [10]the ten sons of Haman the son of Hammedatha, the enemy of the Jews; but they laid no hand on the plunder.

[11]That very day the number of those slain in Susa the capital was reported to the king. [12]And the king said to Queen Esther, "In Susa the capital the Jews have slain five hundred men and also the ten sons of Haman. What then have they done in the rest of the king's provinces! Now what is your petition? It shall be granted you. And what further is your request? It shall be fulfilled." [13]And

---

equivalent of a year's pay for a worker), which the king designated that Haman could keep (cf. 3:9–11). The Jews, on the other hand, took no plunder at all.

And so, just as the Lord manifested his power on behalf of his people on previous occasions, he now gives them a resounding victory over their persecutors—which bears out, yet again, that "the salvation of the righteous is from the Lord; he is their refuge in time of trouble. The Lord helps them and delivers them; he delivers them from the wicked, and saves them, because they take refuge in him" (Ps 37:39–40). For this reason Esther is praised: "In

quod omnes populos invaserat formido eorum. [3]Nam et omnes provinciarum principes et satrapae et procuratores omnisque dignitas, quae singulis locis ac operibus praeerat, sustinebant Iudaeos timore Mardochaei, [4]quem principem esse palatii et plurimum posse cognoverant; fama quoque nominis eius crescebat cotidie et per cunctorum ora volitabat. [5]Itaque percusserunt Iudaei omnes inimicos suos plaga gladii et necis et interitus, reddentes eis, quod sibi paraverant facere. [6]In Susan quingentos viros interfecerunt, extra decem filios Aman Agagitae hostis Iudaeorum, quorum ista sunt nomina: [7]Pharsandatha et Delphon et Esphatha [8]et Phoratha et Adalia et Aridatha [9]et Phermesta et Arisai et Aridai et Iezatha. [10]Quos cum occidissent, praedas de substantiis eorum tangere noluerunt. [11]Statimque numerus eorum, qui occisi erant in Susan, ad regem relatus est. [12]Qui dixit reginae: «In urbe Susan interfecerunt et deleverunt Iudaei quingentos viros et decem filios Aman. Quantam putas eos exercuisse caedem in universis provinciis? Quid ultra postulas et quid vis, ut fieri iubeam?». [13]Cui illa respondit:

Esther said, "If it please the king, let the Jews who are in Susa be allowed tomorrow also to do according to this day's edict. And let the ten sons of Haman be hanged on the gallows." [14]So the king commanded this to be done; a decree was issued in Susa, and the ten sons of Haman were hanged. [15]The Jews who were in Susa gathered also on the fourteenth day of the month of Adar and they slew three hundred men in Susa; but they laid no hands on the plunder.

[16]Now the other Jews who were in the king's provinces also gathered to defend their lives, and got relief from their enemies, and slew seventy-five thousand of those who hated them; but they laid no hands on the plunder. [17]This was on the thirteenth day of the month of Adar, and on the fourteenth day they rested and made that a day of feasting and gladness. [18]But the Jews who were in Susa gathered on the thirteenth day and on the fourteenth, and rested on the fifteenth day, making that a day of feasting and gladness. [19]Therefore the Jews of the villages, who live in the open

Neh 8:10–12
Rev 11:10

order to save the twelve tribes of Israel who were doomed to death, Esther, a woman made perfect by her faith, [. . .] humbled herself and fasted when she prayed that the Lord who sees all things, the God of all ages, would deliver the people for whom she risked her life" (St Clement of Rome, *Ad Corinthios*, 55, 6).

9:20–32. When Haman decided on the extermination of the Jews, he had lots cast to fix the day it should happen, and the day picked was the thirteenth of Adar (3:7). In the language of Babylon the word for "lot" is *pur* (plural, *purim*). And it proved to be the very day that the Jews took revenge on their enemies. They celebrate the following day with feasting and gladness right across the empire, with the exception of Susa, where the slaughter extends to two days (9:17–18).

This is the explanation given for the feast of Purim, which the Jews celebrate every year on the fourteenth and fifteenth of Adar. Purim is a relaxed festival, celebrated with banquets and the exchange of presents.

«Si regi placet, detur potestas Iudaeis, qui in Susan sunt, ut sicut hodie fecerunt, sic et cras faciant, et decem filii Aman in patibulo suspendantur». [14]Praecepitque rex, ut ita fieret. Statimque in Susan pependit edictum, et decem filii Aman suspensi sunt. [15]Congregatis igitur Iudaeis, qui in Susan erant, quarta decima die mensis Adar, interfecti sunt in Susan trecenti viri, nec eorum ab illis direpta substantia est. [16]Reliqui autem Iudaei per omnes provincias, quae dicioni regis subiacebant, congregati pro animabus suis steterunt, ut requiescerent ab hostibus, ac interfecerunt de persecutoribus suis septuaginta quinque milia, sed nullus de substantiis eorum quidquam contigit. [17]Dies autem tertius decimus mensis Adar, dies apud omnes interfectionis fuit, et quarta decima die requieverunt. Quem constituerunt esse diem epularum et laetitiae. [18]At hi, qui in urbe Susan congregati sunt, tertio decimo et quarto decimo die eiusdem mensis in caede versati sunt, quinto decimo autem die requieverunt; et idcirco eundem diem constituerunt sollemnem epularum atque laetitiae. [19]Hi vero Iudaei, qui in oppidis non muratis ac villis morabantur, quartum decimum diem mensis Adar conviviorum et gaudii decreverunt, ita ut exsultent in eo et mittant sibi mutuo partes epularum. Illi autem, qui in urbibus habitant, agunt etiam

towns, hold the fourteenth day of the month of Adar as a day for gladness and feasting and holiday-making, and a day on which they send choice portions to one another.

The feast of Purim commemorates the episode

[20]And Mordecai recorded these things, and sent letters to all the Jews who were in all the provinces of King Ahasu-erus, both near and far, [21]enjoining them that they should keep the fourteenth day of the month Adar and also the fifteenth day of the same, year by year, [22]as the days on which the Jews got relief from their enemies, and as the month that had been turned for them from sorrow into gladness and from mourning into a holiday; that they should make them days of feasting and gladness, days for sending choice portions to one another and gifts to the poor.

Esther 3:7

[23]So the Jews undertook to do as they had begun, and as Mordecai had written to them. [24]For Haman the Agagite, the son of Hammedatha, the enemy of all the Jews, had plotted against the Jews to destroy them, and had cast Pur, that is the lot, to crush and destroy them; [25]but when Esther came before the king, he gave orders in writing that his wicked plot which he had devised against the Jews should come upon his own head, and that he and his sons should be hanged on the gallows. [26]Therefore they called these days Purim, after the term Pur. And therefore, because of all that was written in this letter, and of what they had faced in this matter,

Esther 6:5–13

---

quintum decimum diem mensis Adar cum gaudio et convivio et ut diem festum, in quo mittunt sibi mutuo partes epularum. [19a]Et satrapae provinciarum et principes et scribae regis honorificabant Deum, quia timor Mardochaei eos invaserat. Factum erat enim, ut praeceptum regis in toto regno nominaretur. [20]Scripsit itaque Mardochaeus omnia haec et litteris comprehensa misit ad omnes Iudaeos, qui in omnibus regis provinciis morabantur, tam in vicino positis quam procul, [21]ut quartam decimam et quintam decimam diem mensis Adar pro festis susciperent et, revertente semper anno, sollemni honore celebrarent [22]secundum dies, in quibus requieverunt Iudaei ab inimicis suis, et mensem, qui de luctu atque tristitia in hilaritatem gaudiumque ipsis conversus est, essentque istae dies epularum atque laetitiae, et mitterent sibi invicem ciborum partes et pauperibus munuscula largirentur. [23]Susceperuntque Iudaei in sollemnem ritum cuncta, quae eo tempore facere coeperant, et quae Mardochaeus litteris facienda mandaverat. [24]Aman enim filius Amadathi stirpis Agag, adversarius omnium Iudaeorum, cogitavit contra eos malum, ut deleret illos, et misit Phur, id est sortem, ut eos conturbaret atque deleret. [25]Sed postquam ingressa est Esther ad regem, mandavit ille simul cum litteris, ut malum, quod iste contra Iudaeos cogitaverat, reverteretur in caput eius, et suspenderentur ipse et filii eius in patibulo. [26]Atque ex illo tempore dies isti appellati sunt Phurim propter nomen Phur. Propter cuncta illa, quae in hac epistula continentur, [27]et propter ea, quae de his viderant et quae eis acciderant, statuerunt et in sollemnem ritum numquam mutandum susceperunt Iudaei super se et semen suum et super cunctos, qui religioni eorum voluerint copulari, ut duos hos dies secundum praeceptum et tempus eorum singulis annis celebrarent. [28]Isti dies memorarentur et celebrarentur per singulas generationes in singulis cognationibus, provinciis et civitatibus, nec esset ulla civitas, in qua dies Phurim non observarentur a Iudaeis et ab eorum progenie. [29]Scripseruntque Esther regina filia Abihail et Mardochaeus Iudaeus omni studio ad confirmandam hanc secundam epistulam Phurim. [30]Et miserunt ad omnes Iudaeos, qui in centum viginti septem provinciis regis Asueri versabantur, verba pacis et veritatis, [31]statuentes dies

and of what had befallen them, [27]the Jews ordained and took it upon themselves and their descendants and all who joined them, that without fail they would keep these two days according to what was written and at the time appointed every year, [28]that these days should be remembered and kept throughout every generation, in every family, province, and city, and that these days of Purim should never fall into disuse among the Jews, nor should the commemoration of these days cease among their descendants.

Esther 8:17

[29]Then Queen Esther, the daughter of Abihail, and Mordecai the Jew gave full written authority, confirming this second letter about Purim. [30]Letters were sent to all the Jews, to the hundred and twenty-seven provinces of the kingdom of Ahasu-erus, in words of peace and truth, [31]that these days of Purim should be observed at their appointed seasons, as Mordecai the Jew and Queen Esther enjoined upon the Jews, and as they had laid down for themselves and for their descendants, with regard to their fasts and their lamenting. [32]The command of Queen Esther fixed these practises of Purim, and it was recorded in writing.

Esther 9:23–26

10 [1]King Ashu-erus laid tribute on the land and on the coastlands of the sea. [2]And all the acts of his power and might, and the full account of the high honour of Mordecai, to which the king advanced him, are they not written in the Book of

---

10:1–3; *4–13*; *11:1*. The book ends by giving an interpretation of Mordecai's dream (recorded at the start). Now it is plain to see that the underlying theme is the persecution suffered by the Jews on account of their faithfulness to the one God, and the protection that he extends to them. The noise mentioned in the dream referred to the struggle between the Jews and their enemies. The dragons stood for the two key figures, Haman and Mordecai. When the people cry out to the Lord, he arranges that a humble girl should become queen, just as a tiny spring becomes a river so great that it overflows its banks. And the simple people end up taking revenge on their persecutors. In apocalyptic language appropriate to the genre, the sacred text teaches that God listens to his people's supplications when they humbly invoke him, and he intervenes to deliver them from trials and tribulations.

Verse *1* of chapter *11*, given as an end-piece in the Greek text, is not part of the New Vulgate.

Phurim pro temporibus suis, sicut constituerant Mardochaeus et Esther, et sicut illi statuerant pro seipsis et pro semine suo, praecepta ieiuniorum et clamorum. [32]Et mandatum Esther confirmavit praecepta Phurim et scriptum est in libro. **[10]** [1]Rex vero Asuerus terrae et maris insulis imposuit tributum. [2]Cuius fortitudo et imperium et dignitas atque sublimitas, qua exaltavit Mardochaeum, scripta sunt in libro annalium regum Medorum atque Persarum, [3]et quomodo Mardochaeus Iudaici generis secundus a rege Asuero fuerit et magnus apud Iudaeos et acceptabilis plebi fratrum suorum, quaerens bona populo

2 Mac 15:14

the Chronicles of the kings of Media and Persia? [3]For Mordecai the Jew was next in rank to King Ahasu-erus, and he was great among the Jews and popular with the multitude of his brethren, for he sought the welfare of his people and spoke peace to all his people.

EPILOGUE

Esther *11:2–12*

Interpretation of Mordecai's dream

[4]And Mordecai said, "Those things have come from God. [5]For I remember the dream that I had concernig these matters, and none of them has failed to be fulfilled. [6]The tiny spring which became a river, and there was light and the sun and abundant water—the river is Esther, whom the king married and made queen. [7]The two dragons are Haman and myself. [8]The nations are those that gathered to destroy the name of the Jews. [9]And my nation, this is Israel, who cried out to God and were saved. The Lord has saved his people; the Lord has delivered us from all of these evils; God has done great signs and wonders, which have not occurred among the nations. [10]For this purpose he made two lots, one for the people of God and one for all the nations. [11]And these two lots came to the hour and moment and day of decision before God and among all the nations. [12]And God remembered his people and vindicated his inheritance. [13]So they will observe these days in the month of Adar, on the fourteenth and fifteenth of that month, with an assembly and joy and gladness before God, from generation to generation forever among his people Israel."

11 *[1]In the fourth year of the reign of Ptolemy and Cleopatra, Dositheus, who said that he was a priest and a Levite,*[e] *and Ptolemy his son brought to Egypt*[f] *the preceding Letter of Purim, which they said was genuine and had been translated by Lysimachus the son of Ptolemy, one of the residents of Jerusalem.*

---

suo et loquens ea. quae ad pacem seminis sui pertinerent. [3a]Dixitque Mardochaeus ad omnes: «A Deo facta sunt ista!». [3b]Recordatus est enim Mardochaeus somnii, quod viderat, haec eadem significantis; nec eorum quidquam irritum fuit. [3c]«Quod parvus fons crevit in fluvium, et erat lux et sol et aqua plurima: fons et flumen est Esther, quam rex accepit uxorem et voluit esse reginam; [3d]duo autem dracones, ego sum et Aman; [3e]gentes, quae convenerant, hi sunt, qui conati sunt delere nomen Iudaeorum; [3f]gens autem mea, id est Israel, sunt illi, qui clamaverunt ad Dominum; et salvum fecit Dominus populum suum liberavitque nos de omnibus malis et fecit signa magna atque portenta, quae non sunt facta inter gentes. [3g]Et duas sortes esse praecepit, unam populi Dei et alteram cunctarum gentium. [3h]Venitque utraque sors in statutum tempus et in diem iudicii coram Deo universis gentibus. [3i]Et recordatus est Deus populi sui ac iustificavit hereditatem suam. [3k]Et observabuntur dies isti in mense Adar, quarta decima et quinta decima die eiusdem mensis, dies congregationis et hilaritatis et gaudii coram Deo per vestras deinceps generationes in populo Israel».

e. *Or* priest, and Levitas **f.** Cn: Gk *brought in*

1 MACCABEES

Introduction

Four books have come down to us bearing the title of "Maccabees", but only the first two deal with the struggle against the Seleucid kings which took place in Judea under the leadership of the Maccabees. These two form part of the Christian canon of the Bible; but they are not included in the Jewish canon. Their title derives from the name Maccabeus conferred on Judas, the central figure in the struggle against Antiochus IV Epiphanes (1 Mac 2:4). The two books differ in respect to author, style, date of composition, and purpose, but they deal with the same period of history. Because of the differences, we shall deal with them in separate introductions.

The original text of 1 Maccabees was in Hebrew, and both Origen and St Jerome were familiar with it: but the only texts now conserved are Greek translations. The abundance of Semitic turns of phrase in the Greek show that it is a literal translation of the Hebrew. Second Maccabees, however, was originally written in Greek.

1. STRUCTURE AND CONTENT

The first book of the Maccabees gives the history of the first generation of the Hasmoneans, that is, the sons of Mattathias.[1] It begins with the accession of Antiochus IV Epiphanes to the throne of Syria (175 BC) and ends with the death of Simon Maccabeus, the last surviving son of Mattathias (134 BC). The content of the book is as follows:

1. THE HELLENIZATION OF JERUSALEM (1:1–64). With the collaboration of some influential Jews, Antiochus IV tries to impose Greek customs in Jerusalem. Jewish laws and customs are proscribed, and anyone who fails to give them up is guilty of a capital offence. The temple of Jerusalem is profaned and turned into a pagan temple. The city is fortified and becomes a Syrian citadel (1:33) with a strong Syrian garrison controlling the city and its environs. The Jewish religion seems destined to disappear.

2. MATTATHIAS' ARMED REVOLT (2:1–70). Mattathias and his sons react against the Syrians, their revolt initially taking the form of guerrilla attacks in the hinterland of Jerusalem. The revolt is aimed exclusively at obtaining

1. They are called the Hasmoneans because, according to Flavius Josephus, an ancestor (great-grandfather) of Mattathias was called Hasman (*Antiquitates Judaicae*, 12, 265)

freedom of religion; Mattathias and his friends are joined by a group of people who are still faithful to the Jewish religion—"Hasidaeans", that is to say, devout people (2:42).

3. JUDAS MACCABEUS, LEADER OF THE JEWS (3:1—9:22). On the death of Mattathias, his son Judas Maccabeus takes over as leader of the revolt. He organizes a small army and has successes against local allies of the Syrians; this is followed by victory over the Syrian army based in Judea and commanded by Lysias. As described in the book, Judas inflicts crushing defeats on the enemy. He manages to bring it about that Jewish customs are respected in Judea, and that the temple is restored to Jewish control; the temple is cleansed and rededicated to the Lord. However, Judas does not settle for this relative religious freedom; he embarks on military action in adjacent territories in order to help Jews living there. Meanwhile Antiochus IV dies and is succeeded by his son Antiochus V Eupator who, alarmed by the advances being made by the Maccabees, sends a large army against them, again under the command of Lysias. Judas and his supporters are forced to take refuge in a section of the Holy City; but the arrival in Antioch of Philip, Lysias' political rival, causes Lysias to raise the siege of Jerusalem and arrange for Judas to be offered an armistice. At this point the son of Seleucus IV (Antiochus IV's brother), Demetrius I arrives from Rome and puts Antiochus V and Lysias to death; then, in response to an approach by some Jews who have betrayed the Law, he sends Nicanor to attack Judas Maccabeus. Judas proves victorious again, makes an alliance with the Romans and maintains resistance to the Syrian army until he dies in battle.

4. JONATHAN, JUDAS' SUCCESSOR (9:23—12:53). After Judas' death, his brother Jonathan is made leader of the Jews. With great political skill, and taking advantage of the rivalry between Alexander Epiphanes and Demetrius II for the throne of Syria, Jonathan gets himself appointed high priest, obtains military control of Palestine, and ratifies the treaties with Rome. However, he is murdered in an ambush.

5. SIMON, HIGH PRIEST. JUDEA BECOMES POLITICALLY INDEPENDENT (13:1—16:24). Jonathan is succeeded as leader by his brother Simon, who achieves political independence for Judea, by taking advantage (as Jonathan had done) of a power struggle in Syria—this time between Trypho and Antiochus VII. Simon is assassinated by his son-in-law but is succeeded by his son John Hyrcanus who, when his father was still alive, was a successful military general. With the death of Simon, who is praised by the sacred writer and by the people, the history covered in 1 Maccabees comes to an end.

2. COMPOSITION

The author of 1 Maccabees drew on a variety of sources. Reference is made throughout the book to official documents that he was able to consult in the temple archives (1 Mac 14:49)—the chronicles of the high priests Jonathan and Simon (1 Mac 16:24); the bronze tablets set up in praise of Simon (1 Mac 14:25–49); and some letters from the Seleucid kings and the Roman senate sent to Judas, Jonathan and Simon (1 Mac 5:10–13; 8:22–23; etc.). He also had access to some source to do with the Seleucid kings of Syria. So, the author was certainly a Palestinian Jew, perhaps resident in Jerusalem, and a devout follower of the Law. The book would have been written around 100 BC. From it we can see that the writer was very much a supporter of the Hasmonean dynasty: this can be seen from his attempt to justify the fact that Maccabees' successors hold the titles of high priest and king. He shows how the founders of the dynasty, the Maccabees, came to acquire those titles, and with the people's approval.

Although the author of 1 Maccabees does his best to narrate events in chronological order and to do so objectively (in general he succeeds), some details are incorrect. For example, he gives too late a date for the death of Antiochus IV; he says practically nothing about military reverses suffered by Judas and his brothers, and his reports on treaties made by the Jews with other nations, for example, Sparta, are exaggerated. All this has the effect of enhancing the reputation of Judas and his brothers, and the importance of Judea in the international context. The author of 1 Maccabees does not have the same interest in accuracy that one would expect of a modern historian; he simply tells what he thinks happened, his primary concern being to show that God is the one who guided the course of history in the Seleucid period just as he did in previous times.

3. MESSAGE

In 1 Maccabees, the Law is the central point of reference. The struggle recounted in the book is not so much one between the Seleucids and the Hasmoneans, or even between pagan kings and the Jewish people, as between those who observe the Law and their adversaries. The Law is not simply a list of religious rules and regulations: it derives from the irreversible Covenant that God has made with his people, and which that people must faithfully guard as its greatest treasure.

The history narrated in 1 Maccabees exalts both human and divine values: faith breeds heroism, and service to the nation is one and the same thing as service to God. The best guarantee of victory is reliance on God. Prayer, fasting and reading the word of God (1 Mac 3:48)—these are weapons that cannot be

bested. What matters is not human forces or the size of one's army, but the help that comes from God.

In 1 Maccabees God does not expressly tell the Jews what his plans are: the outcome of their actions done in the name of the Lord will reveal his intentions to them. God's plans are already revealed in the Law and the Prophets, but when situations arise in which they need to ascertain his will, they wait for a prophet to come and tell them—for example, about what to do with the stones of the defiled altar: 1 Mac 4:46. Something similar happens as regards the permanence of the Hasmonean dynasty: God has indeed used it to save his people, and the temple and the Law, but it is still something provisional. Simon is accepted as leader and high priest "until a trustworthy prophet should arise" (1 Mac 14:41). They are waiting for a new situation to emerge, a new kind of relationship between God and his people.

Man's actions are judged and evaluated in terms of his adhesion to the Law; and the criterion for assessing that adhesion is whether or not he supports the Maccabee party. The Maccabees are portrayed as an example of men zealous for the Law and the temple, merciful towards the poor, and generous in placing their life and property at the disposal of the Jewish cause. In 1 Maccabees, involvement in the armed struggle proves that one upholds the Law and Judaism. The cruel acts of vengeance done by the Maccabees which are reported in the book need to be seen in context as acts of zeal to protect the Jewish Law.

4. FIRST MACCABEES IN THE LIGHT OF THE NEW TESTAMENT

In our Lord's time the zeal for the Law evidenced in 1 Maccabees was still very much alive, although it was interpreted differently by the different groups that arose after the religious wars described in the book.

The Pharisees can be traced back to the Hasidaeans, those who initially joined the Maccabee revolt (1 Mac 2:42), but who adopted a different policy later on (1 Mac 7:13); there was also the Sadducee party who were better disposed to the Hasmoneans; whereas the Essenes were at the opposite pole: they even dissociated themselves from temple worship, as we know from extra-biblical sources. However, all these groups were, in their own way, zealous for the Law.

In the light of Christian belief, the history narrated in 1 Maccabees is an inspired testimony to how God was guiding the history of the chosen people right up to the time when he sent the Messiah, his Son Jesus Christ. From the point of view of the history being narrated, no other Old Testament book is as close to the New Testament as 1 Maccabees.

The New Testament does reflect the spiritual values which helped shape the story told in 1 Maccabees; however, Jesus heightened these values and

transformed them, sometimes in a very radical way. Jesus himself was an adherent of the Law of Moses, and he taught that every jot of it would be fulfilled (cf. Mt 5:17–19), but he interpreted and renewed the Law by setting forth a new way of keeping it (cf. Mt 5:20–48), and he established a new law of brotherly love, which outstrips the law of vengeance so much in evidence in the military campaigns of the Maccabees (cf. Mt 5:28–47).

Jesus also showed his zeal for the temple—witness his dramatic expulsion of the moneychangers (cf. Mt 21:12–17). But he also declared that that temple was something provisional and the true worship of God did not depend on the temple but on adoration of the Father in spirit and in truth (cf. Jn 4:23–24). Moreover, the Gospel of St John teaches that the true temple is our Lord's own body (cf. Jn 2:22).

As against the equating of fidelity to the Law with armed rebellion found in 1 Maccabees, the New Testament invites us to offer moral and spiritual resistance to persecution (cf. Mt 10:16–25); and Jesus also establishes separation between political authority and religious allegiance when he proclaims, "Render to Caesar the things that are Caesar's, and to God the things that are God's" (Mt 22:21 and par.).

Read in the light of the New Testament, 1 Maccabees has an additional advantage in that it tells us something about the political and religious context in which Jesus Christ carried out his ministry, and about the difference between the old and the new people of God.

1. THE HELLENIZATION OF JERUSALEM*

Alexander the Great and his successors

1 [1]After Alexander son of Philip, the Macedonian, who came from the land of Kittim, had defeated[a] Darius, king of the Persians and the Medes, he succeeded him as king. (He had previously become king of Greece.) [2]He fought many battles, conquered strongholds, and put to death the kings of the earth. [3]He

***1:1–64.** Greek domination was a terrible trial for the Jewish people. During the Greek period they stayed loyal to the Covenant that God made with the patriarchs, defending it against the Greek religion and culture which were imposed on the East as a result of Alexander the Great's conquests. Pagan customs were introduced into Jerusalem and Judah, firstly, through the infidelity of many Jews who were attracted by the novelty and splendour of Hellenistic culture, and, secondly, because Antiochus Epiphanes tried to weld his territories together politically by imposing Greek civilization and religion. To do this in Judea he attacked the three pillars of the Jewish religion—the temple of Jerusalem; religious customs, particularly circumcision and the sabbath observance; and the books of the Law of Moses. It seemed inevitable that Judaism would disappear or else be merged with the Greek world, as happened in other Eastern nations influenced by Hellenism. But, in fact, Israel kept its religious identity thanks to a special providence of God; this enabled it to continue to be the chosen people from whom would be born the Messiah, Jesus Christ. That is the message of the books of the Maccabees, a message perceived by Church tradition when it acknowledged them as being part of Holy Scripture. When speaking about these books, St Augustine was well aware that the Jews did not regard them as being on the same level as the Law, the Prophets and the Psalms, "but they [these books] will not have been received by the Church in vain if they are read or listened to calmly, and especially those parts that deal with the Maccabees themselves who, for the sake of God's Law, were true martyrs and suffered terrible and humiliating things" (St Augustine, *Contra Gaudentium,* 1, 31, 38).

1:1–10. "The land of Kittim" (in Greek, *khettim*), originally referred to the island of Cyprus, but it also applied to Greece and Macedonia. Alexander the

[1] [1]Et factum est, postquam percussit Alexander Philippi Macedo, qui prius regnavit in Graecia, egressus de terra Cetthim, Darium regem Persarum et Medorum, [2]constituit proelia multa et obtinuit munitiones et interfecit reges terrae; [3]et pertransiit usque ad fines terrae et accepit spolia multitudinis gentium, et siluit terra in conspectu eius, et exaltatum est et elevatum est cor eius. [4]Et congregavit virtutem fortem nimis et obtinuit regiones gentium et tyrannos, et facti sunt illi in tributum. [5]Et post haec decidit in lectum et cognovit quia moreretur; [6]et vocavit pueros suos nobiles, qui secum erant nutriti a iuventute, et divisit illis regnum suum, cum adhuc viveret. [7]Et regnavit Alexander annis duodecim et mortuus est.

a. Gk adds *and he defeated*

advanced to the ends of the earth, and plundered many nations. When the earth became quiet before him, he was exalted, and his heart was lifted up. [4]He gathered a very strong army and ruled over countries, nations, and princes, and they became tributary to him.

[5]After this he fell sick and perceived that he was dying. [6]So he summoned his most honoured officers, who had been brought up with him from youth, and divided his kingdom among them while he was still alive. [7]And after Alexander had reigned twelve years, he died.

[8]Then his officers began to rule, each in his own place. [9]They all put on crowns after his death, and so did their sons after them for many years; and they caused many evils on the earth.

[10]From them came forth a sinful root, Antiochus Epiphanes, son of Antiochus the king; he had been a hostage in Rome. He began to reign in the one hundred and thirty-seventh year of the kingdom of the Greeks.[b]

2 Mac 4:7

Many Jews are led astray

[11]In those days lawless men came forth from Israel, and misled many, saying, "Let us go and make a covenant with the Gentiles round about us, for since we separated from them many evils have come upon us." [12]This proposal pleased them, [13]and some of the

2 Mac 4:9–17

Great died in Babylonia in the year 323 BC. His successors, called the Diadochi, fought among themselves over the division of the empire. Ptolemy I gained control of Egypt, and founded the dynasty of the Lagids. Seleucus, the first of the Seleucid kings, took Babylon. To begin with, Palestine was part of the Ptolemy domains, but in the year 197 BC, after the battle of Baniyas in which Egypt was defeated, it came under the control of the Seleucids. Antiochus IV Epiphanes, son of Antiochus III and brother of Seleucus IV (cf. 2 Mac 4:7), had been sent to Rome by his father as a hostage (in accordance with the treaty of Apamea, 188 BC). The one hundred and thirty-seventh year, counting from 312 BC when the Seleucid dynasty was founded, was 175 BC.

1:11–15. Conforming to Greek ways was equivalent in that situation to

[8]Et obtinuerunt pueri eius regnum, unusquisque in loco suo; [9]et imposuerunt omnes sibi diademata post mortem eius, et filii eorum post eos annis multis. Et multiplicata sunt mala in terra. [10]Et exiit ex eis radix peccatrix, Antiochus Epiphanes filius Antiochi regis, qui fuerat Romae obses, et regnavit in anno centesimo tricesimo septimo regni Graecorum. [11]In diebus illis exierunt ex Israel filii iniqui et suaserunt multis dicentes: «Eamus et disponamus testamentum cum gentibus, quae circa nos sunt, quia, ex quo recessimus ab eis, invenerunt nos multa mala». [12]Et bonus visus est sermo in oculis eorum; [13]et destinaverunt aliqui de populo et abierunt ad regem, et dedit illis potestatem, ut facerent iustitias

b. 175 BC

1 Cor 7:18

people eagerly went to the king. He authorized them to observe the ordinances of the Gentiles. [14]So they built a gymnasium in Jerusalem, according to Gentile custom, [15]and removed the marks of circumcision, and abandoned the holy covenant. They joined with the Gentiles and sold themselves to do evil.

Dan 11:25–28
2 Mac 5:1

Jerusalem sacked by Antiochus Epiphanes

[16]When Antiochus saw that his kingdom was established, he determined to become king of the land of Egypt, that he might reign over both kingdoms. [17]So he invaded Egypt with a strong force, with chariots and elephants and cavalry and with a large fleet. [18]He engaged Ptolemy king of Egypt in battle, and Ptolemy turned and fled before him, and many were wounded and fell. [19]And they captured the fortified cities in the land of Egypt, and he plundered the land of Egypt.

---

turning one's back on the Lord and on the Covenant. Gymnasia were presided over by Greek gods, and "becoming like the Gentiles" involved disguising the signs of circumcision when taking part undressed in gymnasium sports. Belonging to the people of God entailed a moral lifestyle different from that of the Gentiles, just as being a member of the Church, the new people of God, requires a person to avoid practices and attitudes contrary to the natural law and Christian ethics.

Apropos of this, St Paul taught the first Christians: "We beseech and exhort you in the Lord Jesus, that as you learned from us how you ought to live and to please God, just as you are doing, you do so more and more. For you know what instructions we gave you through the Lord Jesus. For this is the will of God, your sanctification: that you abstain from immorality; that each one of you know how to control his own body in holiness and honour, not in the passion of lust like heathen who do not know God" (1 Thess 4:1–5). "Reject the deception of those who appease themselves with the pathetic cry of 'Freedom! Freedom!' Their cry often masks a tragic enslavement, because choices that prefer error do not liberate. Christ alone sets us free, for he alone is the Way, the Truth and the Life" (St J. Escrivá, *Friends of God*, 26).

1:16–28. Antiochus invaded Egypt twice; and on both occasions he sacked Jerusalem on his return journey. The first invasion (the one narrated here) took place in 169 BC; it was a considerable success, but he failed to take Alexandria. The second invasion (narrated in 2 Mac

gentium. [14]Et aedificaverunt gymnasium in Hierosolymis secundum leges nationum; [15]et fecerunt sibi praeputia et recesserunt a testamento sancto et iuncti sunt nationibus et venumdati sunt, ut facerent malum. [16]Et paratum est regnum in conspectu Antiochi, et coepit regnare in terra Aegypti, ut regnaret super duo regna. [17]Et intravit in Aegyptum in multitudine gravi, in curribus et elephantis et equitibus et navium multitudine; [18]et constituit bellum adversus Ptolemaeum regem Aegypti, et veritus est Ptolemaeus a facie eius et fugit, et ceciderunt vulnerati multi. [19]Et comprehenderunt civitates munitas

[20]After subduing Egypt, Antiochus returned in the one hundred and forty-third year.[c] He went up against Israel and came to Jerusalem with a strong force. [21]He arrogantly entered the sanctuary and took the golden altar, the lampstand for the light, and all its utensils. [22]He took also the table for the bread of the Presence, the cups for drink offerings, the bowls, the golden censers, the curtain, the crowns, and the gold decoration on the front of the temple; he stripped it all off. [23]He took the silver and the gold, and the costly vessels; he took also the hidden treasures which he found. [24]Taking them all, he departed to his own land.

2 Mac 5:11–16

2 Mac 5:21

He committed deeds of murder, and spoke with great
arrogance.
[25] Israel mourned deeply in every community,
[26] rulers and elders groaned,
maidens and young men became faint,
the beauty of women faded.
[27] Every bridegroom took up the lament;
she who sat in the bridal chamber was mourning.
[28] Even the land shook for its inhabitants,
and all the house of Jacob was clothed with shame.

Persecution. Construction of the citadel at Jerusalem

[29]Two years later the king sent to the cities of Judah a chief collector of tribute, and he came to Jerusalem with a large force.

5:1, 11–21) came a year later. It was during the second campaign that the Roman legate informed him that Egypt was under the tutelage of Rome; Antiochus angrily withdrew and vented his rage on Jerusalem again. He obtained much plunder on both occasions.

1:29–40. At this point systematic persecution of the Jews begins in Jerusalem itself, with the killing of many of its inhabitants and the plundering of their property. On the high ground on the western part of the city, Antiochus establishes a large garrison, housed in a fortress called the Acra or Citadel, from which he can dominate the temple and the lower part of the city. This means he can control access to the temple and prevent anyone from entering (cf. 2 Mac 5:24–25).

1:29. "Chief collector of tribute": perhaps a "mysarch" (cf. 2 Mac 5:24), a

in terra Aegypti, et accepit spolia terrae Aegypti. [20]Et reversus est Antiochus, postquam percussit Aegyptum in centesimo et quadragesimo tertio anno, et ascendit ad Israel et ad Hierosolyma in multitudine gravi [21]et intravit in sanctificationem cum superbia et accepit altare aureum et candelabrum luminis et universa vasa eius [22]et mensam propositionis et libatoria et phialas et pateras aureas et velum

c. 169 BC

2 Mac 5:24–26

[30]Deceitfully he spoke peaceable words to them, and they believed him; but he suddenly fell upon the city, dealt it a severe blow, and destroyed many people of Israel. [31]He plundered the city, burned it with fire, and tore down its houses and its surrounding walls. [32]And they took captive the women and children, and seized the cattle. [33]Then they fortified the city of David with a great strong wall and strong towers, and it became their citadel. [34]And they stationed there a sinful people, lawless men. These strengthened their position; [35]they stored up arms and food, and collecting the spoils of Jerusalem they stored them there, and became a great snare.

[36] It became an ambush against the sanctuary,
an evil adversary of Israel continually.
[37] On every side of the sanctuary they shed innocent blood;
they even defiled the sanctuary.
[38] Because of them the residents of Jerusalem fled;
she became a dwelling of strangers;
she became strange to her offspring,
and her children forsook her.
[39] Her sanctuary became desolate as a desert;
her feasts were turned into mourning,
her sabbaths into a reproach,
her honour into contempt.
[40] Her dishonour now grew as great as her glory;
her exaltation was turned into mourning.

---

rank in the Seleucid army. Etymologically the word means "chief of Mysian mercenaries" (Mysia being a region in Asia Minor), in Hebrew *sar musim* or *sar misim*, which became distorted into *sar missim*, chief of taxes.

1:41–53. Up to this point the Jews have been governed by their own laws, which were both religious and civil. In order to unify his empire politically, Antiochus wants to impose a single form of religious practice. Those Jews who had a liking for things Greek had no difficulty in accepting the king's laws: they were already conforming to them, and now they became formal apostates of Judaism. Other Jews, maybe the majority, conformed out of fear. But there were others still, whom the sacred writer sees as the true Israel (v. 53), who were forced to go underground to stay loyal to their religion.

et coronas et ornamentum aureum, quod in facie templi erat; et comminuit omnia. [23]Et accepit argentum et aurum et vasa concupiscibilia et accepit thesauros occultos, quos invenit; [24]et, sublatis omnibus, abiit in terram suam et fecit caedem hominum et locutus est superbia magna. [25]Et factus est planctus magnus in Israel et in omni loco eorum; [26]et ingemuerunt principes et seniores, virgines et iuvenes infirmati sunt, et speciositas mulierum immutata est, [27]omnis maritus sumpsit lamentum, et quae sedebat in toro

Observance of the Law is proscribed

[41]Then the king wrote to his whole kingdom that all should be one people, [42]and that each should give up his customs. [43]All the Gentiles accepted the command of the king. Many even from Israel gladly adopted his religion; they sacrificed to idols and profaned the sabbath. [44]And the king sent letters by messengers to Jerusalem and the cities of Judah; he directed them to follow customs strange to the land, [45]to forbid burnt offerings and sacrifices and drink offerings in the sanctuary, to profane sabbaths and feasts, [46]to defile the sanctuary and the priests, [47]to build altars and sacred precincts and shrines for idols, to sacrifice swine and unclean animals, [48]and to leave their sons uncircumcised. They were to make themselves abominable by everything unclean and profane, [49]so that they should forget the law and change all the ordinances. [50]"And whoever does not obey the command of the king shall die."

[51]In such words he wrote to his whole kingdom. And he appointed inspectors over all the people and commanded the cities of Judah to offer sacrifice, city by city. [52]Many of the people, every one who forsook the law, joined them, and they did evil in the

---

maritali, lugebat; [28]et commota est terra super habitantes in ea, et universa domus Iacob induit confusionem. [29]Et post duos annos dierum misit rex principem tributorum in civitates Iudae et venit Ierusalem cum turba magna; [30]et locutus est ad eos verba pacifica in dolo, et crediderunt ei. Et irruit super civitatem repente et percussit eam plaga magna et perdidit populum multum ex Israel. [31]Et accepit spolia civitatis et succendit eam igne et destruxit domos eius et muros eius in circuitu; [32]et captivas duxerunt mulieres et natos et pecora possederunt. [33]Et aedificaverunt civitatem David muro magno et firmo et turribus firmis; et facta est illis in arcem. [34]Et posuerunt illic gentem peccatricem, viros iniquos, et convaluerunt in ea; [35]et posuerunt arma et escas et, congregatis spoliis Ierusalem, reposuerunt illic; et facti sunt in laqueum magnum. [36]Et factum est hoc ad insidias sanctificationi et in diabolum malum in Israel semper; [37]et effuderunt sanguinem innocentem per circuitum sanctificationis et contaminaverunt sanctificationem. [38]Et fugerunt habitatores Ierusalem propter eos, et facta est habitatio exterorum et facta est extera semini suo; et nati eius reliquerunt eam. [39]Sanctificatio eius desolata est sicut solitudo, dies festi eius conversi sunt in luctum, sabbata eius in opprobrium, honor eius in nihilum. [40]Secundum gloriam eius multiplicata est ignominia eius, et sublimitas eius conversa est in luctum. [41]Et scripsit rex Antiochus omni regno suo, ut essent universi populus unus, [42]et relinqueret unusquisque legem suam. Et receperunt omnes gentes secundum verbum regis Antiochi; [43]et multi ex Israel consenserunt cultui eius et sacrificaverunt idolis et coinquinaverunt sabbatum. [44]Et misit rex libros per manus nuntiorum in Ierusalem et in civitates Iudae, ut sequerentur leges gentium terrae, [45]et prohibere holocausta et sacrificia et placationes fieri in templo Dei et contaminare sabbata et dies sollemnes [46]et polluere sancta et sanctos, [47]instruere aras et templa et idola et immolare porcina et pecora communia [48]et relinquere filios suos incircumcisos et polluere animas eorum in omni immundo et abominatione, [49] ita ut obliviscerentur legem et immutarent omnes iustificationes; [50]et, quicumque non fecerit secundum verbum regis Antiochi, morietur. [51]Secundum omnia verba haec scripsit omni regno suo et praeposuit consideratores super omnem populum et mandavit civitatibus Iudae immolare per civitatem et civitatem. [52]Et congregati sunt multi de populo ad eos, omnes, qui dereliquerant legem Domini, et fecerunt mala in terra; [53]et posuerunt Israel in abditis et in absconditis fugitivorum locis. [54]Die quinta decima mensis Casleu, quinto et quadragesimo et centesimo anno, aedificavit abominationem desolationis super altare; et per civitates Iudae in circuitu aedificaverunt aras [55]et ante ianuas domorum et in plateis sacrificabant.

land; [53]they drove Israel into hiding in every place of refuge they had.

The temple profaned, the books of the Law set on fire. Religious persecution

Dan 9:27; 11:31 Mt 24:15

[54]Now on the fifteenth day of Chislev, in the one hundred and forty-fifth year,[d] they erected a desolating sacrilege upon the altar of burnt offering. They also built altars in the surrounding cities of Judah, [55]and burned incense at the doors of the houses and in the streets. [56]The books of the law which they found they tore to pieces and burned with fire. [57]Where the book of the covenant was found in the possession of any one, or if any one adhered to the law, the decree of the king condemned him to death. [58]They kept

---

1:54–64. The author recalls with great sadness the exact day when an altar, or perhaps a statue, dedicated to Zeus Olympus was erected in the temple of Jerusalem—8 December 167 BC. The revulsion God-fearing Jews felt towards that object can be seen from the name used to describe it—"a desolating sacrifice" ("abominatio desolationis", the abomination of desolation: cf. Dan 9:27; 11:31; 12:11). In Hebrew the words used sound like the name of the "Baal of the heavens", the Canaanite idol which Israelites in ancient times found so attractive and against which the prophets strove (cf. 1 Kings 18:20–40). But the phrase also, literally, means something abominable which leads to total perdition. It is, in the last analysis, a symbol of idolatrous worship which seeks to impose itself by force on worship of the true God. Our Lord Jesus Christ will use the very same expression, "desolating sacrifice", "abomination of desolation", to announce the tribulation which will overwhelm Jerusalem (as it indeed did when the Romans destroyed it in 70 AD) and which will be a sign of the tribulations that will happen at the end of time (cf. Mt 24:15–25 and par.).

The events narrated briefly here and the violence done to the Jews, as also exemplary acts of fidelity, are reported in more detail in 2 Maccabees 6:1–11, 18, 31; 7:1–42. It was a very testing time for Israel, a time of purging and purification. When God allows persecution to happen, he does so to elicit fidelity: this is true for Israel and later for the Church.

[56]Et libros legis, quos invenerunt, combusserunt igne scindentes eos; [57]et ubicumque inveniebatur apud aliquem liber testamenti, et si quis consentiebat legi, constitutio regis interficiebat eum. [58]In virtute sua faciebant haec Israeli, omnibus, qui inveniebantur in omni mense et mense in civitatibus. [59]Et quinta et vicesima die mensis sacrificabant super aram, quae erat super altare; [60]et mulieres, quae circumciderant filios suos, interficiebant secundum iussum [61]—et suspendebant infantes a cervicibus eorum—et domos eorum et eos, qui circumciderant illos. [62]Et multi in Israel obtinuerunt et confortati sunt apud se, ut non manducarent immunda, [63]et elegerunt mori, ut non polluerentur escis et non profanarent testamentum sanctum, et moriebantur. [64]Et facta est ira magna super Israel valde.

d. 167 BC

using violence against Israel, against those found month after month in the cities. [59]And on the twenty-fifth day of the month they offered sacrifice on the altar which was upon the altar of burnt offering. [60]According to the decree, they put to death the women who had their children circumcised, [61]and their families and those who circumcised them; and they hung the infants from their mothers' necks.

2 Mac 6:10

[62]But many in Israel stood firm and were resolved in their hearts not to eat unclean food. [63]They chose to die rather than to be defiled by food or to profane the holy covenant; and they did die. [64]And very great wrath came upon Israel.

2. MATTATHIAS' ARMED REVOLT*

Anguish felt by Mattathias and his sons

2 [1]In those days Mattathias as the son of John, son of Simeon, a priest of the sons of Joarib, moved from Jerusalem and settled in Modein. [2]He had five sons, John surnamed Gaddi, [3]Simon called Thassi, [4]Judas called Maccabeus, [5]Eleazar called Avaran, and Jonathan called Apphus. [6]He saw the blasphemies being committed in Judah and Jerusalem, [7]and said,

1 Chron 24:7

Lam 2:5–17

***2:1–70.** Mattathias takes up arms against the king's officers in order to defend his religion and his country, once he realizes that flight, lamentation (vv. 6–14) and passive resistance as shown by the martyrs (vv. 29–38) are not enough. In those times, religion, politics and patriotism were so intertwined as to be inseparable, and the situation was such that the defence of religion called for resort to arms. Given the policies of Antiochus, the only way Judaism could survive was by the Jews getting some degree of political autonomy. Mattathias' revolt was not strictly speaking a "holy war" aimed at imposing a particular religion or wiping out those who practised another; it was a war in defence of Jewish freedoms in the face of an attempt to impose a foreign religion. It was a case, therefore, of a just war.

[2] [1]In diebus illis surrexit Matthathias filius Ioannis filii Simeonis sacerdos ex filiis Ioarib ab Ierusalem et consedit in Modin. [2]Et habebat filios quinque: Ioannem, qui cognominabatur Gaddis, [3]et Simonem, qui vocabatur Thasi, [4]et Iudam, qui vocabatur Maccabaeus, [5]et Eleazarum, qui vocabatur Abaran, et Ionathan, qui vocabatur Apphus. [6]Et vidit blasphemias, quae fiebant in Iuda et in Ierusalem, [7]et dixit «Vae mihi! Ut quid natus sum videre contritionem populi mei et contritionem civitatis sanctae? Et sederunt illic, cum daretur ea in manibus inimicorum, sanctificatio in manu extraneorum. [8]Factum est templum eius sicut homo ignobilis, [9]vasa gloriae eius captiva abducta sunt, trucidati sunt parvuli eius in plateis eius, iuvenes eius in gladio inimicorum. [10]Quae gens non hereditavit regnum eius et non obtinuit spolia eius? [11]Omnis ornatus eius ablatus est; quae erat libera, facta est ancilla. [12] Et ecce sancta nostra et pulchritudo nostra et gloria nostra desolata est, et polluerunt ea gentes. [13]Ut quid nobis adhuc

"Alas! Why was I born to see this,
the ruin of my people, the ruin of the holy city,
and to dwell there when it was given over to the enemy,
the sanctuary given over to aliens?
[8] Her temple has become like a man without honour;[e]
[9] her glorious vessels have been carried into captivity.
Her babes have been killed in her streets,
her youths by the sword of the foe.
[10] What nation has not inherited her palaces[f]
and has not seized her spoils?
[11] All her adornment has been taken away;
no longer free, she has become a slave.
[12] And behold, our holy place, our beauty,
and our glory have been laid waste;
the Gentiles have profaned it.
[13] Why should we live any longer?"

[14]And Mattathias and his sons rent their clothes, put on sackcloth, and mourned greatly.

In its teaching the Church reminds people that they need to work for peace. However, "as long as the danger of war persists and there is no international authority with the necessary competence and power, governments cannot be denied the right of lawful self-defence, once all peace efforts have failed" (Vatican II, *Gaudium et spes*, 79). The Church, in its *Catechism*, tells us that strict conditions need to be met for self-defence by military force to be justified. These conditions are: "the damage inflicted by the aggressor on the nation or community of nations must be lasting, grave and certain; all other means of putting an end to it must have been shown to be impractical or ineffective; there must be serious prospects of success; the use of arms must not produce evils and disorders greater than the evil to be eliminated. The power of modern means of destruction weighs very heavily in evaluating this condition. These are the traditional elements enumerated in what is called the 'just war'" (*Catechism of the Catholic Church*, 2308–2309).

2:1–14. Mattathias may have moved to Mode-in, some 30 km. (19 miles) north-east of Jerusalem, due to the persecution going on in that city (cf. 1:53). The fact that he came from a priestly family (cf. 1 Chron 24:7) is important, because it will later justify

vita?». [14]Et scidit vestimenta sua Matthathias et filii eius et operuerunt se ciliciis et planxerunt valde. [15]Et venerunt, qui ex rege compellebant discessionem, in civitatem Modin, ut sacrificarent. [16]Et multi de Israel accesserunt ad eos, et Matthathias et filii eius congregati sunt. [17]Et responderunt, qui missi erant a rege, et dixerunt Matthathiae: «Princeps et nobilis et magnus es in hac civitate et confirmatus

e. The text of this verse is uncertain **f.** Other authorities read *has not had a part in her kingdom*

Mattathias takes action at Mode-in

[15]Then the king's officers who were enforcing the apostasy came to the city of Modein to make them offer sacrifice. [16]Many from Israel came to them; and Mattathias and his sons were assembled. [17]Then the king's officers spoke to Mattathias as follows: "You are a leader, honoured and great in this city, and supported by sons and brothers. [18]Now be the first to come and do what the king commands, as all the Gentiles and the men of Judah and those that are left in Jerusalem have done. Then you and your sons will be numbered among the friends of the king, and you and your sons will be honoured with silver and gold and many gifts."

---

his son Jonathan becoming high priest (cf. 10:20). The additional names or nicknames given his sons seem to say something about the character of each: *Gaddi* means lucky; *Maccabeus*, hammer; *Thassi*, zealous; *Avaran*, alert; and *Apphus*, cunning. However, by extending Judas' surname, tradition describes them all as the *Maccabees*. The descendants of these men are known as the Hasmoneans because, according to Flavius Josephus the historian, Asmonaeus was a forebear of Mattathias (cf. *De bello Judaica*, 1, 36), perhaps the father of his grandfather Simeon (cf. *Antiquitates Judaicae*, 12, 265).

2:15–28. Mattathias certainly behaves savagely but he has a special reason for acting in this way: it helps to legitimate his leadership and that of his descendants in the liberation of Israel. Due to his priestly background Mattathias was a man of some status; what he did could influence others. Here, in a sense, he represents the people. Not only does he not succumb to the temptation to gain social and financial advantage by being untrue to his conscience and his religion (cf. vv. 17–22); he shows signs of being a saviour of his people. His action is comparable to that of Phinehas (v. 26), that priest who, according to Numbers 25:6–15, ran a spear through an Israelite and a Midianite woman, thereby turning God's wrath back from the people. In reward for his action God gave Phinehas a covenant of peace and

filiis et fratribus. [18]Nunc accede primus et fac iussum regis, sicut fecerunt omnes gentes et viri Iudae et qui remanserunt in Ierusalem, et eris tu et filii tui inter amicos regis et tu et filii tui glorificabimini et argento et auro et muneribus multis». [19]Et respondit Matthathias et dixit magna voce: «Etsi omnes gentes, quae in domo regni sunt, regi oboediunt, ut discedat unusquisque ab officio patrum suorum, et consentiunt mandatis eius, [20]et ego et filii mei et fratres mei ibimus in testamento patrum nostrorum. [21]Propitius sit nobis Dominus, ne derelinquamus legem et iustificationes. [22]Non audiemus verba regis, ut praetereamus officium nostrum dextra vel sinistra». [23]Et, ut cessavit loqui verba haec, accessit quidam Iudaeus in omnium oculis sacrificare super aram in Modin secundum iussum regis. [24]Et vidit Matthathias et zelatus est, et contremuerunt renes eius; et attulit iram secundum iudicium et insiliens trucidavit eum super aram. [25]Et virum regis, qui cogebat immolare, occidit in ipso tempore et aram destruxit; [26]et zelatus est legem, sicut fecit Phinees Zambri filio Salom. [27]Et exclamavit Matthathias voce magna in civitate dicens: «Omnis, qui zelum habet legis statuens testamentum, exeat post me». [28]Et fugit ipse et filii eius in montes, et reliquerunt quaecumque habebant in civitate. [29]Tunc descenderunt multi quaerentes iustitiam et iudicium in desertum, ut sederent ibi, [30]ipsi et filii eorum

[19]But Mattathias answered and said in a loud voice: "Even if all the nations that live under the rule of the king obey him, and have chosen to do his commandments, departing each one from the religion of his fathers, [20]yet I and my sons and my brothers will live by the covenant of our fathers. [21]Far be it from us to desert the law and the ordinances. [22]We will not obey the king's words by turning aside from our religion to the right hand or to the left."

Mt 16:22

[23]When he had finished speaking these words, a Jew came forward in the sight of all to offer sacrifice upon the altar in Modein, according to the king's command. [24]When Mattathias saw it, be burned with zeal and his heart was stirred. He gave vent to righteous anger; he ran and killed him upon the altar. [25]At the same time he killed the king's officer who was forcing them to sacrifice, and he tore down the altar. [26]Thus he burned with zeal for the law, as Phinehas did against Zimri the son of Salu.

Num 25:6–15

[27]Then Mattathias cried out in the city with a loud voice, saying: "Let every one who is zealous for the law and supports the covenant come out with me!" [28]And he and his sons fled to the hills and left all that they had in the city.

2 Mac 5:27
Mt 24:16

---

promised him and his line a perpetual priesthood (cf. v. 54). Moreover, on that occasion God disposed that the Israelites should attack the Midianites and defeat them. The memory of Phinehas endured in Jewish tradition (cf. Ps 106:28–31; Sir 45:23). Although the sacred writer does not expressly say so, the comparison with Phinehas gives us an inkling that Mattathias is becoming someone who has a covenant with God and will be a saviour of the people.

Both Phinehas and Mattathias were motivated by zeal for the Lord and for his Law (vv. 24, 26–27; Num 25:11). Although the way they expressed their zeal was understandable only in that distant context (it would not be acceptable today), their zeal for God and the things of God is still something to be imitated (cf. Origen, *Commentarii in Epistulam ad Romanos*, 8, 1). Our Lord Jesus Christ will also feel zealous for the house of God, the temple, and will perform a symbolic act of violence against those who profaned it (cf. Jn 2:17; Ps 69:9). It is this sort of zeal that leads a Christian to "holy intransigence". "Be uncompromising in doctrine and conduct. But be yielding in manner. A mace of tempered steel, wrapped in a quilted covering. Be uncompromising, but don't be obstinate" (St J. Escrivá, *The Way*, 397).

et mulieres eorum et pecora eorum, quoniam induraverant super eos mala. [31]Et renuntiatum est viris regis et exercitui, qui erat in Ierusalem civitate David, quoniam descenderunt viri quidam, qui dissipaverant mandatum regis, in loca occulta in deserto. [32]Et cucurrerunt post illos multi, et deprehendentes eos applicaverunt contra eos et constituerunt adversus eos proelium in die sabbatorum [33]et dixerunt ad eos: «Usque hoc nunc! Exite et facite secundum verbum regis et vivetis». [34]Et dixerunt:

A decision is taken to fight even on the sabbath. The first guerrillas

[29]Then many who were seeking righteousness and justice went down to the wilderness to dwell there, [30]they, their sons, their wives, and their cattle, because evils pressed heavily upon them. [31]And it was reported to the king's officers, and to the troops in Jerusalem the city of David, that men who had rejected the king's command had gone down to the hiding places in the wilderness. [32]Many pursued them, and overtook them; they encamped opposite them and prepared for battle against them on the sabbath day. [33]And they said to them, "Enough of this! Come out and do what the king commands, and you will live." [34]But they said, "We will not come out, nor will we do what the king commands and so profane the sabbath day." [35]Then the enemy[g] hastened to attack them. [36]But they did not answer them or hurl a stone at them or block up their hiding places, [37]for they said, "Let us all die in our innocence; heaven and earth testify for us that you are killing us unjustly." [38]So they attacked them on the sabbath, and they died, with their wives and children and cattle, to the number of a thousand persons.

2 Mac 6:11

[39]When Mattathias and his friends learned of it, they mourned for them deeply. [40]And each said to his neighbour: "If we all do as our brethren have done and refuse to fight with the Gentiles for our lives and for our ordinances, they will quickly destroy us from the earth." [41]So they made this decision that day: "Let us fight against every man who comes to attack us on the sabbath day; let us not all die as our brethren died in their hiding places."

[42]Then there united with them a company of Hasideans, mighty of Israel, every one who offered himself willingly for the law.

2:29–48. Cf. 2 Mac 6:11. Defence of one's own life had priority over sabbath observance. This can be seen later when our Lord works a cure on the sabbath (cf. Mt 12:9–14 and par.) and proclaims that "the sabbath was made for man, not man for the sabbath" (Mk 2:27).

2:42. The term from which the Hasidaeans get their name means

«Non exibimus neque faciemus verbum regis, ut polluamus diem sabbatorum». [35]Et concitaverunt adversus eos proelium. [36]Et non responderunt eis nec lapidem miserunt in eos nec oppilaverunt loca occulta [37]dicentes: «Moriamur omnes in simplicitate nostra, et testes erunt super nos caelum et terra quod iniuste perditis nos». [38]Et insurrexerunt in eos in bello sabbatis; et mortui sunt ipsi et uxores eorum et filii eorum et pecora eorum usque ad mille animas hominum. [39]Et cognovit Matthathias et amici eius et luctum habuerunt super eos valde; [40]et dixit vir proximo suo: «Si omnes fecerimus, sicut fratres nostri fecerunt, et non pugnaverimus adversus gentes pro animabus nostris et iustificationibus nostris, nunc citius disperdent nos a terra». [41]Et cogitaverunt in die illa dicentes: «Omnis homo, quicumque venerit ad nos in bello die sabbatorum, pugnemus adversus eum et non moriemur omnes, sicut mortui sunt

g. Gk *they*

[43]And all who became fugitives to escape their troubles joined them and reinforced them. [44]They organized an army, and struck down sinners in their anger and lawless men in their wrath; the survivors fled to the Gentiles for safety. [45]And Mattathias and his friends went about and tore down the altars; [46]they forcibly circumcised all the uncircumcised boys that they found within the borders of Israel. [47]They hunted down the arrogant men, and the work prospered in their hands. [48]They rescued the law out of the hands of the Gentiles and kings, and they never let the sinner gain the upper hand.

Testament and death of Mattathias

[49]Now the days drew near for Mattathias to die, and he said to his sons: "Arrogance and reproach have now become strong; it is a time of ruin and furious anger. [50]Now, my children, show zeal for the law, and give your lives for the covenant of our fathers.

[51]"Remember the deeds of the fathers, which they did in their generations; and receive great honour and an everlasting name. [52]Was not Abraham found faithful when tested, and it was

Gen 15:6
Heb 11:17

"faithful", "loyal" or "devout". The group mentioned here is distinct from that of Mattathias and his followers, and it existed before they came on the scene. The Hasidaeans did not start the revolt, but they joined up with the Maccabees (cf. 2 Mac 14:6). However, they did not merge with them (cf. 7:13); from this group will later come the Pharisees and probably also those who withdrew to Qumran.

2:49–70. Like Jacob (cf. Gen 49), Joshua (cf. Josh 24:1–24), and Samuel (cf. 1 Sam 12:1–25) and David (cf. 1 Kings 2:1–9), prior to his death Mattathias leaves his sons a spiritual testament. He reminds them of the famous men in the history of Israel whom they would do well to imitate, and he urges them to be zealous for the Law of God and put their trust in God's help—and also to stick together. But the law of vengeance is still part of Mattathias' mind-set (cf. v. 68); it is a law that will be abolished by our Lord (cf. Mt 5:28–42).

2:52. St Paul and St James recall this same event from the life of Abraham

fratres nostri in occultis». [42]Tunc congregata est ad eos synagoga Asidaeorum fortis viribus ex Israel, omnis voluntarius in lege; [43]et omnes, qui fugiebant a malis, additi sunt ad eos et facti sunt illis ad firmamentum. [44]Et constituerunt exercitum et percusserunt peccatores in ira sua et viros iniquos in indignatione sua; et ceteri fugerunt ad nationes, ut se liberarent. [45]Et circuivit Matthathias et amici eius, et destruxerunt aras; [46]et circumciderunt pueros incircumcisos, quotquot invenerunt in finibus Israel, in fortitudine. [47]Et persecuti sunt filios superbiae, et prosperatum est opus in manu eorum; [48]et obtinuerunt legem de manu gentium et de manu regum et non dederunt cornu peccatori. [49]Et appropinquaverunt dies Matthathiae moriendi, et dixit filiis suis: «Nunc confirmata est superbia et castigatio et tempus eversionis et ira indignationis. [50]Nunc, o filii, aemulatores estote legis; et date animas vestras pro

reckoned to him as righteousness? [53]Joseph in the time of his distress kept the commandment, and became lord of Egypt. [54]Phinehas our father, because he was deeply zealous, received the covenant of everlasting priesthood. [55]Joshua, because he fulfilled the command, became a judge in Israel. [56]Caleb, because he testified in the assembly, received an inheritance in the land. [57]David, because he was merciful, inherited the throne of the kingdom for ever. [58]Elijah because of great zeal for the law was taken up into heaven. [59]Hananiah, Azariah, and Misha-el believed and were saved from the flame. [60]Daniel because of his innocence was delivered from the mouth of the lions.

[61]"And so observe, from generation to generation, that none who put their trust in him will lack strength. [62]Do not fear the words of a sinner, for his splendour will turn into dung and worms. [63]Today he will be exalted, but tomorrow he will not be found, because he has returned to the dust, and his plans will perish. [64]My children, be courageous and grow strong in the law, for by it you will gain honour.

[65]"Now behold, I know that Simeon your brother is wise in counsel; always listen to him; he shall be your father. [66]Judas Maccabeus has been a mighty warrior from his youth; he shall command the army for you and fight the battle against the

Gen 37; 39–41
Num 15:6–13
Num 13:30; 14:24
2 Sam 7
1 Kings 19:10,14
2 Kings 2:11–12
Dan 3
Dan 6
2 Tim 4:17

(cf. Rom 4:3; Jas 2:23), though they do so by quoting Genesis 15:6 literally: "(Abraham) believed the Lord; and he reckoned it to him as righteousness." The author of 1 Maccabees emphasizes the fact that Abraham was faithful when God put him to the test; St Paul, on the other hand, makes the point that what justified Abraham was his trust in God; and St James, for his part, says that Abraham's faith manifested itself in the way he acted, in his "works". These three aspects of faith are inseparable—faithfulness, trust, and works which prove them.

testamento patrum vestrorum: [51]et mementote operum patrum, quae fecerunt in generationibus suis, et accipietis gloriam magnam et nomen aeternum. [52]Abraham, nonne in tentatione inventus est fidelis, et reputatum est ei ad iustitiam? [53]Ioseph in tempore angustiae suae custodivit mandatum et factus est dominus Aegypti. [54]Phinees pater noster zelando zelum Dei accepit testamentum sacerdotii aeterni. [55]Iosue, dum implet verbum, factus est iudex in Israel. [56]Chaleb, dum testificatur in ecclesia, accepit hereditatem. [57]David in sua misericordia consecutus est sedem regni in saecula. [58]Elias, dum zelat zelum legis, receptus est in caelum. [59]Ananias et Azarias et Misael credentes liberati sunt de flamma. [60]Daniel in sua simplicitate liberatus est de ore leonum. [61]Et ita cogitate per generationem et generationem, quia omnes, qui sperant in eum, non infirmabuntur. [62]Et a verbis viri peccatoris ne timueritis, quia gloria eius in stercora et in vermes; [63]hodie extolletur et cras non invenietur, quia conversus est in pulverem suam, et cogitatio eius peribit. [64]Filii, confortamini et viriliter agite in lege, quia in ipsa gloriosi eritis. [65]Et ecce Simon frater vester, scio quod vir consilii est: ipsum audite semper; ipse erit vobis pater. [66]Et Iudas Maccabaeus fortis viribus a iuventute sua erit vobis princeps militiae; et ipse pugnabit bellum populi. [67]Et adducetis ad vos omnes factores legis et vindicate vindictam populi

peoples.[h] [67]You shall rally about you all who observe the law, and avenge the wrong done to your people.[h] [68]Pay back the Gentiles in full, and heed what the law commands."

[69]Then he blessed them, and was gathered to his fathers. [70]He died in the one hundred and forty-sixth year[i] and was buried in the tomb of his fathers at Modein. And all Israel mourned for him with great lamentation.

3. JUDAS MACCABEUS*

Eulogy of Judas Maccabeus

1 Mac 2:1–4

3 [1]Then Judas his son, who was called Maccabeus, took command in his place. [2]All his brothers and all who had joined his father helped him; they gladly fought for Israel.

[3]He extended the glory of his people.
Like a giant he put on his breastplate;
he girded on his armour of war and waged battles,
protecting the host by his sword.
[4]He was like a lion in his deeds,
like a lion's cub roaring for prey.
[5]He searched out and pursued the lawless;

***3:1—9:22.** On Mattathias' death, Judas becomes the military leader (cf. 2:66). He begins by going out to meet (and defeat) Syrian generals based in Judea (3:10–26). This provokes Antiochus to send his two best generals, Nicanor and Gorgias, into Judea; Judas defeats their forces in a battle near Emmaus (3:27—4:25). Then Lysias, the Syrian commander-in-chief, moves in, but when he sees how determined and courageous the Jews are, he withdraws to Antioch to enlist mercenaries (4:26–35). Judas avails himself of the respite to cleanse the temple and reactivate religious worship (4:36–61). He also embarks on campaigns outside Judea to help Jews living in those parts and consolidate his gains (5:1–68). Meanwhile, Antiochus Epiphanes dies and is succeeded by his son Antiochus V Eupator (6:1–17); it is the year 164 BC. When Judas tries to take the Syrian citadel in Jerusalem, the king sends the

vestri; [68]retribuite retributionem gentibus et intendite in praeceptum legis». [69]Et benedixit eos et appositus est ad patres suos. [70]Et defunctus est anno centesimo et quadragesimo sexto; et sepultus est in sepulcris patrum suorum in Modin, et planxerunt eum omnis Israel planctu magno. **[3]** [1]Et surrexit Iudas, qui vocabatur Maccabaeus, filius eius pro eo. [2]Et adiuvabant eum omnes fratres eius et universi, qui se coniunxerant patri eius; et proeliabantur proelium Israel cum laetitia. [3]Et dilatavit gloriam populo suo et induit se loricam sicut gigas et succinxit se arma bellica sua et proelia constituit protegens castra gladio. [4]Similis factus est leoni in operibus suis et sicut catulus leonis rugiens in venationem; [5]et

h. Or *of the people* **i.** 166 BC

he burned those who troubled his people.
[6]Lawless men shrank back for fear of him;
all the evildoers were confounded;
and deliverance prospered by his hand.

Lk 13:27

main body of his army against Jerusalem (6:18–42). Judas is unable to block him, so he falls back and is besieged in a section of the Holy City (6:47–54). But events in Antioch (Philip making a bid for power) force Lysias to return there without delay, so he offers Judas a peace treaty (6:55–63). In 162 BC Demetrius becomes king of Syria, and the pro-Hellenist party in Jerusalem manage to have Alcimus made high priest; Alcimus tries to impose Seleucid policies (7:1–20) but Judas' reaction causes the king to send Nicanor with a large army—which Judas defeats (7:21–50). Then, fearing another Syrian onslaught, Judas makes overtures to Rome and forms an alliance with it (8:1–32); even so, Demetrius attacks again and this time Judas dies in battle (9:1–22).

That is the order of events given in this book. But, in fact, in view of the different sequence found in 2 Maccabees (cf. 2 Mac 9:1–29; 10:1–18; 11:1–15) and the natural logic of events, everything points to Antiochus Epiphanes' dying while Lysias was besieging Jerusalem—and causing Lysias to return to Antioch (and offer peace to Judas before he left). That would have been the point when Judas won a degree of religious freedom for the Jews (6:55–63) and when he had the temple purified (4:36–61; 2 Mac 10:1–8). Both 1 and 2 Maccabees (each in its own way) change the order of events. First Maccabees does so in order to show that the cleansing and rededication of the temple was made possible by Judas' victories, and not by the peace that circumstances forced on Lysias (4:26–61). Second Maccabees, for its part, changes the chronological order because it wants to show that God decided that the temple should be cleansed after the death of the tyrant (2 Mac 9–10). Besides, by delaying Antiochus' death until after the cleansing of the temple, 1 Maccabees is able to link it to his sons' succession to the throne (6:1–17). Still, it is not easy to explain the changes in the chronological order in these two books. As far as the authors' intentions were concerned, chronology was of secondary consideration; what they were mainly interested in was to exalt Judas and all his great successes in the cause of the temple and the deliverance of the Jews.

3:3–9. Judas is praised for two things—pursuing and eliminating the apostate Jews, and delivering the people from

persecutus est iniquos perscrutans et eos, qui conturbabant populum suum, succendit. [6]Et subducti sunt iniqui prae timore eius, et omnes operarii iniquitatis conturbati sunt; et prosperata est salus in manu eius. [7]Et exacerbabat reges multos; et laetificabat Iacob in operibus suis, et in saeculum memoria eius in benedictionem. [8]Et perambulavit in civitatibus Iudae et disperdidit impios ex ea et avertit iram ab Israel; [9]et nominatus est usque ad ultimum terrae et congregavit pereuntes. [10]Et congregavit Apollonius gentes et a Samaria virtutem magnam ad bellandum contra Israel. [11]Et cognovit Iudas et exiit obviam illi; et percussit eum et occidit, et ceciderunt vulnerati multi, et reliqui fugerunt. [12]Et acceperunt spolia eorum,

[7]He embittered many kings,
but he made Jacob glad by his deeds,
and his memory is blessed for ever.
[8]He went through the cities of Judah;
he destroyed the ungodly out of the land;[j]
thus he turned away wrath from Israel.
[9]He was renowned to the ends of the earth;
he gathered in those who were perishing.

2 Mac 8:1–7

Victory over Apollonius and Seron, local army commanders

[10]But Apollonius gathered together Gentiles and a large force from Samaria to fight against Israel. [11]When Judas learned of it, he went out to meet him, and he defeated and killed him. Many were wounded and fell, and the rest fled. [12]Then they seized their spoils; and Judas took the sword of Apollonius, and used it in battle the rest of his life.

[13]Now when Seron, the commander of the Syrian army, heard that Judas had gathered a large company, including a body of faithful men who stayed with him and went out to battle, [14]he said, "I will make a name for myself and win honour in the kingdom. I will make war on Judas and his companions, who scorn the king's command." [15]And again a strong army of ungodly men went up with him to help him, to take vengeance on the sons of Israel.

Seleucid tyranny. The first of these predominates in the panegyric for Judas, and the cleansing of the people is presented as being the reason why God ceased to be angry (v. 8; cf. 2:27). The way in which he went about that cleansing (seeking out and killing the Law's enemies) only makes sense in that historical-religious context. But zeal for the holiness of the community is always something praiseworthy.

3:10–26. According to Flavius Josephus, the battle against Apollonius, governor of Samaria, took place a little north of Jerusalem; whereas Beth-horon (v. 24) is some 8 km. (5 miles) to the north-east of the city. The sacred writer makes much of the military inferiority of Judas, and of his trust in the Lord. The two contenders enter the battle with very different attitudes (vv. 18–22). Judas' attitude anticipates that

et gladium Apollonii accepit Iudas; et erat pugnans in eo omnibus diebus. [13]Et audivit Seron, princeps exercitus Syriae, quod congregavit Iudas congregationem et convocationem fidelium secum et egredientium in proelium, [14]et ait: «Faciam mihi nomen et glorificabor in regno et debellabo Iudam et eos, qui cum ipso sunt, qui spernunt verbum regis». [15]Et accessit, et ascendit cum eo exercitus impiorum fortis auxiliari ei, ut faceret vindictam in filios Israel. [16]Et appropinquavit usque ad ascensum Bethoron, et exivit Iudas obviam illi cum paucis. [17]Ut autem viderunt exercitum venientem sibi obviam dixerunt Iudae: «Quomodo poterimus pauci pugnare contra multitudinem tantam, fortem, et nos fatigati sumus

j. Gk *it*

[16]When he approached the ascent of Beth-horon, Judas went out to meet him with a small company. [17]But when they saw the army coming to meet them, they said to Judas, "How can we, few as we are, fight against so great and strong a multitude? And we are faint, for we have eaten nothing today." [18]Judas replied, "It is easy for many to be hemmed in by few, for in the sight of Heaven there is no difference between saving by many or by few. [19]It is not on the size of the army that victory in battle depends, but strength comes from Heaven. [20]They come against us in great pride and lawlessness to destroy us and our wives and our children, and to despoil us; [21]but we fight for our lives and our laws. [22]He himself will crush them before us; as for you, do not be afraid of them."

1 Mac 2:21

1 Sam 14:6

[23]When he finished speaking, he rushed suddenly against Seron and his army, and they were crushed before him. [24]They pursued them[k] down the descent of Beth-horon to the plain; eight hundred of them fell, and the rest fled into the land of the Philistines. [25]Then Judas and his brothers began to be feared, and terror fell upon the Gentiles round about them. [26]His fame reached the king, and the Gentiles talked of the battles of Judas.

Josh 10:10

Victory over Gorgias near Emmaus*

[27]When King Antiochus heard these reports, he was greatly angered; and he sent and gathered all the forces of his kingdom, a

of a Christian who knows, in the light of Christ's death, that he is a victor: "Remember the concern that Christ the Lord shows for his followers in the Gospel; recall that it is the King of martyrs who furnishes his army with spiritual weapons, who shows them the way to fight, who provides them with his help, who promises them relief, who, having told his disciples, 'In the world you shall have battles,' immediately adds, in order to give them comfort and help them overcome their fear, 'But be of good heart: I have overcome the world'" (St Augustine, *Sermons*, 276, 1).

***3:27—4:25.** Guerrilla warfare has been replaced by a full-scale formal battle between two organized armies. The sacred writer stops to explain the circumstances and preparations of the

ieiunio hodie?». [18]Et ait Iudas: «Facile est concludi multos in manibus paucorum; et non est differentia in conspectu caeli liberare in multis aut in paucis, [19]quoniam non in multitudine exercitus victoria belli, sed de caelo fortitudo est. [20]Ipsi veniunt ad nos in multitudine contumeliae et iniquitatis, ut disperdant nos et uxores nostras et filios nostros et ut spolient nos; [21]nos vero pugnamus pro animabus nostris et pro legitimis nostris, [22]et ipse Dominus conteret eos ante faciem nostram; vos autem ne timueritis eos». [23]Ut cessavit autem loqui, insiluit in eos subito; et contritus est Seron et exercitus eius in conspectu ipsius. [24]Et persequebantur eum in descensu Bethoron usque ad campum, et ceciderunt ex eis octingenti

k. Other authorities read *him*

very strong army. [28]And he opened his coffers and gave a year's pay to his forces, and ordered them to be ready for any need. [29]Then he saw that the money in the treasury was exhausted, and that the revenues from the country were small because of the dissension and disaster which he had caused in the land by abolishing the laws that had existed from the earliest days. [30]He feared that he might not have such funds as he had before for his expenses and for the gifts which he used to give more lavishly than preceding kings. [31]He was greatly perplexed in mind, and determined to go to Persia and collect the revenues from those regions and raise a large fund.

[32]He left Lysias, a distinguished man of royal lineage, in charge of the king's affairs from the river Euphrates to the borders of Egypt. [33]Lysias was also to take care of Antiochus his son until he returned. [34]And he turned over to Lysias[l] half of his troops and the elephants, and gave him orders about all that he wanted done. As for the residents of Judea and Jerusalem, [35]Lysias was to send a force against them to wipe out and destroy the strength of Israel and the remnant of Jerusalem; he was to banish the memory of them from the place, [36]settle aliens in all their territory, and distribute their land. [37]Then the king took the remaining half of his

---

battle—the financial straits Antiochus found himself in on account of the Jewish war (vv. 28–37); the assembling of the Syrian army (vv. 38–41); the preparations on the Jewish side (vv. 42–60); and the victory gained by the Jews (4:1–25).

3:28–37. Antiochus' visit to Persia (which was part of his domains) may have had less to do with the collection of taxes than with the reconquest of Armenia, which had made itself independent. First Maccabees, however, sees Israel as the main and only problem facing the king (v. 36).

viri; reliqui autem fugerunt in terram Philisthim. [25]Et coepit timor Iudae ac fratrum eius, et formido cecidit super gentes in circuitu eorum; [26]et pervenit ad regem nomen eius, et de proeliis Iudae narrabant omnes gentes. [27]Ut audivit autem Antiochus sermones istos, iratus est animo; et misit et congregavit exercitum universi regni sui, castra fortia valde. [28]Et aperuit aerarium suum et dedit stipendia exercitui in annum et mandavit illis, ut essent parati ad omnia. [29]Et vidit quod defecit pecunia de thesauris suis et tributa regionis modica propter dissensionem et plagam, quam fecit in terra, ut tolleret legitima, quae erant a primis diebus; [30]et timuit, ne non haberet ut semel et bis in sumptus et donaria, quae dederat antea larga manu, et abundaverat super reges, qui ante eum fuerant. [31]Et consternatus erat animo valde et cogitavit ire in Persidem et accipere tributa regionum et congregare argentum multum. [32]Et reliquit Lysiam hominem nobilem de genere regali super negotia regia a flumine Euphrate usque ad fines Aegypti [33]et ut nutriret Antiochum filium suum, donec rediret. [34]Et tradidit ei dimidium exercitum et elephantos et mandavit ei de omnibus, quae volebat, et de inhabitantibus Iudaeam et Ierusalem, [35]ut mitteret ad eos exercitum ad conterendam et exstirpandam virtutem Israel et reliquias Ierusalem et auferendam memoriam eorum de loco, [36]et ut constitueret habitatores filios alienigenas in omnibus

l. Gk *him*

troops and departed from Antioch his capital in the one hundred and forty-seventh year.[m] He crossed the Euphrates river and went through the upper provinces.

[38]Lysias chose Ptolemy the son of Dorymenes, and Nicanor and Gorgias, mighty men among the friends of the king, [39]and sent with them forty thousand infantry and seven thousand cavalry to go into the land of Judah and destroy it, as the king had commanded. [40]so they departed with their entire force, and when they arrived they encamped near Emmaus in the plain. [41]When the traders of the region heard what was said to them, they took silver and gold in immense amounts, and fetters,[n] and went to the camp to get the sons of Israel for slaves. And forces from Syria and the land of the Philistines joined with them.

1 Mac 2:18
2 Mac 4:45; 8:8–15; 10:14

3:38–41. Ptolemy was the governor of Coelesyria and Phoenicia; Gorgias, a highly experienced army general; Nicanor, apparently, the man with overall charge of financing and directing operations (cf. 2 Mac 8:8–11). This Emmaus is thought to haave been some 30 km. (19 miles) north-west of Jerusalem, so it is probably not the New Testament Emmaus, which lies about 10 km. from Jerusalem (cf. Lk 24:13).

3:42–60. The Jewish army prepare for battle by means of lamentation, penance and prayer. Since they have no temple to go to, they make their preparations at Mizpah, which had been a place of prayer in the past (cf. Judg 20:1), about 15 km. north of Jerusalem. It was to there that Nazirites were brought (men or women who took a vow not to cut their hair or drink strong drinks) for the rites marking the end of their vows, once the allotted time was over (cf. Num 6:1–21). Because Judah had no prophets at that time, Judas and his men consulted the book of the Law to discover the Lord's will (v. 48) and they put their trust in what heaven decided (v. 60). That is why not everyone is conscripted into the ranks (v. 56; cf. Deut 20:5–9).

finibus eorum et sorte distribueret terram eorum. [37]Et rex assumpsit dimidium exercitum residuum et exivit ab Antiochia de civitate regni sui anno centesimo et quadragesimo septimo et transfretavit Euphratem flumen et perambulabat superiores regiones. [38]Et elegit Lysias Ptolemaeum filium Dorymeni et Nicanorem et Gorgiam viros potentes ex amicis regis [39]et misit cum eis quadraginta milia virorum et septem milia equitum, ut venirent in terram Iudae et disperderent eam secundum verbum regis. [40]Et processerunt cum universa virtute sua; et venerunt et applicaverunt prope Emmaum in terra campestri. [41]Et audierunt mercatores regionis nomen eorum et acceperunt argentum et aurum multum valde et compedes et venerunt in castra, ut acciperent filios Israel in servos, et additi sunt ad eos exercitus Syriae et terrae alienigenarum. [42]Et vidit Iudas et fratres eius quia multiplicata sunt mala, et exercitus applicabant ad fines eorum, et cognoverunt verba regis, quae mandavit facere populo in interitum et consummationem. [43]Et dixerunt unusquisque ad proximum suum: «Erigamus deiectionem populi nostri et pugnemus pro populo nostro et sanctis nostris». [44]Et congregatus est conventus, ut essent parati in proelium et ut orarent et peterent misericordiam et miserationes. [45]Et Ierusalem non habitabatur sicut desertum; non erat qui ingrederetur et egrederetur de natis eius, et sanctum conculcabatur, et filii

m. 165 BC **n.** Syr: Gk *slaves*

[42]Now Judas and his brothers saw that misfortunes had increased and that the forces were encamped in their territory. They also learned what the king had commanded to do to the people to cause their final destruction. [43]But they said to one another, "Let us repair the destruction of our people, and fight for our people and the sanctuary." [44]And the congregation assembled to be ready for battle, and to pray and ask for mercy and compassion.

Is 24:7–12

[45] Jerusalem was uninhabited like a wilderness;
not one of her children went in or out.
The sanctuary was trampled down,
and the sons of aliens held the citadel;
it was a lodging place for the Gentiles.
Joy was taken from Jacob;
the flute and the harp ceased to play.

Judg 20:1–3
1 Sam 7:5–6
2 Mac 8:16–23
2 Mac 8:23
Num 6:1
Acts 21:26
1 Mac 2:21

[46]So they assembled and went to Mizpah, opposite Jerusalem, because Israel formerly had a place of prayer in Mizpah. [47]They fasted that day, put on sackcloth and sprinkled ashes on their heads, and rent their clothes. [48]And they opened the book of the law to inquire into those matters about which the Gentiles were consulting the images of their idols. [49]They also brought the garments of the priesthood and the first fruits and the tithes, and they stirred up the Nazirites who had completed their days; [50]and they cried aloud to Heaven, saying,

"What shall we do with these?
Where shall we take them?
[51] Thy sanctuary is trampled down and profaned,
and thy priests mourn in humiliation.
[52] And behold, the Gentiles are assembled against us
to destroy us;
thou knowest what they plot against us.
[53] How will we be able to withstand them,
if thou dost not help us?"

[54]Then they sounded the trumpets and gave a loud shout.

---

alienigenarum erant in arce; ibi erat habitatio gentibus. Et ablata est voluptas a Iacob, et defecit tibia et cithara. [46]Et congregati sunt et venerunt in Maspha contra Ierusalem, quia in Maspha erat antea locus orationis Israeli; [47]et ieiunaverunt illa die et induerunt se ciliciis et cinerem imposuerunt capiti suo et disciderunt vestimenta sua [48]et expanderunt librum Legis, de quibus scrutabantur gentes similitudines simulacrorum suorum; [49]et attulerunt ornamenta sacerdotalia et primitias et decimas et suscitaverunt nazaraeos, qui impleverunt dies, [50]et clamaverunt voce in caelum dicentes: «Quid faciemus istis et quo eos ducemus? [51]Et sancta tua conculcata sunt et contaminata, et sacerdotes tui in luctu et humiliatione; [52]et ecce nationes convenerunt adversum nos ut nos disperdant: tu scis, quae cogitant in nos. [53]Quomodo poterimus subsistere ante faciem eorum, nisi tu adiuves nos?». [54]Et tubis bucinaverunt et clamaverunt

[55]After this Judas appointed leaders of the people, in charge of thousands and hundreds and fifties and tens. [56]And he said to those who were building houses, or were betrothed, or were planting vineyards, or were fainthearted, that each should return to his home, according to the law. [57]Then the army marched out and encamped to the south of Emmaus.

Deut 20:5–9

[58]And Judas said, "Gird yourselves and be valiant. Be ready early in the morning to fight with these Gentiles who have assembled against us to destroy us and our sanctuary. [59]It is better for us to die in battle than to see the misfortunes of our nation and of the sanctuary. [60]But as his will in heaven may be, so he will do."

1 Mac 2:21
Mt 6:10
2 Mac 8:23–29

4 [1]Now Gorgias took five thousand infantry and a thousand picked cavalry, and this division moved out by night [2]to fall upon the camp of the Jews and attack them suddenly. Men from the citadel were his guides. [3]But Judas heard of it, and he and his mighty men moved out to attack the king's force in Emmaus [4]while the division was still absent from the camp. [5]When Gorgias entered the camp of Judas by night, he found no one there, so he looked for them in the hills, because he said, "These men are fleeing from us."

1 Mac 1:33

[6]At daybreak Judas appeared in the plain with three thousand men, but they did not have armour and swords such as they desired.

[7]And they saw the camp of the Gentiles, strong and fortified, with cavalry round about it; and these men were trained in war. [8]But Judas said to the men who were with him, "Do not fear their numbers or be afraid when they charge. [9]Remember how our

---

4:1–25. Judas is given credit for his intelligent strategy, but what is stressed most is the Jews' conviction that God is the one who will save his people (vv. 10–11, 24–25). God uses Judas and his small and ill-equipped army (v. 6) to give victory to Israel.

voce magna. [55]Et post haec constituit Iudas duces populi, tribunos et centuriones et pentacontarchos et decuriones [56]et dixit his, qui aedificabant domos et sponsabant uxores et plantabant vineas, et formidolosis, ut redirent unusquisque in domum suam secundum legem. [57]Et moverunt castra et collocaverunt ad austrum Emmaum. [58]Et ait Iudas: «Accingimini et estote filii potentes et estote parati in mane, ut pugnetis adversus nationes has, quae convenerunt adversus nos disperdere nos et sancta nostra; [59]quoniam melius est nos mori in bello quam respicere mala gentis nostrae et sanctorum. [60]Sicut autem fuerit voluntas in caelo, sic faciet». **[4]** [1]Et assumpsit Gorgias quinque milia virorum et mille equites electos, et moverunt castra nocte, [2]ut applicarent ad castra Iudaeorum et percuterent eos subito; et, qui erant ex arce, erant illis duces. [3]Et audivit Iudas et surrexit ipse et potentes percutere exercitum regis, qui erat in Emmaum, [4]dum adhuc dispersus esset exercitus a castris. [5]Et venit Gorgias in castra Iudae noctu et neminem invenit; et quaerebat eos in montibus, quoniam dixit: «Fugiunt hi a nobis». [6]Et simul ut dies factus est, apparuit Iudas in campo cum tribus milibus virorum, tantum quod tegumenta et gladios non habebant ut volebant. [7]Et viderunt castra gentium valida et loricatos et equitatus in circuitu

fathers were saved at the Red Sea, when Pharaoh with his forces pursued them. [10]And now let us cry to Heaven, to see whether he will favour us and remember his covenant with our fathers and crush this army before us today. [11]Then all the Gentiles will know that there is one who redeems and saves Israel."

1 Mac 2:21

[12]When the foreigners looked up and saw them coming against them, [13]they went forth from their camp to battle. Then the men with Judas blew their trumpets [14]and engaged in battle. The Gentiles were crushed and fled into the plain, [15]and all those in the rear fell by the sword. They pursued them to Gazara, and to the plains of Idumea, and to Azotus and Jamnia; and three thousand of them fell. [16]Then Judas and his force turned back from pursuing them, [17]and he said to the people, "Do not be greedy for plunder, for there is a battle before us; [18]Gorgias and his force are near us in the hills. But stand now against our enemies and fight them, and afterward seize the plunder boldly."

[19]Just as Judas was finishing this speech, a detachment appeared, coming out of the hills. [20]They saw that their army[o] had been put to flight, and that the Jews[o] were burning the camp, for the smoke that was seen showed what had happened. [21]When they perceived this they were greatly frightened, and when they also saw the army of Judas drawn up in the plain for battle, [22]they all fled into the land of the Philistines. [23]Then Judas returned to plunder the camp, and they seized much gold and silver, and cloth dyed blue and sea purple, and great riches. [24]On their return they sang hymns and praises to Heaven, for he is good, for his mercy endures for ever. [25]Thus Israel had a great deliverance that day.

Ps 118:1–3

---

eorum, et hi docti ad proelium. [8]Et ait Iudas viris, qui secum erant: «Ne timueritis multitudinem eorum et impetum eorum ne formidetis; [9]mementote qualiter salvi facti sunt patres nostri in mari Rubro, cum sequeretur eos pharao cum exercitu. [10]Et nunc clamemus in caelum, si miserebitur nostri et memor erit testamenti patrum nostrorum et conteret exercitum istum ante faciem nostram hodie; [11]et scient omnes gentes quia est, qui redimat et liberet Israel». [12]Et levaverunt alienigenae oculos suos et viderunt eos venientes ex adverso [13]et exierunt de castris in proelium. Et tuba cecinerunt hi, qui erant cum Iuda, [14]et commiserunt bellum; et contritae sunt gentes et fugerunt in campum. [15]Novissimi autem omnes ceciderunt in gladio, et persecuti sunt eos usque Gazeron et usque in campos Idumaeae et Azoti et Iamniae; et ceciderunt ex illis usque ad tria milia virorum. [16]Et reversus est Iudas et exercitus eius a persecutione eorum; [17]dixitque ad populum: «Non concupiscatis spolia, quia bellum contra nos est, [18]et Gorgias et exercitus eius prope nos in monte, sed state nunc contra inimicos nostros et expugnate eos et post haec accipite spolia confidenter». [19]Et, adhuc loquente Iuda haec, apparuit pars quaedam prospiciens de monte. [20]Et vidit quod in fugam conversi sunt sui, et succenderunt castra; fumus enim, qui videbatur, declarabat, quod factum est. [21]Quibus illi conspectis, timuerunt valde; aspicientes vero et Iudae exercitum in campo paratum ad proelium [22]fugerunt omnes in terram alienigenarum. [23]Et Iudas reversus est ad spolia castrorum; et acceperunt aurum multum et argentum et hyacinthum et purpuram marinam et opes magnas. [24]Et conversi hymnum canebant et benedicebant in caelum: «Quoniam

o. Gk *they*

Victory over Lysias at Beth-zur

2 Mac 11:1–12

[26]Those of the foreigners who escaped went and reported to Lysias all that had happened. [27]When he heard it, he was perplexed and discouraged, for things had not happened to Israel as he had intended, nor had they turned out as the king had commanded him. [28]But the next year he mustered sixty thousand picked infantrymen and five thousand cavalry to subdue them. [29]They came into Idumea and encamped at Beth-zur,* and Judas met them with ten thousand men.

1 Sam 14:1–23; 17

[30]When he saw that the army was strong, he prayed, saying, "Blessed art thou, O Saviour of Israel, who didst crush the attack of the mighty warrior by the hand of thy servant David, and didst give the camp of the Philistines into the hands of Jonathan, the son of Saul, and of the man who carried his armour. [31]So do thou hem in this army by the hand of thy people Israel, and let them be

---

4:26–35. The year after Judas' victory at Emmaus, that is, 164 BC, Lysias, who is in charge of the empire during the king's absence from Antioch (cf. 3:32), launches another attack on Judea and Jerusalem, this time from the south-east. Judas goes out to meet him at Beth-zur, a Syrian stronghold 30 km. (19 miles) from Jerusalem, on the Idumean border. First Maccabees gives Judas credit for an overwhelming victory (v. 34); but maybe things were not that simple. Judas may well have come out on top in an encounter with Lysias, as is said here, and the latter may have had to seek reinforcements, but the Syrians eventually got control of the situation and reached Jerusalem, to which they lay siege (cf. 2 Mac 11:13–15; 1 Mac 6:47–54). The author of 1 Maccabees wants to give the impression of a big Jewish victory at this point, because he will go on immediately to tell about the cleansing of the temple.

4:36–61. Now that the enemy threat has been removed, the Maccabees' first priority is to cleanse the temple and reinstate religious worship—which would put their relationship with God on a proper footing, and which was what the war was all about.

The cleansing is entrusted to "blameless priests" as the Law laid down (cf. Lev 22:3–9). The stones of

bonum, quoniam in saeculum misericordia eius». [25]Et facta est salus magna in Israel in die illa. [26]Quicumque autem alienigenarum evaserunt, venerunt et nuntiaverunt Lysiae universa, quae acciderant; [27]quibus ille auditis, consternatus est et animo deficiebat, quod non, qualia voluit, talia contigerant in Israel, et, qualia mandaverat ei rex, evenerant. [28]Et sequenti anno congregavit virorum electorum sexaginta milia et equitum quinque milia, ut debellaret eos. [29]Et venerunt in Idumaeam et castra posuerunt in Bethsuris; et occurrit illis Iudas cum decem milibus viris. [30]Et vidit exercitum fortem et oravit et dixit: «Benedictus es, Salvator Israel, qui contrivisti impetum potentis in manu servi tui David et tradidisti castra alienigenarum in manu Ionathae filii Saul et armigeri eius. [31]Conclude exercitum istum in manu populi tui Israel, et confundantur in exercitu suo et equitibus suis. [32]Da illis formidinem et tabefac audaciam virtutis eorum, et commoveantur contritione sua; [33]deice illos gladio diligentium

ashamed of their troops and their cavalry. [32]Fill them with cowardice; melt the boldness of their strength; let them tremble in their destruction. [33]Strike them down with the sword of those who love thee, and let all who know thy name praise thee with hymns."

[34]Then both sides attacked, and there fell of the army of Lysias five thousand men; they fell in action.[p] [35]And when Lysias saw the rout of his troops and observed the boldness which inspired those of Judas, and how ready they were either to live or to die nobly, he departed to Antioch and enlisted mercenaries, to invade Judea again with an even larger army.

2 Sam 10:1–8

Purification and dedication of the temple

[36]Then said Judas and his brothers, "Behold, our enemies are crushed; let us go up to cleanse the sanctuary and dedicate it." [37]So all the army assembled and they went up to Mount Zion. [38]And

Ps 74:2–7

the altar that Ezra consecrated in his time (cf. Ezra 3:2–5) must be thrown into the Gehenna valley like those from the pagan altars; so they seek a temporary solution until such time as a prophet should come (v. 46; cf. 9:27; 14:41; Dan 3:38). The building of a new altar in line with what Exodus 20:25 laid down reminds us of the dedication of the temple by Solomon (cf. 1 Kings 8:1–66) and the dedication of the temple of Ezra-Nehemiah (cf. Ezra 5:1—6:22). In 2 Maccabees 10:1–8 these events are reported more briefly, but mention is made there of how the fire for the sacrifices was made.

The importance acquired by the feast established to commemorate the dedication of the temple can be seen from 2 Maccabees 1:9, 18; 2:16. In Hebrew this festival is called *Hanukkah* and in Greek *Encenias* because to mark it lamps or candles are lit in people's houses (as is the Jewish practice today) to symbolize the light of the Law. It was on this feast that Jesus told the Jews that he was the Son of God (cf. Jn 10:22–39).

te, et collaudent te omnes, qui noverunt nomen tuum, in hymnis». [34]Et commiserunt invicem proelium, et ceciderunt de exercitu Lysiae quinque milia virorum et prociderunt ex adverso eorum. [35]Videns autem Lysias factam eversionem exercitus sui, Iudae vero audaciam et quemadmodum parati sunt aut vivere aut mori fortiter, abiit Antiochiam et colligebat externos, ut multo numero rursus venirent in Iudaeam. [36]Dixit autem Iudas et fratres eius: «Ecce contriti sunt inimici nostri; ascendamus mundare sancta et renovare». [37]Et congregatus est omnis exercitus, et ascenderunt in montem Sion. [38]Et viderunt sanctificationem desertam et altare profanatum et portas exustas et in atriis virgulta nata, sicut in saltu vel in uno ex montibus, et pastophoria diruta. [39]Et sciderunt vestimenta sua et planxerunt planctu magno et imposuerunt cinerem [40]et ceciderunt in faciem super terram et exclamaverunt tubis signorum et clamaverunt in caelum. [41]Tunc ordinavit Iudas viros, ut pugnarent adversus eos, qui erant in arce, donec mundaret sancta. [42]Et elegit sacerdotes sine macula voluntatem habentes in lege; [43]et mundaverunt sancta et tulerunt lapides contaminationis in locum immundum. [44]Et cogitaverunt de altari holocaustorum, quod profanatum erat, quid de eo facerent. [45]Et incidit illis consilium bonum, ut

p. Or *and some fell on the opposite side*

they saw the sanctuary desolate, the altar profaned, and the gates burned. In the courts they saw bushes sprung up as in a thicket, or as on one of the mountains. They saw also the chambers of the priests in ruins. [39]Then they rent their clothes, and mourned with great lamentation, and sprinkled themselves with ashes. [40]They fell face down on the ground, and sounded the signal on the trumpets, and cried out to Heaven. [41]Then Judas detailed men to fight against those in the citadel until he had cleansed the sanctuary.

1 Mac 2:21

[42]He chose blameless priests devoted to the law, [43]and they cleansed the sanctuary and removed the defiled stones to an unclean place. [44]They deliberated what to do about the altar of burnt offering, which had been profaned. [45]And they thought it best to tear it down, lest it bring reproach upon them, for the Gentiles had defiled it. So they tore down the altar, [46]and stored the stones in a convenient place on the temple hill until there should come a prophet to tell what to do with them. [47]Then they took unhewn[q] stones, as the law directs, and built a new altar like the former one. [48]They also rebuilt the sanctuary and the interior of the temple, and consecrated the courts. [49]They made new holy vessels, and brought the lampstand, the altar of incense, and the table into the temple. [50]Then they burned incense on the altar and lighted the lamps on the lampstand, and these gave light in the temple. [51]They placed the bread on the table and hung up the curtains. Thus they finished all the work they had undertaken.

1 Kings 8:64

Ex 20:25

Ex 25:23–39

Ex 30:1–10

[52]Early in the morning on the twenty-fifth day of the ninth month, which is the month of Chislev, in the one hundred and forty-eighth year,[r] [53]they rose and offered sacrifice, as the law directs, on the new altar of burnt offering which they had built. [54]At the very season and on the very day that the Gentiles had profaned it, it was dedicated with songs and harps and lutes and cymbals. [55]All the people fell on their faces and worshipped and

---

destruerent illud, ne umquam illis esset in opprobrium, quia contaminaverunt illud gentes; et demoliti sunt altare [46]et reposuerunt lapides in monte domus in loco apto, quoadusque veniret propheta, ut responderet de eis. [47]Et acceperunt lapides integros secundum legem et aedificaverunt altare novum secundum illud, quod fuit prius. [48]Et aedificaverunt sancta et, quae intra domum erant, et atria sanctificaverunt. [49]Et fecerunt vasa sancta nova et intulerunt candelabrum et altare incensorum et mensam in templum. [50]Et incenderunt super altare et accenderunt lucernas, quae super candelabrum erant et lucebant in templo, [51]et posuerunt super mensam panes et appenderunt vela et consummaverunt omnia opera, quae fecerant. [52]Et ante lucem surrexerunt quinta et vicesima die mensis noni—hic est mensis Casleu—centesimi quadragesimi octavi anni [53]et obtulerunt sacrificium secundum legem super altare holocaustorum novum, quod fecerunt: [54]secundum tempus et secundum diem, in qua contaminaverunt illud gentes, in ipsa renovatum est in canticis et citharis et cinyris et cymbalis. [55]Et cecidit omnis populus in faciem, et adoraverunt et benedixerunt in caelum eum, qui prosperavit eis; [56]et

q. Gk *whole* **r.** 164 BC

blessed Heaven, who had prospered them. [56]So they celebrated the dedication of the altar for eight days, and offered burnt offerings with gladness; they offered a sacrifice of deliverance and praise. [57]They decorated the front of the temple with golden crowns and small shields; they restored the gates and the chambers for the priests, and furnished them with doors. [58]There was very great gladness among the people, and the reproach of the Gentiles was removed.

Jn 10:22

[59]Then Judas and his brothers and all the assembly of Israel determined that every year at that season the days of dedication of the altar should be observed with gladness and joy for eight days, beginning with the twenty-fifth day of the month of Chislev.

[60]At that time they fortified Mount Zion with high walls and strong towers round about, to keep the Gentiles from coming and trampling them down as they had done before. [61]And he stationed a garrison there to hold it. He also[s] fortified Beth-zur, so that the people might have a stronghold that faced Idumea.

Judas' expedition outside Judea

5 [1]When the Gentiles round about heard that the altar had been built and the sanctuary dedicated as it was before, they became

5:1–54. Judas' campaigns against the neighbouring peoples are justified here because the Jews living among these peoples were being persecuted. The persecution may have been because these neighbours feared a resurgence of Judea, or it could have been that they wanted to help implement Syrian policy. And Judas may have had further reasons for these forays—to settle old scores or to recover territory that had formerly belonged to Israel.

In these campaigns Judas first goes south, to Idumea (the country of Edom or Esau), a traditional enemy of the Jews. He takes punitive action against some semi-nomadic tribes, such as the Baeanites (vv. 3–5), and then he heads east, crossing the Jordan and attacking Ammon (vv. 6–8). He goes on to plan expeditions into the north, and organizes two campaigns in parallel, one on each side of the Jordan—against Galilee to the west and Gilead to the east (vv. 9–19). He sends Simon into Galilee (vv. 21–22) and he himself goes to Gilead (vv. 25–54). But although he gets support there from the Nabateans (v. 25), he

fecerunt dedicationem altaris diebus octo et obtulerunt holocausta cum laetitia et sacrificaverunt sacrificium salutaris et laudis [57]et ornaverunt faciem templi coronis aureis et scutulis et dedicaverunt portas et pastophoria et imposuerunt eis ianuas. [58]Et facta est laetitia in populo magna valde, et aversum est opprobrium gentium. [59]Et statuit Iudas et fratres eius et universa ecclesia Israel, ut agantur dies dedicationis altaris in temporibus suis ab anno in annum per dies octo, a quinta et vicesima die mensis Casleu, cum laetitia et gaudio. [60]Et aedificaverunt in tempore illo montem Sion per circuitum muros altos et turres firmas, ne quando venirent gentes et conculcarent ea, sicut antea fecerunt. [61]Et collocavit

s. Gk adds *to hold it*

very angry, [2]and they determined to destroy the descendants of Jacob who lived among them. So they began to kill and destroy among the people. [3]But Judas made war on the sons of Esau in Idumea, at Akrabattene, because they kept lying in wait for Israel. He dealt them a heavy blow and humbled them and despoiled them. [4]He also remembered the wickedness of the sons of Baean, who were a trap and a snare to the people and ambushed them on the highways. [5]They were shut up by him in their towers; and he encamped against them, vowed their complete destruction, and burned with fire their[t] towers and all who were in them. [6]Then he crossed over to attack the Ammonites, where he found a strong band and many people with Timothy as their leader. [7]He engaged in many battles with them and they were crushed before him; he struck them down. [8]He also took Jazer and its villages; then he returned to Judea.

2 Mac 10:15–23

Josh 6:17

Num 20:23

[9]Now the Gentiles in Gilead gathered together against the Israelites who lived in their territory, and planned to destroy them. But they fled to the stronghold of Dathema, [10]and sent to Judas and his brothers a letter which said, "The Gentiles around us have gathered together against us to destroy us. [11]They are preparing to come and capture the stronghold to which we have fled, and Timothy is leading their forces. [12]Now then come and rescue us from their hands, for many of us have fallen, [13]and all our brethren who were in the land of Tob have been killed; the enemy[u] have

meets strong resistance from the Syrian general Timothy and the cities of the region; these he proceeds to reduce systematically, rigorously applying the rules of law that obtained in that era (vv. 35, 44, 51). Eventually, he returns to Jerusalem. According to the author of 1 Maccabees, these campaigns were designed to rescue the Israelites living in those regions and to bring them back to Judea (vv. 23, 43–54).

illic exercitum, ut servarent eum, et munivit eum ad custodiendam Bethsuram, ut haberet populus munitionem contra faciem Idumaeae. **[5]** [1]Et factum est, ut audierunt gentes in circuitu quia aedificatum est altare et dedicatum est sanctuarium sicut prius, iratae sunt valde [2]et cogitabant tollere genus Iacob, qui erant inter eos, et coeperunt occidere in populo et persequi. [3]Et bellabat Iudas adversus filios Esau in Idumaea, in Acrabattane, quia circumsedebant Israel; et percussit eos plaga magna, compressit eos et cepit spolia eorum. [4]Et recordatus est malitiam filiorum Bean, qui erant populo in laqueum et in scandalum insidiantes eis in viis. [5]Et conclusi sunt ab eo in turribus, et applicuit ad eos et anathematizavit eos et incendit turres eius igne cum omnibus, qui intus erant. [6]Et transivit ad filios Ammon et invenit manum fortem et populum copiosum et Timotheum ducem ipsorum. [7]Et commisit cum eis proelia multa, et contriti sunt in conspectu eius, et percussit eos. [8]Et cepit Iazer et filias eius et reversus est in Iudaeam. [9]Et congregatae sunt gentes, quae sunt in Galaad, adversus Israel, qui erant in finibus eorum, ut tollerent eos; et fugerunt in Datheman munitionem [10]et miserunt litteras ad Iudam et fratres eius dicentes: «Congregatae sunt adversum nos gentes per circuitum, ut nos auferant, [11]et

t. Gk *her* **u.** Gk *they*

captured their wives and children and goods, and have destroyed about a thousand men there."

[14]While the letter was still being read, behold, other messengers, with their garments rent, came from Galilee and made a similar report; [15]they said that against them had gathered together men of Ptolemais and Tyre and Sidon, and all Galilee of the Gentiles,[v] "to annihilate us." [16]When Judas and the people heard these messages, a great assembly was called to determine what they should do for their brethren who were in distress and were being attacked by enemies.[w] [17]Then Judas said to Simon his brother, "Choose your men and go and rescue your brethren in Galilee; I and Jonathan my brother will go to Gilead." [18]But he left Joseph, the son of Zechariah, and Azariah, a leader of the people, with the rest of the forces, in Judea to guard it; [19]and he gave them this command, "Take charge of this people, but do not engage in battle with the Gentiles until we return." [20]Then three thousand men were assigned to Simon to go to Galilee, and eight thousand to Judas for Gilead.

Mt 4:15

[21]So Simon went to Galilee and fought many battles against the Gentiles, and the Gentiles were crushed before him. [22]He pursued them to the gate of Ptolemais, and as many as three thousand of the Gentiles fell, and he despoiled them. [23]Then he took the Jews[x] of Galilee and Arbatta, with their wives and children, and all they possessed, and led them to Judea with great rejoicing.

[24]Judas Maccabeus and Jonathan his brother crossed the Jordan and went three days' journey into the wilderness. [25]They encountered the Nabateans, who met them peaceably and told them all

2 Mac 12:10–31

---

parant venire et occupare munitionem, in quam confugimus, et Timotheus est dux exercitus eorum. [12]Nunc ergo veni et eripe nos de manibus eorum, quia cecidit multitudo de nobis, [13]et omnes fratres nostri, qui erant in locis Tubin, interfecti sunt, et captivas duxerunt uxores eorum et natos et sarcinas et peremerunt illic fere mille viros». [14]Adhuc epistulae legebantur, et ecce alii nuntii venerunt de Galilaea, conscissis tunicis, nuntiantes secundum verba haec, [15]dicentes convenisse adversum se a Ptolemaida et Tyro et Sidone et omnem Galilaeam alienigenarum, ut nos consumant. [16]Ut audivit autem Iudas et populus sermones istos, convenit ecclesia magna cogitare quid facerent fratribus suis, qui in tribulatione erant et expugnabantur ab eis. [17]Dixitque Iudas Simoni fratri suo: «Elige tibi viros et vade et libera fratres tuos, qui sunt in Galilaea; ego autem et frater meus Ionathas ibimus in Galaaditim». [18]Et reliquit Iosephum filium Zachariae et Azariam ducem populi cum residuo exercitu in Iudaea ad custodiam. [19]Et praecepit illis dicens: «Praeestote populo huic et nolite bellum committere adversum gentes, donec revertamur». [20]Et partiti sunt Simoni virorum tria milia, ut iret in Galilaeam, Iudae autem octo milia in Galaaditim. [21]Et abiit Simon in Galilaeam et commisit proelia multa cum gentibus; et contritae sunt gentes a facie eius, [22]et persecutus est eos usque ad portam Ptolemaidis: et ceciderunt de gentibus fere tria milia virorum, et accepit spolia eorum. [23]Et assumpsit eos, qui erant de Galilaea et in Arbattis, cum uxoribus et natis et omnibus, quae erant illis, et adduxit in Iudaeam cum laetitia magna. [24]Et Iudas Maccabaeus et Ionathas frater eius transierunt Iordanem et abierunt viam trium dierum in deserto; [25]et occurrerunt Nabathaeis et obviaverunt eis pacifice et narraverunt eis omnia, quae acciderant fratribus eorum in Galaaditide, [26]et quia multi ex eis comprehensi sunt in Bosora et Bosor in Alimis, Chaspho,

v. Gk *aliens* **w.** Gk *them* **x.** Gk *those*

that had happened to their brethren in Gilead: [26]"Many of them have been shut up in Bozrah and Bosor, in Alema and Chaspho, Maked and Carnaim"—all these cities were strong and large—[27]"and some have been shut up in the other cities of Gilead; the enemy[y] are getting ready to attack the strongholds tomorrow and take and destroy all these men in one day."

[28]Then Judas and his army quickly turned back by the wilderness road to Bozrah; and he took the city, and killed every male by the edge of the sword; then he seized all its spoils and burned it with fire. [29]He departed from there at night, and they went all the way to the stronghold of Dathema.[z] [30]At dawn they looked up, and behold, a large company, that could not be counted, carrying ladders and engines of war to capture the stronghold, and attacking the Jews within.[a] [31]So Judas saw that the battle had begun and that the cry of the city went up to Heaven with trumpets and loud shouts, [32]and he said to the men of his forces, "Fight today for your brethren!" [33]Then he came up behind them in three companies, who sounded their trumpets and cried aloud in prayer. [34]And when the army of Timothy realized that it was Maccabeus, they fled before him, and he dealt them a heavy blow. As many as eight thousand of them fell that day.

[35]Next he turned aside to Alema,[b]* and fought against it and took it; and he killed every male in it, plundered it, and burned it with fire. [36]From there he marched on and took Chaspho, Maked, and Bosor, and the other cities of Gilead.

[37]After these things Timothy gathered another army and encamped opposite Raphon, on the other side of the stream. [38]Judas sent men to spy out the camp, and they reported to him,

---

Maced et Carnain; hae omnes civitates munitae et magnae. [27]Et in ceteris civitatibus Galaaditidis tenentur comprehensi; in crastinum constituerunt admovere ad munitiones et comprehendere et tollere omnes eos in una die. [28]Et convertit Iudas et exercitus eius viam in desertum Bosora repente et occupavit civitatem et occidit omnem masculum in ore gladii et accepit omnia spolia eorum et succendit eam igne; [29]et profectus est inde nocte, et ibant usque ad munitionem. [30]Et factum est diluculo, cum levassent oculos suos, ecce populus multus, cuius non erat numerus, portantes scalas et machinas, ut comprehenderent munitionem, et expugnabant eos. [31]Et vidit Iudas quia coepit bellum, et clamor civitatis ascendit ad caelum sicut tuba et clamor magnus; [32]et dixit viris exercitus: «Pugnate hodie pro fratribus nostris». [33]Et exiit tribus ordinibus post eos, et exclamaverunt tubis et clamaverunt in oratione. [34]Et cognoverunt castra Timothei quia Maccabaeus est, et refugerunt a facie eius; et percussit eos plaga magna, et ceciderunt ex eis in die illa fere octo milia virorum. [35]Et divertit Iudas in Maspha et expugnavit et cepit eam. Et occidit omnem masculinum eius et sumpsit spolia eius et succendit eam igne. [36]Inde perrexit et cepit Chaspho, Maced et Bosor et reliquas civitates Galaaditidis. [37]Post haec autem verba congregavit Timotheus exercitum alium et castra posuit contra Raphon trans torrentem.

y. Gk *they* **z.** Greek lacks *of Dathema*. See verse 9 **a.** Gk *and they were attacking him* **b.** The name is uncertain

"All the Gentiles around us have gathered to him; it is a very large force. [39]They also have hired Arabs to help them, and they are encamped across the stream, ready to come and fight against you." And Judas went to meet them.

1 Sam 14:9–10

[40]Now as Judas and his army drew near to the stream of water, Timothy said to the officers of his forces, "If he crosses over to us first, we will not be able to resist him, for he will surely defeat us. [41]But if he shows fear and camps on the other side of the river, we will cross over to him and defeat him." [42]When Judas approached the stream of water, he stationed the scribes of the people at the stream and gave them this command, "Permit no man to encamp, but make them all enter the battle." [43]Then he crossed over against them first, and the whole army followed him. All the Gentiles were defeated before him, and they threw away their arms and fled into the sacred precincts at Carnaim. [44]But he took the city and burned the sacred precincts with fire, together with all who were in them. Thus Carnaim was conquered; they could stand before Judas no longer.

[45]Then Judas gathered together all the Israelites in Gilead, the small and the great, with their wives and children and goods, a very large company, to go to the land of Judah. [46]So they came to Ephron. This was a large and very strong city on the road, and they could not go round it to the right or to the left; they had to go through it. [47]But the men of the city shut them out and blocked up the gates with stones. [48]And Judas sent them this friendly message, "Let us pass through your land to get to our land. No one will do you harm; we will simply pass by on foot." But they refused to

Num 20:14ff; 21:21ff

---

[38]Et misit Iudas speculari exercitum, et renuntiaverunt ei dicentes: «Convenerunt ad eum omnes gentes, quae in circuitu nostro sunt, exercitus multus nimis; [39]et Arabas conduxit in auxilium sibi, et castra posuerunt trans torrentem, parati ad te venire in proelium». Et abiit Iudas obviam illis. [40]Et ait Timotheus principibus exercitus sui: «Cum appropinquaverit Iudas et exercitus eius ad torrentem aquae, si transierit ad nos prior, non poterimus sustinere eum, quia potens poterit adversum nos; [41]si vero timuerit transire et posuerit castra ultra flumen, transfretemus ad eos et poterimus adversus illum». [42]Ut autem appropinquavit Iudas ad torrentem aquae, statuit scribas populi secus torrentem et mandavit eis dicens: «Neminem hominum reliqueritis, sed veniant omnes in proelium». [43]Et transfretavit ad illos prior, et omnis populus post eum. Et contritae sunt omnes gentes a facie eorum et proiecerunt arma sua et fugerunt ad fanum in Carnain. [44]Et occupaverunt ipsam civitatem et fanum succenderunt igne cum omnibus, qui erant in ipso; et oppressa est Carnain et non potuit sustinere contra faciem Iudae. [45]Et congregavit Iudas universum Israel, qui erant in Galaaditide, a minimo usque ad maximum et uxores eorum et natos et sarcinas, exercitum magnum valde, ut venirent in terram Iudae. [46]Et venerunt usque Ephron. Et haec civitas magna in via, munita valde: non erat declinare ab ea dextera vel sinistra, sed per mediam iter erat. [47]Et incluserunt se, qui erant in civitate, et obstruxerunt portas lapidibus. Et misit ad eos Iudas verbis pacificis [48]dicens: «Transeamus per terram vestram, ut eamus in terram nostram, et nemo vobis nocebit; tantum pedibus transibimus». Et nolebant eis aperire. [49]Et praecepit Iudas praedicare in castris, ut applicarent se unusquisque in quo erat loco. [50]Et applicuerunt se viri virtutis, et oppugnavit civitatem illam tota die et tota nocte; et tradita est civitas in manu eius. [51]Et peremit omnem

open to him. [49]Then Judas ordered proclamation to be made to the army that each should encamp where he was. [50]So the men of the forces encamped, and he fought against the city all that day and all the night, and the city was delivered into his hands. [51]He destroyed every male by the edge of the sword, and razed and plundered the city. Then he passed through the city over the slain.

Josh 6:17

[52]And they crossed the Jordan into the large plain before Beth-shan. [53]And Judas kept rallying the laggards and encouraging the people all the way till he came to the land of Judah. [54]So they went up to Mount Zion with gladness and joy, and offered burnt offerings, because not one of them had fallen before they returned in safety.

Joseph and Azariah routed

[55]Now while Judas and Jonathan were in Gilead and Simon his brother was in Galilee before Ptolemais, [56]Joseph, the son of Zechariah, and Azariah, the commanders of the forces, heard of their brave deeds and of the heroic war they had fought. [57]So they said, "Let us also make a name for ourselves; let us go and make war on the Gentiles around us." [58]And they issued orders to the

---

5:55–68. Joseph and Azariah, who had stayed behind to defend Judea, also yearn for the glory of victory and, disobeying their orders from Judas, they attack Jamnia, to the west of Jerusalem; but they are defeated by Gorgias, for they were not the ones chosen by God to deliver Israel: they did not belong to the Maccabee family (vv. 55–62). Then Judas and his brothers return and win victories to the south and west of Judea; this brings their campaigns to an end (vv. 65–68).

From this account we can see that God reserves victory for Judas and his brothers, and that they are the vehicle of liberation not only for Judea but also for Jews living in the surrounding territories. This is very much in line with the writer's aim—to explain the origin of and to justify the Hasmonean dynasty. Only those who side with the Maccabees and who obey them, the founders of that dynasty, contribute to the deliverance of Israel.

masculinum in ore gladii et eradicavit eam et accepit spolia eius et transivit per civitatem super interfectos. [52]Et transgressi sunt Iordanem in campum magnum contra faciem Bethsan. [53]Et erat Iudas congregans extremos et exhortabatur populum per totam viam, donec veniret in terram Iudae. [54]Et ascenderunt in montem Sion cum laetitia et gaudio et obtulerunt holocausta, quod nemo ex eis cecidisset, donec reverterentur in pace. [55]Et in diebus, quibus erat Iudas et Ionathas in terra Galaad, et Simon frater eius in Galilaea contra faciem Ptolemaidis, [56]audivit Iosephus Zachariae filius et Azarias princeps virtutis res bene gestas et proelia, quae fecerunt, [57]et dixerunt: «Faciamus et ipsi nobis nomen et eamus pugnare adversus gentes, quae in circuitu nostro sunt». [58]Et nuntiaverunt his, qui erant de exercitu suo, et abierunt ad Iamniam. [59]Et exivit Gorgias de civitate et viri eius obviam illis in pugnam;

2 Mac 12:32–46

men of the forces that were with them, and they marched against Jamnia. [59]And Gorgias and his men came out of the city to meet them in battle. [60]Then Joseph and Azariah were routed, and were pursued to the borders of Judea; as many as two thousand of the people of Israel fell that day. [61]Thus the people suffered a great rout because, thinking to do a brave deed, they did not listen to Judas and his brothers. [62]But they did not belong to the family of those men through whom deliverance was given to Israel.

[63]The man Judas and his brothers were greatly honoured in all Israel and among all the Gentiles, wherever their name was heard. [64]Men gathered to them and praised them.

[65]Then Judas and his brothers went forth and fought the sons of Esau in the land to the south. He struck Hebron and its villages and tore down its strongholds and burned its towers round about. [66]Then he marched off to go into the land of the Philistines, *and passed through Marisa.[c]* [67]On that day some priests, who wished to do a brave deed, fell in battle, for they went out to battle unwisely. [68]But Judas turned aside to Azotus in the land of the Philistines;* he tore down their altars, and the graven images of their gods he burned with fire; he plundered the cities and returned to the land of Judah.

2 Mac 1:11–17; 9

Death of Antiochus IV Epiphanes

6 [1]King Antiochus was going through the upper provinces when he heard that Elymais in Persia was a city famed for its wealth in silver and gold. [2]Its temple was very rich, containing golden

---

6:1–17. According to 3:29–31, Antiochus embarked on his expedition to get funds to counter the drain on the empire caused by the war against the Jews. And now we are told that the king's death was brought on by the reports on that war. The information given here about the death of Antiochus

[60]et fugati sunt Iosephus et Azarias et impulsi sunt usque in fines Iudaeae, et ceciderunt illo die de populo Israel ad duo milia viri; et facta est fuga magna in populo, [61]quia non audierunt Iudam et fratres eius existimantes fortiter se facturos. [62]Ipsi autem non erant de semine virorum illorum, per quorum manum salus data est Israel. [63]Et vir Iudas et fratres eius magnificati sunt valde in conspectu omnis Israel et gentium omnium, ubi audiebatur nomen eorum; [64]et conveniebant ad eos fausta acclamantes. [65]Et exivit Iudas et fratres eius et expugnabant filios Esau in terra, quae ad austrum est. Et percussit Hebron et filias eius et destruxit munitiones eius et turres eius succendit in circuitu. [66]Et movit castra, ut iret in terram alienigenarum, et perambulabat Maresam. [67]In die illa ceciderunt sacerdotes in bello, dum volunt fortiter facere, dum sine consilio exeunt in proelium. [68]Et declinavit Iudas in Azotum terram alienigenarum et diruit aras eorum et sculptilia deorum ipsorum succendit igne et exspoliavit exuvias civitatum. Et reversus est in terram Iudae. **[6]** [1]Et rex Antiochus perambulabat superiores regiones et audivit esse Elymaida in Perside civitatem gloriosam divitiis argento et auro [2]templumque in ea locuples

c. Other authorities read *Samaria*

shields, breastplates, and weapons left there by Alexander, the son of Philip, the Macedonian king who first reigned over the Greeks.

[3]So he came and tried to take the city and plunder it, but he could not, because his plan became known to the men of the city [4]and they withstood him in battle. So he fled and in great grief departed from there to return to Babylon.

[5]Then some one came to him in Persia and reported that the armies which had gone into the land of Judah had been routed; [6]that Lysias had gone first with a strong force, but had turned and fled before the Jews;[d] that the Jews[e] had grown strong from the arms, supplies, and abundant spoils which they had taken from the armies they had cut down; [7]that they had torn down the abomination which he had erected upon the altar in Jerusalem; and

1 Mac 1:54; 4:45

agrees with that in 2 Maccabees 9:1–29 only in a very general way. First Maccabees says that Elymais was a city, whereas it was a region in Persia (Elam) where the capital, Susa, was located. The king dies as a result of depression caused by reports of the Jewish victories, and he acknowledges that he has acted wrongly towards the Jews; but, he does not go so far as to invoke the God of Israel (as 2 Maccabees says he did). Second Maccabees, moreover, describes him as suffering a most awful death (not the case here). However, both books make it clear that Antiochus realized that in persecuting the Jews and profaning their temple he was taking on someone much more powerful than himself, and that that was why he was punished by God. In Christian tradition (St Hippolytus, *In Danielem*, 4, 49; St Jerome, *Commentaria in Danielem*, 11), Antiochus is depicted as the first instance of the Antichrist who for a period seeks to take God's place but is eventually overpowered by him.

The death of Antiochus, resulting from his frustration at not being able to eradicate loyalty to and worship of the true God, symbolizes in some way the tragic condition of those who go so far as to try to uproot God from their own lives or that of society.

valde et illic velamina aurea et loricae et scuta, quae reliquit ibi Alexander Philippi rex Macedo, qui regnavit primus in Graecia. [3]Et venit et quaerebat capere civitatem et depraedari eam et non potuit, quoniam innotuit sermo his, qui erant in civitate. [4]Et restiterunt ei in proelium. Et fugit inde et abiit cum tristitia magna, ut reverteretur in Babyloniam. [5]Et venit, qui nuntiaret ei in Perside quia fugata sunt castra, quae iverant in terram Iudae, [6]et quia abiit Lysias cum virtute forti in primis et fugatus est a facie eorum, et invaluerunt armis et viribus et spoliis multis, quae ceperunt de castris quae exciderunt, [7]et quia diruerunt abominationem, quam aedificaverat super altare, quod erat in Ierusalem, et sanctificationem sicut prius circumdederunt muris excelsis et Bethsuram civitatem eius. [8]Et factum est, ut audivit rex sermones istos, expavit et commotus est valde et decidit in lectum et incidit in languorem prae tristitia, quia non factum est ei, sicut cogitabat. [9]Et erat illic per dies multos, quia renovata est in eo tristitia magna, et arbitratus est se mori. [10]Et vocavit omnes amicos suos et dixit illis: «Recessit somnus ab

d. Gk *them* **e.** Gk *they*

that they had surrounded the sanctuary with high walls as before, and also Beth-zur, his city.

[8]When the king heard this news, he was astounded and badly shaken. He took to his bed and became sick from grief, because things had not turned out for him as he had planned. [9]He lay there for many days, because deep grief continually gripped him, and he concluded that he was dying. [10]So he called all his friends and said to them, "Sleep departs from my eyes and I am downhearted with worry. [11]I said to myself, 'To what distress I have come! And into what a great flood I now am plunged! For I was kind and beloved in my power.' [12]But now I remember the evils I did in Jerusalem. I seized all her vessels of silver and gold; and I sent to destroy the inhabitants of Judah without good reason. [13]I know that it is because of this that these evils have come upon me; and behold, I am perishing of deep grief in a strange land."

[14]Then he called for Philip, one of his friends, and made him ruler over all his kingdom. [15]He gave him the crown and his robe and the signet, that he might guide Antiochus his son and bring him up to be king. [16]Thus Antiochus the king died there in the one hundred and forty-ninth year.[f] [17]And when Lysias learned that the

---

6:18–42. Once again the focus is put on those Jews who have betrayed the Law and allied themselves with the Syrians out of self-interest. They ask the king to intervene to prevent Judas from taking over Jerusalem. The sacred writer emphasizes the size, strength and organization of the Syrian army (which makes another attack from the south: cf. 4:28–35) to prepare the reader for what follows—Judas' retreat (cf. v. 47).

oculis meis, et concidi corde prae sollicitudine [11]et dixi in corde meo: Quousque tribulationis deveni et tempestatis magnae, in qua nunc sum? Quia iucundus eram et dilectus in potestate mea! [12]Nunc vero reminiscor malorum, quae feci in Ierusalem, unde et abstuli omnia vasa aurea et argentea, quae erant in ea, et misi auferre habitantes Iudam sine causa. [13]Cognovi quia propterea invenerunt me mala ista; et ecce pereo tristitia magna in terra aliena». [14]Et vocavit Philippum, unum de amicis suis, et praeposuit eum super universum regnum suum; [15]et dedit ei diadema et stolam suam et anulum, ut adduceret Antiochum filium suum et nutriret eum, ut regnaret. [16]Et mortuus est illic Antiochus rex anno centesimo quadragesimo nono. [17]Et cognovit Lysias quoniam mortuus est rex, et constituit regnare Antiochum filium eius pro eo, quem nutrivit adulescentiorem, et vocavit nomen eius Eupatorem. [18]Et hi, qui erant in arce, concluserant Israel in circuitu sanctorum et quaerebant eis mala semper et firmamentum gentium. [19]Et cogitavit Iudas disperdere eos et convocavit universum populum, ut obsiderent eos. [20]Et convenerunt simul et obsederunt eos anno centesimo quinquagesimo et fecerunt ballistas et machinas. [21]Et exierunt quidam ex eis, qui obsidebantur, et adiunxerunt se illis aliqui impii ex Israel [22]et abierunt ad regem et dixerunt: «Quousque non facis iudicium et vindicabis fratres nostros? [23]Nos decrevimus servire patri tuo et ambulare in praeceptis eius et obsequi edictis eius; [24]et filii populi nostri propter hoc obsederunt arcem et alienabant se a nobis, et, quicumque inveniebantur ex nobis, interficiebantur, et hereditates nostrae diripiebantur. [25]Et non ad nos tantum extenderunt manum, sed et in omnes fines

f. 163 BC

king was dead, he set up Antiochus the king's[g] son to reign. Lysias[h] had brought him up as a boy, and he named him Eupator.

The royal army advances on Jerusalem

[18]Now the men in the citadel kept hemming Israel in around the sanctuary. They were trying in every way to harm them and strengthen the Gentiles. [19]So Judas decided to destroy them, and assembled all the people to besiege them. [20]They gathered together and besieged the citadel[i] in the one hundred and fiftieth year;[j] and he built siege towers and other engines of war. [21]But some of the garrison escaped from the siege and some of the ungodly Israelites joined them. [22]They went to the king and said, "How long will you fail to do justice and to avenge our brethren?

[23]We were happy to serve your father, to live by what he said and to follow his commands. [24]For this reason the sons of our people besieged the citadel[k] and became hostile to us; moreover,

1 Mac 1:33–35

suos; [26]et ecce applicuerunt hodie ad arcem in Ierusalem occupare eam et sancta et Bethsuram munierunt. [27]Et, nisi praeveneris eos velocius, maiora quam haec facient, et non poteris continere eos». [28]Et iratus est rex, ut audivit, et convocavit omnes amicos suos et principes exercitus sui et eos, qui super vehicula erant; [29]sed et de regnis aliis et de insulis maritimis venerunt ad eum exercitus conducticii. [30]Et erat numerus exercitus eius centum milia peditum et viginti milia equitum et elephanti triginta duo docti ad proelium. [31]Et venerunt per Idumaeam et applicuerunt ad Bethsuram. Et pugnaverunt dies multos et fecerunt machinas et exierunt et succenderunt eas igne et pugnaverunt viriliter. [32]Et recessit Iudas ab arce et movit castra ad Bethzacharam contra castra regis. [33]Et surrexit rex ante lucem et excitavit exercitum in impetu suo contra viam Bethzacharam, et comparaverunt se exercitus in proelium et tubis cecinerunt [34]et elephantis ostenderunt sanguinem uvae et mori ad acuendos eos in proelium. [35]Et diviserunt bestias per legiones et astiterunt singulis elephantis mille viri in loricis concatenatis, et galeae aereae in capitibus eorum, et quingenti equites ordinati unicuique bestiae electi. [36]Hi ante tempus, ubicumque erat bestia, ibi erant et, quocumque ibat, ibant; non discedebant ab ea. [37]Et turres ligneae super eos firmae, protectae super singulas bestias, praecinctae super eas machinis, et super singulas viri virtutis quattuor, qui pugnabant desuper, et Indus eius. [38]Et residuos equites hinc et inde statuit in duas partes exercitus excitaturos et protecturos in legionibus. [39]Et, ut refulsit sol in clipeos aureos et aereos, resplenduerunt montes ab eis et resplenduerunt sicut lampades ignis. [40]Et distincta est pars exercitus regis super montes excelsos et quidam per loca humilia; et ibant caute et ordinate. [41]Et commovebantur omnes audientes vocem multitudinis et incessum turbae et collisionem armorum; erat enim exercitus magnus valde et fortis. [42]Et appropiavit Iudas et exercitus eius in proelium, et ceciderunt de exercitu regis sescenti viri. [43]Et vidit Eleazar Abaran unam de bestiis loricatam loricis regis, et erat eminens super ceteras bestias, et visum est ei quod in ea esset rex; [44]et dedit se, ut liberaret populum suum et acquireret sibi nomen aeternum. [45]Et cucurrit ad eam audacter, in medio legionis interficiens a dextris et a sinistris, et findebantur ab eo huc atque illuc; [46]et ivit sub elephantum et supposuit se ei et occidit eum; et cecidit in terram super ipsum, et mortuus est illic. [47]Et videntes virtutem regni et impetum exercituum diverterunt se ab eis. [48]Qui autem erant de castris regis, ascenderunt obviam illis in Ierusalem, et applicuit rex ad Iudaeam et montem Sion. [49]Et fecit pacem cum his, qui erant in Bethsura; et exierunt de civitate, quia non erant eis ibi alimenta, eo quod conclusi essent in ea, quia sabbatum erat terrae. [50]Et comprehendit rex Bethsuram et constituit illic custodiam servare eam. [51]Et applicuit castra ad locum sanctificationis dies multos; et statuit illic ballistas et machinas et ignis iacula et tormenta ad lapides iactandos et scorpios ad mittendas sagittas et fundibula. [52]Fecerunt autem et ipsi machinas adversus machinas eorum et pugnaverunt dies multos; [53]escae autem non erant in horreis, eo quod

g. Gk *his* **h.** Gk *He* **i.** Gk *it* **j.** 162 BC **k.** The Greek text underlying *the sons . . . the citadel* is uncertain

they have put to death as many of us as they have caught, and they have seized our inheritances. [25]And not against us alone have they stretched out their hands, but also against all the lands on their borders. [26]And behold, today they have encamped against the citadel in Jerusalem to take it; they have fortified both the sanctuary and Beth-zur; [27]and unless you quickly prevent them, they will do still greater things, and you will not be able to stop them."

[28]The king was enraged when he heard this. He assembled all his friends, the commanders of his forces and those in authority.[l] [29]And mercenary forces came to him from other kingdoms and from islands of the seas. [30]The number of his forces was a hundred thousand foot soldiers, twenty thousand horsemen, and thirty-two elephants accustomed to war. [31]They came through Idumea and encamped against Beth-zur, and for many days they fought and built engines of war; but the Jews[m] sallied out and burned these with fire, and fought manfully.

[32]Then Judas marched away from the citadel and encamped at Beth-zechariah, opposite the camp of the king. [33]Early in the morning the king rose and took his army by a forced march along the road to Beth-zechariah, and his troops made ready for battle and sounded their trumpets. [34]They showed the elephants the juice of grapes and mulberries, to arouse them for battle. [35]And they distributed the beasts among the phalanxes; with each elephant they stationed a thousand men armed with coats of mail, and with brass helmets on their heads; and five hundred picked horsemen were assigned to each beast. [36]These took their position beforehand wherever the beast was; wherever it went they went with it, and they never left it. [37]And upon the elephants[n] were wooden towers, strong and covered; they were fastened upon each beast by special harness,

---

septimus annus esset, et, qui evaserant in Iudaeam de gentibus, consumpserant reliquias repositionis. [54]Et remanserunt in sanctis viri pauci, quoniam obtinuerat eos fames, et dispersi sunt unusquisque in locum suum. [55]Et audivit Lysias quod Philippus, quem constituerat rex Antiochus, cum adhuc viveret, ut nutriret Antiochum filium suum ut regnaret, [56]reversus esset a Perside et Media, et exercitus, qui abierat cum ipso, et quia quaerebat suscipere regni negotia. [57]Festinavit et significavit ire dixitque ad regem et duces exercitus et viros: «Deficimus cotidie, et esca nobis modica est, et locus, quem obsidemus, est munitus, et incumbunt nobis negotia regni. [58]Nunc itaque demus dextras hominibus istis et faciamus cum illis pacem et cum omni gente eorum [59]et constituamus illis, ut ambulent in legitimis suis sicut prius: propter legitima enim ipsorum, quae dispersimus, irati sunt et fecerunt omnia haec». [60]Et placuit sermo in conspectu regis et principum, et misit ad eos pacem facere, et receperunt illam. [61]Et iuravit illis rex et principes. His condicionibus exierunt de munitione. [62]Et intravit rex in montem Sion et vidit munitionem loci et rupit iuramentum, quod iuravit, et mandavit destruere murum in gyro. [63]Et discessit festinanter et reversus est Antiochiam; et invenit Philippum dominantem civitati et pugnavit adversus eum et occupavit civitatem per vim.

l. Gk *those over the reins* **m.** Gk *they* **n.** Gk *them*

and upon each were four[o] armed men who fought from there, and also its Indian driver. [38]The rest of the horsemen were stationed on either side, on the two flanks of the army, to harass the enemy while being themselves protected by the phalanxes. [39]When the sun shone upon the shields of gold and brass, the hills were ablaze with them and gleamed like flaming torches.

[40]Now a part of the king's army was spread out on the high hills, and some troops were on the plain, and they advanced steadily and in good order. [41]All who heard the noise made by their multitude, by the marching of the multitude and the clanking of their arms, trembled, for the army was very large and strong. [42]But Judas and his army advanced to the battle, and six hundred men of the king's army fell.

Eleazar's heroism

[43]And Eleazar, called Avaran, saw that one of the beasts was equipped with royal armour. It was taller than all the others, and he supposed that the king was upon it. [44]So he gave his life to save his people and to win for himself an everlasting name. [45]He courageously ran into the midst of the phalanx to reach it; he killed men right and left, and they parted before him on both sides. [46]He got under the elephant, stabbed it from beneath, and killed it; but it fell to the ground upon him and he died.

6:43–46. Eleazar's heroic action did not have the desired effect, but still he won an "everlasting name". St Gregory the Great draws a spiritual lesson from this episode, making an appeal for humility: "Eleazar fatally wounded the elephant during the battle, but died himself, crushed by the weight of what he had killed. Who does this man, who was vanquished by his own victory, represent, if not those who, having overcome their vice, become proud and fall under those very things they have conquered? He who took pride in the mortal blow he struck was brought to ruin by his dead enemy. We must keep a careful watch so that we do not fail to see that all good things are of no worth unless they protect us from the evils that can advance on us unnoticed. All good deeds perish unless they are closely guarded with humility" (*Moralia in Job*, 19, 21, 34).

6:47–54. The author of 1 Maccabees is careful not to paint the situation as a defeat for the Jews or to blame Judas for the dire situation that his people find themselves in and which eventually forces some of the besieged Jews to take flight (vv. 53–54): he points out that it was "the seventh year", a sabbatical year, when the land was not worked, and this time there was no food in storage.

o. Cn: Some authorities read *thirty*; others *thirty-two*

Judas withdraws. Jerusalem is besieged

[47]And when the Jews[p] saw the royal might and the fierce attack of the forces, they turned away in flight.

[48]The soldiers of the king's army went up to Jerusalem against them, and the king encamped in Judea and at Mount Zion. [49]He made peace with the men of Beth-zur, and they evacuated the city, because they had no provisions there to withstand a siege, since it was a sabbatical year for the land. [50]So the king took Beth-zur and stationed a guard there to hold it. [51]Then he encamped before the sanctuary for many days. He set up siege towers, engines of war to throw fire and stones, machines to shoot arrows, and catapults. [52]The Jews[q] also made engines of war to match theirs, and fought for many days. [53]But they had no food in storage,[r] because it was the seventh year; those who found safety in Judea from the Gentiles had consumed the last of the stores. [54]Few men were left in the sanctuary, because famine had prevailed over the rest and they had been scattered, each to his own place.

Lev 25:1–2

Lysias retires to Antioch. Peace treaty

[55]Then Lysias heard that Philip, whom King Antiochus while still living had appointed to bring up Antiochus his son to be king, [56]had returned from Persia and Media with the forces that had gone with the king, and that he was trying to seize control of the government. [57]So he quickly gave orders to depart, and said to the king, to the commanders of the forces, and to the men, "We daily grow weaker, our food supply is scant, the place against which we are fighting is strong, and the affairs of the kingdom press urgently upon us. [58]Now then let us come to terms with these men, and make peace with them and with all their nation, [59]and agree to let them live by their laws as they did before; for it was on account of

2 Mac 11:13–33

6:55–63. When Philip returns from Persia with regal powers (cf. 6:14–15), Lysias realizes that his position as regent is at risk, so he decides to return to Antioch immediately. But he gives the king very different reasons for his return—the strong resistance being put up by the Jews, and the futility of trying to suppress their traditions. Anyway, the significant thing about the episode is that the Jews are granted freedom to practise their religion. Thus, quite unexpectedly, and due to internal strife in the empire, God comes to the aid of Judas and those besieged in Jerusalem. But the author does not make much of this: he prefers to see divine intervention at work in the spectacular battles won by Judas.

p. Gk *they* **q.** Gk *They* **r.** Other authorities read *in the sanctuary*

their laws which we abolished that they became angry and did all these things."

[60]The speech pleased the king and the commanders, and he sent to the Jews[s] an offer of peace, and they accepted it. [61]So the king and the commanders gave them their oath. On these conditions the Jews[t] evacuated the stronghold. [62]But when the king entered Mount Zion and saw what a strong fortress the place was, he broke the oath he had sworn and gave orders to tear down the wall all around. [63]Then he departed with haste and returned to Antioch. He found Philip in control of the city, but he fought against him, and took the city by force.

Demetrius I, the high priest Alcimus, and Bacchides, the governor of Judea

2 Mac 14:1–10

7 [1]In the one hundred and fifty-first year[u] Demetrius the son of Seleucus set forth from Rome, sailed with a few men to a city by the sea, and there began to reign. [2]As he was entering the royal palace of his fathers, the army seized Antiochus and Lysias to bring them to him. [3]But when this act became known to him, he said, "Do not let me see their faces!" [4]So the army killed them, and Demetrius took his seat upon the throne of his kingdom.

[5]Then there came to him all the lawless and ungodly men of Israel; they were led by Alcimus, who wanted to be high priest. [6]And they brought to the king this accusation against the people: "Judas and his brothers have destroyed all your friends, and have driven us out of our land. [7]Now then send a man whom you trust; let him go and see all the ruin which Judas[v] has brought upon us

7:1–20. Demetrius, son of Seleucus IV (187–175 BC) was the rightful heir to the throne of Syria, but he had not been able to exercise his power because he had been sent to Rome as a hostage to take the place of Antiochus IV Epiphanes (cf. 1:10). Demetrius managed to escape from Rome with the help of his friend the historian Polybius (cf. the latter's *Historiae*, 31, 11ff), and reached Tripolis (north of Beirut) in a Phoenician ship (cf. 2 Mac 14:1), there proclaiming himself king.

The pro-Hellenist party at Jerusalem headed up by Alcimus immediately seek the ear of the new king to get him

[7] [1]Anno centesimo quinquagesimo primo exiit Demetrius Seleuci filius a Roma; et ascendit cum paucis viris in civitatem maritimam et regnavit illic. [2]Et factum est, ut ingressus est domum regni patrum suorum, comprehendit exercitus Antiochum et Lysiam, ut adduceret eos ad eum. [3]Et res ei innotuit, et ait: «Nolite mihi ostendere facies eorum». [4]Et occidit eos exercitus, et sedit Demetrius super sedem regni sui. [5]Et venerunt ad eum viri iniqui et impii ex Israel, et Alcimus dux erat eorum, qui volebat fieri sacerdos; [6]et accusaverunt populum apud regem dicentes: «Perdidit Iudas et fratres eius

s. Gk *them* **t.** Gk *they* **u.** 161 BC **v.** Gk *he*

and upon the land of the king, and let him punish them and all who help them."

1 Mac 2:18

[8]So the king chose Bacchides, one of the king's friends, governor of the province Beyond the River; he was a great man in the kingdom and was faithful to the king. [9]And he sent him, and with him the ungodly Alcimus, whom he made high priest; and he commanded him to take vengeance on the sons of Israel. [10]So they marched away and came with a large force into the land of Judah; and he sent messengers to Judas and his brothers with peaceable but treacherous words. [11]But they paid no attention to their words, for they saw that they had come with a large force.

1 Mac 2:42

[12]Then a group of scribes appeared in a body before Alcimus and Bacchides to ask for just terms. [13]The Hasideans were first among the sons of Israel to seek peace from them, [14]for they said, "A priest of the line of Aaron has come with the army, and he will not harm us." [15]And he spoke peaceable words to them and swore this oath to them, "We will not seek to injure you or your friends." [16]So they trusted him; but he seized sixty of them and killed them in one day, in accordance with the word which was written,

---

to act against Judas and his followers who are imposing the rule of the Law in Jerusalem. Alcimus had been deposed from his position as high priest (cf. 2 Mac 14:3–4), and now he sees an opportunity to regain that position and get control of Jerusalem. The king sees in Alcimus a committed Hellenist, a priest (a descendant of Aaron) and an ambitious man—the ideal person to spearhead Syrian policy in Judea. The Hasideans, too, are deceived in their acceptance of Alcimus, and they dissociate themselves from Judas. For this they suffer the punishment foretold in Psalm 79:2–3 (vv. 13–17). Once again the sacred writer is at pains to point out that those Jews who are unfaithful to God and his cause, that is, those who do not support Judas and his brothers, are responsible for the evils that will soon come about.

omnes amicos tuos et nos dispersit de terra nostra; [7]nunc ergo mitte virum, cui credis, ut eat et videat exterminium omne, quod fecit nobis et regioni regis, et puniat eos et omnes adiutores eorum». [8]Et elegit rex ex amicis suis Bacchidem, qui dominabatur trans flumen, magnum in regno et fidelem regi. Et misit eum [9]et Alcimum impium et constituit ei sacerdotium et mandavit ei facere ultionem in filios Israel. [10]Et surrexerunt et venerunt cum exercitu magno in terram Iudae; et misit nuntios ad Iudam et ad fratres eius verbis pacificis in dolo. [11]Et non intenderunt sermonibus eorum; viderunt enim quia venerunt cum exercitu magno. [12]Et convenerunt ad Alcimum et Bacchidem congregatio scribarum requirere iusta; [13]et primi Asidaei erant in filiis Israel et exquirebant ab eis pacem. [14]Dixerunt enim: «Homo sacerdos de semine Aaron venit et non decipiet nos». [15]Et locutus est cum eis verba pacifica et iuravit illis dicens: «Non inferemus vobis malum neque amicis vestris». [16]Et crediderunt ei. Et comprehendit ex eis sexaginta viros et occidit eos in una die, secundum verbum quod scripsit: [17]«Carnes sanctorum tuorum et sanguinem ipsorum effuderunt in circuitu Ierusalem, et non erat qui sepeliret». [18]Et incubuit timor eorum et tremor in omnem populum, quia dixerunt: «Non est in eis veritas et iudicium; transgressi sunt enim constitutum et iusiurandum, quod iuraverunt». [19]Et movit Bacchides ab Ierusalem et applicuit in

[17]"The flesh of thy saints and their blood
they poured out round about Jerusalem,
and there was none to bury them." Ps 79:2–3

[18]Then the fear and dread of them fell upon all the people, for they said, "There is no truth or justice in them, for they have violated the agreement and the oath which they swore."

[19]Then Bacchides departed from Jerusalem and encamped in Beth-zaith. And he sent and seized many of the men who had deserted to him,[w] and some of the people, and killed them and threw them into a great pit. [20]He placed Alcimus in charge of the country and left with him a force to help him; then Bacchides went back to the king.

Judas' reaction and his victory over Nicanor

[21]Alcimus strove for the high priesthood, [22]and all who were troubling their people joined him. They gained control of the land of Judah and did great damage in Israel. [23]And Judas saw all the

---

7:21–50. Judas' opposition to the policy of Alcimus (a policy which did more harm than that of the Gentiles because it led many Jews astray) and Alcimus' appeal to the king, occasion a new Syrian invasion. The king's army is led by Nicanor, a man already well aware of Judas' courage and military expertise (cf. 3:48—4:27). Nicanor therefore resorts to deception, although according to 2 Maccabees 14:15–33 he was at first well disposed towards Judas and it was only through Alcimus' machinations that he came to hate him. Anyway, Nicanor shows no respect for the people or their religion, and he threatens to destroy the temple (vv. 33–35). The priests react to his arrogance, the sacred writer tells us, by appealing to the Lord (vv. 36–38) and Judas himself calls on God to punish this blasphemy as he did in the past (v. 41; cf. 2 Kings 18:17—19:37). God not only gives victory to Judas, but he inflicts an exemplary punishment on the blasphemer (v. 47). On these events

Bethzaith; et misit et comprehendit multos ex eis, qui ad se refugerant, et quosdam de populo mactavit in puteum magnum. [20]Et commisit regionem Alcimo et reliquit cum eo auxilium in adiutorium ipsi; et abiit Bacchides ad regem. [21]Et contendebat Alcimus pro principatu sacerdotii sui; [22]et convenerunt ad eum omnes, qui perturbabant populum suum, et obtinuerunt terram Iudae et fecerunt plagam magnam in Israel. [23]Et vidit Iudas omnem malitiam, quam fecit Alcimus et, qui cum eo erant, filiis Israel multo plus quam gentes; [24]et exiit in omnes fines Iudaeae in circuitu et fecit vindictam in viros desertores, et cessaverunt ultra exire in regionem. [25]Ut vidit autem Alcimus quod praevaluit Iudas et, qui cum eo erant, et cognovit quia non potest sustinere eos; et regressus est ad regem et accusavit eos criminibus. [26]Et misit rex Nicanorem unum ex principibus suis nobilioribus, qui oderat et inimicitias exercebat contra Israel; et mandavit ei evertere populum. [27]Et venit Nicanor in Ierusalem cum exercitu magno et misit ad Iudam et ad fratres eius verbis pacificis cum dolo [28]dicens: «Non sit pugna inter me et vos; veniam cum viris paucis, ut videam facies vestras cum pace». [29]Et venit ad Iudam, et salutaverunt se invicem

w. Or *many of his men who had deserted*

evil that Alcimus and those with him had done among the sons of Israel; it was more than the Gentiles had done. [24]So Judas[x] went out into all the surrounding parts of Judea, and took vengeance on the men who had deserted, and he prevented those in the city[y] from going out into the country. [25]When Alcimus saw that Judas and those with him had grown strong, and realized that he could not withstand them, he returned to the king and brought wicked charges against them.

1 Mac 3:38; 15:3
2 Mac 8:9,34–36; 14:15–24

[26]Then the king sent Nicanor, one of his honoured princes, who hated and detested Israel, and he commanded him to destroy the people. [27]So Nicanor came to Jerusalem with a large force, and treacherously sent to Judas and his brothers this peaceable message, [28]"Let there be no fighting between me and you; I shall come with a few men to see you face to face in peace." [29]So he came to Judas, and they greeted one another peaceably. But the enemy were ready to seize Judas. [30]It became known to Judas that Nicanor[x] had come to him with treacherous intent, and he was afraid of him and would not meet him again. [31]When Nicanor learned that his plan had been disclosed, he went out to meet Judas

2 Mac 14:29–30

---

and the feast of the "day of Nicanor", see 2 Maccabees 15:25–36.

In this episode Judas is again portrayed as the saviour of Judaism—this time against the attempt by the high priest and his party to give Judaism a Hellenistic stamp, and to do so by force with the help of a powerful foreign army. In the context of 1 Maccabees this new attack on the Jewish religion seems to be brought in as an argument to justify the legitimacy and the policies of the Hasmoneans, the successors of the Maccabees. In the broader context of the Bible, this reassertion of Judaism marks a further step towards the entry on the scene of the true Israel, which will emerge from the faithfulness and obedience to God of Jesus on the cross (cf. Eph 2:14–16; Phil 2:7–9); that new Israel will have to struggle not against human armies but against the wiles of the devil (cf. Eph 6:11–13).

pacifice, et hostes parati erant rapere Iudam. [30]Et innotuit sermo Iudae quoniam cum dolo venerat ad eum, et conterritus est ab eo et amplius noluit videre faciem eius. [31]Et cognovit Nicanor quoniam denudatum est consilium eius et exivit obviam Iudae in pugnam iuxta Chapharsalama; [32]et ceciderunt de Nicanoris exercitu fere quingenti viri, et fugerunt in civitatem David. [33]Et post haec verba ascendit Nicanor in montem Sion; et exierunt quidam ex sacerdotibus de sanctis et quidam ex senioribus populi salutare eum pacifice et demonstrare ei holocaustum, quod offerebatur pro rege. [34]Et irridens sprevit eos et polluit eos et locutus est superbe [35]et iuravit cum ira dicens: «Nisi traditus fuerit Iudas et exercitus eius in manus meas continuo, et erit, si regressus fuero in pace, succendam domum istam». Et exiit cum ira magna. [36]Et intraverunt sacerdotes et steterunt ante faciem altaris et templi et flentes dixerunt: [37]«Tu elegisti domum istam ad invocandum nomen tuum super eam, ut esset domus orationis et obsecrationis populo tuo; [38]fac vindictam in homine isto et exercitu eius, et cadant in gladio. Memento blasphemias

x. Gk *he* **y.** Gk *they were prevented*

in battle near Caphar-salama. [32]About five hundred men of the army of Nicanor fell, and the rest[z] fled into the city of David.

[33]After these events Nicanor went up to Mount Zion. Some of the priests came out of the sanctuary, and some of the elders of the people, to greet him peaceably and to show him the burnt offering that was being offered for the king. [34]But he mocked them and derided them and defiled them and spoke arrogantly, [35]and in anger he swore this oath, "Unless Judas and his army are delivered into my hands this time, then if I return safely I will burn up this house." And he went out in great anger. [36]Then the priests went in and stood before the altar and the temple, and they wept and said,

2 Mac 14:31–36

[37] "Thou didst choose this house to be called by thy name,
and to be for thy people a house of prayer and supplication.
[38] Take vengeance on this man and on his army,
and let them fall by the sword;
remember their blasphemies,
and let them live no longer."

[39]Now Nicanor went out from Jerusalem and encamped in Beth-horon, and the Syrian army joined him. [40]And Judas encamped in Adasa with three thousand men. Then Judas prayed and said, [41]"When the messengers from the king spoke blasphemy, thy angel went forth and struck down one hundred and eighty-five thousand of the Assyrians.[a] [42]So also crush this army before us today; let the rest learn that Nicanor[b] has spoken wickedly against the sanctuary, and judge him according to this wickedness." [43]So the armies met in battle on the thirteenth day of the month of Adar. The army of Nicanor was crushed, and he himself was the first to fall in the battle. [44]When his army saw that Nicanor had fallen, they threw down their arms and fled. [45]The Jews[c] pursued them a day's journey, from Adasa as far as Gazara, and as they followed kept sounding the battle call on the trumpets. [46]And men came out

2 Kings 18:17—19:37
2 Mac 15:22–24
Is 36–37
Acts 12:23

2 Mac 15:25–36

---

eorum et ne dederis eis mansionem». [39]Et exiit Nicanor ab Ierusalem et applicuit ad Bethoron; et occurrit illi exercitus Syriae. [40]Et Iudas applicuit in Hadasa cum tribus milibus viris. Et oravit Iudas et dixit: [41]«Qui missi erant a rege cum male locuti sunt; exiit angelus et percussit in eis centum octoginta quinque milia. [42]Sic contere exercitum istum in conspectu nostro hodie, et sciant ceteri quia male locutus est super sancta tua, et iudica illum secundum malitiam illius». [43]Et commiserunt exercitus proelium tertia decima die mensis Adar; et contrita sunt castra Nicanoris, et cecidit ipse primus in proelio. [44]Ut autem vidit exercitus eius quia cecidit Nicanor, proiecerunt arma et fugerunt. [45]Et persecuti sunt eos viam unius diei ab Hadasa usquequo veniatur in Gazara et tubis cecinerunt post eos cum significationibus. [46]Et exierunt de omnibus castellis Iudaeae in circuitu et ventilabant eos et conversi sunt ad eos; et ceciderunt omnes gladio, et non est relictus ex eis nec unus. [47]Et acceperunt spolia eorum et praedam et caput Nicanoris amputaverunt et dexteram eius, quam extenderat superbe, et attulerunt et suspenderunt contra Ierusalem. [48]Et laetatus est populus valde; et egerunt diem illam in laetitia magna

z. Gk *they* **a.** Gk *of them* **b.** Gk *he* **c.** Gk *They*

of all the villages of Judea round about, and they out-flanked the enemy[d] and drove them back to their pursuers,[e] so that they all fell by the sword; not even one of them was left. [47]Then the Jews[f] seized the spoils and the plunder, and they cut off Nicanor's head and the right hand which he so arrogantly stretched out, and brought them and displayed them just outside Jerusalem. [48]The people rejoiced greatly and celebrated that day as a day of great gladness. [49]And they decreed that this day should be celebrated each year on the thirteenth day of Adar. [50]So the land of Judah had rest for a few days.

Judas' alliance with the Romans

8 [1]Now Judas heard of the fame of the Romans, that they were very strong and were well-disposed toward all who made an alliance with them, that they pledged friendship to those who came to them, [2]and that they were very strong. Men told him of their wars and of the brave deeds which they were doing among the Gauls, how they had defeated them and forced them to pay tribute, [3]and what they had done in the land of Spain to get control of the silver and gold mines there, [4]and how they had gained control of

8:1–32. Judas is acutely aware that, without help, he cannot possibly resist the military might of the Syrian empire. He has obtained religious autonomy, but he aspires to political independence; so, knowing that Rome is attaining ascendancy in East and West, he seeks to form an alliance with that power. He may not, however, realize that there is a price to be paid for Roman help to kingdoms under the sway of other empires—submission to Rome. Even so, in the circumstances, a Roman alliance seems the best solution, and 1 Maccabees interprets it as most creditable to Judas. The sacred writer's high regard for Rome is based mainly on Rome's victories in distant countries such as Spain or against Israel's own enemies, such as Syria (vv. 2–13). As

[49]et constituerunt agere omnibus annis diem istam tertia decima die Adar. [50]Et siluit terra Iudae dies paucos. **[8]** [1]Et audivit Iudas nomen Romanorum quia sunt potentes viribus et consentiunt omnibus, quae postulantur ab eis, et, quicumque accesserint ad eos, statuerunt cum eis amicitiam, [2]et quia sunt potentes viribus. Et narraverunt proelia eorum et virtutes bonas, quas fecerunt in Galatia, quia obtinuerunt eos et duxerunt eos sub tributum, [3]et quanta fecerunt in regione Hispaniae, quod in potestatem redegerunt metalla argenti et auri, quae illic sunt; [4]et possederunt omnem locum consilio suo et patientia—et locus erat longe distans ab eis—et reges, qui supervenerant eis ab extremis terrae, donec contriverunt eos et percusserunt eos plaga magna; ceteri autem dant eis tributum omnibus annis; [5]et Philippum et Persea Citiorum regem et, quotquot adversum eos arma tulerant, contriverunt in bello et obtinuerunt eos; [6]et Antiochum magnum regem Asiae, qui eis pugnam intulerat habens centum viginti elephantos et equitatum et currus et exercitum magnum valde, contritum ab eis: [7]et ceperunt eum vivum et statuerunt, ut eis daret ipse et, qui regnarent post ipsum, tributum magnum et daret obsides et

d. Gk *them* **e.** Gk *these* **f.** Gk *they*

the whole region by their planning and patience, even though the place was far distant from them. They also subdued the kings who came against them from the ends of the earth, until they crushed them and inflicted great disaster upon them; the rest paid them tribute every year. [5]Philip, and Perseus king of the Macedonians,[g] and the others who rose up against them, they crushed in battle and conquered. [6]They also defeated Antiochus the Great, king of Asia, who went to fight against them with a hundred and twenty elephants and with cavalry and chariots and a very large army. He was crushed by them; [7]they took him alive and decreed that he and those who should reign after him should pay a heavy tribute and give hostages and surrender some of their best provinces, [8]the country of India and Media and Lydia. These they took from him and gave to Eumenes the king. [9]The Greeks planned to come and destroy them, [10]but this became known to them, and they sent a general against the Greeks[h] and attacked them. Many of them were wounded and fell, and the Romans[i] took captive their wives and children; they plundered them, conquered the land, tore down their strongholds, and enslaved them to this day. [11]The remaining kingdoms and islands, as many as ever opposed them, they destroyed

---

we read on, we can see how impressed he is by Roman political institutions (vv. 14–16). Although he is not right in everything he says, the Roman model provides a sharp contrast with the despotism of the Seleucid kings.

The alliance with Rome is made in line with standard practice and all due formality. However, from the Roman point of view, given the relative insignificance of Judea and the fact that no solemn oath is involved, it may have been just a treaty of friendship. The Jewish negotiators are men of distinction: on the father of Eupolemus, see 2 Maccabees 4:11; Jason's, see 2 Maccabees 6:18–20. The negotiations work out well, but the treaty means that Judea has entered the sphere of Roman politics. This will ultimately lead to complications and disaster, but for the time being it opens the door to independence from Syria.

constitutum; [8]et regionem Indorum et Mediam et Lydiam et de optimis regionibus eorum et acceptas eas ab illo dederunt Eumeni regi; [9]et quia, qui erant de Hellade, voluerunt ire et tollere eos, et innotuit sermo his, [10]et miserunt ad eos ducem unum et pugnaverunt contra illos et ceciderunt ex eis multi et captivas duxerunt uxores eorum et filios et diripuerunt eos et terram eorum possederunt et destruxerunt munitiones eorum et in servitutem illos redegerunt usque in hunc diem; [11]et residua regna et insulas, quae aliquando restiterant illis, exterminaverunt et in potestatem redegerunt; [12]cum amicis autem suis et, qui in ipsis requiem habebant, conservaverunt amicitiam; et obtinuerunt reges, qui prope et qui longe erant; et quicumque audiebant nomen eorum, timebant eos; [13]quibus vero vellent auxilio esse et regnare, regnabant; quos autem vellent, amovebant: et exaltati sunt valde. [14]Et in omnibus istis nemo portabat diadema, nec induebatur purpura, ut magnificaretur in ea; [15]et curiam fecerunt sibi et cotidie

g. Or *Kittim* **h.** Gk *them* **i.** Gk *they*

and enslaved; [12]but with their friends and those who rely on them they have kept friendship. They have subdued kings far and near, and as many as have heard of their fame have feared them. [13]Those whom they wish to help and to make kings, they make kings, and those whom they wish they depose; and they have been greatly exalted. [14]Yet for all this not one of them has put on a crown or worn purple as a mark of pride, [15]but they have built for themselves a senate chamber, and every day three hundred and twenty senators constantly deliberate concerning the people, to govern them well. [16]They trust one man each year to rule over them and to control all their land; they all heed the one man, and there is no envy or jealousy among them.

Jas 4:2

[17]So Judas chose Eupolemus the son of John, son of Accos, and Jason the son of Eleazar, and sent them to Rome to establish friendship and alliance, [18]and to free themselves from the yoke; for they saw that the kingdom of the Greeks was completely enslaving Israel. [19]They went to Rome, a very long journey; and they entered the senate chamber and spoke as follows: [20]"Judas, who is also called Maccabeus, and his brothers and the people of the Jews have sent us to you to establish alliance and peace with you, that we may be enrolled as your allies and friends." [21]The proposal pleased them, [22]and this is a copy of the letter which they wrote in reply, on bronze tablets, and sent to Jerusalem to remain with them there as a memorial of peace and alliance:

2 Mac 4:11

1 Mac 14:18

[23]"May all go well with the Romans and with the nation of the Jews at sea and on land for ever, and may sword and enemy be far from them. [24]If war comes first to Rome or to any of their allies in all their dominion, [25]the nation of the Jews shall act as their allies wholeheartedly, as the occasion may indicate to them. [26]And to the enemy who makes war they shall not give or supply grain, arms, money, or ships, as Rome has decided; and they shall keep their

---

consulebant trecenti et viginti consulentes semper de multitudine, ut quiete agerent; [16]et committunt uni homini regnare eis per singulos annos et dominari universae terrae suae, et omnes oboediunt uni, et non est invidia neque zelus inter eos. [17]Et elegit Iudas Eupolemum filium Ioannis filii Accos et Iasonem filium Eleazari et misit eos Romam constituere cum illis amicitiam et societatem [18]et ut auferrent ab eis iugum, quia viderunt quod regnum Graecorum in servitutem premeret Israel. [19]Et abierunt Romam—et via multa valde—et introierunt curiam et responderunt et dixerunt: [20]«Iudas Maccabaeus et fratres eius et populus Iudaeorum miserunt nos ad vos statuere vobiscum societatem et pacem et conscribere nos socios et amicos vestros». [21]Et placuit sermo in conspectu eorum. [22]Et hoc est rescriptum epistulae, quam rescripserunt in tabulis aereis et miserunt in Ierusalem, ut esset apud eos ibi memoriale pacis et societatis: [23]«Bene sit Romanis et genti Iudaeorum in mari et in terra in aeternum, gladiusque et hostis procul sit ab eis. [24]Quod si institerit bellum Romanis prius aut omnibus sociis eorum in omni dominatione eorum, [25]auxilium feret gens Iudaeorum, prout tempus dictaverit illis, corde pleno [26]et

obligations without receiving any return. [27]In the same way, if war comes first to the nation of the Jews, the Romans shall willingly act as their allies, as the occasion may indicate to them.

[28]And to the enemy allies shall be given no grain, arms, money, or ships, as Rome has decided; and they shall keep these obligations and do so without deceit. [29]Thus on these terms the Romans make a treaty with the Jewish people. [30]If after these terms are in effect both parties shall determine to add or delete anything, they shall do so at their discretion, and any addition or deletion that they may make shall be valid.

[31]"And concerning the wrongs which King Demetrius is doing to them we have written to him as follows, 'Why have you made your yoke heavy upon our friends and allies the Jews? [32]If now they appeal again for help against you, we will defend their rights and fight you on sea and on land.'"

A new attack on Judea. Death of Judas in battle

9 [1]When Demetrius heard that Nicanor and his army had fallen in battle, he sent Bacchides and Alcimus into the land of Judah a second time, and with them the right wing of the army. [2]They went by the road which leads to Gilgal and encamped against Mesaloth in Arbela, and they took it and killed many people. [3]In the first month of the one hundred and fifty-second year[j] they encamped against Jerusalem; [4]then they marched off and went to Berea with twenty thousand foot soldiers and two thousand cavalry.

9:1–22. King Demetrius is not put off by the death of Nicanor: he sends a new army against Jerusalem, this time from the north. Berea (v. 4) is some 15 km. (9 miles) north of Jerusalem. It is the spring of 160 BC (the first month of the Babylonian calendar ran from mid March to mid April). The sacred writer

proeliantibus non dabunt neque subministrabunt triticum, arma, argentum, naves, sicut placuit Romae; et custodient mandata eorum, nihil accipientes. [27]Similiter autem et si genti Iudaeorum prius acciderit bellum, adiuvabunt Romani ex animo, prout eis tempus permiserit; [28]et adiuvantibus non dabitur triticum, arma, argentum, naves, sicut placuit Romae; et custodient mandata haec absque dolo. [29]Secundum haec verba ita constituerunt Romani populo Iudaeorum. [30]Quod si post haec verba cogitaverint hi aut illi addere aut demere, facient ex proposito suo; et quaecumque addiderint vel dempserint, rata erunt. [31]Et de malis, quae Demetrius rex fecit in eos, scripsimus ei dicentes: "Quare gravasti iugum tuum super amicos nostros, socios Iudaeos? [32]Si ergo iterum adierint nos adversum te, faciemus illis iudicium et pugnabimus tecum mari terraque"». **[9]** [1]Et audivit Demetrius quia cecidit Nicanor et exercitus eius in proelio et apposuit Bacchidem et Alcimum rursum mittere in terram Iudaeae et dextrum cornu cum illis. [2]Et abierunt viam, quae ducit in Galgala, et castra posuerunt in Masaloth, quae est in Arbelis, et occupaverunt eam et peremerunt animas hominum multas. [3]Et mense primo anni

j. 160 BC

[5]Now Judas was encamped in Elasa, and with him were three thousand picked men. [6]When they saw the huge number of the enemy forces, they were greatly frightened, and many slipped away from the camp, until no more than eight hundred of them were left.

[7]When Judas saw that his army had slipped away and the battle was imminent, he was crushed in spirit, for he had no time to assemble them. [8]He became faint, but he said to those who were left, "Let us rise and go up against our enemies. We may be able to fight them." [9]But they tried to dissuade him, saying, "We are not able. Let us rather save our own lives now, and let us come back with our brethren and fight them; we are too few." [10]But Judas said, "Far be it from us to do such a thing as to flee from them. If our time has come, let us die bravely for our brethren, and leave no cause to question our honour."

[11]Then the army of Bacchides[k] marched out from the camp and took its stand for the encounter. The cavalry was divided into two companies, and the slingers and the archers went ahead of the

---

seems to want to make it clear that Judas was acting rashly on this occasion yet he was as brave as ever: he insists on fighting even though most of his force have pulled back; he feels his honour is at stake. Oddly enough, we are not told that Judas appeals for God's help in this battle (vv. 6–10).

The lament on the death of Judas is inspired by David's elegy for Saul and Jonathan (cf. 2 Sam 1:19–27); all his deeds are summed up in the words "the saviour of Israel" (v. 21). Judas was the instrument chosen by divine providence to save Judaism from the syncretism of Hellenist religions, and to protect Israel's identity so that from that people Christ, the Messiah, could emerge.

centesimi et quinquagesimi secundi applicuerunt ad Ierusalem; [4]et surrexerunt et abierunt in Bereth in viginti milibus virorum et duobus milibus equitum. [5]Et Iudas posuerat castra in Elasa, et tria milia viri electi cum eo; [6]et viderunt multitudinem exercitus quia multi sunt et timuerunt valde; et multi subtraxerunt se de castris, et non remanserunt ex eis nisi octingenti viri. [7]Et vidit Iudas quod defluxit exercitus suus, et bellum perurgebat eum; et confractus est corde, quia non habebat tempus congregandi eos, [8]et dissolutus est. Et dixit his, qui residui erant: «Surgamus et ascendamus ad adversarios nostros, si poterimus pugnare adversus eos». [9]Et avertebant eum dicentes: «Non poterimus, sed liberemus animas nostras modo et revertamur nos et fratres nostri et pugnabimus adversus eos; nos autem pauci sumus». [10]Et ait Iudas: «Absit istam rem facere, ut fugiamus ab eis; et si appropiavit tempus nostrum, et moriamur in virtute propter fratres nostros et non inferamus crimen gloriae nostrae». [11]Et movit exercitus de castris, et steterunt illis obviam; et divisi sunt equites in duas partes, et fundibularii et sagittarii praeibant exercitum, et primi certaminis omnes potentes. [12]Bacchides autem erat in dextro cornu; et proximavit legio ex duabus partibus, et clamabant tubis; et clamaverunt hi, qui erant ex parte Iudae, etiam ipsi in tubis; [13]et commota est terra a voce exercituum; et commissum est proelium a mane usque ad vesperam. [14]Et vidit Iudas quod Bacchides et firmior pars exercitus erat in dextris, et

k. Gk *the army*

army, as did all the chief warriors. [12]Bacchides was on the right wing. Flanked by the two companies, the phalanx advanced to the sound of the trumpets; and the men with Judas also blew their trumpets. [13]The earth was shaken by the noise of the armies, and the battle raged from morning till evening.

[14]Judas saw that Bacchides and the strength of his army were on the right; then all the stouthearted men went with him, [15]and they crushed the right wing, and he pursued them as far as Mount Azotus. [16]When those on the left wing saw that the right wing was crushed, they turned and followed close behind Judas and his men. [17]The battle became desperate, and many on both sides were wounded and fell. [18]Judas also fell, and the rest fled.

[19]Then Jonathan and Simon took Judas their brother and buried him in the tomb of their fathers at Modein, [20]and wept for him. And all Israel made great lamentation for him; they mourned many days and said,

1 Mac 2:70
1 Mac 13:25–30

[21] "How is the mighty fallen,
the saviour of Israel!"

2 Sam 1:27

[22]Now the rest of the acts of Judas, and his wars and the brave deeds that he did, and his greatness, have not been recorded, for they were very many.

---

*__9:23—12:53.__ The Jonathan period is marked not so much by military as by diplomatic victories. Jonathan led the Jewish people from 160 to 142 BC. After Judas' death he leads the Jews against the Syrian general Bacchides and defeats him (9:23–73). But the political-military situation changes in 152 BC when a civil war breaks out between the two contenders for the throne of Syria—Alexander Balas, the successor of Antiochus V (cf. 6:17), on one side, and the successors of Seleucus IV, one of whom, Demetrius I, occupied the throne (cf. 7:1), on the other. Both sides want to attract the Jews to their cause, and they make Jonathan tempting offers. Alexander even appoints him high priest (10:20). Jonathan favours Alexander, who

convenerunt cum ipso omnes constantes corde; [15]et contrita est dextera pars ab eis, et persecutus est eos usque ad montem Azoti. [16]Et, qui in sinistro cornu erant, viderunt quod contritum est dextrum cornu, et secuti sunt post Iudam et eos, qui cum ipso erant, a tergo. [17]Et ingravatum est proelium, et ceciderunt vulnerati multi ex his et ex illis; [18]et Iudas cecidit, et ceteri fugerunt. [19]Et Ionathas et Simon tulerunt Iudam fratrem suum et sepelierunt eum in sepulcro patrum suorum in Modin. [20]Et fleverunt eum et planxerunt omnis populus Israel planctu magno et lugebant dies multos [21]et dixerunt: «Quomodo cecidit potens, qui salvum faciebat populum Israel!». [22]Et cetera verborum Iudae et bellorum et virtutum, quas fecit, et magnitudinis eius non sunt descripta; multa enim erant valde. [23]Et factum est, post obitum Iudae emerserunt iniqui in omnibus finibus Israel, et exorti sunt omnes, qui operabantur iniquitatem. [24]In diebus illis facta est fames magna valde, et tradidit se regio cum ipsis. [25]Et elegit Bacchides viros impios et constituit eos dominos regionis; [26]et exquirebant et perscrutabantur amicos Iudae et adducebant eos ad Bacchidem, et vindicabat in illos et illudebat. [27]Et facta est tribulatio magna in Israel, qualis non fuit ex die, qua non est visus propheta illis. [28]Et congregati sunt omnes amici Iudae et dixerunt Ionathae:

4. JONATHAN, JUDAS' SUCCESSOR*

Lawlessness and vengeance. Jonathan's election

[23]After the death of Judas, the lawless emerged in all parts of Israel; all the doers of injustice appeared. [24]In those days a very great famine occurred, and the country deserted with them to the enemy. [25]And Bacchides chose the ungodly and put them in charge of the country. [26]They sought and searched for the friends of Judas, and brought them to Bacchides, and he took vengeance on them and made sport of them. [27]Thus there was great distress in Israel, such as had not been since the time that prophets ceased to appear among them.

1 Mac 4:46

makes him military chief and governor of the Jews (10:48–66); but this leads to a confrontation between Demetrius (the son of Demetrius I) and Jonathan. Jonathan defeats Apollonius, Demetrius' general, in battles on the Mediterranean coast (10:67–88). Eventually, Demetrius secures the throne in 145 BC (as Demetrius II) with the help of Ptolemy, king of Egypt (11:1–19) and, not wanting to have the Jews as enemies, he confirms the concessions made by Alexander and exempts the Jews from payment of tribute (11:20–37). This means that Jonathan is now on Demetrius' side and he sends forces to help keep him on the throne (11:38–53).

However, very soon (in 144 BC) Alexander's son, Antiochus VI, regains his father's throne with the support of Trypho, an ambitious man who will do much harm to the Jews. Jonathan then crosses over to Antiochus VI and fights against the army of Demetrius, winning important battles in Galilee (11:54–74). The circumstances are favourable to renewing treaties with Rome and Sparta, which Jonathan now does (12:1–23), while continuing to engage Demetrius' army. The effect of all this is that he gains control of the northern territories in the region of Hamath; his brother Simon has similar success in the east. Once these regions are secured, the Jews rebuild Jerusalem (12:24–38). But untoward events occur in the court of Antiochus VI: Trypho moves against the king (and in fact kills him) and takes

[29]«Ex quo frater tuus Iudas defunctus est, et vir similis ei non est, qui exeat contra inimicos, et Bacchidem et eos, qui inimici sunt gentis nostrae; [30]nunc itaque te hodie elegimus esse pro eo nobis in principem et ducem ad bellandum bellum nostrum». [31]Et suscepit Ionathas tempore illo principatum et surrexit loco Iudae fratris sui. [32]Et cognovit Bacchides et quaerebat eum occidere; [33]et cognovit Ionathas et Simon frater eius et omnes, qui cum eo erant, et fugerunt in desertum Thecue et consederunt ad aquam lacus Asphar. [34]Et cognovit Bacchides die sabbatorum et venit ipse et omnis exercitus eius trans Iordanem. [35]Et Ionathas misit fratrem suum ducem populi et rogavit Nabathaeos amicos suos, ut commodarent illis apparatum suum, qui erat copiosus. [36]Et exierunt filii Iambri ex Medaba et comprehenderunt Ioannem et omnia, quae habebat, et abierunt habentes ea. [37]Post haec verba renuntiatum est Ionathae et Simoni fratri eius quia filii Iambri faciunt nuptias magnas et ducunt sponsam ex Nadabath filiam unius de magnis principibus Chanaan cum ambitione magna. [38]Et recordati sunt sanguinis Ioannis fratris sui et ascenderunt et absconderunt se sub tegumento montis [39]et elevaverunt oculos suos et viderunt: et ecce tumultus et apparatus multus, et sponsus processit et amici eius et fratres

[28]Then all the friends of Judas assembled and said to Jonathan, [29]"Since the death of your brother Judas there has been no one like him to go against our enemies and Bacchides, and to deal with those of our nation who hate us. [30]So now we have chosen you today to take his place as our ruler and leader, to fight our battle." [31]And Jonathan at that time accepted the leadership and took the place of Judas his brother.

[32]When Bacchides learned of this, he tried to kill him. [33]But Jonathan and Simon his brother and all who were with him heard of it, and they fled into the wilderness of Tekoa and camped by the water of the pool of Asphar. [34]Bacchides found this out on the sabbath day, and he with all his army crossed the Jordan.

The death of John avenged by Jonathan

[35]And Jonathan[1] sent his brother as leader of the multitude and begged the Nabateans, who were his friends, for permission to store with them the great amount of baggage which they had. [36]But the sons of Jambri from Medeba came out and seized John and all that he had, and departed with it.

1 Mac 5:25

the throne; he then sets a trap for Jonathan and imprisons him in Ptolemais (12:39–53;13:31).

With Jonathan as their leader the Jews won not only religious autonomy but political sovereignty; however, they became enmeshed in Syrian politics. Jonathan's remarkable switching of allegiance show his realism and political astuteness. God uses him to guide his people's fortunes.

9:23–34. After the death of Judas the pro-Hellenist party may have had the upper hand for a while. The situation reminds the writer of the difficult times when Jerusalem was being rebuilt after the return from exile, when the last of the prophets were active—Haggai, Zechariah and Malachi. Tekoa is about 20 km. (13 miles) south of Jerusalem.

9:35–42. Seemingly, Jonathan and his followers did not cross the Jordan at that time but he sent his brother John to get the Nabateans to look after the baggage and perhaps also the women and children. Jonathan wreaks vengeance on the men of Jambri (a desert tribe) for their attack on John Maccabeus (v. 42).

eius obviam illis cum tympanis et musicis et armis multis. [40]Et surrexerunt ad eos ex insidiis et occiderunt eos, et ceciderunt vulnerati multi; et residui fugerunt in montes, et acceperunt omnia spolia eorum. [41]Et conversae sunt nuptiae in luctum, et vox musicorum ipsorum in lamentum. [42]Et vindicaverunt vindictam sanguinis fratris sui et reversi sunt ad ripam Iordanis. [43]Et audivit Bacchides et venit die sabbatorum usque ad oram Iordanis in virtute magna. [44]Et dixit ad suos Ionathas: «Surgamus et pugnemus pro animabus nostris; non est enim hodie sicut heri et nudiustertius: [45]ecce enim bellum

1. Gk *he*

[37]After these things it was reported to Jonathan and Simon his brother, "The sons of Jambri are celebrating a great wedding, and are conducting the bride, a daughter of one of the great nobles of Canaan, from Nadabath* with a large escort." [38]And they remembered the blood of John their brother, and went up and hid under cover of the mountain. [39]They raised their eyes and looked, and saw a tumultuous procession with much baggage; and the bridegroom came out with his friends and his brothers to meet them with tambourines and musicians and many weapons. [40]Then they rushed upon them from the ambush and began killing them. Many were wounded and fell, and the rest fled to the mountain; and they took all their goods. [41]Thus the wedding was turned into mourning and the voice of their musicians into a funeral dirge. [42]And when they had fully avenged the blood of their brother, they returned to the marshes of the Jordan.

Jn 3:29

Armed confrontation between Bacchides and Jonathan

[43]When Bacchides heard of this, he came with a large force on the sabbath day to the banks of the Jordan. [44]And Jonathan said to those with him, "Let us rise up now and fight for our lives, for today things are not as they were before. [45]For look! the battle is in front of us and behind us; the water of the Jordan is on this side and on that, with marsh and thicket; there is no place to turn. [46]Cry out now to Heaven that you may be delivered from the hands of our enemies." [47]So the battle began, and Jonathan stretched out his hand to strike Bacchides, but he eluded him and went to the rear. [48]Then Jonathan and the men with him leaped into the Jordan and swam across to the other side, and the enemy[m] did not cross the Jordan to attack them. [49]And about one thousand of Bacchides' men fell that day.

9:43–53. Seemingly (contrary to what was said in v. 34) Bacchides does not cross the Jordan but tries to trap Jonathan on the west bank. A battle ensues which no one wins. Bacchides emerges unscathed, and Jonathan escapes by crossing to the east bank of the Jordan. Bacchides then fortifies the cities around Jerusalem.

9:54–73. The high priest Alcimus tries to dismantle the temple wall dividing

ex adverso nostrum, aqua vero Iordanis hinc et inde, et paludes et saltus, et non est locus divertendi. [46]Nunc ergo clamate in caelum, ut liberemini de manu inimicorum vestrorum». Et commissum est bellum. [47]Et extendit Ionathas manum suam percutere Bacchidem et divertit ab eo retro. [48]Et dissiliit Ionathas et, qui cum eo erant, in Iordanem et transnataverunt in ulteriora; et non transierunt ad eos Iordanem. [49]Et ceciderunt de parte Bacchidis die illa mille viri. Et reversi sunt in Ierusalem. [50]Et

m. Gk *they*

[50]Bacchides[n] then returned to Jerusalem and built strong cities in Judea: the fortress in Jericho, and Emmaus, and Beth-horon, and Bethel, and Timnath, and[o] Pharathon, and Tephon, with high walls and gates and bars. [51]And he placed garrisons in them to harass Israel. [52]He also fortified the city of Beth-zur, and Gazara, and the citadel, and in them he put troops and stores of food. [53]And he took the sons of the leading men of the land as hostages and put them under guard in the citadel at Jerusalem.

Death of Alcimus. Jonathan is persecuted. Bacchides is defeated

[54]In the one hundred and fifty-third year,[p] in the second month, Alcimus gave orders to tear down the wall of the inner court of the sanctuary. He tore down the work of the prophets! [55]But he only began to tear it down, for at that time Alcimus was stricken and his work was hindered; his mouth was stopped and he was paralyzed,

---

the Gentile court from the Jewish inner court, thereby to remove the separation of Jews from Gentiles—an attack on the religious identity of the Israelites as worshippers of the one true God, an identity that the prophets strove so much to protect (v. 54; cf. 1 Kings 18:1–15; etc.). Alcimus' illness and death, which puts a stop to this endeavour, are, implicitly, a punishment from God (vv. 55–56).

Alcimus' attempt to merge Jews and Gentiles was not the way to create a unified people. The time chosen by God for that to happen lay in the future. That union will come about as a gift from God in his good time—and not through infidelity to the Law or by jettisoning the religious identity of the people: it will be achieved by Jesus' sublime obedience on the cross to the will of God, and by mankind's acknowledgment of God as Father, creating a new Israel made up of Jews and Gentiles. In this connexion and using the image of the wall of the temple, St Paul will write: "For he [Christ] is our peace, who has made us both one, and has broken down the dividing wall of hostility, by abolishing in his flesh the law of commandments and ordinances, that he might create in himself one new man in place of the two, so making peace, and might reconcile us both to God in one body through the cross, thereby bringing the hostility to an end" (Eph 2:14–16).

aedificaverunt civitates munitas in Iudaea: munitionem, quae erat in Iericho, et Emmaus et Bethoron et Bethel et Thamnata et Pharathon et Tephon muris excelsis et portis et seris; [51]et posuit custodiam in eis, ut inimicitias exercerent in Israel. [52]Et munivit civitatem Bethsuram et Gazaram et arcem et posuit in eis auxilia et apparatum escarum. [53]Et accepit filios principum regionis obsides et posuit eos in arce in Ierusalem in custodia. [54]Et anno centesimo quinquagesimo tertio, mense secundo, praecepit Alcimus destrui murum atrii sanctorum interioris et destruxit opera prophetarum. Et coepit destruere. [55]In tempore illo percussus est Alcimus, et impedita sunt opera illius, et occlusum est os eius, et dissolutus est, nec ultra poterat loqui verbum et mandare de domo sua; [56]et mortuus est Alcimus in tempore illo

n. Gk *He* **o.** Some authorities omit *and* **p.** 159 BC

so that he could no longer say a word or give commands concerning his house. [56]And Alcimus died at that time in great agony. [57]When Bacchides saw that Alcimus was dead, he returned to the king, and the land of Judah had rest for two years.

[58]Then all the lawless plotted and said, "See! Jonathan and his men are living in quiet and confidence. So now let us bring Bacchides back, and he will capture them all in one night." [59]And they went and consulted with him. [60]He started to come with a large force, and secretly sent letters to all his allies in Judea, telling them to seize Jonathan and his men; but they were unable to do it, because their plan became known. [61]And Jonathan's men[q] seized about fifty of the men of the country who were leaders in this treachery, and killed them.

[62]Then Jonathan with his men, and Simon, withdrew to Bethbasi in the wilderness; he rebuilt the parts of it that had been demolished, and they fortified it. [63]When Bacchides learned of this, he assembled all his forces, and sent orders to the men of Judea. [64]Then he came and encamped against Bethbasi; he fought against it for many days and made machines of war.

[65]But Jonathan left Simon his brother in the city, while he went out into the country; and he went with only a few men. [66]He struck down Odomera and his brothers and the sons of Phasiron in their

---

Alcimus' death was followed by two years of peace (159–157 BC)—peace which, once again, came to an end through the fault of Jews who had turned their back on the Law (vv. 58–59). But this time Jonathan and his followers defeat Bacchides at Beth-basi, near Bethlehem, thanks to Jonathan's military strategy: Jonathan leaves the city on a foray against Arab tribes in league with Bacchides (vv. 65–66) and, by thus reducing Bacchides' support, Simon is able to defeat the Syrians (vv. 67–68). Jonathan offers peace terms to Bacchides, who leaves Judea, never to return; Jonathan establishes his base at Michmash, about 12 km. (7.5 miles) north-west of Jerusalem, keeping his

cum tormento magno. [57]Et vidit Bacchides quoniam mortuus est Alcimus et reversus est ad regem; et siluit terra Iudae annis duobus. [58]Et cogitaverunt omnes iniqui dicentes: «Ecce Ionathas et, qui cum eo sunt, in silentio habitant confidentes; nunc ergo adducamus Bacchidem, et comprehendet eos omnes una nocte». [59]Et abierunt et consilium ei dederunt. [60]Et surrexit, ut veniret cum exercitu multo, et misit occulte epistulas sociis suis, qui erant in Iudaea, ut comprehenderent Ionathan et eos, qui cum eo erant; et non potuerunt, quia innotuit eis consilium eorum. [61]Et apprehenderunt de viris regionis, qui principes erant malitiae, quinquaginta viros et occiderunt eos. [62]Et secessit Ionathas et Simon et, qui cum eo erant, in Bethbasi, quae est in deserto; et exstruxit diruta eius, et firmaverunt eam. [63]Et cognovit Bacchides et congregavit universam multitudinem suam et his, qui de Iudaea erant, denuntiavit; [64]et venit et castra posuit ad Bethbasi et oppugnavit eam dies multos et fecit machinas. [65]Et reliquit Ionathas Simonem fratrem suum in civitate et exiit in regionem et venit cum numero; [66]et percussit Odomera et fratres eius et filios Phasiron in tabernaculo ipsorum et coepit caedere et crescere in virtutibus. [67]Simon vero et, qui

q. Gk *they*

tents. [67]Then he[r] began to attack and went into battle with his forces; and Simon and his men sallied out from the city and set fire to the machines of war. [68]They fought with Bacchides, and he was crushed by them. They distressed him greatly, for his plan and his expedition had been in vain. [69]So he was greatly enraged at the lawless men who had counselled him to come into the country, and he killed many of them. Then he decided to depart to his own land.

[70]When Jonathan learned of this, he sent ambassadors to him to make peace with him and obtain release of the captives. [71]He agreed, and did as he said; and he swore to Jonathan[s] that he would not try to harm him as long as he lived. [72]He restored to him the captives whom he had formerly taken from the land of Judah; then he turned and departed to his own land, and came no more into their territory. [73]Thus the sword ceased from Israel. And Jonathan dwelt in Michmash. And Jonathan began to judge the people, and he destroyed the ungodly out of Israel.

Deut 19:19; 22:22

Jonathan appointed high priest by Alexander. Opposition to Demetrius

10 [1]In the one hundred and sixtieth year[t] Alexander Epiphanes, the son of Antiochus, landed and occupied Ptolemais. They welcomed him, and there he began to reign. [2]When Demetrius the

---

distance from the Syrians who remain installed in the Jerusalem citadel.

10:1–47. Alexander Epiphanes, also known as Alexander Balas, was an upstart who, having won the favour of the Romans, claimed to be the son of Antiochus IV (according to Flavius Josephus, *Antiquitates Judaicae*, 13, 35). Jonathan ably derives advantage from the approaches made to him by the two rival parties. He accepts Demetrius' offer and moves to Jerusalem on condition that the hostages held in the citadel are released (vv. 3–14); but he also accepts from Alexander the offer of the high priesthood (vv. 15–21). Eventually, he takes Alexander's side (vv. 46–47).

cum ipso erant, exierunt de civitate et succenderunt machinas [68]et pugnaverunt contra Bacchidem, et contritus est ab eis, et afflixerunt eum valde, quoniam consilium eius et adventus eius erat inanis. [69]Et iratus est animo contra viros iniquos, qui ei consilium dederant, ut veniret in regionem, et multos ex eis occiderunt et cogitaverunt abire in regionem eius. [70]Et cognovit Ionathas et misit ad eum legatos componere pacem cum ipso et reddere ei captivitatem. [71]Et accepit et fecit secundum verba eius et iuravit se nihil facturum ei mali omnibus diebus vitae eius; [72]et reddidit ei captivitatem, quam prius erat praedatus de terra Iudae, et conversus abiit in terram suam et non apposuit amplius venire in fines eius. [73]Et cessavit gladius ex Israel, et habitavit Ionathas in Machmas; et coepit Ionathas ibi iudicare populum et exterminabat impios ex Israel. **[10]** [1]Et anno centesimo sexagesimo ascendit Alexander Antiochi filius, Epiphanes, et occupavit Ptolemaidam; et receperunt eum, et regnavit illic. [2]Et audivit Demetrius rex et congregavit exercitum copiosum valde et exivit obviam illi in proelium. [3]Et misit Demetrius epistulam ad Ionathan verbis pacificis, ut magnificaret eum. [4]Dixit enim: «Anticipemus facere pacem

r. Other authorities read *they* **s.** Gk *him* **t.** 152 BC

king heard of it, he assembled a very large army and marched out to meet him in battle. [3]And Demetrius sent Jonathan a letter in peaceable words to honour him; [4]for he said, "Let us act first to make peace with him[u] before he makes peace with Alexander against us, [5]for he will remember all the wrongs which we did to him and to his brothers and his nation." [6]So Demetrius[v] gave him authority to recruit troops, to equip them with arms, and to become his ally; and he commanded that the hostages in the citadel should be released to him.

[7]Then Jonathan came to Jerusalem and read the letter in the hearing of all the people and of the men in the citadel. [8]They were greatly alarmed when they heard that the king had given him authority to recruit troops. [9]But the men in the citadel released the hostages to Jonathan, and he returned them to their parents.

[10]And Jonathan dwelt in Jerusalem and began to rebuild and restore the city. [11]He directed those who were doing the work to build the walls and encircle Mount Zion with squared stones, for better fortification; and they did so.

This proved to be the right move, because Alexander prevailed in the end. However, not all Jews would have been as enthusiastic about Jonathan's policy as the author of 1 Maccabees shows himself to be (and maybe that is why Demetrius' letter is addressed to the Jewish people, and not to Jonathan: v. 25), because what Jonathan's appointment in fact involved was taking the high priesthood away from the family of Onias, its traditional holders (cf. 12:7–8, 19–20; 2 Mac 3:1–5; 4:7). We know that Onias IV, the son of Onias III, to whom this office belonged, left for Egypt and there built a replica of the temple of Jerusalem (cf. Flavius Josephus, *Antiquitates Judaicae*, 12, 387; 13, 62–73). It is generally thought that Jonathan is the personage described as the "impious priest" by those who withdrew to Qumran with the "Master of Righteousness".

cum eo, priusquam faciat cum Alexandro adversum nos; [5]recordabitur enim omnium malorum, quae consummavimus in eum et in fratrem eius et in gentem eius». [6]Et dedit ei potestatem congregare exercitum et fabrificare arma et esse ipsum socium eius; et obsides, qui erant in arce, dixit tradi ei. [7]Et venit Ionathas in Ierusalem et legit epistulas in auditu omnis populi et eorum, qui in arce erant; [8]et timuerunt timore magno, cum audirent quoniam dedit ei rex potestatem congregandi exercitum. [9]Et tradiderunt, qui erant in arce, Ionathae obsides, et reddidit eos parentibus ipsorum. [10]Et habitavit Ionathas in Ierusalem et coepit aedificare et innovare civitatem; [11]et dixit facientibus opera, ut exstruerent muros et montem Sion in circuitu lapidibus quadratis ad munitionem: et ita fecerunt. [12]Et fugerunt alienigenae, qui erant in munitionibus, quas Bacchides aedificaverat, [13]et reliquit unusquisque locum suum et abiit in terram suam; [14]tantum in Bethsura remanserunt aliqui ex his, qui reliquerant legem et praecepta; erat enim ad refugium. [15]Et audivit Alexander rex promissa, quae misit Demetrius Ionathae, et narraverunt ei proelia et virtutes, quas ipse fecit et fratres eius, et labores, quos habuerunt. [16]Et ait: «Numquid inveniemus aliquem virum talem? Et nunc faciemus eum amicum et socium nostrum». [17]Et scripsit epistulam et misit ei secundum haec verba dicens: [18]«Rex Alexander fratri

u. Gk *them* **v.** Gk *he*

[12]Then the foreigners who were in the strongholds that Bacchides had built fled; [13]each left his place and departed to his own land. [14]Only in Beth-zur did some remain who had forsaken the law and the commandments, for it served as a place of refuge.

[15]Now Alexander the king heard of all the promises which Demetrius had sent to Jonathan, and men told him of the battles that Jonathan[w] and his brothers had fought, of the brave deeds that they had done, and of the troubles that they had endured. [16]So he said, "Shall we find another such man? Come now, we will make him our friend and ally." [17]And he wrote a letter and sent it to him, in the following words:

[18]"King Alexander to his brother Jonathan, greeting. [19]We have heard about you, that you are a mighty warrior and worthy to be our friend. [20]And so we have appointed you today to be the high priest of your nation; you are to be called the king's friend" (and he sent him a purple robe and a golden crown) "and you are to take our side and keep friendship with us."

1 Mac 2:18

[21]So Jonathan put on the holy garments in the seventh month of the one hundred and sixtieth year,[x] at the feast of tabernacles, and he recruited troops and equipped them with arms in abundance. [22]When Demetrius heard of these things he was grieved and said, [23]"What is this that we have done? Alexander has gotten ahead of

---

Ionathae salutem. [19]Audivimus de te quod vir potens es viribus et aptus es, ut sis amicus noster; [20]et nunc constituimus te hodie summum sacerdotem gentis tuae et ut amicus voceris regis—et misit ei purpuram et coronam auream—et, quae nostra sunt, sentias nobiscum et conserves amicitias ad nos». [21]Et induit se Ionathas stola sancta septimo mense, anno centesimo sexagesimo, in die sollemni Scenopegiae; et congregavit exercitum et fecit arma copiosa. [22]Et audivit Demetrius verba ista et contristatus est nimis et ait: [23]«Quid hoc fecimus quod praeoccupavit nos Alexander apprehendere amicitiam Iudaeorum ad firmamentum? [24]Scribam et ego illis verba deprecatoria et dignitates et dona, ut sint mecum in adiutorium». [25]Et misit eis secundum haec verba: «Rex Demetrius genti Iudaeorum salutem. [26]Quoniam servastis ad nos pactum et mansistis in amicitia nostra et non accessistis ad inimicos nostros, audivimus et gavisi sumus. [27]Et nunc perseverate adhuc conservare ad nos fidem, et retribuemus vobis bona pro his, quae facitis nobiscum, [28]et remittemus vobis praestationes multas et dabimus vobis donationes. [29]Et nunc absolvo vos et remitto Iudaeos a tributis et pretio salis et a coronis; [30]et pro tertia parte seminis et pro dimidia parte fructus ligni, quod debetur mihi accipere, remitto ex hodierno die et deinceps accipere a terra Iudae et a tribus regionibus, quae additae sunt illi ex Samaritide et Galilaea, ex hodierna die et in totum tempus; [31]et Ierusalem sit sancta et libera et fines eius et decimae et tributa. [32]Remitto etiam potestatem arcis, quae est in Ierusalem, et do eam summo sacerdoti, ut constituat in ea viros, quoscumque ipse elegerit, qui custodiant eam. [33]Et omnem animam Iudaeorum, quae captiva est, a terra Iudae in omni regno meo, relinquo liberam gratis, et omnes a tributis solvantur etiam pecorum suorum. [34]Et omnes dies sollemnes et sabbata et neomeniae et dies decreti et tres dies ante diem sollemnem et tres dies post diem sollemnem sint omnes immunitatis et remissionis omnibus Iudaeis, qui sunt in regno meo; [35]et nemo habebit potestatem agere et perturbare aliquem illorum de omni causa. [36]Et ascribantur ex Iudaeis in exercitu regis ad triginta milia virorum, et dabuntur illis copiae, ut oportet omnibus exercitibus regis. [37]Et ex eis constituentur, qui sint in munitionibus regis magnis, et ex his constituentur super negotia regni, quae aguntur ex fide, et praepositi eorum et principes

w. Gk *he* **x.** 152 B.C.

us in forming a friendship with the Jews to strengthen himself. [24]I also will write them words of encouragement and promise them honour and gifts, that I may have their help." [25]So he sent a message to them in the following words:

"King Demetrius to the nation of the Jews, greeting. [26]Since you have kept your agreement with us and have continued your friendship with us, and have not sided with our enemies, we have heard of it and rejoiced. [27]And now continue still to keep faith with us, and we will repay you with good for what you do for us. [28]We will grant you many immunities and give you gifts.

1 Mac 11:34
Lk 15:12

[29]"And now I free you and exempt all the Jews from payment of tribute and salt tax and crown levies, [30]and instead of collecting the third of the grain and the half of the fruit of the trees that I should receive, I release them from this day and henceforth. I will not collect them from the land of Judah or from the three districts added to it from Samaria and Galilee, from this day and for all time. [31]And let Jerusalem and her environs, her tithes and her revenues, be holy and free from tax. [32]I release also my control of the citadel in Jerusalem and give it to the high priest, that he may station in it men of his own choice to guard it. [33]And every one of the Jews taken as a captive from the land of Judah into any part of my kingdom, I set free without payment; and let all officials cancel also the taxes on their cattle.

[34]"And all the feasts and sabbaths and new moons and appointed days, and the three days before a feast and the three after a feast—let them all be days of immunity and release for all the Jews who are in my kingdom. [35]No one shall have authority to exact anything from them or annoy any of them about any matter.

[36]"Let Jews be enrolled in the king's forces to the number of thirty thousand men, and let the maintenance be given them that is

---

sint ex eis et ambulent in legibus suis, sicut praecepit rex in terra Iudae. [38]Et tres regiones, quae additae sunt Iudaeae ex regione Samariae, addatur Iudaeae reputari, ut sint sub uno et non oboediant alii potestati, nisi summi sacerdotis. [39]Ptolemaida et confines eius dedi donum sanctis, quae sunt in Ierusalem, ad necessarios sumptus sanctis. [40]Et ego do singulis annis quindecim milia siclorum argenti de rationibus regis ex locis, quae me contingunt; [41]et omne, quod reliquum fuerit, quod non reddiderant, qui super negotia erant, annis prioribus, ex hoc dabunt in opera domus. [42]Et super haec quinque milia siclorum argenti, quanta accipiebant de sanctorum ratione per singulos annos, et haec remittuntur eo quod ipsa ad sacerdotes pertineant, qui ministerio funguntur. [43]Et quicumque confugerint in templum, quod est Hierosolymis, et in omnibus finibus eius debentes regalia et quamlibet rem, dimittantur, et universa, quae sunt eis in regno meo. [44]Et ad aedificanda vel restauranda opera sanctorum sumptus dabitur de ratione regis; [45]et ad exstruendos muros Ierusalem et communiendum in circuitu sumptus dabitur de ratione regis et ad construendos muros in Iudaea». [46]Ut audivit autem Ionathas et populus sermones istos, non crediderunt eis, nec receperunt, quia recordati sunt malitiae magnae, quam fecerat in Israel et tribulaverat eos valde. [47]Et complacuit eis in Alexandro, quia ipse fuerat eis princeps sermonum pacis, et ipsi auxilium ferebant omnibus diebus. [48]Et congregavit rex Alexander exercitum

due to all the forces of the king. [37]Let some of them be stationed in the great strongholds of the king, and let some of them be put in positions of trust in the kingdom. Let their officers and leaders be of their own number, and let them live by their own laws, just as the king has commanded in the land of Judah.

[38]"As for the three districts that have been added to Judea from the country of Samaria, let them be so annexed to Judea that they are considered to be under one ruler and obey no other authority but the high priest. [39]Ptolemais and the land adjoining it I have given as a gift to the sanctuary in Jerusalem, to meet the necessary expenses of the sanctuary. [40]I also grant fifteen thousand shekels of silver yearly out of the king's revenues from appropriate places. [41]And all the additional funds which the government officials have not paid as they did in the first years,[y] they shall give from now on for the service of the temple.[z] [42]Moreover, the five thousand shekels of silver which my officials[a] have received every year from the income of the services of the temple, this too is canceled, because it belongs to the priests who minister there. [43]And whoever takes refuge at the temple in Jerusalem, or in any of its precincts, because he owes money to the king or has any debt, let him be released and receive back all his property in my kingdom.

[44]"Let the cost of rebuilding and restoring the structures of the sanctuary be paid from the revenues of the king. [45]And let the cost of rebuilding the walls of Jerusalem and fortifying it round about, and the cost of rebuilding the walls in Judea, also be paid from the revenues of the king."

[46]When Jonathan and the people heard these words, they did not believe or accept them, because they remembered the great

---

magnum et admovit castra contra Demetrium. [49]Et commiserunt proelium duo reges, et fugit exercitus Alexandri, et insecutus est eum Demetrius et praevaluit adversus eos; [50]et confirmavit proelium nimis, donec occidit sol, et cecidit Demetrius in die illa. [51]Et misit Alexander ad Ptolemaeum regem Aegypti legatos secundum haec verba dicens: [52]«Quoniam regressus sum in regnum meum et sedi in sede patrum meorum et obtinui principatum et contrivi Demetrium et possedi regionem nostram [53]et commisi pugnam cum eo, et contritus est ipse et castra eius a nobis, et sedimus in sede regni eius; [54]et nunc statuamus ad invicem amicitiam, et da mihi filiam tuam uxorem, et ego ero gener tuus et dabo tibi dona et ipsi digna te». [55]Et respondit rex Ptolemaeus dicens: «Felix dies, in qua reversus es ad terram patrum tuorum et sedisti in sede regni eorum! [56]Et nunc faciam tibi, quae scripsisti, sed occurre in Ptolemaidam, ut videamus invicem nos, et socer fiam tibi sicut dixisti». [57]Et exivit Ptolemaeus de Aegypto, ipse et Cleopatra filia eius, et venit Ptolemaidam anno centesimo sexagesimo secundo. [58]Et occurrit ei Alexander rex, et dedit ei Cleopatram filiam suam et fecit nuptias eius Ptolemaidae sicut reges in magna gloria. [59]Et scripsit rex Alexander Ionathae, ut veniret obviam sibi. [60]Et abiit cum gloria Ptolemaidam et occurrit ibi duobus regibus et dedit illis argentum multum et aurum et dona et invenit gratiam in conspectu eorum. [61]Et convenerunt adversus eum viri pestilentes ex Israel, viri iniqui interpellantes adversus eum; et non intendit ad eos rex. [62]Et iussit rex, et exspoliaverunt Ionathan vestibus suis et

y. The Greek text of this verse is uncertain **z.** Gk *house* **a.** Gk *they*

wrongs which Demetrius[b] had done in Israel and how he had greatly oppressed them. [47]They favoured Alexander, because he had been the first to speak peaceable words to them, and they remained his allies all his days.

Jonathan appointed general and governor

[48]Now Alexander the king assembled large forces and encamped opposite Demetrius. [49]The two kings met in battle, and the army of Demetrius fled, and Alexander[c] pursued him and defeated them. [50]He pressed the battle strongly until the sun set, and Demetrius fell on that day.

[51]Then Alexander sent ambassadors to Ptolemy king of Egypt with the following message: [52]"Since I have returned to my kingdom and have taken my seat on the throne of my fathers, and established my rule—for I crushed Demetrius and gained control of our country; [53]I met him in battle, and he and his army were crushed by us, and we have taken our seat on the throne of his kingdom—[54]now therefore let us establish friendship with one another; give me now your daughter as my wife, and I will become your son-in-law, and will make gifts to you and to her in keeping with your position."

[55]Ptolemy the king replied and said, "Happy was the day on which you returned to the land of your fathers and took your seat on the throne of their kingdom. [56]And now I will do for you as you wrote, but meet me at Ptolemais, so that we may see one another, and I will become your father-in-law, as you have said."

[57]So Ptolemy set out from Egypt, he and Cleopatra his daughter, and came to Ptolemais in the one hundred and sixty-second year.[d] [58]Alexander the king met him, and Ptolemy[e] gave him Cleopatra

---

10:48–66. Despite the pro-Greek party's protests to the king (for it continues to plot against Jonathan), the latter is officially appointed governor of Judea and military chief of the Jews. The Maccabee party and its policy of re-establishing Jewish customs has won the day, and Jonathan wields both civil and religious authority.

induerunt eum purpura; et ita fecerunt. Et collocavit eum rex sedere secum. [63]Dixitque principibus suis: «Exite cum eo in medium civitatis et praedicate, ut nemo adversus eum interpellet de ullo negotio, nec quisquam ei molestus sit de ulla ratione». [64]Et factum est, ut viderunt, qui interpellabant gloriam eius, quae praedicabatur, et opertum eum purpura, fugerunt omnes. [65]Et magnificavit eum rex et scripsit eum inter primos amicos et posuit eum ducem et participem principatus. [66]Et reversus est Ionathas in Ierusalem cum pace et laetitia. [67]In anno centesimo sexagesimo quinto venit Demetrius filius Demetrii

b. Gk *he* **c.** Other authorities read *Alexander fled, and Demetrius* [see New Vg] **d.** 150 BC **e.** Gk *he*

his daughter in marriage, and celebrated her wedding at Ptolemais with great pomp, as kings do.

[59]Then Alexander the king wrote to Jonathan to come to meet him. [60]So he went with pomp to Ptolemais and met the two kings; he gave them and their friends silver and gold and many gifts, and found favour with them. [61]A group of pestilent men from Israel, lawless men, gathered together against him to accuse him; but the king paid no attention to them. [62]The king gave orders to take off Jonathan's garments and to clothe him in purple, and they did so. [63]The king also seated him at his side; and he said to his officers, "Go forth with him into the middle of the city and proclaim that no one is to bring charges against him about any matter, and let no one annoy him for any reason." [64]And when his accusers saw the honour that was paid him, in accordance with the proclamation, and saw him clothed in purple, they all fled. [65]Thus the king honoured him and enrolled him among his chief friends, and made him general and governor of the province. [66]And Jonathan returned to Jerusalem in peace and gladness.

1 Mac 2:18

1 Mac 2:18

Jonathan's victory over Apollonius, Demetrius II's general

[67]In the one hundred and sixty-fifth year[f] Demetrius the son of Demetrius came from Crete to the land of his fathers. [68]When Alexander the king heard of it, he was greatly grieved and returned to Antioch. [69]And Demetrius appointed Apollonius the governor of Coelesyria, and he assembled a large force and encamped against Jamnia. Then he sent the following message to Jonathan the high priest:

[70]"You are the only one to rise up against us, and I have become a laughing-stock and reproach because of you. Why do you assume authority against us in the hill country? [71]If you now have

10:67–89. By siding with Alexander, Jonathan risked confrontation with Demetrius, which was exactly what happened. In 147 BC, king Demetrius' son, Demetrius II Nicator, after establishing himself in Coelesyria, decides to punish Jonathan for his support of Alexander. But Demetrius' general, Apollonius, fails to assess properly the strength of Jonathan's army (he thinks they are no more than guerrillas: vv. 70–71) and he is routed. Jonathan not only obtains a lot of booty but is given Ekron, a city about 35 km. (22 miles) to the west of Jerusalem.

a Creta in terram patrum suorum; [68]et audivit Alexander rex et contristatus est valde et reversus est Antiochiam. [69]Et constituit Demetrius rex Apollonium, qui praeerat Coelesyriae, et congregavit exercitum magnum; et accessit ad Iamniam et misit ad Ionathan summum sacerdotem [70]dicens: «Tu

f. 147 BC

confidence in your forces, come down to the plain to meet us, and let us match strength with each other there, for I have with me the power of the cities. [72]Ask and learn who I am and who the others are that are helping us. Men will tell you that you cannot stand before us, for your fathers were twice put to flight in their own land. [73]And now you will not be able to withstand my cavalry and such an army in the plain, where there is no stone or pebble, or place to flee."

[74]When Jonathan heard the words of Apollonius, his spirit was aroused. He chose ten thousand men and set out from Jerusalem, and Simon his brother met him to help him. [75]He encamped before Joppa, but the men of the city closed its gates, for Apollonius had a garrison in Joppa. [76]So they fought against it, and the men of the city became afraid and opened the gates, and Jonathan gained possession of Joppa.

[77]When Apollonius heard of it, he mustered three thousand cavalry and a large army, and went to Azotus as though he were going farther. At the same time he advanced into the plain, for he had a large troop of cavalry and put confidence in it. [78]Jonathan[g] pursued him to Azotus, and the armies engaged in battle. [79]Now Apollonius had secretly left a thousand cavalry behind them. [80]Jonathan learned that there was an ambush behind him, for they surrounded his army and shot arrows at his men from early morning till late afternoon. [81]But his men stood fast, as Jonathan commanded, and the enemy's[h] horses grew tired.

[82]Then Simon brought forward his force and engaged the phalanx in battle (for the cavalry was exhausted); they were

---

omnino solus resistis nobis; ego autem factus sum in derisum et in opprobrium propter te; et quare tu potestatem adversum nos exerces in montibus? [71]Nunc ergo si confidis in virtutibus tuis, descende ad nos in campum, et comparemus illic invicem, quia mecum est virtus civitatum. [72]Interroga et disce quis sum ego et ceteri, qui auxilio sunt nobis et dicunt: "Non potest stare pes vester ante faciem nostram, quia bis in fugam conversi sunt patres tui in terra sua". [73]Et nunc non poteris sustinere equitatum et exercitum talem in campo, ubi non est lapis neque silex neque locus fugiendi». [74]Ut audivit autem Ionathas sermones Apollonii, motus est animo et elegit decem milia virorum et exiit ab Ierusalem et occurrit ei Simon frater eius in adiutorium. [75]Et applicuit castra in Ioppen; et excluserunt eum, qui erant de civitate, quia custodia Apollonii in Ioppe erat, et oppugnaverunt eam. [76]Et exterriti, qui erant in civitate, aperuerunt ei, et obtinuit Ionathas Ioppen. [77]Et audivit Apollonius et admovit tria milia equitum et exercitum multum. Et abiit Azotum tamquam iter faciens et statim exiit in campum, eo quod haberet multitudinem equitum et confideret in eis. [78]Et insecutus est eum Ionathas in Azotum, et exercitus commiserunt proelium. [79]Et reliquit Apollonius mille equites post eos occulte. [80]Et cognovit Ionathas quoniam insidiae sunt post se; et circuierunt castra eius et iecerunt iacula in populum a mane usque ad vesperam. [81]Populus autem stabat, sicut praeceperat Ionathas, et laboraverunt equi eorum. [82]Et eiecit Simon exercitum suum et commisit contra legionem; equites enim fatigati erant. Et contriti sunt ab eo et fugerunt, [83]et equi dispersi sunt in campo et fugerunt in Azotum et intraverunt in Bethdagon idolum

g. Gk *He* **h.** Gk *their*

overwhelmed by him and fled, [83]and the cavalry was dispersed in the plain. They fled to Azotus and entered Beth-dagon, the temple of their idol, for safety. [84]But Jonathan burned Azotus and the surrounding towns and plundered them; and the temple of Dagon, and those who had taken refuge in it he burned with fire. [85]The number of those who fell by the sword, with those burned alive, came to eight thousand men.

1 Sam 5:1ff
1 Mac 11:4

[86]Then Jonathan departed from there and encamped against Askalon, and the men of the city came out to meet him with great pomp. [87]And Jonathan and those with him returned to Jerusalem with much booty. [88]When Alexander the king heard of these things, he honoured Jonathan still more; [89]and he sent to him a golden buckle, such as it is the custom to give to the kinsmen of kings. He also gave him Ekron and all its environs as his possession.

Fall of Alexander. Demetrius II rules with the support of Egypt

11 [1]Then the king of Egypt gathered great forces, like the sand by the seashore, and many ships; and he tried to get possession of Alexander's kingdom by trickery and add it to his own kingdom. [2]He set out for Syria with peaceable words, and the people of the cities opened their gates to him and went to meet him, for Alexander the king had commanded them to meet him, since he was Alexander's[i] father-in-law. [3]But when Ptolemy entered the cities he stationed forces as a garrison in each city.

11:1–19. The intervention of Ptolemy VI, king of Egypt, is going to change the political situation in Syria. Jonathan wisely gives the king a good reception and escorts him as far as the river Eleutherus, to the north of Lebanon. With Ptolemy's help, Demetrius II regains his throne.

suum, ut ibi se liberarent. [84]Et succendit Ionathas Azotum et civitates, quae erant in circuitu eius, et accepit spolia eorum et templum Dagon et omnes, qui fugerunt in illud, succendit igne. [85]Et fuerunt, qui ceciderunt gladio cum his qui succensi sunt, fere octo milia virorum. [86]Et movit inde Ionathas castra et applicuit ad Ascalonem, et exierunt de civitate obviam illi in magna gloria. [87]Et reversus est Ionathas in Ierusalem cum suis habentibus spolia multa. [88]Et factum est, ut audivit Alexander rex sermones istos, et addidit adhuc glorificare Ionathan [89]et misit ei fibulam auream, sicut consuetudo est dari cognatis regum, et dedit ei Accaron et omnes fines eius in possessionem. **[11]** [1]Et rex Aegypti congregavit exercitum sicut arena, quae est circa oram maris, et naves multas et quaerebat obtinere regnum Alexandri dolo et addere illud regno suo. [2]Et exiit in Syriam verbis pacificis, et aperiebant ei civitates et occurrebant ei, quia mandaverat Alexander rex exire ei obviam, eo quod socer suus esset. [3]Cum autem introiret civitatem, Ptolemaeus ponebat custodias militum in singulis civitatibus. [4]Et, ut appropiavit Azoto, ostenderunt ei templum Dagon succensum et Azotum et suburbana eius demolita et corpora proiecta et combustos, quos combusserat in bello; fecerant enim tumulos eorum in via eius. [5]Et narraverunt regi, quae fecit Ionathas, ut vituperarent eum; et tacuit rex. [6]Et occurrit Ionathas regi in Ioppen cum gloria, et invicem se salutaverunt et dormierunt illic. [7]Et abiit Ionathas cum rege usque ad fluvium, qui vocatur Eleutherus, et reversus est in Ierusalem. [8]Rex autem Ptolemaeus obtinuit dominium

i. Gk *his*

1 Mac 10:84

4When he[j] approached Azotus, they showed him the temple of Dagon burned down, and Azotus and its suburbs destroyed, and the corpses lying about, and the charred bodies of those whom Jonathan[k] had burned in the war, for they had piled them in heaps along his route. 5They also told the king what Jonathan had done, to throw blame on him; but the king kept silent. 6Jonathan met the king at Joppa with pomp, and they greeted one another and spent the night there. 7And Jonathan went with the king as far as the river called Eleutherus; then he returned to Jerusalem.

8So King Ptolemy gained control of the coastal cities as far as Seleucia by the sea, and he kept devising evil designs against Alexander. 9He sent envoys to Demetrius the king, saying, "Come, let us make a covenant with each other, and I will give you in marriage my daughter who was Alexander's wife, and you shall reign over your father's kingdom. 10For I now regret that I gave him my daughter, for he has tried to kill me." 11He threw blame on Alexander[l] because he coveted his kingdom. 12So he took his daughter away from him and gave her to Demetrius. He was estranged from Alexander, and their enmity became manifest.

13Then Ptolemy entered Antioch and put on the crown of Asia. Thus he put two crowns upon his head, the crown of Egypt and that of Asia. 14Now Alexander the king was in Cilicia at that time, because the people of that region were in revolt. 15And Alexander heard of it and came against him in battle. Ptolemy marched out

---

civitatum maritimarum usque Seleuciam maritimam et cogitabat in Alexandrum consilia mala. 9Et misit legatos ad Demetrium dicens: «Veni, componamus inter nos pactum, et dabo tibi filiam meam, quam habet Alexander, et regnabis in regno patris tui; 10paenitet enim me quod dederim illi filiam meam: quaesivit enim me occidere». 11Et vituperavit eum, propterea quod concupisceret regnum eius. 12Et abstulit filiam suam et dedit eam Demetrio et alienavit se ab Alexandro, et manifestatae sunt inimicitiae eorum. 13Et intravit Ptolemaeus Antiochiam et imposuit duo diademata capiti suo, Aegypti et Asiae. 14Alexander autem rex erat in Cilicia illis temporibus, quia rebellabant, qui erant de locis illis; 15et audivit Alexander et venit ad eum in bello. Et produxit Ptolemaeus exercitum et occurrit ei in manu valida et fugavit eum. 16Et fugit Alexander in Arabiam, ut ibi protegeretur; rex autem Ptolemaeus exaltatus est. 17Et abstulit Zabdiel Arabs caput Alexandri et misit Ptolemaeo. 18Et rex Ptolemaeus mortuus est in die tertia; et qui erant in munitionibus, perierunt ab his, qui erant in munitionibus. 19Et regnavit Demetrius anno centesimo sexagesimo septimo. 20In diebus illis congregavit Ionathas eos, qui erant de Iudaea, ut expugnarent arcem, quae est in Ierusalem; et fecerunt contra eam machinas multas. 21Et abierunt quidam, qui oderant gentem suam, viri iniqui ad regem et renuntiaverunt ei quod Ionathas obsideret arcem. 22Et audiens iratus est et statim, ut audivit, movit castra et venit ad Ptolemaidam et scripsit Ionathae, ne obsideret arcem et ut occurreret sibi ad colloquium in Ptolemaidam festinato. 23Ut audivit autem Ionathas, iussit obsidere et elegit de senioribus Israel et de sacerdotibus et dedit se periculo 24et accepit argentum et aurum et vestem et alia xenia multa et abiit ad regem in Ptolemaidam et invenit gratiam in conspectu eius. 25Et interpellabant adversus eum quidam iniqui ex gente sua. 26Et fecit ei rex, sicut fecerant ei qui ante eum fuerant, et exaltavit eum in conspectu omnium amicorum suorum 27et statuit ei principatum sacerdotii et, quaecumque alia habuit prius pretiosa, et fecit eum

j. Other ancient authorities read *they* **k.** Gk *he* **l.** Gk *him*

and met him with a strong force, and put him to flight. [16]So Alexander fled into Arabia to find protection there, and King Ptolemy was exalted. [17]And Zabdiel the Arab cut off the head of Alexander and sent it to Ptolemy. [18]But King Ptolemy died three days later, and his troops in the strongholds were killed by the inhabitants of the strongholds. [19]So Demetrius became king in the one hundred and sixty-seventh year.[m]

Concessions granted by Demetrius II to Jonathan

[20]In those days Jonathan assembled the men of Judea to attack the citadel in Jerusalem, and he built many engines of war to use against it. [21]But certain lawless men who hated their nation went to the king and reported to him that Jonathan was besieging the citadel. [22]When he heard this he was angry, and as soon as he heard it he set out and came to Ptolemais; and he wrote Jonathan not to continue the siege, but to meet him for a conference at Ptolemais as quickly as possible.

[23]When Jonathan heard this, he gave orders to continue the siege; and he chose some of the elders of Israel and some of the

---

11:20–37. Jonathan's attempt to take the citadel reminds us of a previous offer from Demetrius (cf. 10:32, 47), one not yet implemented. Jonathan shows himself to be very noble and courageous in making a personal visit to the king and, although he does not obtain everything he wants (v. 28) he does manage to have Judea exempted from payment of tribute and to have its territory extended: it is given three districts, up to this administered by Samaria (v. 34)—Aphairema (Ephraim), Lydda (Lud), and Rathamin (Ramah). This concession and Jonathan's appointment as a "friend of the king" (cf. vv. 27 and 57) meant that Jonathan's negotiations have been very successful. The citadel, however, was not on the agenda, and it continues to be held by the Syrians.

principem primorum amicorum. [28]Et postulavit Ionathas a rege, ut immunem faceret Iudaeam et tres toparchias et Samaritidem, et promisit ei talenta trecenta. [29]Et consensit rex et scripsit Ionathae epistulas de his omnibus hunc modum continentes: [30]«Rex Demetrius fratri Ionathae salutem et genti Iudaeorum. [31]Exemplum epistulae, quam scripsimus Lastheni parenti nostro de vobis, scripsimus et ad vos, ut sciretis: [32]"Rex Demetrius Lastheni patri salutem. [33]Genti Iudaeorum amicis nostris et conservantibus, quae iusta sunt apud nos, decrevimus benefacere propter benignitatem ipsorum, quam erga nos habent. [34]Statuimus ergo illis fines Iudaeae et tres regiones, Apherema et Lydda et Ramathaim, quae additae sunt Iudaeae ex Samaritide, et omnia confinia earum, omnibus sacrificantibus in Hierosolymis, pro regalibus, quae ab eis prius accipiebat rex per singulos annos de fructibus terrae et pomorum; [35]et alia, quae ad nos pertinent ex hoc tempore decimarum et tributorum pertinentium ad nos, et salis stagna et pertinentes ad nos coronas, omnia ipsis concedimus. [36]Et nihil horum irritum erit ex hoc et in omne tempus. [37]Nunc ergo curate facere horum exemplum, et detur Ionathae et ponatur in monte sancto in loco celebri"». [38]Et videns Demetrius rex quod siluit terra in conspectu suo, et nihil ei resistit, dimisit totum exercitum suum, unumquemque in locum suum, excepto peregrino exercitu, quem contraxit ab

m. 145 BC

priests, and put himself in danger, [24]for he went to the king at Ptolemais, taking silver and gold and clothing and numerous other gifts. And he won his favour. [25]Although certain lawless men of his nation kept making complaints against him, [26]the king treated him as his predecessors had treated him; he exalted him in the presence of all his friends. [27]He confirmed him in the high priesthood and in as many other honours as he had formerly had, and made him to be regarded as one of his chief friends. [28]Then Jonathan asked the king to free Judea and the three districts of Samaria[n] from tribute, and promised him three hundred talents. [29]The king consented, and wrote a letter to Jonathan about all these things; its contents were as follows:

1 Mac 2:18; 10:30,65; 11:34

[30]"King Demetrius to Jonathan his brother and to the nation of the Jews, greeting. [31]This copy of the letter which we wrote concerning you to Lasthenes our kinsman we have written to you also, so that you may know what it says. [32]'King Demetrius to Lasthenes his father, greeting. [33]To the nation of the Jews, who are our friends and fulfil their obligations to us, we have determined to do good, because of the good will they show toward us. [34]We have confirmed as their possession both the territory of Judea and the three districts of Aphairema and Lydda and Rathamin; the latter,

1 Mac 10:26–45

1 Mac 10:30

---

insulis gentium; et inimici erant ei omnes exercitus patrum eius. [39]Tryphon autem erat quidam partium Alexandri prius et vidit quoniam omnis exercitus murmurabat contra Demetrium et ivit ad Imalcue Arabem, qui nutriebat Antiochum filium Alexandri; [40]et assidebat ei, ut traderet eum ipsi, ut regnaret loco patris sui. Et enuntiavit ei quanta constituerat Demetrius et inimicitias exercituum eius adversus illum et mansit ibi diebus multis. [41]Et misit Ionathas ad Demetrium regem, ut eiceret eos, qui in arce erant in Ierusalem et qui in praesidiis erant, quia impugnabant Israel. [42]Et misit Demetrius ad Ionathan dicens: «Non haec tantum faciam tibi et genti tuae, sed gloria illustrabo te et gentem tuam, cum fuerit opportunum; [43]nunc ergo recte feceris, si miseris in auxilium mihi viros, quia discessit omnis exercitus meus». [44]Et misit ei Ionathas tria milia virorum fortium Antiochiam, et venerunt ad regem, et delectatus est rex in adventu eorum. [45]Et convenerunt, qui erant de civitate, centum viginti milia virorum, et volebant interficere regem; [46]et fugit rex in aulam, et occupaverunt, qui erant de civitate, itinera civitatis et coeperunt pugnare. [47]Et vocavit rex Iudaeos in auxilium, et convenerunt omnes simul ad eum et dispersi sunt per civitatem; et occiderunt in illa die centum milia hominum. [48]Et succenderunt civitatem et ceperunt spolia multa in die illa et liberaverunt regem. [49]Et viderunt, qui erant de civitate, quod obtinuissent Iudaei civitatem, sicut volebant, et infirmati sunt mente sua et clamaverunt ad regem cum precibus dicentes: [50]«Da nobis dextras, et cessent Iudaei oppugnare nos et civitatem». [51]Et proiecerunt arma sua et fecerunt pacem; et glorificati sunt Iudaei in conspectu regis et in conspectu omnium, qui erant in regno eius, et nominati sunt in regno et regressi sunt in Ierusalem habentes spolia multa. [52]Et sedit Demetrius rex in sede regni sui, et siluit terra in conspectu eius. [53]Et mentitus est omnia, quaecumque dixit, et abalienavit se a Ionatha et non retribuit ei secundum beneficia, quae sibi tribuerat, et vexabat eum valde. [54]Post haec autem reversus est Tryphon, et Antiochus cum eo puer adulescentior; et regnavit et imposuit sibi diadema. [55]Et congregati sunt ad eum omnes exercitus, quos disperserat Demetrius, et pugnaverunt contra eum, et fugit et terga vertit. [56]Et accepit Tryphon bestias et obtinuit Antiochiam. [57]Et scripsit Antiochus adulescentior Ionathae dicens: «Constituo tibi summum sacerdotium et constituo te super quattuor regiones et ut sis de amicis regis». [58]Et misit illi vasa aurea et ministerium et dedit ei potestatem bibendi in auro et esse in purpura et habere fibulam auream. [59]Et

n. Cn: Gk *the three districts and Samaria*

with all the region bordering them, were added to Judea from Samaria. To all those who offer sacrifice in Jerusalem, we have granted release from[o] the royal taxes which the king formerly received from them each year, from the crops of the land and the fruit of the trees. [35]And the other payments henceforth due to us of the tithes, and the taxes due to us, and the salt pits and the crown taxes due to us—from all these we shall grant them release. [36]And not one of these grants shall be canceled from this time forth for ever. [37]Now therefore take care to make a copy of this, and let it be given to Jonathan and put up in a conspicuous place on the holy mountain.'"

1 Mac 10:29

The Jews come to the aid of Demetrius

[38]Now when Demetrius the king saw that the land was quiet before him and that there was no opposition to him, he dismissed all his troops, each man to his own place, except the foreign troops which he had recruited from the islands of the nations. So all the troops who had served his fathers hated him. [39]Now Trypho had formerly been one of Alexander's supporters. He saw that all the troops were murmuring against Demetrius. So he went to Imalkue the Arab, who was bringing up Antiochus, the young son of Alexander, [40]and insistently urged him to hand Antiochus[p] over to him, to become king in place of his father. He also reported to Imalkue[p] what Demetrius had done and told of the hatred which the troops of Demetrius[p] had for him; and he stayed there many days.

[41]Now Jonathan sent to Demetrius the king the request that he remove the troops of the citadel from Jerusalem, and the troops in the strongholds; for they kept fighting against Israel. [42]And Demetrius sent this message to Jonathan, "Not only will I do these things for you and your nation, but I will confer great honour on

---

11:38–54. As regards Jonathan's relations with Demetrius, the sacred writer keeps stressing Jonathan's determination to get hold of the citadel (v. 41) and at the same time his loyalty to Demetrius (whom he even helps to keep the throne). The episode is an opportunity to underline the courage of the Jewish soldiers, though they were evidently quite brutal (vv. 47–50). But Demetrius did not reciprocate Jonathan's loyalty (v. 53)—which justifies Jonathan's change of allegiance, which we shall now see.

Simonem fratrem eius constituit ducem a descensu Tyri usque ad fines Aegypti. [60]Et exiit Ionathas et perambulabat trans flumen et in civitatibus, et congregatus est ad eum omnis exercitus Syriae in auxilium; et venit Ascalonem, et occurrerunt ei honorifice de civitate. [61]Et abiit inde Gazam, et

o. Or *Samaria, for all those who offer sacrifice in Jerusalem, in place of* **p.** Gk *him*

you and your nation, if I find an opportunity. [43]Now then you will do well to send me men who will help me, for all my troops have revolted." [44]So Jonathan sent three thousand stalwart men to him at Antioch, and when they came to the king, the king rejoiced at their arrival.

[45]Then the men of the city assembled within the city, to the number of a hundred and twenty thousand, and they wanted to kill the king. [46]But the king fled into the palace. Then the men of the city seized the main streets of the city and began to fight. [47]So the king called the Jews to his aid, and they all rallied about him and then spread out through the city; and they killed on that day as many as a hundred thousand men. [48]They set fire to the city and seized much spoil on that day, and they saved the king. [49]When the men of the city saw that the Jews had gained control of the city as they pleased, their courage failed and they cried out to the king with this entreaty, [50]"Grant us peace, and make the Jews stop fighting against us and our city." [51]And they threw down their arms and made peace. So the Jews gained glory in the eyes of the king and of all the people in his kingdom, and they returned to Jerusalem with much spoil.

[52]So Demetrius the king sat on the throne of his kingdom, and the land was quiet before him. [53]But he broke his word about all that he had promised; and he became estranged from Jonathan and did not repay the favours which Jonathan[q] had done him, but oppressed him greatly.

Jonathan takes the side of Antiochus, the son of Alexander. Wars against Demetrius II

[54]After this Trypho returned, and with him the young boy Antiochus who began to reign and put on the crown. [55]All the troops that

---

11:54–74. According to the Roman historian Titus Livy, Antiochus VI was six years old when Trypho took advantage of Demetrius' military weakness to proclaim him king. Jonathan does not hesitate to align himself with the new king, for the latter (or rather his regent) offers not only to confirm concessions already granted but also to appoint Simon the military governor of the

concluserunt, qui erant Gazae; et obsedit eam et succendit, quae erant in circuitu civitatis, et praedatus est ea. [62]Et rogaverunt Gazenses Ionathan, et dedit illis dexteram et accepit filios principum eorum obsides et misit illos in Ierusalem; et perambulavit regionem usque Damascum. [63]Et audivit Ionathas quod aderant principes Demetrii in Cades, quae est in Galilaea, cum exercitu multo volentes eum removere a negotio; [64]et occurrit illis, fratrem autem suum Simonem reliquit in regione. [65]Et applicuit Simon ad Bethsuram et expugnabat eam diebus multis et conclusit eos. [66]Et postulaverunt ab eo dextras accipere, et dedit illis; et eiecit eos inde et cepit civitatem et posuit in ea praesidium. [67]Et Ionathas et

q. Gk *he*

Demetrius had cast off gathered around him, and they fought against Demetrius,[r] and he fled and was routed. [56]And Trypho captured the elephant[s] and gained control of Antioch. [57]Then the young Antiochus wrote to Jonathan, saying, "I confirm you in the high priesthood and set you over the four districts and make you one of the friends of the king." [58]And he sent him gold plate and a table service, and granted him the right to drink from gold cups and dress in purple and wear a gold buckle. [59]Simon his brother he made governor from the Ladder of Tyre to the borders of Egypt.

1 Mac 2:18

[60]Then Jonathan set forth and travelled beyond the river and among the cities, and all the army of Syria gathered to him as allies. When he came to Askalon, the people of the city met him and paid him honour. [61]From there he departed to Gaza, but the men of Gaza shut him out. So he beseiged it and burned its suburbs with fire and plundered them. [62]Then the people of Gaza pleaded with Jonathan, and he made peace with them, and took the sons of their rulers as hostages and sent them to Jerusalem. And he passed through the country as far as Damascus.

[63]Then Jonathan heard that the officers of Demetrius had come to Kadesh in Galilee with a large army, intending to remove him from office. [64]He went to meet them, but left his brother Simon in the country. [65]Simon encamped before Beth-zur and fought against it for many days and hemmed it in. [66]Then they asked him to grant them terms of peace, and he did so. He removed them from there, took possession of the city, and set a garrison over it.

[67]Jonathan and his army encamped by the waters of Gennesaret. Early in the morning they marched to the plain of Hazor, [68]and

---

whole coastal strip, from the border with Egypt in the south to the very north of Palestine, the Ladder of Tyre, a peak accessed by steps in the rock, situated 15 km. (9 miles) south of Tyre (v. 59). This means that the Maccabees take over military control of the region from the Gentiles. Although Simon is the military governor (an appointment that may indicate that Trypho was trying to prevent power being concentrated in Jonathan's hands), Jonathan is the one who takes the initiative and leads the bulk of the army into the areas furthest from Jerusalem, while Simon stays back at Beth-zur (v. 61). Jonathan gets as far as the plains that lie between the Lake of Gennesaret and Lake Hule (near Hazor: v. 67). There he meets difficulties, but prayer and valour win him victory (vv. 71–72). This is the first and only time that 1 Maccabees mentions Jonathan praying. He is a Maccabee distinguished not by his piety but by his skill as a negotiator and his valour in battle.

r. Gk *him* **s.** Gk *beasts*

behold, the army of the foreigners met him in the plain; they had set an ambush against him in the mountains, but they themselves met him face to face. [69]Then the men in ambush emerged from their places and joined battle. [70]All the men with Jonathan fled; not one of them was left except Mattathias the son of Absalom and Judas the son of Chalphi, commanders of the forces of the army. [71]Jonathan rent his garments and put dust on his head, and prayed. [72]Then he turned back to the battle against the enemy[t] and routed them, and they fled. [73]When his men who were fleeing saw this, they returned to him and joined him in the pursuit as far as Kadesh, to their camp, and there they encamped.

[74]As many as three thousand of the foreigners fell that day. And Jonathan returned to Jerusalem.

Jonathan's alliances with Rome and Sparta

1 Mac 8:17–32

12 [1]Now when Jonathan saw that the time was favourable for him, he chose men and sent them to Rome to confirm and renew the friendship with them. [2]He also sent letters to the same effect to the Spartans and to other places. [3]So they went to Rome and entered the senate chamber and said, "Jonathan the high priest

12:1–23. On the treaty with the Romans, see 8:1–32. The treaty with Sparta is mentioned to show Jonathan as the head of a state with international prestige. The agreement with Sparta would have been a treaty of mutual aid (the background to it, on Sparta's side, being the old enmity between Sparta and Athens). Sparta might have been seen as a symbol of resistance to Greek expansionism (the Maccabees' old enemy). The reference to the letter from Arius to Onias I (vv. 7–8) and the content of that letter (vv. 20–23) looks rather like a diplomatic invention on the part of Jonathan or the writer of 1 Maccabees. It is extremely unlikely that around 300 BC (the time of Onias I) and inspired by their racial affinity (vv. 20–21), the Spartans would have taken any interest in Judea, which was then under the dominion of the Lagid kings of Egypt. However,

castra eius applicuerunt ad aquam Gennesar et ante lucem vigilaverunt in campo Asor. [68]Et ecce castra alienigenarum occurrebant ei in campo et tendebant ei insidias in montibus; ipsi autem occurrerunt ex adverso. [69]Insidiae vero exsurrexerunt de locis suis et commiserunt proelium. [70]Et fugerunt, qui erant ex parte Ionathae omnes, et nemo relictus est ex eis, nisi Matthathias filius Absalomi et Iudas filius Chalphi princeps militiae exercitus. [71]Et scidit Ionathas vestimenta sua et posuit terram in capite suo et oravit. [72]Et reversus est ad eos in proelium et convertit eos in fugam; et fugerunt. [73]Et viderunt, qui fugiebant partis illius, et reversi sunt ad eum et insequebantur cum eo usque Cades, usque ad castra ipsorum, et applicuerunt illic. [74]Et ceciderunt de alienigenis in die illa tria milia virorum; et reversus est Ionathas in Ierusalem. **[12]** [1]Et vidit Ionathas quia tempus eum adiuvat; et elegit viros et misit Romam statuere et renovare cum eis amicitiam; [2]et ad Spartiatas et ad alia loca misit epistulas secundum eadem.

t. Gk *them*

and the Jewish nation have sent us to renew the former friendship and alliance with them." [4]And the Romans[u] gave them letters to the people in every place, asking them to provide for the envoys[v] safe conduct to the land of Judah.

[5]This is a copy of the letter which Jonathan wrote to the Spartans: [6]"Jonathan the high priest, the senate of the nation, the priests, and the rest of the Jewish people to their brethren the Spartans, greeting. [7]Already in time past a letter was sent to Onias the high priest from Arius,[w] who was king among you, stating that you are our brethren, as the appended copy shows. [8]Onias welcomed the envoy with honour, and received the letter, which contained a clear declaration of alliance and friendship. [9]Therefore, though we have no need of these things, since we have as encouragement the holy books which are in our hands, [10]we have undertaken to send to

1 Mac 12:20–23
2 Mac 5:9

Rom 15:4

Jonathan's letter to the Spartans does serve to identify where Israel's true strength comes from—the holy books (v. 9) and help from heaven (v. 15). The text does not say what these holy books were, but in the light of 3:48; 2 Maccabees 2:13–14; 8:23 we can take it the books of the Law and the Prophets were regarded as being sacred.

In the letter to the Spartans (irrespective of whether it is fact or fiction) there is an intention which, albeit unclear and in this context unfounded, points to a wonderful state of affairs which will exist later on, when God implements his promises through Jesus Christ. In that economy, not only the Spartans but people of all nations will become children of Abraham through faith in Jesus: "So you see that it is men of faith who are the sons of Abraham. And the scripture, foreseeing that God could justify the Gentiles by faith, preached the gospel beforehand to Abraham, saying, 'In you shall all the nations be blessed.' So then, those who are men of faith are blessed with Abraham who had faith" (Gal 3:7–9; cf. Rom 4:18–25).

[3]Et abierunt Romam et intraverunt curiam et dixerunt: «Ionathas summus sacerdos et gens Iudaeorum miserunt nos renovare amicitiam et societatem secundum pristinum». [4]Et dederunt illis epistulas ad ipsos per loca, ut deducerent eos in terram Iudae cum pace. [5]Et hoc est exemplum epistularum, quas scripsit Ionathas Spartiatis: [6]«Ionathas summus sacerdos et seniores gentis et sacerdotes et reliquus populus Iudaeorum Spartiatis fratribus salutem. [7]Iampridem missae erant epistulae ad Oniam summum sacerdotem ab Ario, qui regnabat apud vos, quoniam estis fratres nostri, sicut rescriptum continet, quod subiectum est. [8]Et suscepit Onias virum, qui missus fuerat, cum honore; et accepit epistulas, in quibus significabatur de societate et amicitia. [9]Nos igitur, cum nullo horum indigeremus, exhortationem habentes sanctos libros, qui sunt in manibus nostris, [10]tentavimus mittere ad vos renovare fraternitatem et amicitiam, ne forte alieni efficiamur a vobis; multa enim tempora transierunt, ex quo misistis ad nos. [11]Nos ergo in omni tempore sine intermissione in diebus sollemnibus et ceteris, quibus oportet, memores sumus vestri in sacrificiis, quae offerimus, et in obsecrationibus, sicut fas est et decet meminisse fratrum. [12]Laetamur itaque de gloria vestra. [13]Nos autem circumdederunt multae tribulationes et multa proelia; et impugnaverunt nos reges, qui sunt in circuitu nostro. [14]Noluimus ergo

u. Gk *they* **v.** Gk *them* **w.** Vg Compare verse 20: Gk *Darius*

renew our brotherhood and friendship with you, so that we may not become estranged from you, for considerable time has passed since you sent your letter to us. [11]We therefore remember you constantly on every occasion, both in our feasts and on other appropriate days, at the sacrifices which we offer and in our prayers, as it is right and proper to remember brethren. [12]And we rejoice in your glory. [13]But as for ourselves, many afflictions and many wars have encircled us; the kings round about us have waged war against us. [14]We were unwilling to annoy you and our other allies and friends with these wars, [15]for we have the help which comes from Heaven for our aid; and we were delivered from our enemies and our enemies were humbled. [16]We therefore have chosen Numenius the son of Antiochus and Antipater the son of Jason, and have sent them to Rome to renew our former friendship and alliance with them. [17]We have commanded them to go also to you and greet you and deliver to you this letter from us concerning

1 Mac 14:22; 15:15

---

vobis molesti esse et ceteris sociis et amicis nostris in his proeliis; [15]habemus enim de caelo auxilium, quod nos adiuvat, et liberati sumus nos ab inimicis nostris, et humiliati sunt inimici nostri. [16]Elegimus itaque Numenium Antiochi filium et Antipatrem Iasonis filium et misimus ad Romanos renovare cum eis amicitiam et societatem pristinam; [17]mandavimus itaque eis, ut veniant etiam ad vos et salutent vos et reddant vobis epistulas nostras de innovatione et fraternitate nostra. [18]Et nunc bene facietis respondentes nobis ad haec». [19]Et hoc est rescriptum epistularum, quas miserunt Oniae: [20]«Arius rex Spartiatarum Oniae sacerdoti magno salutem. [21]Inventum est in scriptura de Spartiatis et Iudaeis quoniam sunt fratres et quod sunt de genere Abraham. [22]Et nunc, ex quo haec cognovimus, bene facietis scribentes nobis de pace vestra. [23]Sed et nos rescribimus vobis. Pecora vestra et possessiones vestrae nostrae sunt, et quae nostra vestra sunt. Mandamus itaque, ut annuntient vobis secundum haec». [24]Et audivit Ionathas quoniam regressi sunt principes Demetrii cum exercitu multo supra quam prius pugnare adversus eum. [25]Et exiit ab Ierusalem et occurrit eis in Amathitem regionem; non enim dedit eis spatium, ut ingrederentur regionem eius. [26]Et misit speculatores in castra eorum, et reversi renuntiaverunt ei quod ita constituunt supervenire illis nocte. [27]Cum occidisset autem sol, praecepit Ionathas suis vigilare et esse in armis paratos ad pugnam tota nocte; et emisit custodes per circuitum castrorum. [28]Et audierunt adversarii quod paratus est Ionathas cum suis in bellum, et timuerunt et formidaverunt in corde suo et accenderunt focos in castris suis. [29]Ionathas autem et, qui cum eo erant, non cognoverunt usque mane; videbant enim luminaria ardentia. [30]Et insecutus est eos Ionathas et non comprehendit eos; transierant enim flumen Eleutherum. [31]Et divertit Ionathas ad Arabas, qui vocantur Zabadaei, et percussit eos et accepit spolia eorum. [32]Et iunxit et venit Damascum et perambulabat omnem regionem illam. [33]Simon autem exiit et venit usque ad Ascalonem et ad proxima praesidia et declinavit in Ioppen et occupavit eam; [34]audivit enim quod vellent praesidium tradere partibus Demetrii, et posuit ibi custodes, ut custodirent eam. [35]Et reversus est Ionathas et convocavit seniores populi et cogitavit cum eis aedificare praesidia in Iudaea [36]et altius extollere muros Ierusalem et exaltare altitudinem magnam inter medium arcis et civitatis, ut separaret eam a civitate, ut esset ipsa singulariter, ut neque emant neque vendant. [37]Et convenerunt, ut aedificarent civitatem; et cecidit de muro, qui erat super torrentem a subsolano, et reparavit eum, qui vocatur Chaphenatha. [38]Et Simon aedificavit Adida in Sephela et munivit eam et imposuit portas et seras. [39]Et quaesivit Tryphon regnare Asiae et imponere sibi diadema et extendere manum in Antiochum regem. [40]Et veritus est, ne forte non permitteret eum Ionathas et ne forte pugnaret adversus eum, et quaerebat comprehendere eum et occidere et exsurgens abiit in Bethsan. [41]Et exivit Ionathas obviam illi cum quadraginta milibus virorum electorum in proelium et venit Bethsan. [42]Et vidit Tryphon quia venit cum exercitu multo et extendere in eum manus timuit [43]et excepit eum cum honore et commendavit eum omnibus amicis suis et dedit ei munera et praecepit exercitibus suis, ut oboedirent ei sicut sibi. [44]Et dixit Ionathae: «Ut quid vexasti universum

the renewal of our brotherhood. [18]And now please send us a reply to this."

[19]This is a copy of the letter which they sent to Onias: [20]"Arius, king of the Spartans, to Onias the high priest, greeting. [21]It has been found in writing concerning the Spartans and the Jews that they are brethren and are of the family of Abraham. [22]And now that we have learned this, please write us concerning your welfare; [23]that your cattle and your property belong to us, and ours belong to you. We therefore command that our envoys[x] report to you accordingly."

Jonathan and Simon, successful generals. Rebuilding at Jerusalem

[24]Now Jonathan heard that the commanders of Demetrius had returned, with a larger force than before, to wage war against him.

[25]So he marched away from Jerusalem and met them in the region of Hamath, for he gave them no opportunity to invade his own country. [26]He sent spies to their camp, and they returned and reported to him that the enemy[y] were being drawn up in formation to fall upon the Jews[z] by night. [27]So when the sun set, Jonathan commanded his men to be alert and to keep their arms at hand so as to be ready all night for battle, and he stationed outposts around the camp. [28]When the enemy heard that Jonathan and his men were prepared for battle, they were afraid and were terrified at heart; so they kindled fires in their camp and withdrew.[a] [29]But Jonathan and his men did not know it until morning, for they saw the fires burning. [30]Then Jonathan pursued them, but he did not overtake them, for they had crossed the Eleutherus river. [31]So Jonathan turned aside against the Arabs who are called Zabadeans, and he crushed them and plundered them. [32]Then he broke camp and went to Damascus, and marched through all that region.

12:24–38. Here we see Jonathan and Simon in their capacities as military chiefs—Jonathan in the northern regions from his base at Hamath (a border city to the north of Canaan) operating towards Damascus; and Simon on the Mediterranean coast. Thus, they are advancing the interests not only of Antiochus VI against Demetrius, but also of the Jews, because their campaigns help secure Judea and the annexed districts. They are able to rebuild and fortify Adida (v. 38), which lay 6 km. (4 miles) to the north-east of Lud, from which they

populum, cum bellum nobis non sit? [45]Et nunc remitte eos in domos suas. Elige autem tibi viros paucos, qui tecum sint, et veni mecum Ptolemaidam, et tradam eam tibi et reliqua praesidia et reliquum exercitum et universos praepositos negotiis et conversus abibo; propterea enim veni». [46]Et credidit ei et fecit, sicut dixit, et dimisit exercitum, et abierunt in terram Iudae. [47]Retinuit autem secum tria milia

x. Gk *they* **y.** Gk *they* **z.** Gk *them* **a.** Other ancient authorities omit *and withdrew*

[33]Simon also went forth and marched through the country as far as Askalon and the neighbouring strongholds. He turned aside to Joppa and took it by surprise, [34]for he had heard that they were ready to hand over the stronghold to the men whom Demetrius had sent. And he stationed a garrison there to guard it.

[35]When Jonathan returned he convened the elders of the people and planned with them to build strongholds in Judea, [36]to build the walls of Jerusalem still higher, and to erect a high barrier between the citadel and the city to separate it from the city, in order to isolate it so that its garrison[b] could neither buy nor sell. [37]So they gathered together to build up the city; part of the wall on the valley to the east had fallen, and he repaired the section called Chaphenatha. [38]And Simon built Adida in the Shephelah; he fortified it and installed gates with bolts.

Trypho takes Jonathan prisoner

1 Mac 11:39ff, 54ff

[39]Then Trypho attempted to become king in Asia and put on the crown, and to raise his hand against Antiochus the king. [40]He feared that Jonathan might not permit him to do so, but might make war on him, so he kept seeking to seize and kill him, and he marched forth and came to Beth-shan. [41]Jonathan went out to meet him with forty thousand picked fighting men, and he came to Beth-shan. [42]When Trypho saw that he had come with a large army, he was afraid to raise his hand against him. [43]So he received him with honour and commended him to all his friends, and he gave him gifts and commanded his friends and his troops to obey him as they would himself. [44]Then he said to Jonathan, "Why have you wearied all these people when we are not at war? [45]Dismiss

---

could dominate the coastal plain (the Shephelah) occupied by the Philistines.

The military strength developed by the Maccabees did not allow them to take over the citadel at Jerusalem (which would have been tantamount to a declaration of war against the king) but it did isolate the citadel and enable them to build up the city, some of its quarters (Chaphenatha), and its walls.

12:39–53. Trypho suspected that Jonathan, who was going from strength to strength, was unlikely to approve of his betrayal of the king and usurpation of the throne. In fact he was wrong,

virorum, ex quibus remisit in Galilaeam duo milia; mille autem venerunt cum eo. [48]Ut autem intravit Ptolemaidam Ionathas, clauserunt portas Ptolemenses et comprehenderunt eum et omnes, qui cum eo intraverant, gladio interfecerunt. [49]Et misit Tryphon exercitum et equites in Galilaeam et in campum magnum, ut perderent omnes socios Ionathae. [50]At illi, cum cognovissent quia comprehensus est

b. Gk *they*

them now to their homes and choose for yourself a few men to stay with you, and come with me to Ptolemais. I will hand it over to you as well as the other strongholds and the remaining troops and all the officials, and will turn round and go home. For that is why I am here."

46Jonathan[c] trusted him and did as he said; he sent away the troops, and they returned to the land of Judah. 47He kept with himself three thousand men, two thousand of whom he left in Galilee, while a thousand accompanied him. 48But when Jonathan entered Ptolemais, the men of Ptolemais closed the gates and seized him, and all who had entered with him they killed with the sword.

49Then Trypho sent troops and cavalry into Galilee and the Great Plain to destroy all Jonathan's soldiers. 50But they realized that Jonathan[c] had been seized and had perished along with his men, and they encouraged one another and kept marching in close formation, ready for battle. 51When their pursuers saw that they would fight for their lives, they turned back. 52So they all reached the land of Judah safely, and they mourned for Jonathan and his companions and were in great fear; and all Israel mourned deeply.

53And all the nations round about them tried to destroy them, for they said, "They have no leader or helper. Now therefore let us make war on them and blot out the memory of them from among men."

---

because all that interested the Maccabee was Judea, and not the internal affairs of the court at Antioch. Therefore, after a stand-off at Beth-shan, on the plain of Esdraelon (vv. 40–41), Jonathan has no qualms about going with quite a small escort to Ptolemais, trusting in Trypho's promise to hand the city over to him (vv. 45–47). But he is being naïve, because Trypho has not changed, and the meeting with Trypho proves to be an appointment with death. All the work done by the Maccabees as military chiefs has backfired (v. 53).

Ionathas et periit, et omnes, qui cum eo erant, hortati sunt semetipsos et ibant conglobati parati in proelium. 51Et videntes hi, qui insecuti fuerant, quia pro anima res est illis, reversi sunt; 52illi autem venerunt omnes cum pace in terram Iudae et planxerunt Ionathan et eos, qui cum ipso fuerant, et timuerunt valde; et luxit Israel luctu magno. 53Et quaesierunt omnes gentes, quae erant in circuitu eorum, conterere eos; dixerunt enim: 54«Non habent principem et adiuvantem; nunc ergo expugnemus illos et tollamus de hominibus memoriam eorum». **[13]** 1Et audivit Simon quod congregavit Tryphon exercitum copiosum, ut veniret in terram Iudae et attereret eam. 2Videns quia in tremore populus est et in timore, ascendit Ierusalem et congregavit populum 3et exhortatus est eos et dixit illis: «Vos scitis quanta ego et fratres mei et domus patris mei fecimus pro legibus et pro sanctis proelia et angustias quales vidimus. 4Horum gratia perierunt fratres mei omnes propter Israel, et relictus sum ego solus. 5Et nunc non mihi contingat parcere animae meae in omni tempore tribulationis; non enim melior sum fratribus meis. 6Vindicabo tamen gentem meam et sancta, uxores quoque et natos vestros, quia congregatae sunt universae gentes conterere nos inimicitiae gratia». 7Et accensus est spiritus populi, simul ut audivit sermones istos, 8et responderunt voce magna dicentes: «Tu es dux noster loco Iudae et

c. Gk *he*

5. SIMON. JUDEA BECOMES POLITICALLY INDEPENDENT*

The people appoint Simon their leader

Heb 12:21

13 [1]Simon heard that Trypho had assembled a large army to invade the land of Judah and destroy it, [2]and he saw that the people were trembling and fearful. So he went up to Jerusalem, and gathering the people together [3]he encouraged them, saying to them, "You yourselves know what great things I and my brothers and the house of my father have done for the laws and the sanctuary; you know also the wars and the difficulties which we have seen. [4]By reason of this all my brothers have perished for the sake of Israel, and I alone am left. [5]And now, far be it from me to spare my life in any time of distress, for I am not better than my brothers. [6]But I will avenge my nation and the sanctuary and your wives and children, for all the nations have gathered together out of hatred to destroy us."

1 Mac 5:2; 12:53

***13:1—16:24.** The period of Simon's leadership is that in which Judea achieves full political independence as a nation. Judas Maccabeus and his brother Jonathan had laid the groundwork for this—Judas by getting religious autonomy, and Jonathan consolidating that gain by obtaining a high degree of autonomy in political and military terms. But Judea continued to be part of the Syrian empire, and the citadel at Jerusalem was still garrisoned by Syrians. The situation will change under Simon Maccabeus.

Simon begins by gathering the people together and asking them to choose him as their leader (13:1–11); with this mandate he prepares to join battle with Trypho, who launches an attack on Judea and puts Jonathan, his captive, to death (13:12–30). Simon then makes approaches to Demetrius (who was in control of some parts of the empire) and is granted complete political independence. He then takes control of Gazara (Gaza)—which gives him access to the sea, and he manages to take over the citadel in Jerusalem (13:31–53). All these achievements merit the glowing tribute paid him by the author of 1 Maccabees (14:4–15). Simon also renews the treaties with Rome and Sparta (16:16–24), and the people record their appreciation of their leader in a lengthy commemorative inscription cast in bronze (14:25–49). For his part, Antiochus VII, the son of Demetrius II, prior to his confrontation with Trypho, confirms Judea's independence and authorizes Simon to mint his own coinage (15:1–24). Meanwhile letters come from Rome recognizing the Jewish nation (15:15–24), but at this point Antiochus feels that the Jews have become too independent and, despite conciliatory overtures from Simon, he decides to invade Judea (15:25–41). This time it is John Hyrcanus, Simon's son, who halts the Syrians' advance (16:1–10). But a conspiracy by one of

[7]The spirit of the people was rekindled when they heard these words, [8]and they answered in a loud voice, “You are our leader in place of Judas and Jonathan your brother. [9]Fight our battles, and all that you say to us we will do.” [10]So he assembled all the warriors and hastened to complete the walls of Jerusalem, and he fortified it on every side. [11]He sent Jonathan the son of Absalom to Joppa, and with him a considerable army; he drove out its occupants and remained there.

Trypho’s threat. Death and burial of Jonathan
[12]Then Trypho departed from Ptolemais with a large army to invade the land of Judah, and Jonathan was with him under guard.
[13]And Simon encamped in Adida, facing the plain. [14]Trypho learned that Simon had risen up in place of Jonathan his brother, and that he was about to join battle with him, so he sent envoys to

---

Simon’s subordinates, Ptolemy, son of Abubus, leads to the assassination of Simon and his sons Mattathias and Judas (16:11–17). John Hyrcanus, however, manages to escape Ptolemy’s net, and he ends up as the new leader of the Jews (16:18–24).

This brings to a close the history of the Maccabees, the sons of Mattathias. Their successors, from John Hyrcanus onwards, are known as the Hasmoneans; what we know about them comes from extra-biblical sources.

13:1–11. Not everyone in Jerusalem may have seen eye-to-eye with Jonathan and Simon’s military enterprises in the service of Syria, or the consequences they would have for the Jews. Therefore Simon reminds them of the sacrifices that have been made (even at the cost of life itself) to defend the Law and the temple, and he shows his determination to follow the course set by his father and brothers. However, his first action is to conquer Joppa, a strategic maritime city (v. 11).

13:12–30. Simon knows how base and treacherous Trypho is, but he agrees to his proposal about ransoming Jonathan, because he does not want to disaffect the people (v. 18). Trypho advances south towards Judea (Adora is 10 km. or 6 miles west of Hebron), and Simon engages in guerrilla warfare again (v. 20). It was the winter of 143 BC, and the snow (not unusual in the Jerusalem area) forces Trypho to retreat—leaving the corpse of Jonathan behind (v. 23). A

Ionathae fratris tui; [9]pugna proelium nostrum, et omnia, quaecumque dixeris nobis, faciemus». [10]Et congregans omnes viros bellatores acceleravit consummare universos muros Ierusalem et munivit eam in gyro. [11]Et misit Ionathan filium Absalomi et cum eo exercitum magnum in Ioppen et, eiectis his, qui erant in ea, remansit illic in ea. [12]Et movit Tryphon a Ptolemaida cum exercitu multo, ut veniret in terram Iudae, et Ionathas cum eo in custodia. [13]Simon autem applicuit in Adidis contra faciem campi. [14]Et ut cognovit Tryphon quia surrexit Simon loco fratris sui Ionathae et quia commissurus esset cum eo proelium, misit ad eum legatos [15]dicens: «Pro argento, quod debebat frater tuus Ionathas fisco regis propter negotia, quae habuit, detinuimus eum; [16]et nunc mitte argenti talenta centum et duos filios eius

him and said, [15]"It is for the money that Jonathan your brother owed the royal treasury, in connection with the offices he held, that we are detaining him. [16]Send now a hundred talents of silver and two of his sons as hostages, so that when released he will not revolt against us, and we will release him."

[17]Simon knew that they were speaking deceitfully to him, but he sent to get the money and the sons, lest he arouse great hostility among the people, who might say, [18]"Because Simon[d] did not send him the money and the sons, he perished." [19]So he sent the sons and the hundred talents, but Trypho[e] broke his word and did not release Jonathan.

[20]After this Trypho came to invade the country and destroy it, and he circled around by the way to Adora. But Simon and his army kept marching along opposite him to every place he went. [21]Now the men in the citadel kept sending envoys to Trypho urging him to come to them by way of the wilderness and to send them

---

family mausoleum of the Maccabees is now built in the Egyptian style at Mode-in (vv. 28–29).

13:31–53. The author of 1 Maccabees condenses events connected with Syria in v. 31, without giving all the facts or paying much attention to chronology. Trypho, in fact, has been operating as king since his return from his invasion of Judea in 142 BC, and he will continue to rule up to 138 BC. But in 139 BC, when Trypho put Antiochus VII to death, Demetrius II (who was probably in control of a part of Syria, and who still hoped to gain the throne), on receiving Simon's appeal, takes it as a sign that he acknowledges neither Trypho nor Antiochus. Maybe for this reason, and not only because of his own weak position, Demetrius makes many concessions to Simon. Specifically, he exempts him from all tribute, which is equivalent to granting Judea full political independence—freeing her from the Gentile yoke; it was the year 142 BC (vv. 41–42; cf. v. 39). Simon takes advantage of the situation to conquer Gazara (Gaza), on the Mediterranean coast, and, at long last, to unseat the Syrians from the citadel, a constant thorn in the side of the Jews at Jerusalem (cf. 1:35–36): the evacuation of the Syrians is celebrated with jubilation and an annual feast is established; it is the fourth of June, 141 BC.

obsides, ut non dimissus fugiat a nobis, et remittemus eum». [17]Et cognovit Simon quia cum dolo loquuntur secum; misit tamen accipere argentum et pueros, ne inimicitiam magnam sumeret ad populum, [18]qui dicerent: «Quia non misit ei argentum et pueros, periit». [19]Et misit pueros et centum talenta. Et mentitus est et non dimisit Ionathan; [20]et post haec venit Tryphon intrare in regionem, ut contereret eam, et gyraverunt per viam, quae ducit Adoram. Et Simon et castra eius ambulabant in omnem locum, quocumque ibant. [21]Qui autem in arce erant, miserunt ad Tryphonem legatos urgentes eum, ut veniret ad eos per desertum et mitteret illis alimonias. [22]Et paravit Tryphon omnem equitatum suum, ut veniret; et in illa nocte fuit nix multa valde, et non venit propter nivem et discessit et abiit in

d. Gk *I* **e.** Gk *he*

food. [22]So Trypho got all his cavalry ready to go, but that night a very heavy snow fell, and he did not go because of the snow. He marched off and went into the land of Gilead. [23]When he approached Baskama, he killed Jonathan, and he was buried there. [24]Then Trypho turned back and departed to his own land.

[25]And Simon sent and took the bones of Jonathan his brother, and buried him in Modein, the city of his fathers. [26]All Israel bewailed him with great lamentation, and mourned for him many days. [27]And Simon built a monument over the tomb of his father and his brothers; he made it high that it might be seen, with polished stone at the front and back. [28]He also erected seven pyramids, opposite one another, for his father and mother and four brothers. [29]And for the pyramids[f] he devised an elaborate setting, erecting about them great columns, and upon the columns he put suits of armour for a permanent memorial, and beside the suits of armour carved ships, so that they could be seen by all who sail the sea. [30]This is the tomb which he built in Modein; it remains to this day.

1 Mac 2:70

1 Mac 12:39–40

Friendship renewed with Demetrius II. Gazara is captured, as is the citadel

[31]Trypho dealt treacherously with the young king Antiochus; he killed him [32]and became king in his place, putting on the crown of Asia; and he brought great calamity upon the land. [33]But Simon built up the strongholds of Judea and walled them all around, with high towers and great walls and gates and bolts, and he stored food in the strongholds. [34]Simon also chose men and sent them to Demetrius the king with a request to grant relief to the country, for all that Trypho did was to plunder. [35]Demetrius the king sent him a favourable reply to this request, and wrote him a letter as follows, [36]"King Demetrius to Simon, the high priest and friend of

1 Mac 12:52

Galaaditim. [23]Et cum appropinquasset Bascaman, occidit Ionathan, et sepultus est illic; [24]et convertit Tryphon et abiit in terram suam. [25]Et misit Simon et accepit ossa Ionathae fratris sui et sepelivit eum in Modin civitate patrum eius. [26]Et planxerunt eum omnis Israel planctu magno et luxerunt eum dies multos. [27]Et aedificavit Simon super sepulcrum patris sui et fratrum suorum et exaltavit illud visu, lapide polito retro et ante; [28]et statuit septem pyramidas, unam contra unam, patri et matri et quattuor fratribus. [29]Et his fecit machinamenta circumponens columnas magnas et super columnas arma ad memoriam aeternam et iuxta arma naves sculptas, quae viderentur ab omnibus navigantibus mare. [30]Hoc est sepulcrum, quod fecit in Modin, usque in hunc diem. [31]Tryphon autem iter faciebat dolo cum Antiocho rege adulescentiore et occidit eum [32]et regnavit loco eius et imposuit sibi diadema Asiae et fecit plagam magnam in terra. [33]Et aedificavit Simon praesidia Iudaeae muniens ea turribus excelsis et muris magnis et portis et seris; et posuit alimenta in munitionibus. [34]Et elegit Simon viros et misit ad Demetrium regem, ut faceret remissionem regioni, quia actus omnes Tryphonis fuerant rapinae. [35]Et Demetrius rex ad verba ista respondit ei et scripsit epistulam talem: [36]«Rex Demetrius Simoni summo sacerdoti et amico regum et senioribus et genti Iudaeorum salutem. [37]Coronam auream et baen, quam misistis,

f. Gk *for these*

kings, and to the elders and nation of the Jews, greeting. [37]We have received the gold crown and the palm branch which you[g] sent, and we are ready to make a general peace with you and to write to our officials to grant you release from tribute. [38]All the grants that we have made to you remain valid, and let the strongholds that you have built be your possession. [39]We pardon any errors and offences committed to this day, and cancel the crown tax which you owe; and whatever other tax has been collected in Jerusalem shall be collected no longer. [40]And if any of you are qualified to be enrolled in our bodyguard,[h] let them be enrolled, and let there be peace between us."

[41]In the one hundred and seventieth year[i] the yoke of the Gentiles was removed from Israel, [42]and the people began to write in their documents and contracts, "In the first year of Simon the great high priest and commander and leader of the Jews."

2 Mac 10:32–38

[43]In those days Simon[j] encamped against Gazara[k] and surrounded it with troops. He made a siege engine, brought it up to the city, and battered and captured one tower. [44]The men in the siege engine leaped out into the city, and a great tumult arose in the city. [45]The men in the city, with their wives and children, went up on the wall with their clothes rent, and they cried out with a loud voice, asking Simon to make peace with them; [46]they said, "Do not treat us according to our wicked acts but according to your mercy." [47]So Simon reached an agreement with them and stopped fighting against them. But he expelled them from the city and cleansed the

---

suscepimus; et parati sumus facere vobiscum pacem magnam et scribere praepositis regis remittere vobis, quae indulsimus. [38]Quaecumque enim constituimus vobis, constant; munitiones, quas aedificastis, vobis sint. [39]Remittimus quoque ignorantias et peccata usque in hodiernum diem et coronam, quam debebatis; et, si quid aliud erat tributarium in Ierusalem, iam non sit tributarium. [40]Et, si qui ex vobis apti sunt conscribi inter nostros, conscribantur, et sit inter nos pax». [41]Anno centesimo septuagesimo ablatum est iugum gentium ab Israel. [42]Et coepit populus Israel scribere in conscriptionibus et commutationibus: «Anno primo sub Simone summo sacerdote magno duce et principe Iudaeorum». [43]In diebus illis applicuit Simon ad Gazaram et circumdedit eam castris et fecit machinam et applicuit ad civitatem et percussit turrim unam et comprehendit. [44]Et eruperant, qui erant intra machinam, in civitatem; et factus est motus magnus in civitate. [45]Et ascenderunt, qui erant in civitate, cum uxoribus et filiis supra murum, scissis tunicis suis, et clamaverunt voce magna postulantes a Simone dextras sibi dari [46]et dixerunt: «Non nobis reddas secundum malitias nostras, sed secundum misericordiam tuam». [47]Et consensit illis Simon et non debellavit eos; eiecit tamen eos de civitate et mundavit aedes, in quibus fuerant simulacra, et tunc intravit in eam canens et benedicens. [48]Et, eiecta ab ea omni immunditia, collocavit in ea viros, qui legem facerent, et munivit eam et aedificavit sibi habitationem. [49]Qui autem erant in arce Ierusalem, prohibebantur egredi et ingredi regionem et emere ac vendere; et esurierunt valde, et multi ex eis fame perierunt. [50]Et clamaverunt ad Simonem, ut dextras acciperent, et dedit illis et eiecit eos inde et mundavit arcem a contaminationibus. [51]Et intraverunt in eam tertia et vicesima die secundi mensis, anno centesimo septuagesimo primo, cum laude et ramis palmarum et cinyris et cymbalis et nablis et hymnis et canticis, quia contritus est inimicus magnus ex Israel. [52]Et constituit, ut

g. The word *you* in verses 37–40 is plural **h.** Or *court* **i.** 142 BC **j.** Gk *he* **k.** Cn: Gk *Gaza*

houses in which the idols were, and then entered it with hymns and praise. [48]He cast out of it all uncleanness, and settled in it men who observed the law. He also strengthened its fortifications and built in it a house for himself.

[49]The men in the citadel at Jerusalem were prevented from going out to the country and back to buy and sell. So they were very hungry, and many of them perished from famine. [50]Then they cried to Simon to make peace with them, and he did so. But he expelled them from there and cleansed the citadel from its pollutions. [51]On the twenty-third day of the second month, in the one hundred and seventy-first year,[l] the Jews[m] entered it with praise and palm branches, and with harps and cymbals and stringed instruments, and with hymns and songs, because a great enemy had been crushed and removed from Israel. [52]And Simon[n] decreed that every year they should celebrate this day with rejoicing. He strengthened the fortifications of the temple hill alongside the citadel, and he and his men dwelt there. [53]And Simon saw that John his son had reached manhood, so he made him commander of all the forces, and he dwelt in Gazara.

Praise of Simon

14 [1]In the one hundred and seventy-second year[o] Demetrius the king assembled his forces and marched into Media to secure help, so that he could make war against Trypho. [2]When Arsaces the king of Persia and Media heard that Demetrius had invaded his

---

14:1–15. With Trypho taken up with affairs at court, and Demetrius the prisoner of the Persians, the Jews at last have peace—all thanks to Simon, whom the author of 1 Maccabees proceeds to eulogize. He celebrates the peace and joy that reign in the country, and the military feats of its leader; he also mentions the consideration shown by Simon to humble folk and the interest he has taken in the temple. Simon is portrayed as having the features of the ideal king.

omnibus annis agerentur dies hi cum laetitia. [53]Et munivit montem templi, qui erat secus arcem, et habitavit ibi ipse et qui cum eo erant. [54]Et vidit Simon Ioannem filium suum quod vir esset et posuit eum ducem virtutum universarum et habitavit in Gazaris. **[14]** [1]Anno centesimo septuagesimo secundo congregavit rex Demetrius exercitum suum et abiit in Mediam ad contrahenda sibi auxilia, ut expugnaret Tryphonem. [2]Et audivit Arsaces rex Persidis et Mediae, quia intravit Demetrius confines suos, et misit unum de principibus suis, ut comprehenderet eum vivum. [3]Et abiit et percussit castra Demetrii et comprehendit eum et duxit eum ad Arsacem et posuit eum in custodiam. [4]Et siluit terra Iudae omnibus diebus Simonis; / et quaesivit bona genti suae, / et placuit illis potestas eius, / et gloria eius omnibus diebus. / [5]Et cum omni gloria sua / accepit Ioppen in portum / et fecit introitum insulis maris. / [6]Et dilatavit fines gentis suae / et obtinuit regionem. / [7]Et congregavit captivitatem multam / et dominatus est Gazarae et Bethsurae et arci; / et abstulit immunditias ex ea, / et non erat qui resisteret ei. / [8]Et unusquisque colebat terram suam cum pace; / et terra dabat fructus suos, / et ligna camporum

l. 141 BC **m.** Gk *they* **n.** Gk *he* **o.** 140 BC

territory, he sent one of his commanders to take him alive. [3]And he went and defeated the army of Demetrius, and seized him and took him to Arsaces, who put him under guard.

1 Mac 3:3–9

[4]The land[p] had rest all the days of Simon.
He sought the good of his nation;
his rule was pleasing to them,
as was the honour shown him, all his days.
[5]To crown all his honours he took Joppa for a harbour,
and opened a way to the isles of the sea.

Ex 34:24

[6]He extended the borders of his nation,
and gained full control of the country.
[7]He gathered a host of captives;
he ruled over Gazara and Beth-zur and the citadel,
and he removed its uncleanness from it;
and there was none to oppose him.

Zech 8:12

[8]They tilled their land in peace;
the ground gave its increase,
and the trees of the plains their fruit.

Zech 8:4–5

[9]Old men sat in the streets;
they all talked together of good things;
and the youths donned the glories and garments of war.

---

fructum suum. / [9]Seniores in plateis sedebant, / omnes de bonis communiter tractabant, / et iuvenes induebant se gloriam / et stolas belli. / [10]Et civitatibus tribuebat alimonias / et constituebat eas, ut essent vasa munitionis, / quoadusque nominatum est nomen gloriae eius / usque ad extremum terrae. / [11]Fecit pacem super terram, / et laetatus est Israel laetitia magna. / [12]Et sedit unusquisque sub vite sua / et sub ficulnea sua, / et non erat qui eos terreret. / [13]Defecit impugnans eos super terram; / reges contriti sunt in diebus illis. / [14]Et confirmavit omnes humiles populi sui / et legem exquisivit et abstulit omnem iniquum et malum. / [15]Sancta glorificavit / et multiplicavit vasa sanctorum. [16]Et auditum est Romae quia defunctus esset Ionathas, et usque in Spartiatas, et contristati sunt valde. [17]Ut audierunt autem quod Simon frater eius factus esset summus sacerdos loco eius et ipse obtineret regionem et civitates in ea, [18]scripserunt ad eum in tabulis aereis, ut renovarent cum eo amicitias et societatem, quam fecerant cum Iuda et cum Ionatha fratribus eius; [19]et lectae sunt in conspectu ecclesiae in Ierusalem. Et hoc exemplum epistularum, quas Spartiatae miserunt: [20]«Spartianorum principes et civitas Simoni sacerdoti magno et senioribus et sacerdotibus et reliquo populo Iudaeorum fratribus salutem. [21]Legati, qui missi sunt ad populum nostrum, nuntiaverunt nobis de vestra gloria et honore, et gavisi sumus in introitu eorum [22]et scripsimus, quae ab eis erant dicta in conciliis populi sic: "Numenius Antiochi et Antipater Iasonis filius, legati Iudaeorum, venerunt ad nos renovantes nobiscum amicitiam". [23]Et placuit populo excipere viros gloriose et ponere exemplum sermonum eorum in segregatis populi libris, ut sit ad memoriam populo Spartiatarum. Exemplum autem horum scripsimus Simoni magno sacerdoti». [24]Post haec autem misit Simon Numenium Romam habentem clipeum aureum magnum pondo mnarum mille ad statuendam cum eis societatem. [25]Cum autem audisset populus sermones istos, dixerunt: «Quam gratiarum actionem reddemus Simoni et filiis eius? [26]Invaluit enim ipse et fratres eius et domus patris eius et expugnavit inimicos Israel ab eis; et statuerunt ei libertatem». Et descripserunt in tabulis aereis et posuerunt in titulis in monte Sion. [27]Et hoc est exemplum scripturae: «Octava decima die Elul, anno centesimo septuagesimo secundo, anno tertio sub Simone sacerdote magno, in Asaramel, [28]in conventu magno sacerdotum et populi et principum gentis et seniorum regionis nota facta sunt nobis haec:

p. Other authorities add *of Judah*

[10] He supplied the cities with food,
and furnished them with the means of defence,
till his renown spread to the ends of the earth.
[11] He established peace in the land,
and Israel rejoiced with great joy.
[12] Each man sat under his vine and his fig tree,
and there was none to make them afraid.
[13] No one was left in the land to fight them,
and the kings were crushed in those days.
[14] He strengthened all the humble of his people;
he sought out the law,
and did away with every lawless and wicked man.
[15] He made the sanctuary glorious,
and added to the vessels of the sanctuary.

1 Kings 5:5
Mic 4:4
Zech 3:10

Renewal of the alliances with Sparta and Rome

1 Mac 8:17–32; 12:1–38

[16]It was heard in Rome, and as far away as Sparta, that Jonathan had died, and they were deeply grieved. [17]When they heard that Simon his brother had become high priest in his place, and that he was ruling over the country and the cities in it, [18]they wrote to him on bronze tablets to renew with him the friendship and alliance

1 Mac 8:17,22; 12:3

14:16–24. The renewal of the treaties of friendship with Rome and Sparta is now presented as being their initiative on learning that Simon is the ruler of Judea. The Spartan letter is written as a reply to the letter reported in 12:6–18. The Roman letter will be transcribed later, in 15:15–21; but it is mentioned here in order to enhance the leading role played by Simon in the making of the treaty with Rome (vv. 16, 24).

[29]Quoniam frequenter facta sunt proelia in regione, Simon autem filius Matthathiae, filius ex filiis Ioarib, et fratres eius dederunt se periculo et restiterunt adversariis gentis suae, ut starent sancta ipsorum et lex; et gloria magna glorificaverunt gentem suam. [30]Et congregavit Ionathas gentem suam et factus est illis sacerdos magnus et appositus est ad populum suum. [31]Et voluerunt inimici eorum calcare et atterere regionem ipsorum et extendere manus in sancta eorum. [32]Tunc restitit Simon et pugnavit pro gente sua et erogavit pecunias multas et armavit viros virtutis gentis suae et dedit illis stipendia. [33]Et munivit civitates Iudaeae et Bethsuram, quae erat in finibus Iudaeae, ubi erant arma hostium antea, et posuit illic praesidium viros Iudaeos; [34]et Ioppen munivit, quae erat ad mare, et Gazaram, quae est in finibus Azoti, in qua hostes antea habitabant, et collocavit illic Iudaeos et, quaecumque apta erant ad correptionem eorum, posuit in eis. [35]Et vidit populus fidem Simonis et gloriam, quam cogitabat facere genti suae; et posuerunt eum ducem suum et principem sacerdotum, eo quod ipse fecerat haec omnia et iustitiam et fidem, quam conservavit genti suae, et exquisivit omni modo exaltare populum suum. [36]Et in diebus eius prosperatum est in manibus eius, ut tollerentur gentes de regione ipsorum et qui in civitate David erant in Ierusalem, qui fecerant sibi arcem, de qua procedebant et contaminabant omnia, quae in circuitu sanctorum sunt, et inferebant plagam magnam castitati; [37]et collocavit in ea viros Iudaeos et munivit eam ad tutamentum regionis et civitatis et exaltavit muros Ierusalem. [38]Et rex Demetrius statuit illi summum sacerdotium secundum haec [39]et fecit eum amicum suum et glorificavit eum gloria magna. [40]Audivit enim quod appellati sunt Iudaei a Romanis amici et socii et fratres, et quia susceperunt legatos

which they had established with Judas and Jonathan his brothers. [19]And these were read before the assembly in Jerusalem.

[20]This is a copy of the letter which the Spartans sent: "The rulers and the city of the Spartans to Simon the high priest and to the elders and the priests and the rest of the Jewish people, our brethren, greeting. [21]The envoys who were sent to our people have told us about your glory and honour, and we rejoiced at their coming. [22]And what they said we have recorded in our public decrees, as follows, 'Numenius the son of Antiochus and Antipater the son of Jason, envoys of the Jews, have come to us to renew their friendship with us. [23]It has pleased our people to receive these men with honour and to put a copy of their words in the public archives, so that the people of the Spartans may have a record of them. And they have sent a copy of this to Simon the high priest.'"

1 Mac 12:16

[24]After this Simon sent Numenius to Rome with a large gold shield weighing a thousand minas, to confirm the alliance with the Romans.[q]

Inscription in honour of Simon

[25]When the people heard these things they said, "How shall we thank Simon and his sons? [26]For he and his brothers and the house

14:25–49. Earlier, the author of 1 Maccabees paid his own tribute to Simon (cf. 14:1–15); now he wants to make the point that the people, too, were full of praise for him and fully supported him. Everything is geared to enhancing the reputation of the Hasmonean dynasty, which begins really with Simon and his son John Hyrcanus; the inscription on the tablets is a sort of constitutional charter of the dynasty. Curiously, no reference is made to Judas Maccabeus, and Jonathan is mentioned only in so far as he was Simon's predecessor (v. 30).

The date of the inscription corresponds to September 140 BC, and the place where the assembly took place, Asaramel, seems to be the outer court of the temple (see the RSV note). The assembly includes representatives of the entire nation (v. 28). As regards the content of the inscription, which includes the themes dealt with in the previous tribute (cf. 14:1–15), there are note-

Simonis gloriose; [41]et quia Iudaei et sacerdotes consenserunt eum esse ducem suum et summum sacerdotem in aeternum, donec surgat propheta fidelis, [42]et ut sit super eos dux, et ut cura esset illi pro sanctis, ut constitueret per eum super opera eorum et super regionem et super arma et super praesidia, [43]et cura sit illi de sanctis, et ut audiatur ab omnibus, et scribantur in nomine eius omnes conscriptiones in regione, et ut operiatur purpura et aurum portet, [44]et ne liceat ulli ex populo et ex sacerdotibus irritum facere aliquid horum et contradicere his, quae ab eo dicuntur, aut convocare conventum in regione sine ipso et vestiri purpura et uti fibula aurea; [45]qui autem fecerit extra haec aut irritum fecerit aliquid horum, reus erit. [46]Et complacuit omni populo statuere Simoni facere secundum verba ista. [47]Et suscepit Simon

q. Gk *them*

of his father have stood firm; they have fought and repulsed Israel's enemies and established its freedom." [27]So they made a record on bronze tablets and put it upon pillars on Mount Zion.

This is a copy of what they wrote: "On the eighteenth day of Elul, in the one hundred and seventy-second year,[r] which is the third year of Simon the great high priest, [28]in Asaramel,[s] in the great assembly of the priests and the people and the rulers of the nation and the elders of the country, the following was proclaimed to us:

[29]"Since wars often occurred in the country, Simon the son of Mattathias, a priest of the sons[t] of Joarib, and his brothers, exposed themselves to danger and resisted the enemies of their nation, in order that their sanctuary and the law might be perserved; and they brought great glory to their nation. [30]Jonathan rallied the[u] nation, and became their high priest, and was gathered to his people. [31]And when their enemies decided to invade their country and lay hands on their sanctuary, [32]then Simon rose up and fought for his nation. He spent great sums of his own money; he armed the men of his nation's forces and paid them wages. [33]He fortified the cities of Judea, and Beth-zur on the borders of Judea, where formerly the arms of the enemy had been stored, and he placed there a garrison of Jews. [34]He also fortified Joppa, which is by the sea, and Gazara, which is on the borders of Azotus, where the enemy formerly dwelt. He settled Jews there, and provided in those cities[v] whatever was necessary for their restoration.

[35]"The people saw Simon's faithfulness[w] and the glory which he had resolved to win for his nation, and they made him their leader and high priest, because he had done all these things and because of the justice and loyalty which he had maintained toward

---

worthy references to Simon's generosity in financing the war (v. 32), his election as high priest and leader on account of his faithfulness to the Law (v. 35), even prior to being confirmed in those positions by the Syrian king (v. 38), and his indisputable authority (vv. 43–44).

Still, v. 41 shows that Simon's leadership and that of his descendants, the Hasmoneans, is something provisional, until such time as a trustworthy prophet shall come. This must surely imply a reference to ancient times when prophets were the ones who picked and anointed

et placuit ei, ut summo sacerdotio fungeretur et esset dux et princeps gentis Iudaeorum et sacerdotum et praeesset omnibus». [48]Et scripturam istam dixerunt ponere in tabulis aereis et ponere eas in peribolo sanctorum in loco celebri; [49]exemplum autem eorum ponere in aerario, ut habeat Simon et filii eius.

r. 140 BC **s.** This word resembles the Hebrew words for *the court of the people of God* or *the prince of the people of God* **t.** The Greek text of this phrase is uncertain **u.** Gk *their* **v.** Gk *them* **w.** Other authorities read *conduct*

his nation. He sought in every way to exalt his people. [36]And in his days things prospered in his hands, so that the Gentiles were put out of the[x] country, as were also the men in the city of David in Jerusalem, who had built themselves a citadel from which they used to sally forth and defile the environs of the sanctuary and do great damage to its purity. [37]He settled Jews in it, and fortified it for the safety of the country and of the city, and built the walls of Jerusalem higher.

[38]"In view of these things King Demetrius confirmed him in the high priesthood, [39]and he made him one of the king's[y] friends and paid him high honours. [40]For he had heard that the Jews were addressed by the Romans[z] as friends and allies and brethren, and that the Romans had received the envoys of Simon with honour.

1 Mac 2:18

[41]"And[a] the Jews and their priests decided that Simon should be their leader and high priest for ever, until a trustworthy prophet should arise, [42]and that he should be governor over them and that he should take charge of the sanctuary and appoint men over its tasks and over the country and the weapons and the strongholds, and that he should take charge of the sanctuary, [43]and that he should be obeyed by all, and that all contracts in the country should be written in his name, and that he should be clothed in purple and wear gold.

Heb 5:6

1 Mac 4:46

[44]"And none of the people or priests shall be permitted to nullify any of these decisions or to oppose what he says, or to convene an assembly in the country without his permission, or to be clothed in purple or put on a gold buckle. [45]Whoever acts contrary to these decisions or nullifies any of them shall be liable to punishment."

---

kings, as Samuel did in the case of David (cf. 1 Sam 16:1–13); but it also includes expectation of an anointed of the Lord, a Messiah, who will be greater than the Hasmoneans. That Messiah anointed by the Spirit of God and having the backing of a prophet like Elijah, whose figure the Gospels associate with John the Baptist (cf. Mt 3:13–17; 17:3–13), is, Christians believe, Jesus Christ, in whom the hopes of Israel find fulfilment.

[15] [1]Et misit rex Antiochus filius Demetrii epistulas ab insulis maris Simoni sacerdoti et principi gentis Iudaeorum et universae genti, [2]et erant continentes hunc modum: «Rex Antiochus Simoni sacerdoti magno et gentis principi et genti Iudaeorum salutem. [3]Quoniam quidam pestilentes obtinuerunt regnum patrum nostrorum, volo autem vindicare regnum, ut restituam illud, sicut erat antea, delectumque feci multitudinis exercitus et feci naves bellicas; [4]volo autem procedere per regionem, ut ulciscar in eos, qui corruperunt regionem nostram et qui desolaverunt civitates multas in regno meo. [5]Nunc ergo statuo tibi omnes oblationes, quas remiserunt tibi ante me reges, et quaecumque alia dona remiserunt tibi. [6]Et

x. Gk *their* **y.** Gk *his* **z.** Gk *they* **a.** Gk *honour; and that*

[46]And all the people agreed to grant Simon the right to act in accord with these decisions. [47]So Simon accepted and agreed to be high priest, to be commander and ethnarch of the Jews and priests, and to be protector of them all.[b] [48]And they gave orders to inscribe this decree upon bronze tablets, to put them up in a conspicuous place in the precincts of the sanctuary, [49]and to deposit copies of them in the treasury, so that Simon and his sons might have them.

Antiochus VII, Demetrius II's successor, tries to regain the throne

1 Mac 8:17; 12:16; 14:22,24

15 [1]Antiochus, the son of Demetrius the king, sent a letter from the islands of the sea to Simon, the priest and ethnarch of the Jews, and to all the nation; [2]its contents were as follows: "King Antiochus to Simon the high priest and ethnarch and to the nation of the Jews, greeting. [3]Whereas certain pestilent men have gained control of the kingdom of our fathers, and I intend to lay claim to the kingdom so that I may restore it as it formerly was, and have recruited a host of mercenary troops and have equipped warships, [4]and intend to make a landing in the country so that I may proceed against those who have destroyed our country and those who have devastated many cities in my kingdom, [5]now therefore I confirm to you all the tax remissions that the kings before me have granted you, and release from all the other payments from which they have released you. [6]I permit you to mint your own coinage as money for your country, [7]and I grant freedom to Jerusalem and the sanctuary. All the weapons which you have prepared and the strongholds

---

15:1–14. This Antiochus was a son of Demetrius I and a brother of Demetrius II. Since the latter continues to be a prisoner of the Persians (cf. 14:3), Antiochus prepares to topple Trypho from the throne. To do this, he tries to win the support of smaller states like Judea, and therefore he does not mind offering tempting concessions; however, he will later try to go back on his word. Specifically he gives Simon authority to mint his own coinage, which is in practice the same as recognizing Judea's political independence (vv. 6–7). Antiochus VII disembarks in Syria in 138 BC and besieges Trypho at Dor, a city 12 km. (7.5 miles) north of Maritime Caesarea.

permisi tibi facere monetam propriam numisma regioni tuae; [7]Ierusalem autem et sancta esse libera, et omnia arma, quae fabricatus es, et praesidia, quae construxisti, quae tenes, maneant tibi; [8]et omne debitum regis et quae futura sunt regi ex hoc et in totum tempus, remittantur tibi. [9]Cum autem obtinuerimus regnum nostrum, glorificabimus te et gentem tuam et templum gloria magna, ita ut manifestetur gloria vestra in universa terra». [10]Anno centesimo septuagesimo quarto exiit Antiochus in terram patrum suorum, et convenerunt ad eum omnes exercitus, ita ut pauci relicti essent cum Tryphone. [11]Et insecutus est eum Antiochus rex, et venit Doram fugiens, quae est ad mare; [12]sciebat enim quod

b. Or *to preside over them all*

which you have built and now hold shall remain yours. [8]Every debt you owe to the royal treasury and any such future debts shall be canceled for you from henceforth and for all time. [9]When we gain control of our kingdom, we will bestow great honour upon you and your nation and the temple, so that your glory will become manifest in all the earth."

[10]In the one hundred and seventy-fourth year[c] Antiochus set out and invaded the land of his fathers. All the troops rallied to him, so that there were few with Trypho. [11]Antiochus pursued him, and he came in his flight to Dor, which is by the sea; [12]for he knew that troubles had converged upon him, and his troops had deserted him. [13]So Antiochus encamped against Dor, and with him were a hundred and twenty thousand warriors and eight thousand cavalry. [14]He surrounded the city, and the ships joined battle from the sea; he pressed the city hard from land and sea, and permitted no one to leave or enter it.

Rome's response to Simon's overtures

[15]Then Numenius and his companions arrived from Rome, with letters to the kings and countries, in which the following was written: [16]"Lucius, consul of the Romans, to King Ptolemy, greeting. [17]The envoys of the Jews have come to us as our friends and allies to renew our ancient friendship and alliance. They had been sent by Simon the high priest and by the people of the Jews,

---

15:15–24. The letter is addressed to the states and cities that were nominally independent but under Roman suzerainty. The copy which is quoted here is the one addressed to the king of Egypt. The Jews are regarded as having the status of any other country, and they are given the right to extradite from other countries people who oppose Simon's rule. The New Vulgate adds (v. 24) that the copy of the letter sent to Simon was also addressed to the Jewish people (the Greek makes no such mention).

congregata sunt mala in eum, et reliquit eum exercitus. [13]Et applicuit Antiochus ad Doram cum centum viginti milibus virorum belligeratorum et octo milibus equitum [14]et circuivit civitatem, et naves a mari accesserunt; et vexabat civitatem a terra et mari et neminem sinebat ingredi vel egredi. [15]Venit autem Numenius et, qui cum eo fuerant, ab urbe Roma habentes epistulas regibus et regionibus scriptas, in quibus continebantur haec: [16]«Lucius consul Romanorum Ptolemaeo regi salutem. [17]Legati Iudaeorum venerunt ad nos amici nostri et socii renovantes pristinam amicitiam et societatem, missi a Simone principe sacerdotum et populo Iudaeorum. [18]Attulerunt autem et clipeum aureum mnarum mille. [19]Placuit itaque nobis scribere regibus et regionibus, ut non exquirant illis mala neque impugnent eos et civitates eorum et regionem eorum et ut non ferant auxilium pugnantibus adversus eos. [20]Visum autem est nobis accipere ab eis clipeum. [21]Si qui ergo pestilentes refugerunt de regione ipsorum ad vos, tradite eos Simoni principi sacerdotum, ut vindicet in eos secundum legem suam». [22]Haec eadem scripsit Demetrio regi et Attalo et Ariarathae et Arsacae [23]et in omnes regiones et Sampsacae et Spartiatis et in

c. 138 BC

[18]and have brought a gold shield weighing a thousand minas. [19]We therefore have decided to write to the kings and countries that they should not seek their harm or make war against them and their cities and their country, or make alliance with those who war against them. [20]And it has seemed good to us to accept the shield from them. [21]Therefore if any pestilent men have fled to you from their country, hand them over to Simon the high priest, that he may punish them according to their law."

Acts 9:2

[22]The consul[d] wrote the same thing to Demetrius the king and to Attalus and Ariarathes and Arsaces, [23]and to all the countries, and to Sampsames,[e] and to the Spartans, and to Delos, and to Myndos, and to Sicyon, and to Caria, and to Samos, and to Pamphylia, and to Lycia, and to Halicarnassus, and to Rhodes, and to Phaselis, and to Cos, and to Side, and to Aradus and Gortyna and Cnidus and Cyprus and Cyrene. [24]They also sent a copy of these things to Simon the high priest.

Antiochus VII turns against Judea and launches an attack

[25]Antiochus the king besieged Dor anew,[f] continually throwing his forces against it and making engines of war; and he shut Trypho up and kept him from going out or in. [26]And Simon sent to Antiochus[g] two thousand picked men, to fight for him, and silver

15:25–41. As was to be expected, now that Antiochus is in Palestine and perhaps sees that Trypho will not cause him any trouble, he retracts the concessions he made to Simon; and he rejects Simon's offer of help. However, Antiochus does treat Simon as an invader and not as a rebellious subject (vv. 28–29). And Simon replies very much as an equal: he is ready to pay only for Joppa and Gazara, which were not part of Judean territory: he offers nothing for the districts whose administration was conferred on him by Demetrius (cf. 11:34, 57), because he regards these as an inheritance that is rightfully his. After Trypho flees to the north of Syria (1 Maccabees does not say how he managed to do that), Antiochus orders an attack on Judea via the west; but his governor, Cendebaeus (v. 38), about whom nothing is known other than what is stated here, spends his time plundering the zone instead. All that he manages to do is to establish himself at Kedron, a few kilometres to the south of Jamnia.

Delum et in Myndum et in Sicyonem et in Carida et in Samum et in Pamphyliam et in Lyciam et in Alicarnassum et in Rhodum et in Phaselidam et in Cho et in Siden et in Aradon et in Gortynam et Cnidum et Cyprum et Cyrenen. [24]Exemplum autem eorum scripserunt Simoni principi sacerdotum et populo Iudaeorum. [25]Antiochus autem rex applicuit castra in Doram in secunda die admovens ei semper manus et machinas faciens et conclusit Tryphonem, ne exiret aut introiret. [26]Et misit ad eum Simon duo milia virorum electorum in auxilium et argentum et aurum et vasa copiosa. [27]Et noluit ea accipere, sed

d. Gk *He* **e.** The name is uncertain **f.** Or *on the second day* **g.** Gk *him*

and gold and much military equipment. [27]But he refused to receive them, and he broke all the agreements he formerly had made with Simon,[g] and became estranged from him. [28]He sent to him Athenobius, one of his friends, to confer with him, saying, "You hold control of Joppa and Gazara and the citadel in Jerusalem; they are cities of my kingdom. [29]You have devastated their territory, you have done great damage in the land, and you have taken possession of many places in my kingdom. [30]Now then, hand over the cities which you have seized and the tribute money of the places which you have conquered outside the borders of Judea; [31]or else give me for them five hundred talents of silver, and for the destruction that you have caused and the tribute money of the cities, five hundred talents more. Otherwise we will come and conquer you."

1 Mac 2:18

[32]So Athenobius the friend of the king came to Jerusalem, and when he saw the splendour of Simon, and the sideboard with its gold and silver plate, and his great magnificence, he was amazed. He reported to him the words of the king, [33]but Simon gave him this reply: "We have neither taken foreign land nor seized foreign property, but only the inheritance of our fathers, which at one time had been unjustly taken by our enemies. [34]Now that we have the opportunity, we are firmly holding the inheritance of our fathers.

[35]As for Joppa and Gazara, which you demand, they were causing great damage among the people and to our land; for them we will give you a hundred talents." Athenobius[h] did not answer him a word, [36]but returned in wrath to the king and reported to him these words and the splendour of Simon and all that he had seen. And the king was greatly angered.

[37]Now Trypho embarked on a ship and escaped to Orthosia. [38]Then the king made Cendebeus commander-in-chief of the

---

rupit omnia, quae pactus est cum eo antea, et alienavit se ab eo. [28]Et misit ad eum Athenobium unum de amicis suis, ut tractaret cum ipso dicens: «Vos tenetis Ioppen et Gazaram et arcem, quae est in Ierusalem, civitates regni mei; [29]fines earum desolastis et fecistis plagam magnam in terra et dominati estis per loca multa in regno meo. [30]Nunc ergo tradite civitates, quas occupastis, et tributa locorum, in quibus dominati estis extra fines Iudaeae; [31]sin autem, date pro illis quingenta talenta argenti, et exterminii, quod exterminastis, et tributorum civitatum alia talenta quingenta: sin autem, veniemus et expugnabimus vos». [32]Et venit Athenobius amicus regis in Ierusalem et vidit gloriam Simonis et claritatem in auro et argento et apparatum copiosum et obstupuit et rettulit ei verba regis. [33]Et respondit ei Simon et dixit ei: «Neque alienam terram sumpsimus neque aliena detinemus, sed hereditatem patrum nostrorum, quae iniuste ab inimicis nostris aliquo tempore possessa est. [34]Nos vero tempus habentes vindicamus hereditatem patrum nostrorum; [35]nam de Ioppe et Gazara, quae expostulas, ipsae faciebant in populo plagam magnam et in regione nostra: horum damus talenta centum». Et non respondit ei verbum. [36]Reversus autem cum ira ad regem renuntiavit ei verba ista et gloriam Simonis et universa, quae vidit, et iratus est rex ira magna. [37]Tryphon autem ascendit in navem et fugit in

h. Gk *He*

coastal country, and gave him troops of infantry and cavalry. [39]He commanded him to encamp against Judea, and commanded him to build up Kedron and fortify its gates, and to make war on the people; but the king pursued Trypho. [40]So Cendebeus came to Jamnia and began to provoke the people and invade Judea and take the people captive and kill them. [41]He built up Kedron and stationed there horsemen and troops, so that they might go out and make raids along the highways of Judea, as the king had ordered him.

John Hyrcanus, a son of Simon, defeats the enemy

16 [1]John went up from Gazara and reported to Simon his father what Cendebeus had done. [2]And Simon called in his two older sons Judas and John, and said to them: "I and my brothers and the house of my father have fought the wars of Israel from our youth until this day, and things have prospered in our hands so that we have delivered Israel many times. [3]But now I have grown old, and you by His mercy are mature in years. Take my place and my brother's, and go out and fight for our nation, and may the help which comes from Heaven be with you."

1 Mac 2:64–68; 13:3; 14:26

16:1–10. By this stage an old man, Simon delegates the mission of defending Israel in the field of battle to two of his sons (vv. 2–3), rather as Mattathias and the other Maccabee brothers had done in their time. It seems very much as if this is a sort of family responsibility that will continue to be exercised by the Hasmonean kings. However, strangely enough, no mention is made of Simon's third son, Mattathias (cf. 16:4).

The battle under John's generalship takes place near Mode-in, where the family mausoleum of the Maccabees was located (cf. 13:26–30). The stream mentioned in v. 6 could be the Wadi Katra, about 25 km. (16 miles) from Mode-in on the way to Azotus. John's bravery in leading his men across the stream is similar to other instances of Maccabee leadership (cf. 5:42–43).

16:11–17. Unlike his brothers (cf. 9:18; 12:48), Simon does not end his days at the hands of the Syrians, Israel's oppressors. He is assassinated by his own son-in-law, Ptolemy. Political reasons may have been behind Ptolemy's marriage

Orthosiam. [38]Et constituit rex Cendebaeum ducem maritimum et exercitum peditum et equitum dedit illi; [39]et mandavit illi movere castra contra faciem Iudaeae et mandavit ei aedificare Cedron et obstruere portas civitatis et ut debellaret populum. Rex autem persequebatur Tryphonem. [40]Et pervenit Cendebaeus Iamniam et coepit irritare plebem et conculcare Iudaeam et captivare populum et interficere. [41]Et aedificavit Cedron et collocavit illic equites et exercitum, ut egressi perambularent vias Iudaeae, sicut constituit ei rex. **[16]** [1]Et ascendit Ioannes de Gazaris et nuntiavit Simoni patri suo, quae fecit Cendebaeus. [2]Et vocavit Simon duos filios seniores, Iudam et Ioannem, et ait illis: «Ego et fratres mei et domus patris mei expugnavimus hostes Israel ab adulescentia usque in hunc diem, et prosperatum est in manibus nostris liberare Israel saepius. [3]Nunc autem senui, vos autem in misericordia sufficientes estis in annis; estote loco meo et fratris mei et egressi pugnate pro gente nostra: auxilium vero de caelo

[4]So John[i] chose out of the country twenty thousand warriors and horsemen, and they marched against Cendebeus and camped for the night in Mode-in. [5]Early in the morning they arose and marched into the plain, and behold, a large force of infantry and horsemen was coming to meet them; and a stream lay between them. [6]Then he and his army lined up against them. And he saw that the soldiers were afraid to cross the stream, so he crossed over first; and when his men saw him, they crossed over after him.

[7]Then he divided the army and placed the horsemen in the midst of the infantry, for the cavalry of the enemy were very numerous.

[8]And they sounded the trumpets, and Cendebeus and his army were put to flight, and many of them were wounded and fell; the rest fled into the stronghold. [9]At that time Judas the brother of John was wounded, but John pursued them until Cendebeus

---

to Simon's daughter. In any case, the assassination, which took place in 134 BC, shows not only the baseness and ambition of Ptolemy, but also the fact that some people felt animosity towards the Maccabees. Ptolemy may have thought he could gain advantage from that disaffection. Dok was about 8 km (5 miles) from Jericho on a hill traditionally associated with Jesus' forty days in the desert.

16:18–24. The author of 1 Maccabees has chosen simply to tell us how John avoided being a victim of the conspiracy. But, the fact that he ends his book (vv. 23–24) in this way (with a formula similar to that used in the books of the Kings at the end of each reign), suggests that he knew about John's subsequent career up to his death in 104 BC. Flavius Josephus, in his *Antiquitates Judaicae*, tells us that John confronted Ptolemy at Jerusalem, and the people sided with John. Ptolemy, forced to flee, took Simon's mother with him as a hostage and put her to death in Kedron. We also know that John was surnamed Hyrcanus, that he rebuilt the walls of Jerusalem, and that under him Judea became a completely independent state. If the author of 1 Maccabees does not mention any of this, it is because he wants to confine his story to the deeds of the Maccabees and the sufferings undergone by the Jewish people to protect their faith and traditions. The history of the successors of the Maccabees is not part of his intention in writing; we must presume that, as he saw it, later events were of no special significance as regards God's relations with his people.

vobiscum sit». [4]Et elegit de regione viginti milia virorum belligeratorum et equites; et profecti sunt ad Cendebaeum et dormierunt in Modin [5]et surrexerunt mane et abierunt in campum. Et ecce exercitus copiosus in obviam illis peditum et equitum, et fluvius torrens erat inter medium ipsorum. [6]Et admovit castra contra faciem eorum ipse et populus eius et vidit populum trepidantem ad transfretandum

i. Other authorities read *he*

reached Kedron, which he had built. [10]They also fled into the towers that were in the fields of Azotus, and John[j] burned it with fire, and about two thousand of them fell. And he returned to Judea safely.

The treachery of Ptolemy, and the death of Simon and two of his sons

[11]Now Ptolemy the son of Abubus had been appointed governor over the plain of Jericho, and he had much silver and gold, [12]for he was son-in-law of the high priest. [13]His heart was lifted up; he determined to get control of the country, and made treacherous plans against Simon and his sons, to do away with them. [14]Now Simon was visiting the cities of the country and attending to their needs, and he went down to Jericho with Mattathias and Judas his sons, in the one hundred and seventy-seventh year,[k] in the eleventh month, which is the month of Shebat. [15]The son of Abubus received them treacherously in the little stronghold called Dok, which he had built; he gave them a great banquet, and hid men there. [16]When Simon and his sons were drunk, Ptolemy and his men rose up, took their weapons, and rushed in against Simon in the banquet hall, and they killed him and his two sons and some of his servants. [17]So he committed an act of great treachery and returned evil for good.

---

torrentem; et transfretavit primus, et viderunt eum viri et transierunt post eum. [7]Et divisit populum, et equites in medio peditum; erat autem equitatus adversariorum copiosus nimis. [8]Et exclamaverunt tubis, et in fugam conversus est Cendebaeus et castra eius, et ceciderunt ex eis multi vulnerati; residui autem in munitionem fugerunt. [9]Tunc vulneratus est Iudas frater Ioannis; Ioannes autem insecutus est eos, donec venit Cedron, quam aedificavit. [10]Et fugerunt usque ad turres, quae erant in agris Azoti, et succendit eas igni; et ceciderunt ex illis duo milia virorum. Et reversus est in Iudaeam in pace. [11]Et Ptolemaeus filius Abubi constitutus erat dux in campo Iericho et habebat argentum et aurum multum; [12]erat enim gener summi sacerdotis. [13]Et exaltatum est cor eius, et volebat obtinere regionem et cogitabat dolum adversus Simonem et filios eius, ut tolleret eos. [14]Simon autem perambulans civitates, quae erant in regione, et sollicitudinem gerens earum descendit in Iericho ipse et Matthathias et Iudas filii eius, anno centesimo septuagesimo septimo, mense undecimo, hic est mensis Sabath. [15]Et suscepit eos filius Abubi in munitiunculam, quae vocatur Doc, cum dolo, quam aedificavit; et fecit eis convivium magnum et abscondit illic viros. [16]Et, cum inebriatus esset Simon et filii eius, surrexit Ptolemaeus cum suis et sumpserunt arma sua et intraverunt in convivium et occiderunt eum et duos filios eius et quosdam pueros eius. [17]Et fecit deceptionem magnam et reddidit mala pro bonis. [18]Et scripsit haec Ptolemaeus et misit regi, ut mitteret ei exercitum in auxilium et traderet ei civitates et regionem. [19]Et misit alios in Gazaram tollere Ioannem; et tribunis misit epistulas, ut venirent ad se, et daret eis argentum et aurum et dona. [20]Et alios misit occupare Ierusalem et montem templi. [21]Et praecurrens quidam nuntiavit Ioanni in Gazara quia periit pater eius et fratres eius et quia: «Misit te quoque interfici». [22]Ut audivit autem, vehementer expavit et comprehendit viros, qui venerant perdere eum, et occidit eos; cognovit enim quia quaerebant eum perdere. [23]Et cetera sermonum Ioannis et bellorum eius et bonarum virtutum, quibus fortiter gessit, et aedificii murorum, quos exstruxit, et rerum gestarum eius, [24]ecce haec scripta sunt in libro dierum sacerdotii eius, ex quo factus est princeps sacerdotum post patrem suum.

j. Gk *he* **k.** 134 BC

Start of the reign of John Hyrcanus

[18]Then Ptolemy wrote a report about these things and sent it to the king, asking him to send troops to aid him and to turn over to him the cities and the country. [19]He sent other men to Gazara to do away with John; he sent letters to the captains asking them to come to him so that he might give them silver and gold and gifts; [20]and he sent other men to take possession of Jerusalem and the temple hill. [21]But some one ran ahead and reported to John at Gazara that his father and brothers had perished, and that "he has sent men to kill you also." [22]When he heard this, he was greatly shocked; and he seized the men who came to destroy him and killed them, for he had found out that they were seeking to destroy him.

[23]The rest of the acts of John and his wars and the brave deeds which he did, and the building of the walls which he built, and his achievements, [24]behold, they are written in the chronicles of his high priesthood, from the time that he became high priest after his father.

2 MACCABEES

Introduction

The second book of the Maccabees is not a continuation of the first; it deals, in a different way and in more detail, with the career of Judas Maccabeus covered in 1 Maccabees 1:1—7:49. The two books were often handed down together and they eventually found their way into the Christian canon. The Codex Sinaiticus does not contain 1 Maccabees, but the Alexandrine Codex has both books, one following on the other; in fact, that is how the book we are now discussing received its name, 2 Maccabees.

1. STRUCTURE AND CONTENT

In 2 Maccabees the actual narrative begins with Seleucus IV, the older brother and predecessor on the Syrian throne of Antiochus IV Epiphanes; and it ends with Judas Maccabeus' victory over Nicanor in 161 BC. The structure of the book is as follows:

INTRODUCTION (1:1—2:32). Prior to the narrative account, we are given two letters sent by the Jews of Jerusalem to the Jews of Egypt urging them to celebrate (as is done in Jerusalem) the feast of the Dedication of the temple (Hanukkah) established by Judas Maccabeus (2 Mac 1:1—2:18). The author then goes on to explain why he is writing this book and how he proposes to approach his subject.

1. PROFANATION AND CLEANSING OF THE TEMPLE (3:1—10:8). Under the devout high priest Onias, the holiness of the temple was inviolable (2 Mac 3:1–40). But when the high priesthood is taken over by men of a Hellenizing bent, such as Jason and Menelaus, God's wrath comes down on Israel and he allows the temple to be profaned and many devout Jews to be martyred—most notably Eleazar and a mother with her seven sons. But the fidelity of the martyrs turns God's anger into mercy. Judas defeats the Syrian generals Nicanor and Gorgias, and Antiochus IV Epiphanes dies in distant Media. At this point the temple is cleansed and rededicated, and the commemorative feast of Hanukkah is established.

2. PEACE AND SECURITY FOR THE JEWS (10:9—15:39). Judas continues the armed struggle—against the royal armies led by Lysias, and Hellenized cities in the region, until eventually Antiochus V grants freedom of worship to the

Jews. Soon after this, Judas leaves Jerusalem to campaign on behalf of Jews living in other cities; once again he has to do battle with Syrian generals and even with Lysias, who is accompanied by the king himself. But Judas' valour forces the Syrians to retreat. When Demetrius I takes over the throne, Alcimus, a Hellenizing Jew, puts himself forward for the high priesthood; he wins the support of the king, who sends Nicanor and an army into Judea. Nicanor blasphemes against the temple but is defeated and slain in battle by Judas. A feast is established to commemorate the victory.

2. COMPOSITION

In 2:19–32 the author spells out his intention and gives the source of his information. His book, he explains, includes a summary of the content of a five-volume history written by Jason of Cyrene, and he gives us to understand that that history formed the background to the previously mentioned letters about the celebration of the feast of the Dedication. We know nothing about the work of Jason of Cyrene other than what we are told here; therefore, it is difficult to assess how accurate a summary is being provided; moreover, there is no further mention of this source in the course of the book. It may well be that Jason's book, like 1 Maccabees, dealt with "Judas and his brothers" (2 Mac 2:19), in which case it could have been written after Simon Maccabeus, the last of Judas' brothers, died—that is, 134 BC. Second Maccabees would have been written around the end of the second century in Alexandria where the letters transcribed at the start of the book were conserved (the first letter is dated 124 BC).

The author's intention is to edify and influence: the book's literary genre is what is called "sentimental history", a genre quite common in Hellenistic literature. History of this sort focuses on the religious significance of events and on the feelings of the personalities involved, but is not greatly concerned with historical precision. It dramatizes certain episodes; speeches it contains are designed to awaken feelings, its criticism of Israel's enemies leaves no doubt about where the writer stands; etc. But despite all this, the history given in the book is basically sound, as can be seen by checking it against that in 1 Maccabees, Flavius Josephus and Seleucid sources.

In the light of those sources one can see that the author of 2 Maccabees changes the order of events to suit his purpose. A good example of this is his setting Lysias' campaign against Judas in the reign of Antiochus V instead of Antiochus IV (when it in fact occurred). This allows him to tie similar events together, to help the reader see their religious significance. In fact, as the author himself says in 2:24–25 (and repeats in 2:30–31), he is not interested in going into details; he wants his book to be an easy and profitable read. Sometimes he gives different accounts of one and the same event: for example, the death of

Antiochus IV is dealt with in one way in the introductory letter (2 Mac 1:13–17) and in another in the body of the book (2 Mac 5:1–27). What the reader should expect to find here is not chronological accuracy but the religious significance of events.

Two episodes that stand out are Judas' cleansing of the temple and the way he obtains religious freedom for the Jews. No mention is made of Mattathias, and Judas' brothers are referred to only in passing (2 Mac 8:22; 14:17). And much importance is given to the priestly figure of Onias III (2 Mac 3:1; 4:4; 15:12). All this seems to indicate that the author of 2 Maccabees does not feel attracted either to the Hasmonean dynasty (the successors of the Maccabees) or to their flaunting of the high priesthood. This, together with its teachings on the resurrection of the dead, means that 2 Maccabees represents a trend in Judaism different from that found in 1 Maccabees.

3. MESSAGE

Second Maccabees contains more explicit religious content than 1 Maccabees. Here political considerations are kept separate from the Law, and the focus of attention is the temple of Jerusalem. Religion has an absolute character deriving from the holiness of God and of the temple. The struggle that Judas engages in has to do with something that is beyond this world: it seeks to bring about the kingdom of the saints. In this connexion the book provides much food for thought about the meaning and value of human life.

Thus, a lot of importance is given to the meaning of martyrdom: human life does have a very high value, but it is not an absolute value. Some things matter more than life—faithfulness to God, the example of irreproachable moral conduct, the freedom necessary for keeping the Law of God, etc.—and therefore death is preferable to renouncing those ideals.

But martyrdom would not fully make sense if death meant the end of everything for man. This book teaches that there is eternal life after death for the righteous, for God will raise them up again. This belief is explicitly stated in the words of the second of the martyr brothers to his executioner: "You accursed wretch, you dismiss us from this present life, but the King of the universe will raise us up to an everlasting renewal of life, because we have died for his laws" (2 Mac 7:9). So, death does not break God's relationship with his faithful.

Nor does death mean a complete breakdown in people's relationships with one another: there continues to be communion between the living and the dead. The living can offer prayers and atoning sacrifices for the dead, as we can see from the passage where Judas orders offerings to be made for those who died in combat (2 Mac 12:38–46).

According to 2 Maccabees, God's action manifests itself in visions or dreams which foreshadow future events, but it is normally to be seen in the form of rewards or punishments. God rewards righteous Jews and punishes sinful Jews and also the enemies of the people. Sometimes God seems to be applying inexorably the law of vengeance: he never forgives Israel's enemies, not even when they repent (2 Mac 9:13). The power of God is infinite; the power of men, even those who consider themselves powerful (such as kings), is insignificant compared with it. God's power is manifested by his creation of all things out of nothing; it is what underpins hope in the resurrection of the just (2 Mac 7:28–29). Sometimes God acts by sending his angels to attend the righteous in their struggles and help them win victory (2 Mac 11:6; 15:22).

Belief in the resurrection of the dead, and in angels, sets 2 Maccabees in the religious world of the Pharisees, as we know from the New Testament (cf. Acts 23:7–8). However, it would not be correct to say that the author was a Pharisee, for he tolerates there being Jewish temples in places other than Jerusalem (2 Mac 6:2), and he praises resort to arms—something that the Pharisees were opposed to.

4. SECOND MACCABEES IN THE LIGHT OF THE NEW TESTAMENT

In the light of the New Testament we can see that 2 Maccabees marks an important step forward in the process of revelation, and it is getting close to teachings which will appear in the New Testament, which corroborates the ideas of 2 Maccabees but transcends and refines them.

Thus, God's ability to raise the dead, and belief in the resurrection are confirmed by the resurrection of Jesus Christ (cf. Acts 2:23–24; Rom 1:4; etc.) and by the hope cherished by the early Christians (cf. 1 Cor 15:1–53). It is true that Jesus corrects the very material notion of the resurrection to be found in 2 Maccabees and steers us to interpret resurrection in another way by saying that in the resurrection men will be like angels in heaven (cf. Mt 22:30 and par.; 1 Cor 15:44–49).

Second Maccabees shows very clearly that the suffering undergone by martyrs redounds to the benefit of the people because it stirs God to intervene on their behalf (cf. 2 Mac 7:38). This truth is borne out fully in Jesus Christ who, by his acceptance of death and his obedience to the Father, redeems us from sin (cf. Mt 26:28) and makes us deserving of salvation (Mt 10:28).

The holiness of the temple and the inviolability of the Law, which come across so forcefully in 2 Maccabees, were deeply appreciated by Jews in our Lord's time. In the Introduction to 1 Maccabees we have referred to how Jesus heightened and transformed those aspects of the Jewish religion. Moreover,

instances of faithfulness to the Law of God at the cost of life itself that are reported in 2 Maccabees can be interpreted by Christians as anticipations of our Lord's demanding teaching: "Do not fear those who kill the body but cannot kill the soul" (Mt 10:28) or "What will it profit a man if he gains the whole world and forfeits his life?" (Mt 16:26).

INTRODUCTION: LETTERS TO THE JEWS OF EGYPT* AND PREFACE

The first letter, quoting another

1 [1]The Jewish brethren in Jerusalem and those in the land of Judea,

To their Jewish brethren in Egypt,

Greeting, and good peace.

Lev 26:42

1 Chron 28:9

Acts 16:14

[2]May God do good to you, and may he remember his covenant with Abraham and Isaac and Jacob, his faithful servants. [3]May he give you all a heart to worship him and to do his will with a strong heart and a willing spirit. [4]May he open your heart to his law and his commandments, and may he bring peace. [5]May he hear your prayers and be reconciled to you, and may he not forsake you in time of evil. [6]We are now praying for you here.

2 Mac 4:7

[7]In the reign of Demetrius, in the one hundred and sixty-ninth year,[a] we Jews wrote to you, in the critical distress which came upon us in those years after Jason and his company revolted from the holy land and the kingdom [8]and burned the gate and shed

---

***1:1—2:32.** To introduce his work, the author of 2 Maccabees includes the text of letters sent by the Jews of Jerusalem to their co-religionists in Egypt (1:1—2:18), and provides a short explanation of what this book is about and why he has written it and chosen the style he uses (2:19–32). This sacred book should be read, then, with the conviction that it is useful for all those who see themselves as members of the chosen people, wherever they may be; the author has the best of intentions and readers should feel well disposed towards him because of his sincerity.

***1:1—2:18.** These two letters date from before the time when 2 Maccabees was written, and they are independent of the source that the author is summarizing in this book (cf. 2:23). However, he has probably modified them a little.

1:1–9. Written in 124 BC, what this letter mainly reveals is the solidarity between the Jews of Jerusalem and those of Egypt, based on the fact that they all share the Covenant that God made with the patriarchs; the Egyptians can show this solidarity by celebrating the feast of the Dedication of the

[1] [1]Fratribus, qui sunt per Aegyptum, Iudaeis salutem dicunt fratres, qui sunt in Hierosolymis Iudaei et qui in regione Iudaeae, pacem bonam. [2]Et benefaciat vobis Deus et meminerit testamenti sui, quod locutus est ad Abraham et Isaac et Iacob servorum suorum fidelium; [3]et det vobis cor omnibus, ut colatis eum et faciatis eius voluntatem corde magno et animo volenti; [4]et adaperiat cor vestrum in lege sua et in praeceptis suis et faciat pacem; [5]et exaudiat orationes vestras et reconcilietur vobis, nec vos deserat in tempore malo. [6]Et nunc hic sumus orantes pro vobis. [7]Regnante Demetrio, anno centesimo sexagesimo nono, nos Iudaei scripsimus vobis in tribulatione et impetu, qui supervenit nobis in istis

a. 143 BC

innocent blood. We besought the Lord and we were heard, and we offered sacrifice and cereal offering, and we lighted the lamps and we set out the loaves. [9]And now see that you keep the feast of booths in the month of Chislev, in the one hundred and eighty-eighth year.[b]

The second letter, from Judas Maccabeus

Acts 5:21

[10]Those in Jerusalem and those in Judea and the senate and Judas,

To Aristobulus, who is of the family of the anointed priests, teacher of Ptolemy the king, and to the Jews in Egypt, Greeting, and good health.

---

temple of Jerusalem ("the feast of booths in the month of Chislev" v. 9, so called because of its resemblance to the feast of Tabernacles: cf. 10:1–8). The letter includes a summary of another letter written in 143 BC in which the Jerusalem Jews notified the Egyptians about the rededication of the temple. Prayer for each other is basic to the relationship between the two communities (v. 6). On this aspect St Augustine comments: "If you pray only for yourself, you will be, as we have already said, the only intercessor in your own favour. On the other hand, if you pray for everybody, you will benefit from the prayers of all, because you too will form part of that one body. In this way, you receive a great reward, for the prayer of one of the people is enriched by the prayer of all the people" (*De Cain et Abel*, 1, 9, 39).

1:10—2:18. Now comes an official letter from the Jerusalem authorities and Judas Maccabeus himself (v. 10) to Aristobulus, a Jewish philosopher of Alexandria who wrote a book dedicated to the Egyptian King Ptolemy Philometor (180–145 BC). Although the letter bears no date, we can see that it was written just after the celebration in Jerusalem of the feast of the Dedication of the temple in 164 BC. The content of the letter is rather complicated and the information it gives about the death of Antiochus IV (vv. 13–16) does not match that given later in 9:1–17 or that in 1 Maccabees 6. However, this is something the author of 2 Maccabees does not worry about, because his reason for bringing the letter in here is to remind the Jews of Egypt that they did receive that invitation to join in the celebration of the feast.

This second letter tells, firstly, about the death of Antiochus IV (possibly confusing him with Antiochus III) and then it moves on to justify the legitimacy of the form of worship re-established in

annis, ex quo recessit Iason et, qui cum eo erant, a sancta terra et a regno, [8]et portam succenderunt et effuderunt sanguinem innocentem; et oravimus ad Dominum et exauditi sumus et obtulimus sacrificia et similaginem et accendimus lucernas et proposuimus panes. [9]Et nunc ut frequentetis dies Scenopegiae mensis Casleu, [10]anno centesimo octogesimo octavo. Qui sunt Hierosolymis et in Iudaea, senatusque et Iudas Aristobulo magistro Ptolemaei regis, qui est de genere christorum sacerdotum, et his, qui in Aegypto sunt, Iudaeis salutem et sanitatem. [11]De magnis periculis a Deo liberati magnifice gratias agimus ipsi, utpote qui adversus regem dimicavimus; [12]ipse enim effervere fecit eos, qui pugnaverunt

b. 124 BC

[11]Having been saved by God out of grave dangers we thank him greatly for taking our side against the king.[c] [12]For he drove out those who fought against the holy city. [13]For when the leader reached Persia with a force that seemed irresistible, they were cut to pieces in the temple of Nanea by a deception employed by the priests of Nanea. [14]For under pretext of intending to marry her, Antiochus came to the place together with his friends, to secure most of its treasures as a dowry. [15]When the priests of the temple of Nanea had set out the treasures and Antiochus had come with a few men inside the wall of the sacred precinct, they closed the temple as soon as he entered it. [16]Opening the secret door in the ceiling, they threw stones and struck down the leader and his men, and dismembered them and cut off their heads and threw them to

1 Mac 6:1–13
2 Mac 9:1–29

Jerusalem, telling how God showed, by means of a miraculous fire, that the sacrifice offered by Nehemiah was acceptable to him (vv. 18–36). Similar confirmation was given the sacrifices of Moses (cf. Lev 9:24), Solomon (cf. 2 Chron 7:1) and Elijah (cf. 2 Kings 18:20–30), all of which were consumed by a miraculous fire. In that fire St Ambrose sees a figure of the Holy Spirit, and he praises the faith, hope and devotion of those priests who hid the fire away: "It was not their intention to bury the gold or to hide the fire-material for their successors to find; but rather, with pure motives, in the middle of a terrible situation, they thought it right to protect the fire from defilement by the wicked: the blood of the martyrs would not extinguish it nor the great weight of ruins put it out. They journeyed to Persia unencumbered but for their religion, for religion is the only thing that they could not be despoiled of during their enslavement" (St Ambrose, *De officiis*, 3, 17, 99–100).

The letter also includes pieces of oral tradition, for example, about how Jeremiah hid the ark and the altar (2:5–8). The sacred writer is not saying that these things happened; he brings them up in order to express his hope that God will soon gather his people together from across the world. For the author of the letter, the fact that the Jews have regained the temple and celebrated the feast of the Dedication is in itself a sign that God will soon intervene to do just that (2:16–18). Read from a Christian perspective, the letter contains an announcement of the one Church in which the new people of God will be assembled.

contra sanctam civitatem. [13]Nam cum in Perside esset dux ipse et qui cum ipso videbatur esse intolerabilis exercitus, concisi sunt in templo Naneae, fraude utentibus sacerdotibus Naneae. [14]Etenim quasi cum ea habitaturus venit ad locum Antiochus et, qui cum ipso erant, amici, ut acciperet pecunias multas dotis nomine. [15]Cumque proposuissent eas sacerdotes Naneae, et ipse cum paucis ingressus esset intra ambitum fani, clauserunt templum; cum intrasset Antiochus, [16]aperto occulto aditu laquearis, mittentes lapides percusserunt ducem et diviserunt membratim et, capitibus amputatis, foras proiecerunt. [17]Per omnia benedictus Deus, qui tradidit eos, qui impie gesserunt. [18]Facturi igitur quinta et vicesima

c. Cn: Gk *as those who array themselves against a king*

the people outside. [17]Blessed in every way be our God, who has brought judgment upon those who have behaved impiously.

[18]Since on the twenty-fifth day of Chislev we shall celebrate the purification of the temple, we thought it necessary to notify you, in order that you also may celebrate the feast of booths and the feast of the fire given when Nehemiah, who built the temple and the altar, offered sacrifices.

[19]For when our fathers were being led captive to Persia, the pious priests of that time took some of the fire of the altar and secretly hid it in the hollow of a dry cistern, where they took such precautions that the place was unknown to any one. [20]But after many years had passed, when it pleased God, Nehemiah, having been commissioned by the king of Persia, sent the descendants of the priests who had hidden the fire to get it. And when they reported to us that they had not found fire but thick liquid, he ordered them to dip it out and bring it. [21]And when the materials for the sacrifices were presented, Nehemiah ordered the priests to sprinkle the liquid on the wood and what was laid upon it. [22]When this was done and some time had passed and the sun, which had been clouded over, shone out, a great fire blazed up, so that all marveled. [23]And while the sacrifice was being consumed, the priests offered prayer—the priests and every one. Jonathan led, and the rest responded, as did Nehemiah. [24]The prayer was to this effect:

1 Pet 4:19

"O Lord, Lord God, Creator of all things, who art awe-inspiring and strong and just and merciful, who alone art King and art kind, [25]who alone art bountiful, who alone art just and almighty and eternal, who dost rescue Israel from every evil, who didst choose the fathers and consecrate them, [26]accept this sacrifice on behalf of all thy people Israel and preserve thy portion and make it holy. [27]Gather together our scattered people, set free those who are slaves among the Gentiles, look upon those who are rejected and

Jas 1:1

---

die mensis Casleu purificationem templi, necessarium duximus significare vobis, ut et vos quoque agatis diem Scenopegiae et ignis, qui datus est, quando Nehemias, aedificato templo et altari, obtulit sacrificia. [19]Nam cum in Persidem ducerentur patres nostri, sacerdotes, qui tunc cultores Dei erant, acceptum ignem de altari occulte absconderunt in cavo putei situm habentis siccum, in quo contutati sunt eum, ita ut omnibus ignotus esset locus. [20]Cum autem praeterissent anni multi, et placuit Deo, ut mitteretur Nehemias a rege Persidis, nepotes sacerdotum illorum, qui absconderant, misit ad ignem. [21]Sicut narraverunt nobis, non invenerunt ignem, sed aquam crassam. Et iussit eos haurire et afferre. Utque imposita sunt sacrificia, iussit sacerdotes Nehemias aspergere aqua et ligna et, quae erant superposita. [22]Utque hoc factum est, et tempus transiit, et sol refulsit, qui prius erat in nubilo, accensus est ignis magnus, ita ut omnes mirarentur. [23]Orationem autem faciebant sacerdotes, dum consummaretur sacrificium, et sacerdotes et omnes, Ionatha inchoante, ceteris autem respondentibus ut Nehemias. [24]Erat autem oratio hunc habens modum: «Domine, Domine Deus, omnium creator, terribilis et fortis, iustus et misericors, qui solus es rex et bonus, [25]solus praestans, solus iustus et omnipotens et aeternus; qui liberas Israel de omni malo, qui fecisti patres electos et sanctificasti eos, [26]accipe sacrificium pro

despised, and let the Gentiles know that thou art our God. [28]Afflict those who oppress and are insolent with pride. [29]Plant thy people in thy holy place, as Moses said."

Deut 30:3–5

[30]Then the priests sang the hymns. [31]And when the materials of the sacrifice were consumed, Nehemiah ordered that the liquid that was left should be poured upon large stones. [32]When this was done, a flame blazed up; but when the light from the altar shone back, it went out. [33]When this matter became known, and it was reported to the king of the Persians that, in the place where the exiled priests had hidden the fire, the liquid had appeared with which Nehemiah and his associates had burned the materials of the sacrifice, [34]the king investigated the matter, and enclosed the place and made it sacred. [35]And with those persons whom the king favoured he exchanged many excellent gifts. [36]Nehemiah and his associates called this "nephthar," which means purification, but by most people it is called naphtha.[d]

Lev 9:24

2 [1]One finds in the records that Jeremiah the prophet ordered those who were being deported to take some of the fire, as has been told, [2]and that the prophet after giving them the law instructed those who were being deported not to forget the commandments of the Lord, nor to be led astray in their thoughts upon seeing the gold and silver statues and their adornment. [3]And with other similar words he exhorted them that the law should not depart from their hearts.

Bar 6

2:19–32. The letters transcribed above already contribute to this book's general purpose—to show how it came about that the Jewish religion was set free from foreign control and how the feast of the Dedication was established. He now goes on to tell us the source he has used for his book (vv. 19–23) and how he proposes to go about writing it (vv. 24–32). We know nothing about Jason the Cyrene other than what it says here. We must presume that the author of 2 Maccabees condensed Jason's work accurately; but we do not know to what extent the religious interpretation of events and of people's feelings (in

universo populo tuo Israel et custodi partem tuam et sanctifica. [27]Congrega dispersionem nostram, libera eos, qui serviunt gentibus, et contemptos et abominatos respice, ut sciant gentes quia tu es Deus noster. [28]Afflige opprimentes nos et contumeliam facientes in superbia. [29]Constitue populum tuum in loco sancto tuo, sicut dixit Moyses». [30]Sacerdotes autem psallebant hymnos. [31]Cum autem consumptum esset sacrificium, ex residua aqua Nehemias iussit lapides maiores perfundi [32]quod ut factum est, flamma accensa est, sed a lumine, quod refulsit ex altari, consumpta est. [33]Ut vero manifestata est res, et renuntiatum est regi Persarum quod in loco, in quo ignem absconderant hi, qui translati fuerant, sacerdotes, aqua apparuit, de qua Nehemias et, qui cum eo erant, purificaverunt ea, quae essent sacrificii, [34]circumsaepiens autem rex et rem diligenter examinans, templum fecit. [35]Et quibus gratificabatur rex, multa dona accipiebat et tribuebat. [36]Appellaverunt autem, qui cum Nehemia erant,

d. Gk *nephthai*

[4]It was also in the writing that the prophet, having received an oracle, ordered that the tent and the ark should follow with him, and that he went out to the mountain where Moses had gone up and had seen the inheritance of God. [5]And Jeremiah came and found a cave, and he brought there the tent and the ark and the altar of incense, and he sealed up the entrance. [6]Some of those who followed him came up to mark the way, but could not find it. [7]When Jeremiah learned of it, he rebuked them and declared: "The place shall be unknown until God gathers his people together again and shows his mercy. [8]And then the Lord will disclose these things, and the glory of the Lord and the cloud will appear, as they were shown in the case of Moses, and as Solomon asked that the place should be specially consecrated."

Rev 2:17; 11:19

2 Thess 2:1

Ex 24:16
1 Kings 8:10–11

---

evidence throughout this book) are his or Jason's; nor do we know whether Jason's work ended with the reign of Antiochus V Eupator (v. 20): 2 Maccabees extends to cover the reign of his successor, Demetrius I (cf. 2 Mac 14–15). Be that as it may, the inspired author of 2 Maccabees takes no responsibility for the historical accuracy of Jason's material (v. 30). His aim is to provide something easy to read, and something that will be useful to the reader (v. 25). Although it seems the sacred writer did not originally intend to go into the reign of Demetrius I, he does devote his two last chapters (14 and 15) to an account of the struggle of Judas Maccabeus against Nicanor, Demetrius' general. Maybe the author of 2 Maccabees decided to include this later period to explain the origin of the feast celebrating the death of Nicanor (the day before Mordecai's day: 15:36).

The fact that the author is so forthcoming about the background to his writing the book (and his admission that he may not have achieved exactitude in the narration of the historical details or events: v. 28) led some Fathers and some Christian writers to doubt the book's veracity and, therefore, its canonicity. However, the author's frankness helps us to understand better how divine inspiration influences a hagiographer—not by miraculously providing him with information, but rather, in a mysterious way, by pressing into service the author's own interests and literary endeavours: "To compose the sacred books, God chose certain men who, all the while he employed them in this task, made full use of their powers and faculties" (Vatican II, *Dei Verbum,* 11).

hunc locum Nephthar, quod interpretatur Purificatio; vocatur autem apud plures Nephthai. **[2]** [1]Invenitur autem in descriptionibus quod Ieremias propheta iussit eos ignem accipere, qui trasmigrabant, ut significatum est [2]et ut mandavit propheta transmigratis dans illis legem, ne obliviscerentur praecepta Domini et ut non exerrarent mentibus videntes simulacra aurea et argentea et ornamenta eorum. [3]Et alia huiusmodi dicens hortabatur, ne legem amoverent a corde suo. [4]Erat autem in ipsa scriptura quomodo tabernaculum et arcam iussit propheta, divino responso ad se facto, comitari secum, usquequo exiit in montem, in quo Moyses ascendit et vidit Dei hereditatem. [5]Et veniens Ieremias invenit domum speluncae; et tabernaculum et arcam et altare incensi intulit illuc et ostium obstruxit. [6]Et accesserunt quidam ex his, qui simul sequebantur, ut notarent viam, et non potuerunt invenire. [7]Ut autem cognovit

[9]It was also made clear that being possessed of wisdom Solomon[e] offered sacrifice for the dedication and completion of the temple. [10]Just as Moses prayed to the Lord, and fire came down from heaven and devoured the sacrifices, so also Solomon prayed, and the fire came down and consumed the whole burnt offerings. [11]And Moses said, "They were consumed because the sin offering had not been eaten." [12]Likewise Solomon also kept the eight days.

Lev 9:24
2 Chron 7:1
Lev 10:16–17
1 Kings 8:65–66

[13]The same things are reported in the records and in the memoirs of Nehemiah, and also that he founded a library and collected the books about the kings and prophets, and the writings of David, and letters of kings about votive offerings. [14]In the same way Judas also collected all the books that had been lost on account of the war which had come upon us, and they are in our possession. [15]So if you have need of them, send people to get them for you.

1 Mac 1:56–57

[16]Since, therefore, we are about to celebrate the purification, we write to you. Will you therefore please keep the days? [17]It is God who has saved all his people, and has returned the inheritance to all, and the kingship and priesthood and consecration, [18]as he promised through the law. For we have hope in God that he will soon have mercy upon us and will gather us from everywhere under heaven into his holy place, for he has rescued us from great evils and has purified the place.

1 Mac 4:59
Deut 30:3–5

Compiler's preface

[19]The story of Judas Maccabeus and his brothers, and the purification of the great temple, and the dedication of the altar, [20]and further the wars against Antiochus Epiphanes and his son Eupator, [21]and the appearances which came from heaven to those

---

Ieremias, culpans illos dixit quod ignotus erit locus, donec congreget Deus congregationem populi et misericordia fiat; [8]et tunc Dominus ostendet haec, et apparebit maiestas Domini, et nubes erit, sicut et sub Moyse manifestabatur, sicut et Salomon petiit, ut locus sanctificaretur magnifice. [9]Manifestabatur autem et ut sapientiam habens obtulit sacrificium dedicationis et consummationis templi. [10]Sicut et Moyses orabat ad Dominum, et descendit ignis de caelo et consumpsit sacrificia, sic et Salomon oravit, et descendit ignis de caelo et consumpsit holocausta. [11]Et dixit Moyses: «Eo quod non sit comestum, quod erat pro peccato, consumptum est». [12]Similiter et Salomon octo dies celebravit. [13]Inferebantur autem in descriptionibus et commentariis secundum Nehemiam haec eadem, et ut construens bibliothecam congregavit libros de regibus et prophetis et libros David et epistulas regum de donariis. [14]Similiter autem et Iudas ea, quae deciderant per bellum, quod nobis acciderat, congregavit omnia, et sunt apud nos. [15]Si ergo desideratis haec, mittite, qui perferant vobis. [16]Acturi itaque purificationem, scripsimus vobis; bene ergo facietis, si egeritis hos dies. [17]Deus autem, qui liberavit universum populum suum et reddidit hereditatem omnibus et regnum et sacerdotium et sanctificationem, [18]sicut promisit in lege. Speramus enim in Deo quod cito nostri miserebitur et congregabit de sub caelo in locum sanctum: eripuit enim nos de magnis periculis et locum purgavit. [19]De Iuda vero Maccabaeo et fratribus eius et de templi magni purificatione et de arae dedicatione, [20]sed et de proeliis, quae pertinent ad Antiochum Epiphanem et filium eius Eupatorem, [21]et de illuminationibus, quae de caelo factae sunt ad eos, qui

e. Gk *he*

who strove zealously on behalf of Judaism, so that though few in number they seized the whole land and pursued the barbarian hordes, [22]and recovered the temple famous throughout the world and freed the city and restored the laws that were about to be abolished, while the Lord with great kindness became gracious to them—[23]all this, which has been set forth by Jason of Cyrene in five volumes, we shall attempt to condense into a single book. [24]For considering the flood of numbers involved and the difficulty there is for those who wish to enter upon the narratives of history because of the mass of material, [25]we have aimed to please those who wish to read, to make it easy for those who are inclined to memorize, and to profit all readers. [26]For us who have undertaken the toil of abbreviating, it is no light matter but calls for sweat and loss of sleep, [27]just as it is not easy for one who prepares a banquet and seeks the benefit of others. However, to secure the gratitude of many we will gladly endure the uncomfortable toil, [28]leaving the responsibility for exact details to the compiler, while devoting our effort to arriving at the outlines of the condensation. [29]For as the master builder of a new house must be concerned with the whole construction, while the one who undertakes its painting and decoration has to consider only what is suitable for its adornment, such in my judgment is the case with us. [30]It is the duty of the original historian to occupy the ground and to discuss matters from every side and to take trouble with details, [31]but the one who recasts the narrative should be allowed to strive for brevity of expression and to forego exhaustive treatment. [32]At this point therefore let us begin our narrative, adding only so much to what has already been said; for it is foolish to lengthen the preface while cutting short the history itself.

2 Mac 5:4

---

generose pro Iudaismo fortiter fecerunt, ita ut universam regionem, cum pauci essent, vindicarent et barbaram multitudinem fugarent [22]et famosissimum in toto orbe templum recuperarent et civitatem liberarent et leges, quae futurum erat ut abolerentur, restituerentur, Domino cum omni clementia propitio facto illis, [23]quae omnia ab Iasone Cyrenaeo quinque libris declarata sunt, tentavimus nos uno volumine breviare. [24]Considerantes enim multitudinem numerorum et difficultatem, quae adest volentibus aggredi narrationes historiarum propter multitudinem rerum, [25]curavimus volentibus quidem legere, ut esset animi oblectatio, studiosis vero, ut facilius possint memoriae commendare, omnibus autem legentibus utilitas conferatur. [26]Et nobis quidem ipsis, qui hoc opus breviandi causa suscepimus, non facilem laborem, immo vero negotium plenum vigiliarum et sudoris assumpsimus. [27]Sicut praeparanti convivium et quaerenti aliorum utilitatem non facile est, tamen propter multorum gratiam libenter laborem sustinebimus, [28]accurate quidem de singulis elaborare auctori concedentes, ipsi autem persequi datam formam brevitati studentes. [29]Sicut enim novae domus architecto de universa structura curandum est, ei vero, qui inurere et pingere curat, quae apta sunt ad ornatum exquirenda sunt, ita aestimo et in nobis. [30]Inire quidem et deambulacrum facere verborum et curiosius partes singulas quasque disquirere historiae congruit auctori; [31]brevitatem vero dictionis sectari et exsecutionem rerum vitare brevianti concedendum est. [32]Hinc ergo narrationem incipiemus, praedictis tantulo subiuncto; stultum etenim est ante historiam effluere, ipsam autem historiam concidere.

1. PROFANATION AND PURIFICATION OF THE TEMPLE*

A foiled attempt by Heliodorus to profane the temple

3 [1]While the holy city was inhabited in unbroken peace and the laws were very well observed because of the piety of the high priest Onias and his hatred of wickedness, [2]it came about that the kings themselves honoured the place and glorified the temple with the finest presents, [3]so that even Seleucus, the king of Asia, defrayed from his own revenues all the expenses connected with the service of the sacrifices. [4]But a man named Simon, of the tribe

---

***3:1—10:8.** Following his source, the author tells how the temple came to be purified and the altar dedicated (2:19). He links this up with the content of the letters used at the beginning of the book (1:1—2:18). But, to grasp the full significance of that purification, one needs to be aware of the whole background, and what purification involved. Therefore, we are told at length about how the temple came to be desecrated (chaps. 3–4), the damage done to it and the sufferings undergone by the martyrs (chaps. 5–7), the valour of Judas and his men as they strove to put things right (chap. 8), how God punished the main culprit, Antiochus (chap. 9), and, finally, how the temple was cleansed and the altar dedicated (10:1–8). The author reports these events, at the same time helping us see their religious dimension. Although the temple was holy and inviolable (3:12, 30), the sin of some (unlawful priests in the main: 4:7—9:24) caused God's wrath to come down on his people, on the temple, which shared the people's lot (5:1–6), and on the martyrs (6:18—7:12), as a temporary chastening punishment. The faithfulness of the martyrs causes God's wrath to cease, and he begins to show the people mercy, by granting victory to Judas (8:1–36), by causing Antiochus to have a change of heart before he dies (9:1–29), and by allowing the Jews to regain and restore the temple (10:1–8).

This first part of 2 Maccabees shows us that faithfulness to God involves heroism, even unto death, and that suffering accepted with faith has a redemptive value, in so far as it moves God to show mercy to his people. These chapters, in this way, help us understand the redemptive value of Christ's death on behalf of all mankind.

3:1–40. In this account the author wants to show that the temple of Jerusalem was

[3] [1]Cum sancta civitas habitaretur cum omni pace, et leges quam optime custodirentur propter Oniae pontificis pietatem et odium malitiae, [2]fiebat ut et ipsi reges locum honorarent et templum maximis muneribus illustrarent, [3]ita ut Seleucus quoque Asiae rex de redditibus suis praestaret omnes sumptus ad ministeria sacrificiorum pertinentes. [4]Simon autem de tribu Belgae praepositus templi constitutus dissentiebat a principe sacerdotum de dispensatione in civitate. [5]Et cum vincere Oniam non posset, venit ad Apollonium Tharseae filium, qui eo tempore erat dux Coelesyriae et Phoenicis, [6]et nuntiavit pecuniis inenarrabilibus plenum esse aerarium Hierosolymis, ita ut multitudo vectigalium innumerabilis esset et

of Benjamin, who had been made captain of the temple, had a disagreement with the high priest about the administration of the city market; [5]and when he could not prevail over Onias he went to Apollonius of Tarsus,[f] who at that time was governor of Coelesyria and Phoenicia. [6]He reported to him that the treasury in Jerusalem was full of untold sums of money, so that the amount of the funds could not be reckoned, and that they did not belong to the account of the sacrifices, but that it was possible for them to fall under the control of the king. [7]When Apollonius met the king, he told him of the money about which he had been informed. The king[g] chose Heliodorus, who was in charge of his affairs, and sent him with commands to effect the removal of the aforesaid money.

[8]Heliodorus at once set out on his journey, ostensibly to make a tour of inspection of the cities of Coelesyria and Phoenicia, but in fact to carry out the king's purpose.

---

inviolable because it was protected by God himself. God's action is depicted by the use of imagery—horses and riders, symbols of his power with which the author of the book was very familiar (cf. 5:2; 10:29; 11:8) and which are to be found in other books of the Bible (cf. Zech 1:8–10; Rev 6:2–8; 19:11–16). We can already see Hellenistically inclined Jews at work, specifically Simon who, seemingly, wants the Jerusalem market to be like Greek markets, unrestricted by Jewish food regulations.

Second Maccabees sees Onias III as a holy man (cf. 4:2–5, 35-37; 15:12); his father, Simon II, is praised in Sirach 50:1–21. Onias' prayer and that of the people moves God to intervene in an extraordinary way. These were times, as the hagiographer points out (v. 1), when the high priest was a devout man, and when, therefore, the Law was well observed and there was peace. God protected his temple. If the temple was later profaned, it was not because God withdrew his protection or because the temple had ceased to be a holy place, but because the high priest failed to keep the Law and had no right to hold the office.

Heliodorus' change of heart, caused by some sudden misfortune, such as an illness or an attack by zealous Jews, shows the power of prayer. Speaking about the power of saints' prayer (they always got what they asked), Origen cites, as one example, the righteous in the times of the Maccabees: "Those who dared to insult the religion of the Jews in the temple of Jerusalem would have to suffer what is written in the book of Maccabees" (*Contra Celsum*, 8, 46).

ea non pertinere ad rationem sacrificiorum; esse autem possibile sub potestate regis haec cadere. [7]Collocutus autem Apollonius cum rege, de indicatis sibi pecuniis aperuit; at ille vocans Heliodorum, qui erat super negotia, misit datis mandatis, ut praedictam pecuniam transportaret. [8]Statimque Heliodorus iter est aggressus, specie quidem quasi per Coelesyriam et Phoenicen civitates esset peragraturus, re vera autem regis propositum perfecturus. [9]Sed cum venisset Hierosolymam et benigne

f. Gk *Apollonius son of Tharseas* **g.** Gk *He*

[9]When he had arrived at Jerusalem and had been kindly welcomed by the high priest of[h] the city, he told about the disclosure that had been made and stated why he had come, and he inquired whether this really was the situation. [10]The high priest explained that there were some deposits belonging to widows and orphans, [11]and also some money of Hyrcanus, son of Tobias, a man of very prominent position, and that it totaled in all four hundred talents of silver and two hundred of gold. To such an extent the impious Simon had misrepresented the facts. [12]And he said that it was utterly impossible that wrong should be done to those people who had trusted in the holiness of the place and in the sanctity and inviolability of the temple which is honoured throughout the whole world. [13]But Heliodorus, because of the king's commands which he had, said that this money must in any case be confiscated for the king's treasury. [14]So he set a day and went in to direct the inspection of these funds.

There was no little distress throughout the whole city. [15]The priests prostrated themselves before the altar in their priestly garments and called toward heaven upon him who had given the law about deposits, that he should keep them safe for those who had deposited them. [16]To see the appearance of the high priest was to be wounded at heart, for his face and the change in his color disclosed the anguish of his soul. [17]For terror and bodily trembling had come over the man, which plainly showed to those who looked at him the pain lodged in his heart. [18]People also hurried out of their houses in crowds to make a general supplication because the holy place was about to be brought into contempt. [19]Women, girded with sackcloth under their breasts, thronged the streets. Some of the maidens who were kept indoors ran together to the gates, and some to the walls, while others peered out of the windows. [20]And holding up their hands to heaven, they all made

---

a summo sacerdote civitatis esset exceptus, narravit de dato indicio, et cuius rei gratia adesset aperuit; interrogabat autem, si vere haec ita essent. [10]Tunc summus sacerdos ostendit deposita esse viduarum et pupillorum; [11]quaedam vero esse Hircani Thobiae, viri valde eminentis, non sicut detulerat obtrectans impius Simon; universa autem argenti talenta esse quadringenta et auri ducenta; [12]decipi vero eos, qui credidissent loci sanctitati et honorati per universum mundum templi venerationi inviolabili tutelae, omnino impossibile esse. [13]At ille, pro his, quae habebat, mandatis a rege, omnino dicebat in regium fiscum ea esse deferenda. [14]Constituta autem die, intrabat de his visitationem ordinaturus. Non modica vero per universam civitatem erat trepidatio. [15]Sacerdotes autem ante altare cum stolis sacerdotalibus iactaverunt se et invocabant in caelum eum, qui de deposito legem posuit, ut his, qui deposuerant, ea salva custodiret. [16]Erat autem, ut qui videret summi sacerdotis vultum, mente vulneraretur: facies enim et color immutatus declarabat internum animi dolorem. [17]Circumfusus enim erat metus quidam viro, et horror corporis, unde manifestus aspicientibus dolor instans cordi efficiebatur. [18]Alii autem de domibus gregatim prosiliebant ad publicam supplicationem, pro eo quod in contemptum locus esset venturus.

h. Some authorities read *and*

entreaty. [21]There was something pitiable in the prostration of the whole populace and the anxiety of the high priest in his great anguish.

[22]While they were calling upon the Almighty Lord that he would keep what had been entrusted safe and secure for those who had entrusted it, [23]Heliodorus went on with what had been decided. [24]But when he arrived at the treasury with his bodyguard, then and there the Sovereign of spirits and of all authority caused so great a manifestation that all who had been so bold as to accompany him were astounded by the power of God, and became faint with terror. [25]For there appeared to them a magnificently caparisoned horse, with a rider of frightening mien, and it rushed furiously at Heliodorus and struck at him with its front hoofs. Its rider was seen to have armour and weapons of gold.

[26]Two young men also appeared to him, remarkably strong, gloriously beautiful and splendidly dressed, who stood on each side of him and scourged him continuously, inflicting many blows on him. [27]When he suddenly fell to the ground and deep darkness came over him, his men took him up and put him on a stretcher [28]and carried him away, this man who had just entered the aforesaid treasury with a great retinue and all his bodyguard but was now unable to help himself; and they recognized clearly the sovereign power of God. [29]While he lay prostrate, speechless because of the divine intervention and deprived of any hope of recovery, [30]they praised the Lord who had acted marvelously for his own place. And the temple, which a little while before was full of fear and disturbance, was filled with joy and gladness, now that the Almighty LORD had appeared.

Heb 12:9
Acts 9:1–29

2 Mac 5:4
Rev 19:11

Lk 24:4
Acts 1:10

Tit 2:11

---

[19]Accinctaeque mulieres ciliciis sub mammis per vias confluebant; sed et virgines, quae conclusae erant, aliae quidem procurrebant ad ianuas, aliae autem ad muros, quaedam vero per fenestras aspiciebant; [20]universae autem protendentes manus in caelum deprecabantur. [21]Erat enim misereri commixtae multitudinis prostrationem et summi sacerdotis in magna agonia constituti exspectationem. [22]Et hi quidem invocabant omnipotentem Dominum, ut credita salva his, qui crediderant, conservaret cum omni tutela. [23]Heliodorus autem, quod fuerat decretum, perficiebat. [24]Eodem loco, ipso cum satellitibus circa aerarium praesente, spirituum et omnis potestatis Dominus magnam fecit ostensionem, ita ut omnes, qui ausi fuerant convenire, perterriti virtute Dei in dissolutionem et formidinem converterentur. [25]Apparuit enim illis quidam equus terribilem habens sessorem et optimo operimento adornatus; isque cum impetu invectus Heliodoro priores calces impegit, qui autem supersedebat videbatur arma habere aurea. [26]Alii etiam apparuerunt duo iuvenes virtute decori, optimi gloria speciosique amictu, qui etiam circumsteterunt eum et ex utraque parte flagellabant sine intermissione multas inferentes ei plagas. [27]Subito autem concidit in terram; eumque multa caligine circumfusum rapuerunt atque in sellam gestatoriam imposuerunt; [28]et eum, qui cum multis cursoribus et satellitibus praedictum ingressus erat aerarium, portabant carentem auxilio ex armis constitutum, manifeste Dei virtutem cognoscentem. [29]Et ille quidem per divinam virtutem iacebat mutus atque omni spe et salute privatus; [30]hi autem Dominum benedicebant, qui magnificabat locum suum et templum, quod paulo ante timore ac tumultu erat

[31]Quickly some of Heliodorus' friends asked Onias to call upon the Most High and to grant life to one who was lying quite at his last breath. [32]And the high priest, fearing that the king might get the notion that some foul play had been perpetrated by the Jews with regard to Heliodorus, offered sacrifice for the man's recovery. [33]While the high priest was making the offering of atonement, the same young men appeared again to Heliodorus dressed in the same clothing, and they stood and said, "Be very grateful to Onias the high priest, since for his sake the Lord has granted you your life. [34]And see that you, who have been scourged by heaven, report to all men the majestic power of God." Having said this they vanished.

Lk 24:31

[35]Then Heliodorus offered sacrifice to the Lord and made very great vows to the Saviour of his life, and having bidden Onias farewell, he marched off with his forces to the king. [36]And he bore testimony to all men of the deeds of the supreme God, which he had seen with his own eyes. [37]When the king asked Heliodorus what sort of person would be suitable to send on another mission to Jerusalem, he replied, [38]"If you have any enemy or plotter against your government, send him there, for you will get him back thoroughly scourged, if he escapes at all, for there certainly is about the place some power of God. [39]For he who has his dwelling in heaven watches over that place himself and brings it aid, and he strikes and destroys those who come to do it injury." [40]This was the outcome of the episode of Heliodorus and the protection of the treasury.

---

plenum, apparente omnipotente Domino, gaudio et laetitia impletum est. [31]Confestim vero ex amicis Heliodori quidam rogabant Oniam, ut invocaret Altissimum, ut vitam donaret ei, qui prorsus in supremo spiritu erat constitutus. [32]Suspectus autem factus summus sacerdos, ne forte rex opinaretur malitiam aliquam ex Iudaeis circa Heliodorum consummatam, obtulit hostiam pro salute viri. [33]Cumque summus sacerdos litationem perficeret, iidem iuvenes rursus apparuerunt Heliodoro eisdem vestibus amicti et astantes dixerunt: «Oniae summo sacerdoti multas gratias age, nam propter eum Dominus tibi vitam donavit; [34]tu autem a caelo flagellatus nuntia omnibus magnam Dei potestatem». Et his dictis, non comparuerunt. [35]Heliodorus autem, hostia Domino oblata et votis magnis promissis ei, qui vivere concessit, et Oniam acceptum habens cum exercitu repedavit ad regem; [36]testabatur autem omnibus ea, quae sub oculis suis viderat, opera maximi Dei. [37]Cum autem rex interrogasset Heliodorum quis esset aptus adhuc semel Hierosolymam mitti, ait: [38]«Si quem habes hostem aut rerum insidiatorem, mitte eum illuc et flagellatum eum recipies, si tamen evaserit, eo quod in loco sit vere Dei quaedam virtus; [39]nam ipse, qui habet in caelis habitationem, visitator et adiutor est loci illius et venientes ad malefaciendum percutit ac perdit». [40]Igitur de Heliodoro et aerarii custodia ita res processerunt. **[4]** [1]Simon autem praedictus, qui pecuniarum et patriae delator exstitit, male loquebatur de Onia, tamquam ipse Heliodorum instigasset et malorum auctor fuisset; [2]benefactoremque civitatis et curatorem gentis suae et aemulatorem legum audebat insidiatorem rerum dicere. [3]Sed cum inimicitia in tantum procederet, ut etiam per quendam eorum, qui a Simone probati essent, homicidia fierent, [4]considerans Onias periculum contentionis et Apollonium Menesthei, ducem Coelesyriae et Phoenicis, augentem malitiam Simonis, [5]ad regem se contulit, non ut civium accusator, sed quod utile esset in commune et singulariter universae multitudinis prospiciens. [6]Videbat enim sine regali providentia impossibile esse pacem adhuc rebus obtingere, nec Simonem cessaturum a stultitia. [7]Sed post Seleuci vitae excessum, cum suscepisset

Jason usurps the high priesthood. The Hellenization of Jerusalem

4 [1]The previously mentioned Simon, who had informed about the money against[i] his own country, slandered Onias, saying that it was he who had incited Heliodorus and had been the real cause of the misfortune. [2]He dared to designate as a plotter against the government the man who was the benefactor of the city, the protector of his fellow countrymen, and a zealot for the laws. [3]When his hatred progressed to such a degree that even murders were committed by one of Simon's approved agents, [4]Onias

---

4:1–22. Tension continues to mount between Onias and Simon. When Onias goes to Antioch, King Seleucus has already been assassinated by Heliodorus, and Antiochus IV is on the throne (175 BC). Antiochus sees in Jason a man he can use to Hellenize Palestine (Jason had already dropped his Jewish name, "Jesus", in favour of a Greek name). Given the status enjoyed by Jerusalem—the author mentions (in v. 11), prior to its happening, the treaty with Rome (cf. 1 Mac 8:17–32)—Jason needed to have a special mandate from the king to do what he planned. The "body of youth" (v. 9) was a place where youths aged eighteen to twenty gathered for athletic and cultural events. The fact that the gymnasium was built alongside the temple meant that it was in some way in competition with it. The "Greek hat" was a cap with wings on it: wearing it was part of the dress-code of the "body of youth". Being enrolled as "citizens of Antioch" (v. 9) meant being nationals of that city. Jerusalem takes part in the games in honour of the pagan gods (vv. 18–20) and acclaims Antiochus as king (vv. 21–22). The entire passage is a description of how life in Jerusalem is becoming that of a pagan city. The events narrated here are dealt with briefly in 1 Maccabees 1:10–15. According to Flavius Josephus, Jason was made high priest after the death of Onias (cf. *Antiquitates Judaicae*, 12, 237). The author of 2 Maccabees says that he supplanted Onias (v. 26)—perhaps to make the point that Jason had no right to be high priest.

As our Lord will often tell us (cf. Mt 10:16–42; 24:9–13; etc.), external difficulties are part and parcel of life for someone who wants to be faithful to God; but a lively hope can turn them into a source of faith and a forge of virtue: "No man, whether he be a Christian or not, has an easy life. To be sure, at certain times it seems as though everything goes as we had planned. But this generally lasts for only a short time. Life is a matter of facing up to difficulties and of

regnum Antiochus, qui Epiphanes appellabatur, ambiebat Iason frater Oniae summum sacerdotium, [8]promittens regi per interpellationem argenti talenta trecenta sexaginta et ex reditu quodam alio talenta octoginta, [9]super haec autem promittebat et alia centum quinquaginta se perscripturum, si concederetur per potestatem eius gymnasium et ephebiam sibi constituere et eos, qui in Hierosolymis erant, Antiochenos scribere. [10]Quod cum rex annuisset et obtinuisset principatum, statim ad Graecam consuetudinem contribules suos transferre coepit. [11]Et, amotis his, quae humanitatis causa Iudaeis a regibus fuerant constituta per Ioannem patrem Eupolemi, qui apud Romanos de amicitia et societate

i. Gk *and*

recognized that the rivalry was serious and that Apollonius, the son of Menestheus[j] and governor of Coelesyria and Phoenicia, was intensifying the malice of Simon. [5]So he betook himself to the king, not accusing his fellow citizens but having in view the welfare, both public and private, of all the people. [6]For he saw that without the king's attention public affairs could not again reach a peaceful settlement, and that Simon would not stop his folly.

1 Mac 1:10

[7]When Seleucus died and Antiochus who was called Epiphanes succeeded to the kingdom, Jason the brother of Onias obtained the high priesthood by corruption, [8]promising the king at an interview[k] three hundred and sixty talents of silver and, from another source of revenue, eighty talents. [9]In addition to this he promised to pay one hundred and fifty more if permission were given to establish by his authority a gymnasium and a body of youth for it, and to enrol the men of Jerusalem as citizens of Antioch. [10]When the king assented and Jason[l] came to office, he at once shifted his countrymen over to the Greek way of life. [11]He set aside the existing royal concessions to the Jews, secured through John the father of Eupolemus, who went on the mission to establish friendship and alliance with the Romans; and he destroyed the lawful ways of living and introduced new customs contrary to the law. [12]For with alacrity he founded a gymnasium right under the citadel, and he induced the noblest of the young men[m] to wear the Greek hat. [13]There was such an extreme of Hellenization and increase in the adoption of foreign ways because of the surpassing wickedness of Jason, who was ungodly and no high priest, [14]that the priests were no longer intent

1 Mac 1:11–51

1 Mac 8:17

experiencing in our hearts both joy and sorrow. It is in this forge that man can acquire fortitude, patience, magnanimity and composure" (St J. Escrivá, *Friends of God*, 77).

4:14. "The call to the discus": we cannot be sure what this means. It may be a call to throw the discus, or a call made with some sort of gong.

functus est legatione, et legitima civium iura destituens, pravos mores innovabat. [12]Prompte enim sub ipsa arce gymnasium constituit et optimos quosque epheborum subigens sub petasum ducebat. [13]Erat autem sic culmen quoddam Graecae conversationis et profectus alienigenarum moris, propter impii et non summi sacerdotis Iasonis inauditam contaminationem, [14]ita ut sacerdotes iam non circa altaris officia dediti essent, sed contempto templo et sacrificiis neglectis, festinarent participes fieri iniquae in palaestra praebitionis post disci provocationem [15]et patrios quidem honores nihil habentes, Graecas autem glorias optimas aestimantes. [16]Quarum gratia periculosa eos contentio habebat, et quorum instituta aemulabantur ac per omnia consimiles esse cupiebant, hos hostes et ultores habuerunt. [17]In leges enim divinas impie agere non est facile, sed haec tempus sequens declarabit. [18]Cum autem quinquennalis agon Tyri celebraretur, et rex praesens esset, [19]misit Iason facinorosus ab Hierosolymis

j. Vg Compare verse 21: Gk uncertain **k.** Or *by a petition* **l.** Gk *he* **m.** Some authorities add *subjecting them*

upon their service at the altar. Despising the sanctuary and neglecting the sacrifices, they hastened to take part in the unlawful proceedings in the wrestling arena after the call to the discus, [15]disdaining the honours prized by their fathers and putting the highest value upon Greek forms of prestige. [16]For this reason heavy disaster overtook them, and those whose ways of living they admired and wished to imitate completely became their enemies and punished them. [17]For it is no light thing to show irreverence to the divine laws—a fact which later events will make clear.

[18]When the quadrennial games were being held at Tyre and the king was present, [19]the vile Jason sent envoys, chosen as being Antiochian citizens from Jerusalem, to carry three hundred silver drachmas for the sacrifice to Hercules. Those who carried the money, however, thought best not to use it for sacrifice, because that was inappropriate, but to expend it for another purpose. [20]So this money was intended by the sender for the sacrifice to Hercules, but by the decision of its carriers it was applied to the construction of triremes.

2 Mac 4:9

[21]When Apollonius the son of Menestheus was sent to Egypt for the coronation[n] of Philometor as king, Antiochus learned that Philometor[o] had become hostile to his government, and he took measures for his own security. Therefore upon arriving at Joppa he proceeded to Jerusalem. [22]He was welcomed magnificently by Jason and the city, and ushered in with a blaze of torches and with shouts. Then he marched into Phoenicia.

The priesthood in the control of Menelaus

[23]After a period of three years Jason sent Menelaus, the brother of the previously mentioned Simon, to carry the money to the king

2 Mac 3:4

4:23–29. Appointment as high priest needed the king's confirmation due to the civil implications of the office. Now the high priesthood has become a purchasable item, and the highest bidder is Menelaus, who is not even a member of the priestly tribe (v. 26). This shows just how degraded Jewish religious institutions have become.

spectatores Antiochenses portantes argenti drachmas trecentas in sacrificium Herculis; quas etiam postulaverunt hi, qui asportaverant, ne in sacrificium erogarentur, quia non oporteret, sed in alium sumptum eas deputari. [20]Sed haec ceciderunt: propter illum quidem, qui miserat, in sacrificium Herculis; propter eos autem, qui afferebant, in fabricam triremium. [21]Misso autem in Aegyptum Apollonio Menesthei filio propter ascensum ad solium Philometoris regis, cum cognovisset Antiochus alienum se ab illius negotiis effectum, propriae securitati consuluit; inde cum Ioppen venisset, se contulit Hierosolymam. [22]Et magnifice ab Iasone et civitate susceptus, cum facularum luminibus et acclamationibus introductus est; deinde sic in Phoenicen exercitum convertit. [23]Et post triennii tempus

n. The exact meaning of the Greek word is uncertain **o.** Gk *he*

and to complete the records of essential business. [24]But he, when presented to the king, extolled him with an air of authority, and secured the high priesthood for himself, outbidding Jason by three hundred talents of silver. [25]After receiving the king's orders he returned, possessing no qualification for the high priesthood, but having the hot temper of a cruel tyrant and the rage of a savage wild beast. [26]So Jason, who after supplanting his own brother was supplanted by another man, was driven as a fugitive into the land of Ammon. [27]And Menelaus held the office, but he did not pay regularly any of the money promised to the king. [28]When Sostratus the captain of the citadel kept requesting payment, for the collection of the revenue was his responsibility, the two of them were summoned by the king on account of this issue. [29]Menelaus left his own brother Lysimachus as deputy in the high priesthood, while Sostratus left Crates, the commander of the Cyprian troops.*

Death of Onias III

[30]While such was the state of affairs, it happened that the people of Tarsus and of Mallus revolted because their cities had been given as a present to Antiochis, the king's concubine. [31]So the king went hastily to settle the trouble, leaving Andronicus, a man of high rank, to act as his deputy. [32]But Menelaus, thinking he had obtained a suitable opportunity, stole some of the gold vessels of the temple and gave them to Andronicus; other vessels, as it happened, he had

Acts 5:2

4:30–38. The sacrilegious bent of Menelaus can be seen from the fact that he steals temple vessels which end up in the markets of pagan cities. King Antiochus' reaction to the murder of Onias is surprising; maybe the king used the opportunity to rid himself of Andronicus. The sacred writer, however, reports these things in order to emphasize what a good man Onias was: even the king had regard for him. The importance of Onias as an intercessor for the people can be seen from the account of a dream Judas Maccabeus has (cf.

misit Iason Menelaum supradicti Simonis fratrem portantem pecunias regi et de negotiis necessariis commonitiones perlaturum. [24]At ille commendatus regi, cum se magnificasset facie potestatis, in semetipsum contulit summum sacerdotium superponens Iasoni talenta argenti trecenta; [25]acceptisque regiis mandatis, venit nihil quidem gerens dignum sacerdotio, animos vero crudelis tyranni et ferae barbarae iram habens. [26]Et Iason quidem, qui proprium fratrem circumvenerat, ipse circumventus ab alio profugus in Ammanitem expulsus est regionem. [27]Menelaus autem principatum quidem obtinuit; de pecuniis vero regi promissis nihil debite agebat, [28]cum vero exactionem faceret Sostratus, qui arci erat praepositus, nam ad hunc exactio vectigalium pertinebat. Quam ob causam utrique a rege sunt advocati; [29]et Menelaus quidem reliquit summi sacerdotii successorem Lysimachum fratrem suum, Sostratus autem Cratetem, qui praeerat Cypriis. [30]Talibus autem constitutis, contigit Tarsenses et Mallotas seditionem movere, eo quod Antiochidi, regis concubinae, dono essent dati. [31]Festinanter itaque rex venit sedare illos, relicto suffecto uno ex iis in dignitate constitutis Andronico. [32]Ratus autem

sold to Tyre and the neighbouring cities. [33]When Onias became fully aware of these acts he publicly exposed them, having first withdrawn to a place of sanctuary at Daphne near Antioch. [34]Therefore Menelaus, taking Andronicus aside, urged him to kill Onias. Andronicus[p] came to Onias, and resorting to treachery offered him sworn pledges and gave him his right hand, and in spite of his suspicion persuaded Onias[q] to come out from the place of sanctuary; then, with no regard for justice, he immediately put him out of the way.* [35]For this reason not only Jews, but many also of other nations, were grieved and displeased at the unjust murder of the man. [36]When the king returned from the region of Cilicia, the Jews in the city[r] appealed to him with regard to the unreasonable murder of Onias, and the Greeks shared their hatred of the crime. [37]Therefore Antiochus was grieved at heart and filled with pity, and wept because of the moderation and good conduct of the deceased; [38]and inflamed with anger, he immediately stripped off the purple robe from Andronicus, tore off his garments, and led him about the whole city to that very place where he had committed the outrage against Onias, and there he dispatched the bloodthirsty fellow. The Lord thus repaid him with the punishment he deserved.

Dan 9:26

15:12), and there is probably a reference to Onias in Daniel 9:26–27 when Daniel sees in the "cutting off of an anointed one" a sign that God's sentence is beginning to be carried out.

4:39–50. The sacred writer has been showing that those who do evil receive the punishment their sin merits. This is what happens to those who had adopted Greek ways (v. 16). Jason is deprived of his office by Menelaus and he has to flee (v. 26); Andronicus, Onias' assassin, is put to death by Antiochus (v. 38); and Lysimachus, the sacrilegious thief, dies at the hands of the crowd (v. 42). However, sometimes evildoers, as in the case of Menelaus, are able to postpone the punishment that is their due. When evil goes unpunished, one needs to be patient and trust in God.

Menelaus accepisse se tempus opportunum, aurea quaedam vasa e templo furatus donavit Andronico et alia vendiderat Tyri et per vicinas civitates. [33]Quod cum certissime cognovisset Onias, arguebat eum, ipse in loco tuto se continens in Daphne secus Antiochiam. [34]Unde Menelaus seorsum apprehendens Andronicum rogabat, ut Oniam interficeret. At vero ille, cum venisset ad Oniam et cum fidem dolo dedisset ac dexteram accepisset dedissetque cum iureiurando, quamvis esset ei suspectus, suasit de asylo procedere, quem statim peremit, non veritus iustitiam. [35]Ob quam causam non solum Iudaei, sed multi quoque ex aliis nationibus indignabantur et moleste ferebant de nece viri iniusta. [36]Sed regressum regem de Ciliciae locis interpellabant, qui erant per civitatem Iudaei, simul et Graecis scelus conquerentibus, de eo quod sine ratione Onias interfectus esset. [37]Contristatus itaque animo Antiochus et flexus ad misericordiam lacrimas fudit, propter defuncti sobrietatem et multam modestiam; [38]accensusque animis, confestim ablata Andronici purpura ac tunicis eius discissis, circumduxit per

p. Gk *He* **q.** Gk *him* **r.** Or *in each city*

A revolt against Menelaus

[39]When many acts of sacrilege had been committed in the city by Lysimachus with the connivance of Menelaus, and when report of them had spread abroad, the populace gathered against Lysimachus, because many of the gold vessels had already been stolen. [40]And since the crowds were becoming aroused and filled with anger, Lysimachus armed about three thousand men and launched an unjust attack, under the leadership of a certain Auranus,* a man advanced in years and no less advanced in folly.

[41]But when the Jews[s] became aware of Lysimachus' attack, some picked up stones, some blocks of wood, and others took handfuls of the ashes that were lying about, and threw them in wild confusion at Lysimachus and his men. [42]As a result, they wounded many of them, and killed some, and put them all to flight; and the temple robber himself they killed close by the treasury.

[43]Charges were brought against Menelaus about this incident. [44]When the king came to Tyre, three men sent by the senate presented the case before him. [45]But Menelaus, already as good as beaten, promised a substantial bribe to Ptolemy son of Dorymenes to win over the king. [46]Therefore Ptolemy, taking the king aside into a colonnade as if for refreshment, induced the king to change his mind. [47]Menelaus, the cause of all the evil, he acquitted of the charges against him, while he sentenced to death those unfortunate men, who would have been freed uncondemned if they had pleaded even before Scythians. [48]And so those who had spoken for the city and the villages[t] and the holy vessels quickly suffered the unjust penalty. [49]Therefore even the Tyrians, showing their hatred of the crime, provided magnificently for their funeral. [50]But

1 Mac 3:38
2 Mac 8:8; 10:12

totam civitatem usque ad eundem locum, in quo in Oniam impietatem commiserat, atque illic sacrilegum interfectorem e mundo sustulit, Domino illi condignam retribuente poenam. [39]Multis autem sacrilegiis per civitatem a Lysimacho commissis Menelai consilio, et divulgata foris fama, congregata est multitudo adversum Lysimachum, vasis aureis iam multis dissipatis. [40]Turbis autem insurgentibus et ira repletis, Lysimachus, armatis fere tribus milibus, iniquis manibus coepit, duce quodam Aurano aetate non minus ac dementia provecto. [41]Sed ut intellexerunt conatum Lysimachi, alii lapides, alii fustes validos arripuere, quidam vero ex adiacente cinere manu apprehenderunt et mixtim iecerunt in eos, qui circa Lysimachum erant. [42]Quam ob causam multos quidem vulneraverunt, quosdam autem et prostraverunt, omnes vero in fugam compulerunt, ipsum vero sacrilegum secus aerarium interfecerunt. [43]De his ergo coepit iudicium adversus Menelaum agitari. [44]Et cum venisset rex Tyrum, apud ipsum causam egerunt missi tres viri a senatu. [45]Et cum iam superaretur Menelaus, promisit Ptolemaeo Dorymenis multas pecunias ad suadendum regi. [46]Unde Ptolemaeus, excipiens seorsum in quoddam atrium columnatum quasi refrigerandi gratia regem, deduxit a sententia. [47]Et Menelaum quidem universae malitiae reum criminibus absolvit; miseros autem, qui etiam si apud Scythas causam dixissent innocentes iudicarentur, hos morte damnavit. [48]Cito ergo iniustam poenam dederunt, qui pro civitate et populo et sacris vasis causam prosecuti sunt, [49]Quam ob rem Tyrii quoque in malefactum indignati, quaeque ad sepulturam eorum necessaria essent, magno sumptu praestiterunt. [50]Menelaus autem propter

s. Gk *they* **t.** Other authorities read *the people*

Menelaus, because of the cupidity of those in power, remained in office, growing in wickedness, having become the chief plotter against his fellow citizens.

Antiochus Epiphanes plunders the temple

5 [1]About this time Antiochus made his second invasion of Egypt. [2]And it happened that over all the city, for almost forty days, there appeared golden-clad horsemen charging through the air, in companies fully armed with lances and drawn swords—[3]troops of horsemen drawn up, attacks and counterattacks made on this side and on that, brandishing of shields, massing of spears, hurling of missiles, the flash of golden trappings, and armour of all sorts. [4]Therefore all men prayed that the apparition might prove to have been a good omen.

2 Mac 3:25

[5]When a false rumor arose that Antiochus was dead, Jason took no less than a thousand men and suddenly made an assault upon the city. When the troops upon the wall had been forced back and

5:1–27. From 1 Maccabees 1:16–24 and Daniel 11:25–31 we know that Antiochus Epiphanes made two expeditions into Egypt. The first was in 169 BC, and things went well for him; on his way back to Antioch he sacked the temple of Jerusalem (cf. 1 Mac 1:16–24; Dan 11:25–28). The second was in 168 BC, and he was forced to withdraw by the Romans. It was after the second campaign that he committed the worst atrocities in the Holy City. Shortly afterwards, in 167 BC, Antiochus ordered that a statue of Zeus be erected in the temple of Jerusalem (cf. 6:1–2; 1 Mac 1:29–64; Dan 11:29–31). The author of 2 Maccabees puts the sack of Jerusalem and Antiochus' atrocity after the second Egyptian campaign. As already pointed out by the author, readers should not expect complete historical precision from him (cf. 2:28). What he is interested in, above all, is to show the underlying causes of events. To do so, he prefaces this passage with a report of a heavenly apparition which announces what is going to befall the city (vv. 2–4; cf. 2:21); then he focuses again on the people's sin, that is, the strife going on inside Jerusalem itself (which resulted from Jason's boundless ambition, and which was the immediate cause of Antiochus' intervention: vv. 5–10); and, finally, he describes the horrific behaviour of Antiochus (vv. 11–26), and makes a reference to Judas

eorum, qui in potentia erant, avaritiam permanebat in potestate, crescens in malitia magnus civium insidiator constitutus. **[5]** [1]Circa hoc autem tempus Antiochus secundam profectionem paravit in Aegyptum. [2]Contigit autem per universam civitatem fere per dies quadraginta videri per aera equites discurrentes, auratas stolas habentes et hastas, ad modum cohortium armatos, et gladiorum evaginationes [3]et turmas equorum per ordinem digestas et congressiones fieri et decursus utrorumque et scutorum motus et contorum multitudinem et telorum iactus et aureorum ornamentorum fulgores omnisque generis loricationes. [4]Quapropter omnes rogabant pro bono factam esse ostensionem. [5]Sed cum falsus rumor exisset tamquam vita excessisset Antiochus, assumptis Iason non minus mille viris

at last the city was being taken, Menelaus took refuge in the citadel. [6]But Jason kept relentlessly slaughtering his fellow citizens, not realizing that success at the cost of one's kindred is the greatest misfortune, but imagining that he was setting up trophies of victory over enemies and not over fellow countrymen.

[7]He did not gain control of the government, however; and in the end got only disgrace from his conspiracy, and fled again into the country of the Ammonites. [8]Finally he met a miserable end.

Maccabeus as a sign of hope on the horizon (v. 27).

The heavenly apparition (vv. 2–4), described by using literary devices of the period (cf. 3:25), is a sort of folk-omen. The account of the death of Jason once again makes the point that evil-doers pay the price of their sins (vv. 9–10; cf. the note on 4:39–50). The sack of the temple was made possible because God had forsaken the sanctuary due to the people's sins (vv. 18–20). Those who backed Hellenization suffer the consequences (vv. 22–26; cf. 4:16).

The words of v. 19 make it plain that what matters to God is the chosen people, and it was for them and their good that he chose to dwell in that sanctuary.

When the people, or, better, the chief priests and their henchmen, reject God, God breaks the special relationship set up with them by his presence in the temple; he will look for a new form of relationship to keep contact with them. Religious institutions, then, are at the service of man and his relationship with God: there is nothing absolute about them. This is something our Lord will say apropos of the sabbath, using a phrase that parallels v. 19: "The sabbath was made for man, not man for the sabbath" (Mk 2:27). By this he means that he, as the Father's envoy, is the way to a new relationship with God; he is therefore "Lord of the sabbath". The sabbath instituted by God at the beginning of the world as an expression of his creative power and his love for man (Gen 2:1–3), as also the temple where his glory dwelt, have given way to the definitive manifestation of God's power and love, and to his new presence among men through Jesus Christ. For the Christian reader of 2 Maccabees, the painful desecration of the throne of Jerusalem was a sign that the presence of God among men was not necessarily linked to that place and that institution. The inspired author of 2 Maccabees is saying as much.

On the "captain of the Mysians", see the note on 1 Mac 1:29.

repente aggressus est civitatem; illis autem, qui erant in muro, compulsis in fugam et ad ultimum iam apprehensa civitate, Menelaus fugit in arcem. [6]Iason vero caedes civium suorum perpetrabat nulli parcens, non intellegens prosperitatem adversum cognatos calamitatem esse maximam, arbitrans autem hostium et non civium se trophaea constituere. [7]Et principatum quidem non obtinuit, finem vero insidiarum suarum confusionem adeptus, profugus iterum abiit in Ammanitidem. [8]Ad ultimum igitur malam reversionem sortitus est; conclusus apud Aretam Arabum tyrannum, fugiens de civitate in civitatem, expulsus ab omnibus, odiosus ut refuga legum et exsecrabilis ut patriae et civium carnifex in

Accused[u] before Aretas the ruler of the Arabs, fleeing from city to city, pursued by all men, hated as a rebel against the laws, and abhorred as the executioner of his country and his fellow citizens, he was cast ashore in Egypt; [9]and he who had driven many from their own country into exile died in exile, having embarked to go to the Lacedaemonians in hope of finding protection because of their kinship. [10]He who had cast out many to lie unburied had no one to mourn for him; he had no funeral of any sort and no place in the tomb of his fathers.

1 Mac 12:7

[11]When news of what had happened reached the king, he took it to mean that Judea was in revolt. So, raging inwardly, he left Egypt and took the city by storm. [12]And he commanded his soldiers to cut down relentlessly every one they met and to slay those who went into the houses. [13]Then there was killing of young and old, destruction of boys, women, and children, and slaughter of virgins and infants. [14]Within the total of three days eighty thousand were destroyed, forty thousand in hand-to-hand fighting; and as many were sold into slavery as were slain.

1 Mac 1:20–24

[15]Not content with this, Antiochus[v] dared to enter the most holy temple in all the world, guided by Menelaus, who had become a traitor both to the laws and to his country. [16]He took the holy vessels with his polluted hands, and swept away with profane hands the votive offerings which other kings had made to enhance the glory and honour of the place. [17]Antiochus was elated in spirit, and did not perceive that the Lord was angered for a little while because of the sins of those who dwelt in the city, and that therefore he was disregarding the holy place. [18]But if it had not happened that they were involved in many sins, this man would have been scourged and turned back from his rash act as soon as

2 Mac 6:12–16; 7:16–19,32–38

2 Mac 3

Aegyptum extrusus est. [9]Et qui multos de patria expulerat, peregre periit ad Lacedaemonios pervectus, quasi pro cognatione habiturus protectionem; [10]et qui insepultos multos abiecerat, ipse illamentatus permansit, nec exsequiis ullis neque patrio sepulcro participavit. [11]Cum autem nuntia ad regem pervenissent de his, quae gesta erant, suspicatus est rex a societate defecturam Iudaeam; et ob hoc profectus ex Aegypto efferatus animo civitatem quidem armis cepit [12]et iussit militibus interficere occursantes nemini parcendo et eos, qui in domos ascenderent, trucidare. [13]Fiebant ergo iuvenum ac seniorum caedes, mulierum et natorum exterminium virginumque et parvulorum neces. [14]Erant autem toto triduo octoginta milia perditi, quadraginta quidem milia in ipso manuum conflictu, non minus autem quam qui iugulati fuerant, venumdati sunt. [15]Non contentus autem his, ausus est intrare templum universae terrae sanctissimum, ducem habens Menelaum, qui legum et patriae fuit proditor, [16]et scelestis manibus sumens sancta vasa et, quae ab aliis regibus et civitatibus erant posita ad augmentum et gloriam loci et honorem, profanis manibus contrectans. [17]Ita extollebatur mente Antiochus non considerans quod propter peccata habitantium civitatem modicum Dominus fuerat iratus; propter quod accidit circa locum despectio. [18]Alioquin nisi contigisset eos multis peccatis esse involutos, sicut Heliodorus, qui missus est a Seleuco rege ad inspectionem aerarii, et ipse, mox ut accessisset, confestim flagellatus repulsus

u. Cn: Gk *Imprisoned* **v.** Gk *he*

1 Chron 17:9
Mk 2:27

he came forward, just as Heliodorus was, whom Seleucus the king sent to inspect the treasury. [19]But the Lord did not choose the nation for the sake of the holy place, but the place for the sake of the nation. [20]Therefore the place itself shared in the misfortunes that befell the nation and afterward participated in its benefits; and what was forsaken in the wrath of the Almighty was restored again in all its glory when the great Lord became reconciled.

[21]So Antiochus carried off eighteen hundred talents from the temple, and hurried away to Antioch, thinking in his arrogance that he could sail on the land and walk on the sea, because his mind was elated. [22]And he left governors to afflict the people: at Jerusalem, Philip, by birth a Phrygian and in character more barbarous than the man who appointed him; [23]and at Gerizim, Andronicus; and besides these Menelaus, who lorded it over his fellow citizens worse than the others did. In his malice toward the Jewish citizens,[w] [24]Antiochus[x] sent Apollonius, the captain of the Mysians, with an army of twenty-two thousand, and commanded him to slay all the grown men and to sell the women and boys as slaves. [25]When this man arrived in Jerusalem, he pretended to be peaceably disposed and waited until the holy sabbath day; then, finding the Jews not at work, he ordered his men to parade under arms. [26]He put to the sword all those who came out to see them, then rushed into the city with his armed men and killed great numbers of people.

1 Mac 1:29–37

1 Mac 1:29–37

1 Mac 2:28

[27]But Judas Maccabeus, with about nine others, got away to the wilderness, and kept himself and his companions alive in the mountains as wild animals do; they continued to live on what grew wild, so that they might not share in the defilement.

---

fuisset ab audacia. [19]Verum non propter locum gentem, sed propter gentem locum Dominus elegit. [20]Ideoque et ipse locus particeps factus populi malorum, postea factus est socius beneficiorum; et, qui derelictus in ira Omnipotentis est, iterum in magni Domini reconciliatione cum omni gloria restitutus est. [21]Igitur Antiochus mille et octingentis ablatis de templo talentis, velocius Antiochiam regressus est, existimans se prae superbia terram ad navigandum, pelagus vero ad ambulandum deducturum propter mentis elationem. [22]Reliquit autem et praepositos ad affligendam gentem: Hierosolymis quidem Philippum, genere Phrygem, moribus barbariorem eo ipso, a quo constitutus est; [23]in Garizim autem Andronicum; praeter autem hos Menelaum, qui gravius quam ceteri imminebat civibus. [24]Misit autem Apollonium Mysarcham cum exercitu—viginti vero et duo milia virorum—praecipiens omnes perfectae aetatis interficere, mulieres autem ac iuniores vendere. [25]Qui cum venisset Hierosolymam et pacificum se simulasset, quievit usque ad diem sanctum sabbati et, cum comprehenderet feriatos Iudaeos, arma capere suis praecepit; [26]omnesque, qui ad spectaculum processerant, trucidavit et civitatem cum armatis discurrens ingentem multitudinem peremit. [27]Iudas autem, qui et Maccabaeus, decimus factus secesserat in eremum et ferarum more in montibus vitam cum suis agebat; et feni cibo vescentes demorabantur, ne participes essent coinquinationis. **[6]** [1]Sed non post multum temporis misit rex senem quendam Atheniensem, qui compelleret Iudaeos, ut se transferrent a patriis legibus et Dei legibus ne uterentur; [2]contaminare etiam, quod in Hierosolymis erat, templum et cognominare Iovis Olympii, et in Garizim,

w. Or *worse than the others did in his malice toward the Jewish citizens.* **x.** Gk *he*

A statue of Zeus is set up in the temple and Judaism is proscribed

1 Mac 1:45–51

6 [1]Not long after this, the king sent an Athenian[y] senator[z] to compel the Jews to forsake the laws of their fathers and cease to live by the laws of God, [2]and also to pollute the temple in Jerusalem and call it the temple of Olympian Zeus, and to call the one in Gerizim the temple of Zeus the Friend of Strangers, as did the people who dwelt in that place.

Rom 1:28

[3]Harsh and utterly grievous was the onslaught of evil. [4]For the temple was filled with debauchery and reveling by the Gentiles, who dallied with harlots and had intercourse with women within the sacred precincts, and besides brought in things for sacrifice that were unfit. [5]The altar was covered with abominable offerings which were forbidden by the laws. [6]A man could neither keep the sabbath, nor observe the feasts of his fathers, nor so much as confess himself to be a Jew.

6:1–11. Hellenist ways are imposed on Jerusalem and other Jewish cities (vv. 1, 8; cf. 1 Mac 1:41–61). In contrast to this, according to Flavius Josephus (*Antiquitates Judaicae*, 12, 257) the Samaritans petitioned Antiochus to dedicate his temple at Gerizim, built by Alexander the Great, to the Greek god Zeus. As the author of 2 Maccabees sees it, both temples, Jerusalem's and Gerizim's, share the same fate—a sign of the temporary nature of each. Jesus will confirm this in his conversation with the Samaritan woman (cf. Jn 4:5–30), though of course without gainsaying the holiness and legitimacy of the temple of Jerusalem (cf. Jn 4:22).

Anyone reading of these atrocities must be helped to see that there is no place for the use of force in religious matters. Conscious of the dignity of every person, the Church "declares that the human person has a right to religious freedom. Freedom of this kind means that all should be immune from coercion on the part of individuals, social groups and every human power so that, within due limits, nobody is forced to act against his convictions nor is anyone to be restrained from acting in accordance with his convictions in religious matters in private or in public, alone or in associations with others. The Council further declares that the right to religious freedom is based on the very dignity of the human person as known through the revealed word of God and by reason itself. This right of the human person to religious freedom must be given such recognition in the

prout erant hi, qui locum inhabitabant, Iovis Hospitalis. [3]Pessima autem et universis gravis erat malorum incursio. [4]Nam templum luxuria et comissationibus gentium erat plenum, scortantium cum meretricibus et in sacratis porticibus mulieribus adhaerentium, insuper et intro inferentium ea, quae non licebat; [5]altare etiam plenum erat illicitis, quae legibus prohibebantur. [6]Neque autem sabbata custodiebantur, neque dies sollemnes patrii servabantur, nec simpliciter Iudaeum se esse quisquam confitebatur. [7]Ducebantur autem cum amara necessitate per singulos menses in die natalis regis ad sacrificium et,

y. Some authorities read *Antiochian* **z.** Or *Geron an Athenian*

[7]On the monthly celebration of the king's birthday, the Jews[a] were taken, under bitter constraint, to partake of the sacrifices; and when the feast of Dionysus came, they were compelled to walk in the procession in honour of Dionysus, wearing wreaths of ivy. [8]At the suggestion of Ptolemy a decree was issued to the neighbouring Greek cities, that they should adopt the same policy toward the Jews and make them partake of the sacrifices, [9]and should slay those who did not choose to change over to Greek customs. One could see, therefore, the misery that had come upon them. [10]For example, two women were brought in for having circumcised their children. These women they publicly paraded about the city, with their babies hung at their breasts, then hurled them down headlong from the wall. [11]Others who had assembled in the caves near by, to observe the seventh day secretly, were betrayed to Philip and were all burned together, because their piety kept them from defending themselves, in view of their regard for that most holy day.

1 Mac 1:60–61

1 Mac 2:32–38

constitutional order of society as will make it a civil right" (Vatican II, *Dignitatis humanae*, 2).

6:12–17. From the text one can sense that God treats his people as a father does his child: he punishes in order to discipline (cf. Deut 8:5). According to the author of 2 Maccabees that is not what happens in the case of pagan peoples. In the New Testament, too, we are told that present trials are a form of discipline by our Father God (cf. Heb 12:6; Rev 3:19). But when the New Testament speaks about divine punishment being deferred, it is not so as to wait "until they have reached the full measure of their sins" (v. 14) but because God wants to give man time to mend his ways (cf. Rom 2:4–5; 2 Pet 3:9). Even so, sins may reach the "full measure", as in the case of those Jews who rejected Christ (cf. Mt 23:32) or those who put obstacles in the way of the Gospel (1 Thess 2:16). But even in those cases the possibility of conversion still exists.

6:18–31. The story of Eleazar carries the lesson that faithfulness to God's law is what matters most to the righteous man, and that the example given by prominent people can have enormous consequences. St Gregory Nazianzen calls Eleazar "the greatest of all those

cum Liberi sacra celebrarentur, cogebantur hedera coronati pompam Libero celebrare. [8]Decretum autem exiit in proximas Graecorum civitates, suggerente Ptolemaeo, ut pari modo et ipsi adversus Iudaeos agerent, ut sacrificarent; [9]eos autem, qui nollent transire ad instituta Graecorum, interficerent: erat ergo videre instantem miseriam. [10]Duae enim mulieres delatae sunt natos suos circumcidisse; quas infantibus ad ubera suspensis, cum publice per civitatem circumduxissent, per muros praecipitaverunt. [11]Alii vero ad proximas coeuntes speluncas, ut latenter septimam diem celebrarent, cum indicati essent Philippo, flammis succensi sunt, eo quod verebantur propter religionem sibimet auxilium ferre pro claritate sanctissimi diei. [12]Obsecro autem eos, qui hunc librum lecturi sunt, ne abhorrescant propter adversos

a. Gk *they*

A religious interpretation of events

[12]Now I urge those who read this book not to be depressed by such calamities, but to recognize that these punishments were designed not to destroy but to discipline our people. [13]In fact, not to let the impious alone for long, but to punish them immediately, is a sign of great kindness. [14]For in the case of the other nations the Lord waits patiently to punish them until they have reached the full measure of their sins; but he does not deal in this way with us, [15]in order that he may not take vengeance on us afterward when our sins have reached their height. [16]Therefore he never withdraws his mercy from us. Though he disciplines us with calamities, he does not forsake his own people. [17]Let what we have said serve as a reminder; we must go on briefly with the story.

2 Mac 5:17–20; 7:16–19,32–38

Wis 11:9–10; 12:2,22

1 Thess 2:16

Martyrdom of Eleazar

[18]Eleazar, one of the scribes in high position, a man now advanced in age and of noble presence, was being forced to open his mouth to eat swine's flesh. [19]But he, welcoming death with honour rather than life with pollution, went up to the the rack of his own accord, spitting out the flesh, [20]as men ought to go who have the courage to refuse things that it is not right to taste, even for the natural love of life.

Lev 11:7–8
Heb 11:35
Dan 11:32–35

---

who suffered before the coming of Christ; as Stephen is first among those who endure suffering after Christ" (*Orationes*, 15, 3). In ascetical tradition, Eleazar continues to be a clear example of fortitude: "The person with fortitude is one who perseveres in doing what his conscience tells him he ought to do. He does not measure the value of a task exclusively by the benefit he receives from it, but rather by the service he renders to others. The strong man will at times suffer, but he stands firm; he may be driven to tears, but he will brush them aside. When difficulties come thick and fast, he does not bend before them. Remember the example given us in the book of the Maccabees: an old man, Eleazar, prefers to die than break God's law. 'By manfully giving up my life now, I will show myself worthy of my old age and leave to the young a noble example of how to die a good death willingly and nobly for the revered and holy laws'" (St J. Escrivá, *Friends of God*, 77).

6:23. The Greco-Roman world called the dwelling-place of the dead "Hades" —in Hebrew "sheol" (cf. the note on 1 Kings 2:6).

casus, sed reputent illas poenas non ad interitum, sed ad correptionem esse generis nostri. [13]Etenim multo tempore non sinere eos, qui gerunt impie, sed statim ultiones adhibere, magni beneficii est indicium. [14]Non enim, sicut et in aliis nationibus, Dominus patienter ferens exspectat, ut eas, cum pervenerint in plenitudinem peccatorum, puniat, ita et in nobis statuit esse, [15]ne, peccatis nostris in finem devolutis, demum in nos vindicet; [16]propter quod numquam quidem a nobis misericordiam suam

[21]Those who were in charge of that unlawful sacrifice took the man aside, because of their long acquaintance with him, and privately urged him to bring meat of his own providing, proper for him to use, and pretend that he was eating the flesh of the sacrificial meal which had been commanded by the king, [22]so that by doing this he might be saved from death, and be treated kindly on account of his old friendship with them. [23]But making a high resolve, worthy of his years and the dignity of his old age and the gray hairs which he had reached with distinction and his excellent life even from childhood, and moreover according to the holy God-given law, he declared himself quickly, telling them to send him to Hades.

[24]"Such pretense is not worthy of our time of life," he said, "lest many of the young should suppose that Eleazar in his ninetieth year has gone over to an alien religion, [25]and through my pretense, for the sake of living a brief moment longer, they should be led astray because of me, while I defile and disgrace my old age. [26]For even if for the present I should avoid the punishment of men, yet whether I live or die I shall not escape the hands of the Almighty. [27]Therefore, by manfully giving up my life now, I will show myself worthy of my old age [28]and leave to the young a noble example of how to die a good death willingly and nobly for the revered and holy laws."

When he had said this, he went[b] at once to the rack. [29]And those who a little before had acted toward him with good will now

---

amovet, corripiens vero per aerumnas populum suum non derelinquit. [17]Sed haec nobis ad commonitionem dicta sint; paucis autem veniendum est ad narrationem. [18]Eleazarus quidam, unus de primoribus scribarum, vir iam aetate provectus et aspectu faciei decorus, aperto ore compellebatur carnem porcinam manducare. [19]At ille magis cum illustri fama mortem quam cum exsecratione vitam complectens, voluntarie praeibat ad supplicium, [20]exspuens autem, quemadmodum oportet accedere eos, qui sustinent non admittere illa, quae non est fas gustare, propter nimium vivendi amorem. [21]Hi autem, qui iniquo sacrificio praepositi erant, propter antiquam cum viro amicitiam tollentes eum secreto rogabant, ut afferret carnes, quibus uti ei liceret quaeque ab ipso paratae essent, et fingeret se eas manducare, quas rex imperaverat de sacrificii carnibus, [22]ut hoc facto a morte liberaretur et propter veterem cum illis amicitiam consequeretur humanitatem. [23]At ille, consilio decoro inito ac digno aetate et senectutis eminentia et acquisita nobilique canitie atque optima a puero vitae disciplina, magis autem sancta et a Deo condita legislatione, consequenter sententiam ostendit: cito, dicens, dimitterent ad inferos. [24]«Non enim aetati nostrae dignum est fingere, ut multi adulescentium arbitrantes Eleazarum nonaginta annorum transisse ad morem alienigenarum [25]et ipsi propter meam simulationem et propter modicum et pusillum vitae tempus decipiantur propter me, et exsecrationem atque maculam meae senectuti conquiram. [26]Nam etsi in praesenti tempore evasero eam, quae ex hominibus est, poenam, manus tamen Omnipotentis nec vivus nec defunctus effugiam. [27]Quam ob rem viriliter nunc vita excedendo senectute quidem dignus apparebo, [28]adulescentibus autem exemplum forte reliquero, ut prompto animo ac fortiter pro sacris ac sanctis legibus honesta morte perfungantur». Et cum haec dixisset, confestim ad supplicium venit, [29]ipsis autem, qui eum ducebant, illam, quam paulo ante

b. Other authorities read *was dragged*

changed to ill will, because the words he had uttered were in their opinion sheer madness.[c] 30When he was about to die under the blows, he groaned aloud and said: "It is clear to the Lord in his holy knowledge that, though I might have been saved from death, I am enduring terrible sufferings in my body under this beating, but in my soul I am glad to suffer these things because I fear him."

31So in this way he died, leaving in his death an example of nobility and a memorial of courage, not only to the young but to the great body of his nation.

Martyrdom of the seven brothers and their mother

7 1It happened also that seven brothers and their mother were arrested and were being compelled by the king, under torture with whips and cords, to partake of unlawful swine's flesh. 2One of them, acting as their spokesman, said, "What do you intend to ask and learn from us? For we are ready to die rather than transgress the laws of our fathers."

Heb 11:35
Jer 15:9

3The king fell into a rage, and gave orders that pans and cauldrons be heated. 4These were heated immediately, and he commanded that the tongue of their spokesman be cut out and that they scalp him and cut off his hands and feet, while the rest of the brothers and the mother looked on. 5When he was utterly helpless,

---

7:1–42. This is one of the most famous and popular passages in the history of the Maccabees—so much so that traditionally (but improperly) these brothers are usually referred to as "the Maccabees". The sacred writer does not tell us the boys' names, or where it all happened; and he brings in the presence of the king to heighten the dramatic effect. The bravery of these young men, it would seem, was inspired by the good example given by Eleazar (cf. 6:28). The mother's intervention divides the scene into two parts—first the martyrdom of the six older brothers (vv. 2–19), and then that of the youngest and the mother herself (vv. 20–41).

In the first part the conviction that the just will rise and evildoers will be punished builds up as the story goes on.

habuerant erga eum benevolentiam, in iram convertentibus, propterea quod sermones dicti, sicut ipsi arbitrabantur, essent amentia. 30Cumque coepisset plagis mori, ingemiscens dixit: «Domino, qui habet sanctam scientiam, manifestum est quia cum a morte possem liberari, duros secundum corpus sustineo dolores flagellatus, secundum animam vero propter ipsius timorem libenter haec patior». 31Et iste quidem hoc modo vita decessit, non solum iuvenibus, sed et plurimis ex gente mortem suam ad exemplum fortitudinis et memoriam virtutis relinquens. **[7]** 1Contigit autem et septem fratres una cum matre apprehensos compelli a rege attingere contra fas carnes porcinas, flagris et nervis cruciatos. 2Unus autem ex illis exstans prior locutor sic ait: «Quid es quaesiturus et quid vis discere a nobis? Parati sumus mori magis quam patrias leges praevaricari». 3Iratus itaque rex iussit sartagines et ollas succendi. 4Quibus statim succensis, iussit ei, qui prior illorum fuerat locutus, amputari linguam et, cute capitis

c. The Greek text of this verse is uncertain

the king[d] ordered them to take him to the fire, still breathing, and to fry him in a pan. The smoke from the pan spread widely, but the brothers[e] and their mother encouraged one another to die nobly, saying, [6]"The Lord God is watching over us and in truth has compassion on us, as Moses declared in his song which bore witness against the people to their faces, when he said, 'And he will have compassion on his servants.'"

Deut 32:36

[7]After the first brother had died in this way, they brought forward the second for their sport. They tore off the skin of his head with the hair, and asked him, "Will you eat rather than have your body punished limb by limb?" [8]He replied in the language of

---

Each of the replies given by the six brothers contains some aspect of that truth. The first says that just men prefer to die rather than sin (v. 2) because God will reward them (v. 6); the second, that God will raise them to a new life (v. 9); the third, that they will rise with their bodies remade (v. 11); the fourth, that for evildoers there will be no "resurrection to life" (v. 14); the fifth, that there will be punishment for evildoers (v. 17); and the sixth, that when just people suffer it is because they are being punished for their own sins (v. 18).

In the second part, both the mother and the youngest brother affirm what the others have said: but the boy adds something new when he says that death accepted by the righteous works as atonement for the whole people (vv. 37–38).

The resurrection of the dead, which "God revealed to his people progressively" (*Catechism of the Catholic Church*, 992), is a teaching that is grounded first on Moses' words about God having compassion on his servants (v. 6; cf. Deut 32:36), and the idea that if they die prematurely they will receive consolation in the next life. This is the point being made by the first brother, and it implies that God "faithfully maintains his covenant with Abraham and his posterity" (ibid.). As the mother sees it (vv. 27–28), belief in the resurrection comes from "faith in God as creator of the whole man, body and soul" (ibid., 992). Our Lord Jesus Christ ratifies this teaching and links it to faith in himself (cf. Jn 5:24–25; 11:25); and he also purifies the Pharisees' notion of the resurrection, which was an interpretation

abstracta, summas quoque manus et pedes ei praescindi, ceteris eius fratribus et matre inspicientibus. [5]Et cum iam per omnia inutilis factus esset, iussit eum igne admoveri adhuc spirantem et torreri in sartagine. Cum autem vapor sartaginis diu diffunderetur, ceteri una cum matre invicem se hortabantur mori fortiter ita dicentes: [6]«Dominus Deus aspicit et veritate in nobis consolatur, quemadmodum per personam contestantis cantici declaravit Moyses: "Et in servis suis consolabitur"». [7]Mortuo itaque illo primo hoc modo, sequentem deducebant ad illudendum; et cute capitis eius cum capillis abstracta, interrogabant, si manducaret prius quam toto corpore per membra singula puniretur. [8]At ille respondens patria voce dixit: «Non faciam». Propter quod et iste, sequenti loco, tormenta suscepit sicut primus. [9]Et in ultimo spiritu constitutus sic ait: «Tu quidem, scelestissime, de praesenti vita nos perdis; sed rex mundi defunctos nos pro suis legibus in aeternam vitae resurrectionem suscitabit». [10]Post hunc tertius

d. Gk *he* **e.** Gk *they*

his fathers, and said to them, "No." Therefore he in turn underwent tortures as the first brother had done. [9]And when he was at his last breath, he said, "You accursed wretch, you dismiss us from this present life, but the King of the universe will raise us up to an everlasting renewal of life,* because we have died for his laws."

[10]After him, the third was the victim of their sport. When it was demanded, he quickly put out his tongue and courageously stretched forth his hands, [11]and said nobly, "I got these from

2 Mac 12:38–46

based only on material terms (cf. Mk 12:18–27; 1 Cor 15:35–53).

In what the mother says (v. 28) we can also see belief in the creation of the world out of nothing "as a truth full of promise and hope" (*Catechism of the Catholic Church*, 297). On the basis of this passage and some New Testament passages, such as John 1:3 and Hebrews 11:3, the Church has formulated its doctrine of creation: "We believe that God needs no pre-existent thing or any help in order to create (cf. Vatican I: DS 3022), nor is creation any sort of necessary emanation from the divine substance (cf. Vatican I: DS 3023–3024). God creates freely 'out of nothing' (DS 800; 3025). If God had drawn the world from pre-existent matter, what would be so extraordinary in that? A human artisan makes from a given material whatever he wants, while God shows his power by starting from nothing to make all he wants" (*Catechism of the Catholic Church*, 296).

The assertion that the death of martyrs has expiatory value (vv. 37–38) prepares us to grasp the redemptive meaning of Christ's death; but we should remember that Christ, by his death, not only deflected the punishment that all men deserve on account of sin, but also, through his grace, makes sinful men righteous in God's sight (cf. Rom 3:21–26).

Many Fathers of the Church, notably St Gregory Nazianzen (*Orationes*, 15, 22), St Ambrose (*De Iacob et vitae beata*, 2, 10, 44–57), St Augustine (*In Epistolam Ioannis*, 8, 7), and St Cyprian (*Ad Fortunatus*, 11) heaped praise on these seven brothers and their mother. St John Chrysostom invites us to imitate them whenever temptation strikes: "All the moderation that they show in the midst of dangers we, too, should imitate by the patience and temperance with which we deal with irrational concupiscence, anger, greed for possessions, bodily passions, vainglory and such like. For if we manage to control their flame, as (the Maccabees) did the flame of the fire, we will be able to be near them and have a share in their confidence and freedom of spirit" (*Homiliae in Maccabaeos*, 1, 3).

illudebatur; et linguam postulatus cito protulit et manus constanter extendit [11]et fortiter ait: «E caelo ista possideo et propter illius leges haec ipsa despicio et ab ipso rursus me ea recepturum spero», [12]ita ut rex et, qui cum ipso erant, mirarentur adulescentis animum, quomodo pro nihilo duceret cruciatus. [13]Et hoc ita defuncto, quartum vexabant similiter torquentes; [14]et, cum iam esset ad mortem, sic ait: «Potius est ab hominibus morti datos spem exspectare a Deo iterum ab ipso resuscitandos; tibi enim resurrectio ad vitam non erit». [15]Et deinceps quintum, cum admovissent, vexabant; [16]at ille respiciens in eum dixit:

Heaven, and because of his laws I disdain them, and from him I hope to get them back again." [12]As a result the king himself and those with him were astonished at the young man's spirit, for he regarded his sufferings as nothing.

[13]When he too had died, they maltreated and tortured the fourth in the same way. [14]And when he was near death, he said, "One cannot but choose to die at the hands of men and to cherish the hope that God gives of being raised again by him. But for you there will be no resurrection to life!"

[15]Next they brought forward the fifth and maltreated him. [16]But he looked at the king,[f] and said, "Because you have authority among men, mortal though you are, you do what you please. But do not think that God has forsaken our people. [17]Keep on, and see how his mighty power will torture you and your descendants!"

2 Mac 5:17–20; 6:12–16

[18]After him they brought forward the sixth. And when he was about to die, he said, "Do not deceive yourself in vain. For we are suffering these things on our own account, because of our sins against our own God. Therefore[g] astounding things have happened. [19]But do not think that you will go unpunished for having tried to fight against God!"

Acts 5:39

[20]The mother was especially admirable and worthy of honourable memory. Though she saw her seven sons perish within a single day, she bore it with good courage because of her hope in the Lord. [21]She encouraged each of them in the language of their fathers. Filled with a noble spirit, she fired her woman's reasoning with a man's courage, and said to them, [22]"I do not know how you came into being in my womb. It was not I who gave you life and breath, nor I who set in order the elements within each of you. [23]Therefore the Creator of the world, who shaped the beginning of man and devised the origin of all things, will in his mercy give life

Job 10:8–12
Ps 139:13–15
Eccles 11:5

«Potestatem inter homines habens, cum sis corruptibilis, facis, quod vis; noli autem putare genus nostrum a Deo esse derelictum: [17]tu autem patienter sustine et videbis maiestatem virtutis ipsius, qualiter te et semen tuum torquebit». [18]Post hunc ducebant sextum, et is mori incipiens ait: «Noli frustra errare; nos enim propter nosmetipsos haec patimur peccantes in Deum nostrum, et digna admiratione facta sunt in nobis: [19]tu autem ne existimes tibi impune futurum quod contra Deum pugnare tentaveris». [20]Supra modum autem mater mirabilis et bona memoria digna, quae pereuntes septem filios sub unius diei tempore conspiciens bono animo ferebat propter spem, quam in Dominum habebat. [21]Singulos illorum hortabatur voce patria, forti repleta sensu et femineam cogitationem masculino excitans animo, dicens ad eos: [22]«Nescio qualiter in utero meo apparuistis neque ego spiritum et vitam donavi vobis et singulorum vestrorum compagem non sum ego modulata; [23]sed enim mundi creator, qui formavit hominis nativitatem quique omnium invenit originem et spiritum et vitam vobis iterum cum misericordia reddet, sicut nunc vosmetipsos despicitis propter leges eius». [24]Antiochus autem contemni

f. Gk *him* **g.** Lat: other authorities omit *Therefore*

and breath back to you again, since you now forget yourselves for the sake of his laws."

[24]Antiochus felt that he was being treated with contempt, and he was suspicious of her reproachful tone. The youngest brother being still alive, Antiochus[h] not only appealed to him in words, but promised with oaths that he would make him rich and enviable if he would turn from the ways of his fathers, and that he would take him for his friend and entrust him with public affairs.

[25]Since the young man would not listen to him at all, the king called the mother to him and urged her to advise the youth to save himself. [26]After much urging on his part, she undertook to persuade her son. [27]But, leaning close to him, she spoke in their native tongue as follows, deriding the cruel tyrant: "My son, have pity on me. I carried you nine months in my womb, and nursed you for three years, and have reared you and brought you up to this point in your life, and have taken care of you.[i] [28] I beseech you, my child, to look at the heaven and the earth and see everything that is in them, and recognize that God did not make them out of things that existed.[j] Thus also mankind comes into being. [29]Do not fear this butcher, but prove worthy of your brothers. Accept death, so that in God's mercy I may get you back again with your brothers."

[30]While she was still speaking, the young man said, "What are you[k] waiting for? I will not obey the king's command, but I obey the command of the law that was given to our fathers through Moses. [31]But you,[l] who have contrived all sorts of evil against the Hebrews, will certainly not escape the hands of God. [32]For we are suffering because of our own sins. [33]And if our living Lord is angry for a little while, to rebuke and discipline us, he will again be reconciled with his own servants. [34]But you, unholy wretch,

2 Mac 5:17–20; 6:12–16

se arbitratus, simul et exprobrantem dedignans vocem, cum adhuc adulescentior superesset, non solum verbis hortabatur, sed et cum iuramento affirmabat se divitem simul et beatum facturum, translatum a patriis legibus, et amicum habiturum et officia ei crediturum. [25]Sed ad haec cum adulescens nequaquam intenderet, vocavit rex matrem et suadebat ei, ut adulescenti fieret suasor in salutem. [26]Cum autem multis eam verbis esset hortatus, promisit suasuram se filio. [27]Itaque inclinata ad illum, irridens crudelem tyrannum sic ait patria voce: «Fili, miserere mei, quae te in utero novem mensibus portavi et lac triennio dedi et alui et in aetatem istam perduxi et nutricem me tibi exhibui. [28]Peto, nate, ut aspicias ad caelum et terram et quae in ipsis sunt, universa videns intellegas quia non ex his, quae erant, fecit illa Deus; et hominum genus ita fit. [29]Ne timeas carnificem istum, sed dignus fratribus tuis effectus suscipe mortem, ut in illa miseratione cum fratribus tuis te recipiam». [30]Cum haec illa adhuc diceret, ait adulescens: «Quem sustinetis? Non oboedio praecepto regis, sed obtempero praecepto legis, quae data est patribus nostris per Moysen. [31]Tu vero, qui inventor omnis malitiae factus es in Hebraeos, non effugies manus Dei. [32]Nos enim pro peccatis nostris haec patimur; [33]et si nobis propter increpationem et correptionem ille vivens Dominus noster modicum iratus est, sed iterum reconciliabitur servis suis.

h. Gk *he* **i.** Or *have borne the burden of your education* **j.** Or *God made them out of things that did not exist* **k.** The Greek here for *you* is plural **l.** The Greek word here for *you* is singular

you most defiled of all men, do not be elated in vain and puffed up by uncertain hopes, when you raise your hand against the children of heaven. [35]You have not yet escaped the judgment of the almighty, all-seeing God. [36]For our brothers after enduring a brief suffering have drunk[m] of everflowing life under God's covenant; but you, by the judgment of God, will receive just punishment for your arrogance. [37]I, like my brothers, give up body and life for the laws of our fathers, appealing to God to show mercy soon to our nation and by afflictions and plagues to make you confess that he alone is God, [38]and through me and my brothers to bring to an end the wrath of the Almighty which has justly fallen on our whole nation."

[39]The king fell into a rage, and handled him worse than the others, being exasperated at his scorn. [40]So he died in his integrity, putting his whole trust in the Lord.

[41]Last of all, the mother died, after her sons.

[42]Let this be enough, then, about the eating of sacrifices and the extreme tortures.

1 Mac 2:42–48

Judas' armed resistance. Early exploits

2 Mac 5:27

8 [1]But Judas, who was also called Maccabeus, and his companions secretly entered the villages and summoned their kinsmen and enlisted those who had continued in the Jewish faith, and so they gathered about six thousand men. [2]They besought the

8:1–36. Cf. 1 Mac 2:42–48. The author of 2 Maccabees focuses all his attention on the activities of Judas, whom he sees as a model of prayer, trust in God, love for his people, a good military strategist, a man of courage and one who is generous to the poor. The battle against Nicanor and Gorgias (vv. 28–29) is recounted in more detail than in 1 Maccabees 3:38—4:25 (where we are told that it took place at Emmaus in 165 BC). The encounter with Timothy took place in Transjordan in 163 BC (cf. 1 Mac 5:6–7), and that with Bacchides in Judah in 161 BC (cf. 1 Mac 7:8–24). In 2 Maccabees these episodes are dealt with (and woven) together, perhaps because they are rather similar and

[34]Tu autem, o sceleste et omnium hominum flagitiosissime, noli frustra extolli elatus vanis spebus, in filios caeli levata manu; [35]nondum enim omnipotentis atque intuitoris Dei iudicium effugisti. [36]Nam fratres nostri, modico nunc dolore sustentato, sub Dei testamentum aeternae vitae reciderunt; tu vero iudicio Dei iustas superbiae tuae poenas exsolves. [37]Ego autem, sicut et fratres mei, et corpus et animam trado pro patriis legibus invocans Deum maturius genti nostrae propitium fieri teque cum tormentis et verberibus confiteri quod ipse est Deus solus, [38]in me vero et in fratribus meis restitit Omnipotentis ira, quae super omne genus nostrum iuste superducta est». [39]Tunc rex accensus ira in hunc super omnes crudelius desaevit, indigne ferens se derisum. [40]Et hic itaque mundus obiit per omnia in Domino confidens. [41]Novissima autem post filios et mater consumpta est. [42]Igitur de sacrificiis et de nimiis crudelitatibus satis sit dictum. **[8]** [1]Iudas vero Maccabaeus et, qui cum illo erant, introeuntes latenter in castella convocabant cognatos et, eos, qui permanserunt in Iudaismo, assumentes, collegerunt circiter

m. Cn: Gk *fallen*

Lord to look upon the people who were oppressed by all, and to have pity on the temple which had been profaned by ungodly men, [3]and to have mercy on the city which was being destroyed and about to be leveled to the ground, and to hearken to the blood that cried out to him, [4]and to remember also the lawless destruction of the innocent babies and the blasphemies committed against his name, and to show his hatred of evil.

[5]As soon as Maccabeus got his army organized, the Gentiles could not withstand him, for the wrath of the Lord had turned to mercy. [6]Coming without warning, he would set fire to towns and villages. He captured strategic positions and put to flight not a few of the enemy. [7]He found the nights most advantageous for such attacks. And talk of his valour spread everywhere.

[8]When Philip saw that the man was gaining ground little by little, and that he was pushing ahead with more frequent successes, he wrote to Ptolemy, the governor of Coelesyria and Phoenicia, for aid to the king's government. [9]And Ptolemy[n] promptly appointed Nicanor the son of Patroclus, one of the king's chief friends, and sent him, in command of no fewer than twenty thousand Gentiles of all nations, to wipe out the whole race of Judea. He associated with him Gorgias, a general and a man of experience in military service. [10]Nicanor determined to make up for the king the tribute

1 Mac 3:3–9

1 Mac 3:38—4:25
2 Mac 4:45; 10:12

1 Mac 2:18; 3:38

---

because the author wants to show the difficulties Judas had to confront before he could cleanse the temple.

As the sacred author reads events, Judas wins his victories because God has "hearkened to the blood that cried out to him" (v. 3), that is, he has accepted the offering made by the martyrs (cf. chaps.6–7); God's wrath has turned to mercy (v. 5). The reading out of the book of the Law (v. 23) substitutes here for listening to the words of the prophets (cf. 1 Mac 3:48). The cruel revenge taken by the Jews on their prisoners (vv. 32–33) must be seen in the context of the law of vengeance and the connexion that the author of 2 Maccabees keeps making between sins committed and punishment of the sinner.

sex milia virorum. [2]Et invocabant Dominum, ut respiceret in populum, qui ab omnibus calcabatur, et misereretur templo, quod contaminabatur ab impiis; [3]et misereretur etiam pereunti civitati et incipienti solo complanari et vocem sanguinis ad se clamantis exaudiret, [4]memoraretur quoque iniquas mortes parvulorum innocentum et blasphemias nomini suo illatas et indignaretur super his. [5]At Maccabaeus, congregata multitudine, intolerabilis iam gentibus efficiebatur, ira Domini in misericordiam conversa. [6]Et civitates et castella superveniens improvisus succendebat et opportuna loca occupans non paucos hostium in fugam convertens, [7]maxime noctes in huiusmodi excursus cooperantes captabat. Et fama virtutis eius ubique diffundebatur. [8]Videns autem Philippus paulatim virum ad profectum venire ac frequentius in prosperitatibus procedere, ad Ptolemaeum ducem Coelesyriae et Phoenicis scripsit, ut auxilium ferret regis negotiis. [9]At ille velociter sumpsit Nicanorem Patrocli de primoribus amicis et

n. Gk *he*

due to the Romans, two thousand talents, by selling the captured Jews into slavery. [11]And he immediately sent to the cities on the seacoast, inviting them to buy Jewish slaves and promising to hand over ninety slaves for a talent, not expecting the judgment from the Almighty that was about to overtake him.

[12]Word came to Judas concerning Nicanor's invasion; and when he told his companions of the arrival of the army, [13]those who were cowardly and distrustful of God's justice ran off and got away. [14]Others sold all their remaining property, and at the same time besought the Lord to rescue those who had been sold by the ungodly Nicanor before he ever met them, [15]if not for their own sake, yet for the sake of the covenants made with their fathers, and because he had called them by his holy and glorious name. [16]But Maccabeus gathered his men together, to the number six thousand, and exhorted them not to be frightened by the enemy and not to fear the great multitude of Gentiles who were wickedly coming against them, but to fight nobly, [17]keeping before their eyes the lawless outrage which the Gentiles[o] had committed against the holy place, and the torture of the derided city, and besides, the overthrow of their ancestral way of life. [18]"For they trust to arms and acts of daring," he said, "but we trust in the Almighty God, who is able with a single nod to strike down those who are coming against us and even the whole world."

Mt 24:15

Ps 20:7

[19]Moreover, he told them of the times when help came to their ancestors; both the time of Sennacherib, when one hundred and eighty-five thousand perished, [20]and the time of the battle with the

2 Kings 19:35
Is 37:36

---

misit, datis ei de permixtis gentibus armatis non minus viginti milibus, ut universum Iudaeorum genus deleret; adiunxit autem ei et Gorgiam virum militarem et in bellicis rebus expertum. [10]Constituit autem Nicanor, ut regi tributum, quod Romanis erat dandum, duo milia talentorum de captivitate Iudaeorum suppleret; [11]statimque ad maritimas civitates misit convocans ad coemptionem Iudaicorum mancipiorum, promittens se nonaginta mancipia talento distracturum non exspectans vindictam, quae eum ab Omnipotente esset consecutura. [12]Iudas autem, ubi comperit de Nicanoris adventu, indicavit his, qui secum erant, exercitus praesentiam; [13]ex quibus quidam formidantes et non credentes Dei iustitiae in fugam vertebantur et in alios locos seipsos transferebant, [14]alii vero omnia, quae eis supererant, vendebant simulque Dominum deprecabantur, ut eriperet eos, qui ab impio Nicanore, prius quam comminus venirent, venumdati essent: [15]et si non propter eos, sed tamen propter testamenta ad patres eorum et propter invocationem sancti et magnifici nominis eius super ipsos. [16]Convocatis autem Maccabaeus sex milibus, qui cum ipso erant, rogabat ne ab hostibus perterrerentur, neque metuerent inique venientium adversum se gentium multitudinem, sed fortiter contenderent, [17]ante oculos habentes contumeliam, quae in locum sanctum ab his iniuste esset consummata, itemque et ludibrio habitae civitatis iniuriam, adhuc etiam veterum instituta convulsa. [18]«Nam illi quidem armis confidunt, ait, simul et audacia; nos autem in omnipotente Deo, qui potest et venientes adversum nos et universum mundum uno nutu delere, confidimus». [19]Cum autem admonuisset eos et de auxiliis, quae facta sunt erga parentes, et de illo sub Sennacherib, ut centum octoginta quinque milia perierunt, [20]et de illo in Babilonia, in proelio quod eis adversus Galatas fuit, ut omnes ad rem venerunt, octo milia cum quattuor

o. Gk *they*

Galatians that took place in Babylonia, when eight thousand in all went into the affair, with four thousand Macedonians; and when the Macedonians were hard pressed, the eight thousand, by the help that came to them from heaven, destroyed one hundred and twenty thousand and took much booty.

[21]With these words he filled them with good courage and made them ready to die for their laws and their country; then he divided his army into four parts. [22]He appointed his brothers also, Simon and Joseph and Jonathan, each to command a division, putting fifteen hundred men under each. [23]Besides, he appointed Elea zar to read aloud[p] from the holy book, and gave the watchword, "God's help"; then, leading the first division himself, he joined battle with Nicanor.

1 Mac 3:48

[24]With the Almighty as their ally, they slew more than nine thousand of the enemy, and wounded and disabled most of Nicanor's army, and forced them all to flee. [25]They captured the money of those who had come to buy them as slaves. After pursuing them for some distance, they were obliged to return because the hour was late. [26]For it was the day before the sabbath, and for that reason they did not continue their pursuit. [27]And when they had collected the arms of the enemy and stripped them of their spoils, they kept the sabbath, giving great praise and thanks to the Lord, who had preserved them for that day and allotted it to them as the beginning of mercy. [28]After the sabbath they gave some of the spoils to those who had been tortured and to the widows and orphans, and distributed the rest among themselves and their children. [29]When they had done this, they made common supplication and besought the merciful Lord to be wholly reconciled with his servants.

[30]In encounters with the forces of Timothy and Bacchides they killed more than twenty thousand of them and got possession of

---

milibus Macedonum—Macedonibus haesitantibus ipsi octo milia peremerunt centum viginti milia propter auxilium illis datum de caelo et beneficia plurima consecuti sunt—; [21]quibus verbis cum eos constantes effecisset et paratos pro legibus et patria mori, in quattuor quasdam partes exercitum divisit. [22]Constitutis itaque fratribus suis ducibus uniuscuiusque ordinis, Simone et Iosepho et Ionatha, subiectis unicuique millenis et quingentenis, [23]insuper et Eleazaro, lecto sancto libro et dato signo adiutorii Dei, primae cohortis ipse ductor commisit cum Nicanore. [24]Et facto sibi adiutore Omnipotente, interfecerunt super novem milia hostium, saucios autem et membris debilitatos maiorem partem exercitus Nicanoris reddiderunt, omnes vero fugere compulerunt. [25]Pecunias autem eorum, qui ad emptionem illorum advenerant, abstulerunt et, cum persecuti eos fuissent satis longe, reversi sunt hora conclusi; [26]nam erat ante sabbatum, quam ob causam non perseveraverunt insequentes eos. [27]Cum autem ipsorum arma collegissent spoliisque hostes exuissent, circa sabbatum versabantur impensius benedicentes et confitentes Domino, qui liberavit eos in isto die misericordiae initium constituens in eos. [28]Post sabbatum vero debilitatis et viduis et orphanis portione de spoliis data, residua ipsi cum pueris partiti

p. The Greek text of this clause is uncertain

some exceedingly high strongholds, and they divided very much plunder, giving to those who had been tortured and to the orphans and widows, and also to the aged, shares equal to their own. [31]Collecting the arms of the enemy,[q] they stored them all carefully in strategic places, and carried the rest of the spoils to Jerusalem. [32]They killed the commander of Timothy's forces, a most unholy man, and one who had greatly troubled the Jews. [33]While they were celebrating the victory in the city of their fathers, they burned those who had set fire to the sacred gates, Callisthenes and some others, who had fled into one little house; so these received the proper recompense for their impiety.[r]

2 Mac 8:23–24

[34]The thrice-accursed Nicanor, who had brought the thousand merchants to buy the Jews, [35]having been humbled with the help of the Lord by opponents whom he regarded as of the least account, took off his splendid uniform and made his way alone like a runaway slave across the country till he reached Antioch, having succeeded chiefly in the destruction of his own army! [36]Thus he who had undertaken to secure tribute for the Romans by the capture of the people of Jerusalem proclaimed that the Jews had a Defender, and that therefore the Jews were invulnerable, because they followed the laws ordained by him.

1 Mac 6:1–16
2 Mac 1:11–17

Death of Antiochus Epiphanes

9 [1]About that time, as it happened, Antiochus had retreated in disorder from the region of Persia. [2]For he had entered the city called Persepolis, and attempted to rob the temples and control the

9:1–29. The death of Antiochus occurred in October–November 164 BC shortly before the purification of the temple, according to what we are told here. However, 1 Maccabees puts it after the purification (cf. 1 Mac 6:1–17), perhaps because that was when the news reached Jerusalem. Although both books agree

sunt. [29]His itaque gestis et communi facta obsecratione, misericordem Dominum postulabant, ut in finem servis suis reconciliaretur. [30]Et contendentes cum his, qui cum Timotheo et Bacchide erant, super viginti milia eorum interfecerunt et munitiones excelsas facile obtinuerunt; et plures praedas diviserunt, aequaliter seipsos participes cum debilitatis et orphanis et viduis, sed et senioribus facientes. [31]Et cum arma eorum diligenter collegissent, omnia composuerunt in locis opportunis, residua vero spolia Hierosolymam detulerunt. [32]Et phylarchen eorum, qui cum Timotheo erant, interfecerunt, virum scelestissimum, qui in multis Iudaeos afflixerat; [33]et cum epinicia agerent in patria, eos, qui sacras ianuas incenderant et Callisthenem succenderunt, qui in quoddam domicilium fugerat; et dignam pro impietate mercedem tulit. [34]Facinorosissimus autem Nicanor, qui mille negotiantes ad Iudaeorum venditionem adduxerat, [35]humiliatus ab his, qui secundum ipsum exsistimabantur exigui esse, auxilio Domini, deposita veste gloriae, per mediterranea fugitivi more solitarius effectus venit Antiochiam, super omnia prosperatus in interitu exercitus. [36]Et, qui Romanis promiserat se tributum de captivitate Hierosolymorum redigere, praedicabat propugnatorem habere Iudaeos et hoc modo invulnerabiles esse,

q. Gk *their arms* **r.** The Greek text of this verse is uncertain

city. Therefore the people rushed to the rescue with arms, and Antiochus and his men were defeated,[s] with the result that Antiochus was put to flight by the inhabitants and beat a shameful retreat. [3]While he was in Ecbatana, news came to him of what had happened to Nicanor and the forces of Timothy. [4]Transported with rage, he conceived the idea of turning upon the Jews the injury done by those who had put him to flight; so he ordered his

---

that the king died as a result of an illness, they differ as to the nature of the illness, the place where the events occur, and the news from Judea that excites the king's anger: in 1 Maccabees it was a report about the defeat of Lysias (whereas that event is not covered in this book until 11:1–12). On this point, 1 Maccabees is the more accurate.

The author of 2 Maccabees wants to make it clear that the purification of the temple was not a consequence of the peace made by the king after the defeat of Lysias, but that it came about as a result of the punishment God inflicted on the king. He also contrasts the king's arrogance with the humiliation that his suffering implies: in fact, so humbled is the king that he acknowledges the God of the Jews and changes his policy towards them. But this conversion comes too late: the king had reached the full measure of his sins and God was not going to show him mercy (vv. 9, 13, 18). God's severity in this instance can be explained by the fact that Antiochus has a change of heart only because he hopes this will avert his punishment. The author interprets the king's terrible death as an application of the law of vengeance. Horrible deaths of this sort are often reported as happening to tyrants: cf. Flavius Josephus' account of the death of Herod the Great (*Antiquitates Judaicae*, 17, 168), and the death of Herod Agrippa recorded in Acts 12:23.

The letter given in vv. 19–23 seems to be the author's version of a letter sent by Antiochus to the Hellenized Jews of Antioch or other cities of the empire. In this version it reads like the testament of a converted pagan king.

Antiochus' arrogance in thinking he was God's equal (vv. 8–12) is an echo and an effect of a temptation that has beset man ever since he was put on this earth: "You will be like God " (cf. Gen 3:5); for, as St Thomas Aquinas explains, pride is the gravest sin of all, since "the aversion to God and his commandments —which is a consequence of other sins —is part of the nature of pride, the essence of which is contempt for God" (*Summa theologiae*, 2, 2, 162, 6).

eo quod sequerentur leges ab ipso constitutas. **[9]** [1]Eodem autem tempore Antiochus inhoneste revertebatur de regionibus circa Persidem. [2]Intraverat enim in eam, quae dicitur Persepolis, et tentavit exspoliare templum et civitatem opprimere; quapropter, multitudine ad armorum auxilium concurrente, in fugam versi sunt, et contigit ut Antiochus in fugam versus ab indigenis turpiter rediret. [3]Et cum esset circa Ecbatana, nuntiata sunt ea, quae erga Nicanorem et Timotheum gesta sunt. [4]Elatus autem ira arbitrabatur se etiam iniuriam illorum, qui se fugaverant, in Iudaeos retorquere; ideoque iussit, ut auriga sine intermissione iter perficeret, caelesti iam eum comitante iudicio. Ita enim superbe locutus erat:

s. Gk *they were defeated*

charioteer to drive without stopping until he completed the journey. But the judgment of heaven rode with him! For in his arrogance he said, "When I get there I will make Jerusalem a cemetery of Jews."

[5]But the all-seeing Lord, the God of Israel, struck him an incurable and unseen blow. As soon as he ceased speaking he was seized with a pain in his bowels for which there was no relief and with sharp internal tortures—[6]and that very justly, for he had tortured the bowels of others with many and strange inflictions. [7]Yet he did not in any way stop his insolence, but was even more filled with arrogance, breathing fire in his rage against the Jews, and giving orders to hasten the journey. And so it came about that he fell out of his chariot as it was rushing along, and the fall was so hard as to torture every limb of his body. [8]Thus he who had just been thinking that he could command the waves of the sea, in his superhuman arrogance, and imagining that he could weigh the high mountains in a balance, was brought down to earth and carried in a litter, making the power of God manifest to all. [9]And so the ungodly man's body swarmed with worms, and while he was still living in anguish and pain, his flesh rotted away, and because of his stench the whole army felt revulsion at his decay. [10]Because of his intolerable stench no one was able to carry the man who a little while before had thought that he could touch the stars of heaven. [11]Then it was that, broken in spirit, he began to lose much of his arrogance and to come to his senses under the scourge of God, for he was tortured with pain every moment. [12]And when he could not endure his own stench, he uttered these words: "It is right to be subject to God, and no mortal should think that he is equal to God."[t]

Job 38:8–11
Ps 65:6–7
Is 40:12; 51:15

Sir 7:17
Acts 12:23

«Congeriem sepulcri Iudaeorum Hierosolymam faciam, cum venero illo». [5]Sed qui universa conspicit, Dominus, Deus Israel, percussit eum insanabili et invisibili plaga; et continuo ut is finivit sermonem, apprehendit eum dolor dirus viscerum et amara internorum tormenta, [6]perquam iuste, quippe qui multis et novis cruciatibus aliorum torserat viscera. [7]Ille vero nullo modo ab arrogantia cessabat; super hoc autem superbia repletus erat, ignem spirans animo in Iudaeos et praecipiens iter accelerari. Contigit autem, ut et ille caderet de curru; qui ferebatur impetu, et gravi lapsu corruens in omnibus corporis membris vexaretur. [8]Isque, qui nuper videbatur fluctibus maris imperare propter super hominem iactantiam et in statera montium altitudines appendere, humiliatus ad terram in gestatorio portabatur manifestam Dei virtutem omnibus ostendens, [9]ita ut de oculis impii vermes scaturirent, ac viventis in doloribus et maeroribus carnes eius diffluerent, illiusque odore totus exercitus gravaretur propter putredinem. [10]Et qui paulo ante sidera caeli contingere se arbitrabatur, eum nemo poterat propter intolerabilem foetoris gravitatem portare. [11]Hinc igitur coepit multum superbiae deponere confractus et ad agnitionem venire divina plaga, per momenta doloribus extensus. [12]Et, cum nec ipse foetorem suum ferre posset, ita ait: «Iustum est subditum esse Deo et mortalem non superbe sentire». [13]Orabat autem hic scelestus Dominum, ei non amplius miserturum, ita dicens: [14]sanctam quidem civitatem, ad quam

t. Or *think thoughts proper only to God*

[13]Then the abominable fellow made a vow to the Lord, who would no longer have mercy on him, stating [14]that the holy city, which he was hastening to level to the ground and to make a cemetery, he was now declaring to be free; [15]and the Jews, whom he had not considered worth burying but had planned to throw out with their children to the beasts, for the birds to pick, he would make, all of them, equal to citizens of Athens; [16]and the holy sanctuary, which he had formerly plundered, he would adorn with the finest offerings; and the holy vessels he would give back, all of them, many times over; and the expenses incurred for the sacrifices he would provide from his own revenues; [17]and in addition to all this he also would become a Jew and would visit every inhabited place to proclaim the power of God. [18]But when his sufferings did not in any way abate, for the judgment of God had justly come upon him, he gave up all hope for himself and wrote to the Jews the following letter, in the form of a supplication. This was its content:

[19]"To his worthy Jewish citizens, Antiochus their king and general sends hearty greetings and good wishes for their health and prosperity. [20]If you and your children are well and your affairs are as you wish, I am glad. As my hope is in heaven, [21]I remember with affection your esteem and good will. On my way back from the region of Persia I suffered an annoying illness, and I have deemed it necessary to take thought for the general security of all. [22]I do not despair of my condition, for I have good hope of recovering from my illness, [23]but I observed that my father, on the occasions when he made expeditions into the upper country, appointed his successor, [24]so that, if anything unexpected happened or any unwelcome news came, the people throughout the realm

---

festinans veniebat, ut eam solo aequalem faceret ac sepulcrum congestorum strueret, liberam ostendere; [15]Iudaeos autem, quos decreverat nec sepultura quidem se dignos habiturum, sed avibus devorandos cum parvulis se feris proiecturum, omnes hos aequales Atheniensibus facturum; [16]templum vero sanctum, quod prius exspoliaverat, pulcherrimis donis ornaturum et sacra vasa multiplicia cuncta se redditurum, et pertinentes ad sacrificia sumptus de redditibus suis praestaturum; [17]super haec autem et Iudaeum se futurum et omnem locum habitabilem perambulaturum praedicantem Dei potestatem. [18]Sed omnino non cessantibus doloribus—supervenerat enim in eum iustum Dei iudicium—semetipsum desperans scripsit ad Iudaeos hanc infra rescriptam epistulam modum deprecationis habentem, haec continentem: [19]«Optimis civibus Iudaeis plurimam salutem et bene valere et esse felices, rex et dux Antiochus. [20]Si bene valetis et filii vestri, et res vestrae ex sententia sunt vobis, precans refero quidem Deo maximam gratiam, in caelum spem habens; [21]ego vero in infirmitate constitutus eram, vestri autem honoris et benevolentiae memineram cum affectione. Reversus de Persidis locis et in infirmitatem incidens molestiam habentem, necessarium duxi pro communi omnium securitate curam habere. [22]Non desperans memetipsum, sed spem multam habens effugiendi infirmitatem, [23]respiciens autem quod et pater meus, quibus temporibus in superiora loca duxit exercitum, ostendit, qui susciperet principatum, [24]ut, si quid contrarium accideret aut etiam quid difficile nuntiaretur, scientes hi, qui circa regionem erant, cui esset rerum summa derelicta, non turbarentur. [25]Ad haec autem considerans de proximo potentes et vicinos regno temporibus insidiantes et eventum exspectantes, designavi filium Antiochum

would not be troubled, for they would know to whom the government was left. [25]Moreover, I understand how the princes along the borders and the neighbours to my kingdom keep watching for opportunities and waiting to see what will happen. So I have appointed my son Antiochus to be king, whom I have often entrusted and commended to most of you when I hastened off to the upper provinces; and I have written to him what is written here. [26]I therefore urge and beseech you to remember the public and private services rendered to you and to maintain your present good will, each of you, toward me and my son. [27]For I am sure that he will follow my policy and will treat you with moderation and kindness."

[28]So the murderer and blasphemer, having endured the more intense suffering, such as he had inflicted on others, came to the end of his life by a most pitiable fate, among the mountains in a strange land. [29]And Philip, one of his courtiers, took his body home; then, fearing the son of Antiochus, he betook himself to Ptolemy Philometor in Egypt.

1 Mac 4:36–61

Purification of the temple. The feast of the Dedication

10 [1]Now Maccabeus and his followers, the Lord leading them on, recovered the temple and the city; [2]and they tore down the altars which had been built in the public square by the foreigners, and also destroyed the sacred precincts. [3]They purified the sanctuary, and made another altar of sacrifice; then, striking fire out of flint, they offered sacrifices, after a lapse of two years,

Mt 12:4

10:1–8. The purification of the temple was one of the main themes the author intended to cover in his book (cf. 2:19) and was the background to the two letters quoted at the start (1:1—2:18). The purification took place in 164 BC. In 1 Maccabees 4:36–61 the actual event is described in more detail, but only here is there mention of how the initial fire for the offerings was made. Although God did not cause fire to come down from heaven as he did on other occasions (cf. 1:19–22; 2:10–11), the fire now being used is not an "unholy" fire, which would have invalidated the offering (cf. Lev 10:1).

regem, quem saepe recurrens in superiora regna plurimis vestrum committebam et commendabam; et scripsi ad eum, quae subiecta sunt. [26]Oro itaque vos et peto memores beneficiorum publice et privatim, ut unusquisque conservet hanc, quam habetis benevolentiam in me et in filium. [27]Confido enim eum modeste et humane, sequentem propositum meum, vobiscum acturum». [28]Igitur homicida et blasphemus pessima perpessus, ut ipse alios tractaverat, peregre in montibus miserabili obitu vita functus est. [29]Transferebat autem corpus Philippus collactaneus eius, qui etiam metuens filium Antiochi ad Ptolemaeum Philometorem in Aegyptum se contulit. **[10]** [1]Maccabaeus autem et, qui cum eo erant, Domino eos praeeunte, templum quidem et civitatem receperunt; [2]aras autem, quas alienigenae per plateam exstruxerant, itemque delubra demoliti sunt [3]et, purgato templo, aliud altare fecerunt et succensis lapidibus igneque de his concepto sacrificia obtulerunt post biennium et incensum et lucernas

and they burned incense and lighted lamps and set out the bread of the Presence. [4]And when they had done this, they fell prostrate and besought the Lord that they might never again fall into such misfortunes, but that, if they should ever sin, they might be disciplined by him with forbearance and not be handed over to blasphemous and barbarous nations. [5]It happened that on the same day on which the sanctuary had been profaned by the foreigners, the purification of the sanctuary took place, that is, on the twenty-fifth day of the same month, which was Chislev. [6]And they celebrated it for eight days with rejoicing, in the manner of the feast of booths, remembering how not long before, during the feast

---

In some way the new feast is like the feast of Tabernacles, which was normally celebrated about two months earlier, but which they had not been able to hold that year. From 1 Maccabees 1:54; 4:52 we can work out that three (not two) years had passed since sacrifices were offered.

The fact that the temple was being used again for the worship of God was a sign that he continued to protect his people and that what he promised was now going to come to pass (cf. 2:18). The Christian reader knows that this purification marked the start of the last stage in the life of the temple of Jerusalem, for worship in this temple will give way to worship "in spirit and truth" (cf. Jn 4:23), which our Lord Jesus Christ will institute. For that reason, the destruction of the temple of Jerusalem in 70 AD does not mean that God has forsaken his people, but simply that the temple had ceased to be the place of God's special presence.

et panum propositionem fecerunt. [4]Quibus autem gestis, rogaverunt Dominum prostrati in ventrem, ne amplius talibus malis inciderent, sed et, si quando peccassent, ut ab ipso cum clementia corriperentur et non blasphemis ac barbaris gentibus traderentur. [5]Qua die autem templum ab alienigenis pollutum fuerat, contigit eadem die purificationem fieri templi vicesima quinta illius mensis, qui est Casleu. [6]Et cum laetitia diebus octo egerunt in modum Tabernaculorum, recordantes quod ante modicum temporis diem sollemnem Tabernaculorum in montibus et in speluncis more bestiarum egerant. [7]Propter quod thyrsos et ramos virides, adhuc et palmas habentes, hymnos tollebant ei, qui prosperavit mundari locum suum. [8]Et decreverunt communi praecepto et decreto universae genti Iudaeorum omnibus annis agere dies istos. [9]Res itaque de fine Antiochi, qui appellatus est Epiphanes, ita se habuerunt. [10]Nunc autem res de Antiocho Eupatore, qui vero filius erat impii, narrabimus, illa breviantes, quae continent bellorum mala. [11]Hic enim, suscepto regno, constituit super negotia regni Lysiam quendam Coelesyriae et Phoenicis ducem primarium. [12]Nam Ptolemaeus, qui dicebatur Macron, quod esset iustum conservare praeferens erga Iudaeos propter in eos factam iniquitatem, conabatur, quae ad illos spectabant, pacifice peragere. [13]Unde accusatus ab amicis apud Eupatorem et cum frequenter se proditorem esse audiret, eo quod Cyprum creditam sibi a Philometore deseruisset et ad Antiochum Epiphanem transiisset, cumque amplius nobilem potestatem digne ferre non posset, veneno hausto vitam finivit. [14]Gorgias autem, cum esset dux locorum, externos milites alebat et frequenter adversus Iudaeos bellum instruebat. [15]Atque una cum ipso etiam Idumaei, qui tenebant opportunas munitiones, exercebant Iudaeos et fugatos ab Hierosolymis suscipientes bellum alere tentabant. [16]Hi vero, qui erant cum Maccabaeo, supplicatione facta et rogato Deo, ut esset sibi adiutor, impetum fecerunt in munitiones Idumaeorum, [17]quas fortiter aggressi, loca obtinuerunt et omnes, qui pugnabant in muris, propulerunt et occurrentes interemerunt et non minus viginti milibus trucidaverunt. [18]Quidam autem, cum confugissent non minus quam novem

Rev 7:9

of booths, they had been wandering in the mountains and caves like wild animals. [7]Therefore bearing ivy-wreathed wands and beautiful branches and also fronds of palm, they offered hymns of thanksgiving to him who had given success to the purifying of his own holy place. [8]They decreed by public ordinance and vote that the whole nation of the Jews should observe these days every year.

2. THE JEWS ENJOY SECURITY AND PEACE*

1 Mac 6:17

Victory over Gorgias and Timothy in the reign of Antiochus V

[9]Such then was the end of Antiochus, who was called Epiphanes.

[10]Now we will tell what took place under Antiochus Eupator, who was the son of that ungodly man, and will give a brief summary of the principal calamities of the wars. [11]This man, when

---

***10:9—15:39.** As he said he would do (cf. 2:20), the sacred author goes on now to deal with the war of Judas Maccabeus against Antiochus V Eupator; this will continue until Judas eventually manages to make agreements which guarantee the peace and security of the Jewish people (10:9—13:26). There were various stages in the war. First, Judas confronts and defeats the local Syrian generals Gorgias and Timothy (10:9–38); then he causes the Syrian commander-in-chief Lysias to withdraw (11:1–12): this leads to initial peace settlements, the terms of which are outlined in letters (11:13–38). However, the local Syrian leaders fail to keep to these terms—which means that the struggle against Gorgias and Timothy continues (12:1–46)—and this causes both Antiochus and Lysias to intervene against Judas; the outcome is victory for Judas, and a Syrian withdrawal; the king offers them new peace terms (13:1–26). In this summarized account, the writer has changed the order of events to suit his purpose (cf. the note on 2:19–32).

Even though he did not say at the start of the book that he would do so, the author extends his account of the deeds of Judas into the reign of the next king, Demetrius I—as far as Judas' victory over Nicanor, which gives the Jews full control over Jerusalem (14:1—15:34). The book then ends with a reminder about how a new feast was established to commemorate that event (15:35–36)—and a few words of farewell (15:37–38).

10:9–38. Antiochus V, the son of Antiochus IV (cf. 9:25), became king in 164 BC and lost the throne three years later (cf. 14:1). As can be seen from the suicide of Ptolemy Macron

milia in duas turres valde munitas et omnia ad repugnandum habentes, [19]Maccabaeus, ad eorum expugnationem relicto Simone et Iosepho itemque Zacchaeo eisque, qui cum ipso erant satis multis, ipse ad ea, quae amplius perurgebant, loca discessit. [20]Hi vero, qui cum Simone erant, cupiditate ducti

he succeeded to the kingdom, appointed one Lysias to have charge of the government and to be chief governor of Coelesyria and Phoenicia. [12]Ptolemy, who was called Macron, took the lead in showing justice to the Jews because of the wrong that had been done to them, and attempted to maintain peaceful relations with them. [13]As a result he was accused before Eupator by the king's friends. He heard himself called a traitor at every turn, because he had abandoned Cyprus, which Philometor had entrusted to him, and had gone over to Antiochus Epiphanes. Unable to command the respect due his office,[u] he took poison and ended his life.

[14]When Gorgias became governor of the region, he maintained a force of mercenaries, and at every turn kept on warring against

1 Mac 5:1–8

(not the same person as the Ptolemy of 4:45 and 8:8), there were differences of opinion at the Syrian court as regards policy towards the Jews. Despite Antiochus IV's death-bed "conversion" (cf. 9:11–17), official policy had not changed much. This meant that Judas had to keep fighting until, with God's help, he won complete freedom for the Jewish people.

To demonstrate this, the author of 2 Maccabees (or the source he is using) brings in here episodes which in fact occurred prior to the death of Antiochus IV and the purification of the temple. Thus, Lysias was put in charge of the government by Antiochus IV (cf. 1 Mac 3:32–33), and the battles reported here against Gorgias and the Idumeans (vv. 14–23), as also Lysias' first campaign (which is reported later: 11:1–12), actually took place in the time of Antiochus IV (cf. 1 Mac 3:38–41; 4:26–35). The author (or his source) has put the events into the reign of Antiochus IV's son, mixing them in with other incidents, such as the one covered in vv. 24–31, because he wants to give the reader to understand that the peace treaty and the withdrawal by the king of Syria were the result of victories won by Judas, whereas the purification of the temple was primarily brought about by God's intervention to punish Antiochus IV (cf. chap. 9). The author has no qualms about changing the order of events if this helps his readers see that God is at work in the purification of the temple, and that Judas' victories are the key to the country's liberation.

For these same reasons the sacred writer does not mind bringing some events forward in time, perhaps because they deal with the subject matter in hand—for example, the taking of the fortress at Gazara (cf. 1 Mac 13:43–48) and the death of Timothy (vv. 32–37), who turns up again when Judas defeats him in Gilead (cf. 2 Mac 12:1–25).

Right through this passage the religious piety of Judas and his followers is being underlined, as also the pride and self-reliance of his enemies, and the aid God gives the Jews—including heavenly apparitions which help them win the day.

u. Cn: The Greek text here is uncertain

the Jews. [15]Besides this, the Idumeans, who had control of important strongholds, were harassing the Jews; they received those who were banished from Jerusalem, and endeavoured to keep up the war. [16]But Maccabeus and his men, after making solemn supplication and beseeching God to fight on their side, rushed to the strongholds of the Idumeans. [17]Attacking them vigorously, they gained possession of the places, and beat off all who fought upon the wall, and slew those whom they encountered, killing no fewer than twenty thousand.

2 Mac 8:23–24

[18]When no less than nine thousand took refuge in two very strong towers well equipped to withstand a siege, [19]Maccabeus left Simon and Joseph, and also Zacchaeus and his men, a force sufficient to besiege them; and he himself set off for places where he was more urgently needed. [20]But the men with Simon, who were money-hungry, were bribed by some of those who were in the towers, and on receiving seventy thousand drachmas let some of them slip away. [21]When word of what had happened came to Maccabeus, he gathered the leaders of the people, and accused these men of having sold their brethren for money by setting their enemies free to fight against them. [22]Then he slew these men who had turned traitor, and immediately captured the two towers. [23]Having success at arms in everything he undertook, he destroyed more than twenty thousand in the two strongholds.

[24]Now Timothy, who had been defeated by the Jews before, gathered a tremendous force of mercenaries and collected the cavalry from Asia in no small number. He came on, intending to take Judea by storm. [25]As he drew near, Maccabeus and his men sprinkled dust upon their heads and girded their loins with sackcloth, in supplication to God. [26]Falling upon the steps before

Ex 23:22

---

a quibusdam, qui in turribus erant, suasi sunt pecunia et, septuaginta milibus drachmis acceptis, dimiserunt quosdam effugere. [21]Cum autem Maccabaeo nuntiatum esset, quod factum est, principibus populi congregatis accusavit quod pecunia fratres vendidissent, adversariis eorum dimissis. [22]Hos igitur proditores factos interfecit et confestim duas turres occupavit. [23]Armis autem in manibus omnia prospere agendo in duabus munitionibus plus quam viginti milia peremit. [24]At Timotheus, qui prius a Iudaeis fuerat superatus, convocatis peregrinis copiis valde multis et congregatis equis, qui erant ex Asia, non paucis, adfuit quasi armis victam Iudaeam capturus. [25]Qui autem cum Maccabaeo erant, appropinquante illo, ad supplicationem Dei terra capita aspergentes lumbosque ciliciis praecincti [26]super crepidinem contra altare provoluti rogabant, ut sibi propitius factus inimicis eorum esset inimicus et adversariis adversaretur, sicut lex declarat. [27]Digressi autem ab oratione, sumptis armis, longius de civitate processerunt et, proximi hostibus effecti, separatim steterunt. [28]Cum autem lux oriens coepisset diffundi, utrique commiserunt, isti quidem prosperitatis et victoriae tamquam sponsorem habentes cum virtute refugium in Dominum, illi autem ut ducem certaminum sibi ipsis statuentes animum. [29]Sed, cum vehemens pugna esset, apparuerunt adversariis de caelo viri quinque in equis, frenis aureis decori et ducatum Iudaeis praestantes; [30]ex quibus duo Maccabaeum medium accipientes suisque armis protegentes incolumem conservabant, in adversarios autem tela et fulmina iaciebant, ex quo caecitate confusi evolaverunt repleti perturbatione. [31]Interfecti sunt autem viginti milia quingenti et equites

the altar, they besought him to be gracious to them and to be an enemy to their enemies and an adversary to their adversaries, as the law declares. [27]And rising from their prayer they took up their arms and advanced a considerable distance from the city; and when they came near to the enemy they halted. [28]Just as dawn was breaking, the two armies joined battle, the one having as pledge of success and victory not only their valour but their reliance upon the Lord, while the other made rage their leader in the fight.

[29]When the battle became fierce, there appeared to the enemy from heaven five resplendent men on horses with golden bridles, and they were leading the Jews. [30]Surrounding Maccabeus and protecting him with their own armour and weapons, they kept him from being wounded. And they showered arrows and thunderbolts upon the enemy, so that, confused and blinded, they were thrown into disorder and cut to pieces. [31]Twenty thousand five hundred were slaughtered, besides six hundred horsemen.

2 Mac 5:4

[32]Timothy himself fled to a stronghold called Gazara, especially well garrisoned, where Chaereas was commander. [33]Then Maccabeus and his men were glad, and they besieged the fort for four days. [34]The men within, relying on the strength of the place, blasphemed terribly and hurled out wicked words. [35]But at dawn of the fifth day, twenty young men in the army of Maccabeus, fired with anger because of the blasphemies, bravely stormed the wall and with savage fury cut down every one they met. [36]Others who came up in the same way wheeled around against the defenders and set fire to the towers; they kindled fires and burned the blasphemers alive. Others broke open the gates and let in the rest of the force, and they occupied the city. [37]They killed Timothy, who was hidden in a cistern, and his brother Chaereas, and Apollophanes. [38]When they had accomplished these things, with hymns and thanksgivings they blessed the Lord who shows great kindness to Israel and gives them the victory.

1 Mac 13:43–48

---

sescenti. [32]Timotheus vero confugit in praesidium, quod Gazara dicitur, optimam munitionem, ducatum illic habente Chaerea. [33]Qui autem cum Maccabaeo erant laetantes obsederunt munitionem diebus quattuor. [34]At hi qui intus erant, loci munimento confisi, supra modum maledicebant et sermones nefandos iactabant; [35]sed, cum dies quinta illucesceret, viginti iuvenes ex his, qui cum Maccabaeo erant, accensi animis propter blasphemias murum viriliter aggressi feroci animo occursantem quemque caedebant; [36]sed et alii similiter ascendentes in circumflexione contra eos, qui intus erant, turres incendebant atque ignes inferentes ipsos maledicos vivos concremabant, alii autem portas concidebant et, recepto residuo exercitu, occupaverunt civitatem [37]et Timotheum occultantem se in quodam lacu peremerunt et fratrem illius Chaeream et Apollophanem. [38]Quibus gestis, in hymnis et confessionibus benedicebant Dominum, qui magnifice Israel benefaciebat et victoriam dabat illis. **[11]** [1]Sed parvo prorsus post tempore Lysias procurator regis et propinquus ac negotiorum praepositus graviter ferens de his, quae acciderant, [2]congregatis octoginta milibus et equitatu universo, veniebat adversus Iudaeos

1 Mac 4:26–35

First campaign of Lysias against the Jews

11 [1]Very soon after this, Lysias, the king's guardian and kinsman, who was in charge of the government, being vexed at what had happened, [2]gathered about eighty thousand men and all his cavalry and came against the Jews. He intended to make the city a home for Greeks, [3]and to levy tribute on the temple as he did on the sacred places of the other nations, and to put up the high priesthood for sale every year. [4]He took no account whatever of the power of God, but was elated with his ten thousands of infantry, and his thousands of cavalry, and his eighty elephants. [5]Invading Judea, he approached Beth-zur, which was a fortified place about five leagues[v] from Jerusalem, and pressed it hard.

Ex 23:20

[6]When Maccabeus and his men got word that Lysias[w] was besieging the strongholds, they and all the people, with lamentations and tears, besought the Lord to send a good angel to save Israel. [7]Maccabeus himself was the first to take up arms, and he urged the others to risk their lives with him to aid their brethren. Then they eagerly rushed off together. [8]And there, while they were still near Jerusalem, a horseman appeared at their head, clothed in white and brandishing weapons of gold. [9]And they all together praised the

2 Mac 5:4

11:1–15. The battle of Beth-zur occurred in the year 164 BC, when Antiochus IV was still alive and before the cleansing of the temple (cf. 1 Mac 4:26–35). Chronologically it should go after 2 Maccabees 8:36. Antiochus had gone on an expedition to Persia, leaving Lysias in charge of the government and of the upbringing of his son, the future Antiochus V (cf. 1 Mac 3:32–36). The king's sudden death far away from his base (chap. 9) means that Lysias has to go back to Antioch even though Judea has not been pacified; but he must have intended to return (cf. 1 Mac 4:35). Seemingly, under pressure from the Romans, to whom the Jews had recourse (cf. 2 Mac 11:34–38), Lysias grants them a respite (cf. 1 Mac 6:55–63). This is the point (around the end of 164 BC) at

---

existimans se civitatem quidem Graecis habitaculum facturum, [3]templum vero in pecuniae quaestum sicut cetera delubra gentium habiturum et per singulos annos venale sacerdotium facturum, [4]nequaquam recogitans Dei potestatem, sed elatus multitudine peditum et milibus equitum et octoginta elephantis. [5]Ingressus autem Iudaeam et appropians Bethsuris, munito quidem praesidio, distanti autem ab Hierosolymis intervallo quinque stadiorum, illud obsidione premebat. [6]Ut autem, qui cum Maccabaeo erant, cognoverunt eum expugnare praesidia, cum fletibus et lacrimis rogabant Dominum et omnis turba simul, ut bonum angelum mitteret ad salutem Israel. [7]Et ipse primus Maccabaeus, sumptis armis, ceteros adhortatus est simul secum periculum subire et ferre auxilium fratribus suis; simul autem et prompto animo impetum fecerunt. [8]Ilico vero, cum prope Hierosolymam essent, apparuit praecedens eos eques in veste candida armaturam auream vibrans. [9]Tunc omnes simul benedixerunt misericordem Deum et convaluerunt animis non solum homines, sed et bestias ferocissimas et muros ferreos parati

v. About twenty miles. The text is uncertain here **w.** Gk *he*

merciful God, and were strengthened in heart, ready to assail not only men but the wildest beasts or walls of iron. [10]They advanced in battle order, having their heavenly ally, for the Lord had mercy on them. [11]They hurled themselves like lions against the enemy, and slew eleven thousand of them and sixteen hundred horsemen, and forced all the rest to flee. [12]Most of them got away stripped and wounded, and Lysias himself escaped by disgraceful flight. [13]And as he was not without intelligence, he pondered over the defeat which had befallen him, and realized that the Hebrews were invincible because the mighty God fought on their side. So he sent to them [14]and persuaded them to settle everything on just terms, promising that he would persuade the king, constraining him to be their friend.[x] [15]Maccabeus, having regard for the common good, agreed to all that Lysias urged. For the king granted every request in behalf of the Jews which Maccabeus delivered to Lysias in writing.

1 Mac 6:57–61

---

which the cleansing of the temple takes place. Both 1 and 2 Maccabees make much of Judas' victory, though each from a different angle: in 1 Maccabees 4:36 it is what makes it possible for the Jews to regain the temple and cleanse it; here, it is what forces Lysias to offer peace terms to the Jews.

penetrare. [10]Praeibant in apparatu de caelo habentes adiutorem, miserante super eos Domino. [11]Leonum autem more impetu irruentes in hostes prostraverunt ex eis undecim milia peditum et equitum mille sescentos, universos autem in fugam verterunt. [12]Plures autem ex eis vulnerati, nudi evaserunt: sed et ipse Lysias turpiter fugiens evasit. [13]Et, quia non insensatus erat, secum ipse reputans factam erga se deminutionem et intellegens invictos esse Hebraeos, potente Deo auxiliante, misit ad eos [14]suasitque eis se consensurum omnibus, quae iusta sunt, et regem quoque persuasurum, ut necessarium crederet se amicum eis esse. [15]Annuit autem Maccabaeus in omnibus, quae Lysias rogabat, utilitati consulens; quaecumque enim Maccabaeus scriptis tradidit Lysiae de Iudaeis, rex concessit. [16]Nam erant scriptae Iudaeis epistulae a Lysia quidem hunc modum continentes: «Lysias populo Iudaeorum salutem. [17]Ioannes et Abessalom, qui missi fuerant a vobis tradentes responsum rescriptum, postulabant circum ea, quae per illud significabantur. [18]Quaecumque igitur oportebat etiam regi perferri, exposui; et quae res permittebat, concessit. [19]Si igitur in negotiis benevolentiam conservaveritis, et deinceps bonorum vobis causa esse tentabo. [20]De ceteris autem per singula mandavi et istis et his, qui a me missi sunt, colloqui vobiscum. [21]Bene valete. Anno centesimo quadragesimo octavo, mensis Iovis Corinthii die vicesima et quarta». [22]Regis autem epistula ista continebat: «Rex Antiochus Lysiae fratri salutem. [23]Patre nostro inter deos translato, nos volentes eos, qui sunt in regno nostro, sine tumultu attendere ad rerum suarum curam, [24]audientes Iudaeos non consensisse patri, ut transferrentur ad Graecas institutiones, sed suo ipsorum instituto adhaerentes postulare sibi concedi legitima sua, [25]cupientes igitur hanc quoque gentem extra tumultum esse iudicamus templum illis restitui remque agi secundum suorum maiorum consuetudinem. [26]Bene igitur feceris, si miseris ad eos et dexteram dederis ut, cognita nostra voluntate, bono animo sint et libenter propriarum rerum instaurationi deserviant». [27]Ad gentem vero regis epistula talis erat: «Rex Antiochus senatui Iudaeorum et ceteris Iudaeis salutem. [28]Si valetis, sic est, ut volumus; sed et ipsi bene valemus. [29]Manifestavit nobis Menelaus velle vos redire et in negotiis propriis versari. [30]His igitur, qui commeant usque ad diem tricesimum mensis Xanthici, erit dextera cum securitate, [31]ut Iudaei utantur cibis et legibus suis sicut et prius, et nemo eorum ullo modo molestiam patietur de his, quae per ignorantiam gesta sunt. [32]Misimus autem et Menelaum, qui vos

x. The Greek text here is corrupt

Letters granting peace to the Jews

[16]The letter written to the Jews by Lysias was to this effect:

"Lysias to the people of the Jews, greeting. [17]John and Absalom, who were sent by you, have delivered your signed communication and have asked about the matters indicated therein. [18]I have informed the king of everything that needed to be brought before him, and he has agreed to what was possible. [19]If you will maintain your good will toward the government, I will endeavour for the future to help promote your welfare. [20]And concerning these matters and their details, I have ordered these men and my representatives to confer with you. [21]Farewell. The one hundred and forty-eighth year,[y] Dioscorinthius twenty-fourth."

[22]The king's letter ran thus:

"King Antiochus to his brother Lysias, greeting. [23]Now that our father has gone on to the gods, we desire that the subjects of the kingdom be undisturbed in caring for their own affairs. [24]We have heard that the Jews do not consent to our father's change to Greek customs but prefer their own way of living and ask that their own customs be allowed them. [25]Accordingly, since we choose that this nation also be free from disturbance, our decision is that their temple be restored to them and that they live according to the customs of their ancestors. [26]You will do well, therefore, to send word to them and give them pledges of friendship, so that they may know our policy and be of good cheer and go on happily in the conduct of their own affairs."

[27]To the nation the king's letter was as follows:

"King Antiochus to the senate of the Jews and to the other Jews, greeting. [28]If you are well, it is as we desire. We also are in good health. [29]Menelaus has informed us that you wish to return home and look after your own affairs. [30]Therefore those who go home by the thirtieth day of Xanthicus will have our pledge of friendship

---

11:16–38. Lysias' letter (vv. 16–21), the king's letter to the Jews (vv. 27–33), and the Romans' letter (vv. 31–38) are dated 164 BC and they all fit in well with the situation after the battle of Beth-zur. But the letter of the king to Lysias (vv. 22–26) bears no date and would fit better in the context of the negotiations after Lysias' second campaign (cf. 13:1–26; 1 Mac 6:28–63). The author has put all four letters together because they all deal with the same sort of material. From them we can see that the Jews are now permitted to keep their own customs and that those who were living in hiding are able to return to their cities (cf. v. 29).

y. 164 BC

and full permission [31]for the Jews to enjoy their own food and laws, just as formerly, and none of them shall be molested in any way for what he may have done in ignorance. [32]And I have also sent Menelaus to encourage you. [33]Farewell. The one hundred and forty-eighth year,[z] Xanthicus fifteenth."

[34]The Romans also sent them a letter, which read thus:

"Quintus Memmius and Titus Manius, envoys of the Romans, to the people of the Jews, greeting. [35]With regard to what Lysias the kinsman of the king has granted you, we also give consent. [36]But as to the matters which he decided are to be referred to the king, as soon as you have considered them, send some one promptly, so that we may make proposals appropriate for you. For we are on our way to Antioch. [37]Therefore make haste and send some men, so that we may have your judgment. [38]Farewell. The one hundred and forty-eighth year,[a] Xanthicus fifteenth."

Just punishment for the men of Joppa and Jamnia

12 [1]When this agreement had been reached, Lysias returned to the king, and the Jews went about their farming.

[2]But some of the governors in various places, Timothy and Apollonius the son of Gennaeus, as well as Hieronymus and Demophon, and in addition to these Nicanor the governor of Cyprus, would not let them live quietly and in peace. [3]And some men of Joppa did so ungodly a deed as this: they invited the Jews who lived among them to embark, with their wives and children,

---

12:1–9. This entire chapter is very much the same in content as 1 Maccabees 5 and deals with the same situation; but 1 Maccabees links these conflicts to Gentile resentment of the fact that the temple is in operation again (cf. 1 Mac 5:1–2), whereas 2 Maccabees sees them as steps on the road to the complete liberation of the Jews. The events at Joppa and Jamnia (not explicitly mentioned in 1 Maccabees) clearly portray Judas as the avenger of his countrymen's blood: he goes to their defence and applies the law of vengeance to their enemies.

alloquatur. [33]Valete. Anno centesimo quadragesimo octavo, Xanthici mensis quinta decima die». [34]Miserunt autem etiam Romani epistulam ita se habentem: «Quintus Memmius, Titus Manius, legati Romanorum populo Iudaeorum salutem. [35]De his, quae Lysias cognatus regis concessit vobis, et nos consentimus. [36]De quibus autem ad regem iudicavit referendum, confestim aliquem mittite inter vos conferentes de his, ut proponamus, sicut congruit vobis; nos enim Antiochiam accedimus. [37]Ideoque festinate et mittite aliquos, ut nos quoque sciamus cuius estis voluntatis. [38]Bene valete. Anno centesimo quadragesimo octavo, quinta decima die mensis Xanthici». **[12]** [1]His factis pactionibus, Lysias pergebat ad regem, Iudaei autem agriculturae operam dabant. [2]Sed ex his, qui duces erant in singulis locis, Timotheus et Apollonius Gennaei filius, sed et Hieronymus et Demophon, super hos et Nicanor

z. 164 BC **a.** 164 BC

on boats which they had provided, as though there were no ill will to the Jews;[b] [4]and this was done by public vote of the city. And when they accepted, because they wished to live peaceably and suspected nothing, the men of Joppa[c] took them out to sea and drowned them, not less than two hundred. [5]When Judas heard of the cruelty visited on his countrymen, he gave orders to his men [6]and, calling upon God the righteous Judge, attacked the murderers of his brethren. He set fire to the harbour by night, and burned the boats, and massacred those who had taken refuge there. [7]Then, because the city's gates were closed, he withdrew, intending to come again and root out the whole community of Joppa. [8]But learning that the men in Jamnia meant in the same way to wipe out the Jews who were living among them, [9]he attacked the people of Jamnia by night and set fire to the harbour and the fleet, so that the glow of the light was seen in Jerusalem, thirty miles[d] distant.

1 Mac 5:24–54

Expedition against Timothy

[10]When they had gone more than a mile[e] from there, on their march against Timothy, not less than five thousand Arabs with five hundred horsemen attacked them. [11]After a hard fight Judas and his men won the victory, by the help of God. The defeated nomads besought Judas to grant them pledges of friendship, promising to give him cattle and to help his people[f] in all other ways. [12]Judas,

---

12:10–31. The scene suddenly changes, and Judas is operating on the other side of the Jordan. According to 1 Maccabees 5:9–13, the Jews of that area sought Judas' help. In 2 Maccabees Judas is in pursuit of Timothy: this takes him first to Caspin, which is about 20 km. (12 miles) east of the Lake of Gennesaret, and then he goes some 140 km (84 miles) to the south (v. 17), into Ammonite territory, from where he goes north again to Carnaim, towards the Jordan; he makes his way back, through Scythopolis (Beth-sin), the city

Cypriarches, non sinebant eos in silentio agere et quiete. [3]Ioppitae vero tale quoddam flagitium perpetrarunt: cum rogavissent Iudaeos, cum quibus habitabant, ascendere scaphas, quas ipsi paraverant, cum uxoribus et filiis, quasi nullis inimicitiis in eos subiacentibus, [4]secundum autem commune civitatis decretum et ipsis acquiescentibus, utpote qui pacem obtinere cuperent et nihil suspectum haberent, eos provectos in altum submerserunt non minus ducentos. [5]Quam crudelitatem Iudas in suae gentis homines factam ut cognovit, praecepit viris, qui erant cum ipso, et, invocato iusto iudice Deo, [6]venit adversus interfectores fratrum et portum quidem noctu succendit, scaphas exussit, eos autem, qui illuc refugerant, gladio peremit. [7]Et, cum conclusus esset locus, discessit quasi iterum reversurus et universam Ioppitarum civitatem eradicaturus. [8]Sed, cum cognovisset et eos, qui erant Iamniae, velle pari modo facere habitantibus secum Iudaeis, [9]Iamnitis quoque nocte supervenit et portum cum navibus succendit, ita ut lumen ignis appareret Hierosolymis a stadiis ducentis quadraginta. [10]Inde, cum iam abiissent novem stadiis et iter facerent ad Timotheum, commiserunt cum eo Arabes non minus quam quinque milia viri et equites quingenti. [11]Cumque pugna valida fieret et hi, qui circa Iudam erant, per auxilium

b. Gk *them* **c.** Gk *they* **d.** Gk *two hundred and forty stadia* **e.** Gk *nine stadia* **f** Gk *them*

thinking that they might really be useful in many ways, agreed to make peace with them; and after receiving his pledges they departed to their tents.

[13]He also attacked a certain city which was strongly fortified with earthworks[g] and walls, and inhabited by all sorts of Gentiles. Its name was Caspin. [14]And those who were within, relying on the strength of the walls and on their supply of provisions, behaved most insolently toward Judas and his men, railing at them and even blaspheming and saying unholy things. [15]But Judas and his men, calling upon the great Sovereign of the world, who without battering-rams or engines of war overthrew Jericho in the days of Joshua, rushed furiously upon the walls. [16]They took the city by the will of God, and slaughtered untold numbers, so that the adjoining lake, a quarter of a mile[h] wide, appeared to be running over with blood.

Josh 6
1 Tim 6:15

[17]When they had gone ninety-five miles[i] from there, they came to Charax, to the Jews who are called Toubiani. [18]They did not find Timothy in that region, for he had by then departed from the

1 Mac 5:37–44
1 Mac 5:13

of the Scyths (v. 29), reaching Jerusalem in time for the feast of Weeks (v. 31). Some Greek codices (and the New Vulgate and the RSV) add that Lysias was in Ephron (v. 27), but that would be highly unlikely, unless another Lysias is being referred to.

Dei prospere gessissent, nomades victi petebant a Iuda dextram sibi dari promittentes se pascua daturos et in ceteris profuturos eis. [12]Iudas autem arbitratus vere in multis eos utiles promisit se pacem acturum cum eis; dextrisque acceptis, discessere ad tabernacula sua. [13]Aggressus est autem et civitatem quandam firmam pontibus murisque circumsaeptam, quae a promiscuis gentibus habitabatur, cui nomen Caspin. [14]Hi vero, qui intus erant, confidentes in stabilitate murorum et apparatu alimoniarum contumeliosius agebant cum eis, qui circa Iudam erant, maledictis lacessentes et blasphemantes ac loquentes, quae fas non est. [15]Qui autem cum Iuda erant, invocato magno mundi Principe, qui sine arietibus et machinis organicis temporibus Iosue praecipitavit Iericho, irruerunt ferociter muris [16]et, capta civitate per Dei voluntatem, inenarrabiles caedes fecerunt, ita ut adiacens stagnum latitudinem habens stadiorum duorum defluere repletum sanguine videretur. [17]Inde autem discesserunt stadia septingenta quinquaginta et pervenerunt in Characa ad eos, qui dicuntur Tubiani, Iudaeos. [18]Et Timotheum quidem in illis locis non comprehenderunt, qui, nullo negotio perfecto, tunc de locis regressus erat, relicto tamen in quodam loco firmissimo praesidio. [19]Dositheus autem et Sosipater, ex ducibus, qui cum Maccabaeo erant, exeuntes peremerunt a Timotheo relictos in praesidio plures quam decem milia viros. [20]At Maccabaeus, ordinato exercitu circum se per cohortes, constituit eos super cohortes et adversus Timotheum processit habentem secum centum viginti milia peditum equitumque duo milia quingentos. [21]Cognito autem Iudae adventu, Timotheus praemisit mulieres et filios et reliquum apparatum in locum, qui Carnion dicitur; erat enim inexpugnabile et accessu difficile praesidium propter locorum angustias. [22]Cumque cohors Iudae prima apparuisset et pavor factus esset super hostes ac timor ex praesentia illius, qui universa conspicit, super eos esset, in fugam exsiluerunt, alius alio se ferens, ita ut saepe a suis laederentur et gladiorum acuminibus configerentur. [23]Iudas autem vehementer instabat confodiens impios et prostravit ad triginta milia virorum. [24]Ipse vero Timotheus incidens in eos, qui erant cum Dositheo et Sosipatre, cum multa adulatione postulabat, ut vivus dimitteretur, eo quod multorum quidem parentes, aliorum autem fratres haberet, et contingeret horum curam non haberi. [25]Et cum

g. The Greek text here is uncertain **h.** Gk *two stadia* **i.** Gk *seven hundred and fifty stadia*

region without accomplishing anything, though in one place he had left a very strong garrison. [19]Dositheus and Sosipater, who were captains under Maccabeus, marched out and destroyed those whom Timothy had left in the stronghold, more than ten thousand men. [20]But Maccabeus arranged his army in divisions, set men[j] in command of the divisions, and hastened after Timothy, who had with him a hundred and twenty thousand infantry and two thousand five hundred cavalry. [21]When Timothy learned of the approach of Judas, he sent off the women and the children and also the baggage to a place called Carnaim; for that place was hard to besiege and difficult of access because of the narrowness of all the approaches. [22]But when Judas' first division appeared, terror and fear came over the enemy at the manifestation to them of him who sees all things; and they rushed off in flight and were swept on, this

1 Mac 5:43

12:32–37. Judas now goes south, into the territory of Idumea, in search of Gorgias, another bitter enemy of the Jews (cf. 8:9; 10:14). As always, the Maccabee has God on his side and he comes out victorious.

12:38–46. Some Jews fell in the battle on account of their sins (v. 42); their comrades pray for them, and Judas orders an atoning sacrifice to be offered (v. 43). These facts, on their own, could simply mean that they wanted to placate God, to ensure that punishment for the men's sins did not fall on the people (cf. Josh 7:1). But the sacred writer provides a deeper and more exact interpretation—that Judas, like the seven martyred brothers and their mother (cf. chap. 7), believed in the future resurrection of those who died in the cause of Judaism. The text makes it clear that Judas shared that belief (v. 44) and on this account he is portrayed as a devout man and an example for others. Reflecting on this doctrine in the light of our Lord's teachings, the Church from the very beginning held that there is a deep communion among the saints and that it is a very good thing to pray for the dead: "the Church in its pilgrim members, from the very earliest days of the Christian religion, has honoured with great respect the memory of the dead; and, 'because it is a holy and a wholesome thought to pray for the dead that they may be loosed from their sins' (2 Mac 12:46), she offers her suffrages for them. The Church has always believed that the apostles and Christ's martyrs, who gave the supreme witness of faith and charity by the shedding of their blood, are closely united with us in Christ; she has always venerated them, together with the Blessed Virgin Mary and the holy angels, with a special love

pluribus modis fidem dedisset secundum hoc constitutum, restituturum se eos illaesos, dimiserunt eum propter fratrum salutem. [26]Egressus autem ad Carnion et Atergation interfecit viginti quinque milia corporum. [27]Post autem horum fugam et necem movit exercitum etiam adversus Ephron civitatem

j. Gk *them*

way and that, so that often they were injured by their own men and pierced by the points of their swords. 23And Judas pressed the pursuit with the utmost vigor, putting the sinners to the sword, and destroyed as many as thirty thousand men.

24Timothy himself fell into the hands of Dositheus and Sosipater and their men. With great guile he besought them to let him go in safety, because he held the parents of most of them and the brothers of some and no consideration would be shown them. 25And when with many words he had confirmed his solemn promise to restore them unharmed, they let him go, for the sake of saving their brethren.

26Then Judas[k] marched against Carnaim and the temple of Atargatis, and slaughtered twenty-five thousand people. 27After the rout and destruction of these, he marched also against Ephron, a fortified city where Lysias dwelt with multitudes of people of all nationalities.[l] Stalwart young men took their stand before the walls and made a vigorous defence; and great stores of war engines and missiles were there. 28But the Jews[m] called upon the Sovereign who with power shatters the might of his enemies, and they got the city into their hands, and killed as many as twenty-five thousand of those who were within it.

29Setting out from there, they hastened to Scythopolis, which is seventy-five miles[n] from Jerusalem. 30But when the Jews who dwelt there bore witness to the good will which the people of Scythopolis had shown them and their kind treatment of them in

---

and has asked piously for the help of their intercession" (Vatican II, *Lumen gentium*, 50).

As the sacred writer sees it, the offering of that sacrifice and the prayer for those who died, mean not only hope in the resurrection, but a conviction that it is possible for a person to be cleansed of sin after death, and that prayers and offerings for the dead can help bring that purification about. That is what the Church believes when it says that there is a Purgatory and that suffrages for the dead have an expiatory value. "From the beginning the Church has honoured the memory of the dead and offered prayers in suffrage for them, above all the Eucharistic sacrifice, so that, thus purified, they may attain the beatific vision of God" (*Catechism of the Catholic Church*, 1032).

munitam, in qua multitudo diversarum gentium inhabitabat, et robusti iuvenes pro muris consistentes fortiter repugnabant; in hac autem machinarum et telorum multi erant apparatus. 28Sed, cum Potentem invocassent, qui potestate sua vires hostium confringit, ceperunt subiectam civitatem et ex eis, qui intus erant, ad viginti quinque milia prostraverunt. 29Inde profecti ad civitatem Scytharum perrexerunt, quae ab Hierosolymis sescentis stadiis aberat. 30Contestantibus autem his, qui erant illic Iudaei,

k. Gk *he* **l.** The Greek text of this sentence is uncertain **m.** Gk *they* **n.** Gk *six hundred stadia*

times of misfortune, [31]they thanked them and exhorted them to be well disposed to their race in the future also. Then they went up to Jerusalem, as the feast of weeks was close at hand.

Expedition against Gorgias

Ex 23:14

2 Mac 8:9; 10:14

[32]After the feast called Pentecost, they hastened against Gorgias, the governor of Idumea. [33]And he came out with three thousand infantry and four hundred cavalry. [34]When they joined battle, it happened that a few of the Jews fell. [35]But a certain Dositheus, one of Bacenor's men, who was on horseback and was a strong man, caught hold of Gorgias, and grasping his cloak was dragging him off by main strength, wishing to take the accursed man alive, when one of the Thracian horsemen bore down upon him and cut off his arm; so Gorgias escaped and reached Marisa.

[36]As Esdris and his men had been fighting for a long time and were weary, Judas called upon the LORD to show himself their ally and leader in the battle. [37]In the language of their fathers he raised the battle cry, with hymns; then he charged against Gorgias' men when they were not expecting it, and put them to flight.

Sin offering for the fallen

[38]Then Judas assembled his army and went to the city of Adullam. As the seventh day was coming on, they purified themselves according to the custom, and they kept the sabbath there.

Deut 7:25

[39]On the next day, as by that time it had become necessary, Judas and his men went to take up the bodies of the fallen and to bring them back to lie with their kinsmen in the sepulchres of their fathers. [40]Then under the tunic of every one of the dead they found sacred tokens of the idols of Jamnia, which the law forbids the Jews to wear. And it became clear to all that this was why these

---

benevolentiam, quam Scythopolitae erga eos habebant, et mitem occursum temporibus infelicitatis, [31]gratias agentes et exhortati etiam de cetero erga genus ipsum benignos esse venerunt Hierosolymam die sollemni Septimanarum instante. [32]Post eam vero, quae dicitur Pentecoste, abierunt contra Gorgiam praepositum Idumaeae. [33]Exivit autem cum peditibus tribus milibus et equitibus quadringentis. [34]Quibus autem congressis, contigit paucos ruere Iudaeorum. [35]Dositheus vero quidam de iis, qui Bacenoris erant, eques vir et fortis, Gorgiam tenuit chlamydeque apprehensum ducebat eum fortiter; et, cum vellet illum capere vivum, eques quidam de Thracibus irruit in eum umerumque amputavit, et Gorgias effugit in Maresa. [36]At illis, qui cum Esdrin erant, diutius pugnantibus et fatigatis, cum invocasset Iudas Dominum, ut adiutorem se ostenderet et ducem belli, [37]incipiens patria voce clamorem cum hymnis, irruens improviso in eos, qui circa Gorgiam erant, fugam eis incussit. [38]Iudas autem, collecto exercitu, venit in civitatem Odollam et, cum septima dies superveniret, secundum consuetudinem purificati in eodem loco sabbatum egerunt. [39]Et sequenti die venerunt, qui cum Iuda erant, eo tempore, quo necessarium factum erat, ut corpora prostratorum tollerent et cum parentibus reponerent in sepulcris paternis. [40]Invenerunt autem sub tunicis uniuscuiusque interfectorum donaria idolorum, quae apud Iamniam fuerunt, a quibus lex prohibet Iudaeos. Omnibus ergo manifestum factum est ob hanc causam

men had fallen. [41]So they all blessed the ways of the Lord, the righteous Judge, who reveals the things that are hidden; [42]and they turned to prayer, beseeching that the sin which had been committed might be wholly blotted out. And the noble Judas exhorted the people to keep themselves free from sin, for they had seen with their own eyes what had happened because of the sin of those who had fallen. [43]He also took up a collection, man by man, to the amount of two thousand drachmas of silver, and sent it to Jerusalem to provide for a sin offering. In doing this he acted very well and honourably, taking account of the resurrection. [44]For if he were not expecting that those who had fallen would rise again, it would have been superfluous and foolish to pray for the dead. [45]But if he was looking to the splendid reward that is laid up for those who fall asleep in godliness, it was a holy and pious thought. Therefore he made atonement for the dead, that they might be delivered from their sin.*

2 Mac 7:9

The king accompanies Lysias in his second campaign. Death of Menelaus

13 [1]In the one hundred and forty-ninth year[o] word came to Judas and his men that Antiochus Eupator was coming with a great army against Judea, [2]and with him Lysias, his guardian, who had charge of the government. Each of them had a Greek force of one hundred and ten thousand infantry, five thousand three hundred cavalry, twenty-two elephants, and three hundred chariots armed with scythes.

1 Mac 6:30

13:1–17. These events took place in 167 BC. According to 1 Maccabees 6:18–28, the reason the king attacked was because Judas laid siege to the citadel where the Syrian garrison of Jerusalem was based. The author of 2 Maccabees, on the other hand, focuses mainly on the treachery of the high priest Menelaus (cf. 4:23–29), which implies that the pro-Greek party was still quite strong and that, as had happened before, some of the Jews themselves were the cause of evils (cf. 4:30–32). Once again the punishment

eos corruisse. [41]Omnes itaque, cum benedixissent, quae sunt iusti iudicis, Domini, qui occulta manifesta facit, [42]ad obsecrationem conversi sunt, rogantes, ut id, quod factum erat, delictum oblivioni ex integro traderetur. At vero fortissimus Iudas hortatus est populum conservare se sine peccato, cum sub oculis vidissent, quae facta sunt propter peccatum eorum, qui prostrati sunt. [43]Et, facta viritim collatione ad duo milia drachmas argenti, misit Hierosolymam offerri pro peccatis sacrificium, valde bene et honeste de resurrectione cogitans. [44]Nisi enim eos, qui ceciderant, resurrecturos speraret, superfluum et vanum esset orare pro mortuis. [45]Deinde considerans quod hi, qui cum pietate dormitionem acceperant, optimum haberent repositum gratiae donum: [46]sancta et pia cogitatio. Unde pro defunctis expiationem fecit, ut a peccato solverentur. **[13]** [1]Anno centesimo quadragesimo nono his, qui erant circa Iudam, notum factum est Antiochum Eupatorem venire cum multitudine adversus Iudaeam [2]et cum eo Lysiam

o. 163 BC

[3]Menelaus also joined them and with utter hypocrisy urged Antiochus on, not for the sake of his country's welfare, but because he thought that he would be established in office. [4]But the King of kings aroused the anger of Antiochus against the scoundrel; and when Lysias informed him that this man was to blame for all the trouble, he ordered them to take him to Beroea and to put him to death by the method which is the custom in that place. [5]For there is a tower in that place, fifty cubits high, full of ashes, and it has a rim running around it which on all sides inclines precipitously into the ashes. [6]There they all push to destruction any man guilty of sacrilege or notorious for other crimes. [7]By such a fate it came about that Menelaus the lawbreaker died, without even burial in the earth. [8]And this was eminently just; because he had committed many sins against the altar whose fire and ashes were holy, he met his death in ashes.

[9]The king with barbarous arrogance was coming to show the Jews things far worse than those that had been done[p] in his father's time. [10]But when Judas heard of this, he ordered the people to call upon the Lord day and night, now if ever to help those who were on the point of being deprived of the law and their country and the

1 Tim 6:15
Rev 17:14; 19:16

1 Mac 4:36

---

of the guilty person is in proportion to his sinfulness (v. 8): Judas' victory is due to divine protection sought through prayer (vv. 10–14).

13:18–26. Comparing this passage with 1 Maccabees 6:48–63, one can see that Judas' victory is being exaggerated here and that what really caused the king to come to terms with the Jews and withdraw from Beth-zur was Philip's rebellion in Antioch (v. 23). Judas now becomes *de facto* governor of Judea, wielding authority recognized by the king. The Jews can practise their religion freely. The king's letter to Lysias given in 11:22–26 really refers to this point. Part of what the king ceded to the Jews had in fact already been gained.

procuratorem et praepositum negotiorum, unumquemque habentem exercitum Graecum peditum centum decem milia et equitum quinque milia trecentos et elephantos viginti duos, currus autem cum falcibus trecentos. [3]Commiscuit autem se illis et Menelaus et cum multa fallacia hortabatur Antiochum non pro patriae salute, sed sperans se constitui in principatum. [4]Sed Rex regum suscitavit animos Antiochi in peccatorem; et, suggerente Lysia hunc esse causam omnium malorum, iussit, ut est consuetudo in loco, adductum in Beroeam necari. [5]Erat autem in loco turris quinquaginta cubitorum, cineris plena, et machinam habebat volubilem undique praecipitem in cinerem. [6]Illic reum sacrilegii vel quorundam etiam aliorum malorum summitatem factum, omnes propellunt ad interitum. [7]Et tali lege praevaricatorem legis contigit mori, nec terram adeptum Menelaum. [8]Valde iuste: nam, quia multa erga aram delicta commisit, cuius ignis et cinis erat sanctus, ipse in cinere mortem reportavit. [9]Sed rex mente efferatus veniebat peiora quam quae sub patre suo facta erant, ostensurus Iudaeis. [10]Quibus Iudas cognitis, praecepit populo, ut die ac nocte Dominum invocarent, si quando et alias etiam nunc adiuvaret

p. Or *the worst of the things that had been done*

holy temple, [11]and not to let the people who had just begun to revive fall into the hands of the blasphemous Gentiles. [12]When they had all joined in the same petition and had besought the merciful Lord with weeping and fasting and lying prostrate for three days without ceasing, Judas exhorted them and ordered them to stand ready.

[13]After consulting privately with the elders, he determined to march out and decide the matter by the help of God before the king's army could enter Judea and get possession of the city. [14]So, committing the decision to the Creator of the world and exhorting his men to fight nobly to the death for the laws, temple, city, country, and commonwealth, he pitched his camp near Mode-in. [15]He have his men the watchword, "God's victory," and with a picked force of the bravest young men, he attacked the king's pavilion at night and slew as many as two thousand men in the camp. He stabbed[q] the leading elephant and its rider. [16]In the end they filled the camp with terror and confusion and withdrew in triumph. [17]This happened, just as day was dawning, because the Lord's help protected him.

Heb 12:4
Rev 2:10

1 Mac 6:43ff
2 Mac 8:23

The king withdraws. A new peace agreement

1 Mac 6:48–63

[18]The king, having had a taste of the daring of the Jews, tried strategy in attacking their positions. [19]He advanced against Beth-zur, a strong fortress of the Jews, was turned back, attacked again,[r] and was defeated. [20]Judas sent in to the garrison whatever was necessary. [21]But Rhodocus, a man from the ranks of the Jews, gave secret information to the enemy; he was sought for, caught, and put in prison. [22]The king negotiated a second time with the people

---

eos, [11]quippe qui lege et patria sanctoque templo in eo essent ut privarentur, ac populum, qui nuper paululum respirasset, ne sineret blasphemis nationibus subdi. [12]Omnibus itaque simul idem facientibus et rogantibus misericordem Dominum cum fletu et ieiuniis et prostratione per triduum sine intermissione hortatus eos Iudas praecepit adesse. [13]Ipse vero seorsum cum senioribus cogitavit, prius quam regis exercitus invaderet Iudaeam et obtinerent civitatem, egressos res adiudicare auxilio Dei. [14]Dans itaque procurationem Creatori mundi, exhortatus suos, ut fortiter dimicarent usque ad mortem pro legibus, templo, civitate, patria, institutionibus, circa Modin exercitum constituit. [15]Cumque suis dedisset signum: «Victoriam Dei», cum iuvenibus fortissimis electis nocte aggressus castra adversus aulam regiam, interfecit viros ad duo milia et primarium elephantorum una cum eo, qui intra habitaculum erat; [16]et postremo metu ac perturbatione castra repleverunt rebusque prospere gestis abierunt. [17]Die autem iam illucescente hoc factum erat, adiuvante eum Domini protectione. [18]Sed rex, accepto gustu audaciae Iudaeorum, artibus loca tentavit. [19]Et Bethsuris, quae erat Iudaeorum praesidium munitum, castra admovebat; sed fugabatur, impingebat, minorabatur. [20]His autem, qui intus erant, Iudas necessaria mittebat. [21]Enuntiavit autem mysteria hostibus Rhodocus quidam de Iudaico exercitu, qui requisitus comprehensus est et conclusus. [22]Iterum rex sermonem habuit ad eos, qui erant in Bethsuris,

q. The Greek text here is uncertain **r.** Or *faltered*

in Beth-zur, gave pledges, received theirs, withdrew, attacked Judas and his men, was defeated; [23]he got word that Philip, who had been left in charge of the government, had revolted in Antioch; he was dismayed, called in the Jews, yielded and swore to observe all their rights, settled with them and offered sacrifice, honoured the sanctuary and showed generosity to the holy place. [24]He received Maccabeus, left Hegemonides as governor from Ptolemais to Gerar, [25]and went to Ptolemais. The people of Ptolemais were indignant over the treaty; in fact they were so angry that they wanted to annul its terms.[s] [26]Lysias took the public platform, made the best possible defence, convinced them, appeased them, gained their good will, and set out for Antioch. This is how the king's attack and withdrawal turned out.

1 Mac 7:1–21

Demetrius I becomes king. Alcimus' intrigues*

14 [1]Three years later, word came to Judas and his men that Demetrius, the son of Seleucus, had sailed into the harbour of Tripolis with a strong army and a fleet, [2]and had taken possession of the country, having made away with Antiochus and his guardian Lysias.

[3]Now a certain Alcimus, who had formerly been high priest but had wilfully defiled himself in the times of separation, realized that there was no way for him to be safe or to have access again to the

***14:1—15:39.** Although the author did not originally plan to deal with events in the reign of Demetrius I (cf. 2:19–23), he now covers at length a new outbreak of persecution and new victories of Judas at the start of that reign (161 BC). As happened at the very beginning (cf. 3:4–6; 4:1–2, 7–8), the root cause was treachery by some Jews; this time Alcimus is the culprit (14:1–36). An elder called Razis (14:37ff) now joins the ranks of the earlier martyrs (cf. 6:18—7:41). The previous persecution ended with the death of the impious Antiochus IV (cf. 9:1–28); this one ends with the death of Nicanor (15:25–34). The feast of the Dedication was established after the first persecution (10:1–8); the new feast of

dextram dedit, accepit, abiit, [23]commisit cum his, qui erant cum Iuda, superatus est, cognovit rebellasse Philippum Antiochiae, qui relictus erat super negotia, confusus est, Iudaeos deprecatus est, subditus est, iuravit de omnibus, quae iusta erant, reconciliatus est et obtulit sacrificium, honoravit templum et loco exhibuit humanitatem; [24]Maccabaeum excepit, reliquit ducem a Ptolemaide usque ad Gerrenos Hegemonidem, [25]venit Ptolemaidam: graviter ferebant Ptolemenses amicitiae conventiones—indignabantur enim supra modum—voluerunt irrita facere pacta. [26]Accessit Lysias ad tribunal, exposuit rationem congruenter, persuasit, sedavit, tranquillos fecit, regressus est Antiochiam. Hoc modo res gestae a rege, adventus et profectionis eius, processerunt. **[14]** [1]Sed post triennii tempus cognoverunt, qui cum Iuda erant, Demetrium Seleuci per portum apud Tripolim adnavigantem cum multitudine valida et navibus, [2]tenuisse regionem sublato Antiocho et procuratore eius Lysia. [3]Alcimus autem quidam, qui

s. The Greek text of this clause is uncertain

holy altar, [4]and went to King Demetrius in about the one hundred and fifty-first year,[t] presenting to him a crown of gold and a palm, and besides these some of the customary olive branches from the temple. During that day he kept quiet. [5]But he found an opportunity that furthered his mad purpose when he was invited by Demetrius to a meeting of the council and was asked about the disposition and intentions of the Jews. He answered:

1 Mac 10:29

[6]"Those of the Jews who are called Hasideans, whose leader is Judas Maccabeus, are keeping up war and stirring up sedition, and will not let the kingdom attain tranquillity. [7]Therefore I have laid aside my ancestral glory—I mean the high priesthood—and have now come here, [8]first because I am genuinely concerned for the interests of the king, and second because I have regard also for my fellow citizens. For through the folly of those whom I have mentioned our whole nation is now in no small misfortune. [9]Since you are acquainted, O king, with the details of this matter, deign to take thought for our country and our hard-pressed nation with the gracious kindness which you show to all. [10]For as long as Judas lives, it is impossible for the government to find peace."

'Nicanor's Day' marks the end of this one. These parallels make for a story well told, in keeping with the author's intentions (cf. 2:25; 15:38–39).

14:1–14. First Maccabees 7:1–50 covers these same events, but more concisely. The new king made his way from Rome to Tripolis, a Phoenician city. The high priesthood had been vacant since the death of Menelaus (13:3–8), and Alcimus, of the pro-Greek faction, plotted very cleverly against Judas. On the Hasidaeans, see the note on 1 Maccabees 2:42.

summus sacerdos fuerat, sed voluntarie coinquinatus temporibus seditionis, considerans nullo modo sibi esse salutem neque accessum ultra ad sanctum altare [4]venit ad regem Demetrium centesimo quinquagesimo primo anno offerens ei coronam auream et palmam, super haec et thallos, qui templi esse videbantur; et ipsa quidem die siluit. [5]Tempus autem opportunum dementiae suae nactus, convocatus a Demetrio ad consilium et interrogatus quo proposito et consilio Iudaei niterentur, [6]ad haec respondit: «Ipsi, qui dicuntur Asidaei, Iudaeorum, quibus praeest Iudas Maccabaeus, bella nutriunt et seditiones movent, nec patiuntur regnum esse quietum. [7]Unde ego defraudatus parentum gloria, dico autem summo sacerdotio, huc nunc veni, [8]primo quidem de his, quae pertinent ad regem, mera fide sentiens, secundo autem etiam civibus meis consulens; nam illorum praedictorum inconsiderantia universum genus nostrum non modice laborat. [9]Sed his singulis, tu rex, cognitis, et regioni et obsesso generi nostro, secundum quam habes omnibus obviam humanitatem, prospice; [10]nam, quamdiu superest Iudas, impossibile est pacem esse negotiis». [11]Talibus autem ab hoc dictis, velocius ceteri amici hostiliter se habentes adversus Iudam inflammaverunt Demetrium. [12]Qui statim assumens Nicanorem, qui fuit praepositus elephantorum, et ducem ostendens Iudaeae misit, [13]datis mandatis, ut ipsum quidem Iudam occideret, eos vero, qui cum illo erant, dispergeret et constitueret Alcimum maximi templi summum sacerdotem. [14]Tunc gentes, quae de Iudaea fugerant Iudam, gregatim se Nicanori miscebant, miserias et clades Iudaeorum prosperitates rerum suarum existimantes fore. [15]Audito itaque Nicanoris

t. 161 BC

1 Mac 2:18; 7:26

[11]When he had said this, the rest of the king's friends, who were hostile to Judas, quickly inflamed Demetrius still more. [12]And he immediately chose Nicanor, who had been in command of the elephants, appointed him governor of Judea, and sent him off [13]with orders to kill Judas and scatter his men, and to set up Alcimus as high priest of the greatest temple. [14]And the Gentiles throughout Judea, who had fled before[u] Judas, flocked to join Nicanor, thinking that the misfortunes and calamities of the Jews would mean prosperity for themselves.

Nicanor and Judas reach an understanding

1 Mac 7:27–28

1 Mac 7:31

[15]When the Jews[v] heard of Nicanor's coming and the gathering of the Gentiles, they sprinkled dust upon their heads and prayed to him who established his own people for ever and always upholds his own heritage by manifesting himself. [16]At the command of the leader, they[w] set out from there immediately and engaged them in battle at a village called Dessau.[x] [17]Simon, the brother of Judas, had encountered Nicanor, but had been temporarily[y] checked because of the sudden consternation created by the enemy.

[18]Nevertheless Nicanor, hearing of the valour of Judas and his men and their courage in battle for their country, shrank from deciding the issue by bloodshed. [19]Therefore he sent Posidonius and Theodotus and Mattathias to give and receive pledges of friendship. [20]When the terms had been fully considered, and the leader had informed the people, and it had appeared that they were of one mind, they agreed to the covenant. [21]And the leaders[z] set a day on which to meet by themselves. A chariot came forward from

---

14:15–25. The pact between Judas and Nicanor, and their friendship (2 Maccabees is our only source for this) shows Judas' valour and also his peaceful nature, throwing into relief the malice of Alcimus, who will manage to undermine that friendship.

adventu et conventu nationum, conspersi terra rogabant eum, qui populum suum constituit usque in aeternum quique suam portionem signis evidentibus protegit. [16]Imperante autem duce, statim inde profectus congreditur eis ad castellum Dessau. [17]Simon vero frater Iudae commiserat cum Nicanore, sed lente ob repentinum adversariorum silentium victus evaserat. [18]Nicanor tamen audiens quam virtutem haberent, qui cum Iuda erant, et animi magnitudinem pro patriae certaminibus, sanguine iudicium facere metuebat. [19]Quam ob rem misit Posidonium et Theodotum et Matthathiam, ut darent dextras atque acciperent. [20]Et, cum diu de his consilium ageretur et ipse dux ad multitudinem rettulisset et paribus suffragiis pareret sententia, sponsionibus pacis annuerunt. [21]Itaque diem constituerunt, qua secreto convenirent eodem, et processit utrumque currus, posuerunt sellas, [22]disposuit Iudas armatos paratos locis opportunis, ne forte ab hostibus repente mali aliquid fieret, congruum colloquium fecerunt.

u. The Greek text is uncertain **v.** Gk *they* **w.** Gk *he* **x.** The name is uncertain **y.** Other authorities read *slowly* **z.** Gk *they*

each army; seats of honour were set in place; Judas[22] posted armed men in readiness at key places to prevent sudden treachery on the part of the enemy; they held the proper conference.

[23]Nicanor stayed on in Jerusalem and did nothing out of the way, but dismissed the flocks of people that had gathered. [24]And he kept Judas always in his presence; he was warmly attached to the man. [25]And he urged him to marry and have children; so he married, settled down, and shared the common life.

Further intrigues by Alcimus. A new outbreak of persecution

[26]But when Alcimus noticed their good will for one another, he took the covenant that had been made and went to Demetrius. He told him that Nicanor was disloyal to the government, for he had appointed that conspirator against the kingdom, Judas, to be his successor. [27]The king became excited and, provoked by the false accusations of that depraved man, wrote to Nicanor, stating that he

---

14:26–36. Judas has behaved very nobly, but Alcimus resorts to lying to accuse Judas and Nicanor of disloyalty to the king; he may have been afraid that Judas would be appointed high priest or a "king's friend". Nicanor reacts very sycophantly to the king and very disloyally to Judas; and his attitude to the temple is worse even than Antiochus IV's, because he threatens not only to profane it but to destroy it.

Nicanor knows very well that Judas has behaved honourably (v. 28) but he makes every effort to kill him. His behaviour is reminiscent of that of Pilate towards our Lord—and of those who come to know the truth but fail to conform their lives to it: "Although each individual has a right to be respected in his own journey in search of the truth, there exists a prior moral obligation, and a grave one at that, to seek the truth and to adhere to it once it is known. As Cardinal John Henry Newman, that outstanding defender of the rights of conscience, forcefully put it: 'conscience has rights because it has duties'" (John Paul II, *Veritatis splendor*, 34).

[23]Morabatur Nicanor Hierosolymis nihilque inique agebat gregesque turbarum, quae congregatae fuerant, dimisit. [24]Habebat autem Iudam semper in conspectu, ex animo erat viro inclinatus. [25]Rogavit eum ducere uxorem filiosque procreare. Nuptias fecit, quiete egit, communiter vivebat. [26]Alcimus autem videns mutuam illorum benevolentiam et factas conventiones accipiens venit ad Demetrium et dicebat Nicanorem aliena sentire a rebus; Iudam enim regni insidiatorem socium sibi designavit. [27]Itaque rex exasperatus et pessimi huius criminationibus irritatus scripsit Nicanori dicens graviter quidem se ferre de conventionibus, iubere tamen Maccabaeum citius vinctum mittere Antiochiam. [28]Quibus cognitis, Nicanor confusus erat et aegre ferebat, si ea, quae convenerant, irrita faceret, nulla a viro facta iniuria; [29]sed, quia regi resisti non poterat, opportunitatem observabat, ut artificio illud perficeret. [30]At Maccabaeus videns secum austerius agere Nicanorem et consuetum occursum ferocius exhibentem, intellegens non ex optimo esse austeritatem, non paucis suorum congregatis, occultavit se a Nicanore. [31]Quod cum ille cognovit fortiter se a viro astutia praeventum, venit ad maximum et sanctum templum et sacerdotibus solitas hostias offerentibus iussit sibi tradi virum. [32]Quibus cum iuramento dicentibus nescire se ubi esset, qui quaerebatur, extendens dexteram ad templum [33]iuravit haec: «Nisi Iudam mihi

was displeased with the covenant and commanding him to send Maccabeus to Antioch as a prisoner without delay.

[28]When this message came to Nicanor, he was troubled and grieved that he had to annul their agreement when the man had done no wrong. [29]Since it was not possible to oppose the king, he watched for an opportunity to accomplish this by a stratagem. [30]But Maccabeus, noticing that Nicanor was more austere in his dealings with him and was meeting him more rudely than had been his custom, concluded that this austerity did not spring from the best motives. So he gathered not a few of his men, and went into hiding from Nicanor.

1 Mac 7:29–30

[31]When the latter became aware that he had been cleverly outwitted by the man, he went to the great[a] and holy temple while the priests were offering the customary sacrifices, and commanded them to hand the man over. [32]And when they declared on oath that they did not know where the man was whom he sought, [33]he stretched out his right hand toward the sanctuary, and swore this oath: "If you do not hand Judas over to me as a prisoner, I will level this precinct of God to the ground and tear down the altar, and I will build here a splendid temple to Dionysus."

1 Mac 7:33–38

[34]Having said this, he went away. Then the priests stretched forth their hands toward heaven and called upon the constant Defender of our nation, in these words: [35]"O Lord of all, who hast need of nothing, thou wast pleased that there be a temple for thy habitation among us; [36]so now, O holy One, Lord of all holiness, keep undefiled for ever this house that has been so recently purified."

---

vinctum tradideritis, istud Dei fanum in planitiem deducam et altare effodiam et templum hic Libero illustre erigam». [34]Et, his dictis, abiit. Sacerdotes autem protendentes manus in caelum invocabant eum, qui semper propugnator fuit gentis nostrae, haec dicentes: [35]«Tu, Domine universorum, qui nullius indiges, voluisti templum habitationis tuae fieri in nobis; [36]et nunc, Sancte, omnis sanctificationis Domine, conserva in aeternum impollutam domum istam, quae nuper mundata est». [37]Razis autem quidam de senioribus ab Hierosolymis delatus est Nicanori, vir amator civitatis et valde bene audiens, qui pro affectu pater Iudaeorum appellabatur. [38]Hic enim pristinis temporibus seditionis iudicium pertulerat Iudaismi corpusque et animam pro Iudaismo tradiderat cum omni perseverantia. [39]Volens autem Nicanor manifestare odium, quod habebat in Iudaeos, misit milites supra quingentos, ut eum comprehenderent; [40]putabat enim, si illum cepisset, se cladem istis illaturum. [41]Turbis autem turrim iam occupaturis et atrii ianuae vim facientibus atque iubentibus ignem admovere et portas incendi, ipse undique comprehensus supposuit sibi gladium [42]volens nobiliter mori potius quam subditus fieri peccatoribus et nobilitate sua indignis iniuriis affici. [43]Sed, cum per contentionis festinationem non certo ictu plagam dedisset, et turbae intra ostia irrumperent, recurrens audacter ad murum praecipitavit semetipsum viriliter in turbas; [44]quibus velociter locum dantibus intervallo facto, venit per medium spatium vacuum. [45]Et, cum adhuc spiraret, accensus animis surrexit et, cum sanguis ad modum fontis deflueret, et gravissima essent vulnera, cursu turbas pertransiens et stans supra quandam petram

a. Gk *greatest*

Death of Razis

[37]A certain Razis, one of the elders of Jerusalem, was denounced to Nicanor as a man who loved his fellow citizens and was very well thought of and for his good will was called father of the Jews. [38]For in former times, when there was no mingling with the Gentiles, he had been accused of Judaism, and for Judaism he had with all zeal risked body and life. [39]Nicanor, wishing to exhibit the enmity which he had for the Jews, sent more than five hundred soldiers to arrest him; [40]for he thought that by arresting[b] him he would do them an injury. [41]When the troops were about to capture the tower and were forcing the door of the courtyard, they ordered that fire be brought and the doors burned. Being surrounded, Razis[c] fell upon his own sword, [42]preferring to die nobly rather than to fall into the hands of sinners and suffer outrages unworthy of his noble birth. [43]But in the heat of the struggle he did not hit exactly, and the crowd was now rushing in through the doors. He bravely ran up on the wall, and manfully threw himself down into

1 Sam 31:4

14:37–46. Here again we can see the author's penchant for dramatizing scenes. There are inaccuracies here as regards time and place. The episode reminds us of the case of Saul, who died in a similar way to Razis to avoid falling into the hands of his enemies (cf. 1 Sam 31:4). This is the only record we have about this elder and his tragic death; the sacred author uses him as an example to show, as he did in his account of earlier martyrs (cf. 6:18—7:41) that it is preferable to die rather than break the law of God or be obliged to do so by the godless. The writer is not justifying suicide (he does not discuss the morality of it here) but presenting an example of heroism and of hope in the resurrection (v. 46). "Suicide is always as morally objectionable as murder. The Church's tradition has always rejected it as a gravely evil choice. Even though a certain psychological, cultural and social conditioning may induce a person to carry out an action which so radically contradicts the innate inclination to life, thus lessening or removing subjective responsibility, *suicide*, when viewed objectively, is a gravely immoral act. In fact, it involves the rejection of love of self and the renunciation of the obligation of justice and charity towards one's neighbour, towards the communities to which one belongs, and towards society as a whole. In its deepest reality, suicide represents a rejection of God's absolute sovereignty over life and death" (John Paul II, *Evangelium vitae*, 66). Cf. also the notes on 1 Sam 31:4–5 and Tob 3:7–10.

praeruptam, [46]prorsus exsanguis iam effectus, proferens intestina et sumens utrisque manibus proiecit super turbas et invocans Dominatorem vitae ac spiritus, ut haec ipsi iterum redderet, ita vita defunctus est. **[15]** [1]Nicanor autem, ut comperit eos, qui cum Iuda erant, in locis esse iuxta Samariam, cogitavit

b. The Greek text here is uncertain **c.** Gk *he*

the crowd. [44]But as they quickly drew back, a space opened and he fell in the middle of the empty space. [45]Still alive and aflame with anger, he rose, and though his blood gushed forth and his wounds were severe he ran through the crowd; and standing upon a steep rock, [46]with his blood now completely drained from him, he tore out his entrails, took them with both hands and hurled them at the crowd, calling upon the Lord of life and spirit to give them back to him again. This was the manner of his death.

2 Mac 7:9

Nicanor and Judas prepare to do battle

15 [1]When Nicanor heard that Judas and his men were in the region of Samaria, he made plans to attack them with complete safety on the day of rest. [2]And when the Jews who were compelled to follow him said, "Do not destroy so savagely and barbarously, but show respect for the day which he who sees all things has honoured and hallowed above other days," [3]the thrice-accursed wretch asked if there were a sovereign in heaven who had commanded the keeping of the sabbath day. [4]And when they

---

15:1–11. In the last event narrated in the book, the author displays all his skill at melodrama. The suspense is created from the start by reporting the terrible blasphemy uttered by Nicanor, who considers himself more powerful on earth than God himself (v. 5), and, by contrast, the attitude of Judas who puts his trust in God, citing the Holy Scriptures and the Jews' own experience of God's mercy (v. 9).The Lord must surely come to their rescue now: his very honour, and the truth of salvation history, is at stake. The confrontation is not so much between Nicanor and Judas, as between Nicanor and God. The writing must be on the wall for Nicanor. These events are covered also in 1 Maccabees 7:33–50, but not nearly so dramatically.

St Paul, in due course, will recommend recourse to "the sacred writings which are able to instruct you for salvation through faith in Christ Jesus" (2 Tim 2:15–16). For that reason, the Church encourages Christians to draw sustenance from them: "all the preaching of the Church, as indeed the entire Christian religion, should be nourished and ruled by Holy Scripture. In the sacred books the Father who is in heaven comes lovingly to meet his

requietionis die cum omni securitate eos aggredi. [2]Iudaeis vero, qui illum per necessitatem sequebantur, dicentibus: «Ne ita ferociter et barbare disperdas, sed honorem tribue praehonoratae diei cum sanctificatione ab eo, qui universa conspicit», [3]ille infelix interrogavit, si est potens in caelo, qui imperavit agi diem sabbatorum. [4]Et respondentibus illis: «Est Dominus vivus ipse in caelo potens, qui iussit colere septimam diem»; [5]at ille ait: «Et ego potens sum super terram, qui impero sumi arma et negotia regis impleri». Tamen non obtinuit, ut nefarium consilium perficeret. [6]Et Nicanor quidem cum summa superbia cervicem erigens cogitaverat commune trophaeum statuere de iis, qui cum Iuda erant. [7]Maccabaeus autem sine intermissione confidebat cum omni spe auxilium se consequi a Domino, [8]et

declared, "It is the living Lord himself, the Sovereign in heaven, who ordered us to observe the seventh day," [5]he replied, "And I am a sovereign also, on earth, and I command you to take up arms and finish the king's business." Nevertheless, he did not succeed in carrying out his abominable design.

[6]This Nicanor in his utter boastfulness and arrogance had determined to erect a public monument of victory over Judas and his men. [7]But Maccabeus did not cease to trust with all confidence that he would get help from the Lord. [8]And he exhorted his men not to fear the attack of the Gentiles, but to keep in mind the former times when help had come to them from heaven, and now to look for the victory which the Almighty would give them. [9]Encouraging them from the law and the prophets, and reminding them also of the struggles they had won, he made them the more eager. [10]And when he had aroused their courage, he gave his orders, at the same time pointing out the perfidy of the Gentiles and their violation of oaths. [11]He armed each of them not so much with confidence in shields and spears as with the inspiration of brave words, and he cheered them all by, relating a dream, a sort of vision,[d] which was worthy of belief.

---

children, and talks with them. And such is the force and power of the Word of God that it can serve the Church as her support and vigour, and the children of the Church as strength for their faith, food for the soul, and a pure and lasting fount of spiritual life" (Vatican II, *Dei Verbum*, 21).

hortabatur suos, ne formidarent adventum nationum, sed in mente habentes adiutoria sibi facta de caelo et nunc sperarent ab Omnipotente sibi affuturam victoriam. [9]Et allocutus eos de Lege et Prophetis, admonens eos etiam de certaminibus, quae perfecerant, promptiores constituit eos. [10]Et, animis eorum excitatis, denuntiavit simul ostendens gentium fallaciam et iuramentorum praevaricationem. [11]Cum autem singulos illorum armavisset, non tam clipeorum et hastarum munitione quam per bonos sermones exhortatione, cumque somnium fide dignum exposuisset, supra modum universos laetificavit. [12]Erat autem huiuscemodi visus eius: Oniam, qui fuerat summus sacerdos, virum honestum et bonum, verecundum occursu, modestum moribus et eloquium digne proferentem et qui a puero omnes virtutes domesticas exercuerat, manus protendentem orare pro omni populo Iudaeorum. [13]Post hoc sic apparuisse virum canitie et gloria praestantem et mirabilem quandam et magni decoris esse eminentiam circa illum. [14]Respondentem vero Oniam dixisse: «Hic est fratrum amator, qui multum orat pro populo et sancta civitate, Ieremias propheta Dei». [15]Protendentem autem Ieremiam dextram dedisse Iudae gladium aureum et, cum daret, dixisse haec: [16]«Accipe sanctum gladium munus a Deo, in quo confringes adversarios». [17]Exhortati itaque Iudae sermonibus bonis valde, et qui poterant ad virtutem incitare et animos iuvenum confortare, statuerunt castra non tendere, sed fortiter inferri et cum omni virtute confligentes de negotiis iudicare, eo quod civitas et sancta et templum periclitarentur. [18]Erat enim timor pro uxoribus et filiis itemque pro fratribus et cognatis in minore parte iacens, maximus vero et primus pro sanctificato templo. [19]Sed et eos, qui in civitate erant comprehensi, non minima sollicitudo habebat propter illum sub aperto concursum. [20]Et, cum iam omnes exspectarent iudicium futurum, hostesque iam committerent, atque exercitus esset ordinatus, et bestiae opportuno in loco constitutae, et equitatus dispositus, [21]considerans Maccabaeus adventum multitudinis et apparatum varium armorum

d. The Greek text here is uncertain

Judas' dream

2 Mac 3:1

[12]What he saw was this: Onias, who had been high priest, a noble and good man, of modest bearing and gentle manner, one who spoke fittingly and had been trained from childhood in all that belongs to excellence, was praying with outstretched hands for the whole body of the Jews. [13]Then likewise a man appeared, distinguished by his gray hair and dignity, and of marvellous majesty and authority. [14]And Onias spoke, saying, "This is a man who loves the brethren and prays much for the people and the holy city, Jeremiah, the prophet of God." [15]Jeremiah stretched out his right hand and gave to Judas a golden sword, and as he gave it he addressed him thus: [16]"Take this holy sword, a gift from God, with which you will strike down your adversaries."

15:12–16. Both Onias and Jeremiah are very relevant to the situation that threatens the people at this point. Onias' prayer prevented the temple from being despoiled (cf. 3:16–21); Jeremiah prayed (cf. Jer 11:20) and later wept over Jerusalem, and he had promised on God's behalf that Judah's fortunes would be restored (cf. Jer 30:1—31:26; 2 Mac 2:1–18). Moreover, Onias, being a priest, stands for the Law, and Jeremiah for the Prophets.

Judas' dream is "worthy of belief" (v. 11) because the sacred writer firmly believes that the righteous who have died help the living by interceding before God on their behalf (vv. 12, 14) and equipping them for battle (v. 15). This teaching links up with that in 12:38–45 about the help that the living can render the dead. This intercommunication between the living and the dead is affirmed and practised in the Church through the communion of saints. Christian tradition has seen this as one of the spiritual passages which confirm that the prayers of the living link up with intercession made by Christ, the angels and the saints: "But it is not only the High Priest who unites himself to the prayer of those who pray as they ought; the angels, too, rejoice in heaven more at the sight of one sinner who repents than at the sight of ninety-

et ferocitatem bestiarum, extendens manus in caelum prodigia facientem Dominum invocavit sciens quoniam non est per arma, sed prout ab ipso iudicatum fuerit dignis tribuit victoriam. [22]Dixit autem invocans hoc modo: «Tu, Domine, qui misisti angelum tuum sub Ezechia rege Iudaeae, et interfecit de castris Sennacherib ad centum octoginta quinque milia, [23]et nunc, Dominator caelorum, mitte angelum bonum ante nos in timorem et tremorem; [24]magnitudine brachii tui exterreantur, qui cum blasphemia veniunt adversus sanctum populum tuum». Et hic quidem in his finem fecit. [25]Qui autem cum Nicanore erant, cum tubis et canticis admovebant; [26]hi vero qui erant cum Iuda, cum invocatione et orationibus congressi sunt cum hostibus. [27]Et manibus quidem pugnantes, sed Dominum cordibus orantes prostraverunt non minus triginta quinque milia praesentia Dei magnifice delectati. [28]Cumque cessassent ab opere et cum gaudio redirent, cognoverunt Nicanorem proruisse cum armis suis; [29]facto itaque clamore et tumultu, patria voce omnipotentem Dominum benedicebant. [30]Et praecepit ille, qui per omnia corpore et animo primus fuerat in certamine pro civibus, qui iuventutis benevolentiam in suam gentem conservaverat, caput Nicanoris abscindi et manum cum umero ac Hierosolymam perferri. [31]Quo

Victory for the Jews

[17]Encouraged by the words of Judas, so noble and so effective in arousing valour and awaking manliness in the souls of the young, they determined not to carry on a campaign but to attack bravely, and to decide the matter, by fighting hand to hand with all courage, because the city and the sanctuary and the temple were in danger. [18]Their concern for wives and children, and also for brethren and relatives, lay upon them less heavily; their greatest and first fear was for the consecrated sanctuary. [19]And those who had to remain in the city were in no little distress, being anxious over the encounter in the open country.

1 Mac 4:36

[20]When all were now looking forward to the coming decision, and the enemy was already close at hand with their army drawn up for battle, the elephants[e] strategically stationed and the cavalry deployed on the flanks, [21]Maccabeus, perceiving the hosts that were before him and the varied supply of arms and the savagery of the elephants, stretched out his hands toward heaven and called upon the Lord who works wonders; for he knew that it is not by arms, but as the Lord[f] decides, that he gains the victory for those who deserve it. [22]And he called upon him in these words: "O Lord, thou

---

nine just men who never sinned; the souls of the saints who already rest in peace are likewise joyful. [. . .] As we read in the book of the Maccabees, Jeremiah appears, marked out by his white hair and glorious dignity, wearing a halo of wonderful and magnificent majesty [. . .] and he stretched out his right hand to give Judas a golden sword. Another saint, who has already has passed away, left this testimony to Jeremiah: "He is the one who prayed much for the people and for the Holy City: Jeremiah, the prophet of God" (Origen, *De oratione*, 11,1).

cum pervenisset, convocatis contribulibus et sacerdotibus, ante altare stans accersiit eos, qui in arce erant, [32]et, ostenso capite iniqui Nicanoris et manu nefarii, quam extendens contra domum sanctam omnipotentis Dei magnifice gloriatus est, [33]linguam etiam impii Nicanoris praecisam dixit particulatim avibus daturum, pretia autem dementiae contra templum suspendere. [34]Omnes igitur in caelum benedixerunt manifestum Dominum dicentes: «Benedictus, qui locum suum incontaminatum servavit!». [35]Alligavit autem Nicanoris caput de summa arce evidens omnibus et manifestum signum auxilii Domini. [36]Itaque omnes communi consilio decreverunt nullo modo diem istum absque celebritate praeterire, habere autem celebrem tertiam decimam diem, mensis duodecimi—Adar dicitur voce Syriaca—pridie Mardochaei diei. [37]Igitur his erga Nicanorem sic gestis, et ex illis temporibus ab Hebraeis civitate possessa, ego quoque hic faciam finem sermonis. [38]Et, siquidem bene et apte compositioni, hoc et ipse volebam; sin autem exigue et modice, hoc est, quod assequi poteram. [39]Sicut enim vinum solummodo bibere, similiter autem rursus et aquam, contrarium est, quemadmodum autem vinum aquae contemperatum iam et delectabilem gratiam perficit, huiusmodi etiam structura sermonis delectat aures eorum, quibus contingat compositionem legere. Hic autem erit finis.

e. Gk *beasts* **f.** Gk *he*

2 Kings 19:35
1 Mac 7:40–42
2 Mac 8:19
Is 37:36
2 Mac 11:6
2 Mac 14:36

didst send thy angel in the time of Hezekiah king of Judea, and he slew fully a hundred and eighty-five thousand in the camp of Sennacherib. [23]So now, O Sovereign of the heavens, send a good angel to carry terror and trembling before us. [24]By the might of thy arm may these blasphemers who come against thy holy people be struck down." With these words he ended his prayer.

1 Mac 7:43–50

[25]Nicanor and his men advanced with trumpets and battle songs; [26]and Judas and his men met the enemy in battle with invocation to God and prayers. [27]So, fighting with their hands and praying to God in their hearts, they laid low no less than thirty-five thousand men, and were greatly gladdened by God's manifestation.

Nicanor's punishment

[28]When the action was over and they were returning with joy, they recognized Nicanor, lying dead, in full armour. [29]Then there was shouting and tumult, and they blessed the Sovereign Lord in the language of their fathers. [30]And the man who was ever in body and soul the defender of his fellow citizens, the man who maintained his youthful good will toward his countrymen, ordered them to cut off Nicanor's head and arm and carry them to Jerusalem. [31]And when he arrived there and had called his countrymen together and stationed the priests before the altar, he sent for those who were in the citadel. [32]He showed them the vile Nicanor's head and that profane man's arm, which had been boastfully stretched out against the holy house of the Almighty; [33]and he cut out the tongue

---

15:17–27. The sacred writer seems to want his readers to concentrate on the spiritual resources being used to prepare for and engage in the battle. What really matters to Judas and his men are the things of God (vv. 17–18), and it is perfectly clear that God's is the victory (vv. 21, 27). Something similar happens in the Christian life, which is a struggle not against armed enemies but against sin.

15:28–36. The gruesome treatment of the dead body of Nicanor needs to be read in the context of the time and remembering that the law of vengeance still applied among the Jews. The author takes it in his stride: as can be seen throughout the book he is convinced that there is a close connexion between sin and the punishment that must be meted out to the sinner (vv. 5–6, 32). Also the description of Nicanor's fate is in line with the author's desire to write a good story; this may be why he points out the connexion with "Mordecai's day", the day which celebrates the vengeance that the Jews took on their enemies in Babylon (cf. Esther 9:1–19). A Christian knows that vengeance no longer has any place, now that revelation has moved on (cf. Mt 5:43–45).

of the ungodly Nicanor and said that he would give it piecemeal to the birds and hang up these rewards of his folly opposite the sanctuary. [34]And they all, looking to heaven, blessed the Lord who had manifested himself, saying, "Blessed is he who has kept his own place undefiled." [35]And he hung Nicanor's head from the citadel, a clear and conspicuous sign to every one of the help of the Lord. [36]And they all decreed by public vote never to let this day go unobserved, but to celebrate the thirteenth day of the twelfth month—which is called Adar in the Syrian language—the day before Mordecai's day.

1 Sam 31:9–10
1 Mac 7:49

Conclusion

[37]This, then, is how matters turned out with Nicanor. And from that time the city has been in the possession of the Hebrews. So I too will here end my story. [38]If it is well told and to the point, that is what I myself desired; if it is poorly done and mediocre, that was the best I could do. [39]For just as it is harmful to drink wine alone, or, again, to drink water alone, while wine mixed with water is sweet and delicious and enhances one's enjoyment, so also the style of the story delights the ears of those who read the work. And here will be the end.

15:37–39. The author of 2 Maccabees is able to say that the city was in the hands of the Jews because they had got control of the temple. But in fact the Syrians were still in control because they were ensconced in the citadel; despite what is said in 15:35, it was another twenty years or so before the Jews took over the citadel (cf. 1 Mac 13:51). Right through the book, reliable historical information (with the chronological order sometimes changed) is interwoven with interpretations of a religious type by the author—much like water mixed into wine (v. 39). His primary objective is to delight and instruct—aspects proper to a literary work of mixed genre and which the Word of God presses into its service.

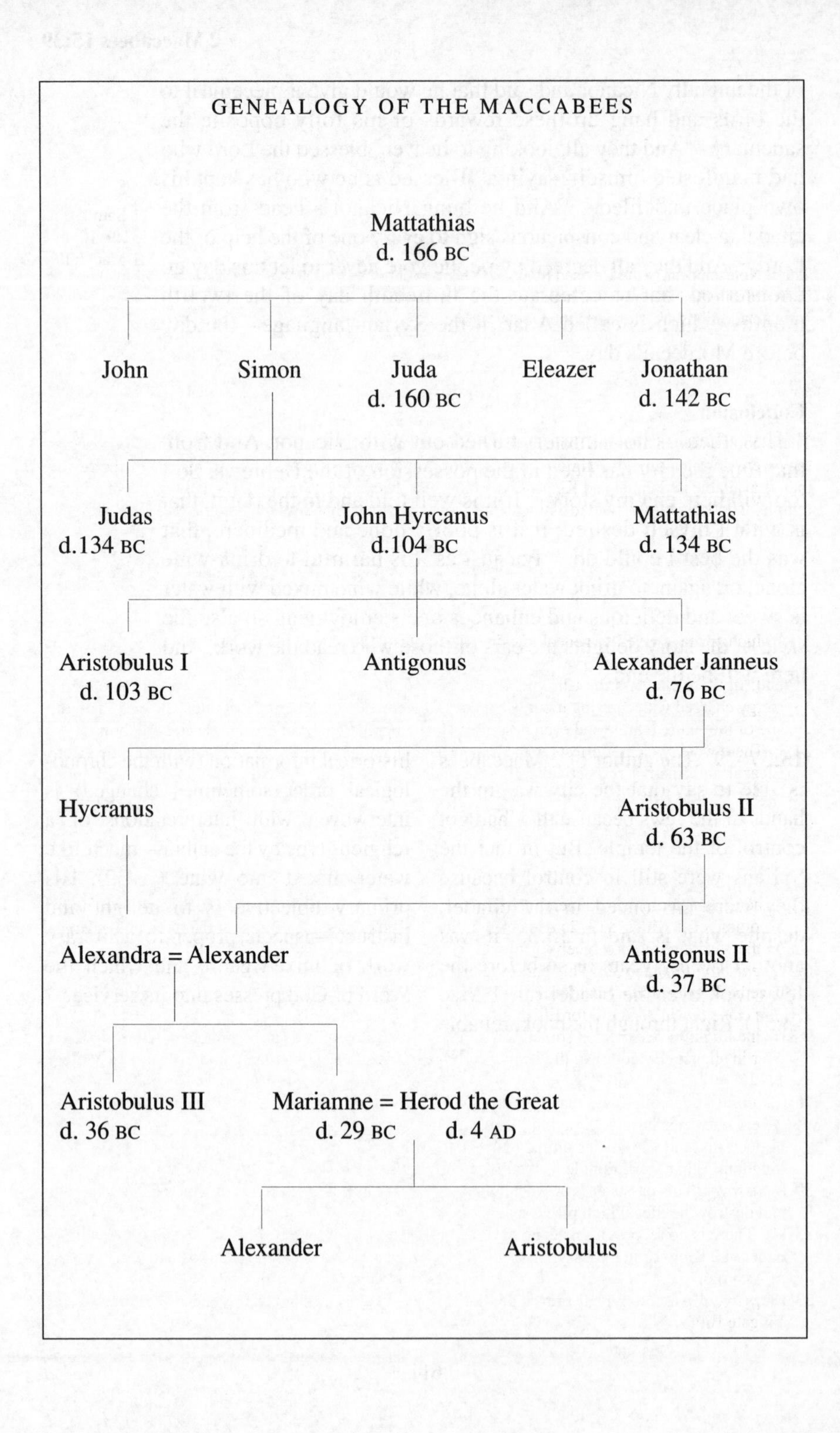
GENEALOGY OF THE MACCABEES
Mattathias
d. 166 BC
John
Simon
Juda
d. 160 BC
Eleazer
Jonathan
d. 142 BC
Judas
d.134 BC
John Hyrcanus
d.104 BC
Mattathias
d. 134 BC
Aristobulus I
d. 103 BC
Antigonus
Alexander Janneus
d. 76 BC
Hycranus
Aristobulus II
d. 63 BC
Alexandra = Alexander
Antigonus II
d. 37 BC
Aristobulus III
d. 36 BC
Mariamne = Herod the Great
d. 29 BC
d. 4 AD
Alexander
Aristobulus

Explanatory Notes

These Notes appear in the Revised Standard Version Catholic Edition. An asterisk *in* the biblical text as distinct from the Navarre Bible headings refers the reader to the Notes given here. N.B. In these Notes, Vulgate additions are quoted in the Douay Version.

1 AND 2 CHRONICLES

These books, written after the Exile, give a second account of the period of the kingship. Composed as they were during a time of religious revival, they aim at giving a more religious history of the period than is available in Samuel and Kings. The author's interest is mainly in Judah and in the worship in the temple. The kingdom of David is idealized and some developments that took place later are here situated in his reign.

1 CHRONICLES

1:1: Much space is given to genealogies in Chronicles. Postexilic Judaism was greatly interested in these in its efforts to preserve the race.

21–end: In these chapters the Chronicler enlarges on the organization of divine worship and of the clergy charged with carrying it out. He records the erection of a (permanent) altar to Yahweh on the site of the future temple and even describes David's preparation for the temple construction.

24:3: There were two chief priests in the time of David, namely, Zadok and Abiathar, descended from Eleazar and Ithamar respectively; cf. 1 Sam 22:20; 2 Sam 15:24. Later, in the time of Solomon, Zadok became sole high priest.

2 CHRONICLES

1:1: The Chronicler makes no mention of the rival claims of Adonijah and of his being put to death by Solomon; cf. 1 Kings 2:13–25. He concentrates on the favourable aspects of the reign and enlarges on the wisdom Solomon received from God.

6:21, *hear thou from heaven*: This phrase recurs like a refrain throughout this prayer, which seems to have been given a liturgical form.

7:1, *fire came down*: As it did for Elijah's sacrifice; cf. 1 Kings 18:38.

9:31: One might have expected something to be said on Solomon's decline in morals, but it is passed over in silence. By contrast, the similar failings of his son Rehoboam are underlined; cf. chapters 11–12.

18:12, *prophets*: Jeremiah says that false prophets usually proclaim what their hearers want them to say: "every one deals falsely … saying, 'Peace, peace,' when there is no peace" (Jer 6:13–14). It will be noticed that the Chronicler omits a large part of 2 Kings which is concerned with the Northern kingdom. Elijah, for example, is mentioned only once, in 21:12.

30:1, *passover*: This passover is not mentioned in Kings. The celebration inspired the people to go out and destroy the illegal high places and altars.

33:11: There is no record of this captivity of Manasseh in Babylon or of his subsequent repentance, either in 2 Kings or in the Assyrian records, though he is known from the latter to have been a vassal of Assyria.

33:18, *prayer*: An apocryphal prayer of Manasseh is usually printed at the end of editions of the Vulgate Bible.

Explanatory Notes

EZRA–NEHEMIAH

These two books were originally one, and were probably by the same author as Chronicles. They deal with the century following the return from the Exile, but it is by no means a complete history that they give. The author's main purpose is to describe the religious and political reorganization after the return, and to underline the workings of God's providence. There is some uncertainty as to the chronology and order of the events described. Two main sources, the memoirs of Ezra and those of Nehemiah, are here intermingled.

EZRA

1:2: The Persians, unlike the Babylonians, pursued a very liberal policy in matters of religion.

4:4: Understandably, the people who had occupied the land in the absence of the exiles now resented their return and, especially, the building of the temple.

5:1: Building is resumed nearly twenty years later, and the temple is completed in four years (515 BC)—but it was a mere shadow of Solomon's temple: cf. 3:12.

7:1: Fifty-seven years later, i.e., about 458 BC, according to one view, Ezra the scribe came with other exiles from Babylonia to carry out a much-needed reform. The total number in this group was some 6,000 or 8,000 persons. Many commentators place Ezra's coming in the reign of Artaxerxes II, 398 BC, and hence after Nehemiah.

9–10: Mixed marriages. Experience had shown that marriage with women of other races involved serious risk of idolatry; cf. Solomon, 1 Kings 11:1–8.

NEHEMIAH

Some years after the arrival of Ezra (cf. Ezra 7), Nehemiah had himself appointed governor of Jerusalem by the Persian king and came to that city to build up its walls (445 BC). As before, the project was opposed by the surrounding peoples (cf. chapters 4 and 6), but this time the work was not interrupted.

8–10: As it was only thirteen years since the reform of Ezra, some scholars think that this passage belongs to the book of Ezra.

8:8: The book was of course written in Hebrew, but the people, since their sojourn in Babylonia, now spoke Aramaic, and it had to be translated for them into that tongue.

TOBIT, JUDITH, ESTHER

These three books appear together in the Greek Bible, usually after the historical books. The complete Aramaic original of Tobit and the Hebrew of Judith have not survived, and neither book was included in the Jewish canon at the end of the first century AD. Existing as they did in the Greek Bible, they would have been used and recognized as Scripture by the first Christians. The Greek "Additions to Esther" were probably written two centuries after the Hebrew text. They were composed in Egypt and they exhibit a strictly Jewish doctrine. All three books have a literary form somewhat strange to the Western mind. They are, in effect, religious tales with the appearance of an historical narrative. They may have an historical basis, but the persons, places, events and dates are woven into the narrative in such a way as to have little resemblance to the actual historical record as we know it from other sources. It would seem, therefore, that the writers are intending, not to write history as we understand that term, but to use historical material to impart a religious message.

TOBIT

The author relates the story of a family living among a pagan people yet trusting fully in God in spite of difficulties. Belief in one God is stressed; marriage between Jews is likewise emphasized and angels

figure prominently in the narrative. The book has much to say, too, about the need for good works. It was written after the Exile at some time during the Persian period, though the story may be a good deal older than that. It shows signs of dependence on earlier writings such as the *Story of Ahikar*, a sixth-century work from Babylon. It also bears a likeness to Genesis in certain points, e.g., Tobit's last injunctions to the family, the important role of angels, the son's search for a wife, and the care given to burial of the dead. It is interesting to note that fragments of the Hebrew and Aramaic texts have been found at Qumran, which favour the longer text of Codex Sinaiticus, the Old Latin and the Vulgate.

2:10: Vulgate adds (verses 12–18): "[12]Now this trial the Lord permitted to happen to him, that an example might be given to posterity of his patience, as also of holy Job. [13]For whereas he had always feared God from his infancy, and kept his commandments, he repined not against God because the evil of blindness had befallen him, [14]but continued immovable in the fear of God, giving thanks to God all the days of his life. [15]For as the kings insulted over holy Job, so his relations and kinsmen mocked at his life, saying: [16]Where is thy hope, for which thou gavest alms, and buriedst the dead? [17]But Tobias rebuked them, saying, Speak not so; [18]for we are the children of saints, and look for that life which God will give to those that never change their faith from him."

3:11–15: The Vulgate version of this prayer (verses 13–23) reads as follows: "[13]She said: Blessed is thy name, O God of our fathers: who when thou hast been angry wilt show mercy, and in the time of tribulation forgivest the sins of them that call upon thee. [14]To thee, O Lord, I turn my face, to thee I direct my eyes. [15]I beg, O Lord, that thou loose me from the bond of this reproach, or else take me away from the earth. [16]Thou knowest, O Lord, that I never coveted a husband, and have kept my soul clean from all lust. [17]Never have I joined myself with them that play; neither have I made myself partaker with them that walk in lightness. [18]But a husband I consented to take, with thy fear, not with my lust. [19]And either I was unworthy of them, or they perhaps were not worthy of me: because perhaps thou hast kept me for another man, [20]for thy counsel is not in man's power. [21]But this every one is sure of that worshippeth thee, that his life, if it be under trial, shall be crowned: and if it be under tribulation, it shall be delivered: and if it be under correction, it shall be allowed to come to thy mercy. [22]For thou art not delighted in our being lost: because after a storm thou makest a calm, and after tears and weeping thou pourest in joyfulness. [23]Be thy name, O God of Israel, blessed for ever."

4:10, *charity*: i.e., almsgiving; cf. also verses 11 and 16.

4:12, *immorality*: i.e., impurity, fornication.

4:17, *Place your bread*: The Greek verb means literally "pour out." The Latin, with its "thy bread and thy wine," preserves better the original text; cf. the *Story of Ahikar:* "Pour out thy wine on the graves of the righteous and drink it not with evil men."

6:15–17: Vulgate differs and gives an exhortation to continence for three nights.

7:13, *and he blessed them*: Vulgate gives the words of the blessing (verse 15): "The God of Abraham, and the God of Isaac, and the God of Jacob be with you, and may he join you together, and fulfil his blessing in you." These words are included in the blessing in the Nuptial Mass.

8:4: Vulgate reads (verses 4–6): "[4]Then Tobias exhorted the virgin, and said to her: Sara, arise, and let us pray to God today, and tomorrow, and the next day: because for these three nights we are joined to God: and when the third night is over, we will be in our own wedlock. [5]For we are the children of God. [6]So they both arose, and prayed earnestly both together that health might be given them."

9:6: Instead of this sentence, Vulgate reads (verses 8–12): "[8]And when he was come into Raguel's house he found Tobias sitting at the table: and he leaped up, and they kissed each other: and Gabelus wept, and blessed God, [9]and said: The God of Israel bless thee, because thou art the son of a very good and just man, and that feareth God, and doth almsdeeds: [10]and may a blessing come upon thy wife and upon your parents: [11]and may you see your children, and your children's children, unto the third and fourth generation: and may your seed be blessed by the God of Israel, who reigneth for ever and ever. [12]And when all had said, Amen, they went to the feast: but the marriage feast they celebrated also with the fear of the Lord."

12:9, *charity*: See note on 4:10.

JUDITH

This is an account of the routine of an army and the freeing of the people of God through a stratagem devised and carried out by a woman (cf. Esther). The story is strongly nationalist in sentiment,

especially the victory song in chapter 16. The writer stresses that Judith's strength comes from God in response to her trust in him, and because she faithfully keeps all the prescriptions of the Law. The Greek version of the book (the basis of this translation) was made from a Hebrew original, now lost. The Latin version was made from an Aramaic text, almost a paraphrase, which is not now extant and which apparently omitted about a fifth of the book.

8:1: The names in this genealogy differ in the various texts and versions.
10:4: The remainder of this verse reads in the Vulgate (verse 4): "And the Lord also gave her more beauty: because all this dressing-up did not proceed from sensuality, but from virtue: and therefore the Lord increased thus her beauty, so that she appeared to all men's eyes incomparably lovely."
13:20: Vulgate adds: "[27]And Achior being called for came, and Judith said to him: The God of Israel, to whom thou gavest testimony, that he revengeth himself of his enemies, he hath cut off the head of all the unbelievers this night by my hand. [28]And that thou mayst find that it is so, behold the head of Holofernes, who in the contempt of his pride despised the God of Israel, and threatened thee with death, saying: When the people of Israel shall be taken, I will command thy sides to be pierced with a sword. [29]Then Achior, seeing the head of Holofernes, being seized with a great fear he fell on his face upon the earth, and his soul swooned away. [30]But after he had recovered his spirits, he fell down at her feet, and reverenced her, and said: [31]Blessed art thou by thy God in every tabernacle of Jacob, for in every nation which shall hear thy name, the God of Israel shall be magnified on occasion of thee."
15:9, *You are the exaltation of Jerusalem*: This passage is included in the office for feasts of the Blessed Virgin Mary, e.g., the little chapter for None on the Assumption, 15 August.
16:25: Vulgate adds (verse 31): "But the day of the festivity of this victory is received by the Hebrews in the number of holy days, and is religiously observed by the Jews from that time until this day."

ESTHER

Set in the Persian capital Susa, this story relates how God saved his people from the hands of an enemy, this time in a foreign country. As in the book of Judith, the deliverance is brought about through the instrumentality of a woman. The book gives details for the keeping of the feast of Purim in memory of this deliverance.

11:2: The disarrangement of the chapter and verse order is due to the insertion of the deuterocanonical portions in their logical place in the story of Esther, as narrated in the Greek version from which they are taken. They are printed in italics to enable the reader to recognize them at once.

In the Vulgate these portions were placed by Jerome immediately after the Hebrew text of Esther, regardless of their logical position, because he himself did not regard them as canonical. Hence they came to be numbered 10:4—16:24. It has been thought best to leave the chapter and verse numbering unchanged in the present edition.

4:8, *and charge her to go to the king to make supplication to him and entreat him for her people*: These words are the equivalent of Vulgate 15:1. The remainder of verse 8, printed in italics, corresponds to Vulgate 15:2–3, but is taken, of course, from the Greek. It is not included in the RSV edition of the Apocrypha, but is listed among the deuterocanonical parts of the book of Esther.
15:1–16: This deuterocanonical passage is a later expansion of the Hebrew text 5:1–2.

1 AND 2 MACCABEES

First Maccabees deals with the history of the Jews in Palestine during the forty years from the accession of the Syrian king Antiochus Epiphanes to the death of Simon in 134 BC. It was a life-and-death struggle between the Jews and the Syrians who wanted to impose Greek religion and culture on them. The book recounts the heroic deeds of the three great leaders. Judas Maccabeus and his brothers Jonathan and Simon, who were in turn at the head of the Jewish people until death overtook them. It was written with a strong religious purpose, and the high point is reached with a description of the rededication of the temple. Originally written in Hebrew, about the year 100 BC, the book now exists only in a Greek translation.

Second Maccabees is quite different. It is not a continuation of 1 Maccabees, but concentrates on the period of about fifteen years covered by 1 Maccabees, chapters 1–7. It aims at bringing out even more strongly the religious lessons of the time, and the story is written in a way that is more like a sermon than a history. The historical facts are arranged to suit the religious purpose of the book. Several passages in the work are well known in reference to particular doctrines, e.g., the resurrection of the body (7:9, 11; 14:46); rewards and punishments after death (6:26); prayers for the dead (12:42–45); the intercession of the saints (15:12–16).

1 MACCABEES

4:29: Vulgate has "Judea" for *Idumea* and "Beth-horon" for *Beth-zur.*
5:35: Vulgate reads "Maspha" (i.e., Mizpah) for *Alema*; cf. note **b.**
5:66, 68: Vulgate has "aliens" and "strangers" for *Philistines*, and "Samaria" for *Marisa*; cf. note **c**.
9:37: Vulgate reads "Madaba" (i.e., Medeba, as in verse 36) for *Nadabath.*

2 MACCABEES

4:29: Vulgate reads: "And Menelaus was removed from the priesthood, Lysimachus his brother succeeding: and Sostratus was made governor of the Cyprians."
4:34, *put him out of the way*: Vulgate has "slew him".
4:40, *Auranus:* Vulgate has "Tyrannus".
7:9, *to an everlasting renewal of life*: Vulgate has: "in the resurrection of eternal life."
12:45: Vulgate has (verses 45–46): "And because he considered that they who had fallen asleep with godliness had great grace laid up for them. It is therefore a holy and wholesome thought to pray for the dead, that they may be loosed from sins."

Sources quoted in the Commentary

1. DOCUMENTS OF THE CHURCH

Vatican, Second Council of the
Sacrosanctum Concilium: Constitution on the Sacred Liturgy, 4 December 1963, AAS 56 (1964) 97–138.
Lumen gentium: Dogmatic Constitution on the Church, 21 November 1964, AAS 57 (1965) 5–71.
Dei Verbum: Dogmatic Constitution on Divine Revelation, 18 November 1965, AAS 58 (1966) 817–835.
Gaudium et spes: Pastoral Constitution on the Church in the Modern World, 7 December 1966, AAS 58 (1966) 1025–1120.
Unitatis redintegratio: Decree on Ecumenism, 21 November 1964, AAS 57 (1965) 90–111.
Nostra aetate: Declaration on the Relation of the Church to non-christian Religions, 28 October 1965, AAS 58 (1966) 740–744.
Dignitatis humanae: Declaration on Religious Freedom, 7 December 1965, AAS 58 (1966) 929–946.
John Paul II
Salvifici doloris, Apostolic Letter on the Christian meaning of human suffering, 11 February 1984, AAS 76 (1984) 201–250.
Sollicitudo rei socialis, Encyclical Letter on the 20th anniversary of *Populorum progressio*, 30 December 1987, AAS 80 (1988) 513–586.
Veritatis splendor: Apostolic Letter on certain fundamental questions of the Church's teaching, 6 August 1993, AAS 85 (1993) 1133–1228.
Evangelium vitae, Encyclical Letter on the value and inviolability of human life, 25 March 1995, AAS 87 (1995) 401–522.

OTHER
Catechism of the Catholic Church, Dublin, 1994.
Roman Catechism: Catechism of the Council of Trent for Parish Priests, trs. McHugh and Callan, reprinted Manila, 1974.

2. LITURGICAL TEXTS

Roman Missal: Missale Romanum, editio typica altera, Vatican City, 1975.
The Divine Office, London, Sydney, Dublin, 1974.

3. THE FATHERS, ECCLESIASTICAL WRITERS AND OTHER AUTHORS

Ambrose, St
De officiis ministrorum libri III, PL 16, 23–184.
De Tobia liber unus, PL 14, 759–794.
De viduis liber unus, PL 16, 233–262.
Augustine, St
Enarrationes in Psalmos, PL 36–37.
Contra duas epistolas pelagianorum. Ad Bonifacium Romanae Ecclesiae episcopum libri IV, PL 44; 549–638.

Contra Gaudentium donatistarum episcopum libri II, PL 43, 707–752.
De Cain et Abel libri II, PL 14, 315–360.
Sermones, PL 38–39.
Bede, St
In Esdram et Nehemiam prophetas allegorica expositio, PL 91, 807–924.
Caesarius of Arles, St
Sermones, CCL 103–104.
Clement of Rome, St
Epistula Clementis ad Corinthios I
Cyprian, St
De oratione dominica, PL 4, 535–562.
Cyril of Alexandria, St
Commentarius in Aggaeum prophetam, PG 71, 1021–1062.
Faustinus Luciferanus
De Trinitate, CCL 69, 293–353.
Fulgentius of Ruspe, St
De remissione peccatorum ad Euthymium libri II, PL 65, 527–574.
Flavius Josephus
Antiquitates Judaicae
Gregory the Great, St
Moralium libri sive expositio in librum Beati Iob, PL 75, 509–76, 782.
Gregory Nazianzen, St
Orationes 15, In Machabeorum laudem, PG 35, 395–36, 664.
John Chrysostom, St
Homiliae III in Sanctos Maccabaeos et in matrem eorum, PG 50, 617–628.
Sermo antequam iret in exilium, PG 52, 427–432.
John Damascene, St
In Assumptionem Domini; Nostri Jesu Christi, PG 96, 817–856.
Expositio fidei orthodoxae, PG 94, 789–1228.
John Mediocre of Naples, St
Sermones, PLS 4, 785–786.
Josemaria Escrivá, St
Friends of God, London etc., 1988.
The Way, Dublin, 1985.
Christ Is Passing By, Dublin etc.1982.
Furrow, London etc., 1987.
Leo the Great, St
Sermones 95. De octo beatitudinibus, PL 54, 117–468.
Origen
Contra Celsum libri VIII, PG 11, 641–1632.
Libellus de oratione, PG 11, 415–562.
Polycarp, St
Epistola ad Philippenses, PG 5, 1005–1024.
Tertullian
Ad uxorem libri II, PL 1, 1385–1418.
Thomas Aquinas, St
Summa theologiae

Headings added to the Biblical Text

1 CHRONICLES

1. GENEALOGIES PRIOR TO THE MONARCHY 1:1
From Adam to Noah 1:1
The Japhethites 1:5
The Hamites 1:8
The Semites 1:17
The Ishmaelites 1:28
Sons of Seir 1:38
Kings of Edom 1:43
Descendants of Judah 2:1
Sons of David 3:1
Sons of Solomon 3:10
Descendants of Judah 4:1
Descendants of Simeon 4:24
Descendants of Reuben 5:1
Descendants of Gad 5:11
Descendants of the half-tribe of Manasseh 5:23
Descendants of Levi 6:1
Other descendants of Levi 6:16
Cantors 6:31
Levite cities 6:54
Descendants of Issachar 7:1
Descendants of Benjamin 7:13
Descendants of Naphtali 7:14
Descendants of Manasseh 7:14
Descendants of Ephraim 7:20
Descendants of Asher 7:30
Descendants of Benjamin 8:1
Descendants of Saul 8:33
Jerusalem after the exile 9:1
The family of Saul 9:35

2. THE REIGN OF DAVID 10:1
Death of Saul 10:1
David is proclaimed king 11:1
Capture of Jerusalem 11:4
David's champions 11:10
David's first supporters 12:1
Warriors who assured David's kingship 12:23
The ark is brought back to Jerusalem 13:1
David at Jerusalem 14:1
Enthronement of the ark in Jerusalem 15:1
The ark is placed in the tent 16:1
The prophecy of Nathan 17:1
David's prayer 17:16
David's victories 18:1
Victories over the Ammonites 19:1
Siege and capture of Rabbah 20:1
Other victories over the Philistines 20:4
The census 21:1
Punishment for holding the census 21:7
Preparations for building the temple 22:1
Orders and functions of Levites 23:1
Classification of the priests 24:1
Other Levites 24:20
Cantors 25:1
Gatekeepers 26:1
Other duties of the Levites 26:20
Military organization 27:1
Civil organization 27:16
Instructions for the building of the temple 28:1
Voluntary offerings 29:1
David's prayer 29:10
Solomon proclaimed king 29:23
Death of David 29:26

2 CHRONICLES

3. THE REIGN OF SOLOMON 1:1
Solomon's gift of wisdom 1:1
Solomon's wealth 1:14
Treaty with the king of Tyre 2:2
Building of the temple 3:1
Furnishings of the temple 4:1
The ark is brought to the temple 5:1
Solomon blesses the people 6:1
Solomon's prayer 6:12
Dedication of the temple 7:1
God's reply to Solomon 7:11
Building of cities 8:1
Solomon's administration 8:7
Visit of the queen of Sheba 9:1
Solomon's wealth 9:13
Death of Solomon 9:29

4. THE KINGS OF JUDAH 10:1
The kingdom is split in two 10:1
Rehoboam, king of Judah 11:1

Rehoboam's supporters 11:13
Rehoboam's wives and family 11:18
Judah invaded by Egypt 12:1
The reign of Abijah 13:1
Victory for Abijah 13:13
The reign of Asa 14:1
Victory over Zerah 14:9
Asa's regulations against idolatry 15:1
Asa's war against Israel 16:1
The reign of Jehoshaphat 17:1
Alliance between Jehoshaphat and Ahab 18:1
Death of Ahab 18:28
Jehoshaphat's legal system 19:1
Jehoshaphat's victory over Ammonites and Moabites 20:1
End of Jehoshaphat's reign 20:31
The reign of Jehoram 21:1
An Edomite rebellion 21:8
Jehoram punished for his infidelity 21:11
The reign of Ahaziah 22:1
The reign of Athaliah 22:10
Joash proclaimed king. Death of Athaliah 23:1
The reign of Joash 24:1
Joash's infidelity 24:17
The reign of Amaziah 25:1
Amaziah punished for his infidelity 25:14
Amaziah defeated by the king of Israel 25:17
End of Amaziah's reign 25:25
The reign of Uzziah 26:1
Uzziah punished for his infidelity 26:16
The reign of Jotham 27:1
The reign of Ahaz 28:1
War against Syria and Ephraim 28:5
Attack by the king of Assyria 28:16

5. THE GREAT REFORMS 29:1
The reign of Hezekiah 29:1
Purification of the temple 29:3
Re-establishment of religious worship 29:20
Celebration of the Passover 30:1
Organization of service in the temple 31:1
Invasion by Sennacherib 32:1
Hezekiah's illness and cure 32:24
Hezekiah's prosperity 32:27
The reign of Manasseh 33:1
The reign of Amon 33:21
The reign of Josiah 34:1
Josiah's early reforms 34:3
Discovery of the book of the Law 34:8
Huldah the prophetess is consulted 34:19
The Covenant is renewed 34:29
Celebration of the Passover 35:1
Death of Josiah 35:20

6. END OF THE KINGDOM OF JUDAH 36:1
The reign of Jehoahaz 36:1
The reign of Jehoiakim 36:5
The reign of Jehoiachin 36:9
The reign of Zedekiah 36:11
Deportation. Destruction of Jerusalem 36:17
Cyrus' edict 36:22

EZRA

1. REBUILDING OF THE TEMPLE 1:1
The exiles return from Babylon 1:1
List of returning exiles 2:1
The exiles arrive in Jerusalem 2:68
The rebuilding of the temple begins 3:7
Opposition to the rebuilding 4:1
A report sent to Artaxerxes 4:8
Artaxerxes orders the building work to stop 4:17
The Jews start building again 5:1
Letter to Darius justifying the building work 5:6
Darius allows the rebuilding to continue 6:1
Completion of the building work 6:13
Dedication of the temple 6:16
Celebration of the Passover 6:19

2. EZRA'S MISSION—TO RE-ESTABLISH THE LAW 7:1
Ezra travels from Babylon to Jerusalem 7:1
Powers given by Artaxerxes to Ezra 7:11
Ezra's gratitude to God 7:27
Key men in Ezra's party 8:1
Ezra's party prepares to leave 8:15
Ezra's party arrives in Jerusalem 8:31
Ezra presents his credentials 8:36
Ezra is pained to find the Law ignored 9:1
The people acknowledge their sin in marrying foreigners 10:1
Ezra calls on the people to assemble at Jerusalem 10:5
The people confess their sin 10:10
Foreign wives are sent away 10:18

Headings added to the Biblical Text

NEHEMIAH

3. NEHEMIAH'S MISSION—TO REBUILD THE CITY 1:1

Nehemiah's prayer for the reunification of Israel 1:1

Nehemiah is authorized to rebuild the wall of Jerusalem 2:1

Those involved in rebuilding the wall 3:1

Enemies oppose the rebuilding of the wall 4:1

Obstacles to rebuilding the wall 4:7

The builders bear arms as they engage in their work 4:15

Nehemiah's administration 5:1

Threats fail to prevent the rebuilding 6:1

Census of the returned exiles 7:1

The Law is read out. The feast of Tabernacles 8:1

Fasting and confession of sins 9:1

Commitment to keep the Law 9:38

Repopulation of Jerusalem and Jordan 11:1

Priests and Levites who returned with Zerubbabel and Jeshua 12:1

Dedication of the wall of Jerusalem 12:27

The people rejoice. Gentiles are kept at a distance 12:44

Nehemiah's second mission—to establish the Law of Moses 13:4

TOBIT

1. TOBIT'S MISFORTUNE. HIS PRAYER IN NINEVEH AND SARAH'S PRAYER IN MEDIA 1:1

Tobit's ancestors and place of origin 1:1

Tobit's religious piety and works of mercy 1:3

Tobit's misfortune 2:1

Tobit's prayer in Nineveh 3:1

Sarah's misfortune 3:7

Sarah's prayer in Media 3:11

The prayers of Tobit and Sarah are heard 3:16

2. TOBIT'S JOURNEY TO MEDIA ACCOMPANIED BY THE ARCHANGEL RAPHAEL 4:1

Tobit's appeal to his son 4:1

Tobias meets the archangel Raphael 5:1

Tobias sets out for Media. The fish from the Tigris river 6:1

Arrival in Media 6:9

Sarah's hand is sought in marriage 7:1

Tobias' and Sarah's wedding night 8:1

Surprise shown by Sarah's parents. Their prayer of thanksgiving 8:13

Further services rendered by Raphael 9:1

Tobias' parents are concerned over his continued absence 10:1

Farewells in Media 10:8

3. IN NINEVEH AGAIN. TOBIT'S CURE. HIS OLD AGE 11:1

Arrival in Nineveh and cure of Tobit 11:1

Tobit blesses Sarah 11:16

The archangel Raphael reveals himself 12:1

Tobias' song of praise 13:1

Tobias' will and death 14:1

Tobit and Sarah move to Media 14:12

JUDITH

1. THE ISRAELITES BESET BY A POWERFUL ENEMY 1:1

Nebuchadnezzar's aggressiveness 1:1

Holofernes' campaign 2:1

Judea on the alert 4:1

Achior proclaims the greatness of the God of Israel 5:1

The Israelites besieged in Bethulia 7:1

2. GOD CONFOUNDS HIS ENEMIES BY MEANS OF JUDITH 8:1

Judith appeals for divine protection 8:1

Judith defeats Holofernes 10:1

Achior's conversion 14:1

The enemy army flees 14:11

Judith's song of praise 15:8

Conclusion 16:18

Headings added to the Biblical Text

ESTHER

PROLOGUE *11:2*
Mordecai's dream *11:2*

1. ESTHER BECOMES QUEEN 1:1
Queen Vashti repudiated 1:1
Ahasu-erus chooses Esther as his queen 2:1

2. MORDECAI AND HAMAN, ENEMIES 2:19
Mordecai exposes a plot against the king 2:19
Mordecai refuses to do obeisance to Haman 3:1

3. A DECREE ORDERING EXTERMINATION OF THE JEWS 3:7
Mordecai asks Esther to intercede for the Jews 4:1
Mordecai's prayer *13:8*
Esther's prayer *14:1*

4. MORDECAI GETS THE BETTER OF HAMAN 5:1
Esther approaches the king 5:1
The king remembers Mordecai 6:1

5. GOD SAVES HIS PEOPLE FROM EXTERMINATION 7:1
Haman is disgraced 7:1
Mordecai is given Haman's position 8:1
The Jews are authorized to defend themselves 8:9
The Jews avenge themselves 9:1
The feast of Purim commemorates the episode 9:20

EPILOGUE 10:5
Interpretation of Mordecai's dream 10:5

1 MACCABEES

1. THE HELLENIZATION OF JERUSALEM 1:1
Alexander the Great and his successors 1:1
Many Jews are led astray 1:11
Jerusalem sacked by Antiochus Epiphanes 1:16
Persecution. Construction of the citadel at Jerusalem 1:29
Observance of the Law is proscribed 1:41
The temple profaned, the books of the Law set on fire. Religious persecution 1:54

2. MATTATHIAS' ARMED REVOLT 2:1
Anguish felt by Mattathias and his sons 2:1
Mattathias takes action at Mode-in 2:15
A decision is taken to fight even on the sabbath. The first guerrillas 2:29
Testament and death of Mattathias 2:49

3. JUDAS MACCABEUS 3:1
Eulogy of Judas Maccabeus 3:1
Victory over Apollonius and Seron, local army commanders 3:10
Victory over Gorgias near Emmaus 3:27
Victory over Lysias at Beth-zur 4:26
Purification and dedication of the temple 4:36
Judas' expedition outside Judea 5:1
Joseph and Azariah routed 5:55
Death of Antiochus IV Epiphanes 6:1
The royal army advances on Jerusalem 6:18
Eleazar's heroism 6:43
Judas withdraws. Jerusalem is besieged 6:47
Lysias retires to Antioch. Peace treaty 6:55
Demetrius I, the high priest Alcimus, and Bacchides, the governor of Judea 7:1
Judas' reaction and his victory over Nicanor 7:21
Judas' alliance with the Romans 8:1
A new attack on Judea. Death of Judas in battle 9:1

4. JONATHAN, JUDAS' SUCCESSOR 9:23
Lawlessness and vengeance. Jonathan's election 9:23
The death of John avenged by Jonathan 9:35
Armed confrontation between Bacchides and Jonathan 9:43
Death of Alcimus. Jonathan is persecuted. Bacchides is defeated 9:54
Jonathan appointed high priest by Alexander. Opposition to Demetrius 10:1
Jonathan appointed general and governor 10:48
Jonathan's victory over Apollonius, Demetrius II's general 10:67
Fall of Alexander. Demetrius II rules with the support of Egypt 11:1
Concessions granted by Demetrius II to Jonathan 11:20
The Jews come to the aid of Demetrius 11:38
Jonathan takes the side of Antiochus, the son of Alexander. Wars against Demetrius II 11:54
Jonathan's alliances with Rome and Sparta 12:1

2 MACCABEES

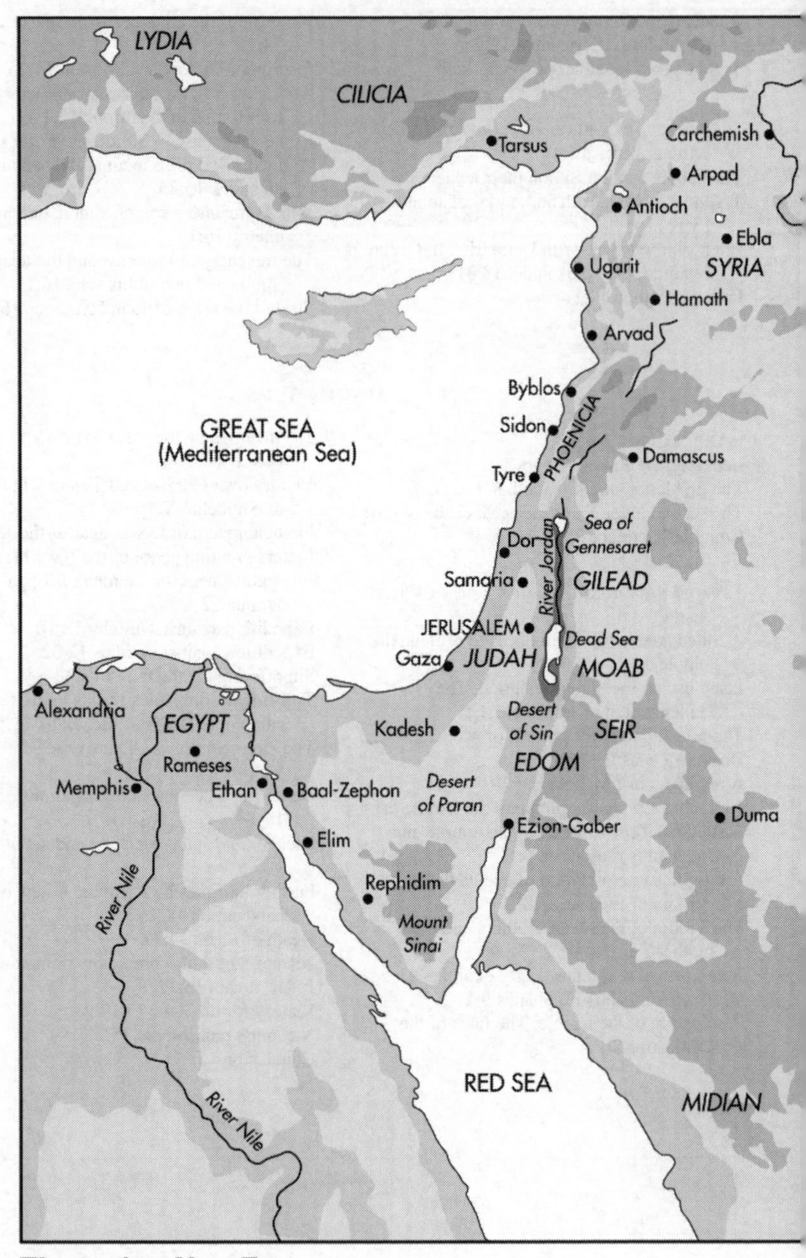

The Ancient Near East

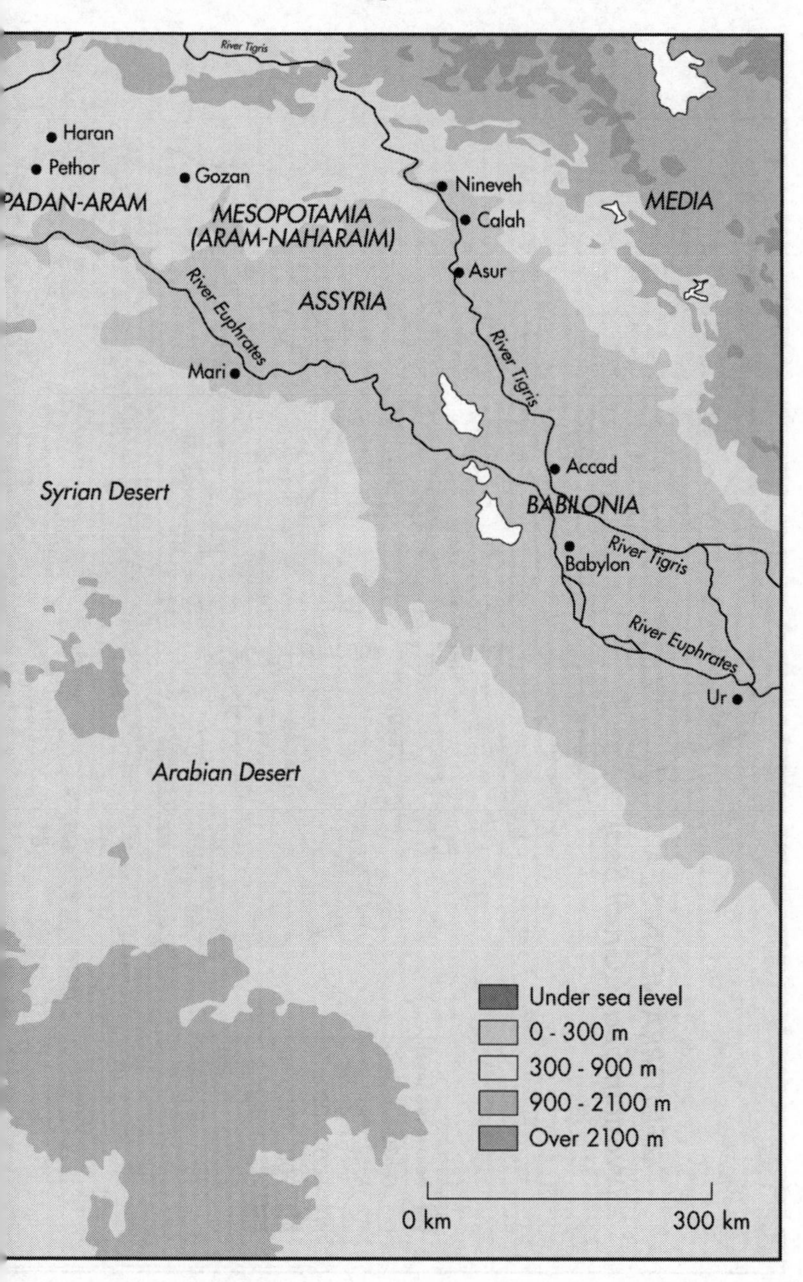
River Tigris
Haran
Pethor
Gozan
PADAN-ARAM
MESOPOTAMIA
(ARAM-NAHARAIM)
Nineveh
Calah
MEDIA
Asur
River Euphrates
ASSYRIA
River Tigris
Mari
Accad
Syrian Desert
BABILONIA
Babylon
River Tigris
River Euphrates
Ur
Arabian Desert
Under sea level
0 - 300 m
300 - 900 m
900 - 2100 m
Over 2100 m
0 km
300 km

MEDITERRANEAN SEA
(Western Sea / Great Sea)
Below sea level
0 - 300 m
300 - 600 m
600 - 900 m
900 - 1200 m
Over 1200 m
Sarepta
LEBANON
Mount Hermon
ARAM
PHOENICIA
DAN
Tyre
Abel-Beth-Maachah
Laish/Dan
MAACHAH
Cana
ASHER
BASHAN
Hammon
Kedesh
Achzib
Yiron
Hazor
Merom
GESHUR
NAPHTALI
Accho
Rehob
Aphek
ZEBULON
Sea of Gennesaret
Ashtaroth
Madon
Golan
Quison
River Yarmuk
Mount Carmel
Shimron-Meron
Mount Tabor
ISACAR
HAVOTH-JAIR
En-dor
Dor
Ophrah
Shunem
Camon
Edrei
Megiddo
Jezreel
Lo-Debar
Rogelim
KINGDOM OF ISRAEL
Taanach
Beth-Shem
MANASSEH
Ramoth-Gilead
MANASSEH
Dothan
GILEAD
Abel-Meholah
Bezek
Socoh
Tirzah
River Jordan
SAMARIA
Mount Ebal
Shechem
Penuel
Pirathon
Succoth
River Jabbok

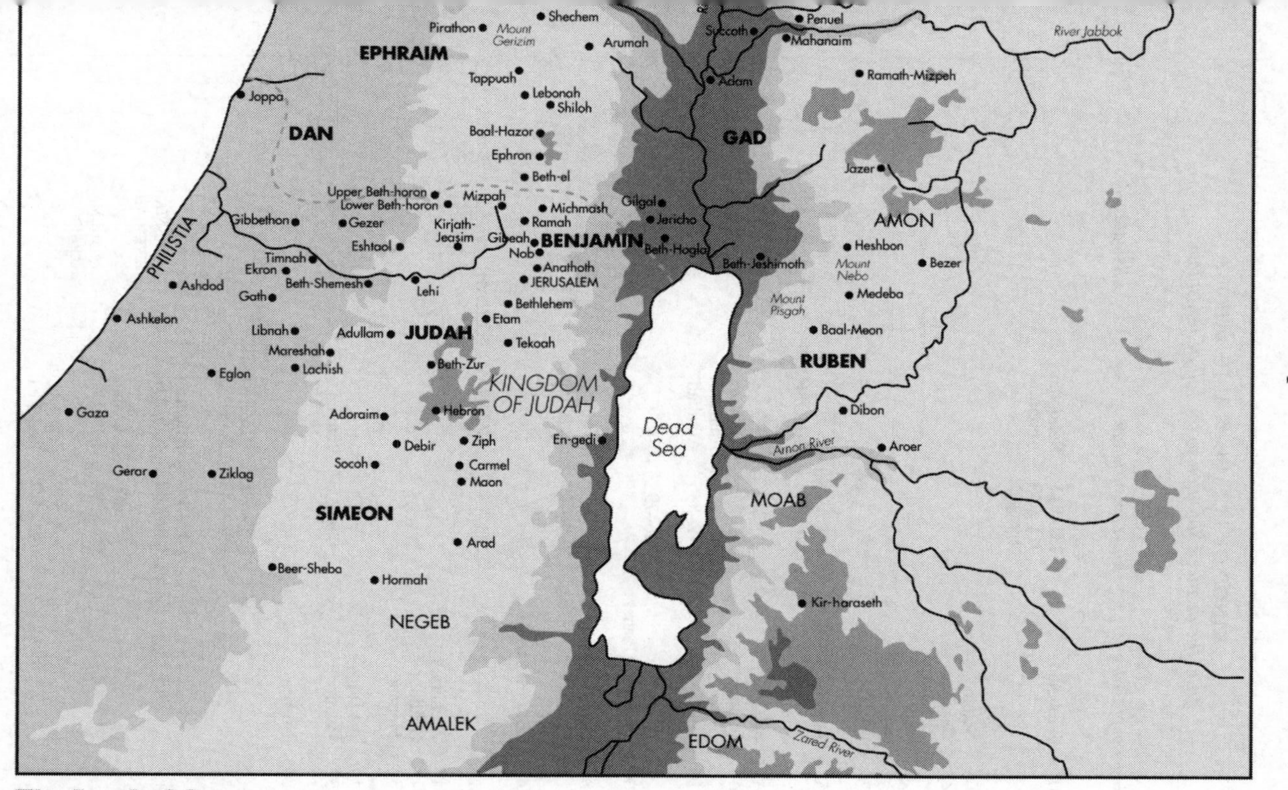

The Land of Canaan

KINGS OF ISRAEL AND JUDAH
from the death of Solomon to the fall of Jerusalem

Kingdom of Israel		*Kingdom of Judah*		*Biblical book*
928–907	Jeroboam	931–911	Rehoboam	
		911–908	Abijam	
		908–867	Asa	
907–906	Nadab			
906–883	Baasha			
883–882	Elah			
882	Zimri			
882–871	OMRI			
873–852	AHAB			
		870–846	JEHOSHAPHAT	
852–851	Ahaziah			
851–842	Joram	851–843*	Jehoram	
		843–842	Ahaziah	
842–814	Jehu	842–836	Athaliah	
		836–798	Joash	
817–800	Jehoahaz (Joahaz)			
800–784	(Jehoash)			
		798–769	Amaziah	
788–747*	JEROBOAM II			
		785–733*	AZARIAH (UZZIAH)	
				AMOS
747	Zechariah			
747	Shallum			
747–737	Menahem			HOSEA
737–735	Pekahiah		Micah	
735–732	Pekah	759–743*	Jotham	MICAH
				ISAIAH
732–724	Hoshea	743–727	Ahaz	
		727–698	HEZEKIAH	
		698–642	Manasseh	
		641–640	Amon	
		639–609	JOSIAH	ZEPHANIAH
				JEREMIAH
		609	Jehoahaz	
		608–598	Jehoiakim	NAHUM
				HABAKKUK
		597	Jehoiachin	
		596–587	Zedekiah	

Note: The biblical books listed on the right contain references to the period of the kings mentioned in the other columns, although some of those books were written later.

The more important kings' names are given in capital letters.

An asterisk indicates that the regnal years include years of regency.